The Grammar of Romanian

The Grammar of Romanian

Edited by
Gabriela Pană Dindelegan

Consultant Editor
Martin Maiden

OXFORD
UNIVERSITY PRESS

Great Clarendon Street, Oxford, OX2 6DP,
United Kingdom

Oxford University Press is a department of the University of Oxford.
It furthers the University's objective of excellence in research, scholarship,
and education by publishing worldwide. Oxford is a registered trade mark of
Oxford University Press in the UK and in certain other countries

© editorial matter and organization Gabriela Pană Dindelegan 2013

© the chapters their several authors 2013

The moral rights of the author have been asserted

First Edition published in 2013

Impression: 1

All rights reserved. No part of this publication may be reproduced, stored in
a retrieval system, or transmitted, in any form or by any means, without the
prior permission in writing of Oxford University Press, or as expressly permitted
by law, by licence, or under terms agreed with the appropriate reprographics
rights organization. Enquiries concerning reproduction outside the scope of the
above should be sent to the Rights Department, Oxford University Press, at the
address above

You must not circulate this work in any other form
and you must impose this same condition on any acquirer

British Library Cataloguing in Publication Data

Data available

ISBN 978-0-19-964492-6

Printed by the MPG Printgroup, UK

Contents

Detailed Contents and Author Attributions vii
Preface xxv
Notes on Style and Format xxvii
Abbreviations and Conventions xxviii
The Contributors xxxii

1 Introduction   1
2 The Verb   18
3 The Structure of Root Clauses   100
4 Non-finite Verb Forms and Non-finite Clauses   204
5 Noun and Noun Phrases   255
6 Pronouns   379
7 Adjectives and Adjectival Phrases   410
8 Adverbs and Adverbial Phrases   432
9 Prepositions and Prepositional Phrases   451
10 The Structure of Complex Clauses. Subordination   466
11 Coordination   514
12 Agreement   526
13 Sentence Organization and Discourse Phenomena   537
14 Derivational Morphology   599
15 Inflectional and Derivational Morphophonological Alternations   607
16 Compounding   612

Sources   621
References   624
Index   649

Detailed Contents and Author Attributions

Preface xxv
Notes on Style and Format xxvii
Abbreviations and Conventions xxviii
The Contributors xxxii

1 Introduction 1
   1.1 Romanian—a brief presentation (Gabriela Pană Dindelegan) 1
      1.1.1 Where Romanian is spoken 1
      1.1.2 The genealogical definition of Romanian 1
      1.1.3 The time and place of the emergence of Romanian 2
      1.1.4 Linguistic contacts 2
      1.1.5 The periodization of Romanian 3
      1.1.6 History of writing in Romanian 5
      1.1.7 Dialectal, socio-professional, and stylistic variation 6
      1.1.8 The individuality of Romanian 7
   1.2 Phonological and orthographic features of Romanian (Camelia Stan) 7
      1.2.1 The phonological system 7
         1.2.1.1 Vowels. The vowels /ə, ɨ/ 7
         1.2.1.2 The word-final post-consonantal glide $[^i]$ 8
         1.2.1.3 Semivowels 8
         1.2.1.4 Consonants 9
      1.2.2 Diphthongs 11
      1.2.3 Triphthongs 12
      1.2.4 Free stress 13
      1.2.5 Phonological orthography 14
         1.2.5.1 The alphabet 14
         1.2.5.2 The letter–phoneme correspondence 14
         1.2.5.3 Etymological spellings 15
         1.2.5.4 Spellings based on grammatical rules 15
         1.2.5.5 Orthographic marks 15
      1.2.6 Pronunciation norms 16
      1.2.7 Punctuation 16
Conclusions 16

2 The Verb   18
　　2.1 Inflectional classes of verbs (Isabela Nedelcu)   18
　　　　2.1.1 Five inflectional classes of verbs   18
　　　　　　2.1.1.1 Two subclasses of the verbs in -*a*: with and without the supplementary suffix -*ez*   19
　　　　　　2.1.1.2 The class of the verbs in -*ea*   20
　　　　　　2.1.1.3 Three subclasses of verbs in -*e*   21
　　　　　　2.1.1.4 Two subclasses of verbs in -*i*: with and without the supplementary suffix -*esc*   21
　　　　　　2.1.1.5 Two subclasses of verbs in -*î*: with and without the supplementary suffix -*ăsc*   22
　　　　2.1.2 Irregular verbs   23
　　2.2 Mood, tense, and aspect (Rodica Zafiu)   24
　　　　2.2.1 Verb morphology   24
　　　　　　2.2.1.1 Synthetic forms   24
　　　　　　2.2.1.2 Analytic forms   37
　　　　2.2.2 Values and uses of verbal moods   43
　　　　　　2.2.2.1 The indicative   43
　　　　　　2.2.2.2 The subjunctive   45
　　　　　　2.2.2.3 The conditional   50
　　　　　　2.2.2.4 The presumptive   53
　　　　　　2.2.2.5 The imperative   54
　　　　2.2.3 The tense–aspect system   55
　　　　2.2.4 Values and uses of verbal tenses   55
　　　　　　2.2.4.1 The present tense of the indicative   55
　　　　　　2.2.4.2 The perfect. The compound past and the simple past   57
　　　　　　2.2.4.3 The present–past distinction for irrealis moods   60
　　　　　　2.2.4.4 The imperfect   60
　　　　　　2.2.4.5 The pluperfect   61
　　　　　　2.2.4.6 The future, the future perfect, and the future in the past   62
　　　　2.2.5 The sequence of tenses   63
　　　　2.2.6 Aspectual periphrases   64
　　2.3 Syntactic and semantic classes of verbs   65
　　　　2.3.1 Transitive verbs (Gabriela Pană Dindelegan)   65
　　　　　　2.3.1.1 Double object verbs   66
　　　　　　2.3.1.2 Complex transitive verbs with an objective predicative complement   70
　　　　2.3.2 Intransitive verbs (Adina Dragomirescu)   72
　　　　　　2.3.2.1 Unaccusatives vs. unergatives   72
　　　　　　2.3.2.2 Copula verbs   78

2.3.3 Experiencer verbs   82
    2.3.3.1 Verbs of perception (Irina Nicula)   82
    2.3.3.2 Verbs of physical sensation (Irina Nicula)   88
    2.3.3.3 Psych verbs (Ana-Maria Iorga Mihail)   92
2.3.4 Verbs of motion (Adina Dragomirescu)   95
    2.3.4.1 Class membership   95
    2.3.4.2 Syntactic features   96

Conclusions   98

3 The Structure of Root Clauses   100

3.1 The subject (Gabriela Pană Dindelegan)   100
  3.1.1 Characteristics   100
  3.1.2 The subject of non-finite forms (lexical vs. controlled / covert)   101
    3.1.2.1 The infinitive   102
    3.1.2.2 The gerund   103
    3.1.2.3 The supine   103
    3.1.2.4 The participle   104
  3.1.3 Non-realization and absence of the subject. Romanian as a pro-drop language   104
    3.1.3.1 Non-realization of the subject   104
    3.1.3.2 The absence of the expletive impersonal pronominal subject   106
    3.1.3.3 The absence of a [+human] non-definite or generic subject. Generic structures   108
    3.1.3.4 Verbs without a subject   109
  3.1.4 The subject realized as a bare noun   111
  3.1.5 The doubly realized subject   112
  3.1.6 The prepositional subject   113
  3.1.7 Finite and non-finite clauses in subject position   114
    3.1.7.1 Relative clauses   114
    3.1.7.2 Non-finite clauses   115
    3.1.7.3 Clauses with a complementizer   116
  3.1.8 Raised subjects (subject-to-subject raising)   117
    3.1.8.1 Syntactically integrated subjects   117
    3.1.8.2 Isolated subjects—hanging topic   118
  3.1.9 Subject word order   119
    3.1.9.1 Word order in the main clause   119
    3.1.9.2 Subject word order in subordinate clauses   123
    3.1.9.3 Romanian, a V–S language?   124

3.2 Objects   125
   3.2.1 The direct object (Gabriela Pană Dindelegan)   125
      3.2.1.1 Characteristics   125
      3.2.1.2 Pronominal clitics in the direct object position vs. bare nominal phrases   127
      3.2.1.3 Prepositional marking. The PE-construction   128
      3.2.1.4 Partitive prepositional constructions   135
      3.2.1.5 Clitic doubling   136
      3.2.1.6 Finite and non-finite clauses in the direct object position   139
      3.2.1.7 Ordinary objects vs. raised objects   140
      3.2.1.8 Direct object word order   142
   3.2.2 The secondary object (Gabriela Pană Dindelegan)   144
      3.2.2.1 Characteristics   144
      3.2.2.2 Realizations   145
      3.2.2.3 Constructions involving overall clausal structure   147
      3.2.2.4 Word order   147
   3.2.3 The indirect object (Ana-Maria Iorga Mihail)   148
      3.2.3.1 Characteristics   148
      3.2.3.2 The indirect object realized as a pronominal clitic   152
      3.2.3.3 Case marking vs. prepositional marking by *la* 'to'   153
      3.2.3.4 Indirect object clitic doubling   154
      3.2.3.5 The indirect object realized as a relative clause   156
      3.2.3.6 Word order   157
   3.2.4 The prepositional object (Dana Niculescu)   157
      3.2.4.1 Characteristics   157
      3.2.4.2 Configurations with the prepositional object   158
3.3 Predicative complements   159
   3.3.1 The subjective predicative complement (Adina Dragomirescu)   160
      3.3.1.1 Characteristics   160
      3.3.1.2 Realizations   161
      3.3.1.3 Word order   165
   3.3.2 The objective predicative complement (Gabriela Pană Dindelegan)   166
      3.3.2.1 Characteristics   166
      3.3.2.2 Realizations   167
      3.3.2.3 Word order   168
3.4 Constructions involving overall clausal structure   169
   3.4.1 Passive and impersonal constructions. *By*-phrases (Adina Dragomirescu)   169
      3.4.1.1 Two types of passive constructions   169
      3.4.1.2 Impersonal constructions   173

3.4.2 Reflexive constructions (Andra Vasilescu) 174
 3.4.2.1 Constructions with syntactic reflexives 174
 3.4.2.2 Constructions with reflexive lexical formatives 178
 3.4.2.3 Constructions with reflexive lexico-grammatical formatives 178
 3.4.2.4 Constructions with reflexive grammatical formatives 179
 3.4.2.5 Reflexive doubling 179
3.4.3 Reciprocal constructions (Andra Vasilescu) 179
 3.4.3.1 Lexical reciprocals 180
 3.4.3.2 Iconic reciprocals 180
 3.4.3.3 The reflexive clitic device 181
 3.4.3.4 The reciprocal pronoun device 182
 3.4.3.5 The redundant device 182
3.4.4 The possessive dative structure. The possessive object (Dana Niculescu) 183
 3.4.4.1 Characteristics 183
 3.4.4.2 The variety of possessive relations encoded by the possessive dative 183
 3.4.4.3 The verbal host 185
 3.4.4.4 Optional vs. obligatory possessive dative clitic 186
 3.4.4.5 Doubling 187
 3.4.4.6 The possessee DP 188
 3.4.4.7 Possessive dative clitic vs. possessive adjective / genitive DP 188
 3.4.4.8 The possessive object 189
3.5 Complex predicates (Adina Dragomirescu) 191
 3.5.1 Definition 191
 3.5.2 Complex predicates with obligatory subject control and obligatory clitic climbing 191
  3.5.2.1 Structures containing a mood and tense auxiliary plus a participle / bare-infinitive 191
  3.5.2.2 The structure *putea* 'can' plus bare-infinitive 194
  3.5.2.3 The structure modal / aspectual verb plus *de*-supine 196
 3.5.3 Complex predicates with subject raising and agreement 197
 3.5.4 Complex predicate-like structures with the subjunctive 200
Conclusions 201

4 Non-finite Verb Forms and Non-finite Clauses 204
 4.1 General features (Gabriela Pană Dindelegan) 204
  4.1.1 Similarities with finite forms 204
  4.1.2 Differences from finite forms. Are non-finite forms mixed categories? 206

4.1.3 Ambiguous non-finite heads 209
4.1.4 The status of the subjunctive 210
4.2 The infinitive (Gabriela Pană Dindelegan) 211
    4.2.1 Mixed marking, suffixal and analytic 211
        4.2.1.1 Five infinitive suffixes: *-a, -ea, -e, -i, -î* 211
        4.2.1.2 The proclitic A as an inflectional marker 212
        4.2.1.3 The DE A sequence 214
    4.2.2 The verbal infinitive vs. the nominal infinitive 215
    4.2.3 The distribution and the internal structure of the non-finite infinitival clause 216
        4.2.3.1 A-infinitival constructions. Syntactic patterns 216
        4.2.3.2 The internal structure of the A-infinitival clause 217
        4.2.3.3 Bare infinitival constructions 218
    4.2.4 Infinitive vs. perfect infinitive 220
    4.2.5 The replacement of the infinitive by the subjunctive 221
4.3 The participle (Gabriela Pană Dindelegan) 222
    4.3.1 Grammatical marking: weak vs. strong participles 223
    4.3.2 The distribution and agreement of the participle 226
        4.3.2.1 The participle as a tense and mood formative 226
        4.3.2.2 The participle as a passive voice formative 226
        4.3.2.3 Participial constructions 227
    4.3.3 A sole auxiliary in the compound past tense 229
    4.3.4 The relation of the participle to the classes of verbs. Ambiguities 229
    4.3.5 Verbal vs. adjectival participles 231
        4.3.5.1 Semantic differences 231
        4.3.5.2 Syntactic differences 232
    4.3.6 Recategorizations: the substantivization and adverbialization of participles 232
4.4 The supine (Gabriela Pană Dindelegan) 233
    4.4.1 The form 234
    4.4.2 The nominal supine vs. the verbal supine 234
    4.4.3 Syntactic patterns with the verbal and the nominal-verbal supine 235
        4.4.3.1 The NP-modifier supine 236
        4.4.3.2 The supine combined with a copula verb 236
        4.4.3.3 The supine clause as a VP prepositional object 237
        4.4.3.4 The supine clause combined with modal and aspectual transitive verbs 237
        4.4.3.5 The supine depending on other transitive verbs 239
        4.4.3.6 The supine clause in impersonal structures 239

                4.4.3.7   Tough-constructions   240
                4.4.3.8   The adjunct supine   241
                4.4.3.9   The supine clause in combination with an adjectival head   241
                4.4.3.10 The 'hanging theme' supine   243
                4.4.3.11 The supine in imperative sentences   243
        4.4.4   The competition between supine, infinitive, and subjunctive   244
    4 5 The gerund (present participle) (Irina Nicula)   245
        4.5.1   Inflectional marking. The structure of the gerund form   245
        4.5.2   The verbal gerund vs. the adjectival gerund   246
        4.5.3   The relation between the verbal gerund and the finite form of the verb   247
        4.5.4   The distribution and functions of the gerund   247
                4.5.4.1   The gerund as a formative   247
                4.5.4.2   The non-finite gerund clause as an adjunct   248
                4.5.4.3   The non-finite gerund clause as a modifier   249
                4.5.4.4   The non-finite gerund clause as an argument   249
                4.5.4.5   Coordinated gerund clauses   249
                4.5.4.6   The gerund construction as a secondary predicate   249
                4.5.4.7   Parenthetical gerund constructions   251
        4.5.5   The ambiguity of the gerund   251
        4.5.6   The internal structure of the non-finite gerund clause   251
        4.5.7   The recategorization of gerund forms   252
Conclusions   253

5 Nouns and Noun Phrases   255
    5.1 Noun morphology   255
        5.1.1   Three genders: masculine, feminine, and neuter (Isabela Nedelcu)   255
                5.1.1.1   The marking of genders   255
                5.1.1.2   The position of the neuter   256
                5.1.1.3   Gender-changing and epicene nouns   258
        5.1.2   Countable and uncountable nouns (Isabela Nedelcu)   258
                5.1.2.1   Plural inflectional endings   258
                5.1.2.2   Alternations in the marking of number distinctions   259
                5.1.2.3   Double plural forms   260
                5.1.2.4   Invariable nouns   260
                5.1.2.5   *Singularia tantum* and *pluralia tantum*   260
        5.1.3   Case forms   261
                5.1.3.1   The nominative and the accusative (Isabela Nedelcu)   261
                5.1.3.2   Genitive and dative case-marking (Camelia Stan)   262
                5.1.3.3   The marking of the vocative (Isabela Nedelcu)   272

xiv *Detailed Contents and Author Attributions*

      5.1.4   Inflectional classes (Isabela Nedelcu)   273
            5.1.4.1   Inflectional subclasses associated with the masculine gender   274
            5.1.4.2   Inflectional subclasses associated with the feminine gender   275
            5.1.4.3   Inflectional subclasses associated with the neuter gender   276
      5.1.5   Nouns with irregular inflection (Isabela Nedelcu)   277
      5.1.6   The inflection of compound nouns (Isabela Nedelcu)   278
  5.2   Semantic-grammatical classes of nouns (Isabela Nedelcu)   278
      5.2.1   Proper names vs. common nouns   279
      5.2.2   Mass nouns   280
      5.2.3   Abstract nouns   281
      5.2.4   Collective nouns   282
      5.2.5   Relational nouns   282
      5.2.6   Deverbal and deadjectival nouns   283
      5.2.7   Picture nouns   284
  5.3   The structure of the nominal phrase   285
      5.3.1   Determiners   285
            5.3.1.1   The enclitic definite article. The proclitic indefinite article (Camelia Stan)   285
            5.3.1.2   Demonstratives (Alexandru Nicolae)   294
            5.3.1.3   Alternative and identity determiners (Alexandru Nicolae)   300
            5.3.1.4   The determiner CEL (Alexandru Nicolae)   309
            5.3.1.5   Polydefinite structures (Alexandru Nicolae)   318
      5.3.2   Quantifiers (Camelia Stan)   319
            5.3.2.1   Numerals   319
            5.3.2.2   Indefinite and negative quantifiers   328
            5.3.2.3   Other quantifiers   330
      5.3.3   Means of encoding nominal phrase internal possession (Alexandru Nicolae)   335
            5.3.3.1   Possessive adjectives   335
            5.3.3.2   The possessive affix   341
            5.3.3.3   The adnominal possessive clitic   343
            5.3.3.4   The possessive relation marked by the preposition DE   347
            5.3.3.5   Possessor deletion by the definite article   348
      5.3.4   The arguments of the noun (Isabela Nedelcu)   349
            5.3.4.1   The arguments of deverbal and deadjectival nouns   349
            5.3.4.2   The arguments of picture nouns   352
            5.3.4.3   The arguments of relational nouns   353

            5.3.5   Restrictive and non-restrictive modifiers   355
                    5.3.5.1   Restrictive modifiers (Camelia Stan)   355
                    5.3.5.2   Non-restrictive modifiers (Camelia Stan)   360
                    5.3.5.3   The inversion pattern [Adjective + *DE* + Noun]
                              (Ana-Maria Iorga Mihail)   365
            5.3.6   Appositions and classifiers (Raluca Brăescu)   366
                    5.3.6.1   Appositions   366
                    5.3.6.2   Classifiers and proper names   369
            5.3.7   Nominal ellipsis and the pronominalization of determiners
                    (Alexandru Nicolae)   370
                    5.3.7.1   Patterns of nominal ellipsis   370
                    5.3.7.2   The range of remnants   372
                    5.3.7.3   The form of the remnant   372
                    5.3.7.4   Focus and ellipsis   374
    Conclusions   375

6   Pronouns (Andra Vasilescu)   379
    6.1   Personal pronouns   379
            6.1.1   The paradigm   379
            6.1.2   Morphological cases   380
            6.1.3   Strong vs. clitic forms   381
                    6.1.3.1   Selection of strong vs. clitic forms   384
                    6.1.3.2   Position of strong and clitic forms   386
                    6.1.3.3   Selection of clitic variants   388
            6.1.4   Clitic clusters   392
            6.1.5   Clitic doubling   394
            6.1.6   Pronominal doubling   395
            6.1.7   Extensions of pronominal heads   395
            6.1.8   Reference: deictic, anaphoric, expletive   396
                    6.1.8.1   Deictic uses   396
                    6.1.8.2   Expletive uses   398
    6.2   Reflexive pronouns   399
    6.3   'Politeness' pronouns   401
            6.3.1   The paradigm   401
            6.3.2   'Politeness' pronouns as social deictics   402
    6.4   Pronominal intensifiers (emphatic pronouns)   404
    6.5   Reciprocal pronouns   407
    Conclusions   408

7 Adjectives and Adjectival Phrases (Raluca Brăescu) 410
   7.1 Characteristics 410
   7.2 Four inflectional classes of adjectives 411
   7.3 The internal make-up of adjectives 414
   7.4 Levels of intensity and degree markers 415
   7.5 Three semantic classes of adjectives 417
      7.5.1 Qualifying adjectives 417
      7.5.2 Relative adjectives 418
      7.5.3 Reference-modifying adjectives 419
   7.6 The structure of the adjectival phrase (AP) 420
      7.6.1 Modifiers 420
      7.6.2 Complements 422
         7.6.2.1 The complement realized as a dative nominal 422
         7.6.2.2 The complement realized as a genitive nominal 423
         7.6.2.3 The complement realized as a PP 424
         7.6.2.4 The direct object 424
         7.6.2.5 The clausal complement 425
         7.6.2.6 The comparative complement 425
      7.6.3 Adjuncts 425
   7.7 The syntactic positions of APs 426
      7.7.1 The adjective as a modifier 426
         7.7.1.1 Postnominal adjectives 427
         7.7.1.2 Prenominal adjectives 427
         7.7.1.3 Free-ordered adjectives 428
      7.7.2 The adjective as a predicative complement 428
      7.7.3 The adjective as an adjunct 430
   7.8 Nominal ellipsis and the substantivization of adjectives 430
Conclusions 431

8 Adverbs and Adverbial Phrases (Carmen Mîrzea Vasile, Andreea Dinică) 432
   8.1 The form of the adverbs 432
      8.1.1 Simple forms 432
      8.1.2 Suffixed forms 432
      8.1.3 Compound forms 434
      8.1.4 Adverbs homophonous with words in other classes 436
         8.1.4.1 Adverbs homophonous with adjectives 436
         8.1.4.2 Adverbs homophonous with verbal forms 436
         8.1.4.3 Nouns with adverbial value 437

       8.1.5   Fixed collocations and adverbial expressions   438
       8.1.6   Non-lexical adverbial formatives   439
   8.2   Adverbial grading   439
   8.3   Semantic classes of adverbs   440
   8.4   The structure of the adverbial phrase (AdvP)   442
       8.4.1   AdvP-internal modifiers   442
       8.4.2   Complements of the adverbial head   442
           8.4.2.1   Prepositional complements of the adverbial head   442
           8.4.2.2   Indirect objects of the adverbial head   443
           8.4.2.3   Dative clitics as indirect objects   443
           8.4.2.4   The comparative complement of the adverbial head   444
       8.4.3   The adjuncts of the adverb   444
   8.5   The external syntax of the adverbial phrase   444
       8.5.1   Adverbs subcategorized by the verbal head   444
       8.5.2   Clausal modal adverbs   445
       8.5.3   *Wh*-adverbs   446
       8.5.4   Adverbs as complements of prepositions and as NP modifiers   446
       8.5.5   Focusing adverbs   446
   8.6   The order of adverbs in the sentence   447
       8.6.1   Adverbial clitics   447
       8.6.2   Manner adverbs   448
       8.6.3   Setting adverbs   449
Conclusions   450

9 Prepositions and Prepositional Phrases (Isabela Nedelcu)   451
   9.1   Simple, compound, and collocated prepositions   451
   9.2   Lexical vs. functional prepositions. Subcategorized prepositions   452
       9.2.1   Lexical prepositions   452
       9.2.2   Functional prepositions   454
       9.2.3   Subcategorized prepositions   457
   9.3   Prepositional phrases   458
       9.3.1   The structure of prepositional phrases   458
       9.3.2   Restrictions imposed by the preposition to its noun complement   458
           9.3.2.1   Case assignment (accusative, genitive, and dative)   458
           9.3.2.2   Restrictions on the usage of the article   459
           9.3.2.3   Number restrictions   461
       9.3.3   Other constituents within the PP   462
   9.4   Parallel forms: with and without an article-like ending   463
Conclusions   465

10 The Structure of Complex Clauses. Subordination 466

- 10.1 Argument clauses (Mihaela Gheorghe) 466
  - 10.1.1 Complementizers 466
    - 10.1.1.1 The complementizers *că* and *să* 467
    - 10.1.1.2 The complementizer *ca...să* 469
    - 10.1.1.3 The complementizers *cum că*, *precum că*, and *cum de* 470
    - 10.1.1.4 The complementizers *dacă* and *de* 471
  - 10.1.2 Argument clauses 473
- 10.2 Conjunctions and clausal adjuncts (Dana Manea) 473
  - 10.2.1 Clausal adjuncts 473
  - 10.2.2 Specific and non-specific subordinating conjunctions 474
    - 10.2.2.1 Clausal adjuncts introduced by specific subordinators 474
    - 10.2.2.2 Clausal adjuncts introduced by non-specific subordinators 475
    - 10.2.2.3 Clausal adjuncts introduced by the subordinating marker *să* 476
    - 10.2.2.4 The structure of complex subordinators 477
  - 10.2.3 Subordinators, prepositions, and focusing particles 477
    - 10.2.3.1 Conjunctions and prepositions 477
    - 10.2.3.2 Conjunctions and focusing particles 478
  - 10.2.4 Clausal adjuncts with covert subordinators 478
  - 10.2.5 Special patterns 478
    - 10.2.5.1 Temporal adjuncts 478
    - 10.2.5.2 Reason adjuncts 479
    - 10.2.5.3 Purpose adjuncts 479
    - 10.2.5.4 Conditional and concessive constructions 480
    - 10.2.5.5 Result adjuncts 481
    - 10.2.5.6 Speech act-related adjuncts 481
  - 10.2.6 Adjuncts with constituent deletion 482
  - 10.2.7 Clausal adjuncts and connective adjuncts 482
  - 10.2.8 Clausal adjuncts word order 483
- 10.3 Relative clauses (relative arguments and relative adjuncts) (Mihaela Gheorghe) 483
  - 10.3.1 Syntactic types of relative constructions 483
  - 10.3.2 Indirect interrogative constructions 486
  - 10.3.3 Relative infinitival constructions 487
  - 10.3.4 Pseudo-cleft constructions 488
  - 10.3.5 The inventory of *wh*-words 489
  - 10.3.6 Features of *wh*-movement in Romanian. Pied-piping 496

10.4 Secondary predication (Blanca Croitor) 497
　10.4.1 General properties 497
　10.4.2 Syntactic and semantic types of SPs 498
　　10.4.2.1 Depictive vs. resultative SPs 498
　　10.4.2.2 Complement vs. adjunct SPs 500
　10.4.3 Main predicates which accept SPs 500
　10.4.4 Types of constituents occurring as SPs 501
10.5 Comparative constructions (Rodica Zafiu) 503
　10.5.1 Comparatives of inequality and equality 503
　　10.5.1.1 Comparison of inequality 504
　　10.5.1.2 Comparison of equality 504
　　10.5.1.3 The structure of the comparative complement 504
　　10.5.1.4 The comparators 506
　　10.5.1.5 Word order 508
　　10.5.1.6 Semantic aspects 510
　10.5.2 Other comparative structures 510
Conclusions 511

11 Coordination (Blanca Croitor) 514
　11.1 Semantic (and logical) types of coordination 514
　　11.1.1 Conjunctive coordination 514
　　　11.1.1.1 Conjunctive coordinators 514
　　　11.1.1.2 Joint vs. disjoint readings of coordinated conjunctive NPs or DPs 515
　　　11.1.1.3 Pseudo-coordination 516
　　11.1.2 Disjunctive coordination 517
　　11.1.3 Adversative coordination 517
　　11.1.4 Conclusive coordination 520
　11.2 Restrictions on the conjuncts 521
　11.3 The structure of the coordinated phrase 522
　　11.3.1 Number of conjuncts 522
　　11.3.2 Juxtaposition 523
　　11.3.3 Asymmetry between conjuncts 523
　11.4 Co-occurrence of coordinators 523
　11.5 Ambiguous readings 524
　11.6 Coordination and ellipsis 525
Conclusions 525

12 Agreement (Blanca Croitor)   526
12.1 DP-internal agreement   526
12.2 Subject–predicate agreement   528
12.2.1 Proper names   528
12.2.2 Inclusive words   528
12.2.3 'Politeness' pronouns   529
12.2.4 Partitive DPs   529
12.2.5 Measure DPs   530
12.2.6 Qualitative DPs   531
12.2.7 Agreement in copular sentences   532
12.2.7.1 Specificational sentences   532
12.2.7.2 Pseudo-cleft sentences   532
12.3 Agreement with coordinated DPs   532
12.3.1 Predicative agreement   532
12.3.1.1 Number agreement   532
12.3.1.2 Gender agreement   533
12.3.1.3 Person agreement   534
12.3.2 Adjectival agreement   534
12.4 Anaphoric agreement   535
Conclusions   536

13 Sentence Organization and Discourse Phenomena   537
13.1 Sentence types (Andra Vasilescu)   537
13.1.1 Declarative sentences   537
13.1.2 Interrogative sentences   539
13.1.2.1 Polar interrogatives   539
13.1.2.2 *Wh*-questions   540
13.1.2.3 Alternative questions   544
13.1.2.4 Tag-questions   545
13.1.2.5 Echo questions   545
13.1.3 Imperative sentences   546
13.1.4 Exclamative sentences and exclamations   548
13.2 Reported speech (Margareta Manu Magda)   551
13.2.1 Specific features   551
13.2.2 Direct speech   551
13.2.3 Indirect speech   553
13.2.4 Changes related to the conversion of direct speech into indirect speech   553

     13.2.4.1 Changes at discourse levels 553
     13.2.4.2 Morphological changes 554
     13.2.4.3 Syntactic changes 555
   13.2.5 Intermediate structures between direct speech and indirect speech 557
 13.3 Negation (Dana Manea) 558
   13.3.1 Negative words 558
   13.3.2 Sentential negation 558
     13.3.2.1 Negative markers within VPs containing clitics 560
     13.3.2.2 Negative markers in complex predicates 560
   13.3.3 Constituent negation 561
   13.3.4 Multiple negation and negative concord 562
   13.3.5 The negative pro-sentence 564
   13.3.6 Covert negation 565
   13.3.7 False negation 565
     13.3.7.1 Double negation 565
     13.3.7.2 Expletive negation 566
     13.3.7.3 Other structures with negative markers 567
 13.4 Information structure (Rodica Zafiu) 568
   13.4.1 Word order 568
   13.4.2 Topicalizing devices 570
     13.4.2.1 Fronting / topicalization 570
     13.4.2.2 Left dislocation 571
     13.4.2.3 Hanging topic 572
     13.4.2.4 Right dislocation 573
   13.4.3 Contrastive topic constructions 573
   13.4.4 Rhematization / foregrounding by pseudo-cleft structures 574
   13.4.5 Focalization 574
 13.5 Modality and evidentiality (Rodica Zafiu) 575
   13.5.1 Verbal moods 575
   13.5.2 Modal verbs 575
     13.5.2.1 The verb *putea* 'be able, can' 576
     13.5.2.2 The verb *trebui* 'must' 578
     13.5.2.3 Other verbs with modal and evidential meaning 580
   13.5.3 Modal adverbials 581
   13.5.4 Other modal markers 583
   13.5.5 'Harmonic' and 'disharmonic' combinations 583
   13.5.6 Evidential markers 584

13.6 Anaphora (Rodica Zafiu)   584
  13.6.1 Anaphorics   584
  13.6.2 Syntactically controlled anaphora and discourse anaphora   585
  13.6.3 Referential anaphora and semantic anaphora   587
  13.6.4 Anaphorics on the grammaticalization cline   589
13.7 Vocative phrases and address (Margareta Manu Magda)   590
  13.7.1 Syntactic particularities of the vocative case   590
  13.7.2 Pragmatic–semantic relations between vocative and other sentence constituents   592
  13.7.3 The expressive function of the vocative   592
  13.7.4 Forms of address   593
Conclusions   596

14 Derivational Morphology (Blanca Croitor)   599
  14.1 Suffixation. Types of suffixes and derivatives   599
    14.1.1 Verb formation   599
      14.1.1.1 Inventory of verbal suffixes   599
      14.1.1.2 Semantic values of the bases and of the derivatives   600
    14.1.2 Noun formation   600
      14.1.2.1 Abstract nouns   600
      14.1.2.2 Nominal gender suffixes   601
      14.1.2.3 Collectives   602
      14.1.2.4 Diminutives   602
      14.1.2.5 Augmentatives   602
      14.1.2.6 Suffixes with other semantic values   603
    14.1.3 Adjective formation   603
    14.1.4 Adverb formation   604
    14.1.5 Semantic relations between suffixes or derivatives   604
  14.2 Prefixation   604
  14.3 Parasynthetic derivation   605
  14.4 Back-formation   605
Conclusions   606

15 Inflectional and Derivational Morphophonological Alternations (Camelia Stan, Mona Moldoveanu Pologea)   607
  15.1 Inflectional alternations   607
    15.1.1 Inventory   607
    15.1.2 Characteristics of alternations   610
  15.2 Derivational alternations   611
Conclusions   611

16 Compounding (Andreea Dinică) 612
    16.1 Types of compounds 612
        16.1.1 Syntactic compounds 612
        16.1.2 Compound lexemes 613
    16.2 Syntactic patterns of compounding in contemporary Romanian 613
        16.2.1 Noun output compounds 613
        16.2.2 Adjective output compounds 617
        16.2.3 Compound lexemes patterns 618
    16.3 Neo-classical compounds 619
Conclusions 619

Sources 621
References 624
Index 649

Preface

The Grammar of Romanian is a descriptive grammar of contemporary literary Romanian. It emphasizes the specific features of Romanian among the Romance languages. The book is intended for use by academic linguists (including advanced students) and specialists in Romance linguistics, as well as advanced learners of Romanian. The book's descriptive framework is modern (in conception, terminology, topics, and bibliography). However, the book avoids overly technical methods in order to be accessible to a wide range of readers. It is neither exhaustive (for reasons of space), nor excessively detailed and should be regarded as an 'essential grammar', covering all the descriptive aspects that are significant and specific to Romanian. The book is based on two very recent Romanian grammars— *Gramatica limbii române* (GALR), Romanian Academy Press, Bucharest, 2008 and *Gramatica de bază a limbii române* (GBLR), Univers Enciclopedic Press, Bucharest, 2010. The former is an academic grammar, and the latter a modern synthesis of it.

As the book is mainly descriptive and its approach synchronic, we have decided to separate the descriptive part from historical and comparative information, as well as from information regarding the present-day usage. Such information will be signalled by the symbols **H**—**history**, **C**—**comparison**, **U**—**usage**, and by specific text formatting. Thus, readers who are interested only in the description of the present-day standard language may choose to read the actual text of the grammar only. Linguists curious about fundamental aspects of the evolution of certain phenomena, as well as aspects of comparative and linguistic variation issues, should consult the special note areas. The historical notes (**H**) focus on phenomena which are specific to Romanian and which are of special diachronic interest to linguists. Comparisons with Latin, Romance, and Balkan languages, and less often with other languages (**C**), are derived from studies in Romance linguistics and in linguistic typology. Again, our goal in these comparisons is to highlight the specific features of Romanian. The book focuses on the standard language. However, linguistic variation (either stylistic or dialectal) as well as aspects of the dynamics of the contemporary language (tendencies of contemporary Romanian, manifested through the infringement of standard norms) are illustrated separately, in the text notes on usage (**U**).

Certain phenomena could have been discussed in many chapters or might even have formed distinct chapters. For example, a special chapter could have been dedicated to deixis, but, for the purposes of economy, we preferred to refer to deixis in the chapters dedicated to pronouns and tense. Word order could also have formed a distinct chapter, but references to word order have been made separately for each component of the syntactic projections (for example, adjectival modifiers placement in the NP, the direct / indirect object placement in the VP, etc.). There is in addition a special discussion of information structure in Section 13.4.

The Grammar of Romanian is a collective work, written by the members of the Grammar Department of the 'Iorgu Iordan—Al. Rosetti' Institute of Linguistics of the Romanian Academy. The editor has been particularly responsible for the conception and organization of the overall structure, as well as the harmonization of the different scientific approaches and of stylistic preferences. The exact contribution of each individual author is specified in the detailed contents. We would like to thank Adina Dragomirescu and Irina Nicula for their hard work in assembling and harmonizing the format of the entire text.

We wish to express our gratitude to Professor Martin Maiden, who, with great generosity and competence, has offered valuable solutions to many questions and puzzles that arose along the way and who has kept a watchful eye on the final revision of the text. His suggestions on content and language have been extremely useful, allowing us, we hope, to improve the final version of the text. We owe an enormous debt of gratitude to OUP's Linguistics Editor Julia Steer for her interest in this line of research, and to Production Editor Victoria Hart for her very competent and useful editorial assistance.

We take full responsibility for any remaining inaccuracies, errors, or inconsistencies.

February 2012   Gabriela Pană Dindelegan

Notes on Style and Format

- Most of the examples have been constructed by the authors, with the exception of those which belong to earlier (older) stages of the language. The inventory of old texts—each one with the period of their dating—is given in the *Sources* at the end of the book.
- Example numbering is reset in each chapter.
- The examples have interlinear glossing and translations; the glosses are not exhaustive—they are adequate for the immediate purpose of the example.
- The cross-referencing system of the book is rich; there are cross-references from one (sub)chapter to another.
- The International Phonetic Alphabet (IPA) has been used in phonetic and phonological transcriptions.

Abbreviations and Conventions

1 ABBREVIATIONS AND CONVENTIONS

1	first person
2	second person
3	third person
a.o.	among others
a.s.o.	and so on
Acc	accusative
Act	active
Adj	adjective
Adv	adverb(ial)
AdvP	adverbial phrase
AP	adjectival phrase
Arom	Aromanian
Art	article
Aug	Augmentative
Aux	auxiliary verb
Bg	Bulgarian
c.	*circa*
Cat	Catalan
Cl	clitic
Coll	collective
Comp	complementizer
ConjP	conjunction phrase (coordinated phrase)
CP	complementizer phrase
CRom	contemporary Romanian
Dat	dative
Def	definite
D	determiner
Dem	demonstrative
Dim	diminutive
DO	direct object
DP	determiner phrase
Engl	English
F	feminine
FinP	finiteness phrase
ForceP	force phrase
Fr	French
Fut	future
Gen	genitive
Ger	gerund / gerundive

Germ	German
Gr	Greek
I	inflection
Imp	imperative
Imperf	imperfect
Impers	impersonal
Ind	indicative
Inf	infinitive
Interj	interjection
Intr	intransitive
IO	indirect object
IP	inflection(al) phrase
It	Italian
Lat	Latin
M	masculine
Mid-Pol	mid-polite
N	noun
Neg	negative
NegV̄O	Negative (marker)–Verb–Object word order
Neut	neuter
Nom	nominative
NP	noun phrase
Nr	Norwegian
Num	numeral
O	object
OPC	objective predicative complement
ORom	old Romanian
P	preposition
Part	partitive
Pass	passive
Perf	perfect
Pl	plural
Pluperf	pluperfect
PO	prepositional object
Pol	polite
PP	prepositional phrase
Pple	participle
Pres	present (tense)
pro	null subject pronoun
PRO	null controlled subject of non-finite forms
Prov	Provençal (= Occitan)
PS	simple past (Fr. *passé simple*)
Ptg	Portuguese
Q	quantifier
QP	quantifier phrase
Refl	reflexive
Rom	Romanian
Ru	Russian

S	subject
S$_A$	the subject of agentive verbs
S$_o$	the subject of non-agentive verbs, occurring in postverbal position
SecO	secondary object
Sg	singular
Sl	Slavic
SOV	Subject–Object–Verb word order
SP	secondary predication
Sp	Spanish
SPC	subjective predicative complement
Spec (, XP)	specifier (of XP)
Subj	subjunctive
Sup	supine
s.v.	*sub voce*
SVO	Subject–Verb–Object word order
TopP	topic phrase
Tk	Turkish
Tr	transitive
V	verb
Voc	vocative
VOS	Verb–Object–Subject word order
VP	verb phrase
VSO	Verb–Subject–Object word order

2 FUNCTIONAL / FREESTANDING MORPHEMES WORDS SPECIFIC TO ROMANIAN

(Given in small capitals both in the text and in the interlinear glosses)

A	functional preposition
A$_{INF}$	marker of infinitive
AL	freestanding syntactic marker of the genitive
CEL	freestanding definite determiner
DE	functional preposition
DE$_{SUP}$	marker of the supine
LUI	freestanding proclitic morpheme of genitive and dative
PE	functional preposition, marker of the direct object
SĂ$_{SUBJ}$	freestanding subjunctive inflectional marker

3 GLOSSING CONVENTIONS; SYMBOLS USED IN EXAMPLES

- \- separates morphs and the corresponding glosses (used in morph-by-morph segmentation)
- . separates multiple glosses of a single morph or word form (used when morph-by-morph segmentation is not necessary); separates syllables
- = separates a clitic from its host

≡	equivalent; marks syncretism (NOM≡ACC indicates that the nominative form is syncretic with the accusative form)
≠	different
/	choice / optionality
//	ambiguous interpretation
[xxxx]	the component deleted in ellipsis
#	prosodically isolated
∅	null argument; zero inflectional ending; the negative term of an alternation
[e]	empty position
t	trace (of movement)
n-word	negative word
wh-word/phrase	word / group extracted and moved in interrogative and relative clauses
*	unattested or ungrammatical example
?	dubious form or usage
(x)	optional element: the example has the same grammatical status with or without X included
(*x)	the example is good without X, but bad when it is included
*(x)	the example is bad unless X is included
SMALL CAPS in examples	contrastive focus / contrastive stress / phrasal stress or for citing Latin forms.

The Contributors

Raluca Brăescu is a Junior Researcher at the Iorgu Iordan—Alexandru Rosetti Institute of Linguistics of the Romanian Academy and Lecturer in Romanian Language and Linguistics at the University of Bucharest, Faculty of Letters.

Blanca Croitor is a Researcher at the Iorgu Iordan—Alexandru Rosetti Institute of Linguistics of the Romanian Academy.

Andreea Dinică is a Researcher at the Iorgu Iordan—Alexandru Rosetti Institute of Linguistics of the Romanian Academy.

Adina Dragomirescu is a Researcher at the Iorgu Iordan—Alexandru Rosetti Institute of Linguistics of the Romanian Academy and Lecturer in Linguistics at the University of Bucharest, Faculty of Letters.

Mihaela Gheorghe is a Professor of Linguistics at the Transilvania University of Braşov and Researcher at the Iorgu Iordan—Alexandru Rosetti Institute of Linguistics of the Romanian Academy.

Ana-Maria Iorga Mihail is a Junior Researcher at the Iorgu Iordan—Alexandru Rosetti Institute of Linguistics of the Romanian Academy.

Dana Manea is a Senior Researcher at the Iorgu Iordan—Alexandru Rosetti Institute of Linguistics of the Romanian Academy.

Margareta Manu Magda is a Researcher at the Iorgu Iordan—Alexandru Rosetti Institute of Linguistics of the Romanian Academy.

Carmen Mîrzea Vasile is a Researcher at the Iorgu Iordan—Alexandru Rosetti Institute of Linguistics of the Romanian Academy and Teaching Assistant in Romanian Language and Linguistics at the University of Bucharest, Faculty of Letters.

Mona Moldoveanu Pologea is a former Junior Researcher at the Iorgu Iordan—Alexandru Rosetti Institute of Linguistics of the Romanian Academy.

Isabela Nedelcu is Lecturer in Linguistics at the University of Bucharest, Faculty of Letters and Junior Researcher at the Iorgu Iordan—Alexandru Rosetti Institute of Linguistics of the Romanian Academy.

Alexandru Nicolae is a Junior Researcher at the Iorgu Iordan—Alexandru Rosetti Institute of Linguistics of the Romanian Academy and Teaching Assistant in Romanian Language and Linguistics at the University of Bucharest.

Irina Nicula is a Junior Researcher at the Iorgu Iordan—Alexandru Rosetti Institute of Linguistics of the Romanian Academy.

Dana Niculescu is Assistant Lecturer in Romanian Language and Linguistics at the University of Amsterdam.

Gabriela Pană Dindelegan is Emeritus Professor of Linguistics at the University of Bucharest, Faculty of Letters and a Senior Researcher at the Iorgu Iordan—Alexandru Rosetti

Institute of Linguistics of the Romanian Academy. She is a Corresponding Member of the Romanian Academy.

Camelia Stan is Associate Professor of Linguistics at the University of Bucharest, Faculty of Letters and a Senior Researcher at the Iorgu Iordan—Alexandru Rosetti Institute of Linguistics of the Romanian Academy.

Andra Vasilescu (Șerbănescu) is Professor of Linguistics and Communication at the University of Bucharest, Faculty of Letters and a Senior Researcher at the Iorgu Iordan—Alexandru Rosetti Institute of Linguistics of the Romanian Academy.

Rodica Zafiu is Professor of Linguistics at the University of Bucharest, Faculty of Letters and Senior Researcher at the Iorgu Iordan—Alexandru Rosetti Institute of Linguistics of the Romanian Academy.

Translators: Alexandru Nicolae (Ch. 1; 4.3; 5; 6; 15), Irina Nicula (Ch. 2; 4; 10.2; 13.3), Dana Niculescu (Ch. 3.1– 3.4.1; 3.4.4; 3.5; 9; 10.5; 13.4–13.6), Blanca Croitor (Ch. 10.4; 11; 12; 14), Andreea Dinică (Ch. 8; 16), Mihaela Gheorghe (Ch. 10.1; 10.3), Margareta Manu Magda (Ch. 13.2; 13.7), Andra Vasilescu (Ch. 3.4.2–3.4.3; 6; 13.3).

Translation revised by: Alexandru Nicolae, Irina Nicula, Dana Niculescu.

1

Introduction

This chapter presents, in the first part, fundamental data on the history of Romanian, and in the last part, the main features of the phonological system of Romanian and the characteristics of the Romanian writing.

1.1 ROMANIAN—A BRIEF PRESENTATION

1.1.1 Where Romanian is spoken

As an official and main language, Romanian is spoken in Eastern Europe, and particularly in Romania and in the Republic of Moldova. As a minority language, it is spoken by speakers that form compact and stable communities of Romanians in the countries surrounding Romania (Ukraine, Hungary, Bulgaria, and Serbia), and by the large Romanian diaspora, spread around the world (Europe, America, Asia, Australia, Africa).

As for the south-Danubian Romanian-speaking area (Aromanian / Macedo-Romanian, Megleno-Romanian, and Istro-Romanian), there are compact areas in Greece, Albania, Bosnia and Herzegovina, and Croatia. The approximate number of Aromanian speakers is 600,000–800,000, of Megleno-Romanian speakers is 5,000–8,000; the Istro-Romanian speakers are the fewest, c.500 (Saramandu 2008: 168).

In 2005, the demographic weight of the Romanian languages was assumed by the Latin Union (an international organization of nations that use Romance languages) to be about 28,000,000 speakers, of whom 24,000,000 are native speakers and represent 0.5 per cent of the world's population (Golopenția 2009: 74; Sala 2010: 864 gives an approximate total of 29,000 000 speakers of Romanian; Alkire and Rosen 2010: 2 record 23,400,000 native speakers). In Europe, Romanian is rated as a medium level language, occupying tenth position among the thirty-seven official languages of the European states, being preceded by English, Russian, German, French, Turkish, Italian, Ukrainian, Spanish, and Portuguese (ELR: 617).

1.1.2 The genealogical definition of Romanian

Romanian is a Romance language, belonging to the Balkan-Romance group of languages; it is the only surviving Eastern-European Romance language. 'Romanian is the Latin language spoken uninterruptedly in the Eastern part of the Roman Empire, consisting of the Romanized Danubian provinces (Dacia, South Pannonia, Dardania, Moesia Superior, and Inferior), from the moment Latin penetrated these provinces until our times' (Rosetti 1986: 75).

Romanian is the descendant of spoken Danubian Latin, the vernacular variant of Latin that emerged as a consequence of the Romanization of the Balkan Peninsula (where the

Romance presence dates back to 229 BC) and of Dacia (which was under Roman domination between 106 AD and 275 AD). Danubian Latin is attested in the almost 3,000 Latin inscriptions discovered in the territory of old Dacia, to which may be added another 3,000 or so inscriptions discovered in the two Moesian regions (Fischer 1985).

1.1.3 The time and place of the emergence of Romanian

The age of formation was between the 7th and the 8th centuries (Rosetti 1986: 323) or between the 6th and the 8th centuries (Sala 2010: 842); it ended before the beginning of the Slavic influence. The most important argument for this periodization is the fact that old Slavic elements (which started to penetrate the language after the 8th century) are no longer subject to the phonetic transformations displayed by the inherited Latin words.

According to some researchers (Coteanu 1981: 75–6; Saramandu 2008: 79–94 and references therein), the famous phrase *torna, torna, fratre* (among the interpretations put forward, 'return, brother')—dating from the year 587 and later reproduced by two Byzantine chroniclers—in which the vocative *frat(r)e* is inconsistent with the Latin inflection, may be considered the oldest attestation of Romanian. According to other researchers (Saramandu 2008: 93), these three words have been interpreted as representing the oldest 'Balkan Romance' sample, a stage which immediately precedes the rise of the Romance idioms in the Balkan area.

As for the place where Romanian was formed, the general view commonly accepted today is that this territory was a large one, consisting of both the north and the south of the Danube (encompassing the regions Dacia and Dobrogea, Moesia Inferior and Superior, possibly Illyria, the regions between the Danube and the Balkans, more precisely, to the north of the Jireček Line, which separates the areas of Roman and Greek influence in the Balkan Peninsula) (Rosetti 1986: 75; Avram and Sala 2001: 59–66; the map of the Romanized region from the Balkan-Danubian area is given in Renzi and Andreose 2003: 296).

1.1.4 Linguistic contacts

The substratum underlying Romanian is represented by the language spoken by the Romanized native population: Thraco-Dacian, a *satem*-type Indo-European. Thraco-Dacian is not directly attested by any surviving texts; it has left only a few uncertain traces. The direct information regarding Thraco-Dacian is limited to a few sporadic notes written down by ancient authors, and also by what is found in Greek or Latin inscriptions or on coins, where a few proper names (anthroponyms, toponyms, hydronyms, and names of mountains) are attested. There are also a few glosses of Dacian medicinal plants recorded in two treaties of Greek and Latin botany and medicine; a few inscriptions, still undeciphered, have also been discovered (Russu 1981; ELR: 546, 584–5).

In order to establish the share of substratum words in Romanian, most researchers (Rosetti 1986: 205–11; Brâncuș 1983, 1995) employ comparison between Romanian and Albanian, which belongs to the same language family as Dacian. Some researchers have tried to reconstruct Thraco-Dacian elements through comparison with other old Indo-European languages.

Research has attributed to the substratum a few hydronyms and a relatively reduced inventory of words, of which only approximately ninety are certain to be of (Thraco-)Dacian origin (Brâncuş 1983; Sala 2010: 846); also, a few elements of phonetics, word formation, and morphosyntactic organization have been attributed to the substratum.

Similarly to substratum of the other Romance languages (Celtic, Iberian, Ligurian), the (Thraco-)Dacian substratum did not change the essential Latin nature of Romanian (Avram and Sala 2001: 54).

The superstratum of Romanian is represented by the old Slavic influence, whose role was significant in the history of Romanian; it is similar to the Germanic superstratum of Western Romance. The result of the Slavic influence on Romanian is a rich inventory of lexical items, together with elements of word formation, phonetics, and morphosyntax (Rosetti 1986: 261–318; Dimitrescu 1978: 88–98 and references therein).

The beginning of the Slavic influence is placed by some researchers in the 6th–7th centuries and by others later, in the 8th–9th centuries. Old Slavic ceases to influence Romanian in the 11th–12th centuries.

Other influences, in approximate chronological order, were: Hungarian, Church Slavonic, Greek in its different stages of evolution (Ancient Greek, manifested through Latin, Medieval Greek, and Modern Greek), Turkish, modern Slavic languages (Bulgarian, Serbian, Polish, Russian, and Ukrainian), dialectal (especially in Transylvania) and literary German, late classical Latin, Italian, French, and English.

The Latin structure of Romanian has not been modified by any of these external factors, all influences being limited to lexis and word formation. The non-Latin grammatical elements underwent a Latino-Romance structural treatment, being adapted to and assimilated by the Romance pattern. The few grammatical borrowings did not bring about new phenomena, but had the role of interrupting the tendencies of late Latin and, at the same time, of preserving and reviving, by external contact, certain categories and features that disappeared in other Romance areas (the preservation of the neuter gender, of two case forms, of the genitive–dative syncretism, of the inflectional marking of the vocative, etc.).

In the mid 20th century, the analysis of the Romanian literary lexis indicated the following etymological composition: inherited Latin words—20 per cent, Slavic (old Slavic, Slavonic Bulgarian, Serbian, Ukrainian, Russian)—11.5 per cent, Turkish—3.60 per cent, Hungarian—2.17 per cent, Modern Greek—2.40 per cent, Romance borrowings—43 per cent (the most: French—38.40 per cent). A similar analysis, carried out on the fundamental lexicon (approximately 2,500 words, which represent the most important words from the point of view of frequency, semantic richness, and productivity), shows a radical change in percentages: first place is occupied by words inherited from Latin, second place by Romance and classical Latin neologisms; Slavic words preserve their proportion, occupying third position.

1.1.5 The periodization of Romanian

In contrast with Western Romance, for which the transition to Romanity and the periodization of this transition can be established within somewhat more stricter boundaries given the continuity of texts, in the case of Romanian, one can only formulate plausible hypotheses, because of the lack of texts for long periods. Entire stages from the history of

Romanian are re-constructed and this is why, instead of some clear-cut limits and strict chronological boundaries, researches have more often than not proposed relative chronologies and loose limits (Ionescu-Ruxăndoiu 2010: 195).

The oldest Romanian period (also known as Common Romanian, Proto-Romanian, Primitive Romanian) is the period prior to the separation of the four Romanian dialects: a north-Danubian dialect (Daco-Romanian) and three south-Danubian dialects (Aromanian / Macedo-Romanian, Megleno-Romanian, and Istro-Romanian).

The separation began in the 10th century and continued in the 11th–12th centuries. It was triggered by the significant establishment of the Slavic population in the Balkan Peninsula and by the foundation of the South Slavic states. The 12th century is considered to be the closing date of this separation (Sala 2010: 855); this idea is supported by the fact that Hungarian loanwords are present only in the Daco-Romanian dialect.

Prior to the separation, there existed a Romanian community, responsible for the common features of the four dialects (inherited from Latin or subsequently developed), features which set Romanian apart, on the one hand, from Latin, and, on the other hand, from the other Romance languages. Among the features that individualize Romanian, common to the four dialects, one should mention at least the following: the nominal declension with two case forms in the singular feminine (*casă* 'house' Nom-Acc vs. *case* Gen-Dat), the enclisis of the definite article, the growth of the plural inflectional ending *-uri* for the neuter gender, the analytic future with an auxiliary derived from Lat. VOLO (*voi cânta* 'I will sing'), the analytic present conditional (*aş cânta* 'I would sing'), and the appearance of the vowel *ă* (Sala 2010: 855).

Given the lack of common attestations, the Common Romanian period can be examined only through comparative reconstruction.

After the 13th century, the four dialects are self standing Romanian enclaves, and have an independent and diverging evolution, which is not ruled by any common norm, a fact which led researchers to acknowledge them as autonomous Romance languages.

After the 13th century, periodization applies exclusively to the history of Daco-Romanian (north-Danubian Romanian), that is what is usually called Romanian. The following phases have been distinguished by researchers:

The first period is the ancient / archaic period (13th–16th century), also named Common Daco-Romanian; this is the period between the split of the Romanian unity and the rise of certain systematic dialectal divergences inside Daco-Romanian, the last of them being placed by researchers in the 16th century. For this period, there are only isolated and fragmentary sources, compiled from texts written in Latin, Hungarian, or Slavonic, in which there occurs a considerable number of Romanian words (for the Romanian words in Slavonic-Romanian documents, see Mihăilă 1974). For this period, the analysis of the few direct sources is supplemented by means of reconstruction (Vasiliu and Ionescu-Ruxăndoiu 1986).

The old period comprises the 16th–18th centuries; more exactly, the landmark dates of this period are 1521 and 1780; 1521 is the year of the first Romanian original text written entirely in Romanian which has survived; 1780 is the year when a very important Romanian grammar—*Elementa linguae daco-romanae sive valahicae*—was printed.

In the 16th century, there appear a series of translations of religious works from Slavonic (manuscripts or works printed in the Cyrillic alphabet). In the next two centuries, the religious texts continue to prevail (the first full translation into Romanian of the Bible is published in 1688); furthermore, there appear the first juridical texts, and writing by chroniclers progresses in parallel to the emergence of the first original literary texts.

The pre-modern period (1780–1830) is characterized by numerous translations, by the appearance of school textbooks, by works in all domains of written culture, by the appearance of the first prescriptive (normative) works on Romanian, and by the beginning of a conscious stage of 'Romanization' / 'Re-Romanization' of Romanian.

The modern period (after 1830) is characterized by the following: stylistic diversification (there is an increasing development of literary styles: scientific, administrative / legal, and belletristic), and increasing productivity of first-hand literary works through the 1848 generation of writers.

The contemporary period (after 1880) is the period in which the processes of literary language modernization and of linguistic rule setting have been brought to a close. Through the express contribution of the school system and of the Romanian Academy, the unique, supradialectal norm prevailed.

The end of the 19th century is a very important moment in the history of Romanian literature as it coincides with the period of activity of the greatest Romanian writers, M. Eminescu, I. Creangă, and I. L. Caragiale.

In the pre-modern and modern periods, the re-Romanization of the Romanian language (Pușcariu 1940: 370–1) is achieved by the massive absorption of borrowings from Romance (especially French and Italian) as well as from late classical Latin. Latino-Romance loanwords often replaced old scholarly Slavonic, Turkish, and Greek terms. Some researchers speak of the Westernization of the Romanian culture (Niculescu 2003: 113–24).

The present-day period (after 1989, i.e. the end of the communist period) is characterized by an extremely rapid rate of change. Openness towards borrowings, especially towards borrowings from English, the emergence of new terminologies, and the dynamic development of the (present-day) journalistic style are the most visible features.

1.1.6 History of writing in Romanian

Between the 16th and the 19th century, the Cyrillic alphabet, borrowed from the Slavs most probably in the 13th century, prevailed; in the transition period 1797–1828, this alphabet underwent various simplifications.

Between 1830 and 1860, the 'transitional' alphabet was used; this is a Cyrillic alphabet with some letters from the Latin one.

In 1860 the Latin alphabet became official. The Latin alphabet had been sporadically employed since the 16th century, using the orthography of foreign languages: Hungarian, Polish, Italian, and German (for the history of writing in Romanian, see Gheție and Mareș 1985; Stan 2012a). The first texts written with the Latin alphabet mainly use etymologizing spellings.

In 1881, Romanian orthography (with Latin letters) was regulated by the Romanian Academy on a fundamentally phonological principle, with few etymological or morpho-syntactic exceptions. Remaining fundamentally phonologically based, Romanian orthography has undergone a few reforms since 1881—the latest one in 1993.

1.1.7 Dialectal, socio-professional, and stylistic variation

As to the stylistic registers of Romanian (oral vs. written, standard vs. non-standard, formal vs. informal), it should be recalled that the written variant of Romanian is a rather late one (see §1.1.5); the first Romanian texts and printings (which enabled the circulation of the written language) date back to the 16th century. Prior to this date there are only isolated Romanian words and fragments in foreign documents.

The standard (standardized / literary) variant is even later, the first attempts to standardize the language (in the first grammars) having begun in the 18th century. However, genuine standardization and enforcement of the supradialectal norm appear in the modern phase of the Romanian culture (the 19th century).

Niculescu (2003: 34–5, 2007: 417–20) characterized Romanian in contrast with other Romance languages as an 'unconstrained language', a feature which derives from the permissiveness of a system that lacked the constraints of the written and standardized language for a long period.

The dialect on which the standard language is based is the Wallachian one, namely the language employed by the deacon Coresi (the first translator and editor in the history of Romanian writing), the language spoken in the north of Wallachia and in the south-east of Transylvania, in which the first printed Romanian texts of the 16th century were written.

As for professional styles and languages, in the present-day language one may distinguish the following styles: artistic, scientific, juridical and administrative, press (media language), and ecclesiastical styles.

After a long period of stylistic domination by what is known in Romanian as 'wooden language', a kind of leaden, formulaic language specific to totalitarian regimes (Thom 1987), the present-day media language is characterized by an informal style, open to colloquial formulae and sometimes to slang (Guțu Romalo 2005: 242–7).

As far as dialectal / territorial variation is concerned, the Daco-Romanian dialect has a five-fold subdialectal configuration (the subdialects of Wallachia, Moldavia, Crișana, Maramureș, and Banat), to which several other transitional varieties are added.

Despite their long-term separation (*c.* 6 centuries) in three different states (Moldova, Țara Românească, Transylvania), the north-Danubian subdialects and varieties are characterized by a remarkable unity, sharply contrasting with most of the dialectal varieties of other Romance areas (Renzi and Andreose 2003: 50). This unity is historically determined, on the one hand, by the cyclic movement of shepherds from the mountains to the plain, and, on the other hand, by the trading, political, and (later) cultural relations between the three Romanian provinces. The Carpathian Mountains were not a real barrier for contact between the three provinces, and thus there are no communication problems for speakers belonging to different dialectal areas.

The differences between the subdialects and varieties faded and continue to do so, with influence and drift in both directions: from the standard language to the subdialects and varieties due to the effect of the press and of schooling, and in the opposite direction, from subdialects and varieties to the supradialectal standard language, as an effect of a 'popularizing' evolution in Romanian literature, that can be seen throughout the entire history of writing, starting with *Anonimul Brâncovenesc* (*The Brâncoveanu Anonymous Chronicle*) and Ion Neculce (a chronicler of the 17th–18th centuries) up to Mihail Sadoveanu and Marin Preda (20th-century writers).

1.1.8 The individuality of Romanian

Among Romance languages, Romanian has a well-marked individuality, which may be attributed to: (a) the geographical and historical condition of the northern- and southern-Danubian Romance community (the periphery of the Romanized area; isolated from the rest of the Romance area until the 18th century); (b) the special sociolinguistic conditions within which this community developed (a multi-ethnic and multi-linguistic space, a 'crossroad of civilizations'—Niculescu 2003: 58); (c) successive acculturation processes through which Romanian-speaking northern- and southern-Danubian groups assimilate and share civilization values and of the non-Latin linguistic heritage of the languages with which they came in contact; (d) permanent contact, during the Middle Ages, with the Balkan populations (the 'Balkan linguistic union', the 'Balkan Sprachbund'—Sandfeld 1930; Rosetti 1986: 225–60).

1.2 PHONOLOGICAL AND ORTHOGRAPHIC FEATURES OF ROMANIAN

1.2.1 The phonological system

All sounds of Romanian are produced using pulmonic egressive air.

The phonological system of standard contemporary Romanian is made up of 33 phonemes: seven vowels, two semivowels, and 24 consonants.

1.2.1.1 Vowels. The vowels /ə, ɨ/

The vocalic system is based on the following distinctions (Table 1.1):

- backness [front / central / back];
- height [high (close) / mid (close-mid) / low (open)];
- rounding [rounded / unrounded].

/o, u/ are rounded vowels while /a, e, i, ə, ɨ/ are unrounded vowels.

(1) /a/   cap 'head'
    /ə/   (orthographically ă)   măr 'apple'
    /e/   pe 'on'
    /i/   din 'from'
    /ɨ/   (orthographically î)   în 'in'
          (orthographically â; see §1.2.5.2)   român 'Romanian'
    /o/   om 'human'
    /u/   cu 'with'

TABLE 1.1 The vowels of Romanian

	FRONT	CENTRAL	BACK
close	i	ɨ	u
close-mid	e	ə	o
open		a	

1 Introduction

H Romanian did not keep Latin vowel quantity distinctions, or the [close / open] distinction in the case of /e/, present in Danubian Latin. Romanian inherited five vowel qualities:

(2) i   u

         e   o

              a

The vowels /ə/ and /ɨ/ emerged later in Romanian.

Of these, the vowel /ə/ is the earlier; its main source is the regular raising of /a/, in the words inherited from Latin, in atonic syllables (*barbă* 'beard' < BARBA) or in accented syllables, in nasal position (ORom *cămp* 'field' < CAMPUS). These phonological laws are prior to the separation of the four dialects (Daco-Romanian, Aromanian, Megleno-Romanian, and Istro-Romanian). The other sources of the vowel /ə/ emerge later.

The vowel /ɨ/ most probably emerged independently in Daco-Romanian and Aromanian. Its sources are the following: the raising of accented /ə/ in nasal position in words inherited from Latin (CRom *câmp* < ORom *cămp*); the evolution of other vowels in words of Latin origin (*vână* 'vein' < VENA); the loan process (*dâmb* 'knoll' < Sl. *do^{n}bŭ*) (for the history of the evolution of Romanian vowels, see Brâncuș 2002: 20–1, 54, 96–102).

C The absence of phonological quantity and nasality (nasal / non-nasal) distinctions for vowels, and the presence of the vowel /ə/ are considered Balkan Sprachbund phenomena; the vowel /ɨ/ is specific to Romanian in the Balkan context (Sandfeld 1930: 12–13, 124–5, 127, and references therein; Feuillet 1986: 45–7). In Romanian, the nasalized vowels are allophones, not distinct phonemes; in this, Romanian differs from Romance languages such as French or Portuguese.

U The present-day norm is for a yod onglide before the initial mid front vowel [e] in the relevant forms of the personal pronoun and of the verb *fi* 'be'. Thus, for instance, the forms *el* 'he' and *este* 'is' are pronounced [jel] and [jeste], respectively.

Pronunciation of /o/ with a labial onglide (*om* [^{w}om] 'human', *dovleac* [d^{w}ovle̯ak] 'pumpkin') occurs in the non-standard language.

Length is not a distinctive feature of vowels in Romanian. Vowels may be long, usually in association with emphasis and are then marked graphically by the repetition of the vowel symbol: *maaare* [ma:re] '(extremely) big'.

1.2.1.2 The word-final post-consonantal glide [^{i}]

The non-syllabic half-voiced sound [^{i}], which appears word-finally, preceded by consonants or consonant clusters, is specific to Romanian (3a). *Muta cum liquida* clusters are excepted from this rule (3b):

(3) a. pomi [pom^i] 'trees', porți [ports^i] 'gates'

  b. tigri [tigri] 'tigers', codri [kodri] 'woods'.

1.2.1.3 Semivowels

Romanian has two semivowels: /e̯/, /o̯/. Semivowels are included in diphthong and triphthong clusters, always in prevocalic position (see §1.2.2–3 and Table 1.2).

TABLE 1.2 The semivowels of Romanian

	FRONT	CENTRAL	BACK
close-mid	e̯		o̯

(4) /e̯/ (*e*) seară 'evening' /o̯/ (*o*) soare 'sun'

The semivowels are distinguished on the basis of backness.

1.2.1.4 Consonants

The consonant system of standard contemporary Romanian is based on the following distinctions (Table 1.3):

- voicing [voiced / voiceless];
- place of articulation [bilabial / labiodental / alveolar / post alveolar / palatal / velar / glottal];
- manner of articulation [plosive / nasal / trill / fricative / affricate / approximant / lateral approximant].

(5)
/b/   **b**an 'coin'
/k/ (*c*)   fo**c** 'fire'
/tʃ/ (orthographically *c + e, i*)   **c**er [tʃer] 'sky', **c**in**c**i [tʃintʃ] 'five'
/c/ (orthographically *c + h + e, i*)   s**ch**imb [scimb] 'exchange'
/d/   po**d** 'bridge'
/f/   **f**ată 'girl'
/g/   **g**ară 'railway station'
/dʒ/ (orthographically *g + e, i*)   min**g**e [mindʒe] 'ball'
/ɟ/ (orthographically *g + h + e, i*)   **gh**eață [ɟatsə] 'ice'
/h/   **h**artă 'map'
/j/ (*i*)   **i**epure 'hare'
/ʒ/ (orthographically *j*)   **j**oi 'Thursday'
/l/   **l**ac 'lake'
/m/   **m**amă 'mother'
/n/   a**n** 'year'
/p/   **p**om '(fruit) tree'
/r/   o**r**aș 'city'
/s/   o**s** 'bone'
/ʃ/ (orthographically *ș*)   po**ș**tă 'post (office)'
/t/   **t**ată 'father'
/ts/ (orthographically *ț*)   **ț**ară 'country'
/v/   **v**ară 'summer'
/w/ (*u*)   no**u**ă 'nine'
/z/   **z**ece 'ten'

10   1 Introduction

TABLE 1.3 The consonants of Romanian

	Bilabial	Labiodental	Alveolar	Post Alveolar	Palatal	Velar	Glottal
plosive	p b		t d		c ɟ	k g	
nasal	m		n				
trill			r				
fricative		f v	s z	ʃ ʒ			h
affricate			ts	tʃ dʒ			
approximant					j		w
lateral approximant			l				

The glides /j/, /w/ display semiconsonant properties in prevocalic position [j], [w] (5), and semivowel features in postvocalic position [i̯], [u̯] (6):

(6) /i̯/ (*i*)   trei   'three'
    /u̯/ (*u*)   leu   'lion'

H The consonant system inherited from Latin was enriched in Romanian. The new consonants are: /tʃ, dʒ, ts, dz, ʃ, ʒ, c, ɟ, h/. The main source of this innovation was the readjustment of the Latin consonant by the action of phonological laws.

   The affricate consonants (a type absent from Latin) developed out of velar and alveolar consonants under the influence of a following front vowel or a yod: [tʃ] < [k, t] (*cer* 'sky' < CAELUM); [dʒ] < [g] (*ger* 'frost' < GELUM); [ts] < [t, k] (*preț* 'price' < PRETIUM); [dz] < [d] (*dzece* 'ten' < DECEM). The consonants [dz, dʒ] also originate in [j]: (*dzăcea* '(to) lie ill' < JACERE; ORom *gioc* 'game' < JOCUS). The consonant [dz] existed also in words from the Thraco-Dacian substratum: *brândză* 'cheese'. The affricate consonant was already present in common Romanian. The affricate consonant [dz] existed in the pre-literary stage and it was maintained in regional Daco-Romanian and in the south Danubian dialects; in Daco-Romanian, [dz] transformed into [z] (ORom *dzece* > CRom *zece*), and thus [z] occurs much more extensively in standard contemporary Romanian than it did in Latin; [z] also entered Romanian through old loanwords (*zid* 'wall' < Sl. *zidŭ*).

   The fricative [ʃ] comes from the Latin [s], followed by a yod (*șapte* 'seven' < */sjepte/ < SEPTEM). The fricative [ʒ] originates in ORom [dʒ + o, u] (ORom *gioc* 'game' > CRom *joc*); this development, later than common Romanian, developed in Daco-Romanian and, to a more limited extent, to the south of the Danube; [dʒ] is regional in contemporary Romanian. The consonant [ʒ] also entered Romanian by means of Slavic loans (*grajd* 'stable').

   The consonants [c, ɟ] are an innovation of Daco-Romanian; they originate in the clusters [kʎ] (< Lat. [kl]), [gʎ] (< Lat. [gl]), where [l] has undergone palatalization: *cheie* [ceje] 'key' < CLAVIS, *gheață* [ɟatsə] 'ice' < GLACIA (GLACIES). The clusters [kʎ, gʎ] were preserved in the south Danubian dialects; they survived in Daco-Romanian until the 15th century.

   The consonant [h], eliminated in words inherited from Latin, penetrated Romanian by means of Old Slavic loanwords (*hrăni* '(to) feed') and, later, through other loans. The consonant [h] also existed in substratum words (*hameș* 'greedy').

   Other phenomena affecting consonants are: loss of the palatal sonorants [ʎ, ɲ], which were maintained only dialectally (*iepure* 'hare' < [ʎepure] < LEPOREM; *călcâi* 'heel' < [kəlkiɲu] < CALCANEUM); betacism (*bătrân* 'old (man)' < VETERANUS); the loss of the labial appendix in the case of the labiovelar *qu, gu* (*cinci* 'five' < QUINQUE); the persistence of the labial appendix in front of [a] and the evolution towards a labial consonant (*apă* 'water' < AQUA); the labialization of the clusters [ks, kt] (*coapsă* 'thigh' < COXA; *opt* 'eight' < OCTO); the rhotacism of intervocalic [l] (> [r]) (*moară* 'mill' < MOLA); the evolution of some consonant clusters, such as [ʃt] < [sk, st + e, i] (also involved in morphophonological alternations; see §15.1; *creștere* 'growth' < CRESCERE) (for the history of the evolution of Romanian consonants, see Brâncuș 2002: 23–4, 55–6, 108–16).

C The specific palatal consonants /c, ɟ/ developed in Romanian. The affricates /tʃ, dʒ, ts, dz/ and the fricatives /ʃ, ʒ, h/ are present in other Romance languages as well (ELIR: 81). Among the specific features of the Romanian consonants are the following: the loss of palatal sonorants (they have been preserved only dialectally); rhotacism of intervocalic [l]; the specific evolution of the Latin clusters [ks, kt, sk]; the great number and complexity of consonant clusters; in exceptional cases (in compound words), the intervocalic clusters may comprise up to five consonants (of which there may be at most three in the same syllable, as a syllable onset): e.g. *optsprezece* ['opt.spre.ze.tʃe] 'eighteen'.

Some consonant clusters (not occurring at morpheme boundaries) are absent from other Romance languages; most are old combinations of Slavic [ml, zd, zg, zgl, zv] or Latin [ʒn] origin; the more recent ones have a learnèd source (Tasmowski-De Ryck 2000: 10–14).

Romanian (unlike Latin or Italian) does not have long consonants with phonological function. Geminate consonants and the consonants [ktʃ] (orthographically *cc*) are separated in the syllabification of the clusters: *înnoi* [in.no.i] 'renew', *accent* [ak.tʃent] 'accent'.

U In Romanian, long consonants are incidental realizations, and are typically associated with emphasis, this being signalled graphically by repetition of the consonant letter: *frrrig* [fr:ig] '(extremely) cold'.

1.2.2 Diphthongs

Romanian has nine rising (or ascending) diphthongs (7a) and thirteen falling (or descending) diphthongs (7b). The structure of rising diphthongs includes the semivowels [e̯, o̯], the semiconsonants [j, w] and the vowels [a, e, ə, o, u]. The structure of falling diphthongs contains the semivowels [i̯, u̯] and any of the vowels.

(7) a. [e̯a]   *sea*ră 'evening'
       [e̯o]   vreo 'around'
       [ja]   *ia*rnă 'winter'
       [je]   *ie*d 'kid'
       [jo]   *io*lă 'yawl'
       [ju]   *iu*bi 'love'
       [o̯a]   *soa*re 'sun'
       [wa]   z*iua* 'day.DEF'
       [wə]   vo*uă* 'you.DAT'

    b. [ai̯] *ai* 'have.PRES.2SG'
       [au̯] s*au* 'or'
       [əi̯] r*ăi* 'bad(PL)'
       [əu̯] s*ău* 'his / her.M.SG'
       [ɨi̯] p*âi*ne 'bread'
       [ɨu̯] r*âu* 'river'
       [ei̯] tr*ei* 'three'
       [eu̯] gr*eu* 'hard / heavy'
       [i̯]   cop*ii* 'children'
       [u̯]   f*iu* 'son'
       [oi̯] d*oi* 'two'

[ou̯]   ou 'egg'
[ui̯]   amărui 'bitter'

H Romanian preserved the Latin diphthong [au̯] (*au* 'or' < AUT), generally pronounced as a hiatus [au]: *aur* 'gold' < AURUM (Rosetti 1986: 109).

The diphthongs [e̯a] and [o̯a] are usually seen as originating in the accented vowels [e] and [o], respectively, followed in the succeeding syllable by [ə] or [e], in words inherited from Latin: *seară* 'evening' < SERA; *soare* 'sun' < SOLEM (Rosetti 1986: 631–6; Avram 2005: 19–65). Diphthongization also took place in contexts in which there is no phonetic conditioning: ē diphthongization to [e̯a] in *dea* < DET (give.SUBJ.PRES.3SG≡PL), *stea* < STET (stay.SUBJ.PRES.3SG≡PL) (Sala 2006: 150; Loporcaro 2011b: 128–30); ['e] diphthongization to [e̯a] in the final segment of Modern Greek (*saltea* 'mattress'), Turkish (*chiftea* 'meatball'), or French (*șosea* 'road') borrowings. The diphthongs [e̯a] and [o̯a] had already occurred in the early phase of Romanian (Brâncuș 2002: 54).

Romanian has developed the other rising diphthongs (a type absent from Latin) and the falling diphthongs through: spontaneous diphthongization (*fier* 'iron' < FERRUM), the reduction of some triphthongs (*piatră* 'stone' < *pieatră*) or the alteration of some Latin consonants (*cui* 'nail' < [kuɲu] < CUNEUM).

The diphthongs /e̯a/, /o̯a/ (Pană Dindelegan 2012) are involved in morphophonological alternations, and play an inflectional role (§15.1): /e̯a/ ~ /e/, in the root (*creadă*$_{\text{SUBJ.PRES.3SG≡PL}}$, *cred*$_{\text{IND.PRES.1SG≡3PL}}$ 'believe') or in the verbal suffix (*lucrează*$_{\text{IND.PRES.3SG≡PL}}$, *lucrez*$_{\text{IND≡SUBJ.PRES.1SG}}$ 'work'; *citească*$_{\text{SUBJ.PRES.3SG≡PL}}$, *citesc*$_{\text{IND.PRES.1SG≡3.PL≡SUBJ.PRES.1SG}}$ 'read'); /o̯a/ ~ /o/, in the root (*roată*$_{\text{SG.NOM≡ACC}}$, *roți*$_{\text{SG.GEN≡DAT≡PL.NOM≡ACC≡GEN≡DAT}}$ 'wheel'). The diphthong /e̯a/ appears in varied phonetic contexts: in the final position of words, bearing stress (*mea* my.F.SG.NOM≡ACC) or not (*asemenea* 'also'), and in medial position, bearing stress (*seară*); the diphthong /o̯a/ always occurs in medial stressed syllables (in initial position, the orthographic sequence *oa-* is pronounced [wa]: *oase* 'bones'). The diphthong /e̯a/ fulfils a varied morphological role: it is an inflectional verb suffix (*avea* have.INF≡IMPERF.3SG), an inflectional marker formed by the enclisis of the definite article -*a* on feminine nouns ending in -*e* (*valea* valley.DEF), or a diminutive suffix (*rămurea* branch.DIM).

C The diphthongs [e̯a] and [o̯a] are a characteristic feature of Romanian.

1.2.3 Triphthongs

Romanian has nine triphthongs. Of these, seven include the vowels [a, e], preceded by [e̯, o̯, j, w] and followed by [i̯, u̯] (8a), and two include the vowel [a], preceded by [j, e̯, o̯] (8b):

(8) a. [e̯ai̯]   citeai read.IND.IMPERF.2SG
    [e̯au̯]   citeau read.IND.IMPERF.3PL
    [jai̯]   suiai climb.IND.IMPERF.2SG
    [jau̯]   iau take.IND.PRES.1SG≡3PL
    [jei̯]   iei take.IND.PRES.2SG
    [jeu̯]   eu I
    [o̯ai̯]   englezoaică Englishwoman

   b. [e̯o̯a] pleoapă eyelid
    [jo̯a] ploioasă rainy

C Similarly to other Romance languages, in Romanian there developed triphthongs (a structure absent from Latin).

1.2.4 Free stress

Romanian has stress accent. Stress is relatively free. It is typically paroxytone (9a) and frequently oxytone (9b) or proparoxytone (9c). Especially in the case of forms with enclitic grammatical marking, the pre-ante-penultimate syllable bears stress. As an effect of postlexical phonological processes, in compound words primary stress may be on the fifth-but-last (9e) or the sixth-but-last (9f) syllable, in which case it is followed by a paroxytone or proparoxytone secondary stress:

(9) a. furnică [fur.'ni.kə] 'ant'
 b. cânta [kɨn.'ta] 'sing'
 c. lingură ['lin.gu.rə] 'spoon'
 d lingurile ['lin.gu.ri.le] 'the spoons'
 e. şaptesprezece ['ʃap.te.spre.ˌze.tʃe] 'seventeen'
 f. şaptesprezecelea ['ʃap.te.spre.ˌze.tʃe.lea] 'seventeenth'

Stress is almost always fixed for nouns and adjectives (9a, c–d), with few exceptions (10a). It is mobile in verb inflection (10b):

(10) a. soră ['so.rə] / surori [su.'rorʲ]
 sister.SG.NOM≡ACC sister.SG.GEN≡DAT.PL.NOM≡ACC≡GEN≡DAT

 b. cobor [ko.'bor] / coborâm [ko.bo.'rɨm]
 descend.IND.PRES.1SG descend.IND.PRES.1PL

Stress plays a phonological role in few cases:

(11) copii ['ko.piʲ] 'copies' / copii [ko.'piʲ] 'children'

H Romanian preserved (pro)paroxytonic stress from Latin (ELIR: 256).
C Romanian fits the general Romance type (except for French), characterized by mobile free stress, with a phonological role. The degree of extension of oxytonic stress in Romanian is similar to that of Spanish and Portuguese (ELIR: 17–18, 226). Romanian is the only Romance language that has stress on the pre-ante-penultimate syllable in simple words (9d) (Loporcaro 2011a: 53, 81, and references therein).

In general, Romanian has preserved the original stress of loanwords; some older loanwords from Hungarian, with etymological stress on the word-initial syllable, have been adjusted to the Romanian stress patterns: *cătană* [kə.'ta.nə] 'soldier'.

In NegPs, the negative marker *nu* ('not') may bear phrasal stress: NU *ştiu* 'I DON'T know'. Romanian thus diverges from languages in which stress is on the verb (TP), such as Italian.

Romanian possesses a metrical structure for the secondary stress; the typical pattern is the trochaic one (12a) (Chiţoran 2002: 86–93). The dactyl is also frequent (12b):

(12) a. mătrăgună [ˌmə.trə]'gu.nə] 'belladonna'
 b. strecurătoare [ˌstre.ku.rə]'toa.re] 'colander'

Romanian is characterized by the variety of its metrical patterns.

1.2.5 Phonological orthography

Romanian has a largely phonological orthography.

1.2.5.1 The alphabet

Contemporary Romanian is written in an adaptation of the Latin alphabet. This contains 31 letters, of which five have diacritical marks ((˘), (^), (,)):

(13)
A, a /a/	F, f /ef/	K, k /ka(ppa)/	Q, q /kju/	U, u /u/
Ă, ă /ə/	G, g /dʒe/	L, l /el/	R, r /er/	V, v /ve/
Â, â /ɨ din a/	H, h /haʃ/	M, m /em/	S, s /es/	W, w /dublu ve/
B, b /be/	I, i /i/	N, n /en/	Ș, ș /ʃe/	X, x /iks/
C, c /tʃe/	Î, î /ɨ din i/	O, o /o/	T, t /te/	Y, y /i grec/
D, d /de/	J, j /ʒe/	P, p /pe/	Ț, ț /tse/	Z, z /zet/
E, e /e/				

C　Romanian is the only language to employ the letter *ț* in its writing system.
U　The letters *k, q, w*, and *y* are often used in the spelling of foreign words. Other letters and diacritical marks (may) occur in the case of foreign words, some of which preserve their original spelling.

1.2.5.2 The letter–phoneme correspondence

In general, the correspondence between letters and phonemes is predictable. The following cases are the exceptions:

(i) letters with multiple values:
  • letters which mark the vowels and their corresponding semivowels or glides (14a)
    e [e, e̯], *i* [i, j, i̯, ʲ], *o* [o, o̯], *u* [u, w, u̯]
  • letters which note different consonants (14b)
    c [tʃ] (in the digraphs *ce, ci*), [c] (in the trigraphs *che, chi*), [k] (in all the other situations)
    g [dʒ] (in the digraphs *ge, gi*), [ɟ] (in the trigraphs *ghe, ghi*), [g] (in all the other situations)
  • ambiguities (letters with multiple values, in the absence of a reading / pronunciation rule) (14c)
    x [ks, gz]
(ii) letters with the same value
  â, î [ɨ] (1), (14d)
  c, k [k, c] (14e)
(iii) sounds which are not graphically marked (14f)
  [j] the yod onglide before *e-*
(iv) letters that mark clusters of sounds (14c)
  x [ks, gz]
(v) diacritical letters (which mark a phonetically null segment) (14g)
  e, i (in the digraphs *ce, ci, ge, gi* and in the trigraphs *che, chi, ghe, ghi*)
  h (in the trigraphs *che, chi, ghe, ghi*).

1.2 Phonological and orthographic features of Romanian

(14) a. in [in] 'flax', iată [jatə] 'look!', oi [oi̯] 'sheep', poți [potsʲ] '(you) can'
b. gem [dʒem] 'jam', ghem [ɟem] 'ball (of thread)', gât [gɨt] 'neck'
c. axă [aksə] 'axis', exemplu [egzemplu] 'example'
d. însă [ɨnsə] 'but, though', reîncepe [rei̯ntʃepe] 'start again', urî [urɨ] 'hate'
   fân [fɨn] 'hay'
e. casă [kasə] 'house', chip [cip] 'face'
   kurd [kurd] 'Kurdish', kilogram [cilogram] 'kilogram'
f. ele [jele] 'they(F)', erau [jerau̯] be.IND.IMPERF.3PL
g. ceai [tʃai̯] 'tea', ochi [oc] 'eye'

U In current orthography, the sound /ɨ/ is represented by the letter *î* at the beginning and at the end of words, and by the letter *â* /ɨ/ word-internally—(1), (14d). Prefixed derived forms whose base-form is spelled with *î*- preserve this spelling of the vowel: *reîncepe* (14d).

C The clusters *ce, ci, ge, gi, che, chi, ghe, ghi* are digraphs and trigraphs, respectively, when they are followed by a vocalic letter different from *e, i* or when they occur word-finally (14g). The clusters *ce, ci, ge, gi, che, chi, ghe, ghi* began to be used at the end of the 18th century and the beginning of the 19th century, on the model of Italian orthography.

1.2.5.3 Etymological spellings

Some etymological spellings are old; this is the case of *e-* [je] in the forms of the personal pronouns and of the verb *fi* 'be' ((iii) above, (14f)). Other etymological spellings are of recent date: Romanian tends to preserve the original spelling of foreign words *(show)*.

1.2.5.4 Spellings based on grammatical rules

Some spellings are based on morphological or syntactical rules. For instance, words that have alternating forms with *e* are written with *ea* (15a), while other words are written with *ia* (15b); homophonic sequences are written together or separately depending on their morphosyntactic structure (15c):

(15) a. ch**ea**mă '(he)calls'   ch**e**m '(I)call'
    b. ch**ia**r 'even'
    c. odată   o dată
       'once, at one time' one time
       'one (single) time'

The share of grammatical rules is relatively limited in the present-day orthography.

1.2.5.5 Orthographic marks

The following marks are used in contemporary Romanian: the hyphen (-), the apostrophe ('), the full stop / period (.), the dash (–), and the slash (/).
  The hyphen is the most important mark. It is mainly used for:

- marking of some syntactic phonetic phenomena; for example, syneresis (16a);
- joining of clitics that lack syllabic independence (16b);
- enclisis of clitics with syllabic independence (16c);
- attachment of formatives in the case of compound words (16d).

(16) a. **ne-a** (spus) [ne̯a]
   CL.DAT.1PL=has told
   b. **i-a** (spus) [ja]
   CL.DAT.3SG=has told
   c. dându-ni-se [din.du.ni.se]
   give.GER=CL.DAT.1PL—CL.REFL.IMPERS
   d. câine-lup
   dog-wolf
   'German shepherd dog'

The period (17a) and the slash are sometimes used in abbreviations (17b), the dash appears in the spelling of compounds (17c), and the apostrophe marks the accidental absence of sounds (17d):

(17) a. C.F.R. (= Căile Ferate Române)
   'Romanian Railways'
   b. c/val (= contravaloarea)
   '(counter)value'
   c. nord–nord-vest
   'north-north-west'
   d. 'neața < bună dimineața
   'mornin'' 'good morning'

Stress is not marked in spelling; this is why forms such as those in (11) are homographic.

1.2.6 Pronunciation norms

The norm for pronunciation is based on the Wallachian subdialect. The model is the pronunciation of middle aged, intellectual speakers from Bucharest. These rules are less firm and less respected than orthographic ones.

1.2.7 Punctuation

The most important rules are the following:

- the absence of the comma before coordinating conjunctions *și* 'and', *sau* 'ori';
- the presence of the comma before adversative conjunctions;
- the question mark (?) is placed at the end of the sentence (not at the beginning).

Quotation marks are of the type („ ").

CONCLUSIONS

The particular phonological features of Romanian are the following: the vowels /ə, ɨ/; the word-final post-consonantal glide [ⁱ] (a half-voiced non-syllabic sound that occurs after consonants, with the exception of the cluster *muta cum liquida* (i.e. consonant + *r* / *l*)); the specific palatal consonants /c, ɟ/; the affricate or fricative consonants /tʃ, dʒ, ts, dz, ʃ, ʒ, h/; the loss of the labial appendix in the case of the labiovelar *qu*, *gu*; the loss of the palatal sonorants [ʎ, ɲ]; the labialization of Latin [ks] (> [ps]), [kt] (> [pt]); the evolution of the cluster Latin [sk] > [ʃt]; the variety and complexity of consonant clusters; the variety of diphthongs; the diphthongs [e̯a, o̯a]; the free stress; the variety of the metrical patterns of the secondary stress.

The orthographic features specific to Romanian are the Latin alphabet, including five letters with diacritical marks and the largely phonological orthography.

2

The Verb

This chapter presents the Romanian verb from a morphological and syntactic-semantic point of view. It contains a description of the five inflectional classes of verbs established depending on the infinitival ending, the grammatical categories of the verb (mood, tense, and aspect) underlying the inflectional subclasses—established in terms of their endings and specific syncretisms, the relation between analytic and synthetic realizations, irregular verbs, and the modal and the temporal-aspectual system. It also contains a description of the typologically important classes of verbs, selected according to syntactic (transitive vs. intransitive) and semantic criteria (experiencer verbs, verbs of perception, verbs of physical sensation, psych verbs, motion verbs).

2.1 INFLECTIONAL CLASSES OF VERBS

2.1.1 Five inflectional classes of verbs

Romanian has five inflectional classes of verbs, characterized by the infinitive endings -*a*, -*ea*, -*e*, -*i*, and -*î*.

C   In contrast to other Romance languages, Romanian not only inherited four inflectional classes (those with the infinitive suffixes -*a*, -*ea*, -*e*, -*i*) from Latin, but also developed a fifth class of verbs, with the suffix -*î* (§2.1.1.5).

Except for the class in -*ea*, all the other classes divide into more subclasses depending on other endings that are inflectionally relevant. Their realization may be influenced by the phonological particularities of the final segment of the root (for a model of verb classification, see Felix 1964).

In each class, the regular inflectional distinctions shown by the grammatical endings may be supplementarily marked by vowel / consonant alternations which affect the root. For example, the consonant alternation /t/ ~ /ts/ and the inflectional ending -*i* mark the 2nd singular present indicative and subjunctive forms (1); the vowel alternation /'e/ ~ /'e̯a/ and the inflectional ending -*ă* mark the present subjunctive form (2a) (in addition, in example (2b), the consonant shift /tʃ/ ~ /k/ also occurs); the consonant alternation /d/ ~ /z/ and the ending -*ând* mark the gerund (3):

(1) cânt /   cânți /   să   cânți
     sing.IND.PRES.1SG   sing.IND.PRES.2SG   să$_{SUBJ}$ sing.SUBJ.2SG

(2) a. începe /   să   înceapă
        begin.IND.PRES.3SG să$_{SUBJ}$ begin.SUBJ.3SG

     b. trece /   să   treacă
        pass.IND.PRES.3SG să$_{SUBJ}$ pass.SUBJ.3SG

(3)   arde /   arzând
      burn.IND.PRES.3SG   burn.GER

2.1.1.1 Two subclasses of the verbs in *-a*: with and without the supplementary suffix *-ez*

In the class of verbs with the infinitive ending *-a*, two subclasses can be distinguished depending on the presence or absence of the suffix *-ez* (with the allomorph *-eaz-*) in the present indicative, present subjunctive, and in the imperative (Table 2.1). The weak present forms (with *-ez*) bear stress on the suffix, whereas the strong ones (without *-ez*) bear stress on the root in all the singular forms and in the 3rd person plural forms.

In contemporary Romanian, the two aforementioned subclasses may overlap. Certain verbs (especially loan verbs) have both variants, with and without the suffix *-ez*, sometimes associated with distinct meanings:

(4)   a. **acord** [atenție]
         'I pay attention'
      b. **acord** [predicatul cu subiectul]
         'I make the predicate agree with the subject'
      c. **acordez** [un instrument muzical]
         'I tune a musical instrument'

(5)   a **ordon** [subalternilor]
         'I give orders to the subordinates'
      b **ordonez** [lucrurile în cameră]
         'I set in order the things in the room'

H The overlaps between the two subclasses are old, and have manifested themselves throughout history. In the 16th century, certain verbs occurred with and without the suffix *-ez*: *întunecază* and *întunecă* 'it is getting dark', *lucreadză* and *lucră* '(s)he / they work(s)', *preveghe* și *preveghează* '(s)he watches / they watch' (Densusianu 1961, II: 130). Between 1640 and 1780, certain forms were also used with apparent free variation: *scurt* and *scurtez* 'I shorten', *ur* and *urez* 'I greet' (Frâncu 2009: 303).

The variations between the two subclasses are present in the modern language as well, speakers using both forms: *aderă—aderează* '(s)he adheres / they adhere', *ignoră—ignorează* '(s)he ignores / they ignore', *perturbă—perturbează* '(s)he perturbs / they perturb' (DOOM recommends only the first form in each pair).

The suffix has only a morphological value, not a semantic one, being equivalent to the suffix *-esc*, which is specific to a subclass of verbs ending in *-i* (see §§2.1.1.4; 2.2.1.1.1). The equivalence of the suffixes *-ez* and *-esc* is shown by the fact that, in the case of certain verbs, it was possible to replace one suffix by the other. This phenomenon was

TABLE 2.1 Class I

CLASS I (VERBS IN *-A*)		
SUBCLASSES	SPECIFIC FEATURES	EXAMPLES
(a)	INF:-'a	învăța 'learn'
	PRES IND, PRES SUBJ, IMP:− -'ez	1SG învăț, 1SG să învăț, 2SG învață! 'learn'
(b)	INF: -'a	lucra 'work'
	PRES IND, PRES SUBJ, IMP: + -'ez	1SG lucrez, 1SG să lucrez, 2SG lucrează! 'work'

recorded in certain stages throughout the history of language and in certain geographical areas: *cucerează*, instead of *cucereşte* '(s)he conquers' (16th century); *(ei) datoresc*, in variation with *(ei) datorează* 'they owe' (both variants are accepted in the contemporary language); *greblesc*, instead of *greblez* 'I rake' (Oltenia); *şchiopătesc*, instead of *şchiopătez* 'I limp' (Transylvania); Maiden (2006–07: 182–3).

In contemporary Romanian, as well as in the other Romance languages, the class of verbs in *-a* and, within it, the subclass of verbs with the suffix *-ez*, is the most productive. The enrichment of the *-ez* subclass of verbs correlates with the productivity of certain borrowed verbal suffixes such as *-iza* and *-iona*, which selects the grammatical suffix *-ez* (Pană Dindelegan 2008b: 557, Dragomirescu 2009: 222).

U   Brâncuş (1976: 488), surveying DEX (1975), shows that 2,065 out of 2,466 verbs which are recent in the language take the suffix *-ez*. For the advantages of inflection with the suffix *-ez*, see §2.2.1.1.1.

2.1.1.2 The class of the verbs in *-ea*

This class is small, comprising 16 old verbs and a few derivatives (Brâncuş 1976: 490) (Table 2.2).

H   Several verbs which, in the old language, belonged to the second class (*rămânea* 'stay', *ţinea* 'keep', *umplea* 'fill') moved, in the standard contemporary language, to the class of verbs with the infinitive ending *-e* (*rămâne* 'stay', *ţine* 'keep', *umple* 'fill').

U   In the modern language, there is a noticeable tendency for verbs ending in *-ea* to shift to the class of verbs ending in *-e* (and more rarely the other way round), given the fact that there are very few differences between the two aforementioned classes. In the spoken (non-standard) language, this shift, accompanied by differences in the position of stress (in the case of the verbs ending in *-ea*, the stress is on the infinitive suffix, while in the case of the verbs ending in *-e*, the stress is on the root), occurs with:

• the infinitive and analytic forms with the infinitive
(6) a. apă'rea—a'pare 'appear'; va apă'rea—va a'pare 'will appear'; ar apă'rea—ar a'pare 'would appear';
      b. 'bate—bă'tea 'beat'; va 'bate—va bă'tea 'will beat'; ar 'bate—ar bă'tea 'would beat';
• the 1st person plural and 2nd person plural present indicative
(7) a. plă'cem—'placem 'we like', plă'ceţi—'placeţi 'you like';
      b. 'facem—fă'cem 'we do', 'faceţi—fă'ceţi 'you do';
• the 2nd person plural imperative when followed by pronominal clitics
(8) spuneţi-mi ['spu.ne.tsimʲ]—spuneţi-mi [spu.'ne.tsimʲ] 'tell me'

Note that stress is not marked in the Romanian orthography.

TABLE 2.2 Class II

CLASS II (VERBS IN *-EA*)	
SPECIFIC FEATURES	EXAMPLES
INF: -'ea	plăcea 'like', tăcea 'keep silent'

2.1.1.3 Three subclasses of verbs in -e

The verbs in -e fall into three subclasses depending on the endings of the simple past and of the participle (Table 2.3).

H In the old language, the verbs *face* 'do' and *întoarce* 'turn' belonged to subclass (c), from the perspective of the participle forms *fapt(u)* 'done', *întort(u)* 'turned'; see §4.3.1.

2.1.1.4 Two subclasses of verbs in -i: with and without the supplementary suffix -esc

The verbs ending in -i fall into two subclasses depending on the presence or absence of the suffix -esc with the allomorph -eșt- in the present indicative and present subjunctive and in the imperative (Table 2.4).

H The 3SG PRESENT INDICATIVE≡3PL PRESENT INDICATIVE syncretism characterizing verbs in subclass (a_3) occurred rather late in Romanian. In the 19th century it had not been generalized, because Moldavian writers used distinct forms for the 3rd person singular and plural forms: *el sufere* 'he suffers' vs. *ei sufăr* 'they suffer', *el acopere* 'he covers' vs. *ei acopăr* 'they cover', *el descopere* 'he discovers' vs. *ei descopăr* 'they discover' (Pană Dindelegan 1987: 95–6). The syncretism that finally prevailed in the literary language may be explained as a consequence of the influence of the large first inflectional class, which has identical forms in the 3rd person singular and plural (Pană Dindelegan 1987: 96–7; Maiden 2009b).

U In the modern language, many verbs have double forms, with and without the suffix -esc: *cheltuiește* vs. *cheltuie* '(s)he spends', *revizuiește* vs. *revizuie* '(s)he revises', *sforăiește* vs. *sforăie* '(s)he snores'. Depending on the verb, DOOM recommends the form with the suffix -esc (*revizuiește* '(s)he revises'), the form without the suffix (*sforăie* '(s)he snores'), or even both forms (*cheltuie, cheltuiește* '(s)he spends').

H There have been variations between the two classes throughout history. In 16th–17th centuries, many verbs (among which *împărți* 'divide; share', *pipăi* 'touch', *slobozi* 'free', *suferi* 'suffer') were attested with both the strong forms and the weak ones (Zamfir 2005: 334–56).

Compared to the modern language, where the productivity of the class of verbs in -i has decreased, in the old language, even until the 19th century, this class of verbs was the most productive, incorporating most of the loan verbs. However, the class of verbs in -i, which consists of both borrowed verbs and regionally used verbs, continues to be productive (Sánchez Miret 2006: 34–45).

TABLE 2.3 Class III

CLASS III (VERBS IN -E)		
SUBCLASSES	SPECIFIC FEATURES	EXAMPLES
(a)	INF: **-e**	*face* 'do'
	PS: -'**u**	*făcui* 'I did'
	PPLE: -'**ut**	*făcut* 'done'
(b)	INF: **-e**	*întoarce* 'turn'
	PS: -(')**se**	*întor'sei* 'I turned', *în'toarse* '(s)he turned'
	PPLE: **-s**	*întors* 'turned'
(c)	INF: **-e**	*rupe* 'tear'
	PS: -(')**se**	*rup'sei* 'I tore', *'rupse* '(s)he tore'
	PPLE: **-t**	*rupt* 'torn'

TABLE 2.4 Class IV

CLASS IV (VERBS IN -*i*)			
SUBCLASSES		SPECIFIC FEATURES	EXAMPLES
(a)	(a₁)	INF: -'i	ieşi 'come out'
		PRES IND, PRES SUBJ, IMP: − -'esc	1SG ies,1SG să ies, 2SG ieşi! 'come out'
		1SG PRES IND inflectional ending≡3PL PRES IND inflectional ending: -Ø	1SG≡3PL ies
	(a₂)	INF.: -'i	sui 'mount'
		PRES IND, PRES SUBJ, IMP: − -'esc	1SG sui, 1SG să sui, 2SG suie!
		3SG / PL PRES IND inflectional ending≡3SG / PL PRES SUBJ inflectional ending: -e [e]	3SG≡3PL suie, 3SG≡3PL să suie
		1SG PRES IND inflectional ending≡2SG PRES IND inflectional ending: -i [i̯]	1SG≡2SG sui
	(a₃)	INF.: -'i	acoperi 'cover'
		PRES IND, PRES SUBJ, IMP: − -'esc	1SG acopăr, 1SG să acopăr, 2SG.IMP acoperă!
		3SG PRES IND inflectional ending≡3PL PRES IND inflectional ending: -ă	3SG≡3PL acoperă
(b)		INF: -'i	citi 'read'
		PRES IND, PRES SUBJ, IMP: + -'esc	1SG citesc, 1SG să citesc, 2SG.IMP citeşte!

2.1.1.5 Two subclasses of verbs in -î: with and without the supplementary suffix -ăsc

Verbs ending in -*î* fall into two subclasses, depending on the presence or absence of the suffix -*ăsc* (with the allomorph -*ăşt*-) in the present indicative and present subjunctive forms and in the imperative (Table 2.5). The two subclasses are also differentiated depending on the position of stress: the verbs with -*ăsc* bear stress on the suffix, whereas the verbs without -*ăsc* bear stress on the root in all the singular forms and in the 3rd person plural.

H The verbs in -*î* originate in Latin verbs (*urî* < vulgar Lat. *HORRĪRE), or in Slavic or Hungarian roots. Some of these verbs take the suffix -*ăsc* (*hotărî* 'decide', *izvorî* 'spring', *ocărî* 'insult'), some others do not (*coborî* 'descend', *doborî* 'knock down', *omorî* 'kill') (Frâncu 2009: 128).

The suffix -*î* evolved from the suffix -*i*, in contexts where the latter was preceded by the geminate sound -*r*. In the 16th–17th centuries there were verbs with parallel forms, in -*i* and -*î*.

TABLE 2.5 Class V

CLASS V (VERBS IN -*î*)		
SUBCLASSES	SPECIFIC FEATURES	EXAMPLES
(a)	INF: -'î	coborî 'descend'
	PRES IND, PRES SUBJ, IMP: − -'ăsc	1SG cobor, 1SG să cobor, 2SG.IMP coboară! 'descend'
(b)	INF: -'î	hotărî 'decide'
	PRES IND, PRES SUBJ, IMP: + -'ăsc	1SG hotărăsc, 1SG să hotărăsc, 2SG.IMP hotărăşte! 'decide'

amări vs. *amărî* 'sadden', *omori* vs. *omorî* 'kill' (Frâncu 2009: 128, 296; see also §4.2.1.1). Given the origin of the class of verbs with the infinitive in *-î*, there are authors who subordinate that class to the fourth class, consisting of verbs with the infinitive suffix *-i* (GLR I: 246; Lombard 1974: 30; Avram 2001: 199, a.o.).

2.1.2 Irregular verbs

A series of verbs which belong to different classes depending on the infinitive endings show irregularities in the realization of the root, of the affixes, and / or of the syncretic forms. These irregularities may be explained in the following ways:

1. etymologically
   - suppletion inherited from Latin: *a fi* 'be' (*sunt* 'I am', *eşti* 'you are', *este* '(s)he is', *fi* 'be', *fiind* 'being', *fost* 'been'), *a da* 'give' (*dădui* 'I gave', *dăduşi* 'you gave'), *a sta* 'stay' (*stătui* 'I stayed', *stătuşi* 'you stayed');
   - suppletion due to regular sound change: *a lua* 'take' (*iau* 'I take', *iei* 'you take', *luăm* 'we take');
   - imperative forms whose irregularities are mainly inherited from Latin: *zi!* 'tell!', *du!* 'bring!';
2. by the membership of certain forms in distinct inflectional classes (compare the present indicative *trebuie* 'must' to the corresponding present subjunctive *să trebuiască*);
3. by the replacement of a form in the paradigm by an atypical variant, recommended by DOOM (*continua* 'continue' has the inflectional ending *-i* in the 1st person singular present indicative, as well as *tăia* 'cut', *mângâia* 'caress', but differs from them in other inflectional forms: 3SG≡3PL (IND) *continuă*, (SUBJ) *să continue*, compared to 3SG≡3PL (IND) *taie*, (SUBJ) *să taie*; 3SG≡3PL (IND) *mângâie*, (SUBJ) *să mângâie*;
4. by the occurrence of specific inflectional endings
   - *avea* 'have': the inflectional endings marking person and number *-m* (*eu am* 'I have'), and *-u* [u̯] (*ei au* 'they have');
   - *bea* 'drink': the inflectional ending *-u* [u̯] (*eu / ei beau* 'I / they drink');
   - *fi* 'be': the imperfect suffix *-a-* (*eram* 'I was', compared to *veneam* 'I was coming');
   - *şti* 'know': the simple past suffix *-u-* (*ştiui* 'I knew', compared to *sări – sării* 'I jumped');
5. by the redundant marking of a grammatical category (in the simple past forms of the verbs *fi* 'be' and *avea* 'have' two endings may occur: *fusei* 'I was', *avusei* 'I had', alongside the forms with a single ending, *fui* 'I was', *avui* 'I had');
6. by the presence of specific syncretic forms:
   - *vrea* 'want': 3SG PRESENT INDICATIVE≡3SG PRESENT SUBJUNCTIVE≡3PL PRESENT SUBJUNCTIVE=-Ø (*el vrea—el / ei să vrea*, compared to *tăcea* 'keep silent': *el tace—el / ei să tacă*);
   - *lua* 'take': 3SG PRESENT INDICATIVE≡3SG PRESENT SUBJUNCTIVE≡3PL PRESENT SUBJUNCTIVE=-Ø (*el ia—el / ei să ia*, compared to *cânta* 'sing': *el / ei cântă—el / ei să cânte*).

2.2 MOOD, TENSE, AND ASPECT

2.2.1 Verb morphology

The Romanian verb marks the categories of mood, tense, and aspect synthetically (by inflection) and analytically (by periphrases). Verbal periphrases show different degrees of grammaticalization.

The moods of Romanian are: the *indicative*, the *subjunctive*, the *conditional*, and the *imperative*. Another paradigm—only partially grammaticalized—deriving from the epistemic future, was called *presumptive* in 20th-century grammars.

Tenses are regularly associated with aspectual values. Certain tenses express primarily temporality (the *present* and the *compound / analytic past*), while some others have predominantly aspectual values (the *imperfect*). The simple temporal distinction present vs. past is marked for all the moods (except for the imperative), as well as for a non-finite verbal form (the *infinitive*). The most complex temporal-aspectual system belongs to the indicative and contains *present*, *past* (the *simple past*, the *compound past*, the *imperfect*, and the *pluperfect*), and *future* forms (the *future*, the *future perfect* and the *future in the past*).

The imperative and most tenses of the indicative (the present, the simple past, the imperfect, and the pluperfect) are simple (synthetic) forms. The present subjunctive is a simple form accompanied almost always by the specific particle să$_{SUBJ}$. Certain tenses of the indicative (the compound past, the future, and the future perfect), the perfect subjunctive, the tenses of the presumptive (present and perfect), and of the conditional (present and perfect) are compound (analytic) forms.

H The modal and temporal-aspectual forms of the Romanian verb either are inherited from Latin (the present indicative, the simple past, the pluperfect, the imperfect, as well as the subjunctive and the imperative), or developed later through the grammaticalization of periphrases (the compound past and the future indicative, the present and perfect conditional).

2.2.1.1 Synthetic forms

Synthetic forms encode mood and tense syncretically, through suffixes ('tense–mood markers'), which are either common to all verbs (such as -*se*- in the pluperfect indicative), or specific to a set of inflectional (sub)classes (e.g. -*a*- and -*ea*- for the imperfect).

H The thematic vowels, specific to the 'long' infinitive (§4.2.1.1) and characterizing the main classes of verbs — -'*a*, -'*e*, -*e*, -'*i*, -'*î* /i/—were inherited from Latin, undergoing various further changes. In Romanian structuralist descriptions they are predominantly treated as inflectional elements, as mood and tense suffixes (Guțu Romalo 1968a: 143–95; Manea 2008b: 403, 420, 433), partially syncretic (common to more moods and tenses), and realized only for some persons.

Suffixes are followed by inflectional endings, which encode person and number. The two categories are expressed cumulatively, but some morphemes are specialized (for example, in the simple past or pluperfect, -*ră*- indicates the plural). Certain endings are unique for all tenses (-*m* for 1st person plural, -*ți* for 2nd person plural); some others contribute to the specification of the modal and temporal form: the ending for the 1st person singular is Ø / -*u* for present indicative and subjunctive, -*i* for simple past, and -*m* for imperfect and pluperfect indicative.

Only a limited number of verbs (in the 2nd and 3rd classes) distinguish between a root for the present (indicative and subjunctive), the imperfect, and the infinitive, and another one for simple past, pluperfect, and participle: *spun-* (*spunem* 'we tell'; *spuneam*, 'we were telling', *spune* '(to) tell') vs. *spu-* (*spusei* 'I told', *spusesem* 'I had told', *spus* 'told'); *ved-* (*vedem* 'we see', *vedeam* 'we were seeing', *vedea* '(to) see') vs. *văz-* (*văzui* 'I saw', *văzusem* 'I had seen', *văzut* 'seen').

H Romanian inherited from Latin the opposition between the *infectum* (the imperfective root) and the *perfectum* (the perfect root), but differences were greatly reduced by the creation of new analogical forms for the perfect.

Verb inflection is also characterized by an extensive root-allomorphy. Root-alternations are 'autonomously morphological', without phonologic conditionings or systematic correlations with semantic or syntactic proprieties, but they follow some very stable patterns (see Maiden 2005, 2009a, 2009c, 2011b).

2.2.1.1.1 The present indicative form of verbs is marked inflectionally, through specific endings. Stress placement is variable (falling either on the root or on the ending), depending on the grammatical person (1–3SG, 3PL vs. 1–2PL) of the verb and on the inflectional class to which verbs belong (III vs. I, II, IV, V).

The present indicative forms for the different inflectional classes are:

Ia	asculta 'listen'	—as'cult—as'culți—as'cultă—ascul'tăm—ascul'tați—as'cultă;
Ib	lucra 'work'	—lu'crez—lu'crezi—lu'crează—lu'crăm—lu'crați—lu'crează;
II	revedea 'revise'	—re'văd—re'vezi—re'vede—reve'dem—reve'deți—re'văd;
III	merge 'go'	—merg—mergi—'merge—'mergem—'mergeți—merg;
IVa₁	sări 'jump'	—sar—sari—'sare—să'rim—să'riți—sar;
IVa₂	sui 'climb'	—sui—sui—'suie—su'im—su'iți—'suie;
IVa₃	suferi 'suffer'	—'sufăr—'suferi—'suferă—sufe'rim—sufe'riți—'suferă;
IVb	iubi 'love'	—iu'besc—iu'bești—iu'bește—iu'bim—iu'biți—iu'besc;
Va	doborî 'knock down'	—do'bor—do'bori—do'boară—dobo'râm—dobo'râți—do'boară;
Vb	hotărî 'decide'	—hotă'răsc—hotă'răști—hotă'răște—hotă'râm—hotă'râți—hotă'răsc.

The thematic vowel of the present indicative (and the present subjunctive, see §2.2.1.1.2) depends on the inflectional class, but also has variant realizations, some of which are conditioned by the phonological context. The thematic vowel ('thematic suffix') occurs only in the 1st and 2nd person plural, and is realized as:

I: -'a (2PL ascul'tați 'you listen'), also in the variant -'ă /ə/ (1PL ascul'tăm 'we listen'); -ă is realized as -e after a yod or a palatalized consonant (1PL tăiem [tə'jem] 'we cut', veghem [ve'ɟem] 'we watch');

II: -'e (2PL ve'deți 'you see', 1PL ve'dem 'we see');

III: (unstressed) -e (2PL 'mergeți 'you go', 1PL 'mergem 'we go');

IVa,b: -'i (2PL dor'miți 'you sleep', 1PL dor'mim 'we sleep');

Va,b: -'â /ɨ/ (2PL cobo'râți 'you descend', 1PL cobo'râm 'we descend').

Verbs in the first inflectional class (with infinitive in -*a*) fall into two subclasses distinguished by the absence / presence of the present supplementary suffix -'*ez*- (also considered an *infix*, see Densusianu 1961, II: 130; Allen 1977), or *stem-extension, stem increment, augment*, etc.): verbs with *strong present forms* (Ia) do not take this suffix, whereas verbs with *weak present forms* (Ib) do take it. The suffix occurs in the 1st, 2nd, 3rd person singular and in the 3rd person plural, with the allomorphs (alongside vowel alternations) *-ez* (1–2SG) and *-eaz-* [e̯az] (3SG, 3PL).

Verbs belonging to the fourth and fifth inflectional classes (with the infinitive in *-i*, or in *-î* respectively) also fall into subclasses of verbs with *strong present forms*, without any supplementary suffix (IVa$_{1,2,3}$, Va), and verbs with *weak present forms*, with the supplementary suffix -'*esc* (IVb) and -'*ăsc* [əsk] (Vb), respectively. The suffix occurs in the 1st, 2nd, and 3rd person singular and in the 3rd person plural, realized (with morphophonological alternations) as *-esc* / *-ăsc* (1SG, 3PL), *-eşt-* / *-ăşt-* (2–3SG).

The weak forms of the present indicative show a high degree of regularity: they do not have vocalic or consonant alternations in the root, and do not change the position of the stress (which constantly falls on the suffix). It is not predictable to which of these inflectional subclasses, with or without *-ez*, or *-esc* / *-ăsc* respectively, a verb belongs, and there are frequent variations between them (§§2.1.1.1, 2.1.1.4, 2.1.1.5).

H The weak present forms developed through the extension and desemanticization of the Latin suffixes (infixes) *-sc-* (either ingressive or denominal) and *-idi-* (denominal) (Rosetti 1986: 79, 141; Hall 1983: 49, 57; Maiden 2004; cf. Meul 2009).

C The series of verbs with the supplementary suffix *-esc* is similar to that found in other Romance languages (see Iliescu and Mourin 1991), which occurs in the same moods as in Romanian (and in the same persons, in the case of the It. *-isc*), and undergo a similar loss of the initial meaning (Maiden 2004; Meul 2009; Costanzo 2011; cf. Schwarze 2009). There are also parallels for the use of the suffix *-ez* in some Italian dialects (Lombard 1954: 486; Maiden 2004).

The inflectional endings for the present indicative—bearing person and number agreement features—are differentiated in the 3rd person according to inflectional class and subclass. In the 1st, 2nd, and 3rd persons singular and plural, they may have distinct phonological realizations depending on the preceding phonological context.

The person and number endings of the present indicative forms are:

1SG: Ø (zero morpheme) (*caut* 'I search'), also realized as *-u* /u/ after a consonant cluster ending in a liquid (*aflu* 'I find out', *mustru* 'I reprimand', *urlu* 'I yell') or as the semi-vowel *-u* /u̯/ in the case of certain irregular verbs: *scriu* [skriu̯] 'I write', *dau* [dau̯] 'I give', *stau* [stau̯] 'I stay';

2SG: non-syllabic *-i* /ʲ/ (*crezi* [krezʲ]) 'you think', also realized as a vowel, when it follows a consonant cluster ending in a liquid (*afli* ['afli] 'you find out', *mustri* 'you reprimand', *urli* 'you yell'), or as a semi-vowel, when it follows a vowel (*dai* [daj] 'you give');

3SG: *-ă* /ə/, for the verbs belonging to the subclasses I, IVa$_3$, Va—*află* '(s)he finds out', *oferă* '(s)he offers', *coboară* '(s)he descends'—or *-e*, for the verbs in the subclasses II, III, IVa$_{1,2}$, b, Vb—*vede, crede, vine, suie, citeşte, urăşte* '(s)he sees, believes, comes, climbs, reads, hates'; *-ă* is also realized as *-e* in a palatal context (see below).

1PL: *-m*—*aflăm* 'we find out', *credem* 'we believe', etc.;

2PL: *-ţi*, with non-syllabic *i* [tsʲ]—*aflaţi* 'you find out', *credeţi* 'you believe', etc.;

3PL: Ø (zero morpheme) and the semi-vowel *-u* /u̯/ (for verbs belonging to the subclasses II, III, IVa$_1$,b,Vb: *văd* 'they see', *vin* 'they come', *citesc* 'they read', *urăsc* 'they hate', or some irregular verbs: *scriu* 'they write') or *-ă* (for the verbs belonging to the subclasses I, IVa$_2$,Va: *află* 'they find out', *acoperă* 'they cover', *coboară* 'they descend').

2.2 Mood, tense, and aspect

The 3rd person forms may be analysed in different ways, as the endings -*ă* and -*e* are considered (a) person and number morphemes (Guțu Romalo 1968a: 171–2; Manea 2008b: 405–6) or (b) allomorphs of the present suffix (which distinguishes the present indicative from present subjunctive) or thematic vowels, part of the stem (Iliescu and Mourin 1991: 138–40); in case (b), the 3rd person forms have a zero personal ending (Pîrvulescu 2006).

H The inflectional endings of the 1st person singular and plural and 3rd person singular and plural and of the 2nd person plural are inherited from Latin, their evolution showing regular phonological changes (the loss of the final consonants and of the final -*u*, the modifications of certain vowels) and certain analogical extensions. Consequently, Lat. -O > -*u*, -MUS > -m; Ø; -AT > -*ă*, -ET, -IT > -*e*; -ANT > -*ă*, -UNT > Ø, -TIS > -*ți*. The final -*u* as an inflectional ending was preserved in certain phonological contexts. In the 2nd person singular, -*i* may be explained in Romanian and Italian as well as an analogical extension of the ending shown by the verbs ending in -*i* (Densusianu 1961, II: 133; but cf. also Maiden 1996).

C In Romanian, phonological changes produced the syncretism between the inflectional endings occurring in the 3rd person plural and those in the 3rd person or 1st person singular; thus, among the Romance languages, Romanian is in between languages like Italian, Spanish, and Portuguese, that have differential person marking, and French, characterized by homonymic extensions. In the 2nd person singular, Romanian and Italian have the inflectional ending -*i*, which is an innovation when compared to the Latin system.

U In the 1st person singular and in the syncretic form of the 3rd person plural, the non-standard use, especially in the southern varieties, preserved the forms modified under the influence of yod, deriving from the alteration of the root-final dentals *t*, *d*, *n* by a palatal element (Lat. -EO): 1SG *scoț* 'I take out', 1SG *văz* 'I see', 1SG *țiu* 'I keep', 1SG *viu* 'I come', etc. or from an analogical extension (1SG *crez* 'I believe', 1SG *spui* 'I say', etc.). In the standard language, these forms were replaced by ones with a reconstructed dental: 1SG *scot*, *văd*, *cred*, *țin*, *spun*. Meanwhile, many variations have been recorded in areas where the first mentioned series of forms were used (Gheție 1975: 594–7; Pană Dindelegan 1987: 11–12; Zamfir 2005: 417–91; Frâncu 2009: 298–300; Maiden 2011b).

Present paradigms show characteristic syncretisms depending on the inflectional classes of verbs. Two situations can be identified:

1. verbs showing 3SG≡3PL syncretism: the inflectional classes I, IVa$_{2,3}$, Va—(*el / ei*) *află* 'he / they find(s) out', (*el / ei*) *suie* 'he / they climb(s)', (*el / ei*) *oferă* 'he / they offer(s)', (*el / ei*) *coboară* 'he / they descend(s)';
2. verbs showing 1SG≡3PL syncretism: the inflectional classes II, III, IVa$_1$,b,Vb—(*eu / ei*) *văd* 'I / they see', (*eu / ei*) *merg* 'I / they go', (*eu / ei*) *dorm* 'I / they sleep', (*eu / ei*) *citesc* 'I / they read', (*eu / ei*) *urăsc* hate 'I / they hate'.

U In regional speech (more exactly, in southern varieties), the 3SG≡3PL syncretism extended to all the subclasses of verbs (*el / ei vede* 'she / they sees', *merge* 'he / they goes', etc.). This extension is stigmatized as a typical non-standard feature.

Supplementary syncretisms (1SG≡2SG) may appear for phonological reasons.
For verbs in the first inflectional class with the semi-vowel [j] occurring in root-final position and for subclass IVa$_2$ (containing a large enough number of members with the derivational suffixes -*(u)i*, -*(ă)i*, -*(â)i*), the inflectional endings have predictable realizations, as required by the phonological context. These verbs are not always recognizable from the orthography: some of them render the semi-vowel—*tăia* [təˈj+a] 'cut'—some others do not,

as the semi-vowel is graphically assimilated by the vowel -*i* in the root—*speria* [speri'j+a] 'frighten' or by the suffix -*i: sui* [su'j+i] 'climb'. The effects of the palatal context are the following:

- the semi-vowel in the root occurs in the 1st person singular, in the context of the zero inflectional ending—*tai* 'I cut', *mângâi* 'I caress', *sperii* 'I frigthen', *sui* 'I climb';
- the semi-vowel in the root is absorbed by the inflectional ending -*i* in the 2nd person singular—2SG *tai* 'you cut', *mângâi* 'you caress', *sperii* 'you frighten', *sui* 'you climb';
- the succeeding vowel is modified by frontness (*ă* > *e*), according to the rule which excludes the diphthong [jə] (*iă* [jə] > *ie* [je]) in standard Romanian: *taie* '(s)he cuts', *tăiem* 'we cut', *suie* '(s)he climbs', etc.

This constraint means that, in the subclasses Ia and IVa₂, the inflectional endings of the 3rd person singular and plural are realized as -*e*, and the inflectional endings of the 1st and 2nd person singular are syncretic:

Ia: *tăia* 'cut'   —tai—tai—'taie—(tă'iem—tă'iaţi)—'taie;
IVa₂: *sui* 'climb' —sui—sui—'suie—(su'im—su'iţi)—'suie.

Vowel alternations in the root are far from systematic, and may be explained as an effect of historical evolution. Verbs with otherwise similar forms may or may not display these types of alternations, depending on whether they are old inherited words (*spăl* 'I wash'—*speli* 'you wash'—*spală* '(s)he / they wash(es)'; *porţi* 'you wear'—*poartă* '(s)he wears'—*purtăm* 'we wear') or modern loanwords (*sper* 'I hope'—*speri* 'you hope'—*speră* '(s)he / they hope (s)'; *suporţi* 'you endure'—*suportă* '(s)he / they endure(s)'—*suportăm* 'we endure'). Some of the alternations occurring in the present indicative originate in effects of vowel harmony and are correlated with the absence or presence in the following syllable of vowels displaying similar features—*plec* / *pleci* 'I / you go' vs. *pleacă* '(s)he / they go(es)', *port* / *porţi* 'I / you wear' vs. *poartă* '(s)he / they wear(s)'; others are due to the differential effects of stress on vowels: 3SG / 3PL 'pleacă vs. 1PL ple'căm, 1SG port vs. 1PL pur'tăm. Many contexts which favoured the occurrence of a certain alternation have changed over time; thus, alternations cannot be described exhaustively only by referring to the modern language.

The inflectional ending -*i* triggers obligatory regular consonant alternations in the root. Some of them are 'hidden' by the orthographic system, through the use of the same grapheme: c /k/ ~ /tʃ/ (*trec* / *treci* 'I / you pass'), g /(g/ ~ /dʒ/ (*rog* / *rogi* 'I / you ask'); others are also graphically visible: t ~ ţ (/t/ ~ /ts/) (*pot* / *poţi* 'I / you can'), s ~ ş (/s/ ~ /ʃ/) (*cos* / *coşi* 'I / you sew'), d ~ z (/d/ ~ /z/) (*văd* / *vezi* 'I / you see').

In conclusion, the present tense paradigm has a wide variety of forms, produced by the existence of several suffixes ('thematic vowels') with the same grammatical values, and by phonological alternations. On the other hand, there are relatively few irregular verbs, most of them being characterized by suppletion following the pattern 1–3SG + 3PL vs. 1–2PL (Maiden 2009a):

lua 'take'   (1SG) **iau**, (2SG) **iei**, (3SG) **ia**, (3PL) **iau** vs. (1PL) **lu'ăm**, (2PL) **lu'aţi**;
mânca   (1SG) **mă'nânc**, (2SG) **mă'nânci**, (3SG, 3PL) **mă'nâncă** vs. (1PL) **mân'căm**,
'eat'   (2PL) **mân'caţi**;
usca 'dry'   (1SG) **u'suc**, (2SG) **u'suci**, (3SG, 3PL) **u'sucă** vs. (1PL) **us'căm**, (2PL) **us'caţi**.

The verb *fi* 'be' has the following present indicative tense forms: 1SG *sunt* [sunt] (standard) / *sânt* [sɨnt] (frequently) / -*s, îs* (non-standard); 2SG *eşti* [jeʃtʲ]; 3SG *este* ['jeste] / *e* [je]; 1PL *suntem* ['suntem] (standard) / *sântem* ['sɨntem] (frequently); 2PL *sunteți* ['suntetsⁱ] (standard) / *sânteți* ['sɨntetsⁱ] (frequently); 3PL *sunt* (standard) / *sânt* (frequently) / *-s, îs* (non-standard) 'they are'.

The verb *avea* 'have' displays the following forms: 1SG *am* [am], 2SG *ai* [ai̯], 3SG *are* ['are], 1PL *avem* [a'vem], 2PL *aveți* [a'vetsⁱ], 3PL *au* [au̯].

2.2.1.1.2 The present subjunctive paradigm is minimally differentiated inflectionally from the present indicative one: inflectional endings differ only in the 3rd person singular and plural, for verbs which do not present supplementary syncretisms produced because of phonological reasons. The main difference is the specialization of the complementizer *să* (SĂ_SUBJ) as a subjunctive marker. Because of the obligatory presence of SĂ_SUBJ, the Romanian present subjunctive is not a simple form *stricto sensu*. However, the 3rd person forms, inflectionally marked, may exceptionally be used without SĂ_SUBJ.

For the distinctive inflectional forms of the subjunctive, 3SG≡3PL syncretism is present in all verbs.

The specific present subjunctive form has *-e* for verbs in the inflectional classes I, IVa₂₋₃ and Va and *-ă* for verbs belonging to the inflectional classes II, III, IVa₁,b and Vb. In effect, the endings for indicative and subjunctive are reversed:

(9)   present subjunctive   present indicative
     -e: să asculte   *-ă*:   ascultă
            SĂ_SUBJ listen.SUBJ.PRES.3SG≡PL   listen.IND.PRES.3SG≡PL
     -ă: să revadă   *-e*:   revede
            SĂ_SUBJ revise.SUBJ. PRES.3SG≡PL   revise.IND.PRES.3SG

The alternation between inflectional endings *-e* and *-ă* is often associated with (vocalic or consonantal) alternations, which additionally mark the difference between the subjunctive and the indicative. Thus, in the 3rd person singular and plural of the verbs with weak present forms, the supplementary suffixes have the variants *-ez-*, *-easc-* [e̯ask] and *-asc-* [ask], distinct from the corresponding variants which occur in the indicative: *-eaz-*, *-eșt-*, and *-ășt-*.

Ia:	să as'cult—să as'culți—să as'culte—să ascul'tăm—să ascul'tați—să as'culte	'listen'
Ib:	să lu'crez—să lu'crezi—să lu'creze—să lu'crăm—să lu'crați—să lu'creze	'work'
II:	să re'văd—să re'vezi—să re'vadă—să reve'dem—să reve'deți—să re'vadă	'revise'
III:	să merg—să mergi—să 'meargă—să 'mergem—să 'mergeți—să 'meargă	'go'
IVa₁:	să sar—să sari—să 'sară—să să'rim—să să'riți—să 'sară	'jump'
IVa₂:	să sui—să sui—să 'suie—să su'im—să su'iți—să 'suie	'climb'
IVa₃:	să 'sufăr—să 'suferi—să 'sufere—să sufe'rim—să sufe'riți—să 'sufere	'suffer'
IVb:	să iu'besc—să iu'bești—să iu'bească—să iu'bim—să iu'biți—să iu'bească	'love'
Va:	să do'bor—să do'bori—să do'boare—să dobo'râm—să dobo'râți—să do'boare	'knock down'
Vb:	să hotă'răsc—să hotă'răști—să hotă'rască—să hotă'râm—să hotă'râți—să hotă'rască	'decide'

For phonological reasons, the difference between the present indicative endings and the present subjunctive ones may be neutralized: verbs of all inflectional classes with root-final [j] have, both in the subjunctive and in the indicative, the ending -*e*:

(10) present subjunctive present indicative
-*e:* să taie -*e:* taie
SĂ_{SUBJ} cut.SUBJ.PRES.3SG≡PL cut.IND.PRES.3SG≡PL
-*e:* să suie -*e:* suie
SĂ_{SUBJ} climb.SUBJ.PRES.3SG≡PL climb.IND.PRES.3SG≡PL

H   The inflectional endings of the 3rd person singular and plural are inherited from Latin (Lat. -ET, -ENT > -e; -AT, -ANT > -ă). The other inflectional forms come from the indicative. Certain 3rd person subjunctive forms preserved an originally palatal alternant of the root-final dentals *t, d, n*: *să scoață* 'take out', *să vază* 'see', *să ție* 'keep', etc. (Pană Dindelegan 1987: 11–2; Frâncu 2009: 298–300); in the present-day language, these forms are archaic or dialectal.

The verbs *fi* 'be' and *avea* 'have' display specific present subjunctive forms (distinguished from the present indicative ones by suppletion). *Fi* has specific subjunctive forms in all persons: 1SG *să fiu*, 2SG *să fii*, 3SG *să fie*, 1PL *să fim*, 2PL *să fiți*, 3PL *să fie*, whereas *avea* displays specific forms only in the 3rd person: 1SG *să am*, 2SG *să ai*, 3SG *să* **aibă**, 1PL *să avem*, 2PL *să aveți*, 3PL *să* **aibă**.

U   In non-standard language, certain variants of the 3rd person forms of the verbs *avea* 'have'—*să aibe* and *să aivă*—are in use (Lombard 1955: 906); these forms may be explained by analogy.

Through a grammaticalization process, the invariable particle SĂ_{SUBJ} became a subjunctive marker, but preserved its functional complementizer features, present in most contexts (§10.1.1.1). In other situations, SĂ_{SUBJ} simultaneously functions as a subjunctive marker and a circumstantial (purpose or conditional) conjunction.

H   The particle SĂ_{SUBJ} comes from the Latin conditional conjunction SI. In the old language, the conditional SĂ (also in the variant *se*) could be followed by indicative (11a) or conditional forms (11b) too:

(11) a. Că   să   ești   și   păcătos,   nu   te   mâhni   (Coresi)
         that SĂ   be.IND.PRES.2SG   also sinful   not   CL.REFL.2SG grieve
         'Don't grieve if you are sinful too'
     b. Ce   folos   e   omului,   să   ară   dobândi   toată
         what   use   is   human.DEF.DAT   SĂ   AUX.COND.3SG   obtain.INF   all
         lumea...?
         world.DEF   (Coresi)
         'What shall it profit a man, if he shall gain the whole world...?'

C   According to the typological parameter mentioned by Giannakidou (2009), Romanian has an intermediary position, between the Romance languages with an inflectionally marked subjunctive, and Balkan languages, which employ an invariable particle. The existence of two complementizers specialized for the distinction *realis / irrealis* is a Balkan feature as well (also present in Greek, Albanian, Macedonian, Bulgarian; see Ammann and van der Auwera 2004: 300–2). Among the Romance languages, only Romanian and southern Italian dialects have a conjunction specialized for subjunctive that is different from the indicative complementizer.

A piece of evidence for the incomplete grammaticalization of să$_{SUBJ}$ is the fact that it can very occasionally be left out in the 3rd person singular and plural forms (which do not necessarily need the analytic marker, as they are already inflectionally differentiated) in matrix clauses (12a) or concessive clausal adjuncts (12b):

(12) a. **Fie** cum zici tu!
 be.SUBJ.3SG how say.IND.PRES.2SG you
 'Be it as you say!'

 b. **Spună** el orice, nu-l ascult
 say.SUBJ.3SG he anything not=CL.ACC.3SG listen.IND.PRES.1SG
 'Whatever he may say, I don't listen to him'

However, the grammaticalization of să$_{SUBJ}$ as a subjunctive marker is very advanced, as shown by the contexts in which the non-complementizer and non-subordinator să$_{SUBJ}$ are obligatory in main clauses in the 1st and 2nd person (13a), and in indirect interrogatives (13b) and relatives in all persons (13c):

(13) a. **Să** vă liniștiți și **să** plecăm!
 să$_{SUBJ}$ CL.REFL.ACC.2PL calm.SUBJ.2PL and să$_{SUBJ}$ go.SUBJ.1PL
 'Calm down and let's go!'

 b. Nu știe **cum să** procedeze
 not knows how să$_{SUBJ}$ act.SUBJ.3SG
 '(S)he doesn't know how to act'

 c. N-am găsit ideea care **să** ne salveze
 not=(we)have found idea.DEF which să$_{SUBJ}$ CL.ACC.1PL save.SUBJ.3SG
 'We didn't find the idea to save us'

Relative clauses with deleted relativizer (14b) are possible in existential, generic sentences, containing bare noun phrases (Farkas 1982; Bužarovska 2004):

(14) a. Nu e om care **să** nu aibă probleme
 not is man which să$_{SUBJ}$ not have.SUBJ.3SG problems

 b. Nu e om **să** nu aibă probleme
 not is man să$_{SUBJ}$ not have.SUBJ.3SG problems
 'There is no man without problems'

Between să$_{SUBJ}$ and the verb, only pronominal clitics, the negative marker *nu*, as well as temporal-aspectual adverbial clitics like *mai* 'more', *și* 'also', *tot* 'always' may intervene, either individually or in sequences of at most five elements (Manea 2008a: 386):

(15) a. să **mai** stea vs. *să **uneori** stea
 să$_{SUBJ}$ more stay.SUBJ.3SG să$_{SUBJ}$ sometimes stay.SUBJ.3SG
 '(s)he should still stay'

 b. Să **nu** ne-o **mai tot** reproșați
 să$_{SUBJ}$ not CL.DAT.1PL=CL.ACC.F.3SG more always reproach.SUBJ.2PL
 'you shouldn't keep on admonishing us'

For the fixed group *ca... să*, see §10.1.1.2.
 Să is also a component of the invariable perfect subjunctive periphrasis (§2.2.1.2.7).

2.2.1.1.3 The forms of the imperfect are made up of the root (usually the same as for the 1st and 2nd person of the present), the specific tense suffix (-'a- or -'ea- [e̯a], depending on the inflectional class, but always stressed), and the inflectional endings -m, -i [i̯], Ø, -m, -ți [tsʲ], -u [u̯].

The suffix -'a- occurs in the verbs with the infinitive in -a and -î:

Ia: asculta 'listen'   ascul'tam—ascul'tai—ascul'ta—ascul'tam—ascul'tați—ascul'tau
V: coborî 'descend' cobo'ram—cobo'rai—cobo'ra—cobo'ram—cobo'rați—cobo'rau

The suffix -'ea- occurs in the verbs with the infinitive in -ea, -e and -i:

II: vedea 'see'   ve'deam—ve'deai—ve'dea—ve'deam—ve'deați—ve'deau
III: spune 'say'   spu'neam—spu'neai—spu'nea—spu'neam—spu'neați—spu'nea
IV: iubi 'love'   iu'beam—iu'beai—iu'bea—iu'beam—iu'beați—iu'bea

In verbs of the fourth inflectional class whose roots end in a vowel followed by a [j] "hidden" by orthography, the palatal element of the root ([j]) absorbs the palatal element of the suffix ([e̯]), and the result is the sequence [ja], rendered orthographically as *ia* or (for the verbs with root-final in [ij]) as *a*:

sui 'climb' [su'j+i]   suiam [su'jam]
mormăi 'mumble' [mormə'j+i]   mormăiam [mormə'jam]
mârâi 'growl' [mɨrɨ'j+i]   mârâiam [mɨrɨ'jam]
(a se) sfii 'be shy' [sfi'j+i] (mă) sfiam [sfi'jam]

H The imperfect is inherited from Latin, but its inflectional endings (with the exception of 1–2PL) are subsequent forms, and some of them are rather late creations. In the 1st person singular, the inflectional ending -m is an analogical extension (probably based on 1st person plural), a late innovation which occurred in the 17th century in the southern dialects, then gradually extended towards the north (Gheție 1972; Zamfir 2007: 173–7). In the old language, the 1SG and 3SG≡PL forms do not display any specific inflectional ending:

(16) a. eu lui   nici de   fărâmele   measeei   meale   nu-i
        I him.DAT nor   from morsels.DEF   meal.DEF.GEN   my.GEN not=CL.DAT.3SG
        da   (Coresi)
        give.IMPERF.1SG
        'I didn't even give him morsel of my meal'
     b. Hristos **grăia**   /   alții **grăia**   (Coresi)
        Christ speak.IMPERF.3SG   others speak.IMPERF.3PL
        'Christ was speaking'   'Others were speaking'

The 3rd person plural inflectional ending -u, initially used regionally (in Banat), was adopted by the literary language only in the 19th century, in order to distinguish singular from plural forms (Gheție and Teodorescu 1965, 1966; Zamfir 2007: 177–9).

Regionally, the suffix -'*iia* [ija] / -'*âia* [ɨja] was also preserved until late for the verbs of the fourth and fifth inflectional classes (*grăiia* 'was / were speaking', *știia* 'knew', *ocărâia* 'was / were cursing') (Theodorescu 1978a: 302–3; Zamfir 2007: 179–88).

In the old language, periphrastic forms of the imperfect were also used (§2.2.6).

2.2 Mood, tense, and aspect

The imperfect forms of the verb *fi* 'be' are based on the suppletive root *er-*: *eram* [jeˈram], *erai* [-jeˈrai̯], *era* [jeˈra], *eram* [jeˈram], *erați* [jeˈratsi̯], *erau* [jeˈrau̯]. For the verbs *da* 'give', *sta* 'stand', alongside the usual modern forms in *dăd-* and *stăt-* (taken over from the perfect): 1SG *dădeam* 'I was giving', 1SG *stăteam* 'I was staying', there still persist older, regular, simple forms (1SG *dam*, *stam*).

2.2.1.1.4 The simple past forms are inflectionally marked by specific endings (suffix + inflectional endings). Stress placement varies depending on the inflectional class to which the verbs belong.

Depending on the inflectional classes, the simple past forms are the following:

Ia,b:	luˈcrai—luˈcrași—luˈcră—luˈcrarăm—luˈcrarăți—luˈcrară	'work'
II:	revăˈzui—revăˈzuși—revăˈzu—revăˈzurăm—revăˈzurăți—revăˈzură	'revise'
IIIa:	făˈcui –făˈcuși—făˈcu—făˈcurăm—făˈcurăți—făˈcură	'make'
IIIb,c:	merˈsei—merˈseși—ˈmerse—ˈmerserăm—ˈmerserăți—ˈmerseră	'go'
IVa₁₋₃,b:	săˈrii—săˈriși—săˈri—săˈrirăm—săˈrirăți—săˈriră	'jump'
Va,b:	doboˈrâi—doboˈrâși—doboˈrî—doboˈrârăm—doboˈrârăți—doboˈrâră	'knock down'

The root of the simple past (the perfective root) is usually identical to the root of the (masculine singular) participle and sometimes (for verbs in the 2nd and 3rd classes) differs from that of the infinitive:

ved+ea$_{INF}$ 'see' vs. **văz**+ui$_{PS}$ 'I saw' / **văz**+ut$_{PPLE}$ 'seen'
coac+e$_{INF}$ 'bake' vs. **cop**+sei$_{PS}$ 'I baked' / **cop**+t$_{PPLE}$ 'baked'

The simple past thematic suffix depends on the inflectional subclass of verbs:

Ia,b:	-ˈa (1SG *asculˈtai* 'I listened'), realized as -ă /ə/ in the 3rd person singular (*asculˈtă*); -ă is realized as -e after a yod (3SG *tăˈie* [təˈje] '(s)he cut';
II, IIIa:	-ˈu (1SG *văˈzui* 'I saw'; 1SG *făˈcui* 'I did');
IIIb,c:	-se (the suffix is stressed in the 1st and 2nd person singular: 1SG *merˈsei* 'I went', 2SG *merˈseși*, and unstressed in the other persons)
IVa₁₋₃,b:	-ˈi (1SG *dorˈmii* 'I slept');
Va,b:	-ˈî (1SG *coboˈrâi* 'I descended').

For all verbs, except for those belonging to subclasses 3b,c, the simple past suffix (the 'thematic vowel') is identical with the vowel of the participle suffix (§4.3.1). Verbs belonging to subclasses 3b,c, with the participle suffixes *-s* or *-t*, take the suffix *-se* in the simple past.

The inflectional endings for the simple past are common to all inflectional classes of verbs. The inflectional endings occurring in the plural are made up of a component expressing number (*-ră-*) and another marking number and person.

The simple past inflectional endings are:

1SG	-*i* [i̯]—*aflai* [aˈflai̯] 'I found out', *crezui* [kreˈzui̯] 'I believed', *mersei* [merˈsei̯] 'I went', *fugii* [fuˈdʒii̯] 'I ran', *coborâi* [koboˈrîi̯] 'I descended';
2SG:	-*și* [ʃi̯]—*aflași* 'you found out';

3SG: Ø—*află* '(s)he found out', *crezu* '(s)he believed', *merse* '(s)he went', *fugi* '(s)he ran', *coborî* '(s)he descended';
1PL: -*ră*+*m*—*aflarăm* 'we found out';
2PL: -*ră*+*ți* [rəts^i]—*aflarăți* 'you found out';
3PL: -*ră*+Ø—*aflară* 'they found out'.

Simple past inflectional endings do not produce alternations, except for -*se*-, which is associated with stress variation: *spăr'sei* 'I broke' vs. *'sparse* '(s)he broke', *sco'sei* 'I took out' vs. *'scoase* '(s)he took out'.

H The simple past forms are inherited from Latin. The distinction between the weak forms (with stress on the suffix) and the strong forms (with stress on the root) was preserved, but the paradigm of the strong simple past forms was gradually levelled by analogy with the weak simple past forms or by the occurrence of the suffix -*se*- corresponding to the sigmatic perfect (Șiadbei 1930; Densusianu 1961, II: 139–40; Theodorescu 1978a: 306–10). In the old language, the etymological strong forms of the simple past were still used: 1SG *merș* 'I went', *ziș* 'I said', *feci* 'I did', etc. (gradually replaced by *mersei*, *zisei*, *făcui*; see Zamfir 2007: 115–58). The inflectional ending -*ră*, which may be explained etymologically only in the 3rd person plural, was extended, in the 18th–19th centuries to the other plural persons (see Pană Dindelegan 1987: 36–8), removing for the verbs in -*a*, -*i*, and -*î* the syncretism of the simple past forms with the present forms (e.g. *lucrăm* 'we worked / work', *auzim* 'we heard / hear').

U For the verbs of the first inflectional class which have the same root for the present and the perfect, the forms of the simple past in the 3rd person singular are written identically to the forms of the present; the only difference consists in the position of the stress: 3SG *cân'tă* (simple past) vs. 3SG *'cântă* (present).

Placement of stress on the suffix -*se*- in the 1st and 2nd person plural: *mer'serăm*—*mer'serăți* (Pană Dindelegan 1987: 39–40) is a non-standard tendency.

The verb *fi* 'be' displays two series of forms:

a. fui—fuși—fu—'furăm—'furăți—'fură
b. fu'sei—fu'seși—'fuse—'fuserăm / fu'serăm—'fuserăți / fu'serăți—'fuseră.

The (b) series, whose forms display two equivalent suffixes (-*u*- and -*se*-), shows stress variations in the 1st and 2nd person plural. *Avea* 'have' also displays two series of forms, one of them regular (*av'ui*), the other one analogical, with two suffixes (*avu'sei*) and similar variations with respect to stress placement (*a'vuserăm / avu'serăm*). The simple past forms of the verbs *da* 'give' and *sta* 'stay' have a special root: 1SG *dădui*, *stătui* (for other forms, see Lombard 1954: 456–8).

2.2.1.1.5 The pluperfect is made up of the perfective root (identical to the root of the participle and of the simple past), to which a suffix composed of two elements is attached—a 'thematic' one, according to inflectional class and identical to the suffix of the simple past (the thematic vowel -'*a*, -'*u*, -'*i*, -'*â*, and -*se* for subclasses 3rd b,c)—and a general one, a specific tense suffix (-*se*-). The inflectional endings (which do not produce alternations) are -*m*, -*și* [ʃ^i], Ø, -*răm*, -*răți* [rəts^i], -*ră*. In the plural, the inflectional endings may be broken down, as in the simple past, into an element expressing number (-*ră*) and a person marker (-*m*, -*ți* [ts^i], Ø).

Stress has a fixed position, falling on the first component of the suffix.

H The Romanian pluperfect indicative continues the Latin pluperfect subjunctive (a unique development in the Romance languages, cf. Theodorescu 1978a). The 3rd person singular form is etymologically transparent (Lat. CANTAVISSET > Rom. *cântase* '(s)he had sung'); in the 2nd person singular, the inflectional ending *-și*, already present in the old language, was probably imposed by analogy with the simple past, under the influence of the prototypical inflectional ending *-i*. In the 1st person singular, the inflectional ending *-m* (absent from the old language—1SG *eu cântase* 'I had sung') was later imposed by analogy as well. The plural forms in the old language (1PL *cântasem*, 2PL *cântaset*, 3PL *cântase*) were modified by the analogical extension of a 2nd person inflectional ending (*cântaseți*) and, further on, by the use of the plural inflectional ending of the simple past (*-ră-*). This inflectional ending (Frâncu 1982b) was initially added to the 3rd person plural form (3PL *cântaseră*), then gradually extended to the 1st and 2nd person plural forms (it became a grammatical norm in DOOM).

The pluperfect is a tense which displays predictable forms with no irregularities, differing from the simple past ones only by the suffix *-se-* and by the inflectional ending in the 1st person singular *-m*.

Depending on the inflectional classes, the pluperfect forms are:

Ia,b:	luˈcrasem—luˈcrasești—luˈcrase—luˈcraserăm—luˈcraserăți—luˈcraseră	'work'
II, IIIa:	văˈzusem—văˈzusești—văˈzuse—văˈzuserăm—văˈzuserăți—văˈzuseră	'see'
	făˈcusem—făˈcusești—făˈcuse—făˈcuserăm—făˈcuserăți—făˈcuseră	'make'
IIIb,c:	merˈsesem—merˈsesești—merˈsese—merˈseserăm—merˈseserăți—merˈseseră	'go'
IVa$_{1-3}$,b:	săˈrisem—săˈrisești—săˈrise—săˈriserăm—săˈriserăți—săˈriseră	'jump'
Va,b:	doboˈrâsem—doboˈrâsești—doboˈrâse—doboˈrâserăm—doboˈrâserăți— doboˈrâseră	'knock down'

H In the old language, periphrases with pluperfect value were frequently used:
(17) a. a fost   venit
           has been   come.PPLE
           'He had come'
      b. era   venit
           was   come.PPLE
           'He had come'

The periphrastic pluperfect containing the verb *fi* 'be' (in the compound past or imperfect) and the participle was preserved until the current stage of language only regionally (in the northern varieties). Certain grammars of the 19th and 20th centuries considered it a literary form. The periphrasis containing the imperfect form of *avea* 'have' is the only pluperfect form existing in Aromanian and Megleno-Romanian.

C The existence of a synthetic pluperfect is a distinctive feature of Romanian (and Portuguese) among the Romance languages, where the pluperfect is predominantly periphrastic.

For the verbs *fi* 'be' and *avea* 'have' the first component of the suffix is *-se-* (as in the past simple forms 1SG *fusei*, *avusei*): 1SG *fusesem*, 1SG *avusesem*; the verbs *da* 'give' and *sta* 'stay' use the special root of the simple past: 1SG *dădusem*, 1SG *stătusem*.

2.2.1.1.6 The main morphological features of the imperative are related to its semantic-pragmatic use. The imperative does not display forms for all grammatical persons, but only for the 2nd person singular and plural, and does not mark the present–past temporal distinction; instead, it displays specific forms for the affirmative–negative distinction.

For morphosyntactic reasons, certain categories of verbs do not allow an imperative form (e.g. unipersonal verbs—meteorological, relational, stative, or perception verbs:

ploua 'rain', *consta* 'consist', *durea* 'hurt', etc.). Not all imperative forms are currently used; in the case of incomplete paradigms, the subjunctive may be used instead of the imperative:

(18) Să   placi   tuturor!
      să_SUBJ   like.SUBJ.2SG   all.DAT
      'May you be liked by everyone!'

      Să   devii   mai   bun!
      să_SUBJ   become.SUBJ.2SG   more   good
      'Become a better person!'

In the 2nd person singular, the affirmative imperative forms have specific inflectional endings, while the negative ones are made up of the negative marker *nu* and the infinitive of the verb. The verbs in the classes Ib, IVb, Vb take the specific suffixes of the indicative and subjunctive (*-ez*, *-esc*, *-ăsc*) in the imperative as well. The inflectional endings of the imperative are: *-ă*, *-i* [ⁱ], *-e*; for the second inflectional class and, partially, for the classes III and IVa$_1$, the 2nd person singular forms are syncretic with the 2nd person singular present indicative forms; for all the other classes of verbs, the 2nd person singular imperative forms are syncretic with the 3rd person singular present indicative forms.

The 2nd person singular imperative forms are shown in Table 2.6.

For the verbs in classes IIIa, b, c and IVa, the variation between the inflectional endings *-e* and *-i* does not depend on the inflectional subclasses. The variation is lexically conditioned, and / or influenced by phonological and prosodic factors. Verbs which take accusative and dative clitics (obligatorily postverbal in the affirmative form) generally have the inflectional ending *-e*: *spune-o!* 'say it!', *spune-mi!* 'tell me!', *înghite-l!* 'swallow it!'. Verbs which do not allow direct or indirect objects (thus, are not followed by clitics) carry the inflectional ending *-i*: *mergi!* 'go!' *fugi!* 'run!'. A verb can also have two variants, depending on the syntactic pattern (Graur 1968: 218–21):

(19) a. Treci mai repede!   vs.   Trece-l strada!
         'Move faster!'   'Help him cross the street!'

      b. Adormi!   vs.   Adoarme-l!
         'Fall asleep!'   'Put him to bed!'

TABLE 2.6 Imperative forms

Ia: pleca 'leave'	'pleacă!	nu **pleca**!
Ib: desena 'draw'	dese'nează!	nu **desena**!
II: tăcea 'keep silent'	taci!	nu **tăcea**!
IIIa,b,c: spune 'say', trece 'pass'	'spune! treci!	nu **spune**! nu **trece**!
IVa$_1$: fugi 'run', înghiți 'swallow'	fugi! în'ghite!	nu **fugi**! nu **înghiți**!
IVa$_2$: sui 'climb'	'suie!	nu **sui**!
IVa$_3$: oferi 'offer'	o'feră!	nu **oferi**!
IVb: citi 'read'	ci'tește!	nu **citi**!
V$_a$: coborî 'descend'	co'boară!	nu **coborî**!
V$_b$: hotărî 'decide'	hotă'răște!	nu **hotărî**!

However, certain verbs allow the construction with clitics even when they have the inflectional ending -*i*: (*auzi-l!* 'oh, listen to him!', *vezi-i!* 'oh, look at them!'). With postverbal clitics, non-syllabic -*i* is obligatorily vocalic:

(20) vezi [vezⁱ]   vs. vezi-l ['ve.zil]
      'See' ('Look!')   'Look at him!'

The 2nd person plural forms are identical to the present indicative and present subjunctive ones. They do not mark the affirmative–negative distinction:

ple'cați! tă'ceți! 'mergeți! fu'giți! cobo'râți!
nu ple'cați! nu tă'ceți! nu 'mergeți! nu fu'giți! nu cobo'râți!

U Shfiting the stress one syllable to the right is frequent (but not accepted by normative grammarians) when the 2nd person plural forms are followed by clitics: *spuneți* ['spunetsⁱ] 'talk!' vs. *spuneți-mi* [spu'netsimⁱ] 'tell me!'.

The Romanian imperative has many unpredictable forms (Maiden 2006), produced by analogy or, in the case of *veni* 'come', under the influence of the vocative forms of nouns, with which they are functionally associated. The verb *fi* 'be' has the 2nd person singular form *fii* and the 2nd person plural form *fiți* (identical to the subjunctive without the marker SĂ_SUBJ, not to the present indicative). Certain verbs display other irregularities in the 2nd person singular: *da* 'give' (2SG *dă!*), *face* 'do' (2SG *fă!*), *zice* 'say' (2SG *zi!*), *duce* 'accompany' (2SG *du!*), *aduce* 'bring' (2SG *'adu!*), *lua* 'take' (2SG *ia!*), *veni* 'come' (2SG *vino!*), etc.

U Non-standard registers show an even greater variation of the 2nd person singular imperative forms, with formations probably created by analogy—2SG *adă!* (< *aduce* 'bring'), 2SG *vină!* (< *veni* 'come').
   The negative forms identical to the infinitive of some irregular verbs are frequently replaced by forms syncretic with the affirmative imperative—*nu fă!* 'don't do!', *nu du!* 'don't bring!', *nu zi!* 'don't say!'; the phenomenon is not recent and represents an alternative inflectional pattern (M. Avram 2005: 198–204). A non-standard negative form of *da* is *nu dădea!* 'don't give / hit!'.

2.2.1.2 Analytic forms

The modal and temporal-aspectual paradigm of the Romanian verb includes a series of periphrases made up of auxiliaries and the participle, the bare infinitive, or subjunctive forms, showing different degrees of grammaticalization (for the tests of syntactic cohesion, see §3.5).

2.2.1.2.1 The compound / analytic past is made up of the auxiliary forms of the verb *avea* 'have' (a reduced form) and the invariable participle of the verb (see §4.3.2.1):

veni 'come' 1SG **am** venit—2SG **ai** venit—3SG **a** venit—1PL **am** venit—2PL **ați** venit—3PL **au** venit

The phonological reduction of the auxiliary with respect to the full lexical verb *avea* is evidence for a high degree of grammaticalization. As an auxiliary, *avea* has only monosyllabic forms: the 3rd person singular form, the 1st and 2nd person plural forms (*a, am, ați* [atsⁱ]) are different from the present forms of the lexical verb (§2.2.1.1.1).

38   2 *The Verb*

C   Romanian patterns with Spanish and Portuguese and differs from French and Italian in using for the analytic past a sole auxiliary *avea* 'have' combined with the invariable participle (§4.3.3).
U   Regionally (in the northern varieties of Romanian), the auxiliary has the 3rd person forms *o* / *or*: *(el) o venit* 'he came', *(ei) or venit* 'they came'.
H   In old Romanian, the form *au* was common to the 3rd person singular and plural (Frâncu 2009: 112, 309–10). After a long period of variation, in the 19th century the form *au* specialized for 3rd person plural.
   Quite often, the auxiliary was placed after the participle:
(21) a. venit-au   domnul
        come=have.3SG ruler.DEF
        'the ruler came'
     b. venit-au   turcii
        come=have.3PL Turks.PL.DEF
        'the Turks came'

The only elements that may intervene between auxiliary and participle are one or more of certain adverbial clitics (*mai, cam, și, tot*), some of which may form clusters:

(22) a   **mai**   **tot**   plecat
      has again   again   leave.PPLE
      '(s)he left again and again'

The compound past forms do not show irregularities: the only differences that occur between the classes of verbs are based on the different participle forms; for the morphology of participle, see §4.3.1.

2.2.1.2.2 The future has more competing series of periphrastic forms, which show different degrees of grammaticalization. These are differentiated sociolinguistically.
   The contemporary language makes use of the standard future form (*voi pleca* 'I will leave' type), with a phonological variant—the so-called regional future (*oi pleca* type)—and two colloquial equivalent periphrases (*o să plec* and *am să plec*).
   The (standard) *voi*-future is made up of an auxiliary deriving from *vrea* 'want', which has the forms 1SG *voi*, 2SG *vei*, 3SG *va*, 1PL *vom*, 2PL *veți*, 3PL *vor*, and the bare infinitive form of the verb: 1SG *voi vedea* 'I will see'.
   The (regional) *oi*-future form has almost the same structure, with the difference that the auxiliary undergoes the phonological reduction of the initial consonant (1SG *oi*, 3PL *o*, 1PL *om*, 3PL *or*) and shows a high degree of vowel instability in the 2nd person singular and plural: 2SG *ăi* (*ei, îi, ii, oi*), 2PL *ăți* (*eți, îți, oți*).
   The (colloquial) *o să*-future form (*o să plec* type) is made up of the particle *o* (which is invariable or has the variant *or* in the 3rd person plural) followed by a sequence identical to the subjunctive form.
   The (colloquial) *am să*-future form (*am să plec* type) is made up of the auxiliary *avea* 'have' (showing similar forms to the lexical verb *avea* 'have') and a sequence identical to the subjunctive form (Table 2.7).
   Future auxiliaries come from verbs which initially had modal meanings: the volitional verb *vrea* 'want' (*voi* / *oi pleca* 'I will leave') and the deontic *avea* + subjunctive 'have to, must' (*am să plec* 'I have to go'; 'I must go'). The periphrasis that contains the auxiliary *avea*

TABLE 2.7 Future periphrastic forms

Standard Future (*voi*-future)	Regional Future (*oi*-future)	Colloquial Future (*o să*-future)	Colloquial Future (*am să*-future)
voi merge	oi merge	o să merg	am să merg
vei merge	ăi / ei / îi / ii /oi merge	o să mergi	ai să mergi
va merge	a / o merge	o să meargă	are să meargă
vom merge	om merge	o să mergem	avem să mergem
veți merge	ăți / eți / îți / oți merge	o să mergeți	aveți să mergeți
vor merge	or merge	o / or să meargă	au să meargă

is not fully grammaticalized: the auxiliary is not phonologically reduced (in contrast to the short forms in the compound past), and it partially preserves the original modal meaning of necessity. Syntactically, it has a medium degree of cohesion; it allows clitics to intervene after SĂ$_{SUBJ}$ (23a), but it does not allow internal negation (23b):

(23) a. am să-l **mai** caut
 have.1SG SĂ$_{SUBJ}$=CL.ACC.3SG more search.SUBJ.1SG
 'I will search for it again'

 b. *am să **nu** plec
 have.1SG SĂ$_{SUBJ}$ not leave.SUBJ.1SG

The periphrasis with the auxiliary *o* shows both a substantial phonological reduction and an abstract meaning. Syntactically, it displays the same features as the *am să*-type:

(24) n-o să-l mai caut
 not=o SĂ$_{SUBJ}$=CL.ACC.3SG more search.SUBJ.1SG
 'I will not search for it anymore'

H In old Romanian (Guțu Romalo 1968b) there were many ways of forming a periphrastic future, with the auxiliaries *vrea* (also in the variant with initial consonant reduction) or *avea*, followed by infinitive or subjunctive:

(25) a. voi(u) găsi
 AUX.FUT.1SG find.INF
 'I will find'

 b. voi(u) să iubesc
 AUX.FUT.1SG SĂ$_{SUBJ}$ love.SUBJ.1SG
 'I will love'

 c. oiu trimite
 AUX.FUT.1SG send.INF
 'I will send'

 d. am a bea
 have.IND.PRES.1SG A$_{INF}$ drink.INF
 'I will drink'

 e. am să caut
 have.IND.PRES.1SG SĂ$_{SUBJ}$ search.SUBJ.1SG
 'I will search'

The forms of the auxiliary *vrea* are the result of a regular phonological evolution from Latin to Romanian. The invariable particle o may be explained as the generalization of the 3SG reduced form of the auxiliary (or, more probably, from the impersonal form *va*, according to Lombard 1939, 1955: 953).

In the old language, the standard future form could also be used with inverted components: *veni-va* '(s)he will come'.

C Romanian differs from western Romance languages and resembles Balkan languages with respect to the periphrastic future form containing a volitional verb. In fact, this is a very frequently mentioned feature of the aforementioned family of languages (Sandfeld 1930; Joseph 1999; Mišeska Tomić 2004: 4–5, 38–42). Another characteristic of the Balkan languages is the presence of the *o să*-future pattern, made up of a particle plus a subjunctive form.

2.2.1.2.3 The future perfect corresponds to the standard future form (the *voi*-type), being made up of the auxiliary *fi* 'be' in the future and the participle form of the verb: 1SG *voi fi plecat* 'I will have left':

pleca 'leave'—1SG voi fi plecat—2SG vei fi plecat—3SG va fi plecat—1PL vom fi plecat—2PL veți fi plecat—3PL vor fi plecat

The *voi fi*-future perfect is a rare, bookish form. The spoken *oi fi*-type is not currently used with the future perfect meaning, as it became specialized for denoting a presumptive perfect meaning (see §2.2.1.2.6).

2.2.1.2.4 The future in the past is an insufficiently grammaticalized periphrastic form, made up of the verb *avea* 'have' in the imperfect and a subjunctive form with the particle SĂ$_{SUBJ}$:

(26) aveam să plec
have.IMPERF.1SG SĂ$_{SUBJ}$ leave.SUBJ.1SG
'I was going to leave'

The future perfect periphrasis comes from the conversion of the periphrasis *am să* (< *am să*-future) into the past.

The periphrasis containing the verb *urma* 'follow' is even less grammaticalized:

(27) urma să plec
follow.IMPERF.3SG SĂ$_{SUBJ}$ leave.SUBJ.1SG
'I was about to leave'

2.2.1.2.5 The present presumptive (or epistemic future) has two variants: (a) a variant identical with the regional future (the *oi*-future); (b) a variant made up of the regional or standard future auxiliary (*oi / voi*) plus the infinitive form *fi* 'be' plus the gerund:

3SG: dormi 'sleep'—(a) o dormi / (b) o fi dormind / va fi dormind

For auxiliaries with persons 1–6, see Table 2.7.

Only the long periphrasis, formed with the gerund (*o / va fi dormind* '(s)he may / might be sleeping'), is specialized for modal values and may appear in variants with or without reduced auxiliary. In the case of the short periphrasis, the form with reduced auxiliary (*o dormi* '(s)he may / might sleep') tends to specialize for the modal value, whereas the other form expresses future values (*va dormi* '(s)he will sleep'). In the case of the variant *o dormi*, the confusion between the epistemic value and the temporal one can only be disambiguated contextually (§2.2.2.4).

C There was much variation in the description of the presumptive, and its status as a mood was denied (Iliescu 1999). The presumptive form gradually and incompletely developed out of the values of the epistemic future (Zafiu 2009). It is considered either a specific Balkan feature (however, the structure and semantic value of the Romanian presumptive distinguish it from the evidential presumptive mood in the Balkan languages; see Friedman 1997; Mišeska Tomić 2004), or a specific Romance feature (the development of an epistemic or conjectural future is a common phenomenon of many Romance languages: Italian, French, etc.; see Rocci 2000; Squartini 2005; Niculescu 2011).

H The specialization of the present presumptive formed with the gerund is the result of a grammaticalization process, which preserved and reanalysed an aspectual periphrasis (§2.2.6). In the old language, periphrases like *voi fi ieşind* 'I will be going out' (*Palia*) had a proper future value (with a progressive component) (Densusianu 1961, II: 146; Guţu Romalo 1968b; Zamfir 2007: 212–19; Zafiu 2009).

U For semantic reasons, presumptive forms are used especially in the 3rd person. There is a preference for using the short periphrasis in the case of the verb *fi* 'be' (*o fi* 'it / (s)he may / might be') and the long one in the case of other verbs (*o fi venind* '(s)he may / might be coming').

2.2.1.2.6 The periphrasis of the perfect presumptive is identical with the future perfect (in spoken and literary varieties), see §2.2.1.2.3.

(28) o fi dormit / va   fi dormit
      o be slept   / AUX.FUT.3SG be slept

The tendency shown by this periphrasis to become specialized for epistemic values is favoured by its extremely limited use with temporal future values. In the contemporary language, the *o fi*-type (specific to spoken varieties) is exclusively a presumptive form.

2.2.1.2.7 Present conditional forms are made up of the auxiliary *aş, ai, ar, am, aţi, ar* plus the bare infinitive form of the verb:

> veni 'come' 1SG aş veni— 2SG ai veni—3SG ar veni—1PL am veni—2PL aţi veni—
> 3PL ar veni

H The origin of the conditional auxiliary is controversial. Certain authors considered the auxiliary to originate in the verb *avea* 'have' which underwent a grammaticalization process (Meyer-Lübke 1895: 114); different explanations were proposed, especially for the anomalous 1SG *aş* (Lat. HABUISSEM, Rosetti 1986: 147; Bugeanu 1970 argued that the auxiliary continued the past of *habere*; see also Zamfir 2007: 359–64). Other authors (Philippide 2011: 525–8) claim that the auxiliary comes from the imperfect of the verb *vrea* 'want'; in the old language, there existed a periphrastic conditional *vrea cânta* 'I would sing', and the periphrasis *vreaş face* 'I would like to do' exists in Istro-Romanian and in the Banat variety too (see also Coene and Tasmowski 2006).

In old Romanian, there existed also a synthetic conditional, inherited from Latin, which was employed until the first half of the 17th century (and, in isolated areas, until even later) (Zamfir 2007: 323): *cântare* 'I would sing'. This form may come from the Latin future perfect, from the perfect subjunctive (Densusianu 1961, II: 147), or from their contamination (Rosetti 1986: 506; Theodorescu 1978b).

C If the hypothesis of the auxiliary development from the verb *vrea* 'want' is valid, then Romanian is the only Romance language whose conditional form developed from periphrases with a volitional verb.

Only the adverbial clitics *mai* 'more', *tot* 'still, repeatedly', *și* 'also', *cam* 'too, rather' (even in clusters) may intervene between the auxiliary and the verb.

(29) ar **mai și** pleca
AUX.COND.3SG≡PL more also leave.INF
'(s)he / they would still leave'

The negation marker and pronominal clitics (except for the feminine singular accusative clitic *o*) precede the periphrasis:

(30) **nu** l-ar căuta
not CL.ACC.3SG=AUX.COND.3SG≡PL search.INF
'(s)he / they would look for it'

U In certain sequences which express greetings or curses, the auxiliary is inverted only if the infinitive occurs in its archaic long form (with the suffix *-re*; (31a)) or combined with a pronominal clitic (31b):
(31) a. Fir-ar al naibii!
be.INF-*RE* =AUX.COND.3SG≡PL AL devil.DEF
'Damn!'
b. Da-ți-ar Dumnezeu sănătate!
give.INF=CL.DAT.2SG=AUX.COND.3SG God health
'May God give you health!'

There is also a periphrasis involving the gerund, scarcely used in the contemporary language (and interpreted by certain authors as an instance of the presumptive mood), which functions as a present conditional form specialized for the (evidential) epistemic value (§2.2.2.3.4). The periphrasis is made up of the auxiliary, the infinitive of the verb *fi* 'be', and the gerund form of the verb:

(32) ar fi plecând
AUX.COND.3SG≡PL be leave.GER
'(s)he / they may / might be leaving'

2.2.1.2.8 The forms of the perfect conditional are made up of the auxiliary *aș, ai, ar, am, ați, ar*, followed by the infinitive of *fi* 'be' and the invariable participle of the verb:

veni 'come' 1SG aș fi venit—2SG ai fi venit—3SG ar fi venit—1PL am fi venit—2PL ați fi venit—3PL ar fi venit

Between the auxiliary and *fi* only the adverbial particles (clitics) *mai* 'more' and *cam* 'a little' may intervene; more particles (*tot* 'always', *și* 'also', etc.) may intervene between *fi* and the participle. The negation marker precedes the whole sequence:

(33) **n-ai mai** fi **și** arătat
not=AUX.COND.2SG more be also shown
'you would not have shown it again'

2.2.1.2.9 Romanian possesses certain subjunctive periphrases. There is an invariable periphrasis of the present subjunctive, made up of the particle să_{SUBJ}, the bare infinitive *fi* 'be' and the gerund of the lexical verb. This form, which is rarely employed, is specialized for the epistemic (evidential) value (§2.2.2.2.1):

(34) să   fi   plecând
      SĂ_{SUBJ}   be   leave.GER
      'I / you / (s)he / we / you / they may / might be leaving'

The perfect subjunctive has a single form for all persons; it is made up of the subjunctive marker SĂ_{SUBJ}, the bare infinitive *fi* and the invariable (masculine singular) participle form of the verb:

veni 'come'   1SG≡2SG≡3SG≡1PL≡2PL≡3PL să fi venit

H In old Romanian, the component *fi* 'be' was inflected for number and person:
(35) să   **fie**   plecat
      SĂ_{SUBJ}   be.SUBJ.3SG≡PL   left.PPLE

2.2.2 Values and uses of verbal moods

2.2.2.1 The indicative

The indicative mood generally expresses reality (referentiality). In simple assertions, with no modalizers, the indicative also has an epistemic modal value (of certainty). In the subordinate clauses selected by an epistemic verb, the indicative is compatible with different degrees of uncertainty (36a). Thus, it may also designate possible, wishful events (36b):

(36) a. Cred   că   **doarme**
         (I)think   that   sleep.IND.PRES.3SG
         'I think (s)he is sleeping'
      b. Sper   că   **va**   **rămâne**   acasă
         (I)hope   that   AUX.FUT.3SG   stay.INF   home
         'I hope (s)he will stay home'

Subordinate clauses in the indicative are introduced by the prototypical declarative complementizer *că* 'that'; for the subordinates which convert a closed interrogative sentence into reported speech, the complementizer is *dacă* 'if, whether' (for more details, see §10.1.1.4):

(37) a. Mi-a   spus **că**   **pleacă**   la   Sinaia
         CL.DAT.1SG=has   told that   leaves   to   Sinaia
         '(S)he told me that (s)he is leaving for Sinaia'
      b. Nu   știu   **dacă**   **a**   **venit**   de la   munte
         not   (I)know   whether   has   come   from   mountain
         'I don't know whether (s)he came from the mountains'

The option between the indicative and the subjunctive is associated with the choice of a specific complementizer. Verbs which take a clausal argument may select: (a) only the complementizer *că* and the indicative mood; (b) only the complementizer *să* and the subjunctive mood; (c) both complementizers and moods, but generally with different semantic and pragmatic values.

Cognitive and declarative verbs that show factual knowledge or express an assertion select the complementizer *că* and the indicative: *descoperi* 'discover', *afla* 'find out', *bănui* 'suppose', *afirma* 'claim', etc. (38a). Volitional verbs—*dori*, *vrea* 'want' (38b), greeting verbs—*ura* 'greet', require verbs—*cere* 'ask', *pretinde* 'pretend', etc., as well as aspectual verbs (*începe* 'begin', *continua* 'continue', etc.), the modal verb *putea* 'can', and factitive verbs (*face* 'do'), etc. select the complementizer *să* and the subjunctive:

(38) a. A aflat **că** **plec**
 has found that (I)leave
 '(S)he found out that I am leaving'

 b. Vrea **să** **plec**
 wants să$_{SUBJ}$ leave.SUBJ.1SG
 '(S)he wants me to leave'

Many verbs select either the indicative or the subjunctive, depending on semantic specialization: for example, the verb *şti* 'know' has either an epistemic meaning (39a) or an ability meaning (39b); the verb *spune* 'say' may introduce an indirect assertion (39c) or a request (39d). In the case of certain epistemic and psych verbs, the use of the future indicative (39e) or of the present indicative displaying a future value (39g) is equivalent to the subjunctive construction (39f, h):

(39) a. Ştiu că el citeşte
 (I)know that he read.IND.PRES.3SG
 'I know he is reading'

 b. Ştiu să citesc
 (I)know să$_{SUBJ}$ read.SUBJ.1SG
 'I know how to read'

 c. I-am spus că a greşit
 CL.DAT.3SG=(I)have said that has made-a-mistake
 'I told him / her (s)he has made a mistake'

 d. I-am spus să-şi corecteze greşeala
 CL.DAT.3SG=(I)have said să$_{SUBJ}$=CL.REFL.DAT correct.SUBJ.3SG mistake.DEF
 'I asked him / her to correct his / her mistake'

 e. Sper că va veni
 (I)hope that AUX.FUT.3SG come.INF

 f. Sper să vină
 (I)hope să$_{SUBJ}$ come.SUBJ.3SG
 'I hope that (s)he will come'

 g. Nu cred că vine mâine
 not (I)think that come.IND.PRES.3SG tomorrow

 h. Nu cred să vină mâine
 not (I)think să$_{SUBJ}$ come.SUBJ.3SG tomorrow
 'I don't think (s)he will come tomorrow'

C   Romance languages show differences in the selection of one mood or the other, especially in the case of the epistemic verbs. In French, Spanish and Italian, epistemic verbs of uncertainty select the subjunctive (e.g. Fr. *douter*, Sp. *dudar*, It. *dubitare* 'doubt'), whereas in Romanian they select the indicative:

(40)   Mă   îndoiesc   că   va   veni
       CL.REFL.ACC1SG doubt.IND.PRES.1SG   that   AUX.FUT.3SG   come.INF
       'I doubt (s)he will come'

In subordinate clauses, Romanian does not show any tendency to extend the use of the indicative instead of the subjunctive.

2.2.2.2   The subjunctive

The subjunctive (also named *conjunctive* in Romanian grammars) is the mood of non-referentiality, of actions or states presented as *irrealis*, as possibilities (potential actions / states). In most cases, the subjunctive is the mood selected within clausal arguments, to which the matrix verb assigns the value of ireality (*Vrea să plece* 'She wants to leave').

2.2.2.2.1   When used in main clauses, the subjunctive is *non-assertive* and has *modal values*: either a mandatory value (in imperative or optative clauses) or an epistemic one—of doubt and supposition regarding an event (in interrogative clauses). These values may be preserved in reported speech and in certain types of relative clauses.

The 'mandatory' subjunctive, with deontic (imperative, hortative) or volitional (optative) values, is used in clauses which express commands or requests (41a), proposals (41b), greetings (41c), or curses (41d):

(41)   a. Să aduci banii!
          'Bring the money!'
       b. Să mergem la masă!
          'Let's go and eat!'
       c. Să fii fericit!
          'May you be happy!'
       d. Ducă-se pe pustii!
          'May it / (s)he go to hell!'

The subjunctive employed in such clauses completes the paradigm of the imperative (which has forms only for the 2nd person) with the *cohortative* 1st person plural form and the *exhortative* 3rd person singular and plural forms. In the 2nd person, there is competition between the subjunctive (42a), which is less direct, and thus less aggressive, and the imperative (42b):

(42)   a. Să-mi   dai   o   carte!
          SĂ_SUBJ=CL.DAT.1SG   give.SUBJ.2SG   a   book
       b. Dă-mi   o   carte!
          give.IMP.2SG=CL.DAT.1SG   a   book!
          'Give me a book!'

C   Ammann and van der Auwera (2004) consider that the existence of a multifunctional volitional mood, which covers optative, imperative, and hortative values, is a general Balkan Sprachbund phenomenon. Other Romance languages distinguish them, for example French: *allons / allez* (cohortative / imperative) vs. *qu'il aille!* (exhortative).

In imprecations, the same verb can be used first in the conditional, then in the subjunctive (43a), or the same verb used first in the subjunctive without the SĂ$_{SUBJ}$ form is repeated in the subjunctive with the SĂ$_{SUBJ}$ form (43b):

(43) a. Fir-ar să fie!
be.INF-*RE*=AUX.COND.3SG SĂ$_{SUBJ}$ be.SUBJ.3SG
'Damn it!'

b. Ducă-se să se ducă!
go.SUBJ.3SG=CL.REFL.ACC.3SG SĂ$_{SUBJ}$ CL.REFL.ACC.3SG go.SUBJ.3SG
'To hell with it!'

When changing commands to reported speech, the subjunctive subordinated to declarative verbs preserves its modal content (and cannot be replaced by the infinitive):

(44) Îi spun să plece
CL.DAT.3SG tell.IND.PRES.1SG SĂ$_{SUBJ}$ leave.SUBJ.3SG
'I tell him / her to go'

In closed or open interrogatives (45a–b), the subjunctive can express a deontic or volitional value (Sandfeld and Olsen 1936: 352):

(45) a. Să plece?
'Should (s)he leave?'

b. Unde să meargă?
'Where should (s)he go?'

This value is preserved in indirect interrogatives (46a,c) and in the non-referential subjunctive relatives as well (46e) (the specific value becoming noticeable in contrast with the indicative, 46b,d,f) (Farkas 1982, 1992; Bužarovska 2004):

(46) a. Îl întreabă unde **să vină**
'(S)he is asking him where (s)he should come'

b. Îl întreabă unde **vine**
'(S)he is asking him where (s)he comes'

c. Mă întreabă dacă **să plece**
'(S)he asks me whether to leave'

d. Mă întreabă dacă **pleacă**
'(S)he asks me whether (s)he leaves'

e. E drumul pe care **să pornești**
'It's the road to set out on'

f. E drumul pe care **pornești**
'It's the road you'll be setting out on'

Thus, deontic and volitional modality seems to be the main value of the Romanian subjunctive (Becker 2010: 257).

2.2 *Mood, tense, and aspect*   47

The epistemic subjunctive generally occurs in interrogative clauses, where it may express suppositions about either present (47a) or past events (47b):

(47) a. Să fie cumva ora 9?
   'Could it be 9 already?'
   b. Să fi plecat oare trenul?
   'Could the train really have left?'

In the same interrogative contexts, the volitional–epistemic distinction is only contextual and depends on the meaning of the verbs.

U   The subjunctive forms of certain verbs developed certain specific values (assumption, approximation) derived from the epistemic ones:
   (48) a. E o idee, **să zicem**, bună
      'Let's say it is a good idea'
      b. **Fie** o dreaptă AB
      'Let there be a straight line AB'
      c. **Să (tot) fie** cam zece kilometri până în centru
      'It may be about ten kilometres to the centre'

The epistemic subjunctive has the gerund periphrasis (§2.2.1.2.9) as a specific means of specialization and disambiguation:

(49) **Să fi fiind** supărat?
   'Could he be angry?'

2.2.2.2.2 When the subjunctive is used as an object in embedded clauses, it expresses certain values of the *irrealis* domain, assigned by the governing head; it tends to simply express the 'notion / concept / idea of the verb' (Maiden and Robustelli 2007: 317) (and is in this respect similar to the infinitive).

The syntactic patterns of this use are the following:

- the subjunctive in contexts of obligatory control;
- the subjunctive embedded in a verb phrase, noun phrase, adverbial phrase, prepositional phrase, without obligatory control.

What is characteristic of Romanian is the frequent use of the subjunctive in argument positions, including the contexts of obligatory control, in competition with the infinitive. This type of subjunctive, which 'names' the event and has a non-referential meaning, may be considered an 'infinitival' subjunctive (see §4.2).

C   The use of the subjunctive in contexts of obligatory control, where other languages (Romance languages above all) use the infinitive, is the most prominent aspect of the general phenomenon of subjunctive extension to the detriment of the infinitive—one of the strongest Balkan Sprachbund features (§4.2.5; see Mišeska Tomić 2004: 31; see also Dyer 1985; Frâncu 2000; Jordan 2009 among others).

In contexts with obligatory control—containing modal or aspectual verbs—both the subjunctive and the infinitive can be used (§4.2.5). Except for the verb *putea* 'can', where both contexts—the subjunctive and the bare infinitive (50a)—are frequent, standard contemporary Romanian prefers the subjunctive (50b):

(50) a. Pot **să** **plec** vs. Pot **pleca**
(I)can SĂ_SUBJ leave.SUBJ.1SG (I)can leave.INF
'I can leave'

b. El începe **să** **vorbească** vs. El începe **a** **vorbi**
he starts SĂ_SUBJ speak.SUBJ.3SG he starts A_INF speak.INF
'He starts talking'

The aspectual verbs *da*, *sta* 'be about (to)', *începe*, *a se apuca* 'begin', as well as the verbs which express volitional controllable actions (*încerca* 'try', *intenționa* 'intend', *reuși* 'succeed', *binevoi* 'be willing') function as obligatory control verbs (51a–c). The same behaviour is shared by certain motion verbs, in which case the subjunctive may be considered obligatory (51d):

(51) a. Dă **să plece**
'(S)he is about to leave'

b. Stă **să plouă**
'It's about to rain'

c. Începe **să citească**
'(S)he starts reading'

d. Maria vine **să** ne **vadă**
'Maria comes to see us'

For the factitive constructions, in which the subjunctive is obligatory, see §3.5.4.
The constructions without obligatory control divide into more subtypes.

(A) In constructions with certain modal and volitional matrix verbs, only the subjunctive can be employed:

(52) a. Trebuie **să** **vină** vs. *Trebuie a veni
must.3SG SĂ_SUBJ come.SUBJ.3SG≡PL must.3SG A_INF come.INF
'(S)he / They must come'

b. Vreau **să** **plec** vs. *Vreau a pleca
want.1SG SĂ_SUBJ leave.SUBJ.1SG want.1SG A_INF leave.INF
'I want to leave'

c. Vreau **să** **plece** toți vs. *Vreau a pleca toți
want.1SG SĂ_SUBJ leave.SUBJ.3PL all want.1SG A_INF leave.INF all
'I want everybody to leave'

C Other Romance languages use the infinitive in control contexts (Fr. *Je veux partir*, It. *Voglio partire* 'I want to leave') and the subjunctive in obviation (disjoint reference) contexts (Fr. *Je veux que tu partes*; It. *Voglio che tu parta* 'I want you to leave'); see §4.2.5.

(B) When it occupies an argument position in the verb phrase or in the noun phrase, the subjunctive is equivalent to a noun denoting an action (e.g. *plecarea* 'the leaving') and to non-finite verb forms (infinitive or supine):

(53) a. **Să   pleci**   e (un lucru) greu / **A   pleca**   e greu / **De**
       SĂ_SUBJ leave.SUBJ.2SG is (a thing) difficult A_INF leave.INF is difficult DE_SUP
       plecat   e   greu
       leave.SUP   is   difficult
       'It is difficult to leave'

   b. Ideea   **să**   **plec**   mi-a   venit   ieri /
      idea.DEF   SĂ_SUBJ   leave.SUBJ.1SG   CL.DAT.1SG=has   come   yesterday
      Ideea   **de**   **a**   **pleca**   mi-a   venit
      idea.DEF   DE   A_INF   leave.INF   CL.DAT.1SG=has   come
      ieri
      yesterday
      'The idea of leaving occurred to me yesterday'

   (C) The clause containing a subjunctive verb may function as the complement of the adjectives *bucuros* 'happy', *dator* 'responsible', *gata* 'ready', etc.:

(54) A   răspuns   repede,   bucuros **să**   **afle**   de   succesul   tău
     has   answered quickly, happy   SĂ_SUBJ   find-out.SUBJ.3SG   about   success.DEF   your
     'He answered quickly, as he was happy to find out about your success'

   (D) When it functions as the complement of *înainte* 'before' (55a) or of *până* 'until' (55b), the subjunctive (in competition with the infinitive) expresses the value of future potentiality; the construction with *fără* 'without' (55c) is counterfactual:

(55) a. Înainte   **să-l**   **cunoască** /   de   a-l   cunoaște,
        before   SĂ_SUBJ=CL.ACC.3SG   know.SUBJ.3SG   DE   A_INF=CL.ACC.3SG   know.INF
        îl   lăuda
        CL.ACC.3SG praise.IMPERF.3SG
        'Before (s)he knew him, (s)he had been praising him'

     b. Până   **să**   **zic**   eu ceva /   până   a   zice
        until   SĂ_SUBJ   say.SUBJ.1SG   I   something   until   A_INF   say.INF
        m-a   întrerupt   eu ceva,
        CL.ACC.1SG=has   interrupted   I   something
        'Before I could say something, (s)he interrupted me'

     c. Vorbește   fără   **să**   **se**   **gândească** /   fără   a
        talks   without   SĂ_SUBJ   CL.REFL.ACC   think.SUBJ.3SG   without   A_INF
        se   gândi
        CL.REFL.ACC   think.INF
        '(S)he talks without thinking'

   (E) The construction with the subjunctive required by the connective *(pentru) ca* 'in order to' (competed by the preposition *pentru* 'for' plus the infinitive) has a purpose meaning, conveying the value of achievable future potentiality:

(56) Citesc   atent   (pentru)   ca   **să**   **înțeleg**
     (I)read   carefully   for   in order   SĂ_SUBJ   understand.SUBJ.1SG
     mai   bine /   pentru   a   înțelege   mai   bine
     more   good   for   A_INF   understand.INF more   good
     'I read carefully to understand better'

H In old Romanian, the sequence *pentru să* was also possible (Avram 2007: 242–3).

The conjunction *să* may also introduce a purpose clause (§2.2.1.1.2). It appears in obligatory adjuncts with obligatory control (51d), but more frequently in ordinary adjuncts, without control:

(57) Au   vorbit încet, să   nu   ne   trezească   zgomotul
     (they)have talked softly să$_{SUBJ}$ not CL.ACC.1PL wake.SUBJ.3SG noise.DEF
     'They talked softly so that the noise should not wake us'

C The association between the subjunctive and the purpose value is current in other Romance languages as well, where certain conjunctions select the subjunctive in the purpose clausal adjunct. What is specific to Romanian is the syncretic use of the particle *să* for the circumstantial value.

2.2.2.2.3 The subjunctive occurs in conditional (58a–b) and concessive structures (58c), in the *protasis*:

(58) a. **Să plece** acum, pierde tot
        'Should he leave now, he would lose everything'
     b. **Să fi știut** asta, plecam mai devreme
        'Had I known this, I would have left earlier'
     c. **Să facă** ce-o vrea, și tot nu ne convinge
        'He may do whatever he wants, but he doesn't convince us'

The subjunctive form in these structures is hypothetical in the present (58a, c), and counterfactual in the perfect (58b).

In this construction, the particle să$_{SUBJ}$ displays its etymological value as a conditional conjunction.

2.2.2.3 The conditional

In optative (59a) and optative and exclamatory clauses (59b), the conditional (also named *conditional-optative* in Romanian grammars) has a optative (modal desiderative) values, while in conditional sentences (59c) it expresses a hypothesis and its consequences. From the conditional value there developed certain pragmatic uses of the mood as a marker of attenuation (59d) and epistemic values, purely hypothetical (59e), or hearsay evidentials (59f):

(59) a. **Aș mânca** o înghețată
        'I would eat an ice-cream'
     b. De-**aș dormi** puțin!
        'If only I slept a little!'
     c. Dacă **ai vrea**, ai putea
        'If you wanted, you could do it'
     d. **Aș dori** un bilet
        'I would like a ticket'
     e. Poartă-te ca și cum **ai fi** vesel
        'Behave as if you were happy'
     f. E bine, **ar fi declarat** el
        '*It's good*, he seems to have said'

In subordination, the conditional occurs in syntactic contexts specific to the indicative, after the complementizers *că* 'that' and *dacă* 'if', but not after să$_{SUBJ}$.

C In Romanian, the conditional does not have a (future in the past) temporal value. Thus, Romanian has (in the model proposed by Thieroff 2010) an 'Eastern conditional', that is a true mood, instead of a 'Western conditional', which is a tense, according to Thieroff.

The perfect conditional usually has a counterfactual meaning, implying the nonaccomplishment of the expressed action:

(60) Dacă **ar fi mers** la mare, ne întâlneam
 'If (s)he / they had gone to the seaside we would have met'

2.2.2.3.1 The values of the optative (desiderative) conditional are not differentiated depending on its occurrence in independent or subordinate clauses. In independent sentences, in the 1st person, the conditional-optative expresses volitional modalization over a possible action controlled by the speaker (61a), while in the 2nd and 3rd persons it describes a desired action from an internal perspective (61b):

(61) a. **Aș** mai **lua** o prăjitură
 'I would have one more cake' ('I want to take...')

 b. Ea **ar merge** la mare
 'She would go to the seaside' ('She wants to go')

In subordinate clauses (either clausal arguments (62a) or clausal adjuncts (62b)), the optative value is preserved:

(62) a. Au aflat că **aș** mai **lua** o prăjitură
 'They found out that I would have one more cake'

 b. Pentru că **ar merge** la mare, a cerut concediu
 'Because she would like to go to the seaside, she asked for a holiday'

In the 2nd and 3rd persons, in main clauses exclusively, the conditional-optative mood has a desiderative-augural value: it expresses the speaker's wish regarding an action (including his own one) he cannot control. These formulas—whether greeting- or imprecation-type—show special marking: by inversion (auxiliaries and clitics follow the main verb) and specific intonation (63a), by expletive negation (63b), or by the initial exclamatory markers *de* 'if only' (and more rarely *dacă*) (63c):

(63) a. Lua-l-ar dracu'!
 take.INF=CL.ACC.3SG=AUX.COND.3SG devil.DEF
 'May he go to hell!'

 b. Nu ți-ar mai veni odată mintea la cap!
 not CL.DAT.2SG=AUX.COND.3SG more come.INF once mind.DEF at head
 'You won't grow up!'

 c. De-ar ajunge mai repede acasă!
 if only=AUX.COND.3SG arrive.INF more quickly home
 'If only he would get home faster!'

The imprecatory pattern with inversion can be followed by a subjunctive form with intensifying value (see (43a) above).

2.2.2.3.2 The conditional proper is characteristically used in conditional sentences, which are made up of a hypothesis plus the formulation of its possible consequences.

The present conditional can be used both in the *apodosis* (matrix clause) and in the *protasis* (subordinate clause) of the hypothetical conditional sentence (64a); in unreal conditional sentences, the perfect conditional (64b) or the imperfect (64c) can be used in both clauses; they may also appear in free variation (64d, e):

(64) a. Dacă **ar vrea,   ar   pleca**
       if AUX.COND.3SG want.INF AUX.COND.3SG leave.INF
       'If (s)he wanted, (s)he would leave'

   b. Dacă **ar   fi vrut,   ar   fi plecat**
      if   AUX.COND.3SG be wanted AUX.COND.3SG be left

   c. Dacă **voia,   pleca**
      if   want.IMPERF.3SG leave.IMPERF.3SG

   d. Dacă **voia,   ar   fi plecat**
      if   want.IMPERF.3SG AUX.COND.3SG be left

   e. Dacă **ar   fi vrut,   pleca**
      if   AUX.COND.3SG be wanted leave.IMPERF.3SG
      'If (s)he had wanted, (s)he would have left'

The conditional also occurs in concessive clause, introduced either by the subordinators *chiar dacă, chiar de, și dacă* 'even if' (65a) or by indefinite pronouns and adverbs (or relative words with indefinite value) (65b):

(65) a. **Chiar dacă ar vrea**, nu poate pleca acum
       'Even if (s)he wanted, (s)he cannot leave now'

   b. **Orice ar face**, nu găsește o soluție
      'Whatever (s)he does, (s)he can't find a solution'

2.2.2.3.3 Some uses of the conditional are based on discourse attenuation effects, regularly associated with certain modal (*trebui* 'must', *putea* 'can', *vrea* 'want', *dori* 'wish') or declarative (*zice, spune* 'say') verbs:

(66) a. **Ar trebui** să plec
       'I should go'

   b. **Aș vrea** să vă întreb
      'I would like to ask you'

   c. **Aș zice** că nu ai dreptate
      'I would say that you are not right'

The conditional has a *hedge* function, because it reduces the illocutionary force of sentences: it converts commands into suggestions (66a), it politely attenuates requests (66b) or it weakens the speaker's commitment to an assertion (66c).

2.2.2.3.4 The conditional has an epistemic value in other cases: in conditioned (counterfactual) hypotheses and in unreal comparisons. In addition, it is a hearsay evidential marker.

In sentences which introduce a hypothesis (with either explicit (67a) or implicit (67b) conditions), the conditional shows achievable or nonachievable possibility:

(67) a. În cazul acesta, el **ar fi / ar fi fost** vinovatul
'In this case, he would be / would have been the guilty one'

b. Asta **ar fi / ar fi fost** problema
'This would be / would have been the problem'

The conditional is used, in variation with the indicative, in unreal comparisons, introduced by the comparative operators *ca şi cum, ca şi când, de parcă* 'as if':

(68) a. Te privea **ca şi cum / ca şi când ar fi vrut** să te omoare
'(S)he was looking at you as if (s)he would have liked to kill you'

b. Te priveşte **de parcă s-ar uita** prin zid
'(S)he is looking at you as if (s)he were looking through the wall'

The counterfactual epistemic value of the constructions is assigned by the comparative operators.

The main epistemic (evidential) value of the conditional is the hearsay one; the conditional expresses lack of commitment to the information taken over from another source (69a–b):

(69) a. (Se zice că) ministrul **ar fi** în Spania
'(It is said that) the minister is apparently in Spain'

b. Autorul **ar fi declarat** că e mulţumit
'The author has apparently declared that he was satisfied'

C   The hearsay evidential conditional occurs in other Romance languages as well (French, Italian, etc.) (Squartini 2008). In Romanian, the conditional does not have an inferential value, unlike French (Dendale 1993; Dendale and Tasmowski 2001).

In contemporary Romanian, the periphrasis with the gerund (70a) (§2.2.1.2.7) is restricted to epistemic uses of the conditional. It functions as a non-ambiguous equivalent of the present conditional (70b), excluding other values (optative, conditional proper, attenuative):

(70) a. Asta   **ar**   **fi**   **fiind**   o   problemă
        this   AUX.COND.3SG   be   be.GER   a   problem

b. Asta   **ar**   **fi**   o   problemă
   this   AUX.COND.3SG   be   a   problem
   'This would be a problem'

2.2.2.4 The presumptive

Generally, the presumptive mood (or the epistemic future) has an evidential value (Reinheimer Rîpeanu 2000; Iliescu 2000; Zafiu 2009), pointing to the fact that a certain assertion is the result of the speaker's mental process (*suppositional evidential*) or of an account to which the speaker does not show commitment (*hearsay evidential*). The purely epistemic value assigned by the evidential function is *uncertainty*.

In main clauses, the presumptive is usually *conjectural, suppositional*, expressing a presupposition about present (71a–b) or past events (71c):

(71) a. Acum **o dormi,** că nu văd lumină
'(S)he may / might sleep now, as I don't see any light'
b. Acum **o fi dormind (va fi dormind)**, că nu văd lumină
'(S)he may / might be sleeping now, as I don't see any light'
c. **O fi rezolvat** toate problemele, că pare mulțumit /
Va fi rezolvat toate problemele, că pare mulțumit
'He may / might have solved all his problems, as he looks satisfied'

The forms syncretic with the regional future and with literary future perfect (72a,b) disambiguate their specific modal value (excluding the future temporal values) by the textual information (adjuncts which exclude the reference to future, the supplementary presence of a modalizer denoting uncertainty, etc.). The specific forms of the presumptive—the gerund periphrasis and the spoken future perfect (72c,d)—do not create confusions:

(72) a. **Probabil** că **o fi** acasă **acum**
'Probably (s)he is home now'
b. **Probabil** că **va fi fost** acasă **atunci**
'Probably (s)he was home then'
c. **O fi venind** primăvara, că începe să fie mai cald
'Probably, spring is coming because the weather is getting warmer'
d. **O fi venit** primăvara, că începe să fie mai cald
'Probably, spring has come, because the weather is getting warmer'

In adversative and concessive structures, the presumptive exhibits a *hearsay evidential value* (showing that the information is not assumed by the speaker and it comes from an external source—'it is said'):

(73) **O fi** el simpatic, dar face multe prostii
'He may be nice, but he does a lot of stupid things'

The presumptive is frequently used in the 3rd person. The suppositions about the direct participants in the communication are less natural, but still they are not impossible (Reinheimer Rîpeanu 2000: 489–90).

2.2.2.5 *The imperative*

The imperative is the mood of directives (commands, requests, advice, etc.), used in imperative sentences and characterized by specific intonation.

The imperative expresses a deontic meaning, which is present only at the clausal level. It cannot occur in subordinate clauses (except for a colloquial construction in which the syntactic relation may be interpreted either as the result of subordination, or as copulative coordination):

(74) Hai, **vino** de **mănâncă**!
'Now come to eat / come and eat!'

Imperative forms (as well as the mandatory subjunctive with imperative or hortative values, §2.2.2.2.1) are frequently accompanied by discourse markers which supplement the appeal function (*hai, ia* 'come (on)', etc.).

2.2.3 The tense–aspect system

The verb contributes to the temporal–aspectual system with its tenses and with some partially grammaticalized periphrases. In the inflection of the verb, the categories of *tense* and *aspect* are syncretically marked: tenses (which set events on the temporal axis) also express aspectual differences. Tense–aspect values interfere with the Aktionsart (the inherent lexical aspectual features) of verbs.

Only the indicative has a complex series of tenses. The absolute (deictic) tenses are: the present, the simple past, the compound past, and the future. The relative (anaphoric) tenses are: the imperfect, the pluperfect, and the future perfect. Absolute tenses have also certain anaphorical uses, with reference points which differ from the speech time.

The mainly aspectual distinction—*perfective* vs. *imperfective*—is partially expressed by past tenses: perfect (the simple past, the compound past, the pluperfect, and the future perfect) vs. imperfect. The present is preponderantly imperfective; the future is neutral to this distinction. The *punctual* vs. *durative (continuous)* aspect are associated with the perfectivity distinction: the imperfect is prototypically *continuous*. The *iterative aspect* is another value of the imperfect.

Other aspectual values—*prospective, inchoative, terminative,* and *resultative*—are not marked mophologically, but only by lexical and syntactic means.

H The main tense–aspect distinctions continue those of the Latin verb system (Salvi 2011: 327–32).
C The Romanian tense–aspect system is similar to those of other Romance languages. This similarity involves, in particular, competition between tenses with close semantic values (simple / compound past), the existence of a progressive tense in the past (the imperfect), the syncretic realization of temporal and aspectual values, and the realization of aspectual values by weakly grammaticalized periphrases. The main differences concern the inventory (e.g. Romanian has a smaller number of temporal forms for irrealis moods than other major Romance languages) and the use of these forms.

2.2.4 Values and uses of verbal tenses

2.2.4.1 The present tense of the indicative

2.2.4.1.1 The present tense has many interrelated temporal values.

Prototypically, the present is an *absolute, deictic* tense, showing that the action takes place in an interval of time that is coextensive with the time of utterance or (75) includes it:

(75) Acum **locuiesc** aici
 'I live here now'

In generic or descriptive sentences, the *omnitemporal* or *atemporal* or *gnomic* present makes reference to states of facts presented as eternal (including thus the speech time) or which are time-insensitive:

(76) Triunghiul **are** trei laturi
'A triangle has three sides'

The present tense can also have *future meaning* when the reference point is not the time of utterance, but an immediately subsequent interval of time. The reference point may be explicit (realized by future adverbials, (77a)) or implicit, inferable from the context (77b).

(77) a. **Mâine**   plec   la   Ploieşti
        tomorrow   leave.IND.PRES.1SG   to   Ploieşti
        'Tomorrow I'm leaving for Ploieşti'

    b. Citesc   şi   eu   toate   textele   trimise
       read.IND.PRES.1SG   also   I   all   texts.DEF   sent
       'I too am reading all the sent texts'

C *The present tense with future meaning* (the '*futurate*'), a widespread linguistic phenomenon (Dahl and Velupillai 2005: 270), is very frequent in Romanian (Sandfeld and Olsen 1936: 312; Manea 2008b: 412). It seems that, among the Romance languages, French uses it less frequently (Rebotier 2009); in Italian, the use is similar to that of Romanian (Salvi and Vanelli 2004: 113).

The future value often occurs in promises or predictions.

The present tense with past meaning (narrative / historic present), which represents a crosslinguistic means of expressing an internal perspective on narrated facts, is used in both informal conversation and fiction.

Frequently, present tense forms occur in extensive sequences, and the past reference point is indicated by the larger discourse context (for example, by the alternation with past tense-sequences, (78a)). Present forms cannot co-occur with past location adverbials (78b), but only with adverbials which contain temporal units of measurement, whose past interpretation is given by the extralinguistic context (78c):

(78) a. [Ieri **am fost** la Ploieşti. **Am mers** cu trenul.] În compartiment, **văd** o figură cunoscută
        [Yesterday I went to Ploieşti. I travelled by train.] In the compartment I see a familiar face

    b. *Ieri   **plec**   la   Ploieşti
       yesterday   leave.IND.PRES.1SG   to   Ploieşti

    c. Cuza   **moare**   în   1873
       'Cuza   dies   in   1873'

In subordinate clauses, the present is generally used as a *relative tense*: it is not directly linked to the time of utterance, but to the temporal interval encoded by the matrix verb. The reference point for the relative present tense may be placed either in the past (79a) or in the future (79b):

(79) a. Acum un an mi-a spus că se **simte**
a year ago CL.DAT.1SG=has told that CL.REFL.3SG feel.IND.PRES.3SG
cam obosit
rather tired
'A year ago he told me that he felt rather tired'

b. Vom vedea ce tren **luăm**
AUX.FUT.1PL see.INF what train take.IND.PRES.1PL
'We will see what train we take'

2.2.4.1.2 The present indicative has a strong affinity for the imperfective aspect, but it is compatible with other aspectual values as well.

The aspectual value of the sentence results from the semantic combination of the *Aktionsart* with the prototypical value of the present and with the information conveyed by contextual markers (usually, adverbials). Hence, sentences with the verb in the present may show *imperfective* and *continuous* (80a), *iterative* (80b), and even *perfective* and *punctual* (80c) aspect:

(80) a. Aşteaptă în stradă
'(S)he is waiting in the street'

b. El îşi verifică mesageria telefonică de trei ori pe zi
'He checks his voicemail three times a day'

c. Deodată, fotografia îi cade din mâini
'Suddenly, the photograph drops from his / her hands'

C Contemporary Romanian, like French (Bertinetto 2000), does not have grammaticalized periphrases with a progressive meaning, contrary to Italian, Spanish, Catalan, and Portuguese (which have periphrases formed of *stare / estar* + gerund); thus, it does not distinguish between a progressive and a non-progressive present. The situation was different in old Romanian (see §2.2.6).

2.2.4.1.3 The present tense can also contribute to the expression of epistemic and deontic modal values. In declarative sentences, the deictic present and especially the present with future meaning (77) expresses a high degree of certainty (if the sentence does not contain any other modalizer with opposite meanings).

A form of *present tense with an imperative or hortative modal value* developed from the present with future meaning:

(81) Mâine pleci la Ploieşti!
'Tomorrow you go to Ploieşti!'

This use of the tense (in the 1st person plural, 2nd and 3rd person singular and plural) usually occurs with the intonation pattern of imperatives.

2.2.4.2   The perfect. The compound past and the simple past

2.2.4.2.1 The temporal values of the two past tenses are similar, but their uses are not identical.

The *compound past* is the most frequently used past tense in Romanian. It designates the action or the state that precedes the time of utterance, without linking to other temporal reference points and irrespective of the temporal distance from the time of utterance:

(82) a. Dan **a venit** de cinci minute și te așteaptă
'Dan came five minutes ago and he has been waiting for you'
b. Basarab I **a trăit** acum șapte sute de ani
'Basarab the 1st lived seven hundred years ago'

Prototypically, the compound past is a *deictic* (*absolute*) tense, which, in certain contexts, can be used as an *anaphoric* (*relative*) tense.

Combined with other temporal markers (temporal adjuncts), especially in the spoken language, the compound past may express an action prior to another action in the past, from a retrospective angle (83a), an action prior to a future action (83b), or an action / state which is simultaneous with another action (83c):

(83) a. A găsit ieri scrisoarea. **A pierdut**-o acum o săptămână
'Yesterday, he found the letter. He had lost it a week ago'
b. O să merg la Ploiești și, când **am terminat** treaba, o să mă întorc
'I will go to Ploiești and, when I will have finished the business, I will come back'
c. Te-am căutat ieri la prânz. Unde-**ai fost**?
'I looked for you yesterday at noon. Where were you?'

In such contexts, the compound past takes over the function of the pluperfect (83a), of the future perfect (83b), or of the imperfect (83c). Its use as a relative tense is frequent in subordinate clauses (see §2.3.2).

In colloquial speech, the compound past may have a special use of anticipation (a future value), by which the speaker expresses his intention to accomplish an action very quickly:

(84) Gata, **am   plecat**!
ready (I)have left
'I'm done and I'm off'

The *simple past (preterite)* is an *absolute tense*, which lost ground in the present-day spoken language, facing competition from and being replaced by, with two important exceptions, the compound past. The simple past is still used in the present-day language in two very different contexts: as a narrative tense, in literary fiction, and as a recent past, in southern regional varieties.

In the written literary language, especially in the 3rd person narratives, it functions as a fictional tense: the tense of 'impersonal' narratives, not assumed by an explicit speaker. It designates actions or states prior to the present, without indicating any relation with the time of utterance:

(85) Monstrul   o   **văzu**   pe prințesă
monster.DEF   CL.ACC.3SG   see.PS.3SG   PE princess
'The monster saw the princess'

When used in fiction, the simple past cannot be subordinated to verbs of declaration:

(86) *Spuse   că   fu   acasă
say.PS.3SG   that   be.PS.3SG   at-home

In fiction, the narrative simple past contrasts with the compound past of the direct speech:

(87) —Am văzut casa, spuse el.
 'I have seen the house, he said'

In the spoken language, in northern varieties, the simple past is no longer used, being completely replaced by the compound past; in southern varieties, especially in the southeast (in Oltenia), the simple past is used with a functional specialization: as a recent past, for events which took place the same day (Brâncuş 1957):

(88) —Unde **fuseşi** de dimineaţă?—Mă **dusei** până la moară
 'Where were you this morning?' 'I went to the mill'

The regional simple past is currently used not only in the 3rd person (like the literary narrative simple past), but also in the 1st and 2nd persons.

C The competition between the old inherited preterite and the compound past periphrasis, which gradually underwent grammaticalization, is present in all Romance languages (see Squartini and Bertinetto 2000). The restriction on the use of the simple past to literary narratives (Weinrich 1964) is common to Romanian and French. The situation in Romanian can be most appropriately compared to that of Italian, where the simple past disappeared in northern dialects, but nevertheless still flourishes in the south and (even more than in Romanian) in the literary language (Renzi and Andreose 2003: 237; Maiden and Robustelli 2007: 301).
U The 'conversational' simple past is regarded as a marker of regional identity, being used (ironically) to characterize the way people speak in Oltenia.

2.2.4.2.2 The main aspectual value of these two tenses is *perfectivity*; they express a completed event.

Both past forms are typically *punctual*, summing up an event (89a), and they show a preference for *momentary* Aktionsart verbs. However, the context may assign other uses to the verb in the past—durative / continuous (89b) or iterative (89c):

(89) a. **A citit / Citi** cartea
 'S(he) read the book'
 b. **A citit / Citi** din carte timp de două ore
 'S(he) read from the book for two hours'
 c. **A venit / Veni** în vizită în fiecare zi
 'S(he) came to visit every day'

The simple past is a *foreground* device, whose prototypical discourse function is to determine the progression of the story:

(90) **Începu** să plouă. Ana îşi **deschise** umbrela
 'It started raining. Ana opened her umbrella'

Similarly, the sequence of verbs in the compound past (which is also a foreground device) indicates a sequence of events (91a), but not in all contexts, because the tense may also have a synthetic, non-successive meaning (91b):

(91) a. **Am ajuns** acolo [T_1]. **Am văzut** dezastrul [T_2]. **Am chemat** poliţia [T_3]
 'I got there. I saw the disaster. I called the Police'

b. **Am ajuns** acolo pe la prânz [T₁]. **A fost** o zi teribilă [Tₙ] [Tₙ includes T₁]
'I got there around noon. It was a terrible day'

2.2.4.3 The present–past distinction for irrealis moods

The perfect subjunctive expresses anteriority and perfectivity in the *irrealis* domain. Certain values (e.g. the mandatory subjunctive, the subjunctive in aspectual and factitive periphrases, §2.2.2.2) exclude the use of the perfect. The perfect conditional does not observe similar restrictions.

In the epistemic uses of the subjunctive, conditional, and presumptive, the perfect denotes a supposition about past events. In conditional structures, the perfect subjunctive and the perfect conditional are counterfactual.

H In old Romanian, the past subjunctive also had a (hearsay) evidential use, in the reported speech:
(92) Dzic să-l fie otrăvit Şerban-vodă (Neculce)
'They say / It is said that Şerban-vodă poisoned him'
This usage disappeared and was replaced by the hearsay use of the conditional.

2.2.4.4 The imperfect

2.2.4.4.1 The temporal value of the imperfect is the past reference: it is the tense of a past action or state, which is partially simultaneous with a specific reference point in the past. Thus, the imperfect is a *relative (anaphoric) tense*, which is tied not only to the present, but also to that reference point. The reference point may be explicit, marked by an adverbial (93a) or by an adjunct temporal clause (93b), or may be implicit, inferable from context (93c):

(93) a. *Atunci* **erai** mai înţelegător
'You were more understanding then'
b. Ana **dormea** *când a sunat telefonul*
'Ana was sleeping when the phone rang'
c. [Am ieşit pe terasă.] Soarele **răsărea**
'I came out on the terrace. The sun was rising'

In fictional narratives, the imperfect is used as the tense of the internal perspective of the character, as 'the present in the past' of the internal monologue:

(94) **Acum îşi amintea** totul cu precizie
'Now he remembered everything accurately'

2.2.4.4.2 Aspectual values are characteristic for the imperfect, which is a means of marking the aspect in the past rather than a proper tense. Its prototypical value is to express the *imperfective* and *durative (continuous)* aspect, to describe a process in progress:

(95) Afară **ploua**, iar tu **stăteai** în casă şi **citeai**
'It was raining outside and you stayed indoors and read'

2.2 Mood, tense, and aspect 61

The imperfect frequently expresses the *iterative* aspect, especially in the case of verbs with punctual meaning:

(96)   **Deschidea şi închidea** uşa de mai multe ori pe zi
'He was opening and closing the door several times a day'

Prototypically, the imperfect is a *background* form, which, in narratives, alternates with *foreground* forms (the simple and the compound past):

(97)   Se **plimbau** prin pădure. Deodată, *auziră / au auzit* un ţipăt
'They were strolling through the forest. Suddenly they heard a scream.'

The imperfect marks a progression of the story only in special narrative contexts (for example, in popular epic poetry, Onu 1958).

2.2.4.4.3 The modal values of the imperfect belong to the *irrealis* domain.

In (unreal) hypothetical conditionals, the imperfect is equivalent to a perfect, counterfactual conditional (see §2.2.2.3.2):

(98)   Dacă **veneai** la petrecere, îţi **povesteam** totul
'If you had come to the party, I would have told you everything'

C   This value, which also exists in Modern Greek, is considered a Balkan Sprachbund feature by some researchers (Mišeska Tomić 2004: 6–7), but it also appears in the Romance languages, for example, in Italian (see Ippolito 2004) and in French. Iatridou (2000) considers that the use of counterfactual perfect and imperfect in conditionals is a very general typological feature.

The so-called 'ludic imperfect', used by children when assigning roles and missions in games, is also marked as 'unreal':

(99)   Acum eu **eram** monstrul şi tu **veneai** cu extratereştrii
'Now (let's pretend that) I am the monster and you are coming with the extraterrestrials'

The imperfect of attenuation occurs in politeness formulas, and it is used to mitigate a request:

(100) **Voiam** să vă întreb ceva
'I wanted to ask you something'

2.2.4.5   *The pluperfect*

2.2.4.5.1 Temporal values are essential for the pluperfect: it is a *relative* tense denoting an action or a state completed before a past reference point, and expressing double anteriority (to the time of utterance and to another moment in the past). As in the case of the imperfect, the reference point may be implicit or explicit (frequently marked by an adverbial):

(101) La ora 5, când l-am sunat, nu **se întorsese** încă acasă
'At five o'clock, when I called him, he hadn't come home yet'

The use of the pluperfect presupposes an interruption of the narrative linearity, a retrospection which is frequently associated with causal explanation. The same sequence can be presented in the natural order of events (102a) or in the reverse order, in the pluperfect (102b):

(102) a. A pierdut adresa. Apoi a rătăcit o oră pe străzi
'(S)he lost the address. Then (s)he wandered in the streets for an hour'
b. A rătăcit o oră pe străzi. **Pierduse** adresa.
'(S)he wandered in the streets for an hour. (S)he had lost the address'

2.2.4.5.2 Aspectual values are secondary. The pluperfect has *perfective* value and displays an affinity for the *punctual* aspect; nevertheless, it may easily combine with verbs with durative meaning (states, activities):

(103) **Stătuse** toată ziua pe teren și apoi **dormise** bine
'(S)he had stayed all the long on the field and then she had slept well'

2.2.4.6 The future, the future perfect, and the future in the past

2.2.4.6.1 From a temporal point of view, the future is an *absolute (deictic) tense*, which encodes events located in a temporal interval subsequent to the speech time.

When subordinated to verbs of declaration or cognitive verbs, the future is used as a relative tense. If the matrix verb is in the past, then the future behaves as the future in the past; it is not possible to decide whether the future event is prior or subsequent to the speech time:

(104) Acum un an mi-a spus că **se va muta** în alt oraș
'A year ago, (s)he told me that (s)he would move to another city' ((a) 'meanwhile, (s)he did it'; (b) '(s)he hasn't moved yet')

In narrative sequences, the future can be used, with the relative value as well, to express an internal perspective, related to a reference point in the past:

(105) În 1852 **se va naște** I.L. Caragiale
'In 1852, I.L. Caragiale was / is born'

The future perfect is a relative tense, which denotes an event which occurs after the moment of utterance, but prior to a future reference point (106a). It is a literary tense, specific to written texts; in the colloquial language, it can be replaced by the analytic past (106b):

(106) a. Când vei ajunge tu aici, eu **voi fi terminat** deja romanul
'When you get here, I will have already finished the novel'
b. Când o să ajungi tu aici, eu **am terminat** deja romanul
'When you get here, I have already finished the novel'

The future in the past is a relative tense as well:

(107) În 1852 **avea să se nască** I.L. Caragiale
(literally) 'In 1852, I.L.Caragiale was to be born'

The future does not have any particular aspectual meaning; the future perfect is perfective.

2.2.4.6.2 The modal meaning is inherent to the future, which expresses unreal, unfulfilled events. The epistemic or conjectural meaning is not conveyed by the main forms of the future (the *voi-*, *o să-* and *am să-* types, see §2.2.1.2.2), but only by the *oi-*type and by the future perfect, which are partially grammaticalized as present and perfect presumptive forms, respectively (§2.2.1.2.5).

U   Certain grammars differentiate modal values of the different future forms (so that, for example, *am să plec* type expresses a higher certainty than *oi pleca* type); these differences have not been confirmed. It is possible that, in the latter case, the impression of uncertainty comes from the contamination between the future temporal meaning and the presumptive meaning.

2.2.5 The sequence of tenses

In Romanian, verbal tenses in subordinate clauses are used as relative, not as deictic tenses: their temporal interpretation relates to the reference point in the matrix clause, not directly to the moment of utterance.

That is why temporal forms in reported speech may remain the same as those in direct speech, only with a difference in meaning.

Thus, the present tense shows partial simultaneity with the events in the matrix clause (108a); the future tense (108b) or the present tense with future meaning (108c) shows posteriority, and the compound past shows anteriority with respect to the time of the matrix clause (108d):

(108) a. Mi-a   spus   că   e   supărat
          CL.DAT.1SG=has   told   that is   angry
          'He told me that he was angry'

       b. Andrei   mi-a   spus   că   **va**   **pleca**   la   Braşov
          Andrei   CL.DAT.1SG=has   told   that   AUX.FUT.3SG   leave.INF   to   Braşov
          'Andrei told me that he would leave for Braşov'

       c. Andrei   mi-a   spus   că   **pleacă**   la   Braşov
          Andrei   CL.DAT.1SG=has   told   that   leaves   to   Braşov
          'Andrei told me that he would leave for Braşov'

       d. Mi-a   spus   că   **a**   **lipsit**   o   lună
          CL.DAT.1SG=has   told   that   has   been away   a   month
          '(S)he told me that he had been away for a month'

This type of construction does not allow inferences about the external deictic system, that is, about the situation in the moment of utterance: (108a) does not imply 'he is still angry'.

Thus, the unmarked option is to use deictic tenses as anaphors, related to the internal reference frame (see Uricaru 2003: 176–91); the option for specific relative tenses (the imperfect, the future in the past, the pluperfect) is possible, but this is the marked option, which presupposes a supplementary reference to the moment of utterance or to another reference point:

(109) a. Mi-a spus că **era** supărat
          'He told me that he was upset'

       b. Mi-a spus că **avea să** plece la Braşov
          'He told me that was going to leave for Braşov'

c. Mi-a spus că **lipsise** o lună
'He told me that he had been away for a month'

From example (109a) it can be inferred that 'he is not upset anymore'. The pluperfect in example (109c) is ambiguous, because the implicit reference point of the pluperfect is not necessarily the present tense of the internal frame.

C The free use of tenses in the subordinate clause, with no strict correspondence, distinguishes Romanian from (the norm in) other Romance languages. The same phenomenon exists in Slavic and in Greek (D'Hulst, Coene, and Avram 2004).

H In the old language, the same system operated (Vasiliu 2007):

(110) a. aceasta   zicea   unii   că   **iaste**
         this   say.IMPERF.3PL   some   that   is
         şi   acelui   fecior,   şi   aşa
         also   that.DAT   lad   and   so
         credea   ei   că-i   **iaste**   (Coresi)
         think.IMPERF.3PL they   that=CL.DAT.3SG is
         'Some said this was to that boy too, and so they believed that it was'
      b. se   credea   că   **va**   **muri**   (Coresi)
         CL.REFL.PASS think.IMPERF.3SG   that   AUX.FUT.3SG die.INF
         'It was believed that (s)he would die'

2.2.6 Aspectual periphrases

Aspectual values are realized by weakly grammaticalized periphrases (§3.5) that generally contain subjunctive forms, and more rarely infinitive or supine forms (Guţu Romalo 1961; Mateica-Igelmann 1989; Manea 2008c: 449–67). That is how *prospective* (111a), *inchoative* (111b), *progressive* (111c), and *terminative* (111d) aspects are realized:

(111) a. Afară **stă să plouă**
         'It's about to rain outside'

   b. Ana **începe să mănânce** / **începe a mânca**
      'Ana starts eating'

   c. Solistul **continuă să cânte**
      'The singer keeps on singing'

   d. Acum **termină de cântat**
      'Now (s)he finishes singing'

Aspectuality may also be expressed by other constructions and by lexical means. For example, the progressive aspect, which is conveyed, by default, by the imperfect, and can also be encoded by certain periphrases (111c), is colloquially marked by (pseudo)coordinating structures with the verb *sta* 'stay' (112a), by adjuncts (112b), or by adverbial clitics (112c):

(112) a. **Stă şi** se uită
         '(S)he sits looking'

   b. Se uită **mai departe** / **în continuare**
      'She keeps on looking'

c. **Tot mai** vorbește?
'Is (s)he still speaking?'

H In the old language, there where numerous periphrases with the verb *fi* and the gerund. The periphrases with the present indicative (113a), with the imperfect (113b), the compound past (113c), the simple past (113d), the future (113e), the present conditional (113f), and the subjunctive (113g), most probably expressed progressive values (Manoliu-Manea 1993: 233–5):

(113) a. sântu   stându   (*Codicele Voronețean*)
         be.IND.PRES.3PL stay.GER
         'they are staying'

      b. era   lăcuind   (Coresi)
         be.   dwell.
         IMPERF.3PL   GER
         'they were dwelling'

      c. au   fost   lăcuind   (Coresi)
         have.3PL   been   dwell.GER
         'they were dwelling'

      d. fuiu   lucrându   (*Codicele Voronețean*)
         be.PS.1SG   work.GER
         'I was working'

      e. va   fi   dzicând   (*Palia*)
         AUX.   be   tell.GER
         FUT.3SG
         'he will tell'

      f. ară   fi   auzind   (*Palia*)
         AUX.COND.3SG be   hear.GER
         '(S)he would have heard'

      g. să   fie   știind   (*Îndreptarea legii*)
         SĂ_SUBJ   be.SUBJ.3SG know.GER
         'had they known'

The periphrasis with the compound past probably had the value of an imperfective past (Densusianu 1961, II: 143; Zamfir 2007: 62–74). The periphrasis with the simple past was very rare, and was probably due to translations (Zamfir 2007: 705–7; Frâncu 2009: 111). Periphrases with the future, the present conditional, and present subjunctive (Densusianu 1961, II: 146; Zamfir 2007: 212–19, 2005: 415–16) specialized for expressing epistemic (conjectural) values; only the first ones are frequent, reorganized in the new paradigm of the presumptive. Some of the others survived until late (see §4.5.4.1).

2.3 SYNTACTIC AND SEMANTIC CLASSES OF VERBS

2.3.1 Transitive verbs

The class of verbs with internal arguments includes verbs with a single internal argument (114) or with two internal arguments (115); within these two classes, two other subclasses can be distinguished depending on the case assigned by the verb to its arguments. More precisely, the distinction regards the opposition direct vs. oblique case. Transitive verbs are verbs which have the ability to select a direct object (114a, 115a, b); (see also DSL : 552–4):

(114) a. Citesc   cartea
         (I)read   book.DEF.ACC
         'I read the book'

   b. Aparține   copiilor
      (It)belongs children.DEF.DAT
      'It belongs to the children'

(115) a. Dau   copiilor   o   carte
         (I)give children.DEF.DAT a   book.ACC
         'I give a book to the children'

   b. Mă   învață   gramatică
      CL.ACC.1SG teaches   grammar
      'He teaches me grammar'

2.3.1.1 Double object verbs

2.3.1.1.1 The largest class of verbs with two objects enters the configuration V + DO + IO (*a da cuiva ceva* 'give something to somebody'), that is, verbs which simultaneously take a direct object and an indirect object. From a semantic point of view, this class is divided into subclasses such as:

- verbs of *giving* (*da* 'give', *atribui* 'confer', *dărui* 'offer', *împrumuta*₁ 'lend', *oferi* 'offer', *trimite* 'send', *vinde* 'sell'), with the thematic grid [Agent + Theme + Recipient] (116a);
- verbs of retrieval (*fura* 'steal', *lua* 'deprive'), with the thematic grid [Agent + Theme + (Source / Possessor)] (116b);
- verbs of saying (*spune* 'tell', *zice* 'say', *mărturisi* 'confess'), with the thematic grid [Agent + Theme + Recipient] (116c);
- verbs of causation (*cauza, face, produce* 'cause'), with the thematic grid [Agent / Cause + Recipient / Benefactive + Result] (116d);
- commissive verbs (*făgădui, promite* 'promise'), with the thematic grid [Agent + Theme + Recipient] (116e);
- verbs expressing actions oriented towards the Benefactive (*cumpăra* 'buy', *pregăti* 'prepare', *repara* 'repair') with the thematic grid [Agent + Theme + (Benefactive)] (116f).

(116) a. Îți **trimit** o carte
         'I send you a book'

   b. I-**am furat** o carte
      'I stole a book from him'

   c. I-**am spus** câteva cuvinte
      'I said a few words to him'

   d. I-**am produs** suferință
      'I produced suffering in him'

e. **I-am promis** ajutor
'I promised to help him'

f. **I-am cumpărat** o maşină
'I bought him a car'

H The syntactic pattern in (116) is inherited from Latin, being well represented, for all semantic subclasses of verbs, in modern as well as in old Romanian:

(117) să   dăruiască   dumitale   multă sănătate   (*Documente*)
      SĂ$_{SUBJ}$ offer.SUBJ.3SG   you.POL.DAT.2SG   much health.ACC
      'to bring you much health'

Given the semantic ambiguity of the morphological dative case and the peculiarity of Romanian verbs to behave as hosts for possessive dative clitics (§3.4.4), the previous pattern may also include some (other) complex thematic roles: Recipient / Possessor, Source / Possessor, Benefactive / Possessor, as in (118a, b):

(118) a. [Ţi]$_{Recipient}$ / $_{Possessor}$-a   trimis   cartea
         'He sent you the book'/ 'He sent you your book'

      b. [Ţi]$_{Benefactive}$ / $_{Possessor}$-a   reparat   maşina
         'He repaired the car for you' / He repaired your car'

Certain features of Romanian, namely the clear distinction between accusative and dative, clitic doubling, and the ability to case-mark objects both inflectionally and analytically (prepositionally or by the proclitic marker LUI), account for the great diversity of configurations: (i) configurations in which objects are marked inflectionally (119a); (ii) configurations only with clitic marking or with double object marking (119b); (iii) configurations with prepositional analytical marking and clitic doubling (119c); (iv) configurations with analytical marking (different types of markers) and doubling (119d):

(119) a. Trimit   **copiilor**   o   **carte**
         (I)send   children.DEF.DAT   a   book.ACC
         'I send a book to the children'

      b. **Li-l**   prezint   (**copiilor**   pe **Ion**)
         CL.DAT.3PL=CL.ACC.M.3SG   (I)introduce   (children.DEF.DAT   PE   Ion.ACC)
         'I introduce Ion to the children'

      c. **Îl**   prezint   (**pe** noul   decan)   (**la doi** dintre ei)
         CL.ACC.M.3SG   (I)introduce   (PE   new.DEF   dean)   (to two   of   them.ACC)
         'I introduce the new dean to two of them'

      d. **I-l**   recomand   (**lui Ion**)   (pe **Gheorghe**)
         CL.DAT.3SG=CL.ACC.M.3SG (I)recommend   (LUI.DAT Ion)   (PE Gheorghe.ACC)
         'I recommend Gheorghe to Ion'

Examining the syntactic variation of this pattern, in which the objects and the verb can be marked simultaneously, the first ones by case marking, prepositional marking, or by the proclitic marker LUI, the latter by clitics, it is clear that Romanian belongs both to the *dependent-marking construction* and to *head-marking construction* type (Ledgeway 2011: 436); simultaneous marking, on the object and on the verb, occurs quite often.

2.3.1.1.2 A smaller class, still representative for Romanian, consists of verbs entering the pattern **V + DO + SecO**. The direct object, displaying the semantic feature [+human], is realized either as an accusative pronominal clitic or as a DP which allows clitic doubling; the secondary object, bearing the [–animate] feature, is not prepositional, being realized as a NP with an unmarked case form (accusative identical with the nominative case form):

(120) Mă_{OD}   învață   matematică_{SecO}
      CL.ACC.1SG teaches   mathematics.ACC≡NOM
      'He teaches me mathematics'

C   The class of verbs taking two objects also existed in Latin (Ernout and Thomas 1959: 37). Unlike Latin, where both objects were overtly marked as accusatives (PUEROS DOCEO GRAMMATICAM), in Romanian only the [+human] object is marked with the accusative, a fact unambiguously shown by the morphology of the pronominal clitic; the other object does not allow clitic doubling.
    In the other Romance languages, this pattern corresponds to a structure containing a dative and an accusative object:
    (121) a. Fr. Je   **lui** enseigne   **les mathématiques**
          b. It. Io   **gli** insegno   **matematica**

    Scholars have mentioned the existence of this syntactic pattern in other Balkan languages too, considering it a Balkan Sprachbund phenomenon (Sandfeld 1930: 201–2; Feuillet 1986: 9; Mišeska Tomić 2004: 6).

H   The aforementioned syntactic pattern has been attested since the earliest Romanian writings:
    (122) a. **Alta**   rog   pre   **domneta**   (*Documente*)
              another.F.SG ask   PE   you.POL.ACC.2SG
              'I want to ask you something else'

          b. Și   **aceasta**   învață   **pre noi**   Dumnezeu: să   nu   ținem
             and   this.F.SG   teaches PE us.ACC   God   să_{SUBJ} not   keep.SUBJ
             pizmă   (*Coresi*)
             envy
             'And this is what God teaches us, not to be envious'

In modern Romanian, the inventory of double object verbs also includes the verbs below:

(123) a. *anunța* 'announce'
         M-a   anunțat   **ora**   **examenului**
         CL.ACC.1SG=has   announced   hour.DEF.ACC≡NOM   exam.DEF.GEN
         '(S)he told me the time of the exam'

      b. *examina* 'examine'
         M-a   examinat   **ultima chestiune**   **predată**
         CL.ACC.1SG=has   examined   last.DEF issue.ACC≡NOM   taught
         '(S)he tested me on the last lesson she taught me'

      c. *învăța* 'teach'
         M-a   învățat   o   **poezie**
         CL.ACC.1SG=has   taught   a   poem.ACC≡NOM
         '(S)he taught me a poem'

      d. *întreba* 'ask'
         M-a   întrebat   **rezultatul**   **meciului**
         CL.ACC.1SG=has   asked   result.DEF.ACC≡NOM   match.DEF.GEN
         '(S)he asked me the score of the match'

2.3 Syntactic and semantic classes of verbs

e. *ruga* 'ask'

   M-a rugat **ceva**
   CL.ACC.1SG=has asked something.ACC≡NOM
   '(S)he asked me to do something'

f. *sfătui* 'advise'

   Asta m-a sfătuit
   this.F.SG.ACC≡NOM CL.ACC.1SG=has advised
   'This is what she advised me to do'

g. *trece* 'pass'

   L-a trecut **strada**
   CL.ACC.3SG=has passed street.DEF.ACC≡NOM
   '(S)he helped him cross the street'

C   In Romanian, the same form of the verb allows two different syntactic and semantic configurations, which correspond to distinct verbs in other languages (Fr. *apprendre, enseigner*; Engl. *learn, teach*):

(124) *învăța₁* 'learn', taking a single object   [V + DO]
     El învață [franceză]_DO
     'He learns French'

(125) *învăța₂*, taking two objects   [V+DO+SecO]
     El [mă]_DO învață [franceză]_SecO
     he CL.ACC.1SG teaches French
     'He teaches me French'

The double object construction is subject to variation, allowing the verbs to occur in different syntactic patterns. They alternate between:

(i) a structure with either a secondary object (i.e. a non-prepositional object), or a prepositional one (V + S + DO + SecO vs. V + S + DO + PrepO):

(126) Mă învață **lucruri rele** vs. **la lucruri rele**
     CL.ACC.1SG teaches things bad   at things bad
     '(S)he teaches me bad things'

(ii) two configurations with different syntactic structures (V + S + DO + SecO vs. V + S + IO + DO):

(127) **Mă** anunță ceva vs. **Îmi** anunță ceva
     CL.ACC.1SG announces something CL.DAT.1SG announces something
     '(S)he tells me something'

Semantically and syntactically, the class of double object verbs is heterogeneous, including:

(i) a subclass of *reporting* verbs: *întreba* 'ask', *anunța* 'announce', *ruga* 'ask', *sfătui* 'advise', which accept various types of reported speech (interrogations, assertions, requests, commands);

(ii) a subclass of *causative* verbs: *învăța* 'make somebody study', *trece* 'make somebody pass', differing from one another in the theta-role grid: *învăța* 'teach'—[V + Agent + Recipient + Theme] vs. *trece* 'help cross'—[V + Agent + Recipient + Path].

The common features of these two subclasses are the identity of the direct object's thematic role and the complex semantic structures: subclass (i) involves the ellipsis of a subordinate component (128a, b), whereas subclass (ii) involves the incorporation of the causative verb *face* 'cause' (129).

(128) a. L-a   întrebat   [care este]   rezultatul
         CL.ACC.3SG=has asked   which is   result.DEF
         '(S)he asked him the result'

   b. L-a   anunțat   [care este]   ziua   examenului
         CL.ACC.3SG=has announced   which is   day.DEF   exam.DEF.GEN
         '(S)he told him the day of the exam'

(129) L-a   învățat [*i.e.* l-a   făcut să   învețe]   matematică
         CL.ACC.3SG=has taught [CL.ACC.3SG=has made să_SUBJ   learn.SUBJ] mathematics
         '(S)he taught him mathematics'

For the various realizations of the secondary object, different from those of the direct object, see §3.2.2.2.

2.3.1.2 Complex transitive verbs with an objective predicative complement

Complex transitive verbs form a class of verbs with two objects (V + DO + OPC), out of which one is realized as an accusative pronominal clitic or as a DP doubled by a clitic, and the other one designates a property of the former one:

(130) a. Îl aleg (ca) **senator**
         'I am appointing him (as a) senator'
   b. Îl numesc **Harry Potter**
         'I am calling him Harry Potter'

They resemble *copula verbs* in terms of the property-denotation encoded by one of the objects. The only difference is that in the case of complex transitives the property refers to the direct object (less often to the indirect object), not to the subject, as happens in the case of copula verbs (§2.3.2.2). Given the resemblance of the two classes, note that verbs with two lexical entries—a transitive and an unaccusative-reflexive one (*a numi pe cineva* 'name somebody' vs. *a se numi* 'be called')—function either as complex transitive verbs (131a) or as copula verbs (131b), depending on what constituent (the direct object or the subject) the property refers to:

(131) a. Ei   îl   [**numesc**]_complex transitive Harry Potter
         they CL.ACC.3SG   call   Harry Potter
         'They call him Harry Potter'

   b. Romanul   [se   **numește**]_copula   Harry Potter
         novel.DEF CL.REFL.ACC.3SG   calls   Harry Potter
         'The novel is called Harry Potter'

H The class of complex transitive verbs continues the class of Latin verbs with double accusative objects (Ernout and Thomas 1959: 35–7). The difference is that in Latin both objects were marked with the accusative (CREARE ALIQUEM CONSULEM 'appoint somebody consul', APPELLARE

ALIQUEM REGEM 'proclaim somebody king'), whereas in Romanian only the object which denotes an entity bears an accusative form; the second object, denoting a property, has an unmarked case form or is realized as a prepositional phrase headed by a preposition of 'quality'.

(132) Îl   aleg   (ca)   **senator**
       CL.ACC.3SG appoint (as)   senator.ACC≡NOM
       'I appoint him (as a) senator'

C   This class is available in other Romance languages too (Salvi 2011: 343).

Complex transitives include two semantic subclasses of verbs: naming verbs and appointing verbs.

2.3.1.2.1 In the case of the naming verbs, the property indicates a metalinguistic feature which concerns the denomination of the entity (i.e. the direct object, and, more rarely, the indirect object) (133a, b). The constituent in the syntactic position of the objective predicative complement (OPC) functions as a property of object denomination, not as a self-referential proper name:

(133) a. L-am numit / L-am poreclit **Surdu**
         'I called / nicknamed him *The deaf guy*'
      b. Îmi zice **Surdu**
         'I am called *The deaf guy*'

The inventory consists of: (i) verbs *of saying*—*zice* 'say', *spune* 'tell', *chema* (meaning here) 'name / give a name'; (ii) *dubbing* verbs—*boteza* 'baptize', *denumi* 'designate', *intitula* 'entitle', *numi* 'name', *porecli* 'nickname', which incorporate the semantic role Theme, present in the periphrastic structures *a pune / a da nume / poreclă* 'give a name / nickname'.

The possible syntactic frames associated with this class of verbs are:

(134) a. S + V + DO + OPC—Ei mă numesc **Nebunu** 'They call me *The mad guy*'
      b. S + V + IO + OPC—Ei îmi zic **Nebunu** 'They call me *The mad guy*'
      c. Ø + V + DO + OPC—Mă cheamă **Ion** 'My name is *Ion*'
      d. Ø + V + IO + OPC—Îmi zice **Ion** 'I am called *Ion*'

The distinction between (134a, b) and (134c, d) regards the subject position; in patterns (134a, b) there is a lexical subject, encoding the Agent thematic role, whereas in the patterns in (134c, d) the subject position is empty, the verbs behaving similarly to subjectless verbs (§3.1.3.4).

H   All the syntactic configurations with complex transitives are old in Romanian, having been attested in early texts:

(135) a. alții   îi   **cheamă**   **papistași**   (Ureche)
         others   CL.ACC.3PL   call   popish
         'Some others call them popish'
      b. cumu-i   **zic**   unii   **Moldova**   (Ureche)
         how=CL.DAT.3SG   say   some   Moldavia
         'As some people call it Moldavia'

2.3.1.2.2 As for appointing verbs, the property predicated of the direct object designates a function, a rank, or a socio-professional category:

(136) L-au ales (ca) **senator**
'They appointed him (as a) senator'

This class divides into two semantic subclasses: (i) *declare* verbs—*alege* 'appoint', *angaja* 'hire', *desemna* 'designate', *unge* 'anoint', all with the meaning 'assign someone to a particular office or position'; (ii) *characterize* verbs—*califica* 'qualify', *caracteriza* 'characterize', *categorisi* 'categorize', *descrie* 'describe', *taxa* 'consider', with the meaning 'assign a certain characteristic to somebody'. These verbs enter different syntactic patterns—they take either a single object, denoting alternatively an entity (137a) or a property (137b), or two objects denoting an entity and a property at the same time (137c):

(137) a. Ei l-au angajat **pe Ion**
'They hired Ion'

   b. Ei au angajat **grădinar**
'They hired a gardener'

   c. Îl angajează pe Ion **grădinar**
'They hire Ion as a gardener'

H Complex transitive verbs are available in old Romanian too:
(138) şi au pus **vezir** pre Uman-paşe   (Neculce)
'And they appointed Uman-pasha vizier'

For the different realizations of the objective predicative complement, see §3.3.2.

2.3.2 Intransitive verbs

In Romanian, there are several subclasses of intransitive verbs, characterized by their inability to take a direct object:

- unaccusative verbs: *curge* 'flow', *a se coace* 'bake', *seca* 'run dry', *veni* 'come, be' (§2.3.2.1);
- unergative verbs: *alerga* 'run', *munci* 'work' (§2.3.2.1);
- copula verbs, many of which behave as unaccusatives: *fi* 'be', *deveni* 'become' (§2.3.2.2);
- experiencer verbs: *a se speria* 'frighten', *a se teme* 'fear' (§2.3.3);
- verbs with symmetric arguments: *a se asemăna* 'resemble', *a se învecina* 'border' (§3.2.4);
- impersonal verbs: *trebui* 'must', *a se cuveni* 'be proper / ought to' (§3.1.3.4).

2.3.2.1 Unaccusatives vs. unergatives

The most relevant distinction which can be drawn within the class of intransitive verbs is the one between unaccusative and unergative verbs. Unaccusative verbs, much more numerous than unergatives, are non-agentive, generally telic verbs. Their sole argument (internal, originating in the position of a direct object) is assigned the thematic role Patient or Theme. Unergative verbs are agentive, generally atelic verbs, and their sole argument (external, originating in the subject position) is assigned the thematic role Agent.

2.3.2.1.1 The class of unaccusative verbs consists of the following semantic subclasses:

- change of state verbs: *adormi* 'fall asleep', *aţipi* 'doze off', *a se altera* 'go bad', *a se caria* 'rot', *a se decolora* 'lose colour', *a se defecta* 'go out of order', *a se deteriora* 'deteriorate', *deveni* 'become', *a (se) îngălbeni* 'turn / make yellow', *a se îngrăşa* 'get fat, gain weight', *a se înnora* 'become cloudy', *a (se) mucegăi* 'get mouldy', *a se răni* 'get hurt', *a se toci* 'get blunt', *a se vindeca* 'recover';
- verbs of spatial configuration: *a se afla* 'be located', *a se apleca* 'bend', *atârna* 'hang', *a se distanţa* 'move off', *a se situa* 'be placed';
- verbs of inherently directed motion: *ajunge* 'arrive', *a se apropia* 'bring / draw near', *a se duce* 'go', *a (se) urca* 'climb';
- verbs of existence, or of appearance / disappearance: *dispărea* 'disappear', *fi* 'be', *a se ivi* 'appear', *muri* 'die', *a se naşte* 'be born';
- verbs of sound, smell, substance emission: *curge* 'flow', *a se infiltra* 'infiltrate', *picura* 'drip', *a se prelinge* 'leak', *a se propaga* 'spread', *transpira* 'sweat';
- aspectual verbs: *a (se) continua* 'continue', *a se declanşa* 'be released', *începe* 'start'.

The class of unergative verbs consists of the following semantic subclasses:

- verbs of voluntary actions: *acţiona* 'act', *insista* 'insist', *a se juca* 'play', *munci* 'work', *renunţa* 'give up';
- verbs of undirected motion: *alerga* 'run', *înota* 'swim', *călători* 'travel', *a se plimba* 'walk';
- verbs of manner of speaking: *chicoti* 'giggle', *chiui* 'shout for joy', *vorbi* 'talk', *ţipa* 'scream';
- verbs of sounds made by animals: *lătra* 'bark', *bâzâi* 'buzz';
- verbs of involuntary, but controllable, body processes: *căsca* 'yawn', *plânge* 'cry', *râde* 'laugh', *strănuta* 'sneeze', *tuşi* 'cough'.

2.3.2.1.2 In Romanian, the syntactic tests for distinguishing unaccusatives from unergatives are weak.

C From this point of view, Romanian resembles modern Spanish or Modern Greek, but differs from Italian, French, Dutch, etc., for which there are more diagnostics that distinguish between unergative and unaccusative verbs (Levin and Rappaport Hovav 1995b; Alexiadou, Anagnostopoulou, and Everaert 2004; Mackenzie 2006, among others).

In Romanian, a verb is considered unaccusative if it takes a single argument, is non-agentive and allows the adjectivization of the participle. The adjectivization of the participle cannot function on its own, because in Romanian this criterion is possible with unaccusatives (139), as well as with transitive verbs (140), psych verbs (141), verbs taking two symmetric arguments (142), but it is not possible with unergative verbs (143).

(139) om **îmbătrânit**
'an aged person'
copil **adormit**
'a child who is asleep'

(140) carte **citită**
'a read book'
om **mâncat**
'a person who has eaten'

(141) femeie **dezamăgită**
'disappointed woman'

(142) om **înrudit** cu mine
'a person related to me'

(143) *femeie **strănutată**
woman sneezed

Like transitive verbs (144), but unlike unaccusatives (145), certain unergatives allow the presence of cognate objects (146) (Hill and Roberge 2006: 10). As a consequence of the small number of unergative verbs allowing this structure, the distinction unaccusative vs. unergative cannot be accounted for in terms of the cognate object construction.

(144) a mânca **mâncarea preferată**
'eat the favourite food'

(145) *a   adormi   un   somn
      A_{INF} fall-asleep.INF   a   sleep
      *a   se   caria   o   carie
      A_{INF} CL.REFL.ACC   grow-carious.INF   a   caries

(146) a dormi **un somn** bun
'to sleep a good sleep'
a munci **o muncă grea**
'to work a hard work'
a plânge **lacrimi amare**
'to cry / shed bitter tears'

H In old Romanian, the occurrence of the cognate object was possible both with verbs considered unaccusative in the current stage of language (147) and with psych verbs (148):

(147) **Adormi** Adam **somnul** cel amar   (Coresi)
'And Adam slept the bitter sleep'

(148) Și   să   veseliră   toți   mare   veselie   (*Alexandria*)
      and CL.REFL.ACC   rejoice.PS.3PL all   big   joy
'And they rejoiced intensely'

In Romanian, past tense auxiliary selection does not function as an unaccusativity diagnostic.

C In Italian, French, Dutch, but also in Old English and old Spanish, the selection of the past tense auxiliary 'have' characterizes unergative verbs, while the selection of the auxiliary 'be' characterizes unaccusative verbs (Burzio 1986; Lamiroy 1999; Kayne 2000; Légendre and Sorace 2003).

Romanian has a split auxiliary system that differs from other Romance languages (Avram and Hill 2007): in Romanian, the selection of 'have' or 'be' depends on the semantic features that determine the sentence interpretation (*irrealis* for 'be', as an auxiliary for the subjunctive, the conditional, the presumptive, the future tense and the infinitive, and *realis* for 'have', as an auxiliary for the past tense), and not on the unaccusative / unergative nature of the verb.

C In the case of other languages, different diagnostic tests for unaccusativity have been put forward: for Italian and French—the test of the partitive pronominal clitics—It. *ne*, Fr. *en*; for Spanish—the test of the postverbal 'bare' subject, allowed by unaccusatives, but not by unergatives (§3.1.9.1.2); and for English—*there*-insertion, locative inversion, and the resultative construction tests. None of these tests works for Romanian (Dragomirescu 2010: 201–23).

2.3.2.1.3 In Romanian, verbs can shift from one syntactic-semantic class to another. This fact strengthens the idea of the transitivity continuum.

Unaccusativity is often a contextual feature. The most important factor that makes an unaccusative verb function, contextually, as an unergative verb is the semantic type of subject—non-human, unable to control the action (associated with the unaccusative behaviour (149a, 150a)) or human, capable of control over the action (associated with the unergative behaviour (149b, 150b)):

(149) a. Sistemul economic **evoluează** încet, dar sigur
'The economic system evolves slowly, but well'
sistem economic **evoluat**
'an evolved economic system'

b. Ion **evoluează** rapid în învăţarea japonezei
Ion evolves rapidly in learning.DEF Japanese.GEN
'Ion makes rapid progress in learning Japanese'
*om **evoluat** în învăţarea japonezei
man evolved in learning.DEF Japanese.GEN

(150) a. Boala **recidivează**
'The disease is recurring'
boală **recidivată**
'recurred disease'

b. Criminalul **recidivează**
'The murderer is relapsing'
*criminal **recidivat**
murderer relapsed

More rarely, and only for verbs of motion, the presence of a delimiting directional phrase causes an unergative verb (151) to function as an unaccusative verb (152) (§2.3.4.2):

(151) În 1980, Ion **a fugit** în străinătate
'In 1980, Ion fled abroad'
om **fugit** în străinătate
man run(PPLE) in abroad
'a man who fled abroad'

(152) Ion **fuge** prin casă
'Ion is running through the house'
*om **fugit** prin casă
man run(PPLE) around house

The occurrence of a cognate object (either with the same lexical root as the verb (153), or in a relation of hyponymy (154)) with an unergative verb makes the latter function as a transitive verb:

(153) a. Ion a **muncit o muncă** grea
Ion has worked a work hard
'Ion worked hard'

b. Ea **a tuşit o tuse** seacă
'She coughed a dry cough'

c. Ion **a dansat un dans**
'Ion danced a dance'

(154) a. Ion **a dansat un vals / un tangou**
'Ion danced a waltz / a tango'

b. Ion şi-**a trăit copilăria** la ţară
Ion CL.REFL.DAT.3SG=has lived childhood.DEF at countryside
'Ion spent his childhood in the countryside'

In some cases, especially in the case of verbs that accept a hyponymic object construction, the diagnostics of transitivity are functional: these verbs can occur in passive constructions (155) and their cognate object can be clitic-doubled or realized as a pronominal clitic (156):

(155) a. Valsul a fost dansat de Ion şi de Maria
'The waltz was danced by Ion and Maria'

b. Dansul acesta l-am dansat cu Ion
dance.DEF this CL.ACC.M.3SG=have danced with Ion
'I danced this dance with Ion'

(156) Copilăria am trăit-o la ţară
childhood.DEF have lived=CL.ACC.F.3SG at countryside
'I lived my childhood in the countryside'

Depending on their ability to participate in the causative alternation (i.e. to have two lexical entries, a transitive and an unaccusative one), unaccusative verbs, irrespective of the semantic subclass they belong to, fall into two classes: *primary* unaccusatives (which do not have a transitive counterpart (157)), and *derived* unaccusatives (with a transitive counterpart (158)). The number of derived unaccusatives is six times greater than that of primary unaccusatives (Dragomirescu 2010: 121).

(157) a. Cerul se înnorează
sky.DEF CL.REFL.ACC becomes-cloudy
'The sky is becoming cloudy'

b. Alunele se râncezesc
hazel-nuts.DEF CL.REFL.ACC languish
'The hazel-nuts are wasting away'

c. Copilul aţipeşte
child.DEF dozes-off
'The child is dozing off'

d. Mărul   cade   din   pom
   apple.DEF   falls   from   apple-tree
   'The apple is falling from the tree'

(158) a. Ion   s-a   accidentat   la   meci
         Ion   CL.REFL.ACC=has   wounded   at   match
         'Ion wounded himself in the match'
         Gheorghe   l-a   accidentat   pe   Ion   la   meci
         Gheorghe   CL.ACC.M.3SG=has   wounded   PE   Ion   at   match
         'Gheorghe wounded Ion in the match'

    b. Uşa   s-a   blocat   din cauza   umidităţii
       door.DEF   CL.REFL.ACC=has   blocked   because   humidity.GEN
       'The door got stuck because of humidity'
       Ion   a   blocat   uşa
       Ion   has   blocked   door.DEF
       'Ion blocked the door'

    c. Tabloul   atârnă   pe   perete
       picture.DEF   hangs   on   wall
       'The picture is hanging on the wall'
       Ion   atârnă   tabloul   pe   perete
       Ion   hangs   picture.DEF   on   wall
       'Ion is hanging the picture on the wall'

    d. Lumânarea   se   stinge   lent
       candle.DEF   CL.REFL.ACC   extinguishes   slowly
       'The candle is going out slowly'
       Ion   stinge   lumânarea
       Ion   extinguishes   candle.DEF
       'Ion is extinguishing the candle'

    e. Naşterea   s-a   declanşat   pe neaşteptate
       birth.DEF   CL.REFL.ACC=has   released   suddenly
       'The birth started suddenly'
       Hormonii   au   declanşat   naşterea
       hormones.DEF   have   released   birth.DEF
       'The hormones triggered the birth'

2.3.2.1.4 In Romanian, there is a special relationship between unaccusative verbs and reflexive verbs: more than three-quarters of unaccusatives can also function as reflexive verbs (Dragomirescu 2010: 121). This situation is favoured by the fact that in Romanian reflexive clitics are multifunctional (§3.4.2).

Another characteristic of Romanian is the large number of unaccusative verbs with two lexical entries, a reflexive and a non-reflexive one; usually, there are (slight) differences in meaning between the two entries (Manoliu-Manea 1993: 83–5; Cornilescu 1998: 320; Dobrovie-Sorin 2006; Calude 2007: 254–7; Dragomirescu 2010: 176–86):

(159) a. Ion   **a   slăbit**   20   de   kilograme
         Ion   has   lost-weight   20   DE   kilos
         'Ion lost 20 kilos'

b. Cureaua **s-a** **slăbit**
   belt.DEF CL.REFL.ACC=has loosened
   'The belt loosened'

(160) a. Copilul **răceşte**
   child.DEF catches a cold
   'The child will catch a cold'

b. Cafeaua **se** **răceşte**
   coffee.DEF CL.REFL.ACC gets-cold
   'The coffee is getting cold'

Change of state verbs (*accelera* 'accelerate', *aclimatiza* 'acclimate', *albi* 'whiten', *anchiloza* 'stiffen', *arde* 'burn', *cangrena* 'become gangrenous', *coace* 'gather', *cocli* 'become coated with verdigris', *condensa* 'condense', *crăpa* 'split; cleave / crack', *cristaliza* 'crystallize', *diminua* 'diminish', *fierbe* 'boil', *îngălbeni* 'turn / make yellow', *împietri* 'harden; turn into stone', *înverzi* 'turn / make green', *mucegăi* 'get / grow / go mouldy', *ologi* '(make) lame', *oxida* 'oxidize', *păli* 'become / turn pale', *putrezi* 'rot', *răci* 'catch a cold; get cold', *râncezi* 'become musty', *rugini* 'rust', *trece* 'heal'), verbs of spatial configuration (*ancora* '(cast an) anchor', *înţepeni* 'stick; get stuck'), verbs of directed motion (*coborî* 'descend; take down', *urca* 'climb'), and aspectual verbs (*continua* 'continue', *porni* 'start; set off', *sfârşi* 'end; finish') display two forms, reflexive and non-reflexive.

2.3.2.2 Copula verbs

Copula verbs form a small and heterogeneous class of units taking a subject and a subjective predicative complement (an adjective (161a), a bare noun (161b), or a noun with the indefinite article (161c), an adverb (161d), a prepositional phrase (161e), a non-finite sentence (161f), or a clausal argument (161g), see §3.3.1). Most copula verbs behave as unaccusatives (§2.3.2.1):

(161) a. Ion este **înalt**
   'Ion is tall'

b. Ei sunt **copii**
   'They are children'

c. El este **un înger**
   'He is an angel'

d. E **bine** să mergi în vacanţă
   'It is good to go on holiday'

e. Masa este **de lemn**
   table.DEF is of wood
   'The table is made of wood'

f. Dorinţa lor este **a scrie**
   wish.DEF their is A$_{INF}$ write.INF
   'Their wish is to write'

g. Credinţa lor este **că vor reuşi**
   'Their belief is that they will succeed'

2.3 Syntactic and semantic classes of verbs

2.3.2.2.1 The typical member of the class of copula verbs is the verb *a fi* 'be', which, semantically speaking, is the most neutral.

U Typically, copula verbs can be gapped:
   (162) Ion este blond, iar fratele lui [este] brunet
          'Ion is blond, and his brother [is] dark haired'

C Like French, Romanian is a Romance language which has a single verb 'be' both for the situative non-copula use and for the copula one (163a, b), contrasting with Spanish, Catalan, and Portuguese, which have two distinct verbs corresponding to the verb 'be' (Feuillet 2006: 155).
   (163) a. **Suntem** într-un cartier elegant al orașului
             'We are in an elegant quarter of the city'
          b. **Suntem** mulțumiți
             'We are satisfied'

The other copula verbs incorporate aspectual or modal semantic information (Avram 2003: 199; Pană Dindelegan 2008f: 285).

Certain copula verbs incorporate aspectual information and, from a semantic point of view, divide into: statives (*însemna* 'mean', *a se numi*, *a se chema* 'be called', *veni*$_1$ 'be' (164)), dynamic and inchoative verbs (*ajunge, deveni, a se face, ieși, a se prinde* 'become', *veni*$_2$ 'become' (165)), durative verbs (*rămâne* 'continue to be' (166)):

(164) a. Renunțarea **înseamnă** inteligență
         renunciation.DEF means intelligence
         'To give up is to be intelligent'

   b. Băiatul **se** **numește** Ion
      boy.DEF CL.REFL.ACC calls Ion
      'The boy is called Ion'

   c. Cum **se** **cheamă** melodia?
      how CL.REFL.ACC calls melody.DEF
      'What is the melody called?'

   d. El îmi **vine** cumnat
      he CL.DAT.1SG comes brother-in-law
      'He is my brother-in-law'

(165) a. Ea **ajunge** ce și-a dorit
         she becomes what CL.REFL.DAT.3SG=has wanted
         'She becomes what she wanted'

   b. El **devine** medic
      'He becomes a doctor'

   c. Fata **s-a** **făcut** mare
      girl.DEF CL.REFL.ACC.3SG=has made big
      'The girl grew up'

   d. El **a** **ieșit** profesor
      he has become professor
      'He became a teacher'

   e. E **s-a** **prins** tovarăș cu Ion
      he CL.REFL.ACC.3SG=has become comrade with Ion
      'He became Ion's friend'

f. El   ne   vine   primar   în   oraş
   he   CL.DAT.1PL   comes   mayor   in   town
   'He will be the mayor of our town'

(166) Ei   au   rămas   prieteni
      they have   remained   friends
      'They continued to be friends'

Other copula verbs incorporate modal information and divide into: factive (*fi* 'be', *însemna* 'mean', *a se numi, a se chema* 'be called' (164)), non-factive (*părea* 'seem', *trece de / drept* 'pass for', *a se ţine* 'be' (167)), or counter-factive (*face pe* 'play', *a se da* 'pretend to be', *a se erija în* 'pretend to be' (168)):

(167) a. El **pare** înţelept
         'He seems wise'

   b. Ea   **trece**   de / drept   frumoasă
      she passes   as   beautiful.F.SG
      'She passes for beautiful'

   c. El   **se**   **ţine**   (de)   văr   cu   Ion
      he   CL.REFL.ACC.3SG   keeps   (as)   cousin   with   Ion
      'He is Ion's cousin'

(168) a. Ea   **face**   pe   proasta
         she makes   PE   stupid.DEF.F.SG
         'She plays stupid'

   b. El   **se**   **dă**   mare
      he   CL.REFL.ACC.3SG   gives   big
      'He is showing off'

   c. Ea   **se**   **erijează**   în   atotcunoscătoare
      she CL.REFL.ACC.3SG   pretends   in   all-knowing.F.SG
      'She sets herself up to be all-knowing'

The verb *arăta* 'look, appear' expresses qualifying and comparative-qualifying predications (Nicula 2012a):

(169) a. Ana **arată** obosită
         'Ana looks tired'

   b. Cum **arată** Ana?
      'What does Anna look like?'

   c. Ana **arată** cum arăta acum 20 de ani
      'Ana looks as she looked 20 years ago'

H Most copula verbs are old in Romanian. The inventory of copula verbs contains only two neological items, *deveni* 'become' and *a se erija în* 'set oneself up as'.

U Some copula verbs are used only in the oral language: *a se da* 'act', *a se prinde* 'become', *a se ţine*, *veni* 'come / be'.

2.3.2.2.2 Certain copula verbs are inherently reflexive (*a se chema* 'be called', *a se erija în* 'set oneself up as', *a se face* 'become', *a se prinde* 'become', *a se numi* 'be called', *a se ține* 'be'), while others are non-reflexive (*ajunge* 'become', *arăta* 'look like', *deveni* 'become', *face pe* 'play the', *fi* 'be', *ieși* 'become', *însemna* 'mean', *părea* 'seem', *trece de / drept* 'pass for', *veni* 'be'). The verbs *face pe* 'play the' and *a se erija în* 'set oneself up as' have a special situation, as they take property-denoting complements and contain in their internal structure the prepositions *pe*, respectively *în*. These prepositions have lost the property of assigning accusative case, and allow a special type of lexical agreement, over the prepositional node (Van Peteghem 1991: 168; Pană Dindelegan 2008a: 353).

(170) Ion **face** pe prostul / Ana **face** pe proasta
Ion makes PE stupid.DEF.M.SG / Ana makes PE stupid.DEF.F.SG
'Ion plays the fool' / 'Anna plays the fool'

(171) Ei se **erijează** în atotcunoscători
they.M.PL CL.REFL.ACC.3PL pretend IN all-knowing.M.PL
Ele se **erijează** în atotcunoscătoare
they.F.PL CL.REFL.ACC.3PL pretend IN all-knowing.F.PL
'They set themselves up as all-knowing'

2.3.2.2.3 Except for the verbs *deveni* 'become' and *a se erija în* 'set oneself up as', which function as copula verbs in all instances, all the other copula verbs are homonymous with (full) lexical verbs:

(172) a. El **este** [în grădină]$_{Adjunct}$
'He is in the yard'

b. Ion **a însemnat** [greșelile]$_{DO}$ [pe o foaie]$_{Adjunct}$
'Ion noted the mistakes on a sheet of paper'

c. Ion **iese** [din cameră]$_{Adjunct}$
'Ion comes out of the room'

Părea 'seem' and *ajunge* 'become' can function both as copula verbs (167a, 165a) and as semi-auxiliaries (173) (Van Peteghem 1991: 167; Pană Dindelegan 2008f: 285):

(173) a. Ea **ajunge** să fie ce și-a dorit
she becomes SĂ$_{SUBJ}$ be.SUBJ.3SG what CL.REFL.DAT.3SG=has wanted
'She becomes what she wanted'

b. El **pare** să fie înțelept
he seems SĂ$_{SUBJ}$ be.SUBJ.3SG wise
'He seems intelligent'

U By raising, the verb *părea* 'seem' changed its categorial status from an impersonal verb into a personal semi-auxiliary or personal copula verb:

(174) **Pare** că el este înțelept > El **pare** că este înțelept > El **pare** înțelept
(it)seems that he is wise > he seems that is wise > he seems wise
'It seems that he is wise' > 'He seems to be wise' > 'He seems wise'

A se numi 'be named', used as a non-reflexive verb, may also function as a complex transitive verb taking an objective predicative complement (§2.3.1.2):

(175) Pe Ion l-**au** **numit** [director]
 PE Ion CL.ACC.3SG=have named director
 'Ion was appointed (as a) director'

2.3.2.2.4 Copula verbs can occur in impersonal structures (with a subjective predicative complement realized as a manner adverb (176) or as an adjective-based adverb (177)), taking subjects realized as clausal arguments or non-finite sentences (Pană Dindelegan 2008a: 353):

(176) **E** **bine** să citeşti / a citi toată bibliografia
 is good SĂ$_{SUBJ}$ read.SUBJ.2SG / A$_{INF}$ read.INF all bibliography.DEF
 'It is good to read all the bibliography'

(177) Mâncarea grasă **este nesănătoasă** > **Este nesănătos** să mănânci
 food.DEF.F.SG greasy is unhealthy.F.SG is unhealthy SĂ$_{SUBJ}$ eat.SUBJ.2SG
 gras
 greasily
 'Fat food is unhealthy' >'It is unhealthy to eat fat food'

2.3.3 Experiencer verbs

2.3.3.1 Verbs of perception

This lexico-grammatical class consists of verbs which incorporate the common inherent semantic feature [+perception], and the individualizing semantic features [+visual], [+auditory], [+tactile], [+olfactory], [+gustatory], corresponding to the sense organs through which perception is formed.

Depending on the presence or absence of the feature [+intentionality of perception], verbs of perception divide into the subclass of verbs of non-intentional perception (*vedea* 'see', *auzi* 'hear', *simţi* 'feel'), with an Experiencer subject, and the subclass of verbs of intentional perception (*privi* 'look, watch', *asculta* 'listen', *mirosi*$_{TR}$ 'smell', *atinge* 'touch', *gusta* 'taste', etc.), with an Agent subject. There is a third class, comprising verbs of evidential perception (*arăta* 'look', *suna* 'sound', *mirosi*$_{INTR}$ 'smell'). For these verbs, the grammatical subject is, from a semantic point of view, the object of perception and bears the semantic role Theme.

2.3.3.1.1 The lexical-semantic fields of the verbs of perception have a heterogeneous structure (Table 2.8).
The structural heterogeneity of the field of perception verbs involves:

- the impossibility of expressing certain types of perceptions by a distinct lexeme. In these situations, periphrastic means of expressing the respective perceptions are used: *avea* 'have' or *simţi* 'feel' + an abstract nominal which denotes a physical property (*avea gust* 'have taste' / *simţi frig* 'be cold');
- the existence of certain verbs which, in the same paradigm, can express two types of perception (*mirosi* 'smell', *vedea* 'see');

TABLE 2.8 Verbs of perception. Inventory and typology

PERCEPTION	NONINTENTIONAL	INTENTIONAL	EVIDENTIAL
VISUAL	Mama **vede** bine 'Mum sees well'	**M-am uitat** la un film 'I watched a movie' **Priveşte** cerul '(S)he looks at the sky' **Vedem** filmul la cinema 'We watch the movie at the cinema'	Andrei **arată** obosit 'Andrei looks tired'
AUDITORY	**Aud** zgomote 'I hear noises'	**Ascult** muzică 'I listen to music'	Muzica **sună** bine 'The music sound fine'
TACTILE	Ø (periphrastically) **Simt** frigul la mâini 'I feel cold in my hands'	**L-a atins** uşor pe umăr ca să-l facă atent '(S)he tapped him softly on the shoulder to make him aware'	Ø
GUSTATORY	Ø (periphrastically) **Simt un gust** amar 'I feel a bitter taste'	**Am gustat** mâncarea 'I tasted the food'	Ø (periphrastically) Prăjitura **are gust** bun 'The cake tastes good'
OLFACTORY	Ø (periphrastically) **Simt miros** de ars 'I can smell something burning'	Câinele **miroase** florile 'The dog smells the flowers'	Florile **miros** puternic 'The flowers smell strong'

- the possibility of expressing certain types of non-intentional perception (tactile, olfactory, and gustatory) with structures which contain the hyperonym *simţi* 'feel' and the abstract nominals which denote the respective physical property (e.g. *gust* 'taste').

2.3.3.1.2 Depending on the type of perception they denote—intentional (i), non-intentional (ii), or evidential (iii)—verbs of perception enter different syntactic patterns.

(i) The verbs of non-intentional perception *vedea* 'see', *auzi* 'hear' can take a sole argument—the NP subject (178a). The verb *simţi* 'feel' cannot occur in this pattern (178b):

(178) a. Aceşti tineri **văd**, dar **nu aud**
'These young people see ("they have the ability to see"), but they do not hear ("are deaf")'
b. *După anestezie, pacienţii nu mai **simt**
after anaesthesia patients.DEF not more feel
(intended meaning: 'do not have sensation')

The verbs *vedea* 'see', *auzi* 'hear', *simţi* 'feel' can take two arguments, an NP subject and a direct object. The direct object can be realized as: a definite nominal (179a), a clausal argument introduced by the complementizer *că* (179b), by the complementizer *să* (179c), or by the complementizer *dacă* 'if' (179d), or a relative clause (179e, f):

(179) a. Văd **casa** / Aud **zgomotele** / Simte **frigul**
'I see the house' / 'I hear the noises' / '(S)he feels cold'

b. Aud **că plouă** / Simt **că Andrei tremură**
'I hear it raining' / 'I feel Andrei shivering'

c. Nu văd **să existe o soluție la această problemă**
'I do not see any solution to this problem'

d. O să văd **dacă mai plouă**
'I will see if it is still raining'

e. Văd **cine intră și iese**
'I can see who is coming in and who is going out'

f. Simt **cum mi se încălzesc picioarele**
'I can feel my feet warming up'

U   In example (179f), the relative *cum* 'how' preserves its modal anaphoric value (Manoliu-Manea 1969: 129):

(180) Simt   (**modul**$_i$)   **cum**$_i$ mi   se   încălzesc   picioarele
      (I)feel (way.DEF)   how   CL.DAT.1SG CL.REFL.ACC   warm-up.3PL   feet.DEF

Its main function is to link two sequences. Thus, *cum* is almost equivalent to the complementizer *că* 'that' (181a, b) (Gheorghe 2004: 154–5):

(181) a. Simt   **cum**   mi   se   încălzesc   picioarele
         (I)feel how   CL.DAT.1SG   CL.REFL.3PL   warm-up.3PL   feet.DEF
         'I can feel my feet warming up'

     b. Simt   **că**   mi   se   încălzesc   picioarele
         (I)feel that   CL.DAT.1SG   CL.REFL.3PL   warm-up.3PL   feet.DEF
         'I can feel that my feet warm up'

The verbs *vedea* 'see', *auzi* 'hear', *simți* 'feel' can function as raising verbs. In these contexts, they take an NP subject, an NP direct object, and a third constituent functioning as a secondary predicate (see also §§10.4.3; 10.4.4). The secondary predicate may be realized as: an adjectival phrase (182a); a bare noun, denoting a socio-human category (182b); a non-finite gerund clause (182c); a prepositional phrase headed by a locative preposition (182d); clauses headed by the complementizers *că* 'that' (182e) or *să* (182f); a pseudo-relative clause (182g):

(182) a. Îl   aud   **răgușit**
         CL.ACC.3SG   hear.1SG   hoarse.M.SG
         'I can hear he is hoarse'

     b. Îl   văd   **profesor**   **universitar**   în   câțiva   ani
         CL.ACC.3SG   see.1SG   professor   university(ADJ)   in   a few   years
         'I see him a university professor in a couple of years'

     c. Îl   aud   **vorbind**   **tare**
         CL.ACC.3SG   hear.1SG   talk.GER   loudly
         'I hear him talking loudly'

     d. Îi   văd   **pe studenți** **în bănci** **și** **pe profesoară** **la** **tablă**
         CL.ACC.3PL see.1SG   PE students   in desks   and   PE teacher   at   table
         'I see the students at the desks and the teacher at the table'

e. Îl   simt   **că**   **tremură**
    CL.ACC.3SG   feel.1SG   that   shivers
    'I feel him shivering'

f. Nu   o   văd   **să**   trăiască   într-o   altă   țară
    not CL.ACC.3SG   see.1SG   să_SUBJ   live.SUBJ.3SG   into=an   other   country
    'I do not imagine her living in another country'

g. Îl   văd   **cum**   roșește
    CL.ACC.3SG   see.1SG   how   blushes
    'I see him blushing'

C The pattern shown in (182c) with a gerund clause corresponds to the Romance pattern 'accusative with infinitive' (183a) or to the pseudo-relative construction (183b), both of which are found in French and Italian:

(183) a. Fr. Je le vois **venir**
         It. La sento **cantare**
      b. Fr. Je le vois **qui** vient
         It. Vedo Gianni **che** canta
                     (in Cinque 2005: 244; Maiden and Robustelli 2007: 390–5)

In Spanish, the gerund (184a) and the infinitive (184b) are used in free variation:

(184) a. Miraba a los niños **jugando**
      b. Miraba **jugar** a los niños

U In these contexts, the adverbial *cum* 'how' diminishes the modal value in favour of a temporal durative value, which enables the equivalence to the gerund (185a, b) (Gheorghe 2004: 245):

(185) a. Îl   simt   **cum**   tremură
         CL.ACC.3SG   feel.1SG   how   shivers
      b. Îl   simt   **tremurând**
         CL.ACC.3SG   feel.1SG   shiver.GER
         'I feel him shivering'

In certain constructions, perception verbs denote cognitive processes, thus they get further away from their primary, physical meaning (see (182b) above).

(ii) Verbs of intentional perception usually take two arguments, the NP subject and the direct object, which can be realized either as an NP (186a) or as a relative clause (186b):

(186) a. **Fata** privește **cerul**
         'The girl looks at the sky'
      b. Ana ascultă **ce e la televizor**
         'Ana listens what is on the television'

Compared to verbs of non-intentional perception, verbs of intentional perception do not select clauses headed by the complementizer *că* 'that':

(187) * Privesc **că** … / *Ascult **că** …
         (I)look that / (I)hear that

Verbs of intentional perception may occur, more restrictively than verbs of non-intentional perception, in raised object structures with secondary predicates. The secondary predicate can be realized as an adjectival phrase (188a) or a non-finite gerund clause (188b):

(188) a. Eu   o   privesc   **speriată**
       I   CL.ACC.F.3SG (I)look   frightened
       'I look at her frightened'

   b. **Îl**   ascult   **cântând**
      CL.ACC.M.3SG   (I)listen   sing.GER
      'I listen to him singing'

In contrast with the structures with verbs of non-intentional perception, in which the participial secondary predicate refers to the direct object of the verb of perception (i.e. object depictive) (189a), in these patterns, the participial secondary predicate can refer only to the NP subject (i.e. subject depictive) (189b):

(189) a. Îl$_j$ **văd**   [supărat t$_j$]
         CL.ACC.M.3SG   (I)see   angry.M.SG

   b. Ana$_i$ mă   **privește**   [și Ana$_i$ este]   plictisită
      Ana   CL.ACC.1SG   looks   [and Ana is]   bored

   (iii) Verbs of evidential perception express certain perceptions from the point of view of an Experiencer whose realization is optional for the verbs *suna* 'sound' (190) and *mirosi* 'smell' (191). In the case of the verb *arăta* 'look' (192), the realization of the Experiencer is not allowed. In such cases, the Experiencer is, implicitly, the speaker:

(190) Fraza   asta   nu   (îmi$_{Experiencer}$)   sună   bine
      sentence.DEF   this   not   CL.DAT.1SG   sounds   good
      'This sentence does not sound good to me'

(191) (Îi$_{Experiencer}$)   miroase   a   ars
      CL.DAT.3SG   smells   like   burnt.PPLE.M.SG
      '(S)he can feel something burning'

(192) Ana   (*îmi)   arată   bine
      Ana   CL.DAT.1SG   looks   good
      'Ana looks good'

The verb *arăta* 'look' takes an NP subject and a property-denoting subjective predicative complement, with different realizations: an adjectival phrase (193a), an adverbial phrase headed by a manner adverbial or by the substitute adverbial *cum* 'how' (193b), a prepositional phrase headed by the comparative prepositions *a* and *ca* 'like' (193c), clauses introduced by the conjunctions *ca și cum, ca și când, de parcă* 'as if' (193d):

(193) a. Ioana arată **obosită**
         'Ioana looks tired'

   b. Copiii arată **bine** / **Cum** arată copiii?
      'The children look fine' / 'What do the children look like?'

   c. Arată **a spaniol** / Arată **ca tine**
      'He looks like a Spaniard' / '(S)he looks like you'

   d. Arată **ca și cum / de parcă** nu ar fi dormit
      '(S)he looks as if she didn't sleep'

The verb *suna* 'sound' has similar syntactic behaviour to *arăta* 'look'. The predicative constituent of the verb *suna* 'sound' has similar realizations to the subjective predicative complement selected by the verb *arăta* 'look'; the only difference is that the predicative of *suna* cannot have an adjectival realization:

(194) a. Franceza lui sună **bine / Cum** sună melodia?
'His French sounds fine' / 'What does the song sound like?'

b. Limba pe care o vorbesc sună **a poloneză**
'The language they are speaking sounds like Polish'

c. Vocea ta sună **ca și când ai fi răcit**
'Your voice sounds as if you had caught a cold'

Mirosi 'smell' enters more diverse syntactic patterns than the other two verbs. When it has the meaning 'have a bad smell', it occurs as a subjectless verb (195a). In the same syntactic pattern, the verb *mirosi* 'smell' can select another type of constituent, realized as a prepositional phrase headed by the preposition *a* 'like'(195b):

(195) a. [Ø]$_S$ În cameră miroase
            in   room   smells
'The room smells bad'

b. [Ø]$_S$ Miroase **a parfum**
         smells   like perfume
'It smells of perfume'

The realization of the Experiencer as a dative clitic is possible only in the (195b) pattern:

(196) Îmi miroase **a parfum**
     CL.DAT.1SG smells like perfume
'I can smell perfume'

The verb *mirosi* 'smell' takes **a sole argument** in the subject position. This argument bears the thematic role Theme:

(197) **Florile** nu miros
     flowers not smell
'The flowers do not smell'

It can also take two arguments, a Locative subject and a prepositional object, headed by the comparative preposition *a* 'like':

(198) **Toată casa** miroase **a fum**
     all house.DEF smells like smoke
'The entire house smells of smoke'

2.3.3.1.3 Depending on the informational structure of the sentences containing verbs of non-intentional perception, Romanian prefers the *se*-passive in the contexts denoting perception of an entity (199a,c) and the *be*-passive in the contexts denoting perception of a process (200a):

(199) a. **Văd** casa din vale > **Se vede** casa din vale
     (I)see house.DEF from valley CL.REFL.PASS see.3SG house.DEF from valley

b. * Casa   din   vale   **este văzută**
   house.DEF   from   valley is   seen

c. **Aud**   melodia >   **Se**   **aude**   melodia
   (I)hear   melody.DEF   CL.REFL.PASS.3SG   hear.3SG   melody.DEF

d. *Melodia   **este   auzită**
   melody.DEF is   heard

(200) a. Îl   **văd**   pe   bătrân   făcând   cumpărături   din   piață >
         CL.ACC.3SG (I)see   PE   old-man doing   shopping.PL   from   market
         Bătrânul   este   **văzut** făcând   cumpărături   din   piață
         old-man.DEF is   seen   doing   shopping.PL   from   market

   b. ***Se**   vede   bătrânul   făcând   cumpărături   din   piață
      CL.REFL.PASS.ACC.3SG   see.3SG old-man.DEF doing   shopping.PL   from   market

Most frequently, the *by*-phrase is not syntactically realized, irrespective of the type of passivization.

2.3.3.2 Verbs of physical sensation

This class is made up of the verbs that can be paraphrased by 'have the physical sensation / state of… (pain, itching, etc.)' or by 'feel… (itching, pain, etc.)' and of verbal constructions equivalent to these verbs—*avea* 'have' or *simți* 'feel', followed by a deverbal noun which designates a physical sensation.

Certain verbs denote physical sensations in their primary use (201a, b), whereas others express physical sensation by means of a verbal metaphor (202a–c).

(201) a. Pe   Ioana   o   **doare**   capul
         PE   Ioana.ACC   CL.ACC.F.3SG   aches   head.DEF.NOM
         'Ioana has a headache'

   b. Pe   mine   mă   **ustură**   pielea   de la soare
      PE   me.ACC   CL.ACC.1SG   smarts   skin.DEF.NOM   from sun
      'My skin smarts because of the sun'

(202) a. Mă   **arde**   în   piept
         CL.ACC.1SG   burns   in   chest
         'I have a burn in my chest'

   b. Mă   **taie**   o   durere   la   inimă
      CL.ACC.1SG   cuts   an   ache.NOM at   heart
      'I have a heartache'

   c. Îi   **vâjâie**   capul
      CL.DAT.3SG   buzzes   head.DEF.NOM
      'I have a buzzing sensation in my head'

2.3.3.2.1 Verbs of physical sensation enter different syntactic patterns. They select an Experiencer / Possessor realized as an accusative personal clitic (201a, b, 202a, b) or an Experiencer / Possessor realized as a dative personal clitic (202c). In these configurations, they encode a part–whole relationship of inalienable possession (body-part–affected person) between the Locative subject (203a, b) or adjunct (203c) and the Experiencer direct object (203a, c) or possessive complement (203b):

(203) a. **Mă** doare **spatele**
CL.ACC.1SG aches back.DEF.NOM
'My back hurts'

b. **Îmi** ard **obrajii**
CL.DAT.1SG burn cheeks.DEF.NOM
'My cheeks burn'

c. **Mă** înjunghie **la inimă**
CL.ACC.1SG stabs at heart
'I have a stitch in my chest'

C In its way of expressing physical sensations, Romanian, which allows Experiencers realized as accusative and dative clitics, differs from Italian and Spanish, in which the Experiencer is realized as a dative clitic (204c, d), and from English or French (Van Peteghem 2007: 572), where the Experiencer is realized as a nominative NP.

(204) a. Pe Ioana o_{ACC} doare spatele
PE Ioana.ACC CL.ACC.3SG aches back.DEF.NOM
'Ioana's back aches'

b. **Îmi**$_{DAT}$ țiuie urechile
CL.DAT.1SG tingle.3PL ears.DEF.NOM
'My ears tingle'

c. It. **Mi**$_{DAT}$ fa male la testa

d. Sp. **Me**$_{DAT}$ duele la cabeza

e. Fr. **J**$_{NOM}$'ai mal à la tête

f. Engl. **I**$_{NOM}$ have a headache

2.3.3.2.2 Depending on their ability to take an accusative clitic (i) or a dative clitic (ii), verbs of physical sensation enter different syntactic patterns. The two classes may overlap (iii).

(i) Verbs of physical sensation may appear in constructions with a sole syntactically realized argument. Usually, this argument is the direct object Experiencer (205) and less often the subject Cause / Source (206):

(205) **Mă** ustură
CL.ACC.1SG itches
'It itches me'
Mă înjunghie
CL.ACC.1SG stabs
'It stabs me'

(206) **Tusea** îneacă
cough.DEF chokes
'The cough chokes'

In such configurations, it is possible that the subject (205) or the direct object (206) remain syntactically unexpressed, even though they are present in the thematic grid of verbs.

Verbs of physical sensation may take two arguments, the Experiencer, in the direct object position, and the Theme (207), Cause / Source (208), or Locative (209), in the postverbal subject position:

(207) **Mă**   roade   **durerea**
       CL.ACC.1SG   rubs   pain.DEF.NOM
       'The pain is gnawing at me'

(208) **Îl**   ustură   **tăietura**
       CL.ACC.3SG   smarts   cut.DEF.NOM
       'The cut is still hurting him'

(209) **Mă**   mănâncă **tot trupul**
       CL.ACC.1SG   itches   all   body.DEF.NOM
       'I am itching all over my body'

The Cause / The Source (210) and the Locative (211) can be realized as prepositional phrases, occupying an adjunct position. In these constructions, the subject remains syntactically unexpressed (see also §3.1.3.4.1).

(210) [Ø]$_S$ O   doare   **de la operație**
                CL.ACC.F.3SG   aches   from   surgery
       'She has pains from the operation'

(211) [Ø]$_S$ O   doare   **în piept**
                CL.ACC.F.3SG   aches   in   chest
       'She has a chest pain'

The syntactic variation between the prepositional Locative and the Locative subject is associated with a semantic distinction. The prepositional construction refers to the internal sensation (212a) compared to the construction in which the Locative occupies the subject position (212b), which expresses either an internal sensation or an external one (Manoliu-Manea 1993: 82–3).

(212) a. Mă   doare   **în gât**
          CL.ACC.1SG   aches   in   throat
          'I have a sore throat'

       b. Mă   doare   **gâtul**
          CL.ACC.1SG   aches   throat.DEF.NOM / neck.DEF.NOM
          'I have a sore throat; My neck aches'

Verbs in this class can enter more extensive constructions, in which they also take optional constituents: Cause / Source (subject) + Experiencer (direct object) + Locative (adjunct) (213); Experiencer (subject) + Theme (direct object) + Locative (adjunct), only with the verbs *avea*, *încerca* 'have', *simți* 'feel' (214).

(213) Pantofii   mă   bat   la   călcâi
       shoes.DEF   CL.ACC.1SG   hurt   at   heel
       'My shoes rub my heel'

(214) Am   o   durere   în   spate
       (I)have   a   pain   in   back
       'I have a back pain'

(ii) Verbs of physical sensation which take a dative clitic do not allow much syntactic variation of the semantic grid. They obligatorily select two arguments—the Experiencer / Possessor in the possessive complement position and the Locative in the subject position:

(215) **Îmi** vâjâie urechile
CL.DAT.1SG buzz ears.DEF.NOM
'I have a buzzing sensation in my ears'

Optionally, the Cause / Source may be expressed; they are realized as a prepositional phrase:

(216) Îmi vâjâie capul **de la febră**
CL.DAT.1SG buzzes head.DEF.NOM from fever
'I have a buzzing sensation in my head from the fever'

(iii) The verbs which typically take an accusative clitic and a nominative Locative (217a) can shift to the possessive dative pattern, in those contexts in which the cause of the physical sensation is realized as a nominal in the nominative (217b):

(217) a. **Mă** gâdilă fruntea
CL.ACC.1SG tickles forehead.DEF.NOM
'I have a tickling sensation in my forehead'

b. Soarele **îmi** gâdilă fruntea
sun.DEF.NOM CL.DAT.1SG tickles forehead.DEF.ACC
'The sun is tickling my forehead'

2.3.3.2.3 Verbs of physical sensations obey certain syntactic restrictions. The configurations in which the Experiencer is realized as an accusative clitic cannot be passivized:

(218) Mă doare stomacul > *Sunt durută de stomac
CL.ACC.1SG aches stomach.DEF.NOM (I)am ached by stomach
'I have a stomach ache'

The Experiencer realized as a pronominal clitic is regularly sentence initial, whereas the Locative, realized as a definite nominal, occurs in postverbal position (219a, b) (see also §3.1.9.1). The Locative nominal can be left-dislocated only under focus (219c, d) (Manoliu-Manea 1993: 82; Van Peteghem 2007: 576):

(219) a. Mă doare **capul**
CL.ACC.1SG aches head.DEF
'I have a headache'

b. Îmi ard **obrajii**
CL.DAT.1SG burn cheeks.DEF
'My cheeks are burning'

c. CAPUL mă doare, nu **spatele**
head.DEF CL.ACC.1SG aches not back.DEF
'I have a headache, not a back pain'

d. OBRAJII îmi ard, nu **fruntea**
cheeks.DEF CL.DAT.1SG burn not forehead.DEF
'My cheeks, not my forehead are burning'

2.3.3.3 Psych verbs

Psych verbs denote a psychological state. This class consists of verbs such as *uimi* 'surprise', *speria* 'frighten', *iubi* 'love', *supăra* 'upset' and of equivalent verbal constructions such as *a(-i) fi* 'be' + noun (*a-i fi teamă* 'be afraid', *a-i fi rușine* 'be ashamed'), which can be paraphrased by 'have the psychological state / the emotional feeling of…' (Manea 2001: 26).

2.3.3.3.1 Psych verbs show a strong correspondence between semantic representation and syntactic structure. They have an 'Experiencer' slot in their thematic grid, which can be realized as a subject (220a, b), a direct object (221), or an indirect object (222) (*experiencer–subject constructions* vs. *experiencer–object constructions*, Crystal 2008: 396).

(220) a. **Câinele** se sperie de lumină
'The dog is frightened by the light'

b. **Ea** adoră parfumurile
'She adores perfumes'

(221) Insuccesul îl deprimă
'Failure depresses him'

(222) Îi convine situația
'The situation suits him'

Certain psych verbs display two forms: the transitive entry is causative, whereas the reflexive one is non-causative—*bucura* 'make happy' vs. *a se bucura* 'enjoy, be happy', *înfuria* 'make somebody furious' vs. *a se înfuria* 'grow furious', *îngrijora* 'make somebody worry' vs. *a se îngrijora* 'become worried'. Either the Stimulus (223a) or the Experiencer (223b) can appear in subject position. Semantically, the two patterns differ with respect to focus placement: either on the quality of the Stimulus or on the state of the Experiencer:

(223)   Stimulus as the subject   Experiencer as the subject
    a. **Pericolul** mă sperie   b. **Eu** mă sperii de pericol
       'Danger frightens me'   'I am frightened by danger'
       Povestea îl amuză   El se amuză de poveste
       'The story amuses him'   'He is amused by the story'

The desiderative verbs *vrea* 'want', *dori* 'wish', *prefera* 'prefer', *spera* 'hope' allow for the Experiencer to be the subject; this feature may be explained as an effect of the fact that psychological processes such as those expressed by such verbs are mentally experienced across cultures as self-originating events (Talmy 2007: 138).

In the semantic domain of cognitive processes, a great number of verbs allow the Experiencer in subject position—*crede, gândi* 'think', *a-și imagina* 'imagine', *a se îndoi* 'doubt', *ști* 'know'—whereas others, less numerous, allow the Stimulus in subject position—*contraria* 'vex', *uimi* 'astonish', *șoca* 'shock'. There are verbs which can appear in both patterns—*a se mira* 'wonder' functions as an Experiencer–subject verb, whereas *mira* 'surprise' functions as an Experiencer–object verb.

The Stimulus is realized as a subject (224) or as a prepositional object (225). In some cases, the Stimulus may remain syntactically unexpressed (226).

(224) a. **Singurătatea** îl sperie
       'Solitude frightens him'

   b. **Amintirile** îl întristează
       'Memories make him be sad'

(225) a. El se teme **de boli**
       'He is afraid of diseases'

   b. Ea se bucură **de întâlnire**
       'She is glad about the meeting'

(226) a. Ion se bucură
       'Ion is glad'

   b. Maria se întristează
       'Maria becomes sad'

C In Romanian, as in other Romance languages, the verbs with two lexical entries, i.e. reflexive and transitive, allow the Stimulus to be realized both as a subject and as an object (223). English seems to favour the realization of the Stimulus as a subject (Talmy 2007: 135): Engl. *This interests me*, *It pleases me*. In English, only a few verbs (*like*, *want*) allow the realization of the Experiencer as a subject.

The Agent is syntactically realized only with the causative verbs expressing a controlled or controllable process:

(227) a. **Mama** îl consolează
       'Mum comforts him'

   b. **Colegii** o enervează
       'Her colleagues annoy her'

The Theme may be realized either as a subject (228a, b) or as a direct object (229a, b):

(228) a. Îi place **filmul**
       'He likes the movie'

   b. Îi convine **situația**
       'The situation suits him'

(229) a. Ea adoră **filmul**
       'She adores the movie'

   b. Ea îl iubește
       'She loves him'

2.3.3.3.2 Psych verbs enter various syntactic patterns. They divide into several syntactic subclasses:

- transitive Experiencer–subject verbs—*adora* 'adore', *detesta* 'detest', *iubi* 'love', *crede* 'think', *ști* 'know' (220b, 229)—and transitive Experiencer–object verbs—*stresa* 'stress', *uimi* 'astonish', *șoca* 'shock', *contraria* 'vex' (221);
- verbs that can function either as reflexive or as transitive: *a (se) alarma* 'be alarmed; alarm', *a (se) amuza* 'be amused; amuse', *a (se) bucura* 'be happy; make happy', *a (se) consola* 'console oneself; comfort', *a (se) descuraja* 'lose courage; discourage', *a (se) enerva* 'become annoyed; annoy', *a (se) entuziasma* 'become enthusiastic; fill with

enthusiasm', *a (se) înfuria* 'become furious; make furious', *a (se) mira* 'wonder; surprise', *a (se) neliniști* 'become worried; worry', *a (se) plictisi* 'become bored; bore', *a (se) speria* 'fear; frighten' (223);
- intransitive verbs that do not select an obligatory pronominal clitic—*deznădăjdui* 'fall into despair', *dispera* 'despair' (230a)—and intransitive verbs with an Experiencer dative obligatory clitic—*a-i plăcea* 'like', *a-i displăcea* 'dislike', *a-i prii* 'be good for', *a-i repugna* 'loathe', *a-i tihni* 'enjoy' (230b):

(230) a. Nu dispera, vom găsi soluții!
'Do not despair, we will find solutions!'

b. Vacanța nu-i tihnește
holiday.DEF.NOM not=CL.DAT.3SG enjoys
'He is not enjoying his holiday'

- obligatorily reflexive verbs that do not allow dative personal clitics: *a se căi* 'repent', *a se sfii* 'be shy, shrink from', *a se sinchisi* 'care', *a se teme* 'fear' (231a) and obligatorily reflexive verbs that take personal dative clitics *a i se urî* 'be fed up', *a i se face* 'feel like doing something; become' (231b):

(231) a. El s-a sfiit să vorbească despre asta
'He shrank from talking about this'

b. Mariei i s-a făcut de plimbare (colloquial)
'Maria felt like a walk'

The intransitive verb *a-i păsa* 'care' (232a), the verb *a-i arde* 'have a desire', obligatorily reflexive verbs which take dative personal clitics (232b), and the structures *a-i părea bine / rău* 'feel happy / sorry' have an empty subject position:

(232) a. Lui Ion îi pasă de studenți
LUI.DAT Ion CL.DAT.3SG cares for students
'Ion cares about the students'

b. I s-a urât de școală
CL.DAT.3SG CL.REFL.ACC.3SG=has been-fed-up with school
'He has got fed up with school'

Certain psych verbs allow parallel syntactic patterns (see 223a, b). The object of a psych verb may become the subject, and the subject in the original structure may show up as a prepositional object (*psych-movement*, Crystal 2008: 396).

H Diachronically, some psych verbs underwent changes in their grammatical selection properties. There are verbs which in old Romanian take an indirect object (233a–c), whereas in the following centuries (contemporary Romanian included) take a direct or a prepositional object—*a se bucura* 'be happy', *a se minuna* 'be surprised', *iubi* 'love':

(233) a. Bucurați-vă **lui dumnedzeu**! (*Psaltirea Hurmuzaki*)
be-happy.IMP.2PL=CL.REFL.ACC.2PL LUI.DAT God
'Be happy to God!'

b. Să se minuneaze **tărieei** Domnului (Coresi)
SĂ.SUBJ CL.REFL.3SG≡PL wonder.SUBJ.3SG≡PL strength.DEF.DAT God.GEN
'Wonder of God's strength'

c. Nu   iubi   **hicleanilor**   (*Psaltirea Hurmuzaki*)
   not love.IMP.2SG   cunning.DEF.DAT.PL
   'Do not love the cunning ones'

2.3.3.3.3 Certain mental states can be expressed compositionally, in stative or dynamic periphrases with the verbs *fi* 'be' or *a se face* 'become' + an abstract nominal (denoting a state) + Experiencer (possessive object): *a-i fi / a i se face teamă / frică / groază* 'be / become afraid', *a-i fi / a i se face rușine* 'be / become ashamed', *a-i fi / a i se face milă* 'feel pity', *a-i fi / a i se face dor* 'miss' (§§3.1.9.1.2, 3.4.4.3).

(234) a. **Ei**   **îi**   este   **teamă** de   fulgere
         her.DAT   CL.DAT.3SG   is   fear   of   lightning.PL
         'She fears / is afraid of lightning'

      b. Ea   **se**   **teme**   de   fulgere
         she   CL.REFL.ACC.3SG   fears   of   lightning.PL
         'She fears / is afraid of lightning'

(235) a. **Lui**   **îi**   este / **i**   **se**   face   rușine
         him.DAT   CL.DAT.3SG   is   CL.DAT.M.3SG   CL.REFL.ACC.3SG   does   shame
         'He is ashamed'

      b. **El se**   **rușinează**
         he CL.REFL.ACC.3SG   is-ashamed
         'He is ashamed'

H   These structures have been compared to an old Latin pattern—the dative with *esse*—where possession was expressed by the verb *esse* plus a dative, in a configuration equivalent with the pattern *habeo* + nominative (Manoliu-Manea 1977: 76; Manea 2001: 76). The configuration with the dative Experiencer and the feeling / state nominal in the nominative is attested in Latin: *Mihi est pudor* (Manoliu-Manea 1977: 76–7).

2.3.4 Verbs of motion

2.3.4.1 Class membership

In a restricted sense, verbs of motion denote events involving a change of object location (236). The class of motion verbs is syntactically relevant.

(236) a. Creionul a căzut de pe masă
         'The pencil fell off the table'

      b. Ion a cărat bagajele în tren
         'Ion carried the luggage into the train'

Besides the information related to the movement of an object in space, verbs of motion can incorporate either spatial features—the path, the starting point of the path, the endpoint of the path, and the localization of the object (*ieși* 'go out', *a se îndrepta* 'head', *pleca* 'leave', *veni* 'come')—or qualia features / the manner of motion (*alerga* 'run / jog', *căra* 'carry', *fugi* 'run', *a se târî* 'crawl', *zbura* 'fly') (Evseev 1974: 71–85; Talmy 2007: 71–2, 88–9).

96   2 The Verb

C   Typologically, Romanian motion verbs, like in other Romance languages, classify both as path-incorporating and manner-incorporating verbs. Romance languages pattern differently from Germanic ones, where verbs of motion usually allow manner incorporation (Talmy 2007: 90).

Even languages belonging to the same family use different means to express the manner of motion: Rom. *ajunge* 'arrive' and *sosi* 'arrive' correspond to Fr. *arriver*, and Rom. *porni* and *pleca* 'leave' correspond to Fr. *partir*, which means that the feature of directionality and of transition from the state of motion to the state of rest is salient in Romanian, but not in French (Reinheimer 1965: 528). Note that *ajunge* and *porni* highlight the perspective of the object of motion, while *sosi* and *pleca* express motion from the endpoint's / speaker's perspective.

The type of the semantic information encoded in motion verbs has syntactic consequences: generally, verbs of directed motion are classified as unaccusatives, while verbs of non-directed motion or manner of motion are classified as unergatives (Levin and Rappaport Hovav 1995b: 147–8). The verb corresponding to the meaning 'fall', including the direction—'down', is unaccusative in Romanian (*cădea*), in French (*tomber*), and in English (*fall*), whereas the verb corresponding to the meaning 'travel', which does not specify the direction, is unergative in Romanian (*călători*), in Italian (*viaggiare*), in French (*voyager*), and in English (*travel*).

2.3.4.2   Syntactic features

Verbs of motion, in particular intransitives, are difficult to classify depending on agentivity or to include in the (semantic-)syntactic classes unaccusative vs. unergative, because their sole argument can be interpreted both as an Agent and as a Patient (Levin 1983: 33).

In Romanian, motion verbs can be divided into the following syntactic subclasses:

- verbs functioning only as transitives, many of which incorporate causative information (*alunga* 'send away', *căra* 'carry', *duce* 'lead; drive', *evacua* 'evacuate', *fugări* 'chase', *introduce* 'insert', *părăsi* 'leave', *transporta* 'carry', etc.):

(237)   a. Ion cară bagajele
           'Ion is carrying the luggage'
        b. Ion alungă ciorile
           'Ion is sending the crows away'

- transitive verbs with an unaccusative counterpart (*a (se) apropia* 'come near', *a (se) clinti* 'move', *coborî* 'take down', *a (se) deplasa* 'move', *a (se) învârti* 'whirl', *a (se) opri* 'stop', *a (se) rostogoli* 'roll', *a (se) sui* 'climb', *urca* 'mount'):

(238)   a. Ion coboară bicicleta / Bicicleta coboară la vale
           'Ion takes down the bicycle' / 'The bicycle is going down hill'
        b. Ion rostogolește piatra / Piatra se rostogolește
           'Ion is rolling the stone' / 'The stone is rolling'

- intransitive unaccusative verbs, incorporating information such as 'directed motion' and / or 'lack of subject's control' (*ajunge* 'arrive', *ateriza* 'land', *cădea* 'fall', *ieși* 'go out', *intra* 'enter', *pătrunde* 'get into', *pleca* 'leave', *reveni* 'come back', *sosi* 'arrive', *veni* 'come'):

(239) a. Ion alunecă pe gheaţă
'Ion is slipping on ice'

b. Creionul cade de pe masă
'The pencil is falling off the table'

- intransitive unergative, agentive verbs (*alerga* 'run', *călători* 'travel', *a se balansa* 'swing', *circula* 'move about', *hoinări* 'stroll', *înota* 'swim', *merge* 'go', *umbla* 'walk', *zbura* 'fly'):

(240) a. Ion aleargă prin parc
'Ion is running in the park'

b. Ion hoinăreşte pe străzi
'Ion is strolling along the streets'

In Romanian, there are no clear-cut syntactic tests to separate the class of unaccusative verbs from that of unergatives (§2.3.2.1.2). The only available test, the adjectivization of the participle, shows that a verb like *fugi* 'run, flee' (incorporating the manner of motion—'rapidly') is unaccusative only when it co-occurs with a delimiting prepositional phrase (enforcing a telic reading), but unergative in the absence of this type of prepositional phrase:

(241) a. Ion **fuge** până acasă / în străinătate
'Ion is running / fleeing home / abroad'

b. om **fugit** până acasă / în străinătate [unaccusative]
man run.PPLE until home / in abroad
'a person who ran / fled home / abroad'

(242) a. Ion **fuge** prin casă
'John is running in the house'

b. *om **fugit** prin casă [unergative]
man run.PPLE through house

C Compared to Italian (243) and English, in which the presence of a delimiting prepositional phrase causes any unergative (agentive) verb to function as an unaccusative, in Romanian, most verbs remain unergative even in the presence of such an adjunct (244, 245):

(243) a. Ugo ha corso meglio ieri [unergative—selection of the auxiliary 'have']
'Ugo ran better yesterday'

b. Ugo è corso a casa [unaccusative—selection of the auxiliary 'be']
'Ugo ran home' (in Levin and Rappaport Hovav 1995b: 186)

(244) a. Ion **a alergat** până la chioşcul de ziare
'Ion ran to the newspaper stall'

b. *omul **alergat** până la chioşcul de ziare [unergative]
man.DEF run.PPLE until to stall.DEF of newspapers

(245) a. Ion **a mers** în mâini până la şcoală
'Ion walked on his hands to school'

b. *omul **mers** în mâini până la şcoală [unergative]
man.DEF walked.PPLE in hands until to school

CONCLUSIONS

1 Romanian created the 5th inflectional class of verbs with the specific infinitive suffix -*î*. In the classes of verbs with the infinitival suffixes -*a*, -*i*, and -*î*, Romanian distinguishes two subclasses, depending on the indicative present suffix: with or without the suffix -*ez* for the verbs in -*a*, with or without the suffix -*esc* for the verbs in -*i*, respectively with or without the suffix -*ăsc* for the verbs in -*î*.

Under Romance influence, the most productive class of Romanian verbs came to be that in -*a* (unlike the old language, where the class of verbs in -*i* was the most productive), and, within it, the specific subclass of the verbs with the suffix -*ez*.

The slight differences between the class of verbs in -*e* and the class of verbs in -*ea* favour shifts from one class to the other.

2 As for realization of the categories of mood, tense, aspect, number, and person, Romanian has a high number of inflectional classes and subclasses, characterized by suffixes and specific syncretisms and by morphophonological alternations; there are a small number of irregular, suppletive verbs. Romanian has a complex of modal forms, realizing the distinctions real vs. unreal and assertive vs. injunctive with a mixed paradigm, which has both purely modal uses and syntactic uses (the subjunctive). Romanian manifests a tendency towards specialization and supplementary marking of epistemic modal values and especially of evidentiality (the presumptive). Temporal–aspectual values have a syncretic realization. Absolute tenses have relative uses, which results in the absence of a system of 'sequence of tenses'.

3 Within the class of verbs with two internal arguments, Romanian, like other Romance languages, distinguishes a subclass of verbs taking a direct and an indirect object, and, unlike other Romance languages, a subclass of verbs taking a direct object and—instead of the indirect object—an argument coded as a nominal phrase with an unmarked form, called *secondary object*.

The classes of Latin verbs which take two accusative objects were preserved in Romanian (verbs with direct and secondary object and verbs with direct object and objective predicative complement). The only change with respect to Latin concerns the morphological status of the secondary object; in Romanian, the secondary object displays an unmarked case form (Acc≡Nom).

Romanian developed certain specific syntactic configurations in which the objective predicative complement occurs with subjectless verbs.

4 There are many more unaccusative than unergative verbs. A verb is unaccusative if it is non-agentive, it has a sole argument, and allows the adjectivization of the participle. Depending on the context, a verb can function either as unaccusative, or as unergative. Unergative verbs easily allow the phenomenon of transitivization by appearing in cognate object constructions. Most unaccusatives allow the causative alternation. Most unaccusatives are reflexive. There are unaccusatives which display two forms—reflexive and non-reflexive—with slight semantic differences between the two forms.

There is only one verb corresponding to the verb 'be'. Romanian has a rich inventory of copula verbs, homonymous with lexical, complex transitive verbs taking objective predicative complements. Some copula verbs belong exclusively to the colloquial language. Two copula verbs, *face pe* 'play the' and *a se erija în* 'set oneself up as' contain a special type of grammaticalized preposition which does not assign case.

5 Compared to English, Romanian has an incomplete paradigm for expressing the three different types of perceptions. Thus, nonintentional tactile, olfactory, and gustatory perceptions are expressed periphrastically, with the verbs *avea* 'have' or *simţi* 'feel' and the abstract nominals denoting the corresponding physical properties. In Romanian there are verbs of perception which, in certain patterns, may function as subjectless. Verbs of perception enter raised object structures, in which they select a subject, an object, and a third constituent, the secondary predicate, with different realizations, including the non-finite gerund clause. The Romanian pattern with non-finite gerund clause corresponds to the Romance pattern 'accusative with infinitive' or to the pseudo-relative construction, both present in French and Italian. Spanish uses both the 'accusative with infinitive' and 'accusative with gerund' patterns in free variation.

In patterns with verbs of physical sensation, the Experiencer is realized either as an accusative clitic or as a dative clitic. In this respect, Romanian differs from Italian and Spanish, which have dative Experiencers, and from French and English, which have nominative Experiencers. Verbs of physical sensation with accusative clitics may enter different syntactic patterns, in which the Locative is realized either as a nominative nominal or as a prepositional phrase. In the contexts with prepositional Locatives, the position of the subject is empty.

There are several subjectless psych verbs which take an Experiencer realized as a dative clitic: *a-i păsa* 'care', *a-i arde* 'have a strong desire', *a i se urî* 'be fed up', *a i se face* 'become; feel like', *a-i părea bine / rău* 'be happy / feel sorry'.

Certain transitive verbs have a reflexive counterpart, in parallel syntactic patterns (Experiencer–subject vs. Stimulus–subject).

6 Like other Romance languages, but unlike Germanic ones, Romanian verbs of motion classify both as path-incorporating and manner-incorporating verbs. In Romanian, unlike English and Italian, the presence of a directional prepositional phrase does not make all unergative verbs function as unaccusative verbs.

3

The Structure of Root Clauses

This chapter presents the syntactic functions of the Romanian root clause: subject, objects (the direct object, the secondary object, the indirect object, and the prepositional object), and predicative complements (the subjective predicative complement and the objective predicative complement). A special section is devoted to constructions involving overall clausal structure (passive and impersonal constructions, reflexive constructions, reciprocal constructions, and the dative possessive structure), as well as to syntactic positions that occur as an effect of syntactic restructuring (*by*-phrases and possessive objects). The final section deals with complex predicates.

3.1 THE SUBJECT

3.1.1 Characteristics

1 The occurrence of a constituent in subject position is conditioned by the verb's capacity to admit this position; Romanian has a number of verbs which are syntactically 'unable' to take a subject (*plouă* 'it rains', *a-i păsa de* 'to care about', *a i se urî de* 'to be fed up with'); they make up grammatical sentences in the absence of the subject position (§3.1.3.4).

2 The subject and the verb impose restrictions on one another; in that, on the one hand, the subject is assigned nominative case by the verbal inflection (*El citeşte* 'He reads') and, on the other hand, the finite verb must agree with the subject in number and person (§12.2).

3 The subject bears the nominative case, a case which has specific markers (different from the accusative) only for the 1st and 2nd person personal pronoun; the other grammatical classes in subject position (noun, non-personal pronouns, finite and non-finite clauses) are inflectionally unmarked.

4 The 'surface' subject can be associated with any type of verb: active transitive (1a), unaccusative (1b), unergative (1c), passive and reflexive-passive (1d, e), inherently impersonal (1f), with a dative or accusative Experiencer (1g, h). In each context the subject bears the nominative case and is responsible for the agreement on the verb; this also holds for the S_O postverbal subject of unaccusative and passive verbs (for the S_O–S_A distinction, see Ledgeway 2011: 469). Only subjectless (§3.1.3.4) and intransitive verbs in restructured configurations with impersonal *se* do not admit a subject (2):

(1) a. **Ion** citeşte o carte
 'Ion is reading a book'
 b. Cresc **preţurile**
 'Prices grow'
 c. **Copiii** aleargă
 'Children run'

d. Sunt enumerate **cauzele**
   'The causes are enumerated'
e. Se numără **greșelile**
   'The mistakes are counted'
f. Se întâmplă **o nenorocire**
   'A misfortune happens'
g. Îmi   place **muzica**
   CL.DAT.1SG likes music.DEF.NOM
   'I like music'
h. Mă   doare **capul**
   CL.ACC.1SG hurts head.DEF.NOM
   'I have a headache'

(2) Se   trăiește bine
  CL.REFL.IMPERS lives well
  'One lives well'

5 The 1st and 2nd person singular and plural subject is usually unrealized, and is retrievable from the verb inflection; the subject of a 3rd person singular or plural verb can also remain unrealized if it can be identified in context. Romanian belongs to the *pro-drop* group of languages (§3.1.3).

6 The subject position is preserved even if the verb cannot agree with it, due to the incomplete inflection of non-finite forms:

(3) înainte de [a ajunge **profesorul /** **eu /** **tu**]
  before A_INF arrive.INF teacher.DEF.NOM I.NOM you.NOM
  'before the teacher / I / you arrived'

C Although subject marking is doubly distributed, both in the subject case form and in the verb agreement, Romanian belongs to those languages with weak subject marking (Pană Dindelegan 2003: 222). This is supported by the fact that the nominative is the least marked of the cases, and that verbs do not always realize agreement with their subject (non-finite verb forms are incapable of agreement).

U In the Wallachian area, the syncretism 3SG≡3PL is general in the present indicative (Caragiu Marioțeanu 1975: 173), so that agreement is not visible in this case (4a). In the non-standard Romanian of other regions, where the verbs with the infinitive in *-ea*, *-e*, and *-i* distinguish 3rd person singular from 3rd person plural, agreement frequently does not take place in the case of a non-agentive postverbal subject (4b).

(4) a. Ei vede /   spune /   vine   [regional]
   they see.3SG≡PL say.3SG≡PL come.3SG≡PL
   'They see / say / come'
  b. Mă   doare picioarele   [non-standard]
   CL.ACC.1SG hurt.3SG legs.DEF.NOM
   'My feet ache'

3.1.2 The subject of non-finite forms (lexical vs. controlled / covert)

Non-finite forms do not generally take subjects, but in specific syntactic conditions can take an overt subject, different from the subject of the matrix verb. This happens more frequently in the case of the infinitive and the gerund, and is less common for the supine and the participle.

3.1.2.1 The infinitive

The lexical subject of the infinitive can occur when the infinitival phrase occupies the following positions: a complement of the noun (5a); the complement of a preposition, when the prepositional phrase functions as an adjunct (5b); a rhematic postverbal subject (5c); and rarely, the object of a verb (5d):

(5) a. speranța [de [a câștiga **candidatul nostru**]]
hope.DEF DE A_{INF} win.INF candidate.DEF.NOM our
'the hope that our candidate will win'

b. până / fără / pentru [a pleca **Ion**]
until / without / for A_{INF} leave.INF Ion.NOM
'until Ion's leaving / without Ion leaving / for Ion to leave'

c. E important [a decide **tu însuți**]
Is important A_{INF} decide.INF you.NOM yourself
'It is important for you yourself to decide'

d. Ion se teme [a nu-l apuca **iarna**]
Ion CL.REFL.ACC fears A_{INF} not=CL.ACC.3SG catch.INF winter.DEF.NOM
cu casa neterminată]
with house.DEF unfinished
'Ion is afraid of winter overtaking him with the house unfinished'

The overt subject of the infinitive is always postverbal.

C Contrary to the 'personal' or 'inflected' infinitive (which has personal endings) found in Portuguese and Galician (Mensching 2000: 27), in Romanian, as in most other Romance languages (Renzi and Andreose 2003: 225–6), the subject of the infinitive is realized in the absence of agreement.

The subject of the infinitive occurs frequently as a controlled, unrealized subject, in the following positions: noun complement (6a); subject (6b, c); direct object (6d). It is either a personal subject in contexts (6a, b, d), or a generic subject, when the infinitival phrase is part of an impersonal construction (6c). It can also occur as a raised subject, in impersonal structures (§3.1.8.1).

(6) a. speranța lui Ion_i [de [a câștiga PRO_i]]
hope.DEF LUI.GEN Ion DE A_{INF} win.INF
'Ion's hope of winning'

b. $Îmi_i$ vine [a plânge PRO_i]
CL.DAT.1SG comes A_{INF} cry.INF
'I feel like crying'

c. E mare păcat [a fura PRO_{ARB}]
is great sin A_{INF} steal.INF
'Stealing is a great sin'

d. Ion_i poate [pleca PRO_i]
Ion can leave.INF
'Ion can leave'

3.1.2.2 The gerund

The lexical subject of the gerund can occur if the gerund clause occupies the following syntactic positions: a non-finite clause adjunct (7a); the direct object of perception verbs ((7b); see also §2.3.3.1); rarely, an instrumental adjunct (7c):

(7) a. [Ajungând **părinții**$_i$ /   **Părinții**$_i$ ajungând   mai   repede],
       arrive.GER parents.DEF.NOM parents.DEF.NOM arrive.GER more quickly
       Ion$_j$ a   rămas   acasă
       Ion   has   remained   home
       'With his parents arriving more quickly, Ion stayed at home'

   b. Ion$_i$ simte   [apropiindu-se   **furtuna**$_j$]
      Ion   feels   come.GER=CL.REFL.ACC.3SG   storm.DEF.NOM
      'Ion feels the storm approaching'

   c. Ion$_i$ a   reușit   [trudind   **alții**$_j$ /
      Ion   has   succeeded   toil.GER   others.NOM
      alții$_j$ trudind   pentru   el]
      others.NOM   toil.GER   for   him
      'Ion has succeeded by others toiling for him'

In (7a, c), the subject can be either post- or preverbal. In (7b), it is postverbal; subject anteposition (8a) makes the construction ambiguous: the nominal phrase *furtuna* 'the storm' can be interpreted as the subject of the non-finite clause or as a raised object (§3.2.1.7). In the case of raised objects, the subject in the gerund clause is not realized (8b):

(8) a. Ion$_i$ [simte [**furtuna**$_j$ apropiindu-se]] vs. Ion$_i$ [simte **furtuna**$_j$ [apropiindu-se]]
       'Ion feels the storm coming'

   b. L$_i$-am   văzut   [*plângând   **Ion**$_i$]
      CL.ACC.3SG=have   seen   cry.GER   Ion.NOM
      'I saw Ion crying'

3.1.2.3 The supine

The lexical subject of the supine rarely occurs and only in impersonal structures in which the supine receives a passive reading and takes a *by*-phrase (9a) or in structures in which the non-finite clause is a nominal modifier and the head noun occurs as an externalization of a locative adjunct (9b):

(9) a. E   dificil   [de   admis   **soluția**   de   toată   lumea]
       is   difficult   DE$_{SUP}$ admit.SUP   solution.DEF.NOM   by   all   people.DEF
       'The solution is hard for everyone to admit'

   b. Am   cumpărat   o   masă$_i$ [de   [mâncat   **patru**
      (I) have   bought   a   table   DE$_{SUP}$ eat.SUP   four
      persoane   (la   ea$_i$)]]
      person.NOM.PL   at   it
      'I bought a dining table for four people to eat at'

H Pattern (9b), although rare in modern Romanian, is old, being attested at the end of the 17th century (Corbea).

3.1.2.4 The participle

The lexical subject of the participle is rarely expressed; it appears either in elliptical structures in which the participial clause functions as a non-finite clause adjunct (10a), or with a few impersonal verbs that allow a passive participle (10b):

(10) a. [(Odată) Plecat **directorul**ᵢ] / [**Directorul**ᵢ plecat], a şi
 once gone director.DEF.NOM director.DEF.NOM gone has already
 început vacarmulⱼ
 started noise.DEF
 'The headmaster having left, the racket had already started'

 b. Trebuie [spus **numai adevărul**]
 must.IMPERS say.PPLE only truth.DEF.NOM
 'Only the truth must be said'

In (10a) only participles that can be adjectivized are allowed (transitive-passives and unaccusatives); the subject word order is free. In (10b), only the participles of passive verbs are allowed, and the subject is obligatorily postverbal. With unergatives, in the context of *trebui*, the subject cannot occur (11):

(11) *Trebuie [vorbit **Ion** repede]
 must.IMPERS speak.PPLE Ion.NOM quickly

3.1.3 Non-realization and absence of the subject. Romanian as a pro-drop language

The fact that the presence of the subject is not obligatory is characteristic of Romanian; its features may be contextually retrieved or may be impossible to recover (fully). The feature label 'null pronominal subject' / 'pro-drop language' is strictly related to the rich verbal inflection, which allows the verb to take over totally or partially, through agreement, the information encoded by the subject. Romanian displays the three characteristics which set apart the pro-drop languages (subject non-realization, free subject inversion, extraction of the subject from the subordinate clause; see Rizzi 1982).

C Romanian differs from French and some northern Italian dialects, where the presence of pronominal clitics in subject position is usually obligatory (Miller and Monachesi 2003: 116–17; Salvi 2011: 344), but resembles Portuguese, Spanish, Catalan, some varieties of Occitan, varieties of central and southern Italian, in which the pronominal subject is not realized (the 'zero' subject; Reinheimer and Tasmowski 2005: 99). Romance languages with non-realized subjects continue the situation of Latin, where the 1st and 2nd person subject was expressed only to add features such as affectedness or emphasis (Ernout and Thomas 1959: 143; Renzi and Andreose 2003: 217).

3.1.3.1 Non-realization of the subject

In Romanian, the 1st and 2nd person singular and plural subject is unrealized in unmarked structures (it is a *pro*), being fully retrieved from verbal inflection (12a). It is realized in stylistically marked constructions, where it has special values of emphasis and / or contrast (12b).

(12) a. Când pro$_i$ ajung acasă, pro$_i$ o iau pe mama$_j$
when arrive.1SG home CL.ACC.F.3SG get.1SG PE mother.DEF
și pro$_{i+j}$ mergem la plimbare
and go.1PL at walk
'When I arrive home, I take mother and we go for a walk'

b. Muncesc și eu, muncești și tu, dar diferența dintre
(I)work also I.NOM (you)work also you.NOM but difference.DEF between
noi este că eu sunt rapid, iar tu ești lent
us is that I.NOM am quick and you.NOM are slow
'We both work, but the difference is that I am quick and you are slow'

The 3rd person singular and plural pronominal subject is also unrealized, if it is fully retrieved in context (13a, b). Subject non-realization occurs both in coordination (13a) and in subordination (13b). The non-realized subject is the most frequent form of zero anaphora (§13.6.2):

(13) a. Ion$_i$ doarme, pro$_i$ se distrează, pro$_i$ nu face nimic altceva
Ion.NOM sleeps CL.REFL.ACC.3SG has-fun not does nothing else
'Ion sleeps, has fun, does nothing else'

b. [Când pro$_i$ a ajuns acasă], mama$_i$ a găsit ușa deschisă
when has arrived home mother.DEF.NOM has found door.DEF open
'When mother arrived home, she found the door open'

Cases of subject control, where subject non-realization is obligatory, occur when the subordinate phrase contains a non-finite clause (§§4.2.3.1, 4.4.3.4). The controller can be the subject of the matrix clause (14a, b) or an internal argument inside the VP (14c) or the DP (14d):

(14) a. Ion$_i$ poate [PRO$_i$ să plece]
Ion.NOM can SĂ$_{SUBJ}$ leave.SUBJ.3SG
'Ion can leave'

b. Ion$_i$ se satură [de învățat PRO$_i$]
Ion.NOM CL.REFL.ACC gets-fed-up DE$_{SUP}$ study.SUP
'Ion gets fed up with studying'

c. Îmi$_i$ vine [PRO$_i$ să plâng]
CL.DAT.1SG comes SĂ$_{SUBJ}$ cry.SUBJ.1SG
'I feel like crying'

d. dorința lui Ion$_i$ [de [a reuși PRO$_i$]]
wish.DEF LUI.GEN Ion DE A$_{INF}$ succeed.INF
'Ion's wish to succeed'

A special case of 3rd person singular and plural unrealized subject occurs when the referent cannot be contextually identified. The impossibility of identifying the referent occurs when the speaker does not want to specify the author of the event (15a), when the author is unknown or generic (15b), or when, from the point of view of the speaker, the identity of the author is of no interest for the communication (15c).

(15) a. —Nu vezi că pro nu adoptă nicio soluție? /
not (you)see that not adopt.3SG≡PL no solution
—Cine? / —Ei, știi tu!
who well (you)know you
'Don't you see that they won't adopt any solution? / —Who? / —Well, you know!'

b. pro Scrie / Spune în ziare
  writes says in newspapers
 'It says in the newspapers'

c. pro Au adus marfă proaspătă
 (they)have delivered merchandise fresh
 'Fresh merchandise has been delivered'

H   In old Romanian, in clauses with verbs of saying, the 3rd person plural form of the verb was frequently employed (16a), a feature carried over from Latin and which exists in all Romance languages, except for French and Rhaeto-Romance (Salvi 2011: 351–2). This old structure with syntactically non-realized subject led to the recategorization of certain verbs, that were initially personal (Pană Dindelegan 2010), as subjectless verbs in the 3rd person singular (16b); see §2.3.1.2.1.

(16)   a. **Zic** că au fost la liturghie arhiepiscopi și
   say.PRES.IND.3PL that have been to liturgy archbishops and
   preoți și diiaconi 64   (Ureche)
   priests and deacons 64
   'They say that 64 archbishops, priests and deacons came to the mass'

   b. [Ø]$_S$ Îi **zice** / **spune** Ion
   CL.DAT.3SG says / says Ion
   'They call him Ion / He is called Ion'

3.1.3.2   The absence of the expletive impersonal pronominal subject

Romanian does not have a non-referential (expletive) pronominal subject of impersonal verbs and constructions. This position remains empty in the following structures:

- subjectless meteorological verbs

(17)   a. [Ø]$_S$ Plouă / Ninge / Tună
   rains snows thunders
   'It rains' / 'It snows' / 'It thunders'

- impersonal verbs with an empty subject position

(17)   b. [Ø]$_S$ Era / Se întâmpla în noiembrie
   be.IMPERF CL.REFL.3SG happen.IMPERF.3SG in November
   'It was / happened in November'

- impersonal verbs with postverbal subjects (S$_O$ type), realized either as a non-finite clause (18a, b), including here a subjunctive clause (18c, d), or as a finite indicative clause (18e):

(18)   a. Trebuie [spus că...]
   must.IMPERS say.PPLE that
   'One must say that...'

   b. Este greu [de spus că...]
   is hard DE$_{SUP}$ say.SUP that
   'It is hard to say that...'

c. Trebuie   [să   citeşti]
   must.IMPERS SĂ_SUBJ   read.SUBJ.2SG
   'You must read'

d. Îmi   place   [să   citesc]
   CL.DAT.1SG   (it)likes SĂ_SUBJ   read.SUBJ.1SG
   'I like reading'

e. Este   sigur   [că   spune   minciuni]
   is   certain   that   (he)tells lies
   'It is certain that he tells lies'

- impersonal verbs with postverbal subjects (S_O type), realized as a nominal phrase headed by an abstract noun or by an equivalent anaphoric pronoun (18f); in these structures, either there is no reference to a person (18f), or the person is referred to by a dative (18g) or accusative clitic (18h):

(18) f. Se   întâmplă   [o nenorocire / asta]
         CL.REFL.ACC.3SG   happens   a tragedy.NOM   this.NOM
         'A misfortune / this is happening'

     g. Îmi   convine   [plecarea]
        CL.DAT.1SG   suits   leaving.DEF.NOM
        'The leaving suits me'

     h. Mă   nelinişteşte [plecarea]
        CL.ACC.1SG   worries   leaving.DEF.NOM
        'The leaving worries me'

The interpretation of contexts (18d–h) as including the subject position is due to the obligatory agreement of the verb with a postposed noun phrase in structures such as (19a, b):

(19) a. S-a   întâmplat   o   nenorocire
        CL.REFL.ACC.3SG=has   happened   a   misfortune
        'A misfortune happened'

     b. S-au   întâmplat   nenorociri
        CL.REFL.ACC.3PL=(they)have   happened   misfortunes
        'Misfortunes happened'

H The structures without an expletive subject correspond to the Latin impersonal constructions with meteorological verbs (20a), with impersonal verbs of feeling (20b), and with impersonal verbs showing necessity or possibility (20c) (Ernout and Thomas 1959: 209–10):

(20) a. PLUIT,   TONAT
        'it rains', 'it thunders'
     b. (ME) MISERET
        'I feel pity'
     c. NECESSE EST, OPORTET, LICET
        'it is necessary', 'it is possible'

C In the Romance family, Romanian belongs to the same group as Italian, Spanish, and Portuguese, but is different from standard French, where an expletive clitic *il* is obligatory in such structures (Renzi and Andreose 2003: 217; Reinheimer and Tasmowski 2005: 105–6; Metzeltin

2011: 84). Note that Romanian does not have presentative-existential structures such as Fr. *il y a*, It. *c'è*, Sp. *hay*, Ptg. *há*, Engl. *there is* (Gawełko 2000: 22).

3.1.3.3 The absence of a [+human] non-definite or generic subject. Generic structures

Romanian does not have a subject-clitic which is specialized for generic structures, such as the French *on*. In order to express a generic subject (which can also include the speaker), Romanian makes use of the structures under (21–25); two of the structures, (21–22), are personal:

- constructions with a 2nd person singular verb (21a, b); if the verb is accompanied by a 2nd person reflexive clitic (21b), the clitic has a generic interpretation:

(21) a. Nu   e   bine   să   pleci$_{generic}$ cu   maşina   obosit
         not   is   good   SĂ$_{SUBJ}$ leave.SUBJ.2SG   with   car.DEF   tired
         'It is not good to drive when one is tired'

      b. Nu   e   bine   să   te   bucuri$_{generic}$ de
          not   is   good   SĂ$_{SUBJ}$ CL.REFL.ACC.2SG   be-happy.SUBJ.2SG   of
          necazul   altuia
          trouble.DEF   another.GEN
          'It is not good to take pleasure in another's trouble'

- constructions with the verb in the 1st person plural:

(22) Nu   e   bine   să   plecăm$_{generic}$ cu   maşina   obosiţi
      not   is   good   SĂ$_{SUBJ}$ leave.SUBJ.1PL   with   car.DEF   tired
      'It is not good to go by car when we are tired'

- impersonal-reflexive constructions (for the difference between (i), (ii), (iii), see §3.4.1):

  (i) derived from a transitive agentive verb (23a);
  (ii) derived from an unergative verb (23b) and from a transitive absolute verb (23c);
  (iii) derived from an unaccusative verb which has a personal subject (23d); copulas and inherently reflexive verbs cannot occur in the construction (iii), because they are not allowed in impersonal-reflexive structures

(23) a. **Se**   **face**   prea   mare   risipă
          CL.REFL.ACC.PASS.3SG   makes   too   big   waste
          'Too much is wasted'

      b. **Se**   **vorbeşte** prea   mult
          CL.REFL.ACC.IMPERS.3SG   talks   too   much
          'There is too much talk'

      c. **Se**   **mănâncă**   prea   mult
          CL.REFL.ACC.IMPERS.3SG   eats   too   much
          'They eat too much'

      d. Iarna   se   **răceşte**   uşor
          winter.DEF   CL.REFL.ACC.IMPERS.3SG   catches-a-cold   easily
          'In the winter one catches a cold easily'

- impersonal-passive structures with *a fi* 'be', from transitive verbs which select a clausal argument:

(24) **Este ştiut** că…
      is   known that…
      'It is known that…'

- structures in which the subject is an NP headed by a generic noun, associated with a definite article with generic reading (25a), or with a universal quantifier (25b):

(25) a. **Lumea /   oamenii**   se   bucură   când
        people.DEF.NOM.SG people.DEF.NOM.PL   CL.REFL.ACC.3SG≡PL   rejoice(s)   when
        vine   primăvara
        comes   spring.DEF.NOM
        'People rejoice when spring comes'

   b. **Tot omul /   Orice om**   se   bucură   când
        all man.DEF.NOM   any man.NOM   CL.REFL.ACC.3SG   rejoices   when
        vine   primăvara
        comes   spring.DEF
        'Every man rejoices when spring comes'

U The structure in (21) is the most frequent pattern, in spite of the ambiguous nature of the 2nd person singular form, which can have both episodic and generic reading in one and the same text.
   The choice of one structure over the other is partially free; it depends on the restrictions set by the impersonal-reflexive constructions. For verbs such as *mânca* 'eat', *pleca* 'leave', there is a free choice (26a); for verbs such as *a se bucura* 'rejoice', *fi* 'be', which do not accept the impersonal-reflexive structure, one of the personal structures has to be chosen (26b):

(26) a. Când   pleci /   plecăm /   se   pleacă   în   vacanţă
         when   leave.2SG   leave.1PL   CL.REFL.ACC.IMPERS   leaves   in   vacation
         'When one goes on vacation'

   b. Când   eşti   obosit /   suntem   obosiţi,   randamentul   este
         when   (you)are   tired   (we)are   tired   efficiency.DEF.NOM   is
         mai   mic
         more   little
         'When one is tired, one's efficiency is lower'

C Except for French, which has a clitic specialized for the position of generic human subject (*on*), all the main Romance languages possess impersonal-reflexive structures with *se / si* (Reinheimer and Tasmowski 2005: 142–8). Structure (21a) is characteristic of Romanian: a personal structure is used for the impersonal reading.
   As far as the *se / si* structure is concerned, there appear to be great differences in the behaviour and status of *se / si* between Romance languages. Romanian and French do not have a *se* corresponding to a nominative subject, while Italian does; Romanian unergative verbs do not allow a nominative *se* functioning as subject (Dobrovie-Sorin 1998: 404–6). For the interpretation of *se* in impersonal structures containing a unergative verb, see §3.4.1.

3.1.3.4 Verbs without a subject

3.1.3.4.1 Romanian has two classes of verbs that make up grammatical sentences in the absence of a subject NP (Pană Dindelegan 2008a: 336–7):

(i) Zero-valent verbs, which leave the subject position unfilled, because Romanian does not have expletive pronominal subjects (§3.1.3.2):

(27) a. Ninge / Plouă / Tună
'It snows' / 'It rains' / 'It thunders'

Just occasionally, the empty position can be filled by a nominal that is an "internal" subject, a Theme or a Result (27b), by a Locative (27c) or by an Agent (27d), which is seen as the author of the action in popular belief:

(27) b. Ploaia plouă
'The rain rains'

c. Cerul tună
'The sky thunders'

d. Sfântul Ilie tună
'Saint Elias thunders'

H The class of zero-valent verbs also occurs in old Romanian, in both variants, without a subject (28a) or with the subject position filled by a DP (28b):

(28) a. şi   [Ø]_S stropiè   de   ploaie   (Neculce)
     and   dripped   of   rain

b. tunră   den   ceriu   **domnulŭ**   cela   de   sus   (*Psaltirea Hurmuzaki*)
   thunders from sky   Lord.DEF.NOM   that   from up
'The Lord from the sky thunders'

C In Latin (Ernout and Thomas 1959: 209), where this class also occurs, it is possible to fill the subject position with nouns that are interpreted as Agents (Lat. IUPPITER TONAT / FULGURAT).

The class of subjectless meteorological verbs is also present in other Romance languages which have null subjects (Italian, Spanish, and Portuguese).

(ii) Psych verbs (§2.3.3.3), which despite the fact that they select two objects (an indirect and a prepositional object), cannot select a nominative NP. Some are not reflexive (29a, b), while others are (29c, d):

(29) a. Îmi   pasă   de   tine
       CL.DAT.1SG   care.3SG   of   you
       'I care about you'

b. Îmi   pare   bine /   pare   rău   de   plecarea   ta
   CL.DAT.1SG   feels well   feels badly   of   leaving.DEF your
   'I am glad / sorry that you are leaving'

c. Mi   s-a   urât   de   singurătate
   CL.DAT.1SG   CL.REFL.ACC=HAVE.3SG   get-fed-up.PPLE   of   loneliness
   'I got fed up with loneliness'

d. I   se   face   de   plimbare
   CL.DAT.3SG   CL.REFL.ACC   feels-like   of   walk
   'He feels like walking'

H The class of subjectless psych verbs is old, being attested in the earliest Romanian texts:

(30) li   să   urâsă   şi   lor   cu   faptele
     CL.DAT.3PL   CL.REFL.ACC.3SG get-fed-up.PLUPERF.3SG   also   them.DAT with   deed.PL.DEF
     lor   (Costin)
     their
     'they also had become fed up with their deeds'

(iii) A group of verbs of physical sensation ((31a); see also §2.3.3.2) and certain psych verbs (31b) enter structures in which they select a subject as well as structures in which they are subjectless:

(31) a. Mă   doare   **gâtul**   vs. Mă   doare   **în   gât**
       CL.ACC.1SG hurts   throat.DEF.NOM   CL.ACC.1SG hurts   in   throat
       'My neck hurts' 'I have a sore throat'
    b. Îmi   plac   **profesorii**   vs. Îmi   place
       CL.DAT.1SG like.3PL teachers.DEF.NOM   CL.DAT.1SG like.3SG
       de   profesori   [non-standard]
       of   teachers
       'I like the teachers'

3.1.3.4.2 Romanian has a type of impersonal construction which is the result of the restructuring of a personal structure containing an intransitive verb (either unergative or unaccusative; see also §3.4.1.2); the verb loses the syntactic position of subject, and becomes contextually zero-valent:

(32) Se   aleargă   prea   lent
     CL.REFL.ACC.IMPERS.3SG   run.3SG   too   slowly
     'One runs too slowly'

3.1.4 The subject realized as a bare noun

In Romanian, although a subject realized as a DP is prototypical, a bare noun subject is not excluded (§5.3.1.1.3), especially if the NP is plural. Romanian does not have strict restrictions regarding the use of bare nouns in subject position (Dragomirescu 2010: 225): a bare noun subject is accepted by any type of verb, especially in postposition (33a–d), but also in anteposition (34a–d):

(33) a. La bibliotecă, citesc   cărți   **studenți**   **din   toți anii**   [transitive]
       at library   read.3PL books   students.NOM   from   all   years
       'In the library, students from all years read books'
    b. Se   aleg   **studenți**   pentru   burse   [passive-reflexive]
       CL.REFL.ACC.PASS   choose.3PL   students.NOM   for   scholarships
       'They are choosing students for scholarships'
    c. În   timp   de   criză,   cresc   **prețuri**,   se
       in   time   of   crisis   increase.3PL prices.NOM   CL.REFL.ACC
       adâncesc   **nemulțumiri**   [unaccusative]
       deepen.3PL discontent.NOM.PL
       'In times of crisis, prices increase, the discontent deepens'
    d. Începe   zgomotul: cântă   **cocoși**,   latră   **câini**,
       starts   noise.DEF   sing.3PL   roosters.NOM   bark.3PL   dogs.NOM
       ciripesc   **păsări**   [unergative]
       chirp.3PL   birds.NOM
       'The noise starts: roosters sing, dogs bark, birds chirp'

(34) a. **Fizicieni din toată Europa** asigură funcționarea reactorului   [transitive]
'Physicists from all over Europe take care of the operation of the reactor'

b. **Studenți eminenți** sunt selectați pentru studii în străinătate   [passive]
'Outstanding students are selected for studies abroad'

c. **Frunze galbene** cad peste tot   [unaccusative]
'Yellow leaves fall all over the place'

d. Zgomotul este infernal: **hamali** urlă, **copii** vorbesc tare   [unergative]
'The noise is terrible: porters yell, children speak loudly'

H   This holds also for old Romanian, where any type of verb (35a, b) accepts a bare noun in the subject position, especially when it has a generic reading:

(35) a. nu-i   trăgea   inima   pe munteni...   să   margă
       not=CL.ACC.3PL   pull.3SG   heart.DEF   PE Wallachians   să$_{SUBJ}$ attack.SUBJ.3SG≡PL
       creștin   asupra   creștinului   (Costin)
       Christian.NOM   over   Christian.DEF.GEN
       'the Wallachians did not like it that a Christian should attack another Christian'

b. cât   să   mânca   **om**   pe om   (Neculce)
   so that   CL.REFL.ACC.3SG≡PL   eat.IMPERF.3SG≡PL   man.NOM   PE   man
   'so that men hurt each other'

3.1.5 The doubly realized subject

Romanian does not display the distinction between clitic and stressed form for the pronominal subject. Functionally, the non-realization of the pronominal subject is equivalent to the situation of a subject expressed through a clitic, whereas its presence is equivalent to a structure with a subject realized as a stressed pronominal form.

C   Romanian behaves like Portuguese, Spanish, Italian, but unlike French; French makes the distinction between pronominal clitic and strong pronominal form in the subject position (Reinheimer and Tasmowski 2005: 99, 103).

The doubly realized subject has two components which relate to the same verb, of which one is referential (a definite NP), and the other is obligatorily anaphoric (a pronoun (36a–c), a lexical anaphora *faptul* 'the fact', or the demonstrative pro-sentence anaphora *asta* 'this', with feminine form and neutral reading (36d)). The double realization of the subject has more stylistically different variants: (36a, b) are colloquial, (36c) is an emphatic structure of the standard language, and (36d) is an emphatic structure of the high register:

(36) a. Vine   [**ea**$_i$ **iarna**$_i$]
       comes   she.NOM   winter.DEF.NOM
       'Winter comes'

b. [**Tânărul împărat**]$_i$ a   mers   [**el**$_i$]   cât   a   mers
   young.DEF emperor.NOM   has   walked   he.NOM   as much as   has   walked
   'The young emperor walked as far as he walked'

c. [**Studenții**]$_i$ au   și   [**ei**$_i$]   dreptatea   lor
   students.DEF.NOM   have   also   they.NOM   right.DEF   their
   'Students too are right'

d. [Că a făcut reclamații]ᵢ, [faptul]ᵢ / [asta]ᵢ este reprobabil
   that has made complaints fact.DEF.NOM this.SG.NOM.F is reprehensible
   'The fact that he has made complaints is reprehensible'

Except for (36a), where the word order is [pronoun + NP], in the other examples, the order is [referential component + anaphora]. In (36a), the unsplit phrase displays a fixed word order, always in postposition; in (36b, c), the phrase is obligatorily split, with the referential component preceding the verb, and the pronominal following it (Cornilescu 2000).

Unlike doubling of the direct and indirect object (§§3.2.1.5, 3.2.3.4), which are grammaticalized phenomena with strict syntactic and semantic rules, the doubling of the subject is optional and strictly limited in use, in all the structures. It is limited to quasi-fixed colloquial constructions and to structures which are stylistically and pragmatically marked (emphatic, focalized, topicalized).

C In Aromanian there exists a clitic doubling pattern which does not exist in Daco-Romanian (Caragiu Marioțeanu 1981); the pattern consists in the emphatic resumption of the subject by a pronominal clitic in the nominative, syncretic with the accusative:
(37)   Arom. **Draclu** tu cărți easte-l / **Draclu** tu cărți l-easte
       devil.DEF in cards is=CL.NOM≡ACC.M.3SG devil.DEF in cards CL.NOM≡ACC.M.3SG=is
       'The devil is in the cards'

3.1.6 The prepositional subject

Realization as a prepositional phrase is not prototypical for the subject; it occurs in a number of constructions which contain: (i) a 'partitive' subject or a *de*-phrase subject; (ii) a locative or temporal subject; (iii) a coordinated subject, when the coordinator is *și cu* 'and with'.

(i) The constructions which contain one of the partitive prepositions *de*, *dintre*, *din* 'of' (38a–c) are interpreted as elliptic structures, with an empty nominal head:

(38) a. Au   murit   și [∅ [**dintre ei**]]
        have died   also   of   them
        'Some of them also died'

     b. S-a   furat   [∅[**din mâncarea   copiilor**]]
        CL.REFL.PASS=has   steal.PPLE   of   food.DEF.ACC   children.DEF.GEN
        'Some of the children's food was stolen'

     c. Au   câștigat și [∅[**de-ai noștri**]]
        (they)have   won   also   of=ours.M.ACC
        'Also some of ours won'

The structure in (38d), where the *de*-phrase has the interpretation 'some which have a certain quality', has an empty nominal head, like the structures above:

(38) d. În   societate, sunt   și [∅   [**de aceia**   [care cred   că
        in   society   (they)are also   of those.ACC   that   think that
        numai   ei   au   dreptate]]]
        only   they   have   right
        'In the society, there are also some people that think that only they are right'

(ii) As far as the locative and temporal structures are concerned, the interpretation of the prepositional phrase as a subject is controversial, as it does not pass the syntactic tests of subjecthood. The PP (or AdvP) is only associated with the non-agentive verb *fi* 'be' (and its synonyms, (39a)) or with an inherently impersonal verb (*îmi convine* 'it suits me', (39b)); examples (39c, d) are structures with metadiscourse resumption, in which the PP functions as a topicalized quotational phrase:

(39) a. **La munte / Acolo** este / înseamnă un loc admirabil
at mountain there is means a place wonderful
pentru odihnă
for rest
'In the mountains / That place is a wonderful place to rest'

b. **În mai** îmi convine
in May CL.DAT.1SG suits
'May suits me'

c. Am decis să mergem **la munte**. [**La munte**] este un loc agreabil pentru mine
'We decided to go to the mountains. In the mountains is a wonderful place for me'

d. Aş vrea să ne vedem **în mai**. [**În mai**] îmi convine
'I would like to see each other in May. May suits me'

(iii) When the subject position is occupied by a copulative coordinated phrase and the conjuncts are animate nominals, the coordinator *şi cu* '(and) with' can occur, in variation with *cu* 'with' (see also §11.1.1.1), and assign the accusative case to the second conjunct (40b):

(40) a. [**Ion (şi) cu Gheorghe**] locuiesc la Paris
Ion.NOM and with Gheorghe.ACC live.3PL at Paris
'Ion and Gheorghe live in Paris'

b. [**Ion şi cu mine**] locuim la Paris
Ion and with me.ACC (we)live at Paris
'Ion and I live in Paris'

The unsplit components and the plural agreement differentiate this structure from the configuration with a comitative adjunct (41):

(41) Ion locuieşte la Paris (*şi) cu Gheorghe / cu mine
Ion.NOM lives at Paris and with Gheorghe.ACC with me.ACC

3.1.7 Finite and non-finite clauses in subject position

3.1.7.1 Relative clauses

Any type of relative can occupy the subject position: indirect interrogative (42a), infinitival relative (42b, c), and headless (free) relative (42d, e); see also §10.3.1:

(42) a. Nu s-a spus [cine a câştigat]
not CL.REFL.PASS=have.3SG say.PPLE who have.3SG win.PPLE

b. Nu-i [ce   mânca]
   not=is what eat.INF
   'There is nothing to eat'
c. N-are   [ce   se   întâmpla]
   not=has what CL.REFL.3SG happen.INF
   'Nothing can happen'
d. Vine   [cine poate]
   comes   who   can.3SG
   'Whoever is able to may come'
e. E   important [cum se   muncește]
   is   important   how CL.REFL.ACC.IMPERS   work.3SG
   'The way one works is important'

3.1.7.2 Non-finite clauses

Any verbal structure headed by a non-finite form can occupy the subject position.

The infinitival structure occurs more frequently as an *A*-infinitival construction (with the proclitic marker A) (43a), and more rarely as a bare-infinitival construction (without the proclitic marker A) (43b). In contemporary standard Romanian, the latter structure is selected only by the impersonal modal verb *se poate*, in constructions with clitic climbing, where the impersonal clitic *se* of the main verb advances to a position in front of the modal verb:

(43) a. E   important   [a-ți   recunoaște   greșeala]$_S$
        is   important   A$_{INF}$=CL.REFL.DAT.2SG   admit.INF   mistake.DEF.ACC
        'It is important to admit your mistake'
     b. [Se   poate   [întârzia]$_S$]$_{Complex\ predicate}$ < Poate
        CL.REFL.IMPERS   can.3SG   be-late.INF   can
        a   se   întârzia
        A$_{INF}$ CL.REFL.IMPERS   be-late.INF
        'One can be late'

For the interpretation of the [*se poate* + infinitive] sequence as a complex predicate, see §3.5.

The gerund structure is selected by a small number of verbs of perception occurring in a reflexive-passive structure (§4.5.4.4):

(44) Se   vede   [apărând   curcubeul]$_S$
     CL.REFL.ACC.PASS   see.3SG   appear.GER   rainbow.DEF.NOM
     'One can see the rainbow appearing'

The supine structure is obligatorily marked by DE$_{SUP}$ and is selected by a small number of verbs: verbs with impersonal use (45a) and modalizing impersonal constructions (45b); for details, see §4.4.3.6:

(45) a. Rămâne /   Este   [de   făcut]$_S$
        remain.3SG   is   DE$_{SUP}$ do.SUP
        'It remains / It is to be done'

b. E   important /   greu /   necesar   [de   **recunoscut**   **adevărul**]s
   is   important   difficult   necessary   DE_SUP   admit.SUP   truth.DEF
   'It is important / difficult / necessary to admit the truth'

The participial structure rarely occurs in subject position and only in relation to impersonal verbs that select a passive participle (for the restructuring of this configuration, see §3.1.8.1):

(46) Trebuie /   Se cuvine   [(să──fie)   **făcut**   acest   **sacrificiu**]s
     must   ought to   SĂ_SUBJ be.SUBJ.3SG make.PPLE   this   sacrifice.NOM
     'This sacrifice must / ought to be made'

3.1.7.3   Clauses with a complementizer

Finite clauses in subject position can occur with any complementizer (*că*-indicative, *să*-subjunctive, *dacă* and their variants), and the selection conditions are the same as for any clause introduced by a complementizer (for details, see §§10.1.1.1–10.1.1.4). SĂ_SUBJ has an intermediate status between an inflectional marker and a complementizer (§2.2.1.1.2).

Some impersonal matrix verbs select only *să* (47a), while others select only *că* (47b):

(47) a. Se cade să..., Se cuvine să...,Merită să..., Trebuie să...,Îmi vine să...
        'It ought to...', 'It ought to...','It is worthy to...','It must...', 'I feel like...'
     b. Din demonstrație decurge / reiese că ...
        'From the demonstration it emerges that...'

Most impersonal epistemic modalizers select *că* (48a), while deontic modalizers select *să* (48b):

(48) a. E sigur că..., E probabil că...
        'It is sure that...', 'It is probable that...'
     b. E obligatoriu să..., E musai să..., E interzis să...
        'It is obligatory to...', 'It must...', 'It is forbidden to...'

Some impersonal matrix verbs allow both *că* and *să*; the structures have different modal interpretations (*realis* vs. *irrealis*):

(49) a. Mă   bucură   **că**   ai   câștigat   **bursa**
        CL.ACC.1SG   makes-happy   that   (you)have   won   scholarship.DEF
        'I am glad that you won the scholarship' [winning the scholarship is a fact]
     b. Mă   bucură   **să**   câștigi   **bursa**
        CL.ACC.1SG   makes-happy   SĂ_SUBJ   win.SUBJ.2SG scholarship.DEF
        'I am glad that you should win the scholarship' [winning the scholarship is possible]

H Old Romanian displays impersonal matrix verbs which select the complementizer *de* (*de*-indicative). *De* was later excluded from the inventory of complementizers of standard Romanian:

(50) Atunce la   mazâlie să   întâmplasă
     then   at   dismissal CL.REFL.ACC.3SG   happen.IND PLUPERF.3SG
     [de   vinisă   sol   din Țara Muntenească Toma] (Neculce)
     that   come.IND.PLUPERF.3SG   messenger from Wallachia   Toma.NOM
     'Then, when he was dethroned, it happened that Toma had come from Wallachia as
     a messenger'

The complementizer ***dacă*** 'if, whether' is selected when a yes / no or alternative interrogation is transposed into indirect speech:

(51) Se   verifică /   Se   urmărește   **dacă**
     CL.REFL.ACC.PASS   verify.3SG   CL.REFL.ACC.PASS   follow.3SG   if
     s-a   procedat   corect
     CL.REFL.ACC.IMPERS=has   acted   correctly
     'One checks / looks whether the procedure was correctly applied'

A different (hypothetical) kind of ***dacă*** is used in two types of structures: in relation to the impersonal copula *înseamnă* 'it means' (52a); as a topicalization and focalization marker, with the function of placing the previously introduced theme in preverbal position; the theme can be resumed by an anaphoric feminine demonstrative with neutral value *asta / aceasta* 'this' (52b):

(52) a. **Dacă** nu vine, înseamnă că nu-i place colaborarea
        'If he does not come, it means that he does not like the collaboration'
     b. **Dacă** n-a venit, (**asta**) a fost / s-a întâmplat pentru că nu i-a plăcut colaborarea
        'If he did not come, this was / happened because he did not like the collaboration'

3.1.8 Raised subjects (subject-to-subject raising)

3.1.8.1 Syntactically integrated subjects

The phenomenon by which the subject is dislocated from the embedded clause and raised to the matrix clause takes place to produce discourse effects (anticipating information, topicalization (53a–c)), or for syntactic reasons (the obligatory fronting of the *wh*-phrase, which includes the interrogative or relative head (53d, e)):

(53) a. [**Copilul**   **nostru**]ᵢ   trebuia   să   vină   tᵢ
        child.DEF.NOM   our   must.IMPERF   SĂ_SUBJ   come.SUBJ.3SG
        'Our child should have come'
     b. [**Copilul**]ᵢ   (mi)   se   părea   a fi tᵢ   răsfățat
        child.DEF.NOM CL.DAT.1SG CL.REFL.ACC.IMPERS seem.IMPERF.3SG A_INF be.INF spoiled
        'The child seemed to me to be spoiled'
     c. [**Ion**]ᵢ   (se)   poate   să   fi   ajuns   tᵢ acum   acasă
        Ion   CL.REFL.IMPERS   can.3SG   SĂ_SUBJ   be   arrive.PPLE now   home
        'Ion may have arrived home now'
     d. [**Ce**]ᵢ   trebuie   să   existe tᵢ   în   bibliotecă?
        what   must   SĂ_SUBJ   exist.SUBJ.3SG   in   library
        'What must exist in the library?'

e. [[**Cine**]ᵢ se dovedeşte a fi tᵢ nevinovat]
    who CL.REFL.ACC.PASS prove.3SG A_INF be.INF NEG-guilty
    nu face închisoare
    not makes prison
    'He who proves to be not guilty does not go to jail'

Subject raising leads to syntactic and inflectional effects on raising verbs, that is 'personalization', which manifests through agreement (54a–d); for the interpretation as a complex predicate, see §3.5.3:

(54) a. **Cărţile** trebuiau / meritau să
    book.F.PL.DEF.NOM have-to.IMPERF.3PL deserve.IMPERF.3PL SĂ_SUBJ
    fie citite
    be.SUBJ.3PL read.PPLE.F.3PL
    'The books had to be read / were worth being read'

   b. **Băieţii** (mi) se **păreau** răsfăţaţi
    boy.M.PL.DEF.NOM CL.DAT.1SG CL.REFL.ACC.IMPERS seem.IMPERF.3PL spoiled.M.PL
    'The boys seemed to me to be spoiled'

   c. **Probele** se dovedeau false
    evidence.F.PL.DEF.NOM CL.REFL.ACC prove.IMPERF.3PL false F.PL
    'The evidence proved to be false'

   d. **Cărţile** erau greu de obţinut
    book.PL.DEF.NOM be.IMPERF.3PL hard(ADV) DE_SUP obtain.SUP
    'The books were hard to obtain'

3.1.8.2 Isolated subjects—hanging topic

The raising and fronting of the subject, that is, its placement in a position which is syntactically and prosodically isolated (55a, b), has a topic discourse effect. It is frequent in the spoken language:

(55) a. **Tu**, # ştiu că tᵢ te-ai chinuit mult
    you.NOM know.1SG that CL.REFL.ACC.2SG=have.2SG suffered a lot
    'As for you, I know that you suffered a lot'

   b. **Ei**ᵢ, # ce bine că tᵢ nu sunt aici!
    they.NOM what good that not (they)are here
    'As for them, how good that they are not here!'

   c. **El**, # la vederea mamei, nu-i mai
    he.NOM at seeing mother.DEF.GEN not=CL.DAT.3SG more
    plăcea nimic [non-standard]
    like.IMPERF.3SG nothing.NOM
    'As for him, when he saw mother, he didn't like anything any more'

The raising and hanging position of the subject can associate with other phenomena which are typical for the spoken language, 'nominativus pendens' and anacoluthon (55c).

3.1.9 Subject word order

3.1.9.1 Word order in the main clause

The subject word order is generally free (S–V / V–S). However, non-marked sentences show word order *preferences* and *restrictions*, and even situations of *fixed word order*. The constraints are syntactic (type of clause and type of predicate).

3.1.9.1.1 The obligatorily preverbal subject is limited to *wh*-sentences, when the *wh*-phrase is part of the subject phrase:

(56) a. [**Ce**] s-a întâmplat?
  'What happened?'

  b. [**Ce carte**] a apărut?
  'Which book appeared?'

  c. [**Ce fel de carne**] îți place?
  'What kind of meat do you like?'

U Although it is less usual, it is possible for the *wh*-phrase to remain *in situ*, in the case of echo-questions (§13.1.2.5):
(57) S-a   întâmplat ce?
   CL.REFL.ACC.3SG=has happened what
   'What has happened?'

3.1.9.1.2 The preference for subject postposition occurs in the following structures:

- As the subject of invective or desiderative sentences; such sentences are sometimes fixed structures, displaying a subjunctive (58a) or optative verb form with a postverbal auxiliary (58b):

(58) a. Arză-l   **focul!**
   burn.SUBJ.3SG=CL.ACC.M.3SG fire.DEF.NOM
   'Damn him!'

  b. Mânca-v-ar   **câinii!**
   eat.INF=CL.ACC.2PL=AUX.COND.3PL dogs.DEF.NOM
   'Damn you!'

- As the non-agentive subject of impersonal and reflexive-passive constructions; the subject is an NP (59a), an embedded finite clause (59b), a non-finite infinitive or supine clause (59c), or a subjunctive clause (59d); postposition also occurs in a passive / reflexive-passive construction (59e):

(59) a. Îmi   trebuie   **liniște**
   CL.DAT.1SG need.3SG rest.NOM
   'I need quiet'

  b. Mă   miră   **că plângi**
   CL.ACC.1SG surprise.3SG that cry.2SG
   'It surprises me that you are crying'

c. E   greu   a   merge   pe   jos /   de   mers   pe   jos
   is   hard   A_INF walk.INF   on   foot   DE_SUP walk.SUP on   foot
   'It is hard to walk'

d. Îmi   vine   să   plâng
   CL.DAT.1SG   comes   SĂ_SUBJ   cry.SUBJ.1SG
   'I feel like crying'

e. Se   ştie /   Este   ştiut   că   a   furat
   CL.REFL.ACC.PASS   know.3SG   be.PRES.3SG   know.PPLE   that   has   stolen
   'It is known that he stole'

- As the non-personal non-agentive subject expressing a body-part; the subject NP enters a relationship of inalienable possession with a dative (60a) or accusative clitic personal pronoun (60b); see also Manoliu (2011: 506):

(60) a. Îmi   cade   părul
        CL.DAT.1SG   fall.3SG hair.DEF.NOM
        'My hair is falling out'

     b. Mă   doare   capul
        CL.ACC.1SG   hurt.3SG head.DEF.NOM
        'I have a headache'

- As the subject of existential verbs (61a); this pattern also includes fixed constructions with *fi* 'be' which express meteorological or temporal states (61b) and physical or psychological states (61c):

(61) a. Aici   e /   există   multă   suferinţă
        here   is   exists   much   sufferance.NOM
        'There is much suffering here'

     b. E   frig /   cald /   secetă /   noapte /
        is   cold.NOM   warm.NOM   drought.NOM   night.NOM
        iarnă /   noiembrie
        winter.NOM   November.NOM
        'It's cold / warm / drought / night time / winter / November'

     c. Îmi   este   frig /   cald /   somn /
        CL.DAT.1SG   is   chilliness.NOM   warm.NOM   sleep.NOM
        ruşine /   dor
        shame.NOM   longing.NOM
        'I am cold / warm / sleepy / ashamed / missing (someone)'

- As the subject of *wh*-questions when a component outside the subject phrase is interrogated (62a), as well as the subject of exclamative sentences which contain a copula (62b):

(62) a. Unde /   Cu   cine   s-a   dus   Ion?
        where /   with who.ACC   CL.REFL.ACC.3SG=has   gone   Ion.NOM
        'Where / With whom did Ion go?'

     b. Ce   frumoşi   sunt   copiii!
        what   beautiful   are   children.DEF.NOM
        'How beautiful the children are!'

- In literary style, the subject of parenthetical sentences with verbs of saying:

(63) 'Hai să ne grăbim!', spuse **primarul**
'Let's hurry! said the mayor'

H Subject postposition is frequent in old Romanian (64a); it is even obligatory when the auxiliary (in perfect and future forms) is postverbal; note that postverbal auxiliaries are frequent in old Romanian (64b):

(64) a. dători-s **vameşii** a plăti (*Documente*)
    indebted=(they)are border-guards.DEF.NOM A$_{INF}$ pay.INF
    'the border guards have to pay'
  b. Rădicatu-s-au **Petriceico-vodă** din Ţara Leşască (Neculce)
    left=CL.REFL.ACC.3SG=has Petriceico-prince from country.DEF Polish
    'Prince Petriceico left Poland'

3.1.9.1.3 Although no rigid rules exist, other word order preferences are at play, which depend on the nature of the predication, the number of arguments, the personal vs. non-personal character of the subject, determination vs. non-determination, and the rhematic nature of the subject. These preferences also occur in other Romance languages except for French, which has a fixed word order (Manoliu 2011: 505–7).

Agentive verbs (65a) occur more frequently with a preposed subject than non-agentive ones (65b,c):

(65) a. **Ion** se antrenează
    Ion.NOM CL.REFL.ACC train.PRES.IND.3SG
    'Ion is training'
  b. A venit **salvarea**
    has come ambulance.DEF.NOM
    'The ambulance arrived'
  c. S-a îmbolnăvit **directorul**
    CL.REFL.ACC.3SG=has become-sick.PPLE director.DEF.NOM
    'The director fell ill'

Verbs with one argument have a 'clearer tendency' towards the V–S word order (66a) (see Suzuki 2010: 40) than those with two or three arguments (66b). This difference probably arises from the fact that, with the exception of unergatives, which are not very numerous, the other verbs that take one argument are non-agentive.

(66) a. A: Ce s-a întâmplat?
      what CL.REFL.ACC.3SG=has happened
      'What has happened?'
    B: A murit **vecinul**, A venit **poştaşul**,
      has died neighbour.DEF.NOM has come postman.DEF.NOM
      'The neighbour has died' 'The postman has come'
      A căzut **tavanul**
      has fallen ceiling.DEF.NOM
      'The ceiling has fallen'

b. A: Ce   s-a   întâmplat? /
      what   CL.REFL.ACC.3SG=has   happened
   'What has happened?'
   B: **Mama**   nu   mi-a   adus   cartea /
      Mother.DEF   not   CL.DAT.1SG=has   brought   book.DEF /
      Ploaia   a   distrus   grădina
      rain.DEF   has destroyed   garden.DEF
   'Mother has not brought me the book'/ 'The rain has destroyed the garden'

The bare subject of all types of verbs, unaccusative (67a), as well as unergative (67b), appears postverbally more frequently than the definite subject (67c, d):

(67) a. Toamna   cad   **frunze**
        autumn.DEF fall   leaves.NOM
        'Leaves fall in the autumn'
     b. Pe   stradă   latră   **câini**,   strigă   **hamali**
        on   street   bark   dogs.NOM   yell   porters.NOM
        'Dogs bark, porters yell, in the street'
     c. **Frunzele**   căzute   acoperă   aleile
        leaves.DEF.NOM   fallen   cover   alleys.DEF
        'The fallen leaves cover the alleys'
     d. **Câinii**   latră,   **hamalii**   strigă
        dogs.DEF.NOM   bark   porters.DEF.NOM   yell
        'The dogs bark, the porters yell'

Rhematic subjects—not only the subject of unaccusative verbs, but also of agentive verbs—appear postverbally more frequently (Manoliu 2011: 505):

(68) A: Cine   ți-a   lucrat   rochia?
        who   CL.DAT.2SG=has worked dress.DEF
     B: Mi-a   lucrat-o   **mama**
        CL.DAT.1SG=has   worked=CL.ACC.F.3SG   mother.DEF.NOM
     'Who made your dress? My mother made it'

U   There are numerous counterexamples to any of these preferences. In a marked word order, the subject of any type of verb can be preverbal, in topic position (69a); when placed in contrastive focus, any subject, as well as any other constituent, can be preverbal (69b–d); see §13.4.3:
(69) a. A: S-a   purtat   urât   cu   tine
           CL.REFL.ACC.3SG=has   treated   badly   with   you
        B: Da,   și   ASTA   nu-mi   place
           yes   and   this.F.SG.NOM not=CL.DAT.1SG   likes
        'He treated you badly' 'Yes, and I don't like it'
     b. **Două,**   NU   TREI   SPARGERI   **s-au**   întâmplat
        two   not   three   break.PL.NOM   CL.REFL.ACC.3PL=have   happened
        'Two, not three break-ins took place'

    c. MÂNA   DREAPTĂ,   NU   CEA   STÂNGĂ   mă   doare
       hand.DEF   right   not   CEL.F.SG.NOM   left   CL.ACC.1SG   hurts
       'My right, not my left hand hurts'
    d. FRICĂ,   NU   RUȘINE   îmi   este!
       fear   not   shame.NOM   CL.DAT.1SG   is
       'I am afraid, not ashamed!'

3.1.9.2 Subject word order in subordinate clauses

3.1.9.2.1 Supplementary constraints manifest in the clauses introduced by complementizers, depending on the type of complementizer (Hill 2004: 349).

- *Că*-indicative admits the S–V and the V–S word order, as well as preverbal Focus (70a–c).
- *Ca(... să)*-subjunctive has the same characteristics as *că* (71a–c).
- *Să*-subjunctive does not allow the S–V word order; it allows only the V–S order, and there is no possibility of preverbal Focus (72a, b).
- *De*-indicative allows neither the S–V nor the V–S word order; it does not admit an overt subject in the unmarked word order (73a, b); when placed in contrastive focus, the subject can be realized postverbally (73c):

(70) a. Sper   că   **Ion**   va   ajunge
       (I)hope   that   Ion   AUX.FUT.3SG   arrive.INF
       'I hope that it is Ion who will arrive'

    b. Sper   că   va   ajunge   **Ion**
       (I)hope   that   AUX.FUT.3SG   arrive.INF   Ion
       'I hope that Ion will arrive'

    c. Sper   că   ION   va   ajunge,   nu   Gheorghe
       (I)hope   that   Ion   AUX.FUT.3SG   arrive   not   Gheorghe
       'I hope it is Ion who arrives, not Gheorghe'

(71) a. Sper ca **Ion** să ajungă
       'I hope that Ion arrrives'

    b. Sper   ca să   ajungă   **Ion**   [non-standard]
       (I)hope   in-order-to   arrive.SUBJ   Ion
       'I hope that Ion arrrives'

    c. Sper   ca   ION   să   ajungă,   nu   Gheorghe
       (I)hope   COMP   Ion   SĂ$_{SUBJ}$ arrive.SUBJ.3SG   not   Gheorghe
       'I hope that Ion, not Gheorghe arrives'

(72) a. *Sper   să   **Ion**   ajungă
       (I)hope   SĂ$_{SUBJ}$ Ion   arrive.SUBJ.3SG

    b. Sper   să   ajungă   **Ion**
       (I)hope   SĂ$_{SUBJ}$ arrive.SUBJ.3SG   ION

(73) a. *Ne-a   făcut de   **noi** am   plecat
        CL.ACC.1PL=has made   that we   have   left
    b. *Ne-a   făcut de   am   plecat **noi**
        CL.ACC.1PL=has made   that have   left   we
    c. Ne-a   făcut [de am   plecat NOI,   NU   CEILALȚI]
        CL.ACC.1PL=has made   that have   left   we   not the-others

3.1.9.2.2 In non-finite clauses, which are prototypically subordinate, when the subject is realized, it appears obligatorily postverbally, with an infinitive or a supine, but accepts both the pre- and postverbal position with a gerund or participle (for examples, see §3.1.2).

In control structures, Romanian may realize the lexical subject only once, in various positions, depending on pragmatic factors (Alboiu 2007; Dragomirescu 2011):

(74) a. (Ion)   se   apucă   (Ion)   a   cânta   (Ion)
        Ion.NOM   CL.REFL.ACC.3SG starts Ion.NOM A$_{INF}$ sing.INF Ion.NOM
    b. (Ion)   se   apucă   (Ion)   de   cântat   (Ion)
        Ion.NOM   CL.REFL.ACC.3SG starts Ion.NOM DE$_{SUP}$ sing.SUP Ion.NOM
        'Ion begins to sing'

3.1.9.2.3 In DP-internal relative clauses, if the subject is not part of the *wh*-phrase, subject–verb inversion is possible (but not obligatory) for any type of verb irrespective of the occurrence of the direct object:

(75) elevul   căruia   **(Ion)**   îi   va   trimite   **(Ion)**
     pupil.DEF   who.DAT   Ion.NOM   CL.DAT.3SG   AUX.FUT.3SG send.INF Ion.NOM
     cartea   **(Ion)**
     book.DEF.ACC Ion.NOM
     'the pupil to whom Ion will send the book'

C   Configuration (75) is different from French, where subject–verb inversion is blocked by a transitive verb with a lexical direct object (see Bonami and Godard 2001: 117).

3.1.9.3 Romanian, a V–S language?

Generally, Romance linguists include Romanian in the S–V–O structural type, together with the other Romance languages; this differs from the Latin S–O–V type (for the change in structural type S–O–V > S–V–O, see Coșeriu 1992–1993: 139–40; Posner 1996: 36, Renzi and Andreose 2003: 220; Ledgeway 2011: 406).

In generative studies (Dobrovie-Sorin 1994: 45, 87, 106; Cornilescu 2000; Alboiu 2002), but also in non-generative research (Renzi 1991), Romanian is considered to belong to the V–S structural type, which sets it apart from other Romance languages.

C   Inside the V–O Romance type, Renzi (1991) distinguishes two subtypes: the VSO type, to which Romanian and (archaic) Sardinian belong, and the S–V–O type, to which French, Italian, etc. belong.

The following arguments have been adduced in favour of the V–S hypothesis:

- Romanian diversified its complementizers; it created *ca... să*, the split variant of *să*, which is specialized for focalization in the subordinate clause, including subject focalization, which is a sign that syntactic word order of the subject and of the object is postverbal.

- Only V–S languages have particles like A (in the structure of the infinitive) and SĂ (in the structure of the subjunctive), which have an ambiguous status between Comp and Inflection; the ambiguity arises from the fact that Comp and Inflection are adjacent (Dobrovie-Sorin 1994: 87, 106).
- An indirect, deductive argument is based on two of Greenberg's quasi-universal implications, i.e.: (i) languages with a dominant V–S–O word order prefer placing the adjective postnominally (N–Adj); (ii) languages with a dominant V–S–O word order place the auxiliary in front of the main verb (Aux–V) (Greenberg 1963: 85).

In his analysis of these two features of Romanian, Renzi (1991) argues that the canonical word order of the qualifying adjective is in postposition; the postposition of the adjective is 'much more constant than in other Romance languages'. Moreover, he discusses the possessive adjectives (*caietul* **meu** 'my notebook'), a class of demonstrative adjectives which is postnominal (*caietul* **acesta** / **acela** 'this / that notebook') and other items which are in free variation, occurring in pre- and in postposition (*mulți oameni–oameni* **mulți** 'many people'). As far as auxiliaries are concerned, Renzi discusses the Romanian future and conditional forms, which differ from the quasi-general Romance forms with postverbal auxiliaries. If we take into consideration features (i) and (ii), Romanian is closer to the VSO type.

Theoretically, one can assert that the deep structure subject is generated in postposition and the preverbal subject is a derived structure. However, if one takes into consideration the 'surface' realizations of the subject, Romanian is not essentially different from other null subject Romance languages, except for the fact that it allows for a greater freedom in the placement of the subject, especially in the main clause.

3.2 OBJECTS

3.2.1 The direct object

3.2.1.1 Characteristics

(i) The direct object is selected by a transitive verb, which can have both a finite (76a) and a non-finite form: infinitive (76b), gerund (76c), supine (76d); the participle does not admit a direct object:

(76) a. El citește o **carte**
'He reads a book'

b. dorința [de [a citi o **carte**]]
wish.DEF DE A$_{INF}$ read.INF a book.ACC
'the wish to read a book'

c. Îl văd [citind o **carte**]
CL.ACC.M.3SG see.1SG read.GER a book.ACC
'I see him reading a book'

d. El se satură [de [citit **cartea**]]
he CL.REFL.ACC gets-tired DE$_{SUP}$ read.SUP book.DEF.ACC
'He is fed up with reading the book'

(ii) Depending on the type of the head verb, the direct object is obligatorily realized (77a) or can be omitted (Gheorghe 2009); in the latter case, either the object is retrieved from the context (77b), or the event has generic reading (77c).

(77) a. *El   consideră Ø, *El   trimite   cuiva Ø
        he   considers   he   sends   someone.DAT
     b. A   terminat   școala? /   A   terminat Ø
        has   finished   school.DEF has   finished
        'Has (s)he finished school?' '(S)he has'
     c. MănâncăØ,   Învață Ø
        eats   studies
        '(S)he is eating' '(S)he is studying'

C   Like Latin (Ernout and Thomas 1959: 212) and other Romance languages, Romanian allows null direct objects (Cole 1987); for the omission of the accusative clitic, see also §3.2.1.5.2.

(iii) The direct object can be either marked or unmarked. It is marked when a pronominal clitic occupies the direct object position, since it has a distinct accusative case marker (78a), and when it occurs with a specific prepositional form, PE (78b). It is unmarked if the nominal phrase is directly connected to the verb, as the form of the head noun is identical to the nominative (78c):

(78) a. El   *mă /*   se   laudă
        he   CL.ACC.1SG   CL.REFL.ACC.3SG   praises
        'He praises me / himself'
     b. Îl   laudă   *pe elev*
        CL.ACC.3SG   praises   PE pupil.ACC
        'He praises the pupil'
     c. Citește   *cărți*
        '(S)he reads books'

C   Romanian has shown a clear tendency towards marking the object, but not the subject (§3.2.1.3; see also Ledgeway 2011: 436). Direct object–subject differentiation, with marking just of the object, can be seen in structure (79):
    (79) Se   mănâncă   **om**   **pe**   **om**
         CL.REFL.ACC.3SG≡PL   eats.3SG≡PL   man.NOM   PE   man.ACC
         'Men hurt one another'

(iv) The direct object accepts doubling by an accusative clitic form, in certain conditions (§3.2.1.5).

(v) The agreement of the participle with the direct object does not occur for verbal forms containing an auxiliary:

(80) cărțile   pe   care   le-am   **cumpărat**
     books.DEF   PE   which   CL.ACC.F.3PL=have.1SG   buy.PPLE
     'the books that I bought'

C   Romanian is one of those Romances languages with an invariable participle in analytic tense forms. This sets it apart from those which display participle agreement with the direct object (Salvi 2011: 341; see also §4.3.2.1):

(81) a. Fr. Ce sont les assiettes que j'ai achetées hier
'These are the plates that I bought yesterday'
b. It. Quanto l'hai aspettata?
'How long did you wait for her?'

(vi) The nominal phrase in direct object position receives one of the following thematic roles: Patient (82a), Theme (82b), Experiencer (82c), Recipient (82d), Path (82e):

(82) a. Loveşte **copilul**
'(S)he is hitting the child'
b. Citeşte **o carte**
'(S)he is reading a book'
c. **Mă** doare capul
'I have a headache'
d. Ei **mă** învaţă ceva
'They teach me something'
e. Trece **strada**
'(S)he crosses the street'

C Configurations (82c, d) are characteristic of Romanian, i.e. encoding the Experiencer (§2.3.3.2) or (in double object structures) the Recipient (§2.3.1.1) as a direct object.

3.2.1.2 Pronominal clitics in the direct object position vs. bare nominal phrases

3.2.1.2.1 In Romanian, the direct object can be realized as a personal (83a) or reflexive pronominal clitic in cases of co-reference with the subject (83b), or when the reflexive has reciprocal value (83c):

(83) a. Am   văzut-**o**
(I)have   seen=CL.ACC.F.3SG
'I saw her'
b. Ion$_i$ **se**$_i$ laudă
Ion   CL.REFL.ACC.3SG   praises
'Ion praises himself'
c. Ei$_{i+j}$ **se**$_{i+j}$ iubesc
they   CL.REFL.ACC.3PL   love
'They love each other'

C Romanian, like all Romance languages, transfers information regarding the object onto the verb by the mediation of the clitic. In constructions with an unmarked direct object (non-prepositional constructions), clitic doubling (84) is the only way in which the object can be distinguished from the subject. Typologically, the phenomenon of cliticization brings Romanian closer to languages with *head-marking constructions* (Ledgeway 2011: 434–5):

(84) [**Noutatea**$_i$ **o**$_i$]$_{DO}$ constituie   [interpretarea]$_S$
novelty.DEF.ACC   CL.ACC.F.3SG   constitutes   interpretation.DEF.NOM
'The interpretation represents the novelty'

3.2.1.2.2 As the 3rd person pronominal clitic is equivalent to a DP, cliticization is blocked when the direct object position is occupied by a bare noun.

Cases of bare nouns as direct objects are less frequent in the singular than in the plural. In the singular, the absence of the article, as well as of other determiners, depends on: the type of noun, mass or abstract (85a, b); its semantic interpretation (*property* or *kind* reading (85c)); the quasi-frozen nature of the phrase, either of the [verb + noun] phrase (85d, e), or of the nominal phrase, which, as a whole, functions as an emphatic negator (85f):

(85) a. Mănânc **carne**
'I eat meat'
b. Doresc **linişte**
'I want silence'
c. Caut **profesor**
(I)search teacher
'I'm looking for a teacher'
d. Am **obicei** să...,
(I)have habit SĂ$_{SUBJ}$
'I have the habit of...'
e. Fac **treabă**
(I)make labour
'I work'
f. N-am văzut **picior** / **ţipenie** de om
not=(I)have seen foot living-creature of man
'I have seen absolutely nobody'

3.2.1.3 Prepositional marking. The PE-construction

3.2.1.3.1 In Romanian, one must distinguish between PE, direct object marker, and lexical *pe* meaning 'on'. In relation to its lexical counterparts (with spatial and temporal value (86a–b)), PE in the direct object structure shares, on the one hand, certain features with lexical *pe* and, on the other hand, it has certain specific features.

(86) a. S-au întâlnit pe stradă
CL.REFL.ACC.3PL=(they)have met on street
'They met in the street'
b. Pleacă **pe** 1 **martie**
leaves on 1 March
'He leaves on the 1st of March'

Shared features with lexical *pe* 'on':

- Both instances of *pe* select the accusative case (87a).
- Like other Romanian prepositions, it blocks the definite article from occurring with otherwise unmodified nouns (87b), but the noun phrase has a definite and specific reading (87c).
- It allows for a relative clause to be its complement (87d):

(87) a. Te-am   rugat   [PE [**tine**]]
       CL.ACC.2SG=(I)have asked   PE   you.ACC
       'I asked you'
   b. Îl   întâlnesc PE *profesorul
       CL.ACC.M.3SG   (I)meet   PE teacher.DEF.ACC
   c. Îl   întâlnesc PE **profesor**
       CL.ACC.M.3SG   (I)meet   PE teacher.ACC
       'I meet the teacher'
   d. Alege   [pe   [cine munceşte bine]]
       chooses PE   who   works   well
       'He chooses those who work well'

Specific features of functional PE:

- It does not assign thematic roles (the thematic role is assigned by the head verb, varying from one verb to another):

(88) a. L-am întâlnit [PE Ion]$_{THEME}$
       'I have met Ion'
   b. L-am bătut [PE Ion]$_{PATIENT}$
       'I have beaten Ion'
   c. Îl doare capul [PE Ion]$_{EXPERIENCER}$
       'Ion has a headache'

- The phrase [PE + NP] can be replaced by an accusative clitic and participates in clitic doubling:

(89) **L$_i$-am**   întâlnit [PE **profesor$_i$**]
       CL.ACC.M.3SG=(I)have met   PE   teacher.ACC

- In passive constructions, the entire [PE + NP] phrase participates in externalization:

(90) Ion îl   salută [PE **profesor**] > [**Profesorul**]   este salutat de Ion
      Ion CL.ACC.M.3SG greets PE   teacher.ACC   teacher.DEF.NOM is   greeted by Ion
      'Ion greets the teacher' 'The teacher is greeted by Ion'

PE has undergone a grammaticalization process, acquiring the features of a functional preposition (§9.2.2). Because PE is necessarily related to the direct object position, leaving aside other selection conditions, PE is a direct object marker.

3.2.1.3.2 The selection of PE is conditioned by the following: **(i)** the NP occupies the DO position; **(ii)** the NP has the feature [+specific] (91a); **(iii)** the head of the NP has the feature [+personal / +animate] (91b).

(91) a. Îl   caută   **pe Ion /**   **pe fratele**   **tău**   vs. Caută
       CL.ACC.M.3SG   searches PE Ion.ACC / PE brother.DEF.ACC   your   searches
       menajeră
       housekeeper
       'He is looking for Ion / your brother' vs. 'He is looking for a housekeeper'

b. Îl   caută   pe   profesor /   **pe**   **Grivei**,   câinele   lui
   CL.ACC.M.3SG searches PE   teacher.ACC / PE   Grivei.ACC dog.DEF his(GEN)
   vs. Caută   o   **carte**
       searches a   book
   'He is looking for the teacher / for Grivei, his dog' vs. 'He is searching for a book'

Besides these conditions (one syntactic, one semantic, and one lexical), it is argued that there is a fourth, epistemic salience (Manoliu-Manea 1993: 202–3; Manoliu and Price 2007: 325–6), which can justify the preferential hierarchy in PE selection, that is: proper name > kinship term > noun denoting a specific person > personal and demonstrative pronoun > personal quantifiers > universal quantifiers > non-specific personal noun > non-personal nouns.

C   Catalan, Spanish, Portuguese, Sardinian, some Franco-Provençal and Italian varieties, as well as Romanian have gone through the same type of innovation, marking the direct object prepositionally, when it is [+specific] and [+human]; only the preposition differs (in Romanian PE is selected (< Lat. PER), while in Ptg., Sp., Sardinian, and southern Italian varieties A is selected (< Lat. AD); see Niculescu (1965: 78), Mardale (2009: 135), Ledgeway (2011: 470–1).

Romanian and Spanish share the features [+specific], [+human], but they also display certain contrasts: in the case of a pronominal direct object with inanimate referent, Romanian employs the prepositional construction more frequently; in the Romanian passive-reflexive structure, a human denoting NP functions as a subject, as verbal agreement takes place, and the insertion of PE is not allowed (92), while in the Spanish construction, the human direct object does not become the grammatical subject, and receives the marker A.

(92) S-a   recunoscut **hoțul** /   *pe **hoț**   după   amprente
     CL.REFL.PASS=has   identified thief.DEF.NOM PE thief.ACC   after   fingerprints
     'The thief was identified by his fingerprints'

From a typological point of view, the creation of a specific DO marker places Romanian among the languages with a strongly marked direct object. The fact that the prepositional construction is related to other features ('high' placement on the animate and on the specificity scale), places Romanian, together with Spanish (Romance languages) and Turkish and Russian in the category of languages that display 'Differential Object Marking' (Tigău 2011: 31–2 and bibliography therein).

Apart from the regular uses, PE also has accidental uses (situations **A–C**), in which at least one of the aforementioned conditions is not observed (Pană Dindelegan 2003: 180):

A. +DO [−animate], [+specific]—Situation (**A**) appears in configurations of the type (93): the direct object position is occupied by an a quotational phrase referring to a non-animate entity (93) or by a pronoun with a non-human referent (94a–c):

(93) L-am   șters   **pe** **'și'**
     CL.ACC.M.3SG=(I)have erased   PE   and
     'I erased "and"'

(94) a. casa   **pe**   **care**   am   cumpărat-o
        house.DEF PE   which.ACC   (I)have   bought=CL.ACC.F.3SG
        'the house that I bought'

    b. **Pe care** dintre case ai vândut-o?
       PE which.ACC of houses (you)have sold=CL.ACC.F.3SG
       'Which of the houses have you sold?'

    c. Le-am reparat **pe toate**
       CL.ACC.F.3PL=(I)have repaired PE all.ACC.F.PL
       'I repaired them all'

B. +DO [−animate], [−specific]—Situation (**B**) occurs in proverbs, where the direct object position is occupied by non-animate nouns with generic reading:

(95) Cui **pe cui** (se) scoate
     nail PE nail.ACC CL.REFL.ACC.3SG pulls-out
     'One nail drives out another'

C. +comparative construction [−animate], [+indefinite]—Situation (**C**) characterizes comparative constructions, where PE occurs irrespective of the [+personal/−animate] feature (96a,b) of the direct object in the reduced comparative clause; for the elliptical nature of comparative structures, see §10.5.

(96) a. O iubește ca **pe tine**
      CL.ACC.F.3SG loves as PE you.ACC
      '(S)he loves her as she loves you'

    b. O iubește ca **pe o floare rară**
      CL.ACC.F.3SG loves as PE a flower rare
      '(S)he loves her like (s)he loves a rare flower'

3.2.1.3.3 In present-day standard Romanian, the syntactic rules distinguish between contexts in which PE is obligatory, optional, and excluded.

In phrases headed by a noun, PE is obligatory for proper names denoting a person or an animal (97a), for relational nouns denoting unique referents (97b–c), for definite determined personal nouns (97d), and for personal articleless nouns, but with specific reading (97e):

(97) a. Îl strig **pe Ion** / **pe Grivei**, cățelul
      CL.ACC.M.3SG (I)call PE Ion.ACC PE Grivei.ACC dog.DEF.NOM
      'I am calling Ion / Grivei the dog'

    b. L-am rugat **pe tata**
      CL.ACC.M.3SG=(I)have asked PE father.DEF.ACC
      'I have asked father'

    c. Am invitat-o **pe maică-sa**
      (I)have invited=CL.ACC.F.3SG PE mother-his≡her.ACC
      'I invited his mother'

    d. L-am rugat **pe profesorul** X
      CL.ACC.M.3SG=(I)have asked PE teacher.DEF.ACC X
      'I have asked teacher X'

    e. L-am rugat **pe profesor**
      CL.ACC.M.3SG=(I)have asked PE teacher.ACC
      'I asked the teacher'

In pronominal constructions, PE is obligatory if the direct object is realized as: a personal and reflexive pronoun, with the strong form (98a,b); politeness pronoun (98c); reciprocal pronoun (98d); pronominal phrases with a demonstrative (98e), except for the feminine pro-sentence demonstrative (see example (103b) below), phrases headed by pronominal CEL (98f) or AL (98g), for any type of referent, personal or non-animate; the interrogative pronouns *cine* 'who', *care* 'which' (98h,i), as well as relative pronouns (98j), and the indefinites based on these forms: *cineva* 'someone', *careva* 'anyone' (98k), *oricine* 'anyone', *oricare* 'any of them' (98l).

(98) a. Te   ajut   **pe tine**
       CL.ACC.2SG (I)help   PE you.ACC
       'I help you'

   b. Se   apără   **pe sine**
      CL.REFL.ACC.3SG   defends   PE self.ACC
      'He defends himself'

   c. Vă   ajută   **pe dumneavoastră**
      CL.ACC.2PL helps   PE you.POL
      'He helps you'

   d. Se   pârăsc   unul   **pe altul** / unul   **pe celălalt**
      CL.REFL.ACC.3PL   tell-on.3PL one   PE other   one   PE another
      'They tell on one another'

   e. Le   repar   **pe acelea** /   **pe celelalte**
      CL.ACC.F.3PL (I)repair   PE those.F.PL   PE the-others.F.PL
      'I repair those / the others'

   f. Le   repar   **pe cele   albastre** / **pe cele   două**
      CL.ACC.F.3PL (I)repair PE CEL.F.PL   blue.F.PL   PE CEL.F.PL   two.F.PL
      'I repair the blue ones / the two'

   g. Le-am   reparat   numai   **pe ale   noastre**
      CL.ACC.F.3PL=(I)have   repaired   only   PE AL.F.PL   our.F.PL
      'I have only repaired our things'

   h. **Pe cine**   ai   întâlnit?
      PE who.ACC   (you)have   met
      'Whom did you meet?'

   i. **Pe care**   l-ai   reparat?
      PE which.ACC   CL.ACC.M.3SG=(you)have   repaired
      'Which one did you repair?'

   j. scaunul   **pe care**   l-ai   cumpărat
      chair.DEF PE which.ACC   CL.ACC.M.3SG=(you)have   bought
      'the chair that you bought'

   k. Aleg   **pe cineva**   cunoscut / **pe careva**   dintre   voi
      (I)choose PE someone.ACC   known /   PE any.ACC   of   you.ACC
      'I choose someone I know / any of you'

   l. Nu greşeşti,   **pe oricine** /   **pe oricare**   ai   alege
      not (you)mistake PE anybody.ACC /   PE anybody.ACC   AUX.COND.2SG   choose.INF
      'You are not mistaken, no matter who you would choose'

U The pronouns *cine* 'who', *oricine* 'anyone' are specialized for human referents, while *care* 'which', *oricare* 'anybody' receive the marker PE, for any type of referent ([+/−human]).

The rule illustrated in (98j) regarding the obligatory use of PE for the relative *care* 'which' is frequently not observed in the non-standard register:

(99) scaunul **care** l-am reparat [non-standard]
chair.DEF which.ACC CL.ACC.M.3SG=(I)have repaired
'the chair that I repaired'

H In old Romanian, the rules regarding the usage of PE were less stable than today.

PE is optional in the following situations:

- for a noun phrase denoting a person, when it associates with indefinite determiners or quantifiers (100a–d), with negative quantifiers (100e), with the interrogative quantifier *câți / câte* 'how many' (100f), and with floating quantifiers (100g):

(100) a. Trimit (pe) câțiva colegi
(I)send PE a few colleagues.ACC
'I am sending a few colleagues'

b. Ajut (pe) trei colegi
(I)help PE three colleagues.ACC
'I am choosing three colleagues'

c. Ajut (pe) un elev
(I)help PE a student.ACC
'I am helping a pupil'

d. Examinez (pe) fiecare copil
(I)examine PE each child.ACC
'I examine each child'

e. N-a găsit (pe) niciun copil
not=has found PE no child.ACC
'He found no child'

f. (Pe) câți dintre ei ai ajutat?
PE how-many.ACC of them (you)have helped
'How many of them have you helped?'

g. Ajută (pe) amândoi / (pe) toți copiii
helps PE both PE all children.DEF.ACC
'He is helping both children / all the children'

The fact that it is 'optional' does not mean that the presence / absence of PE does not have semantic effects; the selection of PE adds specificity information. In the absence of a determiner, PE is the unique specificity marker (101a), while in phrases in which a determiner is present, or two determiners co-occur, it is a supplementary specificity marker (101b):

(101) a. Îl întâlnesc **pe student**
CL.ACC.M.3SG (I)meet PE student.ACC

b. Îl întâlnesc **pe** studentul **cel** nou
CL.ACC.M.3SG (I)meet PE student.DEF.ACC CEL new

U   In structures with optional PE (100a–g), the selection of PE is often associated with clitic doubling (102a,b):

(102) a. Aştept   al   doilea   copil
         (I)expect   the   second   child.ACC
         'I am expecting my second child'
      vs. Îl   aştept   **pe**   al   doilea   copil
         CL.ACC.M.3SG   (I)expect   PE   the   second   child.ACC
         'I am waiting for the second child'
    b. Invit   toţi   copiii
       (I)invite   all   children.DEF.ACC
      vs. Îi   invit   **pe**   toţi   copiii
         CL.ACC.M.3PL   (I)invite   PE   all   children.DEF.ACC
         'I am inviting all the children'

PE is not allowed:

- with an adverbal (bound to the verb) possessive dative clitic (103a);
- with a feminine demonstrative pronoun with neutral value, even in preverbal position (103b);
- with a non-animate noun, with the exception of an quotational noun (103c) (see example (93a) above);
- with a non-specific personal noun with a property or kind reading (103d,e) or a definite personal noun with a generic reading (103f);
- with an indefinite or negative pronoun specialized for non-animate referents: *nimic* 'nothing', *ce* 'what', *ceva* 'what', *orice* 'anything', *ceea ce* 'what' (103g,h).

(103) a. Şi-a   măritat   **fata**
         CL.REFL.DAT.3SG=has   married   daughter.DEF.ACC
         'He married off his daughter'
      vs. *Şi-a   măritat   **pe** fata   sa
         CL.REFL.DAT.3SG=has   married   PE   daughter.DEF.ACC his

    b. **Asta**   o   ştiu   de   mult
       this.ACC   CL.ACC.F.3SG   (I)know   of   long
       'I have known this for a long time'

    c. Repară   **maşina**
       repairs   car.DEF.ACC
       'He repairs the car'

    d. Angajez   **grădinar**
       (I)hire   gardener
       'I am hiring a gardener'

    e. Cumpăr   **casă**
       (I)buy   house
       'I buy a house'

    f. Adoră   **femeia /**   **femeile**
       (he) adores woman.DEF   women.DEF

    g. Nu   înţelege   **nimic**
       'He understands nothing'

    h. Cumpără   **ceva**   **ieftin**
       'He is buying something cheap'

H In a language like Romanian, which has a relatively free word order and displays Acc≡Nom syncretism, the PE construction serves to distinguish between the direct object and the subject ([*Cui*] [*pe cui*] *(se) scoate* 'One nail drives out another') and between the direct object and the obligatory predicative complement (*Aleg* [*pe boier*] [*domn*] 'They elect the boyar as ruler'). The occurrence of the marker PE has been explained as a result of the grammaticalization of the lexical preposition *pe* 'on' (§3.2.1.3.1).

The point of departure was the archaic value of direction of the preposition *pe* (Onu 1959: 187–209); grammaticalization was favoured by the existence of verbs that entered parallel configurations, with a directional adjunct and with a direct object, both realized as personal nouns. Such verbs were *arăta* 'show', *chema* 'call', *striga* 'call', *privi* 'watch':

(104) poate   striga   neștine   **pre** **tălhariu**   (Coresi)
       (he)can call   anybody.NOM   PE   thief.ACC
       'Anybody can call the thief'

Most researchers agree upon a date of emergence later than the separation of the dialects (PE does not occur in any of the South-Danubian varieties), but prior to the 16th century, when the construction is attested in Daco-Romanian. The quasi-general absence of PE in translated religious texts of the 16th century, on the one hand, and its occurrence in original texts, on the other, has been explained through the fact that the structure appeared little before this date. This construction had not yet fully established itself; therefore PE could be suppressed in translated texts, as an effect of the absence of the PE-construction in the original text (Dimitrescu 1973).

3.2.1.4 *Partitive prepositional constructions*

In the absence of the head of the phrase (denoting the 'part'), Romanian allows a partitive prepositional construction in direct object position; a prepositional phrase headed by the partitive prepositions *din, dintre* 'of' is selected:

(105) a. A   băut   [Ø [**din** **vin**]]
         has   drunk   of   wine.ACC
         'he drank some of the wine'

      b. A   pierdut   [Ø [**dintre**   **cărți**]]
         has   lost   of   books.ACC
         'He lost some of the books'

      c. Am   pierdut și   **de-ale**   **prietenilor** /   **de-ale**   **mele**
         (I)have   lost   also   of=AL.F.PL   friend.DEF.GEN.PL   of=AL.F.PL   my.F.PL
         'I also lost some that belong to my friends / some that are mine'

Note that the construction (105c) preserves the archaic partitive preposition *de* (+plural genitive / +plural possessive).

C In Romanian, as in Spanish and Portuguese, but unlike French and Italian (Reinheimer Rîpeanu 1993: 138), there is no partitive article. Accordingly, partitive cliticization of the type Fr. *J'en ai mangé plusieurs / quelques-uns* 'I ate more / some of these' is absent.

U In the absence of the partitive article, a mass noun in direct object position occurs without a determiner (106a); it can also be associated with a partitive quantifier *niște, niscaiva, ceva* 'some'. The canonical partitive construction, in which the part and the whole are both specified (106b), is preferred for countable nouns:

(106) a. Cumpăr   **carne** /   **niște**   **carne**
      (I)buy   meat.ACC / some   meat

    b. Cumpăr   **o**   **parte**   **din**   **cărți**
      (I)buy   a   part.ACC of   books
      'I buy part of the books'

3.2.1.5 Clitic doubling

By doubling (anticipation (107a) and resumption (107b) through a pronominal clitic), the direct object is included in co-referentiality chains which contain two elements selected by the same transitive verb:

(107) a. **Îl**$_i$ văd   **pe**   **Ion**$_i$
      CL.ACC.M.3SG (I)see PE Ion.ACC
      'I see Ion'

    b. **Scrisoarea**$_i$ am   trimis-**o**$_i$
      letter.DEF.ACC (I)have sent=CL.ACC.F.3SG
      'I sent the letter'

Doubling by a pronominal clitic occurs for: an NP headed by a noun (107a,b), an NP headed by different pronouns (108a), including strong personal or reflexive pronouns (108b,c), or an NP headed by a numeral substitute (108d), a relative clause (108e), or a clause introduced by a complementizer (108f).

(108) a. [**Pe** **acesta**$_i$] / [**Pe** **fiecare**$_i$]   **l**$_i$**-am**   ajutat
      PE   this.ACC   PE   each.ACC   CL.ACC.M.3SG=(I)have helped
      'I helped this one / each one'

    b. [**Pe** **mine**$_i$]   **m**$_i$**-au**   ajutat   toți
      PE   me.ACC   CL.ACC.1SG=(they)have helped all
      'Everyone helped me'

    c. **Se**$_i$ cunoaște [**pe** **sine**$_i$]
      CL.REFL.ACC.3SG knows   PE   self.ACC
      'He knows himself'

    d. [**Pe** **trei**$_i$ dintre ei]   **i**$_i$**-am**   ajutat
      PE three.ACC of   them(ACC) CL.ACC.3PL=(I)have helped
      'I helped three of them'

    e. **L**$_i$**-a**   ales   [**pe care**   l-a   dorit]$_i$
      CL.ACC.M.3SG=(he)has chosen PE which.ACC CL.ACC.M.3SG=(he)has wanted
      'He chose the one he wanted'

    f. [**Că** **este** **impertinent**]$_i$, **o**$_i$ știu   de   mult
      that is   impertinent   CL.ACC.F.3SG (I)know for   long
      'I have known for a long time that he is impertinent'

C Doubling places Romanian among the languages that have strong direct object marking: marking is obtained by simultaneously attaching the prepositional marker to the object, and the clitic to the verb (Pană Dindelegan 2003: 226).

3.2.1.5.1 There are important similarities between doubling and the PE-construction, but there are differences too.

Doubling, as opposed to the PE-structure, also occurs when the NP has a [–animate] head (109a), but, like the PE-structure, it is disallowed when the NP has a [–specific] reading (109b–c):

(109) a. **Bibliografia** a citit-**o** de mult
bibliography.DEF.ACC has read=CL.ACC.F.3SG for long
'(S)he read the bibliography long time ago'

b. ***Romane** **le** citeşte zilnic
novels.ACC CL.ACC.F.3PL reads daily

c. ***Grădinar** îl caută
gardener CL.ACC.M.3SG searches

The feature [+specific] links the two phenomena, which allowed for them both to be called 'syntactic specificity means', created inside Romanian.

The preverbal vs. postverbal position of the object is a factor which influences doubling.

Doubling is obligatory for preverbal definite non-animate nouns (110a), but disallowed for postverbal definite non-animate nouns (110b).

(110) a. **Bibliografia** a citit-**o** de mult

b. *A citit-o **bibliografia**
has read=CL.ACC.F.3SG bibliography.DEF.ACC

U In postposition, doubling of a non-animate noun phrase is accepted only if the NP is right dislocated:

(111) A citit-o #, **bibliografia**

Doubling is optional for preverbal indefinite non-animate nouns (112a), but disallowed for the same type of nominal phrase in postposition (112b).

(112) a. **Un exerciţiu util** (**îl**) reprezintă dictarea
an exercise.ACC useful CL.ACC.M.3SG represents dictation.DEF.NOM
'Dictation represents a useful exercise'

b. *Dictarea îl reprezintă **un exerciţiu util**
dictation.DEF.NOM CL.ACC.M.3SG represents an exercise.ACC useful

Drawing a parallel between the rules of obligatory doubling and of the obligatory occurrence of PE, one can notice that the majority coincide. The exception is represented by structures with the interrogative pronoun *cine* 'who' and with the indefinite *cineva* 'someone', which select the PE construction, but do not admit doubling:

(113) a. **Pe cine** (*l)-ai întâlnit?
PE who.ACC CL.ACC.M.3SG=(you)have met

b. (*L)-am ales **pe cineva** cunoscut
CL.ACC.M.3SG=(I)have chosen PE someone.ACC known

C   The co-occurrence of a strong and a clitic pronominal object is also encountered in other Romance languages. Although present in other languages as well, this phenomenon 'is by far more widespread' in Romanian (Sandfeld 1930: 192), a fact considered to be the consequence of the common Balkan base. Clitic doubling is also present in Aromanian, where, in the absence of the PE structure, it represents the only way to distinguish the direct object from the subject (Caragiu Marioțeanu 1975: 241).

Doubling of the direct object headed by a noun phrase through a pronominal clitic is a phenomenon that is also present in other Romance languages, but it is either restricted to dialects (as in some Italian varieties and non-standard Spanish; Reinheimer Rîpeanu 1993: 84; Reinheimer and Tasmowski 2005: 190), or it is a discourse strategy phenomenon. Romanian is the only Romance language that has transformed a discourse strategy tool into a mechanism with syntactic importance.

As a syntactic feature (having a high frequency, obligatory rules), doubling occurs in all Balkan languages (Mišeska Tomić 2004: 47 considers this phenomenon as distinctive of the common Balkan base; it is present in all of the nine Balkan languages that she analyses).

H   Doubling rules have become fixed over time; its use was variable in old Romanian. Some rules, nowadays obligatory in standard Romanian, were optional until quite late. The rule of the doubling of a postverbal PE-nominal phrase has become obligatory in recent decades; the present-day use still shows some fluctuation:

(114)   (Îl)   cunosc   **pe Ion /**   **pe elev**
        CL.ACC.M.3SG   (I)know   PE Ion.ACC   PE student.ACC
        'I know Ion / the pupil'

3.2.1.5.2 The use of the feminine clitic *o* with a neutral value is distinctive of Romanian, which uses the feminine singular *o* with neutral value as a pro-sentence anaphora; it sometimes doubles the feminine demonstratives *asta / aceasta* 'this' with neutral value (see also §13.6):

(115)   a. [Că   este   leneș]$_i$,   **(asta**$_i$**)**   o$_i$ știu   de   mult
            that   is   lazy   this.ACC.F   CL.ACC.F.3SG   (I)know   for   long
            'I have known for a long time that he is lazy'

        b. [S-a   furat   calculatorul]$_i$.   Știu   bine   că   **(asta)**$_i$
            CL.REFL.PASS=has stolen   computer.DEF.NOM   (I)know   well   that   this
            n-ai   făcut-o$_i$ tu
            not=(you)have   done=CL.ACC.F.3SG   you.NOM

The feminine clitic *o* with a neutral value, functioning as a pro-sentence anaphora in the syntactic position of a direct object (115a–b), must be distinguished from the non-anaphoric usage of the same clitic, functioning as an expletive within idiomatic verbal constructions (116a–b); see also §6.1.8.2; Pană Dindelegan 1994:

(116)   a. A luat-**o** razna
            'He has gone mad'

        b. A pornit-**o** spre casă
            'He is on his way home!'

U   There is a stylistic difference between the two constructions (115a–b) and (116a–b): the first one occurs in the standard language, while the second one occurs in colloquial register and in slang.

With respect to use of the clitic as a pro-sentence anaphora, it has been noticed (Iliescu 2007a: 139) that, although Romanian is characterized by clitic doubling, the omission of neutral *o* is more frequent than the omission of the equivalent form in French or German. In present-day Romanian, there are preferences for both the occurrence and the omission of neutral *o:* it is frequently omitted in negative formulas (117a,b), but it is obligatorily expressed after the verbal anaphora *a face* 'do' (115b):

(117) a. Nu   Ø cred
 not   (I)believe
 'I do not believe it'

b. A   acționat   fără   să   Ø știe
 (he)has   acted   without   să$_{SUBJ}$ know.SUBJ.3SG
 'He has acted without knowing'

C   Romance counterparts of the anaphoric clitic *o* ((115a,b) type) are accusative masculine singular (Reinheimer and Tasmowski 2005: 111).

The expletive feminine clitic ((116) type) occurs sporadically in other Romance languages too. Espinal (2009) signals for Catalan, French, Italian, Spanish, and Greek the existence of a pronominal clitic in verbal idiomatic constructions (in the accusative feminine singular or plural, and sporadically in the genitive), similar to the expletive clitic in the idiomatic Romanian constructions. This also occurs in Arom. (*u*; for its use, see DIARO: 307, 326, 425) and in Albanian (Sandfeld 1930: 132–3).

H   The phenomenon of resumption by neutral *o* is old in Romanian (it occurs in the writings of Antim Ivireanul [1692–1714]. In the 20th century, the doubling construction is used more in imitation of the corresponding French structure (Reinheimer and Tasmowski 2005: 112).

3.2.1.6 Finite and non-finite clauses in the direct object position

3.2.1.6.1 The following clauses can occupy the direct object position:

A. any type of relative clause (§10.3.1): free relative (118a), indirect interrogative (118b), infinitival relative (118c);

B. clauses introduced by any type of complementizer (§10.1): with a *bona fide* complementizer (119a), with a complementizer specific to reported speech (119b,c):

(118) a. Mănâncă [**ce i se cere**]
 'He eats what he is asked to'

b. Întreabă [**ce s-a întâmplat**]
 'He asked what happened'

c. El   n-are   [**ce**   **mânca**]
 he   not=has   what   eat.INF
 'He has nothing to eat'

(119) a. El crede [**că a greșit**]
 'He believes that he made a mistake'

b. El întreabă [**dacă sunt șanse de vindecare**]
 'He asks if there are chances of recovery'

c. El mi-a ordonat [**să plec imediat**]
 'He ordered me to leave immediately'

Except for configuration (118c)—possible only if the clause occupies the direct object or subject position (see also §3.1.7.1)—the rest of the configurations may also occur in other positions, with the same complementizers and with the same selection properties for the complementizer, with the same inventory of relatives (pronouns, adjectives, and relative adverbs) and the same construction properties for the relatives.

3.2.1.6.2 Non-finite clauses can also occur in the direct object position: the infinitival clause, as an *A*-infinitival construction (120a) or, in relation to the modal verb *putea* 'can', as a bare infinitival construction (120b); the gerund clause, after verbs of perception (120c); the supine clause, as a DE-supine (120d).

(120) a. Începe   [a   **munci**   din greu]
         (he)starts A_INF   work.INF   hard
         'He starts working hard'

   b. El   [poate   [**alerga**]]
      he   can   run.INF
      'He can run'

   c. El   simte   [**venind**   o   adiere   de   vânt]
      he   feels   come.GER   a   breeze.NOM of   wind
      'He feels a breeze coming'

   d. Ion   termină   [**de**   **parcurs**   bibliografia]
      Ion   finishes   DE_SUP   cover.SUP   bibliography.DEF.ACC
      'Ion finishes covering the bibliography'

C   The following configurations are either specific to Romanian (i), or have a special behaviour in Romanian (ii, iii): (i) non-finite structures with the supine (120d), in which DE functions as an inflectional element (§4.4.3.4); (ii) gerund structures, which occur only after verbs of perception and frequently correspond to infinitive constructions in other Romance languages ((120c); §4.5.4.4); (iii) infinitival structures (120a,b), which occur less frequently in Romanian than in other Romance languages, because the subjunctive has replaced the infinitive (§4.2.5).

3.2.1.7   Ordinary objects vs. raised objects

Unlike prototypical configurations, in which the direct object selected by the matrix verb is located in the VP, in numerous other constructions the direct object does not relate to the head verb, but to a verb which has changed its syntactic frame as an effect of restructuring.

3.2.1.7.1 The *subject-to-object raising* structures occur with transitive verbs; the matrix verb takes a direct object (realized as a clitic or doubled by a clitic), which appears as a result of the raising of the subject from the embedded clause. The former direct object is placed towards the periphery, in the position of a secondary predication (see also §10.4.2.2):

(121)   Vede   [că   **Ion**_i   plânge]_DO   >   [Pe   **Ion**_i   îl_i]_DO   vede
        (he)sees that   Ion   cries   PE   Ion.ACC   CL.ACC.M.3SG   sees
        [că   plânge t_i]_SP
        that   cries
        'He can see that Ion is crying'

Raising verbs differ semantically, belonging to the following classes:

   (i) verbs of perception (§2.3.3.1)

(122)   a.   Îl   văd   că /   cum   plânge
             CL.ACC.M.3SG   (I)see   that   how   cries
             'I see him crying'

b. Îl   simt   (că   e)   supărat
   CL.ACC.M.3SG (I)feel   that is   upset
   'I feel that he is upset'

(ii) verbs expressing cognitive processes

(123) a. Mi-o   imaginez   că / cum pleacă
         CL.DAT.1SG=CL.ACC.F.3SG   (I)imagine that how leaves
         'I imagine her leaving'

      b. Mi-l   amintesc   că / cum pleca   de acasă
         CL.DAT.1SG=CL.ACC.M.3SG   (I)remember that how leave.IMPERF.3SG   from home
         'I remember him leaving from home'

(iii) causative verbs

(124) Îl   face / Îl   lasă / Îl   pune   să   plece
      CL.ACC.M.3SG makes   CL.ACC.M.3SG lets   CL.ACC.M.3SG puts   să_SUBJ leave.SUBJ.3SG
      '(S)he makes him / lets him / forces him to leave'

(iv) desiderative modal verbs

(125) A dorit-o /   A vrut-o   (să   fie)   medic
      has wished=CL.ACC.F.3SG   has wanted= CL.ACC.F.3SG   să_SUBJ be.SUBJ.3SG   doctor
      'He wanted her to become a doctor'

(v) epistemic verbs

(126) Îl   ştiu   (că   e)   plecat / O   crede   (că   e) bolnavă
      CL.ACC.M.3SG (I)know   that is   gone   CL.ACC.F.3SG believes that   is   sick
      'I know he is away' / 'He believes she is sick'

(vi) verbs of appreciation

(127) A socotit-o /   A considerat-o   (că   este) nepregătită
      has considered=CL.ACC.F.3SG   has considered=CL.ACC.F.3SG   that is   unprepared
      'He considered her unprepared'

Syntactic differences exist between the configurations (i)–(vi). The differences regard the structure of the embedded clause:

- (i) and (ii) allow for either a finite or a non-finite gerund clause (128a,b); *că* and *cum* are the complementizers of the finite clause (128c):

(128) a. Îl   văd   [că   plânge] / [plângând]
         CL.ACC.M.3SG (I)see that cries   cry.GER
         'I see him crying'

      b. Mi-l   imaginez [că   pleacă] / plecând]
         CL.DAT.1SG=CL.ACC.M.3SG   (I)imagine that leaves   leave.GER
         'I imagine him leaving'

      c. Îl   văd   [că / cum pleacă]
         CL.ACC.M.3SG (I)see that   how leaves
         'I see him leaving'

C The *raised object* structures are considered a Balkan feature by Sandfeld (1930: 193–4), since they occur in (Daco-)Romanian, Aromanian, Bulgarian, Albanian, and Greek.
  In Latin, there is an infinitival structure corresponding to raised object structures (called *accusativus cum infinitivo*—Lat. SENTIO EUM UENIRE, Ernout and Thomas 1959: 320–1); this does not exist in Romanian, but it occurs in other Romance languages (Gawełko 2003).

- In (iii), a subjunctive clause is allowed.

U In old Romanian and in non-standard present-day Romanian, a *de*-indicative embedded clause can also occur (Hill 2004: 349):
(129) Îl   face /   Îl   pune   [de   pleacă]
       CL.ACC.M.3SG makes CL.ACC.M.3SG puts   that leaves
       'He makes him leave / He forces him to leave'

- In (iv)–(vi) full finite clauses occur, as well as elliptical structures, without the copula, or, more rarely, prepositional phrases headed by *ca* 'as' (a preposition of quality), which select a gerund clause as complement (130c).

(130) a. Îl   știu   [(că e) plecat]
          CL.ACC.M.3SG (I)know   that is   gone
       b. Îl   consider   [(că e) nedreptățit]
          CL.ACC.M.3SG (I)consider that is   wronged
          'I consider him wronged'
       c. Îl   știu /   Îl   consider   [ca   având   talent]
          CL.ACC.M.3SG (I)know   CL.ACC.M.3SG (I)consider as   having   talent
          'I consider him as having talent'

3.2.1.7.2 In other constructions, with impersonal intransitive (131a) and certain transitive personal verbs (131b), the raised direct object occurs isolated to the left (hanging topic).

(131) a. [Pe dânsul$_i$] #, trebuie / se   cuvine   să-l$_i$
          PE he.ACC   must   CL.REFL.ACC   ought.to   SĂ$_{SUBJ}$=CL.ACC.M.3SG
          ajutăm t$_i$
          help.SUBJ.1PL
          'We must / ought to help him'
       b. [iscălitura$_i$] #, învățase   de   o$_i$ făcea t$_i$
          signature.DEF   (he)learn.PLUPERF   that CL.ACC.F.3SG   (he)make.IMPERF
                                                                      (ORom, Neculce)
          'He had learned to sign his name'

3.2.1.8 Direct object word order

Although the direct object is generally postverbal (V–O), its positioning is very free, that is, it does not have to be strictly adjacent to the verb, and it can occur either pre- or postverbally. The only cases of fixed word order concern pronominal clitics, which occupy a fixed position in relation to the verb and also in relation to one another; dative clitics obligatorily precede accusative clitics.

Romanian allows for a sentence to start with a pronominal clitic, which explains the unmarked O–V(–S) structures, in all configurations in which the Experiencer is encoded as a direct object. The O–V configuration is specific for verbs of physical sensation (§2.3.3.2) and for some psych verbs (§2.3.3.3) and occurs either in subjectless sentences (132a) or in structures with postverbal non-agentive subjects (132b,c); see Manoliu (2011: 506).

(132) a. **Mă** doare în gât
CL.ACC.1SG hurts in throat
'I have a sore throat'

b. **Mă** doare capul
CL.ACC.1SG hurts head.DEF.NOM
'I have a headache'

c. **Mă** uimește răspunsul
CL.ACC.1SG surprises answer.DEF.NOM
'The answer surprises me'

Romanian allows for the direct object to be separated from the verb: by different adverbials (133a); or by inserting the second object (indirect (133b), or secondary (133c)) in between.

(133) a. Ion spune **imediat** adevărul
Ion tells immediately truth.DEF.ACC

b. Cumpără **copiilor** pantofi
buys children.DEF.DAT shoes.ACC
'He buys the children shoes'

c. Îl învață **matematică** pe Ion
CL.ACC.M.3SG teaches mathematics PE Ion.ACC
'He teaches Ion mathematics'

In Romanian, direct object fronting is possible for any type of clause: declarative (134a), interrogative (134b), imperative (134c), and exclamative (134d).

(134) a. **Bucureștiul** îl traversez zilnic
București.DEF.ACC CL.ACC.M.3SG (I)cross daily
'I cross Bucharest daily'

b. **Pe cine** ai ajutat?
PE who.ACC (you)have helped
'Whom did you help?'

c. **Cartea,** # citește-o imediat!
book.DEF.ACC read.IMP.2SG=CL.ACC.F.3SG immediately
'Read the book immediately!'

d. **Ce cărți frumoase** citești!
what books.ACC beautiful (you)read
'What nice books you are reading!'

In (134a,c), fronting is optional, and it has discourse effects; in (134c), fronting only occurs in prosodic isolation; in (134b,d), fronting is obligatory, being required by the structural features of the interrogative and exclamative *wh*-phrases.

Romanian has limitations on direct object fronting within embedded clauses: only the *că* / *dacă*-indicative and *ca*-subjunctive complementizers allow fronting (135a,b), while the *să*-subjunctive and *de*-indicative complementizers do not (135c,d):

(135) a. El crede [că pe Ion îl poate ajuta]
 he believes that PE Ion.ACC CL.ACC.M.3SG (he)can help.INF
 'He believes that it is Ion that he can help'

 b. El doreşte [ca pe Ion să-l ajute]
 he wants COMP PE Ion.ACC SĂ$_{SUBJ}$=CL.ACC.M.3SG help.SUBJ.3SG
 'It is Ion he wants to help'

 c. *El doreşte [să pe Ion ajute]
 he wishes SĂ$_{SUBJ}$ PE Ion.ACC help.SUBJ.3SG

 d. *Îl pune [de cartea (o) citeşte]
 CL.ACC.M.3SG puts that book.DEF.ACC CL.ACC.F.3SG reads
 'He makes him read the book'

Other configurations with object raising occur as a result of regular syntactic restructuring phenomena, which lead to the simultaneous change of the DO position related to the verb, and of the hierarchical position of the noun phrase. Such phenomena occur in passive ((136a); §3.4.1) and in pseudo-cleft structures ((136b); §10.3.4):

(136) a. **Cartea** a fost recenzată de specialişti (< Specialiştii au recenzat **cartea**)
 'The book was reviewed by specialists' (< The specialists reviewed the book)

 b. Ceea ce a cumpărat Ion este **o casă veche** (< Ion a cumpărat **o casă veche**)
 'What Ion bought is an old house' (< Ion bought an old house)

3.2.2 The secondary object

3.2.2.1 Characteristics

The secondary object (SecO), called the 'direct object' by older grammars, is a conventional term meant to distinguish between two internal arguments (secondary vs. direct object), which have both common and different features (see point (vi) below).

The secondary object has the following characteristics (Pană Dindelegan 1999: 64–5; Roegiest 1987):

 (i) It is selected by a small class of double object verbs (§3.2.2); the head verb can have finite (137), as well as non-finite form: infinitive, gerund, and participle (§4.1.1):

(137) El mă învaţă o **poezie**
 he.NOM CL.ACC.1SG teaches a poem.ACC≡NOM
 'He teaches me a poem'

 (ii) It occurs in a structure with two internal arguments, i.e. it co-occurs with the direct object (the secondary object requires that the direct object be realized), but it is incompatible with an indirect object.

 (iii) When the direct object is realized as a clitic (or as a clitic doubling structure), the secondary object can be omitted; the consequence is that the verbal event gets a generic reading:

(138) Părinții   l-au   învățat Ø și l-au   sfătuit
      parents.DEF CL.ACC.3SG=have.3PL taught and CL.ACC.3SG=have.3PL advised
      Ø corect
        correctly
      'His parents taught him correctly and gave him good advice'

(iv) The secondary object is directly (non-prepositionally) linked to its head, being realized as a noun phrase which includes an inflectionally unmarked nominal (Acc≡Nom).
(v) The verb generally assigns the role of Theme to the secondary object; the secondary object is frequently included in the thematic grid [Agent + Recipient + Theme]:

(139) Cineva$_{AGENT}$ mă$_{RECIPIENT}$ învață   franceza$_{THEME}$
      someone   CL.ACC.1SG   teaches   French
      'Someone is teaching me French'

(vi) The secondary object shares a number of features with the direct object (§3.2.1); the following features set it apart from the DO:
  • it cannot be realized as an accusative personal or reflexive clitic and, implicitly, it cannot be clitic-doubled (140a);
  • it cannot be coordinated with the direct object (140b);
  • it does not participate in passivization, being a constituent which is not affected by the mechanism of passivization (140c):

(140) a. *Cartea   m-a   învățat-o
         book.DEF.ACC   CL.ACC.1SG=has   taught=CL.ACC.F.3SG
      b. *L-am   învățat pe Ion   sau o   poezie
         CL.ACC.3SG=(I)have   taught   PE Ion.ACC or   a   poem.ACC
      c. *O poezie   a   fost   învățată pe Ion
          a poem.NOM   has   been   taught   PE Ion.ACC

3.2.2.2 Realizations

The following constituents can occur in the position of the secondary, non-animate object (GBLR: 447–53):

  • a definite or indefinite noun phrase (141a); the only verb that allows a bare NP is *învăța* 'teach' (141b):

(141) a. M-a   întrebat **data**   **examenului** / **acest detaliu** /
         CL.ACC.1SG=has asked   date.DEF.ACC≡NOM   exam.DEF.GEN   this detail
         un   **detaliu**
         a   detail
         'He asked me the date of the exam / this detail'
      b. M-a   învățat **gramatică**
         CL.ACC.1SG=has taught   grammar.ACC≡NOM
         'He taught me grammar'

  • a nominal phrase with pronominal head (frequently, an indefinite (142a), a pro-sentence demonstrative with neutral value (142b), an (interrogative) *wh*-element (142c), or a substitute numeral (142d)):

(142) a. M-a   învățat   ceva   nou / orice /   multe / totul
         CL.ACC.1SG=has taught   something   new   anything a lot   everything
     b. M-a   învățat   **asta**:   să   spun
         CL.ACC.1SG=has taught   this.F.SG.ACC≡NOM   SĂ$_{SUBJ}$ tell.SUBJ.1SG
         numai   adevărul
         only   truth.DEF
     c. **Ce**   m-a   învățat?
        what   CL.ACC.1SG=has taught
        'What has he taught me?'
     d. M-a   învățat   numai **două dintre procedee**
        CL.ACC.1SG=has   taught   only   two   of   procedures
        'He has taught me only two of the procedures'

H In old Romanian, to a greater extent than in present-day Romanian, the secondary object structure was syntactically unstable, in that it could be substituted by a dative (143a) or prepositional object (143b):

(143) a. să   ne   învățăm   **adevărului**   (Coresi)
         SĂ$_{SUBJ}$ CL.REFL.ACC.1PL   (we)teach.SUBJ   truth.DEF.DAT
         'to teach ourselves the truth'
     b. așijderea   **spre**   aceaia   ne   învață   (Coresi)
        also   towards   that.ACC.F.SG   CL.ACC.1PL   teaches
        'it teaches us the same thing'

- a relative clause, either an indirect interrogative construction, in the case of the verbal head *întreba* 'ask' (144a), or a headless (free) relative (144b):

(144) a. M-a   întrebat   [**pe cine**$_i$ angajăm t$_i$]
         CL.ACC.1SG=has   asked   PE   who.ACC   (we)hire
         'He has asked me who we were hiring'
     b. M-a   examinat   [**ce**$_i$ mi-a   predat t$_i$ cu   o
        CL.ACC.1SG=has   examined   what   CL.DAT.1SG=has   taught   with a
        zi   înainte]
        day   before
        'He examined me from what he had taught me the day before'

- a subordinate clause introduced by complementizers (145a–c).

All these verbs can introduce reported speech, with the exception of the verb *trece* 'help to cross', which does not allow it; they take subordinate clauses whose complementizers are selected depending on the type of embedded reported speech:

(145) a. M-a   întrebat: ['Mai pleci?'] >   M-a   întrebat   [**dacă**
         CL.ACC.1SG=has   asked   still (you)leave CL.ACC.1SG=has   asked   if
         mai   plec]
         still   (I)leave
         'He asked me: 'Are you still leaving?'' > 'He asked me whether I was still leaving'

3.2 Objects   147

    b. M-a anunțat: ['Examenul începe la ora 15']
       CL.ACC.1SG=has announced exam.DEF NOM starts at hour 15
       'He informed me: "The exam starts at 3 o'clock"'
      > M-a anunțat [că examenul începe la ora 15]
       CL.ACC.1SG=has announced that exam.DEF.NOM starts at hour 15
       'He announced me that the exam starts at 3 o'clock'
    c. M-a rugat: ['Pleacă imediat!'] > M-a rugat
       CL.ACC.1SG=has asked leave.IMP.2SG immediately CL.ACC.1SG=has asked
      [să plec imediat]
      SĂ$_{SUBJ}$ leave.SUBJ.1SG immediately
      '(S)he asked me to leave immediately'

U   The structure with a relative clause or a clause headed by a complementizer is more frequent than the configuration with a nominal phrase; this is a consequence of the fact that these verbs introduce reported speech.

3.2.2.3 Constructions involving overall clausal structure

The secondary object, which obligatorily co-occurs with the direct object, is present in the fundamental structures of the direct object:

- in passive structures, without taking part in passivization (146a);
- in reflexive structures (146b);
- in reciprocal structures, without taking part in the phenomenon of reciprocation (146c);
- in structures with a possessive dative clitic, which enters a relationship with the direct object, and not with the secondary object (146d).

(146) a. Copilul a fost învățat și **limba mamei**
       child.DEF has been taught also language.DEF.ACC≡NOM mother.DEF.GEN
       'The child was also taught his mother's language'
    b. Mă întreb (**care** e) **soluția corectă**
       CL.REFL.ACC.1SG (I)ask which is solution.DEF correct
       'I ask myself what the right answer is'
    c. Se întreabă unul pe altul **câte ceva**
       CL.REFL.ACC.3PL (they)ask one PE another each something
       'They ask one another something'
    d. Și-a învățat fata **o poezie**
       CL.REFL.DAT.3SG=has taught girl.DEF.ACC a poem.ACC≡NOM
       'He taught his daughter a poem'

3.2.2.4 Word order

The secondary object has free word order, that is, it can be placed either pre- or postverbally.

In a neutral word order, the secondary object occurs postverbally, like any other complement; most often it is placed after the direct object (147a), but it can also appear before it (147b):

(147) a. L-am   întrebat   pe   Ion   **tabla**
       CL.ACC.3SG=(I)have   asked   PE   Ion.ACC   table.DEF.ACC≡NOM
       înmulţirii
       multiplication.DEF.GEN
       'I asked Ion the times table'

   b. L-am   întrebat **tabla**   **înmulţirii**   pe
       CL.ACC.3SG=(I)have   asked   table.DEF.ACC≡NOM   multiplication.DEF.GEN   PE
       Ion
       Ion.ACC
       'I asked Ion the times table'

In instances where there is marked word order (topicalization and / or focalization), the secondary object can also precede the verb (148):

(148) Asta   şi   nu   ceea ce   spui   tu,   l-am   întrebat
      this.F.SG.ACC≡NOM   and   not   what   (you)say   you   CL.ACC.3SG=(I)have   asked
      'It is this and not what you are saying, that I asked him'

3.2.3 The indirect object

3.2.3.1 Characteristics

(i) The indirect object is selected by a transitive verb (in structures in which the direct object is usually realized (149a) as well) or by an intransitive verb (in structures in which the indirect object is either the only internal argument (149b) or one of the two arguments, co-occurring with a prepositional phrase (149c)):

(149) a. Ion   oferă   flori   **Mariei**
         Ion.NOM   offers   flowers.ACC   Maria.DAT
         'Ion offers flowers to Maria'

   b. Exemplul   aparţine   **autorului**
      example.DEF.NOM   belongs   author.DEF.DAT
      'The example belongs to the author'

   c. **Îi**   arde   de farse
      CL.DAT.3SG   feels-like   of pranks.ACC
      'He has the urge to play tricks'

(ii) Verbs that select an indirect object divide into two classes, that is, those selecting an obligatory indirect object—*acorda* 'give', *aparţine* 'belong', *a se consacra* 'dedicate oneself', *contraveni* 'conflict with', *datora* 'owe', *dărui* 'give', *dăuna* 'prejudice', *dedica* 'dedicate', *a se deda* 'take to', *plăcea* 'like', *premerge* 'precede' (150), and those selecting an optional indirect object—*citi* 'read', *povesti* 'tell', *spune* 'tell', *zâmbi* 'smile' (151):

(150) a. El   aparţine   comunităţii
         he.NOM   belongs   community.DEF.DAT
         'He belongs to the community'

b. *El   aparține
      he.NOM   belongs

(151) a. El   citește   (copiilor)
         he.NOM   reads   children.DEF.DAT
         'He is reading to the children'

      b. Ea   (le)   spune   o   poveste
         she.NOM CL.DAT.3PL   tells   a   story.ACC
         'She tells them a story'

H In old Romanian many more verbs were able to take indirect objects than is the case today:

(152) a. Să   stăpânească   **zilii**   **și**   **nopții**   (*Biblia*)
         SĂ_SUBJ   own.SUBJ.3SG   day.DEF.DAT   and   night.DEF.DAT
         'to be the master of day and night'

      b. Să   se   atingă   **stricatului**   (Coresi)
         SĂ_SUBJ   CL.REFL.ACC   touch.SUBJ.3SG   depraved.DEF.DAT
         'to touch the depraved'

A fixed syntactic structure in which the verb *a crede* 'believe' selects a dative is preserved in contemporary Romanian:

(153) Nu-și   crede   ochilor   și   urechilor
      NEG=CL.REFL.DAT.3SG   believes   eyes.DEF.DAT   and   ears.DEF.DAT
      'He cannot believe his eyes'

(iii) The following verbs do not take an indirect object: some of the agentive verbs with three arguments, like *învăța* 'teach', *întreba* 'ask' (due to the indirect object–secondary object incompatibility), and non-agentive verbs with two arguments, requiring an Experiencer in direct object position (due to the direct object–indirect object incompatibility (154a,b)):

(154) a. Mă   doare   capul
         CL.ACC.1SG   hurts   head.DEF.NOM
         'I have a headache'

      b. Mă   ustură   degetul
         CL.ACC.1SG   hurts   finger.DEF.NOM
         'My finger hurts'

(iv) The indirect object can be realized as a DP (in Romanian, the inflectional dative marker can only be assigned to a DP) or as a dative personal or reflexive pronominal clitic (§3.2.3.2).

(v) The indirect object is selected by both an active or a passive finite head verb (155a,b) and by non-finite verb forms—the infinitive (156a), the gerund (156b), the participle (156c), and the supine (156d):

(155) a. El   trimite   o   carte   **părinților**
         he   sends   a   book   parents.DEF.DAT
         'He sends a book to his parents'

      b. Cartea   este   trimisă   **părinților**   de către   el
         book.DEF   is   sent   parents.DEF.DAT   by   him
         'The book is sent by him to his parents'

(156) a. ideea   de   a   telefona   **profesorului**
idea.DEF   DE   A$_{INF}$ telephone.INF   teacher.DEF.DAT
'the idea of telephoning the teacher'

b. L-am   văzut   dăruind   **copiilor**   jucării
CL.ACC.M.3SG=have.1SG   seen   giving   children.DEF.DAT   toys
'I saw him giving toys to the children'

c. Cadoul   trimis   **copilului**   a   fost   apreciat
present.DEF   sent   child.DEF.DAT   has   been   appreciated
'The present sent to the child was appreciated'

d. El   a   terminat   de   povestit   **copiilor**
he   has   finished   DE$_{SUP}$ tell.SUP   children.DEF.DAT
'He finished telling stories to the children'

(vi) The indirect object allows for more syntactic variation than the direct object. The dative indirect object structure is either a variant of a direct object structure (157a,b) or of an intransitive prepositional object structure (158a–c):

(157) a. El   succedă   **cuiva** /   **pe cineva**
he   follows   someone.DAT   PE   someone.ACC
'He follows someone'

b. Tehnica   ajută   **lucrătorilor** /   **lucrătorii**
technique.DEF   helps   workers.DEF.DAT   workers.DEF.ACC
'Technique helps workers'

(158) a. El   îi   seamănă   **fratelui**   **lui** /   cu
he   CL.DAT.3SG   resembles   brother.DEF.DAT   his(GEN)   with
fratele   **lui**
brother.DEF.ACC   his(GEN)
'He looks like his brother'

b. Maria   fură   **vecinilor** /   **de la vecini**   maşina
Maria   steals   neighbours.DEF.DAT   from   the   neighbours.ACC   car.DEF.ACC
'Maria steals the car from the neighbours'

c. Ion   dă   mâncare   **animalelor** /   **la animale**
Ion   gives   food   animals.DEF.DAT   to   animals.ACC
'Ion feeds the animals'

(vii) Semantically, the indirect object is assigned one of the following thematic roles: Experiencer (159a), Recipient (159b), Beneficiary (159c), and Source (159d).

(159) a. Îi   place   dansul
CL.DAT.3SG   likes   dance.DEF.NOM
'He likes dancing'

b. El   trimite   **copilului**   o   carte
he.NOM   sends   child.DEF.DAT   a   book.ACC
'He is sending a book to the child'

    c. Bunicul   cumpără   **nepotului**   o   jucărie
       grandfather.DEF.NOM buys   grandson.DEF.DAT a   toy
       'The grandfather buys a toy for his grandson'

    d. **Îi**   cere   **mamei**   un   sfat
       CL.DAT.3SG   asks   mother.DEF.DAT an   advice
       'He asks his mother for some advice'

(viii) When the Experiencer is part of the verb's thematic grid and occupies a different position than that of subject, in most contexts it must be overtly realized. The Experiencer is optional in the context of certain verbs of perception (§2.3.3.1):

(160) (**Îmi**)   miroase a   fum
       CL.DAT.1SG smells   like   smoke.ACC
       'It smells like smoke (to me)'

Rarely, the indirect object has the thematic roles Possessor (161a) and Theme, in symmetric structures (161b):

(161) a. Cartea   îi   aparține   **studentului**
         book.DEF.NOM CL.DAT.3SG belongs   student.DEF.DAT
         'The book belongs to the student'

     b. Mihai   se   aseamănă **lui**   **George**
        Mihai   CL.REFL.ACC.3SG resembles   LUI.DAT George
        'Mihai resembles George'

C   Romanian has a number of obsolete structures with a locative dative; the dative occurs in the context of motion verbs or of stative verbs and does not function as an indirect object, but as an adverbial of place (162):

    (162) Ion   rămâne   **locului**
            Ion   remains   place.DEF.DAT
            'Ion stays put'

    This construction is unique in Romance, and is considered to be a Balkan Sprachbund phenomenon (Brâncuș 1960). In Albanian, this structure is much more frequent. Unlike Romanian and Albanian, in Turkish, Serbian, and Croatian the locative dative occurs only with motion verbs, not with stative verbs.

  (ix) Some of the verbs that select an indirect object can enter possessive structures. Since the indirect object is selected by the head verb, these configurations are ambiguous, that is, the dative clitic can be interpreted either as an indirect object (the possessive reading is absent) or as a possessive dative (163). In the latter case, the clitic cumulates two thematic roles: Possessor and Recipient (§3.4.4.2).

(163) **Îți**   dau   cartea
       CL.DAT.2SG   (I)give   book.DEF
       'I give the book to you / I give your book to you'

  (x) The indirect object can be doubled by a dative pronominal clitic; doubling is in some cases obligatory, in others, optional (see §3.2.3.4).

3.2.3.2 The indirect object realized as a pronominal clitic

The indirect object can be realized as a personal pronominal (164a) or reflexive clitic (164b) which may have a reciprocal reading (164c):

(164) a. **Li**   s-au   acordat   burse
         CL.DAT.3PL CL.RELF.PASS=(they)have granted   scholarships
         'Scholarships were granted to them'

   b. **Ion$_i$ îşi$_i$**   atribuie reuşite   nemeritate
      Ion   CL.REFL.DAT.3SG credits   success.PL   undeserved
      'Ion credits himself with undeserved successes'

   c. Cei   doi   prieteni **îşi**   vorbesc
      CEL.M.PL two   friends   CL.REFL.DAT.3PL talk.3PL
      'The two friends talk to one another'

C In its non-standard variant, Romanian, like Spanish and Portuguese (Reinheimer and Tasmowski 2005: 122), possesses a non-referential dative, which does not occupy the indirect object position, that is the 'dative with neutral value', which is realized as a 3rd person personal pronominal clitic:

(165) a. Ce   să-**i**   faci?
         what   SĂ$_{SUBJ}$=CL.DAT.3SG (you)do
         'What can you do about it?'

   b. Zi-**i**   aşa!
      say.IMP.2SG=CL.DAT.3SG so
      'Say so!'

This dative clitic has a pragmatic role, that is, it places the VP in focus (see §6.1.8.2). Some structures are ambiguous, as they can have a neutral (166b), or referential reading (166a):

(166) a. Ce   să-**i**   faci   (copilului)?   [indirect object]
         what SĂ$_{SUBJ}$=CL.DAT.3SG (you)do child.DEF.DAT
         'What can you do to the child?'

   b. Ce   să-**i**   faci?   [dative with neutral value]
      what SĂ$_{SUBJ}$=CL.DAT.3SG (you)do
      'What can you do about it?'

U Like French (Leclère 1976; Jouitteau and Rezac 2007) and Spanish, colloquial Romanian preserved the Latin 'ethic dative', realized as a 1st or 2nd person non-referential and semantically vacuous dative clitic, which is stylistically and pragmatically marked as [+affected], that is, the speaker displays an affective interest towards one of the characters involved in the verbal event (167a). It is the only Romanian construction which allows the co-occurrence of two clitic forms sharing the same case, but having different person forms (167b) (§6.1.4, §6.1.8.1):

(167) a. Balaurul **mi**-l   ia   pe erou   şi   îl   înghite
         ogre.DEF CL.DAT.1SG=CL.ACC.3SG takes PE hero.ACC and CL.ACC.3SG swallows
         'The ogre lifts the hero up and swallows him'

   b. **Mi**   ţi-l   ia   şi-l   înghite
      CL.DAT.1SG CL.DAT.2SG=CL.ACC.3SG takes and=CL.ACC.3SG swallows
      'He lifts him and swallows him'

The verbs with two objects allow the co-occurrence of two clitic forms, one in the accusative and one in the dative (168). For incompatibilities, see §6.1.4.

(168) Ea   ți-l   trimite
     she.NOM   CL.DAT.2SG=CL.ACC.M.3SG   sends
     'She sends it to you'

3.2.3.3 Case marking vs. prepositional marking by *la* 'to'

An indirect object whose first component of the nominal phrase is invariable (i.e. cannot receive the specific dative case-marker) will be realized as a PP headed by the preposition *la* 'to' (+Acc):

(169) a. Am   dat   premii   **la** **doi**   copii /   dintre copii
        (I)have given   prizes   to   two   children.ACC   of   children
        'I gave prizes to two children / two of the children'

     b. Nu   dau   informații   **la** **astfel de**   oameni
        not (I)give information.PL   to   such   people.PL.ACC
        'I do not give information to such people'

The prepositional phrases functioning as indirect and prepositional objects are separate syntactic structures. There are two tests which apply only to the indirect object realized as a prepositional phrase headed by *la* 'to': clitic doubling (170) and the substitution of the PP with a DP whose determiner is placed at the left of the phrase, so that it can carry the inflectional dative marker (171).

(170) a. **Le**ᵢ   dau   flori   **la** **două**   profesoareᵢ
        CL.DAT.3PL   (I)give   flowers   to   two   teachers.ACC
        'I give flowers to two teachers'

     b. *Li   s-a   gândit   **la** **doi**   elevi
        CL.DAT.3PL   CL.REFL.ACC.3SG=has   thought   to   two.ACC   students.ACC

(171) a. Le   dau   flori   **acestor** /   **aceloraşi** /   **celor**
        CL.DAT.3PL   (I)give   flowers   these.DAT   the-same.DAT   CEL.PL.DAT
        două   profesoare
        two   teachers.DAT
        'I give flowers to these / to the same / to the two teachers'

     b. *Se   gândeşte   **acestor** /   **aceloraşi** /   **celor**   **două**
        CL.REFL.ACC.3SG   thinks   these.DAT   the-same.DAT   CEL.DAT.PL   two
        profesoare
        teachers

U In spoken Romanian, the indirect object is realized as a PP headed by the preposition *la* 'to' even in configurations in which the first component of the phrase has case inflection. The realization by a PP alternates with the realization by a dative DP:

(172) a. Le-am   dat   bomboane   **la copii** /   **copiilor**
        CL.DAT.3PL=(I)have   given   candy.PL.ACC   to   children.ACC   children.DEF.DAT
        'I gave the children candy'

     b. Am   scris   **la** **toți** /   **tuturor**
        (I)have written   to   all.ACC   all.DAT
        'I wrote to all of them'

H In old Romanian, the indirect object could be replaced by a PP headed by the preposition *către* 'towards' (173), when selected by verbs of saying (*spune* 'tell', *zice* 'say', *grăi* 'say'). The *către* 'towards' structure is a regional variant in present-day Romanian.

(173) A zis domnul **către slujitor** să plece
 has said lord.DEF.NOM towards servant să_SUBJ leave.SUBJ.3SG
 'The lord said to the servant to leave'

C Romanian is a language with strong case-marking. For the indirect object, case-marking is doubly distributed, that is, on the indirect object DP (through the case-marker) and on the verb (by the dative clitic attached to it). Indirect object marking is both inflectional and analytic (Manoliu and Price 2007: 321–3).

3.2.3.4 Indirect object clitic doubling

Indirect object doubling is realized by a pronominal clitic which is co-referential with the DP or with the relative clause in indirect object position:

(174) a. Martorul le dă informații **polițiștilor**
 witness.DEF.NOM CL.DAT.3PL gives information.PL.ACC policemen.DEF.DAT
 'The witness gives information to the policemen'

 b. **Președintelui** i s-a acordat încredere
 president.DEF.DAT CL.DAT.3SG CL.REFL.PASS=has given trust
 'The president was given people's trust'

 c. I-am oferit informații **cui a cerut**
 CL.DAT.3SG=(I)have offered information.PL.ACC who.DAT has asked
 'I gave information to whoever asked for it'

Indirect object doubling is impossible, optional, or obligatory, depending on its position relative to the head, the nature of the head, and the type of constituent in the indirect object position (GBLR: 462).

When the indirect object is a DP placed postverbally, doubling is generally optional (175a). Doubling is obligatory when the indirect object is preverbal (175b) (Tasmowski-De Ryck 1987: 387–8). In relative and interrogative clauses, doubling of the pronoun *cine* 'who' is optional (176a), while the doubling of *care* 'which' is obligatory (176b) (Reinheimer and Tasmowski 2005: 197):

(175) a. **(I-)am** dat cărți **studentului**
 CL.DAT.3SG=(I)have given books.ACC student.DEF.DAT

 b. **Copilului / Unui copil / Lui** i-am dat
 child.DEF.DAT a.DAT child him.DAT CL.DAT.3SG=(I)have given
 un cadou
 a present.ACC

(176) a. **Cui** (îi) oferi florile?
 who.DAT CL.DAT.3SG (you)offer flowers.DEF.ACC

 b. Știu **căruia dintre ei** i-ai dat cărți
 (I)know which.DAT of them.ACC CL.DAT.3SG=(you)have given books.ACC

3.2.3.4.1 There are contexts in which doubling is not allowed. The postposed indirect object realized as a DP headed by an [+abstract] noun (177) or as a DP headed by a [+human] noun is not doubled if the head verb is inherently reflexive, when the reflexive pronoun in the accusative is first or second person singular or plural (178a,b):

(177) El (*i) se dedică **studiului**
he CL.DAT.3SG CL.REFL.ACC.3SG dedicates study.DEF.DAT
'He dedicates himself to studying'

(178) a. Mă adresez (*le) **oamenilor / lor**
CL.REFL. (I)address CL.DAT.3PL people.DEF.DAT. them.
ACC.1SG PL DAT
'I address the people / them'
vs. Tu (i) te adresezi **lui**
you.NOM CL. CL.REFL. (you)address him.DAT
DAT.3SG ACC.2SG
'You address him'

b. Ne (*i) prezentăm **directorului**
CL.REFL.ACC.1PL CL.DAT.3SG present.1PL director.DEF.DAT
'We introduce ourselves to the director'
vs. Ea (i) se prezintă **directorului**
she.NOM CL. CL.REFL.ACC.3SG presents director.DEF.DAT
DAT.3SG
'She introduces herself to the director'

3.2.3.4.2 There are contexts in which doubling is obligatory. When it is preverbal, the indirect object occurs in subjectless structures (179a,b) or in structures with postverbal subject (180). In these configurations, doubling is also obligatory when the indirect object is postverbal (181). A strong personal pronoun is always doubled by a clitic (182):

(179) a. **Lui / Anei** îi este rău
him.DAT Ana.DAT CL.DAT.3SG is bad(ADV)
'He / Ana is sick'
b. **Femeii** îi zice Maria
woman.DEF.DAT CL.DAT.3SG says Maria
'The woman is called Maria'

(180) **Câinelui** îi este foame
dog.DEF.DAT CL.DAT.3SG is hunger
'The dog is hungry'

(181) Îi este rău **Anei**
CL.DAT.3SG is bad(ADV) Ana.DAT
'Ana is sick'

(182) **Nouă ne** plac filmele
us.DAT CL.DAT.1PL (they)like films.NOM
'we like films'

3.2.3.4.3 There are contexts in which doubling is optional. Doubling of the postverbal indirect object is optional when it is realized as a DP headed by a [+animate] noun (183) (with the exception of the contexts under §3.2.3.4.1). The doubling of the preverbal indirect object realized as a personal (rarely, reflexive) pronominal clitic is optional; the stressed form occurs for reasons of emphasis (184):

(183) (**Le**) trimitem bani **părinților**
 CL.DAT.3PL (we)send money.PL.ACC parents.DEF.DAT
 'We send money to our parents'

(184) **Vă** ofer (**vouă**) această onoare
 CL.DAT.2PL (I)offer you.DAT this honour
 'I give you this honour'

3.2.3.5 The indirect object realized as a relative clause

The indirect object can be realized as a headless relative clause, usually doubled by a dative clitic occurring in the matrix clause. The indirect object clause is introduced by a relative or indefinite pronoun (185a) and rarely by a relative or indefinite adjective (185b). The connector always displays a dative case form, assigned by the head verb in the matrix clause:

(185) a. **Îi** acordăm premiul **cui / oricui**
 CL.DAT.3SG (we)give prize.DEF.ACC who.DAT whoever.DAT
 îi place competiția
 CL.DAT.3SG likes competition.DEF.NOM
 'We give the prize to the one that / to whoever likes the competition'

 b. (**Îi**) răspunde **oricărui coleg** îl **întreabă**
 CL.DAT.3SG answers any.DAT.M.SG colleague CL.ACC.3SG asks
 'He answers any colleague who asks him'

H The free relative clause in indirect object position is an old Romanian structure:
 (186) Le da bani **cărora** căra **apă**
 CL.DAT.3PL give.IMPERF.3SG money.ACC.PL which.DAT.PL carry.IMPERF.3PL water.ACC
 (Neculce)
 'He gave money to the ones that carried water'

C Like French and Spanish, Romanian also displays the clausal realization of the indirect object as a headless relative:
 (187) a. Fr. Je réponds **à qui j'ai envie de répondre**
 'I answer whomever I feel like answering'
 b. Sp. Doy máximo de puntos **a quien me ayude con estos ejercicios**
 'I give maximum points to whoever helps me with these exercises'

U In colloquial and regional Romanian, the relative clause in indirect object position can be introduced by a PP headed by the preposition *la* 'to' or, less frequently, by *către* 'towards':
 (188) Ea se adresează **la cine** o **cunoaște**
 she CL.REFL.ACC.3SG addresses to who CL.ACC.3SG knows
 'She addresses whoever knows her'

3.2.3.6 Word order

In the unmarked word order, the indirect object DP is postverbal and is not prosodically isolated (graphically, no punctuation mark is present).

With the exception of the realization by clitics, which have a fixed position, realization as a DP leads to a relatively free word order. The indirect object selected by a subjectless verb (189a) or by a verb whose subject is postverbal is preverbal in an unmarked word order (189b):

(189) a. **Băiatului**   îi   pare   rău
            boy.DEF.DAT CL.DAT.3SG seems bad
            'The boy feels sorry'

       b. **Mariei**   îi   place Monet
            Maria.DAT CL.DAT.3SG likes Monet.NOM
            'Maria likes Monet'

3.2.4 The prepositional object

3.2.4.1 Characteristics

(i) The prepositional object is an object headed by a preposition; it functions as an argument of the head.

(190) Ion se   bazează (*pe profesor)
        Ion CL.REFL.ACC.3SG relies   on   teacher
        'Ion relies on his teacher'

(ii) The preposition is selected by the head constituent, therefore it is specific (Huddleston and Pullum 2002: 618).

(iii) The occurrence of the prepositional object in the verb phrase is usually obligatory (190), but it can also be optional (194).

(iv) The thematic role of the prepositional object is transferred from the verb, and not assigned by the preposition. In example (190) the verb assigns the role of Theme to the prepositional object.

(v) Unlike the direct and indirect objects, the prepositional object does not allow substitution with a pronominal clitic form or doubling.

(vi) The status of the preposition in the configuration with prepositional object is different from the status of the preposition *pe* or *la* occurring with the direct and the indirect object, respectively. The prepositional object will always be realized as a prepositional phrase, never as a noun phrase, while the direct and indirect object structures allow both prepositional marking and case marking (§3.2.1, §3.2.3).

(vii) The direct, indirect, and prepositional objects share a feature, that is, the preposition heading the structures has undergone a process of grammaticalization. However, in the prepositional object configuration, the preposition occupies a lower position on the grammaticalization cline than the prepositions which occur in the direct and indirect object structure, respectively (§9.2.3). For example, one can still see the semantic relation between the original locative meaning of *pe* 'on' in (190) and the meaning of the verb *a se baza* 'base oneself', that is, 'rely on'.

3.2.4.2 Configurations with the prepositional object

In a number of Romanian structures, the prepositional object is the only constituent present in the VP adjacent to the verb. The complement of the preposition heading the prepositional object is usually a determiner phrase. Accusative prepositions block the occurrence of the definite article (190) (§9.3.2.2). Besides a DP, the complement of the preposition may be an infinitive (191), a supine (192), or a free relative clause (193) (§10.2.1). A direct object can also be present in the structure, alongside the prepositional object (194). In subjectless configurations, the prepositional object co-occurs with a dative DP (195).

(191) Se   gândește   la   a   demisiona
       CL.REFL.ACC.3SG thinks   about A_{INF} resign.INF
       'He is thinking about resigning'

(192) S-a   săturat   de   spălat   geamuri
       CL.REFL.ACC.3SG=has   got-fed-up DE_{SUP} wash.SUP windows
       'He got fed up with washing windows'

(193) Se   teme   de   cine   vine
       CL.REFL.ACC.3SG fears   of   who   comes
       'He fears the person that is coming'

(194) Ion are un aliat (în George)
       'Ion has an ally (in George)'

(195) Lui   George îi   pasă   de   Maria
       LUI.DAT George CL.DAT.3SG   cares   about   Maria
       'George cares about Maria'

There is a wide range of prepositions which can head a prepositional object in Romanian. The most frequently occurring prepositions are:

- cu 'with': colabora **cu** 'cooperate with', semăna **cu** 'resemble someone'
- de 'of': depinde **de** 'depend on', a se teme **de** 'fear someone'
- din 'from': a se retrage **din** 'retire from', rezulta **din** 'result from'
- în 'in': a se complace **în** 'indulge in', consta **în** 'consist in'
- între 'between': alege **între**... și... 'choose between... and...'
- la 'to': apela **la** 'resort to', a se gândi **la** 'think of', a se referi **la** 'refer to'
- pe 'on': a se baza **pe** 'to rely on', a se supăra **pe** 'get upset with'
- pentru 'for': milita **pentru** 'militate for', mulțumi **pentru** 'thank for'

All the verbs above take a preposition which assigns the accusative case to its complement. A few verbs take a preposition such as *asupra* 'upon', which assigns the genitive case: *a se repezi **asupra** dușmanului* 'fall upon the enemy'.

The preposition can be omitted if the prepositional object is realized as an infinitive with the inflectional head A (196a) or as a free relative clause (196b). The preposition is obligatorily omitted if the prepositional object is realized as a clause headed by a complementizer (197).

(196) a. Se   teme   (de) a   vorbi
          CL.REFL.ACC.3SG fears of A_{INF} talk.INF
          'He is afraid to talk'

       b. Nu îmi   pasă   (de) cine vine
          not CL.DAT.1SG cares of   who   comes
          'I do not care who comes'

(197) Se teme *(de) să vorbească
 CL.REFL.ACC.3SG fears of să_SUBJ talk.SUBJ.3SG
 'He is afraid to talk'

H The structure in which the head verb assigns a specific preposition to its argument is old and productive; neologistic verbs display it too, taking over the pattern from the source language. For example, the Romanian verbs *apela la* 'resort to', *depinde de* 'depend on', *conta pe* 'rely on' are Romance borrowings which take over the original preposition assigned by the verb (Fr. *appeler à, dépendre de, compter sur*).

Certain Romanian verbs have undergone changes in complement selection (Stan 2012b):
- Some of the verbs that selected a dative complement in the 16th century now select a prepositional object: *a se apropia (de)* 'get close to', *a se bucura (de)* 'be happy about' (Pană Dindelegan 1968: 270).
- In old Romanian there are verbs which display free variation in the selection of the preposition: *lua aminte de / la* 'pay attention to'; in modern Romanian, only the latter preposition is selected by the verb.

C Passivization of the prepositional object is not allowed in Romanian (only direct objects of the verb can undergo passivization).

Romanian, like Spanish and Portuguese, but unlike French (Sandfeld 1970: 134), Italian (Renzi, Salvi, and Cardinaletti 2001 II: 523), Catalan (Wheeler, Yates, and Dols 1999: 167), does not have the category of adverbial clitics corresponding to Fr. *y, en*, It. *ne* (Reinheimer and Tasmowski 2005: 17).

Romanian prepositions are always transitive; generally, the absence of their complements is not allowed (Emonds 1985: 274; see also §9.3.1). There are very few exceptions to this rule (§9.3.1).

Romanian, like the other Romance languages, must move its prepositions, unlike English and some other Germanic languages which allow preposition stranding (Koopman 2000; Huddleston and Pullum 2002: 273).

(198) a. Scrisorile **peste care** am dat / *Scrisorile **care** am dat **peste**
 letters.DEF over which (I)have given letters.DEF which (I)have given over
 b. Engl. The letters **which** I came **across**

The selection of the preposition by the verbal head is in some cases specific to Romanian. In the following Romanian and English examples, the preposition selection is different even though the verbs have the same etymon: *depinde de* 'of' vs. Engl. *depend on*, *distinge de* 'of' vs. Engl. *distinguish from*.

3.3 PREDICATIVE COMPLEMENTS

Typical predicative complements are the subjective predicative complement, selected by the copula (§2.3.2.2), and the objective predicative complement, selected by complex transitive verbs (§2.3.1.2).

3.3.1 The subjective predicative complement

3.3.1.1 Characteristics

Syntactically, the subjective predicative complement is selected by a finite (199) or non-finite copula: an infinitive (200), a gerund (201), a supine (202), or a participle (203).

(199) Ana este **frumoasă**
Ana.NOM is beautiful.NOM.F.SG
'Ana is beautiful'

(200) ambiţia de a rămâne **frumoasă**
ambition DE A_{INF} remain.INF beautiful.NOM.F.SG
'the ambition to remain beautiful'

(201) Fiind **frumoasă**, Ana reuşeşte mereu
be.GER beautiful.NOM.F.SG Ana.NOM succeeds always
'Being beautiful, Ana always succeeds'

(202) E greu de ajuns **profesor**
is hard DE_{SUP} become.SUP professor.NOM
'It is hard to become a professor'

(203) ţară fostă **comunistă**
country be.PPLE.F.SG communist.NOM.F.SG
'ex-communist country'

The subjective predicative complement is obligatorily expressed, typically realized as an adjective, which agrees in number and gender with the subject (199). The subjective predicative complement which is realized as an adjective or noun bears the nominative case.

Semantically, the subjective predicative complement has different values: identifying (204), denominative (205), categorizing (206), equating (207), qualifying (208), qualifying-locative (209), restrictive (210), possessive (211), or partitive (212).

(204) Tu eşti **Ana**
'You are Ana'

(205) Ea se numeşte **Ana**
she.NOM CL.REFL.ACC.3SG calls Ana.NOM
'She is called Ana'

(206) Ana este **profesoară**
'Ana is a teacher'

(207) Munca înseamnă **succes**
'Work means success'

(208) Ana este **blondă**
'Ana is blond'

(209) Ana este **din Bucureşti**
'Ana is from Bucharest'

(210) Teoria este **chomskyană**
'The theory is Chomskyan'

(211) Creionul   este **al**   **Anei**
      pencil.DEF.NOM is   AL.M.SG   Ana.GEN
      'The pencil is Ana's'

(212) El   este **de-ai**   **noștri**
      he.NOM   is   of=AL.M.PL   our.M.PL
      'He is one of us'

Besides the semantic information of the subjective predicative complement, the copula contains aspectual and modalizing information (§2.3.2.2.1).

3.3.1.2 Realizations

The subjective predicative complement has different realizations.

  (i) The realization as an adjective ((199), (200), (201), (203), (208), (210)) is typical for the subjective predicative complement and impossible for other complements.
  (ii) As for realization as a nominal, note that the subjective predicative complement may be expressed as a bare noun, with a 'kind' denotation (for other complements, this possibility is rare):

(213) Balena   este **mamifer**
      whale.DEF.NOM   is   mammal.NOM
      'The whale is a mammal'

U   The predicative position is occupied by forms that can be doubly interpreted, as bare nouns or as adjectives:
    (214) a. Ana este **muncitoare**
             'Ana is a worker / hard-working'
          b. Pixurile sunt **consumabile**
             'Pens are consumable objects / consumables'

If the subjective predicative complement is realized as a relational noun (see §5.2.5), the noun can be accompanied by a dative indirect object, which in its turn can be clitic-doubled (215), by a prepositional object (216), or by a genitive complement (217). In the absence of the complement of the relational noun, either a plural (218a) or a multiple subject occurs (218b), otherwise, the noun is recategorized as non-relational (218c).

(215) Ion   (îi)   este frate   lui   Gheorghe
      Ion   CL.DAT.M.3SG   is   brother.NOM   LUI.DAT   Gheorghe

(216) Ion   este frate   cu   Gheorghe
      Ion   is   brother.NOM   with   Gheorghe

(217) Ion   este frate   al   lui   Gheorghe
      Ion   is   brother   AL.M.SG   LUI.GEN   Gheorghe
      'Ion is Gheorghe's brother'

(218) a. Ei sunt frați
         'They are brothers'
      b. Ion și Gheorghe sunt frați
         'Ion and Gheorghe are brothers'

c. După nașterea surorii sale, el a devenit **frate**
after birth.DEF sister.DEF.GEN his.F.SG he has become brother.NOM
mai mare
more old
'After his sister was born, he became the older brother'

In special syntactic structures, certain copulas (*fi* 'be', *veni* 'come, be') accept dative clitics which are the result of the raising of certain complements of the relational noun (219a) or of the adjective (219b):

(219) a. El îi vine văr
he.NOM CL.DAT.3SG comes cousin.NOM
< El vine văr lui
he.NOM comes cousin.NOM him.DAT
'He is his cousin'

b. El îți este drag < El este drag ție
he. CL. is dear.NOM.M. he.NOM is dear.NOM.M. you.DAT.
NOM DAT.2SG SG SG SG
'He is dear to you'

H In old Romanian, the dative configuration was much more frequent; present-day Romanian prefers the prepositional and the genitive complement (216, 217).

C In French and in Spanish, but not in Romanian, the subjective predicative complement can be realized as a neutral accusative pronominal clitic (Reinheimer and Tasmowski 2005: 112):
(220) a. Fr. Je vois ce qui est juste et vrai et ce qui ne l'est pas
b. Sp. Veo lo que es justo y también lo que no **lo** es
'I see what is right and also what is not'

(iii) As far as the prepositional realization is concerned, one must notice that *de*, *drept* 'as', prepositions of quality, accept not only a nominal complement (221), like any other preposition, but also an adjectival one (222):

(221) El se dă drept profesor
he.NOM CL.REFL.ACC.3SG gives as professor
'He pretends to be a professor'

(222) El trece de inteligent
he.NOM passes as intelligent
'He passes as intelligent'

A partitive (223), a complex comparative (224), or a complex quantitative structure (225) can occur in the position of a prepositional subjective predicative complement:

(223) El este **de-ai** **noștri**
he.NOM is of=AL.M.PL our.M.PL
'He is one of us'

(224) El este **ca tine** (**de inteligent**)
he.NOM is as you.ACC.SG as intelligent
'He is as intelligent as you'

(225) Țesătura   este   **de doi   metri**   **(de lungă)**
      fabric.DEF.NOM   is   of   two   metres   DE long.F.SG
      'The fabric is two metres long'

C   In structure (225), *fi* 'be' followed by the preposition *de* can be replaced by *avea* 'have', without a preposition:
    (226) Țesătura   are   doi   metri
          fabric.DEF.NOM   has   two   metres
    The synonymy between *fi* 'be' and *avea* 'have' in structures like (227) is considered a Balkan Sprachbund phenomenon by Sandfeld (1930: 204).
    (227) a. Copilul   este   de   doi   ani
             child.DEF.NOM   is   DE   two   years
          b. Copilul   are   doi   ani
             child.DEF.NOM   has   two   years
          'The child is two years old'

(iv) The AL + genitive or possessive of the subjective predicative complement (228a) is specific to Romanian (§5.3.3.2). In the absence of AL, the occurrence of the genitive or of the possessive in predicative position is impossible (228b).

(228) a. Casa   este   **a**   **Anei** /   **a**   **mea**
         house.DEF.NOM   is   AL.F.SG   Ana.GEN   AL.F.SG   my.NOM.F.SG
         'The book is Ana's / mine'
      b. *Casa   este   **Anei** / **mea**
         house.DEF.NOM   is   Ana.GEN   my.NOM.F.SG

(v) Two configurations are possible when an adverbial is in predicative position. In personal structures, the subjective predicative complement is realized as a substitute adverbial (*așa* 'so', *altfel* 'in another way', *cumva* 'somehow', *oricum* 'any way', *atât* 'this much', *oricât* 'no matter how much', etc.) (229a) or as modal adverbial which generally requires a complement (*asemenea* 'similar to', *aidoma* 'identical to', *împreună* 'together', *laolaltă* 'together') (229b):

(229) a. **Așa**   e   ea!
         so   is   she.NOM
         'That's the way she is!'
      b. Ea   este   **asemenea**   **mamei**   **sale**
         she.NOM   is   like   mother.DEF.DAT   her.DAT.F.SG
         'She is like her mother'

In impersonal constructions in which the subject is realized as a clause headed by a complementizer or non-finite clause, numerous modal and quantitative adverbs can occur (*bine* 'well', *ciudat* 'strange', *destul* 'enough', *exclus* 'excluded', *important* 'important', *musai* 'obligatory', *obligatoriu* 'obligatory', *posibil* 'possible', *sigur* 'certain'):

(230) Este **bine / posibil / exclus** să plecăm
 (it)is good possible excluded să$_{SUBJ}$ leave.SUBJ.1PL
 'It is good / possible / excluded for us to leave'

C In Romanian, modal adverbs are generally homonymous with the masculine singular form of the adjective (§8.1.4.1). The fact that the subjective predicative complement position in impersonal structures such as (230) is occupied by an adverb and not by an adjective is proven by the possibility of a typical adverbial form to occur, such as *bine* 'well', *musai* 'obligatory':

(231) E [$_{AdvP}$ **musai**] să plecăm azi
 is obligatory să$_{SUBJ}$ leave.SUBJ.1PL today
 'It is good for us to leave today'

(232) *om **musai**
 man obligatory

Romanian differs from most other Romance languages and English (which formally differentiate the modal adverb from the singular masculine adjective), as in these languages the subjective predicative complement position is occupied by an adjective:

(233) a. Fr. Il est **sûr** que nous allons partir
 b. Fr. *Il est **sûrement** que nous allons partir

(234) a. Engl. It is **certain** that we will leave
 b. Engl. *It is **certainly** that we will leave

(vi) The subjective predicative complement can be realized as a non-finite clause: infinitival (235), a supine clause (236), and an adjectival participle clause (237):

(235) Intenţia lui este **(de) a pleca**
 intention.DEF.NOM his.GEN is DE A$_{INF}$ leave.INF
 'His intention is to leave'

(236) Maşina este **de spălat**
 machine.DEF.NOM is DE$_{SUP}$ wash.SUP
 'This machine is for washing'

(237) Mâncarea este **stricată**
 food.DEF.NOM is alter.PPLE.F.SG
 'The food is spoiled'

U The infinitive in predicative position is often an A-infinitive sometimes taking the preposition *de* (§4.2.1.3). As in many other contexts, the infinitive is in free variation with the subjunctive (238). In the high register, the infinitive is preferred (Iordan 1956: 411; Sandfeld, Olsen 1962: 131; Stati 1989: 120).

(238) Intenţia lui este **să plece**
 intention.DEF.NOM his is să$_{SUBJ}$ leave.SUBJ.3SG
 'His intention is to leave'

Only the non-passive adjectival participle of unaccusative (237) and of transitive absolute verbs is accepted in predicative position. The participle of verbs that can also occur as causatives can receive both an active and a passive interpretation. It has an active reading with the participle form of the unaccusative verb (*a se coace* 'to ripen') in predicative position (239a), and it has a passive reading with the participle form of the transitive verb (*coace ceva* 'to bake something') in the passive voice (239b) (§4.4.4.4):

(239) a. Mărul   este   **copt**
         apple.DEF.NOM is   ripe.PPLE.M.SG
         'The apple is ripe'
     b. Mărul   este   **copt**   în cuptor de către bucătar
         apple.DEF.NOM is   bake.PPLE.M.SG   in oven   by   cook
         'The apple is baked in the oven by the cook'

Verbal gerunds are excluded in predicative position; gerundial adjectives are, however, allowed:

(240) Valurile   sunt   **spumegânde**
      waves.DEF.NOM are   foam.GER.F.PL
      'The waves are foaming'

(vii) The subjective predicative complement can be realized as a clause headed by a complementizer only in the context of the copulas *fi* 'be', *rămâne* 'remain', and *însemna* 'mean', and only if the subject is an abstract or deverbal noun:

(241) Problema   ta   rămâne   **să**   **câștigi**   mulți bani
      problem.DEF.NOM.F your.F.SG   remains să_SUBJ   earn.SUBJ.2SG   many   money
      'Your problem remains to earn a lot of money'

(242) Speranța   înseamnă **să**   **mergi**   până la   capăt
      hope.DEF.NOM   means   să_SUBJ   go.SUBJ.2SG   till at   end
      'Hope means going until the end'

(viii) The subjective predicative complement can be realized as an indirect interrogative relative clause (243), or as a headless relative, with the *wh*-element in the nominative (244) or in the genitive (245):

(243) Întrebarea   este **cine** **suntem**
      question.DEF.NOM   is   who   (we)are
      'The question is who we are'

(244) El   a   ajuns   **ce**   **și-a**   **dorit**
      he.NOM has arrived what   CL.REFL.DAT.3SG=has   wanted
      'He became what he wanted'

(245) Premiul   este **al**   **cui**   **îl**   **merită**
      prize.DEF.NOM   is   AL.M.SG   who.GEN   CL.ACC.M.3SG   deserves
      'The prize belongs to whoever deserves it'

3.3.1.3 Word order

The typical syntactic position of the subjective predicative complement is postverbal, but, depending on the type of semantic predication and on its occurrence in a main or embedded clause, the following word orders of the components S, V, and subjective predicative complement are possible (Pană Dindelegan 2008f: 289–91): S–V–SPC (246), SPC–V–S (247), V–S–SPC (248), V–SPC–S (249), S–SPC–V (250), SPC–S–V (251):

(246) Eu   sunt **Ion**
       I.NOM am   Ion
       'I am Ion'

(247) Tot   **profesor** a   fost și   tatăl   lui
       also   teacher   has been too father.DEF.NOM his.(GEN)
       'His father was also a teacher'

(248) Voiam   să   ajungi   tu   **director**
       want.IMPERF   SĂ$_{SUBJ}$ arrive.SUBJ.2SG you.NOM.SG director.NOM
       'I wanted for you to become a director'

(249) E   **sănătos** să   alergi
       is   healthy   SĂ$_{SUBJ}$ run.SUBJ.2SG
       'It is healthy to run'

(250) Femeia   tot   **singură**   a   rămas
       woman.DEF.NOM still alone.NOM.F.SG has remained
       'The woman still ended up alone'

(251) **Vinovat**   numai Ion   este
       guilty.NOM.M.SG   only   Ion.NOM is
       'Only Ion is guilty'

3.3.2 The objective predicative complement

3.3.2.1 Characteristics

(i) The objective predicative complement (OPC) is selected by a small class of double object verbs (§2.3.1.2); it designates a *property* of the entity encoded by the first object, which is either a direct (252a,b), or, rarely, an indirect object (252c):

(252) a. **L-au**   angajat **grădinar**
         CL.ACC.3SG=have.3PL   hired   gardener.ACC≡NOM
         'They hired him as a gardener'

     b. **L-au**   botezat   **Ion**
         CL.ACC.3SG=have.3PL   baptized Ion.ACC≡NOM
         'They baptized him Ion'

     c. **I-au**   zis   **Ion**
         CL.DAT.3SG=have.3PL   told   Ion.ACC≡NOM
         'They named him Ion'

(ii) The objective predicative complement shares many features with the direct object, but differs from it in the following respects:
  • it cannot be realized as a personal or reflexive accusative clitic, and, implicitly, it cannot participate in doubling;
  • it does not admit coordination with the (direct or indirect) object with which it co-occurs (253a);
  • it does not participate in passivization, i.e. it is a constituent which is not affected by the mechanism of passivization (253b).

3.3 Predicative complements

(253) a. *L-au ales pe Ion sau deputat
CL.ACC.3SG=have.3PL elected PE Ion or deputy

b. Ion a fost ales **deputat**
Ion has been elected deputy

3.3.2.2 Realizations

The objective predicative complement can be realized as (see Pană Dindelegan 2008g):

- a bare noun, which can take a modifier (254);
- a proper name, when the head is a naming verb (examples (252b,c) above), or a definite noun phrase, when the head is an appointing verb (255).

(254) L-au ales **director (de bancă)**
CL.ACC.3SG=have.3PL elected director of bank
'They elected him as a bank manager'

(255) L-au ales **președintele băncii**
CL.ACC.3SG=have.3PL elected president.DEF bank.DEF.GEN
'They elected him (as a) president of the bank'

In structures in which a proper name or a definite noun phrase occurs, the proper name, as well as the definite noun, receives a special semantic interpretation, which differs from the typical situation: the proper name has a property reading, encoding a denominative characteristic of the noun in the direct (252b) or indirect object position (252c); the definite noun expresses a categorial property of the direct object noun phrase (255). The fact that the definite noun does not have a referential / entity-denoting reading is proven by the possibility of substitution with a bare noun phrase (256a) and by the impossibility of a demonstrative determiner occurring (256b):

(256) a. L-au ales **președinte al băncii / președinte de bancă**
CL.ACC.3SG=have.3PL elected president AL bank.DEF.GEN president of bank

b. *L-au ales **acest președinte**
CL.ACC.3SG=have.3PL elected this president

The objective predicative complement can also be realized as a prepositional phrase headed by a preposition of 'quality' (*ca, drept, de, în calitate de* 'as'), whose characteristic is that it selects a complement with property reading (257a,b):

(257) a. L-au uns [(**ca**) **mitropolit**]
CL.ACC.3SG=have.3PL anointed as metropolitan
'They anointed him a metropolitan'

b. L-au calificat [**de** [**mare fraier**]]
CL.ACC.3SG=have.3PL considered as big sucker
'They considered him a big sucker'

The prepositions of 'quality' (see Pană Dindelegan 2010) allow a complement realized as a noun phrase (257a,b) or as an adjectival phrase (258a), and, in the case of the preposition *ca* 'as', a complement realized as a non-finite gerund clause (258b). In the absence of degree markers, the phrase is categorically ambiguous, because it can be interpreted as either a noun phrase or an adjectival phrase (258c):

(258) a. L-au taxat [de [AP **foarte fraier**]]
        CL.ACC.3SG=have.3PL considered as very stupid
        'They considered him very stupid'

     b. L-au categorisit [ca [VP **neavând viitor**]]
        CL.ACC.3SG=have.3PL considered as NEG-have.GER future
        'They considered him as not having future'

     c. L-au taxat [de [NP//AP **fraier**]]
        CL.ACC.3SG=have.3PL considered as sucker
        'They considered him a sucker'

U   In old Romanian, *de* as a preposition of 'quality' was predominant, while in present-day Romanian, *de* is limited to a small inventory of verbs and *ca* (non-standard, *ca și*) is extending its use.

Further, the objective predicative complement can be realized as an (interrogative or indefinite) pronoun with variable reference, in the series *ce* 'what', *ceva* 'something' (259a,b), an (indefinite interrogative or modal) substitute adverbial in the series *cum* 'how', *astfel* 'so', *cumva* 'somehow', *altcumva* 'somehow different' (260a,b), and, finally, a free relative clause, introduced by an adverbial (261a) or pronominal (261b) *wh*-phrase:

(259) a. **Ce** l-au ales?
        what CL.ACC.3SG=have.3PL elected
        'What did they elect him as?'

     b. L-au ales **ceva important**
        CL.ACC.3SG=have.3PL elected something important
        'They elected him as something important'

(260) a. **Cum** l-au denumit?
        what CL.ACC.3SG=have.3PL named
        'What did they name him?'

     b. L-au denumit **cumva / astfel**
        CL.ACC.3SG=have.3PL named somewhat that
        'They gave him a certain name / They named him so'

(261) a. L-au denumit **cum au dorit**
        CL.ACC.3SG=have.3PL named how have.3PL wished
        'They named him as they wished'

     b. L-au ales **ce au dorit**
        CL.ACC.3SG=have.3PL elected what have.3PL wished
        'They elected him as what they wished'

3.3.2.3 Word order

The objective predicative complement has free word order with respect to the verb. In neutral word order it occurs postverbally, after the object (262a), but also before it (262b). In marked word order, it can occur preverbally (262c):

(262) a. L-au ales pe Ion **decan**
        CL.ACC.3SG=have.3PL elected PE Ion dean
        'They elected Ion as dean'

b. L-au ales **decan** pe Ion
   CL.ACC.3SG=have.3PL elected dean PE Ion

c. **Decan, și nu rector** l-au ales pe Ion
   dean and not rector CL.ACC.3SG=have.3PL elected PE Ion
   'It is as dean not as rector that they elected Ion'

3.4 CONSTRUCTIONS INVOLVING OVERALL CLAUSAL STRUCTURE

3.4.1 Passive and impersonal constructions. *By*-phrases

3.4.1.1 Two types of passive constructions

Romanian has two types of passive constructions: the passive formed with *fi* 'be' plus the participle of the verb, which agrees in gender and number with the subject (263), and the passive bearing the passive-reflexive marker *se* (syncretic with the 3rd person reflexive pronoun), which attaches to the inflected verb (264):

(263) Copilul **este lăudat** de (către) părinți < Părinții îl laudă pe copil
'The child is praised by his parents' < 'The parents praise the child'

(264) **Se construiesc** locuințe noi
CL.REFL.PASS build.3PL houses.NOM new.NOM.PL
'New houses are built'
< (Oamenii) construiesc locuințe noi
'People build new houses'

H Both passive structures are inherited from Latin and are attested in the earliest surviving Romanian texts (Pană Dindelegan 2003: 133; Timotin 2000a: 225), as well as in south-Danubian dialects, which suggests Latin origin (Timotin 2000b: 488).

C The two passive structures also occur in other Romance languages (Posner 1996: 181; Reinheimer Rîpeanu 2001: 305–6). Romanian, however, uses the *se*-passive to a greater extent, a fact which has been explained as the result of Slavic influence (Posner 1996: 181; Timotin 2000b: 488).

U *Fi* 'be' can be replaced, if only rarely, by other verbs, as can the verb 'be' in passives in other Romance languages (e.g. It. *venire, andare*), i.e. *veni* 'come' (265) (Iordan 1950: 277; Fischer 1985: 121; Pană Dindelegan 2008c: 136):

(265) Celălalt bec **vine slăbit**
the-other bulb.NOM comes loosen.PPLE.M.SG
'The other bulb gets loosened'

3.4.1.1.1 Passivization affects transitive verbs that select agentive (263) or non-agentive human subjects (266a), as well as non-human subjects, expressing cause (266b):

(266) a. Banii **au fost pierduți** de Ion
'The money was lost by Ion'

b. Ușa **a fost deschisă** de vânt
'The door was opened by the wind'

Certain transitive verbs do not accept passivization for semantic-syntactic reasons:

(267) *Sunt durut de cap < Mă doare capul
 (I)am hurt.PPLE.M.SG by head CL.ACC.1SG hurts head.DEF.NOM
 'I have a headache'

(268) *Sunt conținute greșeli de carte < Cartea conține greșeli
 are.3PL contain.PPLE.F.PL mistakes by book book.DEF.NOM contains mistakes.ACC
 'The book contains mistakes'

Certain verbs (*dori*, *vrea* 'want', *putea* 'can') which take a sentential complement accept only the *se*-passive, not the *fi* 'be' passive:

(269) Se dorește să se obțină victoria
 CL.REFL.PASS wishes SĂ_SUBJ CL.REFL.PASS obtain.SUBJ.3SG victory.DEF.NOM
 'One wishes to obtain the victory'
 < Jucătorii doresc să obțină victoria
 'The players wish to obtain the victory'

(270) *Este dorit (de către jucători) să se obțină victoria
 is wanted by players SĂ_SUBJ CL.REFL.PASS obtain.SUBJ.3SG victory.DEF.NOM

Transitive verbs with non-realized direct object admit only the *se*-passive, with an impersonal value:

(271) Se mănâncă bine aici < Oamenii mănâncă bine aici
 CL.REFL.PASS//IMPERS eats well here 'People eat well here'
 'One eats well here'

(272) *Este mâncat bine aici
 is eaten well here

3.4.1.1.2 For both structures, passivization has several syntactic effects.

 (i) The transitive structure becomes intransitive. The passive structure is incompatible with a direct object; it only accepts the secondary object of double-object transitive verbs (§2.3.1.1):

(273) Copilul a fost rugat [ceva]_SecO de (către) părinți
 child.DEF.NOM has been asked something by parents
 'The child was asked something by his parents'
 < Părinții [l]_DO-au rugat [pe copil]_DO [ceva]_SecO
 parents.DEF.NOM CL.ACC.M.3SG=have.3PL asked PE child.ACC something
 'The parents asked the child something'

 (ii) The direct object nominal is externalized, and takes the subject position.
 (iii) The subject nominal is marginalized: it either gets in a postverbal position, as a prepositional phrase (*by*-phrase), or it is deleted. What is specific to Romanian is the alternative use of the prepositions *de* (multifunctional) and *de către* 'by' (specialized) to introduce the agent in the passive structure.

In present-day Romanian, the preposition *de* is extensively used. *De către* is used, more rarely, in official styles, with personal nouns (274) and with nouns that are interpreted as personal in the extralinguistic context (275) (Rădulescu Sala 2008: 461). The *by*-phrase can also incorporate a relative clause introduced by a relative pronoun with a human referent (276):

(274) Legea a fost votată de (către) parlamentari
       'The law was voted by the Parliament members'

(275) Legea a fost votată de (către) parlament
       'The law was voted by the Parliament'

(276) Legea a fost votată de (către) cine era prezent la discuții
       'The law was voted by whoever was present at the discussions'

De către 'by' cannot occur with nouns referring to the inanimate force which triggers the action:

(277) Ușa   a   fost   deschisă de   (*către) vânt
       door.DEF.NOM has been   opened   by   wind
       'The door was opened by the wind'

H In the earliest Romanian texts, the *by*-phrase was introduced by the preposition *de*. The preposition *de către* 'by' was grammaticalized for encoding the *by*-phrase from the second half of the 17th century (Stan 2012b).
   In old Romanian, there are contexts in which *de către* 'by' introduces the prepositional object (Diaconescu 1959: 11):
   (278) care trebuie bine a să osăbi **de cătră** alt asemene cuvânt (Budai-Deleanu)
          'which must be distinguished from another such word'

3.4.1.1.3 The coexistence of these two types of passive can be explained through the differences in their frequency and use, although these are tendencies, not rules.

  (i) The *se*-passive is more frequent in old Romanian and in present-day colloquial language than in present-day literary language, which prefers the *fi* 'be' passive (Iordan 1956: 452–3; Berea 1966: 572; Pană Dindelegan 2003: 136).
 (ii) When it is necessary to identify the agent, the *fi* 'be' passive is preferred (279) (Pană Dindelegan 2003: 136; Timotin 2000a: 228); the presence of the *by*-phrase with the *se*-passive is rare (280) (GBLR: 508):

(279) Cartea este citită **de (către) toți studenții**
       'The book is read by all students'

(280) Se știe **de către oricine** că nu putem trăi fără cultură
       'It is known by anyone that we cannot live without culture'

H In old Romanian, up to the 19th century, the realization of the agent in the *se*-passive structure was much more frequent than it is nowadays (Pană Dindelegan 2003: 136):
   (281) Necredinciosu   giudecă-se   **de voi**   (*Codicele Voronețean*)
          unfaithful.DEF.NOM   judge. 3SG=CL.REFL.PASS   by you.PL
          'The infidel is judged by you'

(iii) The *fi* 'be' passive has a complete paradigm, for all persons (282), while the *se*-passive has only a 3rd person form (283):

(282) eu   sunt   lăudat,   tu   eşti   lăudat,   el   este
      I   am   praised   you   are   praised   he   is
      lăudat,   ea   este   lăudată
      praised   she   is   praised.F.SG
      noi   suntem   lăudaţi,   voi   sunteţi lăudaţi,   ei   sunt
      we   are   praised.M.PL   you.PL   are   praised.M.PL   they   are
      lăudaţi, ele   sunt   lăudate
      praised.M.PL they are   praised.F.PL
      'I am / you are / he is / she is / we are / you are / they are praised'

(283) a. Se   aduce   măcar   un   cadou   de   Crăciun
         CL.REFL.PASS   brings   at least   one   present for   Christmas
         'At least one Christmas present is brought'
      b. Se   aduc   multe   cadouri   de   Crăciun
         CL.REFL.PASS   bring.3PL   many   presents for   Christmas
         'Many Christmas presents are brought'

H In old Romanian the passive-reflexive could be used, albeit very rarely, for all persons (Pană Dindelegan 2003: 136):

(284) Eu   trebuescŭ   de   tine   **a**   **mă**   **boteza**   (Coresi)
      I   must.1SG   by   you.SG   A$_{INF}$ CL.REFL.PASS.ACC.1SG baptize.INF
      'I have to be baptized by you'

U Rarely, the personal use of the *se*-passive occurs in present-day colloquial Romanian (Iordan 1956: 452; Pană Dindelegan 2003: 136):

(285) **Te**   **cunoşti**   imediat   când   minţi
      CL.REFL.PASS.ACC.2SG   know.2SG   immediately   when   lie.2SG
      'One realizes immediately that you lie'

(iv) Restricting the distribution of the *se*-passive to the 3rd person led to its impersonal use and furthermore, to the present-day preference for using this construction whenever the agent remains non-realized. However, both types of passive can have impersonal value:

(286) **Este ştiut** că nu putem trăi fără cultură

(287) **Se ştie** că nu putem trăi fără cultură
      'It is known that we cannot live without culture'

(v) The *se*-passive is preferred with postverbal subjects (Pană Dindelegan 2003: 136):

(288) **Se citeşte lecţia** cu glas tare
      'The lesson is read aloud'

(289) Se aşteaptă **vizita** preşedintelui
      'The president's visit is expected'

(vi) The *se*-passive is preferred when the passive subject has a non-entity-denoting reading (generic, massive, or kind denoting nouns) (290), and the *fi* 'be' passive, when the subject has an entity-denoting reading (291) (Pană Dindelegan 2008c: 138):

3.4 Constructions involving overall clausal structure

(290) a. În România, se vânează **lupi**
'In Romania, wolves are hunted'

b. Aici se vinde **carne**
'Meat is sold here'

(291) Ieri, a fost vânat **un lup**
'Yesterday, a wolf was hunted'

3.4.1.2 Impersonal constructions

Romanian has numerous means to express impersonal readings; on the one hand, there are several types of subjectless verbs (§3.1.3.4), and, on the other hand, there are several syntactic constructions specialized for expressing impersonal readings: the use of the 2nd person singular or of the 1st person plural, and the generic subject (*lumea, oamenii* 'people') (§3.1.3.3). Besides this, there is a type of syntactic restructuring with *se*; the impersonal value is obtained by eliminating the subject (§3.1.3.4.2), a phenomenon also interpreted as the passivization of unergative verbs (Dobrovie-Sorin 1998):

(292) a. Oamenii merg pe jos la serviciu > Se   **merge** pe jos   la serviciu
      'People walk to work'   CL.REFL.IMPERS walks on foot to work
                                       'One walks to work'

b. Ei aleargă dimineața >   Se   **aleargă** dimineața
   'They run in the morning'   CL.REFL.IMPERS runs   morning
                                  'One runs in the morning'

C All Romance languages—with the exception of French, which uses the expletive *on* for this type of impersonal constructions—display the *se / si* impersonalization mechanism (Dobrovie-Sorin 1987: 489; Reinheimer and Tasmowski 2005: 107, 142–8). The reflexive structure became a non-agentive marker as early as vulgar Latin, which explains the preference of unaccusative verbs for the reflexive (Salvi 2011: 346; see §2.3.2.1.4). Old Italian had only the *si*-passive structure; the impersonal *si*-construction is a creation of 18th-century modern Italian.

H The *se*-impersonal construction is not attested in the earliest Romanian texts and it is rare in old Romanian:

(293) Așea   **se**   **vorovește**, că...   (Neculce)
      so   CL.REFL.IMPERS   says   that
      'So it is said, that...'

3.4.1.2.1 The *se*-impersonalization occurs for intransitive non-reflexive verbs with human subject, be they unergative (292), unaccusative (294), or psych verbs (295):

(294) a. Ei ajung târziu la serviciu > Se   **ajunge** târziu la   serviciu
      'They arrive late at work'   CL.REFL.IMPERS arrives   late   at   work
                                         'One arrives late at work'

b. Oamenii mor din ignoranță >   Se   **moare** din   ignoranță
   'People die out of ignorance'   CL.REFL.IMPERS dies   from   ignorance
                                   'One dies out of ignorance'

(295) Oamenii **suferă** din cauza sărăciei > Se   **suferă** din cauza sărăciei
      'People suffer because of poverty'   CL.REFL.IMPERS suffers because   poverty.DEF.GEN
                                             'One suffers because of poverty'

C   Unlike Italian (296) and Spanish (297), the Romanian verb *fi* 'be' does not accept *se*-impersonalization:
(296) a. Non **si è** mai contenti   (in Cinque 1988: 522)
          'One is never content'
       b. *Nu **se**   este niciodată mulțumit
          not CL.REFL.IMPERS is   never   content
(297) a. Cuando **se es** tonto, **se es** para siempre   (in Reinheimer and Tasmowski 2005: 144)
          'When one is stupid, one is stupid for ever'
       b. *Când **se**   este prost, **se**   este pentru totdeauna
          when CL.REFL.IMPERS is   stupid CL.REFL.IMPERS is   for   ever

3.4.1.2.2 Although passivization and impersonalization are complementary syntactic mechanisms, the first affecting transitive verbs, and the second one intransitive verbs, there are some passive structures (with *fi* 'be' or with *se*) that can have impersonal value as a result of the fact that they are derived from null-object transitive verbs (§3.4.1.1.1), or a result of the fact that the direct object which became the subject in the passive structure is realized as a clause headed by a complementizer (§3.4.1.1.3).

3.4.2 Reflexive constructions

Romanian displays five types of reflexive constructions, which differ depending on the structural function of the reflexive form: (i) clitic or strong reflexives filling syntactic slots; (ii) reflexive clitics as lexical formatives; (iii) reflexive clitics as lexico-grammatical formatives; (iv) reflexive clitics as grammatical formatives; (v) doubling reflexive clitics (Pană Dindelegan 1999: 97–100, 2008d: 159–67).

C   All the Romance languages show various uses of the reflexive marker. Yet, the phenomenon is far more complex in Romanian, due to the influence of Old Slavic, where the reflexive category extended to inherent reflexives as well.

The reflexive marker can have a dative or an accusative form (§6.2). In non-finite clauses reflexive constructions occur only with the infinitive and the gerund.

3.4.2.1 Constructions with syntactic reflexives

Of the reflexivization devices available crosslinguistically (Faltz 1985), Romanian employs the nominal device, that is a dative or accusative clitic / strong reflexive coreferential with the subject (298a–d). Null form reflexives do not occur (298e).

(298) a. Ion$_i$ se$_i$ spală
          Ion   CL.REFL.ACC.3SG washes
          'Ion washes himself'
      b. Ion$_i$ are   grijă de   sine$_i$
         Ion   has   care   of   self.ACC
         'Ion takes care of himself'

3.4 Constructions involving overall clausal structure

    c. Ion$_i$ își$_i$ cumpără țigări
       Ion CL.REFL.DAT.3SG buys cigarettes
       'Ion is buying cigarettes for himself'

    d. Ion$_i$ a reușit doar datorită sieși$_i$
       Ion has succeeded only thanks to self.DAT
       'Ion succeeded thanks only to himself'

    e. *Ion$_i$ spală e$_i$
       Ion washes (intended meaning: 'Ion washes himself')

The same reflexive forms are used both for confirming the expected identity of the subject and object (299a), and for indicating any unexpected coreferentiality of participant roles (299b,c).

(299) a. Ion$_i$ se$_i$ spală
       Ion CL.REFL.ACC.3SG washes
       'Ion washes himself'

    b. ?Ion$_i$ se$_i$ privește
       Ion CL.REFL.ACC.3SG looks

    c. Ion$_i$ se$_i$ privește în oglindă
       Ion CL.REFL.ACC.3SG looks in mirror
       'Ion is looking at himself in the mirror'

The selection of the clitic over the strong form is predicted by syntactic rules, as shown below.

3.4.2.1.1 In argument positions, accusative and dative reflexive clitics are obligatory whenever, within the same clause, the subject is coreferential with the direct (300a) or the indirect object (300b).

(300) a. El$_i$ se$_i$ spală
       he CL.REFL.ACC.3SG washes
       'He is washing (himself)'

    b. El$_i$ își$_i$ pune multe întrebări
       he CL.REFL.DAT.3SG puts many questions
       'He is asking himself many questions'

Reflexive possessive-dative clitics are obligatory under coreferentiality with the subject (301) (§3.4.4) and in idioms with various degrees of frozenness (302).

(301) El$_i$ și$_i$-a găsit umbrela
     he CL.REFL.DAT.3SG=has found umbrella.DEF
     'He has found his umbrella'

(302) își vede de drum, și-a pus capăt zilelor
     CL.REFL. sees of way, CL.REFL. put end days.DEF.
     DAT.3SG   DAT.3SG=has   DAT
     'He goes his own way, he put an end to his life'

In all other instances, the possessive-dative reflexive is optional, in free variation with other structures (303a,b), showing pragma-semantic and discourse oppositions like topic / comment, part / whole centredness, static / dynamic, agentive / non-agentive (Manoliu-

Manea 1993: 72–87). With verbs of possession, pleonastic possessive-dative reflexive clitics can occur for emphasis (303c).

(303) a. Ion$_i$ își$_i$ iubește copiii / Ion$_i$ îi iubește pe copiii săi$_i$
Ion CL.REFL.DAT.3SG loves children.DEF / Ion CL.ACC.3PL loves PE children.DEF his
'Ion loves his children'

b. Ion$_i$ și$_i$-a pus pe cap o pălărie / Ion a pus pe cap o pălărie
Ion CL.REFL.DAT.3SG=has put on head a hat / Ion has put on head a hat
'Ion put a hat on his head'

c. Ion$_i$ își$_i$ are toți banii la bancă / Ion are toți banii la bancă
Ion CL.REFL.DAT.3SG has all money.DEF at bank / Ion has all money.DEF at bank
'Ion has all his money at the bank'

Some verbs accept both a direct object reflexive clitic (304a) and a possessive object reflexive clitic (304b), the former foregrounding the process–whole relation (i.e. the individual who takes part in the process), the latter, the process–part relation (i.e. the individual's body-part affected in the process).

(304) a. El$_i$ se$_i$ șterge pe picioare
he CL.REFL.ACC.3SG wipes on feet
'He is wiping his feet'

b. El$_i$ își$_i$ sterge picioarele
he CL.REFL.DAT.3SG wipes feet.DET
'He is wiping his feet'

With symmetrical predications, reflexives in the two designated slots display two readings, a reflexive one ('themselves') and a reciprocal one ('each other') (305a,b) (§3.4.3).

(305) a. Maria$_i$ și Ana$_j$ se$_{i+j}$ privesc în oglindă
Maria and Ana CL.REFL.ACC.3PL look in mirror
'Maria and Ana are looking at themselves / at each other in the mirror'

b. Ion$_i$ și Gheorghe$_j$ își$_{i+j}$ cumpără cadouri
Ion and Gheorghe CL.REFL.DAT.3PL buy presents
'Ion and Gheorghe are buying presents for themselves / to each other'

For reflexive clitic doubling, see §3.4.2.5.

3.4.2.1.2 Strong reflexive forms occur as complements of prepositions (306a–d), nouns (306e), adjectives and participles (306f), or adverbs (306g), under coreferentiality with the sentential subject. The accusative / dative case of the strong reflexive is assigned by the preposition, the nominal, or the participial adjective, respectively.

3.4 Constructions involving overall clausal structure   177

(306) a. Ion$_i$ contează   numai   pe   [sine$_i$]
        Ion   relies   only   on   self.ACC
        'Ion relies only on himself'

    b. Ion$_i$ a   reușit   doar   datorită   [sieși$_i$]
        Ion   has   succeeded only   thanks to   self.DAT
        'Ion succeeded thanks to only himself'

    c. Ion$_i$ este   încrezător   în   [sine$_i$]
        Ion   is   confident   in   self.ACC
        'Ion is self-confident'

    d. Ion$_i$ și$_i$-a   pierdut   încrederea   în   [sine$_i$]
        Ion   CL.REFL.DAT.3SG=has   lost   confidence.DEF in   self.ACC
        'Ion lost his self-confidence'

    e. Ion$_i$ a   devenit   dușman   [sieși$_i$]
        Ion   has   become   enemy   self.DAT
        'Ion became his own enemy'

    f. Maria$_i$ are   zilnic   două   ore   rezervate   [sieși$_i$]
        Maria   has   daily   two   hours   reserved   self.DAT
        'Maria has two hours reserved for herself daily'

    g. Ion$_i$ nu   se   mai   recunoștea,
        Ion   not   CL.REFL.ACC.3SG   anymore   recognize.IMPERF.3SG,
        pro$_i$ se$_i$ simțea   departe   de   sine
               CL.REFL.ACC.3SG feel.IMPERF.3SG   far   of   self.ACC
        'Ion did not recognize himself anymore, he felt far from himself'

Although the reflexive construction is the preferred option, a personal pronoun construction is also available, which is ambiguous between a reflexive and a non-reflexive reading, as shown in (307a,b), which transcribe (306a,b). For emphasis, the reflexive / personal pronoun co-occurs with the emphatic intensifier as in (307c,d).

(307) a. Ion$_i$ contează   numai   pe   el$_{i//j}$
        Ion   relies   only   on   him
        'Ion relies only on him / himself'

    b. Ion$_i$ a   reușit   doar   datorită   lui$_{i//j}$
        Ion   has   succeeded   only   thanks   him.DAT
        'Ion succeeded thanks only to him / himself'

    c. Ion$_i$ contează   numai   pe   el$_i$ /   sine$_i$ însuși$_i$
        Ion   relies   only   on   him /   self.ACC   himself.ACC
        'Ion relies only on him / himself'

    d. Ion$_i$ a   reușit   doar   datorită   lui$_i$ /   sieși$_i$ /   lui   însuși$_i$
        Ion   has   succeeded   only   thanks to   him.DAT   self.DAT   lui.DAT himself.DAT
        'Ion succeeded thanks only to himself'

3.4.2.1.3 Most constructions are monoreflexive, as exemplified above. Direflexive constructions are also possible, with an obligatory accusative reflexive clitic in the direct object slot and a strong reflexive in the indirect or in the prepositional object slot (308a–b).

(308) a. El$_i$ s$_i$-a dezvăluit sieși$_i$
he CL.REFL.ACC.3SG=has revealed self.DAT
'He revealed himself to himself'
b. El$_i$ se$_i$ apără de sine$_i$
he CL.REFL.ACC.3SG defends from self.ACC
'He defends himself from himself'

3.4.2.2 Constructions with reflexive lexical formatives

There is a large number of verbs with an accusative (309a) and a smaller number of verbs with a dative (309b) reflexive clitic as an obligatory formative.

(309) a. a se gândi 'think', a se mândri 'be proud of oneself', a se holba 'stare'
b. a-și imagina 'imagine', a-și da seama 'realize'

C In the Romance area, only Romanian has two subclasses of reflexive verbs: accusative and dative reflexives (Niculescu 1965: 31).

The reflexive formative obligatorily marks the verb in all its uses (310a), distinguishes homonymous lexical units (310b), or conveys a register opposition (310c). A few reflexive verbs are inherent impersonals (310d).

(310) a. a se holba / *holba 'stare', a se teme / *teme 'be afraid of'
b. a se aștepta / aștepta 'expect / wait for', a se uita / uita 'look / forget', a se plânge / plânge 'complain / cry', a se duce / duce 'go / carry', a-și da seama / da seama 'realize / account for'
c. (standard) râde 'laugh', divorța 'divorce' / (colloquial, low register) a se râde, a se divorța; (general) a se coagula 'coagulate' / (professional jargon) coagula 'coagulate'
d. a se cuveni / *a cuveni 'ought'

3.4.2.3 Constructions with reflexive lexico-grammatical formatives

Accusative reflexive clitics frequently function as lexico-grammatical formatives, marking a grammatical opposition: (i) intransitive, reciprocal / transitive, agentive (311a); (ii) intransitive, reciprocal / transitive, causative (311b); (iii) intransitive, psych / transitive, causative (311c); (iv) intransitive, inaccusative / transitive, agentive (311d); (v) intransitive, causative / transitive, agentive (311e).

(311) a. a se asemăna cu / a asemăna pe cineva$_i$ cu cineva$_j$ ('resemble / compare somebody$_i$ to somebody$_j$')
b. a se căsători cu cineva / a căsători pe cineva$_i$ cu cineva$_j$ ('get married / marry somebody$_i$ to somebody$_j$'); a se alia cu cineva / a alia pe cineva$_i$ cu cineva$_j$ ('ally oneself with / to ally somebody$_i$ with somebody$_j$')
c. a se supăra / a supăra pe cineva cu ceva ('get angry / make someone angry about something'); a se plictisi de / a plictisi pe cineva cu ceva ('get bored / bore somebody with something')
d. ușa s-a deschis / el a deschis ușa ('the door opened / he opened the door'), motorul s-a oprit / el a oprit motorul ('the engine stopped / he stopped the engine')
e. a se vaccina / a vaccina pe cineva ('get vaccinated / vaccinate someone'); a se tunde / a tunde pe cineva ('cut one's hair / cut somebody's hair')

3.4.2.4 Constructions with reflexive grammatical formatives

Accusative reflexive clitics also function as grammatical formatives in passive and impersonal constructions.

Romanian displays two types of passive constructions, the canonical passive with *be* and the *se*-passive (312), showing pragmatic and semantic differences (§3.4.1).

(312) S-a   hotărât   (de către autoritățile   nipone)   închiderea
       CL.REFL.PASS=has   decided   (by   authorities.DEF Japanese) closing
       centralei   nucleare
       station.DEF.GEN   nuclear
       'The Japanese authorities decided to shut down the nuclear power station'

There are two types of impersonal constructions marked by the accusative clitic *se*: inherent impersonals, with a reflexive lexical formative (§3.4.2.2) and impersonals derived from personal intransitive constructions (313a) or with a non-overt direct object (313b) (§3.4.1).

(313) a. Se   vorbește   mult   aici
          CL.REFL.IMPERS   speaks   much   here
          'They speak a lot here'
       b. Se   mănâncă   bine   în   acest   restaurant
          CL.REFL.IMPERS   eats   well   in   this   restaurant
          'One eats well in this restaurant'

3.4.2.5 Reflexive doubling

Reflexive clitics in direct and indirect object positions admit accusative and dative strong reflexives doubling for emphasis or contrast (314a,b). Possessive / genitive doubling of reflexive clitics in possessive object slots can occur for contrast (314c).

(314) a. Ion se   cunoaște   pe   sine   foarte   bine
          Ion CL.REFL.ACC.3SG   knows   PE   self.ACC   very   well
          'Ion knows himself very well'
       b. Ion își   reproșează doar șieși   eșecul
          Ion CL.REFL.DAT.3SG   blames   only self.DAT   failure.DEF
          'Ion blames only himself for the failure'
       c. Ion își   caută   cărțile   lui
          Ion CL.REFL.DAT.3SG   looks for   books.DEF   his(GEN)
          'Ion is looking for his books'

3.4.3 Reciprocal constructions

Of the devices available crosslinguistically to mark reciprocal meaning (Nedjalkov 2007), Romanian resorts to five: (i) the lexical; (ii) the iconic verbal; (iii) the reflexive clitic; (iv) the reciprocal pronoun; and (v) redundancy, with both a reflexive clitic and a reciprocal pronoun (Pană Dindelegan 1999: 97–100, 2008d: 159–67; Vasilescu 2007a: 221–7).

H   Classical and post-classical Latin used the same five strategies (Nedjalkov 2007: 602–4), which were transmitted to old Romanian.

C Romance languages express the reciprocal meaning via a reflexive clitic or a reciprocal pronoun composed of two indefinite pronouns (Ekkehard and Kokutani 2006: 271–302).

All of the five reciprocal devices occur in gerund and infinitival clauses as well, triggering constituent movements, ellipsis, and control phenomena predicted by non-finite forms construction rules.

3.4.3.1 Lexical reciprocals

Some verbs are inherent reciprocals (315–316). The arguments of symmetric predication occur in subject and direct object positions, respectively (315a) or as plural / coordinated subjects (315b). The two syntactic types correlate with a difference of perspective: a subject to object perspective vs. an equidistant perspective. Some inherently reciprocal verbs are obligatorily marked by the reflexive formative, with no semantic input to the reciprocal relation (316a,b).

(315) a. Ion / el / pro seamănă   cu   Maria / ea
        Ion / he   resembles   with   Maria / her.ACC
        'Ion / he resembles Maria / her'

   b. Ion și   Maria / ei   seamănă
      Ion and   Maria / they   resemble'
      'Ion and Mary / they resemble each other'

(316) a. Ion se   căsătorește cu   Maria
        Ion CL.REFL.ACC.3SG   marries   with   Maria
        'Ion marries Maria'

   b. Ion și   Maria / Ei / pro se   căsătoresc
      Ion and Maria   they   CL.REFL.ACC.3PL   marry
      'Ion and Maria / They are getting married'

3.4.3.2 Iconic reciprocals

Reciprocal structures with two coordinated symmetrical sentences (the same verb and the same two nominals in symmetrical positions) are a possible but infrequent option, alternatively foregrounding each of the actors taking part in the event (317a) or highlighting minimal differences between adjuncts (317b,c). The second clause can be reduced to an adverbial anaphor (317d).

(317) a. Ion salută pe   Gheorghe și   Gheorghe salută pe   Ion
        Ion greets PE   Gheorghe and   Gheorghe greets PE   Ion
        'Ion is greeting Gheorghe and Gheorghe is greeting Ion'

   b. Maria   îi   face   cadouri   Anei,   iar   Ana,   la
      Maria   CL.DAT.3SG   makes   presents   Ana.DAT   and   Ana   at
      rândul ei,   îi   face   cadouri   Mariei
      turn   her(GEN)   CL.DAT.3SG   makes   presents   Maria.DAT
      'Maria gives Ana presents, and Ana, in her turn, gives Maria presents'

c. Părinții   se   bazează   uneori   pe   copii,   dar
   parents   CL.REFL.ACC.3PL rely   sometimes   PE   children but
   copiii.DEF   se   bazează   mereu   pe   părinți
   children   CL.REFL.ACC.3PL rely   always   PE   parents
   'Parents sometimes rely on their children, but children always rely on their parents'

d. Ion salută pe Gheorghe și   invers /   viceversa
   Ion greets   PE Gheorghe and the other way round viceversa
   'Ion is greeting Gheorghe and the other way round / and viceversa'

3.4.3.3 *The reflexive clitic device*

Most often, Romanian resorts to the accusative / dative clitic device. The clitic is uninflected for φ-features (agreement features) and functions as a syntactic anaphor. The accusative clitic occurs whenever the arguments alternatively and symmetrically fill the subject and the direct object slots (318a–b); the dative clitic occurs whenever the arguments alternatively and symmetrically fill the subject and indirect (319a,b) or possessive object (320a,b) slots. The (a) structures show reciprocity between actors presented individually, while the (b) structures show reciprocity in a group.

(318) a. Ion$_i$ și   Gheorghe$_j$ se$_{i+j}$ privesc
        Ion   and   Gheorghe   CL.REFL.ACC.3PL look
        'Ion and Gheorghe are looking at each other'

      b. Ei$_{i+j}$ / pro$_{i+j}$ se$_{i+j}$ privesc
         They   CL.REFL.ACC.3PL look
         'They are looking at each other'

(319) a. Ana$_i$ și   Maria$_j$ își$_{i+j}$ cumpără   cadouri
        Ana   and   Maria   CL.REFL.DAT.3PL   buy   presents
        'Ana and Maria are buying each other presents'

      b. Ele$_{i+j}$ / pro$_{i+j}$ își$_{i+j}$ cumpără   cadouri
         They   CL.REFL.DAT.3PL   buy   presents
         'They are buying each other presents'

(320) a. Ion$_i$ și   Gheorghe$_j$ își$_{i+j}$ citesc   cărțile
        Ion   and   Gheorghe   CL.REFL.DAT.3PL   read   books.DEF
        'Ion and Gheorghe are reading each other's books / the books to each other'

      b. Ei$_{i+j}$ / pro$_{i+j}$ își$_{i+j}$ citesc   cărțile
         They   CL.REFL.DAT.3PL   read   books.DEF
         'They are reading each other's books / the books to each other'

Reciprocity within the group of actors encoded by the subject is implicit, overlapping with the reflexive relation and inferable from the context. Consequently, these structures are ambiguous between a purely reflexive reading ('themselves') and a mixed reflexive–reciprocal reading ('themselves and each other'), contextually disambiguated.

Some verbs with a double syntactic status, that is, transitive and intransitive (*saluta / a se saluta cu*, 'to greet somebody / to greet with somebody') enter two types of reciprocal structures: one with a reflexive-reciprocal clitic filling the direct object slot (321a) and another lexical reciprocal with the reflexive clitic as a formative (321b).

(321) a. Ion$_i$ şi   Gheorghe$_j$ / Ei$_{i+j}$ / pro$_{i+j}$ se$_{i+j}$ saluta
       Ion   and Gheorghe   they   CL.REFL.ACC.3PL greet
       'Ion and Gheorghe / They are greeting each other'

b. Ion / El$_i$ / pro$_i$ se   saluta   cu   Maria / ea$_j$
   Ion   they   CL.REFL.ACC.3SG greet   with Maria   her
   'Ion / He is greeting Maria / her'

3.4.3.4 The reciprocal pronoun device

The obligatory reciprocal pronoun device (*unul... altul*) occurs when the actors of a symmetrical predication fill the slots of the subject and the obligatory prepositional object, respectively (322). For synonyms of *unul... altul* and their selection see §6.5. In some of these reciprocal constructions, the prepositional verb is inherently reflexive (*a se baza pe* 'rely on', 322a), while in others the prepositional verb is non-reflexive (*a avea încredere în* 'trust', 322b). The reciprocal pronoun device is not licensed in genitive / possessive phrases (322c), which, instead, pick up the reflexive possessive dative device (322d) (§3.4.3.3).

(322) a. Ion$_i$ şi   Gheorghe$_j$ / Ei$_{i+j}$ se   bazează [unul pe   altul]$_{i+j}$
       Ion   and Gheorghe   they CL.REFL.ACC.3PL rely   one   on   another
       'Ion and Gheorghe / They rely on each other'

b. Noi avem încredere [unul în   altul]$_{i+j}$
   we   have trust   one   in   another
   'We trust each other'

c. *Ei   admiră casa   unul altuia
    they admire house.DEF one   another.DAT

d. Ei   îşi   admiră casa   unul altuia
   they CL.REFL.DAT.3PL admire house.DEF one   another.DAT
   'They admire each other's house'

3.4.3.5 The redundant device

A redundant device, with a reflexive clitic and a reciprocal pronoun, is also available, either for disambiguation when a reflexive reading is also possible (323a), or for emphasis, by rendering the action / process sequentially (323b). It is also used in structures with a copula and a predicative adjective / adverb (324a,b).

(323) a. Pisicile$_{i+j}$ se$_{i+}$ spală [una pe alta]$_{i+j}$
       cats.DEF   CL.REFL.ACC.3PL wash   one   PE another
       'The cats are washing each other'

b. Băieţii$_{i+j}$ se$_{i+j}$ saluta [unul pe altul]$_{i+j}$
   boys.DEF   CL.REFL.ACC.3PL greet   each   PE another
   'The boys are greeting each other'

(324) a. Băieţii$_{i+j}$ îşi$_{i+j}$ sunt   datori   [unul celuilalt]$_{i+j}$
       boys.DEF   CL.REFL.DAT.3PL are   indebted one   the-other.DAT
       'The boys are indebted to each other'

b. Băieţii$_{i+j}$ îşi$_{i+j}$ sunt alături [unul altuia]$_{i+j}$
   boys.DEF   CL.REFL.DAT.3PL are   next   one   another.DAT
   'The boys are standing by each other'

3.4.4 The possessive dative structure. The possessive object

3.4.4.1 Characteristics

The possessive dative is a widespread construction in Romanian, very frequently used in all the registers of the language to express a relationship of possession.

(i) The possessor is encoded as a dative clitic which takes the verbal complex as its morphophonological support; the DP which expresses the possessee can occupy various syntactic positions in the sentence.
(ii) The occurrence of the dative possessive clitic requires two other components to be expressed in the clause: its verbal host and the DP which encodes the possessed entity.

(325) Îți$_{possessor}$ cunosc sora$_{possessee}$
CL.DAT.2SG (I)know sister.DEF.ACC
'I know your sister'

(iii) The paradigm of the possessive dative includes the clitic forms of the personal and of the reflexive pronoun, which surface in the same position with regard to the verbal host as other dative clitics (§6.1.3).
(iv) The possessive dative has a free and a conjunct clitic form, like the indirect object clitic (§3.2.3).
(v) It has a specific syntactic function in the sentence, that is, it is the possessive object (§3.4.4.8).
(vi) Clitic climbing is possible in the possessive dative construction: the clitic can raise from the IP projected by the head verb and cliticize onto the matrix verb. In (326), the verb *putea* 'can' intervenes between the clitic and its support.

(326) Maria și-ar putea rupe brațul
Maria CL.REFL.DAT.3SG=AUX.COND.3SG can.INF break.INF arm.DEF
'Maria could break her arm'

(vii) The possessive dative clitic can co-occur with another dative DP. This has to be a full argumental DP which is not coreferential with the possessive dative.

(327) Își$_i$ donează bunurile bisericii$_j$
CL.REFL.DAT.3SG donates goods.DEF.ACC church.DEF.DAT
'(S)he donates his / her goods to the church'

(viii) The adverbal possessive dative structure is blocked by the prepositional direct object (§3.2.1.3.2).

(328) Îmi întâlnesc (*pe) colegii
CL.REFL.DAT.1SG (I)meet PE colleagues.DEF.ACC
'I meet my colleagues'

(ix) The possessive dative clitic is in competition with the possessive adjective; the two structures are triggered by different semantic and pragmatic features.

3.4.4.2 The variety of possessive relations encoded by the possessive dative

A rich diversity of relationships of possession can be expressed by the possessive dative structure in Romanian. The full range of inalienably possessed objects occurs in the configuration: kinship terms (329a), body-parts (329b), parts of inanimate entities (expressing the part–whole relationship) (329c), garments worn by the possessor (329d), and behavioural / physical features of the possessor (329e). There are no restrictions on the referents of the two DPs which occur in configurations expressing a relationship of alienable possession: in (330a) the possessor is animate and the possessee, inanimate, in (330b) they are both animate, while in (330c) they are both inanimate.

(I) INALIENABLE POSSESSION

(329)   a. Îmi   pleacă   nepotul
            CL.DAT.1SG   leaves   nephew.DEF.NOM
            'My nephew is leaving'

    b. Maria   și-a   tuns   părul
        Maria   CL.REFL.DAT.3SG=has   cut.PPLE   hair.DEF.ACC
        'Maria cut her hair/ had her hair cut'

    c. Masa   nu   se   poate   folosi,   pentru că   i
        table.DEF   not   CL.REFL.ACC.3SG   can.3SG   use.INF   because   CL.DAT.3SG
        s-a   rupt   un   picior
        CL.REFL.ACC.3SG=has   broken   a   foot.NOM
        'The table can not be used because one foot [leg] has broken'

    d. Îmi   închei   cămașa
        CL.REFL.DAT.1SG   (I)button   shirt.DEF.ACC
        'I button up my shirt'

    e. Îți   admir   curajul
        CL.DAT.2SG   (I)admire   courage.DEF.ACC
        'I admire your courage'

(II) ALIENABLE POSSESSION

(330)   a. I-am   văzut   casa
            CL.DAT.3SG=(I)have   seen   house.DEF
            'I saw his house'

    b. I-am   vizitat   colegul
        CL.DAT.3SG=(I)have   visited   colleague.DEF
        'I visited his colleague'

    c. Am   trecut   pe lângă   mașină.   I-am   văzut   husele
        (I)have   passed   by   car   CL.DAT.3SG=(I)have   seen   covers.DEF
        cele   noi
        CEL.F.PL   new
        'I passed by the car. I saw its new seat covers'

The possessive dative clitic usually has the thematic role of Possessor alone, but it can also simultaneously express two roles (Possessor and Recipient / Goal (331a), Possessor and Source (331b), Possessor and Benefactive (331c), Possessor and Experiencer (331d)) (Van Langendonck and Van Belle 1998).

(331) a. Îți   dau   cartea   (ta)   înapoi
          CL.DAT.2SG (I)give   book.DEF.ACC your.F.SG   back
          'I give you your book back'

   b. Îmi vinde cărțile (mele)
      'He is selling my books'

   c. Ne repară televizorul pe care l-am cumpărat anul trecut
      'He is repairing the TV that we bought last year'

   d. Ochii îi surâd
      'His/her eyes are smiling'

3.4.4.3 *The verbal host*

Any semantic verb class can function as a host for the possessive dative clitic: a verb expressing an activity, an accomplishment, an achievement, or a state (Vendler's typology 1967).

(332) Fetița   îi   merge   de la   un   an   [Activity]
      girl.DEF.NOM   CL.DAT.3SG walks   from   one   year
      'His/her daughter has been walking since she was one year old'

(333) Firma   aceasta mi-a   decorat   casa   [Accomplishment]
      company this   CL.DAT.1SG=has   decorated   house.DEF.ACC
      'This company decorated my house'

(334) Mi-am terminat tema   [Achievement]
      'I have finished my homework'

(335) Copilul îmi stă în poală   [State]
      'The child sits in my lap'

Different syntactic classes of verbs can function as hosts for the possessive dative clitic. Some of its verbal hosts accept a dative complement and some do not.

If the verb assigns the dative case, two configurations are possible. If the dative complement has the thematic role Recipient or Experiencer, the structure admits only for one dative DP to be present (with clitic form), which will bring together the semantic roles of Possessor and Recipient or Experiencer (331a,c,d). If the verbal complex contains a Source DP, then the structure admits two dative DPs, the first one, the possessive dative clitic, bringing together the semantic roles Possessor and Source, and the second one being the Goal ((327), rewritten as (336)).

(336) Își$_{Possessor\ and\ Source}$ donează bunurile **bisericii**$_{Goal}$
      '(S)he donates his / her goods to the church'

If the verb does not take a dative complement, there are no syntactic restrictions on the occurrence of the possessive dative; it can be used in structures which contain both transitive (333) and intransitive verbs (335). The verbal projection can contain an indirect object (336), a prepositional object (347b), an adverbial (335), and a subjective predicative complement (340).

Avea 'have' and *fi* 'be' can both host a dative possessive clitic.

- The verb ***avea*** accepts a reflexive possessive dative in Romanian, in a configuration in which the accusative DP is obligatorily definite and is followed by a secondary predicate. Therefore, the relationship of possession is expressed twice.

186   3 *The Structure of Root Clauses*

(337) Îmi   am   [copiii   departe]
       CL.REFL.DAT.1SG (I)have   children.DEF.ACC   far
       'My children are far away'

- The verb *fi* can also be the host of a possessive dative clitic. The structure continues the Latin SUM PRO HABEO construction, in which the verb *be* could replace *have* to express possession. The fact that the possessee is a bare noun, and not a full DP, is characteristic of these configurations:

(338) Mi-e   foame
       CL.DAT.1SG=is   hunger.NOM
       'I am hungry'

The structure under (338) has an existential reading ('my hunger exists'); the choice of possessed entities is semantically restricted to abstract nouns which refer to a physical or mental state. The postverbal subject NP does not have determiners and has limited combinatorial possibilities. In an alternative structure, the possessee NP can accept an indefinite article, being recategorized as a kind-noun. The presence of the indefinite article is driven by the superlative (339).

(339) Mi-e   o   foame   de   lup!
       CL.DAT.1SG=is   a   hunger.NOM   of   wolf
       'I am terribly hungry'

In another SUM PRO HABEO configuration, the NP that encodes the possessed entity has to be a [+animate] inherently relational bare noun, such as a kinship term, or a noun of the series *prieten* 'friend', *şef* 'boss', *coleg* 'colleague', etc. (340) (§5.2.5). The property-denoting nature of the possessee NP is a consequence of the fact that it occupies the syntactic position of the subjective predicative complement.

(340) Ioana îmi   este   cumnată
       Ioana CL.DAT.1SG   is   sister-in-law
       'Ioana is my sister-in-law'

The verb *fi* also occurs in a configuration like (341), where the possessee *mâinile* 'the hands' takes a determiner and functions as the subject of the sentence.

(341) Mâinile   îmi   sunt   calde
       hands.DEF.NOM   CL.DAT.1SG   are.3PL warm
       'My hands are warm'

3.4.4.4 Optional vs. obligatory possessive dative clitic

Generally, the Romanian possessive dative clitic is optional, being an adjunct to the IP (328); however, in some configurations, it is an obligatory constituent of the IP. The following configurations contain a non-omissible possessive dative:

- the SUM PRO HABEO structures (338), (339);
- configurations with a reflexive dative clitic, in which the possessed entity is a body-part and the host of the clitic is a transitive verb expressing an achievement or an accomplishment ((342a), and (329b), rewritten as (342b));

(342) a. Maria *(și)-a rupt brațul / un braț
Maria CL.REFL.DAT.3SG=has broken arm.DEF an arm
'Maria broke her arm / an arm'

b. Ea *(Și)-a tuns părul
she CL.REFL.DAT.3SG=has cut hair.DEF
'She cut her hair / had her hair cut'

- idiomatic expressions in which the dative clitic is an obligatory constituent:

(343) Nu-și crede ochilor
not=CL.REFL.DAT.3SG believe.3SG eyes.DEF.DAT
'(S)he does not believe his / her eyes'

3.4.4.5 Doubling

The Romanian possessive dative allows the doubling of the clitic by a fully-fledged DP, which can either be assigned the dative case by the verb or the genitive case by the DP encoding the possessee. Therefore, the possessive dative clitic is co-indexed either with a full genitive or with a dative DP.

In the following configurations the possessive dative can only be doubled by a dative DP:

(344) a. Lui$_i$ îi$_i$ trec multe lucruri prin cap
him.DAT CL.DAT.3SG pass many things.NOM through head
'Many things go through his mind'

b. Lui Mihai$_i$ i$_i$-a căzut părul
LUI.DAT Mihai CL.DAT.3SG=has fallen hair.DEF.NOM
'Mihai's hair has fallen out'

H In old Romanian, a configuration similar to (344b), in which the possessee occupies the position of subject, also admitted doubling by a genitive DP.

(345) vădzându că-i s-au svârșit feciorul ei
seeing that=CL.DAT.3SG CL.REFL.ACC.3SG=has died son.DEF.NOM her.GEN
(*Documenta*)
'seeing that her son had died'

The occurrence of a modifier of the possessee DP renders the genitive doubling structure acceptable.

(346) Multe îi$_i$ trec prin capul lui$_i$ cel bolnav
Many.F.PL CL.DAT.3SG pass.3PL through head.DEF his.GEN CEL sick
'Many things pass through his sick mind'

In a number of configurations, only a genitive DP can double the possessive dative clitic.

(347) a. Și$_i$-au pus capăt propriei lor$_i$ vieți
CL.REFL.DAT.3PL=(they)have put end own.DEF.DAT their life.DAT
'They ended their lives'

b. Îmi$_i$ văd de treburile mele$_i$
CL.REFL.DAT.1SG (I)see of business.PL my.F.PL
'I mind my own business'

H In old Romanian, the adverbal possessive dative clitic could also be doubled by an adnominal possessive dative clitic.

(348) că-ş va lăsa împărăteasa-ş
that=CL.REFL.DAT.3SG AUX.FUT.3SG leave.INF empress.DEF=CL.REFL.DAT.3SG
în Iaşi (Neculce)
in Iaşi
'that he will leave his empress in Iaşi'

There are structures which do not admit any type of doubling. They encode a relationship of inalienable possession and the possessee DP is a direct object (349a,b).

(349) a. Şi$_i$-a rupt *(sieşi$_i$) piciorul *(său$_i$)
CL.REFL.DAT.3SG=has broken self.DAT leg.DEF his.M.SG

b. Îi vizitează *(lui) cumnata *(lui)
CL.DAT.3SG visits him.DAT sister-in-law.DEF his.M.SG

H In old Romanian, doubling of a dative possessive encoding a relationship of inalienable possession was possible even if the possessee DP was the direct object (Pană Dindelegan 2009a).

(350) Astăzi îş dă preasfânt sufletul ei în
Today CL.REFL.DAT.3SG gives holy soul.DEF her.GEN in
mâinile fiiului ei (Antim)
hands.DEF son.DEF.GEN her.GEN
'Today she gives up her most holy soul into the hands of her son'

3.4.4.6 The possessee DP

The DP which expresses the possesse is entity-denoting. This translates into the occurrence of the definite or indefinite article with entity-denoting reading (342a).

A property-denoting possessee NP appears in the SUM PRO HABEO structures (338) and (340), being triggered by its predicative position.

Romanian shows no restrictions concerning the syntactic positions that can be occupied by the possessee DP/NP. It can have any function in the sentence, such as direct object (325), subject (329a), adverbial (335), and to a lesser extent indirect object (347a), prepositional object (347b), or predicative (340).

3.4.4.7 Possessive dative clitic vs. possessive adjective / genitive DP

The dative pronominal clitic with a verbal host is the preferred marker of possession in Romanian. The possessive dative is chosen over the possessive adjective in a number of configurations which meet certain pragmatic, semantic, and syntactic conditions (Niculescu 2008a: 208).

The possessive dative clitic is usually the topic of the sentence (351). Topicality is one of the factors which lead to the use of the possessive dative instead of the genitive / possessive adjective structure. Both the dative case and the clitic pronouns occupy a high position in a hierarchy that predicts which nominal element is more likely to become the sentence topic (Manoliu-Manea 1996); therefore, the possessive dative is more likely to take on the role of topic than the genitive / possessive adjective DP.

There are semantic conditions on each of the three constituents of the possessive dative structure which trigger its use. The possessor is encoded as a dative clitic whenever it bears the feature [+affected] (Lamiroy and Delbecque 1998; Salvi 2011: 342). Taking into account the wide range of contexts in which the dative possessive occurs in Romanian (including configurations with the stative verb *fi* 'be' or with DPs encoding an inanimate possessor and possessed entity), the feature [+affected] has to be interpreted in a very broad sense; it has to include any type of effect that an accomplishment or activity can have on the possessor (Niculescu 2008a: 165).

Next to this, the possessive dative structure is triggered by an inanimate possessee, usually a body-part. The verb usually denotes an achievement (326), but it can also denote a state; in this case, it is frequently a verb of perception (330a).

There is also one syntactic condition which needs to be met in order for the possessive dative clitic to be preferred over the possessive adjective: the DP which encodes the possessed entity should have the syntactic function of direct object.

In a context such as (351a), the possessive dative is the unmarked structure, while the genitive in (351b) is emphatic, placing the possessor DP in focus.

(351) a. I-am sărutat mâna
'I kissed her hand'

b. Am sărutat mâna EI
'I kissed HER hand'

H In old Romanian, the possessive adjective was used more frequently in configurations in which an adverbal possessive dative is preferred in modern Romanian (Pană Dindelegan 2009a). The shift from marking the relationship of possession in Romanian at the level of the DP to the level of the IP is to be included in the more general shift from a dependent-marking to a head-marking type of language, which characterizes the evolution from Latin to Romance (Ledgeway 2011: 434).

Certain verbs which take a dative clitic with the thematic role Experiencer do not allow for the clitic to also be interpreted as a possessive, therefore the possessor can be encoded only adnominally (*a-i conveni* 'suit', *a-i plăcea* 'like', *a i se urî de* 'get fed up'). Example (352a) cannot be interpreted as having the meaning of (352b).

(352) a. Îmi place copilul
CL.DAT.1SG likes child.DEF
'I like the child'

b. Îmi place copilul meu
CL.DAT.1SG likes child.DEF my.M.SG
'I like my child'

3.4.4.8 The possessive object

The possessive dative clitic has its own syntactic function in the sentence, that of possessive object. A number of morphosyntactic and semantic characteristics differentiate this function from the indirect object:

- The possessive object is an adjunct in the clause and its thematic role, Possessor, is assigned by the DP possessee, while the indirect object is an argument of the verb and receives the dative case and its thematic role from it.

- The possessive object always occurs in the verb phrase, while an indirect object can occur in an adjectival or adverbial phrase.
- As far as its substitution class is concerned, the possessive object can only take the morphological form of a pronominal clitic, while the indirect object can also be a fully-fledged DP.

H The dative possessive structure is attested from the earliest Romanian texts with the whole range of configurations.

C The adverbal possessive dative (pronominal clitic attached enclitically to the verb) also occurs in Aromanian:

(353) vindică-ńi   sufletlu   ańeu   (in Capidan 1932: 408)
      (you)cure=CL.DAT.1SG soul.DEF   my.M.SG
      'cure my soul'

The possessive dative with a verbal host is a general Romance structure inherited from Latin (Niculescu and Renzi 1991; Salvi 2011: 342). The use of the dative clitic encoding the possessor is not equally spread among Romance languages; for example, in French it is limited to the expression of inalienable possession, with the possessee being a body-part (Reinheimer and Tasmowski 2005: 118). Also, Italian has a rather restricted use of the possessive dative, allowing few perception and emotion verbs as hosts for the clitic (Lamiroy and Delbecque 1998). Spanish uses the possessive dative in a very wide range of configurations. However, Spanish, as opposed to Romanian, does not accept certain stative verbs such as *conocer* 'know' or *ser* 'be' in the possessive dative structure (Dumitrescu 1990a).

Romanian is the only Romance language which preserved the Latin SUM PRO HABEO structure (see Ernout and Thomas 1959: 73).

The widespread use of the adverbal possessive dative in Romanian could be a Balkan Sprachbund feature, since the structure also occurs in Bulgarian, Macedonian, and Serbo-Croat (Pancheva 2004).

Romanian, like the other Romance languages, allows the adverbal dative clitic to remain unrealized with certain directional and locative verbs, in configurations which express a relationship of inalienable possession (*coborî*, *lăsa* 'lower', *pune* 'put', *ridica* 'lift', *ţine* 'hold' etc.) (§ 5.3.3.5).

(354) Ion   (îşi)   coboară   privirea
      Ion   CL.REFL.DAT.3SG lowers   look.DEF
      'Ion looks down'

Unlike other Romance languages, in structures in which a transitive verb expresses an activity, the possessor is the sentence topic and the possessee denotes a body-part, Romanian prefers a configuration with a possessive accusative clitic and a prepositional phrase which encodes the body-part (355a), over a dative possessive configuration (355b) (Manoliu-Manea 1996). In structure (355a) the body-part / process relation is placed in the background, while in (355b), the whole / process relation is placed in the foreground.

(355) a. Mă   spăl   pe   mâini
         CL.REFL.ACC.1SG   (I)wash   PE   hands
      b. Îmi   spăl   mâinile
         CL.REFL.DAT.1SG   (I)wash   hands.DEF
         'I wash my hands'

3.5 COMPLEX PREDICATES

3.5.1 Definition

The complex predicate is a structure made up of two verbs that function as one unit from a syntactic and semantic point of view. The argument structure of the two verbs is characterized by argument composition (Monachesi 1998: 114; 1999: 105), the result of which is a monoclausal verbal complex (Rizzi 1982: 36; Baker and Harvey 2010: 13). The matrix predicate (V1) is a (semi)auxiliary which carries the inflection and which inherits the arguments of the embedded verb (V2)—a non-finite form. Two Romanian structures correspond to this definition; these are, on a descending scale of grammaticalization, the complex predicates with obligatory subject control and obligatory clitic climbing (§3.5.2) and the complex predicates with subject raising and agreement (§3.5.3). The fact that in Romanian the subjunctive (behaving as a non-finite form, see §§4.1.4, 2.2.2.2) replaced the infinitive in many contexts allows for certain subjunctive structures whose behaviour is similar to the complex predicate to be discussed here (§3.5.4).

3.5.2 Complex predicates with obligatory subject control and obligatory clitic climbing

The complex predicate can be identified on the basis of syntactic tests, developed by Guțu (1956), Rizzi (1982), Monachesi (1998), Abeillé and Godard (2003) among others:

- the identity of the subject of the two verbs (obligatory control);
- raising of the argumental clitics of V2 to V1;
- the impossibility for V2 to take the negation marker; negation adjoins to V1, similarly to pronominal clitics.

Romanian complex verbs that pass these three tests contain a mood or tense auxiliary (compound past, perfect conditional, perfect subjunctive, future), a modal or aspectual verb plus a participle, a bare infinitive or a *de*-supine; there are differences of syntactic behaviour between these constructions.

3.5.2.1 Structures containing a mood and tense auxiliary plus a participle / bare-infinitive

The structures containing a mood and tense auxiliary (*fi* 'be', *avea* 'have', *vrea* 'want') plus a participle / bare-infinitive are considered completely grammaticalized periphrastic verb forms, with specific modal and temporal values (§2.2.1.2). Since auxiliary verbs have no argument structure, we can talk sooner of 'inheriting' the arguments from the embedded verb, rather than of argument composition.

The unique subject and the adjunction of the clitics and negation to the auxiliary allow for the structures containing a participle (356–359) or an infinitive (360–361) to be syntactically interpreted as complex predicates:

(356) Am   mâncat   un   măr   [compound past]
      (I)have   eaten   an   apple
      'I ate an apple'
      L-am   mâncat
      CL.ACC.M.3SG=(I)have   eaten
      'I ate it'
      Nu   l-am   mâncat
      not   CL.ACC.M.3SG=(I)have   eaten
      'I did not eat it'
      *L-am   **nu**   mâncat
      CL.ACC.M.3SG=(I)have   not   eaten

(357) **Nu**   l-aş   fi   mâncat   [perfect conditional]
      not   CL.ACC.M.3SG=AUX.COND.1SG   be.INF   eaten
      'I would not have eaten it'

(358) Să   **nu-l**   fi   mâncat   [perfect subjunctive]
      SĂ_SUBJ not=CL.ACC.M.3SG   be.INF   eaten

(359) **Nu-l**   voi   fi   mâncat   [perfect future]
      not=CL.ACC.M.3SG   AUX.FUT.1SG   be.INF   eaten
      'I shall not have eaten it'

(360) a. Voi   mânca   un   măr   [future]
         AUX.FUT.1SG   eat.INF   an   apple
         'I will eat an apple'
      b. Îl   voi   mânca
         CL.ACC.M.3SG   AUX.FUT.1SG   eat.INF
         'I will eat it'
      c. **Nu-l**   voi   mânca
         not=CL.ACC.M.3SG   AUX.FUT.1SG   eat.INF
         'I will not eat it'
      d. *Îl   voi   **nu** mânca
         CL.ACC.M.3SG AUX.FUT.1SG   not   eat.INF

(361) **Nu**   l-aş   mânca   [present conditional]
      not   CL.ACC.M.3SG=AUX.COND.1SG   eat.INF
      'I would not eat it'

C   In modern Romanian, the degree of cohesion between the auxiliary and the embedded verb is high; only monosyllabic adverbial clitics can intervene between them:
    (362) l-am   **mai**   văzut /   îl   voi   **mai**   vedea
          CL.ACC.M.3SG=(I)have   more   seen   CL.ACC.M.3SG   AUX.FUT.1SG   more   see.INF
          'I have seen it before'   'I will see him again'
    This fact, as well as the existence of a complex clitic system, sets Romanian apart from the other Romance languages and brings it closer to south-Slavic languages, that is, Bulgarian and Macedonian (Monachesi 1999: 99–100, 2005: 4–5, 158).
    The participle which enters the complex predicate / periphrastic verb forms is invariable in Romanian, as in Spanish (§4.4.3.2.1). In Italian and French, however, clitic climbing leads to the agreement of the participle, a supplementary mark of group cohesion (Roberts 2010: 76):

(363) a. Fr. Je l'ai peinte, la maison
I CL.ACC.F.3SG=have painted.F.SG the house
b. It. L'ho dipinta, la casa
CL.ACC.F.3SG=(I)have painted.F.SG the house

H The possibilities of dislocation were more varied in old Romanian, which suggests that the structures were not fully grammaticalized:

(364) Biciul carele **au** Dumnezeu **aruncat** (Coresi)
whip.DEF which.M.SG has God thrown
'The whip which God threw'

(365) Deaca nu **va** omul pre ceastă lume, în viiața sa,
if not AUX.FUT.3SG man.DEF on this world in life his.F.SG
purta grije... (Coresi)
carry.INF care
'If man does not take care of..., in this world, in his lifetime'

Contrary to the future with *vrea* 'want' (360), the futures with *o să* (Abeillé and Godard 2003: 126) and with *am să* (§2.2.1.2.2) do not pass the complex predicate tests, as the subjunctive which is present in their structure blocks clitic climbing:

(366) o să îl vedem
O SĂ_SUBJ CL.ACC.M.3SG see.1PL
'we shall see him'
*o îl să vedem
O CL.ACC.M.3SG SĂ_SUBJ see.SUBJ.1PL

(367) am să îl văd
(I)have SĂ_SUBJ CL.ACC.M.3SG see.SUBJ.1SG
'I shall see him'
*am îl să văd
(I)have CL.ACC.M.3SG SĂ_SUBJ see.SUBJ.1SG

U The feminine accusative clitic *o* attaches enclitically to V2 if the host is a past participle (368a) or an infinitive (368b):

(368) a. am mâncat-o
(I)have eaten=CL.ACC.F.3SG
'I ate it'
aș fi mâncat-o
AUX.COND.1SG be eaten=CL.ACC.F.3SG
'I would have eaten it'
b. aș mânca-o
AUX.COND.1SG eat.INF=CL.ACC.F.3SG
'I would eat it'

This situation has been explained by phonological constraints (Monachesi 1999: 110–1, 2005: 169): if the auxiliary has an initial vowel, it cannot host the clitic *o* in contemporary Romanian (369). However, if the auxiliary has an initial consonant, the clitic *o* can be either hosted by V1 (369), or by V2 (370):

(369) o   voi   mânca
       CL.ACC.F.3SG AUX.FUT.1SG   eat.INF

(370) voi   mânca-o
       AUX.FUT.1SG   eat.INF=CL.ACC.F.3SG
       'I will eat it'

C The adjunction of the feminine clitic *o* to V2 instead of V1, in contexts where climbing is obligatory for the other clitics, is a property of Romanian, absent from the other Romance languages (Monachesi 1998: 115), except for some Piedmontese and Franco-Provençal varieties, in which the adjunction of the feminine clitic to the past participle in analytic tenses has been pointed out by Roberts (2010: 229).

Placing the pronominal clitic before the auxiliary brings Romanian closer to the other Romance languages, while placing the pronominal clitic after the auxiliary is a Balkan and Slavic feature (Monachesi 2005: 132).

H Until the 18th century (Stan 2012b), old Romanian did not display this phonological constraint on the placement of the clitic *o*, which behaved like the other clitics (*îl*, *le*), in that it could attach to an auxiliary with an initial vowel:

(371) o   **am**   auzit   (Cantacuzino)
       CL.ACC.F.3SG (I)have   heard
       'I heard it'

In the 16th–19th centuries, the oscillation in the positioning of the clitic is shown by its double realization, before and after the verbal complex (Stan 2012b):

(372) o   au   adus-o   (Neculce)
       CL.ACC.F.3SG (they)have   brought=CL.ACC.F.3SG
       'they brought it'

3.5.2.2 The structure putea 'can' plus bare-infinitive

The structure *putea* 'can' + bare-infinitive is the only complex predicate of the type modal verb + infinitive in Romanian (§§4.2.3.3, 13.5.2.1):

(373) a. Cartea   o   pot   citi   acum
         book.DEF.ACC   CL.ACC.F.3SG   (I)can   read.INF   now
         'I can read the book now'

      b. Ion   se   poate   aștepta   la   orice
         Ion.NOM   CL.REFL.ACC.3SG   can.3SG   expect.INF   at   anything
         < Ion   poate   a   se   aștepta   la   orice
         Ion.NOM   can.3SG   A$_{INF}$ CL.REFL.ACC.3SG expect.INF   at   anything
         'Ion can expect anything'

H Until the 19th century, *putea* 'can' occurred in parallel structures, with a bare-infinitive and with an *a*-infinitive, without clitic climbing:

(374) Să   poată   **a**   le   cuprinde   moșiile   (Neculce)
       SĂ$_{SUBJ}$ can.SUBJ.3SG   A$_{INF}$ CL.DAT.F.3PL   encompass.INF   properties.DEF
       'to be able to encompass their properties'

U In contemporary Romanian, *putea* 'can' rarely selects an *a*-infinitive, and only when the infinitive is under negation. Clitic climbing does not occur in this context (Jordan 2009: 60):

(375) El   putea   **a**   **nu-l**   primi
       he   can.IMPERF.3SG   A$_{INF}$ not=CL.ACC.M.3SG   receive.INF
       'He could refused it'

3.5 Complex predicates

The structure with *putea* 'can', less grammaticalized than the configuration with modal and tense auxiliaries in §3.5.2.1, has the following syntactic features:

(i) It accepts not only accusative clitic raising (373), but also dative clitic raising (376), including raising of the possessive dative (377), and even simultaneous raising of two clitics (378).

(376) Cartea **îți** poate folosi
book.DEF.NOM CL.DAT.2SG can.3SG use.INF
Cartea poate să îți folosească
book.DEF.NOM can.3SG SĂ_SUBJ CL.DAT.2SG use.SUBJ.3SG
'The book can be useful to you'

(377) Copilul **îți** poate fugi de acasă
child.DEF.NOM CL.DAT.2SG can.3SG run.INF from home
Copilul poate să îți fugă de acasă
child.DEF.NOM can. 3SG SĂ_SUBJ CL.DAT.2SG run.SUBJ.3SG from home
'Your child can run away from home'

(378) Cartea **ți-o** poate da
book.DEF.NOM CL.DAT.2SG=CL.ACC.F.3SG can.3SG give.INF
Cartea poate să ți-o dea
book.DEF.NOM can.3SG SĂ_SUBJ CL.DAT.2SG=CL.ACC.F.3SG give.SUBJ.3SG
'He can give the book to you'

(ii) Unlike the structures in §3.5.2.1 (379), the complex predicate with *putea* 'can' accepts the coordination of the embedded verbs (380) (Abeillé and Godard 2003: 152; Guțu 1956: 163–4; Monachesi 2005: 147):

(379) *Ion a **cumpărat** această carte și **citit** primul capitol
Ion has bought this book.ACC and read first.DEF chapter.ACC

(380) Ion poate **cumpăra** această carte și **citi** primul capitol
Ion can.3SG buy.INF this book.ACC and read.INF first.DEF chapter.ACC
'Ion can buy this book and read the first chapter'

(iii) Unlike the structures in §3.5.2.1 (381), it allows for the interposition of modal adverbs (382) (Abeillé and Godard 2003: 154; Monachesi 2005: 134, 208) and of the subject in this configuration (383) (Dobrovie-Sorin 1994: 50), but does not allow the interposition of monosyllabic adverbial clitics (384) (Monachesi 2005: 176):

(381) *Ion îl va **eventual** asculta
Ion.NOM CL.ACC.M.3.SG AUX.FUT.3SG maybe listen.INF

(382) Ion îl poate **eventual** asculta
Ion.NOM CL.ACC.M.3.SG can.IND.PRES.3SG maybe listen.INF
'Ion can maybe listen to him'

(383) Poate **Ion** veni mâine?
can.3SG Ion.NOM come.INF tomorrow
'Can Ion come tomorrow?'

(384) *Ion   îl   poate   **mai**   asculta
      Ion.NOM   CL.ACC.M.3.SG   can.3SG   more   listen.INF

   (iv) It generally accepts *se*-passivization (the direct object of V2 becomes the subject of V1) (Guţu 1956: 61–2):

(385) Cartea   **se**   **poate**   **citi**   de către   oricine   într-o   zi
      book.DEF.NOM   CL.REFL.PASS   can.3SG   read.INF   by   anyone   in=one   day
      'The book can be read by anyone in one day'
      < Oricine   poate   citi   cartea   într-o   zi
      anyone.NOM   can.3SG   read.INF   book.DEF.ACC   in=one   day
      'Anyone can read the book in one day'

3.5.2.3 The structure modal / aspectual verb plus de-*supine*

In the structure modal / aspectual verb + *de*-supine only *avea* 'have' with a dynamic and deontic modal value and the aspectual verbs *termina*, *isprăvi*, pop. *găti* 'finish' (Guţu Romalo 1961) can appear as V1 (§13.5.2.3.1). These verbs share the possibility of being constructed both with the subjunctive (without passing the test of a complex predicate) and with the supine (with clitic climbing and negation attached to V1):

(386) Nu   am   de   citit   cartea
      not   (I)have   DE_SUP   read.SUP   book.DEF.ACC
      > Cartea   **(nu)**   o   am   de   citit
      book.DEF.ACC   not   CL.ACC.F.3SG   (I)have   DE_SUP   read.SUP
      'I do not have to read the book'

(387) Cartea   **(nu)**   o   termin   de   citit
      book.DEF.ACC   not   CL.ACC.F.3SG   (I)finish   DE_SUP   read.SUP
      'The book, I do not finish reading'

U   Attaching negation to V2 is, however, possible in contrastive contexts, which suggests that the structure is not fully grammaticalized:
   (388) Cartea   o   am   **nu**   de   citit,
         book.DEF.ACC   CL.ACC.F.3SG   have.IND.PRES.1SG   not   DE_SUP   read.SUP
         ci   de   cumpărat
         but   DE_SUP   buy.SUP
         'I don't have to read the book, but to buy it'

These structures have the following syntactic features:

   (i) They accept raising of the accusative clitic ((385)–(387)), as V1 is transitive and can take a direct object; raising of the (possessive) dative clitic is conditioned by the capacity of V1 to accept a dative.

(389) *Cartea   **mi-o**   am   de   făcut
      book.DEF.ACC   CL.REFL.DAT.1SG=CL.ACC.F.3SG   (I)have   DE_SUP   make.SUP

(390) Cartea   **ţi-o**   termin   de   citit
      book.DEF.ACC   CL.DAT.2SG=CL.ACC.F.3SG   (I)finish   DE_SUP   read.SUP
      'I finish reading your book'

(ii) Like the constructions in §3.5.2.2, they accept the interposition of modal adverbs (391):

(391) Cartea   o   are **probabil** de   citit
      book.DEF.ACC   CL.ACC.F.3SG   has probably   DE$_{SUP}$ read.SUP
      'He probably has to read the book'

(iii) Like the constructions in §3.5.2.2, but unlike those under §3.5.2.1, the complex predicate containing a modal or aspectual verb + *de*-supine accepts the coordination of V1 with V2 (392) and the interposition of modal adverbs between V1 and V2 (393):

(392) Cartea   o   am   **de**   **citit**   şi
      book.DEF.ACC   CL.ACC.F.3SG   have.IND.PRES.1SG   DE$_{SUP}$ read.SUP   and
      de   **conspectat**
      DE$_{SUP}$ summarize.SUP
      'I have to read and summarize the book'

(393) Cartea   o   termin   **eventual** de   citit
      book.DEF.ACC   CL.ACC.F.3SG   finish.IND.PRES.1SG   maybe   DE$_{SUP}$ read.SUP
      'Maybe I finish reading the book'

(iv) Like the structures in §3.5.2.2, they generally accept *se*-passivization (the direct object of V2 becomes the subject of V1), with the exception of the construction with *avea* (which does not passivize):

(394) Cartea   se   **termină** de   citit   în trei   zile
      book.DEF.NOM   CL.REFL.PASS   finish.3SG   DE$_{SUP}$ read.SUP   in three   days
      de către   oricine
      by   anyone
      < Oricine   termină   de   citit   cartea   în trei   zile
      anyone.NOM   finishes   DE$_{SUP}$ read.SUP   book.DEF.ACC in three   days
      'Anyone can finish reading the book in three days'

U Romanian also has complex predicates with three verbs: modal verb + aspectual verb + embedded verb; clitic(s) and negator attach to the first verb (Pană Dindelegan 2008e: 256):

(395) Casa   **(nu)**   **ţi-o**   poate   termina   de
      house.DEF.ACC   not   CL.DAT.2SG=CL.ACC.F.3SG   can.3SG   finish.INF   DE$_{SUP}$
      construit   în   trei   ani
      build.SUP   in   three   years
      'He can(not) finish building the house in three years'

3.5.3 Complex predicates with subject raising and agreement

Another type of complex predicates is made up of an impersonal verb (which contains modal or aspectual information: *trebui* 'have to / should', *părea* 'seem', *fi* 'be', *urma* 'be going to') + subjunctive; the diagnostic tests are as follows (Pană Dindelegan 2008e: 258–65):

(i) obligatory raising of the subject of V2 before the impersonal V1 and agreement of V1 with the raised subject:

(396) a. Trebuia să citească [ei]
have-to.IMPERF.3SG SĂ_SUBJ read.SUBJ.3PL they.NOM
articolul > Ei trebuiau să
article.DEF.ACC they.NOM have-to.IND.IMPERF.3PL SĂ_SUBJ
citească articolul
read.SUBJ.PRES.3PL article.DEF.ACC
'They had to read / should have read the article'

b. Părea că ei vor câştiga concursul
seem.IMPERF.3SG that they AUX.FUT.3PL win.INF contest.DEF.ACC
> Ei păreau că vor câştiga concursul
they.NOM seem.IMPERF.3PL that AUX.FUT.3PL win.INF contest.DEF.ACC
'They seemed to be winning the contest'

c. Era să uite [ei]
be.IND.IMPERF.3SG SĂ_subj forget.SUBJ.PRES.3PL they.NOM
bagajele acasă
luggage.DEF.ACC.PL home
> Ei erau să uite
they.NOM be.IMPERF.3PL SĂ_SUBJ forget.SUBJ.3PL
bagajele acasă
luggage.DEF.ACC.PL home
'They were about to forget their luggage at home'

d. Urma să citească [ei] romanele
follow.IMPERF.3SG SĂ_SUBJ read.SUBJ.3PL they.NOM novels.DEF.ACC
> Ei urmau să citească romanele
they.NOM follow.IMPERF.3PL SĂ_SUBJ read.SUBJ.3PL novels.DEF.ACC
'They were going to read the novels'

U In the case of *trebui* 'have to, should' and *urma* 'be going to', agreement with the raised subject is accepted by the norm only for 3rd person plural, in the imperfect, the compound past and the future.

(ii) participation of the whole predicate to passivization (if no other constraints exist):

(397) a. Articolul trebuia **să fie** citit (de către ei)
article.DEF.NOM have-to.IMPERF.3SG SĂ_SUBJ be.SUBJ.3SG read.PPLE by them.ACC
'The article had to be read / should have been read (by them)'

b. Concursul părea **să fie** câştigat (de către ei)
contest.DEF.NOM seem.IMPERF.3SG SĂ_SUBJ be.SUBJ.3SG win.PPLE by them.ACC
'The contest seemed to be won (by them)'

U In examples (398a,b) there is ellipsis of the passive operator; the complex predicate contains the modal *trebui* 'have to, should' or *părea* 'seem', agreeing with the passive subject, and the (passive) participle form of V2, agreeing with the subject in gender and number:

(398) a. Articolele trebuiau citite
articles.DEF.NOM have-to.IND.IMPERF.3PL read.PPLE.F.PL
'The articles had to be read / should have been read'

b. Concursurile   păreau   câştigate
   contests.DEF.NOM seem.IMPERF.3PL   win.PPLE.F.SG
   'The contests seemed to be won'

The clitic climbing test does not function for this type of complex predicate (as clitic climbing is blocked by the subjunctive), and neither does the test of negation. The clear indication of argument composition is the agreement of the impersonal verb (recategorized as a personal verb) with the raised subject; *a părea* 'seem' is recategorized as a personal copula (§2.3.2.2):

(399) a. Ei   trebuiau   să   **(nu)** îl   citească
         they.NOM   must.IMPERF.3PL   SĂ_SUBJ   not   CL.ACC.M.3SG   read.SUBJ.3PL
         'They were supposed not to read it'

      b. Ei   păreau   să   **(nu)** îl   câştige
         they.NOM   seem.IMPERF.3PL   SĂ_SUBJ   not   CL.ACC.M.3SG   win.SUBJ.3PL
         'They seemed not to win it'

U There are numerous situations in which the (active or passive) subject is raised even across an impersonal verb, but this does not force the agreement of the impersonal verb with the raised subject (Pană Dindelegan 2008a: 351; Jordan 2009: 227), therefore this cannot be a complex predicate:

(400) a. **Voi**   trebuia   să   îl   citiţi
         you.NOM.PL   have-to.IMPERFF.3SG SĂ_SUBJ   CL.ACC.M.3SG   read.SUBJ.2PL
         < Trebuia   să   îl   citiţi   **voi**
         have-to.IMPERF.3SG SĂ_SUBJ CL.ACC.M.3SG   read.SUBJ.2PL   you.NOM.PL
         'You had to / should read it'

      b. **Romanele**   merita   (să   fie)   citite
         novels.DEF.NOM   deserve.IMPERF.3SG   SĂ_SUBJ   be.SUBJ.PRES.3PL read.PPLE.F.PL
         < Merita   ca   **romanele**   să
         deserve.IMPERF.3SG COMP   novels.DEF.NOM   SĂ_SUBJ
         fie   citite
         be.SUBJ.3PL   read.PPLE.F.PL
         'The novels deserved to be read (by you)'

In colloquial Romanian, other impersonal verbs (*a se întâmpla, a se nimeri* 'happen') can agree with the raised subject:

(401) **Oamenii**   **s-au**   întâmplat   să
      people.DEF.NOM   CL.REFL.ACC.3PL=(they)have   happened   SĂ_SUBJ
      fie   acolo
      be.SUBJ.3PL   there
      'The people happened to be there'
      < S-a   întâmplat   ca   oamenii
      CL.REFL.ACC.3SG=has   happened   COMP   people.DEF.NOM
      să   fie   acolo
      SĂ_SUBJ   be.SUBJ.3PL   there
      'It happened that the people were there'

A special type of complex predicate with subject raising and agreement occurs in the case of the *tough*-constructions plus *de*-supine (Pană Dindelegan 1982):

(402) E   greu   de   citit   cărțile
       is   hard.ADV(≡ADJ.M.SG) DE$_{SUP}$ read.SUP   books.DEF.ACC
       'It is hard to read the books'
       > **Cărțile**   **sunt**   greu   de   citit
       books.DEF.NOM   are.3PL   hard.ADV(≡ADJ.M.SG)   DE$_{SUP}$ read.SUP
       > **Cărțile**   **sunt**   **grele**   de   citit   [non-standard]
       books.DEF.NOM   are.3PL   hard.F.PL   DE$_{SUP}$ read.SUP
       'The books are hard to read'

C   Other Romance languages use the infinitive in *tough*-constructions, while the Balkan languages use the subjunctive (Hill 2002: 497).

3.5.4 Complex predicate-like structures with the subjunctive

If one accepts that obligatory control by the subject of the matrix verb always leads to subject raising (following Hornstein 1999; Pană Dindelegan 2008e, and Alboiu 2007 among others, for Romanian), then all the structures with obligatory control and V2 subjunctive could be considered complex predicates (for the verbs with obligatory controlled subjunctive, see §2.2.2.2.3):

(403) a. Ion$_i$ poate   PRO$_i$ să   plece
          Ion   can.3SG   SĂ$_{SUBJ}$ leave.SUBJ.3SG
          'Ion may leave'
       b. Ion$_i$ începe   PRO$_i$ să   o   mănânce
          Ion   start.3SG   SĂ$_{SUBJ}$ CL.ACC.F.3SG   eat.SUBJ.3SG
          'Ion starts to eat it'

The subjunctive structures are the least grammaticalized and they do not pass the complex predicate tests under §3.5.2 or under §3.5.3, except for the test of obligatory control.

A number of aspectual verbs occur in quasi-frozen constructions. Even if they contain a subjunctive, these structures are more grammaticalized, as the syntactic and semantic cohesion of the group is very strong, and the aspectual verbs are not able any more to select a different type of complement (Pană Dindelegan 2008e: 263):

(404) a. Stă   să   plouă
          stays   SĂ$_{SUBJ}$ rain.SUBJ.3SG
          'It is about to rain'
       b. Ei   dau   să   plece
          they.NOM   give.3PL   SĂ$_{SUBJ}$ leave.SUBJ.3PL
          'They are about to leave'
       c. El   trage   să   moară
          he.NOM   pulls   SĂ$_{SUBJ}$ die.SUBJ.3SG
          'He is about to die'

The fact that in colloquial modern Romanian (405) (Reinheimer and Tasmowski 2005: 203) the clitic can be doubly realized (as in the structures under §3.5.2.1), in that it can attach both to the modal verb and to the subjunctive complement-verb, shows the possibility of the embedded subjunctive structure undergoing the process of argument composition:

(405) Dar cucoana ai putea-o tu
but missus.DEF.ACC AUX.COND.2SG can.INF=CL.ACC.F.3SG you.NOM.SG
să mi-o furi?
SĂ_SUBJ CL.DAT.1SG=CL.ACC.F.3SG steal.SUBJ.2SG
'But could you steal the missus from me?'

The subjunctive construction is also characteristic of the Romanian factitive verbs; the structures are not grammaticalized and do not form complex predicates. The only sign of cohesion between the factitive verb and the clausal argument is the control of the subject of the subjunctive by the direct object of the matrix verb:

(406) O_i fac să plângă [ea]_i
CL.ACC.F.3SG (I)make SĂ_SUBJ cry.SUBJ.3SG she.NOM
'I make her cry'

(407) Îl_i pun să citească [el]_i
CL.ACC.M.3SG (I)put SĂ_SUBJ read.SUBJ.3SG he.NOM
'I make him read'

CONCLUSIONS

1 Romanian is a pro-drop language. The three characteristics of this class (subject non-realization, subject free inversion, the extraction of the subject from the subordinate) have been identified in Romanian. The language lacks an impersonal expletive pronominal subject; Romanian does not display a pronominal clitic in the position of a generic [+human] subject; a large group of verbs form grammatical sentences in the absence of the subject position.

For generic sentences, Romanian uses alternative constructions; the most frequent is a structure with a personal subject (2nd person singular), which leads to the ambiguity between the deictic *tu* 'you' and the generic *tu* 'one'.

Non-finite invariable forms can realize their subject in certain syntactic conditions; this happens more frequently in the case of the infinitive and the gerund, but it is also possible for the supine and the participle; it is more frequent in the syntactic position of adjunct, but it is also not excluded in argument position.

The test of the bare postverbal subject does not represent a diagnostic for unaccusativity in Romanian.

Among the structures which can occupy the subject position, the following are specific to Romanian: (i) non-finite supine structures, in which DE, fully grammaticalized, functions as an inflectional marker; (ii) non-finite gerund structures, functioning as a subject only for a group of verbs of perception in impersonal constructions; (iii) non-finite infinitive structures, which are less frequent in Romanian than in other Romance languages, due to the fact that they are often replaced with the subjunctive.

Subject word order is generally free (S–V / V–S). There are preferences and word order restrictions. Restrictions are syntactically determined (by the sentence types and by the syntactic type of predicate); preferences correlate with the definite vs. non-definite subject type, and with its rhematic vs. thematic nature. In the subordinate clause, supplementary restrictions occur, determined by the complementizer type. In a stylistically marked word order, any type of subject (realized as a noun with or without determiners) associated with any type of verb can occur in preverbal position.

2 Romanian displays specific direct object marking—prepositional marking with PE, which has additional conditions: semantic (the feature [+specific]), lexical (the feature [+human]), pragmatic (the object's high degree of prominence). Romanian is a language characterized by *Differential Object Marking*.

Romanian displays direct object clitic doubling, transforming a tool of emphasis into a mechanism with syntactic relevance, with strict rules allowing and blocking doubling. There is a relationship between doubling and the PE-structure, in that both constructions are united by the feature 'specificity'; Romanian has created two syntactic ways of marking 'specificity' (doubling and the PE-structure).

Romanian is one of those languages that have a special object, but not subject, marking. As far as marking strategies are concerned, it belongs to the type of languages with *dependent-marking constructions* (displaying prepositional marking), and also to the type with *head-marking constructions* (displaying clitic doubling).

Romanian has specific direct object syntactic constructions: the construction with verbs of physical sensation, where the direct object encodes the Experiencer, and the configuration with double object, in which the direct object encodes the Recipient. Among the specific realizations of the direct object, are the gerund clause, the DE-supine, and the infinitival relative clause.

In direct object position, except for the modal *putea* 'can', the subjunctive has won out over the infinitive; for a few head verbs (aspectual, and modal), there is competition between the subjunctive and the supine. Romanian did not preserve 'the accusative and infinitive' structure.

Romanian has a great variety of raised object structures (either with gerund clauses, or with clauses headed by complementizers).

Romanian is characterized by a great freedom in the positioning of the direct object, where separation from the verb and fronting are permitted.

3 Romanian has inherited the construction with personal direct object and non-animate secondary object from Latin. Other Romance languages preferred the corresponding construction with personal indirect object and non-animate direct object.

The construction with direct and secondary object is similar to that with direct and objective predicative complement. The latter structure differs from the first in characteristically using the objective predicative complement to express a *property* of the other object; the property can be denominative or categorizing, with effects on the manner in which it is encoded.

4 Romanian allows clitic realization and clitic doubling of the indirect object. There are strict rules for obligatory, optional, and disallowed doubling. The language strongly marks both the direct and the indirect object. The indirect object is generally case-marked; it is prepositionally marked (with the preposition *la* 'to') when it is realized as a DP whose most leftward constituent is invariable.

5 The prepositional phrase which occupies the position of prepositional object requires the complement of the preposition to be always realized. The prepositional object does not allow passivization, preposition stranding, or substitution by a clitic.

6 The *al* + genitive and the supine realizations of the subjective predicative complement are specific to Romanian. Semantically, the prepositional realizations are highly diverse. The copula *fi* 'be' may be synonymous with *avea* 'have' (this fact is specific to Balkan languages). Impersonal structures display an adverbial subjective predicative complement, while in other languages, it is adjectival. The word order of the subjective predicative complement is highly varied.

7 Like the other Romance languages, Romanian has two passive structures, inherited from Latin. The two types tend to specialize stylistically (the *fi* 'be' passive is preferred by the present-day literary language), and morpho-syntactically (the *se* passive is limited to the 3rd person, which involves the preference for using it in impersonal constructions). At the discourse-pragmatic level, the *se* passive is preferred in structures with postverbal non-individualized subject, and the *fi* 'be' passive, in constructions with preverbal, individualized subject. The *se* passive is more frequent than in other Romance languages. In the passive structure, the *by*-phrase is introduced by *de* or *de către* 'by', depending on the semantic type of the noun.

Romanian has a great variety of impersonal constructions; it does not display an expletive pronominal subject in impersonal constructions. The syntactic mechanism of impersonalization (for intransitive verbs) is rarely attested in old Romanian.

8 There are five types of reflexive constructions and a large number of reflexive verbs. The reflexive marker functions as: (i) a direct, indirect, or possessive complement under coreferentiality with the subject; (ii) a lexical formative of some verbs; (iii) a lexico-grammatical formative, distinguishing lexical meanings via grammatical oppositions; (iv) a grammatical formative for a subtype of passive and impersonal constructions; (v) a doubling reflexive pronoun, used for contrast or emphasis. The selection of strong or clitic reflexives is syntactically predicted. Selection of a dative or accusative reflexive clitic is lexically constrained.

The five reciprocal devices available in Romanian are the lexical, the iconic verbal, the accusative / dative reflexive clitic, the reciprocal pronoun, and redundancy. Each device is syntactically constrained and correlates with pragmatic-discursive effects such as process orientation, globalization / sequentiality, and frequency.

9 Romanian is more permissive than the other Romance languages in its use of the possessive dative clitic, considering the great variety of configurations in which it occurs, such as the Latin SUM PRO HABEO structure. There are hardly any syntactic or semantic restrictions on the use of the possessive dative construction. The DP which encodes the possessed object can occupy any position in the sentence; the host of the clitic can belong to any syntactic class of verbs. A rich diversity of relations of possession can be encoded through the possessive dative structure, be they inalienable or alienable. Finally, any semantic type of verb can function as a host for the clitic, even non-agentive verbs such as *iubi* 'love', *cunoaște* 'know', *admira* 'admire', *avea* 'have', *fi* 'be'.

10 Romanian has a reduced number of complex predicates (in the strict sense of the term), a consequence of the infinitive being substituted by the subjunctive. There are two main types of complex predicates in which argument composition takes place: complex predicates with obligatory subject control and clitic climbing and complex predicates with subject raising and agreement. The complex predicates with the infinitive resemble the structures with the subjunctive, but their cohesion is lower. Romanian does not have complex predicates with causative verbs, or with verbs of perception and of movement. The structure *putea* 'can'+ bare-infinitive has a high degree of grammaticalization, accepting clitic climbing. In *tough*-constructions, Romanian uses the supine.

4

Non-finite Verb Forms and Non-finite Clauses

In the first part of this chapter, the inventory of non-finite verb forms and their common features is presented.

The specific features of each non-finite verb form are then examined and in separate sections, the morphology of non-finite forms (the type of marking, synthetic and/or analytic), as well as the syntax of each type of non-finite clause (internal structure and particularities regarding the incorporation into more extended syntactic phrases) are investigated.

The Romanian non-finite verb forms are: the infinitive, the gerund (present participle), the participle, and the supine. The subjunctive is special in that—despite inflecting for number and person—it sometimes behaves like non-finite forms (§§ 4.1.4, 2.2.2.2).

Each non-finite form has specific semantic, syntactic, and morphological features, but they also have shared features which justify labelling them all *non-finite verb forms* (Huddleston and Pullum 2002: 1173–6).

4.1 GENERAL FEATURES

4.1.1 Similarities with finite forms

Non-finite forms resemble finite forms in their ability to function as heads of syntactic phrases with similar structure, as well as in their capacity to take an overt external argument bearing nominative case.

Besides the frequent contexts with covert subjects, non-finite forms can also take an overt subject which is different from the subject of the matrix verb:

(1) a. [Ajungând **eu** acasă], a început ploaia
 arrive.GER I home has started rain.DEF.NOM
 'When I got home, the rain started'

 b. Dorința lor [de [a câștiga **Ion**]] s-a implinit
 wish.DEF their DE A_{INF} win(INF) Ion.NOM CL.REFL.ACC.3SG=has accomplished
 'Their wish for John to win became reality'

 c. [Odată plecat **profesorul**], elevii au început joaca
 once left(PPLE) teacher.DEF.NOM pupils.DEF.NOM have started play.DEF
 'Once the teacher left, the pupils started to play'

 d. Vreau să cumpăr o masă [de [mâncat **șase persoane** la ea]]
 (I)want $SĂ_{SUBJ}$ buy.SUBJ.1SG a table DE_{SUP} eat.SUP six persons.NOM at it
 'I want to buy a table that six people can eat at'

Non-finite forms can take internal arguments: a direct object (2), a secondary object (3), an indirect object (4). The participle, passive or non-passive, cannot take a direct object, but it can take a secondary object (3c):

(2) a. [Ascultându-**l**], enervarea tuturor creştea
 listen.GER=CL.ACC.3SG irritation.DEF.NOM all.GEN was growing
 'Listening to him, everyone was getting more and more annoyed'

 b. Dorinţa lui Ion este de [a scrie **o carte**]
 wish.DEF LUI.GEN Ion is DE A_INF write.INF a book.ACC
 'John's wish is to write a book'

 c. Mi-e greu [de terminat **cartea**]
 CL.DAT.1SG=is difficult DE_SUP finish.SUP book.DEF.ACC
 'It's difficult for me to finish the book'

(3) a. [Învăţându-l **înmulţirea**], m-am substituit învăţătorului
 teach.GER=CL.ACC.3SG multiplication.DEF.ACC≡NOM CL.REFL.ACC.1SG=have replaced teacher.DEF.DAT
 'Teaching him multiplication, I took the place of the teacher'

 b. Mi-a revenit plăcerea [de [a-l anunţa **rezultatul**]]
 CL.DAT.1SG=has devolved pleasure.DEF DE A_INF=CL.ACC.3SG announce.INF result.DEF
 'The pleasure of telling him the result fell to me'

 c. [Fiind învăţat devreme **scrisul şi cititul**], Ion îşi depăşea colegii
 'Being taught to write and read early, Ion surpassed his collegues'

(4) a. [Dându-se premii **elevilor**], s-a încercat stimularea lor
 'Offering prizes to students was meant to stimulate them'

 b. Se gândeşte la [a oferi diplome **câştigătorilor**]
 'He thinks about offering diplomas to the winners'

 c. E greu [de trimis ajutoare **sinistraţilor**]
 'It is difficult to send aid to the victims of the disaster'

 d. S-au creat premii [destinate **copiilor**]
 'Prizes were created that were meant for children'

Non-finite forms can take predicative complements (5):

(5) a. [Fiind **medic**], nu putea lipsi de la operaţie
 'Being a doctor, he could not miss the surgery'

 b. Încă de mic a simţit dorinţa de [a ajunge **medic**]
 'Since he was a little child he has felt the desire to become a doctor'

 c. Nu e uşor [de ajuns **medic**]
 'It is not easy to become a doctor'

 d. [Devenită **ţară capitalistă**], România are dificultăţi de adaptare
 'Having become a capitalist country, Romania has difficulties in adapting'

The gerund or the infinitive can combine with the passive marker *fi* 'be' (6a,b); the participle and the supine do not accept overt voice markers, but they can incorporate voice values and they allow *by*-phrases (6c,d):

(6) a. Ion a plecat la București, [**fiind trimis de director**]
    Ion has left to Bucharest be.GER sent by director
    'Ion left for Bucharest, sent by the manager'

  b. E important [**a fi ales** chiar **de director**]
    'It is important to be chosen by the manager himself'

  c. Fata [**aleasă de director**] a ratat concursul
    'The girl chosen by the director failed in the competition'

  d. E greu [**de înțeles** situația **de toți cetățenii**]
    is hard DE$_{SUP}$ understand.SUP situation.DEF by all citizens.DEF
    'The situation is difficult for all the citizens to understand'

Non-finite forms can take temporal, aspectual, locative, and modal adjuncts:

(7) a. [Mergând **zilnic spre facultate**], știe bine drumul
    'As (s)he goes to the faculty every day, (s)he knows the way well'

  b. Îmi respect promisiunea de [a veni **zilnic la facultate**]
    'I keep my promise to come to the faculty every day'

  c. E imposibil [de ajuns **la oră fixă la facultate**]
    'It's impossible to get to the faculty at a set time'

  d. Sunt elevi [plecați **din țară temporar**]
    'There are students who have left the country temporarily'

4.1.2 Differences from finite forms. Are non-finite forms mixed categories?

Non-finite forms do not show tense and person inflection. The infinitive can be considered a partial exception, as it does not carry person inflection, but it is inflected for tense, also displaying a perfect form (§4.2.4). The obligatory (selected) subjunctive has a special situation, as it carries person and tense inflection.

Non-finite forms lack autonomy in communication, that is they cannot form independent sentences. The infinitive and the supine are an exception in very rare circumstances: when they head imperative sentences (§§4.2.3.1, 4.4.3.11).

The syntactic phrases they project appear, prototypically, in subordination, being embedded by other syntactic phrases:

(8) a. dorința [de [a reuși]]
    wish.DEF DE A$_{INF}$ succeed.INF
    'the desire to succeed'

  b. El [simte [**venind** un miros greu]]
    he feels come.GER a smell.NOM heavy
    'He feels a strong smell coming'

  c. Se satură [de [**făcut** același lucru]]
    CL.REFL.ACC.3SG is-fed-up DE$_{SUP}$ do.SUP the-same thing
    '(S)he gets fed up with doing the same thing'

The subordinators of non-finite forms are either prepositions (9a,b), or they are simply absent, as in the case of the gerund (10a) and the participle (10b). Relatives are rarely selected by non-finite forms, being possible only in relative infinitival constructions (§§4.2.3.3, 10.3.3).

(9)   a. Se satură [**de** [a pleca mereu ultimul]].
       'He gets fed up with always being the last one to leave'

    b. El se gândeşte [**la** [pregătit examenul]]
       'He thinks about preparing for the exam'

(10) a. Se aude [∅ **tunând**]
       'It can be heard thundering'

    b. Trebuie [∅ **citit** tot ce s-a scris]
       'Everything that has been written must be read'

Except for the infinitive, which shares its negative marker with all the finite forms, the gerund, the participle, and the supine take the prefixal negative marker *ne*-. This prefixal compound may also incorporate the aspectual adverbial clitic *mai* 'more' (12a–c):

(11) gândul de a   **nu** pleca
     thought DE A$_{INF}$ not leave.INF
     'the thought of not leaving'

(12) a. **Ne**(**mai**)citind   de   multă   vreme,   a   uitat   şi   literele
       NEG-more-read.GER for   long   time   has   forgotten also   letters
       'Because (s)he hasn't read anymore for a long time, (s)he forgot even the letters'

    b. lucru   **ne**(**mai**)văzut
       thing   NEG-more-seen(PPLE)
       'thing unseen before'

    c. Aşa   întâmplare   este   de   **ne**(**mai**)auzit
       such   happening   is   DE$_{SUP}$ NEG-more-heard.SUP
       'Such a happening is unheard of'

Non-finite forms can also function as formatives of analytic tenses and moods. When they combine with (semi)auxiliaries, they form monoclausal complex predicates (§3.5.2.1).

The participle is the invariable formative of the compound past (13a), of the perfect subjunctive (13b), perfect presumptive (13c), perfect infinitive (13d), perfect conditional (13e), and future perfect (13f). In combination with the passive marker *fi* 'be', the participle, which in this case displays gender and number agreement with the subject, makes up the passive voice and, in combination with certain modals, complex predicates (13g):

(13) a. am **cântat**
       'I have sung'

    b. să   fi   **cântat**
       SĂ$_{SUBJ}$ be   sung

    c. (v)oi fi **cântat**
       'I shall have sung'

    d. a fi **cântat**
       'to have sung'

e. aş fi **cântat**
   'I would have sung'

f. voi fi **cântat**
   'I shall have sung'

g. Copiii   trebuiau   **pedepsiţi**
   children.DEF.M.PL had-to.IMPERF punished(PPLE)M.PL
   'The children had to be punished'

The infinitive without the inflectional marker A (i.e. the bare infinitive) is an invariable formative of the present conditional (14a) and of the simple future (14b). The bare infinitive also functions as a lexical component of modal complex predicates (14c):

(14) a. aş **cânta**
        'I would sing'

   b. (v)oi **cânta**
        'I shall sing'

   c. El poate **pleca**
        'He can leave'

The gerund is an invariable formative of one of the present presumptive constructions:

(15) va / o fi **cântând**
     '(s)he may / might be singing'

The **supine** does not appear as a formative in analytic moods or tenses, but appears in certain aspectual (16a,b) or modal complex (16c) predicates:

(16) a. Termină **de citit**
        '(S)he finishes reading'

   b. Se apucă **de citit**
        '(S)he begins reading'

   c. Are **de citit**
        '(S)he has to read'

The obligatory (selected) subjunctive is the formative of certain periphrastic future forms (17a–b). It also appears in aspectual and modal periphrastic configurations (17c,d):

(17) a. am **să cânt**
        'I am going to sing'

   b. avea **să plece**
        'He was to leave'

   c. dă **să plece**
        'He is on the point of leaving'

   d. trebuiau **să plece**
        'They had to leave'

In some of their occurrences, non-finite forms display a mixed category behaviour (Bresnan 1997). This status reflects the fact that a single non-finite form can head phrases of two different categorial types.

4.1 General features 209

In modern Romanian, only the participle and, in some of its occurrences, the supine display features of authentic mixed categories. The other non-finite forms (the gerund and the infinitive) are not pure mixed categories, but have similar behaviour.

The participle (18) is characterized by the features [+adjectival inflection, +agreement], [+verbal syntax, i.e. + SecO]:

(18) Copiii   sunt   [învăţaţi   tabla   înmulţirii]
      children.DEF.M.PL are   taught(PPLE)M.PL   table.DEF   multiplication.DEF.GEN
      'The pupils are taught the times table'

The supine (19a–c), in the context of lexical and selected prepositions, is characterized by [+nominal syntax, i.e. +selected by a preposition], [+verbal syntax, i.e. +DO]:

(19) a. Trăieşte   **din**   **strâns**   **gunoaie**
        lives   from   gather.SUP   rubbish
        '(S)he earns a living through scavenging'

    b. Se   satură   **de**   **ţinut**   **regim**
       CL.REFL.ACC.3SG   is-fed-up   DE$_{SUP}$ keep.SUP   diet
       'She gets fed up with keeping to a diet'

    c. Participă   la   **adunat**   **deşeuri**
       participates at   gather.SUP   wastes
       'She takes part in garbage collection'

The infinitive and the gerund are distinguished by [−nominal inflection, i.e. −case, −article], [−verbal inflection, i.e. −person], [+verbal syntax, i.e. +nominative external argument, +accusative internal argument]:

(20) a. [plecând   **el**   primul]
        leave.GER   he.NOM   the first.NOM
        'as he was the first to leave'

    b. dorinţa   de   [a   pleca   **el**   primul]
       wish.DEF   DE   A$_{INF}$ leave.INF   he.NOM   the first.DEF
       'the wish for him to leave first'

    c. [primindu-l]
       receive.GER=CL.ACC.3SG
       'receiving it'

    d. dorinţa   de   [a-l   primi]
       desire.DEF DE   A$_{INF}$=CL.ACC.3SG   receive.INF
       'the desire to receive it'

4.1.3 Ambiguous non-finite heads

Some non-finite forms are ambiguous (in modern Romanian, this is the case with the supine, and, to a certain extent, with the gerund). So, depending on the context, they may head different types of syntactic phrases and admit two readings. As an example, consider the distinction between supine$_1$ (noun), displaying the features [+nominal inflection, +article], [+nominal syntax] (21a), and supine$_2$ (verb), displaying the features [−nominal inflection], [+verbal syntax] (21b):

(21) a. [_DP_**cititul**   revistelor]
     reading.DEF   magazines.DEF.GEN
     'the reading of magazines'

   b. Se   apucă   [de   [_VP_**citit**   **reviste**]]
     CL.REFL.3SG starts   DE_SUP_ read.SUP   magazines.ACC
     '(S)he starts reading magazines'

If the syncretism with the participle is taken into consideration as well (§4.4.1), then the plurifunctionality of a single head is even clearer, as both (verbal and adjectival) participles and (verbal and nominal) supines admit two distinct structures.

The gerund may display verbal behaviour (22a), displaying the features [−adjectival inflection], [+verbal syntax], or adjectival behaviour (22b), having the features [+adjectival inflection, +agreement], [−verbal syntax]:

(22) a. [_VP_**Crescând**   prețul],   patronul   și-a
       raise.GER   price.DEF.ACC≡NOM   owner.DEF CL.REFL.DAT=has
       mărit   profitul
       increased   profit.DEF
       'By raising the price, the owner increased his profit'

   b. grație   producției   [_AP_**crescânde**]   de   petrol
     due   production.F.SG.DAT   increase.GER.F.SG.DAT   of   petrol
     'due to the increasing production of petrol'

4.1.4 The status of the subjunctive

The subjunctive is special, as, depending on the context, it displays variable behaviour. There are certain contexts in which the subjunctive functions as a finite form (23a–c) and there are other contexts in which, despite person and number inflection, and agreement features, it functions in a way similar to non-finite forms (24a–d) (see also §§2.2.2.2.2, 2.2.2.2.3):

(23) a. **Să pleci** imediat!
       'Leave now!'

   b. Oare **să fi venit** Ion?
     'Has John really come?

   c. Caut un apartament care **să mi se potrivească**
     'I look for an apartment that suits me'

(24) a. Are / Avea **să vină**
       'He is / was going to come'

   b. Ion_i_ dă [**să plece** PRO_i_]
     'Ion is on the point of leaving'

   c. El_i_ n-a apucat [**să plece** PRO_i_ înainte de ora 7]
     'He did not manage to leave before 7 o'clock'

   d. Îmi_i_ vine [**să plâng** PRO_i_]
     'I feel like crying'

As a non-finite form, the subjunctive is either a formative in analytic tenses (24a) and in complex predicates (24b,c) or a mood selected by a certain class of verbs (24d). In these configurations, the subjunctive may be replaced by (and competes with) the infinitive or, sometimes, with the supine (25a,b). Even abstract deverbal nouns can replace the infinitive, the subjunctive, or the supine, given the fact that all of them denote events:

(25) a. Se   apucă   să   citească / a   citi /   de   citit   o carte
        CL.REFL.ACC.3SG begins SĂ$_{SUBJ}$ read.SUBJ A$_{INF}$ read.INF DE$_{SUP}$ read.SUP a book
        '(S)he begins to read a book'

   b. Se   gândeşte   să   plece /   a   pleca /   la   plecare
      CL.REFL.ACC.3SG thinks   SĂ$_{SUBJ}$ leave.SUBJ A$_{INF}$ leave.INF at   leaving
      '(S)he thinks of leaving'

C The Romanian subjunctive behaves very similarly to the Modern Greek subjunctive (it occurs in configurations with the particle *na*), which also displays features of a non-finite form (Miller 2002). There are also other phenomena in which the Romanian subjunctive behaves similarly to the Greek one (for the replacement of the infinitive by the subjunctive constructions, see §4.2.5).

4.2 THE INFINITIVE

Among non-finite forms, the infinitive is singled out by the following features:

(a) mixed marking (suffixal and analytic);
(b) the ability to encode a temporal distinction;
(c) its occurrence in contexts common with the subjunctive, which made it possible to replace the infinitive by the subjunctive;
(d) formal differentiation from the nominal infinitive, with which it was originally identical.

4.2.1 Mixed marking, suffixal and analytic

In modern Romanian, the infinitive is characterized by mixed marking. The infinitive form includes a suffixal marker (*-a, -ea, -e, -i, -î*)—dubbed 'thematic vowel' in some works—and an analytical one, the invariable proclitic marker *a*, common to all conjugations.

4.2.1.1 Five infinitive suffixes: -a, -ea, -e, -i, -î

In contemporary Romanian, there are five suffixes of the infinitive, according to which five classes of verbs can be distinguished (§2.1.1): the 1st class: *a...a* (*a cânta* 'sing'), the 2nd class *a...ea* (*a putea* 'be able'), the 3rd class: *a...e* (*a face* 'do'), the 4th class: *a...i* (*a veni* 'come'), and the 5th class: *a...î* (*a urî* 'hate'). All classes except the third take a stressed suffix in the infinitive.

H Romanian inherited the Latin infinitive form with the suffix *-re* (FACERE, CANTARE > Rom. *facere* 'do', *cântare* 'sing'), but this was later lost (*cântare, vedeare, facere, fugire* > *cânta, vedea, face, fugi* 'sing', 'see', 'do', 'run') whence the marking of the infinitive limited to the 'thematic vowel' (*cânta, vedea, face, fugi*). The phenomenon did not occur in Aromanian and Megleno-Romanian, where the infinitive with *-re* has been preserved (Caragiu Marioţeanu 1975: 252, 284).

In Daco-Romanian, *-re* survives only in nominalized infinitives (see §4.2.2).

This phonological reduction of the infinitive is present, although isolated, in other parts of the Romance area as well—in Rhaeto-Romance varieties, in Italian dialects, and in Dalmatian (see Byck 1967: 146). As an effect of the nominalization process, the long form of the infinitive—to which two distinct functions, verbal (26a) and nominal (26b), corresponded—became ambiguous:

(26) a. Încep   a   [_V_ **cântare**]   (old Romanian)
          (I)begin A_INF sing.INF
          'I begin to sing'

      b. Aud   o   [_N_ **cântare**] frumoasă
          (I)hear a   singing   nice
          'I hear a nice singing'

The loss of *-re* made the differentiation of the two homophonous functions possible. The long nominal form of the infinitive (an abstract deverbal noun *cântare* 'singing') was differentiated from the short verbal form (*cânta* 'sing').

Sixteenth-century texts testify to the coexistence of the long and the short verbal infinitival forms (Diaconescu 1977: 105).

The absence of the short form from Aromanian and Megleno-Romanian, as well as the presence of the suffixal marker *-ea* in the second inflectional class make it possible to date the loss of *-re* (*vedeare* > *vedea* 'see') to after the separation of the south-Danubian dialects, but before monophthongation of *ea* to *e* (Diaconescu 1977: 105). Traces of the verbal infinitive with *-re* are present up to a later date in the history of Romanian; in Transylvanian varieties (Mării 2004: 26–31), this form is also mentioned in the mid-20th century both in the configurations (*de*) + *a* + long infinitive and in the inverted forms of the conditional (*vărsare-aș* 'I would spill') or in the future forms with no inversion (*m-oi spălare* 'I would wash myself').

C Romanian has remained close to the Latin infinitive pattern, preserving four infinitival inflectional classes: *-a* (*ara* 'plough'), *-ea* (*putea* 'be able'), *-e* (*merge* 'go'), *-i* (*veni* 'come'); for the way in which infinitive classes were organized in Romance languages, see ELIR: 75–6; Reinheimer Rîpeanu (1998: 283).

Romanian also developed a fifth class, with the infinitive suffix *-î* (older *-îre*). It initially created a phonological variant of the suffix (*i* > variant *î*, after the geminate cluster *rr*-: *HŎRRĪRE > *urâ(re)*), which afterwards transformed into an independent suffix. This change of status (allomorph > distinct suffix) is a late phenomenon (dating back to the 16th century or before; Frâncu 2009: 83), one piece of evidence being the fact that, after the 16th century, both suffixes *-i* and *-î* could appear in the immediate vicinity of *r-* (*hotăr-î* 'decide', *omor-î* 'kill', alongside *măr-i* 'enhance', *călător-i* 'travel'). During the 16th century, frequent variations of the type *amărî—amări* 'sadden', *ocărî—ocări* 'offend' occurred (Diaconescu 1977: 73).

4.2.1.2 The proclitic A as an inflectional marker

In Romanian, proclitic A_INF functions as a morphological marker (Guțu Romalo 1968b: 182), and thus as an inflectional head (Jordan 2009: 181), similarly to the marker TO in English and to the marker SĂ_SUBJ of the Romanian subjunctive. There are several arguments for considering A_INF an inflectional head:

(i) its occurrence is obligatory (27) even when the infinitive appears in subject position (28); its absence is limited to certain situations (§4.2.3.3):

(27) continuă **a citi** / *continuă **citi**
 continues A_INF read.INF continues read.INF
 '(S)he continues reading'

(28) **A învăța** este o datorie / *Î**nvăța** este o datorie
 A_INF learn.INF is a duty read.INF is a duty
 'To learn is a duty'

(ii) its adjacency to the verb is obligatory (29a), except for the cases when pronominal clitics (29b), negative markers (29c), adverbial clitics (29d), or different types of clitics, up to maximum five (29e), intervene between the verb and A_INF:

(29) a. *a **mereu** învăța
 A_INF always learn.INF

 b. a-l citi / a-i spune / a se chinui
 A_INF=CL.ACC read.INF A_INF=CL.DAT say.INF A_INF CL.REFL.ACC torment.INF
 'to read it / to tell him / to torment oneself'

 c. a **nu** pleca
 A_INF not leave.INF
 'to not leave'

 d. a **mai / tot / și** pleca
 A_INF still always immediately leave.INF
 'to leave again / to always leave / to leave immediately'

 e. a **nu și-l mai tot** căuta
 A_INF not CL.REFL.DAT=CL.ACC.3SG more always search.INF
 'to not look for it continuously'

(iii) the presence of an additional complementizer, *de* (§4.2.1.3), as well as the presence of lexical prepositions—*spre a* 'in order to', *până a* 'until', *fără a* 'without', *pentru a* 'for', *în loc de a* 'instead of':

(30) a. Se teme **(de) a** pleca
 CL.REFL.ACC fears of A_INF leave.INF
 '(S)he is afraid of leaving'

 b. Pleacă **pentru / fără a** munci
 leaves for without A_INF work.INF
 '(S)he leaves to work / without working'

(iv) the occurrence of A_INF in raising structures (31a), being fairly well known that any complementizer blocks raising constructions (31b) (Jordan 2009: 247):

(31) a. Copiii **par a fi** fericiți
 children.DEF seem A_INF be.INF happy
 'The children seem happy'

 b. *Copiii **par de a fi** fericiți
 children.DEF seem DE A_INF be.INF happy

H Originally, the analytical marker A_INF (< Lat. AD) functioned as a lexical preposition that introduced purpose adjuncts, and occurred with verbs of motion, as some attestations of the 16th century show:

(32) Merse / ieși **a semăna** (Coresi)
'he went left to sow'

Towards the end of the 16th century, when A-infinitival constructions were also attested in other structures than the purpose ones, as, for example, in the direct object position (33), the status of the proclitic marker *a* had already changed (preposition > inflectional element; Jordan 2009: 51):

(33) Știți **a judecare** (Coresi)
(you)know.PRES.IND A_{INF} judge.INF
'You know how to judge'

Beginning with the 17th century, there have been few verbs which, in configurations with A-infinitivals, preserved their purpose value:

(34) Se pregătește **a pleca**
CL.REFL.ACC prepares A_{INF} leave.INF
'(S)he is getting ready to leave'

4.2.1.3 The DE A sequence

In Romanian, the word *de* behaves as a complementizer (Schulte 2007: 168; Jordan 2009: 174–6), not as an inflectional head, as shown by the fact that (i) it cannot appear in raising structures (see (31b) above); (ii) the DE A structure cannot appear as a fronted infinitival subject (35a); (iii) it cannot co-occur with another lexical preposition (35b):

(35) a. *De a citi este o plăcere
DE A_{INF} read.INF is a pleasure

b. *Se gândește la de a pleca
CL.REFL.3SG thinks at DE A_{INF} leave.INF

H The complementizer *de*, adjacent to the marker A_{INF}, has been attested since the 16th century, when it occurs both in long infinitive (36a) and in short infinitive configurations (36b). In old Romanian the sequence *de a* is much more frequent than in the modern language, occurring in any syntactic position of the infinitive, including the subject and direct object positions:

(36) a. Încetă **de-a grăirea** (Coresi)
finished.PS.3SG DE=A_{INF} speaking.DEF
'(S)he stopped speaking'

b. Stătură **de-a grăi** (Coresi)
stayed.PS.3PL DE=A_{INF} speak.INF
'They stopped speaking'

In contemporary Romanian, the complementizer *de* is allowed in all the structures containing infinitives, with the exception of the infinitive with an imperative value (§4.2.3.1.3), following more restrictive syntactic rules of usage than in the old language. The current standard norm recommends the following: the obligatory selection of *de* when introducing arguments of nouns (37a); the optional selection of *de* when introducing prepositional arguments (37b) and when introducing the subjective predicative complement (37c); the avoidance of the structures containing *de* in the subject and direct object positions (37d); the disallowance of the structure with *de* in the case of impersonal configurations with fronted subjects (37e):

(37) a. gândul **de a** pleca
     thought.DEF DE A_INF leave.INF
     'the thought of leaving'

 b. se teme **(de)** **a** pleca
    CL.REFL.3SG fears OF A_INF leave.INF
    '(s)he is afraid of leaving'

 c. Dorinţa lui este **(de)** **a** pleca
    desire.DEF his(GEN) is DE A_INF leave.INF
    'His desire is to leave'

 d. ?Se cuvine **de a** face asta
    CL.REFL.3SG is-fitting DE A_INF do.INF this
    'It is fitting to do this'

 e. *** De a** face asta, este important
    DE A_INF do.INF this is important

C The complementizer *de* has a similar counterpart (*de* / *di*) in other Romance languages. Depending on the language and, in certain languages (for example, in French), depending also on the governing word, one can choose between *de* / *di* and *a* (Schulte 2007: 339–40). What is specific to Romanian is that *de* obligatorily co-occurs with and before A_INF:

(38) a. dorinţa **de a** pleca
     desire.DEF DE A_INF leave.INF
     'the desire to leave'
 b. *dorinţa de pleca
    desire.DEF DE leave.INF

4.2.2 The verbal infinitive vs. the nominal infinitive

In modern Romanian, the infinitive has two forms: a so-called 'long' form, with the inflection and semantico-syntactic behaviour of an abstract noun (§5.2.3), and a 'short' form, with the semantic and syntactic behaviour of a non-finite verbal form; compare *plecarea* the 'leaving', a DP (39a), with *a pleca* 'leave', a non-finite infinitival clause (39b):

(39) a. consecinţele [_DP**plecării** imediate a lui Ion]
     consequences.DEF leaving.DEF.GEN immediate AL.F.SG LUI.GEN Ion
     'the consequences of John's immediate leaving'
 b. dorinţa de [_VP**a pleca** Ion imediat]
    desire.DEF DE A_INF leave.INF Ion.NOM immediately
    'the desire that John would leave immediately'

H The nominalized 'long' infinitive (40a) was frequent in the 16th century, when it co-occurred with the verbal use of the same form (40b). In old Romanian, the long form of the infinitive behaved ambiguously (§4.1.3):

(40) a. **facerea** ciudeseloru   (Coresi)
     doing.DEF miracles.DEF.GEN
     'the making of miracles'

b. Stătu nărodul **de-a** **aducerea** darure (*Palia*)
  stayed people.DEF DE=A_{INF} bringing.DEF presents.ACC
  'The people stopped bringing presents'

The language evolved in the direction of the formal differentiation of the categorially different heads (in modern Romanian, the long infinitive functions only nominally vs. the short infinitive which functions only verbally).

4.2.3 The distribution and the internal structure of the non-finite infinitival clause

Infinitival structures fall into two classes: *A-infinitival structures* (in which the proclitic marker A occurs), the largest class, and *bare infinitival structures* (the infinitive is marked only by suffix), which are much more syntactically restricted.

4.2.3.1 A-infinitival constructions. Syntactic patterns

4.2.3.1.1 The infinitival clause may appear in the direct object position (41a) or in the secondary object position (41b) of a transitive verb. It may also appear with impersonal verbs, as a rhematic subject, placed postverbally (41c):

(41) a. El_i caută [a mă întâlni PRO_i]
   he searches A_{INF} CL.ACC.1SG meet.INF
   'He is trying to meet me'

  b. L_i-a învățat [a munci PRO_i]
   CL.ACC.3SG=has learned A_{INF} work.INF
   '(S)he taught him to work'

  c. Îmi_i vine [a plânge PRO_i]
   CL.DAT.1SG comes A_{INF} cry.INF
   'I feel like crying'

A-infinitival constructions appear in control structures, selected by the matrix verb (41a–c). More rarely, A-infinitivals can appear in cases of non-coreferentiality of the two subjects (42):

(42) Ion_i dorește [a câștiga **celălalt**_j]
   Ion wants A_{INF} win.INF the-other.NOM
   'Ion wants the other one to win'

4.2.3.1.2 Within the prepositional phrase, the A-infinitive functions as a complement; the prepositional phrase may occupy the following positions:

- prepositional object within a verbal phrase, in which the verb selects different prepositions (43a–b);
- prepositional object within an adjectival (43c) or an adverbial phrase (43d), in which the adjective and the adverb take prepositional objects, selecting a *de*-structure;
- complement within a nominal phrase headed by an abstract nominal derived by nominalization (43e);
- adjunct of a verb, in structures with lexical prepositions (43f).

(43) a. Se   gândește **la** **a**   pleca
       CL.REFL.3SG   thinks   at   A_INF   leave.INF
       'He thinks about leaving'

   b. Regimul   constă   **în** **a**   se   înfometa
      diet.DEF   consists   in   A_INF   CL.REFL.3SG   starve.INF
      'The diet consists of starving yourself'

   c. avid   **de** **a**   câștiga
      greedy   DE   A_INF   win.INF
      'eager to win'

   d. înainte   **de** **a**   pleca
      before   DE   A_INF   leave.INF
      'before leaving'

   e. dorința   **de** **a**   **pleca**
      desire.DEF DE   A_INF   leave.INF
      'the desire to leave'

   f. Pleacă   **pentru** **a**   se   trata
      leaves   for   A_INF   CL.REFL.3SG   treat.INF
      '(S)he leaves for having a treatment'

H   The distribution of the infinitive was wider in old Romanian: *de*-infinitive structures depending on a head noun (43e) also denoted the 'destination', being selected also by nominals with concrete referents (44a); *de*-supine structures were specialized later to denote the value of 'destination' (44b):

(44) a. **apă**   de-a   spălarea   picioarele   (*Palia*)
       water   DE=A_INF   washing.DEF   feet.DEF.ACC
       'water for washing your feet'

   b. **apă**   de   spălat   picioarele
      water   DE_SUP   wash.SUP   legs.DEF.ACC

4.2.3.1.3 The infinitive rarely occurs in imperative sentences with an unspecified addressee (§13.1.3):

(45) A   nu   se   face   gălăgie!
     A_INF not   CL.REFL.PASS   do.INF   noise!
     'Do not make noise! / No noise!'

4.2.3.2   The internal structure of the A-infinitival clause

The infinitive, like the other non-finite verbal forms (§4.1.1), allows any type of object. This, if realized as a pronominal clitic, is obligatorily preverbal, being placed between the marker A_INF and the verbal form (46a,b). The negative particle *nu* 'not' intervenes between the proclitic marker A and pronominal clitics (46c):

(46) a. a-l   vedea
       A_INF=CL.ACC.3SG   see.INF
       'to see him'

   b. a   **mi-o**   impune
      A_INF CL.DAT.1SG=CL.ACC.3SG   impose.INF
      'to impose it to me'

c. a   **nu**   mi-o   impune
    A_INF   not   CL.DAT.1SG=CL.ACC.3SG   impose
    'to not impose it to me'

C Romanian resembles French, but differs from Spanish, where the clitic is placed postverbally, and partially from Italian and Portuguese, where, in certain conditions, the clitic may occur either in a preverbal or in a postverbal position (Reinheimer Rîpeanu 1993: 82).

The infinitive has a subject of its own, bearing the nominative case (for the relation with the controlled subject, see §3.1.2.1), depending on the syntactic position occupied by the infinitival clause:

(i) in structures with personal verbs

(47) Ion_i   se   teme   [(de)   [a   nu   câștiga   **Gheorghe_j**]]
      Ion   CL.REFL.3SG   fears   of   A_INF   not   win   Gheorghe.NOM
      'Ion is afraid of Gheorghe winning'

(ii) in impersonal structures

(48) E   important   [a   câștiga   **Ion**]
      is   important   A_INF   win   Ion.NOM
      'It is important that Ion wins'

(iii) when the infinitival phrase is embedded in a nominal phrase

(49) dorința   [de   [a   câștiga   **noi**   proiectul]]
      desire.DEF   DE   A_INF   win   we(NOM)   project.DEF.ACC
      'the desire that we win the project'

(iv) when the infinitival phrase is embedded in a prepositional or an adverbial phrase

(50) Copiii_i   au   plecat   [până   [a   veni   **mama_j**]]
      children.DEF   have   left   until   A_INF   come.INF   mother.DEF.NOM
      'The children had left before mother came'

C The Romanian infinitive with an overt subject is invariable, differing from the 'personal infinitive' (with personal endings) found in Portuguese and in Galician, in some Sardinian varieties, and in some Italian dialects (Renzi and Andreose 2003: 225–6; Mensching 2000: 27).

4.2.3.3 Bare infinitival constructions

In contemporary standard Romanian, bare infinitival constructions occur in a limited number of contexts:

(i) selected by the modal verb *putea* 'can' (51a);
(ii) in relative infinitival constructions, as the direct object of the personal verb *avea* 'have' (51b) or as the subject of the impersonal verbs *avea* 'have' (51c) and *fi* 'be' (51d); see §10.3.3:

(51) a. El   poate   **pleca**
         he   can   leave
         'He can / may go'

      b. N-am   ce   **face**
         not=have.1SG   what   do.INF
         'I've no alternative'

c. N-are ce **se** **întâmpla**
   not=have.3SG what CL.REFL.3SG happen.INF
   'Nothing can happen'

d. Nu-i cine-l **ajuta**
   not=is who=CL.ACC.M.3SG help.INF
   'There is nobody to help him'

The bare infinitivals under (i) differ from the A-infinitivals in many respects, a fact which accounts for analysing the structure [modal verb + bare infinitive] as a complex predicate (§3.5.2.2).

Bare infinitival constructions allow clitic climbing, that is placing personal and reflexive clitics depending on the infinitive form before the modal verb *putea* 'can'; a single clitic (52a–c) or two clitics (52d) may appear:

(52) a. **O** pot vedea
     CL.ACC. F.3SG can.1SG see.INF
     'I can see her'

b. **Îşi** poate impune părerile
   CL.REFL.DAT.3SG can.3SG impose.INF opinions.DEF.ACC
   '(S)he can impose his / her opinions'

c. **Se** poate apăra
   CL.REFL.ACC.3SG can.3SG defend.INF
   '(S)he can defend himself / herself'

d. **Mi-o** poate spune
   CL.DAT.1SG=CL.ACC.F.3SG can.3SG tell.INF
   '(S)he can say it to me'

Note that the clitic climbing phenomenon is possible only with bare infinitival constructions. The phenomenon does not occur with A-infinitivals (53a) or with the corresponding structures containing subjunctives (53b):

(53) a. *Îl ştiu a citi
     CL.ACC.3SG (I)know A$_{INF}$ read.INF

b. *Îl ştiu să citesc
   CL.ACC.3SG (I)know să$_{SUBJ}$ read.SUBJ.1SG

The bare infinitival structure allows both the *be*-passive (54a) and the reflexive passive (54b):

(54) a. Legea **poate fi adoptată** imediat
     law.DEF.NOM can.3SG be adopted(PPLE)F.SG immediately

b. Legea se **poate adopta** imediat
   law.DEF.NOM CL.REFL.PASS.3SG can.3SG adopt.INF immediately
   'The law can be adopted right away'

Bare infinitivals cannot appear before the matrix verb:

(55) ***Cânta**, pot destul de bine
     sing.INF (I)can enough DE well

The structure does not allow adverbial adjuncts to intervene between the matrix verb and the bare infinitive form:

(56) *Nu pot **devreme** pleca
    not (I)can early leave.INF

H In old Romanian, bare infinitival constructions also occurred with verbs other than *putea* 'can': *vrea* 'want', *şti* 'know', *căuta* 'try', *cuteza* 'dare' (Frâncu 2009: 128):

(57) lui   i   caută   asculta   (*Documente*)
    him.DAT CL.DAT.3SG searches listen.INF
    'He tries to obey him'

These structures disappeared from standard Romanian, initially for the verbs *vrea* 'want' and *cuteza* 'dare' and then for the other verbs (the last attestations for the verb *şti* 'know' date from the first half of the 20th century). In north-western varieties, bare infinitival constructions and clitic climbing with the verbs *vrea* 'want' and *şti* 'know' are also attested in the current stage of the language (Farcaş 2006).

In old Romanian, the verb *putea* 'can' could simultaneously select structures with or without the proclitic marker A (Diaconescu 1977: 157).

4.2.4 Infinitive vs. perfect infinitive

In Romanian, the verbal infinitive developed a new form—the perfect infinitive—with the temporal value [+past, +anteriority in relation to a reference point prior to speech time], introducing a temporal distinction which does not exist in the case of the other non-finite forms (58a). Whereas the perfect infinitive has its own temporal values, the prototypical infinitive is atemporal, and it depends on the temporal value of the context (58b):

(58) a. dorinţa de **a reuşi** vs. dorinţa de **a fi reuşit**
       'the desire to win' vs. 'the desire to have won'

    b. A încercat / Încearcă / Va încerca **a se salva**
       '(S)he tried / tries / will try to save himself / herself'

The perfect infinitive has an analytical form, made up of the proclitic marker A_{INF} plus the invariable auxiliary *fi* 'be' plus the invariable participle of the main verb:

(59) a   fi   reuşit
    A_{INF} be succeeded(PPLE)
    'to have succeeded'

H The perfect infinitive occurs very rarely in old Romanian. The first two attestations date from the 18th century (Frâncu 2009: 321):

(60) Şi   ştiia   a   fi   scris   ca să   se
    and know.IMPERF.3SG A_{INF} be write(PPLE) in order-to CL.REFL.ACC
    curăţească   cei   ce   purta   vasele   Domnului   (Antim)
    clean.SUBJ.3PL CEL.M.PL who wear.IMPERF vessels.DEF God.DEF.GEN

In the general phenomenon of competition between infinitive and subjunctive (§4.2.5), the perfect infinitive occurs in the same contexts as the perfect subjunctive.

U In contemporary Romanian, the perfect infinitive is limited to the language of educated speakers.

4.2.5 The replacement of the infinitive by the subjunctive

The fact that the infinitive shared contexts with the subjunctive, as well as the common meaning of the two verbal forms, made the replacement of the infinitive by the subjunctive possible.

H The replacement phenomenon, which began before the 16th century, has been explained as a Balkan Sprachbund phenomenon with a Modern Greek origin (Sandfeld 1930: 177; Rosetti 1986: 237; Feuillet 1986: 110). Other researchers (Onu 1996; Frâncu 2000: 119) also mention internal reasons that might have caused this phenomenon.

In contemporary Romanian, the infinitive–subjunctive replacement process is far from over (Vulpe 2006: 225). Its stage of evolution depends on: geography (north vs. south); control and the syntactic type of the governing constituent; and register.

(i) The infinitive is best preserved in the northern area of Maramureş and Crişana, especially in quasi-frozen structures, after modal verbs (*putea* 'can', *trebui* 'must', *vrea* 'want', *avea* 'have') and aspectual verbs (*da* 'be on the point of', *începe*, *prinde*, *a se pune* 'begin') (Farcaş 2006).

(ii) When the form in question occurs as an argument of the verb, the degree of replacement by the subjunctive is higher if the subject of the embedded verb is different from the matrix subject (61a). The modal control verb *putea* 'can' is the most conservative, and in contemporary Romanian it selects either the infinitive or the subjunctive in free variation (61b). There are certain verbs which also select the infinitive, but not in the same proportion as *putea* (61c):

(61) a. pro$_i$ Vreau **să plece Ion$_j$** cât mai repede
       (I)want să$_{SUBJ}$ leave.SUBJ.3SG Ion.NOM as more quickly
       'I want Ion to leave as quickly as possible'

    b. Pot **cânta** / Pot **să cânt**
       (I)can sing.INF (I)can să$_{SUBJ}$ sing.SUBJ.1SG
       'I can sing'

    c. Binevoieşte / Caută /Continuă /Începe /Îndrăzneşte / Reuşeşte a **răspunde**
       ((s)he)-is-willing /tries / continues /begins / dares / manages A$_{INF}$ answer.INF
       '(S)he is willing / tries / continues / begins / dares / manages to answer'

(iii) In the case of other syntactic positions—as a complement of a noun (62a), of a preposition (62b), of an adjective (62c), or of an adverb (62d)—but also in relative infinitival constructions (62e), the replacement process was much slower, both forms continuing to be used, with slight variations in percentage depending on the pattern in which they occur: the infinitive is prevalent in pattern (62a), the subjunctive prevails in patterns (62b–e); for notes on the proportions, see Schulte (2007: 292, 294–5, 303–4).

(62) a. dorinţa de a pleca / dorinţa să plece
       desire.DEF DE A$_{INF}$ leave.INF desire.DEF să$_{SUBJ}$ leave.SUBJ.3SG≡PL
       'the desire to leave'

    b. până a veni / până să vină
       until A$_{INF}$ come.INF until să$_{SUBJ}$ come.SUBJ.3SG≡PL
       'before coming'

c. vrednic (de) a fi ales / să fie ales
   worthy DE A_INF be chosen SĂ_SUBJ be.SUBJ.3SG chosen
   'worthy of being chosen'
d. Este uşor a spune asta / Este uşor să spui asta
   is easy A_INF say.INF this is easy SĂ_SUBJ say.SUBJ.2SG this
   'It is easy to say this'
e. N-am unde pleca / N-am unde să plec
   not=have.1SG where go.INF not=have.1SG where SĂ_SUBJ go.SUBJ.1SG
   'I do not have where to go'

(iv) A tendency to return to infinitive structures, on the Romance pattern, can be noted in texts showing educated usage—especially those belonging to journalistic, scientific, juridical, and administrative styles, but also in other types of scholarly texts.

C Note that, in contrast to the Ibero-Romance languages, where the subject coreferentiality requirement is decisive in the selection of the infinitive over the subjunctive, in Romanian, the infinitive can be replaced by the subjunctive under any circumstance, with or without coreferentiality of the subjects (Schulte 2007: 325–6).

The process of replacement is a general Balkan Sprachbund phenomenon, but Balkan languages show different degrees of replacement (Joseph 1983; Mišeska Tomić 2004: 31). In contrast with Macedonian, Tosk Albanian, and Modern Greek, which do not have any type of infinitive, and also with Bulgarian and some Serbian dialects, in which the infinitive has almost disappeared, in Romanian, as well as in standard Croat, standard Serbian, and Gheg Albanian, the infinitive is still used in many syntactic patterns. In the south-Danubian varieties, Aromanian and Megleno-Romanian, the verbal infinitive has almost completely disappeared, while in Istro-Romanian the situation resembles that of Daco-Romanian.

4.3 THE PARTICIPLE

The participle is distinguished among the non-finite forms by the following features:

(a) it possesses a synthetic (suffixal) marker;
(b) it has variable behaviour (adjectival vs. verbal) from one context to another;
(c) in the verbal domain, it has *mixed category* behaviour (Bresnan 1997), simultaneously displaying adjectival inflection and agreement alongside typically verbal features;
(d) in the verbal domain, the verbal participle has limited combinatory capacities in contrast to infinitives and gerunds:
• it cannot host pronominal clitics (compare (63a) and (63b)):

(63) a. carte trimisă lor
        book sent.PPLE.F.SG them.DAT
        'book sent to them'
     b. *carte le trimisă
         book CL.DAT.3PL sent.PPLE.F.SG

• it cannot take voice markers ((64a) vs. (64b)); passive voice is thus marked covertly:

(64) a. carte citită   [+passive]
        book read.PPLE.F.SG
        'a read book'

b. om   băut   [+active]
   man   drunk.PPLE.M.SG
   'drunk man'

- it cannot take the direct object (65a); the non-personal secondary object in double object constructions is accepted (65b):

(65) a. *om   băut   vin
        man   drunk.PPLE.M.SG   wine
     b. fată   învăţată   gramatică
        girl   taught.PPLE.F.SG grammar

- all verbs have participial forms which are used as formatives in analytic tenses; the adjectival participle is not available for all verbs (see §4.3.4).

4.3.1 Grammatical marking: weak vs. strong participles

The stem of the participle is identical to that of the simple past ('the perfect stem') as shown by the root-final palatalization of the stem (d > z $văd_{PRES}$ 'I see'—$văzui_{PS}$ 'I saw'—$văzut_{PPLE}$ 'seen'; $cred_{PRES}$ 'I believe'—$crezui_{PS}$ 'I believed'—$crezut_{PPLE}$ 'believed') and by the morpho-phonological alternation between consonant and ∅, which is of the same type ($şterg_{PRES}$ 'I wipe'—$şter(∅)sei_{PS}$ 'I wiped'—$şter(∅)s_{PPLE}$ 'wiped', $frâng_{PRES}$ 'I break'—$frân(∅)sei_{PS}$ 'I broke'—$frân(∅)t_{PPLE}$ 'broken'). For some verbs (ending in -a, -i, -î), the participial stem is identical with the infinitival one ($cânt$-a_{INF} 'sing'—$cânt$-ai_{PS} 'I sang'—$cânt$-at_{PART} 'sung'); see §2.2.1.1.4.

The participial suffix is -t, with the exception of the subclass of those verbs ending in -e, which take the participial suffix -s. The participial suffix is preceded by the perfect suffix (66a); in the case of verbs ending in -e, the participial suffix attaches directly to the perfect stem (66b,c).

(66) a. văz-u-t
        see-PERF-PPLE
        'seen'
     b. mer-∅-s
        go-PERF-PPLE
        'gone'
     c. cop-∅-t
        bake-PERF-PPLE
        'baked'

Romanian has *weak participles*, which bear the stress on the participial suffix (for verbs with the infinitive ending in -a, -ea, -i, -î and for a number of verbs with the infinitive ending in -e), and a *strong participle*, whose stem bears the stress (for some verbs with an -e infinitive) (Table 4.1).

The negative participle is formed by prefixation of the negative prefix *ne-* (67a); the negative forms can incorporate the adverbial clitic *mai* 'more' (67b):

(67) a. necântat
        NEG-sung
        'unsung'

b. nemaicântat
     NEG-more-sung
     'never sung before'

H Romanian inherited from Latin two types of participles, attested in Danubian Latin: CANTATUS, AUDITUS > Rom. *cântat(u), auzit(u)* 'sung', 'heard', alongside ARSUS, COCTUS > *ars(u), copt(u)* 'burnt', 'baked' (Ionescu-Ruxăndoiu 1978: 333).

   In the evolution of Daco-Romanian, there are frequent shifts between the two subclasses of verbs ending in *-e*: the etymological strong form *fapt(u)* 'made' is replaced by the analogical weak form *făcut*; the weak forms *înțelegut* 'understood', *învăncut / învencut* 'defeated' are replaced by the strong *înțeles, învins*; the strong form *înțelept* 'wise' (< Lat. INTELLECTUS, the participle form of the verb INTELLIGĔRE) appears only as an adjective (*ești înțelept* 'you are wise'—*Documente*); the strong form *întort(u)* 'retorted' becomes *întors*, which is also strong, but uses the suffix *-s* (Diaconescu 1969; Zamfir 2007: 122–57).

In present-day Romanian, the *-t* participle is restricted to a few verbs: *coace* 'bake', *fierbe* 'boil', *frânge* 'break', *frige* 'roast', *înfige* 'thrust', *rupe* 'break', *sparge* 'crack / break', *suge* 'suck', and their derivatives (or the forms including these bases) *răscoace* 'over bake', *înfrânge* 'defeat', *corupe* 'corrupt', *întrerupe* 'interrupt'.

C Like Romanian, Italian, Spanish, and French preserved both kinds of participle (weak and strong); Alkire and Rosen (2010: 176) claim that Italian has preserved many of the strong participle forms and French fewer, whereas in Spanish very few strong participles are preserved.

U Some of the verbs with weak participles in the standard language have, in certain isolated dialectal areas such as Central Transylvania, strong participle variants: *văst / văzut* 'seen', *vint / venit* 'come', *șăst / șezut* 'sat', *găst / găsit* 'found', *piert < pierdut* 'lost' (Todoran 1982; Marin, Mărgărit, and Neagoe 1998: 115).

   Participial suffixes have a variant with a final *u*. This variant was frequent in old Romanian; in the current language it occurs rarely, only in inverted forms; its use is highly marginal:

(68) a. spus**u**-ne-a
        said-*U*=CL.DAT(≡ACC).1PL=has
        'he told us'
     b. dat**u**-mi-s-a
        given-*U*=CL.DAT.1SG=CL.REFL.ACC.3SG=has
        'it was given to me'

In the north-western subdialects (Transylvania, Maramureș, Crișana), in combination with the auxiliary *fi* 'be' and, very rarely, with forms of the auxiliary *avea* 'have', the participial suffix is amplified by the vowel *-ă* (69). This construction has received several explanations (Uritescu 2007: 558–9).

(69) a. aș   fi   cântat**ă**
        AUX.COND.1SG be   sung-*Ă*
        'I would have sung'   [perfect conditional]
     b. să   fi   fost**ă**
        SĂ_SUBJ   be   been-*Ă*   [perfect subjunctive]

In Aromanian, the participle has the invariable vocalic ending *-ă (-î)*: *am^u cântatî* ('I / we have sung') (Caragiu Marioțeanu 1975: 249; Loporcaro 1998: 178). A similar phenomenon is encountered in a restricted North-Danubian area in the north-east of Wallachia and Dobrogea (Marin 1991: 61–3), where the participle form ending in *-ă* occurs after the auxiliary *a avea* (*am luată* 'I / we have taken', *am fostă* 'I / we have been', *a căzută* '(S)he has fallen').

TABLE 4.1 The marking of the participle

CLASSES OF VERBS (THE INFINITIVAL SUFFIX)	THE PARTICIPIAL SUFFIX— WEAK PARTICIPLES	THE PARTICIPIAL SUFFIX— STRONG PARTICIPLES	THE INFINITIVE OF THE VERB	AFFIRMATIVE PARTICIPLE	NEGATIVE PARTICIPLE
-a	*-ˊa+t*		cânta 'sing'	cântat 'sung'	ne(mai)cântat
-ea	*-ˊu+t*		plăcea 'like'	plăcut 'liked'	neplăcut
-e (*-ut* participle)	*-ˊu+t*		face 'make'	făcut 'made'	nefăcut
-e (*-s* participle)		*-Ø+s*	arde 'burn'	ars 'burnt'	nears
-e (*-t* participle)		*-Ø+t*	rupe, frânge 'break'	rupt, frânt 'broken'	nerupt, nefrânt
-i	*-ˊi+t*		auzi 'hear'	auzit 'heard'	neauzit
-î	*-ˊî+t*		omorî 'kill'	omorât 'killed'	neomorât

4.3.2 The distribution and agreement of the participle

The participle occurs either as the formative of the passive voice and of analytic tenses or as the head of a syntactic phrase, embedded in other phrases (Pană Dindelegan 2003: 116–32).

4.3.2.1 The participle as a tense and mood formative

As a formative, the participle is a morphologically invariant component of the following analytic tenses: compound past (70), future perfect, perfect subjunctive, perfect conditional, perfect presumptive, perfect infinitive (for more examples, see §4.1.2).

(70) am cântat
(I)have sung

H In old Romanian, other tenses could also be periphrastic, using the past participle; a case in point is the pluperfect (71a), which is synthetic in the modern language (71b). The analytic type is the only one available in the south-Danubian dialects.
    (71) a. am fost greşit   (old Romanian)
          (I)have been mistaken
          'I had made a mistake'
      b. greşisem   (modern Romanian)
          mistake.PLUPERF.1SG
          'I had made a mistake'

C Alongside Spanish, Portuguese and, to a more limited extent, Catalan and Italian, Romanian is a Romance language in which the participial formative of analytic tenses does not undergo agreement with the subject or the direct object, irrespective of the type of verb / construction, as in (72a–c); for auxiliary selection, see §4.3.3; for the situation of Romanian among the Romance languages, see Loporcaro (1998: 155–6, 160); Salvi (2011: 341).
    (72) a. Ea a **plecat /** *****plecată**
          she has left*(default)* left.F.SG
          'She left'
      b. Ei s-au **speriat /** *****speriaţi**
          they CL.REFL.ACC.3PL=have scared*(default)* scared.M.PL
          'They got scared'
      c. cărţile pe care le-am **citit /** *****citite**
          books.DEF.F.PL PE which CL.ACC.3PL.F=have.1SG read*(default)* read.F.PL
          'The books that I / we read'

In the old language, there are instances of agreeing past participles in the pluperfect, conditional, and subjunctive (analytic tenses), which use the auxiliary *fi* 'be' (Zamfir 2007: 165–6, 209–10; Uriţescu 2007); participial agreement is not available in structures with forms of the auxiliary *have*. The difference between agreeing and non-agreeing participles is still at work in a restricted dialectal area (§4.3.1).

4.3.2.2 The participle as a passive voice formative

Romanian uses only one auxiliary, *fi* 'be' (the *veni* 'come' passive is marginal and has supplementary modal-aspectual values; see §3.4.1). In this structure, similarly to the situation in Romance, the participle is variable, displaying gender and number agreement with the subject (73a). In the impersonal passive structure (73b), there is a default participial form (masculine singular).

(73) a. Elevul /   Eleva /   Elevii /   Elevele
        student.DEF.M.SG   student.DEF.F.SG students.DEF.M.PL students.DEF.F.PL
        este   ajutat / este   ajutată /
        is   helped.M.SG is   helped.F.SG
        sunt   ajutați /   sunt   ajutate de   profesori
        are   helped.M.PL are   helped.F.PL by   professors
        'The student is / Students are helped by professors'

   b. Este   **știut**   că   ai   furat   cartea
      is   known(default≡M.SG)   that (you)have   stolen   book.DEF
      'It is known that you stole the book'

C In modern standard Romanian, the phenomenon of participial agreement, restricted to passive structures, has acquired a different function in contrast to the other Romance languages (where the participle is also variable) in that it distinguishes the passive constructions from periphrastic tense forms (in the feminine and plural).

4.3.2.3 Participial constructions

Participial constructions occur as: DP / NP modifiers; predicative complements of copular verbs or in restructured syntactic configurations; extrasentential adjuncts; rarely, as subjects of impersonal modal verbs.

4.3.2.3.1 As in other Romance languages, the participial DP / NP modifier (§5.3.5) has retained its adjectival meaning from Latin; it displays gender, number, and case agreement ((74)–(75)) with its head:

(74) asupra   acestei   cărți   atât de   **citite**
     on/about   this.GEN.F.SG   book.GEN.F.SG   so   read.PPLE.GEN.F.SG
     'on/about this highly read book'

These constructions are equivalent to a headed relative clause. When they are postnominal, the participle licenses at least a direct internal argument, raised as an antecedent (75a). It may license two arguments, one of which is raised as an antecedent, while the other is a secondary object (75b):

(75) a. cartea   **citită**   de Ion
        book.DEF   read(PPLE)   by Ion
        'the book read by John'

     b. copiii   **învățați**   gramatică
        children.DEF taught(PPLE)   grammar
        'the children (that were) taught grammar'

What is specific to Romanian is the occurrence of the participle with the determiner CEL; in the nominal ellipsis, CEL takes over the function of the elided nominal head (§5.3.1.4):

(76) **Cele   premiate**   au   atras   atenția   publicului
     CEL.F.PL   awarded.F.PL   have   drawn   attention.DEF   public.DEF.GEN
     'The awarded ones drew public attention'

4.3.2.3.2 Modifying participles are predicative complements in copula structures:

(77) Ioana este de mult **plecată**
Ioana.F.SG is for long gone.F.SG
'Ioana has been gone for a long time'

In restructured (raised-object) configurations (§3.2.1.7), the participle relates to the direct object with which it agrees in gender and number:

(78) O știu **plecată**
CL.ACC.F.3SG (I)know gone(PPLE).F.SG
'I know she is gone'

4.3.2.3.3 As an extrasentential adjunct, the participial construction occurs in elliptical isolated structures, where it is a temporal (79a) or reason (79b) adjunct:

(79) a. [**Ajunsă** pro$_i$ acasă], a și început ploaia$_j$
arrived(PPLE).F.SG home has also begun rain.DEF.NOM
'No sooner had she arrived home, than the rain started'

b. [**Plecată** pro$_i$ prea târziu de acasă], pro$_i$ n-a mai găsit bilete
left(PPLE).F.SG too late from home not=has also found tickets
'Having left home too late, she didn't find any more tickets'

As an extrasentential adjunct, the participle displays gender and number agreement with the subject which is either a pro subject, identical to (79b) / different from (79a) the main clause subject, or, more rarely, a lexical subject, different from the main clause subject (80):

(80) [**Ajunsă** mama$_i$ acasă /Mama$_i$ **ajunsă**$_i$ acasă],
acasă], mother.DEF.NOM home mother.DEF.NOM arrived.F home
a și început ploaia$_j$
has also begun rain.DEF.NOM
'With mother having arrived home, it immediately started raining'

4.3.2.3.4 Rarely, the participial clause occurs as the postverbal subject of impersonal modal verbs:

(81) Trebuie [**spus** numai adevărul]$_S$
must said(PPLE) only truth.DEF.NOM
'Only the truth must be said'

U In present-day Romanian, most of the impersonal verbs (82a) and all [*be* + adverbial] impersonal constructions (82b) take a supine clause, as indicated by the occurrence of the supine marker DE$_{SUP}$. As shown in (82c), only a few impersonals (*trebuie* 'must', *se cuvine* 'it is fitting that / ought to', *merită* 'it is worth') take a participial clause. The extension of the DE$_{SUP}$ + supine pattern to the second class of verbs (82d) is not accepted in the standard language. Subject raising (§3.1.8.1) can apply to the pattern in (82c); as an effect, the main verb and the participle undergo agreement with the raised subject (82e).

(82) a. Este / Rămâne **de făcut** încă mult
is / remains DE$_{SUP}$ made.SUP still much
'There is / remains still a lot to be done'

b. Este important **de spus** adevărul
is important DE$_{SUP}$ tell.SUP truth.DEF
'It's important to tell the truth'

c. Trebuie   /Merită   **spus**   adevărul
   must.3SG it-is-worth said.PPLE   truth.DEF
   'The truth must be said / is worth being said'
d. Trebuie   **de**   **spus**   adevărul   [non-standard]
   must.3SG DE_SUP   said.SUP   truth.DEF
   'The truth must be said'
e. Minciunile   trebuiau   **descoperite**   imediat
   lies.DEF.F.PL   must.IND.IMPERF.3PL   unveiled(PPLE).F.PL   immediately
   'The lies had to be immediately unveiled'

4.3.3 A sole auxiliary in the compound past tense

With the compound past, Romanian selects only forms of the auxiliary *avea* ('have'), irrespective of the syntactic type of the verb ((inherently) reflexive or non-reflexive, transitive, unaccusative, or unergative):

(83) a. m-**am**   spălat
        CL.REFL.ACC.1SG=(I)have washed
        'I washed myself'
     b. **am**   spălat   rufe
        (I)have   washed   clothes
        'I washed clothes'
     c. **am**   căzut
        (I)have   fallen
        'I fell'
     d. **am**   înotat
        (I)have   swum
        'I swam'

C Romanian (like Spanish, Portuguese, and Walloon) does not display auxiliary selection in the periphrastic past (Loporcaro 1998). This phenomenon is considered by Sandfeld (1930: 132) to be one area of resemblance between Romanian and Albanian.

Romanian confirms the generalization proposed by Lois (1990: 234), that Romance languages with auxiliary selection (French, Italian, Occitan) display participle agreement, while those without auxiliary selection lack participle agreement.

4.3.4 The relation of the participle to the classes of verbs. Ambiguities

In most cases, transitive verbs yield passive participles (84a,b). Occasionally, these verbs yield active participles, which originate in the absolute use of transitive verbs (84c,d):

(84) a. Cartea   este   citită
        book.DEF.F.SG   is   read.PPLE.F.SG
        'The book is read'
     b. Banii   sunt   incorect   câştigaţi
        money.DEF.M.PL   are   incorrectly   earned.PPLE.M.PL
        'The money is improperly earned'

c. drum   ocolit
   road   go-round.PPLE
   'detour'

d. om   băut
   man   drunk.PPLE
   'drunk man'

The participles of unaccusative verbs are non-passive, irrespective of the type of unaccusativity:

(85) a. fată   plecată /   căzută   pe   gheață
        girl   left(PPLE)   fallen(PPLE)   on   ice
        'girl who has left / fallen on the ice'

   b. om   îmbogăţit
      man   enriched(PPLE)
      'man who became rich'

   c. femeie   rămasă   singură /   devenită   deputat
      woman   remained(PPLE)   single   become(PPLE)   deputy
      'woman who remained single / who became a deputy'

The participle of unergative verbs occurs solely in the structure of analytic tenses. Otherwise, unergative verbs disallow adjectivization of the participle; this is a diagnostic test for distinguishing between unergatives and unaccusatives (§2.3.2.1):

(86) a. *om   tuşit
        man   coughed(PPLE)

   b. *om   înotat
      man   swum(PPLE)

   c. *câine   lătrat
      dog   barked(PPLE)

Given the absence of overt voice markers, there appear ambiguities involving the participles of transitive verbs in the absolute use, which have an active reading, and the participles of *bona fide* transitives, which have a passive reading:

(87) a. om   mâncat
        man   eaten(PPLE.ACT≡PASS)
        'man that has eaten' / 'man that has been eaten (e.g. by a wolf)'

   b. drum   ocolit
      road   go-round(PPLE.ACT) / avoided(PPLE.PASS)
      'road that goes round / road that is avoided'

   c. om   învăţat
      man   learned(PPLE.ACT) / taught(PPLE.PASS)
      'a learnèd man / a taught man'

The existence of unaccusative (reflexive or non-reflexive) / transitive pairs may also give rise to active–passive reading ambiguities for participles:

(88) a. om   oprit   în   faţa   unei   vitrine
       man   stopped(PPLE.ACT≡PASS)   in   front-of a   shop-window
       'a man that stopped in front of a window' / 'a man that was stopped in front of a window'
   b. plante   uscate
      plants   withered(PPLE) / made-dry(PPLE)
      'withered plants' / 'plants that were dried'

4.3.5 Verbal vs. adjectival participles

The *verbal–adjectival* distinction also occurs in other languages (Rivière 1990; Embick 2004). Formally, the verbal and the adjectival participle are identical (89); furthermore, both types display agreement, a characteristic which provides further evidence for taking verbal participles as mixed categories (§4.1.2):

(89) a. Uşa   este închisă   cu   atenţie   de infirmieră   [verbal participle]
       door.F.DEF is   closed.PPLE.F   with   attention by nurse
       'The door is carefully closed by the nurse'
   b. Uşa   a   rămas   închisă   [adjectival participle]
      door.F.DEF   has   remained   closed.PPLE.F
      'The door remained closed'

The differences between the two types of participles are both syntactic and semantic (Nicolae and Dragomirescu 2009).

4.3.5.1 Semantic differences

Verbal participles have the feature [+eventive]. There are two types of adjectival participles, namely *stative participles* (which express a simple state and may occur in comparative constructions, as in (90a)) and *resultative stative participles* (which represent the result of an event and involve adverbial modification, as in (90b)). There is also a third class of adjectival participles, namely participles recategorized as non-intersective deictic or modal adjectives (90c); see §7.5.3:

(90) a. este ca   o   uşă   **înnegrită**
       is   like a   door   blackened(PPLE)
       'It is like a blackened door'
   b. o   uşă   abia /   larg   **deschisă**
      a   door merely   widely opened(PPLE)
      'a merely / widely opened door'
   c. o   **fostă**   directoare
      a   been(PPLE.F.SG)   headmistress.F.SG
      'a former headmistress'
   d. un   **pretins**   savant
      a   claimed(PPLE.M.SG)   scientist.M.SG
      'an alleged scientist'

C In contrast to languages such as English or German (Embick 2004: 358), in Romanian there is no morphophonological distinction between the first two types of adjectival participles (statives vs. resultative statives).

4.3.5.2 Syntactic differences

Only adjectival participles occur with copulas other than *fi* 'be':

(91) a. rămâne   nemâncat
       remains   unfed(PPLE)

   b. ajunge   ofilit
       becomes withered(PPLE)

Adjectival participles accept degree modifiers:

(92) a. mai   nemâncat   decât   alții
       more   unfed(PPLE)   than   others
       'hungrier than others'

   b. foarte   uimit
       very   amazed
       'very amazed'

The syntactic restrictions of adjectival participles may differ from those of the corresponding verb, as shown by the contrast in (93):

(93) a. cărți   [cunoscute   [de   noi   toți]$_{by}$-phrase]   [verbal participle]
       books.F.PL   known.F.PL   by   us   all
       'books known by us all'

   b. cărți   [cunoscute   [copiilor]$_{IO}$]   [adjectival participle]
       books.F.PL   known.F.PL   children.DEF.DAT
       'books familiar to children'

Participial non-intersective adjectives like *fost* 'former', *pretins* 'alleged' are obligatorily prenominal.

Note that certain participles display a mixed behaviour and are thus hard to label (as adjectival or verbal):

(94)   Cartea   este   mai   **cunoscută**   de   medici   decât
       book.DEF.F.SG   is   more   known.PPLE.F.SG   by   physicians   than
       de   lingviști   (degree modifier + *by*-phrase)
       by   linguists
       'The book is better known by physicians than by linguists'

4.3.6 Recategorizations: the substantivization and adverbialization of participles

In the same way as adjectives, participles may also change their category, becoming nouns:

(95) a. spital   de   **arși**
       hospital   of   burned(PPLE.M.PL)
       'hospital for burned people'

b. **spusele** tale
   say(PPLE).DEF.F.PL your
   'your words'

H The substantivization of participles was frequent in old Romanian, where usually the feminine form was selected: *ascunsă* (hidden(PPLE).F 'mystery'); *adusă* (brought(PPLE).F 'sacrifice'), *făgăduită* (pledged(PPLE).F 'promise'), *grăită* (said(PPLE).F 'word, saying'), *porăncită* (commanded (PPLE).F 'command').

The adjectival participle may undergo adverbialization (§8.1.4.2); the masculine singular form of the participle is used as an adverb:

(96) a. om bâlbâit [adjectival participle]
        man stammered(PPLE).M.SG
        'a stammering man'
     b. vorbeşte bâlbâit [manner adverb]
        speaks stammered(PPLE.ADV)
        'he speaks in a stammering way'

4.4 THE SUPINE

Among the non-finite forms, the supine is characterized by the following features:

(a) formal identity with the masculine singular form of the participle;
(b) the presence of a prepositional complementizer, which in some contexts grammaticalizes as an inflectional element;
(c) a variable behaviour—nominal or verbal—from one context to another; when it functions verbally, it displays the features of a mixed category (Bresnan 1997; Soare 2007), simultaneously showing features of nominal and verbal syntax; in some other contexts, it functions as an ambiguous head, which, in the absence of arguments, it may do either nominally or verbally;
(d) it is distinct from the infinitive and gerund, but it resembles verbal participles with respect to the verbal combinatorial abilities, namely: (i) it cannot host pronominal clitics and, consequently, does not allow clitic doubling; (ii) it cannot take overt voice markers, although it may incorporate voice values; (iii) it takes a lexical subject in very few and limited syntactic conditions; (iv) it has common contexts with the infinitive and subjunctive, competing with them.

H Given the weak use of the supine since Latin, where it was in competition with other syntactic patterns (Ernout and Thomas 1959: 262), as well as its absence from all other Romance languages and from Aromanian, the origin of the Romanian supine is uncertain and controversial.

Certain supine forms are sporadically encountered in Megleno-Romanian (Atanasov 2002: 235–6).

There are some linguists who have interpreted it as a survival of the Latin supine (Grandgent 1958: 66; Bourciez 1956: 250, 588; ILR I 1965: 190), while others consider it a late creation of Romanian, deriving from a recategorization of the participle of intransitive verbs (Caragiu Marioțeanu 1962; Brâncuş 2007). Brâncuş explains the formation of the supine through an internal motivation (the supine started to occur instead of the verbal infinitive once the latter nominalized and was replaced by the subjunctive) and mentions the role of the contact with Albanian, which has a unique form corresponding to the Romance infinitive and the perfect participle (see also Manzini and Savoia 2007: 265).

4.4.1 The form

The supine form is identical with the participle; the prefixal negative form allows, as is also the situation with the participle, the incorporation of the adverbial clitic *mai* 'more' (§4.3.1):

(97) a. de văzut
    DE_{SUP} see.SUP(≡PPLE)
    'to be seen'

  b. de nemaivăzut
    DE_{SUP} NEG-more-see.SUP(≡PPLE)
    'which has not been seen before'

U Differentiation of the supine from the past participle has been noted for the verb *fi* 'be' in some localities of Transylvania and Maramureș (see Maiden 2012):

(98) **Fost-ai** la târg? **De fiut, am fost,** dar
    been(PPLE)=have to fair? DE_{SUP} be.SUP (I)have been but
    n-am cumpărat nimic
    not=(I)have bought nothing
    'Have you been to the fair? As for going to the fair, yes, I've been, but I didn't buy anything'

4.4.2 The nominal supine vs. the verbal supine

In modern Romanian, the supine occurs with two different functions: as a nominal, behaving semantically, syntactically, and inflectionally like an abstract deverbal noun (§5.2.6), and as an invariable verbal form, which takes arguments specific to verbs (see also Soare 2002).

The *nominal supine* is characterized by the ability to take the enclitic definite article and also other determiners (99a), by the possibility of expressing case distinctions (99b) and of assigning genitive case to its arguments (99c), or to select a *de* prepositional structure (99d):

(99) a. **mersul /** **acest mers** pe jos
    go.SUP.DEF this go.SUP on down
    'walking' / 'this walking'

  b. contra **mersului** pe jos
    contrary to go.SUP.GEN on down
    'against walking'

  c. **spălatul** **vaselor**
    wash.SUP.DEF dishes.DEF.GEN
    'the washing of the dishes'

  d. **spălatul** de vase
    wash.SUP.DEF of dishes
    'the washing of the dishes'

The *verbal supine*, lacking all the features under (99), is characterized by invariance and by the ability to assign verbal features to its arguments (100):

(100) Mă   satur   **de**   **dat**   **bani**
       CL.REFL.ACC.1SG am-fed-up   DE_SUP   give.SUP   money.PL.ACC
       săracilor   [+DO, +IO]
       poor.DEF.PL.DAT
       'I am fed up with giving money to the poor'

Compare (101a) and (101b), in which the same head supine, in the same prepositional context, is used on one occasion verbally (101a) and on another occasion nominally (101b):

(101) a. Se   plictisește **de** **citit**   aceleași   cărți   [−Art, +DO]
         CL.REFL.ACC.3SG is-fed-up   DE_SUP read.SUP   the-same   books

     b. Se   plictisește **de** **cititul**   acelorași   cărți   [+Art, +Gen]
        CL.REFL.ACC.3SG is-fed-up   DE_SUP read.SUP.DEF   the-same.GEN   books
        '(S)he is fed up with reading the same books'

H The nominal supine is an old creation, attested for all classes of verb since the earliest Romanian writings (Diaconescu 1971; Pană Dindelegan 2011; Dragomirescu 2011). In the old language, the nominal supine was used more frequently than today; for certain verbs, the supine forms were gradually replaced by the corresponding forms of the long nominalized infinitive. The parallel uses—nominal (102a) and verbal (102b)—have been attested since the end of the 17th century.

(102) a. loc   de   **ținutul**   vaselor   (Corbea)
         place DE_SUP keep.SUP.DEF   pots.DEF.GEN
         'a place to keep the pots'

     b. vas   de   **ținut**   ulei   (Corbea)
        pot   DE_SUP keep.SUP   oil.ACC
        'an oil recipient'

There is a third situation (the *nominal-verbal supine*), in which the supine, with no syntactically realized arguments, behaves as an ambiguous head, allowing both the nominal and the verbal interpretation:

(103) a. loc   **de**   **mâncat**
         place DE_SUP eat.SUP
         'place for eating'

     b. Se   gândește   **la**   **plecat**
        CL.REFL.ACC.3SG thinks   at   leave.SUP
        '(S)he thinks about leaving'

     c. Trăiește   **din**   **furat**
        lives   from   steal.SUP
        '(S)he earns a living by stealing'

4.4.3 Syntactic patterns with the verbal and the nominal-verbal supine

The verbal and the nominal-verbal supine occurs in various patterns.

C Certain parallels between the different patterns with the Romanian supine and an Albanian form deriving from the participle introduced by a preposition (Sandfeld 1930: 131) were mentioned above. For most of the patterns below, there are corresponding patterns in Albanian (Brâncuș 2007: 167–73; Manzini and Savoia 2007: 264–97).

4.4.3.1 The NP-modifier supine

Combined with a nominal head, the supine clause modifies the referential content of the noun, denoting a property regarding its origin (104a), its 'purpose' ((104b–f); §5.3.5.1.2), or simply a qualifying property (104g). The supine clause functions as a reduced relative clause, whose head noun occurs as: an externalization of the Patient (104a,b), of the Instrument (104c), of the Theme (104d), or as an externalization of a locative adjunct (104e,f,h). The current preposition is *de*, which is also used in the case of other modifiers (§5.3.5); less frequently, the preposition *pentru* 'for' also occurs (104h).

(104) a. cal   [de   furat]
         horse DE$_{SUP}$ steal.SUP
         'a stolen horse'

     b. vin   [de   vândut]
         wine DE$_{SUP}$ sell.SUP
         'wine for selling'

     c. mașină [de   spălat   rufe]
         machine DE$_{SUP}$ wash.SUP laundry.ACC
         'washing machine'

     d. ajutoare [de   trimis   sinistraților]
         aids DE$_{SUP}$ send.SUP victims.DEF.DAT
         'aids to be sent to the victims of the disaster'

     e. coș$_i$ [de   ținut   cartofii   [(în el$_i$)]]
         basket DE$_{SUP}$ keep.SUP potatoes.DEF.ACC (in it)
         'potato basket'

     f. masă$_i$ [de   stat   cinci persoane (la ea$_i$)]
         table DE$_{SUP}$ sit.SUP five persons.NOM (at it)
         'table for five persons to sit at'

     g. lucru [de   mirat]
         thing DE$_{SUP}$ wonder.SUP
         'curious thing'

     h. coș   **pentru** **ținut** pâine
         basket for keep.SUP bread.ACC
         'bread basket'

Depending on the type of the verb and also on the type of the externalized argument, there are some syntactic patterns (104c–f, h) which accept the realization of a verbal projection, the supine selecting a direct object (104c, e, h), an indirect object (104d), or even a subject of its own (104f).

4.4.3.2 The supine combined with a copula verb

The same structures are also possible with the copula verb *fi* 'be':

(105) a. Calul   este **de** **furat**
         horse.DEF is DE$_{SUP}$ steal.SUP
         'The horse is from stealing'

b. Vinul   este   **de**   **vândut**
      wine.DEF   is   DE_SUP   sell.SUP
      'The wine is for selling'

   c. Maşina   este   **de**   **spălat**   rufe
      machine.DEF is   DE_SUP   wash.SUP   linen.ACC
      'The machine is for washing linen'

4.4.3.3   The supine clause as a VP prepositional object

The supine clause occupies the position of a prepositional object:

(106) a. S-a apucat **de făcut reclamaţii**
         '(S)he started making complaints'

      b. A luat **la puricat acest subiect**
         '(S)he started examining closely this subject'

      c. S-a pus **pe citit cărţi**
         '(S)he started reading books'

The preposition introducing the supine may differ, according to the restriction imposed by the prepositional verb (*de, la, pe*); the same preposition is also selected when the verb combines with a nominal phrase (107):

(107) a. S-a   apucat   **de**   **treabă**
         CL.REFL.ACC.3SG=has   started   of   work
         '(S)he started working'

      b. A   luat   **la**   **control**
         has   taken   at   control
         '(S)he started checking'

      c. S-a   pus   **pe**   **treabă**
         CL.REFL.ACC.3SG=has   put   on   work
         '(S)he started working'

The subject of the supine is controlled by the matrix verb (Dragomirescu 2011):

(108) a. Ion_i s-a apucat [de făcut PRO_i reclamaţii]
         'Ion started making complaints'

      b. Ion_i s-a pus [pe citit PRO_i cărţi]
         'Ion started reading books'

In the context of selected (subcategorized) prepositions (108a,b), the supine functions as a mixed category, being characterized simultaneously by nominal syntax [+prepositional head] and verbal syntax [+internal argument (+DO)].

4.4.3.4   The supine clause combined with modal and aspectual transitive verbs

The supine clause may appear in the context of a transitive verb only with certain modal and aspectual verbs (the modal *avea* 'have' and the aspectual verbs *continua* 'continue', *termina* 'finish', *sfârşi* 'end'):

(109) a. El_i   **are**   [**de**   **citit** PRO_i   zece   romane]
         he   has   DE_SUP   read.SUP   ten   novels
         'He has to read ten novels'

b. Ion$_i$ şi-a **terminat** [de **făcut** PRO$_i$ lecţiile]
Ion CL.REFL.DAT.3SG=has finished DE$_{SUP}$ do.SUP lessons.DEF.ACC
'Ion finished doing his homework'

c. Ion$_i$ **continuă** [de **spus** PRO$_i$ neadevăruri]
Ion continues DE$_{SUP}$ say.SUP NEG-true-things.ACC
'He continues saying untrue things'

In this pattern, the occurrence of the preposition *de* cannot be explained by the governance of the matrix verb; *de* is a proclitic marker of the verbal supine and there are clear arguments to interpret it as an inflectional marker. DE behaves like the infinitive marker A (§4.2.1.2), the only difference being that A functions as an inflectional marker in all the occurrences of the infinitive, while DE does so only in certain contexts of the supine.

The supine forms a complex predicate with the matrix verb (§3.5.2.3), as the following features show:

- the subject of the supine is controlled by the matrix verb and, consequently, cannot be realized (109a–c);
- only one of the components may bear negation (110a,b), except for certain structures with contrastive negation (110c);
- the supine allows clitic climbing (110c–f), with the pronominal clitics raising to the left of the cluster [modal / aspectual verb + supine].

(110) a. Ion **nu are/ nu termină** de citit
Ion not has not finishes DE$_{SUP}$ read.SUP
'Ion does not have to read' / 'Ion does not finish reading'

b. Ion are / termină ***de necitit**
Ion has finishes DE$_{SUP}$ NEG-read.SUP

c. Cartea o are **nu de răsfoit**, ci de comentat
book.DEF CL.ACC.3SG has not DE$_{SUP}$ browse.SUP, but DE$_{SUP}$ comment.SUP
'(S)he does not have to browse the book, but to comment upon it'

d. **Romanele**$_i$ **le**$_i$ are de rezumat t$_i$
novels.DEF CL.ACC.3PL has DE$_{SUP}$ summarize.SUP
'(S)he has to summarize the novels'

e. **Romanele**$_i$ **le**$_i$ termină de citit t$_i$
novels.DEF CL.ACC.3PL finishes DE$_{SUP}$ read.SUP
'(S)he finishes reading the novels'

f. **Lecţiile**$_i$ şi **le**$_i$-a terminat de făcut t$_i$
lessons.DEF CL.REFL.DAT.3SG CL.ACC.3PL=has finished DE$_{SUP}$ do.SUP
'(S)he finished doing her homework'

U Regionally, there are also other verbs with aspectual meaning that may occur with clitic climbing:

(111) clopotele **ni le-au** oprit de tras (Creangă)
bells.DEF CL.DAT.1PL CL.ACC.3PL=have stopped DE$_{SUP}$ pull.SUP
'They stopped pulling the bells for us'

4.4.3.5 The supine depending on other transitive verbs

A configuration similar to the pattern mentioned in §4.4.3.4 is derived by the occurrence of a nominal between the matrix verb and the supine (112a,b). The nominal ends up occupying this position as an effect of the raising of the direct object of the supine:

(112) a. El are **altceva**$_i$ de   citit **t**$_i$
         he has something-else DE$_{SUP}$ read.SUP
         'He has something else to read'

   b. Termină   **ceva**$_i$ de   scris **t**$_i$
      finishes something   DE$_{SUP}$ write.SUP
      'She finishes something to write'

On this pattern, other constructions were created that comprise a transitive verb and a supine clause. In such constructions the subject of the supine is controlled either by the matrix subject (113a,b) or by the matrix indirect object (113c). These structures occur as an effect of the ellipsis of a head noun:

(113) a. El$_i$ capătă [$_{NP}$∅ [de   băut   PRO$_i$]]
         he   gets   DE$_{SUP}$ drink.SUP
         'He gets something to drink'

   b. El$_i$ caută   [$_{NP}$∅ [de   băut PRO$_i$]]
      he   searches   DE$_{SUP}$ drink.SUP
      'He looks for something to drink'

   c. El dă   colegilor$_i$ [$_{NP}$∅ [de   băut   PRO$_i$]]
      he gives colleagues.DEF.DAT   DE$_{SUP}$ drink.SUP
      'He treats his colleagues to a drink'

4.4.3.6 The supine clause in impersonal structures

Combined with an impersonally used verb (*rămâne* 'stay', *fi* 'be') or with an impersonal structure made up of a copula verb plus an adverbial phrase, the supine clause appears, with the most neutral word order, in the position of a rhematic postverbal subject (114a–d):

(114) a. Este / Rămâne   [**de**   **văzut**   PRO$_{ARB}$]
         is   remains DE$_{SUP}$ see.SUP
         'It remains to be seen'

   b. E   sănătos [**de**   **mers** PRO$_{ARB}$ pe jos]
      is   healthy DE$_{SUP}$ go.SUP   on down
      'Walking is healthy'

   c. E   obligatoriu [**de**   **ajuns**   PRO$_{ARB}$ la timp]
      is   obligatory   DE$_{SUP}$ arrive.SUP   at time
      'It is obligatory to arrive in time'

   d. Mi$_i$-e   greu   [**de**   **acceptat** PRO$_i$]
      CL.DAT.1SG=is   difficult   DE$_{SUP}$ accept.SUP
      'It is difficult for me to admit'

These structures display either impersonal control (PRO$_{ARB}$ in examples (114a–c) with a generic interpretation), or indirect object control (114d).

The occurrence of the preposition DE does not depend on the subcategorizing features of the matrix verb; DE functions as a proclitic inflectional marker of the supine, similarly to the contexts mentioned in §4.4.3.4. The fact that DE-supine also occurs when the subject is topicalized (115) is an argument for its inflectional marker status:

(115) [De realizat   totul],#   e   greu
      DE_SUP accomplish.SUP everything is difficult
      'It is difficult to accomplish everything'

In impersonal constructions, the supine clause has an active reading, if the verb is unergative (114b) or unaccusative (114c), and a passive reading, if the *by*-phrase of the verb is syntactically realized (116a). If the supine is realized by a transitive verb and the *by*-phrase is not expressed, it may be interpreted either as active or as passive. In (116a), the argument of the supine functions as the subject of the passive configuration; in (116b), the argument of the supine may be interpreted as subject—for the passive reading—or as an object—for the active reading (Pană Dindelegan 2003: 142–50):

(116) a. Este greu / uşor / cu neputinţă [**de acceptat** [soluţia]_S [de toţi politicienii]_{*by*-phrase}]
         'It is difficult / easy / impossible for the situation to be accepted by all the politicians'
      b. Este greu / lesne / cu neputinţă [**de acceptat** [soluţia]_{DO // S}]
         'It is difficult / easy / impossible to accept the situation'

4.4.3.7 Tough-constructions

Tough-constructions (Postal 1971) are derived from the impersonal structures mentioned in §4.4.3.6 by the raising of the argument of the supine (117a,b) to the left of the cluster [copula verb + adverb + supine]. There is partial agreement between the raised subject and the copula verb, which is a sign of syntactic restructuring (117b) and, implicitly, of the recategorization of the verb:

(117) a. **Minciuna**_i e   greu de   tăinuit t_i
         lie.DEF   is hard DE_SUP hide.SUP
         'The lie is hard to hide'
      b. **Minciunile** **sunt** greu de   tăinuit
         lies.DEF   are   hard DE_SUP hide.SUP
         'Lies are hard to hide'

U In non-standard Romanian (and in 19th-century language, including the high register), there are configurations with 'full' agreement, with the adverb undergoing agreement as well, and behaving, contextually, as an adjective:
   (118) lucrurile   simple   **sunt**   cele   mai   grele   de   priceput
         things.DEF.F.PL   simple   are.3PL   CEL.F.PL   more difficult.F.PL   DE_SUP understand.SUP
         şi   de   primit   (Maiorescu)
         and   DE_SUP   receive.SUP
         'Simple things are the most difficult to understand and accept'
C Even though *tough*-constructions are present in all Romance languages (Roegiest 1981), Romanian is the only Romance language which does not use the infinitive in them.

4.4.3.8 The adjunct supine

The (purpose, locative, restrictive) supine adjuncts appear in constructions such as the following:

(119) a. Ion$_i$ a plecat [la [cules PRO$_i$ mere]]
Ion has left to pick.SUP apples.ACC
'Ion left to pick apples'

b. El$_i$ m-a întrecut [la [făcut PRO$_i$ socoteli]]
he CL.ACC.1SG=has surpassed at do.SUP calculations.ACC
'He surpassed me in doing calculations'

c. Ea a plecat **în peţit**
she has left in woo.SUP
'She's gone wooing'

Different lexical prepositions—each one with its own meaning—are allowed. In (119a,b), the supine functions as a mixed category, simultaneously displaying nominal syntax [+prepositional phrase] and verbal syntax [supine + DO]. In (119c), the nature of the supine is ambiguous—with no syntactically realized arguments, it may be interpreted either as nominal or as verbal.

In (119a–c), the supine is involved in the obligatory control phenomenon.

4.4.3.9 The supine clause in combination with an adjectival head

In combination with a adjective head, the supine clause occurs in different syntactic patterns.

4.4.3.9.1 It functions as the prepositional object of an adjective. In combination with adjectives such as *gata* 'ready', the supine clause has an active reading (120a), whereas combined with other adjectives such as *apt* 'able', *bun* 'good', *demn* 'worthy', *vrednic* 'worthy', it may have either an active (120b) or a passive reading (120c):

(120) a. El$_i$ e **gata** [de intrat PRO$_i$ în concurs]
he is ready / capable DE$_{SUP}$ enter.SUP in contest
'He is ready / able to enter the race'

b. Nu pro$_i$ eşti **bun / apt** [de trăit PRO$_i$ în capitală]
not (you) are good / capable DE$_{SUP}$ live.SUP in capital
'You are not capable of living in the capital'

c. El$_i$ este **bun / demn / vrednic** [de luat în seamă PRO$_i$
he is good / worthy worthy DE$_{SUP}$ take.SUP into consideration
de către noi toţi]
by us all
'He is worthy to be noticed by all of us'

U The preposition *de* is frequently imposed by the selectional feature of the adjective. Other prepositions such as *la* 'at, to' and, in the old language, *spre* 'for' are also possible:
(121) vrednic **spre bătut** cu biciul (Corbea)
deserving for beat.SUP with whip.DEF
'deserving to be beaten with the whip'

C The other Romance languages use the infinitive construction selecting the appropriate preposition (Sala 2006: 134), depending on the language.

4.4.3.9.2 The supine clause may denote a superlative consequence of the degree to which a referent possesses the property denoted by the adjective. Note the occurrence of the intensifier in the structure of the adjectival phrase in (122a), and also its elision in (122b):

(122) a. [aşa de   puternică   [de   nedescris]]
         so   strong   DE$_{SUP}$ NEG-describe.SUP
         'so indescribably strong'

      b. [∅   puternică   [de   neimaginat]]
             strong   DE$_{SUP}$ NEG-imagine.SUP
         'unimaginably strong'

Note that the connector *de*, introducing a result supine clause, is the same as the subordinator which introduces a finite result adjunct (123):

(123)   (atât de)   puternică   [de   nu   se   poate   descrie]
         (so)   strong   DE   not   CL.REFL.PASS can.3SG   describe.INF
         'so undescribably strong'

The adjective may remain unexpressed, in which case the supine clause occupies the predicative position, overlapping with the pattern in §4.4.3.2.

(124)   Durerea   este [$_{AP}$∅   [de   nedescris]]
         pain.DEF   is   DE$_{SUP}$ NEG-describe.SUP
         'The pain is indescribable'

4.4.3.9.3 As a result of inversion and recategorization, the supine may undergo a shift from the postadjectival adjunct position (125a) to the preadjectival superlative intensifier position (125b):

(125) a. fată   frumoasă   de   nedescris
         girl   beautiful   DE$_{SUP}$ NEG-describe.SUP

      b. fată   nedescris   de   frumoasă
         girl   NEG-describe.SUP   DE   beautiful
         'indescribably beautiful girl'

4.4.3.9.4 The supine clause may function as the temporal or restrictive adjunct of the adjective:

(126) a. haină   moale   la   pipăit
         coat   soft   at   touch.SUP
         'a coat soft to the touch'

      b. elev   bun   la   socotit
         pupil   good   at   calculate.SUP
         'pupil good at calculating'

4.4.3.9.5 As an effect of a complete restructuring of the impersonal structure mentioned under §4.4.3.6, a structure like (127) may be derived; here, the supine clause, originally argumental, comes to function as a restrictive adjunct of the adjective. The structure comes to be interpreted as belonging to the pattern deascribed in §4.4.3.9.4, a fact which explains the presence, in some cases, of prepositions other than *de*:

(127) cărți   **greu/**   **grele**   de   citit /   la   citit
       books(F.PL) difficult.ADV / difficult.F.PL   DE_SUP   read.SUP/ at   read.SUP
       'books that are difficult to read'

4.4.3.10 The 'hanging theme' supine

With a discourse role, the supine also occurs in topicalized structures (Pană Dindelegan 2003: 151–64). These patterns are characterized by the syntactic and prosodic left isolation of the supine clause (a *hanging construction*) and by the resumption of the supine form by a finite form in the main clause (128); see also §13.4.2.3.

(128) a. [**De**   **durut**   capul,] #   l-a   durut   toată   ziua
         DE_SUP   hurt.SUP   head.DEF   CL.ACC.3SG=has hurt   all   day.DEF
         'As for having a headache, he had a headache all day long'

      b. [**De**   **citit**,] #   am   citit, dar   n-am   înțeles   nimic
         DE_SUP   read.SUP   (I)have read   but   not=(I)have   understood   anything
         'As for reading, I read, but I haven't understood anything'

De functions as a discourse marker used for the topicalization of the predication, irrespective of the type of predicate (verbal (128a,b), adjectival or nominal (129a,b)):

(129) a. **De** **frumoasă**,   e   frumoasă
         DE   beautiful,   is   beautiful
         'As for being beautiful, she is beautiful'

      b. **De** **frate**,   mi-e   frate,   dar   afacerile   sunt   afaceri
         DE   brother   CL.DAT.1SG=is   brother, but   business   are   business
         'He may be my brother, but business is business'

C   The pattern [*de* + supine] is specific to Daco-Romanian. In other Romance languages and also in Aromanian, there are infinitive constructions corresponding to the aforementioned pattern:

  (130) a. It. Dormire, dormo poco   (in Maiden and Robustelli 2007: 365)
           'As for sleeping, I don't sleep much'
        b. Arom. Ti dureari, nu mi doari multu   (DIARO)
           'As for having pain, I'm not in great pain'

4.4.3.11 The supine in imperative sentences

The non-subordinated supine occurs only in imperative sentences with an unspecified addressee, which can be retrieved in context (131a). The meaning of 'recommendation' and 'urge' occurs as a result of the ellipsis of deontic adverbials in impersonal structures (131b):

(131) a. **De**   **reținut**   ultimul   argument!
         DE_SUP   retain.SUP   last.DEF   argument

      b. [E~~ necesar / recomandabil~~]   **de**   **reținut**   ultimul   argument
         is   necessary recommendable   DE_SUP   retain.SUP   the-last   argument
         '(One should) keep in mind the last argument!'

H   Except for the patterns in §4.4.3.11, whose absence from old Romanian can be explained by the type of text they belong to, all the other patterns, including the ones with a lexical subject (Pană Dindelegan 2011; Dragomirescu 2011), are present in the old language too:

(132) loc   [de   cinat   [șase   înș]ₛ]   (Corbea)
      place DE_SUP   dine.SUP   six   persons
      'place for six persons to dine in'

4.4.4 The competition between supine, infinitive, and subjunctive

The supine shares numerous contexts with the verbal infinitive, contexts in which the subjunctive may also appear. The common contexts and the similar meaning lead to competition between the supine–infinitive–subjunctive. It appears in the following contexts:

(i) noun complement:

(133) dorința   de   citit/   de   a   citi /   să   citești
      desire.DEF   DE_SUP   read.SUP   DE   A_INF read.INF   SĂ_SUBJ   read.SUBJ.2SG
      'the desire to read'

The competition mentioned in (133) is limited to matrix deverbal abstract nouns; compared with the infinitive and subjunctive (functioning as complement of the noun), the distribution of the supine is larger; the supine combines with matrix concrete nouns too functioning as a noun modifier (134):

(134) fată   de   măritat – *fată de a   marita – *fată să   se   mărite
      girl   DE_SUP   marry.SUP   girl   DE A_INF marry.INF girl SĂ_SUBJ   CL.REFL.3SG   marry.SUBJ.3SG
      'girl ready to marry'

(ii) prepositional objects in the verb phrase:

(135) El   se   satură   de   făcut   exerciții / a   face
      he   CL.REFL.3SG   is-fed-up   DE_SUP   do.SUP   exercises / A_INF do.INF
      exerciții /   să   facă   exerciții
      exercises /   SĂ_SUBJ   do.SUBJ.3SG   exercises
      'He is fed up with doing exercises'

(iii) direct objects:

(136) Ei   continuă   de   citit /   a   citi /   să   citească
      they   continue   DE_SUP   read.SUP / A_INF read.INF / SĂ_SUBJ   read.SUBJ.3PL
      'They continue to read'

The class of transitive verbs which take the supine is much more limited than the class of verbs which select the subjunctive (137). Verbs selecting the supine may select the subjunctive as well, but not the other way round:

(137) a. *dorește   de   spus
         wants   DE_SUP   say.SUP

      b. *poate   de   spus
         can.3SG   DE_SUP   say.SUP

      c. *vrea   de   spus
         wants   DE_SUP   say.SUP

(iv) postverbal subjects in impersonal constructions:

(138) E   ușor   de   spus /   a   spune /   să   spui
      is   easy   DE_SUP   say.SUP / A_INF say.INF / SĂ_SUBJ   say.SUBJ.2SG
      'It is easy to say'

All the impersonal constructions with the structure [copula verb + modalizing adverb] select both the supine and the subjunctive or the infinitive.

(v) complements of an adjective:

(139) vrednic **de trimis** la Paris / **(de) a fi trimis** la
worthy DE$_{SUP}$ send.SUP to Paris DE A$_{INF}$ be sent(PPLE) to
Paris / **să fie trimis** la Paris
Paris SĂ$_{SUBJ}$ be.SUBJ.3SG sent(PPLE) to Paris
'deserving to be sent to Paris'

Adjectives selecting the supine allow the subjunctive and the infinitive as well, but not the other way round (Pană Dindelegan 1992: 74):

(140) datoare să înveţe / *de învăţat
obliged SĂ$_{SUBJ}$ study.SUBJ.3SG DE$_{SUP}$ study.SUP
'obliged to study'

(vi) imperative sentences.

(141) **De revăzut /** **A se revedea/ Să**
DE$_{SUP}$ revise.SUP A$_{INF}$ CL.REFL.PASS revise.INF SĂ$_{SUBJ}$
se revadă ultimele două pagini!
CL.REFL.PASS revise.SUBJ.3SG≡PL last.DEF two pages
'Revise the last two pages!'

4.5 THE GERUND (PRESENT PARTICIPLE)

Among the non-finite forms, the gerund is distinguished by the following features:

(i) inflectional marking, by attaching the suffixes *-ând* / *-ind* to the stem of the present;
(ii) direct (non-prepositional) linking to the matrix verb;
(iii) the ability to encode voice distinctions and to select all the arguments specific to finite forms, including the subject and pronominal clitics.

H In Romanian, the gerund probably continues the ablative form of the Latin gerund in *-ndo*. Functionally, the Romanian gerund performs the functions of the Latin present participle, which was not preserved in Romanian, unlike French, Italian, and Spanish.

4.5.1 Inflectional marking. The structure of the gerund form

The gerund is characterized by suffixal marking. The gerundial suffix *-ând* is attached to the present stem of the verbs with the infinitive in *-a* (*lucra* 'work'—*lucrând* 'working'), in *-ea* (*cădea* 'fall'—*căzând* 'falling'), in *-e* (*conduce* 'drive'—*conducând* 'driving'), or in *-î* (*coborî* 'descend'—*coborând* 'descending').

The suffix has the form *-ind* with *-i* infinitive verbs (*a fugi* 'run'—*fug**ind*** 'running'). The suffix *-ind* is also attached to the verbs with the infinitive in *-e*, if the root ends in vocalic *-i* (*scrie* 'write'—*scriind* 'writing'), and to the verbs with the infinitive in *-a*, if the root ends in vocalic *-i* (*apropia* 'bring near'—*apropiind* 'bringing near'), in semivocalic *-i* (*încuia* 'lock'—*încuind* 'locking'), or in the palatal consonants [c], [ɟ] (*îngenunchea* 'kneel'—*îngenunch**ind*** 'kneeling', *veghea* 'watch'– *veghind* 'watching').

U Verbs in the 2nd and 3rd inflectional classes with root-final -*t* or -*d* generally preserve the gerund forms modified under the effect of yod (see also §2.2.1.1.1): *vedea* 'see'—*văzând* 'seeing', *râde* 'laugh'—*râzând* 'laughing', *vinde* 'sell'—*vânzând* 'selling', *crede* 'think'—*crezând* 'thinking', *scoate* 'extract'—*scoțând* 'extracting'. The gerund form of the verb *a bate* (*bătând*) is an exception to this rule.

The forms of the verbs in the 3rd inflectional class with root-final -*n*, modified under the effect of yod, i.e. *spuind* 'telling', *țiind* 'holding', *rămâind* 'staying', etc., which were present in the literary language of the 19th century, are no longer used. The current norm requires the forms with *n*: *spunând*, *ținând*, *rămânând*.

When followed by pronominal clitics (except for the accusative feminine singular clitic *o*), the suffix of the gerund has the forms -*ându* / -*indu*:

(142) a. chemându-l
 call.GER-*U*=CL.ACC.M.3SG
 'calling him'

 b. chemând-o
 call.GER=CL.ACC.F.3SG
 'calling her'

The negative form of the gerund is formed by prefixing *ne*- to the affirmative form:

(143) neputând
 NEG-can.GER
 'not being able'

Adverbial clitics (*mai* 'more' or *prea* 'too') may intervene between the prefixal marker *ne*- and the affirmative gerund form:

(144) a. ne**mai**știind
 NEG-more-know.GER
 'no longer knowing'

 b. ne**prea**știind
 NEG-too-know.GER
 'not knowing too well'

4.5.2 The verbal gerund vs. the adjectival gerund

The gerund developed two forms: one behaving syntactically as a non-finite verbal form (145a) and the other showing gender and number inflection and the semantic and syntactic behaviour of an adjective (145b):

(145) a. Are o rană [VP**sângerând** de două ore]
 has a wound bleed.GER for two hours
 '(S)he has a wound (that has been) bleeding for two hours'

 b. Are o rană [AP**sângerândă**]
 has a wound.F.SG bleeding.GER.F.SG
 '(S)he has a bleeding wound'

The adjectival gerund, frequently used in the literary texts of the 19th century, functioned as the modifier of a noun, either in prenominal or postnominal position:

(146) a. **râzânda**   bucurie   (Bolintineanu)
         laughing.GER.F.SG.DEF joy.F.SG
         'the laughing joy'
    b. umbre   **fuginde**   (Alecsandri)
         shadow.F.PL run.GER.F.PL
         'fleeting shadows'

H The Romanian adjectival gerund, bearing gender, number, and case agreement features with the head noun, is a learnèd reconstruction on the pattern of the French present participle. While frequently used in the literary texts of the 19th century, the adjectival gerund is little used in the 20th century. In the contemporary language, there are only a few adjectival gerunds in use, in quasi-fixed constructions: ordine **crescândă** / **descrescândă** 'ascending / descending order', femeie **suferindă** 'suffering woman', rană **sângerândă** 'bleeding wound', poziție **șezândă** 'sitting position', mână / voce **tremurândă** 'shivering hand / voice'.

Certain adjectival gerunds have been substantivized. The most frequently used in contemporary language is *suferind* 'a suffering person':

(147)   **suferinzii** de inimă
        'those suffering from heart problems'

4.5.3 The relation between the verbal gerund and the finite form of the verb

Compared with the other non-finite forms, the gerund shows the most clearly verb-like behaviour.

(a) It is directly linked to the matrix verb, unlike the supine and the infinitive.
(b) It takes the same arguments as finite forms, including the subject and pronominal clitics (§4.5.6).
(c) It can encode temporal distinctions in the absence of specialized tense forms. In most of its usages, the gerund is semantically and syntactically dependent on a finite verb form. The action expressed by the gerund is simultaneous with the action in the matrix clause (148), or it may precede (149) or follow (150) it. In some of these contexts, the gerund combines with temporal adjuncts (150).

(148) Îl văd **trecând**
      'I see him passing by'

(149) **Greșind** de multe ori, a fost tras la răspundere
      'As he made mistakes many times, he was taken to task'

(150) Ne-am plimbat prin parc, **mergând** apoi acasă
      'We walked in the park, heading home afterwards'

4.5.4 The distribution and functions of the gerund

4.5.4.1 *The gerund as a formative*

The gerund shares with the other non-finite forms the status of being an element in analytic verb forms. The gerund is an element of the present presumptive forms:

(151) a. va   fi   **mergând**
        AUX.FUT.3SG be   go.GER
    b. o   fi   **mergând**
       o   be   go.GER

U   Until the beginning of the 20th century, regional varieties used other periphrastic constructions as well, made up of the gerund form and the auxiliary *fi* 'be' in different tenses. These structures, which had a durative value, have completely disappeared in the contemporary language.

(152)   **erau**   **trecând**   printr-o   pădure   mare   (Ispirescu)
        be.IMPERF.3PL   pass.GER   through=a   forest   big
        'They were crossing a big forest'

4.5.4.2   The non-finite gerund clause as an adjunct

Most frequently, the non-finite gerund clause functions as an adjunct.

In the verb phrase, it functions as modal (153) or instrumental adjunct (154), characterizing the action of the matrix verb:

(153)   Vorbeşte **bolborosind**
        'He talks mumbling'

(154)   A reuşit **furând**
        'He succeeded by stealing'

Extrasententially, the gerund may function as a temporal (155), reason (156), concessive (157), conditional (158), or additive positive (159) adjunct:

(155)   [**Mergând spre casă**], l-a sunat Andrei
        'When he was going home, Andrei phoned him'

(156)   [**Simţindu-se rău**], a plecat acasă
        'As he did not feel well, he left for home'

(157)   [**Chiar şi îngrijindu-se**], tot a răcit
        'Even taking care of himself / herself, (s)he still caught a cold'

(158)   [**Învăţând zi şi noapte**], ar fi reuşit
        'Studying day and night, he would have succeeded'

(159)   Îmi este dator cu cincizeci de lei, [**nemaisocotind tot sprijinul pe care i l-am arătat**]
        'He owes me 50 lei, notwithstanding all the support I showed him'

The gerund clause can also function as an **extrasentential** modal (160) and instrumental adjunct (161), but only if it is prosodically isolated from the rest of the sentence:

(160)   Mergea încet, [**împiedicându-se mereu**]
        '(S)he was walking slowly, stumbling all the time'

(161)   [**Analizând atent situaţia**], a găsit un răspuns la problemele lui
        'By carefully analysing the situation, he found an answer to his problems'

4.5.4.3   The non-finite gerund clause as a modifier

In the noun phrase, the non-finite gerund clause can function as the modifier of the head noun, being semantically equivalent to a relative clause:

(162)   S-au găsit multe [soluții [**vizând** ieșirea din criză]]
'There were found many solutions aiming at a way out of the crisis'

4.5.4.4   The non-finite gerund clause as an argument

In the verb phrase, the non-finite gerund clause is subordinated to the class of perception verbs (§4.5.6), and occupies either the direct object position (163), or the subject position, in configurations with *se*-passive perception verbs (164):

(163)   Aud   [**tunând**]
        (I)hear   thunder.GER
        'I can hear it thundering'

(164)   Se   aude   [**tunând**]
        CL.REFL.PASS   hear.3SG   thunder.GER
        'Thunder can be heard'

In the prepositional phrase, the non-finite gerund clause functions as the complement of the preposition of quality *ca* 'as':

(165)   E   văzut   [ca   [**fiind**   cel   mai   bun   în   domeniu]]
        is   seen   as   be.GER   CEL   more   good   in   domain
        'He is considered to be the best in the field'

U   In these configurations, verbs of evaluation or opinion (*analiza* 'analyse', *considera* 'consider', *judeca* 'judge', *vedea* 'consider'), conjecture verbs (*bănui*, *suspecta* 'suspect') or reporting verbs (*prezenta* 'present', *descrie* 'describe', *recomanda* 'recommend') can appear in the matrix position (Croitor 2008a: 303):
(166)   A prezentat acest volum [ca **fiind** primul lui volum de poezie]
'He presented this volume as being his first poetry volume'

4.5.4.5   Coordinated gerund clauses

The non-finite gerund clause can also denote events that are not subordinated to the matrix predicate. The semantic relation between the gerund construction and the matrix predication is similar to conjunctive coordination (Edelstein 1972: 111; Zafiu 2008a: 532–3). The construction is prosodically isolated and graphically separated from the rest of the clause:

(167)   Ne-am   plimbat   până   spre   seară,
        CL.REFL.ACC.1PL=have   walked   until   towards   evening
        [**luând**-o   apoi   spre   casă]
        head.GER=CL.ACC.3SG   then   towards house
        'We walked until evening, heading home afterwards'

4.5.4.6   The gerund construction as a secondary predicate

The non-finite gerund clause functions as a secondary predicate in raised object structures, with perception verbs in the matrix clause (see also §§10.4.4, 2.3.3.1):

(168) Îi văd [**plimbându-se** în parc]
'I can see them walking in the park'

These configurations with perception verbs and pronominal direct objects are derived by raising the subject of the gerund to the direct object position within the matrix clause, in order to get case marking (§2.3.3.1.2):

(169) Văd   [[**oamenii**]   plimbându-se   în parc] >
      (I)see   people.PL.DEF.NOM   walk.GER=CL.REFL.ACC in park
      [**Îi**   văd]   plimbându-se   în   parc
      CL.ACC.3PL (I)see   walk.GER=CL.REFL.ACC in park
      'I can see people walking in the park' > 'I can see them walking in the park'

C   This type of configuration, called 'the accusative plus gerund construction' (Caragiu 1957; Manoliu-Manea 1977; Drăghicescu 1990) corresponds to 'the accusative plus infinitive' constructions found in other Romance languages (Salvi 2011: 368). In this type of semantico-syntactic relation, Romanian differs from Italian (170) and French (171), which use the infinitive and the pseudo-relative construction, and from Spanish, which uses both forms, the gerund and the infinitive, in free variation (172):

(170) a. Sento **cantare** Gianni / Gianni **cantare**
      b. Sento Gianni **che canta**   (in Maiden and Robustelli 2007: 391–2)
(171) a. Je l'ai entendu **chanter**
      b. Je l'ai entendu **qui chantait** (in Lombard 1974: 298; Manoliu-Manea 1977: 228)
(172) a. Miraba a los niños **jugando**
      b. Miraba **jugar** a los niños

In the case of the verbs of representation like *a-şi imagina, a-şi închipui* 'imagine, fancy', the gerund construction is allowed in most of the Romance languages—Romanian (173a), French (173b), and Portuguese (173c):

(173) a. Mi-o   închipui   **intrând**   aici   pentru   prima   oară
         CL.REFL.DAT.1SG=CL.ACC.3SG   (I)imagine   enter.GER   here   for   the first time
         'I imagine her entering here for the first time'
      b. Je me l'imagine **entrant** ici pour la première fois
      c. Imagino-a **entrando** aqui pela primeira vez (in Reinheimer Rîpeanu 2001: 300–1)

The same pattern is possible with certain event verbs like *descoperi* 'discover', *găsi* 'find', *lăsa* 'leave', *surprinde* 'find':

(174) a. L-am găsit **plângând**
         'I found him crying'
      b. L-am lăsat **dormind**
         'I left him sleeping'
      c. Am surprins-o **vorbind** în somn
         'I caught her talking in her sleep'

These structures with verbs of perception in the matrix are semantically equivalent to the ones in which the aforementioned verbs are followed by pseudo-relative clauses introduced by *cum* 'as' (§§2.3.3.1, 10.1.1.3).

4.5 The gerund (present participle) 251

(175) a. Îi   văd   **îndreptându-se**   spre   școală
         CL.ACC.3PL   (I)see   head.GER=CL.REFL.3PL   towards   school

      b. Îi   văd   **cum** **se**   **îndreaptă** spre   școală
         CL.ACC.3PL   (I)see   as   CL.REFL.3PL   head   towards school
         'I can see them heading to school'

The non-finite gerund clause functions as a secondary predicate in the context of certain prepositional verbs like *a se uita la* 'look at', *a-și aminti de* 'remember'.

(176) M-am tot uitat [la tine [**lucrând**]]
      'I kept on looking at you while you were working'

4.5.4.7 Parenthetical gerund constructions

The gerund constructions *sincer* **vorbind** 'honestly speaking', *teoretic* **vorbind** 'theoretically speaking', *la drept* **vorbind** 'as a matter of fact' are used parenthetically, with a metadiscourse function:

(177) [Teoretic **vorbind**], legea nu permite această măsură
      'Theoretically speaking, the law does not allow this measure'

4.5.5 The ambiguity of the gerund

Configurations with matrix verbs of perception and gerund clauses functioning as secondary predicates allow two readings: the subject of the gerund is coreferential with the subject of the verb of perception (178a); the subject of the gerund is coreferential with the direct object of the verb of perception (178b):

(178) a. Andreea$_i$ îl$_j$ vede [**mergând** PRO$_i$ spre școală]
         'Andreea sees him while she is walking to school'

      b. Andreea$_i$ îl$_j$ vede [**mergând** t$_j$ spre școală]
         'Andreea sees him while he is walking towards school'

C Romanian is different from Italian and French, where the subject of the gerund is coreferential with the subject of the matrix verb (Maiden and Robustelli 2007: 310):
   (179) It. Vidi il ragazzo uscendo dalla chiesa
          'I saw the boy as I came out of the church'

4.5.6 The internal structure of the non-finite gerund clause

The gerund can take any type of argument, in the same way as the other non-finite forms. Object clitics are placed in postverbal position.

(180) a. ajutându-**mă**
         help.GER=CL.ACC.1SG
         'helping me'

      b. spunându-**mi**
         tell.GER=CL.DAT.1SG
         'telling me'

C   With respect to clitic placement, Romanian differs from French, where the clitic is placed in preverbal position, but resembles Spanish and Italian, where the clitic is enclitically attached to the verb.

In certain syntactic conditions, the gerund may take its own nominative subject, distinct from the matrix subject (see also §3.1.2.2). This can happen in the following contexts:

(i) when the gerund clause occupies the extrasentential adjunct position:

(181)   [Venind **copiii**$_i$ de la școală] / [**Copiii**$_i$ venind de la școală], mama$_j$ s-a apucat să așeze masa
'As the children came back from school, mother began to lay the table'

(ii) when the gerund clause occupies the instrumental adjunct position:

(182)   Andrei$_i$ a ocupat această poziție [ajutându-l **părinții**$_j$] / [**părinții**$_j$ ajutându-l]
'Andrei got this position with the help of his parents'

(iii) when the gerund clause occupies the direct object position, depending on a verb of perception:

(183)   Elevii$_i$ aud [sunând **clopoțelul**$_j$]
'The pupils can hear the bell ringing'

4.5.7 The recategorization of gerund forms

Certain gerund forms have been grammaticalized, losing their verbal nature and developing other values.

(i) The form *curând* 'soon' is used in the modern language only as an adverb with temporal value.

(184)   O să vină **curând**
'(S)he will come soon'

H   In the 16th to 18th centuries, *curând* functioned as the gerund form of the verb *cure* 'run' (Dinică 2009: 202–7):
(185)   Și vădzându-l după sine **curând**, mai tare fugiia   (Dosoftei)
'And seeing that he was running after him, he was running even faster'
In the old language, the verbal value coexisted with the temporal one.

(ii) In the contemporary language, the form *privind* (literally 'looking at') may be used as a preposition, with the relational meaning 'as for, regarding':

(186)   **Privind** pensiile, proiectul de lege a trecut
'As for pensions, the bill passed'

H   In the 16th century, the forms *alegând* and *trecând* occurred as components of the prepositional phrases *alegând de* and *trecând de* 'besides, except for' (Frâncu 2009: 144).

(iii) The compound conjunction of reason *fiindcă* 'because' contains the gerund form *fiind* 'being' (< ***fiind*** 'being' + *că* 'that').

H Towards the mid-20th century, the conjunction *fiindcă* 'because' was not always written as one unit. Between the components *fiind* and *că* the adversative conjunction *însă* 'but' could intervene (Avram 1960: 82):

(187) | Fiind | însă | că | ţelul | meu [...] | nu | era | de | a |
|---|---|---|---|---|---|---|---|---|
| be.GER | but | that | goal.DEF | my | not | was | DE | A$_{INF}$ |
| petrece | noaptea | | | | | | | (Alecsandri) |
| spend.INF | night.DEF | | | | | | | |

'But because my goal was not to spend the night'

CONCLUSIONS

1 In Romanian, there are four non-finite verb forms: the infinitive, the gerund (present participle), the participle, and the supine. In contrast to the other Romance languages, Romanian acquired the supine, syncretic with the participle and synonymous with the infinitive. The selected subjunctive has a special situation: in certain occurrences it behaves similarly to non-finite forms despite the fact that it carries person and number inflection.

Non-finite verb forms can have an overt subject (bearing nominative case), distinct from the subject of the matrix verb. The overt subject is more frequent in the case of the infinitive and the gerund, and less common for the supine and the participle.

2 The **infinitive** has mixed marking, both suffixal and analytical. Romanian added a new ending (-*îre*) to the already existent four Latin infinitive endings. The infinitive form underwent phonological reduction, eliminating the final -*re*; it has developed a free proclitic marker A, which historically evolved from the status of lexical preposition, to that of inflectional element.

A new temporal form in the history of Romanian emerged as a late phenomenon: the perfect infinitive.

The infinitive has common contexts and meanings with the personal subjunctive, a fact which favoured the replacement of the infinitive by the subjunctive.

Compared to the categorially ambiguous infinitive in old Romanian, which alternatively functioned either nominally or verbally, Romanian evolved towards the formal differentiation of two distinct heads: a (nominal) 'long' infinitive vs. a (verbal) 'short' infinitive.

3 Romanian is among the Romance languages in which the participle in analytic tenses does not display agreement, irrespective of the type of verb or construction.

In the compound past, the participle selects only the auxiliary 'have', irrespective of the syntactic class of the verb.

Romanian does not formally distinguish between adjectival and verbal participles, on the one hand, and stative and resultative participles, on the other hand.

The verbal participle exhibits mixed category behaviour, simultaneously having adjectival inflection and agreement, as well as verbal syntactic features.

4 Over the history of Romanian, there emerged a diversified scale of degrees of nominalization, distinguishing, as in the case of the infinitive, a verbal supine, similar to the verbal behaviour, and a nominal supine, similar to the nominal behaviour.

The supine form is ambiguous in two respects: it can have, alternatively, nominal and verbal behaviour. There are also constructions in which the supine functions as a mixed category, being characterized simultaneously by the features [+nominal syntax], [+verbal syntax].

The uses and values of the supine diversified: (i) from a nominal supine to a verbal supine; (ii) from the modifier position within the noun phrase to the argument position within the verb phrase; (iii) Romanian created a specific pattern of topicalization, with the supine clause placed in a hanging position.

De, which frequently introduces the supine clause, is ambiguous, displaying variable behaviour from one syntactic context to another; it behaves: (i) as an inflectional marker; (ii) as a lexical or a selected preposition; (iii) as a functional preposition specialized for introducing modifiers in the noun phrase; (iv) as a discourse marker used for the 'hanging theme' construction.

There emerged in Romanian a situation of synonymy between the supine, the infinitive, and the subjunctive, leading to functional competition between them.

5 Among the non-finite forms, the gerund has the most verb-like nature: it may take any type of argument specific to finite verbal forms, including pronominal clitics.

When it follows a verb of perception, the gerund is part of an 'accusative plus gerund', in contrast to the other Romance languages, which select the infinitive instead of the gerund. The 'accusative plus gerund' structures are semantically equivalent to the configurations in which the verb of perception is followed by a pseudo-relative clause, introduced by the adverbial *cum* 'as'.

The 'accusative plus gerund' constructions are ambiguous: (a) the subject of the gerund is co-referential with the matrix subject; (b) the subject of the gerund is co-referential with the direct object of the verb of perception.

5

Nouns and Noun Phrases

In this chapter, we present the main features pertaining to the Romanian nominal phrase: the morphology of nouns and determiners, the semantic-grammatical classes of nouns, and the structure of the nominal phrase (determiners, quantifiers, arguments of the noun, modifiers, and the means of encoding possession within the nominal phrase).

5.1 NOUN MORPHOLOGY

Nouns are inflected for number and case. The inflectional markers are synthetic or analytic. The nominal inflectional characteristics vary depending on the gender of the noun.

5.1.1 Three genders: masculine, feminine, and neuter

Romanian possesses three genders, each of them having subordinate inflectional classes which are separated especially according to their affixes (inflectional endings and the enclitic article) and to the combinations of affixes, as well as to the inflectional syncretisms they display (§5.1.4).

5.1.1.1 *The marking of genders*

Being expressed simultaneously with number, gender may be marked by an inflectional ending, and, in the definite declension, both by an inflectional ending and the definite enclitic article (Tables 5.1 and 5.2).

TABLE 5.1 Gender marking on articleless nouns

		MASCULINE		FEMININE		NEUTER	
		SG	PL	SG	PL	SG	PL
Articleless nouns	NOM≡ACC	elev-∅ pupil-SG	elev-i	fat-ă	fet-e	caiet-∅	caiet-e
	GEN≡DAT	elev-∅ pupil-SG	elev-i	fet-e	fet-e	caiet-∅	caiet-e

TABLE 5.2 Gender marking on nouns bearing the definite article

		MASCULINE		FEMININE		NEUTER	
		SG	PL	SG	PL	SG	PL
Nouns bearing the definite article	NOM≡ACC	elev-**u-l** pupil-SG-DEF	elev-**i-i**	fat-**a**	fet-**e-le**	caiet-**u-l**	caiet-**e-le**
	GEN≡DAT	elev-**u-lui** pupil-SG-DEF GEN≡DAT	elev-**i-lor**	fet-**e-i**	fet-**e-lor**	caiet-**u-lui**	caiet-**e-lor**

H   Throughout the history of Romanian, there have been numerous transitions from one class of gender to another, especially from masculine to neuter and vice versa. These transitions have been influenced by the fact that in the masculine and neuter singular the nouns in question have the same inflectional endings; semantics has also played a part in this process.

On the one hand, nouns like *câmp* 'field' and *roi* 'swarm', which are neuter in the present-day language with the inflectional ending *-uri* in the plural (*câmp**uri***, *roi**uri***), were masculine in previous stages of Romanian, having the typically masculine plural forms *câmpi* (currently preserved in the fixed collocation *a bate câmpii* 'beat about the bush') and *roi* (Diaconescu 1970: 106). On the other hand, masculine nouns such as *stâlp* 'pillar' (PL *stâlpi*), *obraz* 'cheek' (PL *obraji*), *umăr* 'shoulder' (PL *umeri*) belonged to the neuter gender in the 16th century, as shown by their plural forms: *stâlpure*, *obraze*, *umere* (Dimitrescu 1975: 38).

Before their inclusion in a specific gender class, certain nouns were employed with different forms which would allocate them to two gender classes. For instance, in the 16th century, *gruma(d)z* 'neck' was employed either with the plural *grumadzele* (NEUT) (*Psaltirea Hurmuzaki*) or with the plural *gruma(d)zi* (M) (*Palia*) (Diaconescu 1970: 106).

Nouns such as *slugă* 'servant', *vlădică* 'bishop, leader' have raised problems with respect to their inclusion in a specific gender class because of the natural gender of their referent. Thus, the feminine noun *slugă* could appear in old Romanian in masculine contexts: *un slugă* (Coresi) and the masculine noun *vlădică* could change its form on the model of most masculine nouns: *vlădic* (Costin) (Diaconescu 1970: 104–5).

5.1.1.2   The position of the neuter

Alongside masculine and the feminine nouns, marked by specific inflectional endings and by agreement within the NP (§§5.1.4.1, 5.1.4.2), Romanian possesses a third class of nouns, *neuter* nouns. Because of the morphological identity of the neuter with the masculine in the singular and with the feminine in the plural, the neuter is not considered a distinct gender by some scholars, being sometimes called *ambigen* 'ambigeneric' or *eterogen* 'heterogeneric' (Pătruţ 1957; Posner 1996; Bateman and Polinsky 2010, and others).

However that may be, the Romanian neuter is a flourishing class, as testified by the many borrowings that are assigned to the neuter gender (such as *airbaguri* 'airbags', *joburi* 'jobs', *laptopuri* 'laptops', *trenduri* 'trends', *weekenduri* 'weekends').

H   Several hypotheses have been developed as to the origin of the Romanian neuter: inheritance from Latin (e.g. Fischer 1975, 1985: 82; Ivănescu 1957), substratum influence (Nandriş 1961), Slavic influence (Graur 1968: 65), or emergence in Romanian (Rosetti 1986: 597); for an extensive discussion, see ELR: 374–6; Iliescu 2008a: 2647. The Latin origin of the Romanian neuter, a more widely accepted opinion, is also supported by the fact that all the features of the Romanian neuter are also present in late Latin (Fischer 1975).

C   The neuter singles out Romanian among the Romance languages. Some relics of the neuter gender are also found in Italian and in Rhaeto-Romance (Iliescu 2008a: 2647). Unlike Romanian, in Italian there are a few plural forms, considered to be irregular, which may be accounted for starting from the Latin neuter forms. These plural forms are in fact derived with the suffix *-a*, inherited from Latin, and have different meanings with respect to the regular forms which use the inflectional ending *-i*, denoting body parts and other entities occurring in series, parts of masses, and units of measure / quantity: It. *braccia* 'arms (as complex with functionally non-distinct parts)'—*bracci* 'arms', *mura* 'walls (perimeter)'—*muri* 'walls', *ossa* 'bones (as body parts)'—*ossi* 'bones' (as unrelated pieces)'. Some *-a* plurals, such as *uova* 'eggs', *centinaia* 'hundreds', do not have regular counterparts (Acquaviva 2008: 123–61, Loporcaro and Paciaroni 2011: 401–3).

The existence of the neuter gender brings Romanian closer to the Balkan languages, which possess gender forms marked by endings (for instance, in Bulgarian the three genders are distinguished depending on the ending of the noun; Feuillet 1986: 71).

Several semantic-referential and morphosyntactic arguments may be used to support the existence of the neuter as an independent gender in Romanian.

From a semantic-referential point of view, neuter nouns denote only inanimate referents, with the exception of a few generic (*animal* 'animal', *star* '(film) star', *vip* 'VIP') or collective (*popor* 'people', *cârd* 'flock') nouns. Masculine and feminine nouns, in contrast, may denote animate or inanimate referents.

A morphological argument is the inflectional ending -*uri*, which characterizes a subclass of neuter nouns (§5.1.4.3). To a limited extent, -*uri* occurs in feminine nouns as well (e.g. *lipsă* 'gap'—*lipsuri* 'gaps', *treabă* 'affair'—*treburi* 'affairs'), but etymologically, and in the overwhelming majority of cases, it is specific to the class of neuter nouns (see also §5.1.4.2).

H The ending -*uri* continues the final sequence -ORA of certain Latin neuter nouns, morphologically reanalysed as an inflectional ending. Thus, -*or*-, originally a final component of the root, was reanalysed as being part of the inflectional ending: Lat. SG CORPUS, PL CORPOR-A > CORP-ORA, TEMPUS, PL TEMPOR-A > TEMP-ORA (Maiden 2011a: 172).

The Latin neuter final sequence -*ora* evolved in Romanian to -*ure* (frequent in the 16th century) and later to -*uri*. For instance, the Latin plural TEMPORA (SG TEMPUS) became *timpure* (16th century) then *timpuri* (Dimitrescu 1975: 59).

From an inflectional point of view, neuter nouns use the same inflectional endings as masculines (in the singular) and as feminines (in the plural), but what distinguishes neuter is the correlations between inflectional endings; the correlations -Ø— -**e**, -**u**— -**e**, -Ø— -**uri**, -**u**— -**uri** are characteristic of neuters, while masculines show the correlations -Ø— -**i**, -**u**— -**i**, and feminines -**ă**— -**uri** (in the case of feminines, this correlation is limited to very few words) (see Table 5.3; see also §5.1.4).

Similarly, neuter nouns take the same allomorph of the article as masculines in the singular and as feminines in the plural; this results in the correlation -(u)l— -le in the neuter, which contrasts with -(u)l— -i in the masculine and -a— -le in the feminine.

(1)   MASCULINE   NEUTER
   SG   băiatul   (boy.DEF)   creionul (pencil.DEF)
   PL   băieții   (boys.DEF)   —
        FEMININE
   SG   cartea   (book.DEF)   —
   PL   cărțile   (books.DEF)   creioanele (pencils.DEF)

TABLE 5.3 Desinential correlations specific to the neuter gender

NEUTER	MASCULINE	FEMININE
-Ø— -**e** (creion 'pencil'—creioane 'pencils')	-Ø— -**i** (pantof 'shoe'—pantofi 'shoes')	
-**u**— -**e** (registru 'register'—registre 'registers')	-**u**— -**i** (membru 'member'—membri 'members')	
-Ø— -**uri** (pix 'pen'—pix**uri** 'pens')		-**ă**— -**uri** (lipsă 'gap'—lips**uri** 'gaps')
-**u**— -**uri** (titlu 'title'—titl**uri** 'titles')		

For invariable neuter nouns with the inflectional ending -*e* (both in the singular and in the plural), there is also an invariable definite article in the singular and the plural, namely **-le** (2a), which contrasts with the correlation **-le**— **-i** of masculine nouns with the inflectional ending -*e* in the singular (2b) and with the correlation **-a**— **-le** of feminine nouns which have the ending in -*e* in the singular (2c) or which are invariable, their root ending in -*e* (2d):

(2) a. SG num**e**le   — PL num**e**le   (NEUT)
          name.DEF   names.DEF

   b. SG frat**e**le   — PL fraț**ii**   (M)
          brother.DEF   brothers.DEF

   c. SG floar**ea**   — PL flor**ile**   (F)
          flower.DEF   flowers.DEF

   d. SG învățătoar**ea** — PL învățătoar**ele** (F)
          teacher.DEF   teachers.DEF

Although it does not possess specific markers, the neuter is distinct from the masculine and from the feminine precisely because the inflectional endings selected in the neuter are opposed to the feminine in the singular and to the masculine in the plural (Graur 1968: 66). The syntactic consequence of these oppositions is that the neuter forms select agreeing articles and other determiners, quantifiers, and adjectival modifiers with masculine morphology in the singular and feminine morphology in the plural:

(3) NEUT SG **un**   creion **bun**   PL **două**   creioane **bune**
           a.M≡NEUT   pencil good.M≡NEUT   two.F≡NEUT   pencils good.F≡NEUT

5.1.1.3 Gender-changing and epicene nouns

A series of feminine nouns are derived from masculines and, more rarely, vice versa, by means of gender-changing suffixes: -*ă* (*elev* 'student' (M)—*elevă* 'student' (F)), -*că* (*român* 'Romanian' (M)—*româncă* 'Romanian' (F)), -*easă* (*preot* 'priest'—*preoteasă* 'priestess'); -*an* (*gâscă* 'goose'—*gâscan* 'gander'), -*oi* (*vulpe* 'fox'—*vulpoi* 'male fox'), etc. (§14.1.2.2).

Some animate nouns—called 'epicene'—have only one form for both male and female referents: *barză* 'stork', *elefant* 'elephant', *rudă* 'relative', *victimă* 'victim'.

5.1.2 Countable and uncountable nouns

In the case of countable nouns, number marking is realized by the same affixes (inflectional endings and the definite article) that indicate gender (§§5.1.1.1, 5.1.4), which are sometimes reinforced by morphophonological alternations of the stem.

5.1.2.1 Plural inflectional endings

Romanian possesses a variety of plural inflectional endings depending on inflectional classes; the stem-final segment may determine morphophonogical variations (Table 5.4).

C Alongside Dalmatian and Italo-Romance, Romanian belongs to the eastern group of Romance varieties, which use vocalic inflectional endings to mark the plural rather than -*s*, as employed by other varieties (Ibero-Romance, Gallo-Romance, Rhaeto-Romance, and Sardinian); see Maiden (1996) for a discussion of the historical developments.

5.1 Noun morphology

TABLE 5.4 Plural inflectional endings

Gender	Plural Inflectional Endings	Morphophonological Instantiation of the Ending
MASCULINE	-*i*	[-i] codru—codri 'forest(s)' [-i̯] leu—lei 'lion(s)' [-ʲ] pom—pomi 'tree(s)'
FEMININE	-*e* -*le* -*i* -*uri*	[-e] casă—case 'house(s)' [-le] stea—stele 'star(s)' [-ʲ] poartă—porți 'gate(s)' [-i̯] familie—familii 'family' – 'families' [-Ø] baie—băi 'bathroom(s)' [-urʲ] treabă—treburi 'affair(s)'
NEUTER	-*uri* -*e*	[-urʲ] tablou—tablouri 'painting(s)' [-e] teatru—teatre 'theatre(s)' [-i̯] consiliu—consilii 'council(s)'

H The plural inflectional endings in the inflection of the noun are of Latin origin.

The plural ending -*i* originates in the nominative masculine plural ending -I (Lat. ANNI, LUPI > *ani, lupi*) or in -ES (Lat. CANES, NOCTES > *câini, nopți*); the latter probably went through the intermediate stage *[-ei̯] (Maiden 1996: 148–58, Maiden 2011a: 164; Renzi 2002–2003: 199). In the case of feminine plural nouns that end in -*e*, originating in the third Latin declension, the plural inflectional ending -*i* has also been analysed as an extension from masculines (Iordan and Manoliu 1965: 133).

The feminine inflectional ending -*e* has been interpreted as the successor either of the ending Lat. -AE from the nominative plural ending of first declension nouns: Rom. *casa* 'house'—*case* 'houses' < Lat. CASA—CASAE (Iordan and Manoliu 1965: 133), or of -AS, probably having undergone the intermediate stage *[-ai̯] (Maiden 1996: 148–58, Maiden 2011a: 164).

The feminine inflectional ending -*le* is the result of a natural phonological evolution (Lat. PL STELLAE > Rom. *stele* 'stars', see §5.1.4.2).

The neuter inflectional ending -*e* developed out of Lat. -A, which first evolved to -*ă* (Lat. -A > -*ă* > -*e*; Iordan and Manoliu 1965: 134).

The neuter inflectional ending -*uri* clearly derives from Lat. -ORA (§5.1.1.2), and the use of -*uri* with feminines is a later (the earliest attestations date from the 17th century) and rather limited extension from neuter nouns (Graur 1968: 90–2; see also §5.1.4.2).

5.1.2.2 Alternations in the marking of number distinctions

Number distinctions may be supplementarily marked by vowel or consonantal alternations (§15.1).

In present-day language, consonantal alternations in the inflection of the noun are more consistent than vocalic alternations; the former have a regular character, since they continue to function only for borrowings (*bodyguard* 'bodyguard'—*bodyguarzi* 'bodyguards', *byte* 'byte'—*byți* 'bits'), while the latter tend to lose their regular character (*papilom* 'papilloma'—*papiloame* 'papillomas' vs. *simptom* 'symptom'—*simptome* 'symptoms'); see Pană Dindelegan (2009b: 30–2).

5.1.2.3 Double plural forms

Several nouns have double plural forms (§§5.1.1.1, 5.1.4.2, 5.1.4.3).

In the case of certain nouns, the different plural forms have the same meaning and belong either to the same gender class (*cireşe—cireşi* 'cherries', *coperte—coperţi* 'covers' (F), *niveluri—nivele* 'levels' (NEUT)) or to different gender classes (*robinete* (NEUT)—*robineţi* (M) 'taps', *constituente* (NEUT)—*constituenţi* (M) 'constituents', *echivalente* (NEUT)—*echivalenţi* (M) 'equivalents'). However, for other nouns, the different plural forms occurred and were preserved as the effect of semantic specialization: for instance, to the singular *element* 'element' correspond the plurals *elemente* 'components' and *elemenţi* 'parts of a radiator'; similarly, the singular *centru* 'centre' has two plurals, *centre* 'focal points, cities, institutions' and *centri* 'anatomical centres; (sports) players'.

5.1.2.4 Invariable nouns

Certain nouns such as the masculine *pui* 'chicken(s)', *ochi* 'eye(s)', the feminine *judecătoare* 'judge(s)', *învăţătoare* 'teacher(s)' or the neuters *nume* 'name(s)', *codice* 'codex / codices' have only one form for the singular and the plural. In this situation, the enclitic article or other constituents that agree with the noun may disambiguate the syncretism: *învăţătoarea* (teacher.DEF.SG) vs. *învăţătoarele* (teacher.DEF.PL), *învăţătoare **tânără*** (teacher.F.SG young.F.SG) vs. *învăţătoare **tinere*** (teacher.F.PL young.F.PL).

H   The formal identity of the singular with the plural may be explained etymologically and / or phonologically.

   The invariable nouns *pui* 'chicken', *crai* 'king', *ochi* 'eye', *arici* 'hedgehog' originally had a singular inflectional ending -*u*, which has not been written systematically since the 16th century (Diaconescu 1970: 111; Frâncu 2009: 25).

   The noun *nume* had two plural forms in the 16th century: *numere* (< Lat. NOMINA) şi *nume* (Diaconescu 1970: 111; Frâncu 2009: 26). Although *numere* survived into the next two centuries, it has been replaced by *nume*.

   From a historical perspective, the noun *mână* 'hand, arm' is in a totally different situation. In the old language, the noun *mână* had the same form in the singular and in the plural (*mânu*); subsequently, there emerged a distinct singular form, *mână* (recorded as early as the 16th century; Diaconescu 1970: 112; Frâncu 2009: 26–7).

5.1.2.5 Singularia tantum *and* pluralia tantum

Certain nouns occur only in a singular context, while others occur only in the plural, as an effect of their semantic-referential features. Thus, most *singulare tantum* nouns are mass and abstract nouns such as *argint* 'silver', *nisip* 'sand', *vin* 'wine'; *amabilitate* 'kindness', *bunătate* 'goodness', *curaj* 'courage'. In the class of *pluralia tantum* there are a few mass nouns, like *icre* 'roe, caviar', *spaghete* 'spaghetti', *tăieţei* 'noodles', abstract nouns *memorii* 'memoirs', *funeralii* 'funerals', and certain nouns that denote objects made up of two identical parts *ochelari* 'glasses', *ghilimele* 'quotation marks'.

Most *singulare tantum* nouns have a corresponding plural form, which correlates with changes in meaning: the plurals of mass nouns denote sorts (*vinuri* 'sorts of wine'), objects (*arginturi* 'silver objects'); the plural forms of abstract nouns indicate different degrees of transformation from abstract to concrete (*amabilităţi* 'words of kindness', *bunătăţi* 'goodies').

U The plural inflectional ending *-uri* acquired the supplementary value of creating plural nouns denoting sorts. Sometimes, in expressing sorts, the form in *-uri* competes with an older form of plural: SG *blană* 'fur (coat)'—PL *blăni / blănuri*, SG *catifea* 'velvet'—PL *catifele / catifeluri*, SG *vopsea* 'dye'—PL *vopsele / vopseluri*.

Similarly, *plurale tantum* nouns tend to occur in the singular, either displaying the same meaning as the plural form (in the case of mass nouns: PL *icre* 'roe, caviar' > SG *icră*, PL *tărâțe* 'bran' > SG *tărâță*), or indicating a member of a plurality (PL *ochelari* 'glasses' > SG *ochelar*, PL *ghilimele* 'quotation marks' > *ghilimea*).

5.1.3 Case forms

In the inflection of the noun, there are two case forms (§5.1.4). Feminine nouns distinguish a Nom≡Acc form in the singular (*fată*) from a Gen≡Dat singular and Nom≡Acc≡Gen≡Dat plural form (*fete*); these syncretic forms are disambiguated by the definite article (4a–c) or by another element which agrees with the noun (4d–e); see also §5.1.3.2.1.

(4) a. fet-e-i
       girl-GEN≡DAT-DEF.SG

   b. fet-e-le
       girl-PL-DEF.NOM≡ACC

   c. fet-e-lor
       girl-PL-DEF.GEN≡DAT

   d. acestei   fete
       this.GEN≡DAT girl.GEN≡DAT.SG

   e. acestor   fete
       these.GEN≡DAT girls.GEN≡DAT≡NOM≡ACC

C Romanian is the only modern Romance language which has two case forms in nominal inflection (there is also a vocative form, but this is not properly a 'case form') (§13.7).
H Romanian inherited its nominal (noun and adjective) case morphology from Latin (for the adjective, see §7.2), reduced to two distinct case forms: Nom≡Acc and Gen≡Dat (ILR, II: 220 and references therein, Bourciez 1956: 578–80; Renzi 1994: 185–6; Iliescu 2007a: 233). This inflectional feature has also been considered to reflect the influence of the Thracian-Dacian substratum (Sandfeld 1930: 187), which, perhaps, favoured the preservation of the Latin syncretic genitive-dative form (Brâncuș 2002: 25, 56; 2007: 163), or to be an element of Slavic influence (Philippide 2011: 58–9).

5.1.3.1 The nominative and the accusative

In nouns, the nominative and the accusative are identical, unlike the inflection of personal pronouns, where the two cases are distinct: *eu* ('I'), *tu* ('you'), in the nominative vs. the 1st and 2nd person accusative strong forms *mine* and *tine*. In the 3rd person singular, the accusative is identical to the nominative, when strong forms are used (*el* 'he; it', *ea* 'she; it'), or it differs from the nominative, when the clitics *îl* (M) and *o* (F) are used (§6.1.3).

These two cases are distinguished only by their syntactic position, and, implicitly, by the syntactic function fulfilled by the DP of which one of these forms is the head. The diagnostic for the accusative is the replacement of the DP by an accusative clitic:

(5) a. Citesc **cartea** > O   citesc   [accusative]
       (I)read book.DEF   CL.ACC.F.3SG (I)read
       'I'm reading the book / it'
    b. Zugrăvesc **peretele** > Îl   zugrăvesc   [accusative]
       (I)paint   wall.DEF   CL.ACC.M.3SG (I)paint
       'I'm painting the wall / it'

If this test does not go through, one cannot determine the case of the noun. In this situation, the noun has an unmarked case—this is the 'direct' or 'neutral' case (see Pană Dindelegan 2009c; see also Diaconescu 1970: 198, who calls these 'neutral nominal forms'). This situation occurs when the noun is a secondary object (6a), an objective predicative complement (6b), a temporal adjunct (6c), or a quantity adjunct (6d):

(6) a. Mă   învaţă   **gramatică**
       CL.ACC.1SG teaches   grammar
       '(S)he teaches me grammar'
    b. L-au   numit   **director**
       CL.ACC.M.3SG=have   appointed manager
       'They appointed him as a manager'
    c. Citeşte   **nopţile**
       reads   nights.DEF
       '(S)he reads during the night'
    d. Învaţă   multe   **ore**
       studies   many   hours
       '(S)he studies for many hours'

5.1.3.2 Genitive and dative case-marking

While nominative and accusative are not overtly marked on the noun and can be identified only distributionally (§5.1.3.1), the genitive and dative cases are marked inflectionally and syntactically, and sometimes also by morphophonological alternations.

C   Romanian has an intermediate position on the analytic–synthetic scale (Guţu Romalo 2005: 98–100; Iliescu 2007a: 226–7, 233): the prenominal, analytical marking is a Romance characteristic of Romanian; the postnominal, synthetic marking is partly inherited from Latin, and partly a Balkan Sprachbund convergence feature (cf. Manoliu 2011: 484, and reference therein).

5.1.3.2.1 There are two types of genitive and dative inflectional markers:

- synthetic: (i) inflectional endings, (ii) genitive–dative forms of the enclitic definite article;
- analytic: (iii) the proclitic morpheme LUI.

(i) In the regular inflection of nouns (which do not bear the enclitic definite article), the genitive and dative are marked by an inflectional ending distinct from that of the nominative–accusative only in the feminine singular (§5.1.3; for the inventory of inflectional endings, see §5.1.4). Genitive–dative syncretism is general in feminine singular nouns.

5.1 Noun morphology

H Romanian appears to have preserved the syncretism of the genitive with the dative from late Latin (Iliescu 2008b: 3268, and reference therein). This syncretism is shared with the Balkan languages (Feuillet 1986: 78–82).

The old genitive–dative forms *mumâniei* (mother.SG.DEF.GEN≡DAT), *tătânelui* (father.SG.DEF. GEN≡DAT) continue the -N- stem of late Latin -A, -ANIS nouns: MAMMANIS, TATANIS. They are attested with an inflectionally unmarked genitive–dative form, accompanied by a possessive affix (*mumâni-sa* 'his mother', *tătâne-său* 'his father'), with a plural form (*mumâni, tătâni*). The form *frățâni* (brother.SG.GEN≡DAT) is analogical, on the model of *tătâni* (Densusianu 1938: 146–8; CDDE: 128, 183).

(ii) Case can also be marked through the inflection of the enclitic definite article, which attaches either to the head noun or to a prenominal adjectival modifier (§5.3.1.1.1):

(7) a. prieten-u-lui
    friend-SG-DEF.GEN≡DAT
 b. bun-u-lui   prieten
    good-SG-DEF.GEN≡DAT friend

In the definite declension, all nouns distinguish nominative–accusative forms and genitive–dative forms, both in the singular and in the plural (Table 5.2; for the phenomenon of enclisis and for the phonological changes it induces, see §5.3.1.1.1).

H Enclisis of the definite article (which has preserved its case inflection better than the noun; see Table 5.2) offset the loss of the Latin case inflectional endings and consolidated the Latin pattern, characterized by the postposition of case markers (Guțu Romalo 1996: 82).

Feminine proper names ending in *-a* use the genitive–dative inflectional ending *-i* [i̯], like common nouns with the enclitic article; thus, in genitive–dative inflection, these proper names end in *-ei*; for those proper names whose stem-final segment in nominative–accusative is *-ca* and *-ga*, the genitive–dative ending is *-ăi*:

(8) NOM≡ACC   GEN≡DAT
    Ioana (personal name), Transilvania (place name) Ioanei, Transilvaniei
    Rodica (personal name), Praga (place name)   Rodicăi, Pragăi

For some feminine place names with the definite enclitic article *-a* (*Dunărea*) or the stem-final segment *-ca* (*Africa*), the genitive–dative is *-ii*: *Dunării, Africii*.

H In the 16th–17th centuries, there are instances of feminine anthroponyms preceded by the markers *ei, ii* (< *ei*), also written as *i, îi* (with prothetic *î*). These markers have been analysed as definite articles. Proclisis, in these isolated examples, has been explained as reflecting a need to keep proper names morphologically invariant (Coteanu 1969: 119), or as a remnant of an older stage of the language (Densusianu 1938: 175), on a par with the proclisis of the definite article elsewhere in Romance (Dimitrescu 1978: 236):

(9) spuseră   ii   Tamar / zise   Tamareei   (*Palia*)
    told.PS.3PL DAT Tamara   told.PS.3SG   Tamara.DAT
    'They told Tamara'   'He told Tamara'

This pattern can still be found, dialectally, with toponyms and anthroponyms.

In old Romanian, masculine anthroponyms ending in *-u(l)* had enclitically marked genitive–dative forms, in a similar way as common nouns with the enclitic definite article:

(10) Arbanașului   (in Densusianu 1938: 173)
     Arbanaș.GEN≡DAT

Enclitically marked forms (*Arbanașului*, *Radului*) were used for a long period of time, especially in folk writings. However, since the 16th century, proclisis and enclisis have been in free variation: alongside the enclitically marked forms, anthroponyms whose genitive–dative is marked by the proclitic morpheme LUI were also used (see below), the latter generalizing in modern Romanian:

(11) lui   Arbanaș (in Densusianu 1938: 173)
     LUI.GEN≡DAT Arbanaș

(iii) The proclitic free morpheme LUI case-marks masculine singular personal names (irrespective of their final sound) (12a) and feminine singular personal names ending in a sound other than -*a* (12b):

(12) a. (M) lui   Ion
            LUI.GEN≡DAT Ion
     b. (F) lui   Zoe
            LUI.GEN≡DAT Zoe

LUI is also used to case-mark (morphologically) invariable common nouns referring to persons (13), and has extended to invariable common nouns with inanimate referents (names of months, letters, etc.) (14), and to nominal phrases made up of a common noun (a kinship noun or a noun of social relationships) and a possessive affix: *(casa) lui frate-său* 'his brother's house':

(13) lui   nenea (M) / tanti (F)
     LUI.GEN≡DAT   uncle   aunt

(14) (sfârșitul) lui   ianuarie
     end.DEF   LUI.GEN January
     'the end of January'

In a few cases, the proclitic case-marking (by LUI) and the enclitic (by the definite article) are in free distribution (§5.1.5):

(15) a. lui   tata
        LUI.GEN≡DAT   father.DEF
     b. tat-e-i
        father-SG.GEN≡DAT-DEF.GEN≡DAT

U In non-standard present-day Romanian, case-marking by proclitic LUI has also extended to feminine personal names ending in -*a*, to common feminine nouns and to pronouns referring to persons:

(16) a. lui   Maria   (standard language: *Mariei*)
        LUI.GEN≡DAT   Maria
        'of / to Mary'
     b. lui   mama   (standard language: *mamei*)
        LUI.GEN≡DAT   mother.DEF
        'of / to mother'

c. lu(i)   ăsta   mic(ul)   (standard language: *ăstuia mic*)
   LUI.GEN≡DAT this small(DEF)
   'of / to this little one'
   The form is *lu* in non-standard usage.

H   In old and modern Romanian texts, the form *lui* is in variation with the form *lu*. These two forms have been explained as originating in Latin: (a) *lui* (as enclitic *-lui*) < Dat. ĪLLUI (Rosetti 1986: 134), or as being formed from old Romanian *lu* (ILR II: 234–5; Coteanu 1969: 118); (b) *lu* < ĪLLO (Meyer-Lübke 1930: 9; ILR II: 235; Rosetti 1986: 134). Other scholars (e.g. Densusianu 1938: 172) consider these forms to have been created in Romanian from *lui*, in 'phonosyntactic contexts'.

In old Romanian, the genitive–dative of personal names ending in *-a* was marked either proclitically, by the free morpheme LU(I), or enclitically by the ending *-ei* / *-ii*, following the pattern of feminine anthroponyms (see example (8) above). The forms marked enclitically can still be found in idioms (e.g. designating names of holidays):

(17) Duminica   Tomei / Tomii
     Sunday   Thomas.GEN≡DAT

5.1.3.2.2 The syntactic case-marking of the genitive and dative occurs in three types of structures: (i) the structure AL + genitive; (ii) structures with analytic case markers (prepositions); (iii) structures in which case is marked by the inflection of the determiners preceding the noun.

1. AL is a grammaticalized functional element.

H   The functional element AL (an innovation of Romanian) etymologically incorporates the preposition A (see 2 below) and the definite article (Meyer-Lübke 1930: 9; Rosetti 1986: 134–5; Sala 2006: 129; for the alternative etymology based on the demonstrative pronoun *al* / *ăl*, see Coteanu 1969: 138, and references therein).

C   The structure AL + genitive is specific to Romanian.

AL preserves more features from the article component and fewer from the prepositional. In traditional grammars, AL was named *possessive* or *genitival article* (GLR I: 105). The recent analyses of AL (see, e.g., Cornilescu 1992, 1995; GALR I: 235; Niculescu 2008a: 66–76) accord different weights to the similarities with the article, on the one hand, and with the preposition (Grosu 1988; Cornilescu and Nicolae 2009: 657–8), on the other hand.

AL has the feature [+definite]. Syntactically, like the genitive marked (only) by the definite article (18a), the AL-genitive (18b) represents a projection of the determiner, that is a DP (Cornilescu 1992: 242–3); semantically, both types of genitive are referential descriptions:

(18) a. cărţi-le   profesor-u-lui
        book.PL-DEF   profesor-SG-DEF.GEN
        'the professor's books'
     b. aceste   cărţi   ale   profesorului
        these   book.PL   AL.F.PL   professor.SG.DEF.GEN
        'these books of the professor's'

266   5 *Nouns and Noun Phrases*

TABLE 5.5 The forms of AL

	M	F
SG	al	a
PL	ai	ale

AL displays gender and number concord with its governing DP (Table 5.5).

(19) a. niște   cărți   ale   profesorului
        some   book.F.PL AL.F.PL   professor.SG.DEF.GEN
        'some books of the professor's'

   b. un   student   al   profesorului
      a.M.SG   student.M.SG AL.M.SG   professor.SG.DEF.GEN
      'a student of the professor's'

The variable forms of AL have been generalized in contemporary standard Romanian.

U Structures in which AL has the invariable form *a* (20a) occur in most Daco-Romanian sub-dialects, except the southern one (20b):

(20) a. doi   cai   **a**   tat-e-i   (non-standard language)
        two   horse.M.PL AL.M.PL father-SG.GEN-DEF.GEN
     b. doi   cai   **ai**   tatei   (variable AL; standard language)
        'two of father's horses'

H In the 16th century, the variable forms of AL were used in different dialect areas, a fact which suggests that, at an earlier stage of Romanian, variable AL was a general phenomenon; the invariable *a* is an innovation (Gheție and Mareș 1988: 81–3). In the 17th–18th centuries, the variable forms were specific to the southern area, but they are also attested in the northern zone, where invariable *a* prevailed (Frâncu 1997: 327).

The usage of AL in modern Romanian is regulated by a strict adjacency constraint.

AL is compulsory in structures where the adjacency constraint is violated. Violation of the adjacency constraint occurs in the following cases:

(i) The dominating phrase lacks an article (21a); it takes the free proclitic indefinite article morpheme (21b); it has proclitic determiners other than articles—a demonstrative (21c), a quantifier (21d); the article is suffixed to a prenominal adjectival modifier (21e):

(21) a. Am   citit   cărți   ale   profesorului
        have.1SG   read   book.PL   AL.F.PL   professor.SG.DEF.GEN
        'I read books of the professor's'

   b. o carte   a   profesorului
      a book   AL.F.SG   professor.SG.DEF.GEN
      'a book of the professor's'

   c. aceste   cărți   ale   profesorului
      these   book.PL   AL.F.PL   professor.SG.DEF.GEN
      'these books of the professor's'

5.1 Noun morphology

    d. două   cărți   ale   profesorului
       two   book.PL AL.F.PL professor.SG.DEF.GEN
       'two books of the professor's'

    e. noile   cărți   ale   profesorului
       new-PL.DEF book.PL AL.F.PL professor.SG.DEF.GEN
       'the professor's new books'

  (ii) The dominating phrase takes the enclitic definite article, and between it and the genitival phrase there are other elements interpolated (22a); these may include the copula (22b):

(22) a. cărți-le   mai   noi   ale   profesorului
        book-DEF.PL more new AL.F.PL professor.SG.DEF.GEN
        'the professor's newer books'

    b. cărți-le   sunt   ale   profesorului
       book-DEF.PL are   AL.F.PL professor.SG.DEF.GEN
       'the books are the professor's'

  (iii) The genitival phrase occurs before its governing DP (in the present-day language, these structures are rare and stylistically marked):

(23) al   casei   prag
      AL.M.SG house.SG.DEF.GEN threshold
      'the house's threshold'

U AL is used in constructions in which the genitive is syntactically dependent on a deverbal adjective (§7.6.2.2):
    (24) sportiv   câștigător   al   trofeului
           sportsman   winner   AL.M.SG trophy.SG.DEF.GEN
           'a sportsman winner of the trophy'

AL is not used in the structures in which the genitive immediately follows a definite noun phrase; the adjacency constraint is thus observed:

(25) cărți-le   profesorului   / *ale   profesorului
      book-DEF.PL professor.DEF.SG.GEN AL.F.PL professor.SG.GEN
      'the professor's books'

H The rules that regulated the usage of (variable or invariable) AL were not fixed in old Romanian.

At least according to the prescriptive rules of contemporary Romanian, AL must be repeated in case of coordinated genitival phrase (26), except for cases in which the two conjuncts form a (formal and semantic-referential) unit (27):

(26) fondurile   educației   și   ale
      fund.PL.DEF   education.SG.DEF.GEN   and   AL.F.PL
      cercetării   [unique or different referent]
      research.SG.DEF.GEN

(27) Ministerul   Educației   și   Cercetării   [unique referent]
      minister.SG.DEF education.SG.DEF.GEN and research.SG.DEF.GEN

2. In structures with analytic (prepositional) case markers, the genitive relation may be marked in Romanian by the preposition A.

C Prepositional A (< Lat. AD, generalized in Romance as a dative marker) grammaticalized in Romanian as an analytic marker of the genitive relation, and, to a (much more) limited extent, of the dative relation (see example (38)).

In contemporary Romanian, A is a functional preposition, in contexts in which the first constituent of the genitival phrase lacks inflectional case-marking (usually, this element is a cardinal numeral or another quantifier; more rarely, it may be an adjective of an adjectival collocation):

(28) a. (mamă)   a   trei   copii
       mother   A   three   children
       'mother of three children'

   b. (temerile)   a   tot   poporul
       fears.DEF   A   all   nation.DEF
       'the fears of all the nation'

   c. (participarea)   a   numeroşi   sportivi
       participation.DEF   A   numerous   sportsmen
       'the participation of numerous sportsmen'

U In cases of variation between an A-genitive and an inflectional genitive, the A-genitive is preferred in informal contemporary Romanian:
   (29) a. a   câţiva   prieteni
           A   a-few   friends
        b. câtorva   prieteni
           a few.PL.GEN   friends

Prepositional A also marks the syntactic position of the genitive in contexts in which this position is occupied by a relative clause introduced by an invariable *wh*-pronoun (*ce, ceea ce*):

(30) (beneficiul)   a   (ceea) ce   s-a   cheltuit
     benefit.DEF   A   what   CL.REFL.PASS.ACC=has   spent
     'the benefit of what was spent'

U The structures in (30) are found in the high style.
H In old Romanian, A was systematically used to case-mark the genitive relation when the first element of the genitive phrase lacked case inflection and, more rarely, before variable words (a pattern extinct in modern Romanian):
   (31) înaintea   a   domni   (Varlaam)
        before   A   kings
        'before kings'

   Moreover, in the 16th century, there are hybrid structures in which the A-phrase includes a noun inflected for genitive:
   (32) tatăl   a   toţi   ficiorilor   (*Palia*)
        father.DEF   A   all   son.PL.DEF.GEN
        'the father of all boys'

Syntactically, the A-phrase generally represents an NP; semantically, the A-genitive is a non-referential phrase with an intensional, property denotation. Exceptions to this interpretative pattern are the structures in which the head noun of the genitival phrase is definite (28b); these A-phrases are referential expressions and are interpreted extensionally. The relative clause structures introduced by prepositional A have different contextual interpretations: they may have generic or non-generic interpretation in accordance with the referential values of the *wh*-pronoun.

U In informal language, the preposition *la* 'to' is used to introduce referential genitive phrases (DPs), as in (33a), and non-referential genitive phrases (NPs), as in (33b); the preposition *de la* ('of') always introduces a non-referential genitive phrase (33b):

(33) a. (mă-sa)   la   fata   asta
        mother=her to   girl.DEF   this
        'this girl's mother'
     b. (acoperișul)   la /   de la   casă
        roof.DEF   to /   from   house
        'the roof of the house'

H The structures with *la* have been attested since the 16th century; however, this pattern was not frequent in old Romanian.

The old prepositional construction with DE (the Romance genitive following the Latin pattern), representing a possessive phrase, was already a syntactic archaism in 16th century Romanian. The functional preposition was followed either by a bare noun (i.e. an NP), as in (34a), or by a definite noun (i.e. a DP), as in (34b). This structure was replaced by the regular genitive (Densusianu 1938: 143–4; Bourciez 1956: 588):

(34) a. cale(-a)   de   cetate   (*Psaltirea Scheiană*)
        road-DEF   DE   fortress
        'the path of the fortress'
     b. în   dzua   de   rreulu   mieu   (*Psaltirea Hurmuzaki*)
        in   day.DEF.SG   DE   misfortune.DEF   my
        'in the day of my misfortune'

In contemporary Romanian, the preposition DE does not express a genitive relation (§§5.3.3.4, 9.2.2).

The dative relation can be marked in modern Romanian by the prepositions *la* and, more rarely, A.

The preposition *la* is not fully grammaticalized; it still preserves its original allative (directional) value in the structures expressing a dative relation.

H Prepositional *la* etymologically incorporates the Latin preposition AD (*la* < ILLAC AD; Iliescu 2008b: 3268).

The preposition *la* is used in the same contexts as the genitive prepositional marker A, that is, before an element which lacks case inflection—a cardinal numeral (35a) or another quantifier (35b), and, more rarely, an adjective or an adjectival collocation (35c):

(35) a. Dă   mere   la   trei   copii
        gives   apples   to   three   children
        '(S)he gives apples to three children'

b. Trimite   salutări   la   tot   poporul
      sends   greetings   to   all   nation.DEF
      '(S)he sends greetings to the entire nation'
   c. La   astfel   de   oameni   nu   le   pasă   de   nimic
      to   such   of   humans   no   CL.DAT.3PL cares   about nothing
      'This kind of people don't care about anything'

U The *la*-construction (36a) is preferred to the inflectional dative (36b) in informal speech:
(36) a. la   câțiva   prieteni
        to   a-few   friends
     b. câtorva   prieteni
        a few.PL.DAT   friends

The informal prepositional structures, especially with plural common nouns, are tolerated in current standard language (37a). The prepositional structures with singular common nouns (37b) and especially those with proper names (37c) are dialectal:
(37) a. Le   dau   la   copii   să   mănânce
        CL.DAT.3PL   give.1SG   to   children   să$_{SUBJ}$ eat.SUBJ.3PL
        'I feed the children'
     b. Îi   dau   la   copil
        CL.DAT.3SG   give.1SG   to   child
        'I give to the child'
     c. Îi   dau   la   Mihai
        CL.DAT.3SG   give.1SG   to   Mihai
        'I give to Michael'

The *la*-phrase is a non-referential (35a,c) or a referential (35b) expression, which contains either a definite noun (35b) or an inherently definite constituent (i.e. a proper name) (37c). The *la*-phrases with clitic doubling in (37a–b) are referential expressions as well.

H The prepositional *la*-constructions which express a dative relation had relatively low frequency until mid-17th century. Subsequently, these structures extended both in frequency and in areal distribution (Frâncu 1997: 123, 326).

The preposition A marks the syntactic position of dative assigned by the prepositions *grație* 'thanks to, owing to', *datorită* 'because of', *mulțumită* 'thanks to' and by the adverbs / prepositions *conform, potrivit* 'according to', *contrar* 'contrary to'. Prepositional A is used before invariable numerals and in the context in which the dative position is occupied by a relative clause introduced by an invariable *wh*-pronoun (*ce, ceea ce*):

(38) a. (datorită)   a   trei   factori
        because-of   A   three   factors.NOM≡ACC
     b. (contrar)   a   (ceea) ce   știam
        contrary-to   A   what.NOM≡ACC   know.IMPERF.1SG

U The structures in (38) belong to elevated style.

The relative clause structures introduced by prepositional A have different contextual interpretations: they may have generic or non-generic interpretation in conformity with the referential values of the *wh*-pronoun.

H The structures with prepositional A expressing a dative relation were more frequent and more diverse in old Romanian than in modern Romanian. Being in competition with the inflectional dative, they have been gradually replaced by the latter, from the end of the 16th century. In certain redundant structures, the dative relation is double marked, by A and by means of inflection:

(39) cine poate sluji a oamenilor   (Coresi)
    who can serve.INF A human.PL.DEF.DAT
    'who can serve to people'

The preposition A has restricted its syntactic rules of usage.

3. The genitive and the dative may be exclusively syntactically marked, by the inflectional form of the prenominal determiner (indefinite article, demonstrative determiner, etc.):

(40) a. unui băiat
    a.M.GEN≡DAT boy.NOM≡ACC≡GEN≡DAT

   b. acestor prieteni
    this.PL.GEN≡DAT friends.NOM≡ACC≡GEN≡DAT

5.1.3.2.3 Morphophonological alternations in the noun's stem are always a redundant means of inflectional case marking in Romanian, functioning as supplementary genitive and dative markers (§15.1):

- vocalic alternations—/'a/ ~ /'ə/ (*lampă*_{NOM≡ACC}, *lămpi*_{GEN≡DAT}); /'ə/ ~ /'e/ (*cumătră*_{NOM≡ACC}, *cumetre*_{GEN≡DAT}); /ə/ ~ /e/ (*sâmbătă*_{NOM≡ACC}, *sâmbete*_{GEN≡DAT}); /'o̯a/ ~ /'o/ (*floare*_{NOM≡ACC}, *flori*_{GEN≡DAT}); /'e̯a/ ~ /'e/ (*seară*_{NOM≡ACC}, *seri*_{GEN≡DAT}); /'i/ ~ /'ɨi̯/ (*mână*_{NOM≡ACC}, *mâini*_{GEN≡DAT}), etc.
- consonantal alternations—/d/ ~ /z/ (*coadă*_{NOM≡ACC}, *cozi*_{GEN≡DAT}); /t/ ~ /ts/ (*boltă*_{NOM≡ACC}, *bolți*_{GEN≡DAT}); /st/ ~ /ʃt/ (*veste*_{NOM≡ACC}, *vești*_{GEN≡DAT}); /sk/ ~ /ʃt/ (*gâscă*_{NOM≡ACC}, *găște*_{GEN≡DAT}); /l/ ~ /∅/ (*vale*_{NOM≡ACC}, *văi*_{GEN≡DAT}), etc.

U Proper names tend to keep their stem unmodified by morphophonological alternations: *Ioana*_{NOM≡ACC}, *Ioanei*_{GEN≡DAT}; *Leana*_{NOM≡ACC}, *Leanei*_{GEN≡DAT}; *Sanda*_{NOM≡ACC}, *Sandei*_{GEN≡DAT}.

Two morphophonological alternations of the same kind (vocalic or consonantal) do not occur in the same word; there are very few exceptions, e.g. /a/ ~ /ə/, /'a/ ~ /'ə/ (*talangă*_{NOM≡ACC}, *tălăngi*_{GEN≡DAT}). There are however a few nouns which simultaneously exhibit a vocalic alternation and a consonantal; e.g. /'o̯a/ ~ /'o/, /d/ ~ /z/ (*coadă*_{NOM≡ACC}, *cozi*_{GEN≡DAT}); /'a/ ~ /'ə/, /l/ ~ /∅/ (*vale*_{NOM≡ACC}, *văi*_{GEN≡DAT}).

Morphophonological alternations are systematic (in that they represent a type of variation in regular nominal inflection), but not general (in that many neologisms do not show such alternations).

5.1.3.2.4 In modern Romanian there are a few situations in which the genitive occurs without specific marking (i.e. the genitive phrase is invariable). Structures like (41), which contain a bare kinship noun and a possessive affix, are dialectal (§5.3.3.2):

(41) a. ochiul soacră-sa [= soacră-sii] (F)]
    'the eye of his / her mother-in-law'

b. casa taică-său [= lui taică-său (M)]
'the house of his father'

There is a tendency towards extending the unmarked genitive in the case of abbreviations or of other types of invariable proper names:

(42) angajaţii   RADET   [= RADET-u-lui]
     employee.PL.DEF RADET   RADET-SG-DEF.GEN

H In old Romanian, these kinds of structures were more diverse. The genitive could appear without inflectional marking both in the case of common nouns, and in the case of proper names. Moreover, there are a few attestations of this unmarked genitive, always followed by a possessive affix:
   (43) tată   mâne-sa   [= mâne-sii]
        father mother=his / her.NOM≡ACC   mother=his/her.GEN
   'father of his/her mother'
   The inflectionally unmarked genitive–dative form is inherited from Latin in the case of a few nouns: *m(um)âne, tătâne* (§5.1.3.2.1).

5.1.3.3 The marking of the vocative

Besides prosodic marking, the vocative is also marked by specific endings (see also §13.7.1 and Table 5.6).

U Masculine nouns which in the nominative–accusative take, like feminines, the inflectional ending *-ă*, may marginally select *-o* in the vocative (*popo* priest.VOC, *vlădico* bishop.VOC).

Like common nouns, proper names have marked vocative forms as well in non-standard Romanian. Thus, feminine names (*Ana, Ileana, Maria*) and masculine names ending in *-a* (*Costea, Mircea, Toma*) take the inflectional ending *-o* in the vocative (*Ano, Ileano, Mario; Costeo, Mirceo, Tomo*); masculines ending with *-u* or in a consonant (*Popescu, Radu; Ion, Bogdan*) take the ending *-ule* (*Popescule, Radule*) or *-e* (*Ioane, Bogdane*). In the feminine, besides *-o*, the inflectional endings *-ă* or *-e* are also used: *Ană, Ileană, Mărie*.

H The inflectional ending *-e* is inherited from Latin. In the 16th century, it was the most frequent inflectional ending in the masculine singular: *oame* (< Lat. HOMINE), *ome* (man.VOC) (later replaced by *omule*), *drace* (devil.VOC), *împărate* (emperor.VOC), *Avrame* (Avram.VOC), *Iacobe* (Iacob.VOC) (Frâncu 2009: 40).

TABLE 5.6 The marking of the vocative by specific endings

	SINGULAR INFLECTIONAL ENDINGS	PLURAL INFLECTIONAL ENDINGS
MASCULINE	**-e /-ule**: băiete/băiatule (boy.VOC), copile/copilule (child.VOC), codrule (forest.VOC)	**-lor** băieţilor (boys.VOC), copiilor (children.VOC), codrilor (forests.VOC)
	-e (VOC≡NOM≡ACC): frate, părinte	fraţilor (brothers.VOC), părinţilor (parents.VOC)
FEMININE	**-o**: fato (girl.VOC), soro (sister.VOC), vulpeo (fox.VOC)	fetelor (girls.VOC), surorilor (sisters.VOC), vulpilor (foxes.VOC)

The inflectional ending *-ule* emerged in Romanian in the 16th century or shortly before (Frâncu 2009: 40), by adding the inflectional ending *-e* to the article-bearing noun: *copil* (child) > *copilul* (child.DEF) > *copilule* (child.DEF.VOC).

The inflectional ending *-o* is borrowed from Slavic.

The inflectional ending *-lor* is considered to have occurred by an extension of the dative plural definite article identical to constructions which could appear in both the dative and the vocative (Densusianu 1961, II: 94):

(44) o, amar voo,   tâlharilor   (*Texte bogomilice*)
     oh bitter you(DAT) thieves(DAT≡VOC)
     'oh, bitter to you, you thieves!'

C Romanian is marked out among Romance languages by having vocative forms. Traces of vocative marking also occur in Sardinian (for masculine baptismal names), in old Provençal, old French, and Italian (Niculescu 1965: 25). Of the Romance languages, only Romanian inherited the inflectional ending *-e* of the vocative in the second (masculine) declension (Iliescu 2007b: 211–12).

The morphological realization of the vocative is also a Balkan Sprachbund feature, since it also occurs in Macedonian, Bulgarian, Serbo-Croatian, Megleno-Romanian, Aromanian, and Greek (Mišeska Tomić 2004: 9–10).

Besides the forms with specific inflectional markers of the vocative, some of which are interpreted as colloquial in present-day language, forms identical to the nominative–accusative are also employed to mark the vocative:

(45) a. **Copii**,   unde mergeți?
        children(VOC(≡NOM≡ACC)) where (you)go
        'Children, where are you going?'

     b. **Maria**, nu pleca!
        Maria   not leave.INF
        'Maria, don't leave!'

Common nouns bearing no specific vocative inflectional ending are usually accompanied by a modifier (for the description of vocative phrases, see §13.7.1):

(46) **Copil rău**, nu mai face   asta!
     child bad   not more do.INF this
     'Bad child, don't do this anymore!'
     *Copil, nu mai face   asta!
     child not more do.INF this

U In present-day non-standard usage, there are also definite forms of the nouns for the vocative, identical to those in the nominative–accusative:

(47) **Băieții**,   ce   faceți?
     boys.DEF(VOC≡NOM≡ACC) what (you)do
     'Hey, boys, what's up?'

5.1.4 Inflectional classes

The inflectional classes are differentiated according to gender (masculine, feminine, and neuter) and by the identity and patterning of their inflectional endings.

H Romanian, like other Romance languages, inherited the first three Latin declensions: I (*casă* 'house' < CASA), II (*lup* 'wolf' < LUPUS), III (*vale* 'valley' < VALLES); the fourth declension usually blended with the second declension, and the fifth declension with the first one (Graur 1968: 56).

The inflectional classes are well-established. What changes over time is the lexical membership of each class (§5.1.1.1).

5.1.4.1 Inflectional subclasses associated with the masculine gender

The two masculine subclasses both show syncretism for case in the singular and in the plural (i.e. nominative, accusative, genitive, and dative all have the same form), but are distinguished by the desinential marking of the singular and by the form of the definite article (Table 5.7).

The attachment of the definite article -*l* to masculine nouns marked in the singular by the inflectional ending -Ø selects a preceding -*u*- (the old masculine singular inflectional ending) (48b–c); for masculine nouns with the inflectional ending -*e*, the definite article -*le* is attached directly (48e–f):

(48)   a. domn-Ø
       gentleman-SG

   b. domn-u-l
      gentleman-SG-DEF

   c. domn-u-lui
      gentleman-SG-DEF(GEN≡DAT)

   d. frat-e
      brother-SG

   e. frat-e-le
      brother-SG-DEF

   f. frat-e-lui
      brother-SG-DEF(GEN≡DAT)

Table 5.7 Inflectional subclasses of masculine nouns

MASCULINE NOUNS	SYNCRETIC FORMS AND INFLECTIONAL ENDINGS	MORPHOPHONOLOGICAL INSTANTIATIONS OF THE INFLECTIONAL ENDINGS	EXAMPLES
SUBCLASS I	(NOM≡ACC≡GEN≡DAT) SG: -**u** (NOM≡ACC≡GEN≡DAT) PL: -**i**	[-u]—[-i] (the root ends in consonant + r / l) [-u̯]—[-i̯] (the root ends in a vowel) [-Ø]—[-ⁱ] (the root ends in a consonant)	membru—membri 'member(s)' bou—boi 'ox(en)' domn—domni 'gentleman—gentlemen'
SUBCLASS II	(NOM≡ACC≡GEN≡DAT) SG: -**e** (NOM≡ACC≡GEN≡DAT) PL: -**i**	[-e]—[-ⁱ] (the root ends in a consonant)	frate—frați 'brother(s)'

5.1.4.2 Inflectional subclasses associated with the feminine gender

5.1.4.2.1 The feminine nouns typically have two inflectional forms and display syncretisms between nominative and accusative in the singular, and between genitive and dative singular and all forms of the plural; they are subdivided into three subclasses according to the inflectional endings of the singular and the plural (Table 5.8).

H The inflectional pattern [-Ø]—[-le] initially comprised Latin nouns that ended in -LLA (Lat. STELLA > *stea(uă)* 'star', Lat. MAXILLA > *măsea(uă)* 'molar tooth'), and later absorbed feminine borrowings which end in a stressed vowel, usually [a] or [ea] (§1.3.2): *basma* 'headscarf'—*basmale* 'headscarves', *șosea* 'road'—*șosele* 'roads' (Sala 2006: 121). This inflectional pattern, unique in Romance, was very productive in a certain period of the history of Romanian andcomprised inherited nouns (*curea* 'belt'), borrowings from Turkish (*perdea* 'window curtain'), Modern Greek (*saltea* 'mattress'), from French (*bezea* 'meringue'). In current Romanian it is no longer productive (Pană Dindelegan 2007a: 428–9).

5.1.4.2.2 The plural inflectional endings *-e* and *-i* are in competition. Most often, the inflectional ending *-i* prevailed over its competitor *-e* (*străzi* vs. *strade* 'streets', *școli* vs. *școale* 'schools'), and this tendency still holds. The competing *-e* pattern belongs to the literary language; this pattern involves fewer morphophonological alternations in the stem than the *-i* pattern (Graur 1968: 106–27).

H In the 16th century, many nouns had double plural variants, with *-e* and *-i*. In the mid-16th century, the replacement process of *-e* with *-i* was complete for nouns like *biserică* 'church', *inimă* 'heart', *poruncă* 'order', *pâră* 'denunciation', *viață* 'life', which in the previous period had had double forms (Frâncu 2009: 31).

U In present-day language, there are several nouns which have double plural forms; some of them are both accepted by the literary norm (*căpșuni*—*căpșune* 'strawberries', *coperți*—*coperte* 'covers'), others are not (*ciocolate* vs. non-standard *ciocolăți* 'chocolates'; *înghețate* vs. non-standard *înghețăți* 'ice creams').

TABLE 5.8 Inflectional subclasses of two-form feminine nouns

FEMININE NOUNS	SYNCRETIC FORMS AND INFLECTIONAL ENDINGS	MORPHOPHONOLOGICAL INSTANTIATIONS OF THE INFLECTIONAL ENDINGS	EXAMPLES
SUBCLASS I	(NOM≡ACC) SG: -ă (GEN≡DAT) SG ≡(NOM≡ACC≡GEN≡DAT)PL: -e	[-ə]—[-e] (the root ends in a consonant)	casă—case 'house(s)'
SUBCLASS II	(NOM≡ACC) SG: -Ø (GEN≡DAT) SG ≡(NOM≡ACC≡GEN≡DAT)PL: -le	[-Ø]—[-le] (the root ends in a stressed vowel [(e̯)a] or [i])	stea—stele 'star(s)' zi—zile 'day(s)'
SUBCLASS III	(NOM≡ACC) SG: -ă (GEN≡DAT) SG ≡(NOM≡ACC≡GEN≡DAT)PL: -i	[-ə]—[-i̯] (the root ends in a consonant)	poartă—porți 'gate(s)'
SUBCLASS IV	(NOM≡ACC) SG: -e (GEN≡DAT) SG ≡(NOM≡ACC≡GEN≡DAT)PL: -i	[-e]—[-i̯] (the root ends in a consonant) [-e]—[-i̯] (the root ends in [i]) [-e]—[-Ø] (the root ends in the semivowel [-i̯])	floare—flori 'flower(s)' familie—familii 'family—families' odaie—odăi 'room(s)'

TABLE 5.9 Inflectional subclasses of three-form feminine nouns

Syncretic Forms and Inflectional Endings		Morphophonological Instantiations of the Inflectional Endings	Examples
THREE-FORM FEMININE NOUNS	(Nom≡Acc)sg: -ă (Gen≡Dat)sg: -e (Nom≡Acc≡Gen≡Dat)pl: -uri	[-ə]—[-e]—[-ur^i] (the root ends in a consonant)	*lipsă—lipse—lipsuri* 'gap'
	(Nom≡Acc)sg: -ă (Gen≡Dat)sg: -i (Nom≡Acc≡Gen≡Dat)pl: -uri	[-ə]—[-^{i}]—[-ur^i] (the root ends in a consonant)	*treabă—trebi—treburi* 'business'
	(Nom≡Acc)sg: -e (Gen≡Dat)sg: -i (Nom≡Acc≡Gen≡Dat)pl: -uri	[-e]—[-^{i}]—[-ur^i] (the root ends in a consonant)	*vreme—vremi—vremuri* 'time, season'

5.1.4.2.3 A few feminine nouns have three distinct inflectional forms, characterized by syncretisms different from those *of the other classes of nouns*: Nom≡Acc in the singular, Gen≡Dat in the singular, and Nom≡Acc≡Gen≡Dat in the plural (Table 5.9). In contrast to two-form nouns, the nouns in this class take the inflectional ending *-uri* in the plural. Several feminine mass nouns take the inflectional ending *-uri* in the plural, the result being a difference in meaning from the singular, that is the plural denotes sorts or objects: *alamă* '(yellow) brass'—*alămuri* 'objects made of (yellow) brass', *dulceață* 'jam'—*dulcețuri* 'jams', *mătase* 'silk'—*mătăsuri* 'sorts of silk', *verdeață* 'verdure'—*verdețuri* 'greens'.

H The *-uri* plurals started to occur as early as the 17th century (Frâncu 1982a: 199–201), being in competition with the older variants in *-e* or *-i*: *cărni—cărnuri* 'meats' ('sorts of meat'), *lefe / lefi—lefuri* 'salaries'.
   The inflectional ending *-uri* has attached to older roots inflected for plural; this is testified by the alternations of the root: *blană* (SG)—*blăni* (PL)—*blănuri* (PL) 'furs', *bunătate* (SG)—*bunătăți* (PL)—*bunătățuri* (PL) 'sweets, goodies', *treabă* (SG)—*trebi* (PL)—*treburi* (PL) 'affairs' (Avram 2005: 115–16).

5.1.4.3 Inflectional subclasses associated with the neuter gender

5.1.4.3.1 The neuter nouns are distributed into two subclasses, both showing the syncretism between nominative, accusative, genitive, and dative in the singular and nominative, accusative, genitive, and dative in the plural (Table 5.10).

5.1.4.3.2 Plural variants that take the inflectional ending *-e* are in competition with those that take *-uri*. According to Brâncuș (1978: 253–62) on the basis of DEX (1975), 3061 neuter borrowings out of a total of 4586 take the plural inflectional ending *-e* and 1307 take *-uri*, while 57 display dual morphology (taking both *-e* and *-uri*) and 161 have a phonologically conditioned plural with *-i*. Brâncuș draws attention to the fact that *-uri* is extending, because it has the advantage of not modifying the root, contrasting thus with *-e* which can cause alternation in the root (*microfon* 'microphone'—*microfoane* 'microphones', *semiton* 'semitone'—*semitonuri* 'semitones'). Brâncuș' results are confirmed by Pană Dindelegan (2002: 38–9), on the basis of a survey on DCR.
   In present-day language the *-uri* plural of neuters is the most active one, attracting the most borrowings (Pană Dindelegan 2009b: 21–3).

TABLE 5.10 Inflectional subclasses of neuter nouns

NEUTER NOUNS	SYNCRETIC FORMS AND INFLECTIONAL ENDINGS	MORPHOPHONOLOGICAL INSTANTIATIONS OF THE INFLECTIONAL ENDINGS	EXAMPLES
SUBCLASS I	(NOM≡ACC≡GEN≡DAT) SG: **-u** (NOM≡ACC≡GEN≡DAT) PL: **-e**	[-u]—[-e] (the root ends in consonant + r / l) [-u̯]—[-(j)e] (the root ends in a vowel) [-Ø]—[-e] (the root ends in a consonant) [-(j)u]—[-i(i̯)] (the root ends in a semivowel)	*registru—registre* 'register' *brâu—brâie* 'waistband, waist', *frâu—frâie* 'rein' *creion—creioane* 'pencil' *fotoliu—fotolii* 'armchair' *consiliu—consilii* 'council'
SUBCLASS II	(NOM≡ACC≡GEN≡DAT) SG: **-u** (NOM≡ACC≡GEN≡DAT) PL: **-uri**	[-u]—[-urⁱ] (the root ends in consonant + r / l) [-u̯]—[-urⁱ] (the root ends in a vowel) [-Ø]—[-urⁱ] the root ends in a consonant or a stressed vowel)	*titlu—titluri* 'title' *tablou—tablouri* 'painting' *toc—tocuri* 'heel'

U Many neuter nouns have double plural morphology (i.e. with both *-uri* and *-e*). Most often, the literary norm accepts only one variant (e.g. DOOM recommends *aragaze* 'gas stoves', not *aragazuri*; *chibrituri* 'matches', not *chibrite*; *morminte* 'graves', not *morminturi*. In rarer cases, both forms are accepted: *niveluri / nivele* 'levels'.

5.1.5 Nouns with irregular inflection

There are several types of irregularity in the nominal inflection.
Some involve plural inflectional endings, for instance: *-eni* [-enⁱ] ((M) *om* 'man'—*oameni* 'men'), *-ori* [-orⁱ] ((F) *noră* 'daughter-in-law'—*nurori* 'daughters-in-law', *soră* 'sister'—*surori* 'sisters'), *-ete* [-ete] ((NEUT) *cap* 'head'—*capete* 'heads'), which appear only in these words.
Other irregularities concern the definite article form of certain masculine nouns such as *tată* 'father', *papă* 'pope', *pașă* 'pasha'. Because of the inflectional ending *-ă*, which generally characterizes feminine nouns, these masculines take the feminine singular ending *-e*, the feminine singular article *-i* in the Gen≡Dat (*tatei, papei, pașei*), and the singular article *-a* in the Nom≡Acc (*tata, papa, pașa*). In parallel with the aforementioned forms, the noun *tată* has regular masculine forms (Nom≡Acc: *tatăl*, Gen≡Dat: *tatălui*); in the plural, the same nouns behave regularly like masculines (*tați* (Nom≡Acc≡Gen≡Dat), *tații* (Nom≡Acc), *taților* (Gen≡Dat)).
Certain irregularities involve patterns of syncretism. For instance, the noun *tată* displays the syncretism Nom≡Acc singular≡Gen≡Dat singular ((*un*) *tată*≡(*unui*) *tată*) in the indefinite declension, behaving thus like masculine nouns, while in the definite declension, it has two forms in the singular, exactly like feminine nouns (Nom≡Acc *tata*, Gen≡Dat *tatei*). From this point of view, plural defective nouns are also irregular since in the indefinite

declension, they possess only one form for all the morphological cases *cinste* (honour. NOM≡ACC≡GEN≡DAT)—*cinstea* (honour.DEF.NOM≡ACC)—*cinstei* (honour.DEF.GEN≡DAT).

Finally, the feminine nouns *soră*, *noră* have a bisyllabic root in Gen≡Dat singular and Nom≡Acc≡Gen≡Dat plural in which the stress falls on the second syllable: *surori* [su.'ror^i], *nurori* [nu.'ror^i]. In the plural of neuters in root-final unstressed -*o*, the stress shifts onto the *o*: *radio* ['ra.di.o]—*radiouri* [ra.di.'o.ur^i], *zero* ['ze.ro]—*zerouri* [ze.'ro.ur^i].

5.1.6 The inflection of compound nouns

A restricted class of nouns have an analysable structure, being made up either of full words (*floarea-soarelui* flower.DEF-sun.DEF.GEN 'sun flower', *Târgu-Mureș* fair.DEF-Mureș) or of words + lexical components (*teleconferință* 'teleconference', *teatrolog* 'theatre critic').

In the case of compound nouns made up of full words, the degree of cohesion of the components is decisive for the inflection of the compound: both components may be inflected (49), one component may be inflected (50), and, finally, neither component may be inflected (51). For the first two cases, the definite article attaches only to one of the components (52).

(49) a. mamă-mare
    mother.NOM≡ACC-big.NOM≡ACC

b. mame-mari
    mother.SG.GEN≡DAT≡PL-big.GEN≡DAT
    'of / to grandmother'

(50) a. locțiitor
    place-keeper.SG

b. locțiitori
    place-keeper.PL
    'sitter(s)'

(51) pierde-vară ·
    lose-summer.SG≡PL.NOM≡ACC≡GEN≡DAT
    'idler'

(52) a. mama-mare
    mother.NOM≡ACC.DEF-big.NOM≡ACC

b. locțiitorul
    place-keeper.SG.DEF

For details on compound nouns, see §16.2.1.

5.2 SEMANTIC-GRAMMATICAL CLASSES OF NOUNS

All classes of nouns are defined in relation to the prototypical concrete common nouns. In relation to prototypical nouns, other classes distinguish themselves by a series of particular morphosyntactic features which are the reflex of their semantic-referential features.

5.2.1 Proper names vs. common nouns

In contrast to common nouns, whose referents are grouped into classes on the basis of certain common semantic-referential features, proper names are inherently definite and denote unique referents; these inherent properties are reflected by several morphological and syntactic features.

Certain features are characteristic of the entire class, while others are diagnostics for several subclasses of proper names (Tomescu 1998). Within the class of proper names, personal names, which behave more like person-denoting common nouns, can be distinguished from place names, which are more similar in behaviour to non-personal common nouns.

Proper names have a special behaviour with respect to the category of number. On the one hand, proper names display restrictions in the realization of the singular–plural opposition, having either a singular form (*Blagoveștenie, Brașov*) or a plural form (*Rusalii, Carpați*), but not both. On the other hand, when used in the plural, proper names do not denote a set of individuals or entities with common features, as common nouns do, but a plurality of unique individuals that bear the same name:

(53) a. **Mariile** organizează o petrecere
Maria.PL organize a party
'The Marias (= women named Maria) are organizing a party'

b. În România sunt două **Câmpulunguri**
in Romania are two Câmpulung.PL
'In Romanian there are two places named Câmpulung'

H Although they display plural morphology, place names like *București, Ploiești, Humulești* behave as singulars. The forms that take a plural definite article, such as *Bucureștii* (București. DEF(PL)), *Humuleștii* (*Humulești*.DEF(PL)), are obsolete.

Like person-denoting masculine nouns, masculine and a few feminine personal names that end in a consonant or in a vowel other than -*a* are marked for the genitive and dative by the freestanding marker LUI (M *lui Ion*, F *lui Carmen*, *lui Jeni*), thus contrasting with non-personal proper names, which have a regular enclitic marking in the genitive–dative, like common nouns (*Brașovului* Brașov.GEN≡DAT) (§5.1.3.2.1).

The vocative case, which is specific to personal names and to person-denoting common nouns, is either identical to the nominative–accusative form (*Ion* (NOM≡ACC≡VOC), *Maria* (NOM≡ACC≡VOC)) or marked by particular inflectional endings and sometimes additionally by morphophonological alternations (*Ioane* (VOC), *Mario* (VOC)) (§5.1.3.3).

As direct objects, proper names are obligatorily introduced by the functional preposition PE and are subject to clitic doubling:

(54) Îl$_i$ aștept **pe Ion**$_i$
CL.ACC.M.3SG (I)wait PE Ion
'I'm waiting for Ion'

Proper names also have a special behaviour with respect to determination: the article that accompanies the proper name does not have a determination role, but occurs as a consequence of certain syntactic restrictions (§5.3.1.1.1). However, when they are used metaphorically or metonymically—in which case they are recategorized as common nouns—names may take the article (see, for this usage of proper names, Kleiber 1994: 66–133; Jonasson 1994: 214–29; Miron Fulea 2005: 199–206):

(55) a. Am   cumpărat   un   **Enescu**
       (We/I)have   bought   an   Enescu
       'We bought a (record by) Enescu'

   b. **Picasso-ul**   mi-a   plăcut   mult
       Picasso.DEF   CL.DAT.1SG=has   liked   much
       'I liked the (painting by) Picasso a lot'

U Proper names in the plural may take a definite (53a) or indefinite (56) article:
   (56) **Nişte**   **Ane**   organizează   o   petrecere
        some   Ana.PL   organize   a   party
        'Some (girls named) Ana(s) are organizing a party'

Of the constituents of a DP headed by a proper name, the possessor and the modifier show certain particular construction features. Thus, the possessor (a genitive DP or a possessive adjective) is introduced by AL (57), and the (AP or PP) modifier is typically attached with the use of the determiner CEL (58) (§§5.3.1.4.3, 7.7.1.1):

(57) Ion   **al**   Mariei   /   **al**   său
     Ion(M.SG)   AL   Maria.GEN AL   his/her.M.SG
     'Maria's Ion' / 'his / her John'

(58) Ion   **cel**   **frumos** /   **cel**   de   **atunci**
     Ion   CEL   beautiful   CEL   of   then
     'the handsome Ion' / 'the former Ion'

U Because the final sequence -*a* of a feminine proper name is identical to the definite article -*a*, the possessive marker AL can occasionally be omitted (§5.1.3.2.2):
   (59) Ioana   **(a)**   **Mariei**
        Ioana   AL   Maria.GEN
        'Maria's Ioana'

   Especially with feminine proper names, the modifier can attach directly, without the mediation of CEL:
   (60) Ioana   **mică**   este   brunetă,   iar   Ioana   **mare**   este   şatenă
        Ioana   little   is   brunette   but   Ioana   big   is   brown-haired
        'Little Ioana is brunette, while big Ioana is brown-haired'

5.2.2 Mass nouns

The feature [+continuous] which characterizes mass nouns morphosyntactically correlates with the feature [–countable] and with some other syntactic characteristics (for the analysis of mass nouns, see Galmiche 1986: 40–53; Kleiber 2006: 183–202, among others).

Mass nouns combine with singular indefinite quantifiers (*mult* 'much', *puţin* 'few', *destul* 'enough', *atât* 'this much', *câtva* 'some / a little'), which are not accepted by countable nouns:

(61) **mult / puţin**   vin   vs.   *****mult / puţin**   scaun
     much   little   wine   much   little   chair

The specific quantifier of mass nouns is the indefinite adjective *nişte* 'some' (§5.3.1.1.2):

(62) Mănâncă **nişte** brânză!
 eat.IMP.2SG some cheese
 'Eat some cheese!'

Other quantifiers of mass nouns are measure nouns (*kilogram* 'kilo', *litru* 'litre'), container nouns (*sticlă* 'bottle', *cană* 'cup') or partitive nouns (*parte* 'part', *sfert* 'quarter'), which in the pseudopartitive structure take a prepositional NP complement headed by *de*, while in the partitive construction proper they take a prepositional DP headed by the partitive preposition *din* (Nedelcu 2009: 178–90):

(63) a. un litru de vin   b. un litru din (acest) vin
     a litre of wine   a litre of this wine
     'a litre of wine'   'a litre of the wine'

(64) a. o ceaşcă de ceai   b. o ceaşcă din (acest) ceai
     a cup of tea   a cup of this tea
     'a cup of tea'   'a cup of the tea'

(65) a. o jumătate de vin   b. o jumătate din (acest) vin
     a half of wine   a half of this wine
     'a half of wine'   'a half of the wine'

The plurals of mass nouns (most frequently created with use of the inflectional ending *-uri*) denote sorts or objects, or portions (§5.1.2.5).

Mass nouns may occur bare in argument positions:

(66) Se mănâncă **pâine** aici
 CL.REFL.PASS eats bread here
 'Bread is eaten here'

5.2.3 Abstract nouns

Abstract nouns share several grammatical features with mass nouns (for the analysis of abstract nouns, see Anscombre 1996: 257–73; Van de Velde 1996: 275–87, among others). Uncountable abstract nouns (*curaj* 'courage', *pace* 'peace') and a few countable ones which are contextually non-discrete (*grijă* 'care', *talent* 'talent') may combine with singular indefinite quantifiers such as *mult* 'much', *puţin* 'few', *destul* 'enough', *câtva* 'some / a little'; usually *nişte* 'some' is not accepted:

(67) Trebuie să ai **multă grijă** în trafic
 must SĂ_SUBJ have.SUBJ.2SG much care in traffic
 'You must take a lot of care in traffic'

Like mass nouns, abstract nouns may appear bare in argument positions:

(68) a. Are **talent**
       has talent
       '(S)he has talent'

  b. Se cere **atenţie** aici
     CL.REFL.PASS requires attention here
     'Attention is required here'

5.2.4 Collective nouns

The inherent features of these nouns allow them to associate in the singular with a singular quantitative modifier like *numeros* 'numerous' (69) and to combine with a verb like *a se aduna* 'gather / assemble' when they occur in subject position (70) (for the analysis of collective nouns, see Flaux and Van de Velde 2000: 57–61):

(69) grup **numeros** vs. *copil **numeros**
 group numerous child numerous
 'large group'

(70) **S-a adunat un grup** în fața primăriei
 CL.REFL.3SG=has gathered a group in front.DEF town-hall.GEN
 'A group gathered in front of the town hall'

In a binomial noun phrase that contains a generic collective noun in the singular (*grup* 'group', *mulțime* 'multitude, lot', *majoritate* 'majority'), predicate agreement is either in the plural or in the singular (§§5.3.2.3.1, 12.2.5):

(71) Acolo **s-a adunat / s-au adunat** o
 there CL.REFL.ACC=has(3SG) gathered CL.REFL.ACC=have(3PL) gathered a
 mulțime de oameni
 lot of people
 'A lot of people gathered there'

5.2.5 Relational nouns

On account of their inherently relational nature (they establish kinship, social, professional, or part–whole relations), these nouns take arguments, realized as a genitive DP or a possessive adjective (*fratele **Mariei*** brother.DEF Maria.GEN 'Maria's brother'; *fratele **său*** brother.DEF(M.SG) his / her.M.SG 'his / her brother'), as a PP (*frate **cu Maria*** brother with Maria 'brother to Maria') or, more rarely, as a dative (*frate **Mariei*** brother Maria.DAT 'Maria's brother'); for details, see §5.3.4.3.

In Romanian, relational nouns may occur in three types of possessive constructions:

(i) The possessive dative clitic construction; the relational nouns observe certain definiteness restrictions depending on the syntactic-semantic features of the verb (§3.4.4.3):

(72) a. Ți-ai ajutat prietenul
 CL.REFL.DAT.2SG=have helped friend.DEF.ACC
 'You helped your friend'

 b. Îmi țiuie urechile
 CL.DAT.1SG tingle ears.DEF.NOM
 'My ears tingle'

(73) Ion îmi este văr
 Ion CL.DAT.1SG is cousin
 'Ion is my cousin'

(ii) The possessive accusative clitic construction, for relational nouns that denote a part of the body (an inalienable possession structure) (§2.3.3.2.1):

(74) Mă   doare   capul
     CL.ACC.1SG hurts   head.DEF.NOM
     'I have a headache'

(iii) The possessive nominative construction, which involves a relational noun that denotes a part of the body without a subordinate genitive or possessive phrase:

(75) Ion a   ridicat mâna
     Ion has raised hand.DEF.ACC
     'Ion raised his hand'

5.2.6 Deverbal and deadjectival nouns

These nouns present a series of particularities which stem from their derived nature (see Alexiadou 2001; Cornilescu 2001), of which the most general are the following: they preserve the argument structure of the verb / adjective (76), they combine with temporal and aspectual modifiers (77), they allow their arguments to have some realizations in common with the base verb or adjective (78) (for details, see §5.3.4.1):

(76) a. alegerea   **lui**   **Ion** **deputat**
        election.DEF LUI(GEN)   Ion   deputy
        'the election of Ion as a deputy'

  b. egalitatea   **cu**   **bărbații**
     equality.DEF with   men.DEF
     'the equality with men'

(77) a. alegerea   lui   Obama   **ieri**
        election.DEF LUI(GEN)   Obama   yesterday
        'the election of Obama yesterday'

  b. atenția   **în** **permanență**
     attention.DEF   in   permanence
     'permanent attention'

(78) a. dorința   **să**   **plece**
        desire.DEF   SĂ$_{SUBJ}$ leave.SUBJ.3SG
        'his / her desire to leave'

  b. siguranța   **că**   **reușește**
     surety.DEF   that   succeeds
     'the surety that (s)he succeeds'

In Romanian, a series of suffixes are compatible with the nominalization process (*-aș, -ăreț, -eală / -ială, -ință, -ment, -iș, -re, -toare, -tor, -ură*, etc.; see §14.1.2.1.1). Those relevant to the nominalization process are the long infinitive suffix and the supine suffix: unaccusative verbs prefer the long infinitive suffix (which is [+telic]: *venirea* 'the coming', *plecarea* 'the leaving'), while unergative verbs prefer the supine suffix ([–telic]: *plânsul* 'the cry', *râsul* 'the laugh', *mieunatul* 'the mew', *înotatul* 'the swim') (Cornilescu 2001: 468–70). The selection of one suffix over another depends on the stylistic register (Stan 2003: 72–6).

H In the old language, nominalizations could also be based on the participle form of the verb (taking a feminine form):
(79) în agonisâta bunătăţilor   (*Sicriul de aur*)
     in   save.PPLE.F   goods.DEF.GEN
     'hoarding of goods'
This pattern is preserved in certain collocations, such as *Lăsata secului* 'Shrove Tuesday', *fripta* 'hot cockles' (a kids game) (Stan 2003: 58, 104–5).

Event-denoting deverbal nouns (80a,c,e,g) have certain features not shared by those that express results (80b,d,f,h) (see Cornilescu 2001): the realization of the internal argument (80a), combination with a *by*-phrase (80c), with aspectual modifiers (80e) like *constant* 'constant', *frecvent* 'frequent' and the impossibility of combining with locative and temporal modifiers introduced by *de* (80g):

(80)   a. Exprimarea   **sentimentelor**   îi   face   vulnerabili
            expressing.DEF feelings.DEF.GEN CL.ACC.3PL makes   vulnerable
            'Expressing feelings makes them vulnerable'

vs.   b. Exprimarea   din   capitol   este   greşită
           expressing.DEF from   chapter   is   wrong
           'The expression in the chapter is wrong'

     c. Exprimarea   sentimentelor   **de către copii**   îi   face
        expressing.DEF feelings.DEF.GEN by   children   CL.ACC.3PL makes
        vulnerabili
        vulnerable

vs.   d. *Exprimarea **de către Ion** din   capitol   este   greşită
           expressing.DEF by   Ion   from   chapter   is   wrong

     e. Exprimarea   **frecventă**   a sentimentelor   îi   face   vulnerabili
       expressing.DEF frequent.F.SG AL feelings.DEF.GEN CL.ACC.3PL makes vulnerable

vs.   f. *Exprimarea **frecventă**   din   capitol   este   greşită
       expressing.DEF frequent.F.SG from   chapter   is   wrong

     g. *Exprimarea **de acolo** a sentimentelor   îi   face   vulnerabili
       expressing.DEF from there AL feelings.DEF.GEN CL.ACC.3PL makes vulnerable

vs.   h. Exprimarea   **de acolo**   este   greşită
       expressing.DEF from there   is   wrong

5.2.7 Picture nouns

Nouns like *fotografie* 'photo', *imagine* 'image', *portret* 'portrait', *tablou* 'painting' may participate in a possessive structure, denoting the possessed object (81), or in an agentive structure, in which case the picture noun takes arguments such as Agent (82a) or Theme (82b):

(81)   tabloul   lui   Ion
      painting.DEF LUI(GEN) Ion
      'Ion's painting' < 'Ion has a painting'

(82) a. tabloul lui Ion
'the painting by Ion'
b. tabloul lui Ion
'the painting of Ion'

The genitive DP / possessive adjective argument of a 'picture noun' has an ambiguous interpretation in a narrow context (Theme, Agent, or Possessor), contrasting with the *de*-construction, where the *de*-phrase is strictly interpreted as an Agent (83); see also §5.3.4.2.

(83) tabloul   de   Ion
     painting by   Ion
     'the painting by Ion'

5.3 THE STRUCTURE OF THE NOMINAL PHRASE

5.3.1 Determiners

5.3.1.1 The enclitic definite article. The proclitic indefinite article

Romanian possesses a definite article and an indefinite article.

C   Romanian did not develop a partitive article. Romanian thus patterns with languages like Spanish and Portuguese. The partitive article of French and Italian (Posner 1996: 274–6) corresponds in Romanian either to nonpartitive, bare noun structures (84), or to partitive structures with the prepositions *din*, *dintre* ('of, from, out of'), which are based on the preposition *de* (< Lat. DE partitive; Ernout and Thomas 1959: 212)—*din* + singular (85a), *dintre* + plural (85b) (ELIR: 231; Iliescu 2008b: 3271–2):

(84) Rom. Beau   vin   Fr. Je   bois   du   vin
         (I)drink wine   I   drink   ART.PART   wine
(85) a. Rom. Iau   din   pâine Fr. Je   prends   du   pain   [= une partie]
            (I)take   from   bread   I   take   ART.PART   bread   a   part
     b. Rom. unul   dintre sporturi It. uno   degli   sport
            one   of   sports   one   ART.PART   sports

5.3.1.1.1 The definite article varies in gender, number, and case (Table 5.11).

H   The Romanian definite article is inherited form the late Latin unstressed forms of the demonstrative ĪLLE (Densusianu 1901: 143–4), which was a constituent of a nominal phrase (ILR II: 233–4; Rosetti 1986: 134–5; cf. Renzi 2010: 31, 33). According to Coteanu (1969: 141), the definite article most probably emerged in Romanian after the 7th century (cf. also Iliescu 2008b: 3271, and references therein).
C   The preservation of case inflection for the definite article is a characteristic feature of Romanian.

In Romanian, the definite article is enclitic:

(86) calul: cal-u-l
             horse-SG-DEF.NOM≡ACC
             'the horse'

TABLE 5.11 The forms of the definite article

		M	F
SG	NOM≡ACC	-l, -le	-a
	GEN≡DAT	-lui [luị]	-i [ị]
PL	NOM≡ACC	-i [i]	-le
	GEN≡DAT	-lor	

H The enclisis of the definite article has been explained in various ways; the most widely accepted hypotheses are the following: (a) internal evolution in Romanian (Coteanu 1969: 96–7, and references therein; Philippide 2011: 460), on the basis of the primitive structure HOMO ILLE-BONUS or HOMO ILLE + genitive, a continuation of the Latin pattern HOMO ILLE (Bourciez 1956: 248), where ILLE, originally associated with the adjective / genitive, as a DP-internal constituent, was reanalysed and grouped with the noun, in postposition (Graur 1929: 475–7; Graur 1967: 8; Rosetti 1986: 160); (b) inheritance from the Thraco-Dacian substratum, a hypothesis supported by comparison with Albanian (Brâncuș 2002: 56, 2007: 164; Ivănescu 2000: 143-4); (c) enclisis, as a Balkan Sprachbund phenomenon (Sandfeld 1930: 170; Capidan 2006: 128; Feuillet 1986: 72–5). According to some scholars, Romanian influenced Bulgarian with respect to the enclisis of the definite article, because in Bulgarian this phenomenon is attested later than in Romanian (Sandfeld 1930: 170–1).

The enclitic position of the definite article preserves the Latin position of the noun's grammatical markers (Iliescu 2008b: 3271, and references therein). For some interpretations of the grammaticalization of the demonstrative ILLE as a definite article see: Fischer (1985: 90); Coteanu (1969: 101, 141); ILR (II: 230–2); Manoliu (2011: 491–2, and references therein).

Focusing either on the pronominal origin of the article or on its enclisis, various authors have stressed the clitic (Renzi 1993) or the suffixal (Lombard 1974: 192; Ortmann and Popescu 2000; Dobrovie-Sorin and Giurgea 2006; Cornilescu and Nicolae 2011a: 203; Ledgeway 2011: 415) nature of the definite article in Romanian.

C Romanian is the only Romance language that has an enclitic definite article.

The definite article attaches to (1) common nouns, (2) proper names or (3) prenominal adjectives.

1. The enclisis (suffixation) of the definite article to common nouns allows the synthetic marking of the distinction between the nominative–accusative and the genitive–dative syncretic case forms in the definite declension, in the singular and plural (Table 5.2).

In the masculine singular nominative–accusative there exist two forms of the article, selected on the basis of the inflectional ending of the noun: -*l* combines with most nouns, while -*le* is selected only by nouns which take the inflectional ending -*e*:

(87) a. băiat-u-l
   boy-SG-DEF.NOM≡ACC

   b. frat-e-le
   brother-SG-DEF.NOM≡ACC

Neuter nouns in the singular take the masculine forms of the article and in the plural take the feminine forms:

(88) râ-u-l   râu-uri-le
      river-SG-DEF.NOM≡ACC   river-PL-DEF.NOM≡ACC

Neuter nouns with the inflectional ending *-e* select in the singular the definite article form *-le* (*numele* 'name.DEF'), like masculines with the same inflectional ending.

A few common nouns display irregularities in the selection of the definite article forms (§5.1.5).

The feminine singular article *-a* has the following realizations: *-a* [ja] for nouns whose root ends in unstressed [i], and *-ua* [wa] for the noun *zi* 'day' and for nouns ending in stressed *-a* ['a] and *-ea* ['ea̯] (*sanda* 'sandal', *stea* 'star'):

(89) a. famili-a   [familija]
         family-SG-DEF.NOM≡ACC

      b. zi-∅-ua   [ziwa]
         day-SG-DEF.NOM≡ACC

The definite article attaches to the noun in the following ways:

  (i) it may follow the inflectional ending, undergoing no phonological change;
 (ii) it follows the inflectional ending, with phonological changes that are not reflected in the orthography;
(iii) it merges with the inflectional ending, a phonological change which is not reflected by orthography *-ii* [i̯i] > [i];
 (iv) by the realization of the old singular inflectional ending *-u*, for masculine and neuter nouns;
  (v) by the alteration of syllable structure, for masculine and neuter nouns ending in *-i* [i̯];
 (vi) by the substitution of the inflectional ending.

  (i) Following the inflectional ending, undergoing no phonological change—in (90a) the masculine–neuter singular forms *-l*, *-lui* follow the *muta cum liquida* cluster (consonant + *r* / *l*) + *-u* [u]; in (90b) the masculine–neuter singular forms *-le*, *-lui* follow the inflectional ending *-e*; in (90c) the feminine singular form *-i* [i̯] follows the inflectional endings *-e*, *-le*; in (90d) the feminine plural forms *-le*, *-lor* follow the inflectional endings *-e*, *-le*; in (90e) the plural forms *-le*, *-lor* follow the neuter inflectional ending *-e*; the feminine singular form *-ua* [wa] follows the inflectional ending ∅ ((89b) above):

(90) a. (M)   tigr-u-l   tigr-u-lui
               tiger-SG-DEF.NOM≡ACC   tiger-SG-DEF.GEN≡DAT

      b. (NEUT) num-e-le   num-e-lui
               name-SG-DEF.NOM≡ACC   name-SG-DEF.GEN≡DAT

      c. (F)   cas-e-i [i̯]   zi-le-i [i̯]
               house-SG.GEN≡DAT-DEF.GEN≡DAT   day-SG.GEN≡DAT-DEF.GEN≡DAT

d.	(F)	cas-e-le	zi-le-le	
		house-PL-DEF.NOM≡ACC	day-PL-DEF.NOM≡ACC	
		cas-e-lor	zi-le-lor	
		house-PL-DEF.GEN≡DAT	day-PL-DEF.GEN≡DAT	
e.	(NEUT)	num-e-le	num-e-lor	
		name-PL-DEF.NOM≡ACC	name-PL-DEF.GEN≡DAT	

(ii) Following the inflectional ending, with phonological changes that are not reflected in orthography—in (91a) the inflectional ending -*i* [ⁱ] or [i̯] becomes [i], before the masculine plural form -*lor* and the feminine plural forms -*le*, -*lor*; in (91b) the final vowel [ⁱ] of the neuter–feminine plural inflectional ending -*uri* becomes [i] before the forms -*le*, -*lor*; in (91c) the masculine–neuter singular inflectional ending -*u* [w] becomes [u] before -*l*, -*lui*; in (91d) the feminine singular inflectional ending -*e* [e] becomes [e̞] before the article -*a* (-*ea* [e̞a]):

(91) a. (M)   fraț-i [ⁱ]   / fraț-i-lor [i]
           brother-PL   brother-PL-DEF.GEN≡DAT
           te-i [i̯]   / te-i-lor [i]
           linden-PL   linden-PL-DEF.GEN≡DAT
     (F)   ser-i [ⁱ]   / ser-i-le [i]   / ser-i-lor [i]
           evening-PL   evening-PL-DEF.NOM≡ACC   evening-PL-DEF.GEN≡DAT
           che-i [i̯]   / che-i-le [i]   / che-i-lor [i]
           key-PL   key-PL-DEF.NOM≡ACC   key-PL-DEF.GEN≡DAT

    b. (NEUT)   tren-uri [ⁱ]   / tren-uri-le [i]   / tren-uri-lor [i]
           train-PL   train-PL-DEF.NOM≡ACC   train-PL-DEF.GEN≡DAT
     (F)   lips-uri [ⁱ]   / lips-uri-le [i]   / lips-uri-lor [i]
           lack-PL   lack-PL-DEF.NOM≡ACC   lack-PL-DEF.GEN≡DAT

    c. (M)   le-u [u̯]   / le-u-l [u]   / le-u-lui [u]
           lion-SG   lion-SG-DEF.NOM≡ACC   lion-SG-DEF.GEN≡DAT
     (NEUT)   tablo-u [u̯]   / tablo-u-l [u]   / tablo-u-lui [u]
           picture-SG   picture-SG-DEF.NOM≡ACC   picture-SG-DEF.GEN≡DAT

    d. (F)   cart-e [e]   / cart-e-a [e̞a]
           book-SG   book-SG-DEF.NOM≡ACC

(iii) Merging with the inflectional ending, a phonological change which is not reflected by the orthography -*ii* [i̯i] > [i]—the masculine plural, feminine singular definite article -*i* [i̯] merges with the inflectional ending -*i*, which is pronounced as [i] (after the [consonant + *r* / *l*] cluster) (92a), as [ⁱ] (after consonants) (92b), as [i̯] (after vowels) (92c); when it fuses with the definite article, it becomes [i]:

(92) a. (M)   tigr-i [i]   / tigr-i-i   [i̯i] > [i]
           tiger-PL   tiger-PL-DEF.NOM≡ACC

    b. (M)   pom-i [ⁱ]   / pom-i-i   [i̯i] > [i]
           tree-PL   tree-PL-DEF.NOM≡ACC

    c. (F)   che-i [i̯]   / che-i-i   [i̯i] > [i]
           key-PL   key-SG.GEN≡DAT-DEF.GEN≡DAT

5.3 The structure of the nominal phrase 289

H The merger of the article *-ei* with the nominal inflectional ending took place very early (*-eei* > *-ei*, *-ii*; *-iei* > *-ii*, *-ei*); the contracted forms are attested from the 12th to the 15th centuries (so before the appearance of the earliest texts), especially with proper names: *Luminatei* (hydronym, in Vasiliu and Ionescu-Ruxăndoiu 1986: 148); this innovation gradually prevailed. The non-contracted forms became obsolete after the first half of the 17th century (Frâncu 1997: 325): *credinţeei* faith.SG.DEF.GEN≡DAT 'to / of the faith' (*Noul Testament*).

(iv) The realization of the old singular inflectional ending *-u*, for masculine and neuter nouns; in contemporary Romanian, *-u* is uttered only in the presence of an enclitic element:

(93) (M) pom-Ø   pom-u-l   pom-u-lui
         tree-SG tree-SG-DEF.NOM≡ACC   tree-SG-DEF.GEN≡DAT

(v) The alteration of the syllable structure, for masculine and neuter nouns ending in *-i* [i̯]:

(94) (NEUT) pai-Ø [pai̯]   pai-u-l [pa.jul]   pai-u-lui [pa.ju.lui̯]
            straw-SG   straw-SG-DEF.NOM≡ACC straw-SG-DEF.GEN≡DAT

(vi) The substitution of the inflectional ending—the singular nominative–accusative article *-a* replaces the masculine / feminine inflectional ending *-ă* or the feminine inflectional endings *-e* [je] or *-e* [e] preceded by a palatal consonant:

(95) (F) cas-ă   cas-a
         house-SG   house-DEF.NOM≡ACC.SG
         bucuri-e [bukurije] bucuri-a [bukurija]
         joy-SG   joy-DEF.NOM≡ACC.SG
         urech-e [urece]   ureche-a [ureca]
         ear-SG   ear-DEF.NOM≡ACC.SG

U The article *-i* [i̯] is typically not pronounced, but merges with the inflectional ending *i* [i] of the noun; however, the marking of the article in the written language (reflected by forms written with two or three instances of *i*) is obligatory: *pomii* (92b); *fiii* [fii] / [fiii̯] 'the sons'.

The article *-l* is suppressed before a clitic which forms a syllable together with the final segment of the definite noun; the clitic is graphically separated by a hyphen:

(96) la rându-mi
     to turn.SG=CL.1SG
     'on my behalf'

H Omission of the article *-l* is a process that had begun before the 16th century (Vasiliu and Ionescu-Ruxăndoiu 1986: 145).

U The article *-l* is usually not pronounced in present-day language (except in formal speech); however, the marking of the article in the written language is compulsory: *băiatul* [bəjatu] 'the boy'.

The enclitic article is graphically separated by a hyphen in foreign words or in abbreviations that are not adapted to the inflectional system of Romanian; the article *-l* / *-lui* attaches after the inflectional ending *-u*: *show-ul* 'the show', *CV-ului* 'of the CV'.

Some definiteness restrictions are contextually conditioned by the presence of certain quantifiers (§5.3.2) or modifiers (§5.3.5).

The chief function of the article (D [+definite]) is that generally associated with articles in Universal Grammar, and concerns the referentiality of the nominal phrase. The quantificational use of the definite article in generic sentences is also frequent (97a). The distributive value of the definite article is a particular feature of Romanian (97b).

(97) a. Balena este un mamifer
'The whale is a mammal'

b. Costă 2 lei kilogramul
'It costs 2 lei a kilo'

2. The enclisis of the definite article on proper names, which are intrinsically [+definite], is exclusively a formal means of case marking. Recall that certain proper names end in a formative identical to the definite article: *Maria*.

In contemporary standard Romanian, the following proper names may bear the article: place names, abbreviations, and other categories of proper names, which do not include in their final segment the definite article—such as names of institutions, for example *Rapid* (a football club). Place names with a singular / plural masculine form may bear the article in the masculine singular nominative–accusative or genitive–dative (98a,b), and those with a feminine singular form take the article only in the genitive–dative (98c):

(98) a. Olt   Olt-u-l   Olt-u-lui
Olt.SG   Olt.SG-DEF.SG.NOM≡ACC   Olt.SG-DEF.SG.GEN≡DAT

b. Bucureşti   Bucureşti-u-l   Bucureşti-u-lui
Bucureşti.PL   Bucureşti.PL-DEF.SG.NOM≡ACC   Bucureşti.PL-DEF.SG.GEN≡DAT

c. Târgovişte   Târgovişte-i
Târgovişte.SG   Târgovişte.SG-DEF.SG.GEN≡DAT

H The article -*l* frequently combined with (masculine singular) personal names until the end of the 19th century: *Barbul* (CRom *Barbu*). The article -*lu* (masculine singular, genitive–dative) is attested in names in the the old language: *Radulu*[*i*] (ILR II: 234); the form -*lui* (as a genitive–dative inflectional marker) was more frequent than -*lu* even before the 16th century (Vasiliu and Ionescu-Ruxăndoiu 1986: 147): *Radului* (this form is employed in the non-standard language; in the contemporary standard language, the genitive–dative of personal names is marked by the proclitic *lui*; see §5.1.3.2.1).

For certain categories of proper names, such as names of cities, the presence of the definite article is optional in the nominative case (99a); in non-prepositional accusative (99b), and in the genitive–dative (99c) the article obligatorily occurs as a formal case marker:

(99) a. Bucureşti(ul)   este   capitala   României
Bucharest(.DEF)   is   capital.DEF   Romania.GEN
'Bucharest is the capital city of Romania'

b. Vizitez   Bucureştiul
(I)visit   Bucharest.DEF
'I am visiting Bucharest'

c. Străzile   Bucureştiului   sunt   aglomerate
streets.DEF   Bucharest.DEF.GEN   are   crowded
'Bucharest's streets are crowded'

Feminine proper names ending in -*a* sometimes have forms ending in -*ă* / -*e*, on the model of articleless common names; these forms can follow an adjective bearing the definite article (100a), an indefinite article (100b), but not prepositions (100c):

(100) a. Moldova— frumoasa Moldova / Moldovă
Moldavia.DEF—beautiful.DEF Moldavia.DEF Moldavia
'Moldavia—beautiful Moldavia'

b. o Românie nouă
a Romania new
'a new Romania'

c. în România / în *Românie
in Romania.DEF in Romania
'in Romania'

3. The enclisis of the definite article on adjectives occurs only when the adjectival modifier precedes the noun (for the generative interpretation of the structures of this kind, see Cornilescu and Nicolae 2011a: 195–7). In modern Romanian, only the first constituent of the DP bears the enclitic article, no matter whether this constituent is a noun (101a) or an adjective (101b) (for the double definite structures of the old language, see §5.3.1.1.5.2). Structures with certain invariable adjectives are exceptional in that the adjective precedes the article-bearing noun (101c). In structures containing the adjective *întreg* ('whole, entire'), the article may attach either to the adjective, following the general rule (101d), or to the noun, behaving like the quantifier *tot* 'all' (101e):

(101) a. cuvinte-le frumoase
words-DEF beautiful
'the beautiful words'

b. frumoase-le cuvinte
beautiful-DEF words
'the beautiful words'

c. cogeamite / ditamai omu-l
huge enormous man-DEF
'the huge / enormous man'

d. întregu-l secol / zbuciumatu-l secol
whole-DEF century tumultuous-DEF century
'the entire century' 'the tumultuous century'

e. întreg secolu-l / tot secolu-l
whole century-DEF all century-DEF
'the entire century' 'the entire century'

H Structures with articleless adjectives preceding definite nouns were much more varied in the old language; some have been preserved in the present-day religious language: *mare mila lui* (great mercy.DEF his(GEN) 'his great mercy') (Cornilescu and Nicolae 2011a: 199–218).

5.3.1.1.2 The Romanian indefinite article has a heterogeneous paradigm, in terms of its inflection, distribution and semantics.

The indefinite article formally expresses number (singular / plural), gender (masculine / feminine, only in the singular) and case (nominative–accusative / genitive–dative) distinctions. The genitive–dative singular / plural forms are identical to the forms of the indefinite adjective *unii* 'some' (Table 5.24). In the plural nominative–accusative, the suppletive invariable form *niște* is used.

TABLE 5.12 The forms of the indefinite article

		M		F
SG	NOM≡ACC	un		o
	GEN≡DAT	unui		unei
PL	NOM≡ACC		niște	
	GEN≡DAT		unor	

The singular nominative–accusative and genitive–dative forms are identical to those of the adjectival cardinal numeral *un* 'one'.

C In the other Romance languages, the indefinite article is also identical to the cardinal numeral. The indefinite article is identical to the indefinite adjective in Romanian and Spanish. Romanian is the only Romance language that has the suppletive form for the plural *niște* (ELIR: 208; Iliescu 2008b: 3271).

H As in the other Romance languages, the indefinite article is inherited from the Latin cardinal numeral UNUS, UNA, attested with indefinite value as early as the Roman era (Bourciez 1956: 100; ILR II: 236). The original feminine form *ună* has been preserved in Aromanian and Megleno-Romanian, and represents a conservative feature of these varieties; the feminine form *o* is a subsequent innovation, present only in Daco-Romanian and in Istro-Romanian (Caragiu Marioțeanu 1975: 104; Caragiu Marioțeanu *et al.* 1977: 181, 203, 219). The genitive–dative forms *unui*, *unei* appeared at an early stage, on the model of the pronominal declension (ILR II: 236). *Niște* is an indefinite compound word, corresponding to Latin elements NESCIO QUID (Meyer-Lübke 1895: 649; REW: 5899; Pușcariu 1905: 1175).

The indefinite article is proclitic:

(102) (M) un   băiat   unui   băiat
         a.NOM≡ACC.SG boy   a.GEN≡DAT.SG boy
         niște   băieți   unor   băieți
         a.NOM≡ACC.PL boys   a.GEN≡DAT.PL boys
     (F) o   casă   unei   case
         a.NOM≡ACC.SG house   a.GEN≡DAT.SG house
         niște   case   unor   case
         a.NOM≡ACC.PL houses   a.GEN≡DAT.PL houses

Neuter nouns take the masculine forms of the article in the singular:

(103) (NEUT) un   râu   unui   râu
             a.NOM≡ACC.SG river a.GEN≡DAT.SG river

In contrast to the singular forms *un* / *o*, the article *niște* is not a genuinely functional element; rather, it is intermediate between determiner and indefinite pronominal adjective (Stan 2010a):

As a determiner, *niște* has a weak referential function, and can be omitted in many contexts (104a); the [–definite] DP status of referential *niște*-phrases is clearer in contexts in which they participate in anaphoric chains (104d); *niște* does not formally express the Case feature, typically realized at the DP level, the highest projection of the nominal phrase (Giusti 2005: 33–5):

5.3 The structure of the nominal phrase

(104) a. Au sosit [NP ([D niște]) turiști]
have come a.NOM≡ACC.PL tourists
'There arrived (some) tourists'

b. A sosit [DP un turist]
has come a tourist
'There came a tourist'

c. A sosit *[NP turist]
has come tourist
'There came a tourist'

d. [DP Niște turiști] au sosit, [DP alții] întârzie
a.NOM≡ACC.PL tourists have arrived others are-late
'Some tourists came; others are late'

Niște does not display gender and number concord with the head noun; it has an indefinite meaning weaker than other pronominal adjectives (like *câțiva* 'a few'); it does not combine with a null head NP (105) (Cornilescu and Nicolae 2010: 98); it cannot be coordinated with other pronominal adjectives (for the coordination test, see Cardinaletti and Starke 1999: 208):

(105) *niște [NP [e]] unii [NP [e]] / unii [NP oameni]
some some some people

Niște selects as complement a phrase that has a plural countable noun head (104d) or a singular mass noun (106). In some structures with the singular, *niște* is a partitive (106a) (Niculescu 1999: 175–81) or an indefinite (106b) quantifier (Stan 2010a: 569). Like the structures with the plural (104a), *niște* may be an optional indefinite determiner in a phrase with an uncountable singular noun head, having a non-referential semantic interpretation (106c):

(106) a. Bea niște lapte din sticlă!
drink.IMP.2SG some milk from bottle
'Drink some milk from the bottle'

b. Bea niște lapte, dar nu prea mult!
drink.IMP.2SG some milk but not too much
'Drink some milk, but not too much'

c. Bea (niște) lapte!
drink.IMP.2SG some milk
'Drink (some) milk'

C The use of the same element as a partitive article and as an indefinite article in the plural characterizes Italian and French, with some differences between the two languages concerning the degree of grammaticalization and the syntax of articles (Iliescu 2008b: 3272). Romanian is singled out by the very element used in partitive structures (*niște*) and by the syntactic properties of this element: the invariable partitive *niște* is not an article, but a quantifier.

5.3.1.1.3 The absence of the article, in bare noun structures (when the noun is not associated with modifiers, genitives, and other NP constituents), has a few distinctive characteristics in Romanian (Dobrovie-Sorin and Laca 2003).

294   5 *Nouns and Noun Phrases*

In subject position, bare nouns occur postverbally in unmarked sentences; bare plurals are more frequent, while bare singulars (107a) are subject to lexical conditioning (see §3.1.4). Bare nouns also typically occur as subjective predicative complements (107b) (§3.3.1.2). The bare direct object pattern (§3.2.1.2.2) is also characteristic of idioms (107c).

(107) a. Vine   **furtună**
          comes   storm
          'There is a storm coming'

       b. Ion este **inginer**
          'Ion is an engineer'

       c. a   trage   **nădejde**
          A_{INF} pull.INF hope
          'hope'

C   Romanian, Catalan, and Portuguese contrast with French and Italian as to the use of bare nominals in contexts like (107) above. Romanian preserves a syntactic characteristic of the old stage of the evolution of the Romance languages. In old Romanian, bare noun structures were more numerous and more diversified than in the contemporary language (Bourciez 1956: 586; Niculescu 1965: 64–5).

In addition, bare nouns occur in Romanian after most of the prepositions that select the accusative case (for details, see §9.3.2.2):

(108) în   clădire
       in   building
       'in the building'

C   The use of bare nouns after prepositions is a conservative feature of Romanian (Bourciez 1956: 586; Niculescu 1965: 64). For some scholars (Sandfeld 1930: 134), the absence of the article in this type of context represents a Balkan Sprachbund phenomenon.

In structures like (109), bare singulars combine with the preposition *pe* 'per', which expresses a distributive quantificational meaning.

(109) pe lună   pe kilogram   pe oră
       per month   per kilo   per hour

5.3.1.2   Demonstratives

5.3.1.2.1 The demonstrative system of Romanian is based on the proximity distinction: Romanian has proximal demonstratives (*acesta* 'this') and distal demonstratives (*acela* 'that').

C   In contrast to Romance languages such as Portuguese, Spanish, Valencian, and Occitan, but like old and modern French and standard Italian, Romanian does not preserve the tripartite Latin deictic system of the type *near speaker / near addressee / neither*, illustrated by the Latin paradigm HIC, HAEC, HOC / ISTE, ISTA, ISTUD / ILLE, ILLA, ILLUD (Dimitrescu 1975: 161; Fischer 1985: 100; Salvi 2011: 325). Instead, Romanian has developed a system (similar to English) in which the demonstrative elements are distinguished along the *proximity* dimension. However, Romanian contrasts with (modern) French in that the proximity distinction is encoded in the demonstrative lexeme itself (*acesta* 'this' vs. *acela* 'that'), while modern French expresses this distinction syntactically (*celui-ci* 'this one', *celui-là* 'that one'), with the use of adverbial particles (Reinheimer Rîpeanu 2001: 167–8).

Romanian demonstratives inflect for number, gender, and case. They function as prenominal (110a) and postnominal (110b) determiners in non-elliptical DPs, and as 'pronouns' in DPs with elided heads (111).

(110) a. **Acest / Acel** băiat vine
         this   that   boy comes

   b. Băiatul **acesta / acela** vine
       boy.DEF this   that   comes

(111) **Acesta / Acela** vine
       this one that one comes

There is an inflectional distinction between pronominal demonstratives (111) and postnominal demonstrative determiners (110b), on the one hand, and prenominal demonstrative determiners (110a), on the other hand, in that the former display a *long* form differentiated by their final vowel from the *short* form of the latter (see (110a) vs. (110b), (111)).

H This inflectional specialization was not very strict in old Romanian (Dimitrescu 1978: 166–7; Cornilescu and Nicolae 2009: 647). The short forms could appear in contexts where one finds the long form in the modern language: in postnominal position (112a) and in pronominal usages (112b). The long forms could occur prenominally (112c), a position no longer available for them:

(112) a. oamenilor   **acestor**   (Coresi)
           men.DEF.GEN these

   b. **acel** e   frate   mie   (Coresi)
       that   is brother me.DAT

   c. **aceasta** a   noastră carte   (*Documente*)
       this   AL   our   book

The distributional options of modern Romanian were also available in the old language.

Romanian demonstratives are specified as *definite*, and cannot occur in indefinite but [+specific] constructions (e.g. English *There was **this** man*) (Cornilescu 2005b).

5.3.1.2.2 The inventory of demonstratives includes short, long, and unique forms.

The set of proximal demonstratives has two members (*acest(a)* and *ăsta* 'this'), differentiated according to their origin and usage.

Acest(a) is an etymologically complex word (< ECCUM + ISTUM), used in standard written Romanian (Table 5.13). It has both series of forms, short and long. It may appear in all demonstrative positions: prenominal and postnominal determiner, and pronoun.

Ăsta is an etymologically simple word (< ĬSTUS, a vulgar Latin variant of ISTE) (Table 5.14). It is mainly used in standard spoken Romanian. In contrast to *acest(a)*, *ăsta* possesses only *long* forms, being thus excluded from the prenominal determiner position.

TABLE 5.13 The paradigm of *acest(a)* 'this (one)'

CASE	MASCULINE				FEMININE			
	SINGULAR		PLURAL		SINGULAR		PLURAL	
	SHORT	LONG	SHORT	LONG	SHORT	LONG	SHORT	LONG
NOM≡ACC	acest	acesta	acești	aceștia	această	aceasta	aceste	acestea
GEN≡DAT	acestui	acestuia	acestor	acestora	acestei	acesteia	acestor	acestora

TABLE 5.14 The paradigm of *ăsta* 'this (one)'

CASE	MASCULINE		FEMININE	
	SINGULAR	PLURAL	SINGULAR	PLURAL
NOM≡ACC	ăsta	ăștia	asta	astea
GEN≡DAT	ăstuia	ăstora	ăsteia	ăstora

When the demonstrative substitutes a clause (113), only the feminine form *asta* may be used (Nicula 2009: 183). When the demonstrative functions as a substitute within the boundaries of a sentence, both feminine forms, *acesta* and *ăsta*, may be employed (114).

(113) [Ion vrea să urmeze Facultatea de Medicină]$_i$. **Asta**$_i$ / *****Aceasta**$_i$ e
 (Ion wants to go to Medical School) this(F.SG) this(F.SG) is
 interesant
 interesting(M.SG)

(114) [Tipul tuși]$_i$ și după **asta**$_i$ / **aceasta**$_i$ se întoarse
 bloke.DEF coughed and after this this CL.REFL.ACC turn.PS.3SG
 către copil
 to child

Clausal substitution is accompanied by an agreement mismatch: in (113), the postcopular adjective (masculine singular) does not agree with the demonstrative subject (feminine singular).

The inventory of distal demonstratives encompasses two elements (*acel(a)* and *ăla* 'that'), distinguished according to their origin and usage.

Acel(a) is an etymologically complex word (< ECCUM+ILLUM), used in standard written Romanian (Table 5.15). It has both series of forms, short and long. Accordingly, it may function as a prenominal and postnominal determiner and as a pronoun.

Ăla is an etymologically simple word (< ILLE), used in standard spoken Romanian (Table 5.16). In contrast to *acel(a)*, *ăla* possesses only *long* forms and is thus generally excluded from the prenominal determiner position.

5.3 The structure of the nominal phrase

TABLE 5.15 The paradigm of *acel(a)* 'that (one)'

CASE	MASCULINE				FEMININE			
	SINGULAR		PLURAL		SINGULAR		PLURAL	
	SHORT	LONG	SHORT	LONG	SHORT	LONG	SHORT	LONG
NOM≡ACC	acel	acela	acei	aceia	acea	aceea	acele	acelea
GEN≡DAT	acelui	aceluia	acelor	acelora	acelei	aceleia	acelor	acelora

TABLE 5.16 The paradigm of *ăla* 'that (one)'

CASE	MASCULINE		FEMININE	
	SINGULAR	PLURAL	SINGULAR	PLURAL
NOM≡ACC	ăla	ăia	aia	alea
GEN≡DAT	ăluia	ălora	ăleia	ălora

U   In the spoken language the etymologically simple forms are used much more frequently than the etymologically complex ones (Nicula 2008).
  Although demonstratives agree with the head noun, in the spoken language the genitive–dative form of postnominal demonstratives is systematically replaced by the nominative–accusative (Nicula 2009): *băiatului* (GEN≡DAT) *acela* (NOM≡ACC) (non-standard) instead of *băiatului* (GEN≡DAT) *aceluia* (GEN≡DAT) (standard).

5.3.1.2.3 Demonstrative determiners display several distributional and syntactic characteristics.

Prenominal demonstrative take a determinerless (articleless) head-noun complement (115a), while postnominal demonstratives obligatorily occur in DPs with article-bearing noun heads (115b). The postnominal demonstrative construction is thus a polydefinite structure, since definiteness is realized twice (§5.3.1.5), by the article and by the demonstrative.

(115) a. acest   om
         this   man
     b. omul   acesta
         man.DEF   this

Prenominal demonstratives always occupy the DP-initial position. The DP-internal word order is relatively free in DPs headed by prenominal demonstratives, the insertion of any kind of prenominal constituent of the DP between the demonstrative and the head noun being possible:

(116) a. **aceste** două   (interesante) **cărți** (interesante)
         these   two   interesting   books   interesting
     b. **acest** al doilea **concert** al Madonnei
         this   the second   concert   AL Madonna.GEN

By contrast, the distribution of postnominal demonstratives is *severely constrained*. Postnominal demonstratives are *strictly adjacent* to the definite noun head, and the insertion of any constituent between the noun and the demonstrative is strictly barred.

(117) a. copiii   aceştia   frumoşi   vs.   *copiii   frumoşi   aceştia
         children.DEF these beautiful   children.DEF beautiful these
     b. acordarea aceasta   de   burse   vs.   *acordarea   de
        granting.DEF this   of   scholarships   granting.DEF of
        burse   aceasta
        scholarships this

Postnominal demonstratives may only be preceded by nouns bearing the definite article (117). Adjectives suffixed by the definite article cannot precede demonstratives (118):

(118) *frumoasa   aceasta   carte
      beautiful.DEF this   book

H *The adjacency constraint* was not so well-established in old Romanian (Cornilescu and Nicolae 2011a: 214). Complex definite nominal phrases (of the type modifier + noun (119a) or noun + possessor (119b)) could precede the postnominal demonstrative:

(119) a. pă [[ticălosul   pământŭ] **acesta**] să   vie   (Greceanu)
         on wretched.DEF   earth   this   să$_{SUBJ}$ come.SUBJ
     b. Şi   până   la   [[domniia   lui] **aceasta**]   (Costin)
        and until   reign.DEF his this

A definite adjective could also precede the demonstrative, leaving the articleless noun to the right of the demonstrative (Cornilescu and Nicolae 2011a: 215):

(120) întru nenorocitele   **acestea** vremi   (Greceanu)
      in   unfortunate.DEF   these   times

A very important distributional characteristic of postnominal demonstratives is that they license postnominal cardinals (121b), constituents which are otherwise excluded from the postnominal position (121a):

(121) a. *fetele   două
         girls.DEF two
     b. fetele   **acestea** două
        girls.DEF these   two

In sum, Romanian has two complementary paradigms: an adjective paradigm (postnominal demonstratives) and a determiner paradigm (the prenominal demonstrative).

C In this respect, from a Romance comparative perspective, Romanian is, with Catalan, Occitan, and Spanish (Reinheimer Rîpeanu 2001: 201; Ledgeway 2011: 416), a language which preserves two complementary paradigms, one related to the adjective (the postnominal one) and the other to the determiner (the prenominal one). What is specific to Romanian is the strict *adjacency constraint* of the postnominal demonstrative to the definite noun. In Spanish, for instance, adjectives may intervene between the (article plus) noun and the postnominal demonstrative (Brugè 2002: 20). The word order differences have been explained through the different DP-internal movement possibilities of each language: head movement (of the definite noun) in Romanian vs. phrase movement (of the N + A sequence) in Spanish (Cornilescu 2005b).

In predicative position the long form is employed:

(122) Reţeta   este   **aceasta** / *această
      prescription.DEF is   this   this

Finally, both prenominal and postnominal (especially proximal) demonstratives may adjoin to proper names, yielding different interpretations: the postnominal demonstrative (123a) induces a modal (pejorative) evaluation of the proper name, while the prenominal (123b) is ambiguous between a modal evaluative and a mere anaphoric reading.

(123) a. Ionescu **ăsta**   [modal evaluation: pejorative value]
         Ionescu this

   b. **acest** Ionescu   [ambiguous: pejorative or endophoric value]
      this   Ionescu

5.3.1.2.4 The distributional characteristics discussed above show that the two instances of demonstrative determiners have different phrasal statuses (Cornilescu 1992, 2005b; Dumitrescu and Saltarelli 1998): the prenominal demonstrative is a *head*, while the postnominal one is a *phrase*. Besides the adjacency constraint, additional evidence for this comes from nominal ellipsis: only the postnominal form (124a) may occur in elided noun head constructions (124b), this being a hint of its *phrasal* status. Heads cannot be remnants in nominal ellipsis (125b).

(124) a. omul   **acesta**
         man.DEF this

   b. acesta
      this

(125) a. **acest** om
         this   man

   b. *acest
       this

From a functional perspective, the two types of demonstrative determiners are associated with different roles in the information packaging of the DP (Tasmowski 1990; Manoliu 2000; Cornilescu 2005b; Vasilescu 2009b). The prenominal demonstrative is a mere endophoric determiner, a text-cohesion device. By contrast, the postnominal demonstrative is an emphatic element endowed with a specificity feature, and thus behaves like a focus. Consequently, prenominal demonstratives cannot generally be contrastively stressed (126a), while postnominal demonstratives can easily bear nuclear stress (126b):

(126) a. ?ACEASTĂ carte, nu   aceea
         this   book   not that

   b. cartea   ACEASTA, nu   aceea
      book.DEF this   not that

In the subtle interplay of speaker specificity / addressee specificity, the postnominal distal demonstrative presents the referent as being non-specific for the hearer, but specific for the addressee (Manoliu 2000: 592):

(127) spune și   nouă, tată,   cine este **vipera**   **aceea**
      tell also   us   father who   is   viper.DEF   that
      care nu-ți   dă   pace   (Ispirescu)
      who   not=you.DAT give peace
      'Tell us, father, who is that viper who does not leave you alone'

In conclusion, prenominal demonstratives are anaphoric definite determiners, while postnominal demonstratives typically trigger [+specific] readings of the DPs containing them.

5.3.1.3 Alternative and identity determiners

Alternative and identity determiners have an internal non-thematic variable and typically license an argument / complement of identity or difference (Giurgea 2010: 297) introduced by *decât* or *ca / ca și*, a possibility excluded for demonstratives or indefinite determiners:

(128) a. **altul**   decât   mine
         other.DEF   than   me
         'other than me'

   b. **același**   ca   (și)   tine
         same   as   you(ACC)
         'the same as you'

The alternative and identity determiners have joint semantic and syntactic features. They have been traditionally included either in the class of demonstratives, or in that of indefinites. However, they are neither demonstratives (their main function is not to encode proximity / distality dimensions), nor indefinites (they are definite or indefinite).

5.3.1.3.1 The alternative determiners *alt(ul)* ('other / another (one)') and *celălalt* ('the other (one)') have a series of semantic, syntactic, historical features in common.

(a) Semantically, they are both alternative determiners: *alt(ul)* is indefinite, while *celălalt* is (both functionally and etymologically) definite.
(b) Syntactically, they both have pronominal usages (i.e. they appear in nominal ellipsis structures). However, *alt(ul)* has a wider distribution than *celălalt*, a distribution which shows that *alt(ul)* has a double categorization, lexical and functional. Moreover, in nominal ellipsis, *alt(ul)* assumes a special form (incorporating the bound-morpheme definite article). As for their position in nominal phrases with overt heads, *alt* is obligatorily prenominal, while *celălalt* behaves more like a demonstrative: it may precede or follow the nominal head, and, when postnominal, *celălalt* observes the adjacency constraint.
(c) *Alt(ul)* and *celălalt* denote two different types of alterity: 'open alterity' vs. 'closed alterity'.

C Romanian patterns with other languages in grammatically marking the distinction between 'closed alterity' (Lat. ALTER, Fr. *l'autre*, Rom. *celălalt* 'the second of two') and 'open alterity' (Lat. ALIUS, Fr. *un autre*, Rom. *alt(ul)* 'other, another, someone else, something else').

H The distinction between 'closed alterity' and 'open alterity' was expressed in old Romanian by another element, *alalt(ul)* ('the other (one)'), which had the function of modern Romanian *celălalt* ('the other (one)') (Densusianu 1961, II: 123; Rosetti 1986: 499). *Alalt(ul)*, etymologically composed of ILLE (> Rom. *ăl*) + ALTER (> Rom. *alt*), had a full nominal paradigm, with adjectival and nominal ellipsis forms and usage in old Romanian (DA, *s.v. alalt*; Densusianu 1961, II: 123). *Alalt* morphologically behaves similarly to modern Romanian *alt(ul)*: in nominal ellipsis, it incorporates the definite article; in the genitive / dative, singular and plural, the nominal ellipsis forms are distinguished from the forms which appear in overt head structures by the vowel *a*. *Alalalt* ceased to be used at the end of the 18th century (DA, s.v. *alalt*). It is still recognizable in compounds like *alaltăieri* ('the day before yesterday'), *alaltăseară* ('the evening before yesterday evening'), *ăstălalt* ('this other (one)'), *ălălalt* ('the other (one)')—DA, s.v. *alalt*.

Celălalt developed in old Romanian out of the combination of the phonologically reduced, weak demonstrative / determiner *cel* with the element *alalt*. The rise of *celălalt* is simultaneous with the grammaticalization of the determiner CEL from the distal demonstrative *acela* (§5.3.1.4.1). The incorporation of CEL into *alalt* led to the impossibility of postnominally incorporating the definite article in the newly formed element (**celălalt**ul***).

5.3.1.3.2 The distinct properties of *alt* / *altul* (other / other.DEF) are as follows:

(i) *Alt* always occurs prenominally and functions as a determiner, giving an indefinite reading to the nominal phrase:

(129) a. **alt** om
       other man
       'another man' / 'a different man'

Alt contrasts with (some of) its Romance (and Germanic) counterparts, which cannot function as determiners (van Peteghem 1994a, 1994b):

(130) a. Fr. ***autre** home (est venu)
      b. Engl. ***other** man (came)

Under ellipsis, *alt* assumes a special form, incorporating the definite article:

(131) a. **alt** om
       other man

  b. **altul**
     other.DEF

In the earliest written records, *alt* could license nominal ellipsis with (132a) or without (132b) the incorporated definite article (Frâncu 1984; Nicolae 2008):

(132) a. **altul**   ca   Alexandru nu   veți   dobândi   (*Alexandria*)
       other.DEF like Alexandru not AUX.FUT.2PL get.INF
       'you will not get another one like Alexandru'
      b. pre **alți**   i-au   vătămat   (*Documente*)
         PE others CL.DAT.3PL=have hurt
         'He hurt others'

The dialectal area of Bran (Brașov) preserves the situation of the earliest Romanian written records: in binary structures of the type *un(ul)—alt(ul)*, although used in nominal ellipsis constructions, *alt* does not incorporate the definite article, and is closer to its etymological meaning (closed alterity, like ALTER) than to its modern one (Vulpe 1987):

(133) a. lupii   mergea   în flanc unu   după **alt**   (standard Romanian: *altul*)
       wolfs.DEF walk.IMPERF in file one.DEF after other
       'The wolves were walking in a file one after the other'
      b. vorbeam   de ună   și   de **altă**   (standard Romanian: *alta*)
         talk.IMPERF.1SG≡PL of one.F and of other.F
         'I was / We were talking banalities'

(ii) *Alt* displays rich allomorphy, resembling the paradigms of nouns and adjectives (Table 5.17).

TABLE 5.17 The paradigm of *alt(ul)* 'an other (one)'

			SG	PL
M	NOM≡ACC	overt-head structures	alt	alți
		nominal ellipsis structures	altul	alții
	GEN≡DAT	overt-head structures	altui	altor
		nominal ellipsis structures	altuia	altora
F	NOM≡ACC	overt-head structures	altă	alte
		nominal ellipsis structures	alta	altele
	GEN≡DAT	overt-head structures	altei	altor
		nominal ellipsis structures	alteia	altora

(iii) The distribution of *alt* shows that it has a multiple categorization (for a detailed discussion, see Cornilescu and Nicolae 2011d): it is either a prenominal lexical adjective which belongs to the lexical domain of the nominal phrase, roughly having the meaning 'different' (134), or it is a functional adjective, merging in the quantificational domain of the nominal phrase, with the meaning 'other' ((135)–(136)).

(134) deschide   cartea   în **alt**   loc
       opens   book.DEF   in other   place
       '(S)he is opening the book in a different place (= at another page)'

First, *alt* may precede or follow cardinals (irrespective of their internal structure: simple cardinals, as in (135a) and (136a), or complex cardinals with quantified NP structure, as in (135b), (136b):

(135) a. **alți**   doi   copii
         other   two   children
         'other two children'

      b. **alți**   douăzeci   de   copii
         other   twenty   DE   children
         'other twenty children'

(136) a. doi   **alți**   copii
         two   other   children
         'two other children'

      b. douăzeci   de   **alți**   copii
         twenty   DE   other   children
         'twenty other children'

Nominal ellipsis shows that when *alt* precedes the cardinal (135) it is subject to dual interpretation. On the one hand, *alt* is interpreted as the specifier of the cardinal and yields elided structures where the cardinal is the licenser of ellipsis; this is shown by the fact that *alt* does not incorporate the definite article in (137a). On the other hand, *alt* is the head of the construction and is itself specified by the cardinal; the incorporated definite article is an instruction that *alt* is the licenser of ellipsis (137b):

(137) a. **alți**   doi
         other   two

     b. **alții** doi
        other.DEF two

By contrast, when *alt* follows the cardinal, nominal ellipsis is possible only with *alt* bearing the definite article, and, thus, with the cardinal specifying it. More precisely, the construction [simple cardinal + *alt*] has a complex quantifier structure, with *alt(ul)* being the head, and the cardinal being the specifier:

(138) a. doi **alții**
        two other.DEF

      b. *doi **alți**
        two other

Moreover, the licensing of nominal ellipsis by *alt* indicates its functional category behaviour, given that prenominal lexical adjectives do not license nominal ellipsis, but give rise to substantivization.

Nominal ellipsis with morphologically complex cardinals with quantified NP structure (examples (135b), (136b)) provides a slightly different outcome. When *alt* precedes the complex cardinal, nominal ellipsis is possible as above (in (137)), with both the cardinal (139a) and *alt* (139b) as licensors:

(139) a. **alți** douăzeci
        other twenty

      b. **alții** douăzeci
        other.DEF twenty

When *alt* follows the complex cardinal, any form of ellipsis is impossible (140). This indicates that *alt* belongs to the lexical domain of the nominal phrase, behaving like a prenominal lexical adjective:

(140) a. *douăzeci de **alții**
        twenty DE other.DEF

      b. *douăzeci de **alți**
        twenty DE other

Besides the impossibility of licensing nominal ellipsis, the occurrence after the preposition *de* in structures with complex cardinals (136b) goes to show that in the respective structure *alt* belongs to the lexical domain of the nominal phrase.

Alt may precede or follow quantificational adjectives like *mulți* 'many', *puțini* 'few', and *câțiva* 'a few':

(141) **alte** multe lucruri / multe **alte** lucruri
      other many things many other things
      'many other things'

(142) **alte** câteva lucruri / câteva **alte** lucruri
      other a-few things a-few other things
      'a few other things'

Alt rigidly follows quantifiers like *fiecare* 'each, every', *oricare* 'any', *vreun* 'any', *atâţi* 'so many / much', *niciun* 'no':

(143) a. fiecare / oricare / vreun **alt** student
      each   any   any   other student

   b. atâtea   **alte** studente
      so-many other   students

   c. niciun **alt** student
      no   other   student

All these structures have nominal ellipsis counterparts with *alt* as licenser of ellipsis, as the suffixation of the definite article on *alt* indicates:

(144) a. **altele**   multe /   multe   **altele**
         other.DEF.F.PL   many.F   many.F other.DEF.F.PL

   b. **altele**   câteva /   câteva **altele**
      other.DEF.F.PL   few.F   few.F other.DEF.F.PL

(145) a. fiecare / oricare / vreun **altul**
         each   any   any   other.DEF

   b. atâtea   **altele**
      so-many.F   other.DEF.F.PL

Alt may also be specified by the indefinite article with a cardinal interpretation (Nicolae 2008):

(146) un **alt** student
      an other   student

Nominal ellipsis shows that the unit *un* is the indefinite article (147a) and not the indefinite quantifier *un / unul* (147b):

(147) a. un **altul**
         an other.DEF

   b. *unul   **alt** / *unul   **altul**
      an.DEF   other   an.DEF   other.DEF

H The combination of *alt* with the indefinite article has been traditionally interpreted as a French or modern Romance influence on Romanian (Sandfeld and Olsen 1936: 184; Graur 1976: 82, 1988: 328; Iordan 1956: 396–8). Although the differences in meaning between *alt(ul)* and *un alt(ul)* are very subtle, historical surveys (Frâncu 1984; Nicolae 2008) have shown that the structures *un alt* + noun and *un altul* are the outcome of language-internal evolution. The following phases of development have been identified:

(i) (16th–mid-17th century) the articleless (*alt*) (148a) and article-bearing (*altul*) (148b) forms are used pronominally; the articleless form (*alt*) is used adjectivally, as in modern Romanian:

(148) a. văzu   **alţ**   stând   (*Evangheliarul slavo-român de la Sibiu*)
         see.PS.3SG others   staying
         '(S)he saw other ones staying'

	b.	să	puie	**altul**		(*Documente*)
		SĂ_SUBJ	put.SUBJ.3SG	other.DEF		
		'Another one would put it'				

 (ii) (17th century) article-bearing forms (*altul*) systematically replace articleless forms (*alt*) (149a) in nominal ellipsis structures (Frâncu 1984);
 (iii) (the end of the 17th century) the indefinite article specifies overt-head structures with *alt* (149b):

(149)	a.	va	să	hiclenească	pre	**altul**	(*Îndreptarea legii*)
		AUX.FUT.3SG	SĂ_SUBJ	trick.SUBJ	PE	other.DEF	
		'(S)he will trick another one'					
	b.	ca	**o**	**altă**	fire		(*Cantemir*)
		like	a	other	nature		
		'like another nature'					

 (iv) (the end of the 18th century) the indefinite article specifies nominal ellipsis structures with *alt* (i.e. *un altul*):

(150)	Să	nu	rămâie /	Decât	**un**	**altul**	mai	
	SĂ_SUBJ	not	remain.SUBJ.3SG	than	an	other.DEF	more	
	prost							(*Cronica despre domnia lui Mavrogheni*)
	silly							
	'He won't remain sillier than another one'

After the end of the 18th century, the innovation has increasingly spread, and it is part of current usage.

The predicative postcopular position accommodates structures with *alt*, both accompanied and unaccompanied by the indefinite article. The double categorization of *alt* is also apparent here: without the indefinite article (151) the meaning of *alt* is 'different' (Sandfeld and Olsen 1936: 186), while with the indefinite article, the structure receives a quantificational reading (152a), even licensing partitive constructions (152b). The partitive construction is not possible with the example in (151).

(151)	Trebuie	să	iubești	mereu	o	femeie,	dar	femeia	
	must	SĂ_SUBJ	love.SUBJ.2SG	always	a	woman	but	woman.DEF	
	să	fie	mereu	**alta**!					(*Rebreanu*)
	SĂ_SUBJ	be.SUBJ	always	other.DEF					
	'You should always love a woman and the woman should always be different'

(152)	a.	Sodiul	este	un	component	al	sării	
		sodium.DEF	is	a	component	AL	salt.DEF.GEN	
		(cloridul	*este*	**un**	***altul***)			
		chloride.DEF	is	an	other.DEF			
		'Sodium is a component of salt (chloride is another one)'
	b.	**un**	**altul**	dintre	dânșii	i-a	zis	
		an	other.DEF	of	them	CL.DAT.3SG=has	said	
		acestuia	ce	se	mira			(*Sadoveanu*)
		this.DAT	who	CL.REFL.ACC	surprise.IMPERF.3SG			
		'Another one of them talked to this man who was surprised'

Alt may be preceded by demonstratives, which render a definite reading of the nominal phrase:

(153) aceşti **alţi** trei / mulţi copii
 these other three many children
 'these other three / many children'

In combination with the indefinite determiner *unul*, *alt(ul)* gives rise to reciprocal pronominal expressions (§6.5):

(154) Şi-au spus **unul** **altuia** ce
 CL.REFL.DAT.3PL=have said each other.DAT what
 aveau de spus
 have.IMPERF.3PL DE$_{SUP}$ say.SUP
 'They said to each other what they had to say'

Finally, similarly to the feminine indefinite *una* and to the feminine proximal demonstrative *asta*, the pronominal feminine singular and plural forms *alta* and *altele* may have a neuter interpretation:

(155) Una zic şi **alta /** **altele** fac
 one.DEF.F (they)say and other.DEF.F.SG other.DEF.F.PL (they)do
 'They say a thing and do another'

5.3.1.3.3 The properties of *celălalt* ('the other (one)') are as follows:

(i) Like *alt(ul)*, the alternative determiner *celălalt* appears both in overt-head structures (156) and in nominal ellipsis structures (157). Given its [+definite] specification, the distribution of *celălalt* is more similar to that of demonstratives than to that of *alt(ul)*.

In opposition to *alt(ul)*, it does not change its form under ellipsis ((156) vs. (157)); in overt-head structures, it precedes or follows the head noun (156b); when postnominal, *celălalt* observes the adjacency constraint, typical of demonstratives ((156b) vs. (156c)).

(156) a. **celălalt** copil
 the-other child
 b. copi**lul** **celălalt** (frumos)
 child.DEF the-other beautiful
 c. *copi**lul** frumos **celălalt**
 child.DEF beautiful the-other

(157) **celălalt**
 the-other

In overt head structures, *celălalt* always appears in definite noun phrases: when prenominal (156a), *celălalt* itself yields a definite reading of the noun phrase; when postnominal (156b), *celălalt* appears in polydefinite structures (§5.3.1.5), where definiteness is expressed twice (by the definite article, and by *celălalt*).

Prenominally, *celălalt* has a distribution more constrained than *altul*: it precedes cardinal numerals (158) and other quantificational adjectives (159), and does not combine with quantifiers like *fiecare* 'each, every', *oricare* 'any', *vreun* 'any', *atâți* 'so many / much', *niciun* 'no' (160):

(158) **ceilalți**   doi (copii)   (/ *doi **ceilalți**   (copii))
      the-other.PL two children   two the-other.PL children

(159) **ceilalți**   mulți / puțini / câțiva (copii) (/ *mulți / puțini / câțiva
      the other   many   few   few children   many   few   few
      ceilalți   (copii))
      the other   children

(160) (***celălalt**) fiecare / oricare / vreun / niciun (***celălalt**) (student)
      the-other   every   any   any   no   the-other   student

Like *alt(ul)*, *celălalt* gives rise to reciprocal expressions in combination with the indefinite determiner *unul* (§6.5):

(161) Și-au   spus **unul** **celuilalt**   ce   aveau
      CL.REFL.DAT.3PL=has   said each   the-other.DAT   what have.IMPERF.3PL
      de   spus
      DE_SUP   say.SUP
      'They said each other what they had to say'

H In old Romanian, the alternative determiner *alalt* (the counterpart of modern Romanian *celălalt*) also gave rise to reciprocal pronouns in combination with *unul* (DA, s.v. *alalt*):

(162) Urul   **alăltui**   supuindu-se   (*Codicele Voronețean*)
      one.DEF   the-other.DAT   bowing.GER=CL.REFL.ACC

In opposition to *alt(ul)*, *celălalt* does not take a complement of difference because of its internal make-up (**celălalt decât ei* the-other-one than them): the demonstrative / adjectival article initial component (*cel-*) historically incorporated in the structure of *celălalt* (§5.3.1.3.1) binds the internal variable encoded by the alternative component of the item (*-ălalt*).

(ii) *Celălalt* has a rich paradigm (Table 5.18).

U In parallel with the form *celălalt*, there emerged in non-literary Romanian a compound definite alternative determiner whose first component is the distal demonstrative *ăla*: *ălălalt* 'the other (one)'.

Spoken Romanian has extended the *proximity* distinction into the domain of definite alterity. Thus, with the use of the proximal demonstratives *acest(a)* and *ăsta* there emerged two proximal definite determiners of non-identity: *cestălalt* and *ăstălalt* 'this other one'. In present-day language, *ăstălalt* is more frequently used. *Cestălalt* was much more frequent in earlier stages of Romanian (DA, s.v. *cestălalt*).

TABLE 5.18 The paradigm of *celălalt* 'the other (one)'

	M		F	
	SG	PL	SG	PL
NOM≡ACC	celălalt	ceilalți	cealaltă	celelalte
GEN≡DAT	celuilalt	celorlalți	celeilalte	celorlalte

5.3.1.3.4 The properties of the identity determiner *același* 'the same (one)' are reviewed below:

(i) The identity determiner *același* is made up of the distal demonstrative *acela* 'that' and the invariable formative *-și*. Consequently, it displays internal variation, only the first part of the compound (*acela*) varying in gender, number, and case.

Același functions only as prenominal determiner (163a) and in nominal ellipsis structures (163b); it is excluded from the postnominal determiner position.

(163) a. **același** copil
the-same child
'the-same child'

b. **același**
the-same
'the-same one'

Prenominal *același* has a similar distribution to *celălalt*: it rigidly precedes cardinal numerals (164) and other quantificational adjectives (165), and does not combine with quantifiers like *fiecare* 'each, every', *oricare* 'any', *vreun* 'any', *atâți* 'so many / much', *niciun* 'no' (166):

(164) **aceiași** douăzeci (de copii) (/ *douăzeci de **aceiași** (copii))
the-same.M.PL twenty DE children twenty DE the-same.M.PL children

(165) **aceiași** mulți / puțini / câțiva copii (/ *mulți / puțini / câțiva
the-same.M.PL many few a-few children many a-few few
aceiași (copii))
the-same.M.PL children

(166) a. (***același***) fiecare / oricare / vreun / niciun (***același***) (student)
the-same.M.SG every any any no the-same.M.SG student

b. (***aceleași***) atâtea (***aceleași***) studente
the-same.F.PL so many.F the-same.F.PL students(F)

(ii) *Același* has a rich paradigm, as shown in Table 5.19.

C The Romanian demonstrative-based identity determiner *același* corresponds in other Romance languages to prenominal sequences of the type [definite determiner + intensifier] (Reinheimer Rîpeanu 2001: 201); compare Rom. *aceleași greșeli* with It. **gli stessi sbagli**, Fr. **les mêmes fautes**, Sp. **las mismas faltas**, Ptg. **as mesmas faltas**. These intensifiers placed in post-head position are the equivalents of Rom. *însumi, însuți*... ('myself', 'yourself'); thus, compare Rom. *eu însumi* (see §5.3.5.1.1 (ii)) with It. **io stesso**, Fr. **moi-même**, Sp. **yo mismo**, Ptg. **eu mesmo**.

TABLE 5.19 The paradigm of *același* '(the) same (one)'

	M		F	
	SG	PL	SG	PL
NOM≡ACC	același	aceiași	aceeași	aceleași
GEN≡DAT	aceluiași	acelorași	aceleiași	acelorași

H The inventory of identity determiners was richer in the older stages of Romanian. In old Romanian there is an identity determiner made up of the proximal demonstrative *acesta* 'this' and the invariable formative *-și* (e.g. **acestași**—this.MASC.SG+*și*). These analogical forms were regularly used until the mid-19th century; their usage gradually decreased in the second half of the 19th century and in the first decades of the 20th century, finally disappearing (Croitor 2012b; Vasilescu 2012).

(iii) In the current stage of Romanian, *același* is specified as [+definite], yielding a definite reading of the nominal phrase in which it occurs.

H In the 19th century and at the beginning of the 20th century, there are situations when the [+definite] specification may be overridden by the presence of the indefinite article in the nominal phrase:
(167) un **același** drept (Bălcescu)
 a the-same law
 'a law of the same kind'
Indefinite structures with *același* may be found (rarely) in non-literary present-day Romanian.

5.3.1.4 *The determiner* CEL

5.3.1.4.1 One of the special features of the Romanian nominal phrase is the existence of the determiner CEL, which functions both as a freestanding definite article and as an adjectival article.

CEL occurs both in overt head constructions, where it functions as a definite determiner (168), and in elided head constructions, functioning as a pronoun, as in (169):

(168) a. **cei** doi copii b. băiatul **cel** mare
 CEL two children   boy.DEF CEL big
 'the two children'   'the big boy'

(169) a. **cei** doi   b. **cel** mare
 CEL two   CEL big
 'the two of them'   'the big one'

Examples (168a) and (168b) show different instances of CEL. In (168a) CEL is a 'last resort' freestanding definite article, whose insertion is triggered by the intervention of a (morphologically) defective quantifier between the D-position (the initial position of the nominal phrase) and the head noun; CEL is inserted in order to render a definite interpretation to the nominal phrase. In (168b) CEL is an adjectival (/ demonstrative) article, whose optional insertion is triggered by the need to render a distinctive interpretation to the postnominal modifier of the head noun. The structure in (168b) illustrates a double definite construction, since definiteness is expressed twice (by the affixal definite article and by the adjectival article) (see §5.3.1.5), whereas the structure in (168a) is a simple definite construction, in which definiteness is expressed once, by the freestanding definite article CEL. With a few limited exceptions, the two instances of CEL have a different distribution. The freestanding definite article CEL is similar to the freestanding articles of other languages; the adjectival article CEL is however special and typical of Romanian, since it occurs with a special function only in Romanian (§5.3.1.4.3).

H Both instances of CEL developed from the endophoric distal demonstrative *acel* / *acela* (< ECCE / ECCUM + ILLUM, Dimitrescu 1975: 169). According to Iordan and Manoliu (1965: 145), the rise of the determiner CEL—as a different form of the (proximal) demonstrative—took place after the 16th century (see, however, Iliescu 2006 for a different perspective). This historical path of evolution is supported by the survey in Rosetti (1986: 495), where his examples show that the grammaticalizing element displays only aphaeresis (*acela* > *cela*); besides this, the final vowel -*a* is still present and the element still has the distribution of the postnominal demonstrative. From the point of view of grammaticalization theory (e.g. Roberts and Roussou 2003: 132), the change from full demonstrative to article-like determiner implies *semantic bleaching* (i.e. loss of features—in this case, the loss of the [+deictic] feature), *morphophonological reduction* (*acel* / *acela* > CEL), and categorial change (demonstrative > article).

C The rise of the adjectival article CEL is an innovation of Romanian among the Romance languages, supported by contact with other Balkan languages (Niculescu 1965: 19–20; cf. Iliescu 2006: 163), which possess different types of adjectival articles (e.g. Campos 2009, for Albanian) and double definite structures (e.g. Alexiadou and Wilder 1998: 303–4, for Greek). The adjectival article CEL does not have (Romance) counterparts (Reinheimer Rîpeanu 1993: 130, 2001: 189; Vasilescu 2009a: 273).

The grammaticalization of CEL is an example within Romanian of a recurrent Romance typological tendency (Iliescu 2006: 163, 2009: 21), the creation of a new and parallel linguistic form from almost identical material: Lat. ĪLLE (> ILLUM) > Rom. -*(u)l* (demonstrative > definite article) and Rom. *acel* / *acela* > Rom. CEL (demonstrative > adjectival / freestanding article).

The freestanding definite article CEL and the adjectival article CEL have a series of common morphosyntactic traits. First, both instances of CEL have the same paradigm. It is a complete paradigm, similar to that of demonstrative pronouns (Table 5.20).

H In old Romanian, the genitive–dative feminine singular form with which CEL occurs is the etymological one, *cei* (< ECCE / ECCUM + ILAEI, Rosetti 1986: 499). *Celei* is an analogical form, which was generalized after 1780 (Todi 2001: 55).
(170)   credinței   cei   adevărate   (*Anonimul Brâncovenesc*)
        faith.DEF.F.GEN≡DAT CEL.F.GEN≡DAT   true.F.GEN≡DAT
        '(of / to) the true faith'

U In non-literary present-day Romanian, in nominal phrases containing CEL (and demonstratives), case is usually marked on the first constituent of the nominal phrase. Thus, the remaining elements of the phrase usually display only gender and number agreement (171a):
(171) a. omului   cel   / acela   bun   [non-standard]
         man.SG.DEF.GEN≡DAT   CEL.SG.NOM≡ACC   that.SG.NOM≡ACC   good.SG
      b. omului   **celui** /   aceluia   bun   [standard]
         man.SG.DEF.GEN≡DAT   CEL.SG.GEN≡DAT   that.SG.GEN≡DAT   good.SG
         '(of / to) the good man'

TABLE 5.20 The paradigm of CEL

CASE	M		F	
	SG	PL	SG	PL
NOM≡ACC	cel	cei	cea	cele
GEN≡DAT	celui	celor	celei	celor

5.3 *The structure of the nominal phrase* 311

Second, in both instances, CEL is a dependent word (a 'semi-independent pronoun', in Manoliu-Manea 1968: 79, 83, or a 'semi-lexical category', in Vasilescu 2009a). Most syntactic tests indicate that it belongs to the class of clitics (§5.3.1.4.2).

Third, in both instances, CEL licenses nominal ellipsis and, furthermore, CEL-ellipsis may occur even if CEL is excluded in the overt-head counterpart (§5.3.1.4.4).

5.3.1.4.2 In both instances, CEL is a clitic, in need of a right-adjacent host onto which to cliticize; the host of CEL is its right adjacent phrase, since in cases of nominal ellipsis its right-adjacent phrase is pronounced while the head noun, which is left adjacent (when CEL is an adjectival article) or non-adjacent (when CEL is a freestanding definite article), goes unpronounced. In Zwicky and Pullum's (1983: 510) taxonomy (simple vs. special clitics), CEL is a special clitic as it does not have the same distribution as its corresponding full form (the proximal demonstrative *acel / acela* 'that', Pană Dindelegan 2003: 30). The freestanding article CEL patterns with the short form of this demonstrative (***cei / acei** doi copii*) while the adjectival article CEL patterns with the long form (*băiatul **cel / acela** mare*). However, due to semantic bleaching, CEL no longer encodes a distal demonstrative meaning: in the freestanding article variant, CEL has the semantics of a regular, grammaticalized definite article, whereas in the adjectival article construction, it is associated with specific readings attributed to the modifier it precedes (§5.3.1.4.3 (1)).

Both instances of CEL observe, to various degrees, the clitic-hood properties discussed in the relevant literature (Zwicky and Pullum 1983; Bickel and Nichols 2007): (a) *degree of selection*: CEL exhibits a low degree of selection, since it can attach to a variety of hosts belonging to a variety of grammatical categories (see the distribution of CEL in §5.3.1.4.3); (b) CEL *attaches to phrases* (§5.3.1.4.3); (c) *arbitrary gaps*: it is never the case that an expected [CEL+host] combination fails to occur; (d) *morphophonological idiosyncrasies:* the hosts of CEL are never affected by the combination with it; (e) *lack of combinatorial restrictions*: CEL can attach to material containing other clitics, as in (172).

(172) omul **cel** din dreapta-mi
     man.DEF CEL from right.DEF=CL.1SG
     'the man on my right side'

5.3.1.4.3 The determiner CEL has a complex distribution.

1. In the adjectival article construction, the head noun is always definite (bears the affixal definite article) and occupies the first position of the nominal phrase. The adjectival article CEL introduces modifiers belonging to the following categories: APs headed by qualifying adjectives (173a), PPs (173b), the agreeing past participle (173c), and present participles (gerunds) (173d).

(173)   a. vinul **cel** vechi
        wine.DEF CEL old
        'the old wine'

    b. palatul **cel** de cleștar
        palace.DEF CEL of crystal
        'the crystal palace'

    c. copila **cea** pierdută
        girl.DEF CEL lost
        'the lost girl'

d. coşurile   cele fumegânde   [obsolete construction]
   chimneys.DEF   CEL   steaming.GER.F.SG
   'the steaming chimneys'

Different constituents, such as possessive adjectives or genitival personal pronouns (174a) and PPs (174b), may intervene between the definite head noun and the modifier introduced by CEL. Therefore, unlike demonstratives, CEL does not observe *the adjacency constraint* (§5.3.1.2.3).

(174) a. vinul   meu / lui   cel   vechi
         wine.DEF   my   his CEL   old
         'my / his old wine'
      b. palatul   de cleştar   cel   din   poveşti
         palace.DEF of crystal   CEL   from   fairy-tales
         'the crystal palace from fairy tales'

H The distribution of CEL was freer in old Romanian. CEL also introduced APs headed by relative adjectives in overt head noun constructions, a possibility excluded in modern Romanian:
(175) cu   oastea   lui   cea   turcească   (*Letopiseţul Cantacuzinesc*)
      with   army.DEF   his   CEL   Turkish
      'with his Turkish army'

CEL also introduces attributes of proper names, in fixed, conventionalized phrases:

(176) a. Toader   cel   Nebun
         Toader   CEL   mad
      b. Ştefan   cel   Mare
         Stephen   CEL   great

U The conventionalized proper names with CEL are fixed, inflectionally invariable structures. The genitive–dative case of masculine proper names is marked by means of the freestanding inflectional marker *lui*; in the case of feminine proper names, the first term marks GEN≡DAT by means of an inflectional ending. In both genders, CEL is invariable with respect to case inflection:
(177) a. lui   Toader   cel   Nebun
         GEN≡DAT   Toader(NOM≡ACC)   CEL(NOM≡ACC)   mad
      b. Ecaterinei   cea   Mare
         Ecaterina.GEN≡DAT   CEL(NOM≡ACC)   great

Likewise, CEL is used in non-conventionalized structures to introduce modifiers of proper names:

(178) Ioana   cea   mică
      Ioana   CEL   little
      'little Ioana' / 'young Ioana'

In both proper name structures, CEL has the function of licensing the modifier of the proper name (§7.7.1.1).

C The existence of conventionalized proper names with definite determiners is a Romance feature (Iordan 1957: 546–7; Reinheimer Rîpeanu 1993: 131): It. *Lorenzo il Magnifico*, Fr. *Charles le Chauve*, Sp. *Ferdinando el Católico*, Ptg. *Diego Pires o Jovem*. In the Romance languages definite determiners are also used to introduce / license modifiers of proper names: It. *il divino Dante*, *Venezia la bella*; Fr. *le Grand Molière* (cf. Rom. *Ioana cea mică*).

As can be seen from the examples above, CEL insertion is optional. The function of CEL is to signal that the modifier it introduces represents *the most salient property* characterizing the nominal head in the given context. More exactly, when comparing *băiatul mare* (boy.DEF big) and *băiatul cel mare* (boy.DEF CEL big), in the latter case the adjective expresses the identifying property of the boy rather than one property among other possible ones (see Cornilescu and Nicolae 2011c: 60–2 for more details; see also Tasmowki-De Ryck 1994: 18–19; Coene 1999: 180; Vasilescu 2008a: 246–7; GBLR: 140). *Saliency* may be understood here either as *contextual saliency* (the property introduced by CEL serves for contextual identification) or as *strength* (the property introduced by CEL is very characteristic / the most characteristic of the subject so that it serves to identify it). Thus, the relevant properties associated with CEL insertion may be: emphasis and contrast (179a); contextual saliency, the CEL modifier spelling out the identifying property of the referent, without emphasis or contrast (179b); or the signalling of stereotypical properties (179c).

(179) a. Vreau   [bluza   **cea** roşie], nu   pe   cea   galbenă
          (I)want   blouse.DEF   CEL red   not   PE   CEL   yellow
          'I want the red blouse, not the yellow one'

       b. 'Lângă el... un procuror şchiop...
          next to him... a prosecutor lame
          [...]
          —Ce   imbecil! spuse el, cu   adresă   la   [procurorul   **cel**   şchiop]'
          What   idiot   said he with direction at   prosecutor.DEF CEL   lame
          'Next to him sat a lame prosecutor'
          [...]
          —What an idiot! he said, referring to the lame prosecutor'
                                           (Fănuş Neagu, in Tasmowski-De Ryck 1994: 18)

       c. cerul   **cel**   albastru
          sky.DEF   CEL   blue
          'the blue sky'

Finally, the proper name structures with CEL discussed above support the saliency-based interpretation suggested here: the attribute introduced by CEL expresses the identifying property of *Toader* (see example (177a)), which distinguishes the referent from other people baptized 'Toader'. It is clear now why the CEL modifier of the proper name in (178) has an attributive, identifying reading.

2. The freestanding definite article CEL is inserted to render a definite interpretation to the nominal phrase when the first, left-most element of the phrase is a morphologically defective quantifier, which does not and cannot bear the suffixal definite article. In this structure, the head noun is articleless. The defective element may be a cardinal, an ordinal, or an indefinite QP:

(180) a. **cei**   doi   copii
          CEL   two   children
          'the two children'

       b. **cel**   de-al doilea   concurent
          CEL   DE-second   competitor
          'the second competitor'

c. **cele** câteva   fete
   CEL   few   girls
   'the few girls'

The interpretation of the freestanding article CEL structures is not problematic: CEL is the definite determiner of the nominal phrase, behaving like the freestanding articles of other languages (English, for instance). As a freestanding article, CEL (181a) has the distribution of the prenominal (distal) demonstrative determiner (181b):

(181) a. **cei** doi   copii   b. **acei** doi   copii
         CEL   two   children   those   two   children

However, the CEL construction has some word order restrictions not present in the demonstrative construction (Cornilescu 2004: 54–6):

(182) a. **cele** două interesante propuneri /   **acele** două interesante propuneri
         CEL two interesting proposals   those two interesting proposals
      b. ***cele** interesante două propuneri/   **acele** interesante două propuneri
         CEL interesting two proposals   those interesting two proposals

Modal adjectives, which may only precede the head noun, are allowed with prenominal demonstratives, but disallowed with CEL:

(183) a. ***cei** bieți   copii   b. **acei** bieți   copii
         CEL   pitiable   children   those   pitiable   children

3. There are two contexts in which the distribution of the adjectival article CEL and that of the freestanding definite article CEL blend.

First, CEL is a grammatical formative of the superlative (§7.4). The superlative is the result of the combination of CEL with the analytic comparative formatives *mai* 'more' and *mai puțin* 'less'. When the superlative AP is prenominal, CEL has the distribution of the freestanding definite article—that is, it appears in DP-initial position, and the head of the nominal phrase is determinerless:

(184) **cele**   mai   deștepte   fete
      CEL.F.PL   more   smart.F.PL   girl.F.PL
      'the smartest girls'

However, when the superlative AP is postnominal, CEL behaves like an adjectival article (the definite head noun is DP-initial and CEL is postnominal):

(185) fetele   **cele**   mai   deștepte
      girl.DEF.F.PL   CEL.F.PL   more   smart.F.PL
      'the smartest girls'

Second, the freestanding definite article CEL (186a) may occur postnominally and have the distribution of the adjectival article CEL (186b), if the nominal phrase contains a postnominal (usually PP or *wh*-clause) modifier. The modifierless structure is quite atypical (186c).

(186) a. **cele** două   fete   din   Michigan
         CEL   two   girls   from   Michigan

b. fetele **cele** două din Michigan
girls.DEF CEL two from Michigan
'the two girls from Michigan'

c. ??fetele **cele** două
girls.DEF CEL two

4. CEL extended its usage, functioning also as an AdvP-internal constituent. CEL is employed as a grammatical formative of the superlative with adverbs. It may occur as a superlative marker of NP-embedded adverbials (187a) and of sentence-embedded adverbs (187b).

(187) a. [$_{DP}$ cercetarea[[$_{AdvP}$ **cel** mai bine] realizată]]
research.DEF.(F) CEL more fine realized(F)
'the finest realized research'

b. [$_{IP}$ a procedat [$_{AdvP}$ **cel** mai bine]]
has acted CEL more properly
'(s)he acted most properly'

In adverbial contexts (187), CEL is an invariable, adverb-like element, which does not display agreement with the rest of the NP-embedded elements. It occurs with the masculine singular default form CEL.

However, on closer scrutiny, CEL seems not to have fully grammaticalized as an adverbial element. When the AdvP-embedding modifier is prenominal, although invariable, CEL is the determiner of the nominal phrase, since the head noun is determinerless, there is no other determiner-like element in the phrase, and the phrase has a [+definite] interpretation:

(188) **cel** mai bine realizată cercetare
CEL more fine realized research
'the finest realized research'

Furthermore, when the DP embedding an adverbial superlative is in the genitive / dative case and CEL is the first constituent of the phrase, CEL takes over the case inflection, behaving like a *bona fide* determiner:

(189) [[$_{AdvP}$ **celor** mai prost] plătiți] salariați
CEL.GEN≡DAT more under paid employees

In sum, (at least) in some adverbial contexts, CEL stands a dual interpretation / analysis: on the one hand, it is an invariable adverb-like element, and, on the other hand, it is a nominal element, functioning as a determiner.

H The rise of CEL as a relative superlative formative of adverbials is a late phenomenon (after the mid-17th century; Ciompec 1985: 164–6). CEL was first used in NP-embedded adverbial (contexts like (187a) above) where, however, it still kept its nominal properties (i.e. it displays agreement with the other [+N] elements of the nominal phrase):

(190) domnii **cei** mai dănainte (Popescu)
rulers.DEF CEL more before
'the rulers of the past'

U The use of CEL in present-day non-literary Romanian resembles, to a certain extent, the situation in old Romanian. In the DP-embedded usage of adverbials, CEL typically displays agreement with the rest of the [+N] elements or the nominal phrase, irrespective of the position of the adverbial with respect to the head noun (a fact which, again, is a good argument for the dual analysis of CEL):

(191) a. [NP [[AdvP **cea**   mai   bine] cotată]   firmă]
            CEL.F.SG   more well   ranked.F.SG company.F.SG
      'the best ranked company'

   b. [DP calea [[AdvP **cea**   mai   bine] știută   de el]]
           way.DEF.F.SG   CEL.F.SG more well   known.F.SG   by him
      'the way he knows best'

5.3.1.4.4 CEL is the licenser of nominal ellipsis, both as a freestanding definite article and as an adjectival article. However, the discussion of nominal ellipsis with CEL is rather complicated since CEL is a licenser of ellipsis even if it does not occur in the overt counterpart of the structure. As is apparent from the comparison of examples (192a) and (192b), insertion of CEL is not allowed when the postnominal modifier is a relative adjective (recall, however, from (168b), that CEL-insertion is fine with qualifying adjectives). In spite of this, (192c) shows that elided noun-head structures with CEL are perfectly legitimate with relative adjectives.

(192) a. *filmul   **cel** franțuzesc
         movie.DEF   CEL   French

   b. filmul   franțuzesc
      movie.DEF   French
      'the French movie'

   c. filmul   franțuzesc   și   **cel** românesc
      movie.DEF   French   and   CEL   Romanian
      'the French movie and the Romanian one'

Furthermore, while qualifying adjectives may use both the determiner CEL (193a) and the suffixal definite article in elided structures and in substantivization, CEL nominal ellipsis seems to be the only possibility for relative adjectives (193b), where ellipsis with suffixal definite article is ruled out.

(193) a. băiatul   înalt   și   **cel**   scund
         boy.DEF   tall   and   CEL   short
      'the tall boy and the short one'

   b. *Franțues**cul**   a   fost   mai   interesant
       French.DEF   has   been   more   interesting
      intended meaning: 'The French one was more interesting'

This distribution might be explained as a consequence of the fact that relative adjectives do not occur prenominally and, hence, cannot bear the affixal definite article. This view finds further support in the distribution of modal adjectives: these adjectives occur only prenominally (194a) vs. (194b); in definite NPs, they bear the affixal definite article (194c); they are excluded in the (overt head) CEL construction (194d), similarly to relative adjectives (192a):

(194) a. biet   copil
         pitiable   child

b. *copil   biet
child   pitiable

c. bietul   copil
pitiable.DEF   child

d. *copilul   **cel**   biet
child.DEF   CEL   pitiable

In the same way as relative adjectives, modal adjectives only use the affixal definite article (195b) in nominal ellipsis structures. As expected, ellipsis with CEL is excluded (195a):

(195) a. ***cel**   biet
        CEL   pitiable

b. bietul
pitiable.DEF

Furthermore, when an adjective has different readings prenominally and postnominally, only the postnominal reading is kept under CEL-nominal ellipsis. For instance, when used prenominally (196a), *adevărat* has an intensional (modal, evaluative) reading being equivalent with the English 'real', while postnominally (196b) it is ambiguous between a qualifying reading ('true') and an intensional one ('real'). In CEL-ellipsis (196c), only the qualifying (postnominal) reading is kept:

(196) a. o **adevărată**   poveste
        a real.F.SG   story.F.SG
        'a real story'

b. o   poveste   **adevărată**
a   story.F.SG   true.F.SG
'a true / real story'

c. povestea   falsă   și   **cea**   **adevărată**
story.DEF.F   phony.F.SG   and   CEL.F.SG   true.F.SG
'the phony story and the true one'

Another context of disparity between the elided construction and the overt one involves genitives (usually, headed by AL). In the overt structure, CEL cannot be inserted between the definite head-noun and the genitival phrase; however, CEL nominal ellipsis with genitival remnants is very natural:

(197) a. *copilul   **cel**   al   Mariei
child.DEF.M   CEL.M.SG   AL   Maria.GEN

b. copilul   Mariei   și   **cel**   al   Ioanei
child.DEF.M   Maria.GEN   and   CEL.M.SG   AL   Ioana.GEN
'Maria's child and Ioana's one'

c. copilul   cuminte   al   Mariei   și   **cel**   neastâmpărat al Ioanei
child.DEF.M   obedient   AL   Maria.GEN   and   CEL.M   naughty   AL   Ioana.GEN
'Maria's obedient child and Ioana's naughty one'

Finally, CEL may be followed by a *wh*-clause in structures with elided heads (198a). The structure with the overt head expressed is rather odd (198b):

(198) a. **cel** care / ce a venit
    CEL who has come
  b. *omul **cel** care / ce a venit
    man.DEF CEL who has come

5.3.1.5 Polydefinite structures

Romanian possesses several types of polydefinite structures (see the extensive survey in Stan 2012c). We may actually distinguish different types of polydefiniteness taking as criteria the type of determiners involved (the same determiner repeated or different definite determiners) and the interpretation elicited.

5.3.1.5.1 First, polydefiniteness takes the form of double definiteness. In genuine double definite structures, definiteness is expressed twice by means of different definite determiners from the extended projection of the noun, which are associated with different functions and tied to different semantic interpretations. This is the case with the adjectival article construction with *cel* (199a) and of the postnominal demonstrative construction (199b):

(199) a. vinul **cel** vechi
    wine.DEF CEL old
    'the old wine'
  b. vinul **acela** (vechi)
    wine.DEF that old
    'that old wine'

In the adjectival article construction, CEL has the function of triggering a specific interpretation of the postnominal modifier (§5.3.1.4.3; Cornilescu 2004: 57–9). In the postnominal demonstrative construction, the demonstrative is focused (§5.3.1.2.4).

5.3.1.5.2 Second, there is determiner spreading, in which the definite article is realized more than once in the nominal phrase. This type of polydefiniteness is at work in spoken, non-literary Romanian. It has a restricted usage, occurring only with a limited class of (modal) prenominal adjectives, when the head noun is followed by a demonstrative:

(200) săracul băiatul ăla
    pitiable.DEF boy.DEF that
    'that poor boy'

C, H This phenomenon is well investigated for Greek (see Alexiadou and Wilder 1998 among others) and for old Romanian (Croitor 2008b). In old Romanian (201), this double definiteness phenomenon is analysed as an agreement phenomenon (Croitor 2008b):
  (201) **puternica mâna** lui Dumnedzeu (Costin)
    strong.DEF hand.DEF lui(GEN) God
    'God's strong hand'

5.3.1.5.3 Third, Romanian possesses a polydefinite postnominal demonstrative structure (Iordan 1956) in which definiteness is expressed three times: by the definite article suffixed on the head noun, by the postnominal demonstrative, and by the definite article suffixed on the adjective. This structure is typical of the non-literary, usually spoken language.

(202) a. muncitorul **ăla** vrednicul
       worker.DEF that hardworking.DEF
       'that hardworking worker'
    b. săracul băiatul ăla
       poor.DEF boy.DEF that
       'that poor boy'

Furthermore, Romanian, interestingly, has two types of double definite proper names (assuming that proper names are inherently definite), using both the enclitic definite article and the determiner CEL: for example *Mihai Viteazul* (Michael brave.DEF) and *Ecaterina cea Mare* (Ekaterina CEL great); for the CEL proper name, see §5.3.1.4.3).

5.3.2 Quantifiers

The quantifiers of the nominal phrase are numerals and indefinite or negative pronominal adjectives. The Romanian nominal phrase also includes other types of structures with a quantitative meaning.

5.3.2.1 Numerals

There are two types of numeral in Romanian: cardinals and ordinals. Besides these, various other numerical expressions are used (distributive, collective, multiplicative, fractional, or adverbial).

5.3.2.1.1 Cardinal numerals vary in their internal structure and their inflectional and syntactic features.

The simple numerals (those which cannot be further decomposed into lexical morphemes) are: *unu* '1', *doi* '2', *trei* '3', *patru* '4', *cinci* '5', *şase* '6', *şapte* '7', *opt* '8', *nouă* '9', *zece* '10'; *sută* 'hundred', *mie* 'thousand', *milion* 'million', *miliard* 'billion', and *zero* 'zero'. These terms may enter into numerical compounds (*o sută* 'a / one hundred', *şapte mii* 'seven thousand'), and likewise have a simple structure.

H Romanian inherited the numerals 1–10 and the singular *mie* (< MILIA) from Danubian Latin; the form VIGINTI was preserved only in Aromanian (Arom. *yínģiţĭ, yiyinţĭ* '20'; Caragiu Marioţeanu 1975: 243). On this basis, from an early stage Romanian developed a complex cardinal numeral system (see below), made up of elements of Latin origin (ILR II: 64–5), with the exception of the numeral *sută*, a loan from old Slavic (DLR). *Milion, miliard, zero* are modern Romance loanwords.
C Romanian did not inherit Lat. CENTUM, preserved by the other Romance languages.

The numeral *unu* has distinct forms, depending on the NP it quantifies: an overt head phrase (203a) or a null head phrase, where it is used 'pronominally' (203b); the forms *un / o* are identical to the singular form of the indefinite article, and the forms *unul / una* are identical to the singular forms of the indefinite pronouns (§5.3.2.2.1), etymologically incorporating the definite article *-(u)l, -a*:

(203) a. Un băiat a venit, nu doi băieţi
       one boy has come not two boys
       'One boy came, not two boys'

b. Unul   a   venit,   nu   doi
   one.DEF   has   come   not   two
   'One came, not two'

Compound numerals are based on three structural patterns (Stan 2010b: 240–3):

(i) numeral phrase structure—the series *unsprezece* '11', *doisprezece* '12', *treisprezece* '13', *paisprezece* '14', *cincisprezece* ['tʃintʃspreˌzetʃe] '15', *şaisprezece* '16', *şaptesprezece* '17', *optsprezece* '18', *nouăsprezece* '19' (204) (the system of counting by addition);

(ii) quantified NP structure—in the expression of decads (*treizeci* '30'), hundreds (*o sută* '100', *două sute* '200'), thousands (*o mie* '1000', *două mii* '2000'), millions (*un milion* '1,000,000', *două milioane* '2,000,000'), billions (*un miliard* '1,000,000,000', *două miliarde* '2,000,000,000') (205) (the system of counting by multiplication);

(iii) coordinated structure—in joining the units to decads (*douăzeci şi doi* '22'), hundreds ('*două sute trei* '203'), thousands (*trei mii cinci* '3005'), millions (*trei milioane patru* '3,000,004'), billions (*şase miliarde opt* '6,000,000,008') (206) (the system of counting by addition).

(204) a. Num + P (*spre* 'upon') + Num *(zece)*

   b. un-spre-zece
      one-upon-ten
      'eleven'

(205) a. Num + NP

   b. două-zec-i
      two-ten-PL
      'twenty'

(206) a. [Num + NP] (+ *şi* 'and') + Num

   b. două-zec-i   şi   unu
      two-ten-PL   and   one
      'twenty-one'

   c. o   sută   unu
      a   hundred   one
      'a hundred and one'

H The compound numerals have been considered to be a loan translation on the model of Slavic or conceivably of the Thracian substratum (shared by Romanian and Albanian), using Latin material. The expression of decads has been also explained by analogy with the formation of hundreds, made up on the model of a pattern existent in old Latin CENTUM-compounds. Furthermore, it has been claimed that the pattern in (iii) is a continuation of a pattern most probably predominant in Danubian Latin or that it is the outcome of the internal evolution of Romanian, with parallel developments in various non-Romance language (Greek, German, Armenian, the Baltic languages). The structure in (i) contains the preposition *spre* (< sŭPER), which has the archaic meaning 'upon'; the pattern was analogically extended in Aromanian to the series 21–29: *únspríyingiţⁱ* '21' (for the etymology of compound numerals, see Sandfeld 1930: 148–9; Bolocan 1969: 133; FC I: 204–8; Brâncuş 1973; Caragiu Marioţeanu 1975: 244; Fischer 1985: 105; Feuillet 1986: 78; Bauer 2011: 551).

5.3 The structure of the nominal phrase

Of the compound numerals, the series 11–19, with the structure in (i), presents a higher degree of grammaticalization: the internal structure is partially opaque from a semantic point of view since the preposition *spre* no longer has the meaning 'upon'; three compounds display phonologic alterations of the initial element (compare the following contemporary standard Romanian forms: ***patru*** '4'—***paisprezece*** '14', ***șase*** '6'—***șaisprezece*** '16', ***cinci*** '5'—***cin[ci]sprezece*** '15'); all the compounds may display alterations of the final segment in the spoken language: ***unșpe*** '11' (standard language: ***unsprezece***). Of the numerals with the structure in (ii), the ones expressing decads display a higher degree of cohesion: the degree of cohesion is reflected in the orthographic norm (by the fact that they are written as a unit); in one instance, there is a phonological alteration of the initial element, namely in the case of (contemporary standard Romanian) *șaizeci* '60' (contrast to *șase* '6'); in the spoken non-literary language, all compounds display phonological alterations in the final segment consisting in the merger of the embedded conjunction *și* with the final segment in the case of the numerals with the structure in (iii): *douăj doi* '22' (standard *douăzeci și doi*). Of the numerals with the structure in (iii), the ones involving addition to decads display a higher degree of cohesion; they exhibit the phonological alteration pointed out above and a change of stress placement (*șai'zeci*, '*șaizeci și doi*).

The numerals *unu, doi* are the only ones that encode gender distinctions: masculine *un (ul)* / feminine *o (una)*, masculine *doi* / feminine *două*. In the compound numerals in whose structure they occupy the initial position, *un* is invariable, while *doi* preserves (in the standard language) the gender distinction: ***unsprezece, doisprezece*** (M)—***douăsprezece*** (F).

C Like Portuguese, Sardinian, Occitan, and Catalan, Romanian preserves the gender distinction for the numeral 'two', which was present in the earliest phase of all the Romance languages, but disappeared at a later stage or persisted only dialectally (ELIR: 54).

The numeral *un(ul)* also encodes case distinctions; its inflection corresponds to that of the singular indefinite article (Table 5.12) and of the singular indefinite corresponding pronoun, respectively (Table 5.24).

The numerals *zece, sută, mie* have number and case inflection, and they fit the declension of feminine nouns: singular nominative–accusative *zece, sută, mie*; singular genitive–dative, plural nominative–accusative–genitive–dative *zeci, sute, mii*; feminine forms are selected for gender agreement: *o* (F) *sută* 'a / one hundred', *două* (F) *sute* 'two hundred'. *Milion, miliard* have number inflection, and they are included in the declension of neuter nouns: singular nominative–accusative–genitive–dative *milion, miliard*; plural nominative–accusative–genitive–dative *milioane, miliarde*; they display gender agreement with the masculine in the singular and with the feminine in the plural, in compliance with the rule of neuter nouns: *un* (M) *milion* 'one million', *două* (F) *milioane* 'two million'. When they are used as nouns, the numerals *sută, mie, milion, miliard* may bear the enclitic definite article in the singular / plural (*suta* 'the hundred' / *sutele* 'the hundreds', *mia* 'the thousand' / *miile* 'the thousands', *milionul* 'the million' / *milioanele* 'the millions', *miliardul* 'the billion' / *miliardele* 'the billions'); *zece* bears the article only in the plural (*zecile* 'the tens'). In the definite declension, the forms of the article encode the nominative–accusative / genitive–dative case distinction in the singular and in the plural, on the model of the definite declension of nouns:

(207) a. milion-u-l   de dolari /   milion-u-lui   de   dolari
         million-SG-DEF.NOM≡ACC of dollars   million-SG-DEF.GEN≡DAT   of   dollars
         'the million dollars' 'of / to the million dollars'

b. zec-i-le   de cărți /   zec-i-lor   de cărți
   ten-PL-DEF.   of books   ten-PL-DEF.   of books
   NOM≡ACC   GEN≡DAT
   'the tens of books' 'of / to the tens of books'

Simple numerals (208a) and compound numerals with numeral phrase structure (208b) have an adjectival status and attach directly, in prenominal position. Gender agreement is inflectionally marked for *un*, *doi*, *doisprezece* (208a–b), and case agreement is available only for *un* (208a) (see above for the inflectional features of cardinals); for invariable numerals (208c), the genitive–dative case is marked by means of prepositions. *Zero* is a quantifier of the NP only in the singular (209).

(208) a. unei   cărț-i
          a.F.GEN≡DAT   book.F-SG.GEN≡DAT
          'of a / to one book'

       b. douăsprezece   cărț-i
          twelve.F   book.F-PL.NOM≡ACC≡GEN≡DAT
          'twelve books'

       c. mamă   a   trei   copii
          mother A   three   children
          'mother of three children'

(209) zero grade
       'zero degrees'

Compound numerals of the type *douăzeci*, which have a quantified NP structure (ii) (205a,b), those of the type *douăzeci și unu*, which include a quantified NP, expressing addition to decads (iii) (206a,b), and those of the type *o sută douăzeci* '120' (iii) or which include in the final position a numeral with a quantified NP structure have a nominal syntactic structure. These numerals are attached by means of the preposition DE, placed prenominally (210); the preposition DE is in this instance a grammaticalized preposition, that is a functional head. This pattern complies with the Romanian syntactic rule of nominal adjunction: the syntactically subordinated material is adjoined by means of DE (Stan 2010b: 243). The nominal complement of DE has an inflectionally unmarked case form, which is traditionally interpreted as an accusative:

(210) douăzeci /   douăzeci și   una /   o sută   douăzeci de   cărți
       twenty /   twenty and   one /   a hundred twenty   DE   books.ACC
       'twenty / twenty-one / a hundred and twenty books'

C The DE-structure with numerals under a million is specific to Romanian. In other Romance languages, this construction is limited to a few numerals (Fr. *un million d'étudiants*), which have a partitive meaning (Wilmet 2003: 187–8).

H The DE-structure has been explained as a loan from Slavic (Sandfeld 1930: 149); it is possible that the DE-structure be linked to the genitival DE. DE-phrases are used in Aromanian for the series 11–19 as well (Caragiu Marioțeanu 1975: 244–5).

5.3 *The structure of the nominal phrase*　323

The plurals *zeci* 'tens', *sute* 'hundreds', *mii* 'thousands', *milioane* 'millions', *miliarde* 'billions' display noun-like behaviour, have an indefinite quantificational meaning, are compatible with indefinite adjectives such as *câteva* 'a few', and are followed by DE-phrases:

(211)　zeci /　câteva　zeci　de　cărţi
　　　　tens /　a few　tens　DE　books.ACC
　　　　'tens / a few tens of books'

5.3.2.1.2 Ordinal numerals are of two types from the perspective of their internal structure: simple and compound.

The simple ordinal numerals are: *întâi* '1st' and *prim* '1st'.

H　The numeral *întâi* is inherited from the Latin (*ANTANEUS). *Primă* is the only form attested in old Romanian (16th century) of the Latin adjective PRIMUS (Densusianu 1938: 179): *cartea de primă* (book.DEF DE first) 'the first book' (Coresi); the form *primă* is found in compounds inherited from Latin, such as *primăvară* 'spring' (FC I: 27). The full paradigm of *prim* (Table 5.22) was created in the modern language.

The compound ordinal numerals are: *dintâi* '1st', (the non-standard language form) *întâiaşi* '1st', and all the numerals with a higher value than '1st': *al doilea* '2nd'. All compound ordinal numerals are homogenous compounds that display a high degree of cohesion in the contemporary language.

H　The compound ordinal numerals are internal creations of Romanian (FC I: 195–6, 206). The numerals *dintâi* (< prepositional *de* + *întâi*), *întâiaşi* (< *întâi(a)* + the formative *şi*) displayed single unit behaviour as early as old Romanian. All the other ordinal numerals are formed on the cardinal numeral and include the formatives *al* (pre-numeral), and *-le*, *-a* (enclitic). According to a widely accepted interpretation, *al* is etymologically linked to the genitival AL; however, it is a purely morphemic element; *-le* has a controversial origin, probably being related to the definite article (ILR II: 238; Rosetti 1986: 373), a fact which explains the existence of forms such as *al patrul*—which are the typical forms employed in the 16th century (Frâncu 1997: 130); *-a* (in the cluster *-lea*) is a deictic element or a vowel that appeared in certain syntactic contexts (Dimitrescu 1978: 247). The *al*-compounds were not fully fixed / frozen in the old language.

From an inflectional point of view, the numerals *întâi* and *dintâi* are invariable; *întâiaşi* is an invariable feminine singular form. *Întâi* may bear the enclitic definite article (213b); the definite forms express the gender, number, and case distinctions by means of the definite article (Table 5.21).

Prim inflectionally expresses gender, number, and, in the feminine singular, case distinctions (Table 5.22). It may bear the enclitic definite article; the definite forms express the gender, number, and case distinctions by means of the definite article.

TABLE 5.21　The forms of *întâiul*

		M	F
SG	NOM≡ACC	întâiul	întâia
	GEN≡DAT	întâiului	întâii
PL	NOM≡ACC	întâii	întâile
	GEN≡DAT	întâilor	

TABLE 5.22 Forms of *prim / primul*

		M	F
SG	NOM≡ACC	prim / primul	primă / prima
	GEN≡DAT	prim / primului	prime / primei
PL	NOM≡ACC	primi / primii	prime / primele
	GEN≡DAT	primi / primilor	prime / primelor

The *al*-compounds inflectionally encode only the gender distinction: masculine *al... -lea* (*al treilea*), feminine *a... -a* (*a treia*).

Dintâi and the *al*-compounds, preceded by the determiner CEL (always with DE in front of *al*) express gender, number, and case distinctions by the inflection of CEL (Table 5.20): *cel dintâi* (NOM≡ACC) / *celui dintâi* (GEN≡DAT), *cea de(-)a doua* (NOM≡ACC) / *celei de(-)a doua* (GEN≡DAT), etc.

All ordinal numerals are syntactically attached, like adjectives, directly to the noun (without a preposition).

Dintâi is always postnominal (212a); when it is preceded by CEL, it may occur before the noun (212b). The enclisis of the definite article on *întâi* and *prim* occurs when they are prenominal, and it is done in the same way as for adjectives (213), (214c) (see also §5.3.1.1.1). Articleless *prim* is limited to a few (almost) fixed lexical combinations; it is more often prenominal (214a), but the postnominal position is not excluded (214b); when prenominal, it co-occurs with the indefinite article, after the article (214d). Gender, number, and case agreement with the head noun is encoded by the inflection of the numeral *prim* or by the inflection of the accompanying determiners (CEL and the definite article):

(212) a. visul   dintâi
           dream.DEF   first
           'the first dream'

       b. cel   dintâi   vis
          CEL   first   dream
          'the first dream'

(213) a. premiul   întâi
           prize.DEF   first
           'the first prize'

       b. întâiul   premiu
          first.DEF   prize
          'the first prize'

(214) a. de   primă   mână
           of   first   hand
           'first hand'

       b. capitolul   prim,   număr   prim
          chapter   first   number   first
          'first / initial chapter' 'prime number'

    c. primul   capitol
       first.DEF chapter
       'the first chapter'

    d. un   prim   capitol
       a   first chapter
       'a first chapter'

Al-compounds are used only in the singular. The numeral occurs either after a definite noun (215a) or before an articleless noun (215b). Adjacency to the definite article is a major syntactic difference between *al* with numerals and genitive AL (for which, see §5.1.3.2.2).

(215) a. capitolul   al doilea
         chapter.DEF second
         'the second chapter'

      b. al doilea   capitol
        second   chapter
        'the second chapter'

The numerals that bear the definite article and those formed with *al* may have pronominal usages; the article (including the instance incorporated in the formative *al*) licenses a null head:

(216) Primul / al doilea a   sosit
        first.DEF   second   has arrived
        'The first one / the second one arrived'

5.3.2.1.3 The distributive numerical expressions are syntactic clusters, based on the cardinal numerals and the (invariant) adverbial *câte* 'each, apiece':

(217) câte   două   mere
        each   two   apples
        'two apples each / apiece'

H   This pattern continues some structures of vulgar Latin which employed the preposition CATA (CDDE: 81–2; ILR I: 165, 205).

Câte has a wider distribution, also being used in indefinite structures:

(218) câte   unii   oameni
        each   some   people
        'some people'

5.3.2.1.4 The collective numerical expressions are: (i) simple adjectives: *îmbi* 'both', *ambii* 'both', (ii) semitransparent compounds *amândoi* 'both' (where one can recognize the cardinal numeral *doi* '2'), (iii) compounds on the basis of cardinal numerals and the reduced form *tus-* of the indefinite adjective *toți* 'all': *tustrei* 'all three', *tuspatru* 'all four' and structures with *toți* 'all' and any cardinal numeral: *toți trei* 'all three', *toți o sută* 'all one hundred'.

U   In present-day language, only compounds formed on the basis of cardinal numerals 3–7 are used.
H   *Îmbi* and *amândoi* are both inherited from Latin; *ambii* is a modern borrowing and it incorporates the definite article. *Îmbi* is no longer used.

TABLE 5.23 The forms of *ambii*

	M	F
NOM≡ACC	ambii	ambele
GEN≡DAT	ambilor	ambelor

The following forms inflectionally encode gender distinctions: *îmbi* (M) / *îmbe* (F), *amândoi* (M) / *amândouă* (F), *tustrei* (M) / *tustrele* (F). *Ambii* encodes case and gender distinctions by means of the definite article it incorporates (Table 5.23).

Syntactically, *îmbi* and *ambii* (219) are always prenominal (the latter is followed by an indefinite noun, since it already incorporates the definite article); *amândoi* has free word order with respect to the noun (220a,b), it is a floating quantifier (220c) and combines with a definite noun:

(219) ambii copii
 both.DEF children
 'both children'

(220) a. **amândoi** copii-i
 both children-DEF
 'both children'

 b. copii-i **amândoi**
 children-DEF both
 'both children'

 c. copii-i au venit **amândoi**
 children-DEF have come both
 'Both children came'

The *tus*-compounds preserve the floating quantifier syntactic characteristic of *toți* (221a,b); *tus*-compounds also combine with an article-bearing noun; *toți* combines with a definite noun especially in combinations with *trei* (221a,b); in all the other structures, determination by CEL is preferred (221c); in post-numeral DE-phrases, the noun is articleless (221c):

(221) a. Tustrei / toți trei băieți-i au venit
 all-three all three boys-DEF have come

 b. Băieți-i au venit tustrei / toți trei
 boys-DEF have come all-three all three
 'All three boys came'

 c. toți (cei) o sută de copii
 all CEL one hundred DE children
 'all one hundred children'

The clusters which move as whole (*toți* + simple cardinal numeral) display a certain formal solidarity (221a,b). The structures with compound cardinal numerals and especially the ones with CEL do not display homogeneous behaviour; in these cases, *toți* attaches to a quantified NP (QP) or to a DP ((222a) is the representation of (221c)); only *toți* may float in these structures (222b):

(222) a. [toți [(cei) o sută de copii]]
         all   CEL one hundred DE children
     b. (Cei) o sută de copii au primit toți câte un premiu
         CEL one hundred DE children have received all each a prize
        'All one hundred children received a prize each'

With the exception of the old adjective *îmbi*, all collective quantifiers also have pronominal usages:

(223) Ambii / amândoi / tustrei / toți trei au plecat
      both   both   all-three all three have left
      'Both / all three left'

5.3.2.1.5 The multiplicative numerical expressions are adjectives, grammaticalized affixal formations, that have the structure of the participle of a verb formed with the prefix *în-*, which incorporates a cardinal numeral from the series 2–6, 10, 100, and 1,000: *întreit* 'three times more / threefold' *(în-* + *trei* + *-it)* (cf. *întrei* 'treble'). The unmarked word order is postnominal:

(224) un efort înzecit
      an effort tenfold
      'a tenfold effort'

The multiplicative meaning is also expressed by adverbial numerical expressions (§5.3.2.1.7):

(225) de trei ori prețul
      DE three times price.DEF
      'three times the price'

5.3.2.1.6 The fractional numerical expressions are heterogeneous syntactic clusters that include a cardinal numeral and a noun derived from a cardinal numeral with the suffix *-ime*: *trei optimi* 'three eighths'. Other structures include a cardinal numeral and a noun such as *jumătate* 'half', *sfert* 'quarter', *parte* 'part': *trei sferturi* 'three quarters'. These phrases are used in partitive quantification:

(226) trei optimi din averea lui
      three eighths from fortune.DEF his(GEN)
      'three eighths of his fortune'

Expressing percentages involves the preposition *la*: *treizeci la sută* '30%'; these structures occur in different nominal phrases:

(227) a. reducere de 30%
         discount of 30%
         '30% discount'
     b. 30% reducere
        30% discount
        'discount of 30%'
     c. 30% din câștig
        30% from earnings
        '30% of the earnings'

5.3.2.1.7 The adverbial numerical expressions are quasi-fixed collocations, which include a cardinal or ordinal numeral and the singular nouns *dată, oară* 'time' and the plural noun *ori* 'times': *o dată* 'once', *de două ori* 'twice / two times', *(pentru) prima dată* '(for) the first time', *(pentru) a doua oară* '(for) the second time'.

(228) Citește   pentru   prima   dată /   citirea   pentru   prima   dată
      ((s)he)reads   for   first.DEF time   reading.DEF   for   first.DEF time
      'She is reading for the first time' 'reading for the first time'

These expressions are used in nominalized structures, being verbal quantifiers.

5.3.2.2 Indefinite and negative quantifiers

5.3.2.2.1 Indefinite quantifiers are pronominal adjectives.

From the point of view of their internal structure, indefinite adjectives are (i) opaque words (which cannot be further decomposed in present-day language): *un* 'one', *atât(a)* 'so much / many', *tot* 'all', *mult* 'much, a lot of / many', *puțin* 'few, (a) little' or compounds, made up from a *wh*-pronoun and the formatives *fie-, oare-, ori-, -va* or from the formative *vre-* and the indefinite adjective *un: fiecare* 'each, every', *oarecare* 'some, certain', *oricare* 'whatever, any', *orice* 'any', *oricât* 'however, no matter how', *ceva* 'something, anything', *câtva* 'some, a little', *vreun* 'any':

(229) un /   fiecare /   vreun   om
      one   each, every   any   man
      'a / each / any man'

U   Other quantifiers are also available in regional languages: *fiece* 'each, every', *niscai(va)* 'some, any', *oare(și)ce* 'any', etc.

The inflectional characteristics of the indefinite adjectives partially follow from their internal structure.

The indefinite adjective *un* displays gender, number, and case variation; in the singular and in the plural genitive–dative it is homonymous with the indefinite article (compare with Table 5.12); in the singular, it is homonymous with the cardinal numeral *unu* 'one' as well (Table 5.24).

The adjective *vreun* has the same inflection as its base *un*. In the pronominal usage, *un* and *vreun* incorporate the definite article, which licenses a null head:

(230) [unul [e]],   [vreunul [e]]
      one.DEF   one.DEF
      '(any)one'

TABLE 5.24 The forms of *un*

		M	F
SG	NOM≡ACC	un	o
	GEN≡DAT	unui	unei
PL	NOM≡ACC	unii	unele
	GEN≡DAT	unor	

C This incorporation of the definite article in the structure of certain indefinite quantifiers is a typological characteristic of Romanian.

The adjective *atât* (with or without the final element *-a*) displays gender and number variation: masculine singular *atât(a)*, plural *atâţi(a)*; feminine singular *atâta*, plural *atâtea*: *atâtea fete* 'so many girls'.

The adjectives *tot, mult, puţin* display gender and number and, in the plural, case variation: masculine singular *tot, mult, puţin*, plural nominative–accusative *toţi, mulţi, puţini*; feminine singular *toată, multă, puţină*, plural nominative–accusative *toate, multe, puţine*; masculine–feminine plural genitive–dative *tuturor, multor, puţinor*: *tot timpul* 'all the time', *multă oboseală* 'much fatigue', *puţini copii* 'few children', *tuturor oamenilor* 'to / of all the people'.

Compound indefinite adjectives based on *wh*-pronouns have the same inflection as their base (§10.3.5). The *-va* compounds are invariable.

Syntactically, most of the indefinite adjectives show word order and determination restrictions.

Most indefinite adjectives are always prenominal (231a). The exceptions are the following: *tot, mult, puţin* have free word order (231b); *tot* is a floating quantifier (§5.3.2.1.4); *oarecare* has a quantificational meaning when it is prenominal and a qualifying meaning when it is postnominal (231c):

(231) a. unii /   atâţia /   câţiva   oameni
         some   so many   a few   people
         'some people / so many people / a few people'

   b. mulţi   oameni /   oameni   mulţi
      many   people   people   many
      'many people'

   c. un   oarecare   om /   un   om   oarecare
      a   certain / some   human   a   human   ordinary
      'a certain human' 'an ordinary human'

After prenominal indefinite adjectives, the noun (placed in the second position of the noun phrase) does not bear the definite article (231a,b), following the general rule of definite determination (see §5.3.1.1.1); *tot* (221a,b) is exceptional to this rule. Placed postnominally, *mult* and *puţin* may combine with definite or indefinite nouns:

(232) oameni(-i)   mulţi
      humans-DEF   many
      '(the) many people'

From a semantic perspective, *tot* is the typical universal quantifier, and has a globalizing meaning in plural structures: *toţi oamenii* 'all the humans' or a distributive meaning in structures with the singular of count nouns: *tot omul* 'each / every human'; *fiecare* is the distributive universal quantifier: *fiecare om* 'each / every human'.

C Romanian contrasts with other Romance languages in that the definite article is present in the structure of the type *tot omul* 'each / every human' (Niculescu 1965: 66).

The selection of indefinite quantifiers is based on special rules in structures with mass, abstract, and collective nouns (for which, see §5.2.2–4).

5.3.2.2.2 The negative quantifier of the nominal phrase is the pronominal adjective *niciun* 'no'.

It is a compound word, based on the indefinite adjective *un* 'one'; it has only singular forms and it has a declension like *un* (Table 5.24). It is always prenominal and it combines with an indefinite (i.e. articleless) noun:

(233) niciun om
no man
'no man'

As a pronoun, *niciun* incorporates the definite article (234), similarly to its base, *un* (230); it has plural forms.

(234) [niciunul [e]]
NO.DEF
'none'

U The negative quantifiers *niciun, nicio, niciunul, niciuna* have oscillated orthographically between being written separately (*nici un, nici unul*) and being written as one unit; the current orthographic norm recommends the latter.

5.3.2.3 Other quantifiers

5.3.2.3.1 Certain nouns that encode an intrinsic indefinite quantificational (*mulţime* 'lot', *puzderie* 'multitude', *seamă* 'lot', *sumă* 'sum', *sumedenie* 'a great deal') or partitive (*jumătate* 'half', *majoritate* 'majority', *parte* 'part', *rest* 'rest'; §5.3.2.1.6) meaning fulfil a quantifying function in structures in which they are not involved in predicate- (235) or modifier-agreement (236a), that is where agreement is forced by the quantified NP (§12.2.5). Some quantifying nouns may be, in their turn, accompanied by quantitative adjuncts (235c):

(235) a. O mulţime de cetăţeni au votat
a lot(SG) of citizens(PL) have(PL) voted
'A lot of citizens voted'

b. Majoritatea cetăţenilor au votat
majority.DEF(SG) citizens.DEF.GEN(PL) have(PL) voted
'The majority of citizens voted'

c. (O) (mică) parte dintre cetăţeni au votat
a small part(SG) of citizens(PL) have(PL) voted
'A (small) part of the citizens voted'

(236) a. majoritatea deputaţilor liberali [quantificational reading]
majority.DEF(SG) deputies.DEF.GEN(PL) liberal.PL
'the majority of liberal deputies'

b. majoritatea liberală a deputaţilor [non-quantificational reading]
majority.DEF(SG) liberal(SG) AL deputies.DEF.GEN(PL)
'the liberal majority of deputies'

U *Seamă* is obsolete, and *puzderie* and *sumedenie* are typical of the non-standard language:
(237) a. o seamă de însuşiri
a lot of features

b. (o) puzderie / sumedenie de insecte
   a   multitude great deal   of insects
   'a great deal of insects'

Nouns with intrinsic numerical significance (such as *duzină* 'dozen', *pereche* 'pair') and nouns that encode only in certain contexts an indefinite (e.g. *grămadă* 'pile') or partitive (in pseudo-partitive noun phrases: *ceașcă* 'cup', *doză* 'dose', *pic / picătură* 'drop, grain'; see §5.2.2) quantificational meaning also pose predicate- (238a) or adjectival modifier-agreement (238b) problems (§12.2.5). Some nouns of this type may be accompanied by quantitative adjuncts (239):

(238) a. O   duzină   de cămăși   a /   au   costat 100 de dolari
         a   dozen(SG) of shirts(PL) have(SG) have(PL) cost   100 DE dollars
         'A dozen of shirts cost 100 dollars'

      b. o   grămadă   de bani   adunată / adunați
         a   pile(SG)   of money(PL) raised(SG) raised(PL)
         'a pile of collected money'

(239) câteva doze   de alcool
      a-few   doses   of alcohol
      'a few shots of alcohol'

5.3.2.3.2 The interrogative quantifiers are: *care* 'which', *cât* 'how much / many', *ce* 'what', *cine* 'who', *al câtelea* 'which one'.

The operators *care*, *ce*, and *cine* do not inflectionally encode the singular / plural number distinction (§13.1.2.2) and exclusively occur in singular contexts; in spite of this, they may have singular or plural antecedents, thus being able to bind the variable of a nominal expression with a plural reference (240a). Due to the presence of this feature, the interrogatives *care*, *ce*, and *cine* are included in the class of quantifiers (Chierchia 1997: 275; Longobardi 2001: 668). Sometimes, they make reference to a singular nominal expression, but contain the presupposition of existence of a plurality (240b):

(240) a. Cine / care dintre ei a venit, Ion și Maria sau prietenii lor?
         'Who / which of them came, Ion and Maria or their friends?'

      b. Care băiat a venit, Ion?
         'Which boy came, Ion?'

Care and *ce* are used as pronouns (240a), (241a) or as pronominal adjectives (240b), (241b):

(241) a. Ce   citești?
         what   (you)read
         'What are you reading?'

      b. Ce   carte   citești?
         what   book   (you)read
         'What book are you reading?'

Cine is used only as a pronoun; it may referentially bind a masculine (*Ion, prietenii*) or feminine (*Maria*) expression (240a).

Cât is the substitute of cardinal numerals and of certain indefinite quantifiers like *mult* 'much, a lot of / many', *puțin* 'few, (a) little'. It is used as a pronoun (242a) or as a pronominal adjective (242b):

(242) a. Câți   au   venit, doi?
       how-many have   come   two
       'How many of them came, two?'

   b. Câți   băieți au   venit, doi?
      how-many boys   have   come   two
      'How many boys came, two?'

Al câtelea 'which one, the how-manyeth' stands specifically for the ordinal numeral; it includes the formative of the ordinal numeral *al... -lea* and the interrogative pronoun *cât*. It is used as a pronoun (243a) or as a pronominal adjective (243b):

(243) a. Al   câtelea a   venit, al doilea?
        which one   has come   the second
        'Which one came, the second one?'

   b. Al câtelea băiat a   venit, al doilea?
      which   boy   has come   the second
      'Which boy came, the second one?'

C   Like French, Italian, Occitan, Catalan, Spanish, and Portuguese, Romanian expresses the distinction [+animate] *(cine)* / [–animate] *(ce)* by distinct pronominal forms (ELIR: 264); this distinction is not encoded by pronominal adjectives.

5.3.2.3.3 The adverbial quantifiers, specific to the verb phrase, occur in nominalized structures. Formally, these quantifiers are adverbs *(frecvent* 'frequently'), cardinal or ordinal numerical adverbial expressions *(o dată* 'one time', *a doua oară* 'the second time'; see §5.3.2.1.7), and complex phrases *(în două ore* 'in two hours', *timp de două ore* 'for two hours'):

(244) citirea   frecvent / a   doua   oară / timp de două   ore
      reading.DEF frequently   the second time   time for two   hours
      'the frequent reading' / 'the second time reading' / 'reading for two hours'

5.3.2.3.4 Pseudo-quantified NPs include adjectives or nouns with a quantitative meaning.
   Certain adjectival modifiers of the noun phrase are exponents of a quantitative semantic predication.
   The adjectives *complet* 'complete', *global* 'global', *integral* 'integral', *întreg* 'whole, entire', *total* 'total' are quantitative modifiers with a globalizing meaning, partly synonymous with the pronominal adjective *tot* 'all' (the typical universal quantifier):

(245) volumul   complet   al   schimburilor   comerciale
      volume.DEF complete   AL   exchanges.DEF.GEN commercial
      'the complete volume of commercial exchanges'

When it is prenominal, the adjective *întreg* raises problems with respect to the enclisis of the definite article ((101d) above). Furthermore, in prenominal position as well, the adjective *întreg* sometimes has non-quantitative readings (see examples (101d,e) above):

(246) În   vacanță   au   făcut o   întreagă expediție
      in   holiday   (they)have made   a   whole   expedition
      'During the holiday they went on a real / genuine expedition'

The adjective *parțial* is a modifier with partitive meaning:

(247) restaurarea   parțială   a   monumentului
       restoration.DEF partial   AL   monument.DEF.GEN
       'the partial restoration of the monument'

Other (genuine or participial) adjectives express quantitative relations (*echivalent* 'equivalent', *egal* 'equal', *proporțional* 'proportional'), degree values (*crescut* 'increased' / *scăzut* 'decreased', *înalt* 'high (/ tall)', *major* 'major' / *minor* 'minor', *maxim* 'maximum' / *minim* 'minimum', *moderat* 'moderate', *redus* 'reduced'), indefinite values (*multiplu* 'multiple'), etc.:

(248) a. lungimea   echivalentă
          length.DEF   equivalent
          'the equivalent length'

       b. efort   redus
          effort   reduced
          'small effort'

       c. multipli   factori   de   risc
          multiple   factors   of   risk
          'multiple risk factors'

The adjectives *dublu* 'double', *triplu* 'triple', *cvadruplu* 'quadruple', *cvintuplu* 'quintuple', *sextuplu* 'sextuple' are modifiers (249a) that semantically correspond to multiplicative quantifiers: *îndoit* 'twofold', *întreit* 'threefold', *împătrit* 'fourfold', *încincit* 'fivefold', *înșesit* 'sixfold' (§5.3.2.1.5). In the corresponding nominalized structures, the substantivized adjectives *dublu*, *triplu*, etc. are used (249b):

(249) a. distanța   dublă /   îndoită
          distance.DEF   double   twofold
          'the double / twofold distance'

       b. dublul   distanței
          double.DEF   distance.DEF.GEN
          'the double of the distance'

The adjective *ultim* 'last' and the adjectival collocation *cel din urmă* 'the last one' are modifiers that have been semantically associated with ordinal numerals.

5.3.2.3.5 A structure that may be accommodated with quantified NPs is the one where singular DPs are preceded by focusing adverbs with restrictive (*decât, doar, numai* 'only'), cumulative (*și* 'also', *chiar și* 'even'), and negative (*nici* 'not', *nici chiar, nici măcar* 'not even') meaning; semantically, these structures present the presupposition of existence of a plurality (cf. Longobardi 2001: 666–7):

(250) a. doar Ion lucrează
          'only John works' [implicit meaning: 'another one / other ones do(es) not work']

       b. chiar și Ion lucrează
          'even John works' [implicit meaning: 'another one / other ones work(s)']

c. nici măcar Ion nu lucrează
   not even John not works
   'not even John works' [implicit meaning: 'another one / other ones do(es) not work as well]'

5.3.2.3.6 The null quantifiers (Radford 2009: 110) are identifiable in certain coordinate structures, such as the following:

(251) Mănâncă [QP ∅ [legume]], [QP ∅ [fructe]] și [QP mai puține [dulciuri]]
      eats   vegetables   fruits   and   more   less   sweets
      '(S)he eats vegetables, fruits, and less sweets'

5.3.2.3.7 The expression of approximation and vagueness is realized by various means (morphosyntactic, lexical, and semantic): compound numerals containing the indefinite adjective *câteva* 'a few' (252a) or the indefinite pronoun *ceva* 'something' which is, in this instance, a substitute of the numeral (252b); numerals preceded by the prepositions *până în* 'up to', *peste* 'over', *spre* 'towards (~ almost)', *sub* 'under' (253); juxtaposition (254a,b) or coordination with disjunctive conjunctions (254c) of numerals with close values, with the noun being placed after (254a) or between (254b,c) the numerals; adverbs and adverbial collocations with approximation or vagueness meaning—*aproape* 'almost', *aproximativ* 'about', *ca la (vreo)* 'approximately', *cam* 'about', *cel mult* 'at most', *cel puțin* 'at least', *în jur de* 'about', *circa* 'circa, about', *vreo* 'about' (255); structures with the adverbials *maximum* and *minimum*, which come either before the numeral (256a) or after the 'numeral + NP' phrase (256b):

(252) a. **câteva sute** de cuvinte
          a few   hundreds DE words
          'a few hundred words'

   b. **două mii** și **ceva** de dolari
      two thousand and something DE dollars
      'more than two thousand dollars'

(253) **sub două** hectare
      under two hectares
      'less than 2 hectares'

(254) a. **zece-cincisprezece** oameni
         ten-fifteen people
         'ten or fifteen people'

   b. **o** lună, **două**
      one month two
      'one or two months'

   c. pe **un** camion **sau** pe **două**
      on one lorry or on two
      'on one or two lorries'

(255) **cel mult două** zile
      at most two days

(256) a. **maximum** zece zile
maximum ten days

b. **zece** zile **maximum**
ten days maximum
'at most ten days'

5.3.3 Means of encoding nominal phrase internal possession

The following means of encoding possession are found in Romanian: (a) nouns and pronouns in the genitive case; (b) possessive adjectives (including the possessive affix); (c) the adnominal possessive clitic (traditionally known as the adnominal possessive dative); (d) the prepositions DE and A; (e) the definite article. In the current chapter the following are presented: possessive adjectives, adnominal possessive clitics, the preposition DE, and the definite article. The genitive case has been dealt with in the section concerning case-marking (§5.1.3.2; for the ellipsis of the possessee, see §5.3.7.3); similarly, the preposition A is considered an alternative means of introducing genitive phrases (§5.1.3.2).

C   Research on possessive phrases (e.g. Szabolcsi 1984, 1994; Kayne 1994: 85–116; Guéron 1985; for more details, see Cornilescu and Nicolae 2011b: 118–21) has shown that possessive phrases should be viewed as including a predicative relation (i.e. a *subject–predicate* relation) between the possessor and the possessee. Ouhalla (2009) distinguishes two types of languages in terms of the choice of the subject in possessee + possessor construction: *possessor subject languages* and *possessee subject languages*. In the case of *possessor subject languages* (English, Hungarian, Amharic, etc.) the possessive nominal phrase includes a possessor in subject position, while the possessee is the predicate. On the other hand, languages like Romanian (and other Romance languages; Hebrew, Moroccan Arabic, etc.) are *possessee subject languages*.

For instance, in Romanian, the (number and gender) agreement between the possessee and the definite article incorporated on the genitive / possessive marker AL (§5.1.3.2.2) is a clear indication of the *subject–predicate* relation that holds between the subject possessee and the predicate possessor:

(257) a. un   băiat   al   mamei
a   boy.M.SG   AL.M.SG   mother.DEF.GEN

b. două   fete   a**le**   mamei
two   girls.F.PL   AL.F.PL   mother.DEF.GEN
POSSESSEE   SUBJECT   PREDICATE   POSSESSOR

5.3.3.1 *Possessive adjectives*

Romanian possessive adjectives display a hybrid behaviour (adjectival and (pro)nominal (DP-like)) in both overt head and nominal ellipsis contexts (i.e. when there is elision of the possessed object), and have been categorized in the recent literature as 'mixed categories' (Cornilescu and Nicolae 2011b, following Bresnan 1997). The adjectival / pronominal interference is three-fold, as it concerns internal structure, distribution, and syntax. In line with traditional terminology, we will continue to term these words 'possessive adjectives'.

5.3.3.1.1 Possessive adjectives vary morphologically depending on the grammatical person of the possessor and the number of possessors and on the grammatical gender and case of the possessed object and the number of possessed objects, as illustrated in Table 5.25.

336   5 *Nouns and Noun Phrases*

TABLE 5.25 Possessive adjectives

			1ST PERSON		2ND PERSON		3RD PERSON	
			NOM≡ACC	GEN≡DAT	NOM≡ACC	GEN≡DAT	NOM≡ACC	GEN≡DAT
ONE POSSESSOR	ONE POSSESSED OBJECT	M (NEUT)	meu		tău		său	
		F	mea	mele	ta	tale	sa	sale
	MULTIPLE POSSESSED OBJECTS	M	mei		tăi		săi	
		F (NEUT)	mele		tale		sale (see B, C below)	
MULTIPLE POSSESSORS	ONE POSSESSED OBJECT	M (NEUT)	nostru		vostru		—	
		F	noastră	noastre	voastră	voastre	—	
	MULTIPLE POSSESSED OBJECTS	M	noștri		voștri		—	
		F (NEUT)	noastre		voastre		— (see B below)	

A Possessive adjectives do not reflect the (natural) gender of their referent but take over (by agreement) the (grammatical) gender of their governing noun.

B There is a paradigmatic gap in the inventory of possessive adjectives for multiple possessors in the third person; this gap is overridden by the use of the 3rd person plural genitive personal pronoun *lor* 'their'. Furthermore, the 3rd person singular genitive personal pronouns *lui* 'his' and *ei* 'her', on the one hand, and the possessive adjectives denoting a 3rd person referent, on the other hand, are in almost identical distribution (see example (274b) below, for a distributional disparity); however, they differ in that singular 3rd person personal pronouns encode the gender of their antecedent, while possessive adjectives display gender agreement with their governing noun.

C The initial segment of the possessive lexeme (*m-, t-, s-, n-, v-*) indicates the grammatical person and number of possessors; the natural gender of the possessor is not encoded grammatically, but it can be identified contextually (deictically or anaphorically). These initial consonants are also found in the paradigm of personal and reflexive pronouns; thus, compare: ***meu / mea / mei / mele*** (possessive adjective)—***mine*** (strong personal / reflexive pronoun, ACC)—***mă*** (personal / reflexive clitic, ACC). The third person root *s-* historically originates in the paradigm of the reflexive pronoun; its reflexive meaning is no longer present in the paradigm of possessive adjectives.

H There are two major differences between modern and old Romanian with respect to the 3rd person possessive adjective (*său / sa / săi / sale*).

First, there is a clear distributional distinction in the 16th century between the 3rd person forms *lui / ei* and the possessive forms *său / sa / săi / sale*, the latter being reflexive and, in the overwhelming majority of occurrences, binding the subject of the sentence (Berea 1961: 324):

(258) [pământul   nostru]ᵢ va   da   plodul   **său**ᵢ   (*Psaltirea Voroneţeană*)
       land.DEF(NEUT) our   AUX.FUT.3SG give.INF seed.DEF its.NEUT.SG
       'Our land will give its seed'

5.3 The structure of the nominal phrase

By contrast, the personal pronouns *lui* and *ei* may bind either the subject, as in (259a), or another constituent of the sentence: a possessive genitive (259b), a direct object, an indirect object, etc.:

(259) a. Cain$_i$ miră-se   tare   și fața   **lui**$_i$ se   schimbă (*Palia*)
      Cain wonder.PS=CL.REFL.ACC strongly and face.DEF his CL.REFL.ACC change.PS
      'And Cain wondered intensely and his face changed'

   b. Cire sui   în pădurea   Domnului$_i$ și cire stătu în
      who climb.PS in forest.DEF God.GEN   and who stay.PS in
      locu sfântu a **lui**$_i$ (*Psaltirea Scheiană*)
      place sain AL his
      'who climbed up in God's forest and stayed in his sacred place'

The exclusively reflexive usage of these possessive forms has gradually disappeared, beginning with the 17th century (Dimitrescu 1975: 155–58).

Second, in the old language (and true to their Latin etymology), the possessive forms *său / sa / săi / sale* could be used to denote both one possessor and multiple possessors, that is these forms could have plural reference (Densusianu 1961, II: 249), being equivalent to the genitive personal pronoun *lor* (which later took over the plural reference):

(260) mulți$_i$ [...] veriia ispovedindu și   spuindu lucrurele
      many   came   confessing and   telling problems.DEF
      sale$_i$ (*Codicele Voronețean*)
      their.PL
      'Many came confessing and telling their problems'

D The final segment of the possessive lexeme is the locus of adjectival inflection. Morphologically, possessive adjectives are four forms adjectives and observe regular adjectival patterns (§7.2); compare (261a) with (261b) and (261c) with (261d):

(261) a. me**u**   me**a**   me**i**   me**le**   'my'
      b. gre**u**   gre**a**   gre**i**   gre**le**   'hard'
         hard.M.SG   hard.F.SG   hard.M.PL   hard.F.PL

      c. nost**ru**   no**astră**   no**ștri**   no**astre**   'our'
      d. albast**ru** alba**stră** alba**ștri** alba**stre**   'blue'
         blue.M.SG   blue.F.SG   blue.M.PL   blue.F.PL

Moreover, they display the same case syncretism pattern as regular adjectives: in the masculine they have the same form for all cases (NOM≡ACC≡GEN≡DAT), but they show case variation in the singular feminine, where the form of the genitive–dative is different from that of the nominative–accusative, as shown by the opposition (262a–b) vs. (262c–d):

(262) a. cartea   **mea**
         book.F.DEF   my.F.SG

   b. problema   **grea**
      problem.DEF(F)   hard.F.SG

   c. coperta   cărții   **mele**
      cover.DEF book.DEF.GEN(F)   my.GEN.F.SG

   d. soluția   problemei   **grele**
      solution.DEF problem.DEF.GEN(F) hard.GEN.F.SG

H In old Romanian, possessive adjectives could be suffixed by the reflexive particle -ș(i) (Densusianu 1961, II: 120): *ai mieiș, ale meleș, al nostruș, al tăuș, a saș, (ale) saleș* (Coresi).

E Morphophonological alternations from the stem of the possessive adjective are a secondary means of differentiating among different items in the paradigm. For instance, the alternation [str / ʃtr] in *nostru, noștri, vostru, voștri* participates in the opposition 'one possessed object—multiple possessed objects'; similarly, the vowel alternation [o / o̯a] differentiates the masculine and the feminine forms: *nostru—noștri* vs. *noastră—noastre; vostru—voștri* vs. *voastră—voastre*.

5.3.3.1.2 The distributional features and syntactic behaviour of possessive adjectives are varied.

(i) Possessive adjectives are typically postnominal but under certain conditions may also occur prenominally. Like genitive personal pronouns, possessive adjectives either occur 'bare', when they are strictly right-adjacent to a (head) noun or to an adjective bearing the enclitic definite article, as in (263), or are preceded by the functional element AL (§5.1.3.2). Non-adjacency is due to various syntactic contexts: lack of the definite article (264a), intervening adjectives or postnominal demonstratives (264b), prenominal (definite determiner) position (264c) (obsolete in present-day Romanian), or predicative position (264d).

(263) a. copilul **meu** (/ lui / ei)
child.DEF(M) my.M.SG his / her

b. frumoasa **mea** (/ lui / ei) prietenă
beautiful.DEF.F.SG my.F.SG his / her friend(F)

(264) a. un copil **al** **meu**
a child(M) AL.M.SG my.M.SG

b. cartea interesantă / aceasta a **mea**
book.DEF(F) beautiful(F) this(F) AL.F.SG my.F.SG

c. **al** **meu** suflet
AL.M.SG my.M.SG soul

d. Cartea e a **mea**
book.DEF(F) is AL.F.SG my.F.SG

H In old Romanian, the possessive adjective could double an adverbal dative clitic (attached to verb negation) or a full pronoun:

(265) și cine nu-ș$_i$ va lua lui$_i$ crucea
and who not=CL.REFL.DAT.3SG AUX.FUT.3SG take him.DAT cross.DEF
sa$_i$ (Coresi)
his.F.SG
'and who will not take his own cross'
This was possible also for personal pronouns in the genitive case:

(266) păzîndu-și$_i$ tabăra **lor**$_i$ (Costin)
guarding=CL.REFL.DAT.3PL camp.DEF their
'guarding their camp'

In possessed object ellipsis contexts the possessive adjective is always preceded by AL:

(267) Câinele   din   curte e al   Mariei.   Al   **meu** e în casă
      dog.DEF(M) from   yard is AL.M.SG Maria.GEN AL.M.SG my   is in house
      'The dog in the yard is Maria's. Mine is indoors.'

The genitive / possessive analytic marker AL does not display DP-internal agreement in case. However, in nominal ellipsis contexts, AL turns into a pronoun and acquires case morphology, as the comparison between a nominal phrase with an overt noun head in (268a) and its parallel elliptical one in (268b) shows. Also, the 'pronominal' AL-DP may make use of the genitive marker AL, the result being a nominal phrase containing two instances of AL (268c):

(268) a. Am   spus [$_{DP}$ unor   prieteni   **ai**   **mei**]
         (I)have told   some.DAT friends.DAT AL.M.PL   my.M.PL
         'I told (this) to some friends of mine'

     b. Am   spus [$_{DP}$ **alor**   **mei**]
        (I)have told   AL.M.PL.DAT   my.M.PL)
        'I told (this) to my parents / folks'

     c. nişte prietene [$_{DP}$ ale   **alor**   **mei**]
        some friends   AL.F.PL   AL.M.PL.GEN   my.M.PL
        (*alor mei* 'părinţi**lor** mei' ('my parents'))

C   From a distributional point of view, the adjectival character of possessive adjectives is not so obvious in Romanian, because of AL. In some languages (e.g. Italian), possessive adjectives have a non-ambiguous adjectival distribution (Longobardi 1994: 623); in others (French, Spanish), possessives are definite determiners (Antrim 2003). The dual adjectival–determiner paradigm seems to have historically underlain all Romance varieties, but has been lost in most languages by the jettisoning of one paradigm in favour of the other (Ledgeway 2011: 417). Furthermore, in some languages and varieties (Romanian, Spanish, Occitan, Catalan, Algherese), there emerged a distinction between the clitic or affixal forms (see §5.3.3.2 for Romanian), which are specified as [+definite] on account of the lexicalization of the D position, and the tonic adjectival forms, which are underspecified for definiteness.

  (ii) The interpretation of possessive adjectives in predicative position (264d) is somehow controversial since, unlike other languages, the morphology does not indicate whether this is a nominal ellipsis context (hence, a 'pronominal' usage of the possessive adjective) or a mere adjectival context (the insertion of AL being taken as the result of non-adjacency to a definite article).

C   Languages like French distinguish possessive adjectives, which are always prenominal definite determiners, and (morphologically complex) possessive pronouns that may appear in predicative position (Price 2008: 158, 162).
    As remarked by many authors (Antrim 2003; Dobrovie-Sorin and Giurgea 2011; Cornilescu and Nicolae 2011b), although possessives have been classified as adjectives, they fail to satisfy the general properties of adjectives: to function as an attribute, to function as a predicate, to allow modification by an intensifier, to be used in the comparative or in the superlative. The fact that Romanian possessives occur in predicative position only preceded by AL, corroborated with data from other languages and with the fact that, in the case of quantifiers, the long ('pronominal') form is the one occurring in predicative position (e.g. *El este altul* / **alt* he is other.DEF / other), all these indicate that, at least in the case of Romanian, possessives in predicative position are to be interpreted as 'pronominal', that is as being instances of nominal phrases with elided (possessee) noun heads.

(iii) Possessive adjectives have *pronominal* properties in the sense that, like nouns, they have a referential index and behave like referential phrases. This accounts for the following properties of Romanian possessive adjectives (Vasilescu 2007b; Dobrovie-Sorin and Giurgea 2011; Cornilescu and Nicolae 2011b).

A Possessive adjectives do not assign, but are assigned thematic roles (typical adjectives assign rather than being assigned thematic roles):

(269) a. mâna   **mea**   (Possessor)
          hand.DEF   my

       b. dormitul   **meu** ore întregi   (Agent)
          sleeping.DEF my for hours

       c. îmbătrânirea **mea**   (Patient)
          ageing.DEF   my

       d. plecarea   **mea**   (Theme)
          leaving.DEF my

       e. cartea   **mea**   (ambiguous: Possessor or Agent)
          book.DEF   my
          'my book' / 'the book written by me'

B Possessive adjectives are in complementary distribution with (lexical or pronominal) genitive DPs. This is visible in nominalizations, where only one genitive thematic position is available: it can be filled in either by a genitive (270a–b) or by a possessive adjective (270c), but never by both:

(270) a. mângâierea   **copilului** (Theme) de către mamă   (Agent)
          caressing.DEF child.SG.GEN   by   mother

       b. mângâierea   **lui** (Theme)   de către mamă   (Agent)
          caressing.DEF he.GEN   by   mother

       c. mângâierea   **sa** (Theme)   de către mamă   (Agent)
          caressing.DEF his / her.SG.F.NOM≡ACC   by   mother

C Furthermore, possessive adjectives may bind reflexive expressions (271), take secondary predicates (272), and control a small clause subject (273), syntactic phenomena available only for arguments / referential phrases (Dobrovie-Sorin and Giurgea 2011; Cornilescu and Nicolae 2011b):

(271) părerea   **noastră**$_i$ despre [noi înşine]$_i$
       opinion.DEF(F) our.F.SG   about   us   ourselves

(272) o poză   **a**   **mea**   [blond(ă)]
       a picture(F)   AL   my.F.SG   blond.M/F.SG
       'a picture of me blond'

(273) vizita   **sa**   [înarmat(ă)] până în dinţi]
       visit.DEF(F)   his / her.F.SG   armed.M/F   to   in teeth

D Finally, as can be seen in Table 5.25, possessive adjectives exhibit variation for person, a striking pronominal property.

5.3.3.2 The possessive affix

Weak forms of possessive adjectives (274b) may be affixed onto bare (i.e. articleless) noun roots, this being one of the few contexts where possessive adjectives and genitival pronouns do not show the same distribution and behaviour ((274a) vs. (274b)):

(274) a. tatăl   lui /   ei /   **său**
      father.DEF(M.SG)   his(GEN)   her(GEN)   his/her.M.SG

     b. tac-**su** /   *tac-**lui**
      father-his / her.M.SG   father-his
      'his/her father'

C   The phenomenon of possessive adjective affixation is also attested in central and southern Italian dialects (Salvi 2011: 337).

The affixation of the possessive adjective is restricted to kinship and social relation nouns (*mamă* 'mother', *tată* 'father', *frate* 'brother', etc.; *stăpân* 'master', *moașă* 'midwife', etc.; see §5.2.5), and is typically found in non-standard Romanian. Like full non-affixal possessive adjectives, the possessive affix displays agreement with the possessee noun. The possessive adjective may be suffixed only to a noun root; any other root (prenominal adjectives, for instance) is excluded.

From a syntactic perspective, the possessive affix construction is a *construct state* structure (Cornilescu 1995).

5.3.3.2.1 There are various degrees of boundedness of the affix to the nominal host, reflected in the case-marking possibilities of the compound:

   A The combinations containing masculine nouns mark the genitive and dative by the proclitic morpheme *lui*:

(275)   lui   frate-**miu**
        LUI.GEN≡DAT   brother-my.M.SG

   B The combinations containing feminine nouns have three possibilities of marking the genitive and dative: by the proclitic morpheme *lui* (276); by means of a nominal inflectional ending which is suffixed at the end of the compound (277); finally, both components of the compound (the noun and the possessive adjective) may display case variation (278):

(276)   lui   soră-mea
       LUI.GEN≡DAT   sister-my.F.SG

(277)   soră-**tii**   (vs. NOM≡ACC: soră-ta)
       sister(NOM≡ACC)-your.F.SG.GEN≡DAT

(278)   nevesti-**sii**   (vs. NOM≡ACC: nevastă-sa)
       wife.GEN≡DAT-his / her.F.SG.GEN≡DAT

   C The possessive affix may take over other inflectional case endings, such as those of the vocative:

(279)   sor-**meo**!
       sister-my.F.SG.VOC

The combination of the bare noun with the affixal possessive adjective represents a phonological word (Niculescu 2008b); the possessive component cannot be (contrastively) stressed:

(280) *sor-MEA
       sister-my

5.3.3.2.2 The possessive affix displays a rich morphological and morphophonological variation. It is available only for 1st–3rd persons singular, displaying the following forms (Vasilescu 2008a: 194–5): *-meu / -miu, -mea, -mei / -mii* (1st person), *-tău / -to / -tu, -ta, -tei / -tii* (2nd person), *-său / -so / -su, -sa, -sei, -sii* (3rd person).

The combination of the affixal possessive with the articleless noun results in internal sandhi and other phonological phenomena (Avram 1986; Vasilescu 2008a: 194–5; Niculescu 2008b: 137): *frac-tu, frac-su* (*frate* > *frac*), *naşi-su* (*naş* > *naşi*), *socră-miu* (*socru* > *socră*), *mă-ta* (*mamă* > *mă*).

5.3.3.2.3 Possessive affixation is exclusively postnominal. The definite article is excluded from nominal phrases containing possessive affixes. The [noun + possessive affix] phrase is a definite description (GBLR: 368, 370). Additional evidence for the definiteness of nominal phrases containing possessive affixes comes from the following facts: they cannot take the indefinite article, as in (281); on the other hand, they allow the presence of demonstratives, which are specified as [+definite] (see (283) below):

(281) *o mamă-**sa**
       a mother-his/her.F.SG

Structures with the possessive affix participate in doubling phenomena (Avram and Coene 2008: 380); the possessive affix may be doubled by full (nominal or pronominal) possessive DPs in the genitive case (282a,c):

(282) a. măsă-**sa**$_i$ lui   Ion$_i$
           mother-his.F.SG   LUI.GEN   Ion
       b. *măsa-**sa**   a   lui   Ion
           mother-his.F.SG   AL   LUI.GEN   Ion
       c. tac-**su**$_i$ ei$_i$
           father-her.M.SG   her
       d. *tac-**su**   al   ei
           father-her.M.SG   AL   her

The possessive affix seems to have taken over the syntactic functions of the definite article, since full genitive DPs need not be preceded by the marker AL when they are left-adjacent to the [noun + possessive affix] phrase ((282a,c) vs. (282b,d) above). Also, postnominal demonstratives can occur when they are strictly adjacent to the possessive affix; recall that postnominal demonstratives need to be strictly adjacent to the definite article (§5.3.1.2.3):

(283) a. frac-**su**   ăsta   mic
           brother-his/her.M.SG   this(M.SG)   little
       b. sor-**sa**$_i$ asta   a ei$_i$
           sister-her.F.SG   this(F.SG)   AL her

5.3 The structure of the nominal phrase

In opposition to full possessive adjectives (284a) and adnominal clitics (284b), possessive affixes cannot take two coordinated nominals in their scope (284c):

(284) a. [părinţii şi fraţii]   **mei**
       parents.DEF and brothers.DEF my.M.PL

   b. propriile-**mi**   [priceperi şi îndoieli]
      own.DEF=CL.1SG skills   and doubts

   c. *[mamă şi soră]-**mea**
       mother and sister-my.F.SG

Finally, in opposition to adnominal clitics, possessive adjectives, and nominal phrases in the genitive case, which may fill thematic positions other than that of the Possessor, the possessive affix is specialized for the Possessor role, being an argument of the kinship / social relation noun (§5.3.4.3).

5.3.3.3 The adnominal possessive clitic

Besides full and affixal possessive adjectives, Romanian also has the possibility of marking nominal phrase internal possession by means of genuine adnominal clitics.

H Agreement has not been reached with respect to the case value of the adnominal possessive clitic. Two main solutions have been advanced in the literature:
  (i) on morphological and diachronic grounds, some researchers claim that they are dative clitics (GLR I: 141–4; Avram 2001: 161; Vasilescu 2008a: 202);
  (ii) on distributional and thematic grounds, others claim that adnominal clitics are distinct from dative indirect object clitics, being genitive clitics (Manoliu 1967; Grosu 1988; Cornilescu 1995; Avram 2000; Avram and Coene 2002, 2008).

The adnominal clitic is obsolete in contemporary Romanian; it is used for stylistic and rhetorical purposes, mainly in poetic texts. The adnominal clitic was present from the earliest Romanian written texts (Densusianu 1961, II: 120–1; Rosetti 1986: 543); it was at its most productive in the literary language of the 19th century (Niculescu 2008a: 78).

C Adnominal possessive clitics are also found in Aromanian (Capidan 2005: 536), and more rarely in Italian (Serianni 1997: 117) and other Romance languages. In Romance, the adnominal clitic pattern obligatorily presupposes the existence of a verb (Niculescu 2008a: 78; Serianni 1997: 117).
  The existence of adnominal possessive clitics is considered a Balkan Sprachbund phenomenon (Sandfeld 1930: 188; Niculescu 1965: 36–7; Mišeska Tomić 2006: 6–7) but the Balkan languages do not behave uniformly with respect to this phenomenon (Pancheva 2004: 176). As in Romanian, in Bulgarian and Macedonian adnominal clitics display second position behaviour.
  Balkan adnominal clitics externalize (Pancheva 2004: 180; but cf. Tasmowski and Pană Dindelegan 2009), adjoining to the clausal domain, in which situation they lose their second position behaviour and display indirect object properties (Avram and Coene 2008: 364).

H The adnominal clitic is considered an internal creation of Romanian, dating back to the period of the emergence of the language (Rizescu 1959; Dimitrescu 1978: 251; Ivănescu 2000: 230).

5.3.3.3.1 Adnominal possessive clitics have a very constrained distribution (Pană Dindelegan 2003: 90) and display second-position (Wackernagel) clitic behaviour (cf. Avram and Coene 2008: 363–4); more exactly, the clitic is always postnominal and strictly adjoins to the D(eterminer) position, being a second-position clitic of the D position. The base onto which they cliticize must be in the nominative or accusative case (Niculescu 2008b: 134). If the nominal phrase contains a definite article, the clitic right-adjoins the definite article (285):

(285)   cartea-i
        book.DEF=CL.3SG
        'his / her book'

If the head noun is preceded by a prenominal adjective, which takes over the article, the clitic adjoins to the article:

(286)   frumoasa-i   carte
        beautiful.DEF=CL.3SG   book
        'his / her beautiful book'

However, when the prenominal adjective is preceded by degree words, the clitic maintains its adjunct-to-the article position (287a), and does not raise to the second position of the nominal phrase (287b):

(287)   a. atât de / foarte   frumoasa-i   casă
           so   very   beautiful.DEF=CL.3SG   house
        b. *atât-i de   frumoasa   casă
           so=CL.3SG   beautiful.DEF   house
           *foarte-i   frumoasa   casă
           very=CL.3SG   beautiful.DEF   house

More rarely, when the head noun is articleless, the clitic directly adjoins to the bare noun:

(288)   din   parte-mi
        from   part=CL.1SG
        'on my behalf'

To sum up, the adnominal clitic displays second position effects; it is not, however, a nominal phrase second position clitic (as in other Balkan languages, cf. Pancheva 2004: 178), but a second position clitic of the element which occupies the D(eterminer) position of the nominal phrase.

H   The nominative–accusative condition on the host of the adnominal clitic was not obligatory in old Romanian. There are various instances in which there is cliticization onto genitive or dative hosts (Densusianu 1961, II: 120):

(289)   rudeloru-ți   (Coresi)
        relatives.GEN≡DAT=CL.2SG
        'to / of your relatives'

Additionally, as shown in (290a) and (290b), the adnominal clitic may adjoin to 'definite' prepositions (prepositions etymologically containing the definite article), which typically select genitive phrases (cf. (290c)):

(290)   a. deasupra-mi
           above=CL.1SG

b. în juru-**i**
   around=CL.3SG

c. deasupra / în jurul **casei** /   **lui**
   above   around house.DEF.GEN his(GEN)

Also, there is a definiteness requirement on nominal phrases (Avram and Coene 2008: 364) containing adnominal clitics: adnominal clitics cannot occur in indefinite phrases.

The adnominal clitic also occurs in double definite structures with postnominal demonstratives:

(291) ochii-**i**   aceştia frumoşi
     eyes.DEF=CL.3SG these   beautiful

5.3.3.3.2 Compared to dative and accusative verbal clitics, adnominal clitics currently have a reduced inventory, with forms only for singular (persons 1 to 3), non-reflexive. Adnominal clitics do not encode the gender of their referent. From a typological perspective, in Cardinaletti and Starke's (1995) classification (*strong pronouns / weak pronouns / clitic pronouns*), Romanian adnominal clitics always appear as clitic pronouns, never as weak forms (Avram 2000).

Adnominal possessive clitics are syncretic with dative clausal personal clitics (but not with dative weak or strong pronouns). Their inventory is as follows:

(292) a. casa-**mi**   1st person
        house.DEF=CL.1SG

     b. mâna-**ţi**   2nd person
        hand.DEF=CL.2SG

     c. cartea-**i**   3rd person
        book.DEF=CL.3SG

Reflexive clitics do not occur in this position.

H   Modern Romanian differs from old Romanian in two important respects. First, old Romanian possessed a full inventory (persons 1 singular to 3 plural) of adnominal clitics (Densusianu 1961, II: 120), which could cliticize onto definite or bare nominal roots (the combinations in (293) are no longer available). Second, in old Romanian, the reflexive clitic also occurred in this position (294).

    (293) a. casa-**ne**   (Coresi)   1st person plural
              house.DEF=CL.1PL

         b. părinţi-**vă**   (*Texte măhăcene*)   2nd person plural
            parents=CL.2PL

         c. maşteha-**le**   (Coresi)   3rd person plural
            stepmother=CL.3PL

    (294) bărbatulu-**şi**   (Coresi)   3rd person singular reflexive
         husband.DEF=CL.REFL.3SG

The plural adnominal clitics (293) are very restricted in modern Romanian.

Phonologically, adnominal clitics may be cliticized only on vowel bases; when they adjoin to (nominal and adjectival) bases containing the masculine definite article, the final consonant of the article is obligatory deleted (295a,b); the full vowel -*u*- takes over the function of the definite article:

(295) a. curaj**u**-i   vs.   *curaj**ul**-i
           courage.DEF=CL.3SG   courage.DEF=CL.3SG
       b. frumos**u**-i   băiat   vs.   *frumos**ul**-i   băiat
           beautiful.DEF =CL.3SG boy   beautiful.DEF=CL.3SG   boy

The adnominal possessive clitic cannot be (contrastively) stressed:

(296) *cartea-MI
       book.DEF=CL.1SG

5.3.3.3.3 Morphology aside, one of the most pervasive arguments in favour of considering adnominal clitics as genitives is the fact that they occur in complementary distribution with full (nominal and pronominal) genitives and possessive adjectives (Avram and Coene 2008). Consequently, adnominal clitics do not participate in the possessor doubling phenomena:

(297) a. casa-**i**
           house.DEF=CL.3SG

       b. casa   **lui /**   **ei /**   **sa /**   **băiatului /**   **Mariei**
           house.DEF(F.SG) his(GEN)   her(GEN)   his/her.F.SG   boy.DEF.GEN   Maria.GEN

       c. *casa-**i**   **lui /**   **ei /**   **sa/**   **băiatului / Mariei**
           house.DEF=CL.3SG his(GEN)   her(GEN)   his/her.F.SG   boy.DEF.GEN Maria.GEN

H Old Romanian occasionally allowed the doubling of the adnominal clitic by a genitival phrase / possessive adjective:

(298) a. au   prinsu   pe   Heizăr   ghenărarul   la   mâna-i$_i$ [lui
           have   caught   PE   Heiser   general.DEF   at   hand.DEF=CL.3SG   LUI.GEN
           Tupil-grof]$_i$ (Neculce)
           Tupil-count
           'they caught general Heiser at Count Tulip's hand'
       b. înfrumusețarea   sufletului-ş$_i$ său$_i$ (Coresi)
           adornment.DEF   soul.DEF.GEN(NEUT)=CL.REFL.3SG   his / her.M.SG
           'the adornment of his / her own soul'

One other genitive distributional characteristic is adjacency to the definite article ((285)–(286)). Furthermore, adnominal clitics may be selected by genitive-selecting prepositions (299a–b), a position from which datives are excluded (299c):

(299) a. contra-**i**
           against=CL.3SG

       b. contra   **lui /**   **băiatului**
           against   his(GEN) /   boy.DEF.GEN

       c. *contra   **mie**
           against   me(DAT)

5.3 The structure of the nominal phrase

When cliticized onto a prenominal adjective, the adnominal clitic may take scope over more than one noun:

(300)   admirabilele-**i**   [intenţii   şi   dorinţe]
        admirable.DEF=CL.3SG   purposes   and   wishes

In opposition to the possessive affix, which is exclusively specialized for the Possessor thematic role, the adnominal clitic may fill other thematic roles when it adjoins nominal phrases whose heads are argument-structure nouns:

(301)   a. sora-**mi**   (POSSESSOR)
           sister.DEF=CL.1SG

        b. cererea-**ţi**   (AGENT)
           asking.DEF=CL.2SG

        c. suferinţa-**i**   (EXPERIENCER)
           suffering.DEF=CL.3SG

H   The adnominal clitic occupied non-Possessor thematic positions in old Romanian as well (Densusianu 1961, II: 120; Tasmowski and Pană Dindelegan 2009: 339–40):

(302)   i-au   trimis [...]   întru   întâmpinare-**i**   (Neculce)
        CL.DAT.3SG=have.3PL   sent   to   welcoming=CL.3SG
        'they sent them to welcome him'

5.3.3.4 The possessive relation marked by the preposition DE

In order to introduce a special type of possessive relation (a 'belonging' relation), Romanian uses the preposition DE 'of'.

(303)   a. mână   **de**   copil
           hand   DE   child
           'child's hand'

        b. mijloc   **de**   codru
           middle   DE   forest
           'middle of forest'

The Romance preposition DE did not disappear in Romanian; rather, it is found in limited and highly specialized constructions which have been analysed as *kind* or *property*-denoting genitives (Cornilescu 2006; Pană Dindelegan 2008h; Cornilescu and Nicolae 2009). From the more general, typological perspective put forth by Koptjevskaja-Tamm (2002, 2005), which distinguishes *anchoring* (referential) and *non-anchoring* (kind and property) genitives, Romanian DE-structures may be considered *non-anchoring* genitives.

C   The DE-structures of modern Romanian differ from the prepositional DE-genitive of Romance languages. The old Romanian DE-structures, discussed in §5.1.3.2.2 (see example (34)), illustrate the Romance pattern.

Prepositional DE-structures have the following characteristics:

(i) DE selects a bare noun phrase (a singular noun) (304a) or a number phrase (a plural noun) (304b) (GBLR: 60):

(304) a. fată **de** [negustor(SG)]   [property denoting]
         girl DE merchant
     b. fată **de** [negustori(PL)]   [kind denoting]
         girl DE merchants

(ii) The nominal complement of DE is incompatible with determiners or quantifiers:

(305) a. *fată **de** acest negustor
         girl   DE this merchant
     b. *fată **de** doi negustori
         girl   DE two merchants

(iii) The DE-phrase may occur after the copula:

(306) **Fata**   este **de negustori**
      girl.DEF   is   DE merchants

Although the complement of DE does not denote an entity (it denotes a kind or a property), the possessive meaning is obtained presuppositionally (Niculescu 2008a: 87): in *fată de negustor / negustori* ('girl *of* merchant / merchants') the existence of the possessor is presupposed and implicit, namely, there must be 'a merchant / some merchants' such that there exists 'a girl of a merchant / merchants'.

H In old Romanian, the inflectional genitive and the DE-phrases (§5.1.3.2.2) were not specialized as they are in modern Romanian, where the inflectional genitive has an entity-type, referential denotation while the complement of DE denotes kinds or properties (Pană Dindelegan 2008h; Cornilescu and Nicolae 2009).

Other quasi-similar nominal patterns containing prepositional DE and proper names have been included in this class of structures (Niculescu 2008a: 89):

(307) a. Iancu **de** Hunedoara
         Iancu of Hunedoara
     b. vin **de** Odobeşti
         wine of Odobeşti

The relation marked by DE in (307) above is more likely to be analysed as locative rather than possessive.

5.3.3.5 Possessor deletion by the definite article

The Romanian definite article has an advanced degree of deicticity, which favours possessor deletion and allows for its identification contextually (Şerbănescu 2000: 137). Consequently, kinships nouns and nouns expressing inalienable possession relations (e.g. nouns denoting body-parts) may be used in Romanian only with the definite article:

(308) a. tat**a**
         father.DEF
         'my father'
     b. închide ochi**i**   şi deschide gur**a**
         close   eyes.DEF and open   mouth.DEF
         'Close your eyes and open your mouth'

5.3 The structure of the nominal phrase 349

With kinship and social relation nouns, the possessive definite article occurs after the preposition (309a), although the noun is not followed by modifiers; compare this with (309b), where the article disappears after the preposition:

(309) a. mă   gândesc la tat**a** / vecin**ul**
   CL.REFL.ACC think of father.DEF neighbour.DEF

  b. mă   gândesc la copil / doctor
   CL.REFL.ACC think of child doctor

5.3.4 The arguments of the noun

The following types of nouns take arguments: deverbal and deadjectival nouns, picture nouns and relational nouns. Deverbal nouns, deadjectival nouns and picture nouns resemble each other from the point of view of argument realization. Relational nouns have a different argument structure.

5.3.4.1 The arguments of deverbal and deadjectival nouns

Deverbal and deadjectival nouns (for their description, see §5.2.6) can take the following types of arguments:

(i) a genitive DP which corresponds to the direct object (310a,b) or to the subject (311a,b):

(310) a. spălatul **rufelor**
   washing.DEF clothes.DEF.GEN
   'the washing of clothes'

  b. inițiatorul **proiectului**
   initiator.DEF project.DEF.GEN
   'the initiator of the project'

(311) a. sosirea **Mariei**
   arrival.DEF Maria.GEN
   'Maria's arrival'

  b. atenția **ei**
   attention.DEF her(GEN)
   'her attention'

(ii) a possessive adjective (312a,b) or an adnominal possessive clitic, in obsolete constructions (313a,b):

(312) a. venirea   **sa**
   coming.DEF(F.SG.NOM) his/her.F.SG.NOM
   'his/her coming'

  b. tristețea   **sa**
   sadness.DEF(F.SG.NOM) his/her.F.SG.NOM
   'his/her sadness'

(313) a. plecarea-ți
       leaving.DEF=CL.2SG
       'your leaving'
    b. tristețea-i
       sadness=CL.3SG
       'his/her sadness'

(iii) a headless relative clause:

(314) a. plecarea   cui   mi-e   drag
       leaving.DEF   who.GEN   CL.DAT.1SG=is   dear
       'the departure of one who is dear to me'
    b. curiozitatea cui   ne-a   chemat
       curiosity.DEF who.GEN   CL.ACC.1PL=has   called
       'the curiosity of one who called us'

(iv) a dative DP, licensed by an argument that corresponds to a direct object, realized as a PP (315a) or as a genitive DP (315b):

(315) a. acordarea   *de burse*   **studenților**
       granting.DEF   of scholarships students.DEF.DAT
       'the granting of scholarships to students'
    b. predarea   *limbii*   *române*   **străinilor**
       teaching.DEF   language.DEF.GEN   Romanian.GEN   foreigners.DAT
       'the teaching of Romanian to foreigners'

(v) a PP which:

- corresponds to a prepositional object:

(316) a. dependența   **de medicamente** < depinde   **de medicamente**
       dependence.DEF   on drugs   ((s)he)depends   on drugs
       'the dependence on drugs'
    b. atenția   **la detalii** <   atent   **la detalii**
       attention.DEF   to details   attentive to   details
       'the attention to details'

- originates in a VP whose argument is a kind-denoting bare noun (317a–b) or an infinitive (317c); the PP is introduced by the preposition *de*:

(317) a. citirea   **de romane** <   citește   **romane**
       reading.DEF   of novels   reads   novels
       'the reading of novels'
    b. vânzătorul   **de suveniruri** < vinde   **suveniruri**
       seller.DEF   of souvenirs   sells   souvenirs
       'the souvenir seller'
    c. plăcerea   **de a   citi** <   îi   place   **a   citi**
       pleasure.DEF   DE   A_INF   read.INF   CL.DAT.3SG   likes   A_INF   read.INF
       'the pleasure of reading'

- a PP whose governor is a deverbal noun that originates in an inherently reciprocal verb; it is introduced by the preposition *între* ('between, among'), preserved from the VP (318a), or by *dintre* ('between, among'), which does not occur in the VP, but it is selected by deverbal nouns (318b) (see Pană Dindelegan 1999: 117; Stan 2003: 145):

(318) a. alianța **între** **ei** < se aliază **între** **ei**
 alliance.DEF between them CL.REFL.ACC (they)ally between them
 'the alliance between them'

 b. asemănarea **dintre** **ei** vs. *seamănă **dintre** **ei**
 resemblance.DEF between them (they)resemble between them
 'the resemblance between them'

(vi) an indirect interrogative clause:

(319) a. întrebarea **când vom** **ajunge**
 question.DEF when AUX.FUT.1PL arrive.INF
 'the question when we arrive'

 b. curiozitatea **unde au** **mers**
 curiosity.DEF where (they)have gone
 'the curiosity about where they went'

(vii) a CP introduced by a complementizer:

(320) a. dorința **să** **pleci**
 desire.DEF SĂ_SUBJ (you)leave
 'your desire to leave'

 b. întrebarea **dacă** **plecăm**
 question.DEF whether (we)leave
 'the question whether we are leaving'

 c. siguranța **că** **reușește**
 surety.DEF that succeeds
 'the surety that (s)he succeeds'

H In the old language, there are rare instances of deverbal (long infinitive) nouns which take an accusative complement, corresponding to the direct object in the VP (Stan 2003: 126–32):

(321) a. ascultarea **pre** **Hristos** (*Noul Testament*)
 obey.INF.DEF PE Christ
 'obeying Christ'

 b. împărțirea **cei** **buni** din cei răi (Varlaam)
 divide.INF.DEF CEL.PL.ACC good(PL.ACC) from CEL.PL.ACC mean(PL.ACC)
 'the separation of the good from the bad'

Also, in the old texts, there are rare instances of a bare deverbal noun (a long infinitive) taking a dative complement:

(322) iertare **păcatelor** noastre să luăm (Varlaam)
 forgive.INF sins.DEF.DAT≡GEN our(DAT) SĂ_SUBJ take.SUBJ
 'to be forgiven for our sins'

Since it is uncertain whether the head noun bears the article (in the old texts, the article was not consistently written down), the interpretation as a dative or as a genitive of the noun in boldface in (322) is ambiguous (Stan 2003: 119–21).

U There is a tendency to replace the dative argument (323b) by a directional PP (323a) when the arguments of the head are realized by genitive and dative DPs, as an effect of the genitive–dative syncretism:

(323) a. acordarea **premiilor** **la** **copii**
granting.DEF prizes.DEF.GEN to children(ACC)
b. acordarea **premiilor** **copiilor**
granting.DEF prizes.DEF.GEN children.DAT
'the granting of prizes to children'

The realization of arguments is compulsory in the VP, but it is optional in the corresponding nominalization (Pană Dindelegan 1999: 118):

(324) a. Juriul selectează **concurenții**
committee.DEF selects competitors.DEF
'The committee selects the competitors'
> Selecția **(concurenților)** este riguroasă
selection.DEF (competitors.DEF.GEN) is rigorous
'The selection (of the competitors) is rigorous'
b. Autoritățile reabilitează **imobilele**
authorities.DEF rehabilitate buildings.DEF
'The authorities are rehabilitating the buildings'
> Reabilitarea **(imobilelor)** este gratuită
rehabilitation.DEF (buildings.DEF.GEN) is free
'The rehabilitation (of the buildings) is free'

In the case of deverbal nouns, the realization or non-realization of the arguments correlates with the *event–result* distinction (Grimshaw 1990); for other criteria of distinguishing these two readings, see §5.2.6. Thus, only event-denoting deverbal nouns ((325), unlike (326)) obligatorily lexicalize their internal argument and / or *by*-phrase:

(325) Redactarea **textului** **de către elevi** este îngrijită [event reading]
editing.DEF text.DEF.GEN by students is careful
'The editing of the text by the students is careful'

(326) *Redactarea **de către elevi** din caiet este îngrijită [result reading]
editing.DEF by students from notebook is careful

5.3.4.2 The arguments of picture nouns

The arguments of picture nouns, such as *fotografie* 'photo', *imagine* 'image', *tablou* 'painting', share certain features with the arguments of deverbal and deadjectival nouns.

Some actualizations of the arguments of picture nouns are the same as those of deverbal and deadjectival nouns (see §5.3.4.1):

(i) a genitive DP corresponding to a direct object (327a) or to a subject (327b):

(327) a. fotografia **lui** **Ion** ('L-am fotografiat **pe Ion**')
photo.DEF LUI.GEN Ion CL.ACC.M.3SG=(I)have photographed PE Ion
'the photo of Ion'

b. fotografia **lui** **Ion** ('Ion a făcut fotografia')
photo.DEF LUI.GEN Ion Ion has taken photo.DEF
'the photo by Ion'

(ii) a possessive adjective:

(328) fotografia **sa**
photo.DEF(F.SG) his/her.F.SG
'photo of/by him/her'

(iii) a headless relative clause:

(329) fotografia **cui** **mi-e** **drag**
photo.DEF who.GEN CL.DAT.1SG=is dear
'the photo of / by one who is dear to me'

(iv) a PP headed by *de* 'by':

(330) o fotografie **de** **Ion**
a photo by Ion
'a photo by Ion'

Picture nouns do not always actualize the argument structure. They may have a common noun reading, expressing possessed objects and taking a non-selected Possessor (§5.3.3.1.2):

(331) fotografia **lui** **Ion**
photo.DEF LUI.GEN Ion
'the photo that Ion has'

C In Romanian, as in the case of the English and Dutch prenominal genitive (see Alexiadou, Haegeman, and Stavrou 2007: 586), the genitive complement to picture nouns may be interpreted as an Agent, a Theme, or a Possessor when it is the sole complement to the noun; however, two genitive complements are unambiguously interpreted as a Theme (the first complement) and as a Possessor or an Agent (the second complement):

(332) [portretul [**Mariei**]$_{\text{THEME}}$ **al** **lui** **Ion**]$_{\text{POSSESSOR//AGENT}}$
portrait Maria.GEN AL LUI.GEN Ion
'Ion's portrait of Maria' / 'the portrait of Maria by Ion'

In Romanian, there exists a rare structure which is also found in French, with all three thematic roles hierarchically ordered (Theme > Agent > Possessor):

(333) a. Rom. Portretul **lui** **Aristotel** **de** **Rembrandt** **al** **lui** **Petre**
portrait.DEF LUI.GEN Aristotle by Rembrandt AL LUI.GEN Petre
'the portrait of Aristotle by Rembrandt owned by Petre'

b. Fr. le portrait d'Aristote de Rembrandt de Pierre (in Alexiadou, Haegeman, and Stavrou 2007: 583)

5.3.4.3 The arguments of relational nouns

Relational nous are defined in connection to a correlative term, as part of an obligatory relation: kinship (*tată* 'father', *văr* 'cousin'), social (*prieten* 'friend', *vecin* 'neighbour', *șef* 'chief'), part—whole (*parte* 'part', *fragment* 'fragment', *mână* 'hand', *acoperiș* 'roof').

The arguments of relational nouns can be expressed as:

(i) a genitive DP:

(334) El   este fratele   **Mariei**
       he   is   brother.DEF Maria.GEN
       'He is Maria's brother'

(ii) a possessive adjective (335a–b) or, in the non-standard language and only for kinship nouns, a possessive affix (336) (for the analysis of the possessive in both cases, see §5.3.3.1, 5.3.3.2):

(335) a. Prietenul   **meu**   citeşte mult
         friend.DEF(M.SG)   my.M.SG   reads   a-lot
         'My (boy)friend reads a lot'

      b. Mâna   **sa**   este fină
         hand.DEF(F.SG)   his/her.F.SG   is   soft
         'His hand is soft'

(336) Soră-**sa**   e   mică
       sister-his/her   is   little
       'His / her sister is little'

C Like French, but unlike English, in Romanian, the genitival or possessive argument of a part-denoting noun that co-occurs with a possessive nominative is obligatorily omitted (Dobrovie-Sorin 2001: 220):

(337) a. Ion a   ridicat **mâna**   vs. *Ion_i a   ridicat **mâna lui**_i   (Romanian)
         Ion has   raised hand.DEF   Ion   has   raised hand his
         'John raised his hand'
      b. J'ai levé **la main**   (French)
      c. I raised **my hand**   vs. *I raised **the hand**   (English)

(iii) a PP headed by the preposition *cu* ('with'); this pattern is available when the relational noun in a predicative position denotes a referent of the same order with the referent indicated by the argument (Giurgea 2006: 46):

(338) a. Ion este văr   **cu**   Gheorghe
         Ion is   cousin   with   Gheorghe
         'John and Gheorghe are cousins'

      b. Reporterul   vorbeşte cu   câţiva   angajaţi,   colegi   **cu**
         reporter.DEF   talks   with   a few   employees   colleagues with
         persoana   dispărută
         person.DEF   missing
         'The reporter is talking to a few employees, colleagues of the missing person'

      c. *Ion este şef   **cu**   Gheorghe
          Ion is   chief   with   Gheorghe

(iv) in the non-standard language, a phrase in the dative; this construction is obsolete:

(339) Ion este frate   **lui**   Gheorghe
       Ion is   brother LUI.DAT   Gheorghe
       'Ion is Gheorghe's brother'

The non-realization of the argument of relational nouns (Nedelcu 2010: 122–3) is possible if the relational noun:

(i) denotes an unique referent:

(340)   Mergem   la   **tata**
        (we)go   at   father.DEF
        'We are going to father'

(ii) takes an identifying modifier:

(341)   A   venit   **vecinul**   **cel rău**
        has   come   neighbour.DEF   CEL mean
        'The mean neighbour came'

(iii) establishes an anaphoric (inalienable possession) connection with a coreferential term:

(342)   **Maşina**   intrase   în   şanţ,   pentru că   **roata**   sărise
        car.DEF   enter.PLUPERF   in   ditch   because   wheel.DEF   jump.PLUPERF.3SG
        'The car had entered the ditch because the wheel had come off'

(iv) has a kind / property reading:

(343)   Ion   a   devenit   **tată**
        Ion   has   become   father
        'Ion became a father'

(v) has an arbitrary reference:

(344)   Profesorul   vrea   să   participe   şi   un   **tată**   la   discuţii
        professor.DEF   wants   să_SUBJ   participate   also   a   father   in   discussions
        'The professor wants a father to participate in the discussions as well'

(vi) occurs in a generic sentence:

(345)   **Fratele**   e   tot   frate
        brother.DEF   is   still   brother
        'A brother is still a brother'

5.3.5 Restrictive and non-restrictive modifiers

5.3.5.1 Restrictive modifiers

Restrictive modifiers, which restrict the potential reference of the noun phrase in which they are included and identify the referent (according to a widely accepted definition which stems from Bolinger 1967), are realized as APs, PPs, DPs, and clauses.

Romanian is characterized by the postnominal positioning of restrictive modifiers. In this respect, certain genitive phrases (which are focused and placed to the left of the head-noun (see example (355c) below)) and prenominal eventive passive participles (which do not have a complete clausal structure (see (356b) below) are exceptional.

5.3.5.1.1 The typical restrictive modifiers are APs.

(i) Non-descriptive adjectives, kind phrases, or kind-level modifiers (Truswell 2004: 141; Cornilescu and Nicolae 2011c, and references therein), classifying adjectives, which are reference- (not referent-)modifying and set up a denotational unit with the head noun, are usually 'contrastive':

(346) a. ardei   gras /   iute
           pepper fat   spicy
           'pepper'

        b. făină   albă /   integrală
           flour   white   integral
           'whole / white flour'

C   The postposition of classifying adjectives is a Romance characteristic of Romanian (see also §5.3.5.2.1). Focusing and placement to the left of the head for these adjectives is not allowed in contemporary Romanian.

In the case of participles, the loss of theta-role assignment and the formation, alongside the noun, of a denotational unit are indications of the participles' recategorization as adjectives; compare: adjectival (347a) vs. verbal participle (347b):

(347) a. lapte   bătut
           milk   beaten
           'buttermilk'

        b. câinele   bătut   (de   dresor)
           dog.DEF   beaten   by   trainer
           'the dog beaten by the trainer' [Passive Agent]

(ii) The pronominal adjective *însuşi* 'oneself' (§6.4) is used in contemporary Romanian as an external restrictive modifier; it is an intensifier of the definite article (in Bolinger's (1967: 19) terms), a focal constituent of the DP, which occurs either before or after the (obligatorily) definite noun:

(348) a. însuşi   profesorul
           himself   professor.DEF

        b. profesorul   însuşi
           professor.DEF himself
           'the professor himself'

Only the 3rd person singular and plural forms (348) are used in structures with nouns. The 1st and 2nd person forms are used in pronominal DPs:

(349)   eu   însămi
           I   myself

5.3.5.1.2 The PPs that make up a denotational unit with the nouns (being analogous to kind-level AP modifiers (346)) are introduced by the preposition *de*; the complement of *de* is an NP (350a) or a supine clause (350b):

(350) a. coleg   **de**   **şcoală**
           colleague of   school
           'a schoolmate'

    b. maşină **de tuns gazonul**
       machine DE_SUP mow.SUP lawn.DEF
       'a lawnmower'

C According to some linguists (e.g. Bourciez 1956: 250, 588), the NP-internal supine construction continues a primitive Romance pattern, specific to eastern Romance, which developed out of a destination / purpose meaning:

(351) Rom. câine **de vânat**   <   *CANIS DE VENATU
            dog   DE_SUP   hunt.SUP
            'hunting dog'   'hunting dog > dog for hunting'

Other prepositional modifiers are more varied from a formal point of view, both with respect to the inventory of prepositions employed and to the categorial status of the complement of the preposition—e.g. NP (352a), DP (352b), AdvP (352c):

(352) a. fata **cu ochi albaştri**
        girl.DEF with eyes blue
        'the blue-eyed girl'

      b. cadoul **de la tine**
        gift.DEF from you
        'the gift from you'

      c. ziua **de ieri** / fereastra **de sus**
        day.DEF of yesterday window.DEF of up
        'yesterday / the day before' 'the top window'

The PP headed by the preposition *de* may include an infinitival clause. Modifiers of this type are always dependent on abstract nominals:

(353) ideea **de a încerca ceva nou**
       idea.DEF DE A_INF try.INF something new
       'the idea of trying something new'

H In old Romanian, the infinitival restrictive modifier also occurs with the 'long' *-re* form (§4.2.1.1). The preposition *de* is occasionally missing before the infinitive (with or without *-re*):

(354) a. puterea **a stare**   (Costin)
        power A_INF stay.INF
        'the power to stay'

      b. au darul **a vesti**   (*Noul Testament*)
        (they)have gift A_INF announce.INF
        'they have the gift of bringing news'

The infinitive's distribution was wider in the old language: the *de*-structures also expressed 'destination / purpose', being selected by nouns with a concrete referent as well (in a later stage of Romanian, the *de*-supine got specialized for the 'destination / purpose meaning'; see example (351) above and §4.2.3.1.2).

C The prepositional *de*-structure is an original Romance pattern (Bourciez 1956: 249). The *de a* structure is specific to Romanian (§4.2.1.3).

PPs may embed a relative clause (§5.3.5.1.4).

5.3.5.1.3 Genitive (DP) phrases and *de*-phrases equivalent to a genitive (§5.1.3.2.1–2) modify aspectual (355a) or spatial positioning (355b–c) nouns:

(355) a. miezul   **nopții /**   miez   **de**   **noapte**
         middle.DEF   night.DEF.GEN   middle   of   night
         'the middle of the night / midnight'

   b. începutul   **drumului /**   început   **de**   **drum**
      beginning.DEF way.GEN.DEF   beginning   of   road
      '(the) beginning of the way'

   c. **al**   **vieții**   început
      AL   life.DEF.GEN   beginning
      'the beginning of life'

5.3.5.1.4 (i) Non-finite clauses in modifier position are participial (356a–b) or gerundial (356c); for the infinitive and supine modifiers, which are obligatorily introduced by prepositions, see §5.3.5.1.2 (examples (351), (353)). Romanian eventive passive participles display the properties determined by Sleeman (2008) for other languages: they are interpretable as reduced relative clauses; postnominal eventive participles may be replaced by a full relative clause, have a complete clausal structure, and license at least a direct internal argument, which is raised as an antecedent (*filmul* in (356a)); prenominal eventive participles do not have a full clausal structure (356b). Modification of prenominal participles by adverbials of the *recent*-type indicates their eventive reading:

(356) a. filmul   (care   a   fost)   **premiat**   **recent**   **de**   **juriu**
         film.DEF   which   has   been   awarded   recently   by   jury
         'the film (that was) recently awarded by the jury'

   b. **recent**   **premiatul**   (***de**   **juriu**)   film
      recently   awarded.DEF   by   jury   film
      'the recently awarded (*by the jury) film'

   c. lista   **cuprinzând**   **semnăturile**
      list.DEF   contain.GER   signatures.DEF
      'the list containing the signatures'

(ii) Finite clauses in modifier position require a complementizer or a relative (*wh-*) marker.

The clausal modifiers introduced by complementizers (*că, să, ca... să, cum că, dacă*; §10.1.1), as well as the infinitival clauses (353–354) are always dependent on abstract nouns:

(357) a. faptul   **că**   **încerci**
         fact.DEF that   (you)try
         'the fact that you try / are trying'

   b. problema   **dacă**   **merită**   **să**   **încerci**
      problem.def whether   worth.3SG   SĂ_SUBJ   try.SUBJ.2SG
      'the problem of whether it is worth trying'

Wh-clausal modifiers are introduced by *wh*-pronouns (*care, ce, de* 'who, which') and by *wh*-adverbs (*când, cum, unde* 'when, how, where') (§10.3.5). The antecedent of *wh*-pronouns is the head of the noun phrase (§10.3.1.1). The pronoun *care* displays the gender and the number of the antecedent, while its case or preposition correspond to the base generation position, being required by the relativized category: dative, corresponding to a relativized indirect object (358a); accusative, corresponding to a relativized complement of a preposition (358b), etc. *Wh*-adverbs are semantically equivalent to *wh*-pronouns in headed relative clauses (358b). In nominalized structures, question nouns take only free relative clauses, which are headed by any *wh*-interrogative pronoun (*cine* 'who', *ce* 'what', *care* 'which', *cât* 'how much / many', *al câtelea* 'which one') (358c–d), adjectival *wh*-interrogatives *(ce, care, cât, al câtelea)* (358e) or adverbial *wh*-interrogatives (*când* 'when', *cât* 'how much', *cum* 'how', *încotro, unde* 'where') (358f); the interrogative pronouns display the case or preposition corresponding to the base-generation position: the subject in the nominative case (358c); the complement of the preposition in the genitive case (358d):

(358) a. băiatul **căruia mă adresez**
       boy.DEF who.DAT CL.REFL.ACC.1SG speak
       'the boy to whom I'm speaking'

   b. ziua **când / în care** a **venit**
      day.DEF when in which has come
      'the day when / in which (s)he came'

   c. întrebarea **cine vine**
      question who comes
      'the question who comes / is coming'

   d. întrebarea **împotriva cui lupți**
      question.DEF against who.GEN (you)fight
      'the question who you are fighting against'

   e. întrebarea **din ce țară ești**
      question.DEF from which country (you)are
      'the question what country you are from'

   f. întrebarea **cum te numești**
      question.DEF how CL.REFL.ACC.2SG (you)name
      'the question what your name is'

C Romanian is distinguished by the evolution of the Latin pronoun QUALIS > *care* (Bourciez 1956: 598). In old Romanian, the pronoun *care* incorporated the definite article, both in relative and in interrogative structures. The forms with enclitic article, which displayed gender and number variation (masculine singular *carele*, plural *carii*; feminine singular *carea*, plural *carele*), competed with the form *care*; the definite forms were more widely used in the northern area, but were jettisoned after the 18th century (Frâncu 1997: 129, 331). Romanian contrasts with languages like French and Italian, where the pronoun that incorporates the definite article is always a relative pronoun. In contemporary Romanian, *care* has lost the article and consequently no longer has nominative–accusative inflection. It is used in the same conditions as the descendants of QUI in Western Romance; thus, Romanian does not possess the relative pronominal doublet QUI / (ILLE) QUALIS: Fr. *qui / lequel*, It. *chi / (il) quale*, Sp. *que / (el) qual* (Niculescu 1965: 38; Posner 1996: 306).

H The pronoun *ce*, etymologically characterized by [–human] reference, has extended to [+human] referents:

(359) omul **ce** vine
      man that comes
      'the man that is coming'

In structures where a prenominal genitive is relativized (§10.3.5.1, §10.3.6) (i.e. an AL genitive), AL displays gender and number agreement with its governing phrase, and the pronoun *care* with its referential antecedent (360a,c); the genitive may occur in a postnominal position only in a DP selected by a preposition (360b):

(360) a. băiatul   cu   a   cărui   soră   am   vorbit
         boy.DEF(M)   with   AL.F.SG   who.M.SG.GEN   sister(F)   (I)have   spoken

   b. băiatul   cu   sora   căruia   am   vorbit
      boy.DEF(M)   with   sister.DEF(F) whose.M.SG.GEN   (I)have   spoken
      'the boy whose sister I spoke to'

   c. băiatul   a   cărui   soră   mă   cunoaşte
      boy.DEF(M)   AL.F.SG   who.M.SG.GEN   sister(F)   CL.ACC.1SG   knows
      'the boy whose sister knows me'

   d. *băiatul   sora   căruia   mă   cunoaşte
      boy.DEF(M)   sister.DEF(F) whose.M.SG.GEN   CL.ACC.1SG   knows

H   In old Romanian, the genitive forms of the pronoun *care*, which ended in *-a*, occurred both in a prenominal (361) and in a postnominal position; at a later stage, the distribution of these forms became more restrictive, with the forms ending in *-a* in postnominal position (360b) and those without *-a* in prenominal position (360a,c):
   (361) în cărora   mână (Coresi) (genitive without AL) / (CRom) în a căror   mână
         in whose.GEN   hand   in AL whose.GEN hand
         'in whose hand'

5.3.5.2 Non-restrictive modifiers

Non-restrictive modifiers are realized as: APs, PPs, comparative constructions (*ca*-phrases), AdvPs, and clauses.

Romanian is characterized by prevalent postnominal positioning of non-restrictive modifiers. Most modifiers are always placed at the right of their head (PPs, *ca*-phrases, AdvPs, and clauses). Most types of APs are postnominal; the prenominal position is possible only with certain types of adjectives, which contextually actualize a special meaning or which contextually incorporate certain semantic features (§5.3.5.2.1). A special characteristic of Romanian is the very restrictive nature of the preposing of modifiers in unmarked word order.

5.3.5.2.1 The typical non-restrictive modifiers are APs.
The distribution of APs is dependent on the interpretation on the AP, according to the following parameters: argumental or thematic vs. non-argumental; intersective vs. non-intersective; individual-level vs. stage-level; modal-reading or quantificational-reading vs. implicit relative reading; stylistically marked vs. unmarked; with respect to the closeness to the N head: direct vs. indirect modification, NP-modification / DP-modification, internal vs. external modification, etc. (see, among others, Giorgi 2001: 318–19; Laenzlinger 2005; Haumann 2010: 63–73, and references therein).

   (i) Argumental APs or thematic adjectives, which fill semantic roles licensed by a head, are either Possessor thematic adjectives (362a), or correspond to arguments in nominalized structures: Agent adjectives (362b), Theme adjectives (362c), etc. (for the interpretation of thematic adjectives as arguments of deverbal nouns, see Marchis 2010; §5.3.3, §5.3.4):

(362) a. casa **părintească** [= casa **părinților**]
　　　　house.DEF parental　　house.DEF parents.DEF.GEN
　　　　'the parental house (= the parents' house)'

　　　b. asuprirea **otomană** [= asuprirea **otomanilor**]
　　　　oppression Ottoman(ADJ)　oppression.DEF Ottomans.DEF.GEN
　　　　'the Ottoman oppression (= the Ottomans' oppression)'

　　　c. pierderile **omenești** [= pierderile **de oameni**]
　　　　losses.DEF human(ADJ)　losses.DEF of humans ('humans perished')]
　　　　'the human losses (= the losses of humans)'

Agent / Theme adjectives have a fixed word order, occurring at the right of the head. Possessor adjectives may sometimes be prenominal.

　(ii) Of the non-argumental APs, those whose head is a qualifying-descriptive adjective have some syntactic particularities. The internal structure of these APs is essentially clausal; some adjectival heads may take arguments, which are case-marked with the dative and theta-marked by the adjective or whose preposition is assigned by the adjective (363a–b); other adjectival heads may only take adverbial adjuncts (363c) (§7.6.3):

(363) a. carte [$_{AP}$ utilă [$_{DP}$ **părinților**]]　　　　　　　　　　　　　　(Goal)
　　　　book　　useful　　parents.DEF.DAT
　　　　'book useful to the parents'

　　　b. un om [$_{AP}$ capabil [$_{PP}$ **de orice**]]　　　　　　　　　　　　　(Theme)
　　　　a human capable　of anything
　　　　'a human capable of anything'

　　　c. coloană [$_{AP}$ îngustă [$_{AdvP}$ **sus**]] și [$_{AP}$ lată [$_{AdvP}$ **jos**]]
　　　　column　　narrow　　above　and　wide　　down
　　　　'a column narrow at the top and wide at the bottom'

Adjectives compatible with adverbial adjuncts display this syntactic property only when they occur as non-restrictive modifiers (364a), not as restrictive modifiers (364b):

(364) a. obelisc **negru sus**
　　　　obelisk black above
　　　　'obelisk black at the top'

　　　b. diamant **negru**
　　　　diamond black
　　　　'black diamond'

The adjectives that take a prepositional or dative complement (syntactically realized or not) are typically used (in the NP) only as non-restrictive modifiers.

　The APs with a complex internal structure (with complements or adjuncts of the adjectival head) are placed at the right of the nominal head.

　(iii) Intersective adjectives (365), which combine with the noun by set-intersection, have been interpreted (Cornilescu 2009; Cornilescu and Nicolae 2011c, and references therein) as NP-adjectives ('direct' modifiers of the NP), linearized in post-head position, and non-intersective adjectives like *fost* 'former', *pretins* 'alleged', etc. have been considered kind-level adjectives (§5.3.5.1.1), with pre-head fixed position. Generally, intersective adjectives (colour-, form-, substance-, origin-, nationality-adjectives) cannot be focused and placed to the left of the head noun:

(365) fustă   **albastră**
       skirt   blue
       'blue skirt'

Subsective adjectives whose interpretation is relative to a comparison class (Truswell 2004: 139) are also postnominal (366a). Some subsective adjectives may be focused, placed to the left of the noun and prosodically marked by accent (366b). The syntactic relation between subsective and intersective adjectives is not based on a strict rule, word order being generally free (366c):

(366) a. fustă **lungă**, câine **bătrân**
         skirt long   dog   old
         'long skirt' 'old dog'

      b. o MARE problemă / *o LUNGĂ fustă
         a big   problem   a   long   skirt

      c. fustă **lungă albastră** / fustă **albastră lungă**
         skirt long   blue   skirt blue   long
         'blue long skirt'   'long blue skirt'

C Romanian contrasts with English, where intersective and subsective adjectives have a relatively free word order in prenominal position, and subsective adjectives precede in surface linear order the intersective ones (Truswell 2004: 139–40, for the description of English structures).

(iv) The distributional differences between individual-level and stage-level adjectives (see Cornilescu 2005a, for a generative analysis of Romanian data) particularly concern their relative word order, in the contexts in which they co-occur—in post-head position, the individual-level adjective is closer to the head noun than the stage-level one:

(367) o fată **înaltă** **bolnavă**
       a girl tall   sick
       'a sick tall girl'

(v) A few adjectives have variable word order, occurring both in prenominal (368a,c) and in postnominal position (368b,d); they display certain subtle interpretative differences: modal (368a) or quantificational (368c) vs. qualifying (368b,d).

(368) a. **săracul** / **sărmanul** om
         poor.DEF   poor.DEF   man
         'the pitiable man'

      b. omul   **sărac** / **sărman**
         man.DEF   poor   poor
         'the poor (= i.e. penniless) man'

      c. **vechea**   maşină
         old.DEF   car
         'the former car' (in contrast with other cars)

    d. maşina   **veche**
       car.DEF   old
       'the old / ancient car'

Intrinsically modal (369a) or quantificational (369b) adjectives are always prenominal:

(369) a. **bietul**   om
         pitiable.DEF man
         'the pitiable man'

       b. **cogeamite /**   **ditamai**   omul
         extremely-big extremely-big man.DEF
         'the extremely big man'

(vi) Qualifying adjectives are postnominal in the unmarked word order (370a). Adjectives of this type are, however, sensitive to pragmatic and stylistic interface conditions. The epithet adjective may be focused and placed in a prenominal position (370b), as a DP-modifier (Cornilescu and Nicolae 2011c).

(370) a. un   copac   **frumos**
         a   tree   beautiful
         'a beautiful tree'

       b. un   **frumos**   copac
         a   beautiful tree

C   The postnominal placement of qualifying adjectives is more extensive in Romanian than in other Romance languages, such as French (Lombard 1974: 98–9; Iliescu 2008b: 3271, and references therein; Posner 1996: 146).

    The prenominal placement of the epithet adjective is a parameter of typological variation. In Romanian, the prenominal placement (Niculescu 1991: 293–4) is a continuation of the Latin [Adj-N] pattern, the most widely used in vulgar Latin (Bourciez 1956: 99, 587). With respect to the extension of this phenomenon, there are some differences among the Romance languages (see Laenzlinger 2005: 646–70, with reference to French, Italian, and Spanish). In standard Romanian, the prenominal placement pattern (370b) might have been consolidated by the French influence (Posner 1996: 147) of the 19th century.

In postnominal position, qualifying adjectives are preceded by classifying adjectives (§5.3.5.1.1; see also Giurgea 2005: 53–6):

(371) substanţă **chimică**   **periculoasă**
       substance   chemical   dangerous
       'dangerous chemical substance'

5.3.5.2.2 PPs modifiers are most frequently introduced by the prepositions *de* 'of', *cu* 'with', *fără* 'without':

(372) a. cutie **de**   **lemn**
         box   of   wood
         'wooden box'

       b. pantofi **cu /**   **fără**   **cataramă**
         shoes   with   without buckle
         'shoes with / without buckle'

De-phrases sometimes incorporate PPs, *de* being a means of integrating PPs in the NP:

(373) a. casa   [_PP_ **de** [_PP_ **la**   **munte**]]
      house.DEF   of   at   mountain
      'the house in the mountains'

     b. casa   (care)   este   **la munte**
      house.DEF   (which)   is   at mountain
      'the house (which) is in the mountains'

In nominalized structures, there occur PPs corresponding to adverbial adjuncts in the VP. The structures are more varied both with respect to the preposition employed (*din* 'from, out of', *în* 'in', *la* 'at', *pe* 'on', etc.) and to the complement of the preposition—DP / NP (374a–d), infinitival clause (374e):

(374) a. ieşirea   **din**   **Bucureşti**
      leaving.DEF   from   Bucharest
      'going out of Bucharest'

     b. plecarea   **în**   **ziua**   **următoare**
      leaving.DEF   in   day.DEF   following
      'leaving the following day'

     c. sosirea   **la aeroport**
      arriving.DEF   at   airport
      'arriving at the airport'

     d. mersul   **pe**   **bicicletă**
      riding.DEF   on   bike
      'riding a bike'

     e. prezentarea   dovezilor   **fără**   **a**   **omite**   **nimic**
      presentation.DEF   proofs.DEF.GEN   without A_{INF} omit.INF   nothing
      'the presentation of the proofs without omitting anything'

5.3.5.2.3 Comparative constructions (*ca*-phrases) are generally descriptive, qualifying:

(375) un copil **ca tine** / **ca** un **înger**
      a   child   like   you   like   an   angel

5.3.5.2.4 AdvPs occur in nominalized structures and correspond to VP adverbial adjuncts:

(376) plecarea   **acolo** /   **astăzi** /   **degrabă**
      leaving.DEF   there   today   quickly
      'leaving there / today / quickly'

5.3.5.2.5 (i) Non-finite clauses in modifier positions are participial (377a) or gerundial (377b):

(377) a. magazin **deschis recent**
      shop   opened   recently
      'recently opened shop'

     b. ţărani   **mâncând**   **cartofi**
      peasants   eat.GER   potatoes
      'potato eating peasants'

(ii) Finite clauses in modifier position require a conjunction or a relative *(wh-)*marker.

Clausal modifiers introduced by conjunctions occur only in nominalized structures and correspond to VP adverbial adjuncts:

(378) plecarea   **îndată**   **ce**   **e**   **posibil**
       leaving.DEF as soon   as   is   possible
       'leaving as soon as it is possible'

Non-restrictive relative clausal modifiers (like restrictives; see also §5.3.5.1.4) are headed by *wh*-pronouns (*care, ce* 'who, which') and by *wh*-adverbs (*când, cum, încotro, unde* 'when, how, where'). The antecedent of the *wh*-pronoun is the head of the noun phrase. The pronoun *care* displays the gender and the number of the antecedent, while its case or preposition correspond to the base generation position, being required by the relativized category: nominative, corresponding to a relativized subject (379a); accusative, corresponding to a relativized complement of a preposition (379b), etc. *Wh*-adverbs are semantically equivalent to *wh*-pronouns from headed relative clauses (379b):

(379) a. Am   cumpărat mere,   **care** **nu** **i-au**   **plăcut**
         (I)have bought   apples which   not   CL.DAT.3SG=have   liked
         'I bought apples, which he did not like'
      b. Are o casă   **unde /** **în** **care** se   **simte** **bine**
         has a house where   in   which   CL.REFL.ACC.3SG feels   good
         '(S)he has a house where (s)he feels good'

In contrast to restrictive relative clauses, non-restrictive relative clauses may also be introduced by the adjectival *wh*-element *care* 'which':

(380) A   stat   în oraș două zile, **în** **care** **timp** **și-a**
       has stayed in town two   days   in   which   time   CL.REFL.DAT.3SG=has
       vizitat **prietenii**
       visited   friends.DEF
       '(S)he stayed in town for two days, during which time (s)he visited his/her friends'

Relative clauses may correspond to VP adverbial adjuncts:

(381) sosirea   **când** **am**   **stabilit**
       arriving.DEF when   (we)have   set
       'the arrival when we agreed'

This type of usage is specific to nominalized structures.

5.3.5.3 *The inversion pattern [Adjective + DE + Noun]*

The inversion of the internal constituents of the nominal phrase correlates with a change of the syntactic relations among these constituents: the syntactically dependent adjective becomes the head of phrase. There are two patterns of this kind. First of all, there are patterns attested since old Romanian, which target animate referents and actualize in the DP-initial position adjectives that display an intermediary stage of substantivization; these adjectives express insults (382) or have an affective, emotive content (383). Second, in this pattern there occur structures based on a comparison; the first position is occupied by an adjective-based noun (384).

(382) prostul de Mihai
stupid.DEF DE Mihai
'stupid Mihai'

(383) săracul de tine
poor.DEF DE you
'you poor fellow'

(384) o frumusețe de rochie
a beauty DE dress
'a beauty of a dress'

H Historically, this structure is considered a Romance pattern originating in a Latin structure of the type MONSTRUM HOMINIS. Initially, the second component of the structure was a noun in the genitive. The genitive occurred only when the first component of the structure expressed a spiritual or physical quality of an individual (Diez 1876: 131). This structure later evolved towards the Romance DE-pattern. In Romanian, this structure is attested as early as the 16th century.

C In contrast to Spanish, where the DP-initial adjective may, to a limited extent, take comparison markers, in Romanian the category of comparison is totally disallowed with adjectives in this position (Mihail 2009b: 98).

(385) *foarte prostul de Mihai
very stupid.DEF DE Mihai

U The structures based on a comparative pattern may include in the first position a prototypical noun, appreciative (386) or depreciative (387):

(386) o comoară de băiat
a treasure DE boy
'a treasure of a boy'

(387) un monstru de femeie
a monster DE woman
'a monster of a woman'

5.3.6 Appositions and classifiers

5.3.6.1 Appositions

The prototypical appositive pattern is made up of two coreferential nominals: the base, which identifies the referent, and the *apposition*, which is a predicate of the base (Forsgren 2000):

(388) Aceasta este **fiica** **mea,** *Maria*
this is daughter.DEF(F.SG) my.F.SG Maria(F)

5.3.6.1.1 The structure of the appositive syntagm is diversified because, practically, each constituent may be extended by an apposition. In general, the apposition replicates the syntactic category of the base: DP ((389a,b)), AP (390), VP (391), and IP (392)):

(389) a. [DP **Prietenul** meu], [DP *Andrei*], ne însoțește
friend.DEF(M.SG) my.M.SG Andrei CL.ACC.1PL accompanies

b. [DP **Ei**], [DP *autoarei*], îi mulțumesc
    her.DAT authoress.DEF.DAT CL.DAT.3SG (I)thank
    'I thank her, the authoress'

(390) Pare [AP **năucită**], adică [AP *intimidată*]
     seems distraught.DEF that is intimidated.FEM
     'She seems distraught, that is intimidated'

(391) A câștigat respectul [VP **muncind**], adică [VP *scriind zi și noapte*]
     has earned respect.DEF work.GER that is write.GER day and night
     '(S)he earned his / her respect by working, that is, by writing day and night'

(392) [IP **Era un om foarte serios**], adică [IP *își*
     be.IMPERF.3SG a man very serious that is CL.REFL.DAT.3SG
     rezolva atent problemele]
     solve.IMPERF.3SG carefully problems.DEF
     'He was a very serious man, that is, he carefully solved his problems'

The apposition and the base may sometimes be expressed by different syntactic categories:

(393) [AdvP **Atunci**], [PP *în ziua aceea*], am stabilit întâlnirea
     then in day.DEF that (we)have set-up meeting.DEF
     'Then, on that day, we set up the meeting'

(394) Avea [DP**o problemă**]: [IP *își pierduse portofelul*]
     have.IMPERF.3SG a problem CL.REFL.DAT.3SG lose.PLUPERF.3SG wallet.DEF
     'He had a problem: he had lost his wallet'

Although they are not syntactically dependent on the base, appositive clauses may be headed by complementizers (*că, să, ca... să*) or by *wh*-adverbs (*unde* 'where', *când* 'when', *cum* 'how'):

(395) a. Ea a înțeles **un lucru**: *că nu va*
       she has understood a thing: that not AUX.FUT.3SG
       reveni niciodată acasă
       return.INF never home
       'She has understood one thing: that (s)he will never return home'

    b. Ne-am întâlnit **acolo**, *unde am hotărât*
       CL.REFL.ACC.1PL=have.1PL met there where (we)-have decided
       'We met there, where we had decided'

5.3.6.1.2 Apposition is signalled by appositive markers (pause, low intonation, independent stress), which are graphically realized by the comma (,), the colon (:) or the dash (–). The apposition may also be accompanied by lexical markers (adverbials: *adică* 'that is', *anume* 'namely', *respectiv* 'respectively', *mai exact* 'namely') or by metadiscourse procedures (the insertion of quotatives / *verba dicendi*: *altfel spus* 'put differently', *mai bine zis* 'in other words'):

(396) a. **Amintirile** – *refugiul ei spiritual* – erau intacte
       memories.DEF refuge.DEF her(GEN) spiritual were untouched
       'Her memories – her spiritual refuge – were untouched'

b. **Ana,** *adică prietena mea,* lipsea
   Ana that is friend.DEF(F.SG) my.F.SG miss.IMPERF.3SG
   'Ana, my friend, was missing'

c. **Fuga** *de la accident, mai bine zis*
   running.DEF from accident more well said
   lașitatea, este condamnabilă
   cowardice.DEF is condemnable
   'Running from the accident, in other words the cowardice, is condemnable'

5.3.6.1.3 Depending on the criterion assumed, there are several types of apposition (Brăescu 2008: 664–6).

(i) Depending on the degree of complexity of the appositive structure, one may distinguish between simple appositions (397a) and chained appositions (397b):

(397) a. **Vecinul** *meu, Andrei,* face sport
     neighbour.DEF(M.SG) my.M.SG Andrei makes sport
     'My neighbour, Andrew, practices sports'

b. **Se** vorbea mult **despre Elena,** *vecina lui, o*
   CL.REFL.ACC speak.IMPERF.3SG much about Elena neighbour.DEF his a
   sportivă celebră
   sportswoman famous
   'There was a lot of talking about Elena, his neighbour, a famous sportswoman'

(ii) Depending on the semantic relation between the two components, one may distinguish: appositions of equivalence (398a), identifying appositions (398b), qualifying appositions (398c), and classifying appositions (398d).

(398) a. **Prietenul** *meu, confidentul meu,* era acolo
     friend.DEF(M.SG) my.M.SG confidant.DEF(M.SG) my.M.SG was there
     'My friend, my confidant, was there'

b. **Ne** ajută **ele,** *prietenele tale*
   CL.ACC.1PL help they.F friends.DEF(F.PL) your.F.PL
   'They, your friends, will help us'

c. **Ana,** *blonda înaltă,* a câștigat
   Ana blonde.DEF tall has won
   'Ana, the tall blonde girl, won'

d. **Vi-l** prezint **pe Ion Popescu,** *președinte*
   CL.DAT.2PL=CL.ACC.M.3SG introduce PE Ion Popescu president
   al asociației
   AL association.GEN
   'Let me introduce to you Ion Popescu, president of the association'

(iii) Depending on the lexical reinterpretation of the base, one may distinguish multiple appositions (399a) and summarizing appositions (399b):

(399) a. **I-am** cunoscut **familia:** *mama, soția și copiii*
     CL.DAT.3SG =(I)have met family.DEF mother.DEF wife.DEF and children.DEF
     'I met his family: his mother, wife and children'

b. I-am revăzut **pe Liviu, pe Mara, pe**
   CL.ACC.M.3PL=(I)have met-again PE Liviu PE Mara PE
   Anca, *adică* *pe* *toți*
   Anca that-is PE all
   'I met again Liviu, Mara, Anca, that is, all of them'

5.3.6.1.4 The syntactic features of the apposition are established by comparison with the base of the syntagm.

The apposition is always postposed to the base. Word order change entails the inversion of the function of the two constituents of the syntagm:

(400) a. **Prietena mea,** *Ana,* locuiește la parter
         friend.DEF(F.SG) my.F.SG Ana lives at ground flour
         'My friend, Ana, lives on the ground floor'

   b. **Ana,** *prietena mea,* locuiește la parter
      Ana friend.DEF(F.SG) my.F.SG lives at ground flour
      'Ana, my friend, lives on the ground floor'

The apposition may optionally agree for case with the base:

(401) a. I-a vorbit **Mariei,**
         CL.DAT.3SG=has spoken Maria.DAT
         colega *sa*
         colleague.DEF.NOM≡ACC(F.SG) his/her.F.SG.NOM≡ACC

   b. I-a vorbit **Mariei,** *colegei* *sale*
      CL.DAT.3SG=has spoken Maria.DAT colleague.DEF.DAT(F.SG) his / her.F.SG.DAT
      '(S)he spoke to Maria, his / her colleague'

C   Romanian preserved the Latin pattern of case-agreeing appositions. In the present language, there is a preference for non-agreeing appositions, which surface in the nominative–accusative case, a fact which reflects the tendency towards inflectional impoverishment. Modern Romanian is thus closer to the Romance type, which preserves a vernacular Latin structure (ELR: 52).

The apposition may preserve the prepositional construction of the base (402a). Classifying appositions are exceptional in this respect, due to their property-denoting character (402b):

(402) a. Am discutat <u>**cu**</u> **prietena ta,** *(cu)* *Ana*
         (I)have discussed with friend.DEF(F.SG) your.F.SG with Ana
         'I discussed with your friend, (with) Ana'

   b. Vi-l prezint **pe Ion Popescu, (*_pe_)** *medic* *sportiv*
      CL.DAT.2PL=CL.ACC.M.3SG introduce PE Ion Popescu PE physician sportive
      'Let me introduce to you Ion Popescu, sport physician'

5.3.6.2 *Classifiers and proper names*

The pattern in which the first constituent is a common noun bearing the definite article, fulfilling a classifier role (Cornilescu 2007), and the second constituent is a proper name also occurs:

(403) a. regele Arthur
         king.DEF Arthur

   b. orașul București
      city.DEF Bucharest

370   5 Nouns and Noun Phrases

TABLE 5.26 Diagnostics for appositions and classifiers

DIAGNOSTIC	APPOSITIVE SYNTAGM	CLASSIFIER STRUCTURE
The suspension of the constituent	ALLOWED Vorbesc **cu prietenul meu**, *Andrei* talk(I) to friend.DEF my Andrei 'I'm talking to my friend, Andrei'	DISALLOWED *Locuiesc **în oraşul**, *Braşov* live(I) in city.DEF Braşov
The possibility to leave out the constituent	ALLOWED Vorbesc **cu prietenul meu** talk(I) to friend.DEF my 'I'm talking to my friend	DISALLOWED *Locuiesc **în oraşul** live(I) in city.DEF
Word-order/function change of the constituents	ALLOWED Vorbesc **cu** *Andrei,* **prietenul meu** (I)talk to Andrei friend.DEF my 'I'm talking to Andrei, my friend'	DISALLOWED *Locuiesc **în** *Braşov,* **oraşul** (I)live in Braşov city.DEF
The occurrence of appositive markers	ALLOWED Vorbesc **cu prietenul meu**, *adică Andrei* (I)talk to friend.DEF my that is Andrei	DISALLOWED *Locuiesc **în oraşul**, *adică Braşov* (I)live in city.DEF that is Braşov
Case agreement	ALLOWED Am spus **prietenului meu**, (I)have said friend.DEF.DAT my *lui Andrei* LUI(DAT) Andrei 'I told my friend Andrei'	DISALLOWED *A acordat ajutoare **oraşului** (he)has given help.PL city.DEF.DAT *Braşovului* Braşov.DAT

The proper name that accompanies the classifier is not an apposition, as previously assumed in traditional descriptions. This is testified by the diagnostics shown in Table 5.26.

H   The genitive of designation (*cetatea Sucevei* fortress.DEF Suceava.GEN) is an ancient pattern. The classifier nominative structure was generalized in modern Romanian.
C   The competition between the pattern with a noun in the genitive and the one with a noun in the nominative (*urbs Romae / urbs Roma*), attested since vulgar Latin (Rosetti 1986: 157), was not inherited by the other Romance languages, where the *de*-prepositional structures prevailed: Fr. *la ville de Paris*.

5.3.7 Nominal ellipsis and the pronominalization of determiners

5.3.7.1 Patterns of nominal ellipsis

Romanian displays a variety of patterns of nominal ellipsis ('pronominal uses' of determiners), which are given below (with the notation [ ] indicating the gap, the strikethrough showing the ellipsis site, and the words in boldface indicating the remnant).

The remnant is a purely lexical element, i.e. an AP (404a) or a PP (404b):

(404) a. Ion   vrea   maşină roşie, iar   Petru vrea   [maşină]   **galbenă**
         John wants car   red,   but   Peter wants   car   yellow
         'John wants a red car, and Peter wants a yellow one'

b. Ion   vrea   maşină   de   curse,   iar   Petre   îşi   doreşte
   John   wants   car   of   race,   but   Peter   CL.REFL.DAT.3SG desires
   [maşină] de   teren
   car   of   terrain
   'John wants a racing car, and Peter wants an off-road one'

The remnant is a functional element, i.e. a determiner (405a) or a quantifier (405b–d):

(405) a. Dă-mi   cărţile   acestea   şi   ia-le
         give.IMP.2SG=CL.DAT.1SG   books.DEF   these   and   take.IMP.2SG=CL.ACC.F.3PL
         pe   [cărţile] acelea!
         PE   books.DEF those
         'Give me these books and take those!'

      b. Au   venit   mulţi   studenţi,   dar   nu   îi   cunosc
         have   come   many   students   but   not   CL.ACC.M.3PL   (I)know
         pe   toţi   [studenţii]
         PE   all   students.DEF
         'A lot of students came, but I do not know all (of them)'

      c. Maria   a   cumpărat   puţine   cărţi,   iar   Petru   a
         Maria   has   bought   few   books   but   Peter   has
         luat   (mai)   multe   [cărţi]
         taken   more   many   books
         'Maria bought few books, and Peter bought more'

      d. Tu   poţi   lua   două   mere,   iar   Maria   trei   [mere]
         you   can   take.INF   two   apples   and   Maria   three   apples
         'You may take two apples and Maria three'

The remnant sequence may contain two or even three functional (prenominal) elements, with distinct roles in the DP:

(406) A   vorbit   de   trei   studenţi   buni.   Din păcate,   nu-i
      has   spoken   of   three   students   good   unfortunately,   not=CL.ACC.M.3PL
      cunosc   pe   cei   trei   [studenţi buni] /   pe   toţi   cei   trei [studenţi buni]
      (I)know   PE   CEL   three   students good   PE   all   CEL   three students good
      '(S)he told me about three good students. Unfortunately, I do not know (all) the three good ones'

Finally, the remnant sequence may be complex and discontinuous, containing both prenominal and postnominal elements:

(407) a. două   capitole   ale   Ralucăi   şi   trei   [capitole]   ale   Irinei
         two   chapters   AL.F.PL   Raluca.GEN   and   three   chapters   AL.F.PL   Irina.GEN
         'two chapters by Raluca and three by Irina'

      b. două   vile   la   mare   şi   trei   [vile]   la   munte
         two   villas   at   sea   and   three   villas   at   mountain
         'two villas at the seaside and three in the mountains'

4.3.7.2 The range of remnants

Romanian provides interesting data with regard to the range of remnants allowed in nominal ellipsis, since the remnant may freely be an argument: a subcategorized PP (408a) and a PP or genitival argument in nominalizations (408b,c):

(408) a. abuzul   de   băutură   şi   **cel**   **de**   **tutun**
abuse.DEF of   alcohol and CEL of   tobacco
'the abuse of alcohol and tobacco'

    b. acordarea   de   burse   şi   **cea** **de** **premii**
granting.DEF of scholarships and CEL of prizes
'the granting of scholarships and prizes'

    c. acordarea   burselor   şi   **cea** **a** **premiilor**
granting.DEF scholarships.GEN and CEL AL prizes.GEN
'the granting of scholarships and prizes'

C It has often been claimed that nominal ellipsis, like VP-ellipsis, targets the whole NP; thus any argument will be part of the elided constituent (see Sleeman 1996 for French; Ticio 2010 for Spanish; Lobeck 1995 and Llombart-Huesca 2002 for English). However, at least for Romance languages (French and Spanish), the same researchers (Sleeman 1996; Ticio 2010) acknowledge that the data regarding the impossibility of argumental remnants are not clear-cut, and provide counterexamples (Sleeman 1996: 31; Ticio 2010: 179–80). What is important here is that the existence of the determiner CEL enables Romanian to display a wider variety of ellipsis patterns with argumental remnants (408).

5.3.7.3 The form of the remnant

Another problematic aspect of nominal ellipsis concerns the form that the remnant takes in elided structures. Remnants roughly fall into two large classes, each of which comprises several subclasses.

A. There are *remnants whose form does not change* under ellipsis. This class includes, on the one hand, lexical AP and PP remnants (see §5.3.7.1) and, on the other hand, functional remnants which belong to several classes:

- quantifiers: cardinals (409a), ordinals (409b), and other quantifiers (409c):

(409) a. două (/   două   cărţi)
two (ones) two   books

    b. al   doilea   (/ al   doilea copil / copilul   al   doilea)
the second (one)   the second child child.DEF the second

    c. mulţi (/ mulţi copii / copii(i)   mulţi)
many   many chidren children(DEF) many

- identity and alternative determiners:

(410) acelaşi /   celălalt   (/ acelaşi / celălalt copil)
the-same-one the-other-one the-same / other   child

- the clitic determiner CEL (411)—see also §5.3.1.4.4:

(411) a. cel bun (/copilul cel bun)
       CEL good   child.DEF CEL good
    b. cei   doi (/cei   doi copii)
       CEL.M.PL two   CEL.M.PL   two children

B. The second class is represented by remnants whose form changes under ellipsis; this class is further subdivided into three subclasses.

There are determiner and quantifier remnants which acquire a special (i.e. strong) form under ellipsis, represented by the enclisis of the (deictic) particle *-a* onto the non-elliptical form:

- demonstratives, which have a short/weak form in prenominal position and a long/strong form in post-head position and under ellipsis:

(412) acest**a**   (/omul   acest**a** /acest om)
      this (one)   man.DEF   this   this man

- indefinite quantifiers and *wh*-elements in genitive–dative plural (413a) or singular (413b):

(413) a. tuturor(**a**)   (/tuturor (*tuturora)   oamenilor)
         all.GEN≡DAT   all.GEN≡DAT   humans.DEF.GEN≡DAT
     b. fiecărui**a**   (/ fiecărui (*fiecăruia)   om)
        each / every.GEN≡DAT   each / every. GEN≡DAT   human.GEN≡DAT≡NOM≡ACC

H This functional difference was not available in old Romanian in the case of indefinite quantifiers and *wh*-elements: the formative *-a* did not distinguish between the nominal ellipsis form and the form which appeared in overt head structures.

There is a restricted class of elements which, under ellipsis, acquire the definite article, although their meaning is, in most cases, indefinite. All these (morphologically paradoxical) forms have adjectival morphology, and this is what allows them to take over the definite article:

- the indefinites *un* ('a / one') and *alt* ('other') become *unul* (one.DEF) and *altul* (other.DEF):

(414) Unul   a   intrat   în clasă, altul   a   ieşit
      one.DEF   has entered in class   other.DEF   has gone out
      'One (of them) entered the classroom, another went out'

- scalar adjectives such as *primul* (first.DEF 'the first one'), *ultimul* (last.DEF 'the last one'), *următorul* (next.DEF 'the next/following one'), and the negative quantifier *niciunul* (no.DEF 'none') display the same behaviour.

Finally, it is worth mentioning the situation of genitive and possessive adjective remnants which behave under ellipsis (415a) in the same way as in the context of non-adjacency to a definite noun (415b), always being preceded by the functional element AL:

(415) a. Câinele   din   curte e   **al**   Mariei.   **Al**   meu e   în casă.
         dog.DEF(M) from yard   is   AL.M.SG   Maria.GEN   AL.M.SG   my   is in house
         'The dog in the yard is Maria's. Mine is indoors'

b. câinele   frumos   **al**   Mariei /   **al**   meu
   dog.DEF(M)   beautiful   AL.M.SG   Maria.GEN   AL.M.SG   my

In genitive–dative plural contexts, with possessive adjectives in ellipsis, the element AL takes the form *alor* (416a), not shared by the overt head construction (416b). Therefore, the functional element AL acquires the genitive–dative plural inflectional ending *-or* from the paradigm of nouns and pronouns: *al + or > alor*. Recall that in non-elliptical structures, AL does display gender and number, but not case concord with the head noun (§5.1.3.2.2).

(416) a. Le-am   spus   **alor**   mei
        CL.DAT.3.PL=have   told   AL.DAT.PL   my
        'I told my folks'

      b. Le-am   spus   unor   prieteni   **ai**   mei
        CL.DAT.3.PL=have   told   some.DAT   friends.DAT   AL.PL   my
        'I told that to some of my friends'

5.3.7.4 Focus and ellipsis

It has often been claimed in the general literature on ellipsis (Merchant 2001; Winkler 2005; Giurgea 2010) and in the nominal ellipsis literature (Eguren 2010; Cornilescu and Nicolae 2010) that the process of non-pronunciation is tied to the (contrastive) focalization of the remnant; structurally, this may trigger differences in the internal structures of elided vs. overt head constructions. Romanian provides pervasive (formal and functional) evidence that this is the case, and that the internal structure of DPs with ellipsis is different from the internal structure of DPs with overt nominal heads.

Formal evidence consists of distributional disparities between ellipsis DPs and overt head DPs. In overt head constructions, the clitic definite determiner CEL cannot be followed by relative (i.e. thematic and classifying) adjectives, as in (417a); by contrast, elided noun head structures with CEL are perfectly legitimate with this type of adjectives (§5.3.1.3.4), as in (417b):

(417) a. *filmul   **cel**   franţuzesc
         movie.DEF   CEL   French

      b. filmul   franţuzesc   şi   **cel** românesc
         movie.DEF   French   and   CEL Romanian
         'the French movie and the Romanian one'

Also, all the formal changes that affect the remnants (there is a wide class of remnants whose form changes under ellipsis, discussed above in §5.3.7.3.B) may be taken as evidence for focus; the particles that are added to the remnant may be taken as focus particles (see examples (412–413) above).

Functional evidence is given by demonstratives. These are nominal remnants / licensers of nominal ellipsis which appear in elided structures only with their long form. It has been shown in the chapter on demonstratives (§5.3.1.2.4) that in overt head constructions, the long (i.e. postnominal) form of demonstratives is associated with emphatic readings, may be stressed, and behaves like a contrastive focus.

CONCLUSIONS

1 The noun has number and, more limited, case inflection.

Nouns are grouped into three classes of gender: masculine, feminine, and neuter. Each gender class is characterized by specific syncretisms and particular inflectional ending correlations. The neuter distinguishes from the masculine and the feminine: (i) semantically, by the feature [–animate]; (ii) syntactically, by the specific agreement imposed to adjectives and articles—masculine in the singular, and feminine in the plural.

Romanian preserved the syncretism of the genitive with the dative from late Latin. This syncretism is also specific to Balkan languages.

Romanian inherited from Latin a case inflection characterized by the opposition of two feminine singular forms, in the articleless declension of nouns (and adjectives): nominative–accusative vs. genitive–dative.

The Romanian feminine is characterized by the syncretism of the genitive–dative singular form with the unique (nominative–accusative–genitive–dative) plural form. In the case of the masculine and of the neuter, there is no trace of case form distinctions—there exist only singular / plural distinctions, case syncretism being thus total.

As for the means of marking the genitive and the dative, Romanian has an intermediate position on the synthetic–analytic scale, possessing both synthetic (inflectional) and analytic (prepositional) case markers.

Romanian diversified its inflectional case markers, adding to its inventory of inflectional endings (a restricted one, however, if compared to Latin) the forms of the enclitic definite article, which is fused with the noun, and which is also involved in case marking, besides functioning as a determiner.

There appeared a new case marker (the proclitic morpheme LUI), specific to (masculine) anthroponyms, a fact which highlights the importance of the animate (human) / inanimate distinction. The contexts of LUI have broadened from anthroponyms to certain inanimate common nouns.

Contemporary Romanian uses specialized prepositions for marking the genitive and the dative relation. The preposition A grammaticalized as a syntactic marker of the genitive relation, and, to a (much more) limited extent, of the dative one. The preposition *la*, which etymologically incorporates the Latin preposition AD, is an incompletely grammaticalized dative marker. The prepositions A and *la* observe several usage rules, some of them obligatory (system rules), some of them optional (tied to a specific language register).

On the basis of the Latin preposition AD, there emerged a supplementary syntactic marker of the genitive (i.e. AL), which in some contexts allows double case marking, synthetic and analytic. The syntactic marking of the genitive by AL contextually cancels out the genitive–dative syncretism (general in the inflection of nouns and adjectives).

There is a strong rivalry between the feminine plural inflectional endings *-e* and *-i* (the latter more frequently triggers morphophonological alternations), on the one hand, and the neuter inflectional endings *-e* and *-uri*, on the other hand.

There are special vocative endings for the masculine and the feminine.

The inflectional distinctions are sometimes accompanied by morphophonological alternations, which modify the root of the noun, as well as that of adjectives and, more rarely, of pronouns in the DP.

2 Anthroponyms behave like person-denoting common nouns while toponyms resemble to a larger extent non-personal common nouns. The modifiers of anthroponyms are attached

with the use of the determiner CEL. The direct object of person-denoting nouns (anthroponyms and relational nouns) is introduced by the functional preposition PE and it is clitic doubled. A particular feature of proper names is the articulation of toponyms but the lack of articles with anthroponyms.

Mass nouns and abstract nouns combine with specific indefinite quantifiers or occur bare in argument position.

Romanian contrasts with certain languages, in which singular collective nouns impose plural agreement of the verb.

The genitive DP / possessive adjective argument of a picture noun has an ambiguous interpretation in a narrow context (Theme, Agent, or Possessor), contrasting with the *de*-construction, where the *de*-phrase is strictly interpreted as an Agent.

3 The definite article is enclitic, and the indefinite article is proclitic.

The definite and indefinite articles display case inflection. The indefinite article is homonymous in the singular with the indefinite adjective *un*. The indefinite article has a heterogeneous inflectional paradigm, which includes a suppletive form: *niște* (NOM≡ACC, PL).

The very same element (*niște*) has a double role: it functions as an indefinite article (when it combines with plural NPs) and as an (adjectival) partitive or indefinite quantifier (in singular NPs headed by mass nouns).

Romanian allows bare nouns as subjects (in certain lexically and syntactically conditioned contexts) and as direct objects. Certain structures with bare predicatives correspond in other languages to structures with the indefinite article. The definite article is excluded in DPs selected by certain prepositions.

4 The demonstrative system of Romanian is based on the proximity distinction: Romanian has proximal demonstratives (*acest(a)*, *ăsta* 'this') and distal demonstratives (*acel(a)*, *ăla* 'that').

Romanian demonstratives occur in three syntactic instances: as prenominal and postnominal determiners and as pronouns. Postnominal demonstrative determiners display a long form differentiated by a distinctive vowel from the short form of prenominal demonstratives.

There are distributional and functional differences between prenominal and postnominal demonstrative determiners. Postnominal demonstratives are strictly right-adjacent to a definite nominal head; prenominal demonstratives do not observe this restriction, and DP-internal word order in phrases with prenominal demonstratives is relatively free. Prenominal demonstratives are anaphoric definite determiners, while postnominal demonstratives are focused and typically trigger [+specific] readings of the DPs containing them.

5 Romanian possesses two alternative determiners, which denote two different types of alterity: open alterity (*alt(ul)* '(an) other') vs. closed alterity (*celălalt* 'the other (one)'). From a syntactic point of view, these determiners have the following features: *alt(ul)* behaves like a prenominal indefinite determiner, while *celălalt* has the distribution of a demonstrative (it occurs prenominally and postnominally, and, when postnominal, it observes the adjacency constraint, typical of demonstratives); *alt(ul)* has a double categorization, lexical and functional.

The identity determiner of Romanian is *același* ('the same one'); *același* is made up of the distal demonstrative *acela* 'that' and the invariable formative *și*; *același* displays internal variation. It is disallowed in postnominal position; it functions only as a prenominal determiner and as a pronoun.

6 There has emerged a special determiner (CEL) which distinguishes the Romanian nominal phrase in the Romance family. CEL is a special clitic; it has a special distribution (it behaves like a freestanding definite article and like an adjectival article), and it is associated, in each distributional pattern, with a particular interpretation. As a freestanding article, CEL is a 'last resort' element, inserted as the effect of the intervention of a (morphologically) defective quantifier (indefinite QP) between the DP-initial position and the head noun; interpretatively, it behaves like the freestanding definite article of other languages. As an adjectival article, CEL has an atypical distribution (it follows a definite noun and it precedes a variety of types of phrases—APs, PPs, present, and past participial phrases), and a special interpretation: its function is to signal that the modifier it introduces is the most salient property of the nominal head. In nominal ellipsis contexts, CEL has a wider distribution than in overt head structures.

7 Romanian possesses several types of polydefinite structures: double definite structures, determiner spreading structures and the polydefinite postnominal demonstrative structures. In this respect, Romanian resembles languages of other families, such as Greek and certain Scandinavian varieties.

8 Romanian is distinguished by the variety of the types of numerical expressions with a quantificational meaning.

Romanian did not preserve the Latin numeral CENTUM, which was replaced by *sută* 'hundred' (an old Slavic borrowing). The compound numerals are made up of elements of Latin origin (with the exception of *sută*) on a Balkan pattern.

The gender distinction for the numeral *doi* 'two' was preserved (and lost in most other Romance languages). There emerged a nominal inflectional paradigm for the numerals (F) *zece* 'ten', *sută* 'hundred', *mie* 'thousand', (NEUT) *milion* 'million', *miliard* 'billion'.

Cardinal numerals above 19 combine with the noun with the use of DE.

The indefinite quantifiers have a diversified internal structure and inflection.

The opposition [+animate] / [−animate] is marked by distinct forms in interrogative and relative pronouns: *cine* 'who' vs. *ce* 'what'.

The expression of approximation and vagueness is achieved by various means.

9 Typologically, if possession is conceived as a predicative (subject–predicate) relation, then Romanian is a possessee-subject language.

All types of pronouns are used as a means of encoding possession: full pronouns (possessive adjectives or pronouns in the genitive case), clitics (the adnominal possessive clitic), and affixes (the possessive affix and the definite article).

Romanian preserved a dual adjectival–determiner paradigm, which seems historically to have underlain all Romance varieties, but has been lost in most languages; the possessive adjective belongs to the adjectival paradigm, while the possessive affix belongs to the determiner paradigm.

Romanian possesses an adnominal possessive clitic, which right-adjoins to the D-position, making it a second-position (Wackernagel) clitic.

10 Deverbal nouns do not allow the co-occurrence of two genitives corresponding to the direct object and to the subject in the matching VP structure.

In the nominative possessive construction, the part-denoting relational noun does not allow syntactic realization of the genitival / possessive argument.

11 Qualifying adjectives are predominantly postnominal, a Romance feature; the postposition is more extended in Romanian than in other Romance languages. The prenominal position of epithet adjectives is the effect of the preservation of the old [Adj-N] pattern.

Likewise, the primitive Romance pattern *de* + infinitive was preserved in Romanian as well as in western Romance. What is specific to Romanian is the co-occurrence of the preposition DE with the infinitive marker A_{INF}.

The pronoun QUALIS transformed into a true relative pronoun (*care*) and is used without an article, in the same circumstances as the descendants of QUI in western Romance; the western Romance relative pronominal doublet that originates in QUI / (ILLE) QUALIS was not preserved in Romanian.

12 Appositions may agree for case with their coreferential base. However in contemporary Romanian the preferred structures are those without case-agreement, with the apposition in the nominative.

13 There is a restricted class of elements which, under ellipsis, acquire the definite article, although their meaning is, in most cases, indefinite: *unul* 'one' and *altul* 'another'.

Thanks to the determiner CEL, Romanian displays a wider variety of ellipsis patterns with argumental and adjectival remnants than the other Romance languages.

Romanian provides (functional and formal) evidence for the hypothesis that the ellipsis of the head involves the focalization of the remnant.

6

Pronouns

This chapter presents the four classes of pronouns which mark person distinctions: personal pronouns, which index the communicative roles of speaker / group of the speaker, hearer / group of the hearer, and observer(s), that is non-speaker(s), non-hearer(s); reflexive pronouns, which simultaneously encode the communicative roles and subject–object coreferentiality; politeness pronouns, which simultaneously encode the communicative roles, and the social distance and hierarchy between interlocutors; emphatic pronouns, which function as pronominal intensifiers.

A fifth class is included here, reciprocal pronouns which do not encode the grammatical category of person, but reflect the relation between the (usually) [+human / +animate] arguments of the symmetrical predication, thus indirectly evoking the category of person.

The description below highlights the morphosyntactic, semantic, referential, and pragma-discursive features of these classes.

6.1 PERSONAL PRONOUNS

6.1.1 The paradigm

The 1st and the 2nd person singular and plural pronouns index the communicative roles by different lexemes, unmarked overtly for gender. The 3rd person pronouns do not mark the [+/– animate] distinction, but they 'simultaneously' mark number and gender distinctions. The paradigm of personal pronouns in their nominative forms is presented in Table 6.1.

H The forms for the 1st and the 2nd person have cognate counterparts inherited from Latin, throughout Romance. Like the other Romance languages, Romanian inherited the 3rd person forms from the Latin demonstrative pronouns (Dimitrescu 1978: 249–61). Consequently, in Romanian both the 3rd person personal pronouns and the demonstrative pronouns can substitute [+/–human] nominals, and the masculine / feminine grammatical opposition reflects both natural and grammatical gender.

TABLE 6.1 Personal pronouns

Person	M	F
1SG	eu 'I'	
2SG	tu 'you'	
3SG	el 'he'	ea 'she'
1PL	noi 'we'	
2PL	voi 'you'	
3PL	ei 'they'	ele 'they'

C   All Romance languages inherited the Latin suppletive morphology of the 1st and the 2nd person and developed 3rd person singular and plural forms based on the demonstrative ILLE, which replaced Lat. HIC, ISTE, ILLE, IPSE, SE (Reinheimer and Tasmowski 2005: 15, 21; Maiden 2011a: 159). While the referent of an NP already introduced in discourse is encoded by an anaphoric demonstrative in Latin and by an anaphoric personal pronoun in western Romance languages, both a personal pronoun (focusing the actor) and a demonstrative (introducing a new vantage point in presenting the referent, Manoliu 2011: 480) can occur in Romanian.

The lexical paradigm of the personal pronouns includes the pronoun *dânsul* for the 3rd person. *Dânsul* marks number, gender, and case distinctions as nouns do, by inflectional endings and by the incorporated definite article (Table 6.2).

H   *Dânsul* seems to be a late Romanian compound (*de* + *însul*) dating from the end of the 16th century / the beginning of the 17th century (Dimitrescu 1978: 261–5; Niculescu 1999: 144–74; see also ELR: 432). For the 3rd person, old Romanian also used *însul* (descending from Lat. *IPSE, Dimitrescu 1978: 257–8); it still occurs in contemporary Romanian, but only in prepositional contexts: *într-însul* / *într-însa* 'in it / him / her', *dintr-însul* / *dintr-însa* 'from it / him / her', *printr-însul* / *printr-însa* 'through it / him / her'.

Dânsul was a personal pronoun in earlier stages, but functions as a social deictic in contemporary Romanian (§6.3).

U   *Dânsul* shows regional and register variation: regionally (in Moldavia) and in the non-standard use it still functions as a personal pronoun, while in standard Romanian it has been attracted to the politeness value (see §6.3.2). Its first uses as a social deictic were recorded at the end of the 19th century in the region of Muntenia, which favoured its penetration into standard Romanian (Dimitrescu 1978: 261–5; Niculescu 1999: 144–74).

6.1.2   Morphological cases

Romanian pronouns have distinct forms for the nominative, dative, and accusative. For the genitive / possessive, see §5.3.3.1.

Morphological cases are most clearly marked for the 1st and the 2nd person singular, while the other forms show a nominative–accusative syncretism for the strong forms (Table 6.3).

H   Romanian dative forms continue those of Latin. According to some authors, the accusative forms (*mine* 'me', *tine* 'you') were formed in old Romanian with the particle *-ne*, by analogy with the relative pronoun *cine* ('who(m)'); according to others, they are the result of a substratum influence (ELR: 431–3; Dimitrescu 1978: 255–6; Feuillet 1986: 19).

TABLE 6.2 Personal pronouns

GENDER / NUMBER	M	F
SG	dânsul 'he'	dânsa 'she'
PL	dânşii 'they'	dânsele 'they'

TABLE 6.3 Case forms of the personal pronouns

PERSON		NOM	ACC	DAT
1SG		eu 'I'	mine 'me'	mie 'to me'
2SG		tu 'you'	tine 'you'	ție 'to you'
1PL		noi 'we / us'		nouă 'to us'
2PL		voi 'you'		vouă 'to you'
3SG	M	el 'he / him'		lui 'to him'
	F	ea 'she / her'		ei 'to her'
3PL	M	ei 'they / them'		lor 'to them'
	F	ele 'they / them'		

C In all Romance languages pronouns preserved declensional distinctions better than nouns (Sornicola 2011: 38–9; Salvi 2011: 322–5). In Romanian, personal pronouns mark the nominative–accusative distinction by suppletive forms, while nouns do not make this distinction.

Pronouns in the 3rd person have strong forms for the genitive as well. Pronominal genitive forms are syncretic with the dative forms (M.SG *lui* 'his', F.SG *ei* 'her', M≡F.PL *lor* 'their'), an inflectional feature they share with nouns. For the synonymy between the genitive forms of the personal pronouns and the possessive forms, see §5.3.3.1.

6.1.3 Strong vs. clitic forms

Personal pronouns in the accusative and dative have two series of forms: strong and clitic (Table 6.4).

H The emergence of two series of pronouns, clitic and strong, is an innovation of Romance languages (Reinheimer and Tasmowski 2005: 23) with respect to Latin, where weak pronouns were variants of the strong forms with the same range of syntactic functions, and did not modify the stress of their hosts (Salvi 2011: 326–7). Old Romanian dative and accusative clitics have Latin etyma (Dimitrescu 1978: 249–61).

C Romanian has several features distinguishing it from other Romance languages: a large number of morphologically and phonologically induced clitic variants, the prothetic *î* series, and distinct accusative and dative forms. Romanian, like Spanish, Italian, and Portuguese, but unlike French, does not have nominative clitics (Reinheimer and Tasmowski 2005). A double series of clitic and strong pronouns also occur in Balkan languages (Feuillet 1986: 84).

Romanian does not have partitive clitics, like Latin, Spanish, and Portuguese, and unlike French (*en*) and Italian (*ne*). Like Portuguese and Spanish, Romanian does not have locative clitics, corresponding to Fr. *y* and It. *ci* (Reinheimer and Tasmowski 2005: 221). Nor does it have clitics for deleted predicative complements (nouns and adjectives) (cf. Fr. *Il l'est*, Sp. *Lo es*) (Niculescu 1978: 233; Posner 1996: 168).

TABLE 6.4 Dative and accusative strong and clitic forms

CASE NUMBER GENDER	FORMS		PERSON 1 SG M≡F	PL M≡F	PERSON 2 SG M≡F	PL M≡F	PERSON 3 SG M	F	PL M	F
DAT	STRONG		mie [mie]	nouă [nowə]	ţie [tsie]	vouă [vowə]	lui [luj]	ei [jej]	lor [lor]	
	CLITIC	FREE / BOUND	mi [mi] -mi [mʲ] mi- [mi, mj] -mi- [mi, mj]	ne [ne], ni [ni] -ne ne- [ne, nę], ni- -ne- [ne, nę] -ni-	ţi [tsi] -ţi [tsʲ] ţi- [tsi, tsj] -ţi- [tsi, tsj]	vă [və], vi [vi] -vă vă-, vi- -vă-, -vi-	i [i] -i [j] i- [i / j] -i- [i / j]		le [le], li [li] -le le- [le, lę], li- -le- [le, lę] -li-	
	BOUND				v- [v]					
	FREE		îmi [imʲ]		îţi [itsʲ]		îi [ij]			
ACC	STRONG		mine [mine]	noi [noj]	tine [tine]	voi [voj]	el [jel]	ea [ja]	ei [jej]	ele [jele]
	CLITIC	FREE / BOUND	mă [mə] -mă mă-	ne [ne] -ne ne- [ne, nę] -ne- [ne, nę]	te [te] -te te- [te, tę] -te- [te, tę]	vă [və] -vă	o [o] -o o- -o- [o, ǫ]		le [le] -le le- [le, lę] -le- [le, lę]	
	BOUND		m- [m] -m-		v- [v] -v-	-l [l] l- -l-	-i [j] i- [j] -i- [j]			
	FREE					îl [il]	îi [ij]			

Clitics do not bear stress and must have a phonological host, which may or may not be the syntactic host. Most clitics can be both free from and bound to the host; some of them are obligatorily free, others are obligatorily bound.

The phonological hosts can be verbs (1a), auxiliaries (1b), verbal interjections (1c), nouns (1d), adjectives (1e), adverbs (1f), prepositions with article-like endings (1g), relative and interrogative adverbs (1h) and pronouns (1i), conjunctions (1j), the A infinitive and the SĂ subjunctive markers (1k), the negative marker *nu* (1l), or another pronominal clitic (1m) (§6.1.4).

(1) a. îi spun, îl cunosc
   CL.DAT.3SG tell.1SG, CL.ACC.M.3SG know.1SG
   'I'm telling him', 'I know him'

  b. i-am spus, l-am văzut
   CL.DAT.3SG=(I)have told, CL.ACC.M.3SG=(I)have seen
   'I told him', 'I saw him'

  c. iată-l!
   look=CL.ACC.M.3SG
   'here he is!'

d. inima-i
   heart.DEF=CL.3SG
   'his / her heart'

e. frumoasa-i   carte
   beautiful.DEF=CL.3SG book
   'his / her nice book'

f. deasupra-mi
   above=CL.1SG
   'above me'

g. împotriva-mi
   against=CL.1SG
   'against me'

h. unde-l   pune
   where=CL.ACC.M.3SG   puts
   'where he puts it'

i. cine-i   spune
   who=CL.DAT.3SG   tells
   'who tells him'

j. dacă-l   vezi,   c-o   cunosc
   if=CL.ACC.M.3SG   see,   that=CL.ACC.F.3SG   know
   'if you see him', 'that I know her'

k. a-i   spune,   să-l   văd
   A_INF=CL.DAT.3SG   tell.INF,   SĂ_SUBJ=CL.ACC.M.3SG   see.SUBJ
   'to tell him', '(I) should see him'

l. nu-i   spun,   nu-l   văd
   not=CL.DAT.3SG   tell,   not=CL.ACC.M.3SG   see
   'I'm not telling him', 'I do not see him'

m. mi-l   dă
   CL.DAT.1SG=CL.ACC.M.3SG   gives
   'he's giving it to me'

In writing, the link between the clitic and the host is marked by a hyphen to the right, to the left or both to the right and to the left of the clitic (§6.1.3.3).

Some clitic forms show phonologically conditioned allophones, as showed in Table 6.5. Compared to their strong forms, there are numerous and irregular syncretisms of clitics: the gender syncretism of the 3rd person singular dative clitics (*îi, i*); the dative–accusative syncretisms of the 1st and the 2nd person plural clitics (*ne* and *vă, v-*, respectively); the crossed-case syncretisms of the 3rd person, that is the dative singular–accusative plural masculine (*îi, i*) and dative plural–accusative, plural, feminine (*le*). The hierarchy of persons with regard to syncretisms is 1st, 2nd singular > 1st, 2nd plural > 3rd singular > 3rd plural.

TABLE 6.5 Allomorphs of accusative and dative clitics

Clitic	Allophone	Phonological context	Example
mi ți	[mi] [tsi]	Followed by a consonant in the word adjacent to its right	[mi] le dă, [mi]-l dă [tsi] le dă, [tsi]-l dă
	[mj] [tsj]	Part of a diphthong formed with the initial vowel of the word adjacent to its right	[mj]-a spus [tsj]-a spus
	[m^i] [ts^i]	Final element in a syllable formed with the conjunct host	nu-[m^i] spune nu-[ts^i] spune
ne te le	[ne] [te] [le]	Followed by a consonant or a vowel in the word adjacent to its right with which it forms a hiatus	nu [ne] vede nu [ne] aude nu [te] vede nu [te] aude nu [le] vede nu [le] aude
	ne [ne̯] te [te̯] le [le̯]	Part of a diphthong formed with the initial vowel of the word adjacent to its right	[ne̯]-a întrebat [te̯]-a întrebat [le̯]-a întrebat
i	[i]	Forming an independent syllable	nu [i] le dau
	[j]	Forming a diphthong with the vowel of the host adjacent to its left / right	nu-[i̯] spun [j]-am adus

C   Romanian strong pronominal forms show fewer syncretisms than western Romance languages. Accordingly, the 1st and the 2nd person singular have the Nom≠Acc≠Dat configuration in Romanian, but the Nom≠(Acc≡Dat) configuration in Italian, Spanish, Portuguese, and the Nom≡Acc≡Dat configuration in French; the 1st and the 2nd person plural have the Nom≡Acc≠Dat configuration in Romanian and the Nom≡Acc≡Dat configuration in western Romance languages; the 3rd person singular and plural pattern as Nom≡Acc≠Dat in Romanian, and as Nom≡Acc≡Dat in Italian, Spanish, French, and Portuguese. For the clitic forms, syncretisms in Romanian are similar to other Romance languages, except for the 1st and 2nd person singular, where Acc≠Dat (Niculescu 1965: 30; Reinheimer and Tasmowski 2005: 87; Salvi 2011: 322–3).

6.1.3.1   Selection of strong vs. clitic forms

Strong and clitic forms show complementary distribution. Strong forms behave like DPs, while clitics are constrained by various distributional rules.

6.1.3.1.1 Strong dative forms are used in verbless elliptical sentences (2a,b), as complements in NPs (2c), APs (2d), PPs (2e), and as appositions (2f).

(2) a. A: Cui   i-o   dai? // B: Ție /   lui
       A: Whom CL.DAT.3SG=CL.ACC.F.3SG give // B: you.DAT / him.DAT
       A: 'To whom are you giving it? // B: To you / To him'
    b. Cinste   lor!
       honour   them.DAT
       'Congratulations to them!'

c. cumnat   nouă
   brother-in-law   us.DAT
   'our brother-in-law'

d. util   nouă
   useful   us.DAT
   'useful to us'

e. datorită   vouă
   thanks to   you.DAT
   'owing to you'

f. O   dau   primeia,   adică   ție
   CL.ACC.F.3SG   give   the-first.DAT   namely   you.DAT
   'I'm giving it to the first one, namely to you'

In VPs, strong pronouns co-occur with an accusative clitic (3a; §6.1.4). In combination with a participle (3b), a supine (3c), or an interjection (3d), only the long forms are ruled in.

(3) a. m-a   prezentat   lui
       CL.ACC.1SG=has   introduced   him.DAT
       'he introduced me to him'

   b. acordate   nouă
      awarded   us.DAT
      'awarded to us'

   c. de   adus   lor
      DE_SUP   bring.SUP   them.DAT
      'to bring them'

   d. bravo   lor!
      bravo   them.DAT
      'well done them'

Accusative strong forms occur as complements in PPs.

(4) pe   mine,   cu   tine,   despre   el,   pentru   noi
    PE   me.ACC,   with   you.ACC,   about   him.ACC,   for   us.ACC
    'me', 'with you', 'about him', 'for us'

6.1.3.1.2 Dative clitics prototypically occur in VPs filling the indirect object (5a) or the possessive object (5b) slot. There is also a dative / genitive clitic which occurs in DPs (5c), NPs (5d), and PPs (5e) (see §5.3.3.3).

(5) a. îmi   spune
       CL.DAT.1SG   tells
       'he tells me'

   b. îmi   curge   nasul
      CL.DAT.1SG   drips   nose.DEF.NOM
      'my nose is running'

   c. cartea-mi,   minunata-i   carte
      book.DEF=CL.1SG   wonderful.DEF=CL.3SG book
      'my book', 'his wonderful book'

d. în   inimă-mi
   in   heart=CL.1SG
   'in my heart'

e. deasupra-mi
   above=CL.1SG
   'above me'

Accusative clitics occur only in VPs with verbs (6a) or verbal interjections (6b) as lexical heads.

(6) a. O   citeşte
       CL.ACC.F.3SG   reads
       'he is reading it'

    b. Uite-o!
       look=CL.ACC.F.3SG
       'here it is!'

6.1.3.2 Position of strong and clitic forms

The position of strong and clitic forms is complementary.

6.1.3.2.1 Dative strong forms are normally postposed to their hosts, but the order may be reversed and the pronominal stressed for emphasis and contrast (7a). Inversion is blocked in PPs (7b).

(7) a. utilă   nouă /   nouă   utilă;   cumnat   mie /   mie   cumnat
       useful us.DAT / us.DAT useful   brother-in-law   me.DAT   me.DAT brother-in-law
       'useful to us', 'brother-in-law to me'

    b. datorită   ţie /   *ţie   datorită
       thanks-to   you.DAT   you.DAT   thanks-to
       'thanks to you'

6.1.3.2.2 The position of clitics depends on the morphological class of the host. In DPs (8a), NPs (8b), and PPs (8c), clitics are postposed, and inversion is ruled out. In VPs, both dative and accusative clitics are normally preposed to the lexical verb (8d,e).

(8) a. cartea-mi,   minunata-i   carte
       book.DEF=CL.1SG,   wonderful.DEF=CL.3SG   book
       'my book'   'his / her wonderful book'

    b. în   minte-mi
       in   mind=CL.1SG
       'in my mind'

    c. deasupra-mi
       above=CL.1SG
       'above me'

    d. înainte-ne
       before=CL.1PL
       'before / in front of us'

e. îi spun, îl întreb
   CL.DAT.3SG tell.1SG, CL.ACC.3SG ask.1SG
   'I'm telling him', 'I'm asking him'

Only verbal auxiliaries and adverbial clitics can split the clitic–lexical verb complex (9a,b). For clitic climbing with modal and aspectual complex predicates, see §3.5.2.

(9) a. I-am (mai și) spus
     CL.DAT.3SG=have (more also) said
     'above all / even more, I have told him'

   b. L-aș (tot) întreba
     CL.ACC.3SG=AUX.COND.1SG (continuously) ask.INF
     'I would continuously ask him'

There are several exceptions to the rule. Dative and accusative clitics are postposed when they are hosted by gerunds (10a), imperatives (10b), inverted optatives (10c), and the subjunctive without să (10d).

(10) a. spunându-i, întrebându-l
      telling=CL.DAT.3SG asking=CL.ACC.M.3SG
      'telling him', 'asking him'

    b. spune-i!, întreabă-l!
      tell.IMP=CL.DAT.3SG ask.IMP=CL.ACC.M.3SG
      'tell him!', 'ask him!'

    c. lua-l-ar dracu'!
      take.INF=CL.ACC.M.3SG=AUX.COND.3SG devil.DEF
      'to Hell with him!'

    d. bată-l Dumnezeu!
      beat.SUBJ=CL.ACC.M.3SG God
      'May God punish him!'

For phonological reasons (Monachesi 1999: 110–1, 2005: 169), the clitic *o* is obligatorily postposed in combination with the compound past and the conditional (11) (§3.5.2.1).

(11) am întrebat-o, aș ruga-o
    have.1SG asked=CL.ACC.F.3SG would beg=CL.ACC.F.3SG
    'I asked her' 'I would ask her'

H The position of clitics with respect to the verb has changed over time: in old Romanian the postposition of clitics was rather frequent, while the feminine singular clitic *o* occurred preposed to the pluperfect and the conditional auxiliary. Clitic reduplication (12) was also frequent (Reinheimer and Tasmowski 2005: 76).

  (12) de o au adus-o (Neculce)
      which CL.ACC.F.3SG have brought=CL.ACC.F.3SG
      'which they brought'

U With two coordinated imperatives, the second clitic may occasionally be preposed in colloquial speech, for emphasis.

  (13) Du-te și îi spune!
      go.IMP=CL.REFL.ACC.2SG and CL.DAT.3SG tell.IMP
      'Go and tell him!'

In the context of an A-infinitive or a negative verb form, clitics occur between the infinitive marker and the verb (14a) or between the negator and the verb (14b), respectively.

(14) a. a-i spune, a-l întreba
 A_{INF}=CL.DAT.3SG tell.INF A_{INF}=CL.ACC.3SG ask.INF
 'to tell him', 'to ask him'

    b. nu-i spun, nu-l văd
 not=CL.DAT.3SG tell not=CL.ACC.3SG see
 'I'm not telling him / her', 'I do not see him'

C In informal registers, Romanian (as do other Romance languages) allows auxiliary and second clitic deletion in coordinated structures (15). Unlike other Romance languages, gapping of the verb is allowed if it is repeated in the two coordinated structures (16).

(15) L-a crezut și iertat
 CL.ACC.3SG=has believed and forgiven
 'He believed and forgave him'

(16) Îmi și îți dă dreptate
 CL.DAT.1SG and CL.DAT.2SG gives right
 'He thinks that you and I are right'

6.1.3.3 Selection of clitic variants

Free and bound clitics form series of allomorphs. The selection of these series is contextually conditioned by morphosyntactic rules (adjacency to an auxiliary), by phonological rules (the vowel adjacent to the right and / or to the left of the clitic) and by register rules (formal / informal).

The phonological constraints are subject to three general phonological principles: (i) the presence of a vocalic host for consonant clitics; (ii) the conversion of a hiatus into one of the diphthongs in the phonological inventory of Romanian (§1.3.2); (iii) the differentiation of dative and accusative forms in clitic clusters. The intersection of a large number of variables with a rich inventory of clitics produces many rules which underlie the conditioned realization of allomorphs.

6.1.3.3.1 Free dative and accusative clitics follow similar distributional rules.

A dative clitic in the series {îmi, îți, îi, ne, vă, le} is obligatorily selected if the clitic is adjacent to a pause (#) or to a consonant both to its left and to its right (17a); it is selected only in the formal register if it is adjacent to a vowel to its left or / and to its right (17b), while the informal register prefers the conjunct forms. For clitic clusters, see §6.1.4.

(17) a. îmi spune, când îmi spune
 CL.DAT.1SG tells, when CL.DAT.1SG tells
 'he tells me', 'when he tells me'

    b. ce îmi arată
 what CL.DAT.1SG shows
 'what he shows me'

The selection rules for the accusative clitics in the series {mă, te, îl, o, ne, vă, îi, le} are the following: a form in this series is obligatorily selected if it is adjacent to a consonant or to e, i, u both to its left and to its right (18a,b); a clitic form which starts with the prothetic vowel {îl, îi} is selected only in the formal register if it is adjacent to a vowel to its left (18c), while a conjunct form occurs in the informal register (§6.1.3.3.2); a clitic ending in a vowel {*mă, te, ne, vă, le*} adjacent to *a, o* to its right is selected only in the formal register, while a conjunct form is used in the informal register (§6.1.3.3.2); the vocalic clitic *o* is generally free (18e), although the conjunct form is not excluded, especially in the context of the negator *nu* and the subjunctive marker să (18f) (§6.1.3.3.2).

(18) a. când mă vede, când îl vede
 when CL.ACC.1SG sees when CL.ACC.M.3SG sees
 'when he sees me', 'when she sees him'

 b. mă educă, te iubește, vă uită
 CL.ACC.1SG educates CL.ACC.2SG loves CL.ACC.2PL forgets
 'he educates me', 'he loves you', 'he forgets you'

 c. nu îl cunosc
 not CL.ACC.M.3SG know
 'I do not know him'

 d. mă aude, te observă
 CL.ACC.1SG hears CL.ACC.2SG observes
 'he hears me' 'he observes you'

 e. o aude, o întreb
 CL.ACC.F.3SG hears, CL.ACC.F.3SG ask
 'He hears her', 'I'm asking her'

 f. n-o cunosc, s-o văd
 not=CL.ACC.F.3SG know SĂ$_{SUBJ}$=CL.ACC.F.3SG see.SUBJ
 'I do not know her' 'to see her'

6.1.3.3.2 The distributional rules for bound dative and accusative clitics are similar.

Dative or dative / genitive clitics linked to their left {*-mi, -ți, -i, -ne, -vă, -le*} are obligatorily postposed, both in VPs (19a), and in DPs (19b), NPs (19c), AdvPs (19d), and PPs (19e). The insertion of the archaic ending *-u* after a consonant (19f) and the diphthongization of the final vowel (19g) are contextual strategies of phonological accommodation. The allomorphs {*-mi, -ți, -i*} are obligatorily selected in the context of the infinitive A and of the subjunctive SĂ markers (19h). In the informal register, these allomorphs are frequently selected in the context of the negator *nu* (19i), of the coordinating (19j) and of the subordinating (19k) conjunctions; less often, they combine with relative or interrogative pronouns / adverbs (19l) and interjections ending in a vowel (19m).

(19) a. spune-i, spunându-i
 tell.IMP=CL.DAT.3SG telling=CL.DAT.3SG
 'tell him', 'telling him'

 b. cartea-mi, măiastra-ți carte
 book.DEF=CL.1SG wonderful.DEF=CL.2SG book
 'my book', 'your wonderful book'

 c. în inimă-ți
 in heart=CL.2SG
 'in your heart'

 d. înainte-ne
 before=CL.1PL
 'before / in front of us'

e. deasupra-i
   above=CL.3SG
   'above him'

f. spunându-mi
   telling=CL.DAT.1SG
   'telling me'

g. cere-i
   ask.IMP.2SG=CL.DAT.3SG
   'ask him'

h. a-mi   spune,   să-i   spun
   A_INF=CL.DAT.1SG tell.INF SĂ_SUBJ=CL.DAT.3SG   tell.SUBJ
   'to tell me', 'to tell him'

i. nu-mi   spune,   nu-ți   amintești
   not=CL.DAT.1SG tell   not=CL.REFL.DAT.2SG   remember
   'do not tell me', 'you do not remember'

j. și-l   văd,   fie-i   dai
   and=CL.ACC.M.3SG   see   or=CL.DAT.3SG   give
   'and I see him', 'or you give him'

k. dacă-ți   dă,   că-i   arăt
   if=CL.DAT.2SG   gives   that=CL.DAT.3SG   show
   'if he gives you', 'that I show him'

l. unde-mi   pun   hainele?,   ce-ți   trebuie
   where=CL.DAT.1SG   put   clothes.DEF what=CL.DAT.2SG   need
   'where do I put my clothes?', 'what you need'

m. na-ți   banii!
   take(INTERJ)=CL.DAT.2SG   money.DEF
   'here is your money'

A dative clitic in the series {*mi-, ți-, i-, ne-, v-, le-, mi-, ți-, i-, ne-, v-, le-*}, linked to its right, obligatorily occurs when it precedes a vowel-initial auxiliary (20a); in this context two phonological strategies for avoiding hiatus are available: deletion of the final vowel of the clitic form (20b) or diphthongization (20c). These forms also occur in informal registers when they are adjacent to a verb which starts with *a* or *o* to avoid hiatus (20d); the 2nd person plural clitic selects the allomorph *vă-* (not *v-*) which deletes the vowel *î* of the adjacent verb (20e).

(20) a. mi-a   spus,   ți-ar   da
        CL.DAT.1SG=has   told   CL.DAT.2SG=AUX.COND.3SG   give
        'he told me', 'he would give you'

     b. v-a   cerut
        CL.DAT.2SG=has   asked
        'he asked you'

     c. mi-a   spus,   ți-a   dat
        CL.DAT.1SG=has   told,   CL.DAT.2SG=has   given
        'he told me', 'he gave you'

    d. vă   aduce   bani >   v-aduce   bani   [spoken language]
        CL.DAT.2PL   brings   money > CL.DAT.2PL=brings money
        'he brings you money'

    e. vă   împarte banii >   vă-mparte   banii   [spoken language]
        CL.DAT.2PL   splits   money.DEF > CL.DAT.2PL=splits money.DEF
        '(s)he splits the money between you'

Dative 'mesoclitics' (those linked to the left and to the right) are postposed in clitic clusters (§6.1.4) and rarely inverted in imprecations (21a) and in archaic forms (21b).

(21) a. Da-ţi-ar   Dumnezeu   sănătate!
            give.INF=CL.DAT.2SG=AUX.COND.3SG God   health
            'God bless you!'

      b. spusu-i-am
           told-*U*=CL.DAT.3SG=(I)have
           'I told him'

Left bound accusative clitics in the series {-*mă*, -*te*, -*l*, -*o*, -*ne*, -*vă*, -*i*, -*le*} are obligatorily bound when they are adjacent to a verb in the imperative or in the gerund (22a); the bound clitic -*o* also occurs in the context of analytic verbal forms with an auxiliary starting in a vowel (i.e. pluperfect, conditional) (22b).

(22) a. ajută-mă,   ajutându-mă
            help.IMP=CL.ACC.1SG helping=CL.ACC.1SG
            'help me', 'helping me'

      b. *o   a   văzut >   a văzut-o,
            CL.ACC.F.3SG has   seen >   has seen=CL.ACC.F.3SG
            *o   aş   întreba >   aş   întreba-o
            CL.ACC.F.3SG AUX.COND.1SG ask.INF > AUX.COND.1SG   ask.INF=CL.ACC.F.3SG

Right bound accusative clitics {*m-*, *te-*, *l-*, *ne-*, *v-*, *i-*, *le-*} obligatorily occur for hiatus avoidance when they precede an auxiliary starting with a vowel (23a). Rarely, they occur for hiatus avoidance in the informal register if they are adjacent to a verb which starts in *a* or *o* (23b); the allomorphs *mă-* and *o-* occur in front of a verb that starts with *î*, which is deleted in the context of the respective clitics (23c,d).

(23) a. m-a   întrebat,   te-ar   întreba
            CL.ACC.1SG=has asked   CL.ACC.2SG=AUX.COND.3SG ask.INF
            'he asked me', 'he would ask you'

      b. m-ameninţă,   te-opreşte   (spoken language)
            CL.ACC.1SG=threatens CL.ACC.2SG=stops
            'he threatens me'   'he stops you'

      c. mă întreabă >   mă-ntreabă   (spoken language)
            CL.ACC.1SG asks > CL.ACC.1SG=asks
            'She asks me'

      d. o întreb >   o-ntreb   (spoken language)
            CL.ACC.F.3SG ask > CL.ACC.F.3SG=ask.1SG
            'I ask her a question'

Accusative mesoclitics (those linked to the left and to the right) occasionally occur in imprecations (24a) and in inverted archaic forms (24b).

(24) a. Bătu-l-ar　　　　　　　　　　　　Dumnezeu!
　　　　beat-*U*=CL.ACC.M.3SG=AUX.COND.3SG　God
　　　　'May God punish him!'

　　　b. cerutu-l-am
　　　　asked-*U*=CL.ACC.M.3SG=have
　　　　'I asked for it'

6.1.4 Clitic clusters

A dative and an accusative clitic may co-occur with double object verbs (a direct and an indirect object). They occur both pre- (25a) and postverbally (25b).

(25) a. mi-l　　　　　　　　　　　prezintă,　　mi-o　　　　　　　　　　　arată
　　　　CL.DAT.1SG=CL.ACC.M.3SG　introduces　CL.DAT.1SG=CL.ACC.F.3SG　shows
　　　　'she introduces him to me'　　　　　　'he is showing it to me'

　　　b. prezentându-mi-l,　　　　　　　　　　　　arată-mi-o!
　　　　introducing=CL.DAT.1SG=CL.ACC.M.3SG　　show.IMP=CL.DAT.1SG=CL.ACC.F.3SG
　　　　'introducing him to me'　　　　　　　　　'show it to me'

The selection of allomorphs in the clitic clusters is subject to phonological rules: (i) a dative free form in the series {*mi, ţi, i, ni, vi, li*} occurs when the dative clitic is adjacent on its right to an accusative syllabic clitic starting with a consonant: *mi te, ţi le, vi le, i te*, etc.; (ii) a dative form linked on its right, in the series {*mi-, ţi-, i-, ni-, vi, li-*} occurs under adjacency with one of the accusative clitics *l* or *i*, with which it forms a syllable; from the available plural dative forms, *ne / ni, vă / vi / v-, le / li*, the second one is selected because it avoids the dative≡accusative syncretism in clitic clusters. The possible clitic combinations are presented in Table 6.6, where /?/ marks a small(er) degree of acceptability (Avram 2001: 160; Săvescu Ciucivara 2011).

The combination of clitics is constrained by morphosyntactic, semantic, referential, and phonological rules producing clusters with various degrees of acceptability.

According to the morphosyntactic rules (i) the dative clitic precedes the accusative clitic, both in anteposition (26a) and in postposition (26b); (ii) strings of two clitics of the same person (1st or 2nd person) are excluded (26c); (iii) 1st person singular and plural clitics obligatorily precede 2nd person singular and plural clitics (26d). However, the co-occurrence of two pronominal forms of the same person is allowed if the accusative clitic is preposed to the verb, and the dative is postposed as a strong form (26e). Moreover, while the accusative clitic remains preverbal, the dative can move in postposition to the verb as a strong form (26f).

(26) a. mi-l　　　　　　　　　　　prezintă
　　　　CL.DAT.1SG=CL.ACC.M.3SG　introduces
　　　　'she introduces him to me'

　　　b. prezintă-mi-l!,　　　　　　　　　　　　　　　prezentându-mi-l,
　　　　introduce.IMP=CL.DAT.1SG=CL.ACC.M.3SG　introducing=CL.DAT.1SG=CL.ACC.M.3SG
　　　　'introduce him to me!',　　　　　　　　　　　'introducing him to me'

TABLE 6.6 Clitic clusters

	MĂ	TE	L	O	NE	VĂ	I	LE
mi	–	+	+	+	–	?+	+	+
ți	–	–	+	+	–	–	+	+
i	?+	+	+	+	?+	?+	+	+
ne/ni	–	+	+	+	–	?+	+	+
vă/vi/v-	–	–	+	+	–	–	+	+
le/li	?+	+	+	+	?+	?+	?+	?+

    c. *mi   mă   arată,   *ți   te   redă
       CL.DAT.1SG CL.ACC.1SG shows CL.DAT.2SG CL.ACC.2SG restore

    d. *ți   mă,   *ți   ne,
       CL.DAT.2SG CL.ACC.1SG   CL.DAT.2SG CL.ACC.1PL
       *vi   mă,   *vi   ne
       CL.DAT.2PL CL.ACC.1SG   CL.DAT.2PL CL.ACC.1PL

    e. mă   arată   mie
      CL.ACC.1SG shows   me.DAT
      'it reveals me to myself'

    f. mă   spune   ție
      CL.ACC.1SG tells   you.DAT
      'he denounces me to you'

According to the semantic-referential rule, pronominal clitics in inclusion relations cannot cluster (27).

(27) *mi   ne   arată,   *ți   vă   spune
     CL.DAT.1SG CL.ACC.1PL show   CL.DAT.2SG CL.ACC.2PL say

The phonological rule applies to clitic clusters marked with /?/ in Table 6.6 and exemplified below in (28a). These clusters are not excluded either by the syntactic rule or by the semantic-referential rule, but they yield odd, less common strings of sounds. Such strings become more acceptable if a phonological host for the clitic occurs (28b) and are fully acceptable if the dative is postposed to the verb as a strong pronoun (28c) or in combinations with obligatorily postverbal clitics (28d).

(28) a. ?i   mă   prezintă
         CL.DAT.3SG CL.ACC.1SG introduces
         'He introduces me to him'

      b. ?i   ne-a   prezentat
          CL.DAT.3SG CL.ACC.1PL=has introduced
          'He introduced us to him'

      c. mă   prezintă   lui
          CL.ACC.1SG introduces him.DAT
          'he is introducing me to him'

      d. prezentându-i-ne
         introducing=CL.DAT.3SG=CL.ACC.1PL
         'introducing us to him'

C Romanian patterns with Portuguese, Spanish, and Italian as far as the dative–accusative order of clitics is concerned, while French allows both the dative–accusative and the accusative–dative order. Romanian rejects the co-occurrence of the impersonal reflexive in clitic clusters, unlike French and unlike Portuguese and Spanish, where *se* + *dative* + *accusative* strings are grammatical, or Italian, where *dative* + *accusative* + *si* is licensed (Reinheimer and Tasmowski 2005: 219). While Romanian and Italian allow the co-occurrence of three personal clitics, one of them an ethic dative, French allows only strings of two personal clitics (Niculescu 1978: 237). In Romanian, person restrictions are fewer and weaker than in other Romance languages: the 3rd person singular dative does not co-occur with accusative persons 1 and 2 in western Romance languages, but such combinations have various degrees of acceptability in Romanian, in a way similar to Slavic languages; 1st and 2nd persons cannot co-occur in western Romance languages, except for some Spanish and Italian dialects (Niculescu 1978: 238–40; Dobrovie-Sorin 2000; Săvescu Ciucivara 2011).

6.1.5 Clitic doubling

Romanian displays clitic doubling of the direct and indirect object, involving accusative and dative clitics, respectively. Romanian clitic doubling has two variants: resumptive doubling (29a) and anticipation (29b). Agreement between the noun and the clitic in the chain is overt (29c) or covert (29d,e), depending on the inherent features of the clitic.

(29) a. pe care$_i$ nu-l$_i$ cunosc, cui$_i$ nu   i$_i$-a   spus
       PE which not=CL.ACC.M.3SG know   whom.DAT not CL.DAT.3SG=has told
       'which I do not know', 'to whom she didn't tell'

   b. l$_i$-a   văzut   pe Ion$_i$,   i$_i$-a   spus lui   Ion$_i$
       CL.ACC.M.3SG=has seen   PE Ion   CL.DAT.3SG=has told LUI.DAT   Ion
       'she saw Ion' 'she told Ion'

   c. îl$_i$ văd   pe Ion$_i$,   o$_i$ văd   pe   Ioana$_j$,
       CL.ACC.M.3SG see   PE Ion   CL.ACC.F.3SG see   PE   Ioana
       'I see Ion' 'I see Ioana'

   d. îi$_{i+j}$ văd   pe   Ion$_i$ și   Ioana$_j$
       CL.ACC.3PL   see   PE   Ion   and Ioana
       'I see Ion and Ioana'

   e. le$_i$ spun   băieților$_i$,   le$_i$ spun   fetelor$_i$
       CL.DAT.3PL tell   boys.DEF.DAT   CL.DAT.3PL tell   girls.DEF.DAT
       'I'm telling the boys' 'I'm telling the girls'

Clitic doubling of the direct and indirect object correlates with individualization: doubling occurs for nominals with the [+specific] feature, whether inherent to the clitic or contextually acquired (§3.2.1.5, §3.2.3.4).

C Among Romance languages, only Romanian and some Spanish dialects display grammaticalized clitic doubling (Reinheimer and Tasmowski 2005: 219, 287).

Nominal direct and indirect objects are doubled by 3rd person singular and plural clitics; demonstrative and indefinite object pronouns designating the group of the hearer / speaker are doubled by 1st and 2nd person plural clitics (30a–c) (§12.2.3).

(30) a. I$_i$-a   ajutat   pe   aceştia$_i$ /   pe   fiecare$_i$ /   pe   toţi$_i$
      CL.DAT.M.3PL=has   helped   PE   these /   PE   each /   PE   all
      '(S)he helped these ones / each of them / them all'

b. Ne$_i$-a   ajutat   pe   aceştia$_i$ care… /   pe   fiecare$_i$ /   pe   toţi$_i$
      CL.DAT.1PL=has   helped   PE   these   who… /   PE   each /   PE   all
      '(S)he helped us who… / each one / everybody'

c. V$_i$-a   ajutat   pe   aceştia$_i$ care… /   pe   fiecare$_i$ /   pe   toţi$_i$
      CL.DAT.2PL=has   helped   PE   these   who… /   PE   each /   PE   all
      'She helped you who… / each one / everybody'

6.1.6 Pronominal doubling

Accusative and dative 1st and 2nd person strong pronouns optionally double the direct and indirect clitic objects for emphasis (31).

(31) a. Mă$_i$ întreabă   (pe   mine$_i$)
      CL.ACC.1SG   asks   (PE   me.ACC)
      'He is asking *me*'

b. Îmi$_i$ spune   (mie$_i$)
      CL.DAT.1SG   tells   (me.DAT)
      'He is telling *me*'

6.1.7 Extensions of pronominal heads

Pronouns do not combine with complements or determiners (§5.3). Some pronouns enter appositive constructions, and sometimes accept isolated modifiers and adjuncts: appositive constructions with proper names (32a), categorizing nominals (32b), definite numeric (32c), or indefinite (32d) quantifiers (Vasilescu 2009b); some modifiers or adjuncts are relative (32e), elliptical (32f), or non-finite (32g) clauses, optionally headed by *cel* (32h); focus adverbials can precede pronouns (32i).

(32) a. Eu, Ion, am hotărât asta
     'I, Ion, have decided that'

b. noi   profesorii
     we   teachers.DEF
     'we teachers'

c. eu   unul,   noi   trei
     I   one.DEF.M   we   three
     'I for one' 'we three'

d. noi   toţi,   ei   câţiva
     we   all   they   few
     'we all' 'the few of them'

e. eu,   care   te   iubesc
     I   who   CL.ACC.2SG   love
     'I who love you'

f. el   de   acolo
    he   from there
    'him over there'
g. în   poza   aceea eşti tu,   înotând
    in   picture.DEF that are you   swimming
    'in that picture it's you, swimming'
h. el, cel de   ieri,   tu,   cel   muncind zi   şi   noapte
    he   CEL of   yesterday you   CEL   working day and night
    'he, the one he used to be' 'you, the one working day and night'
i. chiar eu,   tocmai tu,   exact el
    'I myself / even me' 'just you' 'exactly him'

6.1.8 Reference: deictic, anaphoric, expletive

Depending on the context, personal pronouns can function as deictics, anaphorics, and expletives.

6.1.8.1 Deictic uses

The 1st and the 2nd person pronouns function as deictics, while the 3rd person pronouns function as deictics or anaphorics, depending on the context. Personal deixis sometimes overlaps with social and empathetic deixis.

Several features of Romanian culture, for example orality (as defined in Tannen 1981), contextualism (as defined in Hall 1976), and intense 'face-work' (as conceived in Brown and Levinson 1978) predict a heavy use of deictics as cues for the participants' interactional involvement in the speech event and as discourse coherence markers (Manoliu-Manea 2001).

Being a pro-drop language, Romanian relies on verb inflection to mark person deixis rather than on personal pronouns. Personal pronouns occur for emphasis, contrast, topicalization, and foregrounding, as presupposition triggers, speech act hedges, or intensifiers, and discourse-break markers (Vasilescu 2009c).

Personal pronouns occur in structures with double or multiple deictics: pronominal subject + inflection (33a); personal pronoun + pronominal intensifier (+ inflection) (33b); (personal pronoun +) reflexive + inflection (33c); clitic + strong pronoun, that is pronominal doubling (33d); possessive dative + possessive (+ personal pronoun) + inflection (33e).

(33) a. eu   citesc,   tu   citeşti
        I   read.1SG   you   read.2SG
        'I am reading'   'You are reading'
     b. eu   însumi i-am   spus, am   plecat cu   el   însuşi
        I   myself CL.DAT.3SG=have   told   have left   with him himself
        'I told him myself'   'I left with him'
     c. tu   te   gândeşti,   eu   mă   spăl
        you   CL.REFL.ACC.2SG   think.2SG   I   CL.REFL.ACC.1SG wash.1SG
        'you are thinking'   'I am washing'

d. te   ajut   pe   tine,   îți   spun   ție
    CL.ACC.2SG   help   PE   you.ACC CL.DAT.2SG   tell   you.DAT
    'I am helping you'   'I am telling you'

e. tu   ți-ai   mâncat   porția   ta
    you   CL.REFL.DAT.2SG=have   eaten   portion.DEF   your
    'You have eaten your portion'

Some instances of multiple deictics, that is emphatic pronoun structures, inherent reflexives, and reflexive possessive datives, have grammaticalized.

Person shifts produce special deictic uses. The 'collective plural' (34a) functions as a strategy to express group inclusion and non-assertiveness in colloquial speech. The 'solidarity plural' shows empathy with the interlocutor and functions as a strategy of persuasion (34b). In the written register, the 'editorial plural' (34c) voices shared attitudes and alignment. The 'authorial plural' (34d) in scientific texts is a strategy of objective or of author–reader shared stance. In class interactions and in school books the 'didactic plural' (34e) is the unmarked option.

(34) a. Așteptăm de la Guvern pensii mai mari
         'We expect higher pensions from the Government'

     b. Acum luăm pastilele
         'Now we are taking the pills'

     c. Parcurgem o perioadă de criză
         'We are going through a period of crisis'

     d. Vom descrie în continuare cliticele românești
         'Next we are going to describe Romanian clitics'

     e. Citiți lecția!
         'Read the lesson!'

The switch from the 1st person singular (*I*) to the 1st person plural (*we*) marks, depending on the context, either hierarchic inferiority ('modesty plural') or hierarchic superiority ('authority plural'). Both uses are ever less frequent in contemporary Romanian and occur mostly in the speech of less educated people.

The 2nd person pronouns and inflections have shifted to non-deictic uses and have grammaticalized as the basic strategies for encoding the generic and the impersonal meaning in colloquial speech ((35a); see also §3.1.3.3) while the formal style has adopted the reflexive passive strategy (35b). Colloquially, first person singular (35c) can convey the generic, impersonal meaning, as well.

(35) a. Nu pleci fără să spui 'bună ziua'
         'You are not leaving without saying *good bye*'

     b. Nu se pleacă fără a spune 'bună ziua'
         'One doesn't leave without saying *good bye*'

     c. Când nu știu, întreb!
         'When I do not know, I ask'

Contextual uses of pronouns are associated with various empathetic values. The 1st and the 2nd person dative clitics have grammaticalized as markers of affective stance or empathy, the so-called 'ethic dative' (36a). The use of the personal pronoun / possessive *nostru* 'our' to express location is a strategy of affiliation by building an inside-perspective (36b). Person shifts in the use of personal pronouns (2nd singular > 1st singular; 2nd plural > 1st plural) convey a patronizing attitude (36c,d). The use of a noun to designate the 1st person expresses distant self-reference (36e). Reversed address forms, common to several Balkan and Romance languages (Renzi 1968; Beyrer 1979), are frequent in Romanian when adults address children; a relational or a proper name will sometimes substitute a pronoun to convey an affective stance (36f,g). Pronominal subject doubling functions as a linguistic marker of indirect speech acts, changing an assertion into a warning, threat, etc. (36h).

(36) a. Și   mi-(ți)-l   ia   la întrebări
        and   CL.DAT.1SG=CL.DAT.2SG=CL.ACC.M.3SG   takes at questions
        'And (s)he starts questioning him'

   b. la noi în   țară
      at us   in   country
      'in our country'

   c. Eu sunt băiat inteligent
      'I am an intelligent boy'

   d. Noi suntem copii cuminți
      'We are good children'

   e. Și s-a pus Maria / fata pe învățat...
      'And Mary / the girl started to study'

   f. Andrei, hai cu bunica / cu Ioana! (It is the grandmother / Ioana who addresses Andrei)
      'Andrei, come with granny / Ioana'

   g. Ce   faci   acolo, mamă?   (mother to her child)
      What do.2SG   there, mother?
      'What are you doing there, honey?'

   h. Vine   ea,   mama!
      comes   she   mother.DEF
      'I am warning you, mom is coming!'

For anaphoric uses see §13.6.

6.1.8.2 Expletive uses

Romanian displays zero reference pronouns in non-argumental positions, that is expletives with pragmatic functions on the borderline between empathetic and discourse deixis: the 'neuter dative' (37a) and the 'neuter accusative' ((37b); see also §3.2.1.5.2) in colloquial and slang idiomatic expressions. They mark the small psychological distance among the interlocutors. Some are obligatory, others are optional.

(37) a. Dă-i   cu   bere, dă-i   cu   vin!
        give.IMP=CL.DAT.3SG   with beer, give.IMP=CL.DAT.3SG   with wine
        'They keep drinking glasses of beer and wine, one after another'

   b. A   luat-o   la   fugă
      has taken=CL.ACC.F.SG   at   run
      'He ran away'

6.2 REFLEXIVE PRONOUNS

The Romanian reflexive pronouns have three persons, singular and plural, overtly marked for the dative–accusative opposition. They display syncretisms with persons 1 and 2 singular and plural of the personal pronouns ((38a,b); §6.1.3), and have dedicated forms for person 3, unmarked for gender and number, as shown in Table 6.7.

(38) a. eu$_i$ mă$_i$ spăl,   tu$_i$ te$_i$ speli
     I   CL.REFL.ACC.1SG   wash.1SG   you   CL.REFL.ACC.2SG   wash.2SG
     'I wash myself'   'you wash yourself'

  b. eu$_i$ îmi$_i$ spun,   tu$_i$ îți$_i$ spui
     I   CL.REFL.DAT.1SG   say.1SG   you   CL.REFL.DAT.2SG   say.2SG
     'I say to myself'   'you say to yourself'

Reflexives have strong and clitic forms, the latter being either free or bound. In contemporary Romanian they occur only in VPs; the constructions with reflexives in NPs (39a), AdvPs (39b) and PPs (39c) are archaic (§5.3.3.3).

(39) a. în   cale-și
       in   way=CL.REFL.3SG
       'on his way'

  b. asupră-și
     over=CL.REFL.3SG
     'over himself'

  c. a   luat   asupră-și
     has   taken   over=CL.REFL.3SG
     'he assumed it / took it on himself'

H Romanian reflexives continue those of Latin (ELR: 477–8; Ernout and Thomas 1959: 182–6). Some forms in ORom on the border between reflexives and intensifiers (*șie, șieși, eluși, țieși, loruși*) have disappeared in modern Romanian (Dimitrescu 1978: 266–7).

C All Romance languages continue the Latin reflexive *se* (Maiden 2011a: 159). The strong–clitic opposition has been inherited by other Romance languages, as well (It. *si / sé*, Fr. *se / soi*), but only Romanian marks the dative–accusative opposition (cf. Niculescu 1965: 31).

TABLE 6.7 Reflexive pronouns

CASE		PERSON 3	
FORMS		SINGULAR M≡F	PLURAL M≡F
D	STRONG		sie(și) [sie(ʃⁱ)]
	CLITIC	FREE	îşi [iʃⁱ]
		BOUND	și [ʃi] -și [ʃⁱ] și- [ʃi, ʃj] -și- [ʃi, ʃj]
ACC	STRONG		sine [sine]
	CLITIC	FREE / BOUND	se [se] -se se- [se, sę] -se-
		BOUND	s- -s-

The selection rules for the allomorphs of *și* [ʃi, ʃj, ʃⁱ] (40a) and *se* [se, ș] (40b) are the same with the personal pronouns *mi* and *ne*, respectively. The selection of strong vs. clitic forms for the 3rd person and their position in the VP follow the same rules as personal pronouns do (§6.1.3.3).

(40) a. [ʃi] le spală, [ʃja]-a spălat hainele, nu-[ʃⁱ] spală hainele
   b. [se]vede, [se̦a]șteaptă

The same morphosyntactic, phonological, and register rules constrain the selection of both personal and reflexive pronouns (§6.1.3.3), as shown in (41a–f).

(41) a. s-a   gândit,   s-ar   gândi
       CL.REFL.ACC.3SG=has   thought   CL.REFL.ACC.3SG=AUX.COND.3SG   think
       'he thought' 'he would think'

   b. Ducă-s-ar   pe pustii!, gânditu-s-a
      go=CL.REFL.ACC.3SG=AUX.COND.3SG on deserts thought=CL.REFL.ACC.3SG=have
      'May he go to Hell',   'He thought'

   c. gândindu-se
      thinking=CL.REFL.ACC.3SG
      'thinking'

   d. se   ascunde >   [se̦a]scunde
      CL.REFL.ACC.3SG   hides >   CL.REFL.ACC.3SG=hides
      'he hides'

   e. se   oprește >   [se̦o]prește
      CL.REFL.ACC.3SG   stops >   CL.REFL.ACC.3SG=stops
      'he stops'

   f. se   întreabă >   se-ntreabă
      CL.REFL.ACC.3SG   asks >   CL.REFL.ACC.3SG=asks
      'he asks himself'

The strong forms of the reflexive pronouns are synonyms of phrases that combine a personal pronoun and an intensifier:

(42) a. pe   sine≡pe el   însuși
       PE   self≡PE   him.ACC   himself
       'himself'

   b. sieși≡lui   însuși
      self.DAT≡him.DAT   himself
      'to himself'

For emphasis the reflexive clitic, dative, and accusative, can be doubled by the reflexive strong form (43a,b), by the personal pronoun (43c,d), or by the reflexive / personal pronoun and an intensifier simultaneously (43e–h).

(43) a. Își   reproșează   sieși
       CL.REFL.DAT.3SG   reproaches   himself.DAT
       'He reproaches himself'

   b. Se   cunoaște   pe   sine
      CL.REFL.ACC.3SG   knows   PE   himself
      'He knows himself'

c. Îşi   reproşează lui
   CL.REFL.DAT.3SG reproaches him.DAT
   'He reproaches himself'

d. Se   cunoaşte pe el
   CL.REFL.ACC.3SG knows   PE him
   'He knows himself'

e. Îşi   reproşează sie   însuşi
   CL.REFL.DAT.3SG reproaches self.DAT himself
   'He reproaches himself'

f. Se   cunoaşte pe sine însuşi
   CL.REFL.ACC.3SG knows   PE self himself
   'He knows himself'

g. Îşi   reproşează lui   însuşi
   CL.REFL.DAT.3SG reproaches him.DAT himself
   'He reproaches himself'

h. Se   cunoaşte pe el însuşi
   CL.REFL.ACC.3SG knows   PE him himself
   'He knows himself'

In high registers of contemporary Romanian the prefix *auto* is increasingly used with reflexive verbs, redundantly, to express the reflexive meaning (44).

(44) a se autoproclama, a se autointitula, a se autocaracteriza
     'self-proclaim' 'self-call' 'self-characterize'

Romanian reflexive pronouns are multifunctional (§3.4.2).
   Reflexive head–modifier relations are similar to personal pronoun head–modifier relations (§6.1.7).

6.3 'POLITENESS' PRONOUNS

Romanian displays politeness pronouns for the 2nd and 3rd persons singular and plural.

6.3.1 The paradigm

Politeness pronouns for the 2nd person are *dumneata* (Table 6.8) and *dumneavoastră* (Table 6.9), and for the 3rd person *dumnealui* (Table 6.10).
   They show case, gender, and number syncretisms.
   Syncretisms are disambiguated situationally and / or contextually by other inflected words in sentence (45a,b).

(45) a. Dumneavoastră, doamnă, sunteţi obosită
        'You, lady, are tired'
     b. Dumneavoastră, doamnelor, sunteţi obosite
        'You, ladies, are tired'

TABLE 6.8 Politeness pronouns (a)

	Singular Person 2 sg		Person 2pl	
	M	F	M	F
NOM≡ACC	dumneata		–	
GEN≡DAT	dumitale			

TABLE 6.9 Politeness pronouns (b)

	Singular Person 2 sg≡2 pl
	M≡F
NOM≡ACC	dumneavoastră
GEN≡DAT	

TABLE 6.10 Politeness pronouns (c)

	Singular Person 3 sg		Person 3 pl	
	M	F	M	F
NOM≡ACC	dumnealui	dumneaei	dumnealor	
GEN≡DAT				

C The Romanian politeness pronominal system is the most complex in the Romance area. Among Romance languages, Romanian has a politeness pronoun for the 3rd person (Reinheimer and Tasmowski 2005: 149).

H In the Romanian pronominal system, politeness pronouns were the last to emerge, as late as the 16th century, with several lexical variants (*domneata, domneta, domniata, domnia-voastră, dumniile voastre, domniia sa, domnisale, domnesa*), first in private documents, and later, in the 18th century, in religious texts (Dimitrescu 1978: 265–6). In the 2nd person, *dumneavoastră* ('your lordship') served as a basis for new lexemes (*Domnia Voastră, Domniile Voastre*). Forms for the 3rd person emerged by analogy (*Domnia Sa, Domniile Sale* 'thy lordship').

Politeness pronouns have the same distributional and combinatorial properties as strong personal pronouns (§6.1.3.1). Head–modifiers relations are similar for personal and reflexive pronouns (§6.1.7).

6.3.2 'Politeness' pronouns as social deictics

Politeness pronouns function as social deictics and together with personal pronouns they form a four-term politeness continuum. Degrees of politeness (zero–minimum–high–maximum) overlap with the informal / formal and solidarity / distance oppositions (Table 6.11).

TABLE 6.11 The politeness continuum

PERSON	PERSONAL PRONOUN ZERO DEGREE (I)	POLITENESS PRONOUN MINIMUM DEGREE, INFORMAL, SOLIDARITY (II)	HIGH DEGREE FORMAL, +/− SOLIDARITY (III)	MAXIMUM DEGREE, FORMAL, DISTANCE (IV)
2 SG	tu 'you'	dumneata, mata	dumneavoastră	Domnia Voastră
3 SG	el 'he' ea 'she'	dânsul (M) dânsa (F)	dumnealui (M) dumneaei (F)	Domnia Sa
2 PL	voi 'you'	—	dumneavoastră	Domniile Voastre
3 PL	ei 'they' (M) ele 'they' (F)	dânşii (M) dânsele (F)	dumnealor	Domniile Lor

C While Spanish, French, and Italian have a binary politeness system, Romanian and Portuguese (*tu–você–senhor*) have a gradual system (Niculescu 1965: 43; Reinheimer and Tasmowski 2005: 149).

The contextual parameters that underlie the use of social deictics are social distance (social class, education, age, sex, and status), hierarchic asymmetry and degree of intimacy / solidarity between the interlocutors (Vasilescu 2008a: 212–18). The selection of the politeness pronoun depends on the contextual negotiation of relations among the participants in the speech event; marked options function as strategies of persuasion or generate conversational implicatures like assumed equality with the interlocutor, minimized / maximized hierarchic asymmetries or social distance, a change in the discourse relations dynamics, power shifts, irony, etc.

Contextually, the 2nd person reflexive pronouns can acquire the [+deferent] feature, showing the [+/−deferent] opposition as in (46a) and (46b), respectively. *Dumneata*, which includes in its structure the 2nd person possessive *ta* (*dumneata* < *domnia* + *ta*) agrees with the 2nd person singular of the verb and conveys a lower degree of politeness (46c).

(46) a. Te   temi   de   câini, Maria?
       CL.REFL.ACC.2SG fear.2SG of dogs, Maria?
       'Are you afraid of dogs, Maria?'

   b. Vă   temeţi   de   câini, domnule?
      CL.REFL.ACC.2PL fear.2PL of dogs, gentleman.DEF.VOC?
      'Are you afraid of dogs, sir?'

   c. Dumneata   te   temi de câini, domnule?
      you.MID.POL.2SG CL.REFL.ACC.2SG fear of dogs gentleman.DEF.VOC?
      'Are you afraid of dogs, sir?'

H The agreement of politeness pronouns in subject position with the 2nd person plural as a grammaticalized deference strategy (*dumneavoastră sunteţi*) emerged at the beginning of the 19th century, following intense contact with the French culture. In rural areas, less educated people would still use politeness terms of address in the context of the 2nd person singular (47a) instead of the 2nd person plural (47b).

(47) a. Domnul   doctor,   ești   om   cu   carte!
       gentleman.DEF doctor,   are.2SG   man   with book!
       'Doctor, you are an educated person!'
    b. Domnul   doctor,   sunteți   om   cu   carte!
       gentleman.DEF doctor,   are.PRES.2PL   man   with book!
       'Doctor, you are an educated person!'

Romanian honorifics are organized in a closed system of historically created terms. They index social or institutional (clergy) hierarchy. For social positions, pronominal expressions, that is compounds of a noun and a possessive, are used (48a). Often, adjectives function as pragmatic intensifiers (48b). Related to this semantic field there are terms still used in diplomacy (48c). Expressions for clergy hierarchic positions are composed with nominal / adjectival pragmatic intensifiers and a possessive (48d) (Vasileanu 2009).

(48) a. Măria Ta, Domnia Ta, Majestatea Ta / Voastră, Sfinția Ta
       'My Lord', 'Your Highness', 'Your Majesty', 'Your Holiness'
    b. Luminate Împărate, Preasfințite Împărate
       'Enlightened Emperor', 'Holy Emperor'
    c. Excelența Voastră
       'Your Excellency'
    d. Preasfinția Sa, Cucernicia Sa
       'His Holiness'

Romanian has two options for the agreement of honorifics with the verb, which correlate with different degrees of politeness: syntactic agreement with the 2nd person plural of the verb (lower degree of politeness, 49a,b), and semantic agreement with the 3rd person singular (higher degree of politeness, 49c,d).

(49) a. Alteța   Voastră   ați   spus...
       highness   your.2PL   have.2PL   said
       'Your highness has said...'
    b. Domnule,   doriți   o   bere?
       gentleman.DEF.VOC   wish.2PL   a   beer?
       'Sir, would you like a beer?'
    c. Alteța   Voastră   a   spus...
       highness   your.2PL   has.3SG   said...
       'Your highness has said...'
    d. Domnul   dorește   o   bere?
       gentleman.DEF wishes   a   beer?
       'Would Sir like a beer?'

6.4 PRONOMINAL INTENSIFIERS (EMPHATIC PRONOUNS)

Pronominal intensifiers (emphatic pronouns / adjectives) form a lexico-grammatical paradigm distinct from the paradigm of reflexives. They overtly mark person, number, gender, and partly case, as shown in Table 6.12.

TABLE 6.12 The emphatic pronoun

Case	1 Sg		1 Pl		2 Sg		2 Pl		3 Sg		3 Pl	
	M	F	M	F	M	F	M	F	M	F	M	F
NOM≡ACC	însumi	însămi	înşine	însene	însuţi	însăţi	înşivă	însevă	însuşi	însăşi	înşişi	înseşi
GEN≡DAT		însemi				înseţi				înseşi		însele

H   In Latin the emphatic meaning was conveyed by the 'intensive demonstrative' IPSE (*ipse Caesar*), which expressed the opposition to an entity explicitly or implicitly evoked in the context (Ernout and Thomas 1959: 189); the demonstrative also accepted an adverbial use (UALUE SE IPSE APERUERUNT 'the door opened by itself'; ET IPSE 'he too'). Compared to Latin, the Romanian correspondent (Old Romanian *însu*) loosened its indexical value and became a focal particle pointing to a salient constituent in the co-text (Manoliu 2011: 478).

C   In the Romance area, only Romanian developed an emphatic pronoun, which is a compound of the pronoun *însu* (descending from the Lat. IPSE) + a personal / reflexive dative clitic (*mi, ţi, şi, ne, vă, şi / le*). Other Romance languages (Fr. *même*, It. *stesso*, Sp. *mismo*, Ptg. *mesmo*) use a unique form both as an intensifier and as a determiner of identity (Manoliu-Manea 1993: 122–3, 1994).

U   Of the two forms available for the 3rd person feminine, modern Romanian prefers *însele*, probably due to the analogy with the plural forms of the (pro)nouns they intensify (50).
   (50)   fetele   însele,   ele   însele
          girls.DEF   themselves,   they   themselves
          'the girls themselves',   'they themselves'

Person and number oppositions are marked on the intensifier by the (suppletive) forms of the reflexive clitic; gender (and number) oppositions are marked on the first constituent in the structure by inflectional endings common with those of adjectives (M.SG -*u*; F.SG -*ă*; M.PL -*i*; F.PL -*e*). The case opposition is marked only in the feminine singular.

U   Contemporary Romanian shows a tendency to simplify the inflectional system of the intensifiers. The 3rd person masculine forms in particular tend to be generalized in sub-standard Romanian.
   Emphatic pronouns occur especially in written language; in spoken language adverbial (51a), adjectival (51b), numeral (51c), and idiomatic (51d) synonyms are preferred.
   (51)   a. chiar / tocmai el,   eu personal
             'he himself',   'I personally'
          b. propria mea mamă,   tu singură
             'my own mother',   'you yourself'
          c. eu   una
             I   one.DEF.F
             'as for me'
          d. cu urechile mele,   cu ochii mei,   cu mâna mea
             'with my own ears', 'with my own eyes', 'with my own hands'

Intensifiers copy the gender and number features of the (pro)nominal in the structure. Normally they relate to [+human] nominals, but increasingly to [–animate] ones as well (52a,b).

(52) a. omul   însuşi
       man.DEF himsef
       'the man himself'

   b. discursul însuşi
      speech.DEF himself
      'the speech itself'

The (pro)noun and its intensifier form an intonation unit, with the semantic stress on either of the two terms; a higher degree of emphasis is conveyed when both terms are stressed.

H In old Romanian intensifiers frequently functioned as substitutes for personal pronouns in the subject position; today this use is peripheral (53).

(53) însumi l-am   văzut
     myself CL.ACC.M.3SG=have seen
     'I saw him / it myself'

Intensifiers can precede or follow the DP (54a,b); their position correlates with a pragmatic difference, that is (a) infirming an expectation which does not include the value of the intensified nominal or (b) the negation of the possibility that the predication does not apply to the value of the variable expressed by the intensified argument (Manoliu-Manea 1993: 120–1).

(54) a. însuşi   copilul,   însuşi Ion, însumi eu
        himself   child.DEF himself Ion   myself I
        'the child himself' 'Ion himself' 'I myself'

    b. copilul   însuşi,   Ion însuşi,   eu însumi
       child.DEF himself   Ion himself   I   myself
       'the child himself' 'Ion himself' 'I myself'

Intensifiers occur in postposition exclusively when they intensify a (pro)noun marked for the genitive or the dative (55a,b); with plural pronouns preposed intensifiers seem less acceptable (55c).

(55) a. Mi-a   spus mie   însemi /   *însemi   mie
        CL.DAT.1SG=has told me.DAT myself.F.DAT myself.F.DAT me.DAT
        'She told me'

    b. casa   lui   Cosmin însuşi / *lui   însuşi   Cosmin
       house.DEF LUI.GEN   Cosmin himself   LUI.GEN   himself Cosmin
       'the house of Cosmin himself'

    c. noi înşine /   ?înşine   noi
       we   ourselves ourselves we
       'we ourselves'

Normally the intensifier is adjacent to the intensified term, but inserted words are not excluded, yet they are limited (56a,b).

(56) a. Profesorul vine   însuşi   să   vadă   ce   se   întâmplă
        teacher.DEF comes   himself SĂ_SUBJ   see.SUBJ   what CL.REFL.3SG happens
        'The professor comes himself to see what is going on'

    b. După cum însuşi   mărturiseşte autorul
       as   how himself confesses   author.DEF
       'As the author himself confesses'

6.5 RECIPROCAL PRONOUNS

Romanian shows several reciprocal pronouns realized as compounds of two indefinite pronouns (57a) or a preposition and a personal pronoun (57b). They have adverbial synonyms (57c).

(57) a. unul... altul,   unul... celălalt,   fiecare... fiecare
       one... another   one... the-other   each   each
       'each... other', 'one... another'

   b. între   noi / voi / ei /   ele
      among we   you   they.M they.F
      'each... other', 'one... another'

   c. reciproc
      reciprocally
      'reciprocally'

Unul... altul 'each other' is the most frequent and also the unmarked term of the paradigm. *Unul... celălalt* 'one another' is selected for groups of two entities individually foregrounded. *Fiecare... fiecare* 'one another' distributively emphasizes the entities which form the group of the subject. *Între noi / voi / ei / ele* 'each other' is used to foreground the group expressed by the subject. The adverb *reciproc* 'reciprocally' foregrounds the relation of reciprocity and leaves in the background the actors involved in the relation.

The reciprocal pronoun *unul... altul* functions as an anaphor whose antecedents are the terms of the multiple / plural subject (58).

(58) Ion$_i$ și Gheorghe$_j$ se   salută unul$_{i/j}$ pe altul$_{i/j}$
     Ion and Gheorghe   CL.REFL.ACC.3PL greet one.M.SG   PE other.M.SG
     'Ion and Gheorghe are greeting each other'

Despite its semantic unity, *unul... altul* has internal inflection. The indefinite pronouns in the structure copy the gender features of the antecedents (59a,b); when the terms display different gender features, the masculine prevails over the feminine (59c); when the terms display different number features, the formal or semantic plural prevails over the singular (59d).

(59) a. Maria$_i$ și Ana$_j$ se   salută una$_{i/j}$ pe alta$_{j/i}$
        Maria and Ana   CL.REFL.ACC.3PL greet one.F.SG   PE other.F.SG
        'Maria and Ana greet each other'

   b. Ion$_i$ și Gheorghe$_{i/j}$ se   salută unul$_{i/j}$ pe altul$_{j/i}$
      Ion and Gheorghe   CL.REFL.ACC.3PL greet one.M.SG   PE other.M.SG
      'Ion and Gheorghe greet each other'

   c. Ion$_i$ și Ana$_j$ se   salută unul$_{i/j}$ pe altul$_{i/j}$
      Ion and Ana   CL.REFL.ACC.3PL greet one.M.SG   PE other.M.SG
      'Ion and Ana are greeting each other'

   d. Antrenorul$_i$ și echipa$_j$ se   felicită   unii$_{i/j}$ pe alții$_{i/j}$
      coach.DEF   and team.DEF CL.REFL.ACC.3PL congratulate one.M.PL   PE other.M.PL
      'The coach and the team are congratulating each other'

The reciprocal phrase reflects the morphological cases and the obligatory prepositions in the corresponding bi-propositional structure (60a,b).

(60) a. Maria   salută   pe   Ion   și   Ion   salută   pe Maria
       Maria   greets   PE   Ion   and   Ion   greets   PE Maria
       'Maria greets Ion and Ion greets Maria'
       >Maria   și   Ion se   salută unul   pe   altul
       Maria   and   Ion CL.REFL.ACC.3PL greet one.M.SG PE   other.M.SG
       'Maria and Ion greets each other'
   b. Maria   îi   dă   cadouri   lui   Gheorghe și
       Maria   CL.DAT.3SG gives   presents   to   Gheorghe and
       Gheorghe îi   dă   cadouri   Mariei
       Gheorghe CL.DAT.3SG gives   presents   Maria.DAT
       'Maria gives presents to Gheorghe and Gheorghe gives presents to Maria'
       > Maria   și   Gheorghe își   dau   cadouri
       Maria   and   Gheorghe CL.REFL.DAT.3PL give presents
       unul   altuia
       one.M.SG other.DAT.M.SG
       'Maria and Gheorghe give presents to each other'

Unul... celălalt and *fiecare... fiecare* function analogously; the latter is avoided if the second argument has an oblique case (?*fiecare... fiecăruia*). *Între noi / voi / ei / ele* copies the person features of the arguments, that is 1st / 2nd / 3rd person plural, and also the gender for the 3rd person; it does not occur in the context of a prepositional verb (*a se baza pe* 'rely on', *a avea grijă de* 'take care of').

The reciprocal pronouns are obligatory or optional depending on the structure in which they occur (for the reciprocal pronoun device and other devices used to express reciprocal meaning, see §3.4.3).

CONCLUSIONS

1 Personal pronouns display three grammatical persons, singular and plural, showing suppletion for persons 1 and 2, and marking gender distinctions overtly only in the 3rd person, but not the [+/−animate] opposition. First person plural functions contextually as an inclusive or an exclusive plural. Case distinctions are overtly marked, that is nominative ≠ accusative ≠ dative. Third persons singular and plural have forms for the genitive, syncretic with the dative forms, and parallel with possessives. In the dative and the accusative, personal pronouns have two series of forms, strong and clitic, with many allomorphs and syncretisms arranged along a hierarchy, that is persons 1, 2 sg > 1, 2 pl > 3 sg > 3 pl. Strong forms are postposed in NPs, APs, PPs, and occasionally in VPs; clitics are postposed in DPs, NPs, PPs, and in VPs marked for the gerund and the imperative, and preposed in all other VPs. The selection of clitic variants is governed by numerous morphosyntactic, phonological, and register rules. Clitic clusters are governed by less rigid morphosyntactic, referential, and phonological rules than in other Romance languages. Clitic doubling of direct and indirect objects is partly grammaticalized, and has two variants: resumptive doubling and anticipation. Pronominal doubling is available for emphasis and disambiguation. As deictics, personal pronouns index a wide range of contextual meanings, mostly based on person switches. The neuter dative, the neuter accusative and the ethic dative are expletives with pragmatic functions.

2 Reflexive pronouns have dedicated strong and clitic forms in the 3rd person accusative and dative. For persons 1 and 2, singular and plural, the forms of the reflexive pronoun are syncretic with the forms of the personal pronoun. The free and bound reflexive clitics follow the same allomorphy conditions as the personal clitics. Pronominal doubling is also available. Romanian reflexives are multifunctional.

3 'Politeness' pronouns have forms for persons 2 and 3 and show many gender, number, and case syncretisms. They share the distributive and combinatory features with the personal pronouns. As social deictics they form a four-degree politeness continuum, which overlaps with the formal / informal opposition.

4 The compound forms of the intensifiers are an innovation of Romanian, which is the only Romance language with intensifiers that are formally different from the identity determiners. Their rich inflection shows on one or another or on both formatives and overtly marks person, number, and gender oppositions.

5 As in all Romance languages, reciprocals are compounds of two indefinite pronouns. They overtly mark the gender, number, and case features of the (pro)nominals with which they are coindexed. They are obligatory or optional constituents in the sentence structure depending on the syntactic slot they fill.

7

Adjectives and Adjectival Phrases

This chapter presents the Romanian adjectives from a threefold perspective: morphological (inflectional categories: gender, number, and case; inflectional classes; the classes of adjectives from the point of view of their internal make-up), semantic (the semantic types of adjectives), and syntactic (the internal structure of APs, levels of intensity and degree markers, the distribution of APs, and nominal ellipsis with adjectives).

7.1 CHARACTERISTICS

The Romanian adjective is an open class of words, varying in gender, number, and case and agreeing morphosyntactically with a noun or pronoun.

Agreement is marked by inflectional endings (1a,b), by the definite article, which may or may not merge with the inflectional endings (for prenominal adjectives) (1c,d), and additionally by morphophonological alternations (1e–g):

(1)   a.   fată   mic-**ă**
           girl(F.SG.NOM≡ACC)   little-F.SG.NOM≡ACC

    b.   băieți   bun-**i**
        boy(M.PL.NOM≡ACC≡GEN≡DAT)   good-M.PL.NOM≡ACC≡GEN≡DAT

    c.   simpl-**a**   intenție   —   simpl-**e-le**   intenții
       mere-DEF.F.SG   intention(F.SG)   mere-F.PL-DEF   intention(F.PL)

    d.   bun-**u-l**   prieten   —   bun-**i-i**   prieteni
       good-M.SG-DEF   friend(M.SG)   good-M.PL-DEF   friend(M.PL)

    e.   ver**de**   —   verzi
       green.SG   green.PL

    f.   român**esc**   —   români**ești**
       Romanian.M.SG   Romanian.M.PL

    g.   negru   —   neagră
       black.M.SG   black.F.SG

Adjectives share a series of inflectional affixes with nouns, and the variation of the stem generally displays morphophonological alternations common to both classes. There also exist dissimilarities between the inflection of the noun and that of the adjective: some inflectional endings (*-uri* for plural, *-o* for vocative (2c)) never occur with adjectives.

(2)   a.   **Scumpă**   fată!   [adjective]
       dear.NOM≡ACC≡VOC   girl.NOM≡ACC≡VOC

    b.   **Scumpo!**   [noun]
       dear.VOC

c. ***Scumpo** fată! [adjective]
   dear.VOC girl.NOM≡ACC≡VOC

Some alternations are typical only of adjectives ((['ə / 'e / 'e̯a]—*rău* (M.SG) / *rele* (F.PL / F.SG. GEN≡DAT) / *rea* (F.SG) 'bad') (see also §15.1).

H Similarly to nouns, adjectives of the ancient lexical stock of Romanian display a large number of morphophonological alternations (3a). A part of neological adjectives lose the consonantal and vocalic alternations (3b–c), showing fewer additional markers in comparison to old adjectives (for details, see §15.1.2).

(3) a. gol   goală   goi   goale
       empty.M.SG empty.F.SG empty.M.PL empty.F.PL
    b. fidel   fidelă   fideli   fidele
       loyal.M.SG loyal.F.SG loyal.M.PL loyal.F.PL
    c. prompt   promptă   prompți   prompte
       prompt.M.SG prompt.F.SG prompt.M.PL prompt.F.PL

With neuter nouns, adjectives have masculine inflection in the singular and feminine inflection in the plural (§5.1.2):

(4) a. un   tablou   interesant
       a(M) painting(NEUT) interesting(M)
    b. două tablouri   interesante
       two(F) paintings(NEUT) interesting(F)

By agreement, adjectives (5a) are distinguished from the homonymous adverbs (5b):

(5) a. Ea conduce [_Adj**vesel-ă**]
       she drives cheerful-F.SG
       'She is cheerful as she drives'
    b. Ea conduce [_Adv**vesel**]
       she drives cheerfully

7.2 FOUR INFLECTIONAL CLASSES OF ADJECTIVES

Romanian adjectives are divided into four inflectional classes (Table 7.1), depending on the number of distinct forms. The following syncretisms are general:

- masculine singular (NOM≡ACC≡GEN≡DAT);
- masculine plural (NOM≡ACC≡GEN≡DAT);
- feminine (GEN.SG≡DAT.SG≡NOM.PL≡ACC.PL≡GEN.PL≡DAT.PL).

Four-form adjectives represent the richest class in Romanian. Participial adjectives also follow this pattern (§4.4):

(6) adus   adusă   aduși   aduse
    brought.M.SG brought.F.SG brought.M.PL brought.F.PL

TABLE 7.1 The inflectional classes of adjectives

INFLECTIONAL CLASSES OF ADJECTIVES	ADDITIONAL INFLECTIONAL SYNCRETISMS	MORPHOPHONOLOGICAL REALIZATIONS OF INFLECTIONAL ENDINGS	EXAMPLES			
			SG		PL	
			MASC	FEM	MASC	FEM
FOUR-FORM ADJECTIVES		[-∅] – [-ə] – [-ʲ] – [-e]	bun 'good'	bună	buni	bune
		[-∅] – [-ə] – [-ʲ] – [-e]	gol 'empty'	goală	goi	goale
		[-u] – [-ə] – [-ʲ] – [-e]	aspru 'harsh'	aspră	aspri	aspre
		[-u̯] – [-∅] – [-ʲ] – [-le]	rău 'bad'	rea	răi	rele
THREE-FORM ADJECTIVES	F.SG≡F.PL	[-∅] – [-e] – [-ʲ] – [-e]	visător 'dreamy'	visătoare	visători	visătoare
	M.PL≡F.PL	[-u] – [-e] – [-ʲ] – [-ʲ]	cenușiu 'gray'	cenușie	cenușii	cenușii
		[-u] – [-e] – [-ʲ] – [-ʲ]	straniu 'eerie'	stranie	stranii	stranii
		[-∅] – [-ə] – [-ʲ] – [-ʲ]	românesc 'Romanian'	românească	românești	românești
TWO-FORM ADJECTIVES	M.SG≡F.SG; M.PL≡F.PL	[-e] [-e] [-ʲ] – [-ʲ]	mare 'big'	mare	mari	mari
	M.SG≡M.PL; F.SG≡F.PL	[-∅] – [-e] – [-∅] – [-e]	greoi 'heavy'	greoaie	greoi	greoaie
	M.SG≡M.PL≡F.PL	[-∅] – [-e] – [-∅] – [-∅]	gălbui 'yellowish'	gălbuie	gălbui	gălbui
	M.SG≡F.SG≡F.PL	[-e] – [-e] – [-∅] – [-e]	tenace 'tenacious'	tenace	tenaci	tenace
INVARIABLE ADJECTIVES	M.SG≡F.SG≡M.PL≡F.PL		sadea 'genuine', doldora 'chock-full', cumsecade 'nice', grena 'garnet red', feroce 'ferocious', negru-abanos 'ebony black'			

H Some modern four-form adjectives ending in -*c* or -*g* (the type *puternic, puternică, puternici, puternice* 'strong') had three forms in the old language, realizing only the inflectional ending -*i* and thus displaying a feminine plural≡masculine plural syncretism (7a, b). Some of the modern three-form adjectives ending in -*c* or -*g* (the type *lung, lungă, lungi* 'long') had four inflectional forms; the -*i* feminine plural form (syncretic with the masculine plural one) alternated with the -*e* form (8a,b). Some two-form adjectives (the type *tare, tari* 'strong') were generally invariable (9a,b) (Frâncu 2009: 48; Mîrzea Vasile 2012b; Nicula 2012b):

(7) a. cântările   jalnici
      songs.DEF(F)   pathetic.F.PL(≡M.PL)
   b. tainici   oftări
      secretive.F.PL(≡M.PL)   sorrows(F)

(8) a. adânce   //   adânci
      deep.F.PL   deep.M.PL≡F.PL
   b. drage   //   dragi
      dear.F.PL   dear.M.PL≡F.PL

(9) a. cai   mare
      horses(M) big.M.PL
   b. casele   cele mare
      houses.DEF(F) CEL big.F.PL

Some adjectives remain in the same inflectional paradigm (show the same number of distinct forms), but change their syncretisms. In old Romanian, the adjective *nou* 'new' displayed the syncretism feminine singular≡feminine plural (10a,b); in the present-day language, the plural forms (feminine and masculine) are syncretic (10c,d):

(10) a. învățătură   nouă
       learning(F)   new.F.SG
    b. învățături   nouă (ORom)
       learnings(F)   new.F.PL
    c. cărți   noi
       books(F)   new.F
    d. pantofi   noi
       shoes(M)   new.M

In present-day Romanian, the class of invariable adjectives is open. The adjectives ending in -*ce* (*atroce* 'atrocious', *eficace* 'efficient', *perspicace* 'shrewd', *precoce* 'precocious', *propice* 'propitious') have a special behaviour; when they are prenominal, they take over the noun's definite article, thus explicitly marking the grammatical categories:

(11) a. atroce**le**   război
       atrocious.DEF.M.SG war
    b. ineficace**le**   mijlocaș
       inefficient.DEF.M.SG midfielder

In the vocative, adjectives, like nouns, may occur in the same form as the nominative:

(12) a. Oameni   buni!
       men(VOC≡NOM)   good(VOC≡NOM)
    b. Fată   frumoasă!
       girl(VOC≡NOM)   beautiful(VOC≡NOM)

H In old Romanian, there are frequent cases in which both the adjective and the noun bear vocative inflection, irrespective of their position (13a,b). In the present-day language, this construction is limited to the epistolary style (13c,d):

(13) a. Mărite împărate!
     great.VOC emperor.VOC
  b. O, craiule înălțate!
     oh, king.DEF.VOC high.VOC
  c. Iubite prietene!
     dear.VOC friend.VOC
  d. Stimate domnule!
     esteemed.VOC sir.DEF.VOC

The adjective *drag* 'dear' has two parallel forms in the vocative singular: *drag* (M.SG)—*dragă* (F.SG) (14a,b) and *dragă* (M≡F.SG) (14c,d).

(14) a. Drag prieten! / Prieten drag!
     dear.M.VOC friend.M friend.M dear.M.VOC
  b. Dragă prietenă! / Prietenă dragă!
     dear.VOC friend.F friend.F dear.VOC
  c. Dragă vecine! / Vecine dragă!
     dear.VOC neighbour.M.VOC neighbour.M.VOC dear.VOC
  d. Dragă Ion și Maria!
     dear.M≡F.SG.VOC Ion and Maria

7.3 THE INTERNAL MAKE-UP OF ADJECTIVES

From the point of view of their morphological structure, the following classes of adjectives may be distinguished:

(i) Simple (non-derived) adjectives: *bun* 'good', *mare* 'big', *roșu* 'red'.
(ii) Adjectives derived by means of suffixes from nominal bases (*săptămânal* 'weekly', *arădean* 'from Arad', *omenesc* 'human(ADJ)') or verbal bases (*vorbăreț* 'talkative, chatty', *preferabil* 'preferable', *premergător* 'preceding') (see also §§14.1.3, 14.2.1).

Like nouns, adjectives may be suffixed by diminutive and augmentative suffixes (*hărnicel* diligent.DIM, *plinuț* fat.DIM, *grăsan* fat.AUG).

(iii) Adjectives derived by means of prefixes: *străvechi* 'ancient', *arhiplin* 'overcrowded', *neatent* 'unattentive'.
(iv) Compound adjectives (inflection is marked on the last component: *cuminte* 'obedient' (< *cu* 'with' + *minte* 'mind'), *sociocultural* 'sociocultural', *clarvăzător* 'clairvoyant', *literar-artistic* 'literary-artistic' or the compound has an invariable form: *cumsecade* 'kind' < *cum* 'how' + *se cade* 'ought'); see §16.2.2.

7.4 Levels of intensity and degree markers

By compounding, some originally variable adjectives become invariable: *nuanță alb-murdar* 'off-white shade'.

(v) Adjectives obtained by conversion from past participles or gerunds (present participles):

(15)   a. zi   plăcută
           day(F)   pleasant.F

       b. persoane   suferinde
           person(F.PL) suffering.F.PL

(vi) Fixed lexical collocations (inflectionless clusters, which display an adjectival syntactic behaviour): *oameni de seamă* 'people of note', *oameni de geniu* 'people of genius', *oameni în floarea vârstei* 'people in the prime of their age'.

7.4 LEVELS OF INTENSITY AND DEGREE MARKERS

The category of comparison is expressed analytically, by more or less grammaticalized markers; the following degrees of comparison are available: the comparative of superiority (16a), of inferiority (16b), and of equality (16c); the relative superlative of superiority (16d) and of inferiority (16e). In the Romanian terminological tradition, this paradigm includes the absolute superlative forms (16f), a category which expresses the maximum degree of intensity, but not the comparison:

(16)   a. **mai**   frumos
           more   beautiful
           'more beautiful'

       b. **mai   puțin** frumos
           more   less   beautiful
           'less beautiful'

       c. **la fel de / tot așa de / tot atât de**   frumos
           equally   beautiful
           'equally beautiful'

       d. **cel   mai**   frumos
           CEL   more   beautiful
           'the most beautiful'

       e. **cel   mai   puțin** frumos
           CEL   more   less   beautiful
           'the least beautiful'

       f. **foarte** frumos
           very   beautiful
           'very beautiful'

H   In old Romanian, the intensifier *foarte* 'very' was not completely grammaticalized as a superlative marker; it functioned as an adverb (17a) or adjective (17b) as well, with the meaning 'intense(ly)', 'a lot', 'very much':

(17) a. **foarte** i   se   rupe   inema de fecioru-i   (Coresi)
       very CL.DAT.3SG CL.REFL.ACC breaks heart of son.DEF=CL.3SG
       '(S)he is very sad because of his/her son'
   b. cufundară   ca   plumbul într-o   apă   **foarte**   (Coresi)
      immersed.PS.3PL like   lead   in=a   water very
      'They sank like lead in a very deep water'

In old Romanian, strong intensity was also marked by means of the adverbials *tare* 'intensely' and *prea* 'too'. In the present language, *prea* indicates an excess (18a), and *tare* is limited to non-standard, colloquial Romanian (18b):

(18) a. o pauză prea mare
       a   break too   big
       'an excessively long break'
   b. o fată tare drăguță
       a   girl very pretty
       'a very pretty girl'

C   In Latin, the category of comparison was expressed mainly synthetically. All the Romance languages, with the exception of Romanian, possess relics of the synthetic pattern (It. *migliore*, Sp. *mejor*, Fr. *meilleur*, Ptg. *melhor* 'better') (Maiden 2011b: 223).

The means by which the analytical category of comparison is expressed differ in the Romance languages. For the comparative, Romanian uses the formative *mai* 'more' < MAGIS, while French and Italian use *plus*. Like other Romance languages, but unlike Latin, Romanian distinguishes two types of superlative, relative and absolute. The first type is made up of the comparative, preceded by the definite article (Fr. *le plus fort*, Sp. *el más fuerte*) or the determiner CEL (§5.3.1.4). The latter is obtained by means of grammaticalized adverbials: Rom. *foarte inteligent*, Fr. *très intelligent*, It. *molto intelligente*, Sp. *muy inteligente* (Iordan and Manoliu 1965: 152).

Romanian has a rich inventory of lexical (non-grammaticalized) means for marking the variation of intensity (Pană Dindelegan 1992: 85–117; Mîrzea Vasile 2012a): the construction [adverbial + DE + adjective] (19a), the preposed supine construction (19b), the adverbialized noun construction (19c), repetitive structures (19d), or prefixal means (19e), etc.:

(19) a. un   om   **excesiv**   de   **politicos**
       a   man   excessively   DE   polite
       'an excessively polite man'
   b. o fată **nespus**   de   **frumoasă**
       a   girl un-speak.SUP   DE   beautiful
       'an unutterably beautiful girl'
   c. un copil **scump** foc
       a child sweet   fire(ADV)
       'a very sweet child'
   d. adevărul **gol**   **goluț**
       truth.DEF naked   -naked(DIM)
       'the naked truth'
   e. un magazin **arhiplin**
       a   store   overfull
       'an overfull store'

Some adjectives intrinsically contain the intensity information: former Latin superlatives (*optim* 'optimum', *maxim* 'maximum') or adjectives which contain in their lexical structure superlative features (*excelent* 'excellent', *enorm* 'enormous').

U Although the present literary norm recommends the usage of these adjectives without the intensity markers, structures of this type are found in non-standard usage:

(20) a. candidatul   mai   optim
        candidate.DEF   more   optimum

   b. traducerile   cele   mai   perfecte
      translations.DEF   CEL   more   perfect

Some adjectives do not allow intensity variation because they do not express properties of the referents (§§7.4.2, 7.4.3):

(21) a. *foarte   clorhidric
        very   hydrochloric

   b. *foarte   terorist
      very   terrorist

   c. *cel   mai   viitor
      CEL   more   future

7.5 THREE SEMANTIC CLASSES OF ADJECTIVES

There are three semantic classes of adjectives: qualifying, relative, and reference-modifying adjectives.

7.5.1 Qualifying adjectives

Qualifying adjectives denote properties of entities (they are *object-level adjectives* (McNally and Boleda 2004)). They are intersective, appear in predicative positions (22a), are compatible with degree markers (22b), occur in exclamative constructions (22c), occur in the CEL-construction (22d) (for details, see §5.3.1.4.3), and may serve as input for adjective-based nouns (22e):

(22) a. Fata   este   **frumoasă**
        girl.DEF   is   beautiful
        'The girl is beautiful'

   b. **foarte   frumoasă**
      very   beautiful

   c. Ce   **frumoasă**   e   fata!
      what   beautiful   is   girl.DEF
      'How beautiful the girl is!'

   d. fata   cea   **frumoasă**
      girl.DEF   CEL   beautiful
      'the beautiful girl'

   e. **frumusețe**
      beauty

7.5.2 Relative adjectives

Relative adjectives denote sets of properties (they are *kind-level adjectives* (McNally and Boleda 2004)) and have an identificational function (they operate a non-deictic localization in time and space) (23a,b) or a classifying function (they describe species of the referent denoted by the head noun) (24a,b):

(23) a. unelte   preistorice
        tools   prehistoric(al)
 b. roman   interbelic
        novel   interwar

(24) a. dramă   muzicală
        drama   musical
 b. arte   plastice
        arts   plastic

Some relative adjectives are thematic (Bosque and Picallo 1996) and function as arguments of non-prototypical nouns, filling diverse thematic positions: Agent (25a), Cause (25b), and Theme (25c) (§5.3.5.2.1):

(25) a. atac   terorist
        attack   terrorist
 b. discriminare   rasială
        discrimination   racial
 c. producție   petrolieră
        production   petrol(ADJ)

Relative adjectives do not typically occur in predicative positions (26a), they are not compatible with degree markers (26b), they do not occur in exclamative constructions (26c), they do not combine with the determiner CEL in overt-head structures (26d) (§5.3.1.4.3), they do not serve as input for adjective-based nouns (26e):

(26) a. *Atacul   este   **terorist**
        attack.DEF   is   terrorist
 b. *atac   **foarte**   **terorist**
        attack   very   terrorist
 c. *Ce   **terorist**   e   atacul!
        what   terrorist   is   attack.DEF
 d. *atacul   **cel**   **terorist**
        attack.DEF   CEL   terrorist
 e. ***teroristicitate**

H   In old Romanian, the relative adjectives could combine with the determiner CEL.
       (27) letopisețul   cel   leșescu   (Costin)
             chronicle   CEL   Polish

Numerous adjectives that were originally relative adjectives are recategorized into qualifying adjectives, illustrating the *mixed adjective* type (Bartning and Noailly 1993):

(28) a. universitate [Relative provincială] vs. atitudine [Qualifying(foarte) provincială]
        university   provincial   attitude   (very)   provincial

    b. ceas [Relative mecanic] vs. zâmbet [Qualifying (foarte) mecanic]
        watch   mechanical   smile   (very)   mechanical

7.5.3 Reference-modifying adjectives

Reference-modifying adjectives (Bolinger 1967) are either lexemes with a vague meaning or partly semantically bleached, recategorized lexemes, which neither necessarily identify the referent, nor denote properties, but function as mere operators (Brăescu 2012: 54–68) which realize:

(i) the process of spatial and temporal anchoring—deictic adjectives:

(29) a. o **viitoare** mamă
       a future mother

    b. campania **actuală**
       campaign.DEF present

    c. pagina **anterioară**
       page.DEF previous

    d. **precedenta** discuție
       previous.DEF discussion

(ii) the pragmatic adjustment of the denomination—modal adjectives:

(30) a. un **simplu** accident
       a mere accident

    b. o **pură** întâmplare
       a mere happening

    c. o **adevărată** tragedie
       a real tragedy

    d. un **pretins** faliment
       an alleged bankruptcy

(iii) the scaling of entities—contrastive adjectives:

(31) a. trăsătură **specifică**
       feature specific

    b. mașină **personală**
       car personal

(iv) the scaling of intensity—intensive adjectives:

(32) a. un **vechi** prieten
       an old friend

    b. un **mare** fumător
       a great smoker

(v) the evaluation of expressivity—affective adjectives:

(33) a. **blestemata** taxă
　　　 damn.DEF　 tax

　　 b. **biata**　 fată
　　　 poor.DEF　 girl

The adjectives in this class display a heterogeneous syntactic behaviour; they may or may not occur in the predicative position (34) and they may or may not accommodate intensity markers (35):

(34) a. Afacerea　　este **personală**
　　　 business.DEF is　 personal

　　 b. *Mama　　 este **viitoare**
　　　 mother.DEF is　 future

(35) a. un **foarte vechi** prieten
　　　 a　 very　 old　 friend

　　 b. *o **foarte pură** coincidenţă
　　　 a　 very　 mere　 coincidence

U　In present-day Romanian, there are two adjectives corresponding to English 'old':
(36) a. vin　 vechi　 vs. *vin bătrân
　　　 wine　 old
　　　 'old wine'
　　 b. om　 bătrân　 vs. *om vechi
　　　 man　 old
　　　 'old man'
In context (36a) the antonym is *nou* 'new', while in context (36b) the antonym is *tânăr* 'young'.

7.6 THE STRUCTURE OF THE ADJECTIVAL PHRASE (AP)

The adjective may be accompanied by modifiers, complements, and adjuncts.

7.6.1 Modifiers

The modifiers of the adjective may be the following:

(i) intensifiers, which fall into two classes: amplifiers (37a–c) and downtoners (37d–e);

(37) a. o femeie **foarte** frumoasă
　　　 a woman very　 beautiful

　　 b. un om　 obosit **rău**
　　　 a　 man tired　 badly

　　 c. un vecin　　 supărat **peste măsură**
　　　 a　 neighbour upset　　 beyond measure

7.6 The structure of the adjectival phrase (AP)

    d. un comportament **un pic** ciudat
       a   behaviour   a little   strange

    e. un vecin **puțin** nervos
       a   neighbour slightly irritated

(ii) approximators:

(38) a. păr **cam**   alb
         hair somewhat white

     b. fată **oarecum** frumoasă
        girl   somewhat beautiful

     c. un sunet **abia**   perceptibil
        a   sound almost perceptible

(iii) modalizers:

(39) a. o sugestie **sigur**   bună
         a suggestion certainly good

     b. o colegă **cică**   bolnavă
        a colleague allegedly ill

(iv) categorizers:

(40) a. un obicei **tipic**   american
         a   habit   typically American

     b. o situație **teoretic** dificilă
        a situation theoretically difficult

     c. o situație **practic**   imposibilă
        a situation practically impossible

(v) negators:

(41) a. un anturaj **deloc**   potrivit
         a   entourage not-at-all suitable

     b. o fată **nu**   prea rea
        a girl   not   too   bad

(vi) degree markers:

(42) a. un om   **mai**   bun
         a   person more good

     b. copilul **cel mai** cuminte
        child.DEF CEL more obedient

Both postnominal and prenominal adjectives may be accompanied by modifiers:

(43) a. un om [pe deplin fericit]
         a person fully   happy

     b. [o prea bună] vecină
        a   too   good   neighbour

Modification is hierarchical (stacked), if a modifier takes scope over an already modified adjective:

(44) a. o comportare [ocazional   [foarte agresivă]]
        a behaviour   occasionally   very   aggressive
     b. un pahar   [încă   [aproape   plin]]
        a   glass   still   almost   full

7.6.2 Complements

The complementation relation is not licensed by the entire class of adjectives. Some adjectives obligatorily take complements (45a), other adjectives may take complements (45b), still other adjectives do not license complements at all (45c):

(45) a. suferință **premergătoare** **morții**
        suffering   prior-to   death
     b. un personaj   **ironic**   (**cu**   **ceilalți**)
        a   character   ironic   with   the-others
     c. fată   **frumoasă**
        girl   beautiful

The deletion of the complement may induce a supplementary effect of ambiguity (46a) or may trigger a change of the semantic class of the adjective (46b):

(46) a. El merge   într-o   direcție   **necunoscută** vs. **necunoscută** **nouă**
        he goes   in=a   direction   unknown   unknown   us.DAT
        'He goes in a direction unknown (to us)'
     b. Prăjitura   este **bună** vs. **bună** **de** **aruncat**
        cake.DEF   is   good   good   to   throw
        'The cake is good (to throw)'

C   In contemporary Romanian, as in English (Alexiadou and Wilder 1998), only postnominal adjectives license complements:

(47) *mândra   de fiul   său mamă   vs. mamă   mândră de fiul   său
      proud.DEF of son.DEF   her mother   mother proud   of son.DEF her

7.6.2.1 The complement realized as a dative nominal

The following adjectives take a dative complement: prototypical adjectives (48a), postverbal adjectives which retain the combinatorial possibilities of the verbs from which they originate (48b), and postverbal adjectives that have selectional properties different from their corresponding verb (48c):

(48) a. angajat   **loial**   **firmei**
        employee   loyal   company.DEF.DAT
        'employee loyal to the company'
     b. om   **folositor** **celorlalți**   vs. [$_{VP}$ **folosește** **celorlalți**]
        man   useful   the-others.DAT   uses   the-others.DAT
        'man useful to the others'

    c. atitudine **păgubitoare** **societăţii** vs. [$_{VP}$ **păgubeşte** **societatea**]
       attitude harmful society.DEF.DAT harms society.DEF.ACC
       'attitude harmful to the society'

H The pattern [adjective + noun in the dative case] is an old pattern which has been reinforced by borrowed adjectives (Pană Dindelegan 1992: 41):

(49) a. program accesibil tuturor
       programme accessible everybody.DAT
       'a program accessible to everybody'
    b. fiu ostil tatălui
       son hostile father.DEF.DAT
       'son hostile to his father'

U Variation between a dative complement and a PP complement is frequent:

(50) a. un act similar acestuia / cu acesta
       a document similar this.DAT with this
       'a document similar to this one'
    b. comportament caracteristic lui / pentru el
       behaviour characteristic him.DAT for him.ACC
       'behaviour characteristic of him'

7.6.2.2 The complement realized as a genitive nominal

The genitive complement is licensed only by postverbal adjectives that originate in transitive verbs with a [+definite] direct object:

(51) a. echipă **deţinătoare** a trofeului vs. [$_{VP}$ **deţine trofeul**]
       team holding AL trophy.DEF.GEN owns trophy.DEF.ACC
       'team holding the trophy'
    b. eleve **câştigătoare** ale concursului vs. [$_{VP}$ **câştigă concursul**]
       students winning AL contest.DEF.GEN wins contest.DEF.ACC
       'student that won the contest'

The corresponding prepositional construction (52) yields a different reading of the complement: the genitival complement (51) is entity-denoting, while the prepositional complement (52) is generic, kind-denoting:

(52) a. echipă **deţinătoare** de trofee
       team holding DE trophies
       'team holding trophies'
    b. elevă **câştigătoare** de concursuri
       student winning DE contests
       'student who wins contests'

These genitive-licensing adjectives are recategorized as nouns in the presence of modifiers (Rădulescu 1992; GBLR: 225):

(53) a. echipă **deținătoare** certă   a   trofeului
       team(F) holding(F) certain(F) AL trophy.DEF.GEN
       'team that will certainly take the trophy'
   vs.   *echipă   certă   a   trofeului
          team(F) certain(F) AL trophy.DEF.GEN
   b. elevă **câștigătoare** clară   a   concursului
      student(F) winning(F) clear(F) AL contest.DEF.GEN
      'student that will clearly win the contest'
   vs.   *elevă   clară   a   concursului
          student(F) clear(F) AL contest.DEF.GEN

7.6.2.3 The complement realized as a PP

The selection of a particular preposition depends on the adjectival head:

(54) a. om   capabil   **de**   iubire
       human capable   of   love
   b. copil   sensibil   **la**   frumusețe
      child sensitive   to   beauty
   c. program   conform   **cu**   regulamentul
      programme conforming with regulation.DEF
   d. soț   gelos   **pe**   soție
      husband jealous on wife

The postverbal derived adjectives or the participles retain the selectional features of the verbal base:

(55) a. persoană   temătoare **de** orice   (< a se teme **de** 'fear **of**')
       person   fearing   of   everything
   b. angajat   obligat   **la** multe   călătorii   (< a obliga **la** 'force / oblige **to**')
      employee   obliged   to   many   trips

7.6.2.4 The direct object

A single transitive adjective in Romanian licenses the direct object:

(56) El   îmi   este **dator**   viața
     he   CL.DAT.1SG is   indebted   life.DEF.ACC
     'He owes me his life'

The structures *furios pe* 'furious with', *supărat pe* 'upset with', *mânios pe* 'angry with' license a prepositional object (not a direct object), according to the selectional features of the verbs they originate from (*a se înfuria pe* 'become furious with', *a se supăra pe* 'become upset with', *a se mânia pe* 'be angry with').

7.6.2.5 The clausal complement

The adjectival head may select complementizers: *că* 'that', *să* + SUBJ 'that' (for assertive or non-assertive subordinate clauses) or *dacă* 'whether, if' (for the conversion of an interrogative, from direct speech into reported speech).

(57) a. sportivă   sigură   **că**   a   reușit
sportswoman certain that has succeeded

b. soldat gata **să** moară în luptă
soldier ready SĂ$_{SUBJ}$ die.SUBJ in battle

c. concurent curios **dacă** a câștigat
contestant curious whether has won

The non-finite forms of the verb may also be complements of adjectives; the supine is obligatorily preceded by the preposition, and, in the case of the infinitive, the preposition is optional (§§4.2, 4.5):

(58) a. capabil (de) a lucra
capable of A$_{INF}$ work.INF

b. bun de aruncat
good DE$_{SUP}$ throw.SUP

7.6.2.6 The comparative complement

The comparative complement is licensed by the degree modifier of the adjectival head; it is realized either as a PP (59a–c) or as a comparative sentence (60a,b) (§10.5):

(59) a. <u>mai</u> frumoasă **decât** mine
more beautiful than me

b. <u>la fel de</u> bun **ca** ieri
equally good as yesterday

c. <u>cel mai</u> cuminte **din** clasă
CEL more obedient from classroom

(60) a. Ioana e <u>mai</u> înaltă **decât** a fost mama ei
Ioana is more tall than has been mother.DEF her

b. Scrie la fel de ușor **precum** vorbește
writes equally easy as ((s)he)speaks

7.6.3 Adjuncts

Adjectives (especially postverbal ones) have adjuncts with various semantic values: locative (61a), temporal (61b), manner (61c), instrument (61d), purpose (61e), result (61f), reason (61g) (§10.2).

(61) a. copil murdar **pe** mâini
child dirty on hands

b. persoană **ieri** veselă
person yesterday cheerful

c. casă **prost** întreţinută
   house poorly maintained

d. fată obligată **prin şantaj**
   girl forced through blackmail

e. studentă plecată **pentru studiu**
   student left for study

f. prietenă aşa de tristă **încât rămâne acasă**
   friend so sad that stays home

g. femeie avară **din sărăcie**
   woman miserly because-of poverty

U In the case of some postnominal adjectives, adjuncts typically precede the head:
(62) a. uşă [larg deschisă]
        door widely open
     b. un copil [bine crescut]
        a   child well raised
     c. fată veselă
        girl cheerful

7.7 THE SYNTACTIC POSITIONS OF APs

Adjectives may function as modifiers, complements, adjuncts, or may occur in appositive constructions.

7.7.1 The adjective as a modifier

Prototypically, the adjective is a modifier of a nominal head. Adjectives typically follow the head noun (§5.3.5):

(63) fată veselă
     girl cheerful

C In classical Latin, adjectives were either prenominal or postnominal. In Romance, there is a preference for postposition: Rom. *pisica neagră*, It. *il gatto nero*, Fr. *le chat noir*, Sp. *el gato negro* (the black cat). In Germanic and Slavic, adjectives typically precede the head: Germ. *die schwarze Katze*, Engl. *the black cat*, Pol. *czarny kot* (Copceag 1998: 86).

Postnominal adjectives in Romance (64b,c) display the mirror image order of the English prenominal adjectives (64a) (Cinque 2010):

(64) a. The most probable main cause of his death   (English)
     b. La causa prima più probabile della sua morte   (Italian)
     c. Cauza principală cea mai probabilă a morţii sale   (Romanian)

7.7.1.1 Postnominal adjectives

Postnominal adjectives function as restrictive or non-restrictive modifiers (§§5.3.5.1.1, 5.3.5.2.1).

The following classes of adjectives are exclusively postnominal: invariable adjectives (65a), with the exception of those ending in *-ce* (see (11) above); adjectives in the CEL adjectival article construction (65b); relative adjectives (65c), and some reference-modifying adjectives (65d):

(65) a. o femeie   **sexy**
        a woman   sexy

 b. fata   cea   **mică**
    girl.DEF CEL   little

 c. arte **plastice**
    arts plastic

 d. munca   **individuală**
    labour individual

H In old Romanian, relative adjectives could also precede the head:
(66) **romana**   monarhie   (Cantacuzino)
     Roman.DEF   monarchy

When it combines with a proper name, the postnominal adjective has an identifying value, implying a contrast either between two referents (67a) or between two instances of the same referent (67b):

(67) a. Silvia blondă și   Silvia brunetă
        Silvia blonde and Silvia dark-haired

 b. Matei cel bun
    Matei CEL good

Juxtaposed adjectives enter stacking relations:

(68) a. [[costume țărănești] românești]
        costumes   rustic   Romanian

 b. [[costume românești] țărănești]
    costumes   Romanian   rustic

C Of the Romance languages, Romanian most frequently accepts the postnominal position for descriptive adjectives (Lombard 1974: 98).

7.7.1.2 Prenominal adjectives

Prenominal adjectives are non-restrictive, non-intersective, non-predicative, and realize a modal subjective evaluation (for the situations of marked word order, see §5.3.5.2.1).

The class of exclusively prenominal adjectives is quite limited in Romanian:

(69) a. un **fost / biet**   coleg
        a   former poor   colleague

 b. un **așa-zis / pretins** prieten
    a   so-called alleged   friend

U Some adjectives have fixed word order in evaluative collocations:
(70) a. act   de   **mare**   **curaj**
        deed   of   great   courage
    b. prilej   de   **tristă** **amintire**
        occasion of   sad   memory
    c. prin   **viu**   **grai**
        through   living   speech

When it combines with a proper name, the prenominal adjective denotes an intrinsic, descriptive feature of the referent:

(71) a. bunul   Matei
        good.DEF   Matei
    b. blonda   Silvia
        blond.DEF   Silvia

7.7.1.3 Free-ordered adjectives

Although they are prototypically postnominal, numerous adjectives may precede or follow the head noun:

(72) a. o fată   frumoasă
        a girl   beautiful
    b. o frumoasă fată
        a beautiful girl

The change of position sometimes triggers type-shifting: some adjectives are qualifying when they follow the head (73a,c) and reference-modifying when they precede the head (73b,d) (§5.3.5.2.1):

(73) a. o afirmație   **simplă**
        a statement   simple / mere
    b. o **simplă**   afirmație
        a mere   statement
    c. o poveste   **adevărată**
        a story   true / real
    d. o **adevărată** poveste
        a real / proper story

7.7.2 The adjective as a predicative complement

In the VP, the adjective may be a subjective predicative complement (74a) or it may be incorporated in a PP (containing a preposition 'of quality') which occupies the position of an objective predicative complement (74b):

(74) a. El   este **isteț**
        he   is   smart
    b. O   ia   de   **proastă**
        CL.ACC.F.3SG   takes   DE   fool.F
        'He takes her to be a fool'

7.7 The syntactic positions of APs

As an effect of syntactic restructuring, the adjective occurs as a secondary predicate:

(75) a. Fata   venea   **veselă** <Fata   venea și fata   era   **veselă**
        girl.DEF came   cheerful.F girl.DEF came and girl.DEF was cheerful.F

   b. Ana bea   cafeaua   **fierbinte** <Ana bea   cafeaua   când /
      Ana drinks coffee.DEF.F hot.F   Ana drinks coffee.DEF.F when /
      dacă este **fierbinte**
      if   is   hot.F

Evaluative, subjective adjectives are secondary predications that cannot be left out in combination with propositional attitude verbs (*considera* 'consider', etc.), causative verbs (*lăsa* 'leave', *ține* 'keep') or the verb *avea* ('have'):

(76) a. Îl   crede   pe Luca **bolnav**
        CL.ACC.M.3SG   believes PE Luca ill.M
        'He believes that Luc is ill'

   b. Mama   ține   casa   **curată**
      mother.DEF keeps house.DEF(F)   clean.F

   c. Ea   are sotul   **bolnav**
      she has husband.DEF   ill
      'Her husband is ill'

Descriptive and resultative adjectives (77a,b) are secondary predications that may be omitted (Rothstein 2003):

(77) a. Maria a   condus mașina   **furioasă**
        Maria has driven car.DEF furious.F
        'Maria was furious as she drove the car'

   b. Ion a   vopsit gardul   **verde**
      Ion has painted fence.DEF green
      'Ion painted the fence green'

C In contrast to English (Svenonius 2008), Romanian has only the weak resultative pattern, in which the adjective in predicative position is a canonical result of the event denoted by the verb; the relation between the argument and the verb (*vopsi* 'paint', *fierbe* 'boil') is determined by the meaning of the verb, therefore it is lexically determined (§10.4.2.1):

   (78) a. A   vopsit scaunul   **roșu**
           has painted chair.DEF(M) red.M
           'He painted the chair red'
      b. Am   fiert   ouăle   **moi**
         (I)have boiled eggs.DEF(F)   soft
         'I have boiled the eggs (leaving them) soft'

Adjectives function as secondary predicates in appositive detached patterns; in such structures, they enter equivalence relations with the adjectival base:

(79) Bun, **adică amabil**, așa îl   știau   toți
     kind that is courteous, so CL.ACC.3M.SG   knew.IMPERF.3PL   all
     'They all knew that he was kind, that is courteous'

7.7.3 The adjective as an adjunct

In elliptical structures, adjectives, either alone or incorporated into PPs, may be adjuncts; they display the following values: reason (80a), additive negative (80b), additive positive (80c), substractive (80d), and condition (80e) (§10.2):

(80) a. Nu mai putea vorbi **de tristă și supărată**
not more could speak of sad and upset
'She could no longer speak so sad and upset was she'

b. **În loc de roșii,** merele erau galbene
instead-of red apples.DEF were yellow
'Instead of being red the apples were yellow'

c. **Pe lângă leneșă**, mai era și mincinoasă
besides lazy also (she)was also mendacious
'On top of being lazy, she was also a liar'

d. Cafeaua nu-mi place altfel **decât amară**
coffee.DEF not=CL.DAT.1SG likes otherwise than bitter
'I do not like any coffee other than bitter'

e. **Singură,** nu vreau să plec
alone not (I)want să_SUBJ leave.SUBJ
'I do not want to leave alone'

7.8 NOMINAL ELLIPSIS AND THE SUBSTANTIVIZATION OF ADJECTIVES

The ellipsis of the head involves the occurrence of the adjective in the noun's position and triggers an anaphoric connection with an antecedent:

(81) a. Candidații vor bifa răspunsurile corecte cu pixul
candidates.DEF AUX.FUT.3PL tick answers.DEF correct with pen.DEF
albastru sau **cu** [pixul] **negru**
blue or with pen.DEF black
'The candidates are going to tick the right answers with a blue or black pen'

b. A: Speli legumele cu apă caldă?
(you)wash vegetables.DEF with water hot
'Do you wash vegetables with warm water?'
B: Nu, **cu** [apă] **rece**
no with water cold
'No, with cold'

The substantivized adjective selects the inflectional markers typical of nouns, taking over the gender and the number features of the elided referent. Typically, adjectives with a [+human] feature undergo substantivization:

(82) a. micuța
little.DEF
'the little one (girl)'

b. liberalii
      liberal.PL.DEF
      'the liberals'

U Participle-based substantivized adjectives are very frequent in the present-day language:
   (83) a. invitați
           invited.PL
           'guests'
        b. travestiți
           disguised.PL
           'masked one'
        c. admiși
           accepted.PL
           'accepted ones'
   Adjectives in the absolute superlative constructions generally cannot substantivize (84a). The cases of substantivization are limited to fixed constructions, such as (84b).
   (84) a. *foarte   nefericiții
           very   unhappy.PL.DEF
        b. mult-prea-nefericiții
           way-too-unhappy.PL.DEF
           'the ones that are very unhappy'
   Nominal ellipsis with the determiner CEL is possible with both qualifying and relative adjectives (see §5.3.1.4.4):
   (85) a. fata   frumoasă   și   **cea**   **urâtă**
           girl.DEF   beautiful and   CEL   ugly
           'the beautiful girl and the ugly one'
        b. acidul   sulfuric   și   **cel**   **cianhidric**
           acid.DEF   sulphuric and   CEL   cyanhydric
           'the sulphuric and the cyanhydric acids'

C Nominal ellipsis with adjectival remnants is more productive in Romanian than in other Romance languages (Cornilescu and Nicolae 2010).

CONCLUSIONS

The adjective displays gender, number, and case variation. The morphological categories are marked by inflectional endings, the definite article (in the case of prenominal adjectives), and morphophonological alternations. Adjectival inflection is rich and has many features in common with the nominal one.

The means by which the category of comparison is marked are analytic and partially grammaticalized.

Postnominal qualifying adjectives generate extended adjectival phrases, with modifiers, complements, and adjuncts.

In general, the adjective is postnominal, but many adjectives exhibit free word order with respect to the head noun. Word order changes may trigger meaning variations.

The deletion of the head noun may trigger the substantivization of adjectives or the occurrence of nominal ellipsis patterns, headed by the determiner CEL.

8

Adverbs and Adverbial Phrases

This chapter presents the forms of the adverb, the structure of the adverbial phrase, and its position in the sentence. It also presents the semantic types of adverbs and gradable adverbs. Romanian adverbs are either simple, monomorphemic, or derivationally created with the suffixes *-eşte* / *-iceşte*, *-iş (-îş)*, and *-mente*. Most adverbs are identical to the masculine singular form of the adjective, and a few coincide with forms in other classes of words. There also exist compound adverbs, fixed collocations, and adverbials such as *în mod* ('in a way / in a manner') plus an adjective. The description also covers emphatic non-lexical formatives of adverbs. Several other syntactic problems are discussed: the characteristics of adverbs as heads (extended by adjuncts, complements, and modifiers), adverbs as clause-embedded constituents (complements of verbs, prepositions, or modifiers of the noun phrase), and adverbs as extrasentential constituents, displaying different degrees of independence.

8.1 THE FORM OF THE ADVERBS

8.1.1 Simple forms

Simple adverbs are not obviously analysable into smaller constituents in present-day Romanian: *abia* 'just', *acum* 'now', *acolo* 'there', *aşa* 'this way', *atunci* 'then', *azi* 'today', *chiar* 'really', *când* 'when', *ieri* 'yesterday', *încă* 'still', *jos* 'down', *nici* 'neither', *nu* 'no', *şi* 'also', *unde* 'where' (all of Latin origin); *da* 'yes', *lesne* 'easily' (both of Slavic origin); *musai* 'necessarily' (of Hungarian origin); *başca* 'separately', *taman* 'just' (both of Turkish origin); *agale* 'slowly', *anapoda* 'topsy-turvy' (both of Greek origin); *deja* 'already', *eventual* 'likely', *probabil* 'maybe; probably', *vizavi* 'opposite' (all late borrowings from other Romance languages).

8.1.2 Suffixed forms

There is a small set of adverbs (nowadays infrequently used, but see Haneş 1960 and Chircu 2006 for old Romanian) containing the suffixes *-eşte* / *-iceşte*, *-iş (-îş)*, and *-mente*.

The adverbs ending in **-eşte** / **-iceşte** were and still are the most numerous (in current dictionaries, over 175 lexemes end in *-eşte*, and almost 25 in *-iceşte*). These usually have an adjectival counterpart ending in *-esc*.

H The etymology of *-eşte* is controversial: (a) it is made up of the adjectival suffix *-esc* plus the Latin adverbial suffix *-e* (Pascu 1916: 179; Haneş 1960: 141), preserved in adverbs like *bine* 'well', *limpede* 'clearly', *foarte* 'very', *repede* 'quickly', *mâine* 'tomorrow', etc.; (b) it originates in the Latin suffix *-isce* (Meyer-Lübke 1900: 686); (c) it is of Thracian origin (Graur 1936: 84).

C This suffix is also present in Megleno-Romanian (Atanasov 2002: 253) and Aromanian (Papahagi 1963), but is not attested in Istro-Romanian (Chircu 2008: 125). In Albanian, there exists a similar adverbial suffix -*isht* (Sandfeld 1930: 128; Rosetti 1986: 239; Duchet 1991: 190).

The derivational base for the adverbs in -*este* can be a noun or an adjective ending in -*esc* (in the latter case, there is affix substitution):

(1) a. frăţeşte 'like a brother, fraternally' < *frate* (N) 'brother' or < *frăţesc* (ADJ) 'brotherly'
    b. englezeşte 'like an Englishman, in the English manner; (in) English' < *englez* (N) 'English' or < *englezesc* (ADJ) 'English'

H The suffix -*iceşte* resulted from a reanalysis of the final part of adjectives containing -*ic* (2a):

(2) a. teoreticeşte 'theoretically' (obsolete) < *teoretic[esc]* (obsolete) + -*este* or < *teoretic* + -*este*
    b. spiritualiceşte 'spiritually' (obsolete) < *spiritualic[esc]* (obsolete) + -*este* [*spiritualic] or < *spiritual* + -*iceşte*

Many adverbs ending in -*este* express comparisons (1). Most of the adverbs ending in -*iceşte* and a few of those ending in -*este* express point of view (3).

(3) a. Stă prost **băneşte**
       'He's badly off, money-wise'
    b. **Istoriceşte**, acest summit este important
       'From a historical point of view, this summit is important'

U In contemporary Romanian, the adverbs in -*este* are more frequent than those in -*iceşte*, which are obsolete and may be replaced by ordinary adverbs (4).

(4) a. **Juridiceşte**, cazul este rezolvat
    b. **Juridic**, cazul este rezolvat
       'From the juridical point of view / Juridically, the case is solved'

Ethnic derivatives have a typically adverbial value (5a) or a nominal value (5b,c). In the latter case, they may be headed by prepositions (5c):

(5) a. S-a   tuns   **franţuzeşte**
       CL.REFL.3SG=has clipped   French-*EŞTE*
       '(S)he had a French haircut'
    b. Ea ştie   **româneşte** /   (limba)   română   / româna
       she knows Romanian-*EŞTE*   language Romanian   Romanian.DEF
       'She knows Romanian'
    c. Elevul   recită o poezie **în franţuzeşte** / în (limba) franceză
       schoolboy.DEF recites a poem in French-*EŞTE*   in language French
       'The schoolboy recites a poem in French'

U In the contemporary language, the non-prepositional usage of -*este* adverbs denoting languages is restricted to verbs meaning 'talk', 'know', 'understand', 'learn' (5b). In general, the prepositions *în* 'in', *pe* 'on', or *din* 'from' are employed (5c).

C Romanian differs from the rest of Romance (Arvinte 1983: 81, 91–2) and resembles Latin (6a), but one cannot assume a direct relation between Latin and Romanian. Romanian also resembles Albanian (6b) in this respect.

(6) a. **Latine** / **graece** (Latin)
loquitur
'(S)he speaks Latin / Greek'
b. Flet ti **anglisht**? (Albanian; in Mëniku and Campos 2011: 19)
'Do you speak English?'

The prepositional use is probably the result of Slavic influence (for Czech, see Stone 1993: 478; for Lower Sorbian, see Short 1993: 631); in Russian, it covers manner adverbs (Wade 2011: 396–7).

The adverbs ending in *-iş (-îş)* number only 25 in current dictionaries, and the suffix is not currently productive. They are used in regional and colloquial language, and tend to become fixed in idiomatic structures. Usually, they are adjuncts of verbs of motion, localization, and intentional visual perception.

(7) pieptiş 'abruptly': *a urca* **pieptiş** 'climb abruptly'
cruciş 'crosswise': *a (se) pune* **cruciş** 'oppose', *a se uita* **cruciş** 'squint / look askance'

H The etymology of *-iş* is uncertain (Densusianu 1901: 364–5). Pascu (1916: 367) relates it to the adjectival suffix *-iş*.

The derivational base for *-iş (-îş)* is usually a noun (8a) or a verb (8b):

(8) a. cruciş 'crosswise' < *cruce* 'cross', făţiş 'frankly' < *faţă* 'face', pieptiş 'abruptly' < *piept* 'chest'
b. târâş 'crawling, on all fours' < *a (se) târî* 'crawl'

The adverbs ending in *-mente* number 20–35 in modern dictionaries. These are Romance borrowings (mainly from French and Italian) beginning with the mid-19th century, used in formal language (Dănăilă 1960; Dinică 2008: 588).

(9) actualmente 'at present', realmente 'actually', eminamente 'eminently', literalmente 'literally', finalmente 'finally', totalmente 'totally', esenţialmente 'essentially', moralmente 'morally', necesarmente 'necessarily'

C In contrast to the rest of Romance, the adverbs in *-mente* were not inherited in Romanian (Bauer 2011: 552) and in the dialects of southern Italy (Posner 1996: 83). The only Romanian adverb inherited from Latin which contains the ablative *mente* is *altminteri* 'otherwise' (Puşcariu 1940: 54; Bauer 2011: 553). This adverb exhibits great diachronic variation in form (*aimintre, aiminteri, aminterea; altminte, altminterea, altmintrelea*, etc.); most of these forms have in common the *-r-*, probably a remnant of the Latin adverbial suffix *-(i)ter* (Bauer 2011: 553).

Diminutive forms of adverbs are derived with the suffixes *-i(ş)or, -(ic)el, -uc(ă), -uleţ, -uş, -uţ(a)*.

(10) binişor 'quite well' (< *bine* 'well'), târzior 'latish' (< *târziu* 'late'); uşurel 'quite easily' (< *uşor* 'eas(il)y'); acăsucă (DIM) 'at home' (< *acasă* 'at home'); greuleţ 'ticklishly' (< *greu* 'difficult(ly)')

8.1.3 Compound forms

Many adverbial forms are the result of compounding; they may be more (12) or less (11) transparent in the modern language:

(11) devreme 'early', deasupra 'above', decât 'only', demult 'long ago', dedesubt 'beneath', deseori 'often', rareori 'rarely, seldom', câteodată 'sometimes', numaidecât 'immediately', astăzi 'today', altădată 'formerly', totodată 'simultaneously', cică 'allegedly; they say (that)', parcă '(as) it seems' (§13.5.3).

(12) astă-vară 'last summer', azi-noapte 'last night', târâş-grăpiş 'gropingly', încet-încet 'slowly', mâine-poimâine 'sooner or later', ici-colo 'here and there'.

H A few adverbs (originally fixed phrases) contain a reflex of the Latin preposition AD; some are inherited from Latin (*abia* 'just', *afară* 'outside', *apoi* 'then', *aproape* 'close, almost'), others are created in Romanian (*acasă* '(at) home', *alocuri* 'here and there', *alene* 'slowly', *anevoie* 'slowly', *anume* 'namely'). The obsolete preposition *a* is also included in fixed collocations such as: *de-a dreptul* 'well and truly', *de-a binelea* 'completely, really', *de-a lungul* 'along'.

The use of multiple (semantically redundant) prepositions is a frequent way of creating compound adverbs: *de-a dreapta* 'to the right', *pe de-a-ntregul* 'wholly', *cu dinadins* 'purposely' (Ciobanu 1957: 62–6; Ciompec 1985: 86–9, 94).

The adverbial pro-forms are displayed in series and show formal variation at the lexical and phonological level (Table 8.1).

Beside these, there are also forms used regionally or emphatically:

- The adverbs *oarecât* 'a little', *oareunde* 'somewhere', *oarecând* 'sometime', *oarecum* (the most frequent) 'somewhat' are made up with the element **oare-** (< conj. *oare* < *oare(-)* < *VOLET (= VULT), Ciorănescu 2002; TDRG³), and correspond semantically to the **-va** series (< *va* < *vare* < *voare < *VOLET, Lombard 1938: 204).
- The adverbs *fiecât* 'however much', *fieunde* 'anywhere', *fiecând* 'anytime', *fiecum* 'anyway' contain **fie-** (< *(să) fie*, SUBJ.3SG of *fi* 'be'), with formal variations (*fieşte-*, *fite-*, *fişte-*), and are synonymous with the **ori-** forms (< *veri*, IND.PRES.2SG of *vrea* 'want', TDRG³).

C The Romanian compound series may formally correspond to similar series found in the Balkan languages (Sandfeld 1930: 128; Rosetti 1986: 233; Djamo-Diaconiţă 1976: 161–7). The resemblance between the *-va* series of Romanian and the *-do* series of Albanian (*do, dua* 'want', Djamo-Diaconiţă 1976: 163) is however only formal; unlike Romanian, the Albanian forms have a free-choice value. They have been partially loan-translated into Aromanian (*iuţido* 'anywhere', *cândţido* 'anytime').

TABLE 8.1 Adverbial pro-forms

SEMANTIC TYPE	SIMPLE ADVERB	COMPOUND ADVERB			
	RELATIVE-INTERROGATIVE	EXISTENTIAL	'FREE-CHOICE'	ALTERNATIVE	NEGATIVE
QUANTITY	cât 'how much'	câtva 'a little'	oricât 'however much'	—	nicicât 'not at all'
PLACE	unde 'where'	undeva 'somewhere'	oriunde 'anywhere'	altundeva 'elsewhere'	niciunde 'nowhere'
TIME	când 'when'	cândva 'sometimes'	oricând 'any time'	altcândva 'another time'	nicicând 'never'
MANNER	cum 'how'	cumva 'somehow'	oricum 'anyway'	altcumva 'otherwise'	nicicum 'in no way, nohow'

Romanian indefinites exhibit formal similarities to non-Romance languages, according to Lombard (1938), but also fit the Romance pattern (i.e. there are compound series based on verbs meaning 'be' and 'want'; forms including a reflexive: Rom. *orişicine, cinevaşi*; Cat. and Prov. *quisvol*, Sp. *Quiensequiere*, It. *qualsivoglia*).

8.1.4 Adverbs homophonous with words in other classes

8.1.4.1 Adverbs homophonous with adjectives

Most adverbs are formally identical to the masculine singular form of the adjective; these adverbs most frequently indicate manner, quantification, or discourse evaluation.

(13) a. Fetele   răspund   **corect**
       girls.DEF   answer   correct.ADV≡ADJ.M.SG
       'The girls answer correctly'

    b. Rezolv **legal**   problema
       (I)solve legal.ADV≡ADJ.M.SG problem.F.DEF
       'I solve the problem legally'

C This phenomenon is generalized in Romanian. Elsewhere in Romance, this adjective-as-adverb usage is restricted to a few stable contexts; these shorter forms are preferred to suffixed adverbs in non-standard varieties and are normal in some Italo-Romance dialects (Grundt 1972; Maiden and Robustelli 2007: 201–2, 210–1; Bauer 2011: 556).

    In Istro-Romanian, the distinction between the adjectival and the adverbial usage of the same lexeme may be morphologically marked by the ending *-o* borrowed from Croatian: (ADJ) *plin* – (ADV) *plino* (Frăţilă and Bărdăşan 2010: 49).

8.1.4.2 Adverbs homophonous with verbal forms

The past participles of transitive verbs may be used as adverbs (14a). A few non-finite unergative verbs (with ambiguous interpretation: non-prepositional supine or active participle) can modify verbs of saying or verbs of motion (14b, c).

(14) a. Întreb **deschis**
       (I)ask   open.ADV≡PPLE
       'I ask frankly'

    b. Ea   vorbeşte   **răstit**
       she   speaks   shouted.ADV≡SUP/PPLE
       'She speaks shouting'

    c. Bătrâna   merge   **şchiopătat**
       old-lady.DEF   walks   limped.ADV≡SUP/PPLE
       'The old lady limps'

In preadjectival position, the negative supine may be interpreted as an adverb. This structure has a superlative reading (§4.4.3.9.3).

(15) o casă   [[**nemaipomenit**   de] mare]
       a house NEG-more-mentioned.ADV≡SUP DE big
       'an extremely big house'

8.1 The form of the adverbs

Other verb forms may supply adverbial constructions. For instance, the adverb *curând* 'soon' is based on the gerund of the old verb *cure* 'run' (Dinică 2009). The adverb *poate* 'maybe' (obsolete *poate (a) fi* 'may be') is the 3rd person singular present indicative of the verb *a putea* 'can, may' (Zafiu 2006).

8.1.4.3 Nouns with adverbial value

A noun can lose certain specific nominal features to acquire an adverbial value (Neamțu 1979; Rădulescu 1985) in two typical circumstances:
In the non-standard language some adverbial nouns express form (16a–b) or intensity (16c–e), in certain fixed structures.

(16) a. Câinele   doarme   **covrig**
       dog.DEF   sleeps   coil.ADV≡N
       'The dog sleeps coiled up / curled up'

   b. Copiii   s-au   strâns   **ciorchine**   în jurul clovnului
      children.DEF CL.REFL.ACC=have.3PL gathered bunch.ADV≡N around clown.DEF.GEN
      'The children clustered around the clown'

   c. Fata   e frumoasă **foc**
      girl.DEF is beautiful fire.ADV≡N
      'The girl is extremely beautiful'

   d. Sticlele   sunt înghețate   **tun**
      bottles.DEF are frozen   canon.ADV≡N
      'The bottles are completely frozen'

   e. Camera   e curată **lună**
      room.DEF is clean moonlight.ADV≡N
      'The room is as clean as a new pin'

In the standard language, units of time (parts of the day, seasons, days of the week) are nouns with an iterative (17a) or non-iterative reading (17b), when they take the (singular or, more rarely, plural) definite article (*seara* evening.DEF 'in the evening / every evening', *serile* evenings.DEF 'every evening'; *vara* summer.DEF 'in the summer / every summer', *verile* summers.DEF 'every summer'; *duminica* Sunday.DEF 'on Sundays / every Sunday', *duminicile* Sundays.DEF 'every Sunday'), and quantitative value (18) especially when they are used in the plural without any modifiers.

(17) a. **Vara** (= verile) merg la mare
       'Every / In the summer I go to the seaside'

   b. E născut **vara**
      'He was born in the summer'

(18) Ion a muncit din greu **ani / ore**
     'Ion worked hard for years / hours'

U   In this structure, certain nouns can take demonstrative determiners (*dimineața asta* 'this morning'), quantifiers (*două veri* 'two summers', *tot anul* 'the whole year', *nicio zi* 'not a day'), restrictive modifiers (*anul trecut* 'last year'), or emphatic non-restrictive modifiers (*ani de zile* 'years and years', literally 'years of days'; *luni de zile* 'for months', literally 'months of days', *ore întregi* 'hours and hours', literally 'full hours'). This type of noun does not accept *fiecare* 'every', unlike in English or French.

The plural definite form of the noun *chip* 'manner, way' became an evidential adverb with the meaning 'allegedly, ostensibly, apparently':

(19) A venit, **chipurile**, să ne ajute
 '(S)he came ostensibly to give us a hand'

8.1.5 Fixed collocations and adverbial expressions

The adverbial expressions or paraphrases comprise a preposition (*în*, *din*, sometimes *la*), a noun meaning 'way, manner' (*mod*, *manieră*, of Romance origin; *chip*, *fel*, of Hungarian origin, see Balázs 1988) or a nominal collocation (*punct de vedere* 'point of view') and, generally, a following adjective. The most frequent type is (20a–b):

(20) a. în mod inteligent / asemănător
 in way intelligent.ADJ similar.ADJ
 'intelligently / alike'

 b. din punct de vedere fizic / teoretic
 from point of view physical.ADJ theoretical.ADJ
 'from a physical / theoretical point of view'

 c. în acest chip, în chip sistematic
 in this way in way systematic.ADJ
 'this way', 'systematically'

 d. într-o manieră elegantă / diferită
 in=a manner elegant.ADJ different.ADJ
 'elegantly', 'differently'

 e. la modul sincer / teoretic
 at way.DEF sincere.ADJ theoretical.ADJ
 'sincerely', 'theoretically'

 f. în acest / acelaşi fel
 in this the same way
 'this way', 'the same way'

Fixed adverbial collocations exhibit great structural variation:

(21) a. din păcate 'unfortunately', din fericire 'fortunately', cu de-a sila 'forcibly', din timp în timp 'from time to time', de jur împrejur 'all around', de-a rostogolul 'by rolling'

 b. pe ascuns 'stealthily', pe alese 'at choice', pe apucate 'at random', pe dibuite 'fumblingly', pe înserate 'at dusk', pe nesimţite 'imperceptibly', pe sărite 'by hops and skips / by jumps'

C The fixed collocations in (21b) are based on a recursive structure: the compulsory preposition *pe* literally 'on', plus a form homophonous with the participle / supine plus the optional adverbial formative *-e* (identical to the feminine / neuter plural inflectional ending *-e*).
 These structures have formal or semantic counterparts in the Romance languages: It. *(a) tastoni, (a) saltelloni*; Fr. *à tâtons, à reculons*; Sp. *a reculones, a tropezones*; Ptg. *aos tropeções, aos trambolhões*, etc. (Reinheimer Rîpeanu and Leahu 1983: 451; Pharies 1997).

8.1.6 Non-lexical adverbial formatives

In non-standard, colloquial modern Romanian, as well as in old Romanian, adverbs, pronouns, and, rarely, numerals and conjunctions contain non-lexical particles like *-a, -le, -și(-)* (the most frequent), *-i, -te-, re(-)* (Ciompec 1980). These elements occur in final position (22a), except for *-te-* (22b); *-ș(i)-* can also occur inside pro-forms (22b). They can often be stacked (22c):

(22) a. acum**a**   pururi**le**   acuș**(i)**
         now-*A*   always-*LE*   now-*Ș(I)*
         'now'   'always'   'now'

   b. fi**te**cine   fi**te**cum   oriș**(i)**cum   fi**teș**cum
      any-*TE*-who   any-*TE*-how   any- *Ș(I)*-how   any-*TE-Ș(I)*-how
      'anybody'   'anyhow'   'anyway'   'anyhow'

   c. aci**lea**   pururi**lea**   cumvași**lea**
      here-*LE-A*   always-*LE-A*   somehow-*ȘI-LE-A*
      'here'   'always'   'somehow'

These particles are generally deictic and non-referential. They are highly expressive and non-predictable. In certain situations, they have become obligatory constituents (23a). The elements *-a*, *-le* and, stacked, *-lea* can also hypercharacterize a fixed adverbial collocation containing a preposition (23b).

(23) a. tocm**ai**   aiure**a**   aieve**a**
         just-*I*   elsewhere-*RE-A*   really-*A*

   b. de-**a**   buși**le**   pe apuca**tea**   pe sări**telea**
      DE=*A*   fists-*LE*   on gripped-*E-A*   on skipped-*E-LE-A*
      'on all fours' 'at random'   'by hops and skips / by jumps'

8.2 ADVERBIAL GRADING

Modal, quantitative, and a few locative and temporal adverbs display the same comparison system as adjectives (§§7.4, 10.5):

U When an adverb in the superlative is the adjunct of a (generally participial) adjective, the degree marker usually displays agreement (24b). If the AP is DP-initial, and the DP is in the genitive / dative, agreement must occur (24c) (see also §5.3.1.4.3).

(24) a. angajații   **cel mai bine** plătiți   (standard)
         employees.DEF   CEL more well   paid

   b. angajații   **cei   mai   bine** plătiți
      employees.DEF   CEL.M.PL more well   paid   (non-standard)
      'the best paid employees'

   c. Greva   **celor**   (*cel) **mai prost** plătiți angajați începe mâine
      strike.DEF   CEL.PL.GEN   CEL   more bad   paid   employees starts tomorrow
      'The strike of the worst paid employees starts tomorrow'

8.3 SEMANTIC CLASSES OF ADVERBS

The semantic classes of adverbs comprise words that are heterogeneous from a formal point of view.

(i) Manner adverbs, like adjectives, have either qualifying meaning (*frumos* 'beautifully', *bine* 'well', *așa* 'so') or a meaning related to instrument or means (*discutăm telefonic* 'we discuss on the phone', *rezolvă problema matematic* '(s)he solves the problem mathematically').

(ii) Modal adverbs (§13.5.3; Zafiu 2008d: 702–26) are either formally identical to manner adverbs or have designated forms: *bineînțeles* 'naturally', *firește* 'naturally', *pasămite* 'apparently', *poate* 'maybe', *musai* 'necessarily'.

(iii) Quantifying adverbs give instructions regarding quantity (*mult* 'much', *puțin* 'a little', *câtva* 'a little', *oricât* 'however', *atât* 'so much / long'), duration and frequency (*zilnic* 'daily', *lunar* 'monthly', *anual* 'yearly', *duminica* 'on Sunday / every Sunday', *mereu* 'always', *într-una* 'uninterruptedly', *iarăși* 'again').

(iv) Setting adverbs are locative (*acasă* '(at) home', *aici* 'here', *departe* 'far', *undeva* 'somewhere') and temporal (*azi* 'today', *mâine* 'tomorrow', *întotdeauna* 'always', *niciodată* 'never').

The system of spatial adverbial deictics is organized around two terms, *aici* 'here' and *acolo* 'there', endowed with the feature [+localization]. There are in addition terms encoding the feature [+movement], [+direction], such as *încoace* 'hither', *încolo* 'thither', which are compatible only with verbs of movement (Manoliu 2011: 487):

(25) a. Vino **aici / încoace!**
 'Come here / hither!'
 b. Stai **aici / * încoace!**
 'Stay here!'

A special interrogative–relative indicating direction and historically based on Lat. CONTRA is *încotro* 'whither':

(26) a. **Încotro** mergi?
 'Where / In what direction are you going?'
 b. Nu știu **încotro** s-o iau
 'I don't know which way to go'

C Despite a few adverbs encoding the feature [+direction] (*încotro* 'whither', *încolo* 'thither', *încoace* 'hither', *dincolo* 'over there', *dincoace* 'over here'), Romanian did not inherit from Classical Latin the general lexical-syntactic distinction of *localization / direction* (*ubi / quo, ibi / eo, foris / foras, Romae sum / Romam eo*, etc.). The localization / direction merger also occurs in Macedonian, Bulgarian, Aromanian, Albanian, Megleno-Romanian, and Modern Greek and it has been attributed to the Balkan Sprachbund (Sandfeld 1930: 191–2; Mišeska Tomić 2004: 47). In Latin, the features [+direction] [+localization] are sometimes expressed identically (Ernout and Thomas 1959: 111–14), and this characteristic has persisted into the Romance languages (Sandfeld 1930: 192).

H Romanian inherited Lat. UBI in the adverb *i(u)o*, frequent in the 16th century (27a), in parallel with *unde*, which also displays the localization / direction merger; the adverb *i(u)o* was subsequently abandoned (Ciompec 1985: 51; Frâncu 2009: 134). In the south-Danubian varieties, the descendents of UBI (27b) were preferred to the descendents of UNDE.

(27) a. **Io** e Dumnezeul lor? (*Psaltirea Scheiană*)
'Where is their God?'
b. Arom. **Ĭu** bea pul'i apă?
'Where do the chicks drink water?' (Papahagi 1963)

Temporal deixis expressed by means of adverbials displays a few recurrent lexical and syntactic patterns.

Temporal deictic adverbs denoting the days of the week are organized in a threefold manner (28). These forms can appear in compounds expressing moments of the day, some of them with a recursive structure and meaning (29a); other temporal compounds are less transparent in contemporary Romanian (29b).

(28) răsalaltăieri (obsolete) 'three days ago'–alaltăieri 'the day before yesterday'–ieri 'yesterday'–azi / astăzi 'today'–mâine 'tomorrow'–poimâine 'the day after tomorrow'–răspoimâine 'two days after tomorrow'

(29) a. ieri-dimineaţă 'yesterday morning', alaltăieri-seară 'two evenings ago', mâine-noapte 'tomorrow night'
b. aseară 'yesterday evening', azi-noapte 'last night', diseară 'this evening, tonight'

The adverbial expressions for seasons display a regular frozen structure for past (30a) and future (30b) reference and a less frozen structure for the present (30c). The preposition *la* for future reference can also occur in other structures except for names of seasons (31).

(30) a. astă-primăvară 'last spring', astă-iarnă 'last winter'
b. la primăvară 'next spring', la iarnă 'next winter'
c. (în) vara asta / aceasta vs. *această vară
(in) summer.DEF this this summer
'this summer' 'this summer'

(31) la noapte 'tonight', la anu(l) 'next year'

For specific past (32a) or future (32b) reference there are two main series, using *acum*, literally 'now' and *peste* 'over, on':

(32) a. acum două minute 'two minutes ago', acum trei ani 'three years ago'
b. peste două minute 'in two minutes' time', peste trei ani 'in three years' time'

(v) Adverbs encoding logical relations such as concession (33) or condition (34) are rare.

(33) Fac sport şi **totuşi / tot** nu slăbesc
'I do sport, but still I don't lose weight'

(34) Citeşte cartea, **altfel / altminteri** nu vei înţelege!
'Read the book, otherwise you won't understand!'

(vi) The adverbs of neutral affirmation and negation are *da* 'yes' and *no* 'nu'. The positive answer (Zafiu 2008b: 671–9) as well as the negative one (§13.3; Zafiu 2008c: 680–701) can be enhanced / substituted by modal adverbs:

(35) a. (de)sigur 'sure', bineînţeles 'of course', fireşte 'naturally', evident 'obviously', de bună seamă 'for sure', fără îndoială 'without a doubt'
b. nicidecum 'not at all', deloc 'not at all', nici vorbă 'not in the least'

C The *da* affirmation has multiple Slavic origins (Bulgarian, Russian, and Serbo-Croatian) and has been used in Romanian since the late 17th century, in parallel with *dar(ă)*, *aşa*, *iacă*. The adverb *aşa*, which contains Lat. SIC (inherited by Italian, Portuguese, and French) for a long time represented the main affirmative marker in the northern and western Daco-Romanian varieties, and did so sporadically in Aromanian (Niculescu 1965; Dominte 2003: 39–41).

8.4 THE STRUCTURE OF THE ADVERBIAL PHRASE (AdvP)

The prototypical way of extending an AdvP is modification. Complementation and adjunction are rarer, and are lexically and / or syntactically constrained.

8.4.1 AdvP-internal modifiers

Like the adjectival head, the modifiers of the adverbial head may be adverbs with different values: degree (36a–c), gradual progression (37), approximation (38), modality (39), etc.:

(36) a. **mai** / **foarte** târziu
       more / very late
       'later / very late'

   b. **extrem**   de aproape, **imens de** departe
      extremely DE close   huge DE far
      'extremely close', 'immensely far'

   c. **îngrozitor de** dificil,   **regretabil de** târziu
      terribly   DE difficult regretably DE late
      'terribly difficult', 'regrettably late'

(37) **din ce în ce** mai târziu, **tot mai** greu
     'later and later', 'increasingly difficult'

(38) **cam** devreme, **oarecum** aproape, **relativ**   bine,
     'rather early', 'quite   close', 'relatively well'

(39) **probabil** aici,   **cică** mâine,   **pesemne** acolo
     'probably here', 'allegedly tomorrow', 'probably there'

Certain pre-head superlative modifiers, such as those in (36b,c), are attached by means of the functional preposition DE. In stacked modification, the degree and approximation constituents modify the head, and the modal modifiers take scope over the whole phrase:

(40) **probabil** [**extrem**   de [târziu]]
     probably extremely DE late
     'probably extremely late'

8.4.2 Complements of the adverbial head

8.4.2.1 Prepositional complements of the adverbial head

A few adverbs license a prepositional complement, frequently linked to the head by the preposition *de* and, sporadically, by *cu* or *la*:

(41) a. [**aproape** [de aici]], [**indiferent** [de situație]]
close   DE here   irrespectively DE situation
'close to here', 'no matter what the situation'

b. [**concomitent** [cu ședința]]
concomitantly with meeting.DEF
'concomitantly with the meeting'

c. [**relativ**   [la raportul   anterior]]
relatively   to report.DEF previous
'in relation to the previous report'

8.4.2.2   Indirect objects of the adverbial head

A few adverbs based on a reference-modifying adjective can license an indirect object in the dative: *aidoma* 'similarly', *asemenea* 'like', *anterior* 'previously', *posterior* 'subsequently', *ulterior* 'afterwards', etc.

(42) a. Ion se   poartă   [**aidoma**   [tatălui]]
Ion CL.REFL.ACC.3SG behaves similarly father.DEF.DAT
'Ion behaves like his father'

b. [**Anterior** [concursului]],   elevii   au   primit   instrucțiuni
previously contest.DEF.DAT pupils.DEF have received instructions
'Before the competition, the pupils received instructions'

8.4.2.3   Dative clitics as indirect objects

The indirect objects surfacing as free (43) or bound (44) pronominal personal or reflexive clitics in the dative are licensed by a few adverbs and fixed collocations with an initially locative meaning: *înainte* 'before', *împrejur* 'around', *dedesubt* 'beneath', *în față* 'in front', *în spate* 'behind', etc. The structures in (44), where is is not clear if these clitics are true datives or genitives (see §5.3.3.3), are typical of old Romanian and have counterparts in structures with a prepositional head (45), associated with the article-like ending (§9.4).

(43) a. **îmi**   stă   **împotrivă**
CL.DAT.1SG stands against
'(S)he stands against me'

b. **I-au**   ieșit   **înainte**
CL.DAT.3SG=(they)have gone   front
'They went out to meet him / her'

(44) a. Stă   **împotrivă-mi**
stands against=CL.1SG
'(S)he stands against me'

b. Au   ieșit   **înainte-i**
(they)have   gone   front=CL.3SG
'They went out to meet him / her'

(45) a. Stă   **împotriva-mi /   mea**
stands against-*A*=CL.1SG my.F.SG
'(S)he stands against me'

b. Au ieşit **înaintea-i/** **lui /** **ei /** **sa**
(they)have gone front-*A*=CL.3SG his(GEN) her(GEN) his / her
'They went out to meet him / her'

8.4.2.4 The comparative complement of the adverbial head

As with adjectives, the comparative complement of the adverb can be expressed in the presence of comparative and superlative markers (§§7.6.2.6, 10.5).

(46) a. Aleargă [mai repede [**decât ceilalţi concurenţi**]]
runs more fast than the-other competitors
'(S)he runs faster than the other competitors'

b. Aleargă [cel mai repede [**dintre concurenţi**]]
runs CEL more fast of competitors
'(S)he runs the fastest of the competitors'

8.4.3 The adjuncts of the adverb

The adjuncts of the adverbial head express either quantity (47a) or consequence / result (47b).

(47) a. A plătit [mai mult [**cu 300 de lei**]]
'(S)he paid 300 lei more'

b. Mănâncă [repede [**de speriat**]]
eats fast DE$_{SUP}$ scare.SUP
'(S)he eats frighteningly fast'

8.5 THE EXTERNAL SYNTAX OF THE ADVERBIAL PHRASE

AdvPs are typically VP adjuncts and, on rare occasions, AP (§7.6.3) and AdvP (§8.4.3) adjuncts. The situations below characterize only certain adverbial classes.

8.5.1 Adverbs subcategorized by the verbal head

A few verbs require an adverbial complement:

(48) a. a se comporta / a proceda **bine / rău / aşa**
'behave / do right / wrong / this way'

b. a dura / a valora / a costa **mult / puţin**
'last / be worth / cost much / little'

c. a locui **aici / acolo / departe / aproape**
'live here / there / far / close'

Except for the adverbial complements licensed by the verb, the adverbial constituents are optional.

(49) a. Aude **clar** muzica
 hears clearly music.DEF
 '(S)he hears the music clearly'

 b. Deschide ferestrele **larg**
 opens windows.DEF widely
 '(S)he opens the windows wide'

 c. Vopseşte **verde** scaunele
 paints green.ADV chairs.DEF
 '(S)he paints the chairs green'

8.5.2 Clausal modal adverbs

Modal adverbs (§13.5.3) and a few approximation / degree adverbs (*aproape* 'almost', *mai* 'more', etc.) usually modify either a single constituent or the entire sentence, with which they can be connected directly (52) or by a complementizer—the epistemic and evaluation adverbs are generally connected by *că* 'that' (50) and deontic adverbs by *să* (51).

(50) a. **(E) probabil / sigur / adevărat / bine** [că a plecat]
 (is) probable sure true good that has left
 '(S)he probably / surely / left; it is true / good that (s)he left'

 b. lucrare [**poate că** [bună]]
 paper maybe that good
 'a probably good paper'

(51) E **bine / musai / necesar** [să iei medicamente]
 is good compulsory necessary SĂ_SUBJ take.SUBJ.2SG medicines
 'It is good / compulsory / necessary to take medicines'

(52) a. **Probabil / sigur / fireşte / poate** [a plecat]
 probably surely of course perhaps has left
 'Probably / surely / of course / perhaps (s)he has left'

 b. femeie [**probabil / sigur / poate** [bolnavă]]
 woman probably surely maybe ill
 'a woman who is probably / surely / perhaps ill'

The complentizers *că* or *să* give rise to different readings of the same adverb (§10.1.1.1):

(53) a. E **bine / important** că ai rămas [evaluative]
 'It is good / important that you stayed'

 b. E **bine / important** să rămâi [deontic]
 'It is good / important to stay'

The copula is optional for most of these adverbs (50a) and is disallowed for a few: *fireşte* 'naturally', *pesemne* 'probably', *poate* 'maybe', *negreşit* 'for sure', *desigur* 'certainly'. For the analysis of adverbs functioning as subjective predicative complements, see §3.3.1.2(v).

8.5.3 *Wh*-adverbs

The adverbs *când* 'when', *cât* 'how much', *cum* 'how', *încotro* 'whither', *unde* 'where' introduce finite (54a) and infinitival (54b) free (headless) relatives (§10.3.3), or headed relatives ((55); see also §5.3.5.2.5). The adverbs *oricând* 'at any time', *oricât* 'however much', *oricum* 'anyhow', *oriunde* 'anywhere', *oriîncotro* 'anywhere, in any direction, whithersoever' introduce only free relatives.

(54) a. Merg **unde** m-ai   trimis
         (I)go where CL.ACC.1SG=have.2SG sent
         'I'm going where you sent me'

      b. N-am   **cum** te   ajuta
         not=(I)have how CL.ACC.2SG help.INF
         'I have no way of helping you'

(55) Îmi plac zilele **când** plouă
      'I like days when it rains'

8.5.4 Adverbs as complements of prepositions and as NP modifiers

Setting adverbs can act as complements of prepositions.

(56) Citește **de aici până acolo**
      '(S)he reads from here to there'

Setting adverbs are generally non-restrictive modifiers of a nominal head. If the head is a prototypical noun, the AdvP is introduced by the preposition *de* ((57); see also §5.3.5.1.2); in the case of a deverbal noun, the AdvP can be adjoined to the head directly (58a) or by means of the preposition *de* (58b) (see also §§5.3.5.2.4, 5.3.2.3.3; Stan 2003: 197–204).

(57) cartea   **de**   **acolo**
      book.DEF   from   there
      'the book from there'

(58) a. plecarea   **azi**
         leaving.DEF   today
         'leaving today'

      b. plecarea   **de**   **azi**
         departure.DEF from   today
         'departure today'

8.5.5 Focusing adverbs

The focusing adverbs *doar* 'only', *numai* 'only', *decât* 'only', *și* 'too', *chiar (și)* 'even', *tocmai* 'just', *mai ales* 'especially', *măcar* 'at least', *nici* 'neither' adjoin to different kinds of phrases: AdvPs (59), DPs (when they also have quantification value, §5.3.2.3.5), PPs (60), clausal adjuncts, etc. They usually occur in the left periphery (*și* 'too', *decât* 'only', *nici* 'neither' have only this possibility). A modal adverb that takes scope over the whole phrase is external to the focus phrase:

(59) **posibil** [**chiar** [mai [departe [de aici]]]]
    possibly even more far from here
    'possibly even farther from here'

U In relation to a PP, the focusing adverbs are usually preposed to the head; they may also occur after the head; postposition is more often than not tied to or associated with quantification:

(60) a. Mama șterge praful **și** în camera ta
       mother.DEF wipes dust.DEF too in room.DEF your
    b. Vorbim **inclusiv** despre copii ((,) **inclusiv**)
       (we)speak inclusively about children inclusively
    c. Scriu articolul (**numai**) în **numai** două zile (**numai**)
       (I)write article.DEF only in only two days only

8.6 THE ORDER OF ADVERBS IN THE SENTENCE

In modern standard Romanian, *mai* '(any) more, still', *și* 'immediately, also', *tot* 'still, also', *prea* 'too', *cam* 'rather' are the only adverbs that occur in a fixed position, following the auxiliary.

8.6.1 Adverbial clitics

The adverbs *mai* '(any) more, still, also' (61), *și* 'immediately, also' (62), *prea* 'too' (63), *cam* 'rather' (64), *tot* 'still, also' (65), which display context-dependent meanings, can split analytic verbal forms according to criteria of semantic compatibility. They typically occur in preverbal position, after auxiliaries or the infinitive inflectional head A and / or negation. This has been an important argument for considering them clitics (Dobrovie-Sorin 1999: 522; Reinheimer Rîpeanu 2004: 225).

(61) a. Ion a **mai** vizitat România în 2001   [standard]
       Ion has also visited Romania in 2001
    b. Ion **mai** a vizitat România în 2001   [non-standard]
       Ion also has visited Romania in 2001
    'Ion has already visited Romania in 2001'

(62) După ședință, Ion a **și** plecat
    after meeting Ion has immediately left
    'Ion left immediately after the meeting'

(63) Ion nu se **prea** descurcă la matematică
    Ion not CL.REFL.ACC.3SG too manages at maths
    'Ion is not too good at maths'

(64) Ion s-a **cam** plictisit la film
    Ion CL.REFL.ACC.3SG=has rather bored at film
    'Ion got rather bored at the film'

U Positional variation usually reflects semantic specialization (Tasmowski and Reinheimer Rîpeanu 2003; Barbu 2004; Reinheimer Rîpeanu 2004, 2005, 2010; Donazzan and Mardale 2010):

(65) a. Deși   s-a   simțit foarte rău   ieri,   Ion   **tot**
        although CL.REFL.ACC.3SG=has felt very   bad   yesterday   Ion   still
        a   (***tot**)
        has   still   venit   la   spital singur
                                   come   to   hospital alone
        'Although Ion felt very bad yesterday, he still came to the hospital alone'

   b. În   ultimul   an,   Ion   (**tot**)   a   **tot**   venit la   spital
      in   the-last year, Ion   repeatedly   has   repeatedly   come   to   hospital
      'In the last year, Ion has repeatedly come to the hospital'

In the Wallachian subdialect, the position of *mai* '(any)more, still, also' is less rigid ((61b), see also Avram 1977: 29–31).

The adverb *mai* '(any) more, still, yet, also' can be incorporated within the adjectival participle (66a), supine (66b), and gerund (66c), being preceded by the negative prefix *ne-*. The adverb *prea* 'too' can split the negative gerund (spelling being oscillatory in this case) (67):

(66) a. poveste ne**mai**pomenită
        story   NEG-more-mentioned.PPLE
        'incredible story'

   b. poveste ne**mai**pomenit   de   lungă
      story   NEG-more-mentioned.PPLE   DE   long
      'incredibly long story'

   c. Ne**mai**putând   respira,   a   murit
      NEG-more-be-able.GER   breathe.INF   has   died
      'Not being able to breathe anymore, (s)he died'

(67) Ne **prea** plăcându-i /   ne**prea**plăcându-i   matematica, a
     NEG too   like.GER=CL.DAT.3SG   NEG-too-like.GER=CL.DAT.3SG   maths   has
     pierdut   bursa
     lost   scholarship.DEF
     'Not much liking mathematics, he lost the scholarship'

8.6.2 Manner adverbs

The order of VP-internal manner adverbs is related to the class-internal semantic variation. In the unmarked position, they immediately follow the verbal head or the direct object (68a), but never split an analytic verbal form (68b).

(68) a. Maria a   povestit **frumos**   întâmplarea   (**frumos**)
        Maria has told   beautifully   story.DEF   beautifully
        'Maria has told the story beautifully'

   b. *Maria a   **frumos**   povestit
      Maria   has beautifully   told

Romanian does not require the manner adverb to come immediately before or after the subject, which is typically an adjective position (69).

(69) **Precaută**, Maria a plecat din clasă
 cautious.F.SG Maria has left from classroom
 'Cautiously, Maria left the classroom'

Usually, the VP-internal adverbs such as *tehnic* 'technically', *politic* 'politically', *diplomatic* 'diplomatically' immediately follow the verbal head:

(70) Şi-au depăşit **tehnic** adversarii
 CL.REFL.DAT.3PL=(they)have defeated technically competitors.DEF
 'They defeated their competitors technically'

Placed sentence-initially, these adverbs operate at IP level, semantically restricting the meaning of the sentence (71). The same type of restriction can also occur at AP level (72), but the position of the adverb is free, preferably preceding the adjectival head.

(71) **Tehnic**, [soluţia este imposibilă]
 technically solution.DEF is impossible
 'From a technical point of view, the solution is impossible'

(72) Ai găsit o soluţie **tehnic** imposibilă (**tehnic**)
 (you)have found a solution technically impossible technically
 'You found a solution which is impossible from a technical point of view'

8.6.3 Setting adverbs

Place and time adverbs frequently follow the head (73). If they are licensed by the verbal head, they immediately follow it (74).

(73) a. Cumpăr pâine **diseară**
 'I buy bread tonight'

 b. Pun cartea **acolo**
 'I put the book there'

(74) Locuieşte **aici** împreună cu familia
 '(S)he lives here with his / her family'

Adverbs are not rigidly ordered with respect to one another (Cinque 1999: 28):

(75) Soseşte **devreme aici (devreme)**
 '(S)he arrives early here (early)'

When they refer to the whole sentence, setting adverbs have a very flexible position. They frequently occur in clause-initial position, and are not rigidly ordered with respect to one another.

(76) **Ieri, aici / Aici, ieri** [a avut loc un eveniment cultural]
 yesterday here here yesterday has taken place an event cultural

CONCLUSIONS

Most manner Romanian adverbs are identical to the masculine singular form of adjectives. There are few adverbs with special forms (with adverbial suffixes). The Latin ablative *mente* was not employed in Romanian adverbial derivation.

A number of non-lexical formatives can be used in adverbial derivation (or for pronouns, and sporadically for numerals and conjunctions).

Adverbs expressing the names of languages behave syntactically like nouns.

Motion verbs and verbs of saying may select an unergative non-finite form (a participle or a supine) recategorized as adverbial adjuncts.

Adverbs in certain non-comparative superlative structures are introduced by the functional preposition *de*. As a non-restrictive modifier of a nominal head, the adverb is also headed by a preposition (usually *de*); adverbs may attach directly (i.e. without a preposition) to deverbal nominal heads.

The adverbs *mai* '(any) more, still, also', *și* 'immediately, also', *tot* 'still, also', *prea* 'too', *cam* 'rather' behave like clitics and can split analytic verb forms.

9

Prepositions and Prepositional Phrases

This chapter presents the inventory and the internal structure of the Romanian prepositions (simple, compound, and collocations), the semantico-syntactic types of prepositions (lexical, functional, and a mixed group, selected by different heads), the components of the PP and the restrictions imposed by the preposition to its complements, as well as parallels between certain prepositions and adverbs.

9.1 SIMPLE, COMPOUND, AND COLLOCATED PREPOSITIONS

The class of prepositions contains many items inherited from Latin (*a* 'like', *ca* 'as', *cu* 'with', *către* 'towards', *de* 'of', *după* 'after', *în* 'in', *la* 'at / to', *pe* 'on'), a series of loans (*grație* 'thanks to', *per* 'per', *pro* 'for'), and prepositions formed in Romanian (*datorită* 'due to', *mulțumită* 'thanks to').

H Certain prepositions that are attested in old Romanian, such as *adins* 'between', *na* 'at / to', *de-aleanul* 'against' (occurring in the 16th century, Densusianu 1961, II: 177–81), disappeared, while others became restricted in use (§9.2).

In Romanian, most prepositions are simple, made up of just one word (*a* 'like', *cu* 'with', *de* 'of', *grație* 'thanks to', *în* 'in', *la* 'at; to', *lângă* 'near', *pe* 'on', *până* 'until').

H A series of prepositions, written as one word according to current orthographic norms, are originally compound prepositions: *despre* 'about' (< *de* 'of' + *spre* 'towards'), *din* 'from' (< *de* 'of' + *în* 'in'), *dinspre* 'from' (< *de* 'of' + *în* 'in' + *spre* 'towards'), *dintre* 'between; among' (< *de* 'of' + *între* 'between / among'), *înspre* 'towards' (< *în* 'in' + *spre* 'towards').

There are relatively few compound prepositions (*de-a* 'of', *de către* 'by', *de la* 'from'):

(1) a. jocul **de-a** trenul
    game DE=A train.DEF.ACC
    'the train game'
   b. textul scris **de către** Ion
    text.DEF writen by Ion.ACC
    'the text written by Ion'
   c. a oprit-o **de la** sinucidere
    has stopped=CL.ACC.F.3SG from suicide.ACC
    'this stopped her from committing suicide'

Besides the simple and compound prepositions, Romanian displays a large number of prepositional collocations, which obligatorily contain at least one preposition: *în fața* 'in front of', *în jurul* 'around', *față de* 'relative to', (*în*) *afară de* 'besides; except for', *cu privire la* 'regarding'. The class of collocations is open; many word sequences tend to become frozen phrases: *cu excepţia* 'except for', *cu scopul* 'in order to'.

9.2 LEXICAL VS. FUNCTIONAL PREPOSITIONS. SUBCATEGORIZED PREPOSITIONS

Prepositions are a semilexical category; they have an intermediate status between lexical and functional elements (Corver and Van Riemsdijk 2001). Within the heterogeneous preposition class, two types of preposition can be distinguished, depending on their syntactic and semantic characteristics: functional and lexical. Besides these, the subcategorized prepositions (obligatorily selected by a lexical head) belong to a special type, with mixed, functional, and lexical characteristics.

9.2.1 Lexical prepositions

Prepositions such as *din* 'from', *după* 'after', *graţie* 'thanks to', *împotriva* 'against', *în* 'in', *la* 'at; to', *lângă* 'near', *pentru* 'for', *spre* 'towards', *sub* 'under' contribute to establishing semantic relations within the phrase; the substitution of one preposition with another generally involves changes in meaning:

(2) a. Merge **în** magazin [localization]
      walks in store
      '(S)he walks in the store'

   b. Merge **spre** magazin [direction]
      goes towards store
      'S/he goes towards the store'

(3) a. Te aştept **la** ora trei [temporal localization]
      CL.ACC.2SG (I) expect at hour three
      'I am expecting you at three o'clock'

   b. Te aştept **după** ora trei [posteriority]
      CL.ACC.2SG (I) expect after hour three
      'I am expecting you after three o'clock'

Two lexical prepositions may be semantically equivalent, in rare cases. This is true of prepositions such as *contra* and *împotriva* 'against', *în faţa* and *înaintea* 'in front of', *spre* and *pentru* 'for' (indicating purpose):

(4) L-a lăudat **pentru** /**spre** a-i da încredere
    CL.ACC.M.3SG=has praised for A_{INF}=CL.DAT.3SG give.INF trust
    '(S)he praised him in order to boost his confidence'

Certain lexical prepositions, which were initially synonymous, and therefore in competition, became specialized for certain contexts. Of the pairs *în—întru* 'in', *din—dintru* 'from', *prin—printru* 'through', the second member is selected—in the form *într-*, *dintr-*, *printr-* — when followed by the indefinite article *un / o* 'a' (5a), the indefinite pronoun *unul / una* 'other; one' (5b), or the old personal pronoun *însul* 'he' / *însa* 'she' (5c).

9.2 Lexical vs. functional prepositions. Subcategorized prepositions

(5) a. în   casă   vs.   într-o   casă
       in   house.ACC   in=a   house.ACC

   b. într-una   din   zile
      in=one   of   days

   c. dintr-însul /   dintr-însa
      from=he.DEF.ACC /   from=she.DEF.ACC

U The prepositions *întru*, *dintru*, and *printru* are the contextual variants of *în*, *din*, and *prin* (5a) and must be differentiated from *între*, *dintre*, *printre*, which combine with a plural nominal or a coordinated structure (§9.3.2.3).

Lexical prepositions assign different thematic roles, such as Beneficiary (6a), Locative (6b), Path (6c), Source (6d), and Instrument (6e):

(6) a. A muncit **pentru ea**
       '(S)he worked for her'

   b. Lampa este **pe podea**
      'The lamp is on the floor'

   c. Trece **prin parc**
      '(S)he passes through the park'

   d. Vine **din străinătate**
      '(S)he comes from abroad'

   e. Citește **cu ochelarii**
      '(S)he reads with glasses'

Certain lexical prepositions are polysemous.

The preposition *după* 'after' can indicate the space behind an object (7a), but it can also express posteriority (3b), purpose (7b), conformity (7c):

(7) a. Stă   **după**   ușă
       stays   after   door.ACC
       '(S)he stays behind the door'

   b. S-a   dus   **după** cumpărături
      CL.REFL.ACC.3SG=has   gone   after   shopping.ACC
      '(S)he went shopping'

   c. A   făcut   totul   **după**   dorința   ei
      has   done   everything   after   wish.DEF.ACC   her(GEN)
      '(S)he did everything according to her wish'

The preposition *spre* 'towards' indicates direction (2b), purpose (4), or closeness to a certain moment in time (8):

(8) Vom   ajunge   **spre**   seară
    AUX.FUT.1PL   arrive.INF   towards   evening.ACC
    'We will arrive towards evening'

C Romanian is the only Romance language in which the descendant of Lat. SŬPER 'above'—*spre*—evolved towards a directional meaning ('towards') (Niculescu 1965: 116). *Spre* is rarely attested with this meaning in the 16th century, old Romanian *spre* displaying meanings similar to those of the descendants of Lat. sŭper in other Romance languages (Niculescu 1965: 110–13). The purpose meaning of *spre* occurs exclusively in Romanian, and has been attributed to Slavic influence (Niculescu 1965: 131–7).

The preposition *din* 'from', made up of the prepositions *de* 'of' (with the initial meaning of point of departure) and *în* 'in', can express the locative source (9a)—from which derives the partitive meaning (9b)—the temporal source (9c), or the cause (9d):

(9) a. sportivii **din** România
 athletes.DEF from Romania.ACC
 'The athletes from Romania'

 b. un student **din** grup
 a student from group.ACC
 'a student in the group'

 c. Revoluția **din** 1989
 revolution.DEF from 1989
 'The revolution of 1989'

 d. A căzut **din** neatenție
 has fallen from lack-of-attention.ACC
 '(S)he fell because (s)he did not pay attention'

H In old Romanian, the preposition *a* had lexical uses ('to; at', 'like'). The locative *a* no longer occurs in Romanian, but it can be recognized in compounds like *acasă* '(at) home', *alături* 'next to', *alocuri* 'here and there'. *A* occurs in contemporary Romanian, in rare quasi-fixed constructions expressing likeness or similarity (*miroase a tei* 'it smells like lime', *calcă a popă* 'he walks like a priest').

9.2.2 Functional prepositions

Functional prepositions, which have only a grammatical role and no lexical meaning, are *a*, *de*, *la*, *pe* (for the analysis of functional prepositions, see Van Riemsdijk 1990; Mardale 2009). As they do not have the capacity to assign thematic roles, their complement receives its role from the lexical head. In (10a), the Patient role of the noun is assigned by the verb *bate* 'beat', not by the preposition *pe* (§3.2.1.3.1); the noun is assigned the same role in the absence of the preposition (10b):

(10) a. Ion îl bate pe Gheorghe
 Ion CL.ACC.3SG beats PE Gheorghe.ACC
 'Ion beats Gheorghe'

 b. Ion bate măgarul
 Ion beats donkey.DEF.ACC
 'Ion beats the donkey'

Functional prepositions have the following uses, each discussed in turn:
- where *a* and *la* are case markers;
- where the preposition *pe* is the [+specific] direct object marker;
- where the preposition *de* appears in certain structures, in which it takes specific functions.

9.2 Lexical vs. functional prepositions. Subcategorized prepositions 455

As functional prepositions, *a* and *la* are case markers. In addition to the prototypical inflectional genitive marker, Romanian employs the preposition *a* (11a, b); as well as the dative case marker it employs the prepositions *la* (12a) and *a* (12b). Prepositional marking is triggered by the lack of case inflection of the leftmost constituent of the DP (11a, 12a, b); it can also occur as a free variant of the inflectional marker (11b) (for further details, see §5.1.3.2.2):

(11) a. cărţile   a   doi   copii
books.DEF A two children.NOM≡ACC
'the books of two children'

b. contra a mai multe persoane /   contra mai multor persoane
against A more many persons.NOM≡ACC against more many.GEN persons
'against more persons'

(12) a. Am   oferit   cărţi   la   cinci   copii
(I)have offered books to five children.NOM≡ACC

b. datorită   a   ceea ce   ne-a   învăţat
thanks-to A what CL.ACC.1PL=has taught
'thanks to what (s)he taught us'

C Apart from the aforementioned syntactically restricted configurations, Romanian does not employ a descendant of Lat. AD as a dative marker or as a preposition of direction, unlike the other Romance languages (Posner 1996: 124). In old Romanian, *a* is attested as a dative case marker (§5.1.3.2.2).

In their evolution from Latin, the other Romance languages extended prepositional case marking to the detriment of inflectional marking (Salvi 2011: 338–9). Prototypically, Romanian marks the genitive and the dative synthetically.

The preposition *pe* is the [+specific] direct object marker, assigning the accusative case (§3.2.1.3.2):

(13) a. Te   aşteaptă pe tine
CL.ACC.2SG waits PE you.ACC
'(S)he is waiting for you'

b. Ia-l   pe acesta
take.IMP.2SG=CL.ACC.M.3SG PE this.ACC
'Take this one!'

The capacity to assign the accusative case proves the prepositional nature of *pe*, the head of a PP.

De has a number of functional uses:

(i) in structures with a cardinal number above 19 (§5.3.2.1.1):

(14) a. douăzeci de oameni
twenty DE persons
'twenty people'

b. cincizeci şi unu de oameni
fifty-one DE persons
'fifty-one people'

(ii) in pseudopartitive structures (Kupferman 2004: 301–3; for Romanian, Tănase-Dogaru 2009: 67–128; Nedelcu 2009: 178–90):

(15) un kilogram de mere
 a kilogram of apples

(iii) in structures similar to standard partitive structures (marked by *din* or *dintre* 'of', as in example (20)), in which the complement of the preposition is a genitive / possessive in the singular with a property reading (16), a genitive / possessive in the plural with an entity reading (17a) or with a double reading, entity or property (17b) (Cornilescu 2006: 28–36; Nedelcu 2009: 162–78):

(16) o carte **de-a** ei / **de-a** mea
 a book of=AL.F.SG her(GEN) of=AL.F.SG my.F.SG
 'a book of hers' 'a book of mine'

(17) a. o prietenă **de-ale** Mariei / **de-ale** mele
 a friend of=AL.F.PL Maria.GEN of=AL.F.PL my.F.PL
 'a friend of Mary's' 'a friend of mine'

 b. două **de-ale** mele
 two of=AL.F.PL my.F.PL
 'two of mine'

H In old Romanian, partitive *de* occurred in constructions in which the noun referring to the 'whole' had an unmarked nominative≡accusative form:
 (18) ura **de sâmbăte** (*Codicele Voronețean*)
 one of Saturdays
 'one of the Saturdays'
 In old Romanian, functional *de* was also a genitive case marker (§5.1.3.2.2):
 (19) neguțătorii și mișeii **de aiasta țară** (*Documente*)
 traitors.DEF and villains.DEF of this country

U In present-day Romanian, *de* is no longer used in the partitive structure, the prepositions *din*, *dintre* 'of' being used instead:
 (20) două **dintre / din cărți**
 two of books
 'two of the books'

(iv) in structures with an ordinal numeral formed with *al*, headed by the determiner *cel*:

(21) Cel **de-al doilea** este colorat
 CEL DE=AL second is colourful
 'The second one is colourful'

(v) in structures with predicate inversion (§5.3.5.3):

(22) măgarul **de Ion**
 donkey.DEF DE Ion
 'that donkey Ion'

(vi) in adjectival or adverbial phrases, when a degree marker is placed to the left of the head:

(23) Prăjitura este **extraordinar** **de** bună
 cake.DEF is extraordinarily DE good
 'The cake is extremely good'

(vii) as the head of a *by*-phrase (§3.4.1.1.2):

(24) Bibliografia a fost citită **de** **studenți**
 bibliography.DEF has been read by students
 'The bibliography was read by the students'

(viii) when it links the argument of a deverbal noun (25) or the modifier (26) to the head (§5.3.4.1, §9.3.5.2):

(25) citirea **de** **texte** **vechi** < citește **texte** **vechi**
 reading DE texts old reads texts old
 'the reading of old texts' '(S)he reads old texts'

(26) casa [**de** [**lângă** **deal**]] < casa este **lângă** **deal**
 house.DEF DE near hill house.DEF is near hill
 'the house next to the hill' 'the house is next to the hill'

9.2.3 Subcategorized prepositions

Certain prepositions are selected by the head of the phrase, which can be a verb (*a apela la* 'resort to', *a se asocia cu* 'associate with', *a se bizui pe* 'rely on'), an adjective (*atent la* 'careful at', *capabil de* 'capable of', *gelos pe* 'jealous of'), an adverb (*conform cu* 'in accordance with', *aidoma cu* 'identically to / just like'), or a deverbal noun (*asocierea cu* 'association with', *apelarea la* 'the appeal to', *supărarea pe* 'anger at').

On the one hand, they resemble lexical prepositions in two respects: they do have a lexical meaning (even if it is less transparent than the meaning of lexical prepositions) and they are involved in theta role assignment, compositionally, that is together with the lexical category which is their head (Rauh Wuppertal 1994: 51, 74; Pană Dindelegan 2003: 171)—Theme (27a), Beneficiary (27b), Goal (27c,d):

(27) a. Frumusețea [constă în armonie]
 'Beauty consists in harmony'

 b. Manualul este [util pentru studenți]
 'The manual is useful for the students'

 c. [Apelează la mama] pentru a o ajuta
 'She turns to her mother for help'

 d. Ion este [gelos pe Gheorghe]
 'Ion is jealous of Gheorghe'

On the other hand, they resemble functional prepositions because they mark a prepositional object which has an obligatory preposition (§3.2.4).

458   9 Prepositions and Prepositional Phrases

9.3 PREPOSITIONAL PHRASES

9.3.1 The structure of prepositional phrases

The extended structure of PPs is [[Modifier] [Prep [Complement]]]:

(28) [[pe]   [lângă]   [perete]]]
     on   near   wall
     'along / next to the wall'

Focusing particles (certain adverbs with emphatic or restrictive role) can attach to the left of the PP:

(29) a. și /   nici / tot /   chiar   despre   tine
        Also   nor   still   precisely   about   you.ACC

     b. **Doar / numai**   cu   trenul
        Only   with   train.DEF.ACC
        'only by train'

Modifiers are preposed to the preposition and have the role of approximation:

(30) a. **pe**   la   prânz
        on   at   lunch
        'around lunchtime'

     b. **cam**   cu   teamă
        around   with   fear
        'quite frightened'

The complements of the preposition are obligatorily realized lexically. In the rare situations in which complements remain unexpressed, they can always be retrieved from context:

(31) Putem   să   ne   vedem   **după**
     (we)can   să$_{SUBJ}$ CL.REFL.ACC.1PL   see.SUBJ.1PL   after
     'We can see each other afterwards'

9.3.2 Restrictions imposed by the preposition to its noun complement

9.3.2.1 Case assignment (accusative, genitive, and dative)

Prepositions such as *cu* 'with', *de* 'of', *despre* 'about', *din* 'from', *dintre* 'between', *în* 'in', *la* 'at; to', *pentru* 'for', *printre* 'among', *spre* 'towards', *sub* 'under' and collocations which display one of these prepositions as their last component (*față de* 'in comparison with', *în loc de* 'instead of', *cu privire la x* 'as far as x is concerned') assign the accusative:

(32) a. cu   **tine**   b. față de   **tine**
        with you.ACC   in-comparison-with   you.ACC
        'with you'   'in comparison with you'

Prepositions whose final segment is identical to the definite article (*dedesubtul* 'under', *împotriva* 'against', *înaintea* 'before', *înapoia* 'behind') and collocations whose last component is definite or whose final segment is identical to the article (*în fața* 'in front of', *în jurul* 'around', *în afara* 'except (for)') select a constituent that is marked with the genitive (33a, b), just as definite nouns do (33c):

(33) a. dedesubtul **mesei**
    under.DEF table.DEF.GEN
    'under the table'

   b. în fața **casei**
    in front.DEF house.DEF.GEN
    'in front of the house'

   c. cartea **fetei**
    book.DEF girl.DEF.GEN
    'the girl's book'

The prepositions *datorită, grație, mulțumită* 'thanks to' assign the dative case:

(34) grație **ție**
    thanks-to you.DAT
    'thanks to you'

The borrowings *per* 'per', *pro* 'for', *supra* 'on', *versus* 'versus', *via* 'via' select an NP unmarked for case, formally identical to the nominative≡accusative:

(35) per **articol**
    per article.NOM≡ACC

9.3.2.2 Restrictions on the usage of the article

The prepositions assigning the genitive and the dative select a noun suffixed by the definite article or which takes a different determiner; the DP always has an entity reading:

(36) a. împotriva **dușmanului / acestui dușman**
    against enemy.GEN this.GEN enemy
    'against the enemy / this enemy'

   b. grație **profesoarei / acestei profesoare**
    thanks-to teacher.DEF.DAT this.DAT teacher.DAT
    'thanks to the teacher/ this teacher'

Most of the prepositions assigning the accusative select a noun whose definite article remains unrealized (37a–c); when the noun takes a modifier, a possessor, or a complement, the article is realized (38a–c):

(37) a. Merge la **magazin**
    goes to store.ACC
    '(S)he goes to the store'

   b. Pisica stă pe **fotoliu**
    cat.DEF sits on armchair.ACC
    'The cat sits in the armchair'

   c. Unul dintre **copii** este student
    one of children is student
    'One of the children is a student'

(38) a. Merge la **magazinul** central / de vizavi
     goes to store.DEF.ACC central DE across
     '(S)he goes to the central store / the store across the street'

   b. Pisica stă pe **fotoliul** Mariei
      cat.DEF sits on armchair.DEF.ACC Maria.GEN
      'The cat sits in Maria's armchair'

   c. unul dintre **copiii** ei
      one of children.DEF.ACC her(GEN)
      'one of her children'

The bare noun (37a–c) has a definite, entity reading, the same as the noun with a determiner (38a–c).

C   The non-realization of the article in the context of a preposition is specific to Romanian. Elsewhere in Romance, the preposition usually requires the presence of the definite article: compare It. *sulla tavola*, Fr. *sur la table*, Sp. *sobre la mesa*, Ptg. *sobre a mesa* with Rom. *pe masă* 'on the table' (Reinheimer Rîpeanu 2001: 196–7).

The general rule of the definite article 'deletion' has a number of exceptions, which are due to the semantic-referential characteristics of the noun or to the semantic and configurational properties of the preposition.

If the noun denotes unique persons, it takes the definite article (39a):

(39) a. Merge la **mama** / la **bunica**
     goes to mother.DEF.ACC to grandmother.DEF.ACC
     '(S)he goes to mother / grandmother'

   vs.

   b. Merge la **facultate**
      goes to faculty.ACC
      '(S)he goes to the faculty'

Instrumental and comitative *cu* selects a definite noun (40a,b). However, the article of a mass or an abstract noun (41a,b) is not expressed when the noun does not have any constituents subordinated to it:

(40) a. Scriu **cu** **creionul**
     (I)write with pencil.DEF.ACC
     'I write with a pencil'

   b. Merg **cu** **copilul**
      (I)walk with child.DEF.ACC
      'I am walking with the child'

(41) a. Îndulceşte cafeaua **cu** **zahăr** / cu **zahărul** din **pliculeţ**
     sweetens coffee.DEF with sugar.ACC with sugar.DEF.ACC from packet.DIM
     '(S)he sweetens the coffee with sugar / with the sugar in the packet'

   b. Acţionează **cu** **prudenţă** / cu **prudenţa** dobândită în timp
      acts with caution.ACC with caution.DEF.ACC acquired in time
      '(S)he acts with caution / with the caution (s)he acquired over time'

The prepositions *decât* 'than', *ca, cât, precum* 'as' in comparative constructions require the realization of the definite article (§10.5.1):

(42) Crinul   este   mai   frumos   **decât** **trandafirul**
     lily.DEF   is   more   beautiful than   rose.DEF.ACC
     'The lily is more beautiful than the rose'

In many contexts, the articled, as well as the bare noun, correlates with a definite, entity reading. The noun complement of the preposition is bare in certain contexts, because it has property reading.

The prepositions of 'quality' (*ca, drept, de* 'as') select a bare noun with a *property* reading (Pană Dindelegan 2007b):

(43) Prepoziția   funcționează **drept** **cap** **de** **grup**
     preposition.DEF   functions   as   head   of   phrase
     'The preposition functions as the head of the phrase'

Other prepositions, which contextually take a non-referential complement, select a bare noun, as in (44), where the PP is in the position of a modifier (44a) or of a predicative complement (44b):

(44) a. fetele   **cu**   **ochelari**
        girls.DEF   with   glasses
        'Girls with glasses'

    b. Cutia   este   **din**   **plastic**
       box.DEF   is   of   plastic
       'The box is made of plastic'

Nouns whose definite form is required by the preposition may occasionally have a property reading; this is true of the complement of prepositions *pe* 'like' and *de-a* 'of' in configurations such as:

(45) a. Face   **pe**   **prostul**
        makes   like   fool.DEF
        'He plays the fool'

    b. jocul **de-a** **școala** / **de-a** **v-ați**   **ascunselea**
       game   DE=A   school.DEF / DE=A   CL.REFL.ACC=have.2PL   hidden.F.PL-*LE-A*
       'the game of playing school' / 'the game of hide and seek'

9.3.2.3 Number restrictions

The locative, partitive, and symmetric prepositions *dintre* 'between / among / of' (and *din* 'of' in variation with *dintre*), *între* 'between', *printre* 'among' obligatorily select a plural noun (46) or two coordinated nouns (47):

(46) a. florile   **dintre**   **copaci**
        flowers.DEF   among / between   trees

    b. unul **dintre** / **din**   **jucători**
       one   of   of   players
       'one of the players'

(47) o discuție **între** şef şi angajat
     a talk   between   boss and employee

Partitive *de* also requires a plural genitive or a possessive DP complement:

(48) un coleg   **de-ai**   **noştri**
     a   colleague   of=AL.M.PL   our.M.PL
     'a colleague of ours'

H In old Romanian and as late as the 19th century, the prepositions *între* and *dintre* 'among; between' appeared before each member of the coordination:

(49) iaste sol   **între**   noi   şi   **între**   Dumnezeu   (Varlaam)
     is   messenger between   us.ACC   and between   God.ACC
     'He is an intermediary between us and God'

9.3.3 Other constituents within the PP

The complement of the preposition can be a headless relative clause:

(50) Stă **la cine îl invită**
     'He stays at who invites him'

A PP may occasionally contain an AP when its head is a preposition of quality, such as *ca, drept, de* 'as':

(51) Apreciem   **ca / drept oportună**   această măsură
     (we)appreciate as   opportune   this   measure

The infinitival (52), supine (53), and gerund clause (54) can also occur in the PP, the gerund clause being selected by the preposition of quality *ca* 'as':

(52) Renunţă **la** **a-i**   **mai** **scrie**
     gives-up at   A_INF=CL.DAT.3SG   more   write.INF
     '(S)he gives up writing to him / her again'

(53) S-au   creat   locuri **pentru** **fumat**
     CL.REFL.PASS=have   created places for   smoke.SUP
     'Smoking places were created'

(54) O   consideră   **ca** **fiind** perfectă **pentru** acest serviciu
     CL.ACC.F.3SG   considers   as   be.GER   perfect   for   this   job
     '(S)he considers her to be perfect for this job'

The infinitival clause is equivalent to a clause headed by a complementizer when the head of the PP is a preposition such as *până* 'until', *fără* 'without', *pentru* 'for':

(55) Mai   are   de   aşteptat   **până** **a**   **ajunge**   **acolo /** **până**   **să**
     more   has   DE_SUP wait.SUP   until   A_INF   arrive.INF   there   until   SĂ_SUBJ
     ajungă   **acolo**
     arrive.SUBJ.3SG   there
     '(S)he still has to wait until (s)he gets there'

The prepositions *până* 'until' and *fără* 'without' select the complementizer *să* (subjunctive marker); the preposition *pentru* 'for' selects the split complementizer *ca... să*.

H In old Romanian, *pentru* 'for' also selected the complementizer *să*:
(56) câte   nevoi   au   răbdat   **pentru să**   întărească
     how-many   hardships (they)have   endured for să_SUBJ   strengthen.SUBJ.3PL
     credința   lui   Hristos   (Varlaam)
     belief.DEF LUI.GEN   Christ
     'how many hardships they endured to strengthen their belief in Christ'

There are cases when a PP embeds another PP; for instance, the PP headed by *până* 'until' includes another PP headed by *la* 'at':

(57) a. până [la anul]   b. până [la școală]
        until at year.DEF.ACC   until at school.ACC
        'until next year'   'until one is at school'

The PP headed by the preposition *la* 'at' can be subordinated to a PP headed by the lexical (or subcategorized) preposition *de* 'of / from':

(58) a. Vine   **de**   [la   Brașov]]
        comes   of   at   Brașov
        'She comes from Brașov'

  b. datează [**de** [la mijlocul   secolului   trecut]]
     dates   of   at   middle.DEF   century.DEF.GEN   previous
     'It dates from the middle of the last century'

A PP (originally part of a VP) is embedded in another PP, when the latter is, in turn, incorporated in a DP. The embedding is realized by the functional preposition *de* (§9.2.2, §5.3.5.2):

(59) Cartea   este   **pe banc膬**   >   cartea   [**de**   [pe   bancă]]
     book.DEF is   on desk   book.DEF DE   on   desk
     'The book is on the desk' 'the book on the desk'

9.4 PARALLEL FORMS: WITH AND WITHOUT AN ARTICLE-LIKE ENDING

Certain prepositions have an ending which is identical to the definite article; they also display a parallel adverbial form, without the article-like ending (§8.4.2.3):

(60) a. asupr**a**   vs. asupră
        over.DEF   over

  b. deasupr**a**   vs. deasupră
     above.DEF   above

  c. împotriv**a**   vs. împotrivă
     against.DEF   against

  d. înaint**ea**   vs. înainte
     before.DEF   before

  e. împreju**rul**   vs. împrejur
     around.DEF   around

f. dedesubt**ul** vs. dedesubt
   under.DEF   under

g. în faț**a** vs. în față
   in front.DEF   in front

h. în jur**ul** vs. în jur
   around.DEF   around

U Some forms without the article-like particles, such as *asupră* and *deasupră*, are obsolete.

The presence or absence of the complement distinguishes the forms with and without article-like endings. The forms with article-like ending obligatorily take a complement, and they assign the genitive case:

(61) Au   acționat **împotriva** **măsurilor**   **nedrepte** / *****împotriva**
     (they)have   acted   against   measures.DEF.GEN   unfair /   against
     'They acted against the unfair measures'

Like nouns, the forms with an article-like ending take complements realized by: genitive or possessive DPs (62), quantified NPs or relative clauses displaying the genitive marker A (63a–b), and a pronominal clitic (64) (§5.3.3.3):

(62) A   venit **înaintea** Mariei /   **mea**
     has   come   before   Maria.GEN   my.F.SG
     '(S)he came before Maria / me'

(63) a. Au   acționat **împotriva** **a** **două** **măsuri**   **nedrepte**
        (they)have acted   against   A   two   measures   unfair
        'They acted against two unfair measures'

     b. Au   acționat **împotriva** **a** **ceea ce** **s-a**   **propus**
        (they)have acted   against   A   what   CL.REFL.PASS=has   proposed
        'They acted against what was proposed'

(64) Au   acționat **împotriva-mi**
     (they)have   acted   against=CL.1SG
     'They acted against me'

The forms without the article-like ending may also occur without a complement, a fact which led to their categorization as adverbs:

(65) Au   venit **înainte** (de   ora   stabilită)
     (they)have   come   before   of   hour.DEF   established
     'They arrived before the time scheduled'

H The obsolete form *asupră* has a special behaviour, requiring the presence of the complement, realized as a clitic:
   (66) Au   năvălit **asupră-ne** / *****asupră**
        (they)have   rushed   over=CL.1PL /   over

In old Romanian, the complement realized as a dative clitic can have the main verb as its host:
   (67) nevoia   ce i-au   venitu **asupră**   (Ureche)
        constraint.DEF that CL.DAT.3SG=have   come   over
        'the constraints that are laid upon him'

CONCLUSIONS

Romanian prepositions assign the accusative, the genitive, or the dative case.

Generally, the prepositions that assign the accusative case select a bare noun (when the noun complement occurs without a modifier or any other constituent); this noun can receive a definite reading.

A preposition can combine with another preposition; the resulting sequence functions as a compound preposition in some contexts; in other contexts, one preposition embeds another.

Romanian displays a series of prepositions with an article-like ending, and parallel adverbial forms, without the article-like ending.

10

The Structure of Complex Clauses. Subordination

This chapter presents some aspects of the structure of complex clauses, paying special attention to subordination: argument clauses, conjunctions and clausal adjuncts, relative clauses, secondary predication, and comparative structures.

10.1 ARGUMENT CLAUSES

Like many other languages, in Romanian, argumental syntactic positions are required by the semantico-syntactic structure of the matrix head (verb, adjective, adverb, interjection, noun). They are nominal syntactic positions, but can also be clauses: (i) finite subordinate clauses introduced by complementizers (§10.2.1), (ii) integrated relative clauses (§10.3.1.3) or (iii) non-finite clauses (Chapter 4).

10.1.1 Complementizers

Că, să, ca...să, and *dacă* are the prototypical complementizers. Their main features are their high degree of abstractness as well as occurrence in various syntactic configurations. They are not specialized for the clausal expression of particular syntactic positions.

(1) a. Ei   sunt [AP mândri [**că**   au   reușit]]
       they are   proud   that   have.3PL   succeeded
       'They are proud that they have succeeded'

   b. [VP Începe   [**să**   plouă]]
          starts   SĂ$_{SUBJ}$ rain.SUBJ
          'It starts raining'

   c. E [AdvP bine   [**ca**   tu   **să**   vii   cu   noi]]
        is   fine   COMP you   SĂ$_{SUBJ}$ come.SUBJ   with   us
        'It is fine that you come with us'

   d. [VP Nu   știu   [**dacă**   au   sosit]]
          not know   if   have.3PL   arrived
          'I don't know whether they have arrived'

Other complementizers such as: *de* (the equivalent of *dacă* 'if, whether'), *cum că, precum că* 'that', and *cum de* 'how come' occur in contexts with certain stylistic features (§10.1.1.3).

Like other Romance languages, Romanian does not allow headless complement clauses. Complementizers are always overt. Omission of complementizers is possible only in complex structures consisting of two or more coordinated complement clauses, under the same C-head:

(2) Credeam [că [IP el are dreptate] și [IP ea se înșală]]
'I thought that he was right and she was wrong'

With the complementizer *să*, a structure like (2) is ungrammatical, as shown in (3). In spite of some Comp features such as the selection of complement clauses, invariability, and precedence with respect to clitics and negators, *să* also exhibits inflectional features (§2.2.2.2, §13.1.3). Coordination of two IPs under a common head *să* is ruled out because both verbs need the subjunctive marker *să*.

(3) *Vreau [CP să [IP plece   Ion și [IP mama   rămână]
     Want   SĂ_SUBJ leave.SUBJ Ion and   mother stay.SUBJ

Coordinated constructions with *să* are possible with topicalized subjects and in the presence of complementizer *ca*, as a part of the group *ca...să* (§10.1.1.2, §2.2.2.1).

(4) Vreau [ca   [Ion să   plece]   și [mama   să   rămână]]
     want COMP Ion   SĂ_SUBJ   leave.SUBJ and mother SĂ_SUBJ   stay.SUBJ

The selection of complementizers is determined either *syntactically*, by the class of verbs in the matrix clause (for the selection of *să₂*, see §10.1.1.1; for the selection of *dacă₁*, see §10.1.1.4), or *semantico-syntactically*, by the modality features of the subordinate clause (for the selection of *să* vs. *că*, see §10.1.1.1).

10.1.1.1 The complementizers că *and* să

The choice between *să* or *că* is semantico-syntactically governed. It depends either on the nature of the matrix verb, or on contextual features to do with the speaker's commitment towards the certainty of the event in the argument clause. Given the complexity of the syntactic status of *să* (subjunctive marker and functional constituent of Comp), the selection of complementizers is correlated with the mood features of the verb in the argument clause: *să*—for subjunctive, *că*—for the other verbal moods (§2.2.1).

C   Complementizer selection as a function of the subordinate clause ((*ca*...) *să* for the subjunctive and *că* for the indicative) is different from most other Romance languages (French, Spanish, standard Italian), where mood selection is not associated with a specific complementizer. The situation in Romanian is similar to that of certain southern Italian dialects, where the complementizers *mu / mi / ma* vs. *ca* are distributed depending on the semantico-syntactic features of the matrix verb. Standard Italian employs either *che* or the infinitive (Roberts and Roussou 2003: 88; Ledgeway 2000: 70–4, 2005: 365–6). The contexts described for *mu / mi / ma*—volitive and epistemic verbs, possibility of co-occurrence with the interrogative complementizer *si* 'if'—are the same as the contexts of *să* in Romanian. The fact that the Greek particle *na* (Roussou 2010: 583) is used in similar contexts suggests a Balkan origin for the phenomenon (Mišeska Tomić 2004: 32–4; Rooryck 2000: 71).

Subordinate clauses introduced by *că* are usually assertive. Semantically, the matrix verbs of the argument clauses introduced by *că* are factive predicates: (*se*) *afirmă că*... 'they say that...', (*se*) *dovedește că*... 'it is proved that...', counterfactive predicates: *minte că*... 'he lies that...', *inventează că*... 'he pretends that...', or non-factive predicates: (*se*) *pare că*... 'it seems that...', (*se*) *presupune că*... 'they suppose that...'.

(5) a. Faptele lui au dovedit **că** nu ţi-e prieten
'His actions proved that he is not your friend'

b. A minţit **că** n-a văzut filmul
'He lied in saying that he hadn't seen the film'

c. Se pare **că** nu mai vine
'It seems that he will not come'

Să is selected by lexical modal verbs or adverbs (*a se cuveni* 'ought to', *a se cădea* 'be appropriate', *trebui* 'must', *(fi) obligatoriu / necesar / permis* '(be) compulsory / necessary / allowed'), verbs with deontic value (*cere* 'require', *ruga* 'ask', *sfătui* 'advise'), volitive modal verbs (*dori* 'wish', *spera* 'hope', *vrea* 'want'), modalizers of evaluation (*detesta* 'hate', *plăcea* 'like', *merita* 'deserve'), aspectual and modal verbs (inherently aspectual: *continua* 'continue, keep', *începe* 'start', inherently modal: *putea* 'can', or contextually aspectual: *da, sta* 'be about to ...'):

(6) a. Se cuvine / trebuie / putem **să** fim gata până joi
'We should / must / can be ready by Thursday'

b. Te roagă / doreşte / îi place **să**-l ajuţi
'He asks you to help him / He wants you to help him / He likes you to help him'

c. Continuă / începe / stă **să** plouă
'It keeps / starts raining / it's about to rain'

The contrast between *assertive / non-assertive* (7a–b), *affirmative / negative* (7c–d) and *interrogative / non-interrogative* (7e–f) determines the modal selection associated with *că* or *să*:

(7) a. E   bine   **că**   vii
    is   fine   that   come.2SG
    'It is fine that you come'

b. E   bine   **să**   vii
   is   well   SĂ$_{SUBJ}$ come.SUBJ.2SG
   'It is fine that you should come'

c. Ştiu   **că**   a   primit   premiul
   know.1SG   that   has   received   prize.DEF
   'I know that he received the prize'

d. Nu   ştiu   **să**   fi   primit   premiul
   not   know.1SG   SĂ$_{SUBJ}$ be   received   prize.DEF
   'I am unaware of his receiving the prize'

e. Am   aflat   **că**   Ion   a   fost   dat   afară
   have.1SG   found-out   that   Ion   has   been   given   out
   'I found out that Ion had been sacked'

f. Ai   aflat   **să**   fi   fost   dat   afară   Ion?
   have.2SG   found-out   SĂ$_{SUBJ}$ be   been   given   out   Ion
   'Are you aware of Ion's having been sacked?'

Romanian, like other Romance languages, shows a *polarity subjunctive*, but the semantic conditions for the occurrence of the subjunctive are distinct. In Romanian, the choice of the indicative in a negative context is associated with the fact that the subject of the matrix clause believes in the truth of the negated subordinate clause, whereas the choice of the subjunctive expresses a certain degree of uncertainty in this respect (8a–b). Balkan languages such as Bulgarian or Modern Greek also show this contrast (Siegel 2009: 1871–5).

(8) a. Ion   nu   crede   **că**   **a**   **venit**   **Ana**
       Ion   not   believes that   has   come   Ana
       'Ion doesn't believe that Ana came' (i.e. 'Ion believes it to be a fact that Ana did not come')

   b. Ion   nu   crede   **să**   **fi**   **venit**   **Ana**
      Ion   not   believes SĂ$_{SUBJ}$ be   come   Ana
      'Ion doesn't believe that Ana came' (i.e. 'Ion does not believe it to be a fact that Ana came')

The complementizer *să$_2$* (with a different value from *să$_1$*) is selected by verbs of communication (*spune* 'say', *sugera* 'suggest', *scrie* 'write') as a marker of the reported imperative sentence (§13.2).

(9) a. Terminați lucrarea până mâine!
       'Finish the paper by tomorrow!'

   b. El   a   spus   **să**   **terminăm**   **lucrarea**   **până**   **mâine**
      he   has said   SĂ$_{SUBJ}$ finish.SUBJ.1PL   paper.DEF   until   tomorrow
      'He said we should finish the paper by the next day'

U When the main verb is missing, the subjunctive gets the value of a hedged imperative (10a). The same effect is obtained by the topicalization of the subordinate clause (10b) (§2.2.2.2.1).

   (10) a. Să   terminați   lucrarea!
           SĂ$_{SUBJ}$ finish.SUBJ.2PL   paper.DEF
           'Finish the paper!'
        b. Să terminați lucrarea, vă rog!
           'Finish the paper, please!'

10.1.1.2 The complementizer ca...să

Apart from the complementizer *să*, Romanian uses the fixed group *ca... să*, whose occurrence is syntactically dependent on the movement of a constituent in the subordinate clause (the subject (11a), the direct object (11b), the indirect object (11c), or an adjunct (11d)) to a position in front of the subordinate verb. The moved constituent may be topic (11a–b) or focus (11c–d).

(11) a. Vrea   **să**-i   spui   o poveste   >
        want.3.SG   SĂ$_{SUBJ}$=CL.DAT.3.SG   tell.SUBJ.2SG   a story
        Vrea   **ca**   **tu**   **să**-i   spui   o poveste
        want.3.SG   COMP   you   SĂ$_{SUBJ}$=CL.DAT.3SG   tell.SUBJ.2SG   a story
        'He wants **you** to tell her a story'

   b. E   necesar   **să**   te   ajute   cineva   >
      is   necessary   SĂ$_{SUBJ}$ CL.DAT.2.SG help.SUBJ.3SG   someone
      E necesar   **ca**   **pe**   **tine**   **să**   te   ajute   cineva
      is necessary   COMP   PE   you   SĂ$_{SUBJ}$ CL.ACC.2SG   help.SUBJ.3SG someone
      'It is necessary that someone should help you'

c. Trebuie   să-i   spui   tot   >
    must   SĂ_SUBJ=CL.DAT.3.SG   tell.SUBJ   everything
    Trebuie   ca   LUI   să-i   spui
    must   COMP   him.DAT   SĂ_SUBJ=CL.DAT.3SG   tell.SUBJ.2SG
    tot,   nu   mie
    everything   not   me.DAT
    'You have to tell HIM everything'

d. Trebuie   să   rezolvi   problema   astăzi   >   Trebuie   ca
    must   SĂ_SUBJ   solve.SUBJ.2SG problem.DEF   today   must   COMP
    ASTĂZI   să   rezolvi   problema,   nu   mâine
    today   SĂ_SUBJ   solve.SUBJ   problem.DEF   not   tomorrow
    'You have to solve the problem TODAY'

Romanian is one of those Romance languages with a dual system of complementizers, which are able to exploit the whole C domain. Such languages employ a complementizer for the indicative, that expresses the higher position—*Force*—and precedes topics and foci, in contrast to a complementizer for the subjunctive, that expresses lower positions—*Fin* (*Finiteness head*), following topics and foci (Ledgeway 2011: 431–2; for the split-analysis of the CP, see Rizzi 1997). In Romanian, this contrast is achieved simultaneously (Barbosa 2001; Stan 2007), through the complex complementizer *ca... să*, whose first component *ca* is *Force*, whereas *să* expresses the head *Fin*:

(12) Vreau [_CP [_ForceP **ca** [_TopP Ion_i [_FinP **să** [_VP vină t_i]]]]]
      want.1SG   COMP   Ion   SĂ_SUBJ   come.SUBJ.3SG
      'I want Ion to come'

H Old Romanian used *ca să* in variation with *să* (for the value of *ca să* as subordinator for clausal adjuncts, see §10.2.2). The complex complementizer *ca... să*, whose occurrence involves movement of a constituent marked as a topic or focus to the left, was sporadic in the old language. The specialization of *ca... să* for argument clauses is quite recent (the beginning of the 20th century) and is the result of prescriptive rules (Graur 1968: 335).

10.1.1.3 *The complementizers* cum că, precum că, *and* cum de

Unlike the complementizer *că*, which can be used as a subordinator (§10.2.2), the fixed collocations *cum că*, *precum că*, and *cum de* introduce only argument clauses in the positions of subject (13a), direct object (13b), secondary object (13c), prepositional object (13d), and complement of a noun (13e):

(13) a. Se zvonește **cum că** ar fi fost colaborator al securității
         'The rumour is **that** he was a collaborator of the Securitate'
      b. L-am rugat să-mi spună **cum de** nu te-a avertizat că o să plece
         'I asked him to tell me **how come** he didn't warn you that he was going to leave'
      c. Mă întreb **cum de** n-ai venit cu noi
         'I wonder **how come** you didn't come with us'
      d. Mă mir **cum de** n-ai aflat asta
         'I wonder **how come** you didn't find that out'

e. Ion a infirmat zvonul **cum că** ar fi fost forțat să demisioneze
'John rejected the rumour **that** he was forced to resign'

H In old Romanian, *cum* had the value of a complementizer, especially after verbs of perception (14a) or of saying (14b), in pseudo-relative clauses (Manoliu-Manea 1977: 221). In such contexts, *cum* is the equivalent of *că*:

(14) a. Îl văd **cum** vine
him see how comes
'I see him coming'

b. Duca-vodă au scris și el la hanul **cum** și el iaste robu (Neculce)
Duca-vodă has written also he to khan.DEF how also he is prisoner
'Duca-vodă has also written a letter to the khan, (saying) that he was a prisoner too'

The fixed collocations *cum că*, *precum că*, and *pecum că* are contaminations of *cum* with the complementizers *că* and *să*. *Cum să* has limited use even in old Romanian:

(15) Au socotit niște dumnezăești părinți **cum să** nu
have.3.PL decided some holy fathers how să_SUBJ not
oprească acela post (in DA)
stop.SUBJ that fasting
'Some holy fathers decided not to stop that fasting'

In text books of the 18th century and the beginning of the 19th century, *cum că* and *p(r)ecum că* were markers specialized for reported speech. After *verba dicendi* and the related deverbal nouns, they occured more frequently than the complementizer *că*.

(16) a. Au dzis **cum că**-i greșit (Neculce)
have.3PL said how that=is wrong
'They said that it is wrong'

b. Au pârât pe veziriul, **precum că** s-au
have.3PL denounced PE vizier.DEF how that CL.REFL.ACC.3SG=have
agiuns cu moscalii (Neculce)
made a covenant with Russians.DEF
'They have denounced the vizier for having made a covenant with the Russians'

Cum de is the result of the adjacency of two connectors—the head of a deleted indirect interrogative clause and the complementizer *de* (§10.1.1.4, §10.2.2):

(17) Mă întreb **cum** (a fost posibil) / (s-a
CL.REFL.ACC.1SG wonder how (has been possible) (CL.REFL=have.3SG
întâmplat) **de** n-ai aflat
happened) that not=have.2SG found out
'I wonder how come you haven't found out'

U In contemporary Romanian, *cum că* and *precum că* are employed as evidential markers, with counterfactive or non-factive predicates (see also §13.5.6), or in the administrative register:

(18) statuarea Curții Constituționale **precum că** art. III din lege este constituțional
'the decision of the Constitutional Court that article III of the law is constitutional'

10.1.1.4 *The complementizers* dacă *and* de

Dacă has two values: *dacă₁*—selected by words of saying: verbs, adjectives, nouns (19a–c), as markers of indirect questions (*yes–no* or alternative), and *dacă₂*—a connector with hypothetical value, introducing events that are projected in the future (19d) or with non-hypothetical value (19e), introducing events that are already accomplished, but which contradict the expectations of the hearer:

(19) a. M-a întrebat **dacă** venim
CL.ACC.1SG=has asked if come.1PL
'He asked me if we would come'

b. Era nedumerită **dacă au înțeles corect** ce le-a spus
was confused if have.3PL understood correctly what CL.DAT.3PL=has said
'She was not sure whether they understood correctly what she had said to them'

c. Întrebarea **dacă vine și ministrul** era pe buzele tuturor
question.DEF if comes also minister.DEF was on lips.DEF everybody.GEN
'The question about the (hypothetical) coming of the minister was on everybody's lips'

d. **Dacă vine**, înseamnă că mă iubește
if comes means that CL.ACC.1SG loves
'If he comes, it means that he loves me'

e. **Dacă am plecat**, am făcut-o ca să te ajut
if have left have done=CL.ACC.F.3SG in-order să$_{SUBJ}$ CL.ACC.2SG help.SUBJ.1SG
'If I left, I did it in order to help you'

H *Dacă* is a multifunctional clausal connector (derived from the grammaticalization of *de* + *că* (DA, Cioranescu 2002: 281) or of *de* + *ca* (TDRG 1911: 4). As a complementizer, it functions with the two values described above (*dacă$_1$* and *dacă$_2$*), while as an adjunct subordinator it is multifunctional (§10.2.2).

De has three different values in Romanian: (i) *de$_1$*—a subordinator for clausal adjuncts, which has grammaticalized the temporal meaning of the preposition *de*, inherited from Latin, to which other meanings were subsequently added: purpose and result (§10.2.2); (ii) complementizer, with three meanings: *de$_2$*—an obsolete equivalent of *dacă*, *de$_3$*—an equivalent of *să*, which occurs with verbs in the indicative, as in (20a) (Niculescu 1965: 24, 75; Hill 2004: 345–6), and *de$_4$*—a functional head on the border between coordination and subordination, which can be substituted by both *să*, and *și*, as in (20b); (iii) *de$_5$*—a regional and non-standard relative word (20c), see §10.3.5.5, probably deriving from the contamination of *de$_1$* with a complementizer of Bulgarian origin (Krapova 2010).

(20) a. Ne-a făcut / s-a întâmplat **de** am
CL.DAT.1PL=has made CL.REFL.ACC.3SG=have3SG happened that have.1PL
curățat grădina
cleaned garden.DEF
'He made us clean the garden' / 'It happened so that we cleaned the garden'

b. Ion se duse **de** luă mașina din garaj
Ion CL.REFL.ACC.3SG went that took car.DEF from garage
'Ion went to get his car from the garage'

c. fata aia **de**-am trimis-o la tine
girl.DEF that that=have.1SG sent=CL.ACC.3SG to you
'that girl that I have sent to you'

U The complementizer *de* is a functional equivalent of *dacă*. The difference between *dacă* and *de* is stylistic. *De* is no longer used in literary Romanian, it may be found only in the spoken language.

(21) N-am   să   mă   mai   întreb   **de**-i   bine ori nu
     not=have1.SG SĂ$_{SUBJ}$ CL.REFL.ACC.1SG more ask.SUBJ whether=is good or not
     'I won't ask myself any more whether it's right or not'

10.1.2 Argument clauses

Subordinate clauses introduced by *complementizers* are selected by verbs (a), adjectives (b), adverbs (c), verbal interjections (d), and nouns (e):

(22) a. Ea [crede [**că ai dreptate**]] / Ana [nu ştie [**dacă va veni**]]
        'She thinks that you are right' / 'Ana doesn't know if she will come'

   b. [Atentă [**să-şi rezolve problemele**]], a uitat de voi
      'Focused on solving her own problems, she forgot about you'

   c. [Sigur [**că ai dreptate**]]
      'Of course you are right'

   d. [Iată [**că a ajuns**]]
      'Look, she arrived'

   e. [Ideea [**ca ea să fie promovată**]] nu e respinsă de nimeni
      'The idea of her being promoted is not rejected by anyone'

Prototypical complementizers introduce all kinds of argument clauses (§3.1–5, §5.3.4), except for the indirect object clause, which is always a relative clause (§3.2.3.5).

10.2 CONJUNCTIONS AND CLAUSAL ADJUNCTS

10.2.1 Clausal adjuncts

Clausal adjuncts (called, 'circumstantial clauses' in Romanian grammatical terminology) can be realized as: clauses introduced by subordinating conjunctions (§10.2.2), relative clauses (§10.3), and non-finite clauses, directly linked to the matrix clause (23a) or embedded in prepositional phrases (23b), or in adverbial phrases (23c) (Manea 2010):

(23) a. [Plecând Ion]$_{Temporal / Reason}$, Ana a fost mai relaxată
        'When / As John left, Anna was more relaxed'

   b. Ion merge deseori [**la** pescuit calcani]$_{Purpose}$
      'Ion frequently goes fishing for plaice'

   c. A venit [**înainte** de a fi gata masa]$_{Temporal}$
      '(S)he had come before the dinner was ready'

Non-finite adjuncts with an infinitival (24a) or a supine head (24b) are embedded in prepositional phrases, like adjuncts with a subjunctive head (24c):

(24) a. [În afară de   a   scrie   cărți]_{Substractive}, nu-l   interesează nimic
       except-for   A_{INF} write.INF books,   not=CL.ACC.3SG interests   nothing
   b. [În afară   de   scris   cărți]_{Substractive}, nu-l   interesează nimic
       except-for DE_{SUP} write.SUP books,   not=CL.ACC.3SG interests   nothing
   c. [În afară   să   scrie   cărți]_{Substractive}, nu-l   interesează nimic
       except-for SĂ_{SUBJ} write.SUBJ books,   not=CL.ACC.3SG interests   nothing
   'Except for writing books, he is not interested in anything'

There are certain adjuncts—reason, purpose, conditional, additive positive, substractive, and additive negative—which can be realized only by clauses introduced by subordinating conjunctions. There are others which cannot be realized by clauses introduced by subordinating conjunctions—instrument, manner, locative, and additive positive. Connective adjuncts often link units smaller than the clause (Huddleston and Pullum 2002: 665, 775).

10.2.2 Specific and non-specific subordinating conjunctions

10.2.2.1 Clausal adjuncts introduced by specific subordinators

The adjuncts mentioned below are introduced by specific subordinators (either simple or complex): manner (*precum* 'such as', *ca și cum, ca și când, de parcă* 'as if', *după cum* 'as'), temporal (*imediat ce, (de) îndată ce, pe dată ce* 'as soon as', *până ce* 'until', *abia ce* 'hardly', *(ori) de câte ori* 'every time when'), reason (*căci, deoarece, fiindcă, întrucât, din pricină că, din cauză că, pentru că, pe motiv că, de vreme ce, din moment ce* 'because, as, since'), conditional (*în caz că* 'if'), concessive (*deși, chiar dacă, chiar de, cu toate că, chit că,* (colloquially) *măcar că* 'although, even though', (colloquially) *măcar să* 'if only'), result (*așa că* 'so', *încât* '(so...) that'), quantity (*pe cât* 'as...(as...)', *cu cât* 'the more...(the more...)*'), additive negative (*în loc să* 'instead of'), additive positive (*pe lângă că, după ce că,* (regionally) *las' că* [< *lasă că*] 'besides'), purpose (*pentru ca să* 'in order that').

The subordinators *deși* 'although', *întrucât* 'as', *încât* 'so that', *din moment ce* 'since', *deoarece, pe motiv că* 'because', *precum* '(such) as' are preferred in the contemporary standard language and are avoided in the non-standard language.

H In old Romanian (16th century), the concessive subordinator *deși* functioned as a split subordinator—*și... de* or *de... și*. The complex subordinator was first attested in the 17th century (Călărașu 1978: 354–67; Todi 2001: 184).
   From the 17th century, the meaning and the autonomous use of *ca* disappeared. The subordinator started to combine with the subjunctive preceded by *să* (< Lat. SI). The sequence *ca să* grammaticalized and specialized for denoting the resultative relation (ILR II: 290–1). A similar phenomenon of grammaticalization—by incorporating the subjunctive marker—happened with other specific subordinators, such as *măcar să* 'if only', *în loc să* 'instead of', or non-specific subordinators, such as *fără să* 'without; unless' (§10.2.2.2).
   At the end of the 19th century, *fiindcă* 'because' (< *fiind* 'being' + *că*) and *deoarece* 'because' (< *de* + *oare* + *ce*) became grammaticalized.
   In the 16th–19th centuries, *căci* 'because' (< *că* + *ce*) occurred in structures with the preposition *pentru* 'for' and with the conjunction *că* 'that': *pentru căci, căci că* 'because' (Todi 2001: 172).
   The reason subordinator *întrucât* 'as' originates in the manner subordinator *întru cât* 'to what extent'. At the end of the 20th century, the reason subordinator *întrucât* 'as' started to gain ground.

The result subordinator *încât* '(so...) that' occurred at the end of the 18th century, prevailing over *cât* and *cât să* 'so that', which are currently used only in non-standard Romanian.

The result subordinator *aşa că* 'so' began to be used frequently in the first half of the 19th century.

10.2.2.2 Clausal adjuncts introduced by non-specific subordinators

The following adjuncts are introduced by non-specific, either simple or complex subordinators: additive positive, substractive ((*în*) *afară că* 'besides; except, apart from'), temporal, additive positive (*după ce* 'after; besides', *în timp ce, în vreme ce, pe când, (pe) câtă vreme* 'while; whereas'), conditional, concessive, reason, additive negative (*când* 'if; when; since'), temporal, reason (*cum* 'as soon as; as'), reason, conditional, temporal (*odată ce* 'since; if; once'), reason, additive negative (*unde* 'as; while'), concessive, conditional, additive negative (*de unde* 'although; while'), temporal, quantity (*până* 'until; up to'), manner, conditional, concessive (*fără să* 'without; unless; although'), substractive, additive positive (*decât* 'except (for); besides').

Certain multifunctional subordinators—*că* (temporal, reason, concessive), *ca să* (purposive, resultative, additive negative), *dacă* (conditional, concessive, temporal, reason, additive negative), *de* (conditional, resultative, purposive, concessive)—also function as complementizers (§10.1.1).

C   The complementizers *ca, că* are inherited from Latin, and also occur in other Romance languages (ILR II: 290–2; Sala 2006: 137).

Note that Romanian, French, Spanish, and Italian preserved QUOD (Rom. *că*) expressing the resultative and reason relation, used as such in Latin too (ILR I: 355–6, 343).

Cum < Lat. QUOMODO continues the range of meanings it had in Latin, where it could function as a manner, temporal, and reason subordinator. In the 16th–18th centuries, *cum* was used with concessive and resultative meaning as well. Using a subordinator with a primary manner meaning (similar to the Rom. *cum*) in resultative structures is a phenomenon found in other Balkan languages as well (Cugno 1996: 28).

It is generally accepted that *de* comes from the Latin DE, probably influenced by South-Slavic *da* or Turkish *de* (Călăraşu 1978: 367). The intermediate coordinator–subordinator status of the resultative *de* (Niculescu 1965: 24, 75) is a feature specific to Romanian (26b). Sandfeld (1930: 196) noted the use of the resultative coordinator *de* in interrogative structures, in the context of Balkan languages' preference for paratactic structures:

(25)   Ce-ai   uitat   [de   te-ai   întors]$_{Result}$?
what=(you)have forgotten that CL.REFL.2SG=(you)have returned
'What did you forget that made you come back?'

H   The usage of the subordinator *de* with resultative, purposive, and conditional values was attested in the writings of the 16th–17th centuries. The resultative *de* (with the connective *aşa* 'so, such' in the matrix) is frequent in the 16th century. Since the mid-19th century, the resultative *de* has been used especially in the non-standard (regional and spoken) language, while in the literary texts the subordinator *încât* (< *în* + *cât*) is preferred.

Clausal adjuncts introduced by the subordinators resultative *de* 'that' (26a), purposive *de* 'in order to' (26b), resultative *că* 'that' (26c), concessive *că* 'even though' (26d), reason *că* 'because, as' (36a–b), and additive negative *de unde* 'since' (26e)—occur frequently in the non-standard and colloquial language.

(26) a. Era așa frumoasă, [de te   minunezi]_Result
        was so   beautiful   that CL.REFL.ACC wonder.2SG
        'She was amazingly beautiful!'

   b. Fugi [de adu apă !]_Purpose
      'Go and fetch some water!'

   c. Este atât de frig, [că au înghețat ferestrele]_Result
      'It is so cold that the windows have frozen over'

   d. Și mama, [că e mamă]_Concessive, și tot nu înțelege
      'And mother, even though she is a mother, still doesn't understand'

   e. [De unde credea că va fi promovat]_Additive negative, a fost (în schimb) concediat
      'While he thought he would be promoted, he was fired instead!'

In the regional and colloquial language, the subordinators *cum* 'how' and *când* 'when' are general in declaratives (27a), but more frequent in basic interrogatives, in rhetorical interrogatives (27b), or in exclamatives (27c):

(27) a. [**Cum** nu   suportă soarele]_Reason, nu   merge la mare
        how   not stands   sun.DEF   not goes   to seaside
        'As (s)he cannot stand the sun, (s)he doesn't go to the seaside'

   b. Cum   să   mintă,   [**când** el   însuși văzuse   accidentul]_Reason?
      how   SĂ_SUBJ lie.SUBJ when   he   himself see.PLUPERF.3SG accident.DEF
      'How can he be lying when he had seen the accident himself?'

   c. Continuă să   vorbească [**când** știe   [cât   enervează]]_Concessive!
      continues SĂ_SUBJ talk.SUBJ when   knows how-much   annoys
      'He keeps on talking when he knows how annoying he is!'

10.2.2.3 Clausal adjuncts introduced by the subordinating marker *să*

The subjunctive marker *să* may additionally function as a subordinator when it introduces conditional (28a) or concessive clausal adjuncts (28b):

(28) a. [**Să** fi luat examenul]_Conditional, ar fi fost o surpriză
        'Had he passed the exam, it would have been a surprise!'

   b. [(Chiar) **să** vreau]_Concessive, nu aș putea face nimic
      'No matter how much I want to, I couldn't do anything'

H In the old language, *să* (< Lat. SI), originally meaning 'if', was frequently followed by the indicative form of the verb:

(29) **Să** ești   cărtular, învață   tu   însuți   pre el   (Coresi)
     if   (you)are.IND.PRES.2SG   scholar   learn.IMP.2SG you yourself PE   him
     'If you are a scholar you teach him yourself'

Să may also introduce result (30a) and purpose clausal adjuncts (30b), in free variation with specialized conjunctions.

(30) a. Fumul   era   atât de gros [(**încât**) să-l   tai
        smoke.DEF was   so   thick that   SĂ_SUBJ=CL.ACC.3SG cut.SUBJ.2SG
        cu   cuțitul]_Result
        with   knife.DEF
        'The smoke was so thick that you could cut it with a knife'

b. Pleacă   [(**ca**)   să   culeagă   mure]_Purpose
   leaves   in-order   să_SUBJ   pick.SUBJ   blackberries
   'He goes to pick blackberries'

10.2.2.4   The structure of complex subordinators

In contemporary standard Romanian, complex subordinators are formed according to the following patterns:

   (i) [preposition + noun + *că*]: *din cauză că, din pricină că, în caz că, pe / sub / cu motiv că* 'because, as a consequence';
   (ii) [preposition + *că*]: *pentru că* 'because';
   (iii) [the gerund of the verb *a fi* 'be' + *că*]: *fiindcă* 'because';
   (iv) [adverb + *că, dacă, de, să*]: *măcar că* 'although';
   (v) [intensifier + subordinator]: *şi dacă* 'even if', *chiar dacă* 'even if';
   (vi) [preposition + adverbial + *că*]: *în afară că* 'besides, apart from, in addition to';
   (vii) [preposition + temporal noun + relative pronominal]: *în vreme ce, în timp ce, pe câtă vreme* 'while, whereas'.

The subordinators in (vii) are used particularly for introducing additive negative clauses (31a) or result clauses (31b):

(31) a. Ana e blondă, [**în timp ce / în vreme ce / pe când / (pe) câtă vreme** Maria e
                                                                        brunetă]_Additive negative
         'Ana is blonde, while / whereas Maria is dark-haired'
      b. [**De vreme ce / odată ce** i-ai promis]_Reason, scrie-i!
         'Since you promised him, write to him!'

10.2.3   Subordinators, prepositions, and focusing particles

10.2.3.1   Conjunctions and prepositions

Certain subordinators (subordinating conjunctions) are also used as prepositions: manner (*fără să* vs. *fără* 'without'), temporal (*până (să)* 'until'— subordinating conjunction (32a) vs. *până* 'until'—preposition (32b)), reason (*din cauză că, din pricină că* 'because' vs. *din cauza, din pricina* 'because of'), conditional (*în caz(ul) că, cu condiţia să* 'on the condition that', *fără să* 'unless' vs. *în cazul / în caz de* 'in case of', *cu condiţia de* 'on the condition that', *fără* 'but for'), additive positive (*pe lângă că, în afară că* 'besides' vs. *pe lângă* 'in addition to', (*în) afară de* 'apart from'), substractive ((*în) afară că, (în) afară să* 'except (for)', *decât să* 'but (for)' vs. (*în) afară de* 'except (for)', *decât* 'but (for)'), additive negative (*în loc să* vs. *în loc de* 'instead of').

(32) a. [**Până** a intrat el], nu a spus nimic
         '(S)he didn't say anything until he entered'
      b. [**Până** acum], nu a spus nimic
         '(S)he didn't say anything until now'

10.2.3.2 Conjunctions and focusing particles

Certain subordinators—reason (33a), purpose (33b), and conditional subordinators (33c)—can be accompanied by focusing particles:

(33) a. Nu plâng, [**că** *doar* înțeleg situația]$_{Reason}$!
'I am not crying, because I do understand the situation'

b. Se purta frumos, [**ca** *nu (care) cumva* să fie pedepsit]$_{Purpose}$
'He was behaving well so that he should not somehow be punished'

c. Vin [*numai / doar* **dacă / de** mă invită Maria]$_{Conditional}$
'I will come only if Maria invites me'

10.2.4 Clausal adjuncts with covert subordinators

In certain syntactic situations, some adjuncts realized by finite clauses have a covert subordinator: the reason adjunct (34a), the purpose adjunct (34b), and the concessive adjunct in antithetical symmetric structures (34c).

(34) a. E mai bine pentru el: [(**fiindcă**) nu se mai amăgește]$_{Reason}$
'It is better for him: he does not keep fooling himself'

b. [(**Dacă**) vrei cartea]$_{Conditional}$, împrumut-o de la bibliotecă!
'You want the book, borrow it from the library!'

c. [(**Chiar dacă / de**) îi explici]$_{Concessive1}$, [(**chiar dacă / de**) nu-i explici]$_{Concessive2}$, el tot nu te va crede
'Whether you explain it to him or not, he still will not believe you!'

10.2.5 Special patterns

10.2.5.1 Temporal adjuncts

Depending on the point of reference, temporal adjuncts may be introduced by different subordinators.

If the event in the matrix clause is simultaneous with the event in the subordinate clause, the two events may be connected by: *în timp ce, pe când, în vreme ce* 'while', *câtă vreme, cât timp* 'as long as', *(ori) de câte ori* 'every time (when)' (35a).

If the event expressed in the subordinate clause is prior to the matrix event, the anteriority relation may be expressed by the following subordinators: *după ce* 'after', *(de) îndată ce, imediat ce, cum* 'as soon as', *odată ce* 'once' (35b).

If the subordinate event is subsequent to the matrix event, the two clauses may be connected by the following subordinators: *până să, până (ce)* 'until' (35d).

To express temporal proximity, the following subordinators may be used: *(de) îndată ce, imediat ce* 'as soon as', *cum* '(as soon) as', *nici că* 'hardly... when'; the last one is a temporal adjunct used in constructions with inverted word order (35c).

(35) a. [În timp ce lucram]_{Temporal}, a sunat telefonul
'While we were working, the phone rang'

b. Plecăm [(de) îndată ce vine Ion]_{Temporal}
'We are leaving as soon as Ion arrives'

c. Nici nu am ajuns bine acasă, [că a și sunat la ușă]_{Temporal}
'Hardly had we got home when the doorbell rang'

d. A lucrat până (ce) s-a înserat
'(S)he worked until the evening came'

H The specialization of subordinators for a certain temporal relations only occurred in the 19th century. In old Romanian (16th–17th centuries), the subordinators *ca*, *dacă*, *până* could express almost any temporal relationship. Of these, only *până* 'until' is present in modern Romanian (Avram 1960: 62). The complex subordinators *în vreme ce*, *în timp ce* 'while', *îndată ce*, *imediat ce* 'as soon as' emerged in the 19th century.

10.2.5.2 Reason adjuncts

Clausal reason adjuncts fall into two semantic subtypes: ordinary reason adjuncts (36a) and speech act-related reason adjuncts, regularly introduced by the subordinator *că* 'because' (36b):

(36) a. Bunicul a obosit, [că a mers mult pe jos]_{Reason}
'Grandfather got tired because he walked a lot'

b. E obosit, [că e galben la față!]_{Reason}
'He is tired, because he is yellow in the face'
('I claim that he is tired because he is yellow in the face')

C In the Balkan area speech act-related reason adjuncts occur in Albanian, Bulgarian, and in Modern Greek (Cugno 1996: 15).

The reason adjunct introduced by the subordinator *cum* 'because' (37a) can be split, by moving a constituent to a higher position (37b):

(37) a. [**Cum** stă departe]_{Reason}, întârzie întotdeauna
how lives far   is-late always

b. [Departe **cum** stă]_{Reason}, întârzie întotdeauna
far   how lives   is-late always
'Because (s)he lives far away, (s)he is always late'

10.2.5.3 Purpose adjuncts

The configurations which contain the purposive subordinator *de* have a symmetrical structure (38a,b). The matrix and the subordinate verbs are in the same grammatical mood and tense. In these structures, used especially in the colloquial and regional language, the verbs may be in the imperative too (38b):

(38) a. Mergea   la   piață [**de**   cumpăra   fructe și
go.IMPERF.3SG to   market in-order-to buy.IMPERF.3SG fruits and
legume   proaspete]_{Purpose}
vegetables   fresh
'(S)he was going to the market place to buy fresh fruit and vegetables'

b. Mergi   la   piață   [**de**   cumpără   fructe   și
    go.IMP.2SG to   market   in-order-to   buy.IMP.2SG fruits   and
    legume   proaspete]_Purpose!
    vegetables fresh
    'Go to the market place to buy fresh fruit and vegetables!'

The purpose adjunct introduced by the subordinator *(pentru) ca să* 'in order to' may occur in adversative, elliptical structures:

(39) Nu veniserăm [**ca să ne relaxăm**]_Purpose, ci ~~veniserăm~~ [**ca să lucrăm**]_Purpose
      'We had not come to relax, but to work'

10.2.5.4 Conditional and concessive constructions

In *if*-clauses the matrix and the subordinate verb are symmetrical: both the protasis (the subordinate clause) and the apodosis (the matrix clause) display the same grammatical mood or the same tense form (40a–c), (41a), (42a). Mood selection is imposed by the type of conditional construction: *realis*—V (PRES, PERF, FUT) IND (40a), *potential*—V (PRES) COND, (PRES) SUBJ (40b), *irrealis*—V (PERF) COND / (PERF) SUBJ, (IMPERF) IND (40c).

(40) a. [Dacă va cânta Ionescu], [biletele se vor vinde]
         'If Ionescu sings, the tickets will be sold'

     b. [Dacă ar cânta Ionescu], [biletele s-ar vinde]
         'If Ionescu sang, the tickets would be sold'

     c. [Dacă ar fi cântat Ionescu], [biletele s-ar fi vândut]
         'If Ionescu had sung, the tickets would have been sold'

C Colloquial Italian also uses the imperfect indicative for *irrealis* constructions. The symmetry of the verbal forms in the matrix and the subordinate clause is a general feature of the Balkan languages (Cugno 1996: 50). What is specific to Romanian is the asymmetric construction (see examples (43a,b) below) with the conditional and the imperfect indicative (Cugno 1996: 54).

The concessive adjunct and the matrix clause form a complex sentence similar to conditional constructions. The two configurations resemble each other in the selection of grammatical moods. The only difference between them resides in the affirmative / negative form of the verb.

(41) a. [Dacă   plângi]_Conditional, [îl   înduioșezi]
         if   cry.PRES.IND.2SG   CL.ACC.3SG   impress.PRES.IND.2SG
         'If you cry, you impress him'

     b. [Chiar dacă / deși   plângi]_Concessive, [**nu** îl   înduioșezi]
         even if   although   cry.PRES.IND.2SG   not   CL.ACC.3SG impress.PRES.IND.2SG
         'Even if / Although you cry, you do not impress him'

(42) a. [Dacă   tu   îl   rugai]_Conditional, [el   semna   cererea]
         if   you CL.ACC.3SG   ask.IMPERF.2SG   he   sign.IMPERF.3SG   petition.DEF
         'If you had asked him, he would have signed the petition'

     b. [Chiar dacă /   deși   tu   **nu** îl   rugai]_Concessive, [el
         even if   although   you not   CL.ACC.3SG   ask.IMPERF.2SG   he
         (tot) semna   cererea]
         still sign.IMPERF.3SG petition.DEF
         'Even if / Even though you had not asked him, he still would have signed the petition'

(43) a. [Dacă citea   cartea]$_{Conditional}$, [el ar   fi intervenit în discuție]
        if   read.IMPERF.3SG book.DEF   he AUX.COND.3SG be intervened in discussion
        'If he had read the book, he would have intervened in the discussion'
    b. [Chiar dacă / deși   ar   fi citit   cartea]$_{Concessive}$,
        even if   although AUX.COND.3SG be read   book.DEF
        [el   (tot) **nu** intervenea   în discuție]
        he   still not   intervene.IMPERF.3SG in discussion
        'Even if / Even though he had read the book, he would still not have intervened in the discussion'

An old and frequently used construction is the one in which the conditional adjunct containing a pro-sentence negative adverb is part of an exclamative reason construction:

(44) Vino   și   tu, [că   [de /dacă   nu]$_{Conditional}$,
     come.IMP.2SG   also you because if   not
     mă   supăr]$_{Reason}$!
     CL.REFL.ACC.1SG   get-angry
     'You come too, because I will get angry at you if you do not!'

Concessive adjuncts may occur in antithetic symmetric patterns:

(45) a. [**De unde are**]$_{Concessive1}$, [**de unde n-are**]$_{Concessive2}$, ea plătește impozitele
        'Whether she has money or not, she still pays the taxes'
    b. [**(Fie) că minte**]$_{Concessive1}$, [**(fie) că nu minte**]$_{Concessive2}$, el tot nu o crede
        'Whether she is lying or not, he still does not believe her'

10.2.5.5 Result adjuncts

In Romanian there are two types of result adjuncts. One denotes the consequence of a process (46a), whereas the other denotes the consequence and the intensity of a process (46b):

(46) a. Sunt obosită, [**așa că** voi rămâne acasă]
        'I am tired, so I will stay home'
    b. Se îmbrăca așa de elegant, [**încât** toți îl admirau]
        'He used to dress so elegantly that everybody admired him'

10.2.5.6 Speech act-related adjuncts

Manner, reason, purpose, conditional, and concessive adjuncts, introduced by specific subordinators, can function as speech act-related adjuncts, with metalinguistic function:

(47) a. [**Pentru că tot vorbim despre asta**]$_{Reason}$, coafura ei era impecabilă
        'Since we are talking about it, her hair-do was perfect'
    b. Coafura ei era impecabilă, [**ca să nu spun mai mult**]$_{Purpose}$
        'Her hair-do was perfect, not to say more'
    c. Coafura ei era impecabilă, [**deși impresia mea nu contează**]$_{Concessive}$
        'Her hair-do was perfect, though my opinion does not matter'

10.2.6 Adjuncts with constituent deletion

With certain adjuncts—concessive, reason, and conditional—the deletion of certain constituents may occur: the copula *fi* 'be' (48), the copula *fi* 'be' + the subordinator (49), the tense auxiliary + the subordinator (50).

(48)   [Chiar (şi) (dacă ar fi) aşa]$_{Concessive}$, (tot) nu m-ai convins
       'Even so, you still didn't convince me'

(49)   [(Pentru că era) fericită de rezultatul la examen]$_{Reason}$, [a plecat în excursie]
       'Because she was happy about the result of the exam, she left on a trip'

(50)   [(Dacă ar fi) sănătos]$_{Conditional}$, s-ar mobiliza mai mult
       'If he were healthy, he would try harder'

10.2.7 Clausal adjuncts and connective adjuncts

Depending on the subordinators they are introduced by, certain clausal adjuncts may co-occur with connective adjuncts, which are usually placed in the matrix clause. Connectives are often optional, but there are contexts in which they are obligatory (54a,b).

(51)   Copiii sunt (**aşa**) [(**pre**)**cum** îi creşti]$_{Manner}$
       'Children are the way you raise them'

(52)   [(**Ori**) de câte ori îl certai]$_{Temporal}$, (**de atâtea ori**) plângea
       'Every time you scolded him he was crying'

(53)   a. (**De-**)**abia** am ajuns acasă, [că a şi sunat la uşă]$_{Temporal}$
          'No sooner had I got home, than the doorbell rang'

       b. [**Cum** m-a văzut]$_{Temporal}$, (**cum**) a început să plângă
          'No sooner did (s)he see me than (s)he started crying'

(54)   a. [**Pe cât** e de deşteaptă]$_{Quantity}$, **pe atât** e de frumoasă
          'She is just as clever as she is beautiful'

       b. [**Cu cât** îl lauzi]$_{Quantity}$ [**cu atât** e mai obraznic]
          'The more you praise him, the more cheeky he is'

(55)   (**De aceea**) s-a supărat, [**fiindcă** nu l-ai invitat]$_{Reason}$
       'That is why he got angry, because you didn't invite him'

(56)   A venit (**de aceea / pentru aceea**) [ca să ne ajute]$_{Purpose}$
       'That is why he came, to help us'

(57)   [**Dacă** plouă]$_{Conditional}$, (**atunci**) îmi iau umbrela
       'If it rains, then I will take my umbrella'

(58)   [**Deşi** plouă]$_{Concessive}$, (**totuşi / tot**) nu-mi iau umbrela
       'Even though it is raining, I am still not taking my umbrella'

(59)   [**Dacă** Petre e deştept]$_{Additive\ negative}$, (**apoi / atunci**) Ion e genial
       'If Petre is clever, then Ion is a genius'

(60) [**După ce că** e prost]$_{\text{Additive positive}}$, (**mai**) are și pretenții
'Besides being stupid, he also gives himself airs'

(61) Ion se plictisise **până într-atât** [**încât** adormise în timpul prelegerii]$_{\text{Result}}$
'Ion had become bored to such an extent that he had fallen asleep during the speech'

10.2.8 Clausal adjuncts word order

Clausal adjuncts generally display free word order.

The following adjunct clauses always follow the matrix clause: adjuncts of temporal proximity (occuring with inverted word order) introduced by the subordinator *că* 'when' (35c); reason adjuncts introduced by the subordinators *căci, că* 'because, as' (36a,b); result adjuncts introduced by the subordinators *încât* '(so...) that', *de* 'that', *așa că* 'so' ((25), (26a,c), (30a), (46a,b)); reason adjuncts with covert subordinators (34a, 49).

Certain adjuncts are always placed before the matrix clause: the quantity adjunct introduced by the subordinator *pe cât* 'as (...as)' (54a); the reason adjunct introduced by the subordinator *cum* 'because' (27a); the additive negative adjunct introduced by the subordinators *unde, de unde, dacă* 'since' (26e); the conditional adjunct with a covert subordinator, occurring in exclamations (34b).

10.3 RELATIVE CLAUSES (RELATIVE ARGUMENTS AND RELATIVE ADJUNCTS)

10.3.1 Syntactic types of relative constructions

In Romanian, as in most European languages, the relative clause formation is based on *relativization* (Huddleston and Pullum 2002: 1037), a syntactic mechanism involving the movement of a relativizer *wh*-element to the left, in *Spec, CP*. The moved component leaves a coindexed trace (*t*) in its position of origin.

(62) Aceasta   este   **casa**$_i$ [[despre   **care**$_i$]   ți-am   vorbit **t**$_i$]
     this   is   house.DEF   about   which   CL.DAT.2SG=have.1SG   told
     'This is the house which I have told you about'

In prototypical relative clauses, the *wh*-word is always overt. Deletion of the relativizer is possible only under certain semantic and syntactic circumstances: (i) in volitive, hypothetical or superlative contexts that trigger the occurence of the subjunctive in the subordinate clause; in this case, the subjunctive marker *să* acts like a connector for the subordinate clause (ii) in situations in which the antecedent of the relative clause is a quantifier (63a–c), a definite or an indefinite NP, explicitely or implicitly modified (63d,e).

(63) a. Nu-i   **nimeni**   (**care**)   să-l   ajute
        not=is   nobody   (which)   SĂ$_{\text{SUBJ}}$=CL.ACC.3SG   help.SUBJ
        'There is nobody to help him'

    b. Va   fi   **primul**   (**care**)   să-l   ajute
       AUX.FUT.3SG   be   first.DEF   which   SĂ$_{\text{SUBJ}}$=CL.ACC.3SG   help.SUBJ
       'He will be the first to help me'

c. De-aş   avea   **pe cineva**   (**care**)   să   mă   ajute!
   if=AUX.COND.1SG have.INF PE someone   which   să_SUBJ CL.ACC.1SG help.SUBJ
   'If I had someone to help me'

d. Nu   e   el   **omul**   (**care**)   să   se   sperie   de un refuz
   Not is he   man.DEF   which   să_SUBJ CL.REFL.ACC.3SG scare.SUBJ of a   refusal
   'He is not the man to be afraid of a refusal'

e. Nu   există   **moment mai   bun**   (**în care**)   să   întrebi   asta
   not exist.3SG   moment   more good   in which   să_SUBJ ask.SUBJ.2SG that
   'There is no better moment to ask that'

C Subjunctive relatives (with optional deletion of the relativizer) also occur in languages such as Macedonian, Albanian, Modern Greek, and Aromanian (Bužarovska 2004: 377). Romanian subjunctive relatives display a wider application range than their counterparts in the other Balkan languages. Thus, subjunctive relatives modifying a definite subject NP (63d) and existential relatives (63a,e) are possible in Romanian, but not in Modern Greek, Macedonian, Aromanian, and Albanian (Bužarovska 2004: 400).

10.3.1.1 Headed relative clauses are embedded into the matrix clauses and restrictively (64a) or non-restrictively (64b) modify one of the constituents of that clause (§5.3.5.1):

(64) a. Am   văzut ieri   **filmul**$_i$ **care**$_i$ a   luat t_i Oscarul   anul   trecut
         have.1SG seen yesterday movie.DEF   which   has taken   Oscar.DEF year.DEF last
         'Yesterday I saw the movie that took the Oscar last year'

    b. [**Filmul   acesta**]$_i$,   **care**$_i$ a   luat t_i Oscarul   anul   trecut,
        movie.DEF   this   which   has   taken   Oscar.DEF year.DEF   last
        nu   m-a   prea   impresionat
        not   CL.ACC.1SG=has   too   impressed
        'I was not very impressed by this movie, which took the Oscar last year'

10.3.1.2 Headless (free) relative clauses occur in the positions of direct object (65a,d), subject (65b), indirect object (65c), or prepositional object (65e); in the examples below, their missing head is signalled by the symbol [e]. Syntactically, they are DPs containing a CP (van Rijemsdik 2006: 340).

(65) a. Am   văzut [$_{DP}$ [e$_i$]   [**ce**$_i$ mi-ai   adus t_i]]
         have.1SG seen   what   CL.DAT.1SG=have.2SG brought
         'I saw what you brought me'

    b. Scapă [$_{DP}$ [e$_i$]   [**cine**$_i$ poate t_i]]
        escapes   who   can
        'Whoever can escapes'

    c. Dau   explicaţii [$_{DP}$ [e$_i$]   [**cui**$_i$ le   cere t_i]]
        give.1SG   explanations   who.DAT   CL.ACC.3PL   asks
        'I'll give explanations to whoever will ask for them'

10.3 Relative clauses (relative arguments and relative adjuncts) 485

    d. Văd [$_{PP}$ **pe** [$_{DP}$ [e$_i$] [**cine**$_i$ intră t$_i$]]]
        see.1SG   PE   who enters
        'I can see whoever will enter here'
    e. Soluția   depinde   [$_{PP}$ **de** [$_{DP}$ [e$_i$] [**ce**$_i$ vrei   tu t$_i$]]]
        solution.DEF depends   on   what want you
        'The solution depends on what you want'

The inflectional features of the Romanian relative words, correlated with the parametric features of a pro-drop language, allow the simultaneous expression of divergent constraints from both the matrix clause and the embedded clause. In (65c) and (65d), the VP in which the relative clause is embedded selects the dative and the prepositional case construction, respectively, while in the subordinate clause, given the subject position of the relativized category, the required case is the nominative. The relative pronoun will thus observe the formal restriction imposed from the matrix clause (*cui*$_{DAT}$, respectively *pe cine*$_{ACC}$). In (65d) and in (65e), the relative pronoun is embedded in a PP belonging to the matrix clause, in the position occupied by a deleted DP; formally, the relative pronoun will receive the accusative case from this prepositional head, while in the subordinate clause it is in the subject and the direct object position, respectively.

10.3.1.3 **Integrated relative clauses** modify an overt NP (66a) or a covert DP / NP (66b–c), occupying argumental or predicative positions in the matrix clause:

(66) a. [$_{DP}$ Acei   câțiva [$_{NP}$ turiști$_i$ [care$_i$ [au   vizitat orașul   tău t$_i$]]]]
        those   few   tourists   which have.3PL visited town.DEF your
        au   fost   impresionați
        have.3PL been   impressed
    b. Adu [$_{DP}$ [e$_i$] [ce$_i$ [ai   scris t$_i$]]]!
        bring.2SG   what   have.2SG written
    c. El a   devenit [$_{NP}$ [e$_i$] [ce$_i$ [și-a   dorit t$_i$]]]
        he have.3SG become   what   CL.REFL.DAT.3SG=have3.SG wanted

10.3.1.4 **Supplementary relative clauses** are embedded in appositions (67a) or in the position of a non-restrictive modifier (67b) for a constituent in the matrix clause. The modified constituent may be overt (67a,b), or covert (67c).

(67) a. S-au   dus   acolo$_i$, [**unde**$_i$ îi   aștepta
        CL.REFL.ACC.3PL=have.3PL gone there where CL.ACC.3PL wait.IMPERF.3SG
        fiul   lor]
        son.DEF.NOM   their
        'They went where their son was waiting for them'
    b. Ion   a   urmat   [studii de istorie]$_i$, [**pe care**$_i$ le$_i$-a   abandonat
        Ion   has followed   studies of history PE which CL.ACC.3PL=has abandoned
        pentru a   deveni   pictor]
        for   A$_{INF}$ become.INF painter
        'Ion studied history, which he abandoned to become a painter'

c. A telefonat [e_i], [când_i a ajuns]
   has called   when   has arrived
   'He called when he arrived'

10.3.2 Indirect interrogative constructions

The *wh*-questions in reported speech are selected by (i) verbs of communication *întreba* 'ask', *răspunde* 'answer', *spune* 'tell', *zice* 'say', *povesti* 'narrate', *explica* 'explain' (68a), or by verbs expressing cognitive processes: *şti* 'know', (*nu*) *avea habar* 'have no idea', *afla* 'find out', *descoperi* 'discover', *stabili* 'establish', *a-şi aminti* 'remember', *a-şi aduce aminte* 'recall', *vedea* 'see' (with cognitive meaning, in a metaphoric use) (68b); (ii) verbs of attitude or uncertainty: *a* (*nu-*)*i păsa* '(not) care about', *a se frământa* 'bother' (68c); (iii) nouns or adjectives semantically related to the verbs above: *întrebarea* 'the question', *răspunsul* 'the answer', *spusa* 'the saying' (68d), *curios* 'curious', *mirat* 'astonished', *nelămurit* 'confused' (68e).

Syntactically, indirect questions are 'pure clauses', CPs occupying the position of DPs (van Rijemsdik 2006: 340).

(68) a. **Mă   întreb [e_i]   [cu   cine   vine   la   petrecere]_i**
        CL.REFL.ACC.1SG wonder   with   who   comes   to   party
        'I wonder who he will come to the party with'

   b. **Nu   văd [e_i]   [ce   mai   are   de   spus   acum]_i**
        not see.1SG   what   more   has   DE_SUP say.SUP   now
        'I can't see what else he has to say now'

   c. **Se   frământă [_PP Ø [e_i]]   [ce   să   facă]_i**
        CL.REFL.ACC.3SG   worries   what   SĂ_SUBJ   do.SUBJ
        'He worries at not knowing what to do'

   d. Mi-am   pus   întrebarea [e_i]   [**cine** mai vine   la   petrecere]_i
        CL.REFL.DAT.1SG=have.1SG put   question.DEF   who   else comes   to   party
        'I have been asking myself who else will come to the party'

   e. Eram   **curioasă** [_PP Ø [e_i]] [**ce**-ai   mai   făcut]_i
        was.1SG curious   what=have.2SG   else   done
        'I was curious about what you have done lately'

Some of the terms belonging to the semantic class described above can select both indirect questions and headless relative clauses. The *wh*-word of a headless relative clause is coindexed with the DP in the matrix clause (69b,d), while the *wh*-word of an indirect question has divergent reference (69a,c).

(69) a. A   întrebat pe   cine   se   afla   acolo [_DP **ceva_j**]
        has   asked   PE   who   CL.REFL.ACC.3SG   be.IMPERF.3SG there (something)
        [[**ce   muzică**]_i să   **pună** t_i]_j
         what   music   SĂ_SUBJ   put.SUBJ.3SG
        '(S)he asked the people who were there what music (s)he should play'

   b. A   întrebat [_PP **pe** [_DP [e_i] [**cine**_i [se   afla   t_i   acolo]]]]
        has   asked   PE   who   CL.REFL.ACC.3SG   be.IMPERF.3SG   there
        ce muzică   să   pună
        what music   SĂ_SUBJ   put.SUBJ
        '(S)he asked the people who were there what music (s)he should play'

c. Nu-mi pasă [PP de [DP ceva_j]] [cine mă vede t_i]_j
   not=CL.DAT.1SG care of something who CL.ACC.1SG sees
   'I do not care who will see me'

d. Nu-mi pasă [PP de [DP [e_i] [cine_i [mă vede t_i]]]]
   not=CL.DAT.1SG care of who CL.ACC.1SG sees
   'I do not care about who sees me'

10.3.3 Relative infinitival constructions

This kind of relative clause is atypical from two points of view: (i) it is always selected by the impersonal verb *fi* 'be' (70h) or by the verb *avea* 'have', with personal (70a–d) or impersonal (70e–g) value, and (ii) its predicate is a non-finite verbal form—the short infinitive, without the analytical marker A.

(70) a. N-am ce_i face t_i
   not=have.1SG what do.INF
   'I have nothing to do'

b. Fata asta n-are la cine_i merge t_i
   girl.DEF this not=has to who go.INF
   'This girl has nobody to go to'

c. Am unde_i merge t_i
   have.1SG where go.INF
   'I have where to go'

d. Ei n-au cum_i câştiga t_i
   they not=have.3PL how win.INF
   'They have no way of winning'

e. N-are ce_i se-ntâmpla t_i
   not=have.3SG what CL.REFL.ACC.3SG=happen.INF
   'Nothing can happen'

f. N-are cine_i-l ajuta t_i
   Not=has who=CL.ACC.3SG help.INF
   'There is nobody to help him'

g. N-are unde_i / cum_i / când_i se petrece aşa ceva t_i
   not=has where how when CL.REFL.ACC.3SG happen.INF so something
   'There is no place / no way / no time for such a thing to happen'

h. Nu-i cine_i-l ajuta t_i
   not=is who=CL.ACC.M.3SG help.INF
   'There is nobody to help him'

C The construction belongs to a semantico-syntactic pattern with non-indicative verbs, which can be found in many Romance and Balkan languages, recently described as *modal existential constructions* (MEC) (Grosu 2004; Šimík 2011). Usually, the infinitive is the primary MEC mood, but there are languages in which the verb in the MEC is always a subjunctive, while in others the only option is the infinitive. Romanian allows both types: infinitive-MEC and subjunctive-MEC (Šimík 2011: 45).

H The infinitival relative constructions are old syntactic structures of Latin origin, their use in contemporary Romanian being almost exclusively limited to the spoken language. The construction is quasi-fixed, and it is limited to a small number of contexts of occurrence; for the hypothesis that the infinitive employed in indirect relative-interogative constructions in Romance originates in the Latin imperfective subjunctive, see Scida 2004: 89.

The early evidence of this construction in Romanian dates back to the 16th century (Diaconescu 1967, 1977). A *wh*-word associated with an infinitive occurs in old Romanian in syntactic patterns similar to those employed in contemporary Romanian, in subject or direct object positions of the verbs *a avea* 'have' or *fi* 'be'. In old Romanian, the relative pronoun *ce* 'what' has the highest frequence of occurence, followed by *unde* 'where'. Later, the pattern is extended to other *wh*-words: *cine* 'who', *cum* 'how', *când* 'when'.

Relative clauses and indirect questions share most of the inventory of their connectors. Except for the fixed adverbial collocation *de ce* 'why', the entire range of *wh*-words that are used in indirect questions can be employed with relative clauses as well. On the other hand, *ceea ce* 'what', *de* 'which' and some compound indefinite pronouns (*oricine* 'whoever', *orice* 'whatever') occur only in relative clauses and are disallowed in relative-interrogatives. The range of *wh*-words that are employed for the relative infinitival constructions overlaps with that employed for indirect questions, including the specific *de ce*. The use of the *wh*-pronoun *care* in infinitival relative clauses is possible only in extended configurations, under a partitive anaphoric relation with the antecedent (Pomian 2008: 202):

(71) S-au întors și Ion$_i$, și Petre$_j$. N-ai [de care$_{i/j}$ te teme t$_i$ / t$_j$], că amândoi sunt serioși
'Both Ion and Petre are back. You shouldn't fear any of them, because they are both reliable'

Like indirect questions, infinitival relative constructions allow stacking:

(72) N-am   cui   ce   spune
     not=have.1SG who.DAT what say.INF
     'I have nobody to say anything to'

10.3.4 Pseudo-cleft constructions

In the absence of expletive subjects, the strategy of clefting in Romanian involves *pseudo-clefts*. In a narrow sense, pseudo-clefts are nominal relative clauses introduced by *what* in position of subject / theme (Prince 1978: 883). In a wider sense, besides the identifying constructions with a headless relative clause, *pseudo-clefts* also include relative clauses with a nominal antecedent: *the + thing, one, place, time, reason, way* (Collins 1991: 27).

The most frequent patterns are illustrated in (73):

(73) a. [Ce   mă   deranjează cel mai   tare] e că nu ai   răbdare
        what CL.ACC.1SG bothers   CEL more badly is that not have.2SG patience
        'What bothers me the most is that you are impatient'

   b. [Ceea ce   l-a   supărat pe Ion] a fost că
       what   CL.ACC.3.SG=has upset   PE Ion   has been that
       n-ai   anunțat   întârzierea
       not=have.2SG announced   delay.DEF
       'What upset Ion was that you didn't tell him you would be late'

c. **Cel** [**care** a anunțat întârzierea] a fost Paul
CEL which have.3SG announced delay.DEF have.3SG been Paul
'The one that announced the delay was Paul'

d. Chestia [**care** mă supără cel mai tare] este că
thing.DEF which CL.ACC.1SG bothers CEL more badly is that
nu ai răbdare
not have.2SG patience
'The thing that upsets me the most is that you don't have patience'

10.3.5 The inventory of *wh*-words

The inventory of relative words in Romanian includes pronouns (*care* 'which', *cine* 'who', *ce* 'what', *cât* 'how many', *ceea ce* 'what', *de* 'which'), adjectives (*care* 'which', *ce* 'what', *cât* 'how many'), and adverbs (*unde* 'where', *când* 'when', *cum* 'how', *cât* 'how much'). Except for the compound pronoun *ceea ce* (§10.3.5.3) and for *de* (a pronoun used in the colloquial and regional language, §10.3.5.5), which are employed only in relative clauses, the Romanian *wh*-system is common to both relative and indirect interrogative constructions (§13.1.2.2). Disambiguation is possible only in the following syntactic context: the relative words, belonging to the relative clauses, are always coreferential to a constituent in the matrix clause, while the interrogative *wh*-words, occurring in *wh*-questions, are not involved in any external referential relation (§10.3.2).

10.3.5.1 **Care** (< Lat. QUALIS, Cioranescu 2002) is the most frequent of the relative clauses connectors in Romanian. It has the same privilege of occurrence in indirect questions as well. In its pronominal (74) or adjectival (75) usage, as an anaphoric for [+/−animate] antecedents, *care* displays case, number, and gender inflection (Table 10.1).

H In old Romanian and later, *care* displayed a richer morphology than in the contemporary language (§5.3.5.1.4).

(74) a. Tânărul$_i$ [**care**$_i$ a intrat t$_i$] este fiul Marei
young.DEF which has entered is son.DEF Mara.GEN
'The young man who has entered is Mara's son'

b. Muntele$_i$ [**pe care**$_i$ îl$_i$ vezi în fotografie t$_i$] este Piatra Craiului
mountain.DEF PE which CL.ACC.3SG see.2SG in picture is Piatra Craiului
'The mountain which you see in the picture is Piatra Craiului'

TABLE 10.1 Forms of *care*

	SG		PL	
	M	F	M	F
NOM≡ACC	care			
GEN≡DAT	cărui(a)	cărei(a)	căror(a)	

c. Tânărul_i / Tânăra_j [căruia_i / căreia_j] i_{i/j}-am dat
   young.M.DEF young.F.DEF which.M which.F CL.DAT.3SG=have.1SG given
   cartea t_{i/j}] este fiul / fiica Marei
   book.DEF is son.DEF daughter.DEF Mara.GEN
   'The young man/woman to whom I've given the book is Mara's son / daughter'

d. Tinerii_i [cărora_i le_i-am dat cartea t_i] sunt
   young.PL.DEF which.PL CL.DAT.3PL=have.1SG given book.DEF are.3PL
   children.DEF Mara.GEN
   copiii Marei
   'The young people to whom I've given the book are Mara's children'

(75) Au adus covorul_i, [[care covor]_i nu se potrivea în
      have.3PL brought carpet.DEF which carpet not CL.REFL.ACC.3SG fit.IMPERF.3SG in
      noul decor t_i]
      new.DEF decor
      'They brought the carpet, which did not fit in the new decor'

The genitival *wh*-phrase has two forms: (76a), with the relative pronoun inflected for genitive case and article-like ending *a* (*căruia* / *căreia*), and (76b), with the possesive marker *al* and inflectional form (*al cărui* / *al cărei*):

(76) a. El este tânărul_i [_PP cu [_DP fratele **căruia**_i]_j] am fost coleg t_j
        he is young.DEF with brother.DEF which.M.SG.GEN have.1SG been classmate
        'He is the young man with whose brother I was at school'

     b. Acesta este tânărul_i [_PP cu [_DP **al cărui**_i frate]_j]
        this be.3SG young.DEF with AL which.GEN.M.SG brother.DEF
        am fost coleg t_j
        have.1SG been classmate
        'This is the young man with whose brother I was at school'

U In spoken Romanian, *care* is often employed uninflected (without the dummy preposition PE, the direct object marker) or with markers of analytic inflection:

   (77) a. mobilă potrivită pentru garsoniera_i **care**_i o_i au
           furniture suitable for studio.DEF which CL.ACC.3SG have.3PL
           'furniture suitable for the studio they own'

        b. Omul **la care**_i nu-i_i place munca nu știe ce-i bucuria
           man.DEF to which not=CL.DAT.3SG likes work not knows what=is joy.DEF
           'The man who does not like work doesn't know what joy is'

        c. mândră, mândrulița mea, **care**_i m-am iubit **cu ea**_i
           dear dear.DIM.DEF my which CL.REFL.ACC.1SG=have.1SG loved with her.ACC
           'my dearest one, whom I used to love'

   The loss of inflection would make the construction opaque. The retrieval of the missing information is made either by the doubling of the relative pronoun in direct / indirect object position by a clitic (77a–b), or by using a 'pronoun-retention type' strategy (Comrie 2003: 20) occurring exclusively in the informal, spoken register (77c).

H Romanian has shown in its history a general tendency to replace synthetic inflection by analytic (Diaconescu 1970: 222–3) or to use invariable relative pronouns. The invariable relative pronoun and the inflected pronoun have most probably coexisted since the earliest stages. The prevalence of the inflected forms in the contemporary language is due to normative influence (Vulpe 1980: 169).

10.3 Relative clauses (relative arguments and relative adjuncts)

TABLE 10.2 Forms of *cine*

	SG / PL	
	M	F
Nom≡Acc	cine	
Gen≡Dat	cui	

10.3.5.2 The **relative pronoun** *cine* (< Lat. QUE(M)NE *QUENE (QUEM), Cioränescu 2002: 189), always employed in headless relative clauses or in indirect questions, has exclusively pronominal use and is inflected only for case (Table 10.2).

(78) a. Vine la petrecere [[e$_i$] [**cine**$_i$ a fost invitat t$_i$]]
  'Whoever was invited will come to the party'

   b. Voi da cartea [[e$_i$] [**cui**$_i$ mi-o va cere t$_i$ primul]]
  'I will give the book to whoever will ask me first'

   c. [**Cine**$_i$ te iubește t$_i$] te înțelege [e$_i$]
  'Whoever loves you understands you'

Cine is semantically [+specific] and is a substitute for [+human] nominals. With generic meaning, like in (78c), it refers either to the 'whole' or to a part of the 'whole' (Manoliu-Manea 1968: 101–2).

H The use of the interrogative *cine* in relative clauses comes quite late in Romanian (Rizescu 1962: 54), and this fact explains why speakers often felt it necessary to double the relative pronoun *cine* by another pronoun in the matrix clause (79a–b). In emphatic contexts, the reduplication is also possible in contemporary Romanian (79c).

(79) a. **Cine** ascunde vrajba, **el** strânge hitlenșug (ORom)
  who hides discontent.DEF he gathers deviousness
  'The ones who hide their discontent will attract deviousness'

   b. **Cine** ari strica logodna, **acela** să piardză acei 12.000 de galbini (ORom)
  who AUX.COND.3SG break.INF engagement.DEF that să$_{SUBJ}$ lose.SUBJ those 12.000 of coins
  'He who breaks the engagement, let him lose the 12,000 coins'

   c. **Cine** te-a trimis acolo, **ăla** să te ajute acum
  who CL.ACC.2SG=has sent there that să$_{SUBJ}$ CL.ACC.2SG help.SUBJ now
  'He who sent you there, let him help you now'

In the old language, *cine* was a synonym of *care* (Densusianu 1961, II: 122) and it could be employed in headed relative clauses as well (80). As an isolated phenomenon, *cine* following a nominal antecedent could be found in texts from the beginning of the 20th century (Nilsson 1969: 73).

(80) Acela om [**cine** în Hs. crede] (ORom)
That man who in Christ believes
'That man who believes in Christ'

U In present-day Romanian, constructions in which *cine* has a nominal antecedent (81a–b) are not accepted.
(81) a. *Nu era nimeni [pe cine să întrebe]
not was nobody PE who SĂ_SUBJ ask.SUBJ
'There was nobody whom he could ask'
b. *copilul [ai cui părinți...]
child.DEF AL.M.PL who.GEN parents
'the child whose parents...'

C In other Romance languages, the equivalent of the Romanian *cine* is used in contexts both with non-referential (82a) and referential antecedent (82b). In the second context, present-day Romanian always employs *care* (82c):
(82) a. Fr. J'aime **qui** m'aime
'I love whoever loves me'
b. Fr. J'aime l'homme **qui** m'a choisie
'I love the man who chose me'
c. Rom. Îl iubesc pe cel / pe omul **care** mă iubește
'I love the one / the man that loves me'

In Romanian, the indefinites *cine* and *ce* are widely used when the antecedent is non-referential (83a–b), while in other Romance languages it occurs as a definite antecedent (83c) (Manoliu-Manea 1977: 306).
(83) a. Rom. Iubesc pe **cine** mă iubește
love.1SG PE who CL.ACC.1SG loves
'I love him who / whoever loves me'
b. Rom. Dă-i **cui** vrei
give.IMP.2SG=CL.DAT.3SG who.DAT want.2SG
'Give it to whoever you want'
c. Fr. J'aime **celui qui** m'a choisie
'I love the one who chose me'

Frequently, *cine* is associated to the preposition *cu*, selected by the verb in the subordinate clause, but it may also join other prepositions, selected by a head in the matrix clause: *de către cine* 'by whom', *de la cine* 'from whom', *la cine* 'to whom', *în funcție de cine* 'depending on whom', *pentru cine* 'for whom'.

In indirect questions, *cine* is more frequent than in relative clauses, and probably it is its interrogative origin that explains this contrast.

10.3.5.3 Ce (< Lat. QUID) is an invariable pronoun / adjective. It is usually a substitute for inanimates (84a), but can also be employed for animate referents (84b–c):

(84) a. Săptămâna_i [ce_i vine] o să fiu la Cluj
week.DEF what comes o să_SUBJ be.SUBJ.1SG at Cluj
'Next week I will be in Cluj'

b. Cel_i [ce_i a intrat] este fiul Marei
CEL who has entered is son.DEF Mara.GEN
'The one who entered is Mara's son'

c. Fata_i [ce_i ți-am prezentat-o ieri] este
girl.DEF what CL.DAT.2SG=have.1SG introduced=CL.ACC.3SG yesterday is
sora ei
sister.DEF her(GEN)
'The girl that I introduced to you yesterday is her sister'

U *Ce* is most frequently the head of a relative clause that modifies the pronominal *cel*. The frequency of this context determined the interpretation of *cel ce* as a compound relative pronoun. Recent research has shown that the agglutination of the group is not yet complete.

The collocation *ceea ce* displays a deeper stage of grammaticalization, manifested by the invariability of the fosilized demonstrative *ceea* and by the impossibility of its dissociation from *ce*.

The relative pronoun *ce* is also frequently associated to the universal quantifier *tot* 'every'. *Ceea ce* can freely share the same contexts, the only difference between the two variants of the relative *ce* being the level of emphasis (Nilsson 1969: 45; Lombard 1974: 199).

(85) Tot (**ceea**) **ce** mi-ai spus este adevărat
'Everything you told me is true'

Compared to the distribution of *care*, the distribution of *ce* does not generally exhibit important restrictions (except for the ones regarding the case inflection). When the relative clause is embedded in a PP, *care* is still preferred, because of a difference in acceptability displayed in examples like (86) (see Lombard 1974: 200):

(86) a. Asta e ceva **ce** mă privește
this is something what CL.ACC.1SG concerns
'This is something that concerns me'

b. ?Asta e ceva **la ce** m-am gândit
this is something at what CL.REFL.ACC.1SG=have.1SG thought
'This is something I have thought of'

c. Asta e ceva **la care** m-am gândit
this is something at which CL.REFL.ACC.1SG=have.1SG thought
'This is something I have thought of'

As an adjective, *ce* occurs only in headless relative clauses:

(87) Nu avem **ce** reacții aștepta de la ea
'We don't have any reactions to expect from her'

10.3.5.4 The pronoun and the adjective **cât** (< Lat. QUANTUS, contaminated with QUOTUS, Ciorănescu 2002: 204) shows gender, number, and case inflection (Table 10.3).

TABLE 10.3 Forms of *cât*

	SG		PL	
	M	F	M	F
Nom≡Acc	cât	câtă	câți	câte
Gen≡Dat	–	–	cător	

The forms of *cât* are usually used for denoting quantity, duration, proportion. *Cât* is employed as a pronoun (88) and as an adjective (89).

(88) a. În   timpul   **cât**   a   stat   cu   noi   s-a   simțit
        in   time.DEF   how-much   has   stayed   with   us   CL.REFL.ACC.3SG=has   felt
        foarte   bine
        very   well
        'For as long as (s)he stayed with us (s)he felt very well'

   b. Toate   **câte**   ți   le-a   spus   sunt   adevarate
      all   how-many   CL.DAT.2SG   CL.ACC.3PL=has   told   are   true
      'Everything (s)he told you is true'

(89) a. **Câte**   zile   am   să   mai   am,   voi   avea
        how-many   days   AUX.FUT.1SG   SĂ_SUBJ   more   have.SUBJ.1SG   AUX.FUT.1SG   take.INF
        grijă   de   ea
        care   of   her
        'For as many days as I have left, I will take care of her'

   b. Mă   întreb   **câtor**   oameni   li   s-o
      CL.REFL.ACC.1SG   ask   how-many.DAT   people   CL.DAT.3PL   CL.REFL.ACC.3SG=O
      mai   fi   întâmplat   asta
      more   be   happened   this
      'I wonder to how many people something like this might have happened'

For the genitive–dative in the singular, analytic constructions are employed:

(90) **La**   **câți**   le-a   cerut   părerea,   toți   au
      to   how-many   CL.DAT.3PL=has   asked   oppinion.DEF   all   have3.PL
      răspuns   la fel
      answered   the-same
      'Everyone whom he asked for an opinion answered the same'

Unlike the interrogative *cât*, which can freely combine with a wide range of prepositions (Șerbănescu 2002; §13.1.2.2), the relative pronoun *cât* is associated mostly with *din* 'from' and *după* 'after'.

10.3.5.5 The relative pronoun *de* is employed in the colloquial register, as an invariable equivalent of *care*. Usually, its antecedent is [+personal], mostly the colloquial demonstrative *ăl(a)* (91a). The usage of *de* in other registers is obsolete (91b).

(91) a. Nebun   e   ăl   **de**   te-o   mai   crede   vreodată
       crazy   is that who CL.ACC.2SG=O more believe.INF   ever
       'Crazy is the one who will ever believe you again'

   b. În toți anii   **de**   trecură,   am   aflat   câte   ceva
      in all years.DEF which pass.PS.3PL have.1SG found-out how-many something
      'In all the years that went by, I found out some things'

H The origin of *de* is uncertain. Most sources refer to its Latin origin (< Lat. DE), but it could also be the result of contamination with the Bulgarian connector *deto* (see also §10.1.1.3, §10.2.2, Krapova 2010).

The use of *de* as an equivalent of *care*, especially in those stages of the language in which *care* displayed rich inflection, had the advantage of invariability. With *de*, rather than *care*, the speaker had an invariant relativizer whose syntactic function could simply be performed by means of a clitic:

(92) a. cheile$_i$ **de**$_i$ le$_i$ ținea t$_i$ în   mână
       keys.DEF   which   CL.ACC.3PL hold.IMPERF.3SG   in   hand
   b. cheile$_i$ pe   **care**$_i$ le$_i$ ținea t$_i$ în   mână
      keys.DEF   PE   which   CL.ACC.3PL held   in   hand
      'The keys that he held in his hand'

10.3.5.6 The relative adverbs ***unde, când, cum, cât*** mark the relative junction when the relativized category is a semantically compatible adverb or a noun with locative, temporal, modal, or quantity meaning (93a–d). The relative adverbs are, therefore, adverbial anaphors having their referential source in the matrix clause. The fixed collocation *de ce* 'why', corresponding to an adjunct of cause or purpose, occurs only in indirect questions (93e) and is distinct from the free association [$_{PP}$ de [$_{DP}$ ce]] 'of what', that can also occur in relative clauses (93f).

(93) a. locul   **unde**   ne-am   întâlnit prima oară
       place.DEF where   CL.REFL.ACC.1PL=have.1PL   met   first   time
       'the place where we first met'

   b. ziua   **când**   te-am   văzut
      day.DEF   when   CL.ACC.2SG=have.1SG   seen
      'the day I saw you'

   c. modul   **cum**   ai   procedat
      way.DEF   how   have.2SG   acted
      'the way you acted'

   d. În timpul   **cât**   tu   erai   la   școală,   eu   am   terminat   treaba
      in time.DEF while   you were at   school   I   have   finished   job.DEF
      'while you were at school, I finished my job'

   e. N-a   întrebat [e$_i$]   [**de ce**   nu   vii]$_i$
      not=has   asked   why   not   come.2SG
      'He did not ask why you were not coming'

f. Agață haina [de [eᵢ] [ceᵢ ai agățat-o tᵢ și ieri]]]
hang.IMP.2SG coat.DEF of what have.2SG hanged=CL.ACC.3SG also yesterday
'Hang the coat on what you hung it on yesterday'

In certain contexts, some of the relative connectors underwent a process of grammaticalization. Employed with bleached circumstantial meaning, the relative adverbs *unde*, *când*, *cum* lost their syntactic function, and function contextually as subordinators expressing reason (Guțu 1957: 168–9, see also §10.2.2.2).

(94) **Cum** n-avea timp de povești, a plecat
'As he had no time for stories, he left'

U In context, some relative pronouns may also loosen their relativizer function and act almost like subordinators, without being fully grammaticalized as shown in example (94). Relators (Gheorghe 2008: 216–18) have a light relation to the matrix clause, both as far as the anaphoric relation to the host is concerned, and with respect to the degree of embedding. The relator repositions a large syntactic sequence, sometimes a whole sentence, functioning as a structural device employed for assuring discourse continuity. See the *continuative* relative clauses in (95a–b), that were frequent in Latin prose and that are available in other Romance languages as well (Lambrecht 2000: 52). The relative pronoun *care* occurring in some deviant constructions in spoken non-literary Romanian (95c) is also a relator:

(95) a. Și i-am spus că am stat și mi-am
and CL.DAT.3SG=have.1SG told that have.1SG stayed and CL.REFL.DAT.1SG=have.1SG
făcut temele, **la care** el a reacționat imediat
done homework.DEF at which he has reacted immediately
'And I told him that I stayed there, doing my homework, at which he reacted immediately'

b. Animalul se scutură, privi în jur, **după care**
animal.DEF CL.REFL.ACC.3SG shake.PS.3SG looked around after which
dispăru în pădure
disappeared in woods
'The animal shook itself, looked around, after which it disappeared in the woods'

c. Era lume multă acolo, **care** nu se putea
was people much there which not CL.REFL.3SG could
să facem scandal
să_SUBJ make.SUBJ.1PL noise
'There were a lot of people there, so we could not make a fuss'

10.3.6 Features of *wh*-movement in Romanian. Pied-piping

When the interrogative, the relative, or the relative–interrogative word is embedded into a phrase, the [*wh*] feature percolates, causing the movement of the entire group (96a–c). Romanian does not allow *preposition stranding*. Cases of prepositional heads remaining *in situ* are impossible (96d,e).

(96) a. [**Care** nepot]ᵢ vine tᵢ în vizită? [interrogative clause]
'Which nephew comes to visit?'

b. Ia [**ce** păpușă]ᵢ vrei tᵢ! [relative clause]
'Take which(ever) doll you want'

c. Nu ştiu [ce funcţionar]ᵢ te-a ajutat tᵢ   [relative–interrogative clause]
   'I don't know which clerk helped you'

d. *[*Ce* **funcţionar**]ᵢ depinde rezolvarea problemei [*de* tᵢ]?
   what clerk depends solving.DEF problem.DEF of
   vs. **De** *ce* **funcţionar** depinde rezolvarea problemei?
   of what clerk depends solving.DEF problem.DEF

e. *maşina [**portbagajul** *căreia*]ᵢ ai pus valizele [*în* tᵢ]
   car.DEF trunk.DEF which.GEN have put suitcases.DEF in
   vs. maşina **în portbagajul** *căreia* ai pus valizele
   car.DEF in trunk.DEF which.GEN have put suitcases.DEF
   'The car in the trunk of which you put the suitcases'

10.4 SECONDARY PREDICATION

10.4.1 General properties

The secondary predicate (SP) is a syntactically non-autonomous semantic predicate, syntactically attached to a main predicate. The main predicate is a verb, in a finite or non-finite form, a verbal interjection (97a–c) or a noun (98) in the semantic class of 'picture nouns' (§5.2.7):

(97) a. Ioana pleacă **fericită**
        Ioana leaves **happy**.F.SG
        'Ioana leaves happy'

   b. Plecând **supărată**, Ioana...
      leaving **upset**.F.SG Ioana.F
      'Leaving upset, Ioana...'

   c. Iată-i **ajunşi** la destinaţie!
      look=CL.ACC.M.PL arrived.M.PL at destination
      'Here they are, at their destination'

(98) Fotografia / tabloul / filmul cu Maria **blondă** era pe masă
     photo.DEF painting.DEF film.DEF with Maria blonde.F.SG was on table
     'The photo / The painting / The film with Maria (as a) blonde was on the table'

SP applies semantically to an argument or an adjunct of the main predicate, which can be:

(99) a. SUBJECT:
        Aici e **Maria** *tânără*
        here is Maria young.F.SG
        'Here is Maria (when she was) young'

   b. DIRECT OBJECT:
      Mi-l imaginez **pe bunicul** meu *tânăr*
      CL.DAT.1SG=CL.ACC.M.3SG imagine PE grandfather.M.SG.DEF my young.M.SG
      'I imagine my grandfather (when he was) young'

c. PREPOSITIONAL OBJECT:
Îmi amintesc **de bunicul** meu *tânăr*
CL.DAT.1SG remember of grandfather.M.SG.DEF my young.M.SG
'I remember my grandfather (when he was) young'

d. SUBJECTIVE PREDICATIVE COMPLEMENT:
Ea este **studenta** admisă *prima*
she is student.DEF(F) admitted.F.SG first.F.SG
'She is the student (who was) admitted first'

e. INDIRECT OBJECT:
Dăm bonusuri **cumpărătorilor** veniți *primii* la magazin
give.1PL bonuses buyer.M.PL.DAT come.M.PL first.M.PL at store
'We give bonuses to the buyers who arrive at the store first'

f. BY-PHRASE:
Casa a fost construită **de bunicul** meu *tânăr*
house.DEF has been built by grandfather.M.SG.DEF my young.M.SG
'The house was built by my grandfather when he was young'

g. COMITATIVE ADJUNCT:
A plecat **cu** **ea** *sănătoasă* și s-a
has left with her.ACC healthy.F.SG and CL.REFL.ACC.3SG=has
întors **cu** **ea** *bolnavă*
returned with her.ACC ill.F.SG
'He left with her healthy and came back with her ill'

The most productive SPs are those whose semantic subject is the subject or the direct object of the main verb.

With the exception of SPs whose semantic subject is the subject or the direct object of the main verb, SPs cannot precede their semantic subject:

(100) *Îmi amintesc *tânăr* **de bunicul** meu
CL.DAT.1SG remember young.M.SG of grandfather.DEF my

Prototypically, SPs are optional constituents (unlike predicative complements), as the sentence is grammatical and the main verb is semantically complete without the SP. However, some SPs cannot be omitted from the sentence, a property which points to their complement status (§10.4.2.2).

Adjectival SPs agree with their semantic subject in gender and number (see examples (97) and (98) above).

10.4.2 Syntactic and semantic types of SPs

10.4.2.1 Depictive vs. resultative SPs

There are two major semantic types of SPs, differentiated by their relation to the event or the state denoted by main verb:

(i) depictive (descriptive):

(101) a. Ion a tăiat pâinea **aproape necoaptă**
Ion has cut bread.F.SG.DEF almost NEG-baked.F.SG

b. Ion   a   vopsit   casa   **netencuită**   bine
      Ion   has   painted   house.F.SG.DEF   NEG-plastered.F.SG   well
      'Ion painted the house when it was not well plastered'

(ii) resultative:

(102) a. Ion   a   tăiat   pâinea   **felii**
         Ion   has   cut   bread.DEF   slices
         'Ion cut the bread into slices'

      b. Ion   a   vopsit   casa   **albastră**
         Ion   has   painted   house.F.SG.DEF   blue.F.SG
         'Ion painted the house blue'

Depictive SPs express a property of the nominal which is valid during the entire temporal frame of the main predicate. The adjectival depictive SPs denote a non-inherent, stage-level property, in general. Exceptions are possible, as the restriction is pragmatic rather than semantic (Rothstein 2006: 223):

(103) a. *Ion   a   tăiat   pâinea   **integrală**   (vs. (101a))
         Ion   has   cut   bread.F.SG.DEF   whole-grained.F.SG
      b. Ion a comandat pâinea   **integrală**   şi   chiflele   **albe**
         Ion has ordered bread.F.SG.DEF   whole-grained.F.SG   and bun.F.PL.DEF   white.F.PL
         'Ion ordered whole-grained bread and white buns'

Resultative SPs denote a property which is the result of the event expressed by the main predicate. The subject of depictive SPs is the subject, an object, or an adjunct of the main verb. The subject of resultative SPs is the direct object of the main predicate (see examples (102a,b) above).

C   In Romanian, as well as in French, Italian or Spanish, resultative SPs are not very frequent, unlike in English, German, or Chinese (Folli and Ramchand 2005). Only some accomplishment verbs allow resultative SPs, such as *vopsi* 'to paint', *tăia* 'to cut', *strânge, aduna* 'to gather', *coace* 'to bake', *găti* 'to cook', etc. Generally, Romance languages lack resultative SPs (Levin and Rappaport Hovav 1995a), both adjectival, like the ones in (102b), and prepositional, subject-oriented ones, like *John kicked the dog into the bathroom* (Mateu 2001: 240). This is related to the fact that in Romance languages the meaning associated with the path is incorporated into the verb, while English expresses the path by means of a PP (Talmy 1985; see also §2.3.4).

In relation to their semantic subject, depictive SPs can express a quality (104a), as well as the category (104b), the identification (104c), the possession (104d), the partition (104e), and the circumstance of the event (104f–h):

(104) a. Beau   ceaiul   **rece**
         drink.1SG   tea.DEF   cold
         'I drink the tea cold'

      b. Ion   e   considerat   **un   geniu**
         Ion   is   considered   a   genius
         'Ion is considered a genius'

      c. Îl   bănuiau   **spionul   trimis   de   duşmani**
         CL.ACC.M.3SG=suspected.3PL   spy.DEF   sent   by   enemies
         'They suspected him to be the spy sent by the enemies'

d. Imobilul   îl   ştiam   **al   lui   Ion**
   building.NEUT.SG.DEF CL.ACC.M.3SG knew.1SG AL   LUI.GEN Ion
   'I knew that the building was Ion's'

e. Te   credeam   **de-ai**   **noştri**
   CL.ACC.2SG believe.1PL of=AL.M.PL   our.M.PL
   'I thought you were one of ours'

f. A   trăit   **bolnav** de diabet   încă mulţi ani
   has   lived   ill.M.SG   of diabetes still many   years
   'He lived with diabetes for many years'

g. Te   vrem   **alături** de   noi
   CL.ACC.2SG want.1PL   beside   DE   us
   'We want you beside us'

h. Maria era   frumoasă   **tânără**
   Maria was   beautiful.F.SG young.F.SG
   'Maria was beautiful when she was young'

Depictive SPs are distinguished from absolutive adjunct APs, which are prosodically isolated and have a much freer semantic distribution (Rothstein 2006: 223). Sometimes, they have a circumstantial meaning: cause (105a), concession (105b).

(105) a. Maria   a   plecat,   **supărată**
         Maria   has   left   upset.F.SG
         'Maria left, upset'

   b. **Rănit**   la picior, soldatul   a reuşit   să   ajungă   în tranşee
      injured.M.SG   to leg   soldier.M.SG.DEF has managed să$_{SUBJ}$ arrive.SUBJ   in trenches
      'Injured in the leg, the soldier managed to get to the trenches'

10.4.2.2 Complement vs. adjunct SPs

In general, depictive SPs are considered adjuncts, while resultative SPs are analysed as complements. However, the distinction of complement vs. adjunct is not so clear cut. The SP in (106) can be omitted, while the SPs in (107) cannot be omitted without making the sentence ungrammatical:

(106) Am   tăiat   pâinea   **(felii)**
      have.1SG   cut   bread.DEF   (slices)
      'I cut the bread (into slices)'

(107) a. Îl   consider   pe   Ion   **foarte** **harnic**
         CL.ACC.M.3SG consider.1SG   PE   Ion   very   hard-working
         'I consider Ion to be very hard-working'

   b. *Îl   consider   pe   Ion
      CL.ACC.M.3SG consider.1SG   PE   Ion

10.4.3 Main predicates which accept SPs

In general, any type of verb can accept at least one type of SP, including copula verbs (108a) and complex transitive verbs with obligatory predicative complements (108b):

(108) a. Ioana e mai drăguță **blondă**
Ioana is more cute.F.SG blonde.F.SG
'Ioana is cuter (as a) blonde'

b. L-au uns domn **tânăr**
CL.ACC.M.3SG=have enthroned ruler young.M.SG
'They anointed him as lord when he was young'

Some classes of verbs more frequently take SPs whose semantic subject is the direct object of the main verb: some perception verbs (*auzi* 'hear', *simți* 'feel', *vedea* 'see'), the verbs which denote cognitive processes (*a-și aminti* 'remember', *crede* 'believe', *cunoaște* 'know', *imagina* 'imagine', *recunoaște* 'recognize', *ști* 'know'), doubt (*bănui* 'suspect', *suspecta* 'suspect'), volition (*dori* 'want', *prefera* 'prefer', *vrea* 'want'), appreciation (*considera* 'consider'), presentational verbs (*arăta* 'show', *prezenta* 'present'), verbs like *avea* 'have', *mânca* 'eat', and *bea* 'drink'.

The main verb can be finite or non-finite, in the active or passive voice (including reflexive passives):

(109) a. Suspecții sunt cunoscuți **cu antecedente penale**
suspect.M.PL are known.M.PL with antecedents penal
'The suspects are known to have criminal records'

b. Măsurile luate s-au dovedit **ineficiente**
measure.F.PL.DEF taken.F.PL CL.REFL.PASS=have proved inefficient.F.PL
'The measures taken proved to be inefficient'

If the main verb is transitive, the subject of the depictive SP can be the subject or the direct object of the main verb (within the confines of agreement) (110a,b). For some verbs, the preferred reading is the latter ((111a); see also §2.3.3.1):

(110) a. L-am întâlnit pe Ion **supărat**
CL.ACC.M.3SG=have.1SG met PE Ion upset
'I met Ion when I / he was upset'

b. Am cunoscut-o pe Ioana **tânără**
have.1SG known=CL.ACC.F.3SG PE Ioana young.F.SG
'I met Ioana when I / she was young'

(111) a. Am văzut-o pe Ioana **supărată**
have.1SG seen=CL.ACC.F.3SG PE Ioana upset.F.SG
'Ioana was upset when I saw her' (instead of 'I was upset when I saw Ioana')

vs. b. Am privit-o pe Ioana **supărată**
have.1SG looked=CL.ACC.F.3SG PE Ioana upset.F.SG
'I looked at Ioana upset'

10.4.4 Types of constituents occurring as SPs

The prototypical constituent occurring as an SP is the AP (see example (97) above). Secondary predicates can also be PPs (112), NPs with a non-referential, property reading (113), nominative or genitive DPs (114), pronouns (115a,b), AdvPs (116), non-finite clauses (117), CPs (118), and *wh*-clauses (119):

(112) Mi-am   imaginat-o   **cu   pălărie**
       CL.REFL.DAT.1SG=have.1SG   imagined=CL.ACC.F.3SG   with   hat
       'I imagined her with a hat'

(113) Ion a   plecat în Spania **muncitor necalificat**
       Ion has left   in Spain   worker   unqualified
       'Ion left for Spain to work as an unqualified worker'

(114) a. Nu mi-l   imaginam **bărbatul** care a   devenit ulterior
          not CL.REFL.DAT.1SG=CL.ACC.M.3SG imagined man.DEF   which has become later
          'I did not imagine him to be the man that he became later'

       b. Casa   o   ştiam **a**   **bunicii**
          house.F.SG.DEF   CL.ACC.F.3SG   knew   AL.F.SG   grandmother.DEF.GEN
          'I knew the house was my grandmother's'

(115) a. Nu   eşti   profetul   **care** te   crezi
          not are.2SG prophet.DEF   which   CL.REFL.ACC   believe.2SG
          'You are not the prophet you think you are'

       b. **Cine** se   crede   el?
          who   CL.REFL.ACC.3SG believes   he
          'Who does he think he is?'

(116) Pe Ion şi   Maria i-am   văzut **împreună**
       PE Ion and Maria CL.ACC.3PL=have.1SG   seen   together
       'I saw Ion and Maria together'

(117) a. L-am   văzut **fumând**
          CL.ACC.3SG=have.1SG seen   smoking
          'I saw him smoking'

       b. Pe Maria o   credeau   **de**   **măritat**
          PE Maria CL.ACC.F.3SG believe.IMPERF.3PL DE_SUP marry.SUP
          'They thought it was the right time for Maria to get married'

       c. Am   găsit-o   **plânsă** toată
          have.1SG found=CL.ACC.F.3SG   cried.F.SG all.F.SG
          'I found her all in tears'

       d. Îl   consider   **a**   **fi**   cel mai   potrivit   pentru
          CL.ACC.M.3SG   consider.1SG   A_INF   be.INF   CEL more appropriate for
          această   slujbă
          this   job
          'I consider him the most appropriate for this job'

(118) Îl   bănuiam   **că**   bea
       CL.ACC.M.3SG   suspected.1SG that   drinks
       'I suspected him of drinking'

(119) O   ştiu   **ce**   **persoană** **serioasă** e
       CL.ACC.F.3SG   know.1SG   what   person   serious   is
       'I know what a serious person she is'

H In contemporary Romanian, only the infinitive of the verb *a fi* can be an SP. In the 19th century, under the influence of French, other infinitives could also occur as SPs:

(120) vedem   ideea   de   unitate   **a**   **se**   **arăta**   (Bălcescu)
      see.1PL   idea.DEF   of   unity   A_INF   CL.REFL.ACC.3SG   show
      'we see the idea of unity forming'

Some SPs are formed with a preposition or a fixed prepositional sequence denoting the quality—most commonly *ca*, but also *de* (mostly colloquially), *drept* or *în calitate de* 'as':

(121) a. Ion lucrează în Spania **ca** **profesor** de muzică
         Ion works   in Spain   as   teacher   of music
         'Ion works in Spain as a music teacher'

   b. Ea   s-a   prezentat   **drept** **Violeta** **Popescu**
      she CL.REFL.ACC.3SG=has   presented   as   Violeta   Popescu
      'She introduced herself as Violeta Popescu'

   c. L-am   pierdut **de** **muşteriu**
      CL.ACC.M.3SG=have.1SG   lost   as   customer
      'We have lost him as a customer'

   d. Ion a   ţinut prima conferinţă de presă **în** **calitate** **de** **preşedinte**
      Ion has held   first conference of press in   quality   of   president
      'Ion held his first press conference as president'

These prepositions are not always interchangeable; some verbs accept only *de* or *ca*. For instance, in (121c) only *de* is possible. When the qualitative NP is preceded by the copula verb *fi*, in the gerund or in the infinitive, only *ca* is accepted:

(122) Lumea   te   percepe   **ca** *a*   *fi* /   *fiind*   o persoană vulnerabilă
      people.DEF CL.ACC.2SG   perceives   as   A_INF   be.INF   be.GER   a person   vulnerable
      'People perceive you as a vulnerable person'

PPs headed by *ca* can take a gerund as a complement, most frequently of the verbs *fi* or *avea*. It is the only context in Romanian where a preposition can have a gerund as a complement (§4.5.4.4):

(123) a. O   ştiam **ca fiind** una dintre cele mai   apreciate   profesoare
         CL.ACC.F.3SG   knew   as be.GER   one of   CEL   more appreciated teachers
         'I knew her to be one of the most appreciated teachers'

   b. Nucile   sunt   cunoscute   **ca** **având**   multe vitamine
      walnut.F.PL.DEF are   known.F.PL   as   having.GER many   vitamins
      'Walnuts are known as having many vitamins'

10.5 COMPARATIVE CONSTRUCTIONS

10.5.1 Comparatives of inequality and equality

Comparative structures are licensed by gradable predicates (adjectival and adverbial heads) and have a high degree of complexity, because they are based on clausal ellipsis and on syntactic reorganization.

The main types of comparison are the comparison of inequality (quantitative) and of equality (predominantly quantitative, but also qualitative).

This construction includes a comparative complement headed by an adjective or an adverb in the comparative degree (§7.4), licensed by the comparative marker.

10.5.1.1 Comparison of inequality

The (degree and) comparative markers which license the comparison of inequality are *mai* 'more' and *mai puțin* 'less'. The quantitative comparison expresses the common property of the compared entities, and can even specify the difference (by means of a measure adjunct):

(124)   Scândura este **(cu 2 centimetri) mai lungă decât ușa**
'The board is (two centimetres) longer than the door'

The prototypical comparator (connector) of inequality is *decât* 'than', which is, to a certain extent, in competition with *ca* (see §10.5.1.4.2).

10.5.1.2 Comparison of equality

Comparison of equality is less grammaticalized than the comparison of inequality: this structure displays a number of synonymous degree markers (*la fel de, tot așa de, tot atât de* 'as'), whose presence is optional and emphatic:

(125)   Ciuperca   e   **(tot așa de)** mare ca o   umbrelă
        mushroom.DEF   is as   big   as an umbrella
        'The mushroom is as big as an umbrella'

The main comparator is *ca* 'as', but there is a rich series of similar connectors: *precum* 'like', *cât* 'as much as', *cum* 'how / as', (more rarely) *aidoma* 'just like'.

10.5.1.3 The structure of the comparative complement

The comparative construction can contain all the components of the comparison, except for the gradable predicate, which is not repeated. The elements which encode the semantic differentiation of the comparison are preserved from the reduced clause.

The complement can be a finite verb clause or a reduced clause or, in the most fixed pattern of reorganization, a prepositional phrase (headed by a comparator).

The clausal realization is specific to the more complex comparisons (in which there are many different constituents), or to emphatic structures:

(126)   a. Am ajuns acum cu mașina **mai repede decât am ajuns [repede] atunci cu trenul**
        'Now I arrived by car quicker than I arrived then by train'
        b. Sunt **mai bucuros azi   decât   erai   tu   [bucuros] ieri**
           (I)am more happy   today   than   be.IMPERF   you.NOM   happy   yesterday
           'I am happier today than you were yesterday'
        c. Sunt **la fel de bucuros cum   ești   tu   [bucuros]**
           (I)am as   happy   as   are   you.NOM   happy
           'I am as happy as you are'

The components of the reduced clause are syntactically realized as adverbial phrases (127a), as prepositional phrases (127b), as noun phrases (127c), or as sequences of different constituents (127d):

(127) a. Sunt mai bucuros **decât ieri**
'I am happier than yesterday'
b. Alergam mai repede **decât pe stadion**
'I was running faster than in the stadium'
c. Îmi merge mai bine **decât prietenei tale**
'It's going much better for me than for your friend'
d. Am ajuns acum cu mașina mai repede **decât atunci cu trenul**
'Now I arrived by car quicker than I arrived then by train'

The comparators (*decât* 'than', *ca* 'as; than', *cât* 'as much as', *precum* 'like') have a complex behaviour: they are comparative connectors, prepositions and (except *ca*) conjunctions. They assign case only to the subject of the reduced comparative clause.

Nominal remnants of the reduced clause can have the same case as the compared term (128a), in *derived-case comparatives* (Stassen 2005), or (as ex-subjects) they become complements of the comparator, and are assigned accusative case, in *fixed-case comparatives* (128b):

(128) a. Mi-a   fost   mai   bun   prieten   **mie**   **decât**   **țîe**
       CL.DAT.1SG=has   been   more good   friend   me.DAT   than   you.DAT
       'He was a better friend to me than to you'
b. **Eu**   sunt   mai   bun   **decât**   **tine**
   I.NOM   am   more   good   than   you.ACC
   'I am better than you'

C Latin also allowed both types of comparative structures, but with other syntactic restrictions. In Romanian, the fixed-case comparatives are the result of a process of grammaticalization, by which some comparators, originally subordinating conjunctions, became prepositions, assigning accusative case: *decât tine*$_{\text{ACC}}$.

When a complex comparative construction occurs, including, besides the subject, other constituents, two configurations are possible (Van Peteghem 2009): a hybrid one, in which the noun or pronoun is assigned the accusative (129a), and a purely elliptical one, with a noun or pronoun in the nominative (129b):

(129) a. (Eu)   sunt   mai   bucuros   azi   decât   **tine**   ieri
       I   am   more   happy   today   than   you.ACC   yesterday
b. Eu   sunt   mai   bucuros   azi   decât   **tu**   ieri
   I   am   more   happy   today   than   you.NOM   yesterday
   'I am happier today than you were yesterday'

When comparison is headed by a manner adverbial, the direct object of the reduced clause can receive (130a) or not (130b) the marker PE, with a function of disambiguation, irrespective of the presence of the marker in the compared term:

(130) a. Îngrijește   **casa**   mai   bine   decât   **pe**   o   **floare**
       takes-care   house.DEF   more   well   than   PE   a   flower.ACC
       '(S)he takes care of the house better than (s)he does of a flower'
b. Citește   **teza**   mai   repede   decât   **un**   **roman**   **polițist**
   reads   thesis.DEF   more   quickly   than   a   novel.ACC   police(ADJ)
   '(S)he reads the thesis quicker than a detective novel'

The adverbs that are part of impersonal evaluative structures can take a comparative complement realized as an infinitival or subjunctive clause:

(131) a. E   mai   greu   a   face   decât a   spune
         is   more hard   A_INF   do.INF   than   A_INF   say.INF
         'It is harder to do than to say'

   b. Mai   bine   să   greșești   decât   să   nu   faci   nimic
      more   well   SĂ_SUBJ   mistake.SUBJ.2SG   than   SĂ_SUBJ   not   do.SUBJ.2SG   nothing
      'It is better to make a mistake than to do nothing'

The comparative complement can be a modalized expression, often elliptical (only the modal verb is preserved):

(132) Prețul   e   mai   mare decât ar   trebui   (să   fie)
      price.DEF   is   more   big   than   AUX.COND.3SG   must.INF SĂ_SUBJ   be.SUBJ.3SG
      'The price is bigger than it should be'

Reducing a sentence can create syntactic ambiguities, when the comparison refers to different predicates within the compared sentence:

(133) Ana are o soră mai frumoasă **decât Maria**
   a. decât   este   Maria   frumoasă
      than   is   Maria   beautiful
      'Ana has a sister more beautiful than Maria'
   b. decât   are   Maria   o soră
      than   has   Maria   a sister
      'Ana has a sister more beautiful than Maria's sister'

10.5.1.4 The comparators

10.5.1.4.1 *Decât* is specialized for the comparison of inequality and it is multifunctional: it functions as a clausal connector introducing a clausal comparative (126a,b), as a comparator for *derived-case comparatives*, introducing remnants of the clause (127a–d, 128a, 129b), and as a preposition which assigns the accusative case to the head noun (the former subject of the clause) in the derived structure (128b); some uses are hybrid (129a).

H *Decât* is made up of the preposition *de* 'of' + the relative element *cât* 'how much'. In the 16th century, the comparison of inequality often occurred with the comparative connector *de* 'than' (134a), in competition with *decât* 'than' (134b):

(134) a. mai mare *de* toți oamenii   (Coresi)
         'greater than all the people'
   b. mai dulci *decât* miearea   (Coresi)
      'sweeter than honey'

In the 17th–18th centuries, *decât* gradually became more frequent (Ciobanu 2007: 170; Frâncu 2009: 198), completely replacing *de*. In present-day Romanian, *de* is preserved in fixed structures (*mai presus de* 'above') and in numerical expressions:

(135) mai mult de 2 ore
       'more than two hours'

Decât as a clausal connector can still be analysed (into a relative element, *de*, and a quantitative component, *cât*, Cornilescu 2008). The similar comparative marker *de cum* 'than' is even less grammaticalized, behaving as an exclusively clausal connector:
(136) mai bine *de cum* credeam
'better than I thought'

10.5.1.4.2 The main comparative connector of equality is *ca* 'as'. *Ca* is grammaticalized as a preposition, assigning accusative (137a), but functions as an comparator for *derived-case comparatives* too (137b,c); unlike *decât*, in complex structures which are reduced clauses, *ca* only allows hybrid constructions in which the former subject (bearing the accusative) co-occurs with another constituent (137d), but not with a nominative case form (137e). *Ca* does not function a clausal connector (137f).

(137) a. Eşti   (tot atât de) deştept **ca mine**
         (you)are   as   smart   as me.ACC
         'You are as smart as me'
    b. Îţi   e (la fel de) frig **ca mie**
       CL.DAT.2SG is as   cold as me.DAT
       'You are as cold as me'
    c. Te   sperie (tot aşa de) tare **ca pe mine**
       CL.ACC.2SG scares as   much as PE me.ACC
       'It scares you as much as me'
    d. Azi   sunt   (la fel de) bucuros **ca tine**   ieri
       today (I)am as   happy   as you.ACC yesterday
       'Today I am as happy as you were yesterday'
    e. *Azi   sunt   (la fel de) bucuros **ca tu**   ieri
       today (I)am as   happy   as you.NOM yesterday
    f. *Azi   sunt   (la fel de) bucuros **ca erai   tu**   ieri
       today (I)am as   happy   as be.IMPERF.2SG you.NOM yesterday

Complementarily, *cum* 'as' occurs only as a clausal connector and is never prepositional:

(138) a. Sunt (la fel de) bucuros **cum erai tu**
         'I am as happy as you were'
    b. *Sunt (la fel de) bucuros **cum tu**

The comparative connector *ca* 'than' is used for the comparison of inequality too; it occurs in the same contexts as *decât* 'than' (except for the case in which the comparing element is a clause with an expressed verb):

(139) Eşti   mai   deştept **ca   mine**
      (you)are more smart   than me.ACC
      'You are smarter than me'

H *Ca* 'than, as' comes from the Lat. QUAM. In old Romanian, *ca* was specific for the comparison of equality; it could also take a clause as its complement:
  (140) a. tare **ca o grăunţă de muştari**   (Coresi)
          'hard as a mustard seed'
       b. **Ca este tatăl,**   aşa şi   fiiul   (*Psaltirea Scheianǎ*)
          as is   father.DEF so   also   son.DEF
          'Like father, like son'

Its occurrence in the comparison of inequality does not seem to directly continue the situation in Latin, but it is likely to be a later re-expansion, attested since the 17th century (DA, s.v. *ca*); see Frâncu 1979. The present-day norm accepts this use (Avram 2001: 122), although in the standard language *decât* tends to become specialized for the comparison of inequality and *ca* for equality).

Other operators are *cât* 'as much as' and *precum* 'like', which function both as clausal connectors, taking a clause as their complement, and as case-assigning prepositions; *cât* is, however, rarely used as a clausal connector, and *precum*—rarely as a preposition:

(141) a. tot atât de mic cât ar fi un purice
just as little as AUX.COND.3SG be.INF a flee
'as small as a flee'

b. tot atât de mic cât tine
just as little as you.ACC
'as little as you'

c. la fel de tânăr precum sunt colegii lui
as young as are.3PL colleagues his.GEN
'as young as his colleagues'

d. la fel de tânăr precum mine
as young as me.ACC

10.5.1.5 *Word order*

10.5.1.5.1 Generally, the comparative structure immediately follows the adjectival or adverbial head. However, (when topicalized) the adjective in the predicative complement position allows the comparative complement to be placed at a distance from it (142a,b). Comparative adverbial phrases have a freer word order (142c,d). The comparative complement of the quantifiers *mult* 'much' and *puțin* 'little' is placed after the quantified noun phrase and takes scope over it as a whole (142e,f):

(142) a. Mai important e omul decât opera
more important is man.DEF than work.DEF
'Man is more important than his work'

b. La fel de important e omul ca și opera
as important is man.DEF as also work.DEF
'The man is as important as his work'

c. Mai tare sună toba decât chitara
more loud sounds drum.DEF than guitar.DEF
'The drum sounds louder than the guitar'

d. La fel de mult îmi place supa ca și ciorba
as much CL.DAT.1SG likes soup.DEF as also sour-soup.DEF
'I like soup as much as ciorba'

e. Are mai multe calități decât defecte
has more many qualities than defects
'(S)he has more qualities than defects'

  f. Vin   la fel de   mulți   oameni   câți   am   invitat
    come.3PL   as   many   men   as   (I)have   invited
    'There are coming as many people as I invited'

H   In old Romanian the comparative sequence could precede the head:
   (143)   acel   ce   în   oaste   e   **decât toți mai**   tare   (Alexandrescu)
       that   which   in   army   is   than   all   more   strong
       'the one that is the strongest in the army'

C   According to the typological parameter for word order of constituents of comparative structures (Crookston 1999), Romanian displays the predominant order adjective / adverb + comparative connector + reference point (*mai bun* 'better' + *decât* 'than'+ *el* 'him'), as expected for SVO and VSO languages; what is specific to Romanian is the greater freedom of placement of the *connector + reference point* construction.

10.5.1.5.2 The comparative complement of equality generally occurs immediately after the head adjective or adverb (144a); there is also a variant of this comparative structure with the complement occurring in quantifier (intensifier) position, preposed and connected to its head by DE (144b):

(144)   a. Movila   e   mare   **cât**   **casa**
      heap.DEF   is   big   as   house.DEF
    b. Movila   e   **cât**   **casa**   **de**   mare
      hillock.DEF   is   as   house.DEF   DE   big
    'The hillock is as big as the house'

In comparatives of equality, the comparative connector can be preceded by the focusing particles such as *tocmai* 'precisely', *la fel* 'identically', *exact* 'exactly', etc. placed to its left (145a). A supplementary focalization (often disambiguating) is realized through the particle *și*, placed after the connectors *ca* 'as', *cât* 'as much as', *precum* 'like', which take the form *ca și* (145b), *cât și*, *precum și*:

(145)   a. mic   exact   **cât**   **un**   **purice**
      little   exactly   as   a   flee
    b. la fel de   mic   **ca**   **și**   **puricele**
      as   little   as   also   flee.DEF
    'as small as a flee'

In this structure, the markers of the comparison of equality, which emphasize the comparison—*tot atât (de)* 'just so' / *tot așa (de)* 'just so' / *la fel (de)* 'identical'—can occur not only as quantifiers of the adjective or adverb, but may also be preposed to the comparator:

(146)   a. Cafeaua   e   la fel   de   bună   **ca**   **ceaiul**
      coffee.DEF   is   identical   DE   good   as   tea.DEF
    b. Cafeaua   e   la fel   **ca**   **ceaiul**   de   bună
      coffee.DEF   is   identical   as   tea.DEF   DE   good
    'Coffee is as good as tea'

10.5.1.5.3 Comparators impose certain word order constraints: the noun to which they assign case is obligatorily adjacent to them (147a), and the sentence preserves the word order of the relative (comparative) clause—introduced by *(de)cât, (pre)cum*—with the subject being placed postverbally (147b):

(147) a. (El)   vorbise   despre reguli mai   mult decât **mine**
         he   speak.PLUPERF.3SG   about   rules   more much than   me.ACC
         despre excepţii
         about   exceptions
         'He had spoken about rules more than I had about exceptions'

   b. Am   aşteptat mai   mult decât a   aşteptat **el**
      (I)have   waited   more much than   has   waited   he.NOM
      'I waited more than him'

10.5.1.6 Semantic aspects

The term of comparison can be the prototype of a quality; in this case, the comparison enters the domain of quantification and induces a superlative reading (148a,b). The term of comparison can also be ambiguous, contextually identifiable (148c); in this case, the comparison has a slightly quantifying role:

(148) a. alb ca zăpada
         '(as) white as snow'
   b. limpede ca ziua
      '(as) clear as daylight'
   c. bun ca Ion
      'as good as Ion'

10.5.2 Other comparative structures

10.5.2.1 The 'proportional' structures equate two scalar predicates and obligatorily contain a correlative element (*pe cât... pe atât; cu cât... cu atât*):

(149) a. E   un lucru pe cât de dificil,   pe atât de necesar
         is   a   thing how   difficult   as much   necessary
         'It is just as difficult a thing as it is necessary'

   b. Cu   cât   e   mai   dificil   lucrul,   cu   atât   e   mai   necesar
      with how is more   difficult thing.DEF   with   as-much   is more   necessary
      'The more difficult (a thing is), the more necessary (it is)'

10.5.2.2 Non-scalar equating comparison can be expressed by the identity determiner *acelaşi* ('the same') and the comparator *ca* (in focalized structures *ca şi*; in some structures, *cu*); see also §5.3.1.3.4:

(150) a. Gardul   are   aceeaşi   lungime   ca   grădina
         fence.DEF has   the-same   length   as   garden.DEF

b. Gardul   este   de   aceeași   lungime   cu   grădina
   fence.DEF is   DE   the-same length   with   garden.DEF
   'The fence has the same length as the garden'

Non-scalar non-identity comparison uses the alternative determiner *alt(ul)* and the comparator *decât* (§5.3.1.3.4):

(151) altul decât el
       '(some) other than him'

10.5.2.3 A comparison which does not syntactically depend on a degree marker can enter very different syntactic structures, outside of the adjectival and adverbial phrase: manner adjunct (152a), modifier in the nominal phrase (152b), subjective predicative complement (152c), etc.:

(152) a. Ne   plimbăm   cum   vă   plimbați   și   voi
         CL.REFL.ACC.1PL walk.1PL how   CL.REFL.ACC.2PL   walk.2PL   also   you.PL
         'We walk as you walk'
      b. A   fost   o   zi   ca   oricare   alta
         has been   a   day   like   any   other
         'It was a day like any other day'
      c. Pâinea   e   ca   o   piatră
         bread.DEF is   like a   stone
         'The bread is like a stone'

10.5.2.4 The superlative structure can receive a prepositional complement which encodes the domain of the comparison:

(153) a. E cel mai bun **din lume**
         'It is the best in the world'
      b. Înoată cel mai bine **dintre noi toți**
         'He swims the best of all of us'

CONCLUSIONS

1 Romanian complementizers are always overt. Deletion is allowed only for the second complementizer of two coordinated IPs, if they share the same C-head.

Selection of complementizers is determined either syntactically or semantico-syntactically.

Unlike the subjunctive in other Romance languages, the Romanian subjunctive is not exclusively affixal, but it involves the presence of an independent particle (*să*), as in some Balkan languages. Selection of *să* is strongly related to the semantic conditions of occurrence for the subjunctive (a mix of Romance and Balkan features). The syntactic status of *să* is ambiguous. It exhibits both Comp and Infl features.

Romanian is one of those Romance languages with a dual system of complementizers, which are able to exploit the whole C-domain, before or after topicalized or focalized constituents. A special case is the complementizer *ca... să*, which simultaneously expresses two positions: *Force* and *Fin*.

The prototypical complementizers in Romanian are *că*, *să*, *ca... să*, and *dacă*. Besides them, other connectors are employed: the multifunctional complementizer *de* and a series of grammaticalized collocations (*cum că*, *precum că*, *cum de*), specialized as supplementary markers (besides the modal ones) for expressing the speaker's commitment towards the truth of the argument clause or specialized in a certain stylistic register.

All kinds of argument clauses can be introduced by complementizers, except for the clausal indirect object, which is always a headless relative clause.

2 In contemporary Romanian, not all the adjuncts can be realized as subordinate clauses.

Note the large number of multifunctional non-specific subordinators and the lesser number of specific subordinators. Certain clausal adjuncts require or allow the occurrence of connective adjuncts in the matrix. The presence of connectives helps distinguish clausal adjuncts introduced by multifunctional subordinators. Alongside conjunctions, there are numerous complex sequences (collocations) functioning as subordinators.

The verbs of the subordinate clause usually do not show tense and mood constraints although reason and the quantity adjuncts do not allow the subjunctive while verbs in temporal posteriority adjuncts, introduced by the subordinator *până* 'until', and in the protoypical purpose adjunct, are in the subjunctive. Only if they are introduced by the conjunction *de* (with an intermediate status between coordinator and subordinator) are their verbs in the indicative or imperative.

Alongside the symmetry of the verbal forms in the two clauses which form conditional and concessive constructions, two peculiarities regarding *irrealis* configurations should be noticed: the use of the imperfect indicative and the presence of asymmetric structures with the structure [perfect conditional + imperfect indicative].

Adjuncts generally display free word order, but postposition is preferred, while there are some adjuncts which have fixed word order (either preposed or postposed to the matrix clause).

3 Movement of the *wh*-word together with the phrase in which it is embedded is obligatory, both in relative clauses and in indirect questions. The presence of the relative word is also obligatory. Cases of omission are marginal and are strictly semantically conditioned.

In headless relative clauses, the *wh*-word accommodates to the constraints of the syntactic phrase to which it belongs, so that its case inflection could be different from that required by its syntactic position in the subordinate clause.

Romanian has preserved relative infinitival constructions, originating in the Latin imperfect subjunctive. The infinitival construction is in free variation with the subjunctive construction, unlike other Romance languages, which allow only one of the variants.

The clefting strategy is possible only in pseudo-cleft patterns.

Certain relative connectors have lost their relativizer features, becoming multifunctional subordinators.

4 Structures with SPs show great syntactic variety. Verbs which accept SPs are quite numerous and diverse. Descriptive SPs are much more frequent than resultative SPs. Many types of constituents can be SPs, but the most frequent are APs, PPs, and DPs denoting a quality or a property. The subject of the SPs is coreferential with an argument or, less frequently, with an adjunct of the main predicate.

5 Romanian has comparative connectors which allow derived-case comparatives and assign case to the subject of the derived comparative clause, as happens in fixed-case comparatives.

For comparison of inequality, the multifunctional connector *decât* 'than' is employed, which functions both as a preposition and as a subordinating conjunction. The comparison of equality also has multifunctional connectors (*cât* 'as', *precum* 'like'), but more frequently resorts to distinct means for the two constructions: the preposition *ca* 'as' and the subordinating conjunction *cum* 'as'. Multifunctional connectors come from relative words and preserve some of their properties.

The structures that express the comparison of equality are not completely grammaticalized and frequently do not express the comparative markers.

The prevailing order in comparative structures is head + comparative connector + reference point. However, the comparative complement has a relatively free order, allowing topicalization.

11

Coordination

In this chapter, we describe the semantic types of coordination in Romanian, the coordinators that express them and their syntactic or semantic characteristics. Prototypically, by coordination the same syntactic position is extended by adding a complement of the same type, an adjunct of a certain type, etc. The resulting conjuncts belong to the same semantic type (for instance, a qualifying adjective cannot be coordinated with a classifying one). In general, each of the conjuncts can occupy the same syntactic position alone, with some adjustments involving agreement or anaphoric terms.

11.1 SEMANTIC (AND LOGICAL) TYPES OF COORDINATION

Traditionally, four semantic types of coordination are described in Romanian grammars (GALR I: 638–9): conjunctive, disjunctive, adversative, and conclusive. The constraints on coordination and the conjuncts are restricted to a specific type of coordination.

11.1.1 Conjunctive coordination

11.1.1.1 Conjunctive coordinators

The prototypical conjunctive coordinator is *şi* 'and'. The coordinators *ca şi*, *precum şi* ('as well as') and *nici* ('nor') have a contrastive meaning, placing the focus on the conjunct they precede. The correlatives *şi... şi...*, *atât... cât şi...* ('both... and...'), *nici... nici...* ('neither... nor...') have a contrastive, focalizing meaning as well.

The most widespread coordinator is *şi*, which can link phrases and clauses. The coordinators *ca şi*, *precum şi*, and *nici* can link only clauses; correlatives *şi... şi...*, *atât..., cât şi...*, *nici... nici...* can link both phrases and clauses:

(1) a. **Şi** Ion, **şi** Maria au telefonat
    and Ion and Maria have phoned
    'Both Ion and Maria phoned'

 b. Ion nu a venit, **nici** nu a telefonat
    Ion not has come, neither not has phoned
    'Ion did not come, neither did he phone'

 c. **Nici** Ion, **nici** Maria nu au venit
    neither Ion neither Maria not have come
    'Neither Ion nor Maria came'

Nici is the equivalent of *şi* in negative sentences, when both clausal conjuncts are negative. The replacement of *şi* with *nici* in negative sentences is not obligatory so that the two coordinators may co-occur:

(2) Ion   nu   a   venit   și /   **nici** /   și   **nici**   nu   a
    Ion   not   has come   and   neither   and neither   not has
    telefonat   că   întârzie
    phoned   that is late
    'Ion didn't come, neither did he phone to say he was late'

If the conjoined phrase (ConjP) is the subject of the sentence, *și* can be followed by the comitative preposition *cu* 'with'. Sometimes, only *cu* marks the conjunctive coordination, even if the verb does not have a comitative or a reciprocal meaning. The element introduced by *cu* cannot be analysed as a fronted comitative adjunct, since it cannot be moved to a postverbal position:

(3) a. **Ion**   (și)   **cu**   Dan   au   telefonat   la   minister   să
       Ion   (and)   with   Dan   have phoned   at   ministry   să$_{\text{SUBJ}}$
       rezolve   problema
       solve.SUBJ   problem.DEF
       'Ion and Dan phoned the ministry to solve the problem'

    b. ***Ion**   a   telefonat   **cu**   Dan   la   minister...
        Ion   has   phoned   with   Dan   at   ministry...

With propositional conjuncts, conjunctive coordination can be pragmatically enriched with adversative (4a), conclusive or consecutive values (4b), resulting from the content of the conjuncts (not from the coordinator itself):

(4) a. Am   dat   zeci   de telefoane   și   n-am   rezolvat   nimic
       have.1SG   given   dozens of phone calls   and   not=have.1SG   solved   nothing
       'I made dozens of phone calls, but I didn't solve anything'

    b. A   lucrat   sub   presiune   și   a   făcut   greșeli
       has   worked   under   pressure   and   has   made   mistakes
       'He worked under pressure and he made mistakes'

Inherently reciprocal predicates (5a) and predicates with an inherently plural meaning (5b) do not accept ConjPs headed by correlatives as subjects:

(5) a. *Și   Ion,   și   Maria   **s-au**   **căsătorit** /   sunt   **vecini**
       and   Ion   and   Maria   CL.REFL.ACC.3PL=have   married   are   neighbours
       de   cinci   ani
       for   five   years

    b. *Și   ziua,   și   noaptea   **alternează**
       and   day.DEF   and   night.DEF   alternate

11.1.1.2 Joint vs. disjoint readings of coordinated conjunctive NPs or DPs

Coordinated NPs or DPs can have a joint reading (the conjuncts have the same referent) or a disjoint reading (the conjuncts have different referents). If ConjP has a joint reading, the definite article has to attach to every noun inside the ConjP. The indefinite article can appear before every conjunct or only once (its presence being determined by the syntactic context):

(6) a. coleg**ul**   și   priten**ul**   meu   [joint or disjoint reading]
       colleague.DEF   and   friend.DEF   my.SG
       'my colleague and friend / my colleague and my friend'

b. Invităm **un medic și profesor** universitar, Ion Popescu, să
invite.1PL a doctor and teacher academic Ion Popescu să.SUBJ
țină o conferință
hold.SUBJ a conference
'We invite a doctor and university teacher, Ion Popescu, to present a conference'

c. Maria este **o mamă și o soție** foarte bună
Maria is a mother and a wife very good.FEM
'Maria is a very good mother and wife'

Other determiners appear only once, before the whole ConjP with joint reading:

(7) acest / alt coleg și (*acest / *alt) prieten
this / other colleague and (this / other) friend
'this colleague and friend'

11.1.1.3 Pseudo-coordination

In pseudo-coordinated ConjPs, the conjunction *și* has the function of subordinator, linking two verbs which behave like a syntactic unit: the first verb is the equivalent of an injunction or has an aspectual value (for aspectual verbs in Romanian, see Guțu Romalo 1961).

Injunctive verbs are verbs of motion (*merge* 'go', *a se duce* 'go', *veni* 'come', *trece* 'pass'), the interjection *hai* 'let's' and the verb *lua* 'take' (8a). In these structures, *și* is equivalent to the conjunction *de* (§10.1.1.4):

The second imperative verb may be either followed (8b) or preceded (8c) by the reflexive clitic:

(8) a. Treci / vino / hai / ia și spală vasele!
pass.IMP.2SG come.IMP.2SG let's.INTERJ take.IMP.2SG and wash.IMP.2SG dishes.DEF
'Come and wash the dishes!'

b. Du-te și culcă-te!
go.IMP.2SG=CL.REFL.ACC.2SG and lie-down.IMP.2SG=CL.REFL.ACC.2SG

c. Du-te și te culcă!
go.IMP.2SG=CL.REFL.2SG and CL.REFL.2SG sleep.IMP.2SG
'Go to bed!'

Inherent aspectual verbs (*începe* 'begin', *a se apuca* 'begin', etc.) or contextually aspectual verbs (*sta* 'stay') can occur in these constructions:

(9) Începe / se apucă / stă
start.IND.PRES.3SG CL.REFL.ACC.3SG begin.IND.PRES.3SG stay.IND.PRES.3SG
și scrie
and write.IND.PRES.3SG
'He is writing / He starts writing'

With pseudo-coordinated ConjPs, both verbs have the same mood and tense, the order of the conjuncts cannot be changed, and the conjuncts cannot be linked by a correlative of the type *atât... cât și...* ('both...and...')(Johannessen 1998).

11.1.2 Disjunctive coordination

The prototypical disjunctive coordinators are *sau* 'or' and, slightly less frequently, *ori*. As correlatives, the coordinators *fie...fie...* ('either...or...') and, slightly less frequently, *sau....sau...*, *ori...ori...* are employed.

The disjunction can be exclusive (10a) (the primary meaning) or inclusive (10b). The latter meaning is derived from the first one. Usually, agreement can help differentiate between the two types:

(10) a. Ministrul   Muncii   va   fi   Ion sau George
        minister.DEF   work.DEF.GEN   AUX.FUT.3SG   be   Ion or   George
        'The Minister of Labour will be Ion or George'

  b. **Un deputat sau un senator** au   multe privilegii
     a   deputy   or   a   senator   have   many   privileges

With correlative disjunction, the exclusion is stronger than with the simple (non-correlative) disjunctive ConjP. Although correlative disjunctive ConjPs have an exclusive reading *per se* (11a), in certain contexts it is possible to derive a cumulative (i.e. inclusive) meaning by temporal adverbs of frequency (11b):

(11) a. **Fie   Ion, fie Dan**   va   ține   discursul
        either Ion   or   Dan   AUX.FUT.3SG   hold   discourse.DEF
        'Either Ion or Dan will deliver the speech'

  b. Diminețile   bea   **fie**   ceai, **fie** cafea
     mornings.DEF   drinks   either   tea   or   coffee
     'In the morning he drinks either tea or coffee'

A particular subtype of correlative disjunction is the so-called 'alternative' coordination, realized by correlative coordinators, such as *ba...ba...* (colloquial), *când...când...* (literally 'when...when...', meaning 'sometimes...sometimes...'). The term *alternative* points to the fact that conjuncts participate alternatively in the event(s) denoted by the verb; thus, the general meaning is cumulative, making alternative coordination an intermediate type, between disjunction and conjunction. The conjuncts are arguments (12a) or adjuncts (12b):

(12) a. Diminețile   bea   **ba**   **cafea,** **ba**   **ceai**
        mornings.DEF   drink.IND.PRES.3SG   now   coffee   then   tea
        'In the morning he drinks sometimes tea, sometimes coffee'

  b. Mergea   la   spital   **când**   **dimineața,**   **când**   **seara**
     go.IMPERF.3SG to   hospital   when   morning.DEF   when   evening.DEF
     '(S)he went to the hospital sometimes in the morning, sometimes in the evening'

11.1.3 Adversative coordination

The Romanian adversative system is organized on three levels (Niculescu 1965; Zafiu 2005), differentiated by the strength of the adversative relation, by the type of conjuncts and by the pragmatic and thematic context in which they are found. The strength of the adversative relation is more or less dependent on the context and on the meaning of the conjuncts, not necessarily derived from the meaning of the conjunction itself. These three types of adversative relations are associated with different conjunctions, which are not interchangeable—proof that the difference between the three types is not merely related to the intensity of the adversative relation, but that there are other pragmatic and thematic factors involved (Zafiu 2005). Generally speaking, the three types are: (A) contrast, (B) correction, and (C) thematic change:

A. The coordinators used to express contrast are the conjunction *dar* and the adverb *însă*, which can float inside the second conjunct. The first type of contrast is between the semantic content of the conjuncts. This contrast can be more or less subjective, related to the speaker's point of view:

(13) a. Produsul   e   scump,   **dar** nu   e   de   calitate
        product.DEF is   expensive but   not is   of   quality
        'The product is expensive but not of quality'

   b. Produsul   e   scump,   **însă** nu   e   **(însă)** de   calitate   **(însă)**
      product.DEF is   expensive but   not   is   but   of   quality   but

The second type of contrast is between the expectation expressed by the first conjunct and the argument expressed by the second conjunct (Zafiu 2005):

(14) Am   venit   mai   devreme, **dar/** **însă** nu   am   mai
     have.1SG   come   more   early   but   but   not   have.1SG   more
     găsit   pe   nimeni
     found   PE   nobody
     'I came earlier, but I didn't find anyone'

Dar and *însă* are semantically interchangeable, but *însă* is found more frequently in the literary than in the spoken language.

The conjuncts can be clauses or phrases, usually APs, AdvPs, PPs, in adjunct positions. NPs and DPs cannot be coordinated by *dar* and *însă*; what looks like DP adversative coordination is, in fact, clausal coordination involving gapping:

(15) Ar   trebui   să   cumpărăm   o   **maşină,** **dar** **nu**   o   **Dacia**—
     AUX.COND.3SG   must   SĂ_SUBJ   buy.SUBJ   a   car   but   not   a   Dacia
     dar   nu   o   [maşină]   Dacia
     but   not   a   car   Dacia
     'We should buy a car, but not a Dacia'

The coordination of categorially different constituents is possible, but the structures are, in fact, elliptical:

(16) Vreau   să   cumpăr   o   **maşină, dar nu scumpă**—... dar nu
     want.1SG   SĂ_SUBJ   buy.SUBJ.1SG   a   car   but not expensive   but not
     [o maşină]   scumpă
     a car   expensive
     'I want to buy a car, but not an expensive one'

B. The second conjunct corrects and substitutes a hypothesis expressed by the first conjunct, which is overtly negated; the coordinator specialized for this type of adversative relation is the conjunction *ci*:

(17) Nu plec   mâine,   **ci** peste trei zile
     not leave.1SG tomorrow but after three days
     'I'm not leaving tomorrow, but in three days'

The negated element in the first conjunct can be the predicate, an argument (18a) or an adjunct (18b). The presence of clausal or constituent negation in the first conjunct is obligatory:

(18) a. **Nu Ion** a   venit, **ci** Dan
        not Ion has come but   Dan
        'It wasn't Ion that came, but Dan'

   b. Plec   **nu** **mâine**,   **ci**   **vineri**
      leave.1SG not tomorrow but   Friday
      'I'm leaving not tomorrow, but Friday'

The opposite correction is expressed by *şi nu* 'and not'; in this case, the order of the conjuncts is reversed, and the rejected hypothesis is in second position. This type of coordination is possible only when the correction applies to arguments or adjuncts of the clause (19a), not to the predicate (19b):

(19) a. Vine   Dan, **şi** **nu** Ion
        come.3SG Dan and not Ion
        'Dan comes, not Ion'

   b. *Ion a   rămas   acasă, **şi** **nu** a   venit
       Ion has remained home   and not has come
       'What Ion did was stay at home, not come'

A particular subtype of correction is expressed by the correlative *nu numai / nu doar... ci şi / dar şi...* ('not only... but also...'), with the conjunctions *dar* and *ci* being interchangeable. The first conjunct negates or rejects a hypothesis and the second conjunct expresses a correction of the hypothesis and an addition. The general meaning is a cumulative one, as this type of ConjP could be equivalent with a ConjP coordinated by *atât... cât şi...* ('both... and...').

(20) a. Maria este **nu** **numai /** **nu** **doar** o profesoară, **dar** **şi**
        Maria is   not   only   not   only   a teacher   but   and
        o cercetătoare   foarte buna
        a researcher   very   good
        'Maria is not only a very good teacher, but also a very good researcher'

   b. **Nu** **numai /** **Nu** **doar** Maria, **ci** **şi** Ion a   venit
      not   only   not   only   Maria but and Ion has come
      'Not only Maria but also Ion came'

Nu numai... ci şi / dar şi... coordinates phrases or clauses with obligatory gapping (21a). By contrast, *nu numai că..., dar...* can coordinate clauses without gapping (21b):

(21) a. Nu numai Ion a   lipsit,   dar şi   Gheorghe (*a întârziat)
        not only Ion has been absent but also Gheorghe (has been-late)

   b. Nu numai că   Ion a   plecat, dar şi   Gheorghe a   întârziat
      not only that Ion has left   but also Gheorghe has been-late
      'Not only did Ion leave, but Gheorghe was late'

C. In the third type of adversative relation, the second conjunct expresses thematic contrast, signalling the fact that the theme of the sentence has changed; the conjunction *iar* is specialized for this type of relation. The adversative meaning of *iar* is very weak; this type of coordination is often described as an intermediate one, between conjunctive and adversative (Niculescu 1965: 104):

(22) Ion merge la cinema, **iar** Andrei la teatru
     Ion goes to cinema but / and Andrei to theatre

C Romance languages fall into two large groups, according to the adversative relations that they express: Romanian and Spanish, like Latin, have two types of adversative relations, contrast (Sp. *pero*, Rom. *dar*, *însă*) vs. correction (Sp. *sino*, Rom. *ci*), while French and Italian have one type (Zafiu 2010). Moreover, Romanian has a third type of adversative relation, not found in the other Romance languages (Niculescu 1965: 100–6). Other Romance languages do not have a coordinator specialized for a minimal adversative relation like the Rom. *iar*. For the first two types of adversative relations, other Romance languages use descendants of Lat. MAGIS 'more' (Sp. *más*, Fr. *mais*, It. *ma*, Ptg. *mes*, Prov. *mas*, Cat. *mes*) or other conjunctions. Romanian did not inherit the Latin adverb MAGIS as a marker of the adversative relation (Niculescu 1965: 102).

U In the spoken language, some speakers mark the adversative relation pleonastically with *dar însă*, another argument for taking *însă* to be an adverb rather than a conjunction.

It is possible to concatenate two adversative conjuncts, as long as they involve different types of adversative relations:

(23) Am   cumpărat o maşină, **dar** nu un Logan, **ci** o Skoda
     have.1SG bought   a car   but not a Logan but a Skoda
     'I bought a car, not a Logan, but a Skoda'

11.1.4 Conclusive coordination

Conclusive coordinators are adverbs and grammaticalized PPs, with full or partial lexical meaning. The most common is the adverb *deci*, followed by *aşadar* and *(care)vasăzică* 'so' (colloquial). Coordinative PPs with conclusive meaning are *prin urmare*, *în concluzie*, *în consecinţă*, *ca atare* 'therefore'. The conjuncts can be phrases or clauses:

(24) Ion,   **deci** / **prin   urmare**   şi   soţia   lui   ştiau   de
     Ion   so   through consequence and wife.DEF   his(GEN) knew.3PL   about
     plecările   de acasă ale   lui
     leaving.PL.DEF from home AL.PL   LUI.GEN Dan
     'Ion, and therefore also his wife, knew about Dan's departures from home'

H Romanian conjunctions are inherited from Latin: *şi* < adv. SIC, *nici* < conj. NEQUE, *însă* < pron. IPSA or IPSE or developed in Romanian: *sau* < conj. *să* + conj. *au* 'or' (< Lat. AUT), *fie* < vb. *(să) fie* (3rd person subjunctive form of *fi* 'be'), *ci* < pron. *ce* (< Lat. QUID), *aşadar* < adv. *aşa* 'so' + conj. *dar*, *deci* < preposition *de* + adv. *aci* (variant of *aici* 'here'). The etymology of conjunctions *iar*, *dar*, and *ori* is controversial, but most authors agree that they derive from Latin words (CDDE).

The disjunctive conjunction *au* is obsolete. It is attested in the written language until the beginning of the 19th century (Nedelcu 2012). The conjunctive conjunction *i*, borrowed from Slavic, was used in the administrative texts until the 19th century (Nedelcu 2012). The conjunctive conjunction *e* (< Lat. ET), attested in the 16th century, was lost in the following centuries (ELR: 142; Rizescu 2007: 195). Other conjunctions attested only in old Romanian are the disjunctive pairs *oare... oare* (*vare... vare...*, *veri... veri...*), a variant of *ori... ori...* (which comes from the Latin verb form VOLET; Toma 1978: 361–2), and *săva(i)... săva(i)* (ELR: 142).

Some coordinators can establish supplementary semantic or pragmatic relations between sentences (*și* 'and', *sau, ori* 'or', *dar, însă* 'but', *deci, așadar* 'so' etc.). The coordinator *or* (borrowed from Fr. *or*) is specialized for the adversative relations between sentences:

(25) Era sigur că va obține o notă foarte bună; **or**, așteptările lui nu s-au împlinit
  'He was sure that he would get a very good mark, but his expectations were not fulfilled'

11.2 RESTRICTIONS ON THE CONJUNCTS

Any syntactic position can be extended by conjunctive or disjunctive coordination. The coordination of different syntactic positions (Avram 1957) is possible especially if the conjuncts belong to certain morphological categories (adverbs of space, time, and manner (26a), indefinites (26b), *wh*-elements (26c)):

(26) a. Trebuie să   ne   oprim   **aici și   acum** / ***la Ploiești și**
        must   SĂ$_{SUBJ}$ CL.ACC.1PL stop.SUBJ.1PL here   and now   at Ploiești and
        peste o   oră
        in   one hour
        'We must stop here and now / at Ploiești and in one hour'

  b. Poți   slăbi mâncând **orice**   **și** **oricând** / ***legume** **și** **seara**!
     can.2SG slim eating   anything   and   anytime   vegetables and   evening.DEF
     'You can lose weight by eating anything anytime'

  c. Va   veni   **când** **și** **unde** îl   invită
     AUX.FUT.3SG come.INF   when   and   where   CL.ACC.3SG invite
     'He will come whenever and wherever they invite him'

Although the conjuncts are generally of the same syntactic category, co-ordination of different constituents is possible, as long as they occupy the same syntactic position:

(27) a. Tricoul   este larg   și   cu   dungi   orizontale   (AP and PP)
        T-shirt.DEF is   large and with   stripes horizontal

  b. De ziua   ei,   Maria   dorește o   mașină
     for birthday   her.GEN   Maria   wants   a   car
     nouă și   să   plece   într-o   croazieră pe Mediterană (DP and CP)
     new and SĂ$_{SUBJ}$ leave.SUBJ.3sg in=a   cruise   on Mediterranean
     'For her birthday Maria wants a new car and to go on a Mediterranean cruise'

The conjuncts can be prefixes (28) or prepositions (29), in contexts with ellipsis:

(28) terapie **pre-** **și** **postoperatorie**
      therapy   pre-   and   postsurgical

(29) Avem   pâine   cu   şi   fără   sare
     have.1PL bread with and   without   salt

A DP can be coordinated with a *wh*-interrogative word, if they have the same syntactic function and the interrogative word is not fronted. Often, the sentence is more acceptable if the interrogative word is preceded by the adverbial clitic *mai* 'more':

(30) a. **Maria şi mai cine** pleacă mâine?
        Maria and more who leaves tomorrow
        'Maria and who else leaves tomorrow?'
     b. Mergi **la Paris, la Londra şi mai unde**?
        go.2SG to Paris to London and more where
        'You go to Paris, London and where else?'
     c. Acolo i-ai   văzut **pe Ion, Dan, Maria şi pe mai cine**?
        There CL.ACC.3PL=have.2SG seen PE Ion Dan Maria and PE more who?
        'There you saw Ion, Dan, Maria and who else?'

Coordination cannot apply to clitics or determiners in the standard language.

11.3 THE STRUCTURE OF THE COORDINATED PHRASE

11.3.1 Number of conjuncts

The general, cross-linguistic distinction between binary and multiple ConjPs (Haspelmath 2007) is found in Romanian. Binary coordination involves: (i) correlative conjunctive ConjPs with *atât... cât şi...*; (ii) adversative ConjPs; (iii) conclusive ConjPs.

In binary ConjPs, each conjunct can contain a ConjP, the result being a layered ConjP, such as:

(31) a. [**atât**   [Ion   şi   Maria], **cât**   **şi**   [Dan   şi   Andreea]]
        [so-much [Ion   and   Maria]   as-much and   [Dan   and   Andreea]]
     b. [Ion e   inginer,   **dar**   [nu   are   loc   de   muncă   şi   nici   nu   caută]]
        [Ion is engineer but   [not has place of   work   and   neither not searches]]

The interpretation is sometimes ambiguous:

(32) a. Vor   participa   Ion şi   Paul sau Dan
        AUX.FUT.3PL participate Ion and   Paul or   Dan
     b. [[Ion şi Paul] sau Dan]   [*sau* 'or' has scope over *şi* 'and']
     c. [Ion şi [Paul sau Dan]]   [*şi* is higher in the structure and has scope over *sau*]

A conclusive ConjP can be followed by another conclusive conjunct, giving the impression of a multiple ConjP. In fact, the third conjunct stands in relation with the last conjunct of the first ConjP; therefore, the structure contains two binary ConjPs:

(33) Nu   am   găsit   bilete,   **deci**   trebuie   să   amânăm
     not have.1SG found   tickets so   must.3SG să_{SUBJ} postpone.SUBJ
     plecarea,   **deci** nu   vom   ajunge   la   timp
     leaving.DEF so   not AUX.FUT.1PL arrive.INF   at   time

With the exception of correlative ConjPs, the coordinator prototypically occurs only before the last conjunct. In emphatic contexts, the coordinator can occur before each conjunct, except the first (but not if there is a large number of conjuncts).

11.3.2 Juxtaposition

Usually, juxtaposition occurs in non-correlative ConjPs, where the coordinator precedes only the last conjunct. These ConjPs are conjunctive or disjunctive:

(34) a. Ar   putea   participa   **Ion, Gheorghe, Dan, Marius**...
         AUX.COND can.INF participate.INF Ion Gheorghe   Dan Marius
                                                    [two readings: conjunctive and disjunctive]
        'Ion, Gheorghe, Dan, and / or Marius could participate.'
    b. Vreți   o mașină **albă, roșie, albastră**...?
        want.2PL a car   white red   blue   [disjunctive interpretation]
        'Do you want a white, a red or a blue car?'

ConjPs in which juxtaposition is the only means of relating the conjuncts usually form lists.

11.3.3 Asymmetry between conjuncts

In most adversative ConjPs and in conclusive ConjP, the order of the conjuncts is not reversible, for semantic reasons. The order of conjuncts is also constrained in anaphoric contexts or by pragmatic relations between the conjuncts:

(35) a. Ion$_i$ și   nevasta lui$_i$ au   plecat vs. *Nevasta lui$_i$ și
        Ion   and   wife.DEF his(GEN) have.3PL   left   wife.DEF his(GEN) and
        Ion$_i$ au   plecat
        Ion   have.PL   left
        'Ion and his wife left.'
    b. Intri   pe   site   și   te   înscrii
        enter.2SG on   site   and CL.REFL.ACC.2SG   register.2SG
        'You go on the site and sign up'
        vs.   *Te   înscrii   și   intri   pe   site
                CL.REFL.ACC.2SG   register.2SG   and enter.2SG   on   site

11.4 CO-OCCURRENCE OF COORDINATORS

The conjuncts can be linked by more than one coordinator. Usually, these contexts involve: correlative ConjPs in which the linking coordinator (an adverb) is supplemented by *și* or *dar* (36a,b); conclusive ConjPs in which the conclusive coordinator *deci* (an adverb) is supplemented by *și* (37):

(36) a. **Și**   Ion,   **dar și**   Maria   au   contribuit   la
        and   Ion   but and   Maria   have   contributed   to
        realizarea   proiectului
        realization.DEF   project.DEF.GEN
        'Both Ion and Maria contributed to the realization of the project'

b. **Nici** Ion, **dar nici** Maria nu au contribuit
neither Ion but neither Maria not have.3PL contributed
la realizarea proiectului
to realization.DEF project.DEF.GEN
'Neither Ion nor Maria contributed to the realization of the project'

(37) N-a învăţat cât trebuie **şi deci** n-a luat examenul
not=has studied how-much must.3SG and so not=has taken exam.DEF
'He hasn't studied as much as he had to, so he failed the exam'

11.5 AMBIGUOUS READINGS

An adjectival or prepositional ConjP adjoined to a DP or an NP can have two types of readings: discrete or non-discrete. In the discrete interpretation, the conjuncts apply separately to a subset of the entities denoted by the NP or the DP (38a). In the non-discrete interpretation, the entire ConjP applies to the NP or the DP, so that all the entities have the property denoted by ConjP (38b):

(38) a. Avem maşini noi şi uzate [discrete reading: there are two types of cars]
have.1PL cars new and used
'We have new and used cars'

b. Avem cărţi noi şi interesante [non-discrete reading: only one type of books]
have.1PL books new and interesting
'We have new and interesting books'

The structure is more ambiguous when a subject ConjP is applied to a predicate ConjP:

(39) Ion şi Andrei au fost miniştri de Finanţe şi de Externe
Ion and Andrei have.3PL been ministers of Finance and of External

a. 'Ion was minister of Finance and Andrei was minister of [discrete reading]
External Affairs'

b. 'Ion was minister of Finance and External Affairs and [non-discrete reading]
Andrei was minister of Finance and External Affairs'

The same types of reading occur when a verbal predicate is applied to a ConjP:

(40) Am împrumutat 10 lei lui Ion, Vasile şi Dan
have.1PL lend 10 lei LUI.DAT Ion Vasile and Dan

a. 'I lent 10 lei to Ion, 10 lei to Vasile and 10 lei to Dan' [discrete reading]

b. 'I lent 10 lei in total, to Ion, Vasile and Dan' [non-discrete reading]

When the predicate is applied to each entity individually, the repetition of case markers or prepositions with each conjunct is preferred:

(41) Am împrumutat 10 lei lui Ion, **lui** Vasile şi **lui** Dan
have.1SG lent 10 lei LUI.DAT Ion LUI.DAT Vasile and LUI.DAT Dan
'I lent 10 lei to Ion, to Vasile, and to Dan'

(42) a. Ieri   am   discutat   **cu**   Ion   și   Maria
       yesterday   have.1SG   discussed   with   Ion   and   Maria
    b. Ieri   am   discutat   **cu**   Ion   și   **cu**   Maria
       yesterday   have.1SG   discussed   with   Ion   and   with   Maria

11.6 COORDINATION AND ELLIPSIS

Several types of coordinative ellipsis, cross-linguistically attested, are possible in Romanian (Bîlbîie 2009): gapping (43), right node raising (44), argument cluster coordination (45), sluicing (46), end-attachment coordination (47):

(43) Ea   merge   la   film,   el   la   teatru
     she   goes   to   film   he   to   theatre

(44) Eu   am   cumpărat,   iar   tu   ai   vândut   un   apartament   cu   4   camere
     I   have   bought   and   you   have   sold   an   apartment   with   four   rooms

(45) a. Îi   ofer   lui   Dan   un   tricou   și   Mariei   o   bluză
        CL.DAT.3SG   offer   LUI.DAT   Dan   a   T-shirt   and   Maria.DAT   a   blouse
        'I offer Dan a T-shirt and Maria a blouse'
    b. Ion   merge   la   bunici   sâmbătă   și   la   părinți   duminică
       Ion   goes   to   grandparents   Saturday   and   to   parents   Sunday

(46) Cineva   a   rănit   pe   altcineva,   dar   nu   știu   cine   pe   cine
     Somebody   has   hurt   PE   somebody-else   but   not   know.1SG   who   PE   who
     'Somebody hurt somebody else, but I don't know who hurt who'

(47) a. Ion   nu   va   pleca,   și   nici   Dan
        Ion   not   AUX.FUT.3SG   leave.INF   and   neither   Dan
        'Ion will not leave, and neither will Dan'
    b. Ion   mai   mănâncă   dulciuri,   dar   Maria   niciodată
       Ion   more   eats   sweets   but   Maria   never
       'Ion does eat sweets sometimes, but Maria never'

CONCLUSIONS

Romanian is the only Romance language with a three-level adversative system, with specialized coordinators expressing contrast (*dar*, *însă*), correction (*ci*) and thematic change (*iar*). Other Romance languages do not have an equivalent of *iar*. Moreover, Romanian has different coordinators for the other two adversative relations, a distinction also found in Spanish (*pero* vs. *sino*). Due to this three-level distinction which extends to the coordinators employed, in Romanian two adversative conjuncts can concatenate.

Și, the prototypical conjunctive coordinator, functions in other contexts as an adverb expressing cumulativity.

Some coordinators are found only in correlative pairs (e.g. *fie...fie...*).

The coordination of categorially different constituents is possible, with certain restrictions.

12

Agreement

We discuss here various types of agreement: DP-internal, subject–predicate, with coordinated DPs, and anaphoric. Agreement is generally purely formal, and based on the morphosyntactic features of the source noun, but under certain syntactic and semantic conditions agreement may be semantic (based on the semantic features of the source noun). If the source of agreement has no formal or semantic features (from which agreement can otherwise be predicted), default forms are used (3rd person singular, for the verb, and masculine singular for the adjective). Pronouns display concord in gender, and sometimes in number with their nominal antecedent.

12.1 DP-INTERNAL AGREEMENT

In the DP, any word with inflection which determines or modifies the noun head agrees with it in gender, number, and case. Agreement is based on the formal features of the noun. Semantic agreement in the DP can never override grammatical agreement.

For prototypical adjectives, case agreement is visible only in the feminine, singular, genitive / dative form, which is syncretic with the plural form (1b), and distinct from the nominative / accusative form (1a):

(1) a. (o) fată **înaltă**
 a.F.SG.NOM≡ACC girl.F.SG.NOM≡ACC tall.F.SG.NOM≡ACC
 b. (unei) fete **înalte**
 a.F.SG.GEN≡DAT girl.F.SG.GEN≡DAT tall.F.SG.GEN≡DAT
 c. (unei) fete **văzută** (non-standard)
 a.F.SG.GEN≡DAT girl.F.SG.GEN≡DAT seen.F.SG.NOM≡ACC

There is a tendency to lose case agreement, which goes back to the 16th century (Vasiliu 1965). In contemporary Romanian, this tendency mostly affects participial adjectives, especially in the spoken language (1c) (Croitor *et al.* 2009).

In the paradigm of pronominal adjectives, case agreement is better marked. Some pronominal adjectives (the indefinite, the negative (§5.3.2.2), the relative and interrogative (§5.3.5.5), and the demonstrative (§5.3.2.1)) mark the distinction genitive–dative vs. nominative–accusative for masculine and feminine, singular and plural.

U Postnominal demonstratives tend to lose case agreement (Iordan 1947: 424; Graur 1968: 299):
 (2) producția anului acesta (non-standard) / acestuia (standard)
 production.DEF year.DEF.GEN this.NOM≡ACC≡GEN≡DAT this.GEN≡DAT
 'the production of this year'

For the intensifier pronoun (§6.5) and the possessive (§6.3.3.1), case agreement is visible only in the feminine singular, genitive–dative form:

(3) a. fata **însăşi** / fetei **înseşi**
      girl.DEF.NOM≡ACC herself.NOM≡ACC girl.DEF.GEN≡DAT herself.GEN≡DAT
   b. fiica **mea** / fiicei **mele**
      daughter.DEF.NOM≡ACC my.NOM≡ACC daughter.DEF.GEN≡DAT my.GEN≡DAT

U By virtue of being an inflectional morpheme, *al* does not mark case agreement in the standard language, unlike the possessive adjectives which it precedes:

(4) acestei profesoare a mele (standard)
    this.GEN≡DAT teacher.GEN≡DAT AL.F.SG.NOM≡ACC≡GEN≡DAT my.GEN≡DAT

In the colloquial register, speakers tend to eliminate this asymmetry between *al* and *meu*, either by extending case agreement to *al* (5a) or by not marking case agreement on *meu* (5b):

(5) a. acestei profesoare ale mele (non-standard)
       this.GEN≡DAT teacher.GEN≡DAT AL.F.PL.GEN≡DAT my.GEN≡DAT
    b. acestei profesoare a
       this.GEN≡DAT teacher.GEN≡DAT AL.F.SG.NOM≡ACC≡GEN≡DAT
       mea (non-standard)
       my.NOM≡ACC≡GEN≡DAT

Compound numerals (§5.3.2.1) tend to lose gender agreement in the spoken register; the masculine form is frequently used instead of the feminine (especially with *doisprezece* and numerals ending in *unu*):

(6) a. **doisprezece** fete (non-standard) vs. **douăsprezece** fete (standard)
       twelve.M girls.F twelve.F girls.F
       'twelve girls'
    b. treizeci şi **unu** de mii (non-standard) vs. **treizeci şi una**
       thirty and one.M DE thousands.F thirty and one.F
       de mii (standard)
       DE thousands.F
       'thirty-one thousand'

The definite and the indefinite article (except *nişte*) agree in gender and number with the noun which heads the DP (§5.3.1.1):

(7) carte**a** băiatu**l** cărţi**le** băieţi**i** o carte un băiat
    book.F.SG.DEF boy.M.SG.DEF books.F.PL.DEF boys.M.PL.DEF a.F book.F a.M boy.M

The only term displaying referential person agreement inside the DP is the intensifier pronoun (§6.5), which marks gender, number, and case on its first component (*însu-*) and person on the second component (*-mi* for the 1st person singular, *-ţi*, for the 2nd person singular, etc.).

(8) a. eu **însămi** — mie **însemi**
       I myself.F.SG.NOM me.DAT myself.F.SG.DAT
    b. eu **însumi** — tu **însuţi**
       I myself.M.SG.NOM you yourself.M.SG.NOM

When an adverb in the superlative modifies a participle within the DP, the determiner CEL of the adverb's superlative degree is sometimes variable in the spoken language, displaying agreement by attraction with the head noun (see also §5.3.1.4):

(9) a. angajaţii   cel /   cei   mai   prost   plătiţi
       employee.M.PL   CEL.M.SG   CEL.M.PL   more   badly   paid.M.PL
   b. cel /   cei   mai   prost   plătiţi   angajaţi
      cel.M.SG   CEL.M.PL   more   badly   paid   employee.M.PL
      'the worst paid employees'

12.2 SUBJECT–PREDICATE AGREEMENT

Romanian is a pro-drop language, with rich verbal inflection. In the 1st and 2nd person, the subject is 'included' in the verbal form.

Verbs without a nominal subject (§3.1.3.4) have an unmarked, default form, which is the 3rd person singular.

In most contexts, the verb agrees with the subject on the basis of the latter's formal features, but semantic agreement is allowed in certain contexts, mentioned below.

H In old Romanian, collective nouns could also trigger semantic agreement (Carabulea 1965). In present-day Romanian, collective nouns trigger formal agreement.

(10) Nărodul   văzură   Hristos   în   codru   suind   (Coresi)
      people.COLL.DEF   saw.3PL   Christ   in   forest   going up

12.2.1 Proper names

Names of persons agree semantically, based on the referential features of the noun.

(11) Toma   este   înalt,   dar   şi   Ingrid   este   înaltă
     Toma   is   tall.M.SG.NOM≡ACC   but   also   Ingrid   is   tall.F.SG.NOM≡ACC

Some place names, names of companies, institutions, and organizations display two agreement possibilities: formal or conceptual (i.e. based on the features of the common noun denoting the concept related to the proper name $oraş_{NEUT}$ 'city', $ţară_F$ 'country', $insulă_F$ 'island', $munte_M$ 'mountain', $companie_F$ 'company').

(12) a. **Tulcea**   a   fost   **întemeiată /**   **întemeiat**   în
        Tulcea.F   has   been   founded.F.SG /   founded.M.SG   in
        anul...   — [oraşul]   Tulcea
        year...   — [city.NEUT.SG] Tulcea   (formal agreement is preferred)
     b. 'Rulmentul'   a   fost   vândută — [compania]   'Rulmentul'
        'Rulmentul'.M.SG   has   been   sold.F.SG — company.F.SG   'Rulmentul'

12.2.2 Inclusive words

Inclusive words are indefinite, negative, interrogative, and relative pronouns, as well as DPs in subject position, which optionally accept the verb in the first and second person plural (Gruiţă 1981; Croitor 2012). The reading of the sentence is the following: the speaker or the hearer is included in the entities denoted by the subject. This type of subject–predicate agreement is 'semantic', since the nominal itself does not have the feature [+person]:

(13) a. Câțiva / unii   au   **am /**   **ați**   adus   un   cadou
         several some   have.3PL   have.1PL   have.2PL   brought   a   gift

   b. Aceia   care   **am /**   **ați**   venit...
      those   which   have.1PL /   have.2PL   come...

   c. Oricare / toți   **am /**   **ați**   **putea**   face   asta
      anybody   all   AUX.COND.1PL   AUX.COND.2PL   can.INF   do.INF   this

   d. Niciunul   nu   **vom /**   **veți**   **rămâne**   aici
      none   not   AUX.FUT.1PL   AUX.FUT.2PL   remain   here

(14) a. Zece   persoane   **am**   **semnat**   contract   cu   această   companie
         ten   persons   have.1PL   signed   contract   with   this   company

   b. Toate   fetele   **am**   **plecat**   la   film
      all.F.PL   girl.F.PL   have.1PL   left   to   film

12.2.3 'Politeness' pronouns

With second person 'politeness' pronouns, the participle and the adjective in a predicative position agree on the basis of the referential features of the subject pronoun, while the verb agrees on the basis of the formal features of the subject. This may give rise to sentences in which the verb and the adjective / participle have different number features:

(15) a. Dumneata   **ești**   **invitat /**   **invitată**   la   primărie
         you.MID.POL   are.2SG   invited.M.SG   invited.F.SG   to   city-hall

   b. Dumneavoastră   **sunteți**   **invitat /**   **invitată /**   **invitați /**   **invitate**
      you.POL   are.2PL   invited.M.SG   invited.F.SG   invited.M.PL   invited.F.PL
      la   primărie
      to   city-hall

Politeness DPs such as *Majestatea Voastră* 'Your Majesty', *Alteța Voastră* 'Your Highness', made up of a noun and a possessive in the 2nd person plural, admit two types of verbal agreement: in the 3rd person singular (formal agreement with the head noun) or in the 2nd person plural (referential agreement). In the formal language, the 3rd person is preferred by some speakers, who consider it more polite, because it avoids addressing the hearer directly:

(16) Alteța   Voastră   **a /**   **ați**   **primit**   o   scrisoare
     Highness.DEF   Your   has   have.2PL   received   a   letter

12.2.4 Partitive DPs

Complex DPs with a partitive DP or NP in the first position (*parte* 'part', *jumătate* 'half', *o treime* 'one third', etc.) followed by a partitive PP containing a plural noun (*din(tre) studenți* 'of the students') or a plural pronoun (*din(tre) ei* 'of them') may trigger plural agreement on the verb, irrespective of word order. Thus plural agreement is not an instance of 'attraction agreement' or a result of word order:

(17) **Au** /   **a**   **votat**   o   parte   dintre   studenți
    have.3PL   has   voted   a   part   of   students

When the partitive PP contains a 1st or 2nd person plural pronoun, person agreement of the verb usually reflects the inclusion of the speaker or of the hearer, respectively, in the event denoted by the verb. If the verb is in the 3rd person, the speaker or the hearer is not included in the event.

(18) Jumătate dintre   noi   **am** /   **au**   **plecat**
    half   of   us   have.1PL   have.3PL   left

In complex partitive DPs, the quantifier in the first position can be a singular indefinite or negative pronoun (*vreunul* 'anyone', *oricare* 'anyone', *fiecare* 'each', *niciunul* 'no one') which allows plural (semantic) agreement of the verb, irrespective of word order:

(19) Aceste   întâmplări   le-**am**   **trăit**   fiecare   dintre   noi
    these   happenings   CL.ACC.3PL=have.1PL   lived   each   of   us

Plural agreement is also triggered in contexts with ellipsis of the partitive PP:

(20) Studenții$_i$ sunt   în   laborator.   O   parte   [dintre ei$_i$]
    students.DEF   are   in   laboratory   a   part   [of them]
    vor   **da**   test   mâine
    AUX.FUT.3PL   give   test   tomorrow

When the partitive PP contains a singular noun, the participle (or the subjective predicative complement) can agree with the partitive DP / NP in the first position or with the NP in the partitive PP (the latter type of agreement is preferred):

(21) O   jumătate   din   perete   a   fost   **zugrăvit** /   **zugrăvită**
    one half.F.SG   of   wall.M.SG   has   been   painted.M.SG   painted.F.SG

U When the partitive PP contains a collective noun, plural agreement of the verb is accepted by some speakers. This is an instance of semantic agreement, since none of the nouns is morphologically marked for plural (Croitor and Dobrovie-Sorin 2011):

(22) O   parte   din   guvern   **au**   **demisionat** /   **sunt**   **corupți**
    a   part   of   government   have.3PL   resigned   are   corrupted.M.PL

12.2.5 Measure DPs

Measure DPs, made up of a measure noun and a PP headed by the functional preposition DE, usually trigger number agreement with the second NP, if it is in the plural:

(23) O   armată   de   furnici   **au**   **invadat**   bucătăria
    an   army   DE   ants   have.3PL   invaded   kitchen.DEF

If the predicate applies to the measured entities as a 'whole', agreement can be in the singular:

(24) Un   kilogram   de   mere   **a**   **costat**   3   lei
    a   kilogram   DE   apples   has   cost   3   lei

Gender agreement can be with the first or the second noun, if they are both in the singular:

(25) O tonă de zahăr a fost
 a ton.F.SG DE sugar.M.SG has been
 donată / **donat** unor orfelinate
 donated.F.SG donated.M.SG some.DAT orphanage.PL.DAT

Some measure DPs trigger agreement with the measure noun, if it is in the plural:

(26) Două tone de zahăr **au** **fost** **donate /**
 two ton.F.PL DE sugar.M.SG have.3PL been donated.F.PL
 *****a** **fost** **donat**
 has been donated.M.SG

This difference between gender agreement and number agreement with measure DPs (compare (25) to (26)) is an indication that in Romanian number marking is stronger than gender marking (Graur 1968: 313).

If the first noun has full referential meaning (i.e. it does not function as a measure noun), it triggers agreement on the verb (27a):

(27) a. *O grămadă* de cărţi **era** în mijlocul
 a heap of book.PL was in middle.DEF
 camerei   [the books formed a heap]
 room.DEF.GEN
 'A heap of books was in the middle of the room'

 b. *O grămadă* de cărţi **erau** în mijlocul camerei [many books]
 a heap of book.PL were in middle.DEF room.DEF.GEN
 'A load of books were in the middle of the room'

12.2.6 Qualitative DPs

The agreement of qualitative DPs N1 *de* N2 (§5.3.5.3) depends on the [+/–animate] feature of N2. If N2 is [+animate], it triggers gender agreement, while if N2 is [–animate], agreement oscillates (Vişan 2004):

(28) a. *Un munte de femeie* a fost **transportată /** *****transportat**
 a mountain.M of woman.F has been transported.F transported.M
 cu ambulanţa la spital
 with ambulance.DEF to hospital
 'A hulk of a woman was transported by ambulance to hospital'

 b. *O bijuterie de automobil* a fost **expus /** **expusă**
 a jewel.F of car.M has been shown.M shown.F
 de Renault la târg
 by Renault at fair

If N1 is not fully referential, as in superlative and zero-degree qualitative DPs (Doetjes and Rooryck 2003; Mihail 2009a, 2009b), then it loses its ability to trigger agreement on the verb:

(29) | Prostia | | asta | de | roman | e | foarte | *plictisitoare / | plictisitor
| stupidity.F.DEF | this | of | novel.N | is | very | boring.F | boring.M

When N2 is a 1st or 2nd person pronoun, agreement can be with N1 or N2:

(30) Deșteptul de mine a / am uitat ușa descuiată
smart.DEF of me has have.1SG forgotten door.DEF open
'Stupid me left the door open'

12.2.7 Agreement in copular sentences

12.2.7.1 Specificational sentences

In specificational sentences (N1 + *fi* 'be' + N2), the copula verb agrees with N2:

(31) a. Vinovatul **sunt** / *este eu
culprit.DEF am / is I

b. Prioritatea ministrului **sunt** / *este pensiile
priority.SG.DEF minister.DEF.GEN are.3PL is pension.PL.DEF

Agreement is influenced by the presence of the definite determiner on N2. If N2 is a bare plural, it does not trigger agreement. The bare plural functions as a 'label'. Compare (32a) to (32b) below:

(32) a. Cina mea preferată **este** / *sunt cartofi prăjiți
dinner.DEF my favorite is are potatoes fried

b. Cina mea preferată *este / **sunt** cartofii prăjiți
dinner.DEF my favorite is are potatoes.DEF fried

12.2.7.2 Pseudo-cleft sentences

In pseudo-cleft and inverted pseudo-cleft sentences, verbal agreement depends on the presence of the determiner on the focused post-copular plural noun. If this is a bare noun, it does not trigger agreement; if it is a DP, it triggers plural agreement on the verb:

(33) a. Ceea ce aș mânca acum e / *sunt cartofi
what AUX.COND.1SG eat now is are chips.NOM

b. Ceea ce aș mânca acum *e / sunt cartofii
what AUX.COND.1SG eat now is are potatoes.DEF
rămași de la prânz
left from lunch

12.3 AGREEMENT WITH COORDINATED DPs

12.3.1 Predicative agreement

12.3.1.1 Number agreement

When a conjunctive ConjP is in subject position, the verb can agree with the closest conjunct (GALR II: 386–7) in some contexts.

12.3 Agreement with coordinated DPs

In V–S sentences, singular agreement is justified as a processing phenomenon; singular agreement is not allowed by predicates with an inherently plural meaning:

(34) a. A **luat cuvântul** președintele țării și premierul
have.3SG taken word president.DEF country.DEF.GEN and prime-minister.DEF
'The president of the country and the prime-minister have spoken'

b. *Ieri **s-a căsătorit** Ion și Maria
yesterday CL.REFL.ACC.3SG=has married Ion and Maria
'Ion and Maria married yesterday'

When the conjuncts are bare mass or abstract nouns, the copula verb can agree in the singular or plural, depending on the degree of individualization of each conjunct; in (35a), the two nouns have a higher degree of individualization, while in (35b), the conjuncts form a semantic unit:

(35) a. Lapte și unt **sunt / e** în frigider
milk and butter are is in refrigerator

b. La Constanța **e / *sunt** frig și ceață în acest moment
at Constanța is are cold and fog in this moment

If the conjuncts form a semantic unit, the verb can agree in the singular:

(36) *Secera și ciocanul,* un simbol al comunismului,
sickle.DEF and hammer.DEF a symbol of communism.GEN.DEF
a / au dispărut după 1990
has have.3PL disappeared after 1990

With **disjunctive** ConjPs, the reading of the disjunction (exclusive vs. inclusive) is reflected by agreement (singular vs. plural):

(37) a. Ion sau Dan **va fi ales** președintele României
Ion or Dan AUX.FUT.3SG be elected.M.SG president.DEF Romania.GEN

b. Ion sau Dan **vor fi aleși** deputați la toamnă
Ion or Dan AUX.FUT.3PL be elected.M.PL deputy.M.PL at autumn

12.3.1.2 Gender agreement

Generally, gender agreement with ConjPs can be described as semantic. When both conjuncts are [+animate], the adjective in a predicative position and the participle agree in the masculine if at least one of the referents is masculine. This generalization includes ConjPs in which all the conjuncts are inflectionally feminine, and one of them has a masculine referent (Farkas and Zec 1995); formal agreement, in the feminine, is ungrammatical:

(38) a. Prietenul meu și surorile lui sunt **plecați** la munte
friend.M.SG.DEF my and sister.F.PL.DEF his(GEN) are gone.M.PL to mountain
'My friend and his sisters are gone to the mountains'

b. Ordonanța și soția sa au fost **capturați / *capturate**
orderly.F.SG.DEF and wife.DEF his have.3PL been captured.M.PL captured.F.PL
'The orderly and his wife were captured'

If only one of the conjuncts is [+animate], that conjunct triggers the gender agreement:

(39) Bărbatul   și   mașina   au   fost   **implicați** /
     man.M.SG.DEF   and   car.F.SG.DEF have.3PL   been   involved.M.PL
     *implicate   într-un accident
     involved.F.PL in an   accident
     'The man and his car were involved in an accident'

When both conjuncts are [–animate], agreement cannot be referential and is based on certain resolution rules. In many contexts, the unmarked form is used, namely the feminine plural. The masculine plural form is used if: all the conjuncts are masculine (40a) (but in the spoken language feminine agreement is also possible); one of the conjuncts is masculine plural (40b); the masculine conjunct is closer to the verb (40c). In other contexts, the unmarked feminine plural form is preferred (Croitor and Giurgea 2009):

(40) a. *Morcovul*   *și*   *ardeiul*   sunt   **gustoși** /
        carrot.M.SG.DEF and   pepper.M.SG.DEF   are   tasty.M.PL
        gustoase   [M.SG. + M.SG.]
        tasty.F.PL

     b. *Pantofii*   *și*   *rochia*   sunt   **puși** /   **puse**
        shoe.DEF.M.PL   and   dress.DEF.F.SG   are   put.M.PL   put.F.PL
        în   valiză   [M.PL. + F.SG.]
        in   suitcase

     c. *Gardul*   *și*   *cireșul*   sunt   **tăiate** /
        fence.DEF.NEUT.SG and   cherry-tree.DEF.M.SG are   cut.F.PL
        tăiați   [NEUT.SG. + M.SG.]
        cut.M.PL

12.3.1.3 Person agreement

The hierarchy of person agreement in Romanian is 1st > 2nd > 3rd, as in many other languages (Corbett 2006): if one of the conjuncts is in the 1st person, the verb agrees in the 1st person plural (41a); otherwise, if one of the conjuncts is in the 2nd person, the verb agrees in the 2nd person plural (41b):

(41) a. Eu și   tu   **am**   fost   **chemați**   la   interviu
        I   and you have.1PL   been   called   to   interview
     b. Tu și   el   **plecați**   mâine
        you and he   leave.2PL   tomorrow

12.3.2 Adjectival agreement

In Romanian, the adjective agrees with the closest conjunct (42a). Under the influence of other Romance languages (Avram 2001: 358), since the 19th century, in the literary language the adjective agrees with the entire ConjP (42b):

(42) a. vin   și   țuică   **fiartă**
       wine.NEUT.SG and   brandy.F.SG   boiled.F.SG

   b. vinul   și   țuica   **fierte**
      wine.NEUT.SG.DEF and brandy.F.SG.DEF boiled.F.PL

The resolution rules when the conjuncts have different gender features are the same as for the adjective in predicative position. Sometimes, speakers prefer to avoid using the adjective (43a), for two reasons: (i) agreement with the entire ConjP seems unnatural or ungrammatical; (ii) agreement with the closest conjunct is ambiguous (it is not clear whether the semantic domain of the adjective is the ConjP or the closest conjunct). Speakers prefer to use a relative clause instead (43b):

(43) a. automobilul   și   casa   **cumpărată / cumpărate**
       car.DEF.NEUT.SG and   house.DEF.F.SG bought.F.SG   bought.F.PL

   b. automobilul   și   casa   care   au   fost   cumpărate
      car.DEF.NEUT.SG and   house.DEF.F.SG which have.PL been   bought.F.PL

The possessive can only agree with the closest conjunct (44a). In order to avoid any ambiguity, the possessive is repeated after each conjunct (44b).

(44) a. casa   și   mașina   **mea/   *mele**
       house.F.SG.DEF and car.F.SG.DEF   my.F.SG   my.F.PL

   b. casa   mea   și   mașina   mea
      house.DEF my.F.SG and   car.DEF my.F.SG

A plural DP can be followed by singular coordinated adjectives, if they belong to certain semantic types. Examples with adjectives expressing nationality are the most frequent:

(45) a. limbile   **română**   și   **maghiară**
       language.F.PL Romanian.F.SG   and   Hungarian.F.SG

   b. președinții   **român**   și   **francez**
      president.M.PL. Romanian.M.SG and   French.M.SG

   c. *rochiile   **albă**   și   **neagră**
      dress.F.PL   white.F.SG   and   black.F.SG

H Until the 19th century, agreement between the verbal predicate and the subject displayed a higher degree of variability, because the language was less subject to the normative influence of grammars, manuals, etc.

12.4 ANAPHORIC AGREEMENT

The relative pronoun *care* in the genitive case, preceded by *al*, has a complex agreement pattern: *al* agrees with the possessee in the relative clause, while the relative pronoun, which encodes the possessor, displays agreement with the antecedent in the main clause:

(46) ...**prieteni**$_i$ a_j **căror**$_i$ **vizită**$_j$ ne-a   bucurat   mult
      ...friend.PL   al.F.SG   which.GEN.PL   visit.F.SG   CL.ACC.1PL=has pleased   much

Generally speaking, anaphoric pronouns either agree with their antecedent according to the gender of the referent, or display grammatical (formal) gender:

(47) Toată lumea_i e preocupată doar de problemele **lui**_i / **ei**_i
all.F.SG people.F.SG is concerned.F.SG only of problems.DEF his(GEN) her(GEN)
'Everybody is concerned only with their own problems'

CONCLUSIONS

In Romanian, agreement can be characterized as principally formal, that is, based on the morphosyntactic features of the source noun. Agreement is well marked, due to the rich morphology of verbs and adjectives.

In the nominal phrase, all the inflectible words depending on the head noun agree with it in gender, number, and case, based on formal, that is morphosyntactic features. Intensifier pronouns also display person agreement. All determiners agree with the noun which heads the DP.

Verb agreement is based on the formal features of the subject noun but in some contexts semantic agreement is possible.

With ConjPs agreement is mostly semantic, that is, referential. When agreement in gender cannot be based on the semantic features of the conjuncts, the two other agreement possibilities are agreement with the closest conjunct or the use of a default form. Agreement in number with the closest conjunct is possible in some contexts: in V–S sentences; when the conjuncts form a semantic unit; in existential sentences; when the conjuncts are bare mass or abstract nouns.

13

Sentence Organization and Discourse Phenomena

In this chapter, we present the main aspects of sentence organization: sentence types (declarative, interrogative, imperative, and exclamative), reported speech, negation, information structure, modality and evidentiality, anaphora, vocative phrases, and address strategies.

13.1 SENTENCE TYPES

13.1.1 Declarative sentences

Romanian displays both SVO and VSO word order. The former is more frequent, the latter occurs with verbs in certain semantic classes (2a,b), in rhematic sentences (2c), in embedded sentences headed by relatives (2d) or by complementizers (2e) (§3.1.9, Manoliu 2011: 505–6).

(1) Ion citește ziarul
    Ion reads newspaper.DEF
    'Ion reads the newspaper'

(2) a. Mă doare capul
       me.ACC aches head.DEF
       'My head aches'
    b. Îmi place muzica
       me.DAT likes music.DEF
       'I like music'
    c. —Ce s-a întâmplat? / —A venit vecinul
       what CL.REFL.ACC.3SG=has happened / has come neighbour.DEF
       '—What happened? /—The neighbour came'
    d. Nu știu ce face Ion
       not know.1SG what does Ion
       'I don't know what Ion is doing'
    e. Vreau să vină Ion
       want.1SG SĂ_SUBJ come.SUBJ Ion
       'I want Ion to come'

Declarative sentences have falling intonation. Changes in the information structure of the sentence syntactically marked by inversion, fronting, left dislocation, right dislocation, and sometimes clitic doubling of the direct / indirect object trigger changes in the pitch contour (Dascălu Jinga 2008: 949–54).

Since Romanian is a pro-drop language, the realization of the subject correlates with discourse phenomena, that is discourse continuity / break, discourse contrast, emphasis, etc. (Manoliu 2011: 480; Vasilescu 2009c).

Romanian is a discourse configurational language. Hence there are few syntactic constraints on word order. They involve the position of auxiliaries / modals / aspectual verbs, as well as the position of negation, pronominal, and adverbial clitics relative to the verb. The position of the subject, direct object, indirect object, and adjuncts is free. Word order changes trigger modifications of the intonation contour and generate pragmatic and discourse effects like topic / comment, focus / background, discourse prominence, perspective effects, stance, etc. (§13.4). Examples (3a–e) show free word order for the sentence 'Ion is reading the newspaper' and its pragmatic and discourse correlates, while examples (3f–k) show free and constrained word order for the sentence 'I don't have a headache'.

(3) a. Ion citeşte ziarul
Ion.NOM reads newspaper.DEF.ACC
'Ion is reading the newspaper' (this is what Ion is doing)

b. Citeşte Ion ziarul
reads Ion.NOM newspaper.DEF.ACC
'Ion is reading the newspaper' (this is what is going on)

c. Ziarul îl citeşte Ion
newspaper.DEF.ACC CL.ACC.M.3SG reads Ion.NOM
'What is happening to the newspaper is that Ion is reading it'

d. Ziarul Ion îl citeşte
newspaper.DEF.ACC Ion.NOM CL.ACC.M.3SG reads
'As for the newspaper, the person who is reading it is Ion'

e. Ion ziarul (îl) citeşte (nu revista)
Ion.NOM newspaper.DEF.ACC CL.ACC.M.3SG reads not magazine.DEF
'Ion is reading the newspaper (not the magazine)'

f. Nu mă doare capul
not CL.ACC.1SG aches head.DEF.NOM
'I don't have a headache'

g. Capul nu mă doare
head.DEF.NOM not CL.ACC.1SG aches
'It's not my head that aches (but something else)'

h. Nu capul mă doare
not head.DEF.NOM CL.ACC.1SG aches
'It's not my head that aches (but something else)'

i. *Nu doare mă capul
not aches CL.ACC.1SG head.DEF.NOM

j. *Mă capul nu doare
CL.ACC.1SG head.DEF.NOM not aches

k. *Doare nu mă capul
aches not CL.ACC.1SG head.DEF.NOM

Romanian does not have cleft constructions. Pseudo-clefting produces several structural variants with focalization and thematization (§10.3.4, §13.4.3).

13.1.2 Interrogative sentences

Romanian displays all major interrogative structures (polar interrogatives, *wh*-interrogatives, alternative interrogatives) and minor types (tag questions, echo questions). For an extensive syntactic, pragmatic, and semantic approach, see Șerbănescu 2002, Vasilescu 2008b.

13.1.2.1 Polar interrogatives

Compared to declaratives (4a), polar interrogatives, both affirmative and negative, have a special pitch contour and show subject–predicate inversion (4b).

(4) a. Ion (nu) a venit
 Ion (not) has come
 'Ion didn't come'

 b. (Nu) a venit Ion?
 (not) has come Ion
 'Didn't Ion come?'

They generally have rising intonation and stress on the focused constituent. Pitch variation in the intonation contour reflects differences in the information structure of the sentence (5a–c), as well as differences in presuppositions and implicatures (Dascălu Jinga 2008: 957–64). In negative interrogatives there is less of a height difference between the initial and the final part of the sentence than in affirmatives. Interrogatives with topicalized subjects have the same structure as declaratives (5d). The negator *nu* (*n-*) attached to polar questions functions as a pragmatic hedge, that is a negative politeness strategy (5e).

(5) a. **A citit** Ion cartea?
 has read Ion book.DEF
 '**Did** Ion **read** the book?'

 b. A citit **Ion** cartea?
 has read Ion book.DEF
 'Did **Ion** read the book?'

 c. A citit Ion **cartea**?
 has read Ion book.DEF
 'Did Ion read the **book**?'

 d. **Ion** a citit cartea?
 Ion has read book.DEF
 'Did **Ion** read the book?'

 e. N-a citit **Ion** cartea? / **Ion** n-a citit cartea?
 not=has read Ion book.DEF? / Ion not=has read book.DEF
 'Didn't **Ion** read the book?'

H In the 16th–18th centuries most polar interrogatives were marked by the adverbial particles *au*, *doară, au doară, oare, au nu, au nu... doară* (Carabulea 2007: 277). In contemporary Romanian only *oare* 'indeed' (6a) and *doar nu* 'surely' (6b) have been preserved and function as modal intensifiers.

(6) a. Oare   vine?
     indeed   comes
     'Is he coming, indeed?'
  b. Doar   nu   vine?
     surely not comes
     'Don't tell me he's coming!'

Questions that elicit directives are marked by the subjunctive particle *să* (7).

(7) Să   plec?
   SĂ$_{SUBJ}$ leave.SUBJ
   'Shall I leave?', 'Do you want me to leave?'

The standard answer to polar questions is elliptical, that is the pro-phrases *da* 'yes', *nu* 'no'. Alternative positive answer strategies include modal adverbials (*evident* 'of course', *poate* 'perhaps', *normal* 'naturally', etc.), repetition of the predicate or of the focused word(s) in the sentence, as well as paraverbal and nonverbal elements. Frequent negative answer strategies include negative intensifiers (*în niciun caz* 'in no case', *sub nicio formă*, 'by no means', *nicidecum* 'no way', etc.), the repetition of the verbal predicate, paraverbal, and nonverbal elements, etc. (§13.3.5, Zafiu 2008c: 700–1). A special particle, *ba*, heads affirmative answers (*da* 'yes') to hedged negative questions.

(8) —N-a   venit Ion? —Ba da! /—Ba a   venit!
   not=has come Ion   nay yes nay has come
   —'Didn't John come?—Yes, he did'

Phatic interrogatives involve perception (9a) or cognition (9b) verbs, as well as the pro-phrases *da* and *nu* (9c).

(9) a. Vezi?,   Auzi?
     see.2SG   hear.2SG
     'Do you see?', 'Do you hear?'
  b. Știi?,   Înțelegi?
     know.2SG   understand.2SG
     'Do you know?', 'Do you understand?'
  c. Da?, Nu?
     'Yes?', 'No?'

13.1.2.2 Wh-*questions*

In *wh*-questions the interrogative word is fronted. The intonation contour is falling and the interrogative word has a higher pitch (Dascălu Jinga 2008: 954–7). Pitch height varies with the information structure of the sentence. If the interrogative word fills the subject slot, the falling pitch contour is the only element which distinguishes interrogatives from declaratives (10a). If the interrogative word fills other syntactic slots, the subject–predicate inversion occurs alongside the falling intonation (10b). *Wh*-questions display adjacency effects ((10c) vs. (10d)).

(10) a. Cine a venit?
   who has come
   'Who came?'

   b. Ce$_i$ a citit Ion t$_i$?
   what has read Ion
   'What did Ion read?'

   c. Pe cine$_i$ ajută Ion t$_i$?
   PE who helps Ion
   'Whom is Ion helping?'

   d. *Pe cine Ion ajută t$_i$?

Wh-questions that elicit directives are marked by the subjunctive particle (11a,b).

(11) a. Cine să vină?
   who SĂ$_{SUBJ}$ come.SUBJ
   'Who should come? / Who do you want to come?'

   b. Unde să vină?
   where SĂ$_{SUBJ}$ come.SUBJ
   'Where should he come? / Where do you want him to come?'

Romanian interrogative words are interrogative pronouns (12a), interrogative pronominal adjectives (12b), and interrogative adverbs (12c).

(12) a. cine?, ce?, care?, cât$_1$?, al câtelea?
   'who?, what?, which?, how much?, what rank? which one (in a numerical order)?'

   b. ce?, care?, cât$_1$?, al câtelea?, ce fel de?
   'what?, which?, how much?, which one (in a numerical order)?, what sort / kind of?'

   c. unde?, când?, cum?, cât$_2$?, de ce?, încotro?
   'where?, when?, how?, how much?, why?, in which direction / whither?'

Interrogative pronouns / adjectives display the same inflection as relative pronouns / adjectives (§10.3.5). The singular masculine form of the pronoun / adjective *cât* ('how much?') is syncretic with the form of the adverb *cât* ('how much?'). *Ce* ('what?') functions both pronominally and adjectivally, but also as a formative in the reason and purpose adverbial fixed sequence *de ce* 'why?'. Interrogative quantifiers bind entities with the following semantic features: *cine* [+animate]; *ce* [–animate]; *care* [+partitive, +/–animate], *cât* [quantified NPs]; *al câtelea* [ranked NPs]. *Ce* also stands for VPs (13).

(13) Ce s-a întâmplat?, Ce ai făcut?
   'What happened?', 'What have you done?'

U In non-standard Romanian *care* can substitute *cine*:
   (14) Cine este acolo? > Care este acolo?
   'Who's there?'

Interrogative adjectives differ little from interrogative pronouns: *ce* stands for [+/–animate] DPs with categorial and identification readings only (15a,b); *care?, cât?, al câtelea?* function much like their pronominal counterparts; *ce fel de* is always an interrogative adjective with no pronominal counterpart and triggers a qualificative (15c) or a categorial (15d) reading.

(15) a. Ce   elev   a   făcut   asta?   [Ion]
         what   student has   done   this
         'Which student did this?'

   b. Ce   carte   vrei?   [Pirații din Caraibe]
      what   book   want.2SG
      'Which book do you want?'   [The Pirates of the Caribbean]

   c. Ce   fel   de   om   e   el?   [un om rău]
      what kind of   man   is   he
      'What kind of man is he?' [a bad man]

   d. Ce   fel   de   cărți   preferi?   [cărți SF / facile]
      what kind of   books   prefer.2SG
      'What sort of books do you prefer?'   [SF books / easy books]

Interrogative adverbs bind entities with the following semantic features: *unde* [+place, +point of arrival]; *când* [+time]; *cum* [+manner]; *cât* [+quantity]; *de ce* [+reason / purpose]; *încotro* [+direction]. Interrogative pronouns / adjectives / adverbs combine with a large number of prepositions (16).

(16)   cu cine, despre ce, pentru care, fără câte, de unde, până când, despre cât, etc.
       'with whom, about what, for which one, without how many, from where / whence,
       until when, about how much', etc.

The interrogative pronouns *cine, care, cât* differ with respect to clitic doubling (17a–c) (§3.3.2.1.5).

(17) a. Pe cine   ai   văzut? / *Pe cine   l-ai   văzut?
        PE who   have   seen   PE who   CL.ACC.3SG=have.2SG   seen
        'Whom did you see?'

   b. *Pe care   ai   văzut? /   Pe care   l-ai   văzut?
      PE   which   have   seen   PE   which   CL.ACC.3SG=have.2SG   seen

   c. Pe câți   (i)-ai   întrebat?
      PE how many   CL.ACC.3PL=have.2SG   asked
      'How many of them did you ask?'

In multiple questions all the interrogative words, irrespective of their morphosyntactic category, can be fronted. Optionally, they admit conjunctive coordination of the last term (18a,b).

(18) a. Cine   ce   (și)   cui   i-a   dat?
        who   what   (and)   whom   CL.DAT.3SG=has   given
        'Who gave whom what?'

   b. Cine   unde   (și)   când   a   plecat?
      who   where   (and)   when   has   left
      'Who left and where and when?'

Multiple questions show a 'superiority effect', that is the *wh*-subject obligatorily precedes *wh*-objects and *wh*-adjuncts (19a,b).

(19) a. Cine ce face?
     who what does
   b. *Ce cine face?
      what who does
      'Who does what?'

Romanian privileges *wh*-movement. Nevertheless, interrogatives with the *wh*-word *in situ* occur in echo questions to focus the theme (20a), in multiple questions, optionally (20b), with obligatory *island constraints* (i.e. the interrogative element cannot be moved out of a subordinate clause, according to Chomsky 1986) (20c). The pitch contour is rising and *ce* is stressed.

(20) a. Ce a mâncat? / A mâncat ce?
        what has eaten has eaten what
        'What did (s)he eat?' / '(S)he ate what?'
   b. Cine ce ţi-a spus / Cine ţi-a spus ce?
      who what CL.DAT.2SG=has told who CL.DAT.2SG=has told what
      'Who told you what?'
   c. *Ce$_i$ ai venit la bibliotecă să citeşti t$_i$? / Ai venit
      what have come at library să$_{SUBJ}$ read.SUBJ / have come
      la bibliotecă să citeşti ce?
      at library să$_{SUBJ}$ read.SUBJ what
      'You came to the library to read what?'

Pied-piping (i.e. the effect by which movement of one element is accompanied by that of all the others related to it, according to Ross 1986: 126) is obligatory in all circumstances (21a,b) and preposition stranding is blocked (21c). *Wh*-elements allow long-distance unbounded dependencies (21d) (§10.3.6.1).

(21) a. [Ce carte]$_i$ citeşte Ion t$_i$? vs. *Ce$_i$ citeşte Ion t$_i$ carte?
        what book reads Ion   what reads Ion book
        'What book is Ion reading?'
   b. [Ai cui prieteni]$_i$ sunt ei t$_i$? vs. *Ai cui$_i$ sunt ei prieteni t$_i$?
      AL.M.PL who.GEN friends are they   AL.M.PL who.GEN are they friends
      'Whose friends are they?'
   c. Pe cine$_i$ se bazează t$_i$ Ion? vs. *Cine$_i$
      on who CL.REFL.ACC.3SG relies Ion /   who
      se bazează Ion pe t$_i$?
      CL.REFL.ACC.3SG relies Ion on
      'Whom is Ion relying on?'
   d. Pe cine$_i$ crezi [că a spus Ion [că vrea [să vadă t$_i$]]]
      PE who think.2SG that has said Ion that wants să$_{SUBJ}$ see.SUBJ
      'Whom do you think Ion said he wanted to see?'

In Romanian the major island constraints are: adjunct islands (22a), *wh*-islands (22b), complex NP constraint (22c), and coordinate structure constraint (22d).

(22) a. *Ce$_i$ a întârziat   Ion [pentru   că a   pierdut t$_i$]?
       what has been-late   Ion because   has lost

   b. *Cui$_i$ nu-ţi   place [ce   i-a   spus t$_i$ Ion]?
       who.DAT   not=CL.DAT.2SG   likes what CL.DAT.3SG=has   said   Ion

   c. *Cine$_i$ mi-a   arătat   Maria [cartea   pe   care
       who   CL.DAT.1SG=has   shown   Maria book.DEF   PE   which
       a   scris-o t$_i$]?
       has   written=CL.ACC.F.3SG

   d. *Ce$_i$ a   cumpărat   Ion   caiete   şi t$_i$?
       what   has bought   Ion   notebooks   and

The 'complementizer-trace' effect is not in force. That is to say that both subjects and objects can be extracted from the embedded clause (23a,b), and null complementizer sentences are not allowed (23c).

(23) a. Pe cine$_i$ crezi   [că   [a   văzut   Dan t$_i$]]?
       PE who   think.2SG   that   has   seen   Dan.NOM
       'Whom do you think Dan saw?'

   b. Cine$_i$ crezi   [că   [l-a   văzut t$_i$ pe   Dan]]?
       who   think.2SG   that   CL.M.3SG=has   seen   PE   Dan.ACC?
       Who do you think saw Dan?

   c. *Pe cine$_i$ crezi [Ø   [a   văzut   Dan t$_i$]]?
       PE who   think.2SG has   seen   Dan

The unmarked option for answers to *wh*-questions is the elliptical sentence, which preserves the interrogated constituent only (24a); the non-elliptical sentence (24b) generates conversational implicatures (as defined in Grice 1975).

(24)   —Cine a venit?
       who has come
       'Who came?'
   a. —Ion
       'Ion'
   b. —Ion   a   venit
       Ion has   come
       'Ion came'

13.1.2.3 Alternative questions

Alternative questions are coordinated by *sau* or *ori* 'or', the former being preferred in contemporary Romanian. Two or more clausal or non-clausal constituents may be coordinated (25a–c). In symmetrical alternative questions the preferred order is positive—negative; the reversed order (25d) is possible, yet not frequent, and signals a change in expectations regarding the answer. The pitch contour is rise–fall (Dascălu Jinga 2008: 964–5).

(25) a. Mănânci   mere   sau / ori   pere?
       eat.2SG   apples   or   pears
       'Are you eating apples or pears?'

b. Vii   sau / ori   nu   vii?
   come.2SG   or   not   come.2SG
   'Are you coming or are you not coming?'

c. Citeşti,   scrii   sau / ori   mănânci?
   read.2SG write.2SG   or   eat.2SG
   'Are you reading, writing or eating?'

d. ??Nu   vii   sau / ori   vii?
   not   come.2SG   or   come.2SG
   'You're not coming? Or are you?'

13.1.2.4 Tag-questions

Romanian tag-questions have a fixed structure (26), with several elliptical variants (27). The selection of the negative (26a) or positive (26b) form of the tag is free, and not induced by the positive / negative structure of the base. Differences occur on the pragmatic level: the negative tag is hedged and functions as a negative politeness strategy, while the positive tag is intrusive and functions as a positive politeness strategy.

(26) a. (Nu)   a   venit,   **nu-i**   **aşa**?
        (not) has   come,   not=is   so

   b. (Nu)   a   venit,   **aşa**   **e** /   **aşa-i**?
      (not) has   come,   so   is /   so=is
      'He didn't come, did he? / He came, didn't he?'

(27) aşa?,   e?,   nu?,   da?
     so?,   is?,   no?,   yes?
     'Right?'

Tags have a fall–rise intonation; the information structure of the sentence correlates with slight differences in the pitch contour (Dascălu Jinga 2008: 963–4).

13.1.2.5 Echo questions

Several echo-question devices are available: the repetition of (a part of) the sentence uttered by the interlocutor, a higher pitch on the echo part of the sentence, a fronted or *in situ* interrogative word, pro-phrases (28a–d), etc. (for a detailed description, see Dumitrescu 1990b).

(28) A plecat luni
     'He left on Monday'

   a. A plecat luni?
      'He left on Monday?'

   b. Când a plecat? / A plecat când?
      'When did he leave?' / 'He left when?'

   c. Ce?,   Cum?
      what   how
      'What?'

   d. Ce   face?,   Poftim?
      what does   pardon
      'Sorry?'

Echo *ce* can be embedded as a complement of a complementizer (29a) or of an auxiliary (29b).

(29) A spus că va pleca
'He said that he would leave'

    a. A   spus   că   ce?
       has   said   that   what
       'He said that what?'

    b. A   spus   că   va   ce?
       has   said   that   AUX.FUT.3SG   what
       'He said that he would what?'

Echo questions have rising intonation and the echo word is stressed (Dascălu Jinga 2008: 960–3).

13.1.3 Imperative sentences

Imperative sentences (Pîrvulescu and Roberge 2000) can be structured around (i) an overt imperative, with dedicated forms for the 2nd person, singular and plural, affirmative and negative (30a,b) (§2.2.1.1.6) or (ii) a surrogate imperative, that is the present subjunctive (30c), the present (30d) and future (30e) indicative, and, for some uses, the infinitive (30f) and the supine (30g). Predicative interjections may stand in for imperative verbs (30h).

(30) a. Pleacă!,   Plecaţi!
         leave.IMP.2SG   leave.IMP.2PL
         'Leave!'

      b. Nu   pleca!,   Nu   plecaţi!
        not   leave.INF.2SG not leave.IMP.2PL
        'Don't leave!'

      c. Să   (nu)   pleci,   Să   (nu)   plecaţi!
        SĂ_SUBJ not   leave.SUBJ.2SG SĂ_SUBJ not   leave.SUBJ.2PL
        '(Don't) leave!'

      d. (Nu)   Pleci!,   (Nu)   plecaţi!
        not   leave.IND.PRES.2SG not   leave.IND.PRES.2PL
        'You are (not) leaving!'

      e. (Nu)   vei   pleca! / (Nu)   veţi   pleca!
        not   AUX.FUT.2SG leave.INF (not) AUX.FUT.2PL leave.INF
        'You will (not) leave!'

      f. A   (nu)   se   păstra   la   loc   uscat!
        A_INF not   CL.REFL.PASS keep.INF at   place dry
        '(Do not) keep in a dry place!'

      g. De   reţinut!
        DE_SUP remember.SUP
        'Remember!'

      h. Na! / Uite! / Hai! / Ssssttt!
        'Here you are! / Look! / Let's! / Hush!'

Subjunctive forms render the desiderative–hortative meaning for the 1st and 3rd persons singular and plural (31a–c).

(31) a. Să mănânc ceva!
 să$_{SUBJ}$ eat.SUBJ.1SG something
 'Let me eat something! /I'll eat something!'
 b. Să mâncăm ceva!
 să$_{SUBJ}$ eat.SUBJ.1PL something
 'Let's eat something!'
 c. Să mănânce ceva!
 să$_{SUBJ}$ eat.SUBJ.3SG≡PL something
 'Let him eat something!'

In complex sentences the imperative occurs in the main clause (32a). Two or several imperative sentences can be coordinated (32b).

(32) a. Ia ce-ţi dau eu!
 take.IMP what=CL.DAT.2SG give I
 'Take what I'm giving you!'
 b. Stai aici şi taci!
 stay.IMP here and keep silent.IMP
 'Stay here and keep silent!'

Imperatives have a falling intonation, with a pitch on the imperative form (Dascălu Jinga 2008: 965). Generally, imperatives are subjectless (33a); the subject occurs for contrast (33b) or focus (33c).

(33) a. Vino!
 come.IMP.2SG
 'Come!'
 b. Vino tu! (nu Ion)
 come.IMP.2SG you not Ion
 'You come! (not Ion)'
 c. Vino şi / doar tu!
 come.IMP.2SG and / only you
 'Come you too! / Only you come!'

Often, imperatives co-occur with vocatives (34a) and interjections (34b) (§13.7).

(34) a. Pleacă, Ioane / Ion!
 leave.IMP.2SG Ion.VOC Ion.VOC≡NOM
 'Go away, Ion!'
 b. Băi, pleacă!
 hey leave.IMP.2SG
 'Hey you, go away!'

Imperatives coordinated with declaratives by means of conjunctions function as conditional structures (35).

(35) Întârzie şi vei fi concediat! ['Dacă întârzii vei fi concediat']
 'Be late and you'll be fired!' ['If you're late you'll be fired']

13.1.4 Exclamative sentences and exclamations

Exclamatives share the features [+assertive, +factive, +evaluative, +gradual] and are headed by *wh*-exclamative words. They have rising intonation that varies in order to reflect the information structure of the sentence and the emotions expressed (Vişan 2002; Dascălu Jinga: 2008: 967–78).

Romanian *wh*-exclamative words are *ce* 'what', *câţi, câte* 'how many', *cum / cum... de* 'how', *cât / cât de / cât... de* 'how much'. *Ce* is embedded in NP or AP and moves alone or with its nominal / adjectival head; $cât_1$ originates in the QP; *cum* in the AdvP, and *cum... de* in Spec, AdvP, in the gradation adverbial position; $cât_2$ in the AdvP, and $cât_2$ *de / cât_2... de* in Spec, AdvP, in the gradation adverbial position, as shown in (36a–g). Optatives and conditionals with *ce* or *cum* form a special subclass of exclamatives (36h).

(36) a. Ce$_i$ fată t$_i$!
       what girl
       'What a girl!'

   b. Ce$_i$ fată [t$_i$ frumoasă]! / [Ce   frumoasă]$_i$ fată t$_i$!
      what girl   beautiful   what   beautiful   girl
      'What a beautiful girl!'

   c. Câte$_i$ [t$_i$ cărţi]!
      how-many   books
      'How many books!'

   d. Cum$_i$ scrie t$_i$!
      how   write.3SG
      'How he writes!'

   e. Cum$_i$ scrie   de [t$_i$ frumos]!
      how   write.3SG   DE   beautiful
      'How nicely he writes'

   f. Cât   mănâncă t$_i$!
      what   eat.3SG
      'How much he eats!'

   g. Cât$_i$ mănâncă t$_i$ de   mult! / [Cât   de]$_i$ mult   mănâncă!
      how   eat.3SG   DE   much / how   DE   much   eat.3SG
      'How much he's eating!/ What a lot he's eating!'

   h. Ce /   Cum aş   (mai)   mânca o   prăjitură!
      what / how AUX.COND.1SG   (more)   eat   a   cake
      'How I could eat a cake!'

U   In non-standard Romanian *ce de* and *ce* are used as synonyms of $cât_1$ and $cât_2$ (37).
   (37) a. Ce   de   cărţi!
           what DE   books
           'How many books!'
        b. Ce   de   mănâncă!
           what DE   eat.3SG
        c. Ce   mănâncă!
           what   eat.3SG
           'How much he is eating!'

In focal structures, *mai* can be placed immediately to the left of the NP / VP (the adjectival *câte* is excluded) (38a–c).

(38) a. Ce mai fată (frumoasă)!
 what more girl (beautiful)
 'What a (beautiful) girl!'

 b. Cum mai vorbeşte (de tare)!
 how more speaks (DE loud)
 'How loudly (s)he speaks!'

 c. *Câte mai cărţi a cumpărat!
 How-many more books has bought

Exclamative constructions can be independent, coordinated, or complex sentences, with one (39a,b) or several *wh*-element(s) in front of each of the coordinated clauses (39c).

(39) a. Ce frumos cântă!
 what beautiful sings
 'How beautifully (s)he sings!'

 b. Ce frumos cânta când avea 4 ani!
 what beautiful sing.IMPERF.3SG when had 4 years
 'How beautifully (s)he sang when (s)he was four!'

 c. Ce frumos cântă şi (ce frumos) dansează!
 what beautifully sings and what beautifully dances
 'How beautifully (s)he sings and dances!'

Apart from these prototypical exclamatives, shared with other Romance languages and English, Romanian displays three other types: constructions marked by inversion and optionally headed by the complementizer *că* (40a); affirmative / negative constructions with an argument rendered as a fronted *wh*-constituent (40b); verbless constructions with a reversed adjectival modifier (40c).

(40) a. (Că) frumoasă (mai) e! (Că) bine (mai) scrie!
 that beautiful more is that well more writes
 'How beautiful she is!' 'How well she writes!'

 b. Ce a spus! / Ce n-a spus!
 what has said what not=has said
 'She said so many / terrible things!'

 c. Frumoasă fată!
 beautiful girl
 'What a beautiful girl!'

Various affective intonations (joy, dissatisfaction, amazement, anger, despair, etc.) can be attached to declarative and interrogative sentences, without any supplementary syntactic markers, yielding exclamations (41a–d).

(41) a. A venit Ion!
 has come Ion
 'Ion has come!'

b. A venit Ion?!
   has come Ion
   'Did Ion come?!'

c. Cine a venit?!?
   who has come
   'Who came?!?'

d. Vii sau pleci?!
   come.2SG or leave.2SG
   'Are you coming or going?'

Some exclamations display a special structure: the subjunctive without *să* (42a), the reversed conditional (42b), elliptical conditionals (42c), a main clause with a dummy relative (42d), and juxtaposed symmetrical subordinate clauses (42e).

(42) a. Trăiască regele!
       live.SUBJ king.DEF
       'Long live the king!'

   b. Lua-te-ar dracu'!
      take=CL.ACC.2SG=AUX.COND.3SG devil.DEF
      'Go to Hell!'

   c. Dacă aş fi ştiut înainte!
      if AUX.COND.1SG be known before
      'Had I known before!'

   d. Unde nu m-ar invita pe mine?!
      where not CL.ACC.1SG=AUX.COND.3SG invite PE me.ACC
      'I wish he invited me!'

   e. Vrei, nu vrei, pleci!
      want.2SG not want.2SG leave.2SG
      'Whether you want to or not, you must leave!'

There are several types of verbless exclamations: one-constituent elliptical sentences (43a), symmetrical elliptical sentences (43b), idiomatic phrases (43c), semantically bleached NP structures, functioning as interjections (43d), and pro-sentence interjections (43e).

(43) a. Afară!
       'Out!'

   b. Cu cât mai repede, cu atât mai bine!
      'The sooner, the better!'

   c. Cum să nu?!
      'Of course!'

   d. Sfinte Sisoe!
      'Holy cow!'

   e. Ei!!!
      'Hey!'

13.2 REPORTED SPEECH

13.2.1 Specific features

The reported speech system includes citation indicators in the citing discourse (external to the investigated structure) and the actual (reported) cited discourse (in basic forms—direct speech and indirect speech—and in combined forms—free indirect discourse, bound direct speech). These forms are defined by semantic dependency on a reporting word. The main reporting verbs in Romanian are: *spune* 'say' and *zice* 'utter' (Fischer and Vasiliu 1953; Popa 2007; Barbu 2008).

13.2.2 Direct speech

In direct speech, the quoted discourse retains the same intonation, addressed discourse forms, deictic words, and pragmatic markers as those used when the direct discourse is uttered. It is independent from quotation indicators in terms of syntactic subordination.

Reporting indicators are:

(i) Verbs: primary declarative verbs (elements from the *verba dicendi* category (44) as well as equivalent idioms and phrases (45)) and secondary declarative verbs (contextual substitutes of a *verbum dicendi*: communication verbs (46), attitude verbs (47), verbs that express non-verbal sound-making (48) or gestures (49)).

(44) spune 'say', vorbi 'speak', zice 'utter', întreba 'ask', răspunde 'answer'

(45) arunca o vorbă 'drop a hint', întoarce vorba 'talk back'

(46) întrerupe 'interrupt', relua 'resume'

(47) a se bucura 'rejoice', a se mira 'be surprised'

(48) ofta 'sigh', plânge 'cry', tuna, fulgera 'thunder, rage'

(49) zâmbi 'smile', a se încrunta 'frown'

(ii) Nominal elements: nouns (appellatives (50a), terms naming the linguistic acts that are being performed (50b,c)), words semantically related to declarative verbs (51a–c) and pronouns (52)).

(50) a. **Ion:**   'Vii?'   **Vasile**:   'Da'
       Ion   (you)come   Vasile   yes
       Ion: 'Are you coming?' Vasile: 'Yes, I am'

   b. **Afirmația**   'Ion   învață'
      statement.DEF   Ion   studies
      'The statement *Ion is studying*'

   c. **Întrebarea**   'Când   vii?'
      question.DEF   when   (you)come
      'The question *When are you coming?*'

(51) a. **Cuvintele**   'Ai   grijă!'   l-au   speriat
       words.DEF.NOM   have.IMP.2SG   care   CL.ACC.3SG=have.3PL   scared
       'The words *Take care!* scared him'

  b. **Citatul**   'Era odată...'
    quotation.DEF was once
    'The quotation: Once upon a time, there was...'

  c. **Vorba**   **(a)ceea** 'Nimic nou sub soare'
    word.DEF that   nothing new under sun
    'As the saying goes: Nothing new under the sun'

(52) **El:**   'Vrei   apă?'   **Ea:**   'Nu'
   he   (you)want water   she   no
   'He says: "Do you want some water?" She says: "No"'

 (iii) Transphrastic connectors:

(53) Zise: 'Pleacă!'
   (he)said go-away.IMP.2SG
   'He said: Go away!'
   Şi   ea: 'Nu vreau!' **Dar:**   'Să   nu te   întorci!'
   and she[said] not want (I) but   SĂ$_{SUBJ}$ not CL.REFL.ACC.2SG come-back
   'She answers: I don't want to!' 'But don't come back!'

U In Romanian, the colloquial quoted speech indicators are: the adverb *cică* 'reportedly' (54a), the citation paraphrase *vorba ăluia* 'as they say' (54b), the verb *face* 'do' instead of *spune* 'say' (54c), alternating *zic / zice* 'I say / he says' to mark discourse roles (speaker-listener) when shifting from one deictic framework to another in reported speech (54d).

 (54) a. **Cică:**   'Iarna   e grea'
     reportedly winter.DEF is hard
     'They say winter time is harsh'

   b. **Vorba** **ăluia:**   'Lucrăm cu   materialul clientului!'
     word.DEF that.GEN (we)work with material.DEF client.GEN
     'As they say: We work with the client's material'

   c. **Face:** 'Vino   acasă!'
     does: come.IMP.2SG home
     '(S)he goes: Come home!'

   d. 'Poftim', **zic,**   'banii!'   'Mulţumesc!', **zice**
     look   (I)say money.DEF (I)thank   (he)says
     '*Here is the money*, I say. *Thank you*, he says'

Quotation indicators are placed before (55a), in between (incidental position) (55b), or after reporting words (55c):

(55) a. Mama   **zise:** 'Deschide   fereastra!'
    mother.DEF said open.IMP.2SG window.DEF
    'Mother said: Open the window!'

   b. 'Deschide,   **zise** mama,   fereastra!'
    open.IMP.2SG said mother.DEF window.DEF

   c. 'Deschide   fereastra!', **zise** mama
    open.IMP.2SG window.DEF said mother.DEF
    'Open the window, mother said'

Some indicators (the verbs *crede* 'believe', *pretinde* 'claim') can only be postposed to the cited discourse:

(56) 'Cunosc situația', **pretinde** el
 (I)know situation.DEF claims he
 'I know the situation, he claims'

13.2.3 Indirect speech

Indirect speech reports the content of an utterance using syntactic subordination to a primary or secondary declarative verb (for this distinction, see §13.2.2).

Verbs such as *decide* 'decide', *a se gândi* 'think', *crede* 'believe' may turn up as secondary declarative verbs:

(57) **Am decis** să plecăm
 (we)have decided să$_{SUBJ}$ go.SUBJ.1PL
 'We decided to leave'

U The following verbs do not accept indirect speech, but only direct speech: (transitive) listener-oriented declarative verbs (realized as an indirect object in the dative case)—*expune* 'expose', *prezenta* 'present' (58a); associative verbs—*delibera* 'deliberate', *negocia* 'negotiate' (58b); verbs pointing to iterative actions such as *cicăli* 'nag' (58c); dubbing verbs—*boteza* 'baptize', *numi* 'name', *porecli* 'nickname' (58d); verbs denoting a speaker's repetitive gestures and facial expression—*imita* 'imitate', *maimuțări* 'monkey' (58e).

(58) a. *A **expus** că a înțeles
   has exposed that has understood
 b. ***Negociază** că îl vinde mai ieftin
   negotiates that CL.ACC.M.3SG sells more cheaply
 c. *El l-a **cicălit** că a vorbit
   he CL.ACC.3SG=has nagged that has spoken
 d. *L-a **poreclit** că este un 'Popescu'
   CL.ACC.3SG=has nicknamed that is a 'Popescu'
 e. *L-a **imitat** că urlă
   CL.ACC.3SG=has imitated that yells

Dicendi expressions from the citing discourse are placed (with rare exceptions) before the reported discourse:

(59) **Spune** că o să plece
 says that o să$_{SUBJ}$ leave.SUBJ.3SG
 '(S)he says that she would leave'

13.2.4 Changes related to the conversion of direct speech into indirect speech

13.2.4.1 Changes at discourse levels

When transforming direct speech into indirect speech, the uttered intonation changes and direct address mechanisms vanish either through syntactic reorganization (the noun in the vocative becomes the indirect object and the imperative mood changes to the subjunctive with imperative value) or by removing them (in the case of affective forms):

(60) a. Mama   i-a   spus: '**Fetițo**   **dragă**,   învață!'
       mother.DEF CL.DAT.3SG=has told   girl.VOC dear   study.IMP.2SG
       'Mother told her: Dear girl, study!'

    b. Mama   i-a   spus **fetiței**   să   învețe
       mother CL.DAT.3SG=has told girl.DEF.DAT SĂ_{SUBJ} learn.SUBJ.3SG
       'The mother told the little girl to study'

Exclamative sentences lose their affective charge, which is then rendered by other (lexical-grammatical) means:

(61) a. '**Cât** ești **de** frumoasă!'
       how (you)are DE beautiful
       'How beautiful you are!'

    b. Mi-a   spus că   sunt   **foarte** frumoasă
       CL.DAT.1SG=has told that (I)am very   beautiful
       'He told me that I was very beautiful'

Interjections (+ the relative *ce* 'what' with adjectival or adverbial value, the exclamative adverbs *cât de* 'how', *cum* 'how') are replaced by verbs that describe the state they suggest and / or by grammatical mechanisms:

(62) a. '**Vai! Ce cald** e **afară!**'
       oh how hot (it)is outside
       'Oh, dear, how hot it is outside!'

    b. S-a   plâns   **că** **afară** e **foarte** **cald**
       CL.REFL.ACC.3SG=has complained that outside is very   hot
       '(S)he complained that outside it was very hot'

13.2.4.2 Morphological changes

Personal pronouns or possessive adjectives in the 1st person are replaced with 3rd person forms (63), 2nd person is replaced by 1st or 3rd person (64), personal pronouns and verbs in the 3rd person remain unchanged (65):

(63) a. '**Merg** la teatru'
       (I)go to   theatre
       'I am going to the theatre'

    b. El mi-a   spus că   **merge** la   teatru
       he CL.DAT.1SG=has told that goes   to   theatre
       'He told me that he was going to the theatre'

(64) a. 'Am găsit creionul **tău**'
       (I)have found pencil.DEF your
       'I found your pencil'

    b. Mi-a   spus că   a   găsit   creionul   **meu** / **său**
       CL.DAT.1SG=has told that has found pencil.DEF my   his
       '(S)he told me that (s)he had found my / his / her pencil'

(65) a. **'Ei au mințit'**
　　　they have lied
　　　'They lied'

　　b. A spus că **ei au mințit**
　　　has said that they have lied
　　　'(S)he said that they had lied'

Adverbs of place and time change: *aici* 'here' > *acolo* 'there'; *acum* 'now' > *atunci* 'then'; *mâine* 'tomorrow' > *a doua zi* 'the following day'. Proximal demonstrative pronouns and adjectives are replaced by distal demonstrative adverbs / pronouns and vice versa (*acesta* 'this' > *acela* 'that'; *asta* 'this' > *aia* 'that').

The only verbal mood that must change is the imperative, which transposes into the subjunctive:

(66) a. **'Vino!'**
　　　come.IMP.2SG
　　　'Come!'

　　b. Îi spune **să vină**
　　　CL.DAT.3SG tells SĂ_SUBJ come.SUBJ.3SG
　　　'He tells him / her to come'

C Unlike other Romance languages, in Romanian the tense-forms of the original utterance may be maintained in indirect speech, although this is not a strict rule.

13.2.4.3 Syntactic changes

In indirect speech, the discourse form depends on the type of sentence used in the original utterance, denoting the attitude / communicative intention adopted by the speaker (Manu Magda 1993; Vulpe 1993).

In declarative sentences, the main constituent in reported sentences, as well as the linking elements that introduce them (*că* 'that' vs. *să*) depend on the type of the speech act they express.

The same main constituent (*verba dicendi* such as *spune* 'say', perception verbs such as *auzi* 'hear', potentially performative verbs used for commissive acts, such as *promite* 'promise', *a se angaja* 'commit', *făgădui* 'pledge, promise', or for directive acts, such as *sugera* 'suggest') has a choice between the complementizers *că* and *să*, based on the opposition between assertive (*că*) and non-assertive (*să*) (§10.1.1.1).

(67) a. El (ne) spune **că** afară este cald
　　　he CL.ACC.1PL tells that outside is warm
　　　'He tells us that it is warm outside'

　　b. El (ne) spune **să** plecăm
　　　he CL.ACC.1PL tells SĂ_SUBJ leave.SUBJ.1PL
　　　'He tells us to leave'

U The complementizer *cum că* 'that' marks an epistemic distance (§13.5.6):
　　(68) Circulă zvonul **cum că** a mințit
　　　　circulates rumour.DEF how that has lied
　　　　'There's a rumour that he has lied'

In optative clauses with an implicit conditional, the affective marker (e.g. the intonation) is implied either by the subordinate verbal mood (69b)—the conditional—or by lexical means, using a desiderative verb such as *dori* 'want' (69c).

(69) a. 'Ce aş   mai cânta!' (dacă aş   putea)
       how AUX.COND.1SG more sing.INF if AUX.COND.1SG can.INF
       'How I would sing if I could'

   b. Mi-a   spus că ar   cânta
      CL.DAT.1SG=has   told that AUX.COND.3SG sing.INF
      '(S)he told me that he would sing'

   c. Mi-a   spus că ar   dori   să   cânte
      CL.DAT.1SG=has   told that AUX.COND.3SG want.INF SĂ_SUBJ sing.SUBJ.3SG
      '(S)he told me that he would like to sing'

Conditional clauses with an unexpressed main clause become explicit conditionals subordinated to the reporting word in an expressed main clause:

(70) a. 'De ar   veni   vara!'
       if AUX.COND.3SG   come.INF summer
       'If only summer would came!'

   b. Mi-a   spus **că ar   fi bucuros** să
      CL.DAT.1SG=has   told that AUX.COND.3SG be happy   SĂ_SUBJ
      vină   vara
      come.SUBJ.3SG   summer.DEF
      'He told me that he would be happy if summer would come'

Total direct interrogatives and alternative interrogatives, having as a main constituent a verb of saying, become argument clauses introduced by the complementizer *dacă* or colloquial *de* 'if'.

(71) a. 'Ai   înţeles?'
       (you)have   understood
       'Did you understand?'

   b. M-a   întrebat **dacă** am   înţeles
      CL.ACC.1SG=has   asked   if   (I)have   understood
      '(S)he asked me if I had understood'

Partial direct interrogatives become relative clauses and the reported speech is introduced by interrogative pronouns, adjectives and adverbs (*unde* 'where', *când* 'when', *cum* 'how', *cine* 'who', *ce* 'what', etc.) which thus change to relative-interrogative elements:

(72) a. '**Ce**   doreşti?'
       what   (you)want
       'What do you want?'

   b. M-a   întrebat **ce**   doresc
      CL.ACC.1SG=has   asked   what   (I)want
      '(S)he asked me what I wanted'

In indirect speech, directive structures with predicates that take personal verbal forms (imperative (73a), indicative (73b), subjunctive (73c)) are built on forms of the subjunctive, with the particle *să*, and directive verbs as matrix constituents—*cere* 'ask', *interzice* 'forbid', *recomanda* 'recommend' (74).

(73) a. **Vino** repede!
          'Come quickly!'
      b. **Vii** repede!
          'You come quickly!'
      c. **Să vii** repede!
          'Come quickly!'

(74) I-am   cerut să   vină   repede
      CL.DAT.3SG=have.1SG asked să$_{SUBJ}$ come.SUBJ.3SG   quickly
      'I asked him / her to come quickly'

13.2.5 Intermediate structures between direct speech and indirect speech

13.2.5.1 In free indirect style, the citing discourse does not contain a reporting verb and the cited discourse is not involved in a syntactically dependent relation with the former one (Mancaş 1972).

Free indirect style features the same change in grammatical person of the direct speech pronoun and verb as in indirect speech; any such changes are purely stylistic.

In a text where the speaker is a narrator, 1st and 2nd persons switch to 3rd person:

(75) Ion se frământa neîncetat. Da, **n-o s-o ierte** niciodată
      'Ion was continuously fretting. Indeed, he would never forgive her'

In a text where the speaker is a character, 2nd person switches to 1st person:

(76) El a mărturisit, **contând pe discreţia noastră,** că a vândut grădina
      'He confessed, counting on our discretion, that he had sold the garden'

13.2.5.2 Bound direct speech is a combined form, used in colloquial communication, which maintains all the features of direct speech, but introduces the reported sentence through the complementizer *că*; the sentence becomes syntactically dependent on the reporting words.

In bound direct speech, the discourse follows the intonation pattern specific to the various sentence types they include:

(77) Mama spune **că** 'Fetelor, masa este gata!' / 'Fetelor, veniţi la masă?' / 'Fetelor, veniţi la masă!'
      'Mother says: 'Girls, dinner is ready! / Girls, are you coming to dinner? / Girls, come to dinner!'

U   Colloquial Romanian shows some variations with respect to the rules of the standard language, keeping the same intonation when converting an interrogative utterance into indirect speech, introduced by *că* 'that' (Golopenţia 1959):
    (78) a. I-a   spus   că   să   plece!
             CL.DAT.3SG=has   told   that   să$_{SUBJ}$ leave.SUBJ.3SG
             '(S)he told him / her to leave'
          b. L-a   întrebat că   ce   caută   acolo?
             CL.ACC.3SG=has   asked   that   what   seeks   there
             '(S)he asked him / her what she was doing there'
    In colloquial language, one can also maintain in indirect speech deictic words that need to be removed or modified in the standard language:

(79) a. 'Amână examenul pe mâine!'
   postpone.IMP.2SG exam.DEF on tomorrow
   'Postpone the exam for tomorrow'
 b. I-a spus să amâne examenul pe mâine
   CL.DAT.3SG=has told să_SUBJ postpone.SUBJ.3SG exam.DEF for tomorrow
   '(S)he told her / him to postpone the exam for the next day'

13.3 NEGATION

13.3.1 Negative words

Simple negation (both sentential and constituent negation) is expressed by the negative marker *nu* 'no; not', by the negative prefixal marker *ne-*, and by the preposition / subordinator *fără* 'without' (with privative meaning).

Double or multiple negation is expressed by the combination of the aforementioned elements with *n*-words:

(i) negative adverbs: *nicăieri, niciunde* 'nowhere' (locative adverbs); *niciodată, nicicând* 'never' (temporal adverbs); *nicicum* 'no way', *nicidecum* 'not at all', *nicicât, nicidecât* 'not at all, no way'(manner adverbs); *nici* 'neither' (adverbial clitic);
(ii) negative pronominal (or adjectival) quantifiers: *nimeni* 'nobody', *nimic* 'nothing', *niciunul, niciuna* 'none', *niciun (băiat) / nicio (fată)* 'no boy / girl'(§5.3.2.2.2).

Simple constituent negation can be lexically expressed by the following prefixes: *ne-* (*neciteț* 'illegible'), *in-* (*incorect* 'incorrect'), *non-* (*nonfigurativ* 'nonfigurative'), *a-* (*anormal* 'abnormal').

H Some negative words (or at any rate their constituent elements) come from Latin: *nimeni* 'nobody' (with the regional and colloquial form *nimenea* and the old and non-standard variants *nime, nimene* < Lat. NĒMĪNEM, *nimic* 'nothing', with the non-standard and colloquial form *nimica* (and its old variant *nemică*) < Lat. NEC MĪCA (CDDE: 191), *fără* 'without' < Lat. FŎRĀS, *niciunul, niciuna* 'not one, none' (< non-standard Lat. NĔQUĔ UNUS (-UM /A), *nicăieri* 'nowhere', non-stardard *nicăierea* (with the old variant *nicăiure*) < non-standard Lat. NEC ALIUBI (CDDE: 31). All the other lexical units are formed in Romanian, by compounding.
Of the negative prefixes, *ne-* comes from Slavic, while the others (*non-, a-*) are recent borrowings from other Romance languages.

Negative markers can be accompanied, especially in the spoken language, by emphasizers, or by non-autonomous negators, whose function is to reinforce negation: *deloc, defel, neam* 'not at all', *pentru nimic în lume* 'for anything in the world', *câtuși de puțin* 'not at all', *nici vorbă* 'no way'; see also §13.3.5.

U *Neam* (< Bg. *nema, neama*) 'not at all' is a Wallachian regionalism.

13.3.2 Sentential negation

Sentential negation is expressed by means of a single marker, either the autonomous marker *nu* 'not' or as the prefixal marker *ne-*. The marker *nu* 'not' may accompany the indicative (80a), the conditional (80b), and the imperative (80c), as well as the subjunctive (80d) or the infinitive (80e):

(80) a. **Nu** a cântat
   not has sung
   'He didn't sing'

   b. **Nu** ar cânta
   not AUX.COND.3SG sing.INF
   '(S)he wouldn't sing'

   c. **Nu** cânta!
   not sing.INF
   'Do not sing!'

   d. A plecat ca să **nu** ne deranjeze
   has left in-order SĂ_SUBJ not CL.ACC.1PL bother.SUBJ.3SG
   '(S)he left to not bother us'

   e. a **nu** cânta
   A_INF not sing.INF

U In the colloquial and non-standard language, the marker *nu* 'not' may also take the form *n-* before the verbal forms beginning with *a*:
(81) **nu** am plecat vs. **n-**am plecat
   not (I)have left   not=(I)have left
   'I haven't gone'

The prefixal negative marker *ne-* attaches to the remaining non-finite forms—the gerund (82a), the participle (82b), and the supine (82c):

(82) a. Îl convingi **ne**contrazicându-l
   CL.ACC.3SG convince.IND.PRES.2SG NEG-contradict.GER=CL.ACC.3SG
   'You convince him by not contradicting him'

   b. **Ne**însoțită de primar, nu vizitează satul
   NEG-accompanied.PPLE.F.SG by mayor not visits village.DEF
   'She will not visit the village unaccompanied by the mayor'

   c. Peisajul era de **ne**imaginat
   scenery.DEF was DE_SUP NEG-imagine.SUP
   'The scenery was unimaginable'

Sentence negative markers are always preposed to the verb (see examples (80), (82), (84)), irrespective of the subject position. Typologically, Romanian displays the order NegVO.

C The same phenomenon is recorded in standard Italian, Spanish, Catalan, Portuguese, in certain Southern Italian dialects, and in certain Rhaeto-Romance varieties. Several other Romance languages or varieties, such as Occitan and Piedmontese, have only postverbal negative markers (Zanuttini 1997: 3–8; de Swart 2010: 92–7).

In the infinitive (83a), subjunctive (83b), and supine (83c), the negative marker intervenes between the markers *a, să, de*, and the lexical verb.

(83) a. a **nu** spune / a **nu** fi spus
        A$_{INF}$ not say.INF A$_{INF}$ not be say.PPLE
        'to not say' / 'to not have said'

     b. să **nu** spună / să **nu** fi spus
        SĂ$_{SUBJ}$ not say.SUBJ.3SG SĂ$_{SUBJ}$ not be say.PPLE

     c. frumoasă de **ne**imaginat
        beautiful DE$_{SUP}$ NEG-imagine.SUP
        'unimaginably beautiful'

When preceded by negative markers, verbs do not change their form (84a). Negative verb forms are identical to the affirmative ones, except for the negative imperative 2nd person singular, which is syncretic with the infinitive (84b).

(84) a. Cântaţi! vs. **Nu** cântaţi!
        sing.IMP.2PL   not sing.IMP≡IND.PRES.2PL
        'Sing!'   'Do not sing!'

     b. Cântă! vs. **Nu** cânta!
        sing.IMP.2SG   not sing.IMP≡INF
        'Sing!'   'Do not sing!'

13.3.2.1 Negative markers within VPs containing clitics

The negative marker *nu* 'not' precedes pronominal clitics (reflexive and non-reflexive, which are followed by auxiliaries and / or adverbial clitics (85a,b)). The 3rd singular feminine clitic is an exception, because when combined with the compound past indicative form or with conditional forms, it is placed after the past participle or infinitive (85c).

(85) a. **nu** se (prea) gândeşte
        not CL.REFL.ACC.3SG too think.IND.PRES.3SG

     b. **nu** l-ai mai căuta
        not CL.ACC.3SG=AUX.COND.2SG more search.INF

     c. **nu** am (mai) văzut-o
        not (I)have more seen=CL.ACC.F.SG

The prefixal negative marker *ne-* precedes adverbial clitics (86a), whereas pronominal clitics are placed in postverbal position (86b):

(86) a. **ne***mai*auzit
        NEG-more-heard.PPLE

     b. **ne**spunându-mi
        NEG-tell.GER=CL.DAT.1SG

13.3.2.2 Negative markers in complex predicates

A structure with a matrix verb and an embedded verb can be interpreted as a complex predicate if the negative marker *nu* precedes the matrix verb, as in (80a–c), (81), (85b,c), and (87) (for other tests, see §3.5.2).

(87) a. Ion **nu** [poate solicita] un credit bancar
        John not can request a loan bank
        'John cannot request a bank loan'

b. Maria **nu** [are de scris] un articol
   Mary not has DE_SUP write.SUP an article
   'Mary doesn't have to write an article'

c. Discuțiile **nu** [trebuiau (să fie)
   speech.F.PL not should.IMPERF.3PL SĂ_SUBJ be.SUBJ.3PL
   pregătite] din timp
   prepared.PPLE.F.PL from time
   'The speeches did not have to be prepared in advance'

The strategy of placing the negative marker within the complex predicate emphasizes the interaction between negation and modality. For example, the placement of negation before the main verb (88a) triggers a dynamic reading, and double negation (88b), before the main verb and before the embedded verb, triggers a deontic reading (Borchin 1999: 70; de Haan 2006; Manea 2012):

(88) a. Ea **nu**-l putea citi
     she not=CL.ACC.M.3SG can.IMPERF.3SG read.INF
     'She could not read it'

   b. Ea **nu** putea a **nu**-l citi
      she not can.IMPERF.3SG A_INF not=CL.ACC.M.3SG read.INF
      'She could not afford not to read it'

13.3.3 Constituent negation

Constituent negation is realized by placing the negative marker *nu* 'not' in front of the phrase, irrespective of the syntactic type of phrase. Generally, this type of negation occurs in contexts expressing a relation of opposition—either explicit (89a,b,g,h) or implicit (89c–f).

(89) a. [**Nu** [acești studenți]] sunt vinovați, ci ceilalți
     'It is not these students who are guilty, but the other ones'

   b. Mă întreb [**nu** [dacă va pleca]], ci dacă va rămâne
     'I'm asking myself not whether (s)he'll leave, but whether (s)he'll stay'

   c. [**Nu** [ripostând agresiv]] te impui
     'It's not by retorting aggressively that you impose yourself'

   d. [**Nu** [la tine]] îi este gândul
     'It is not you (s)he is thinking of'

   e. [**Nu** [pentru a te încuraja]] te laud
     'It's not to encourage you that I praise you'

   f. [**Nu** [totdeauna]] este așa amabil
     'He is not always so kind'

   g. Scria [**nu** bine], ci foarte bine
     '(S)he was writing not well, but very well'

   h. Ea era [**nu** foarte] generoasă, ci extrem de generoasă
     'She was not very generous, but extremely generous'

13.3.4 Multiple negation and negative concord

Romanian displays strict negative concord. Negative constituents are licensed only by the negative markers which express sentential negation, irrespective of their pre- or postverbal position. In (90) and (91), double and multiple negation does not change the negative reading of the clause.

(90) a. **Nimeni** şi **nimic** nu l-a înduioşat
nobody and nothing not CL.ACC.3SG=has impressed

b. **Nu** l-a înduioşat **nimeni** şi **nimic**
not CL.ACC.3SG=has impressed nobody and nothing
'Nobody and nothing impressed him'

c. *****Nimeni** şi **nimic** l-a înduioşat
nobody and nothing CL.ACC.3SG=has impressed

(91) a. **Niciodată nimeni** nereproşându-i **nimic**, acum era surprins
never nobody NEG=reproach.GER=CL.DAT.3SG nothing now was surprised
'As nobody had ever reproached him for anything, now he was surprised'

b. *****Nimeni** reproşându-i **nimic niciodată**, acum era surprins
nobody reproach.GER=CL.DAT.3SG nothing never now was surprised

C All Romance languages continue the phenomenon of double negation which was already attested in vulgar Latin. Romanian differs from other Romance languages such as Italian, Spanish, European Portuguese, and Sardinian, which belong to the non-strict negative concord group of languages: the sentence negative marker is obligatory only if the *n*-word occurs in postverbal position (Zanuttini 1997: 3–14; Déprez 2000: 254–9).

Romanian, as a strict negative-concord language, behaves like Balkan languages such as Greek and Bulgarian (Sandfeld 1930: 36), and also like Polish, Hungarian, Japanese.

H In the 16th century, negative concord was not strict. *N*-words did not obligatorily select the sentential negative marker *nu* 'not':

(92) Aceasta ştiindŭ, fraţilorŭ, **nimică** să ne mâhnimŭ (Coresi)
this know.GER brothers.VOC nothing să$_{SUBJ}$ CL.REFL.ACC.1PL grieve.SUBJ.1PL
'As we all know this, brothers, there is nothing that we should grieve for'

Simple negation (specific to Classical Latin) and double negation were in free variation in vulgar Latin (Toma 1978: 202). In old Romanian (the 17th–18th centuries), simple negation becomes rarer: only *nici* 'neither' and its compounds could function as absolute negative markers (Ciompec 1969: 202):

(93) **Niceodată** asupra ei oşti să facă (Costin)
never over her armies să$_{SUBJ}$ do.SUBJ.3SG
'Never set armies against it'

Negative concord is optional in contexts where positive polarity items are also accepted (*cineva* 'somebody', *ceva* 'something', *vreunul*, *vreuna* 'anybody', *vreun*, *vreo* 'any', *oriunde* 'everywhere', *totdeauna* 'always', *şi* 'also'):

(94) a. **Nu** se prezintă **vreunul / cineva** mai pregătit
not CL.REFL.ACC.3SG comes-along anybody / somebody more prepared
'None more suited comes along'

b. A venit **ne**silit de **cineva** anume
has come NEG-obliged.PPLE.M.SG by somebody precisely
'He came of his own will'

Negative concord does not apply in the following contexts:

- in non-interrogative clauses introduced by the complementizer *că* 'that', in which the verb is in the indicative (95);
- in interrogative clauses introduced by *dacă* 'whether' (96);
- in structures with adjectives derived with negative prefixes (97):

(95) a. *****Nu** am crezut că ai cumpărat **nimic**
not (I)have believed that (you)have bought nothing

b. **Nu** am crezut că ai cumpărat **ceva**
not (I)have believed that (you)have bought something
'I did not believe that you bought something'

(96) a. *****Nu** l-am întrebat dacă a fost anunțat de **nimeni**
not CL.ACC.3SG=(I)have asked if has been announced by nobody

b. **Nu** l-am întrebat dacă a fost anunțat de **cineva**
not CL.ACC.3SG=(I)have asked if has been announced by someone
'I did not ask him if he was announced by anybody'

(97) a. *****Era o veste **ne*importantă*** pentru **nimeni**
was a news unimportant for nobody

vs. b. Era o veste **ne*importantă*** pentru **oricine**
was a news unimportant for anybody
'It was unimportant news for anyone'

Apart from occurring in contexts with negative concord, *n*-words appear only in: high literary style, preposed to non-finite affirmative verbal forms (98); in comparative configurations which behave like idiomatic constructions (99); in configurations which contain minimizers recategorized as nouns (100):

(98) a. aspect de **nimeni** adus în discuție
issue by nobody brought into discussion
'issue brought into discussion by nobody'

b. atitudine **nicicum** de ignorat
attitude anyway DE ignored.SUP
'attitude which shouldn't be ignored under any circumstance'

(99) a. a fost odată **ca niciodată**
has been once as never
'once upon a time'

b. frumoasă **ca nimeni alta / ca nimeni altcineva**
beautiful.F.SG as nobody other as nobody someone else
'beautiful as anyone else'

(100) a. El e **un nimeni** / Ăsta e **un nimic**
he is a nobody this is a nothing
'He's a nobody' 'This is a trifle'

b. A   vândut   casa   **pe   nimic**
   has sold   house.DEF   on   nothing
   '(S)he sold the house for a song'

c. E   **o   nimica   toată**
   (it)is a   nothing.F.SG.DEF   all.F.SG
   'It is a mere trifle'

In dialogue, *n*-words are used independently as answers to different types of interrogatives. In these contexts, their occurrence is the result of an ellipsis:

(101) A: Cine te-a așteptat la aeroport?
          'Who waited for you at the airport?'

       B: **Nimeni** [nu m-a așteptat]
          'Nobody waited for me'

13.3.5 The negative pro-sentence

The marker *nu* 'no' can be used completely autonomously as a pro-sentence in independent (102a), coordinated (102b,c), matrix (102d), or embedded clauses (102e):

(102) A: Danei i-a plăcut filmul ?
          'Did Dana like the movie?'

       B: a. **Nu!**
             'No!'

          b. Și   da,   și   **nu**
             and   yes   and   no
             'yes and no'

          c. Nici   da,   nici   **nu**
             neither yes   neither   no
             'Neither yes nor no'

          d. **Nu,** fiindcă nu îi plac filmele SF
             'No, because she does not like SF movies'

          e. Cred   că   **nu**
             (I)think that   not
             'I think she did not'

U In colloquial language, especially in dialogue, there are also other emphasizing / intensifying lexical items functioning as pro-sentences—certain proper *n*-words (*nicidecum* 'not at all', *nici vorbă, nici gând* 'no way', *în niciun caz* 'under no account') and contextual *n*-words (*deloc, defel* 'not at all', *câtuși de puțin* 'not in the least'):

(103) a. A: Te-ai simțit jignit?
             'Did you feel offended?'
          B: **Nicidecum! / Nici vorbă! / Nici gând!**
             'Not at all!'

b. A: Te-ai supărat?
'Did you get upset?'
B: **Deloc / Câtuși de puțin**
'Not at all' / 'Not in the least'

The negative pro-sentence also occurs in special discourse situations: in coordinated structures, *nu* 'no' expresses intensification (104a); in combination with *ba* 'no, nay', *nu* 'not' expresses the contradiction of an assertion (104b); in interrogative structures, *nu* 'not' does not express negation anymore, but surprise (106a) or request for approval (106b).

(104) a. Am insistat, dar ea **nu și nu! / nu! / nu, nu! / nu, nu, nu! / nu, nu și iar nu!**
'I insisted, but she repeatedly said *no*!'
b. A: M-ai mințit
'You lied to me'
B: Ba **nu!**
'Oh, no, I did not'

H In non-standard contemporary Romanian, the particle *ba* (< Bg. *ba*) has a different usage, functioning as an archaic and colloquial variant of *nu* 'no'. It occurs especially with interrogative disjunctive clauses:
(105) Ai fost la școală sau **ba**?
'Have you been to school or not?'
(106) a. A: Radu n-a citit cartea
'Radu did not read the book'
B: **Nu?**
'Didn't he?' ('Really?', 'I expected that he would have read it')
b. E frumoasă, **nu**?
'She is beautiful, isn't she?' ('I am right, aren't I?', 'Don't you agree?')

13.3.6 Covert negation

Negation may also be expressed by certain positive lexical items or syntactic phrases. Non-finite infinitival clauses headed by the adverbial sequence *departe de* 'far from' express negative meanings (107). Covert negation also occurs in the case of rhetorical questions in the affirmative (108).

(107) [**Departe de** a fi mulțumit], a încheiat totuși contractul
'Far from being satisfied, he still signed the contract' ('Although he was not satisfied, he signed the contract')
(108) Dar cine îl crede?
'But who believes him?' ('Nobody believes him')

13.3.7 False negation

13.3.7.1 Double negation

In Romanian, double negation is realized in the following patterns:

(i) negative marker + matrix verb (deontic modal verb) + negative marker + embedded verb:

(109) **Nu** trebuie să **nu** vii cu noi
'You do not have to not come with us' ('You can come with us')

(ii) negative marker + matrix verb (epistemic modal verb) + negative marker + embedded verb:

(110) **Nu** credeam că **nu** vei pleca din București
'I did not think that you were not going to leave Bucharest'
('I thought you were going to leave Bucharest')

(iii) negative marker + matrix verb + adjunct introduced by a subordinator with privative meaning:

(111) **Nu** a plecat în vacanță **fără** copii niciodată
'(S)he has never gone on holiday without her children'
('Whenever she went on holiday, she took her children')

(iv) negative marker + copula verb + adjective derived with a negative prefix, functioning as a subjective predicative complement:

(112) Legea asta **nu** este **ne**dreaptă / **nu** este **in**completă
'The law is not unfair / incomplete' ('The law is fair / complete')

(v) NPs containing negative intensifiers (emphasizers) + lexical units derived with negative prefixes:

(113) Este o discuție **defel** /**deloc** /**câtuși de puțin ne**plăcută = 'Este o discuție plăcută'
'It is a not at all / not in the least unpleasant discussion' ('It a pleasant discussion')

13.3.7.2 Expletive negation

There are two types of structures with expletive negation:

(i) structures with obligatory sentential negation—in rhetorical questions (114a), with the clausal object of the verb *a se teme* 'fear' (114b), in temporal adjuncts introduced by the subordinator *până* 'until, before' (114c), in exclamative clauses introduced by *ce* 'what', *cât* 'how many' (114d,e), and in structures with *nu* 'not' + *decât* 'except for, but' ((114f); see Zafiu (2008c: 698)).

(114) a. Cine **nu** știe lucrul acesta?
who not knows thing this
'Who doesn't know this?' ('Everybody knows this')

b. Se   teme   să   **nu** afle   Ion
CL.REFL.3SG fears   SĂ_SUBJ   not   find.SUBJ.3SG out Ion
'She fears that John should find out'

c. **Nu** se   lasă   până **nu** găsește răspunsul   corect
not   CL.REFL.ACC.3SG   give up.3SG until not   finds   answer.DEF correct
'(S)he won't give up before she finds the correct answer'

       d. Ce   **nu**   mi-a   **zis**!
          what   not   CL.DAT.1SG=has   said
          'What didn't he say to me!'
       e. Câte   prostii   **nu**   a   **făcut**!
          how   many.F.PL   foolish-things   not   has   done!
          'How many foolish things didn't he do!'
       f. **Nu**   te   ascultă   **decât**   pe   tine
          not   CL.ACC.2SG   listens   only   PE   you.ACC
          'She obeys nobody else but you'

   (ii) interrogative structures with optional sentential negation (i.e. 'removable expletive negation', Barbu Mititelu and Maftei Ciolăneanu 2004: 42):

(115) (**Nu**) vii și tu cu noi?
       'Aren't you coming with us?'

13.3.7.3   Other structures with negative markers

Sentential negation (116a) and constituent negation (116b) may also occur in coordinated structures (§11.1.3).

(116) a. **Nu** a venit **nici** Ion, **nici** Gheorghe
          'Neither Ion nor Gheorghe came'
       b. **Nu** cadouri vrea, ci afecțiune
          'It is not gifts that she wants, but affection'

Certain verbs, which in the affirmative select only the complementizer *că* 'that' (+ indicative), may also select the complementizer *să* (+ subjunctive) in the negative. The selection of one complementizer or another entails subtle modal differences (§10.1.1.1).

(117) a. Cred   **că**   vine
          (I)think   that   come.IND.PRES.3SG
          'I think (s)he comes'
       b. Nu   cred   **că**   vine
          not   (I)think   that   come.IND.PRES.3SG
          'I do not think (s)he will come'
       c. **Nu**   cred   **să**   vină
          not   (I)think   să_{SUBJ}   come.SUBJ.PRES.3SG
          'I do not think (s)he will come'

(118) **Nu** am muncit atât ca să fiu umilit
       'I did not work so hard to be humiliated now'
       ('I worked hard, but not to be humiliated')

Contexts such as (118) are formally similar to the structures with expletive negation. In such contexts, the negation raising phenomenon occurs (Ionescu (ed.) 2004: 44).

13.4 INFORMATION STRUCTURE

13.4.1 Word order

As a 'discourse configurational language' (Kiss 1995), Romanian displays a relatively high freedom of constituent placement within the sentence, which serves discourse purposes: to mark the *topic-comment* informational structure (which leads to discourse coherence) and to produce emphatic effects (focalization).

13.4.1.1 In Romanian, the dominant unmarked word order of the body of the sentence is SVO (Dryer 2005: 332; Ledgeway 2011: 408, §3.1.9.3); it occurs in declarative main clauses in which the grammatical subject corresponds to the topic (§13.1.1).

C SVO word order is common to Romance languages; relative word order freedom is a feature of 'null subject' languages. The SVO order of Romanian has been challenged by some scholars (Dobrovie Sorin 1994; Cornilescu 2000; Alboiu 2002; see also the discussion in Manoliu 2011: 508), but their arguments more probably illustrate word order flexibility; the SVO pattern remains dominant. Balkan languages are also discourse configurational (Krapova 2004).

The left periphery is reserved for connectors, focusing adverbs, modalizers, and certain (e.g. situational) adjuncts; it is also the specific position for *topicalization* (marking topic continuity and contrastive topic) and for *contrastive focus*.

13.4.1.2 The subject is frequently postverbal when it is a rhematic element, together with the verb—in 'what happened?' contexts, such as (119a), including existential structures, such as (119b)—and in configurations in which another constituent is topicalized (119c):

(119) a. Ce   se   întâmplă?—Trece o **maşină**
         what   CL.REFL.ACC   happens   passes a car.NOM
         'What is going on?' 'A car is passing'

   b. Sunt   **multe   greşeli**   în   text
      are.3PL   many   mistakes.NOM   in   text
      'There are many mistakes in the text'

   c. Cartea   mi-a   dat-o   **Ion**
      book.DEF.ACC   CL.DAT.1SG=has   given=CL.ACC.3SG   Ion.NOM
      'Ion gave me the book'

The subject realized as an indefinite NP or the subject which is assigned a different role than Agent has certain affinities with the rheme position, that is, it is usually postverbal (§3.1.9.1.2); this word order is also displayed by subjects realized as full embedded clauses or as infinitival / supine clauses. Bare nominal subjects are usually rhematic and postverbal.

13.4.1.3 In *wh*-interrogatives, the *wh*-phrase is placed in initial position and the subject (when different from the *wh*-word or from the *wh*-phrase) is obligatorily postverbal (120a). Exclamatives with markers which are originally interrogative elements display the same word order restrictions (120b):

(120) a. Ce   a   găsit **Ion**? vs. *Ce   Ion   a   găsit?
         what has found Ion.NOM   what Ion.NOM has found
         'What did Ion find?'
   b. Ce   mare e   **grădina**! vs. *Ce   mare grădina   e!
         what big   is garden.DEF.NOM   what big   garden.DEF.NOM is
         'How big the garden is!'

13.4.1.4 In embedded clauses, the complementizer *că* does not impose word order restrictions, while *să* allows for a constituent to occur in initial position only when *să* is part of the complex complementizer *ca... să* (§3.1.9.2.1):

(121) a. Știe   **că** Ion   a   venit / Știe   **că** a   venit Ion
         knows   that   Ion.NOM has come   knows   that   has come Ion.NOM
         '(S)he knows that Ion came'
   b. Vrea   **să**   vină   Ion /   Vrea   **ca**   Ion   **să**   vină
         wants SĂ_SUBJ come.SUBJ.3SG Ion.NOM wants COMP   Ion.NOM SĂ_SUBJ come.SUBJ.3SG
         '(S)he wants Ion to come'

13.4.1.5 Indirect *wh*-interrogatives obligatorily have the word order of direct interrogatives, while relative clauses do not display this restriction:

(122) a. Nu   știu   unde   așteaptă **ei**   vs. *Nu   știu   unde
         not   (I)know   where wait.3PL they.NOM   not   (I)know   where
         ei   așteaptă
         they   wait.3PL
         'I do not know where they are waiting'
   b. Acesta e locul   unde   așteaptă **ei** / Acesta e locul   unde   **ei** așteaptă
         this   is place.DEF where wait.3PL they   this   is place.DEF where they   wait.3PL
         'This is the place where they are waiting'

13.4.1.6 It is not clear whether there exists a dominant word order for objects. The *indirect before direct* object word order is often preferred when the objects are DPs (to avoid the genitive–dative ambiguity), but the inverse order is also frequent (123a). The *dative before accusative* word order is obligatory only for pronominal clitics (123b), see §6.1:

(123) a. Arăt   **publicului**   **tabloul** /   Arăt
         (I)show   public.DEF.DAT   painting.DEF.ACC   (I)show
         tabloul   **publicului**
         painting.DEF.ACC   public.DEF.DAT
         'I show the painting to the public'
   b. **I-l**   arăt
         CL.DAT.3SG=CL.ACC.3SG   (I)show
         'I show it to him / her'

The prepositional object is generally placed after the direct or the indirect object.

13.4.1.7 The position of adverbial / prepositional adjuncts is relatively free, depending on their semantic connection with the verb. Situational adjuncts generally occupy the first position in the sentence (124a), instrumental or manner adjuncts are usually postverbal (124b):

(124) a. **Azi** **la** **ora** **5** are loc întâlnirea
today at hour.DEF five has place meeting.DEF
'The meeting takes place today at 5 o'clock'

b. Scrie **bine** **cu** **creionul**
writes well with pencil.DEF
'(S)he can write well with the pencil'

Clausal adjuncts headed by a subordinator have specific word order restrictions, see §10.2.8.

13.4.2 Topicalizing devices

Topicalization—placing a constituent in initial position (at the left periphery) to mark its *topic* role—is realized by a number of different *fronting constructions*: (a) *fronting* or proper *topicalization*, a simple change in word order; (b) *left dislocation*, accompanied by clitic or demonstrative doubling; (c) *hanging topic*, a suspended theme, accompanied or not by specific markers. The topicalization of the direct object is also favoured by the syntactic restructuring which results from passivization (§3.4.1).

Left dislocation is an extremely frequent topicalization mechanism, and certain structures are grammaticalized.

13.4.2.1 Fronting / topicalization

The topicalization of prepositional objects and of adverbials which are typically postverbal is obtained by simply changing the word order (125a,b). The same behaviour is displayed by predicative objects (in the rare cases in which they are topicalized (125c)), as well as by those subjects which are normally postverbal (125d):

(125) a. Îi mai ții minte pe frații mei? **La**
CL.ACC.3PL still remember PE brothers.DEF my.M.PL at
ei mă gândeam acum
them.ACC CL.REFL.ACC.1SG think.IMPERF.1SG now
'Do you remember my brothers? It is them that I was thinking of just now'

b. —De ce vorbește tare? —**Tare** vorbește pentru că e surd
why speaks loudly loudly speaks because is deaf
'Why does he speak loudly?' 'He speaks loudly because he is deaf'

c. Rochia e albă și albastră. **Albă** e doar pe margini
dress.DEF is white and blue white is only on margins
'The dress is white and blue. It is white only on the margins'

d. **Ceață** e, dar avioanele pot decola
fog is but planes.DEF can.3PL take off
'It is foggy, but planes can take off'

The aforementioned constituents can advance from an embedded clause to a position in front of the matrix verb, producing embedded topicalization constructions:

(126) **Ceață** s-ar putea să fie
fog CL.REFL.ACC.3SG=AUX.COND.3SG can.INF SĂ_SUBJ be.SUBJ.3SG
'Fog there might be'

Certain objects (realized as bare NPs, indefinite pronouns, etc.) do not occur in clitic doubling structures; they therefore can also produce a topicalized structure:

(127) a. **Oameni pricepuți** au și ei
people skilled have.3PL also they.NOM
'They too have skilled people'

b. **Multe** așteaptă el de la noi
many expects he.NOM from us.ACC
'He expects many things from us'

13.4.2.2 Left dislocation

The direct and indirect objects realized as DPs and as strong pronouns are placed in initial position only in the presence of clitic doubling (the phenomenon of clitic left dislocation, Cinque 1990). In Romanian, these constituents occur as left dislocations, with obligatory clitic resumption:

(128) a. Citesc cartea / **Cartea** o citesc
(I)read book.DEF.ACC book.DEF.ACC CL.ACC.3SG (I)read
'I read the book' 'It is the book that I read'

b. (Îi) scriu băiatului / **Băiatului** îi scriu
CL.DAT.3SG (I)write boy.DEF.DAT boy.DEF.DAT CL.DAT.3SG (I)write
'I write to the boy' 'It is the boy to whom I write'

The left dislocated constituent is sometimes prosodically isolated (by 'comma intonation'). The extension of clitic doubling to structures with unmarked word order, as an optional (in the case of indirect objects headed by nouns (128b)) or obligatory mechanism (in the case of direct objects marked by PE, with nominal or pronominal head (129a,b) and of pronominal indirect objects (129c)) is a specific feature of Romanian (§3.2.1–2.2):

(129) a. Îl văd pe Ion / **Pe Ion** îl văd
CL.ACC.3SG (I)see PE Ion.ACC PE Ion.ACC CL.ACC.3SG (I)see
'I see Ion' 'It is Ion that I see'

b. Te văd pe tine / **Pe tine** te văd
CL.ACC.2SG (I)see PE you.ACC PE you.ACC CL.ACC.2SG (I)see
'I see you' 'It is you that I see'

c. Îți scriu ție / **Ție** îți scriu
CL.ACC.2SG (I)write you.DAT you.DAT CL.ACC.2SG (I)write
'I write to you' 'It is to you that I write'

C   Left dislocation with clitic doubling is a pan-Romance and a Balkan phenomenon (Krapova 2004); differences occur only in the degree of grammaticalization of doubling in contexts without dislocation.

H   In old Romanian, topicalization (without clitic resumption) was more frequent in cases where the modern language requires dislocation (with clitic resumption); it also occurred in configurations with *p(r)e*:

(130) a. **singurătatea** **şi** **viaţă îngerească** iubiră   (Coresi)
loneliness.DEF and life angelic love.PS.3PL
'Loneliness and angelic life is what they liked'

b. **pre Dumnezeu** uită   (Coresi)
PE God forgets
'(S)he forgets God'

The subject DPs / NPs which normally occur postverbally (§13.4.1.2) can be left dislocated (with pronominal resumption) in colloquial speech (Cornilescu 2000; see also §3.1.5):

(131) **Supărarea** trece **ea** cum trece…
anger.DEF.NOM passes she.NOM how passes
'Anger will eventually pass'

Embedded argument clauses are topicalized (132a) or left dislocated, with clitic, demonstrative, or clitic + demonstrative resumption (132b):

(132) a. **Că e bun**, ştie oricine
that is good knows anybody

b. **Că e bun**, (asta) (o) ştie oricine
that is good this.F.SG.NOM CL.ACC.F.3SG knows anybody
'Everybody knows that he is good'

Constituents can advance from the embedded clause to a position in front of the matrix verb, producing overlapping constructions with left dislocation:

(133) Cartea, ştii că ţi-am dat-o
book.DEF.ACC (you)know that CL.DAT.2SG=(I)have given=CL.ACC.F.3SG
'As for the book, you know that I gave it to you'

13.4.2.3 Hanging topic

The *hanging topic* is realized by syntactic discontinuity and prosodic isolation or by specialized constructions (with specific markers).

The *hanging topic* without specific markers is typical of oral constructions (Merlan 1998). Sometimes it displays pronominal or lexical resumption (134b):

(134) a. **Cafea**, să n-aud
coffee SĂ_SUBJ not=(I)hear

b. **Cafea**, să n-aud de **ea / asta / cafea**
coffee SĂ_SUBJ not=(I)hear of it this coffee
'As for coffee, I do not want to hear about it'

The *hanging topic* is signalled by specific markers. NP topicalization can receive specific markers —*cât despre, dacă e vorba de, în privinţa, în ceea ce priveşte, referitor la* 'as far as x is concerned', *din punct de vedere* 'from the point of view of', etc., which associate with movement to topic position. The topicalized constituent does not have the expected regular case form and does not enter the configuration that it would have entered as part of the sentence; nor is it pronominally or lexically resumed. The connection with its original position is only referential (anaphoric):

(135) a. **Cât despre cafea**$_i$, $\emptyset_i$ este destul de proastă
       as   for   coffee   is   quite   bad
       'As for the coffee, it is quite bad'

   b. **Dacă e vorba de cafea**$_i$, nu vreau să beau $\emptyset_i$
      if is talk of coffee not (I)want să$_{SUBJ}$ drink.SUBJ.1SG
      'As far as coffee is concerned, I do not want to drink it'

Certain markers such as *cât despre* 'as for' have the role of changing the topic and even of introducing a new element in the topic position of the sentence, connecting it to the context as if it were already known.

Specific predicate topicalization structures (which are typically oral, colloquial) are the ones with the supine ((136a); see §4.4.3.10) and with the preposition DE followed by the adjectival predicate (136b):

(136) a. **De dormit**,# a dormit
       DE$_{SUP}$ sleep.SUP has slept
       'As for sleeping, (s)he slept'

   b. **De frumoasă**,# e frumoasă
      DE beautiful.F.SG is beautiful.F.SG
      'As far as beauty is concerned, she is beautiful'

Both constructions require the lexical resumption of the topicalized constituent.

13.4.2.4 Right dislocation

Right dislocation, as a way of pointing to the topic, is an addition which is prosodically isolated and often accompanied by a clitic (137a) or by null subject doubling (137b):

(137) a. Îl$_i$ cunosc de mult, # [pe fratele   tău]$_i$
       CL.ACC.3SG (I)know of much   PE brother.DEF your.M.SG
       'I have known him for a long time, your brother'

   b. pro$_i$ E foarte simpatic, # [fratele   tău]$_i$
            is very   nice   brother.DEF your.M.SG
      'He is very nice, your brother'

13.4.3 Contrastive topic constructions

Romanian has a weak adversative connector with the specific role of marking the contrastive topic: *iar* 'and; while' (Zafiu 2005; Vasilescu 2010). A finite verb form cannot be placed directly after *iar*:

(138) a. Trenurile   merg   bine, iar   autobuzele merg   prost
         trains.DEF   ride   well   while buses.DEF   ride   badly
         'Trains are going well, while buses are going badly'
     b. *Trenurile   merg   bine, iar   merg   prost autobuzele
         trains.DEF ride.3PL   well   while ride.3PL   badly buses.DEF

13.4.4 Rhematization / foregrounding by pseudo-cleft structures

The typical rhematization structure isolates the topic (by means of a relative clause in subject position), emphasizing the rheme (in subjective predicative complement position):

(139) [**Ceea ce** vreau   să   spun   e]   [că   ai   greşit]
       what   (I)want   SĂ   say.SUBJ.1SG is   that (you)have mistaken
       'What I want to say is that you made a mistake'

C   Romanian pseudo-cleft constructions (§10.3.4) are relatively new, of learnèd origin (probably loan translations) and belong to the standard and high register.

13.4.5 Focalization

The (contrastive) focus (which introduces a contrast with the expectations of the informational background) activates presuppositions; it is marked by intonation (phrasal stress), sometimes associated with word order changes (fronting) or with focusing adverbs.

The preferred focalization position is the beginning of the sentence. Both the topic and the emphatic rheme (the focus) tend therefore to occur in initial position; the difference is that the topic is unmarked while the focus bears phrasal stress and can take focusing adverbs to its left.

13.4.5.1 Focalization through phrasal stress allows the free placement of constituents in the sentence:

(140)   Deocamdată   au   mâncat   [FOCUSCIREŞELE]   (şi
        So far   (they)have   eaten   cherries.DEF   and
                     au   lăsat   căpşunile)
                     (they)have   left   strawberries.DEF
        'For now they have eaten the cherries (and they have left the strawberries)'

13.4.5.2 Word order change (movement to initial position) associates with phrasal stress:

(141)   [FOCUS**Cu trenul**]   merg   la   mare,   nu   cu   maşina
              by train.DEF   (I)go   to   seaside, not   by   car.DEF
        'It is by train that I go to the seaside, not by car'

Movement to initial position can also be a type of left dislocation, accompanied by syntactic doubling (by clitic or other anaphors) in the case of the direct and indirect objects:

(142) [FOCUS**Pe polițiști**] i-au   chemat vecinii,   nu pe pompieri
      PE policemen CL.ACC.3PL=have called neighbours.DEF not PE firemen
      'It is the police that the neighbours called, not the firemen'

13.4.5.3 Marking by focusing adverbs (*chiar* 'self / in person', *și* 'also', *tocmai* 'self / precisely', etc.), including the constituent negation *nu* 'not', requires phrasal stress and allows for the constituent to be freely placed in the sentence:

(143) Au   venit **chiar**   [FOCUS **proprietarii**]
      have.3PL   come in-person   owners.DEF.NOM
      'The owners came themselves'

Besides the role of emphasizing a rhematic constituent, focusing adverbs also have specific semantic-pragmatic values (§8.5.5).

13.5 MODALITY AND EVIDENTIALITY

Modality is encoded by grammatical and lexical means: verbal moods, adverbials, and modal verbs (*trebui* 'must', *putea* 'can') which are undergoing a grammaticalization process.

Evidentiality is rather strongly marked (mostly in spoken Romanian): by the (partial) grammaticalization of the epistemic future (the presumptive mood) and by a series of hearsay markers.

13.5.1 Verbal moods

Verbal moods have epistemic, as well as deontic (and volitional) values (§2.2.2). Prototypically, the indicative is epistemically associated with the *realis* value and certainty, while the subjunctive, the conditional, and the presumptive, with the *irrealis* value and uncertainty. The imperative and the 'mandatory' subjunctive have a deontic value, indicating obligation; the optative conditional and, sometimes, the subjunctive are volitional.

Some tenses of the indicative have special modal values (§2.2.3): the present associates with an epistemic reading (certainty) or with a deontic one (hortative); the future marks uncertainty or deontic and volitional meaning, the imperfect can be used as an *irrealis* marker.

13.5.2 Modal verbs

The prototypical modal verbs, which are undergoing a slow grammaticalization process, acquiring certain restrictions and structural particularities, are *putea* 'can' and *trebui* 'must'.
They have *root* readings (dynamic and deontic modality) and *epistemic* readings.

H In the area of obligation and of certainty, the inventory of verbs with modal meaning was quite different in the old language. While *putea* (< vulgar Lat. *POTĒRE) occurred frequently in the 16th century, as the main verb expressing permission and probability, *trebui* (< old Slavic *trěbovati*), often used with the etymological meaning 'need', was rivalled by *(a) se cădea* (< Lat. CADĒRE), and *(a) se cuveni* 'ought'. Similar modal values are conveyed also by *fi* and *avea* structures:

(144) unde **iaste** de **trebuiaște**, **cade-se** mainte ce e de folos a grăi (Coresi)
'if it is necessary, one must say beforehand what needs to be said'

13.5.2.1 The verb **putea** 'be able, can'

13.5.2.1.1 The modal verb *putea* has a dynamic reading, expressing the ability of the agent or the favourable circumstances of an event (145a), a deontic reading, indicating permission (145b), and an epistemic meaning, indicating likelihood and possibility / probability (145c):

(145) a. Ion e   puternic: **poate**   ridica 100 de   kg
         Ion is   strong   (he)can   lift   100 DE   kg
         'Ion is strong: he is able to lift 100 kilos'

   b. Acum, cine vrea   **poate**   pleca
      now   who   wants can.3SG   leave
      'Anyone who wants may leave now'

   c. Din   câte   înțeleg,   Ion **poate**   fi   acum la Cluj
      from how-much.F.PL (I)understand   Ion can.3SG   be   now   at Cluj
      'From what I understand, Ion may now be in Cluj'

13.5.2.1.2 The verb *putea* has three different main constructions: with subject and object (146a), with an impersonal clausal subject (146b), and (restricted to the 3rd person singular) with the reflexive-impersonal clitic *se* (146c). The situations in which the verb occurs without an object (146d) are cases of contextually retrievable ellipsis:

(146) a. El   **poate**   să   citească
         he   can   SĂ$_{SUBJ}$ read.SUBJ.3SG
         'He can read'

   b. **Poate**   să   plouă
      can.3SG   SĂ$_{SUBJ}$ rain.SUBJ.3SG
      'It may rain'

   c. **Se**   **poate**   să   plouă
      CL.REFL.ACC.3SG   can.3SG   SĂ$_{SUBJ}$ rain.SUBJ.3SG
      'It may rain'

   d. Fiecare   face   ce   **poate**   [face]
      everyone   does   what   can.3SG   do.INF
      'Each one does what (s)he can'

U In spoken Romanian, the truncation of the 3rd person present indicative verb form is very frequent when followed by the complementizer *să* (*poa' să* ['pwasə]).

The modal verb accepts either a bare infinitive (147a,b) or a subjunctive (146a,b) in the first two constructions, but only the subjunctive in the third (147c):

(147) a. El **poate** citi
         'He can read'

   b. **Poate**   ploua
      can.3SG   rain
      'It may rain'

   c. *****Se**   **poate**   (a)   ploua
      CL.REFL.ACC.3SG   can.3SG   A$_{INF}$ rain.INF

Apparent exceptions to this restriction are the cases in which the clitic *se* is raised from the embedded clause, where it had reflexive (148a), reflexive-passive (148b) or impersonal values (148c):

(148) a. Ion se poate spăla
 Ion CL.REFL.ACC.3SG can.3SG wash.INF
 'Ion can wash himself'

 b. Uşa se poate deschide cu cheia
 door.DEF CL.REFL.PASS can.3SG open.INF with key.DEF
 'One can open doors by key'

 c. Se poate pleca
 CL.REFL.IMPERS can.3SG leave.INF
 'People can go'

Together with a bare infinitive form, the verb *putea* forms a complex predicate (Abeillé and Godard 2003) or even 'a complex inflectional form' (Hill 2009, §2.5.2.2).

H The use of the bare infinitive instead of the A-infinitive in the context of *putea* is a quite recent phenomenon. In the regional language, the pattern with *putea* and the A-infinitive (*poate a veni* '(s)he can come') was preserved until the 19th century.

C Clitic raising is obligatory for the modal construction with bare infinitive (see §2.5.2.2). In Italian, clitics can be placed both in front of the modal construction and within it, which indicates a lower degree of grammaticalization of the construction: *può vederlo / lo può vedere* '(S)he can see him'. The same situation occurs in Spanish, Catalan, and Portuguese (Reinheimer and Tasmowski 2005). Standard French allows only clitic placement within the structure (*il peut le voir*), but the construction *il le peut voir* existed in old French, and is still recorded (Rowlett 2007).

13.5.2.1.3 There are only partial correspondences between the syntactic structures and the semantic values of the modal verb. With the root meanings (dynamic—'having the ability' and deontic—'be allowed'), the subject is an argument of the verb *putea*. In its epistemic meaning (of supposition regarding the sentence), *putea* is either impersonal or a personal subject-raising verb.

For the epistemic value, Romanian most frequently uses the impersonal structure with the clitic *se*, *(a) se putea* (with subject fronting in the matrix (149a) or in the argument clause (149b)):

(149) a. Ion **se** **poate** să taie acum lemnele
 Ion CL.REFL.ACC.3SG can.3SG SĂ$_{SUBJ}$ chop.SUBJ.3SG now wood.PL.DEF

 b. **Se** **poate** ca Ion să taie acum lemnele
 CL.REFL.ACC.3SG can.3SG COMP Ion SĂ$_{SUBJ}$ chop.SUBJ.3SG now wood.PL.DEF
 'Ion may be chopping the wood now'

The form without *se* is more ambiguous: the epistemic reading depends on the semantics of the verb, on the tense, and on the context. The epistemic meaning is less probable for *agentive* verbs (150a) than for *state* verbs (150b):

(150) a. Ion **poate** să **taie** lemnele
 Ion can.3SG SĂ$_{SUBJ}$ chop.SUBJ.3SG wood.DEF

 b. Ion **poate** să **fie** acasă
 Ion may.3SG SĂ$_{SUBJ}$ be.SUBJ.3SG at-home

If *putea* is in the present or imperfect indicative, and the subordinate verb is in the perfect subjunctive, the epistemic reading (supposition about a past event) occurs more readily (151a) or is the sole option (151b):

(151) a. Ion **putea** să fi tăiat lemnele
Ion can.IMPERF.3SG SĂ$_{SUBJ}$ be chopped wood.PL.DEF
'Ion could / might have chopped the wood yesterday'
b. Ion **poate** să fi tăiat lemnele
Ion can.3SG SĂ$_{SUBJ}$ be chopped wood.PL.DEF
'Ion may have chopped the wood'

There are no significant semantic differences between the construction of *putea* with a bare infinitive (as a complex predicate, see §3.5.2.2) and with the subjunctive (§2.2.2.2, §4.2.5). However, the bare infinitive does not accept tense variation, so constructions similar to (151) are not possible. The highly grammaticalized syntactic status of *putea* as a component of a complex predicate occurs more frequently in dynamic and deontic contexts, but only rarely in the epistemic ones.

13.5.2.1.4 A form of the verb *putea*—the 3rd person present indicative *poate*—is grammaticalized as an adverb of epistemic modality (uncertainty). The adverb is either incidental or takes a complement introduced by *că*:

(152) a. S-a greşit, **poate**, la numărătoare
CL.REFL.PASS=has mistaken maybe at counting
b. **Poate** s-a greşit la numărătoare
maybe CL.REFL.PASS.ACC=has mistaken at counting
c. **Poate** că s-a greşit la numărătoare
maybe that CL.REFL.PASS.ACC=has mistaken at counting
'Maybe there was a mistake in counting'

H The adverb may have appeared through the abbreviation of the modal marker *poate-fi* (Zafiu 2006), present in older texts (153a), which is originally an impersonal construction (153b):
(153) a. acest om **poate-fi** este trebuitoriu (Neculce)
'This man is maybe useful'
b. cronicariul leşescu de aceste poveşti foarte pre scurt scrie, că **poate fi** *că* nu au ştiut di toate (Ureche)
'The Polish chronicler writes very briefly about these stories, because it is possible that he did not know all these'
The origin of the adverb in the impersonal construction accounts for its epistemic value and for the compatibility with the complementizer *că*.

13.5.2.2 The verb **trebui** *'must'*

13.5.2.2.1 The modal verb *trebui* has a dynamic reading, expressing objective necessity or circumstances that obligatorily lead to an event (154a), a deontic reading, expressing obligation (154b), and an epistemic and evidential meaning, expressing probability and conjecture (154c):

(154) a. Am pus scrisoarea la poştă: **trebuie** să sosească
(I)have put letter.DEF at post must.3SG SĂ$_{SUBJ}$ arrive.SUBJ.3SG
'I put the letter in the post: it has to arrive'

 b. **Trebuie** ca fiecare să-şi plătească impozitul
  must.3SG COMP everyone SĂ$_{SUBJ}$=CL.REFL.DAT.3SG pay.SUBJ.3SG tax.DEF
  'Everyone must pay their taxes'

 c. **Trebuie** să aibă el ceva de
  must.3SG SĂ$_{SUBJ}$ have.SUBJ.3SG he something DE$_{SUP}$
  întrebat, din moment ce a ridicat mâna
  ask.SUP since has raised hand.DEF
  'He must have something to ask, since he raised his hand'

13.5.2.2.2 In its modal uses, *trebui* enters an impersonal construction, with a clausal subject (155a), in which subject fronting and subject raising (with agreement) are possible (155b); the non-realization of the embedded clause is a case of ellipsis (155c):

(155) a. **Trebuie** să fie o greşeală
  must.3SG SĂ$_{SUBJ}$ be.SUBJ.3SG a mistake
  'It must be a mistake'

 b. Ei **trebuiau / trebuia** să vină
  they must.IMPERF.3PL must.IMPERF.3SG SĂ$_{SUBJ}$ come.SUBJ.3PL
  'They had to come'

 c. Fiecare face ce **trebuie** [să facă]
  everyone does what must.3SG SĂ$_{SUBJ}$ do.SUBJ.3SG
  'Everyone is doing what they have to'

The construction with a nominal postverbal subject (*Îmi trebuie bani* 'I need money') is never modal.

 The embedded clause selects the complementizer *să* and the subjunctive mood; the infinitive is not used in this structure any more.

H In old Romanian, *trebui* also admitted an infinitive:
 (156) atunce mai vârtos **trebuiaşte a ne teame şi a ne cutremura** (Coresi)
  'then we have to be more afraid and tremble'

Trebui has fewer of the syntactic characteristics of a grammaticalized modal verb than *putea*. It enters a complex predicate with subject raising and agreement (157a) or with subject raising, agreement, and an elliptical passive construction (157b) (§3.5.3).

(157) a. Copiii **trebuiau** să plece
  children.DEF must.IMPERF.3PL SĂ$_{SUBJ}$ leave.SUBJ.3PL
  'The children had to leave'

 b. Florile **trebuiau** [să fie] udate
  flowers.DEF must.IMPERF.3PL SĂ$_{SUBJ}$ be.SUBJ.3PL watered.F.PL
  'The flowers had to be watered'

13.5.2.2.3 The verb has an epistemic reading (of supposition regarding the sentence content), mainly in impersonal constructions with a clausal SĂ$_{SUBJ}$ subject (158a) or (less frequently) in raising constructions (158b):

(158) a. **Trebuie** să fi greşit noi undeva
  must.3SG SĂ$_{SUBJ}$ be mistaken we somewhere
  'We must have erred somewhere'

b. Ei **trebuie** să fi greşit undeva
   they must.3SG≡PL SĂ_SUBJ be mistaken somewhere
   'They must have erred somewhere'

This structure only occurs with the present tense of the verb, which led to the interpretation of the invariable form as a clausal adverb. However, *trebuie*, unlike other Romanian clausal adverbials, is never used parenthetically and without a complementizer.

H In the 16th–17th centuries, *trebui* had only root meanings; the epistemic reading is relatively recent (Avram 2008).

U In spoken Romanian, the verb *trebui* also frequently occurs with a truncated 3rd person present indicative form, followed by the complementizer *să*: *tre' să...* 'I/you/he/, etc must'. This form is also independent of the verb's modal value.

The modal *trebuie* has an epistemic value almost exclusively in the present tense (and only rarely in the imperfect). The epistemic reading is favoured by the use of the perfect subjunctive in the subordinate clause:

(159) a. **Trebuie** să fi tăiat cineva lemnele
         must.PRES.3SG SĂ_SUBJ be chopped someone wood.PL.DEF
         'Someone must have chopped the wood'
      b. **Trebuia** să fi tăiat cineva lemnele
         must.IMPERF.3SG SĂ_SUBJ be chopped someone wood.PL.DEF
         'Someone must have chopped the wood'

The construction of the impersonal *trebui* with the complementizer *că*, specialized for the epistemic-evidential doubt or supposition value, is more recent:

(160) **Trebuie** că au greşit ei undeva
      must.3SG that have.3PL mistaken they somewhere
      'They must have erred somewhere'

13.5.2.3 Other verbs with modal and evidential meaning

13.5.2.3.1 The personal verb *avea* 'have' taking a prepositional supine complement, which displays subject control and accusative clitic raising, has only root modal meaning (dynamic and deontic):

(161) El o are de scris mâine
      he CL.ACC.F.3SG has DE_SUP write.SUP tomorrow
      'He has to write it tomorrow'

H The corresponding subjunctive structure is largely grammaticalized, and has become one of the future tense paradigms (*are să scrie* 'he will write').

13.5.2.3.2 The impersonal verb *fi* 'be', with a prepositional supine, has the same root modal meaning (especially deontic):

(162) E de vorbit mâine
      is DE_SUP talk.SUP tomorrow
      'We have to talk tomorrow'

This verb also shows a root (especially dynamic) construction with the subjunctive, mainly in conditional (163a) and temporal clauses (163b):

(163) a. Dacă e să plecăm, închidem uşa
　　　　if is sĂ_SUBJ go.1PL close.1PL door.DEF
　　　　'If we must go, we will close the door'

　　　b. Când e să se întâmple, se întâmplă
　　　　when is sĂ_SUBJ CL.REFL.ACC.3SG happen.SUBJ.3SG CL.REFL.ACC.3SG happens
　　　　'When it has to happen, it just happens'

13.5.2.3.3 The verb *părea* 'seem' (§3.5.3) is both impersonal and personal (the construction with subject raising and agreement became fixed), taking either an A-infinitive / sĂ-subjunctive (164a,b) complement, or an indicative or epistemic conditional complement introduced by the complementizer *că* (164c); ellipsis of the embedded verb is allowed in the case of copula verbs (164d):

(164) a. Pare a ploua / să plouă
　　　　seems A_INF rain.INF sĂ_SUBJ rain.SUBJ.3SG
　　　　'It seems that it is raining'

　　　b. Ei par a fi obosiţi / să fie obosiţi
　　　　they seem.3PL A_INF be.INF tired.M.PL sĂ_SUBJ be.SUBJ.3PL tired
　　　　'They seem to be tired'

　　　c. El pare că doarme / ar dormi
　　　　he seems that sleeps / AUX.COND.3SG sleep.INF
　　　　'It seems that he is sleeping'

　　　d. El pare obosit
　　　　he seems tired.M.SG
　　　　'He seems tired'

The meaning of the verb is epistemic-evidential: it marks uncertainty produced by a visual pseudo-perception.

The reflexive-impersonal construction has a mainly evidential reportative value ('it is said') and manifests a tendency to be used incidentally, as a marker in fixed patterns:

(165) a. **Se** **pare** că au plecat toţi
　　　　CL.REFL.ACC.3SG seems that (they)have left all

　　　b. Au plecat, **se** **pare**, toţi
　　　　have left CL.REFL.ACC.3SG seems all

　　　c. Au plecat, **pare-se**, toţi
　　　　have left seems=CL.REFL.ACC.3SG all
　　　　'It seems that they have all left'

13.5.3 Modal adverbials

13.5.3.1 Modal adverbials (mainly adverbs, and prepositional phrases, see §8.5.2) have certain construction (and word order) particularities: they can be prosodically integrated (166a) or parenthetic (166b); they can be followed by the complementizer CĂ, which subordinates a clause (166c), with subject fronting (166d) or which tends to become a component of a lexical item (*desigur că* (166e)):

(166) a. un   om   **desigur**   onest
        a   man certainly   honest
        'a man (who is) certainly honest'

   b. un om, **desigur**, onest
      'certainly an honest man'

   c. **Desigur   că**   Ion   e   un   om   onest
      certainly that Ion   is   a   man   honest

   d. Ion **desigur**   că   e   un   om   onest
      Ion certainly   that is   a   man   honest

   e. Ion e   un   om   **desigur   că**   onest
      Ion is   a   man   certainly that honest
      'Ion is certainly an honest man'

13.5.3.2 Most modal adverbials are epistemic, placed (also mediated by intensity modifiers, approximators, etc.) on the uncertainty / certainty scale (*oarecum sigur* 'somewhat certain', *destul de sigur* 'quite certain', *foarte sigur* 'very certain', *cât se poate de sigur* 'as certain as can be' *mai mult ca sigur* 'more than certain', etc.).

Certainty is expressed by adverbials such as *desigur* 'certainly', *evident* 'obviously', *sigur* 'surely', *bineînțeles* 'of course', *firește* 'certainly'; *de bună seamă* 'certainly', *cu siguranță* 'surely', *fără îndoială, fără nicio îndoială, fără doar și poate* 'undoubtedly', *mai mult ca sigur* 'absolutely certain', and by the sequences *în* 'in'+ *mod* 'way' (or *în* 'in'+ *chip* 'way') + adjective: *în mod cert* 'certainly', *în mod sigur* 'surely', *în chip evident* 'obviously'.

There are fewer adverbials of uncertainty: *poate* 'maybe', *probabil* 'probably', *eventual* 'in case of need', *parcă* 'seemingly'; there are no sequences containing the nouns *mod* or *chip* 'way' with uncertain meaning. Some of the adverbs that mark uncertainty mainly indicate the source of knowledge, and thus are also evidential (§13.5.6).

13.5.3.3 There are fewer deontic adverbials. According to their meaning, there are modalizers of obligation—*obligatoriu, neapărat, negreșit*, (colloquial) *musai* 'obligatorily', sequences such as *în mod / chip necesar* 'necessarily', *în mod / chip obligatoriu* 'obligatorily'—and fewer of permission—*eventual* 'maybe'. Deontic adverbs do not display a clearly clausal behaviour: they can function as independent pro-sentences, but not as heads. They are generally integrated, more rarely parenthetical.

Adverbials can also express evaluative or appreciative modality (Lyons 1977; Pană Dindelegan 1985), which is realized only lexically; they are fewer than the epistemic adverbials and occur exclusively as heads: *bine că* 'it's a good job that; thank God that', *noroc că* 'it's lucky that', *păcat că* 'it's a pity that', *ciudat că* 'it's strange that', etc. or exclusively as incident / integrated elements: *din fericire* 'fortunately', *din păcate / din nenorocire / din nefericire* 'unfortunately'.

13.5.4 Other modal markers

13.5.4.1 The copular non-grammaticalized structures, such as *e sigur* 'it is sure' (epistemic), *e necesar* 'it is necessary' (deontic), *e bine* 'it is good' (appreciative) generally occur in initial position, followed by *că* (167a); some may also be parenthetically used (167b):

(167) a. **E clar** că vor pleca mâine
is clear that AUX.FUT.3PL leave.INF tomorrow
 b. Vor pleca, **e clar**, mâine
AUX.FUT.3PL leave.INF is clear tomorrow
'It is clear that they will leave tomorrow'

Some of them are in variation with modal adverbials which can also occur independently (*e sigur* 'it is certain'/ *sigur* 'certainly').

13.5.4.2 Modal epistemic particles are used in interrogatives: *oare* 'I wonder / maybe', *cumva* 'may be / happen to'.

H Old Romanian had other modal adverbs of possibility with particle behaviour; some disappeared (*cândai* 'perhaps'), others changed their meaning (*doar* became a restrictive focalizer).

13.5.4.3 A series of verbs with modal meaning (especially epistemic) are used in constructions that tend to become fixed as pragmatic markers, especially as hedges (*nu știu* 'I do not know', *știu eu?* 'what do I know?') or modalizers (*se știe* 'it is known').

U In colloquial Romanian, the sequence *cre'că* (< *cred că*... 'I think that...') is undergoing a process of transformation into a modal marker.

13.5.5 'Harmonic' and 'disharmonic' combinations

The combination of 'harmonic' or 'disharmonic' modal markers (those with similar or contrary meaning, respectively) is quite frequent. The markers can be grammatically different, for example an adverb and a verbal mood (conditional (168a), presumptive (168b)):

(168) a. Cică ar veni mâine (harmonic use)
allegedly AUX.COND.3SG come.INF tomorrow
'Apparently, he is coming tomorrow'
 b. Sigur că poate o fi greșit (disharmonic use)
certainly that maybe o be.INF mistaken
'It is certain that he may have erred'

13.5.6 Evidential markers

The most important Romanian evidential markers are the verbal moods: the subjunctive is suppositional, especially in interrogative sentences, the conditional is predominantly reportative and sometimes inferential, and the presumptive is generally suppositional, but also reportative in adversative structures, then, a 'non-first-hand evidential' (Aikhenvald 2004: 288). The ongoing grammaticalization of the presumptive provides Romanian with a specialized evidential device (Reinheimer Rîpeanu 2000; Zafiu 2002).

Modal verbs have some predominantly evidential readings (Cuniță 2004): the epistemic uses of *trebui* 'must' and especially the construction *trebuie că* (§13.5.2.2.3) are inferential.

The collocational complementizer *cum că* (§10.1.1.3) displays a tendency to specialization as a reportive / hearsay marker (which indicates the non-assumption of the reported content).

In the colloquial language, there are many reportative markers—*cică, pasămite, chipurile* (Scripnic 2010), *vezi Doamne* 'apparently', etc.—which indicate the fact that the information taken over is not assumed. They are either prosodically integrated or parenthetic:

(169) a. A   câştigat **cică**   un premiu
         has won   allegedly   a prize
         '(S)he apparently won a prize'

   b. Are, **chipurile**,   20 de   ani
         has apparently   20 DE   years
         '(S)he is apparently 20 years old'

C   The marker *cică* < *zice că* 'they say that' has a counterpart in Sp. *dizque* 'apparently' (Dumitrescu 2012; Cruschina and Remberger 2008).

Other declarative verbs tend to produce hearsay markers in fixed structures (e.g. *zice-se* 'it is said', Ganea 2010). An adverb which has become an inferential marker is *pesemne* 'seemingly'.

Perceptual evidentiality is marked especially by presentative interjections (*iată, uite* 'look'). Like the modal verb *părea* 'seem' (§13.5.2.3.3), the adverbial derived from it *parcă* (< *pare că* 'it seems that') is a pseudo-perceptual which marks uncertainty and excludes the supposition and the reportative values.

13.6 ANAPHORA

13.6.1 Anaphorics

Non-ambiguous grammatical means of indicating coreference are the reflexive, reciprocal-reflexive, and possessive-reflexive clitics, relative pronouns, and the zero anaphora in syntactic constructions with obligatory control and in coordinated structures. When it is not grammatically constrained, anaphora allows competition between several realizations—zero anaphora, personal pronouns, demonstrative pronouns and adverbs, referential DPs. The selection of a certain realization depends on antecedent accessibility and influences anaphora resolution.

13.6.2 Syntactically controlled anaphora and discourse anaphora

13.6.2.1 Reflexive, reciprocal-reflexive, and possessive-reflexive clitics (§3.4.2-4, §6.2, §6.5) are means for the realization of bound anaphora, that is, they mark the obligatory coreference of the subject and the direct (170a), indirect (170b), or possessive object (170c):

(170) a. Ion$_i$ se$_i$ admiră în oglindă
Ion CL.REFL.ACC.3SG admires in mirror
'Ion admires himself in the mirror'

b. Ion$_i$ şi Maria$_j$ îşi$_{i+j}$ trimit flori
Ion and Maria CL.REFL.DAT.3PL send flowers
'Ion and Maria send flowers to one another'

c. Ion$_i$ îşi$_i$ admiră părinţii t$_i$
Ion CL.REFL.DAT.3SG admires parents.DEF
'Ion admires his parents'

d. Ion$_i$ îl$_j$ admiră
Ion CL.ACC.3SG admires
'Ion admires him'

e. Ion$_i$ îi$_j$ admiră părinţii t$_j$
Ion CL.DAT.3SG admires parents.DEF
'Ion admires his parents'

In examples (170d,e), the personal pronominal clitics indicate disjoint reference, that is, non-identity with the subject.

Reflexive clitics also occur in (emphatic or disambiguating) doubling structures, alongside the strong forms of the reflexive or personal pronoun; the strong form occurs either alone, bearing phrasal stress (*sine* self.ACC, *el* him.ACC; *sieşi* self.DAT, *lui* him.DAT), or accompanied by the intensifier *însuşi* 'himself' (§6.4), with which it tends to form frozen phrases; these structures are evolving towards compound reflexives (*sine însuşi, el însuşi* himself.ACC; *sie însuşi, lui însuşi* himself.DAT) (171a); the forms *sine, sieşi* and the compound forms *el însuşi, sine însuşi* are coreferential with the subject irrespective of the syntactic position they occupy (they function as long-distance reflexives) (171b). The strong forms of the personal pronoun are ambiguous, as they allow both coreference and disjoint reference (171c):

(171) a. Ion$_i$ se$_i$ admiră pe sine$_i$ / pe el$_i$ / pe
Ion CL.REFL.ACC. admires PE self.ACC PE him.ACC PE
[sine însuşi]$_i$ / pe [el însuşi]$_i$
self.ACC himself PE him.ACC himself
'Ion admires himself'

b. Ion$_i$ e prieten cu Andrei$_j$ dar [pro]$_i$ are o părere
Ion is friend with Andrei but has an opinion
bună numai despre sine$_i$ / [el însuşi$_i$]
good only about self.ACC him.ACC himself
'Ion is Andrei's friend, but has a good opinion only of himself'

c. Ion$_i$ are o părere bună despre el$_{i//j}$
Ion has an opinion good about him.ACC
'Ion has a good opinion of himself / him'

Like all pro-drop languages, Romanian very often uses zero anaphora when the subject is coreferential with an antecedent: in coordination (172a) and in subordination (172b).

(172) a. Ion$_i$ salută și [pro]$_i$ pleacă (și el$_i$)
Ion greets and leaves also he
'Ion says hello and he leaves (too)'

b. Ion$_i$ încearcă să citească PRO$_i$ / a citi PRO$_i$
Ion tries SĂ$_{SUBJ}$ read.SUBJ.3SG A$_{INF}$ read.INF
'Ion tries to read'

13.6.2.2 Discourse anaphora reflects the universal accessibility hierarchy, in which the more reduced the form of the anaphor is, that is, the closer it is to zero anaphora, the more probable is coreference. In Romanian the main hierarchy levels (in a very simplified form of Ariel's 1990 hierarchy) are:

zero anaphora > personal pronoun > demonstrative > referential DP

In a sentence, the realization of the subject as zero anaphora generally indicates coreference with a highly accessible antecedent, which occupies the same syntactic position (subject); the personal pronoun can be used for both disjoint reference and coreference (173b); the demonstrative clearly marks disjoint reference and the fact that a closer antecedent is selected, occupying a different position than the subject (173c). The DP marks disjoint reference and its antecedent either occupies a different syntactic position than the DP, or is placed at an even greater distance (173d):

(173) Ion$_i$ s-a întâlnit cu Dan$_j$.
Ion CL.REFL.ACC.3SG=has met with Dan
'Ion met Dan'

a. [**pro**]$_i$ I$_j$-a dat o carte
CL.DAT.3SG=has given a book

b. **El**$_{j//i}$ i$_{i//j}$-a dat o carte
he CL.DAT.3SG=has given a book

c. **Acesta**$_j$ i$_i$-a dat o carte
this CL.DAT.3SG=has given a book
'He gave him a book'

d. [**Colegul de facultate**]$_{k//j}$ i$_i$-a dat o carte
colleague.DEF of faculty CL.DAT.3SG=has given a book
'His faculty colleague gave him a book'

The coreferentiality can be indicated by the zero anaphora when that has the same thematic role as the antecedent (Experiencer as in 174), even if the syntactic positions are different:

(174) Pe Ion$_i$ îl$_i$ doare capul. [**pro**]$_i$ Suferă îngrozitor
PE Ion CL.ACC.3SG aches head.DEF.NOM suffers terribly
'Ion has a headache. He suffers terribly'

The syntactic–pragmatic preferences for discourse anaphora do not always hold in the colloquial, especially oral, language, where ambiguities are solved on the basis of cognitive and contextual factors.

The cataphoric use of pronouns is also possible, especially in subordinate clauses placed in front of the matrix clause:

(175) Când   l$_i$-am   văzut   eu,   Dan$_i$ era   vesel
       when   CL.ACC.3SG=(I)have   seen   I   Dan   be.IMPERF.3SG   happy
       'When I saw him, Dan was happy'

13.6.3 Referential anaphora and semantic anaphora

13.6.3.1 Referential nominal anaphora (which presupposes coreference with an antecedent) is realized as a nominal substitute (zero anaphora, personal, reflexive, possessive, and demonstrative pronoun) (176a) or by means of a determiner (definite article, demonstrative, or identity determiner, see §5.3.1) which triggers coreference with the antecedent (176b):

(176) Ana a mai scris [o carte]$_i$
       'Ana wrote another book'

   a. [**pro**]$_i$ A   fost   publicată   anul   trecut
                     has   been   published   year.DEF   past
      'It was published last year'

   b. [Volumul]$_i$ /   [**acest**   volum]$_i$ /   [**același**   volum]$_i$ a   fost
      volume.DEF   this   volume   the-same   volume   has   been
      publicat   anul   trecut
      published   year.DEF   past
      'The / this / the same volume was published last year'

Adverbial anaphorics (*atunci* 'then', *acolo* 'there') and zero anaphora can have adverbial antecedents:

(177) a. A ajuns [la Ploiești]$_i$ și de **acolo**$_i$ a luat trenul
          'He arrived in Ploiești and from there he took the train'
       b. A plecat [la Ploiești]$_i$. A ajuns Ø$_i$ la ora 5
          'He left for Ploiești. He arrived at 5 o'clock'

Referential resumption can be either integral or partial, i.e. in partitive structures:

(178) [Supa]$_i$ e   bună.   Mai   vreau Ø$_i$
       soup.DEF   is   good   more   (I)want
       'The soup is good. I want more'

Romanian demonstratives (§5.3.1.2) do not follow a deictic model (that of textual deixis), in which the proximal demonstrative has a closer antecedent and the distal demonstrative is placed further away in the text. In the standard language the anaphoric used to point to a referent which is different from the subject of the previous sentence (i.e. with change of topic) is usually *acesta* 'this' (173c).

The distal demonstrative *acela* 'that' occurs in order to additionally mark narrative distance (Zafiu 2004):

(179) Poliția   îl   caută   pe   Ion$_i$.   Se   pare   că
      police.DEF   CL.ACC.3SG   searches   PE   ION   CL.REFL.IMPERS   seems that
      acesta$_i$ / **acela$_i$**   era   criminalul
      this   that   be.IMPERF   criminal.DEF

Textual deixis employs the sequence *acesta din urmă* 'this last one, the latter', as well as ordinal and alternative substitutes (*primul*... 'the first, the former', *al doilea* 'the second, the latter'/ *celălalt* 'the other').

U   In the spoken language, *ăsta* 'this' and *ăla* 'that' are frequently used as 'deixis ad phantasma' (Manoliu Manea 1995), with no reference to the external world, but to the representation created by the utterance, and depending on the cognitive prominence of the referents. In standard written Romanian, the demonstrative *acesta* 'this' is very much used, even in situations in which coreference would have been sufficiently marked by the personal pronoun or by the definite article.

13.6.3.2 The anaphora which summarizes a clausal content (and is considered *textual deixis* by some authors) is realized (also depending on the syntactic position) as a feminine pronoun with neutral value: *o* 'it' (180a), *asta* 'this' (180b), *ceea ce* 'what' (180c), as zero anaphora (180d), or as a pro-sentence adverb (180e):

(180) a. [A   plecat   devreme]$_i$.   I-am   reproșat-o$_i$ imediat
          has   left   early   CL.DAT=have   reproached=CL.ACC.F.3SG   immediately
          '(S)he left early'   'I immediately reproached him / her for it'

      b. [A   plecat   devreme]$_i$.   **Asta$_i$**   i-am   reproșat
          has   left   early   this.F.SG   CL.DAT.3SG=(I)have   reproached
          '(S)he left early'   'This is what I reproached him / her for'

      c. [A   plecat   devreme]$_i$,   [**ceea ce**]$_i$ i-am   reproșat
          has   left   early   what   CL.DAT.3SG=(I)have   reproached
          '(S)he left early'   'What I reproached to him / her'

      d. [A   plecat   devreme]$_i$.   [**pro**]$_i$ A   fost   o   greșeală
          has   left   early   has   been   a   mistake
          '(S)he left early'   'It was a mistake'

      e. [A   plecat   devreme]$_i$.   —Mă   tem   că   **da$_i$**
          has   left   early   CL.ACC.1SG   (I)fear   that   yes
          '(S)he left early'   'I am afraid so'

13.6.3.3 Semantic anaphora (which differs from the referential anaphora by introducing a new referent, similar to the antecedent from a semantic point of view) has many possibilities of realization, among which are the specialized determiners AL and CEL (used pronominally).

For the nominal semantic anaphora, personal clitics, as well as AL (181a), the distal demonstrative (181b), and the determiner CEL (181c) are employed as 'lazy pronouns' (which avoid repetition, being used without co-referentiality):

(181) a. Ana îşi   ia   **banii**   azi,   iar Ion şi-**i**
         Ana CL.REFL.DAT.3SG takes money.DEF today, and Ion CL.REFL.DAT.3SG=CL.ACC.3PL
         primeşte mâine   pe   **ai**   lui
         receives tomorrow PE   AL.M.PL   his.GEN
         'Ana receives her money today, and Ion receives his tomorrow'
     b. Îi   plac   **ziariştii**   echilibraţi   şi   îi
        CL.DAT.3SG   like.3PL journalists.DEF   balanced   and   CL.DAT.3SG
        displac   **aceia**   care   exagerează
        dislike.3PL   those.M.PL   that   exaggerate.3PL
        'He likes balanced journalists and dislikes those that exaggerate'
     c. Ana stă   în   **cortul**   galben, iar Ion în   **cel**   albastru
        Ana stays in   tent.M.SG.DEF   yellow   and Ion in   CEL.M.SG   blue
        'Ana stays in the yellow tent and Ion in the blue one'

AL sometimes produces ambiguity between the semantic and the coreferential reading:

(182) Cadourile   sunt   pentru   **vărul**   meu   şi   **al**   Danei
      presents.DEF   are   for   cousin.DEF   my.M.SG.DEF   and   AL.M.SG   Dana.GEN
      'The presents are for my and Dana's cousin / for my cousin and for Dana's'

Adjectival predicative semantic anaphora is realized either as zero anaphora (ellipsis), or by the substitutes *(tot) aşa, la fel* 'identical' (183a). Verbal anaphora is generally realized as zero anaphora (ellipsis). For certain semantic classes of verbs, it may be realized as the verb *face* 'do' which has the direct object clitic *o* attached to it (183b):

(183) a. Ion   e   **vesel**.   Şi   Maria   e Ø /   [**la fel**]
         Ion   is   happy   and   Maria   is   the-same
         'Ion is happy. And so is Maria'
     b. Ion   [a   **demisionat**]   ieri.   Maria   Ø /   [a   **făcut-o**]
        Ion   has   quitted   yesterday   Maria   has   done=CL.ACC.F.3SG
        a   doua   zi
        the- second day
        'Ion quitted yesterday. Maria did so the second day'

13.6.4 Anaphorics on the grammaticalization cline

Coreference is supplementally marked (emphatically, for disambiguating purposes) by lexical markers which are on the way to grammaticalization—the modifiers *respectiv* 'particular; very', *numit* 'named', *pomenit* 'mentioned', *în cauză* 'involved', etc.:

(184) A   cumpărat   [o   maşină]$_i$ şi   a   plecat.
      has   bought   a   car   and   has   left
      [Maşin*a*   **respectivă**]$_i$ / [**Respectiva**   maşină]$_i$ i-a   fost   furată
      car.DEF   particular   particular.DEF   car   CL.DAT.3SG=has been   stolen
      'He bought a car and left. That particular / very car was stolen'

Respectivul (masculine singular) are *respectiva* (feminine singular) are also on the way to grammaticalization as an anaphoric pronoun (Halvorsen 2002).

The adjective *propriul* 'own', suffixed by the definite article, functions as an emphasizer of the coreference between the possessive and the subject, and it can be used instead of the possessive:

(185) a. Ion$_i$ nu   mai   vorbește   cu   [propriul   său]$_i$ frate
         Ion   not   more   speaks   with   own.DEF   his.M.SG   brother
     b. Ion$_i$ nu   mai   vorbește   cu   **propriul**$_i$ frate
         Ion   not   more   speaks   with   own.DEF   brother
        'Ion does not speak to his own brother any more'

13.7 VOCATIVE PHRASES AND ADDRESS

13.7.1 Syntactic particularities of the vocative case

The vocative is a non-syntactic case, and its main function is address, expressing the *allocutive* pragmatic role. It either has its own specific form or is identical to the nominative–accusative form (§5.1.3.3). Unlike the other cases, it is always intonationally marked and generally isolated from the rest of the sentence with a pause, marked in writing by a comma.

The vocative appears in many syntactic contexts: it may stand on its own as a unanalysable, syntactically unstructured sentence, accompanying another declarative (186a), interrogative (186b), or imperative (186c) sentence, without being syntactically linked to it, or it may stand on its own (187). In other contexts, it can play the role of an apposition that agrees (188a) or not with a vocative, whose first element is a 2nd person pronominal DP (188b) or a 2nd person unexpressed subject (188c) and it may also appear in classifier structures (189) (§5.3.6.2).

(186) a. **Ioane**,   este   târziu
         Ion.VOC   is   late
        'Ion, it is late'
     b. **Ioane**,   când   vii?
         Ion.VOC   when   (you)come
        'Ion, when are you coming?'
     c. **Ioane**,   vino   repede!
         Ion.VOC   come.IMP.2SG   quickly
        'Ion, come quickly!'

(187) Ioane!
      Ion.VOC
      'Ion!'

(188) a. tu,   **Ioane**
         you.VOC≡NOM   Ion.VOC
        'You, Ion'
     b. Vorbesc   cu   tine,   **Ioane**!
        (I)speak   with   you.ACC   Ion.VOC
        'I'm talking to you, Ion!'

c. Răspunde, **Ioane!**
answer.IMP.2SG Ion.VOC
'Answer, Ion!'

(189) frate **Ioane**
brother.VOC(≡NOM≡ACC) Ion.VOC
'brother Ion'

The vocative cannot take argumental positions specific to the noun (GBLR: 127), but it may be the head of an extended nominal phrase. The phrase comprises: determiners (the definite article when followed by a genitive or a possessive adjective (190a,b), but not with a prenominal demonstrative (190c)), quantifiers (191a,b), possessive phrases (which come second, when the first element is a DP (192a–d)), modifiers (adjectives (193a–e), prepositional phrases (193f), or relative clauses (193g)).

(190) a. Fat**a** mamei!
girl.DEF.VOC(≡NOM≡ACC) mother.DEF.GEN

b. Băiatul meu!
boy.DEF.VOC(≡NOM≡ACC) my.M.SG.VOC(≡NOM≡ACC)

c. *Această fată, vino!
this.F.SG girl come.IMP.2SG

(191) a. **Toată** lumea, la masă! / **Toți** băieții,
all people.DEF.VOC(≡NOM≡ACC) at table all boys.DEF.VOC(≡NOM≡ACC)
la sport!
at sport

b. **Amândoi** concurenții, pe scenă!
both competitors.DEF on scene

(192) a. Fata / Fetele **mamei!**
girl.DEF.VOC(≡NOM≡ACC) girl.DEF.VOC(≡NOM≡ACC) mother.DEF.GEN

b. Fata **mea!**
girl.DEF.VOC(≡NOM≡ACC) my.F.SG.DEF.VOC(≡NOM≡ACC)

c. Maria **mea!**
Maria.VOC(≡NOM≡ACC) my.F.SG.DEF.VOC(≡NOM≡ACC)

d. Frumosul **meu!**
beautiful.M.SG.DEF.VOC(≡NOM≡ACC) my.M.SG.VOC(≡NOM≡ACC)

(193) a. Fetiță **frumoasă!**
girl.SG.VOC(≡NOM≡ACC) beautiful.F.SG.VOC(≡NOM≡ACC)

b. Fetițo / Mario **dragă!**
girl.SG.VOC Maria.VOC dear.F.SG.VOC(≡NOM≡ACC)

c. **Stimate** domn!
esteemed.M.SG.VOC sir.SG.VOC(≡NOM≡ACC)

d. Măi, ăla **mic!**
Hey that.M.SG.VOC(≡NOM≡ACC) little.M.SG.VOC(≡NOM≡ACC)

e. Tu   **urâtule!**
you.VOC(≡NOM)   ugly.M.AG.DEF.VOC

f. Băiatul /   Tu   **din**   **banca**   **întâi!**
boy.DEF.SG.VOC≡NOM≡ACC   you.VOC(≡NOM)   from   desk   first

g. Fetițo /   Tu   **care**   **stai**   **în**   **picioare!**
girl.VOC   you.VOC(≡NOM)   who   (you)stay   in   feet

13.7.2 Pragmatic–semantic relations between vocative and other sentence constituents

The vocative is normally associated with other allocutives: interjections of interpellation (*mă(i)*, *bă(i)*, *fă*, *bre*) (Manu Magda 2004) (194), imperative forms (195), hortatory interjections (196) (Manu Magda 2003, 2009), cumulative forms of direct address (197).

(194)   **Măi**   Ioane!
             hey   Ion.VOC

(195)   **Vino,**   Ioane!
             come.IMP.2SG   Ion.VOC

(196)   **Hai,**   Ioane!
             come-on   Ion.VOC

(197)   a. Dragul   meu
               dear.DEF.M.SG.VOC(≡NOM≡ACC)   my.M.SG.VOC(≡NOM≡ACC)
               domn   consilier
               sir.SG.VOC(≡NOM≡ACC)   adviser.M.SG.VOC(≡NOM≡ACC)
               general   Ionuț Popescu!
               general.M.SG.VOC(≡NOM≡ACC)   Ionuț Popescu.VOC≡NOM≡ACC

         b. Hei,   tu,   fata
               hey   you.VOC(≡NOM)   girl.DEF.SG.VOC(≡NOM≡ACC)
               mea   frumoasă   din   prima   bancă!
               my.F.SG.VOC(≡NOM≡ACC)   beautiful.F.SG.VOC(≡NOM≡ACC)   from   the-first   desk

U   Interjections of interpellation, playing the same role as a vocative in speech, very frequently appear on their own in familiar registers.
        (198)   **Măi**   (băiatule),   pleacă!
                   Hey   boy.DEF.VOC   leave.IMP.2SG

13.7.3 The expressive function of the vocative

The vocative, a form of direct address, has an expressive function (Stan 2005: 157) and as such is very distinct from other Romanian case forms. It conveys the speaker's various states of mind (the vocative of concern / reproach / hesitation) by intonation.

U   The derivatives of *dragă* 'dear' have particular stylistic values: *drăguță* (obsolete, initially hypocoristic, especially in old people's address to young people) is currently used with a slightly ironic or pejorative value:

(199) Drăguță,   vorbește   mai   rar!
      dear.DIM.SG.VOC(≡NOM≡ACC) speak.IMP.2SG more slow
      'Darling, talk more slowly!'

Feminine forms of address such as *iubita* 'sweetheart' (200), *scumpa* 'darling' or *șefa* 'boss' are frequently encountered in the language of less educated people.

(200) Ce   faci,   iubita?
      what (you)do sweetheart.F.SG.DEF.VOC(≡NOM≡ACC)
      'What are you doing sweetheart?'

13.7.4 Forms of address

Romanian has a strongly differentiated system of address elements, comprising the pronominal system, the address term system, and interpellations (Manu Magda 2008: 887–91).

U Present-day Romanian is undergoing a revival of inflectionally marked vocative forms, as well as their tendency to change into interpellatory interjections (*domnule* Mr.DEF.VOC, with its syncopated variant *dom'le* (201a), *frate* brother.VOC, *soro* sister.VOC (201b), *nene* uncle.VOC, terms used to designate different categories of speakers, irrespective of gender).

(201) a. Mama   i-a   zis   fetei: **'Dom'le,** cumpără   un telefon!'
         mother.DEF CL.DAT.3SG=has said girl.DEF.DAT   Mr.DEF.VOC   buy.IMP.2SG a phone
         'Mother said to the girl: Hey, buy a phone!'
      b. Ce   spui,   **soro**?   (wife to her husband)   (Caragiale)
         what   say.2SG sister.VOC
         'What are you saying, man?'

Some religious nouns have an interjectional value when used in the vocative:

(202) Dumnezeule! / Doamne!   / Sfinte!
      God.DEF.VOC   Lord.DEF.VOC   saint.VOC
      'Oh, my God', 'Oh, Lord!', 'Oh, Holy Saint!'

13.7.4.1 The pronominal address system includes informal address variants—*tu* you.SG, *voi* you.PL and semiformal ones—*dumneata* you.MID.POL (with the versions *mata, tale, tălică*), as well as reverential forms of address: *dumneavoastră* you.POL (*Domnia Ta* you.POL, *Domnia Voastră* you.POL, *Măria Ta* 'Your Highness', etc.) (§6.3).

13.7.4.2 According to the interlocutors' social status and role relations, we find: (i) generic formal *terms of address* (*domnule* 'mister /sir', *doamnă* 'Mrs. / madam', *domnișoară* 'miss', *duduie* 'young lady / madam'), associated or not with an indicator of function (203a); (ii) informal terms, such as proper name vocatives (*Ioana, Vasile*) and common nouns, associated with 2nd person singular verbal / pronominal forms (203b).

(203) a. Domnule   inspector
         Mr.DEF.VOC   inspector.VOC(≡NOM≡ACC)
      b. Auzi   tu,   fată,   bei   ceai?
         hear.IMP.2SG   you   girl.VOC(≡NOM≡ACC)   (you)drink   tea

U In the literary language, function- or title-based address implies the exclusive use of plural verb forms:
(204) Domnule   profesor,   **veniți**   mâine?
       Mr.DEF.VOC   teacher   (you)come   tomorrow

In the familiar language, such formulae may be associated with singular verb forms:
(205) Domnule   Trăiene,   **dă**-mi   niște   lemne
       Mr.DEF.VOC   Traian.VOC   give.IMP.2SG=CL.DAT.1SG   some   woods

Honorary titles are associated either with a 2nd person plural verb (206a), in which case they function as vocatives or, more often, with a 3rd person singular verb (206b), when they function as nominatives (§12.2.3):
(206) a. Alteța   Voastră,   **ați**   **spus**
          highness   your   (you)have   said
       b. Alteța   Voastră   a   spus
          highness   your   has   said

A more frequently used address formula has the vocative identical to the definite nominative, unaccompanied by a surname:
(207) Atenție,   **domnu'**/   **doamna**!
       attention   Mr.DEF.VOC(≡NOM≡ACC)   Mrs.DEF.VOC(≡NOM≡ACC)

The contracted form *dom'* is sometimes accepted as a polite term of address when associated with a title (*dom' profesor* sir.VOC professor).

The term *duduie* is used in cities as an address term for a female and has no particular sociolinguistic connotation:
(208) **Duduie,**   aveți   stilouri?
       madam.VOC(≡NOM≡ACC)   (you)have   pencils

The generic terms of address used during the communist period, *tovarășe* comrade.M.VOC, *tovarășă* comrade.F.VOC, became obsolete when the social and political situation changed.

Social and professional status requires the use of terms that designate functions (*președinte* 'president', *primar* 'mayor', *ministru* 'minister'), occupations (*inginer* 'engineer', *maistru* 'master') or professional titles (*doctor, academician*).

Age requires reverential forms (literary: *domnule* 'sir', *doamnă* 'madam'; familiar: *nene* 'uncle', *unchiule* 'uncle', *tanti* 'auntie', *tataie* 'grandpa', *mamaie* 'grandma', *șefule* 'boss', *șefa* 'boss' or regionally: *babule, bade, dodă, gagă, lele, leliță, liță*, etc.), associated with pronouns expressing relations of equality or inequality between interlocutors (*tu* 'you', *dumneata* you.MIS.POL, *mata, matale, tale, tălică*):

(209) A. Unde   stai,   **tataie**?
          where   (you)stay   grandpa.VOC(≡NOM≡ACC)

       B. **Dom'**   **doctor,**   departe
          mister.VOC≡NOM≡ACC   doctor.VOC(≡NOM≡ACC)   far

U Older people address younger people by name or by using address terms such as *băiete* 'boy', *fată* 'girl', *omule* 'man', *dragă* 'dear' (210a) or 'reversed forms of address' (210b,c) (Renzi 1968).
(210) a. **Băiete,**   adu   apă!
          boy.VOC   bring.IMP.2SG   water
          'You, boy, bring some water!'
       b. **Mamă,**   n-ai   voie!   (mother to her child)
          mother.VOC(≡NOM≡ACC)   not=(you)have   permission
          'Sweetheart, you are not allowed!'

13.7 Vocative phrases and address

    c. **Tată,** fii mai ascultător! (father to his son)
       father.VOC(≡NOM≡ACC) be.IMP.2SG more obedient!
       'Son, be more obedient!'

In familiar address, specific community-given names for various degrees of kinship are very often used: *mamă!* 'mum', *tată!* 'dad', *bunico!* 'grandmother', *bunicule!* 'grandfather', *unchiule!* 'uncle', *mătușă!* 'aunt', *nepoate!* 'nephew', *vere!* 'cousin', *nevastă!* 'wife', *bărbate!* 'husband' (with the stylistically marked variants *mămică* 'mummy', *mami* 'mum', *tăticule* 'daddy', *tati* 'dad', *buni* 'grandma', etc.); to these, *tanti!* and, less frequently, *nene!* are added, used by the speaker to address both a person who is a more distant relative and an older person:

(211)   'Săru' mâna, **tanti!'** /   'Bună, **nene Tică'**
      (I)kiss hand.DEF aunt.VOC(≡NOM≡ACC) hi uncle.VOC Tică.VOC(≡NOM≡ACC)

The gradation of phatic elements depends on the formality of the communication context.

U Formal types of address, associated with second person plural verbal forms + terms expressing the subjective appreciation of the interlocutors' relation (*drag* 'dear', *iubit* 'sweetheart', *onorat* 'honorary', *scump* 'darling', *stimat* 'esteemed'), are specific to more or less formal communication contexts, such as the academic environment (212a,b), the media or conferences (212c,d).

(212)   a. Stimați colegi
      esteemed.M.PL.VOC≡NOM≡ACC colleagues.VOC(≡NOM≡ACC)
      'Dear Colleagues'
    b. Onorată asistență
      honoured.F.SG.VOC(≡NOM≡ACC) audience.VOC(≡NOM≡ACC)
      'Honoured Audience'
    c. Stimați spectatori,
      esteemed.M.PL.VOC(≡NOM≡ACC) viewers.VOC(≡NOM≡ACC)
      'Dear Audience'
    d. Onorat auditoriu
      honoured.M.SG.VOC(≡NOM≡ACC) audience.VOC(≡NOM≡ACC)
      'Honoured Audience'

As the relation between the interlocutors becomes closer, the speaker resorts to proper names or common noun vocatives, pronouns, and even interjections:

(213)   **Măi Ioane,** hai la treabă!
      hey Ion.VOC come-on to work

The choice of vocative forms tends to depend on the symmetry or asymmetry of the relationship: mutual address with title + surname (214), mutual pronominal address (215), non-mutual address (216).

(214)   A. **Domnu' Ionescu,** am terminat
         mister.DEF.VOC(≡NOM≡ACC) Ionescu.VOC(≡NOM≡ACC) (I)have finished

      B. Bine, **doamnă Popescu**
         right Mrs.VOC(≡NOM≡ACC) Popescu.VOC(≡NOM≡ACC)

(215)   A. **Angela,** deschide!
         Angela.VOC(≡NOM≡ACC) open.IMP.2SG

      B. Imediat, **Iulia**
         Immediately Iulia.VOC(≡NOM≡ACC)
         'Angela, open up!' 'Just a moment, Julia'

(216) A. **Ioane**, dă-mi cartea
Ion.VOC give.IMP.2SG=CL.DAT.1SG book.DEF

B. Da, **domnu' Popescu**
yes mister.DEF.VOC(≡NOM≡ACC) Popescu.VOC(≡NOM≡ACC)

13.7.4.3 Interjections used to hail people are *măi, mă, fă, bre*. 'Allocutive' interjections with a phatic role, such as *bre, mă(i), bă!, fă!*, indicate that the speaker belongs to a socio-cultural group that lacks prestige: *mă!, măi!* are an exception as they show up even in the familiar speech of educated speakers, for example in broadcast media language (217). More recently, the use of *mă(i)* has been extended to address females, which shows the loss of its initial function and its specificity as a *marker of familiar address* (218).

(217) **Măi**! Eu spun o chestie foarte serioasă! Dă bine, **mă**
'Man! I'm saying a very serious thing! Man, this looks right'

(218) **Mă**, fată, nu știu dacă ți-e de folos ce ți-am spus eu (conversation between two female colleagues)
'Well, dear, I don't know if what I told you is any use to you'

CONCLUSIONS

1 Romanian is a pro-drop 'discourse configurational language' displaying both SVO and VSO word order and no expletive subject. The relatively free order of constituents correlates with various pragmatic and discourse oppositions.

Polar questions are marked by subject—predicate inversion and specific intonation. In *wh*-questions, the interrogative word is moved to sentence-initial position except when it is the sentential subject. *Wh*-constituents *in situ* are also allowed under specific syntactic and pragmatic-discourse circumstances. In multiple questions all *wh*-constituents may remain *in situ* or be fronted. Pied-piping is obligatory, preposition stranding is not allowed, long-distance unbounded dependencies are. Major island constraints are adjunct islands, *wh*-islands, coordinate structure constraint, the complex NP constraint. Subject island constraints and complementizer trace effects are not in force. Alternative questions are coordinated by *sau / ori* 'or' and display the affirmative—negative unmarked order. Tag-questions have a fixed lexical structure and a low degree of grammaticalization. Echo questions follow the pan-Romance patterns.

Imperative sentences are built on overt imperative forms or on various surrogate structures. The subject is covert in unmarked sentences, and overt when it is contrasted or focused.

Exclamatives are marked by fronted *wh*-words and sometimes by predicate–argument inversion. Some exclamations have morphosyntactic markers.

2 When converting direct into indirect speech, personal deictic words are modified (changing pronominal and verbal forms), while modification of verbal moods and tenses is optional (except for the imperative, which becomes subjunctive).

Romanian features special complementizers or relative adverbs for reporting each clause type: *că* 'that', for assertive declarative sentences; *să*, for non-assertive declarative sentences and for imperatives; *dacă* 'if, whether', for total and alternative direct interrogatives; *unde* 'where', *când* 'when', *cum* 'how', *cine* 'who', *ce* 'what' for partial direct interrogatives.

3 Sentential negation is expressed by a sole negative marker placed in preverbal position— *nu* 'no' (in the case of finite clauses and of the infinitival clause) or by the prefix *ne-* (in the case of the other non-finite clauses); thus, Romanian belongs to the NegFirst type of languages.

Constituent negation is primarily realized by the negative marker *nu* 'not' placed before the constituent. *Nu* (< Lat. NON) is used for sentential negation, constituent negation (if preposed to the constituent), and may also function as an adverbial pro-sentence.

Negative pro-sentence and the sentential negation may co-occur.

Contemporary Romanian displays strict negative concord: *n-words* are licensed by the sentential negative marker. It allows non-strict negative concord in certain stylistically marked contexts.

Romanian allows double and multiple negations, without changing the negative reading of the clause.

There are contexts in which the double negation yields affirmative clauses.

There are three strategies for placing the negative marker within the complex predicates containing modal verbs.

4 Romanian displays a relatively high freedom in constituent placement.

Fronting is employed both for topicalization and for contrastive focus.

Left dislocation produces constructions with obligatory clitic doubling. Clitic doubling, extended even to structures showing no dislocation, plays an important role in syntactic disambiguation.

The main means for the realization of contrastive focalization is phrasal stress, associated with fronting.

5 Modality is generally realized lexically (as adverbial markers) or by grammatical moods; modal verbs occupy an intermediate position, because they are only partially grammaticalized.

Evidentiality is relatively strongly marked through verbal moods (of which only the presumptive is specialized) and through specialized adverbial markers.

6 Zero anaphora is very frequent; among other functions, it plays the role of clitic substitutes with partitive or local meaning in other Romance languages.

Semantic anaphora is realized by numerous grammaticalized means, of which CEL and AL are specialized for this purpose.

Anaphora summarizing clausal content is realized as a feminine pronoun with neutral value.

Certain lexical devices tend to be grammaticalized as coreferentiality markers or even as anaphoric substitutes.

7 Romanian has a vocative, marked by suprasegmental means (intonation) and morphological means (specific inflectional endings). Colloquially it is very often accompanied (or

even replaced) by a set of interpellatory interjections (*hei, ei, e, măi, mă, băi, bă, bre, fa, fă, făi, tu*) and hortatory interjections (*hai* 'come on', *stai* 'wait'). A phenomenon typical of the familiar register is reverse address, whereby adults addressing younger persons use forms normally associated with the way children address parents or grandparents. Being regularly used in modern communication, some vocatives and 'allocutive' interjections (such as *dom'le, măi*), specific to oral expression, have become markers of the speaker's orientation to the listener. The complexity of the address system, with the vocative as its key functional form, marks Romanian out among Romance languages.

14

Derivational Morphology

This chapter contains a description of suffixation and prefixation in Romanian, as well as a brief presentation of back-formation and parasynthetic derivation.

Derivation is the most productive means of word formation, both in old Romanian and in the modern language. Suffixation is much more productive than prefixation. Romanian has a large number of suffixes, inherited or borrowed from Slavic, Turkish, Hungarian, or Romance languages, which are attached to old or new bases. Some suffixes were more productive in the old language, others were borrowed in the modern period and have created numerous derivatives in contemporary Romanian, so that derivation remained very productive. Unlike prefixation, suffixation frequently involves phonological alternations, many of which are also found in inflection (for phonological alternations occurring in derivation, see §15.2).

14.1 SUFFIXATION. TYPES OF SUFFIXES AND DERIVATIVES

14.1.1 Verb formation

14.1.1.1 Inventory of verbal suffixes

Most verbal suffixes attach to nouns and adjectives. Verbal bases are less numerous and their derivatives have less semantic values.

The infinitive suffixes *-a*, *-i*, and *-î* are also derivational suffixes. They can attach to nouns and adjectives. The most productive, throughout the attested periods of Romanian, are *-a* and *-i*:

- **N > V:** *felie* 'slice' > *felia* 'slice', *fragment* 'fragment' > *fragmenta* 'fragment', *coajă* 'peel' > *coji* 'peel', *killer* > *killeri* 'kill', *izvor* 'spring' > *izvorî* 'spring';
- **Adj > V:** *urât* 'ugly' > *urâţi* 'uglify'; *amar* 'bitter' > *amărî* 'embitter'.

Less often, the suffix *-a* attaches to adverbs and onomatopoeia, and *-i* attaches to numerals and onomatopoeia:

- **Adv > V:** *departe* 'far' > *a (se) depărta* 'move away';
- **Interj > V:** *guiţ* 'oink' > *guiţa* 'oink';
- **Num > V:** *zece* 'ten' > *înzeci* 'multiply by ten'.

The causative suffixes *-iza* and *-ifica*, borrowed from French (*-iser*, *-ifier*) and Italian (*-izzare*, *-ificare*), are very productive in contemporary Romanian. They attach to old or new adjectival and nominal bases:

- **Adj > V:** *marginal* 'marginal' > *marginaliza* 'marginalize', *simplu* 'simple' > *simplifica* 'simplify';

- **N > V:** *alfabet* 'alphabet'> *alfabetiza* 'alphabetize, educate', *deșert* 'desert' > *deșertifica* 'turn into desert'.

The most productive of the two is the suffix *-iza*, which can attach to proper names as well: *McDonald's* > *macdolnadiza* 'McDonald's-ize, globalize'.

Other productive suffixes are *-(i)ona* and *-ui*. The suffix *-(i)ona*, borrowed from French and Italian, attaches to nouns and is productive in the contemporary language: *concluzie* 'conclusion' > *concluziona* 'conclude'. The suffix *-ui* was productive in the old language and has been revived in contemporary Romanian. It attaches to nouns, some of which are very recent loanwords: *ceară* 'wax' > *cerui* 'wax', *viață* 'life' > *viețui* 'live', *cârmă* 'helm' > *cârmui* 'helm, rule', *sfat* 'advice'> *sfătui* 'advise', *bip* 'beep' > *bipui* 'beep', *brand* 'brand' > *brandui* 'brand', *chat* 'chat' > *chatui* 'chat', *țeapă* 'trickery'> *țepui* 'trick' (slang).

The suffixes *-ăi* (/ *-âi*) and *-(ă)ni* attach mostly to onomatopoeic words: *balang* 'ding-dong'> *bălăngăni* 'ding-dong', *bee(h)* 'baa'> *behăi* 'baa', *mac* 'quack' > *măcăni* 'quack', *mâr* 'growl' > *mârâi* 'growl', *mor* 'grrr' > *mormăi* 'grumble', *scârț* 'creak'> *scârțâi* 'creak'.

Deverbal suffixes are rare: *bate* 'beat' > *bătuci* 'batter', *linge* 'lick'> *linguși* 'flatter'.

14.1.1.2 Semantic values of the bases and of the derivatives

Verbs derived from nouns and adjectives can incorporate:

(i) the result expressed by the base; these derivatives are frequently organized into causative and unaccusative pairs (the unaccusative is usually reflexive):
- **N > V:** *a (se) cocoșa* 'hump' (< *cocoașă* 'hump'), *a (se) fărâmița* 'crumble' (< *fărâmiță* 'crumb'), *a (se) înfrumuseța* 'beautify' (< *frumusețe* 'beauty'), *a (se) mucegăi* 'mould' (< *mucegai* 'mould'), *rugini* 'rust' (< *rugină* 'rust');
- **Adj > V:** *a (se) ieftini* 'cheapen' (< *ieftin* 'cheap'), *a (se) îngălbeni* 'grow / turn yellow' (< *galben* 'yellow'), *înverzi* 'turn / make green' (< *verde* 'green');

(ii) the instrument, expressed by the nominal base: *ciocăni* 'hammer' (< *ciocan* 'hammer'), *mătura* 'sweep' (< *mătură* 'broom');

(iii) the agent, expressed by the nominal base: *tâlhări* 'rob' (< *tâlhar* 'thief');

(iv) a comparison: *a (se) ghemui* 'crouch' (< *ghem* 'ball');

(v) a relation: *a se înrudi* 'be related' (< *rudă* 'relative');

(vi) location, in a broad sense (destination, source, distance), expressed by the adverbial base: *înainta* 'go forward' (< *înainte* 'forward').

For a comprehensive study of verbal suffixes in Romanian, see FC III.

14.1.2 Noun formation

The bases are mainly nouns, verbs, and adjectives. Sometimes they are cardinal numerals, in derivatives with *-ime*, with a partitive value (*trei* 'three'> *treime* 'one third', *patru* 'four' > *pătrime* 'one fourth', etc.).

14.1.2.1 Abstract nouns

Romanian has many abstract nominal suffixes. The most productive nominal suffix is *-re*, inherited from Latin, which denotes the action or the state and can attach to most verbs (*plecare* 'leaving' < *pleca* 'leave'; *citire* 'reading' < *citi* 'read'). Some verbs do not accept this suffix: *înotare (vs. înot 'swimming'), *trebuire (vs. trebuinţă 'need, necessity'), *fugire (vs. fugă 'running'), *murire (vs. moarte 'death'), *dormire (vs. dormit 'sleeping'). All neological verbs can take the suffix -re. The derivatives with -re are in competition with the nominalized supine (for nominalizations in Romanian, see Cornilescu 2001; Stan 2003).

Abstract nominal derivatives fall into two large groups: those which denote an action, a state or the result, formed from verbs, and those which denote a quality, formed from verbs and adjectives.

14.1.2.1.1 Many abstract nominal suffixes found in derivatives which denote actions, states, or results are old and productive in regional and colloquial language: *-anie / -enie* (*vedenie* 'vision' < *vedea* 'see'), *-are* (*vânzare* 'sale' < *vinde* 'sell'), *-ciune* (*sfiiciune* 'shyness' < *a se sfii* 'be shy'), *-eală / -ială* (*cheltuială* 'expense' < *cheltui* 'expend'), *-inţă* (*voinţă* 'will' < *voi* 'want'), *-iş / -âş* (*seceriş* 'harvest' < *secera* 'harvest'), *-mânt* (*jurământ* 'vow' < *jura* 'make a vow'), *-toare* (*vânătoare* 'hunting' < *vâna* 'hunt'), *-ură* (attached only to participial bases: *fiertură* 'broth' < *fiert* 'boiled', *ruptură* 'break, tear' < *rupt* 'broken'), *-uş* (*frecuş* 'rubbing' < *freca* 'rub').

Some suffixes are neological borrowings, which can attach to old or neological bases, with various origins: *-ment*, which is the learnèd variant of the inherited *-mânt* (*antrenament* 'training' < *a se antrena* 'train'), *-ţie* (*administraţie* 'administration, management' < *administra* 'administrate'), borrowed from Russian (ELIR), found mostly in neologistic analysable borrowings, which is the learnèd variant of the inherited *-ciune*.

Many derivatives are found in regional language (*petrecanie* 'death; party' < *petrece* 'party'), in the colloquial register (*bumbăceală* 'beating' < *bumbăci* 'beat'), or in slang (*ciordeală* 'theft' < *ciordi* 'steal'). For the properties of deverbal formations, see §5.3.4; Stan 2003.

14.1.2.1.2 Many derivatives are formed from adjectives, with various suffixes: *-anţă* (*siguranţă* 'safety' < *sigur* 'safe'), *-ete* (*scumpete* 'dearness' < *scump* 'dear'), *-ie* (*mândrie* 'pride' < *mândru* 'proud'), *-ime* (*frăgezime* 'tenderness' < *fraged* 'tender'), *-(i / ă)tate* (*fermitate* 'firmness' < *ferm* 'firm').

14.1.2.1.3 Two or even three abstract derivatives can quite frequently be formed from the same base: *cheltuire—cheltuit—cheltuială* 'spending' (< *cheltui* 'spend'), *urcare—urcat—urcuş* 'climbing' (< *urca* 'climb'), *împărţire—împărţit—împărţeală* 'division' (< *împărţi* 'divide'), *cerere—cerut—cerinţă* 'request' (< *cere* 'request'). The derivatives are partially synonyms, with different degrees of abstraction.

Some of the suffixes above can form derivatives with concrete meaning: *-re* (*mâncare* 'food' < *mânca* 'eat', *avere* 'fortune' < *avea* 'have'), *-inţă* (*adeverinţă* 'certificate' < *adeveri* 'certify').

14.1.2.2 Nominal gender suffixes

Most gender suffixes derive a feminine noun from a masculine one. The derivatives denote persons, animals, and plants. The most productive suffix is *-ă*, homonymous with the inflectional ending for feminine singular, nominative and accusative, found in most feminine nouns (§5.1.1): *inginer* 'engineer' > *ingineră* 'female engineer', *profesor* 'teacher' > *profesoară* 'female teacher'.

Ethnic names may be derived with *-că* (*român* 'Romanian' > *româncă* 'Romanian woman'), *-ă* (*azer* 'Azeri' > *azeră* 'Azeri woman'), or *-oaică* (*englez* 'English' > *englezoaică*

'English woman'). Occupational names are derived with *-easă* (*bucătar* 'cook' > *bucătăreasă* 'female cook') or *-iţă* (*barman* 'bartender'> *barmaniţă* 'female bartender', *doctor* 'doctor' > *doctoriţă* 'female doctor'. Feminine nouns derived from masculine occupational nouns may denote occupations (*croitoreasă* 'female tailor' < *croitor* 'tailor') or the wife of the referent denoted by the nominal base (*preoteasă* 'the priest's wife' < *preot* 'priest').

For occupational names, in formal registers the masculine noun is sometimes preferred, as the feminine is not officially required (*Ioana*$_F$ *e inginer*$_M$, 'Ioana is an engineer'; *doamna*$_F$ *deputat*$_M$ *Ionescu* 'Mrs. deputy Ionescu').

Some bases form two derivatives: *americană—americancă* 'American woman', *vulturoaie—vulturoaică* 'female eagle' (in the regional language), *doctoriţă—doctoră* 'woman doctor'; *ministră—ministreasă* (both colloquial).

A masculine noun is, less commonly, derived from a feminine one, with *-an* (*curcan* 'male turkey' < *curcă* 'turkey hen') or *-oi* (*broscoi* 'male frog' < *broască* 'frog').

14.1.2.3 Collectives

The most productive suffixes are *-ime* (especially for [+human] referents: *student* 'student' > *studenţime* 'student body', *prost* 'stupid' > *prostime* 'rabble'), *-iş* (*frunză* 'leaf' > *frunziş* 'foliage'), and *-et* (*brad* 'fir tree' > *brădet* 'fir wood'). These suffixes attach to nominal and adjectival bases.

14.1.2.4 Diminutives

Romanian has many diminutive suffixes, some of them inherited from Latin, others borrowed into the old language. The most productive of them are *-uţ* (*pat* 'bed' > *pătuţ* 'small bed'), *-el* (*scaun* 'chair' > *scăunel* 'small chair'), *-uşor* (*porc* 'pig' > *porcuşor* 'small pig'), and *-aş* (*butoi* 'barrel' > *butoiaş* 'small barrel'), for masculine and neuter nouns, and *-iţă* (*rochie* 'dress' > *rochiţă* 'short dress'), *-uţă* (*umbrelă* 'umbrella'> *umbreluţă* 'small umbrella'), *-ică* (*mamă* 'mother' > *mămică* 'mammy'), for feminine nouns. Proper names are frequent bases for diminutives (*Dănuţ* < *Dan*, *Alinuţa* < *Alina*).

A base can form two diminutives: *puişor—puiuţ* 'small chicken / cub', *porcuşor—porculeţ* 'small pig', *ciobănaş—ciobănel* 'little shepherd'. Two diminutive suffixes can concatenate: *mămicuţă* 'mammy' < *mamă* 'mother'+ *-ică* + *-uţă*.

Some derivatives formed with a diminutive suffix have lost their diminutive meaning: *bunic* 'grandfather', *bunică* 'grandmother' (< *bun* 'grandfather', *bună* 'grandmother').

Diminutive derivatives have many pragmatic and stylistic values, such as hypocorism, affection, contempt, smallness. Many derivatives are spontaneous creations, occurring in everyday conversations, given that diminutives are very productive in contemporary spoken language (especially when adults talk to children).

14.1.2.5 Augmentatives

Augmentative suffixes are less productive than diminutives, and their derivatives have fewer semantic and pragmatic values, similarly to other Romance languages (Bauer 2011: 539). For feminine bases, the most productive suffixes are *-oaie* (*casă* 'house' > *căsoaie* 'big house') and *-oi*, which creates neuter derivatives (*cămaşă* 'shirt' > *cămăşoi* 'big shirt'). For masculine bases, the most productive suffixes are *-an* (*băiat* 'boy' > *băietan* 'big boy') and *-andru* (*băiat* > *băiețandru* 'big boy'). Augmentatives tend to acquire pejorative connotations (*gol* 'naked' > *golan* 'ruffian').

14.1.2.6 Suffixes with other semantic values

Other semantic values, more or less productive, of nominal derivatives are agent, instrument, location, origin or relation, and division. Romanian has several suffixes which denote the agent (generally speaking), which can attach to verbs or nouns. The most productive of them are: *-ar* (*bere* 'beer' > *berar* 'brewer'), *-tor* (*munci* 'work' > *muncitor* 'worker'), *-or* (*dirija* 'conduct' > *dirijor* 'conductor'), *-ist* (*tractor* 'tractor' > *tractorist* 'tractor-driver') and *-ant* (*specula* 'speculate' > *speculant* 'speculator').

The most productive instrument suffix is *-(ă)tor*, *-(ă)toare*, attached to verbal bases (*bate* 'beat' > *bătător* 'carpet beater', *spânzura* 'hang' > *spânzurătoare* 'gallows', *strecura* 'strain' > *strecurătoare* 'strainer').

The suffixes which derive locative nouns can be attached to nouns and verbs. The suffixes *-ărie* and *-ie* attach only to nouns (*covrig* 'pretzel' > *covrigărie* 'pretzel shop', *brutar* 'baker' > *brutărie* 'bakery'), while the suffixes *-toare*, *-ție* attach to verbs (*trece* 'pass' > *trecătoare* 'gorge').

Other semantic values of nominal derivatives are period (*copilărie* 'childhood' < *copil* 'child') and division (*sutime* 'one hundredth' < *sută* 'hundred').

14.1.3 Adjective formation

Romanian has many adjectival suffixes, attached to nouns, verbs, or adjectives:

- N > Adj: *-al: cameră* 'room'> *cameral* 'cameral'; *-ar: școală* 'school' > *școlar* 'educational'; *-aș: margine* 'edge' > *mărginaș* 'peripheral'; *-at: buză* 'lip' > *buzat* 'thick-lipped'; *-ean: Constanța* [city] > *constănțean* 'person from Constanța'; *munte* 'mountain' > *muntean* 'highlander'; *-ian: Eminescu* > *eminescian* 'in the manner of / relating to Eminescu'; *-esc: om* 'man' > *omenesc* 'human'; *-ist: ochelari* 'glasses' > *ochelarist* 'person who wears glasses'; *-istic: calendar* 'calendar' > *calendaristic* 'according to the calendar'; *-iu: cenușă* 'ash' > *cenușiu* 'greyish, ashen'; *-nic: casă* 'house' > *casnic* 'domestic'; *-os: ban* 'money'> *bănos* 'lucrative'.
- V > Adj: *-os / -ios / -cios / -ăcios: tăia* 'cut' > *tăios* 'sharp / cutting'; *a se supăra* 'upset' > *supărăcios* 'grumpy'; *-ăreț: a se descurca* 'manage' > *descurcăreț* 'resourceful'; *-uc: uita* 'forget' > *uituc* 'forgetful'; *-(ălali)tor: cauza* 'cause' > *cauzator* 'causative'; *-ant / -ent: participa* 'participate' > *participant* 'participant'; *-nic: dori* 'wish' > *dornic* 'eager'; *-bil: utiliza* 'utilize' > *utilizabil* 'utilizable'.
- Adj > Adj: *-atic: singur* 'alone' > *singuratic* 'lonely', *-iu: galben* 'yellow' > *gălbeniu* 'yellowish', *-ui: verde* 'green' > *verzui* 'greenish', *-nic: amar* 'bitter' > *amarnic* 'bitter'.

Some derivatives are formed with diminutive suffixes. They denote a lower degree of intensity of the quality expressed by the base: *-el* (*voinic* 'robust' > *voinicel*), *-ică* (*harnică* 'diligent' > *hărnicică*), *-uț* (*prost* 'stupid' > *prostuț*).

- **acronyms > Adj**: *-ist*: *IT-ist* 'IT worker', pronounced [aitist], *PNL-ist* 'member of PNL (National Liberal Party)', pronounced [penelist], *CFR-ist* 'worker of the CFR (Romanian railways) company', pronounced [tʃeferist].

14.1.4 Adverb formation

The most productive adverbial suffix, both in old and in contemporary Romanian, is *-eşte*, attached to nominal bases (*oameni* 'men' > *omeneşte* 'humanly', *american* 'American' > *americăneşte* 'Americanly'). Other adverbial suffixes are *-iş* and *-âş* (*cruce* 'cross' > *cruciş* 'crosswise', *chior* 'blind in one eye' > *chiorâş* 'squinting'). See also §8.1.2.

Some adverbs can take the diminutive suffix *-işor*, to express a lower degree of intensity (*bine* 'well' > *binişor* 'quite well', *departe* 'far' > *depărtişor* 'quite far, farish').

14.1.5 Semantic relations between suffixes or derivatives

Some suffixes are polysemous or homonymous: *-ime* derives collectives (*studenţime* 'student body'), partitives (*pătrime* 'quarter'), or abstract nouns (*frăgezime* 'tenderness'); *-iţă* derives feminine nouns from masculine ones (*doctoriţă* 'female doctor') or diminutives (*lădiţă* 'small bin'); *-toare* creates feminine names of agents (*muncitoare* 'female worker'), names of instruments (*strecurătoare* 'strainer'), or abstract names (*vânătoare* 'hunting'), but the derivatives are differentiated by the plural ending: *-e* for [+human] feminine derivatives (*semănătoare* (SG≡PL) 'a woman who sows'), *-i* for [–human] feminine derivatives (*semănătoare* (SG)—*semănători* (PL) 'the instrument used for sowing').

Some derivatives have several semantic values. For instance, *seceriş* (*secera* 'harvest' + *-iş*) denotes: (i) the action of harvesting; (ii) the period when the harvesting takes places; (3) the harvest.

H   The origin and the history of Romanian suffixes is complex (Pascu 1916; Popescu-Marin 2007).
Some suffixes were inherited from Latin: *-ar*, *-at*, *-atic*, *-ă*, *-ciune*, *-easă*, *-el*, *-et*, *-ime*, *-inţă*, *-mânt*, *-os*, *-(ă)tate*, *-tor*, *-(t)ură*. The adjectival suffix *-esc* is believed to have been inherited from Latin, although according to some, it was inherited from Thraco-Dacian.

Many suffixes were borrowed into the old language from Slavic languages (*-an*, *-anie* / *-enie*, *-că*, *-eală*, *-ean*, *-iţă*, *-nic*, the verbal suffix *-ui*), Hungarian (*-ău*, *-(ălu)lui*), Greek (*-isi*), and Turkish (*-giu*). Many are no longer productive.

Some suffixes were borrowed into modern Romanian from Romance languages (French and Italian): *-ism*, *-ist*, *-iza*, *-itate*, *-ţiune*, *-al*. They are very productive and can be recognized in many analysable words. The Latin suffix -TIO was borrowed in Romanian through Russian, as *-ţie*, and also through Romance languages, as *-ţiune*; the two suffixes formed many parallel derivatives (*naţie*, *naţiune* 'nation'), but nowadays *-ţie* is the more productive (Pană Dindelegan 2008i).

Some suffixes were formed in Romanian, such as the adverbial *-eşte* (made up of the adjectival suffix *-esc* plus the adverbial suffix *-e*; §8.1.2).

Some suffixes are compounds: *-oaică* (*-oa(i)e* + *-că*), *-icel* (*-ic* + *-el*), *-icea* (*-ic* + *-ea*), *-ărie* (*-ar* + *-ie*) (Pascu 1916).

14.2 PREFIXATION

Most formations with prefixes are verbs, as in other Romance languages (Bauer 2011: 532). In the history of Romanian few prefixes have been productive: *în-*, *ne-*, *de-₁*, *des-* / *dez-* / *de-₂*, *prea-*, *re-*, *stră-*. In contemporary Romanian, only *ne-* and *re-* are still productive. Prefixes do not change the morphological class of the base. (For a comprehensive study of Romanian prefixes, see FC II).

The negative prefixes are the old and very productive *ne-* and the neological *in-*, occurring in the literary language. They attach to nouns, adjectives, and verbs:

(i) nouns: *claritate* 'clarity' > *neclaritate* 'vagueness';
(ii) adjectives: *bun* 'good' > *nebun* 'crazy'; *capabil* 'capable' > *incapabil* 'incapable'; many bases for the derivatives with *ne-* are participles: *găsit* 'found' > *negăsit* 'not found', *bărbierit* 'shaved' > *nebărbierit* 'unshaven';
(iii) verbs: *socoti* 'account / esteem' > *nesocoti* 'ignore'.

The verbal prefix *în- / îm-* forms unaccusative or causative formations. The bases are very frequently nouns, adjectives (in parasynthetic derivatives) or verbs: *împietri* 'petrify' < *piatră* 'stone', *înfiora* 'shiver' < *fior* 'shiver', *înăspri* 'harden' < *aspru* 'stiff, harsh'.

The prefix *pre-* expresses temporal relations, in verbal derivatives: *vedea* 'see' > *prevedea* 'foresee'.

The superlative prefix *stră-* attaches to adjectival and nominal bases: *vechi* 'old' > *strămoșchi* 'ancient', *bunic* 'grandfather' > *străbunic* 'great grandfather'.

The neological prefix *re-* expresses repetition and it is very productive: *reciti* 'read again' < *citi* 'read', *rescrie* 'to write again' < *scrie* 'write' a.s.o.

The prefixes which express reversion are *des- / dez- / de-*, and *răs- / răz-*, attached to verbal bases: *desface* 'undo' < *face* 'do', *a se răzgândi* 'change one's mind' < *a se gândi* 'think'.

H Several prefixes were inherited from Latin: *de-, des- / dez-, în- / îm-, pre-, re-, stră-*. The prefix *re-* was revived by neological borrowings from Romance languages. Some prefixes were borrowed from Slavic languages into the old language (*ne-, pre-, răs- / răz-*), or from Romance languages into modern Romanian (the negative suffix *in-*, the privative suffix *a-*, found in derivatives like *agramatical* 'ungrammatical', *apolitic* 'apolitical').

14.3 PARASYNTHETIC DERIVATION

Parasynthetic formations, obtained by the simultaneous attachment of a suffix and a prefix, are verbs, with nominal or adjectival bases: *îndurera* 'grieve' < *în-* + *durere* 'grief' + *-a*, *a (se) înnegri* 'turn black' < *în-* + *negru* 'black' + *-i* (for parasynthetic derivation in Romance languages, see Reinheimer-Rîpeanu 1974).

14.4 BACK-FORMATION

The derivatives obtained by back formation (the removal of a suffix-like element) are not very numerous. They fall into several main categories:

(i) neuter nouns derived from verbs: *alint* 'caress' < *alinta* 'caress', *auz* 'hearing' < *auzi* 'hear', *înot* 'swimming' < *înota* 'swim', *zbor* 'flight' < *zbura* 'fly';
(ii) feminine nouns derived from verbs, with the feminine inflectional ending *-ă*: *bârfă* 'gossip' < *bârfi* 'gossip', *dovadă* 'proof' < *dovedi* 'prove', *poruncă* 'order' < *porunci* 'order', *rugă* 'prayer' < *ruga* 'pray';
(iii) [+animate] masculine nouns derived from their feminine counterparts: *pisic* 'tomcat' < *pisică* 'cat', *moș* 'old man' < *moașă* 'midwife, old woman'.

(iv) masculine names of fruit trees and shrubs, created from the feminine name of the fruit (following a pattern inherited from Latin): *alun* 'hazelnut tree' < *alună* 'hazelnut', *cais* 'apricot tree' < *caisă* 'apricot', *vișin* 'sour cherry tree' < *vișină* 'sour cherry'.

There are various other derivatives obtained by the removal of an ending interpreted as a suffix, like *-ie* (*biolog* 'biologist' < *biologie* 'biology', *ecolog* 'ecologist' < *ecologie* 'ecology'), *-re* (*întrajutora* 'help' < *întrajutorare* 'help'). For back-formation in Romanian, see Hristea 1984.

CONCLUSIONS

Suffixation is much more productive than prefixation or compounding. This generalization refers to the large number of suffixes and formations obtained by derivation, in all attested periods of the language. Romanian has a large number of suffixes, with various origins: inherited from Latin, borrowed into the old language from Slavic, Turkish, Greek, Hungarian, and in the modern period from Romance languages (French, Italian), or formed in Romanian. They attach to old or neological bases and give rise to many new formations.

Some of the most productive suffixes are those which form abstract nouns, diminutives, collective nouns, adjectives with verbal and nominal bases, and the verbal suffixes *-iza* and *-ifica*. Some derivational suffixes are also grammatical suffixes: the verbal (infinitival) suffixes *-a* and *-i*, the nominal suffix *-ă* (homonymous with the feminine singular inflectional ending).

15

Inflectional and Derivational Morphophonological Alternations

This chapter gives the inventory of vocalic and consonantal alternations.

In the inflectional system, morphophonological alternations are supplementary markers which co-occur with the affixal morphosyntactic markers (1a); they are occasionally the sole markers (although they co-occur *orthographically* with an affixal marker (1b)):

(1) a. du**d**-∅ / du**z**-i /d/ ~ /z/
 mulberry-SG mulberry-PL
 'mulberry tree(s)'
 b. ra**c**-∅ [rak] /ra**c**-i [ratʃ] /k/ ~ /tʃ/
 crayfish-SG crayfish-PL

Most such alternations are the result of differences of stress and phonological structure among paradigmatic forms.

15.1 INFLECTIONAL ALTERNATIONS

There are:

- vocalic alternations: between vowels (/a/ ~ /e/ *fată*$_{\text{SG.NOM≡ACC}}$, *fete*$_{\text{SG.GEN≡DAT≡PL.NOM≡ACC≡GEN≡DAT}}$ 'girl'), between a vowel and a diphthong (/o/ ~ /o̯a/ *rod*$_{\text{SG}}$, *roade*$_{\text{PL}}$ 'fruit'), between diphthongs (/ja/ ~ /je/ *băiat*$_{\text{SG}}$, *băieți*$_{\text{PL}}$ 'boy');
- consonantal alternations: between consonants (/t/ ~ /ts/ *frate*$_{\text{SG}}$, *frați*$_{\text{PL}}$ 'brother'), between consonant clusters (/sk/ ~ /ʃt/ *gâscă*$_{\text{SG.NOM≡ACC}}$, *gâște*$_{\text{SG.GEN≡DAT≡PL.NOM≡ACC≡GEN≡DAT}}$ 'goose'), between a consonant and zero (/l/ ~ /∅/ *cal*$_{\text{SG}}$, *cai*$_{\text{PL}}$ 'horse').

15.1.1 Inventory

Vocalic alternations occur:

1. in stressed syllables:
   - /'a/ ~ /'ə/ (N *mare*$_{\text{SG.NOM≡ACC}}$, *mări*$_{\text{SG.GEN≡DAT≡PL.NOM≡ACC≡GEN≡DAT}}$ 'sea'; Adj *călare*$_{\text{SG}}$, *călări*$_{\text{PL}}$ 'on horseback'; V *agață*$_{\text{IND.PRES.3SG≡PL}}$, *agăț*$_{\text{IND≡SUBJ.PRES.1SG}}$ 'hang');
   - /'a/ ~ /'e/ (N *șarpe*$_{\text{SG}}$, *șerpi*$_{\text{PL}}$ 'snake'; Adj *deșartă*$_{\text{F.SG.NOM≡ACC}}$, *deșert*$_{\text{M.SG}}$ 'vain'; V *șade*$_{\text{IND.PRES.3SG}}$, *șed*$_{\text{IND.PRES1SG≡3PL≡SUBJ.PRES.1SG}}$ 'sit');
   - /'ə/ ~ /'e/ (N *văr*$_{\text{SG}}$, *veri*$_{\text{PL}}$ 'cousin');
   - /'ə/ ~ /'e/ ~ /'e̯a/ (Adj *rău*$_{\text{M.SG}}$, *rele*$_{\text{F.SG.GEN≡DAT≡PL.NOM≡ACC≡GEN≡DAT}}$, *rea*$_{\text{F.SG.NOM≡ACC}}$ 'mean');

- /'e̯a/ ~ /'e/ (N creastă_SG.NOM≡ACC, creste_SG.GEN≡DAT≡PL.NOM≡ACC≡GEN≡DAT 'crest'; Adj țărănească_F.SG.NOM≡ACC, țărănesc_M.SG 'rural'; V aleargă_IND.PRES.3SG≡PL, alerg_IND≡SUBJ.PRES.1SG 'run');
- /'ja/ ~ /'je/ (N băiat, băieți; Adj biată_F.SG.NOM≡ACC, biet_M.SG 'pitiable'; V piaptănă_IND.PRES.3SG≡PL, pieptăn_IND≡SUBJ.PRES.1SG 'comb');
- /'ɨ/ ~ /'a/ (N pârâu_SG, pâraie_PL 'stream');
- /'ɨ/ ~ /'ɨi̯/ (N mână_SG.NOM≡ACC, mâini_SG.GEN≡DAT≡PL.NOM≡ACC≡GEN≡DAT 'hand');
- /'ɨ/ ~ /'i/ (N cuvânt_SG, cuvinte_PL 'word'; Adj vânăt_M.SG, vineți_M.PL 'purple'; V vând_IND.PRES.1SG≡3PL≡SUBJ.PRES.1SG, vinde_INF≡IND.PRES.3SG 'sell');
- /'o̯a/ ~ /'o/ (N floare_SG.NOM≡ACC, flori_SG.GEN≡DAT≡PL.NOM≡ACC≡GEN≡DAT 'flower'; Adj groasă_F.SG.NOM≡ACC, gros_M.SG 'thick'; V rod_IND.PRES.1SG≡3PL≡SUBJ.PRES.1SG, roade_INF≡IND.PRES.3SG 'gnaw');
- /'o/ ~ /'u/ (Num amândoi_M.NOM≡ACC, amânduror_M≡F.GEN≡DAT 'both').

2. in unstressed syllables:
- /a/ ~ /ə/ (N talangă_SG.NOM≡ACC, tălăngi_SG.GEN≡DAT≡PL.NOM≡ACC≡GEN≡DAT 'cowbell');
- /ə/ ~ /e/ (N tabără_SG.NOM≡ACC, tabere_SG.GEN≡DAT≡PL.NOM≡ACC≡GEN≡DAT 'camp'; Adj proaspăt_M.SG, proaspeți_M.PL 'fresh'; V apăr_IND≡SUBJ.PRES.1SG, aperi_IND≡SUBJ.PRES.2SG 'defend');
- /o̯a/ ~ /o/ (N mijloace_PL, mijloc_SG 'middle').

U The current standard norm admits the following stress variants: ['miʒlok], ['miʒlo̯atʃe], with alternation /o/ ~ /o̯a/ in unstressed syllable and, respectively, [miʒ'lok], [miʒ'lo̯atʃe], with alternation /o/ ~ /o̯a/ in stressed syllable.

Vowel alternations may involve the change of the position of the accent:

- /'a/ ~ /ə/ (V bag_IND≡SUBJ.PRES.1SG, băgăm_IND≡SUBJ.PRES.1PL 'put');
- /'a/ ~ /'ə/ ~ /'e/ ~ /ə/ (V spală_IND.PRES.3SG≡PL, spăl_IND≡SUBJ.PRES.1SG, speli_IND≡SUBJ.PRES.2SG, spălăm_IND≡SUBJ.PRES.1PL 'wash');
- /'a/ ~ /'ə/ ~ /'e/ ~ /ə/ ~ /e/ (V vadă_SUBJ.PRES.3SG≡PL, văd_IND.PRES.1SG≡3PL, vede_IND.PRES.3SG, văzui_PS.1SG, vedem_IND≡SUBJ.PRES.1PL 'see');
- /'a/ ~ /ə/ ~ /'ɨ/ (V rămas_PPLE, rămăsei_PS.1SG, rămân_IND.PRES.1SG≡3PL≡SUBJ.PRES.1SG 'remain');
- /'i/ ~ /e/ (V prezint_IND≡SUBJ.PRES.1SG, prezentăm_IND≡SUBJ.PRES.1PL 'present');
- /'o/ ~ /'o̯a/ ~ /u/ (Pron tot_M.SG, toată_F.SG.NOM≡ACC, tuturor_PL.GEN≡DAT 'all'; V port_IND≡SUBJ.PRES.1SG, poartă_IND.PRES.3SG≡PL, purta_INF≡IMPERF.3SG 'bear; wear');
- /'o/ ~ /u/ (N soră_SG.NOM≡ACC, surori_SG.GEN≡DAT≡PL.NOM≡ACC≡GEN≡DAT 'sister');
- /'u/ ~ /Ø/ (V usuc_IND≡SUBJ.PRES.1SG, uscăm_IND≡SUBJ.PRES.1PL 'dry').

The consonantal alternations are as follows:

- /b/ ~ /Ø/ (V fierbe_INF≡IND.PRES.3SG, fierse_PS.3SG 'boil');
- /k/ ~ /tʃ/ (N berbec_SG, berbeci_PL 'ram'; Adj adânc_M.SG, adânci_M≡F.PL≡F.SG.GEN≡DAT 'deep'; V calca_INF≡IMPERF.3SG, calce_SUBJ.PRES.3SG≡PL 'step on');
- /k/ ~ /tʃ/ ~ /Ø/ (V ducând_GER, duce_INF≡IND.PRES.3SG, duse_PS.3SG 'lead');
- /k/ ~ /tʃ/ ~ /p/ (V cocând_GER, coace_INF≡IND.PRES.3SG, copsei_PS.1SG 'bake');
- /d/ ~ /z/ (N brad_SG, brazi_PL 'fir tree'; Adj blând_M.SG, blânzi_M.PL 'kind'; V cădea_INF≡IMPERF.3SG, căzând_GER 'fall');

- /d/ ~ /z/ ~ /Ø/ (V arde_INF≡IND.PRES.3SG, arzând_GER, arse_PS.3SG 'burn');
- /g/ ~ /dʒ/ (N covrig_SG, covrigi_PL 'pretzel'; Adj stâng_M.SG, stângi_M≡F.PL≡F.SG.GEN≡DAT 'left'; V adăugând_GER, adauge_SUBJ.PRES.3SG≡PL 'add');
- /g/ ~ /dʒ/ ~ /Ø/ (V spărgând_GER, sparge_INF≡IND.PRES.3SG, sparse_PS.3.SG 'break');
- /g/ ~ /dʒ/ ~ /p/ (V înfigând_GER, înfige_INF≡IND.PRES.3SG, înfipsei_PS.1.SG 'thrust');
- /l/ ~ /Ø/ (N cal, cai; Adj destul_M.SG, destui_M.PL 'enough');
- /n/ ~ /Ø/ (V rămân_IND.PRES.1SG≡3PL≡SUBJ.PRES.1SG, rămâi_IND≡SUBJ.PRES.2SG);
- /s/ ~ /ʃ/ (N urs_SG, urși_PL 'bear(s)'; Adj des_M.SG, deși_M.PL 'frequent'; V coase_INF≡IND.PRES.3SG, coși_IND≡SUBJ.PRES.2SG 'sew');
- /sk/ ~ /ʃt/ (N gâscă, gâște; Adj orășenesc_M.SG, orășenești_M≡F.PL≡F.SG.GEN≡DAT 'urban'; V cresc_IND.PRES.1SG≡3PL≡SUBJ.PRES.1SG, crești_IND.PRES.2SG 'grow');
- /s(t)/ ~ /ʃ(t)/ (N veste_SG.NOM≡ACC, vești_SG.GEN≡DAT≡PL.NOM≡ACC≡GEN≡DAT 'news'; Adj trist_M.SG, triști_M.PL 'sad'; Pron acesta_M.SG, aceștia_M.PL 'this / these'; V gusta_INF≡IMPERF.3SG, guști_IND≡SUBJ.PRES.2SG 'taste');
- /s(tr)/ ~ /ʃ(tr)/ (N ministru_SG, miniștri_PL 'minister'; Adj albastru_M.SG, albaștri_M.PL 'blue'; Pron nostru_M.SG, noștri_M.PL 'our');
- /(ʃ)k/ ~ /(ʃ)t/ (N pușcă_SG.NOM≡ACC, puști_SG.GEN≡DAT≡PL.NOM≡ACC≡GEN≡DAT 'gun'; V mușca_INF≡IMPERF.3SG, muști_IND≡SUBJ.PRES.2SG 'bite');
- /t/ ~ /ts/ (N burete_SG, bureți_PL 'sponge'; Adj bogat_M.SG, bogați_M.PL 'rich'; V bate_INF≡IND.PRES.3SG, bați_IND≡SUBJ.PRES.2SG 'beat');
- /t/ ~ /ts/ ~ /Ø/ (V scoate_INF≡IND.PRES.3SG, scoțând_GER, scoase_PS.3SG 'take out');
- /z/ ~ /ʒ/ (N obraz_SG, obraji_PL 'cheek'; Adj viteaz_M.SG, viteji_M.PL 'courageous').

H Most of the alternations are the outcome of the phonological rules specific to the history of Romanian (Vasiliu and Ionescu-Ruxăndoiu 1986: 120–5, 133, and references therein; Brâncuș 2002: 96–116). The main causes of the emergence of alternations are stress differences in Latin inflection, which produced the raising of certain vowels, and palatalization of root-final consonants under the influence of the inflectional affix (Sala 2006: 130–1).

The oldest alternations probably emerged in an early stage of Romanian; these involve (clusters of) sounds (non-)existent in Latin (§1.2): /'a/ ~ (/a/ >) /ə/; /'o/ ~ (/o/ >) /u/; /'ə/ ~ /'a/ (ORom părău_SG, părae_PL 'stream'); /'e̯a/ ~ /'e/; /'o/ ~ /'o̯a/; /k/ ~ /tʃ/; /g/ ~ /dʒ/; /s/ ~ /ʃ/; /sk/ ~ /ʃt/; /s(t)/ ~ /ʃ(t)/; /(ʃ)k/ ~ /(ʃ)t/; /t/ ~ /ts/; /d/ ~ /dz/ became /d/ ~ /z/ by the change of the affricate /dz/, in southern Daco-Romanian; this form was adopted in standard Romanian (putred_M.SG, putrezi_M.PL 'rotten').

Other alternations emerged later. The alternation /'a/ ~ /'ə/ probably emerged before the 12th century, in southern Daco-Romanian. The alternation /'ə/ ~ /'ɨ/ (ORom cuvăntu_SG, cuvinte_PL 'word') was followed by the raising of ['ə] > ['ɨ] (ORom cuvăntu > cuvânt): CRom /'ɨ/ ~ /'i/ (cuvânt, cuvinte). The alternation /'ə/ ~ /'e/ appeared after the transformation ['e] > ['ə] (*peru_SG > ORom păr(u), peri_PL 'hair'). The alternations /'e̯a/ ~ /'a/, /'a/ ~ /'e/ occurred (in Daco-Romanian) by monophthongization: ['e̯a] > ['a], after labials, before a nonpalatal vowel in the succeeding syllable (until the 16th century); ['e̯a] > ['e], before [e] in the succeeding syllable (a process not yet finished in the 16th century): *measă_SG.NOM≡ACC / *mease_SG.GEN≡DAT≡PL.NOM≡ACC≡GEN≡DAT > ORom masă / mese 'table' (Avram 2005: 65–71). The monophthongization process led to the disappearance of the alternation /'e̯a/ ~ /'e/, especially in southern Daco-Romanian, in words such as the ORom leage_SG.NOM≡ACC > lege, legi_SG.GEN≡DAT≡PL.NOM≡ACC≡GEN≡DAT 'law'. The alternation /l/ ~ /Ø/ is the consequence of the change [l] > [ʎ] > [Ø]. The alternation /(d)z/ ~ /ʒ/, initially present in Slavic loanwords (cneaz_SG, cneji_PL 'knez'), was extended after the

15th century. The alternation /s(tr)/ ~ /ʃ(tr)/ is not attested before the 16th century: ORom *fiastru*_{SG}, *fiastri*_{PL} > *fiaștri* 'stepson'.

C   The variety and extension of the alternations (e.g. velar–palatal alternations) mark out Romanian in the Romance family (Maiden 2011b: 220).

In terms of the morphological importance of the alternations, Romanian resembles the Slavic languages, so that they have been considered by some scholars to reflect Slavic influence (ELR: 39).

15.1.2 Characteristics of alternations

Many alternations are common to nouns, adjectives, and verbs. The alternation /'ə/ ~ /'e/ occurs only with nouns, /z/ ~ /ʒ/ with nouns and adjectives, /(ʃ)k/ ~ /(ʃ)t/ with nouns and verbs. Certain alternations are lexically restricted: /'i̯/ ~ /'ii̯/ to the noun *mână* 'hand', /o/ ~ /o̯a/ (in an unstressed syllable), to the noun *mijloc* 'middle', /'ə/ ~ /'e/ ~ /'e̯a/, to the adjective *rău* 'bad'. The alternation /'a/ ~ /'ə/ does not occur with adjectives (compare N *mare*_{SG}, *mări*_{PL} 'sea' to Adj *mare*_{M.SG≡F.SG.NOM≡ACC}, *mari*_{M≡F.PL≡F.SG.GEN≡DAT} 'big').

Most alternations are binary; three-term alternations occur only with verbs; taking into account the position of stress, a few verbs have four alternating vowels: /'ə/ ~ /'e/ ~ /'a/ ~ /ə/, and *vedea* 'see' has five: /'ə/ ~ /'e/ ~ /'a/ ~ /e/ ~ /ə/.

Alternations involving ∅ are consonantal, with the exception of vocalic /'u/ ~ /∅/; the alternation /l/ ~ /∅/ occurs with nouns and adjectives, and the rest occur with verbs.

The alternations alter the root of the word (1) or certain verbal inflectional suffixes:

(2)   lucr-ez   -∅ /   lucr-eaz   -ă   /e/ ~ /e̯a/
      work-IND.PRES-1SG   work-IND.PRES   -3SG≡PL
      'work'

The consonantal alternations occur at the end of the root, and the vowel alternations occur within the root, with some exceptions (Adj *grea*_{SG.NOM≡ACC}, *grele*_{SG.GEN≡DAT≡PL.NOM≡ACC≡GEN≡DAT} 'hard; heavy').

Words may contain a vowel alternation (N *șarpe*, *șerpi*), a consonant alternation (Adj *blând*, *blânzi*) or a vowel alternation plus a consonantal (N *noapte*_{SG.NOM≡ACC}, *nopți*_{SG.GEN≡DAT≡PL.NOM≡ACC≡GEN≡DAT} 'night'). In the case of a few adjectives and verbs, there occur two vowel alternations (Adj *geamăn*_{M.SG}, *gemeni*_{M.PL} 'twin', V *seamănă*_{IND.PRES.3SG≡PL}, *semeni*_{IND≡SUBJ.PRES.2SG} 'resemble') and a consonant alternation (Adj *vânăt*, *vineți* 'purple'; V *leapădă*_{IND.PRES.3SG≡PL}, *lepezi*_{IND≡SUBJ.PRES.2SG} 'hurl').

Most vowel alternations occur in stressed syllables. There are few alternations which occur in unstressed syllables: /ə/ ~ /e/ (for nouns and adjectives) and /o/ ~ /o̯a/ (for nouns). With verbs, the alternations are usually associated with stress shift; since nouns overwhelmingly have fixed stress (§1.2.4), this situation occurs only rarely: /'o/ ~ /u/ (*soră*, *surori*).

Most alternations are phonologically conditioned. Many consonant alternations result from the alteration of the consonant before [i], and, for /k/ ~ /tʃ/, /g/ ~ /dʒ/, /sk/ ~ /ʃt/, also before [e] (§1.2.1.4); the alternations /'e̯a/ ~ /'e/, /'o̯a/ ~ /'o/ are conditioned by the aperture of the final vowel (§1.2.2); /'ə/ ~ /'e/, /ə/ ~ /e/, /'ɨ/ ~ /'i/ are produced after labial consonants in the case of nouns, and also after dentals in the case of adjectives. In the case of nouns and verbs, there are also inflectional class restrictions: /ə/ ~ /e/ occurs in the feminine and neuter; /'a/ ~ /'ə/ occurs with feminines (*cetate*_{SG.NOM≡ACC}, *cetăți*_{SG.GEN≡DAT≡PL.NOM≡ACC≡GEN≡DAT}

'fortress'), but not with masculines in the very same phonological environment (*frate, fraţi*); /n/ ~ /Ø/ appears before a nonsyllabic [i], with verbs whose infinitive ends in *-e, -i* (*veni*_{INF≡PS.3SG}, *vii*_{IND≡SUBJ.PRES.2SG} 'come'), but not also those whose infinitives end in *-a*, in the very same phonological conditions (*aduna*_{INF≡IMPERF.3SG}, *aduni*_{IND≡SUBJ.PRES.2SG} 'collect'). Of the plural inflectional endings of nouns, *-uri* does not trigger alternations. A few alternations are lexically conditioned: /'i/ ~ /'ii̯/, /'i/ ~ /'a/, /o/ ~ /o̯a/, /'u/ ~ /Ø/, etc.

The phenomenon of vowel harmony is manifested in nouns, adjectives, and verbs: some alternating vowels agree with the vowels in the succeeding syllables with respect to one or more features (*tânăr*_{M.SG}, *tineri*_{M.PL} 'young man').

The complexity of the conditions that govern the system of alternations and its dynamics make it impossible to formulate precise rules (for contemporary Romanian). The enrichment of the system of alternations, which has assumed an inflectional function (often redundantly), reflects the tendency to multiple marking of morphosyntactic categories, characteristic of Romanian (Brâncuş 2007: 12).

U In contemporary standard Romanian, there is a tendency to reduce alternations in the case of newer loanwords, where the alternation functions as a redundant inflectional marker: *remarcă*_{SG.NOM≡ACC}, *remarci*_{SG.GEN≡DAT≡PL.NOM≡ACC≡GEN≡DAT} 'remark' vs. *marcă*_{SG.NOM≡ACC}, *mărci*_{SG.GEN≡DAT≡PL.NOM≡ACC≡GEN≡DAT} 'mark(er); brand' (/'a/ ~ /'ə/); *transport*_{IND≡SUBJ.PRES.1SG}, *transportă*_{IND.PRES.3SG≡PL}, *transporta*_{INF≡IMPERF.3SG} 'transport' vs. *port, poartă, purta* (/'o/ ~ /'o̯a/ ~ /u/); *englez*_{SG}, *englezi*_{PL} vs. (obsolete) *engleji*_{PL} 'English' (/z/ ~ /ʒ/); *menestrel*_{SG}, *menestreli*_{PL} 'minstrel' vs. *colonel*_{SG}, *colonei*_{PL} 'colonel(s)' (/l/ ~ /Ø/).

15.2 DERIVATIONAL ALTERNATIONS

Most alternations are common to inflection and derivation, because they are or were subject to the same phonological conditionings. The main causes of derivational alternations are a change of the final consonant of the base under the influence of the palatal (semi-)vowels which occur at the beginning of the derivative suffix: /k/ ~ /tʃ/ (*porc, purcel* 'pig, piglet'), /d/ ~ /z/ (*crud, cruzime* 'cruel, cruelty') and the loss of stress as an effect of selection by a stressed suffix, with raising of the vowel that has become unstressed: /'a/ ~ /ə/ (*brad, brădet* 'fir tree, fir wood'), /'o/ ~ /u/ (*frumos, frumuşel* 'beautiful, pretty'). A few alternations occur only in derivation (ELR: 171): /d/ ~ /ʒ/ (Adj *rotund*, V *rotunji*, Adj *rotunjor* 'round, (to) round, rounded'), /ts/ ~ /tʃ/ (N *căruţ*, N *cărucior* 'cart, stroller'). The alternation /'a/ ~ /ə/ triggers the occurrence of the alternation /a/ ~ /ə/ in pretonic syllables, by vowel harmony (*pa'har, păhă'rel* 'glass, small glass'; Avram 1993: 383–4).

CONCLUSIONS

Romanian developed at an early stage a complex system of morphophonological alternations, which marks it out in the Romance family.

The alternations occur in inflection (with nouns, adjectives, and verbs) and in suffixal derivation.

The alternations have the role of supplementary inflectional markers (co-occurring with affixal markers); occasionally they may be the sole markers. The tendency to accumulate markers is specific to Romanian. There is a tendency to avoid this type of redundancy in the case of borrowings in contemporary standard Romanian.

Although systematic, the alternations do not have a general application, which makes it impossible to give absolute rules for their occurrence.

16

Compounding

This chapter presents the types of compounds available in Romanian—syntactic compounds and compound lexemes—and the patterns of compounding associated with each type. These two types differ formally in their degree of cohesion, with morphological and syntactic consequences. Syntactic compounds are based on patterns generally attested in Romance languages. In the contemporary language, certain patterns of compounding are more productive, under the influence of the language used in the media. Compound lexemes are the result of agglutination in older stages of the language; they display numerous patterns and are no longer productive.

16.1 TYPES OF COMPOUNDS

16.1.1 Syntactic compounds

Syntactic compounds (Lyons 1977: 534–5) are the result of the 'petrifaction' of certain syntactic phrases. The distinction between syntactic compounds and free syntactic phrases is based on semantic criteria. Syntactic compounds have semantic autonomy, their meaning differing from that of their individual components. The meaning of the compound is often compositional; in this case, the semantic relation between the compound and the 'dominant' component (FC I: 30) is one of hyponymy, i.e. the compound is a subclass of the main component (*câine-lup* dog-wolf 'wolfhound' is a breed of dog, *floarea-soarelui* flower.DEF-sun.DEF.GEN 'sunflower' is a flower).

In compounding, several semantic processes may be involved: semantic deviation or metaphorical or metonymical transfer, which have the effect of making the meaning of the compound opaque in relation to the meaning of its internal components: *coada-șoricelului* tail.DEF-mouse.DIM.DEF.GEN 'yarrow' (plant), *bou-de-baltă* ox-of-swamp 'water beetle' (insect). The meaning of the compound is not transparent; it cannot be inferred from that of the components. In regional language, many compounds denoting plants, insects, and animals are the result of a metaphorical transfer (*traista-ciobanului* bag.DEF-shepherd.DEF.GEN 'shepherd's purse', *gura-leului* mouth.DEF.-lion.DEF.GEN 'snap dragon').

Syntactic compounds have a different morphological behaviour depending on the base syntactic pattern. This behaviour is heterogeneous even within the same pattern of compounding. The difference is due to the different degree of cohesion and the degree of transparency of the compounds. These features are determined by the age and the frequency of the compounds ('institutionalization', Lyons 1977: 535), by the language they come from, and by the orthographic tradition.

16.1.2 Compound lexemes

Compound lexemes are the result of the agglutination of uninflected elements to a nominal (*fărădelege* without-DE-law 'wrongdoing'), adjectival (*dreptcredincios* right-**believer** 'believer'), verbal (*binecuvânta* well-**say** 'to bless'), or adverbial base (*niciodată* not-**once** 'never'). Compounds may be made up by the attachment of fossilized elements (originating in verbal forms) to pronominal (*cineva* who-VA 'somebody': *va* < *vare* < **voare* < Lat. **volet*, *fiecare* be.SUBJ-which 'each'), adverbial (*oriunde* ORI-where 'anywhere', *ori* < *veri*. IND.PRES.2SG < *vrea* 'want') or conjunctional bases (*fiindcă* be.GER-that 'because'). Prepositions can also be the result of agglutination (*dintre* 'between' < *de* 'of' + *între* 'between, among', *despre* 'about' < *de* 'of' + *spre* 'to'). These compounds are entirely assimilated to the new lexical and grammatical classes to which they belong; their morphological and syntactic behaviour is similar to that of the single elements of the respective class. For most speakers of Romanian, they have lost their (near-)totally analysable nature: *dintre* 'between' (*de* 'of' + *între* 'between, among'), *deseară* 'tonight' (*de* 'of' + *seară* 'evening'). The tendency to agglutinate prepositions and adverbs to each other or to various bases is inherited from Latin and was productive all over Romance (Bourciez 1956; ELIR: 67; Bauer 2011: 542). In contemporary Romanian, these types of compounding are no longer productive.

H In the time of Slavic influence, loan translations were rare (*Bunavestire* good.DEF.F.SG-news.F.SG 'The Annunciation', *atotputernic* A-all-powerful 'almighty'), and they consolidated the patterns inherited from Latin (Hasan and Popescu-Marin 2007: 233). For the second half of the 20th century, Iordan (1947: 227) notes that there is intense activity in the field of compounding, and that contemporary Romanian has a relatively large number of compounds and is prepared to accept new ones.

U There is no consistent rule for writing compounds. *Compound lexemes* are written without spaces. Most *syntactic compounds* are written with a hyphen. The writing rule has been determined by a complex of factors, morphological (morphological class of the internal elements of the compound, type of inflection), syntactic (the syntactic relations which govern the compound), and historical (age of the compound, orthographic tradition).

16.2 SYNTACTIC PATTERNS OF COMPOUNDING IN CONTEMPORARY ROMANIAN

Different patterns of compounding show differences in morphological and syntactic behaviour, frequency, and productivity.

16.2.1 Noun output compounds

The following structural patterns are found in compound nouns:

1. [N + N$_{GEN}$]$_N$ (*floarea-soarelui* flower.DEF-sun.DEF.GEN 'sunflower', *gura-leului* mouth.DEF-lion.DEF.GEN 'snap dragon').

This pattern is endocentric; the elements of the compounds are in a head–possessor relation, with the head to the left of the compound. The inflection of the compound is

mostly internal, due to the fact that the head of the phrase is inflected: *florii-soarelui* flower.
DEF.GEN-sun.DEF.GEN 'sunflower', *gurii-leului* mouth.DEF.GEN-lion.DEF.GEN 'snap dragon'.
These compounds do not usually have a plural form: **cozile-șoricelului* tails.DEF-mouse.
DEF.GEN 'milfoils' (*Am cules niște (flori de) coada-șoricelului* 'I have picked up some milfoils'). A plural form is occasionally possible: ?*florile-soarelui* flowers.DEF.PL-sun.DEF.
GEN 'sunflowers'.

C   This pattern was inherited from Latin in all Romance languages (ELIR: 67), but nowadays these compounds appear in Romanian because it is the only Romance language to have maintained case inflection (Bauer 2011: 544). In western Romance, where nouns do not have synthetic inflection, the equivalent pattern is [N + [Prep + Art] + N] (It. *fiore del latte*, Fr. *bonheur du jour*, Sp. *lengua del ciervo*) (Giurescu 1975: 62).

This type of compounding is frequent especially in regional language. Today its productivity is weak.

2. [N + de + N]ₙ (*floare-de-colț* flower-of-corner 'edelweiss', *viță-de-vie* vine-of-vineyard 'grape-vine', *gură-de-lup* mouth-of-wolf 'crow-bar').

The head of the phrase is inflected: *florii-de-colț* flower.DEF.GEN-of-jut 'of the edelweiss', *viței-de-vie* vine.DEF.GEN-of-vineyard 'of the grape-vine'.

The pattern is well represented in Romanian, with many compounds in regional varieties. It is an innovation of Latin, and the compounds are frequent in all Romance languages (Giurescu 1975: 63; ELIR: 67).

This pattern is not productive in the contemporary language.

3. [N + N]ₙ.

Compounds with this structure can be divided into three sub-patterns, depending on their inflectional behaviour and semantic interpretation.

(i) [N + N]ₙ (*mamă-soacră* mother-mother.in.law 'mother-in-law', *tată-socru* father-father. in.law 'father-in-law', *inginer-șef* engineer-chief 'chief engineer', *locotenent-colonel* lieutenant-colonel 'lieutenant colonel', *general-maior* general-major 'major general')

The pattern in (i) is old. The inflection is of various kinds:

- both elements are inflected: *mamei-soacre* mother.DEF.GEN-mother.GEN-in-law 'of mother-in-law', *mame-soacre* mothers-mothers-in-law 'mothers-in-law'; the enclitic article is attached only to the first element: *mama-soacră* mother.DEF-mother-in-law 'the mother-in-law', *tata-socru* father.DEF-father-in-law 'the father-in-law'; *ingineri-șefi* engineers-chiefs 'chief engineers', *inginerului-șef* engineer.DEF.GEN-chief 'chief engineer's';
- both elements are inflected, the enclitic article being attached to the last element: *locotenenți-colonei* lieutenants-colonels 'lieutenant colonels', *locotenent-colonelului* lieutenant-colonel.DEF.GEN 'lieutenant colonel's';
- the plural is marked on both elements, the attachment of the enclitic article has no consistent rules; both situations are possible (the article can be suffixed on the first or on the last element): *generali-maiori* generals-majors 'major generals', *generalului-maior* general.DEF.GEN-major 'major general's' / *general-maiorului* general-major.DEF. GEN 'major general's');

(ii) [N + N]ₙ (*cuvânt-cheie* word-key 'keyword', *știre-bombă* news-bomb '(news) bombshell', *război-fulger* war-lightening 'blitzkrieg', *pește-spadă* fish-sword 'swordfish').

In compounds of type (ii), the head of the phrase is inflected: *cuvinte*~PL~-*cheie*~SG~ words-key 'keywords'. The second element of the compound acquires a qualifying value, expressing a superlative value (*cheie* 'key'—'very important', *bombă* 'bomb'—'out of the ordinary', *fulger* 'lightening'—'fast'). In these contexts, the second term can be interpreted as the result of conversion into an invariable adjective. This syntactic relation, although not marked, can be subsumed to the head–modifier type.

This pattern is more productive in the press: *știre-bombă* news-bomb 'bombshell', *dezvăluire-șoc* disclosure-shock 'shock disclosure', *invitat-surpriză* guest-surprise 'surprise-guest' (Stoichițoiu Ichim 2006; Barbu 2010).

The second term of the compound can be seen either as a modifying adjective (as in the examples above) or as a relative adjective inducing a semantic limitation. These compounds are based on a metaphorical transfer, but their meaning is denotative, and used in specialized terminologies: *rechin-ciocan* shark-hammer 'hammer head', *pește-spadă* fish-sword 'swordfish'. The first element is inflected: *rechini-ciocan* sharks-hammer, *pești-spadă* fish.PL-sword.

U   An exception to the pattern in (ii) is the compound *câine-lup* dog-wolf 'wolf hound', which is formally and semantically similar to the ones above, but for which the norm recommends plural marking on both elements: *câini-lupi* dogs-wolves 'wolf hounds'. In colloquial language, the plural may be marked only on the first element: *câini-lup* dogs-wolf 'wolf hounds' (*pui de **câini-lup** gratis* cubs of dogs-wolf free 'free wolf hound cubs').

(iii) [N + N]~N~ (*antrenor-jucător* trainer-player, *președinte-[director-general]* president-general manager).

Compounds of this type are obtained from the juxtaposition of two nouns in the nominative–accusative, and are analysable as derived from conjunctive coordinated phrases: *antrenor și jucător* 'trainer and player'. The compounds lack morphological unity, both terms being inflected. This pattern is literary, recent and very productive; such compounds are frequently ad-hoc creations, determined by the need for concision in formal registers (*asigurare-reasigurare* insurance-reinsurance, *cercetare-dezvoltare* research-development—Barbu 2010: 17).

4. [N + Adj]~N~ (*mamă-mare* mother-great 'grandmother', *gulere-albe* collars-white 'white-collar workers').

This class is heterogeneous, comprising old compounds (*mamă-mare* mother-great 'grandmother', *fată-mare* girl-big 'virgin') and new formations, especially loan translations (*gulere-albe* collars-white 'white-collars', *capete-rase* heads-shaved 'skinheads', *berete-verzi* berets-green 'green-berets').

Their heterogeneity is manifested at the inflectional level as well:

- older terms are inflected on both elements: *mamei-mari* mother.DEF.GEN-great.GEN 'grandmother's', *fetei-mari* girl.DEF.GEN-big.GEN 'the virgin's' or are not inflected at all: *un / o / niște gură-spartă* a.M / a.F / some mouth-broken 'a / some blabbermouth'
- the enclitic article is attached only to the first element: *mamele-mari* mothers.DEF-great 'the grandmothers', *fetele-mari* girls.DEF-big 'the virgins', *gulerele-albe* collars.DEF-white 'the white-collars'.

Most compounds are exocentric.

This pattern is productive, as many new loan translations are made up on this model (*capete-rase* heads-shaved 'skinheads', *berete-verzi* berets-green 'green-berets').

5. [Adj + N]_N (*bună-cuviință* good-decency 'decency', *rea-voință* ill-will 'malevolence', *prim-ministru* prime-minister 'prime-minister').

These compounds display internal inflection (*bunei-cuviințe* good.DEF.GEN-decency.GEN, *relei-voințe* ill.DEF.GEN-will.GEN), in compliance with the norm, but in colloquial registers only the last element is sometimes inflected: *rea-voinței* bad.NOM-will.DEF.GEN.

Compounds like *prim-solist* 'principal soloist', *prim-balerin* 'principal dancer' have inflection on the last element, following the grammatical norm. For a similar compound, *prim-ministru* 'prime-minister', the norm recommends inflection on the last element, but colloquially, especially in the spoken language, the adjective in the first position is inflected (*primului-ministru* prime.DEF.GEN-minister 'the prime-minister's'). This pattern has a low productivity.

6. [V + N]_N (*încurcă-lume* tangle-world 'muddler', *pierde-vară* lose-summer 'idler', *papă-lapte* eat-milk 'mollycoddle', *linge-blide* lick-plates 'sponger', *fluieră-vânt* whistle-wind 'idler').

From a morphological point of view, this structure is fixed, as the elements do not inflect. In the contemporary language, these compounds are specific to regional or familiar varieties, and have various stylistic connotations. For instance, those which denote persons are pejorative. In older stages of Romanian, compounds of this type were more numerous (Drăganu 1998: 107).

They are exocentric compounds, in which one can recognize the structure predicate–argument. The argument can be in the first position: *soare-apune* sun-set 'sunset', *gură-cască* mouth-yawn 'lay-about'.

C This type of compound is very frequent in Romance, where it developed independently from Latin (Meyer-Lübke 1895: 630) and had a high degree of productivity. Found initially in place names, this pattern has become more frequent and productive with common nouns in Spanish, Italian, and French (Bourciez 1956). Archaic Latin had a type of *root compounding* in which the second element was a verb. The productivity of the pattern [V + N]_N in western Romance is attributed to the fact that it replaces the Latin type of *root compounding* (Bourciez 1956).

H The nature of the verbal element of these compounds has been much discussed. Meyer-Lübke (1895: 630–2) analyses this construction from the oldest attestations of topical names, in the 9th century, in French and Italian, and shows that this pattern was frequently made up of the verb in the imperative, 2nd person singular, and a noun functioning as a subject or direct object. Drăganu (1998: 105–7) also analyses this verbal form as an imperative, adding to the place-names arguments other Romanian structures in which the imperative is more obvious: *toacă-gură* bother.IMP.2SG-mouth 'talkative'. Other analyses are mentioned in FC I: 106–7; Maiden 2006: 47–59; Ralli Patras 2008: 25–7.

In Romanian, this pattern is no longer productive. Sporadically, spontaneous formations are found in colloquial language: *un plimbă hârtia* a walk paper.DEF 'a pen pusher'.

U Sentence-like compounds ('conglomerates') can be assigned to this type (Benveniste 2000: 130–1)—*tace-și-face* shuts up.IND.PRES.3SG-and-does.IND.PRES.3SG 'a person who acts on the sly', *lasă-mă-să-te-las* let.IMP.2.SG=CL.ACC.1SG-SĂ_{SUBJ}-CL.ACC.2SG-let.SUBJ.1SG 'stick in the mud', *du-te-vino* go.IMP.2SG-CL.REFL.ACC.2SG-come.IMP.2SG 'hustle and bustle'. They are mainly verbal forms representing fixed structures, used as nominals:

(1) e   un   lasă-mă-să-te-las
    is   a   let.IMP.2SG=CL.ACC.1SG-SĂ_SUBJ-CL.ACC.2SG-let.SUBJ.1SG
    'He is a stick-in-the-mud'
(2) e   un   du-te-vino
    is   a   go.IMP.2SG-CL.REFL.ACC.2SG-come.IMP.2SG
    'There is a hustle and bustle'

16.2.2 Adjective output compounds

1. [Adj + Adj]_Adj (*social-democrat* social-democratic, *alb-vișinii* white-dark red).

These compounds are formed by the juxtaposition of two adjectives.
Inflection is marked on the second element: *măsuri social-democrate* measures.F social-democratic.F.PL 'social-democratic measures'. Certain compounds may become nouns:

(3) Social-democrații   au   inițiat   moțiunea   de   cenzură
    Social-democrat.M.PL.DEF   have   initiated motion.DEF of   censorship
    'The social-democrats moved the censorship motion'

These forms are frequently used in the contemporary language, and the pattern is productive.

2. [Adj + Adv / Pple]_Adj (*roșu-aprins* red-fired 'scarlet', *verde-deschis* green-open 'light green', *albastru electric* blue electric 'electric blue').

For the compounds of this type the norm does not admit inflection (*bluze verde-deschis* blouses green-open 'light-green blouses', *pantofi roșu-aprins* shoes red-fired 'scarlet shoes'). These constructions can be analysed as elliptical (*bluze de culoare verde-deschis* 'light green coloured blouses'). The pattern is similar to the [N + N]_N (ii) nominal pattern, in which the modifier marks a unique semantic feature of the head. The pattern is open to new formations, most of them recent.

3. [Adj + N]_Adj (*albastru-cerneală* blue-ink, *verde-praz* green-leek, *gri-șobolan* grey-rat).

This compounding pattern is the result of ellipsis, *albastru ca cerneala* 'blue like ink'. The construction does not inflect (*pălării galben-pai* hats yellow-straw 'straw yellow hats'), the whole compound behaving like an invariable adjective. The pattern is productive.

4. [N + Adj]_Adj (*nord-african* north-African, *cap-sec* head-empty 'blockhead').

The last element of the compound carries inflectional markers: *nord-africanii* North-Africans.DEF, *sud-dunărenii* South-Danubians.DEF.
The pattern is productive.
Some old exocentric compounds, from regional varieties, which display an affective semuantic value, are built on the same pattern: *gură-spartă* mouth-broken 'chatty', *mațe-fripte* guts-fried 'pinchpenny', *cap-sec* head-empty 'blockhead'. They frequently become nouns.

5. [Adv + Adj / Pple]_Adj (*nou-născut* newly-born, *liber-cugetător* free-thinker).

Only the adjective / participle is inflected (*nou-născuți* newly-born.PL, *liber-cugetători* free-thinkers).

U   In colloquial language, the adverb may also be inflected (*noi(i)-născuți* new.PL.(DEF)-born.PL).

Some compounds become nouns:

(4) Nou-născuții   au   fost   salvați
     newly-born.PL.DEF   have   been   saved
     'The newborns were saved'

(5) Liber-cugetătorii   sunt   priviți   cu   neîncredere
     free-thinkers.DEF   are   regarded   with   disbelief
     'Free-thinkers are regarded with disbelief'

This pattern is productive, the compounds with *bine* 'well', *rău* 'badly', and *nou* 'newly' acting like an analogical model for other compounds which may, thus, become 'institutionalized' (*nou venit* newly come 'newcomer', *rău platnic* badly payer 'bad payer'). Phrases like *bine-crescut* well-raised, *bine-cunoscut* well-known, *bine-venit* well-come, previously considered 'free' adjectival phrases, are nowadays regarded as compound words.

16.2.3   Compound lexemes patterns

Compound lexemes are based on the agglutination of elements belonging to various lexical and grammatical classes, on patterns which are not recurrent or productive. Many elements are loan translations on a Slavic or Romance model.

1. **Nouns**
   - [Adj + N]$_N$ *primăvară* first-summer 'spring';
   - [Prep + Prep + N]$_N$ *fărădelege* without-of-law 'wrongdoing';
   - [Prep + Pron + Adj / N]$_N$ (in loan translations on Slavic model) *atotputernic* A-all-powerful 'almighty' [N + N]$_N$ (loan translations on Romance model) *omucidere* man-slaughter 'homicide'.

2. **Adjectives**
   - [Adv + Adj]$_{Adj}$ *clarvăzător* clear-seeing 'long-sighted', *dreptcredincios* right-believer 'orthodox';
   - [N + Adj]$_{Adj}$ *codalb* (< *coadă albă* tail white) 'white-tailed';
   - [Prep + N]$_{Adj}$ *cuminte* with-mind 'well behaved';
   - [Negative particle + Adv + Pple]$_{Adj}$ *nemaipomenit* not-more-happend 'unprecedented'.

3. **Pronouns**
   - [Pron + Pron]$_{Pron}$ *altcineva* (< *alt + cineva* else-somebody 'somebody else');
   - [Prep + Pron]$_{Pron}$ *dânsul* (< *de + însul* of-he 'he');
   - ['fossilized' verbal form + Pron]$_{Pron}$ *fiecare* (< *fie + care* be.SUBJ-which 'every'; *oricare* (< *ori + care* want-which 'any') (§5.3.2.2.1);
   - [Pron + 'fossilized' verbal form]$_{Pron}$ *cineva* (< *cine + va* who-want 'somebody') (§5.3.2.2.1);
   - [N + Possessive]$_{Pron}$ *dumneata* (< *domnia ta* Highness-your 'you' (formal)) (§6.3.1);
   - [Adv + Pron]$_{Pron}$ *niciunul* (< *nici + unul* neither-one.DEF 'none') (§5.3.2.2.2).

4. **Numerals** (§5.3.2.1.1)
   - [Num + Prep + Num]$_{Num}$ *unsprezece* (unu + spre + zece one-upon-ten 'eleven');
   - [Num + Num]$_{Num}$ *douăzeci* (< *două* + *zeci* two.FEM-tens 'twenty');
   - [Num + Conj + Num]$_{Num}$ *treizeci și unu* (thirty-and-one 'thirty-one').

5. **Verbs**
   - [Adv+V]$_V$ *binevoi* well-want 'agree', *binecuvânta* well-say 'bless'.

6. **Adverbs** (§8.1.3)
   - [Adv + N]$_{Adv}$ *ieri-seară* yesterday-evening, *mâine-dimineață* tomorrow-morning;
   - [Prep + Adv]$_{Adv}$ *demult* of-long 'long time ago', *dinafară* from-outside 'from outside';
   - [Prep + N]$_{Adv}$ *acasă* (< *a* + *casă* at-home), *aminte* (< *a* + *minte* at-mind, in *a-și aduce aminte* 'remember').

7. **Prepositions**
   - [Prep + Prep]$_{Prep}$ *dintre* (< *de* 'of' + *între* 'between, among'), *din* (< *de* 'of' + *în* 'in').

16.3 NEO-CLASSICAL COMPOUNDS

Neo-classical compounds are made up of an initial or final compounding term of Greek or Latin origin, attached to a base (*supra-*, *mega-*, *tele-*, *bio-*; *-fil*, *-log*, etc.). Most compounds of this type are loans. The inventory of compounds and elements of compounding is very rich and constantly increasing through loans: *virusologie* 'virusology', *sacrosant* 'sacrosanct'.

H Romanian has borrowed elements of compounding from other languages as well: Slavic (*proto-*: *protopop* 'archpriest'), Turkish and Modern Greek, mainly in proper names (Tk. *cara-*: Caramarin, Gr. *papa-*: Papahagi) (ELIR: 67).

Elements of compounding isolated from neo-classical compounds may be combined with Romanian bases, giving rise to playful formations: *secretomanie* (< secret-o-mania 'secretiveness'), *spionofobie* (< spy-o-phobia 'spy phobia'), *zvonotecă* (< rumour-o-teca 'a rumour mill'). Neo-classical compounds may constitute bases for derivatives: *hidroelectrician* 'hydro-electrician' < *hidroelectric* 'hydro-electric'.

Another particularity is the isolation of the compounding marker *o* from the structure of some neo-classical compounds (*tehnico-științific* technical-scientific) and its usage in new formations: *monarho-republica* monarchy-republic, *turistico-sălbatic* tourist-wild, *vinoterapie* wine-therapy. This type is unproductive, but is current in the language of the media.

CONCLUSIONS

Romanian compounding is less productive than derivation and the language is not very open to compounding (the latter feature is inherited from Latin). The number of compounds increased during the last century through borrowing of compounding patterns which have become productive.

The pattern [N + N$_{\text{GEN}}$]$_{\text{N}}$, inherited in all Romance languages (in non-analysable compounds), has been productive only in Romanian.

The most productive patterns in contemporary Romanian are [N + N]$_{\text{N}}$ and [Adj + Adj]$_{\text{Adj}}$.

The inflection of compounds is heterogeneous, differing from one pattern to another, and inconsistent from one compound to another within the same class.

Romanian can detach the compounding marker *o* from neo-classical compounds and create new compounds, most frequently adjectival.

Sources

The years given between [...] represent the dating of the text or the period during which the author published his or her work. The year indicated in the second part represents the year of the modern edition, which is the most recent or the best edition from the contemporary period.

Alecsandri [1840–1888] = Alecsandri, Vasile, *Opere*, I–X. Bucharest, Minerva, 1966–1985.
Alexandria [1620] = Academia Română, *Cele mai vechi cărți populare în literatura română*, XI, *Alexandria*, Cea mai veche versiune păstrată. Edited by Florentina Zgraon. Bucharest, Fundația Națională pentru Știință și Artă, 2006.
Anonimul Brâncovenesc [1706–1717]= *Istoria Țării Rumânești de la octombrie 1688 pînă la martie 1717 (Cronica anonimă despre Brîncoveanu / Anonimul Brîncovenesc)*. In *Cronicari munteni*, II, edited by Mihail Gregorian. Bucharest, Editura pentru Literatură, 1961.
Anonimul Cantacuzinesc [1690] = *Anonimul Cantacuzinesc*. In *Cronicari munteni*, I, edited by Mihail Gregorian. Bucharest, Editura pentru Literatură, 1961.
Antim [1692–1714] = Antim Ivireanul, *Opere*. Edited by Gabriel Ștrempel. Bucharest, Minerva, 1972.
Axinte Uricariul [1730] = Axinte Uricariul, *Cronica paralelă a Țării Românești și a Moldovei*. Edited by Gabriel Ștrempel. Bucharest, Minerva, 1993.
Bălcescu [1861–1863] = Bălcescu, Nicolae, *Românii supt Mihai Voievod Viteazul*. Bucharest, Editura Academiei Române, 1953.
Biblia [1688] = *Biblia, adecă dumnezeiasca scriptură ale cei vechi și ale cei noao leage toate, care s-au tălmăcit dupre limba elinească spre înțeleagerea limbii rumânești cu porunca prea bunului creștin și luminatului domn Ioan Șărban Cantacozino Basarab Voievod și cu îndemnarea dumnealui Costadin Brâncoveanul mare logofăt*. Bucharest.
Bolintineanu [1842–1870] = Bolintineanu, Dimitrie, *Opere*. Bucharest, Editura de Stat pentru Literatură și Artă, 1951.
Budai-Deleanu [1800–1812] = Budai-Deleanu, Ioan, *Țiganiada*. Edited by Florea Fugariu. Bucharest, Minerva, 1981.
Cantacuzino [1678–1688] = Cantacuzino, Constantin, *Istoria Țării Rumânești*. In *Cronicari munteni*, I, edited by Mihail Gregorian. Bucharest, Editura pentru Literatură, 1961.
Cantemir [1798] = Cantemir, Dimitrie, *Divanul sau Gâlceava înțeleptului cu lumea*. Edited by Virgil Cândea. Bucharest, Editura pentru Literatură, 1969.
Caragiale [1880] = Caragiale, Ion Luca, *Opere complete*. Bucharest, Minerva, 1908.
Codicele Voronețean [1563–1583] = *Codicele Voronețean*. Edited by Mariana Costinescu. Bucharest, Minerva, 1981.
Corbea [1691–1697] = Corbea, Teodor, *Dictiones latinae cum valachica interpretatione*. Edited by Alin-Mihai Gherman. Cluj, Clusium, 2001.
Coresi [16th century] = Coresi, *Tâlcul evangheliilor (Cazania I). Molitevnic rumânesc* [1567–1568]. Edited by Vladimir Drimba. Bucharest, Editura Academiei Române, 1998.
Coresi, *Evanghelia cu învățătură* [1581]. Edited by Sextil Pușcariu and Alexie Procopovici. Bucharest, Atelierele Grafice Socec, 1914.
Coresi, *Praxiul* [1563]. Edited by Ion Bianu. Bucharest, Tiparul Cultura Națională, 1930.
Coresi, *Tetraevanghelul* [1561]. Edited by Florica Dimitrescu. Bucharest, Editura Academiei Române, 1963.
Costin [1675] = Costin, Miron, *Letopisețul Țării Moldovei*. In *Opere alese*. Edited by P. P. Panaitescu. Bucharest, Editura Tineretului, 1966.
Creangă [1881] = Creangă, Ion, *Amintiri din copilărie*. Bucharest, Minerva, 1978.

Cronica despre domnia lui Mavrogheni [1790] = *Cronica despre domnia lui Mavrogheni*. In *Cronici și povestiri românești versificate*. Edited by Dan Simionescu. Bucharest, Editura Academiei Române, 1967.

DEX [1975] = Academia Română, Institutul de Lingvistică 'Iorgu Iordan', *Dicționarul explicativ al limbii române*. Bucharest, Editura Academiei Române.

DIARO [1997] = Matilda Caragiu Marioțeanu, *Dicționar aromân (macedo-vlah)*, A–D. Bucharest, Editura Enciclopedică.

Documenta [19th century] = *Documenta Romaniae Historica*, A. Moldova, XIX. Edited by C. Cihodaru, I. Caprosu, and L. Simanschi. Bucharest, Editura Academiei Române, 1965–1977.

Documente [1521–1600] = *Documente și însemnări românești din secolul al XVI-lea*. Edited by Gheorghe Chivu, Magdalena Georgescu, Magdalena Ioniță, Alexandru Mareș, and Alexandra Roman-Moraru. Bucharest, Editura Academiei Române, 1979.

Dosoftei [1682] = Dosoftei, *Viața și petreacerea svinților*. In *Opere*, Bucharest, Minerva, 1978.

Evangheliarul slavo-român de la Sibiu [1551–1553] = *Evangheliarul slavo-român de la Sibiu*. Edited by E. Petrovici and L. Demény. Bucharest, Editura Academiei Române, 1971.

Greceanu [1711] = Greceanu, Radu, *Cronica*. In *Cronicarii Munteni*, edited by Al. Piru. Bucharest, Editura Tineretului, 1964.

Hasdeu [1878–1879] = Hasdeu, Bogdan Petriceicu, *Cuvente den bătrâni*. Bucharest, Editura Didactică și Pedagogică, 1984.

Îndreptarea legii [1652] = *Îndreptarea legii*. Edited by Andrei Rădulescu. Bucharest, Editura Academiei Române, 1962.

Ispirescu [1862–1887] = Ispirescu, Petre, *Opere*. Edited by Aristița Avramescu. I, Bucharest, Editura pentru literatură, 1969; II, Bucharest, Minerva, 1971.

Letopisețul Cantacuzinesc [1690] = *Istoria Țării Rumânești de când au descălecat pravoslavnicii creștini (Letopisețul Cantacuzinesc)*. In *Cronicari munteni*, I, edited by Mihail Gregorian, Bucharest, Editura pentru Literatură, 1961.

Maiorescu [1874] = Maiorescu, Titu, *Critice*. Bucharest, Editura Fundației Culturale Române, 1996.

Neculce [cca 1743] = Neculce, Ion, *Letopisețul Țării Moldovei and O samă de cuvinte*. Edited by Iorgu Iordan, Bucharest, Editura de Stat pentru Literatură și Artă, 1959.

Negruzzi [1836–1868] = Negruzzi, Costache, *Opere alese*, I–II. Bucharest, Editura de Stat pentru Literatură și Artă, 1955.

Noul Testament [1648] = *Noul Testament*, tipărit pentru prima dată în limba română la 1648 de către Simion Ștefan, Mitropolitul Transilvaniei. Reeditat după 340 de ani din inițiativa și purtarea de grijă a prea Sfințitului Emilian, Episcop al Alba Iuliei. Alba Iulia, Editura Episcopiei Ortodoxe Române a Albei Iuliei, 1988.

Palia [1581–1582] = *Palia de la Orăștie*. Edited by Viorica Pamfil, Bucharest, Editura Academiei Române, 1968.

Popescu [1723–1729] = Popescu, Radu, *Istoriile domnilor Țărâi Rumânești*. In *Cronicari munteni*, I, edited by Mihail Gregorian. Bucharest, Editura pentru Literatură, 1961.

Pravolniceasca condică [1780] = *Pravolniceasca condică*. Bucharest, Editura Academiei Române, 1957.

Psaltirea Hurmuzachi [1490–1516] = *Psaltirea Hurmuzachi*. Edited by Ion Gheție and Mirela Teodorescu. Bucharest, Editura Academiei Române, 2005.

Psaltirea Scheiană [1573–1578] = *Psaltirea Scheiană*. Edited by I.-A. Candrea. Bucharest, Socec, 1916.

Psaltirea Voronețeană [1551–1558] = *Psaltirea Voronețeană*. Edited by C. Gălușcă. Halle, 1913.

Rebreanu [1909–1943] = Rebreanu, Liviu, *Opere*. Bucharest, Univers Enciclopedic, 2001.

Sadoveanu [1904–1954] = Sadoveanu, Mihail, *Opere*, I–VIII. Bucharest, Minerva, 1981–1997.

Sicriul de aur [1683] = Ioan Zoba din Vinț, *Sicriul de aur*. Edited by Anton Goția. Bucharest, Minerva, 1984.

Tetraevanghel [1560–1561] = *Tetraevanghel*, Brașov. Edited by Florica Dimitrescu. Bucharest, Editura Academiei Române, 1963.

Texte bogomilice [1580–1619] = *Texte bogomilice*. In Hasdeu, *Cuvente den bătrâni*.

Texte măhăcene [1580–1619] = *Texte măhăcene*. In Hasdeu, *Cuvente den bătrâni*.
Ureche [1642–1647] = Ureche, Grigore, *Letopisețul Țării Moldovei*. Edited by Liviu Onu. Bucharest, Editura Științifică, 1967.
Varlaam [1643] = Varlaam. *Cazania*, Iași. Edited by J. Byck. Bucharest, Editura Academiei Române, 1966.

References

ABEILLÉ, A., and GODARD, D. (2003). 'Les Prédicats complexes dans les langues romanes', in D. Godard (ed.), 125–84.
ACQUAVIVA, P. (2008). *Lexical Plurals: A Morphosemantic Approach*. Oxford: Oxford University Press.
AIKHENVALD, A. (2004). *Evidentiality*. Oxford: Oxford University Press.
ALBOIU, G. (2002). *The Features of Movement in Romanian*. Bucharest: Editura Universității din București.
ALBOIU, G. (2007). 'Moving Forward with Romanian Backward Control and Raising', in W. D. Davies, and S. Dubinsky (eds), *New Horizons in the Analysis of Control and Raising*. Dordrecht: Springer, 187–211.
ALEXIADOU, A. (2001). *Functional Structure in Nominals: Nominalization and Ergativity*. Amsterdam: John Benjamins.
ALEXIADOU, A., and WILDER, C. (1998). 'Adjectival Modification and Multiple Determiners', in A. Alexiadou and C. Wilder (eds), *Possessors, Predicates and Movement in the Determiner Phrase*: Amsterdam / Philadelphia: John Benjamins, 303–32.
ALEXIADOU, A., HAEGEMAN, L., and STAVROU, M. (2007). *Noun Phrase in the Generative Perspective*. Berlin: Mouton de Gruyter.
ALEXIADOU, A., ANAGNOSTOPOULOU, E., and EVERAERT, M. (eds) (2004). *The Unaccusativity Puzzle: Explorations of the Syntax–Lexicon Interface*. Oxford: Oxford University Press.
ALKIRE, T., and ROSEN, C. (2010). *Romance Languages: A Historical Introduction*. Cambridge: Cambridge University Press.
ALLEN, A. S. (1977). 'The Interfix I/ESC in Catalan and Rumanian', *Romance Philology* 31, 2: 203–11.
AMMANN, A., and VAN DER AUWERA, J. (2004). 'Complementizer-Headed Main Clauses for Volitional Moods in the Languages of South-Eastern Europe: A Balkanism?', in O. Mišeska Tomić (ed.), 293–314.
ANSCOMBRE, J.-C. (1996). 'Noms de sentiment, noms d'attitude et noms abstraits', in N. Flaux, M. Glatigny, and D. Samain (eds), 257–73.
ANTRIM, N. M. (2003). 'Number, Gender and Person Agreement in Prenominal Possessives', in W. E. Griffin (ed.), *The Role of Agreement in Natural Language*. Texas: Texas Linguistic Forum, 1–12.
ARIEL, M. (1990). *Accessing Noun Phrase Antecedents*. London: Routledge.
ARVINTE, V. (1983). *Român, românesc, România. Studiu filologic*. Bucharest: Editura Științifică și Enciclopedică.
ATANASOV, P. (2002). *Meglenoromâna astăzi*. Bucharest: Editura Academiei Române.
AVRAM, A. (1986). 'Sandhi Phenomena in Romanian', in A. Henning (ed.), *Sandhi Phenomena in the Languages of Europe*. Berlin / New York: Mouton de Gruyter, 551–74.
AVRAM, A. (1993). 'Alternanțe vocalice și armonie vocalică în limba română', *Studii și cercetări lingvistice* 44: 377–87.
AVRAM, A. (2005). *Metafonia și fenomenele conexe în limba română*. Bucharest: Editura Academiei Române.
AVRAM, L. (2000). 'From Possessive Clitics to Object Clitics: A Unifying Analysis', in L. Tasmowski (ed.), 83–100.
AVRAM, L. (2003). *English Syntax: The Structure of Root Clauses*. Bucharest: Oscar Print.
AVRAM, L. (2008). '*A trebui*: de la modalitate de tip deontic la implicatură epistemică', in G. Pană Dindelegan (ed.), 195–202.
AVRAM, L., and COENE, M. (2002). 'Dative / Genitive Clitics as Last Resort', *Balkanistica* 15: 1–34.

AVRAM, L., and COENE, M. (2008). 'Romanian Possessive Clitics Revisited', in L. Tasmowski, and D. Kalluli (eds), *Clitic Doubling in the Balkan Languages*. Amsterdam / Philadelphia: John Benjamins, 361–87.

AVRAM, L., and HILL, V. (2007). 'An Irrealis *BE* Auxiliary in Romanian', in R. Aranovich (ed.), *Split Auxiliary System: A Cross-Linguistic Perspective*. Amsterdam: John Benjamins, 47–64.

AVRAM, M. (1957). 'Observații asupra coordonării', in A. Graur, and J. Byck (eds), 151–9.

AVRAM, M. (1960). *Evoluția subordonării circumstanțiale cu elemente conjuncționale în limba română*. Bucharest: Editura Academiei Române.

AVRAM, M. (1977). 'Particularități sintactice regionale în dacoromână', *Studii și cercetări lingvistice* 28: 29–35.

AVRAM, M. (1987). *Probleme ale exprimării corecte*. Bucharest: Editura Academiei Române.

AVRAM, M. (2001). *Gramatica pentru toți*. Bucharest: Humanitas.

AVRAM, M. (2005). *Studii de morfologie a limbii române*. Bucharest: Editura Academiei Române.

AVRAM, M. (2007). 'Propozițiile subordonate', in M. Avram (ed.), 219–76.

AVRAM, M. (ed.) (2007). *Sintaxa limbii române în secolele al XVI-lea–al XVIII-lea*. Bucharest: Editura Academiei Române.

AVRAM, M., and SALA, M. (2001). *Faceți cunoștință cu limba română*. Cluj: Echinox.

BAKER, B., and HARVEY, M. (2010). 'Complex Predicate Formation', in M. Amberder, B. Baker, and M. Harvey (eds), *Complex Predicates: Cross-Linguistic Perspectives on Event Structure*. Cambridge / New York: Cambridge University Press, 13–46.

BALÁZS, L. (1988). 'Rom. *fel* și *chip*', *Studia Universitatis Babeș–Bolyai. Philologia* 33: 76–81.

BARBOSA, P. (2001). 'On Inversion in Wh-questions in Romance', in A. Hulk, and J.-Y. Pollock (eds), *Subject Inversion in Romance and the Theory of Universal Grammar*. Oxford: Oxford University Press, 20–59.

BARBU, A.-M. (2004). 'Statutul semiadverbelor din cadrul complexului verbal', in G. Pană Dindelegan (ed.), 625–34.

BARBU, A.-M. (2010). 'Baza de date românească din cadrul platfomei Neorom', *Limba română* 59: 13–30.

BARBU, X. I. (2008). *Verbele dicendi în limba română: aspecte etimologice, semantice și sintactice*. Ph.D. Thesis, Universitatea din București.

BARBU MITITELU, V., and MAFTEI CIOLĂNEANU, R. (2004). 'The Main Aspects of the Grammar of Negation in Romanian', in E. Ionescu (ed.), 32–67.

BARTNING, I., and NOAILLY, M. (1993). 'Du Relationnel au qualificatif: flux et reflux', *L'Information grammaticale* 58: 27–32.

BATEMAN, N., and POLINSKY, M. (2010). 'Romanian as a Two-Gender Language', in D. B. Gerdts, J. C. Moore, and M. Polinsky (eds), *Hypothesis A / Hypothesis B: Linguistic Explorations in Honor of David M. Pelmutter*. Cambridge, MA: MIT Press, 41–77.

BAUER, B. L. M. (2011). 'Word Formation', in M. Maiden, J. Ch. Smith, and A. Ledgeway (eds), 532–63.

BĂLĂȘOIU C. (2004). *Discursul raportat în textele dialectale românești*: Bucharest: Editura Universității din București.

BECKER, M. (2010). 'Mood in Romanian', in B. Rothstein, and R. Thieroff (eds), 251–69.

BENVENISTE, E. (2000 [1967]). 'Fundamentele sintactice ale compunerii nominale', *Probleme de lingvistică generală*. L. M. Dumitru (transl.). Bucharest: Universitas.

BEREA, E. (1961). 'Din istoria posesivului *său-lui* în limba română', *Studii și cercetări lingvistice* 12: 319–33.

BEREA, E. (1966). 'Observații asupra diatezei pasive în limba română', *Studii și cercetări lingvistice* 17: 567–78.

BERTINETTO, P. M. (2000). 'The Progressive in Romance, as Compared with English', in Ö. Dahl (ed.), 559–604.

BEYRER, A. (1979). 'Adresse inverse en roumain', *Limba română* 28: 91–4.

BICKEL, B., and NICHOLS, J. (2007). 'Inflectional Morphology', in T. Shopen (ed.), 169–240.

BÎLBÎIE, G. (2009). 'Spre o tipologie a construcţiilor eliptice în raportul de coordonare', in R. Zafiu, G. Stoica, and M. Constantinescu (eds) 23–32.

BOLINGER, D. (1967). 'Adjectives in English: Attribution and Predication', *Lingua* 18: 1–34.

BOLOCAN, G. (1969). 'Observaţii asupra originii numeralelor româneşti', *Limba română* 18: 133–5.

BONAMI, O., and GODARD, D. (2001). 'Inversion du Sujet. Constituance et ordre des mots', in J.-M. Marandin (ed.), *Cahier Jean-Claude Milner*. Paris: Vivier, 117–306.

BORCHIN, I.-M. (1999). *Modalitatea şi predicatul verbal compus*. Timişoara: Editura Helicon.

BOSQUE, I., and PICALLO, C. (1996). 'Postnominal Adjectives in Spanish DPs, *Journal of Linguistics* 32: 349–85.

BOSQUE, I. (ed.) (2010). *Nueva gramática de la lengua española. Manual*. Asociación de Academias de la Lengua Espanola. Madrid: Espasa Libros S.L.

BOSQUE, I., and DEMONTE, V. (eds) (1999). *Gramática descriptiva de la lengua española*. Real Academia Española, Colección Nebrija y Bello. Madrid: Espasa.

BOURCIEZ, E. (1956). *Éléments de linguistique romane*. Paris: Klincksieck.

BRĂESCU, R. (2008). 'Apoziţia', in GALR II, 655–68.

BRĂESCU, R. (2012). *Adjectivul în română. Sintaxă şi semantică*. Bucharest: Editura Universităţii din Bucureşti.

BRÂNCUŞ, G. (1957). 'Sur la valeur du passé simple en roumain', in I. Iordan, E. Petrovici, and A. Rosetti (eds), *Mélanges linguistiques*. Bucarest: Éditions de l'Académie Roumaine, 159–73.

BRÂNCUŞ, G. (1960). 'Despre dativul locativ', *Studii şi cercetări lingvistice* 11: 381–5.

BRÂNCUŞ, G. (1973). 'Originea structurii numeralului românesc', *Studii şi cercetări lingvistice* 24: 507–10.

BRÂNCUŞ, G. (1976). 'Productivitatea conjugărilor în româna actuală', *Studii şi cercetări lingvistice* 27: 485–92.

BRÂNCUŞ, G. (1978). 'Pluralul neutrelor în româna actuală', *Studii şi cercetări lingvistice* 29: 253–62.

BRÂNCUŞ, G. (1983). *Vocabularul autohton al limbii române*. Bucharest: Editura Ştiinţifică şi Enciclopedică.

BRÂNCUŞ, G. (1995). *Cercetări asupra fondului traco-dac al limbii române*. Bucharest: Ministerul Învăţământului, Institutul Român de tracologie, Biblioteca thracologica VIII.

BRÂNCUŞ, G. (2002). *Introducere în istoria limbii române*. I. Bucharest: Editura Fundaţiei 'România de Mâine'.

BRÂNCUŞ, G. (2007, 2008). *Studii de istorie a limbii române*. Bucharest: Editura Academiei Române.

BRESNAN, J. (1997). 'Mixed Categories as Head Sharing Constructions', in M. Butt, and T. Holloway King (eds), *Proceedings of the LFG97 Conference*. San Diego: University of California. On-line: CSLI Publications.

BROWN, P., and LEVINSON, S. C. (1978). *Politeness: Some Universals in Language Usage*. Cambridge: Cambridge University Press.

BRUGÈ, L. (2002). 'The Positions of Demonstratives in the Extended Nominal Projection', in G. Cinque (ed.), *Functional Structure in DP and IP: The Cartography of Syntactic Structures I*. Oxford: Oxford University Press.

BUGEANU, D. (1970). 'Viitorul cu *habeo* în limba română. I. Paradigma *habeo cantare*', *Studii şi cercetări lingvistice* 21: 621–44.

BURZIO, L. (1986). *Italian Syntax: A Government-Binding Approach*. Dordrecht: D. Reidel.

BUŽAROVSKA, E. (2004). 'Subjunctive Relatives in Balkan Languages', in O. Mišeska Tomić (ed.), 377–404.

BYCK, J. (1967). *Studii şi articole*. Bucharest: Editura Ştiinţifică.

CALUDE, A. S. (2007). 'Light and Heavy Reflexive Marking: The Middle Domain in Romanian', *Annual Review of Cognitive Linguistics* 5: 239–69.

CAMPOS, H. (2009). 'Some Notes on Adjectival Articles in Albanian', *Lingua* 119: 1009–34.

CAPIDAN, T. (2005 [1932]). *Aromânii. Dialectul aromân*. Bucharest: Editura Fundaţiei Culturale Aromâne 'Dimândarea Părintească'.

CAPIDAN, T. (2006 [1937]). *Macedoromânii. Etnografie, istorie, limbă*. Bucharest: Editura Fundaţiei Culturale Aromâne 'Dimândarea Părintească'.
CARABULEA, E. (1965). 'Acordul după înţeles şi prin atracţie în limba română veche', *Limba română* 14: 593–608.
CARABULEA, E. (2007). 'Propoziţiile interogative', in M. Avram (ed.), 277–84.
CARAGIU, M. (1957). 'Sintaxa gerunziului românesc', in A. Graur, and J. Byck (eds), 61–89.
CARAGIU MARIOŢEANU, M. (1962). 'Moduri nepersonale', *Studii şi cercetări lingvistice* 13: 29–42.
CARAGIU MARIOŢEANU, M. (1975). *Compendiu de dialectologie română*. Bucharest: Editura Ştiinţifică şi Enciclopedică.
CARAGIU MARIOŢEANU, M. (1981). 'Un cas d'emphase pronominale en aroumain: la reprise du sujet par des formes atones', *Logos Semantikos. Studia Linguistica in Honorem Eugenio Coşeriu*, IV: 155–60.
CARAGIU MARIOŢEANU, M., GIOSU, Ş., IONESCU-RUXĂNDOIU, L., and TODORAN, R. (1977). *Dialectologie română*. Bucharest: Editura Didactică şi Pedagogică.
CARDINALETTI, A., and STARKE, M. (1999). 'The Typology of Structural Deficiency', in H. van Riemsdijk (ed.), 145–233.
CĂLĂRAŞU, C. (1978). 'Conjuncţia', in F. Dimitrescu (ed.), 358–67.
CDDE. CANDREA, I.-A., and DENSUSIANU, O. (2003 [1907]). *Dicţionarul etimologic al limbii române. Elementele latine*. G. Brâncuş (ed.). Bucharest: Paralela 45.
CHIERCHIA, G. (1997). *Semantica*. Bologna: il Mulino.
CHIRCU, A. (2006). 'Adverbele româneşti în *-iş (-âş)*', in G. Pană Dindelegan (ed.), 57–66.
CHIRCU, A. (2008). *L'Adverbe dans les langues romanes: Études étymologique, lexicale et morphologique*. Cluj-Napoca: Casa Cărţii de Ştiinţă.
CHIŢORAN, I. (2002). *The Phonology of Romanian: A Constraint-Based Approach*. Berlin / New York: Mouton de Gruyter.
CHIVU, G., PANĂ DINDELEGAN, G., DRAGOMIRESCU, A., NEDELCU, I., and NICULA, I. (eds). (2012). *Studii de istorie a limbii române. Morfosintaxa limbii literare în secolele al XIX-lea şi al XX-lea*. Bucharest: Editura Academiei Române.
CHOMSKY, N. (1986). *Barriers*. Cambridge, MA: MIT Press.
CINQUE, G. (1988). 'On Si Constructions and the Theory of Arb', *Linguistic Inquiry* 19, 4: 521–81.
CINQUE, G. (1990). *Types of A'-Dependencies*. Cambridge, MA: MIT Press.
CINQUE, G. (1999). *Adverbs and Functional Heads*. Oxford: Oxford University Press.
CINQUE, G. (2005). *Italian Syntax and Universal Grammar*. Cambridge: Cambridge University Press.
CINQUE, G. (2010). *The Syntax of Adjectives*. Cambridge: MIT Press.
CINQUE, G., and GIUSTI, G. (eds) (1995). *Advances in Roumanian Linguistics*. Amsterdam / Philadelphia: John Benjamins.
CIOBANU, F. (1957). 'Valorile prepoziţiilor în construcţiile cu adverbe', in A. Graur, and J. Byck (eds), 43–66.
CIOBANU, F. (2007). 'Complementul', in M. Avram (ed.), 117–88.
CIOMPEC, G. (1969). 'Observaţii asupra exprimării negaţiei în limba română din secolele al XVI-lea–al XVIII-lea', *Studii şi cercetări lingvistice* 20: 197–209.
CIOMPEC, G. (1980). 'Particulele adverbiale în limba română', *Limba română* 29: 85–95.
CIOMPEC, G. (1985). *Morfosintaxa adverbului românesc. Sincronie şi diacronie*. Bucharest: Editura Ştiinţifică şi Enciclopedică.
CIORĂNESCU, A. (1954–1966). *Diccionario Etimológico Rumano*, Biblioteca Filológica, Universidad de La Laguna, Tenerife. Rom. edn.
CIORĂNESCU, A. (2002). *Dicţionarul etimologic al limbii române*. Bucharest: Saeculum I. O.
COENE, M. (1999). *Definite Null Nominals in Romanian and Spanish: A Generative Approach to the Internal Syntax of DP*. Antwerpen: Universitaire Instelline Antwerpen.
COENE, M., and TASMOWSKI, L. (eds) (2005). *On Space and Time in Language*. Cluj-Napoca: Clusium.
COENE, M., and TASMOWSKI, L. (2006). 'On the Balkan–Slavic Origins of the Romanian Conditional', *Revue roumaine de linguistique* 51: 321–40.

COENE, M., DE MULDER, W., DENDALE, P., and D'HULST, Y. (eds) (2000). *Traiani Augusti vestigia pressa sequamur. Studia lingvistica in honorem Lilianae Tasmowski*. Padua: Unipress.
COLE, P. (1987). 'Null Objects in Universal Grammar'. *Linguistic Inquiry* 18, 4: 577–612.
COLLINS, P. (1991). *Cleft and Pseudo-Cleft Constructions in English*. London: Routledge.
COMRIE, B. (2003). 'Typology and Language Aquisition: The Case of Relative Clauses', in A. Ramat Giacalone (ed.), *Typology and Second Language Acquisition*. New York: Mouton de Gruyter, 19–35.
COMRIE, B., and CORBETT, G. G. (eds) (1993). *The Slavonic Languages*. London / New York: Routledge.
COPCEAG, D. (1998). *Tipologia limbilor romanice*. Cluj-Napoca: Clusium.
CORBETT, G. G. (2006). *Agreement*. Cambridge: Cambridge University Press.
CORNILESCU, A. (1992). 'Remarks on the Determiner System of Rumanian', *Probus* 4, 3: 189–260.
CORNILESCU, A. (1995). 'Romanian Genitive Constructions', in G. Cinque, and G. Giusti (eds), 1–54.
CORNILESCU, A. (1998). 'Remarks on Syntax and the Interpretation of Romanian Middle Passive *SE* sentences', *Revue roumaine de linguistique* 43: 317–42.
CORNILESCU, A. (2000). 'The Double Subject Construction in Romanian', in V. Motapanyane (ed.), 83–124.
CORNILESCU, A. (2001). 'Romanian Nominalizations: Case and Aspectual Structure', *Journal of Linguistics* 37, 3: 467–501.
CORNILESCU, A. (2004). 'În legătură cu conceptul de pronume semiindependent. Observații asupra articolului adjectival *cel*', in G. Pană Dindelegan (ed.), 51–62.
CORNILESCU, A. (2005a). 'Romanian Adjectives and the Stage Level / Individual Level Contrast', in M. Coene, and L. Tasmowski (eds), 75–91.
CORNILESCU, A. (2005b). 'Demonstratives and Minimality', *Bucharest Working Papers in Linguistics* 7, 1: 102–17.
CORNILESCU, A. (2006). 'Din nou despre *un prieten de-al meu*', in G. Pană Dindelegan (ed.), 25–37.
CORNILESCU, A. (2007). 'On Classifiers and Proper Names', *Bucharest Working Papers in Linguistics* 9, 1: 61–75.
CORNILESCU, A. (2008). 'Reanaliză și interpretare: structura lui *decât*', in G. Pană Dindelegan (ed.), 203–12.
CORNILESCU, A. (2009). 'On the Linearization of Adjectives in Romanian', in D. Torck, and L. Wetzels (eds), *Romance Languages and Linguistic Theory 2006*. Amsterdam / Philadelphia: John Benjamins, 33–52.
CORNILESCU, A., and NICOLAE, A. (2009). 'Evoluția articolului hotărât și genitivul în româna veche', in R. Zafiu, G. Stoica, and M. Constantinescu (eds), 647–67.
CORNILESCU, A., and NICOLAE, A. (2010). 'On Nominal Ellipsis and the Valuation of Definiteness in Romanian', *Bucharest Working Papers in Linguistics* 12, 1: 93–125.
CORNILESCU, A., and NICOLAE, A. (2011a). 'On the Syntax of Romanian Definite Phrases: Changes in the Patterns of Definiteness Checking', in P. Sleeman, and H. Perridon (eds), *The Noun Phrase in Romance and Germanic. Structure, Variation, and Change*. Amsterdam / Philadelphia: John Benjamins, 193–221.
CORNILESCU, A., and NICOLAE, A. (2011b). 'Romanian Possessives: Adjectives or Pronouns? A comparative perspective', in I. Nedelcu, A. Nicolae, A. Toma, and R. Zafiu (eds), *Studii de lingvistică. Omagiu doamnei profesoare Angela Bidu-Vrănceanu*. Bucharest: Editura Universității din București, 111–43.
CORNILESCU, A., and NICOLAE, A. (2011c). 'Nominal Peripheries and Phase Structure in the Romanian DP', *Revue roumaine de linguistique* 56: 35–68.
CORNILESCU, A., and NICOLAE, A. (2011d). 'On the Syntax of the Romanian Indefinite Pronouns *unul* and *altul*', in R. Zafiu, C. Ușurelu, and H. Bogdan Oprea (eds), 67–94.
CORVER, N., and VAN RIEMSDIJK, H. (2001). *Semi-lexical Categories: The Function of Content Words and the Content of Function Words*. Berlin / New York: Mouton de Gruyter.

COSTANZO, A. R. (2011). *Romance Conjugational Classes: Learning from the Peripheries*. Ph.D. Thesis, The Ohio State University.

COȘERIU, E. (1992–1993). 'Tipologia limbilor romanice. Prelegeri și conferințe', *Anuar de lingvistică și istorie literară* 33: 119–44.

COTEANU, I. (1969). *Morfologia numelui în protoromână (româna comună)*. Bucharest: Editura Academiei Române.

COTEANU, I. (1981). *Structura și evoluția limbii române (de la origini până la 1860)*. Bucharest: Editura Academiei Române.

COTEANU, I. (ed.) (1985). *Limba română contemporană. Fonetica. Fonologia. Morfologia*. Bucharest: Editura Didactică și Pedagogică.

CROOKSTON, I. (1999). 'Comparative Constructions', in K. Brown, and J. Miller (eds), *Concise Encyclopedia of Grammatical Categories*. Oxford: Elsevier, 76–81.

CROITOR, B. (2008a). 'Predicativul suplimentar', in GALR II, 301–17.

CROITOR, B. (2008b). 'Aspecte privind acordul în determinare în limba română veche', in G. Pană Dindelegan (ed.), 213–18.

CROITOR, B. (2012a). *Acordul în limba română*. Bucharest: Editura Universității din București.

CROITOR, B. (2012b). 'Pronumele în secolul al XIX-lea', in G. Chivu, G. Pană Dindelegan, A. Dragomirescu, I. Nedelcu, and I. Nicula (eds), 121–72.

CROITOR, B., and DOBROVIE-SORIN, C. (2011). 'The Agreement of Collective DPs in Romanian', in J. Herschensohn (ed.), *Romance Linguistics 2010: Selected Papers from the 40th Linguistic Symposium on Romance Languages*. Amsterdam: John Benjamins.

CROITOR, B., and GIURGEA, I. (2009). 'On the So-Called Romanian *neuter*', *Bucharest Working Papers in Linguistics* 11, 2: 21–39.

CROITOR, B., DINICĂ, A., DRAGOMIRESCU, A., MÎRZEA VASILE, C., NEDELCU, I., NICOLAE, A., NICULA, I., RĂDULESCU SALA, M., and ZAFIU, R. (2009). 'Tendințe morfosintactice ale limbii române actuale manifestate în mass-media audiovizuală', in G. Pană Dindelegan (ed.), 493–512.

CRUSCHINA, S., and REMBERGER, E. (2008). 'Hearsay and Reported Speech: Evidentiality in Romance', *Rivista di Grammatica Generativa* 33: 99–120.

CRYSTAL, D. (2008). *Dictionary of Linguistics and Phonetics*. (6th edn.). Malden / Oxford / Victoria: Blackwell Publishing.

CUGNO, F. (1996). *Strutture sintattiche subordinate nelle lingue balcaniche: causali, condizionali, concessive*. Alessandria: Edizione dell' Orso.

CUNIȚĂ, A. (2004). 'Les Verbes roumains *a trebui* et *a putea*—marqueurs de modalité et indices évidentiels', *Revue belge de philologie et d'histoire* 82: 717–32.

D'HULST, Y., COENE, M., and AVRAM, L. (2004). 'Syncretic and Analytic Tenses in Romanian. The Balkan Setting of Romance', in O. Mišeska Tomić (ed.), 355–74.

D'HULST, Y., ROORYCK, J., and SCHROTEN, J. (eds) (2001). *Romance Languages and Linguistic Theory 1999*. Amsterdam: John Benjamins.

DA / DLR. ACADEMIA ROMÂNĂ. *Dicționarul limbii române*. (1913–1948). Bucharest: Socec, Universul, Monitorul Oficial; (1965–2010), serie nouă. Bucharest: Editura Academiei Române.

DAHL, Ö. (ed.) (2000). *Tense and Aspect in the Languages of Europe*. Berlin / New York: Mouton de Gruyter.

DAHL, Ö., and VELLUPILLAI, V. (2005). 'Tense and Aspect', in WALS, 266–81.

DASCĂLU JINGA, L. (2008). 'Organizarea prozodică a enunțului', in GALR II, 946–91.

DĂNĂILĂ, I. (1960). 'Sufixul *-mente* în limba română', in A. Graur, and J. Byck (eds), *Studii și materiale privitoare la formarea cuvintelor în limba română*. II. Bucharest: Editura Academiei Române, 185–99.

DCR. DIMITRESCU, F. (1997). *Dicționar de cuvinte recente*. Bucharest: Logos.

DE HAAN, F. (2006). 'Typological Approaches to Modality', in W. Frawley (ed.), *The Expression of Modality*. Berlin: Walter de Gruyter, 27–70.

DE SWART, H. (2010). *Expression and Interpretation of Negation: An OT Typology*. Springer: Dordrecht.

DEN DIKKEN, M. (2006). *Relators and Linkers: The Syntax of Predication, Predicate Inversion, and Copulas*. Cambridge, MA: MIT Press.

DENDALE, P. (1993). 'Le Conditionnel de l'information incertaine: marqueur modal ou marqueur évidentiel?', in G. Hilty (ed.), *Actes du XXe Congrès international de linguistique et philologie romanes*, 1. Tübingen and Basel: Francke, 163–76.

DENDALE, P., and TASMOWSKI, L. (eds) (2001). *Le Conditionnel en français*. Metz: Université de Metz.

DENSUSIANU, O. (1901, 1938). *Histoire de la langue roumaine*. I, II. Paris: Ernest Leroux. Rom. edn.: J. Byck (ed.) (1961). *Istoria limbii române*. I, II. Bucharest: Editura Științifică.

DÉPREZ, V. (2000). 'Parallel (A)symmetries and the Internal Structure of Negative Expressions?', *Natural Language and Linguistic Theory* 18: 253–342.

DIACONESCU, I. (1967). 'Propoziția relativă infinitivală', *Analele Universității București. Limba și literatura română* 16: 143–8.

DIACONESCU, I. (1969). 'Modul participiu în limba română din secolele al XVI-lea, al XVII-lea și al XVIII-lea', *Analele Universității București. Limba și literatura română* 18: 25–39.

DIACONESCU I. (1971). 'Supinul în limba română din secolul al XVI-lea, al XVII-lea și al XVIII-lea', *Analele Universității București. Limba și literatura română* 20: 151–63.

DIACONESCU, I. (1977). *Infinitivul în limba română*. Bucharest: Editura Științifică și Enciclopedică.

DIACONESCU, P. (1959). 'Exprimarea complementului de agent în limba română', *Limba română* 8: 3–17.

DIACONESCU, P. (1970). *Structură și evoluție în morfologia substantivului românesc*. Bucharest: Editura Academiei Române.

DIMITRESCU, F. (1973). 'Despre *pre* la acuzativ în limba textelor traduse din slavă în secolul al XVI-lea', in F. Dimitrescu (ed.), *Contribuții la istoria limbii române vechi*. Bucharest: Editura Didactică și Pedagogică, 38–43.

DIMITRESCU, F. (1975). *Introducere în morfosintaxa istorică a limbii române*. Bucharest: Universitatea din București.

DIMITRESCU, F. (ed.) (1978). *Istoria limbii române*. Bucharest: Editura Didactică și Pedagogică.

DINICĂ, A. (2008). 'Adverbul', in GALR I, 585–605.

DINICĂ, A. (2009). '*Curând*—adverb indepedent sau formă a verbului *a cure*?', *Limba română* 58: 202–7.

DJAMO-DIACONIȚA, L. (1976). 'Përema dhe ndajfolje të formuara me ndihmen e foljes "dua" në rumanisht dhe në shqip', *Studime Filologjike* 3: 161–9.

DOBROVIE-SORIN, C. (1987). *Syntaxe du roumain*. Ph.D. Thesis. Université Paris 7.

DOBROVIE-SORIN, C. (1994). *The Syntax of Romanian*. Berlin: Mouton de Gruyter. Rom. edn: 2000. *Sintaxa limbii române. Studii de sintaxă comparată a limbilor romanice*. Bucharest: Editura Univers.

DOBROVIE-SORIN, C. (1995). 'Romanian Clitic Clusters: Dériving Linear Order from Hierarchical Structure', in G. Cinque, and G. Giusti (eds), 55–82.

DOBROVIE-SORIN, C. (1998). 'Impersonal *se* Constructions in Romance and the Passivization of Unergatives', *Linguistic Inquiry* 29, 3: 399–437.

DOBROVIE-SORIN, C. (1999). 'Clitics across Categories: The Case of Romanian', in H. van Riemsdijk (ed.), 515–42.

DOBROVIE-SORIN, C. (2001). 'Génitifs et déterminants', in G. Kleiber, B. Laca, and L. Tasmowski (eds), *Typologie des Groupes Nominaux*, Presses Universitaires de Rennes, 205–31.

DOBROVIE-SORIN, C. (2006). 'The SE-Anaphor and its Role in Argument Realization', in M. Everaert, H. van Riemsdijk, R. Goedemans, and B. Hollebrandse (eds), 118–77.

DOBROVIE-SORIN, C., and GIURGEA, I. (2006). 'The Suffixation of Definite Articles in Balkan Languages', *Revue roumaine de linguistique* 51: 73–104.

DOBROVIE-SORIN, C., and GIURGEA, I. (2011). 'Pronominal Possessors and Feature Uniqueness', *Language* 87: 126–57.

DOBROVIE-SORIN, C., and LACA, B. (2003). 'Les Noms sans déterminant dans les langues romanes', in D. Godard (ed.), 235–79.

DOETJES, J., and ROORYCK, J. (2003). 'Generalizing Over Quantitative and Qualitative Constructions', in M. Coene, and Y. D'Hulst (eds), *From NP to DP: The Syntax and Semantics of Noun Phrases*. Amsterdam: John Benjamins, 277–95.

DOMINTE, C. (2003). *Negația în limba română*. Bucharest: Editura Fundației 'România de Mâine'.

DONAZZAN, M., and MARDALE, A. (2010). 'Additive and Aspectual Adverbs: Towards an Analysis of Romanian *mai*', *Revue roumaine de linguistique* 55: 247–69.

DOOM. ACADEMIA ROMÂNĂ. I. VINTILĂ RĂDULESCU (ed.). (2005). *Dicționarul ortografic, ortoepic și morfologic al limbii române*. (2nd edn). Bucharest: Editura Univers Enciclopedic.

DRAGOMIRESCU, A. (2009). 'Dinamica normei lingvistice. Observații statistice asupra verbelor din DOOM^2, in G. Pană Dindelegan (ed.), 219–26.

DRAGOMIRESCU, A. (2010). *Ergativitatea. Tipologie, sintaxă, semantică*. Bucharest: Editura Universității din București.

DRAGOMIRESCU, A. (2011). 'The Subject of the Supine Clause in Romanian and A-Chains', *Revue roumaine de linguistique* 56: 571–92.

DRĂGANU, N. (1998 [1906]). *Compunerea cuvintelor în limba română*. Timișoara: Amphora.

DRĂGHICESCU, J. (1990). 'Remarques sur la construction *gerunziu cu acuzativ*', *Revue roumaine de linguistique* 35: 303–7.

DRYER, M. S. (2005). 'Order of Subject, Object, and Verb', in WALS, 330–33.

DSL. BIDU-VRĂNCEANU, A., CĂLĂRAȘU, C., IONESCU-RUXĂNDOIU, L., MANCAȘ, M., and PANĂ DINDELEGAN, G. (2005). *Dicționar general de științe. Științe ale limbii*. Bucharest: Nemira.

DUCHET, J. L. (1991). 'La Génèse de l'adverbe: le cas de l'albanais', *Travaux linguistiques du CERLICO* 4: 189–95.

DUMITRESCU, D. (1990a). 'El dativo posesivo en español y en rumano', *Revista española de lingüística* 2: 403–30.

DUMITRESCU, D. (1990b). *The Grammar of Echo Questions in Spanish and Romanian*. Ph.D. Thesis, University of Southern California. Los Angeles.

DUMITRESCU, D. (2012). 'Rum. *Cică* vs. esp. *Dizque*: Polifonía e intertextualidad. *Oralia*', Anejo 6, *Polifonía e intertextualidad en el diálogo*, ed. by Clara Ubaldina Lorda (to appear).

DUMITRESCU, D., and SALTARELLI, M. (1998). 'Two Types of Predicate Modification: Evidence from the Articulated Adjectives of Romanian', in J. Lema, and E. Treviño (eds), *Theoretical Analyses on Romance Languages*. Amsterdam: John Benjamins, 175–92.

DYER, D. L. (1985). 'The Interplay of Subjunctive and Infinitive Complements in Romanian', *Folia slavica* 7: 362–80.

EDELSTEIN, F. (1972). *Sintaxa gerunziului românesc*. Bucharest: Editura Academiei Române.

EGUREN, L. (2010). 'Contrastive Focus and Nominal Ellipsis in Spanish', *Lingua* 120: 435–57.

EGUREN, L., and FERNÁNDEZ SORIANO, O. (eds) (2007). *Coreference, Modality, and Focus: Studies on the Syntax–Semantics Interface*. Amsterdam: John Benjamins.

EKKEHARD, K., and KOKUTANI, S. (2006). 'Reciprocity', *Linguistics* 44, 2: 271–302.

ELIR. SALA, M. (ed.) (1989). *Enciclopedia limbilor romanice*. Bucharest: Editura Științifică și Enciclopedică.

ELR. SALA, M. (ed.) (2001). *Enciclopedia limbii române*. Bucharest: Univers Enciclopedic.

EMBICK, D. (2004). 'On the Structure of Resultative Participles in English', *Linguistic Inquiry* 35, 3: 355–92.

EMONDS, J. (1985). *A Unified Theory of Syntactic Categories*. Dordrecht: Foris.

ERNOUT, A., and THOMAS, Fr. (1959). *Syntaxe latine*. Paris: Klincksieck.

ERNST, G., GLEßGEN, M.-D., SCHMITT, C., and SCHWEICKARD, W. (eds) (2008). *Romanische Sprachgeschichte / Histoire linguistique de la Romania*. III. Berlin / New York: Walter de Gruyter.

ESPINAL, T. (2009). 'Clitic Incorporation and Abstract Semantic Objects in Idiomatic Constructions', *Linguistics* 47, 6: 1221–71.

EVERAERT, M., VAN RIEMSDIJK, H., GOEDEMANS, R., and HOLLEBRANDSE, B. (eds) (2006). *The Blackwell Companion to Syntax IV*. Oxford: Blackwell Publishing Ltd.

EVSEEV, I. (1974). *Semantica verbului*. Timișoara: Facla.

FALTZ, L. (1985). *Reflexivization: A Study in Universal Syntax*. London / New York: Garland.
FARCAȘ, M. (2006). 'Infinitivul în subdialectul maramureșean', *Lucrările celui de al XII-lea simpozion național de dialectologie*. Cluj-Napoca: Mega, 195–202.
FARKAS, D. F. (1982). *Intensional Descriptions and the Romance Subjunctive Mood*. New York / London: Garland Publishing.
FARKAS, D. (1992). 'On the Semantics of Subjunctive Complements', in P. Hirschbühler, and E. F. K. Koerner (eds), *Romance Languages and Modern Linguistic Theory*. Amsterdam: John Benjamins, 69–104.
FARKAS, D. F., and ZEC, D. (1995). 'Agreement and Pronominal Reference', in G. Cinque, and G. Giusti (eds), 83–101.
FC. *Formarea cuvintelor în limba română*. CIOBANU, F., and HASAN, F. (1970). I. *Compunerea*. AVRAM, M., CARABULEA, E., CIOBANU, F., FICȘINESCU, F., GHERMAN, C., HASAN, F., POPESCU-MARIN, M., RĂDULESCU, M., RIZESCU, I., and VASILIU, L. (1978). II. *Prefixele*. VASILIU, L. (1989). III. *Sufixele*. Bucharest: Editura Academiei Române.
FELIX, J. (1964). 'Classification des verbes roumains', *Philologica Pragensia* 7, 3: 291–9.
FEUILLET, J. (1986). 'La linguistique balkanique', *Cahiers balkaniques* 10: 3–121.
FEUILLET, J. (2006). *Introduction à la typologie linguistique*. Paris: Honoré Champion.
FISCHER, I. (1975). 'Originea latină a neutrului românesc', *Studii și cercetări lingvistice* 26: 569–75.
FISCHER, I. (1985). *Latina dunăreană. Introducere în istoria limbii române*. Bucharest: Editura Științifică și Enciclopedică.
FISCHER, I., and VASILIU, E. (1953). 'Vorbirea directă și indirectă', *Limba română* 4: 35–40.
FLAUX, N., and VAN DE VELDE, D. (2000). *Les Noms en français: esquisse de classement*. Paris: Ophrys.
FLAUX, N., GLATIGNY, M., and SAMAIN, D. (eds) (1996). *Les Noms abstraits: histoire et théorie*. Villeneuve d'Ascq: Presses Universitaires du Septentrion.
FOLLI, R., and RAMCHAND, G. (2005). 'Prepositions and Results in Italian and English: An Analysis from Event Decomposition.', in A. VAN Hout, H. de Swart, and H. J. Verkuyl (eds), *Perspectives on Aspect*. Springer: Dordrecht, 81–105.
FORSGREN, M. (2000). 'Apposition, attribut, épithète: même combat prédicatif?', *Langue française* 125: 30–45.
FRĂȚILĂ, V., and BĂRDĂȘAN G. (2010). *Dialectul istroromân. Straturi etimologice*. I. Timișoara: Editura Universității de Vest.
FRÂNCU, C. (1979). 'Vechimea și răspândirea comparativului de neegalitate exprimat prin *ca*', *Limbă și literatură* 24: 50–5.
FRÂNCU, C. (1982a). 'Vechimea și difuziunea lexicală a unei inovații comune dialectelor limbii române: desinența *-uri* la pluralul femininelor', *Limba română* 31: 199–212.
FRÂNCU, C. (1982b). 'Vechimea formelor de mai mult ca perfect, perfect compus, prezent indicativ și conjunctiv cu *-ră*', *Limba română* 31: 281–93.
FRÂNCU, C. (1984). 'Vechimea și răspândirea unor pronume, adjective pronominale și numerale cu articolul nehotărât: *un alt(ul)*, *un al doilea*, *un același*', *Analele științifice ale Universității 'Alexandru Ioan Cuza' din Iași* 30: 33–43.
FRÂNCU, C. (1997). 'Morfologia. Sintaxa', in ILRL, 113–74, 319–75.
FRÂNCU, C. (2000). *Conjunctivul românesc și raporturile lui cu alte moduri*. Iași: Casa Editorială 'Demiurg'.
FRÂNCU, C. (2009). *Gramatica limbii române vechi (1521–1780)*. Iași: Casa Editorială 'Demiurg'.
FRIEDMAN, V. A. (1997). 'On the Number of Paradigms in the Romanian Presumptive Mood (modul prezumtiv)', *Studii și cercetări lingvistice* 48: 173–9.
GALMICHE, M. (1986). 'Note sur les noms de masse et le partitif', *Langue française* 72: 40–53.
GALR. ACADEMIA ROMÂNĂ, V. GUȚU ROMALO, (ed.) (2008 [2005]). *Gramatica limbii române*. I *Cuvântul*, II *Enunțul*. Bucharest: Editura Academiei Române.
GANEA, A. (2010). '*Se zice* et *zice-se*: une unité ou deux? Sémantisme évidentiel et fonctionnement contextuel', in R. Zafiu, A. Dragomirescu, and A. Nicolae (eds), 67–74.

GAWEŁKO, M. (2000). 'Sur la spécificité typologique du roumain', *Revue roumaine de linguistique* 45: 9–27.
GAWEŁKO, M. (2003). 'Sur la proposition infinitive romane introduite par un verbe de perception', *Studii și cercetări lingvistice* 54: 53–67.
GBLR. PANĂ DINDELEGAN, G. (ed.) (2010). *Gramatica de bază a limbii române*. Bucharest: Univers Enciclopedic Gold.
GHEORGHE, M. (2004). *Propoziția relativă*. Pitești: Paralela 45.
GHEORGHE, M. (2008). 'Construcții cu propoziții relative', in GALR II, 208–33.
GHEORGHE, M. (2009). 'Observații cu privire la utilizarea absolută a unor verbe tranzitive', in: R. Zafiu, B. Croitor, and A.-M. Mihail (eds), *Studii de gramatică. Omagiu Doamnei Profesoare Valeria Guțu Romalo*. Bucharest: Editura Universității din București, 81–4.
GHEȚIE, I. (1972). 'Vechimea formelor în *-m* de la pers. I sg. a imperfectului', *Studii și cercetări lingvistice* 23: 59-61.
GHEȚIE, I. (1975). *Baza dialectală a românei literare*. Bucharest: Editura Academiei Române.
GHEȚIE, I., and MAREȘ, A. (1985). *Originile scrisului în limba română*. Bucharest: Editura Științifică și Enciclopedică.
GHEȚIE, I., and MAREȘ, A. (1988). 'În legătură cu istoria articolului genitival din dacoromână', *Limba română* 37: 81–3.
GHEȚIE, I., and TEODORESCU, M. (1965). 'L'Influence de la langue littéraire sur les parlers dacoroumains—à propos de la désinence *-u* de la 3ᵉ personne du pluriel de l'imparfait de l'indicatif', *Revue roumaine de linguistique* 10: 183–91.
GHEȚIE, I., and TEODORESCU, M. (1966). 'À propos de la désinence *-u* de la 3ᵉ personne du pluriel de l'imparfait de l'indicatif: nouvelles contributions', *Revue roumaine de linguistique* 11: 183–91.
GIANNAKIDOU, A. (2009). 'The Dependency of the Subjunctive Revisited: Temporal Semantics and Polarity', *Lingua* 120: 1883–908.
GIORGI, A. (2001). 'La struttura interna dei sintagmi nominali', in L. Renzi, G. Salvi, and A. Cardinaletti (eds), 287–329.
GIURESCU, A., (1975). *Les Mots composés dans les langues romanes*. Paris: Mouton, The Hague.
GIURGEA, I. (2005). 'La Linéarisation des adjectifs en roumain: mouvement ou contraintes sémantiques?', in M. Coene, and L. Tasmowski (eds), 51–73.
GIURGEA, I. (2006). 'Nouns and Symmetric Relations', *Bucharest Working Papers in Linguistics* 8, 1, University of Bucharest, 46–55.
GIURGEA, I. T. (2010). *Pronoms, déterminants et ellipse nominale: Une approche minimaliste*. Bucharest: Editura Universității din București.
GIUSTI, G. (2005). 'At the Left Periphery of the Romanian Noun Phrase', in M. Coene, and L. Tasmowski (eds), 23–49.
GLR. ACADEMIA ROMÂNĂ. A. GRAUR, M. AVRAM, and L. VASILIU (eds) (1966 [1963]). *Gramatica limbii române*. I, II. Bucharest: Editura Academiei Române.
GODARD, D. (ed.) (2003). *Les Langues romanes: Problèmes de la phrase simple*. Paris: CNRS Éditions.
GOLOPENȚIA, S. (1959). 'Despre o variantă a vorbirii indirecte', *Studii și cercetări lingvistice* 10: 593–4.
GOLOPENȚIA, S. (2009). *Româna globală. Limba română și vorbitorii ei în afara României*. Bucharest: Fundația Culturală 'Secolul 21'.
GRANDGENT, C. H. (1958). *Introducere în latina vulgară*. E. Tănase (transl.). Cluj: Editura Universității 'Victor Babeș'.
GRAUR, A. (1929). 'À propos de l'article postposé en roumain', *Romania* 55: 475–80.
GRAUR, A. (1936). *Mélanges linguistiques 1*. Paris–Bucharest: Droz.
GRAUR, A. (1967). 'De nouveau sur l'article postposé en roumain', *Revue roumaine de linguistique* 12: 3–18.
GRAUR, A. (1968). *Tendințele actuale ale limbii române*. Bucharest: Editura Științifică.
GRAUR, A. (1976). *Capcanele limbii române*. Bucharest: Editura Științifică și Enciclopedică.
GRAUR, A. (1988). *Puțină gramatică*. II. Bucharest: Editura Academiei Române.

GRAUR, A., and BYCK, J. (eds) (1956, 1957). *Studii de Gramatică*. I, II. Bucharest: Editura Academiei Române.
GREENBERG, J. H. (1963). 'Some Universals of Grammar with Particular Reference to the Order of Meaningful Elements', in J. H. Greenberg (ed.), *Universals of Language*. Cambridge, MA: MIT Press, 73–113.
GRICE, P. (1975). 'Logic and Conversation', in P. Cole, and J. Morgan (eds), *Syntax and Semantics* 3: *Speech Acts*. New York: Academic Press, 41–58.
GRIMSHAW, J. (1990). *Argument Structure*. Cambridge, MA: MIT Press.
GROSU, A. (1988). 'On the Distribution of Genitive Phrases in Romanian', *Linguistics* 26: 931–49.
GROSU, A. (2004). 'The Syntax-Semantics of Modal Existential Wh Constructions', in O. Mišeska Tomić (ed.), 419–49.
GRUIȚĂ, G. (1981). *Acordul în limba română*. Bucharest: Editura Științifică și Enciclopedică.
GRUNDT, L.-O. (1972). *Études sur l'adjectif invarié en français*. Bergen / Oslo / Tromsø: Universitetsforlaget.
GUÉRON, J. (1985). 'Inalienable Possession, PRO-Inclusion and Lexical Chains', in J. Guéron, H.-G. Obenauer, and J.-Y. Pollock (eds), *Grammatical Representation*. Dordrecht: Foris, 42–86.
GUȚU, V. (1956), 'Semiauxiliarele de mod', in A. Graur, and J. Byck (eds), 57–81.
GUȚU, V. (1957). 'Propoziții relative', in A. Graur, and J. Byck (eds), 161–71.
GUȚU ROMALO, V. (1961). 'Semiauxiliare de aspect?', *Limba română* 1: 3–15.
GUȚU ROMALO, V. (1968a). *Morfologie structurală a limbii române*. Bucharest: Editura Academiei Române.
GUȚU ROMALO, V. (1968b). 'Le Futur en roumain aux XVIe–XVIIIe siècles', *Revue roumaine de linguistique* 13: 427–31.
GUȚU ROMALO, V. (1996). 'Le Nom roumain—évolution et typologie', in M. Iliescu, and S. Sora (eds), 77–83.
GUȚU ROMALO, V. (2005). *Aspecte ale evoluției limbii române*. Bucharest: Humanitas Educațional.
HALL, E. T. (1976). *Beyond Culture*. New York: Double Day.
HALL, R. A. Jr. (1983) *Proto-Romance Morphology*. Amsterdam / Philadepphia: John Benjamins.
HALVORSEN, A. (2002). 'Le Cas du roumain *respectivul*', *Romansk Forum* 16, 2: 1063–71.
HANEȘ, Gh. (1960). 'Sufixele adverbiale *-ește* și *-icește*', in A. Graur, and J. Byck (eds), *Studii și materiale privitoare la formarea cuvintelor în limba română*. II. Bucharest: Editura Academiei Române, 139–47.
HASAN, F., and POPESCU-MARIN, M. (2007). 'Compunerea', in M. Popescu-Marin (ed.), 225–70.
HASPELMATH, M. (1997). *Indefinite Pronouns*. Oxford: Clarendon Press.
HASPELMATH, M. (2007). 'Coordination', in T. Shopen (ed.), 1–51.
HAUMANN, D. (2010). 'Adnominal Adjectives in Old English', *English Language and Linguistics* 14, 1: 53–81.
HILL, V. (2002). 'The Gray Area of Supine Clauses', *Linguistics* 40, 3: 495–517.
HILL, V. (2004). 'On Left Periphery and Focus', in O. Mišeska Tomić (ed.), 339–54.
HILL, V. (2009). 'Stages of Grammaticalization for the Modal *putea*', *Revue roumaine de linguistique*, 54: 63–82.
HILL, V., and ROBERGE, I. (2006). 'A Locally Determined Verb Typology', *Revue roumaine de linguistique* 51: 5–22.
HOLTUS, G., METZELTIN, M., SCHMITT, M. C., and NIEMEYER, M. (eds) (1988–2004). *Lexikon der Romanistischen Linguistik*. Tübingen: Niemeyer.
HORNSTEIN, N. (1999). 'Movement and Control', *Linguistic Inquiry* 30: 69–96.
HRISTEA, T. (ed.) (1984). *Sinteze de limba română*. Bucharest: Albatros.
HUDDLESTON, R., and PULLUM, G. K. (2002). *The Cambridge Grammar of the English Language*. Cambridge: Cambridge University Press.
IATRIDOU, S. (2000). 'The Grammatical Ingredients of Counterfactuality', *Linguistic Inquiry* 31: 231–70.

ILIESCU, M. (1999). 'Pour un statut sémantique et syntaxique du "présomptif" roumain', in R. Brusegan, and M. A. Cortelazzo (eds), *Il tempo, i tempi: omaggio a Lorenzo Renzi*. Padova: Esedra. 97–112.

ILIESCU, M. (2000). 'Grammaticalisation et modalités en roumain: le futur déictique et épistémique', in M. Coene, W. De Mulder, P. Dendale, and Y. D'Hulst (eds), 429–42.

ILIESCU, M. (2006). 'L'Article adjectival roumain: un exemple de recurrence typologique ciclique', *Revue roumaine de linguistique* 51: 159–63.

ILIESCU, M. (2007a). *Româna din perspectivă romanică*. Bucharest: Editura Academiei Române.

ILIESCU, M. (2007b). 'Notă asupra *genului personal* în limba română', in S. Reinheimer Rîpeanu, and I. Vintilă-Rădulescu (eds), 211–14.

ILIESCU, M. (2008a), 'Histoire interne du roumain: morphosyntaxe et syntaxe', in G. Ernst, M.-D. Gleßgen, C. Schmitt, and W. Schweickard (eds), 2646–52.

ILIESCU, M. (2008b). 'Phénomènes de convergence et de divergence dans la Romania: morphosyntaxe et syntaxe', in G. Ernst, M.-D. Gleßgen, C. Schmitt, and W. Schweickard (eds.), 3266–81.

ILIESCU, M. (2009). 'Aspects de l'évolution de l'article défini en français et en roumain', *Travaux de linguistique* 59, 2: 13–23.

ILIESCU, M., and MOURIN, L. (1991). *Typologie de la morphologie verbale romane*. Innsbruck: Amoe.

ILIESCU, M., and SORA, S. (eds) (1996). *Rumänisch: Typologie, Klassifikation, Sprachcharakteristik*. München, Würzburg: Wissenschaftlicher A. Lehmann.

ILIESCU, M., SILLER-RUNGGALDIER, H., and DANLER, P. (eds) (2010). *Actes du XXVe Congrès International de Linguistique et de Philologie Romanes*. Berlin / New York: De Gruyter.

ILR. ACADEMIA ROMÂNĂ. *Istoria limbii române*. I. (1965). A. GRAUR (ed.). II. (1969). I. COTEANU (ed.). Bucharest: Editura Academiei Române.

ILRL. GHEȚIE, I. (ed.) (1997). *Istoria limbii române literare. Epoca veche (1532–1780)*. Bucharest: Editura Academiei Române.

IONESCU, E. (2004). 'The Semantic Status of Romanian N-words in Negative Concord Constructions', in E. Ionescu (ed.), 83–118.

IONESCU, E. (ed.) (2004). *Understanding Romanian Negation: Syntactic and Semantic Approaches in a Declarative Perspective*. Bucharest: Editura Universității din București.

IONESCU-RUXĂNDOIU, L. (1978). 'Participiul', in F. Dimitrescu (ed.), 332–5.

IONESCU-RUXĂNDOIU, L. (2010). 'Tradiție și modernitate. Puncte de vedere asupra volumului I din noul Tratat de istorie a limbii române', in G. Chivu, and O. Bărbulescu (eds), *Studii de limba română. Omagiu profesorului Grigore Brâncuș*. Bucharest: Editura Universității din București, 195–201.

IORDAN, I. (1947 [1943]). *Limba română actuală. O gramatică a greșelilor*. Bucharest: Socec.

IORDAN, I. (1950). 'Note sintactice', *Studii și cercetări lingvistice* 1: 269–79.

IORDAN, I. (1956). *Limba română contemporană*. Bucharest: Editura Ministerului Învățământului.

IORDAN, I. (1957). *Introducere în lingvistica romanică*. Bucharest: Editura Ministerului Învățământului.

IORDAN, I., and MANOLIU, M. (1965). *Introducere în lingvistica romanică*. Bucharest: Editura Didactică și Pedagogică.

IPPOLITO, M. (2004). 'Imperfect Modality', in J. Guéron, and J. Lecarme (eds), *The Syntax of Time*. Cambridge, MA: MIT Press, 359–87.

IVĂNESCU, G. (1957). 'Soarta neutrului latin clasic în latina populară și în limbile romanice', *Studii și cercetări lingvistice* 8: 299–313.

IVĂNESCU, G. (2000). *Istoria limbii române*. Iași: Junimea.

JOHANNESSEN, J. B. (1998). *Coordination*. Oxford: Oxford University Press.

JONASSON, K. (1994). *Le Nom propre: constructions et interprétations*. Louvain-la-Neuve: Duculot.

JORDAN, M. (2009). *Loss of Infinitival Complementation in Romanian Diachronic Syntax*. Ph.D. Thesis, University of Florida.

JOSEPH, B. D. (1983). *The Synchrony and Diachrony of the Balkan Infinitive*. Cambridge: Cambridge University Press.

JOSEPH, B. D. (1999). 'Romanian and the Balkans: Some Comparative Perspectives', in S. Embleton, J. Joseph, and H.-J. Niederehe (eds), *The Emergence of the Modern Language Sciences. Studies on the Transition from Historical-Comparative to Structural Linguistics in Honour of E.F.K. Koerner.* II. *Methodological Perspectives and Applications.* Amsterdam: John Benjamins, 218–35.

JOUITTEAU, M., and RÉZAC, M. (2007). 'The French Ethical Dative. 13 Syntactic Tests', *Bucharest Working Papers in Linguistics* 9, 1: 97–108.

KAYNE, R. (1994). *The Antisymmetry of Syntax.* Cambridge, MA / MIT Press.

KAYNE, R. S. (2000). *Parameters and Universals.* Oxford: Oxford University Press.

KISS, K. É. (1995). 'Introduction', in K. É. Kiss (ed.), *Discourse Configurational Languages.* New York / Oxford: Oxford University Press, 3–27.

KLEIBER, G. (1994). *Nominales: essais de sémantique référentielle.* Paris: Armand Colin.

KLEIBER, G. (2006). 'Du Massif au comptable: le cas des N massifs concrets modifiés', in F. Corblin, S. Ferrando, and L. Kupferman (eds), *Indéfini et prédication.* Paris: Presses de l'Université Paris / Sorbonne, 183–202.

KOOPMAN, H. (2000). 'The Structure of Dutch PPs', in H. Koopman (ed.), *The Syntax of Specifiers and Heads.* London: Routledge, 198–256.

KOPTJEVSKAJA-TAMM, M. (2002) 'Adnominal Possession in the European Languages: Form and Function', *Sprachtypologie und Universalienforschung* 55: 141–72.

KOPTJEVSKAYA-TAMM, M. (2005). '*Maria's ring of gold:* Adnominal Possession and Non-anchoring Relations in European Languages', in K. Ji-Young, B. H. Partee, and Y. A. Lander (eds), *Possessives and Beyond: Semantics and Syntax.* University of Massachusetts Occasional Papers: Amherst, 155–81.

KRAPOVA, I. (2004). 'Word Order in Topic–Focus Structures in the Balkan Languages', *Romània Orientale* 17: 139–62.

KRAPOVA, I. (2010). 'Bulgarian Relative and Factive Clauses with an Invariant Complementizer', *Lingua* 120: 1240–72.

KUPFERMAN, L. (2004). *Le Mot 'de'.* Bruxelles: Duculot.

LAENZLINGER, C. (2005). 'French Adjective Ordering: Perspectives on DP-Internal Movement Types', *Lingua* 115, 5: 645–89.

LAMBRECHT, K. (2000). 'Prédication seconde et structure informationnelle: la relative de perception comme construction présentative', *Langue française* 127: 49–66.

LAMIROY, B. (1999). 'Auxiliaires, langues romanes et grammaticalisation', *Langages* 33, 135: 33–45.

LAMIROY, B., and DELBEQUE, N. (1998). 'The Possessive Dative in Romance and Germanic Languages', in W. Van Langendonck, and W. Van Belle (eds), 29–74.

LECLÈRE, C. (1976). 'Datifs syntaxiques et datif éthique', in J.-C. Chevalier, and M. Gross (eds), *Méthodes en grammaire française.* Paris: Klincksieck, 73–96.

LEDGEWAY, A. (2000). *A Comparative Syntax of the Dialects of Southern Italy: A Minimalist Approach.* Oxford: Blackwell.

LEDGEWAY, A. (2005). 'Moving through the Left Periphery: The Dual Complementiser System in the Dialects of Southern Italy', *Transactions of the Philological Society* 103: 339–96.

LEDGEWAY, A. (2011). 'Syntactic and Morphosyntactic Typology and Change', in M. Maiden, J. C. Smith, and A. Ledgeway (eds), 382–471.

LÉGENDRE, G., and SORACE, A. (2003). 'Auxiliaires et intransitivité en français et dans les langues romanes', in D. Godard (ed.), 183–233.

LEVIN, B. C. (1983). *On the Nature of Ergativity.* Ph.D. Thesis, Cambridge, MA: MIT.

LEVIN, B., and RAPPAPORT HOVAV, M. (1995a). *Argument Realization.* Cambridge: Cambridge University Press.

LEVIN, B., and RAPPAPORT HOVAV, M. (1995b). *Unaccusativity: At the Syntax–Lexical Semantics Interface.* Cambridge / London: Cambridge University Press.

LLOMBART-HUESCA, A. (2002). 'Anaphoric *one* and NP-Ellipsis', *Studia linguistica* 56: 59–89.

LOBECK, A. (1995). *Ellipsis: Functional Heads, Licensing, and Identification.* Oxford: Oxford University Press.

Lois, X. (1990). 'Auxiliary Selection and Past Participle Agreement in Romance', *Probus* 2, 2: 233–55.
Lombard, A. (1938). 'Une Classe spéciale des termes indéfinis dans les langues romanes', *Studia Neophilologica* 1–2: 186–209.
Lombard, A. (1939). 'Le Futur roumain du type *o să cânt*', *Bulletin linguistique* 7: 5–28.
Lombard, A. (1954, 1955). *Le Verbe roumain: étude morphologique*. I, II. Lund: C. W. K. Gleerup.
Lombard, A. (1974). *La Langue roumaine. Une présentation*. Paris: Klincksieck.
Longobardi, G. (1994). 'Reference and Proper Names: A Theory of N-movement in Syntax and Logical Form', *Linguistic Inquiry* 25, 4: 609–65.
Longobardi, G. (2001). 'I quantificatori', in L. Renzi, G. Salvi, and A. Cardinaletti (eds), 659–710.
Loporcaro, M. (1998). *Sintassi comparata dell' accordo participiale romanzo*. Turin: Rosenberg & Sellier.
Loporcaro, M. (2011a). 'Syllable, Segment and Prosody', in M. Maiden, J. C. Smith, and A. Ledgeway (eds), 50–108.
Loporcaro, M. (2011b). 'Phonological Processes', in M. Maiden, J. C. Smith, and A. Ledgeway (eds), 109–54.
Loporcaro, M., and Paciaroni, T. (2011). 'Four-Gender Systems in Indo-European', *Folia Linguistica* 45, 2: 389–433.
Lorda, C.-U. (ed.) (2012). *Polifonía e intertextualidad en el diálogo*, Madrid: Arco Libros.
Lyons, J. (1977). *Semantics*. II. Cambridge: Cambridge University Press.
Mackenzie, I. (2006). *Unaccusative Verbs in Romance Languages*. New York: Palgrave Macmillan.
Maiden, M. (1996). 'On the Romance Inflectional Endings *-i* and *-e*', *Romance Philology* 50, 2: 147–82.
Maiden, M. (2004). 'Verb Augments and Meaninglessness in Romance Morphology', *Studi di grammatica italiana* 22: 1–61.
Maiden, M. (2005) 'Morphological Autonomy and Diachrony', *Yearbook of Morphology 2004*: 137–75.
Maiden, M. (2006). 'On Romanian Imperatives', *Philologica Jassyensia* 2: 47–59.
Maiden, M. (2006–2007). 'Despre unele elemente "goale" în sistemul morfologic al limbii române normate și al graiurilor românești', *Dacoromania* 11–12: 179–86.
Maiden, M. (2009a). 'From Pure Phonology to Pure Morphology: The Reshaping of the Romance Verb', *Recherches linguistiques de Vincennes* 38: 45–82.
Maiden, M. (2009b). 'On Number Syncretism in Romanian Third Person Verb Forms', in F. Sánchez Miret (ed.), *Romanística sin complejos. Homenaje a Carmen Pensado*. Bern: Lang, 381–407.
Maiden, M. (2009c). 'Un capitolo di morfologia storica del romeno: preterito e tempi affini', *Zeitschrift für romanische Philologie* 125: 273–309.
Maiden, M. (2011a). 'Morphological Persistence', in M. Maiden, J. C. Smith, and A. Ledgeway (eds), 155–215.
Maiden, M. (2011b). 'Morphophonological Innovation', in M. Maiden, J. C. Smith, and A. Ledgeway (eds), 216–67.
Maiden, M. (2011c). 'Allomorphy, Autonomous Morphology and Phonological Conditioning in the History of the Daco-Romance Present and Subjunctive', *Transactions of the Philological Society* 109, 1: 59–91.
Maiden, M. (2012). 'Supin și participiu trecut în morfologia istorică a limbii române', in R. Zafiu, A. Dragomirescu, and A. Nicolae (eds), 11–8.
Maiden, M., and Robustelli, C. (2007). *A Reference Grammar of Modern Italian*. London: Hodder Arnold.
Maiden, M., Smith, J. C., and Ledgeway, A. (eds) (2011). *The Cambridge History of Romance Languages*. I. *Structures*. Cambridge / New York: Cambridge University Press.
Mancaș, M. (1972). *Stilul indirect liber în româna literară*. Bucharest: Editura Didactică și Pedagogică.
Manea, D. (2001). *Structura semantico-sintactică a verbului românesc. Verbele psihologice*. Bucharest: Editura Arhiepiscopiei Romano-Catolice de București.

MANEA, D. (2008a). 'Modul', in GALR I, 358–93.
MANEA, D. (2008b). 'Timpul', in GALR I, 394–448.
MANEA, D. (2008c). 'Categoria aspectului', in GALR I, 449–67.
MANEA, D. (2010). 'Aspecte ale realizării adjuncților în româna contemporană', in R. Zafiu, A. Dragomirescu, and A. Nicolae (eds), 93–101.
MANEA, D. (2012). 'Modalitate și negație în limba română contemporană', in R. Zafiu, A. Dragomirescu, and A. Nicolae (eds), 137–44.
MANOLIU, M. (1967). 'Genitivul pronumelui personal în limba română contemporană', in I. Coteanu (ed.), *Elemente de lingvistică structurală*. Bucharest: Editura Științifică, 274–90.
MANOLIU, M. (2000). 'Demonstratives, Story-World and Talk-Interaction', in M. Coene, W. De Mulder, P. Dendale, and Y. D'Hulst (eds), 583–600.
MANOLIU, M. M. (2011). 'Pragmatic and Discourse Changes', in M. Maiden, J. Ch. Smith, and A. Ledgeway (eds), 472–531.
MANOLIU, M., and PRICE G. (2007). 'Convergence in Divergence: Romanian and the Romance Type', in S. Reinheimer Rîpeanu, and I. Vintilă-Rădulescu (eds), 319–29.
MANOLIU-MANEA, M. (1968). *Sistematica substitutelor în româna standard*. Bucharest: Editura Academiei Române.
MANOLIU-MANEA, M. (1969), 'Accusativus cum infinitivo dans les langues romanes (complétive ou relative?)', *Cahiers de linguistique théorique et apliquée* 7: 125–36.
MANOLIU-MANEA, M. (1977). *Elemente de sintaxă comparată romanică. Tipologie și istorie*. Bucharest: Universitatea din București.
MANOLIU-MANEA, M. (1993). *Gramatică, pragmasemantică, discurs*. Bucharest: Litera.
MANOLIU-MANEA, M. (1994). 'La Pragma-sémantique de l'identité', *Revue roumaine de linguistique* 39: 441–55.
MANOLIU-MANEA, M. (1995). 'From *deixis ad oculos* to discourse markers via *deixis ad phantasma*', *Revue roumaine de linguistique* 40: 57–73.
MANOLIU-MANEA, M. (1996). 'Inalienability and Topicality in Romanian: Pragma-semantics of Syntax', in H. Chappell, and W. McGregor (eds), *The Grammar of Inalienability: A Typological Perspective on Body Part Terms and the Part–Whole Relation*. Berlin: Mouton de Gruyter, 711–43.
MANOLIU-MANEA, M. (2001). 'The Conversational Factor in Language Change. From Prenominal to Postnominal Demonstratives', in J. L. Brinton (ed.), *Selected Papers from the 14th International Conference on Historical Linguistics*. Amsterdam: John Benjamins, 187–205.
MANU MAGDA, M. (1993). 'Dialogue dans le dialogue', in H. Löffler (ed.), *Dialoganalyse* IV, I. Tübingen: Niemeyer, 79–88.
MANU MAGDA, M. (2003). 'Expresii ale mobilizării și demobilizării verbale în dialogul social românesc', in L. Dascălu Jinga, and L. Pop (eds), *Dialogul în româna vorbită*. Bucharest: Oscar Print, 73–95.
MANU MAGDA, M. (2004). 'Suporturi verbale ale "tipului vocativ" în limba română actuală', in G. Duda, and D. Tomescu (eds), *Direcții în cercetarea lingvistică actuală. In memoriam Magdalena Vulpe*. Ploiești: Editura Universității din Ploiești, 101–17.
MANU MAGDA, M. (2008). 'Limba română vorbită', in GALR II: 869–904.
MANU MAGDA, M. (2009). 'Indici de alocutivitate în limba română actuală (clasa alocutivelor interjecționale)', in G. Pană Dindelegan (ed.), 459–90.
MANZINI, M., and SAVOIA, L. M. (2007). *A Unification of Morphology and Syntax. Investigations into Romance and Albanian dialects*. London / New York: Routledge.
MARCHIS, M. (2010). 'On the Morpho-Syntactic Properties of Relational Adjectives in Romanian and Spanish', *Bucharest Working Papers in Linguistics* 12, 1: 77–91.
MARDALE, A. (2009). *Les Prépositions fonctionnelles du roumain: études comparatives sur le marquage casuel*. Paris: L'Harmattan.
MARIN, M. (1991). 'Morfologia verbului în graiurile muntenești', *Fonetică și dialectologie* 10: 45–65.
MARIN, M., MĂRGĂRIT, I., and NEAGOE V. (1998). 'Graiuri românești din Ucraina și Republica Moldova', *Fonetică și dialectologie* 17: 69–155.

MATEICA-IGELMANN, M. (1989). *Moyens d'exprimer les aspects de la phrase verbale en roumain contemporain*. Bochum: Brockmeyer.

MATEU, J. (2001). 'Locative and Locatum Verbs Revisited: Evidence from Romance', in Y. D'Hulst, J. Rooryck, and J. Schroten (eds), 223–44.

MĂRII, I. (2004). *Contribuții la lingvistica limbii române*, Cluj: Clusium.

MCNALLY, L., and BOLEDA, G. (2004). 'Relational Adjectives as Properties of Kinds', in O. Bonami, and P. Cabredo Hofherr (eds), *Empirical Issues in Formal Syntax and Semantics* 5: 179–96.

MËNIKU, L., and CAMPOS, H. (2011). *Discovering Albanian 1. Textbook*. University of Wisconsin Press.

MENSCHING, G. (2000). *Infinitive Constructions with Specified Subjects: A Syntactic Analysis of the Romance Languages*. Oxford: Oxford University Press.

MERCHANT, J. (2001). *The Syntax of Silence: Sluicing, Islands, and the Theory of Ellipsis*. Oxford: Oxford University Press.

MERLAN, A. (1998). *Sintaxa și semantica-pragmatica limbii române vorbite. Discontinuitatea*. Iași: Editura Universității 'Alexandru Ioan Cuza'.

METZELTIN, M. (2011). *Gramatica explicativă a limbilor romanice. Sintaxă și semantică*. Iași: Editura Universității 'Alexandru Ioan Cuza'.

MEUL, C. (2009). 'The Intra-Paradigmatic Expansion of the Infix -I/ESC- from Latin to Modern Romance: Morphomic Patterning and beyond', *Morphology* 20, 1: 1–40.

MEYER-LÜBKE, W. (1895, 1900). *Grammaire des langues romanes. II. Morphologie. III. Syntaxe*. Paris: H. Welter.

MEYER-LÜBKE, W. (1930). 'Rumänisch und romanisch', *Analele Academiei Române, Memoriile Secțiunii literare* III, 5: 1–36.

MIHAIL, A.-M. (2009a). 'Tiparul sintactic afectiv (Det) N_1 de N_2: origine și realizări în limba română veche (*amărâtul de om, această ticăloasă de țară*)', in R. Zafiu, B. Croitor, and A.-M. Mihail (eds), 125–34.

MIHAIL, A.-M. (2009b). 'Utilizările tiparului afectiv (Det) N_1 de N_2 (*nebunul de Ion*) în limba română actuală', in G. Pană Dindelegan (ed.), 95–112.

MIHĂILĂ, G. (1974). *Dicționar al limbii române vechi (sfârșitul sec. al X-lea–începutul sec. al XVI-lea)*. Bucharest: Editura Enciclopedică Română.

MILLER, D. G. (2002). *Nonfinite Structures in Theory and Change*. Oxford: Oxford University Press.

MILLER, P., and MONACHESI, P. (2003). 'Les pronoms clitiques dans les langues romanes', in D. Godard (ed.), 67–123.

MIRON-FULEA, M. (2005). *Numele proprii. Interfața semantică–sintaxă*. Bucharest: Editura Universității din București.

MIŠESKA TOMIĆ, O. (2004). 'The Balkan Sprachbund Properties', in O. Mišeska Tomić (ed.), 1–55.

MIŠESKA TOMIĆ, O. (ed.) (2004). *Balkan Syntax and Semantics*. Amsterdam: John Benjamins.

MIŠESKA TOMIĆ, O. (2006). *Balkan Sprachbund Morpho-syntactic features*. Dordrecht: Springer.

MÎRZEA VASILE, C. (2012a). *Eterogenitatea adverbului românesc: tipologie și descriere*. Bucharest: Editura Universității din București.

MÎRZEA VASILE, C. (2012b). 'Adjectivul în secolul al XIX-lea', in G. Chivu, G. Pană Dindelegan, A. Dragomirescu, I. Nedelcu, and I. Nicula (eds), 63–110.

MONACHESI, P. (1998). 'The Morphosyntax of Romanian Cliticization', in P. Coppen, H. van Halteren, and L. Teunissen (eds), *Proceedings of Computational Linguistics in The Netherlands 1997*. Amsterdam / Atlanta: Rodopi, 99–118.

MONACHESI, P. (1999). 'The Syntactic Structure of Romanian Auxiliary (and modal) verbs', in G. Bouma, E. Hinrichs, G. J. M. Kruijff, and R. Oehrle (eds), *Constraints and Resources in Natural Language Syntax and Semantics*. Stanford: CSLI Publications, 101–18.

MONACHESI, P. (2005). *The Verbal Complex in Romance: A Case Study in Grammatical Interfaces*. Oxford / New York: Oxford University Press.

MOTAPANYANE, V. (ed.) (2000). *Comparative Studies in Romance Syntax*. Amsterdam: Elsevier.

NANDRIȘ, O. (1961). 'Le Genre, ses réalisations et le genre personnel en roumain', *Revue de linguistique romane* 25: 47–74.

NEAMȚU, G. G. (1979). 'Despre acuzativul timpului în limba română', *Cercetări de lingvistică* 24: 63–71.

NEDELCU, I. (2009). *Categoria partitivului în limba română*. Bucharest: Editura Universității din București.

NEDELCU, I. (2010). 'Observații asupra numelor (uni)relaționale', in R. Zafiu, A. Dragomirescu, and A. Nicolae (eds), 121–29.

NEDELCU, I. (2012). 'Conjuncția în secolul al XIX-lea', in G. Chivu, G. Pană Dindelegan, A. Dragomirescu, I. Nedelcu, and I. Nicula (eds), 261–74.

NEDJALKOV, V. (2007). *Reciprocal Constructions*. Amsterdam: John Benjamins.

NICOLAE, A. (2008). '*Altul* vs *un altul*. Noi explicații', in G. Pană Dindelegan (ed.), 119–26.

NICOLAE, A., and DRAGOMIRESCU, A. (2009). 'Omonimia sintactică a participiilor românești', in R. Zafiu, B. Croitor, and A.-M. Mihail (eds), 193–205.

NICULA, I. (2008). 'Utilizări pragmatice ale demonstrativului în limba vorbită actuală: *asta* vs *aceasta*', in G. Pană Dindelegan (ed.), 127–32.

NICULA, I. (2009). 'Dinamica pronumelor și a adjectivelor demonstrative în limba română actuală. Observații pe corpusurile de română vorbită', in G. Pană Dindelegan (ed.), 181–94.

NICULA, I. (2012a). *Modalități de exprimare a percepțiilor fizice. Verbele de percepție în limba română*. Bucharest: Editura Universității din București.

NICULA, I. (2012b). 'Adjectivul în secolul al XX-lea', in G. Chivu, G. Pană Dindelegan, A. Dragomirescu, I. Nedelcu, and I. Nicula (eds), 449–68.

NICULESCU, A. (1965, 1999, 1978, 2003). *Individualitatea limbii române între limbile romanice* I, II. Bucharest: Editura Științifică. III, IV. Cluj-Napoca: Clusium.

NICULESCU, A. (1991). 'L'ordine delle parole in rumeno', in G. Borghello, M. Cortelazzo, and G. Padoan (eds), *Saggi di linguistica e di letteratura in memoria di Paolo Zolli*. Padova: Antenore, 289–99.

NICULESCU, A. (2007). 'Permisivitatea limbii române—o problemă culturală', in C. Stan, R. Zafiu, and A. Nicolae (eds), 417–20.

NICULESCU, A., and RENZI, L. (1991). 'Pronoms personnels clitiques possessifs en roumain et dans les langues balcaniques', *Modèles linguistiques* 2: 123–142.

NICULESCU, D. (2008a). *Mijloace lingvistice de exprimare a posesiei în limba română*. Bucharest: Editura Universității din București.

NICULESCU, D. (2008b). 'Cliticele posesive din grupul nominal', in G. Pană Dindelegan (ed.), 133–40.

NICULESCU, D. (2011). 'The Grammaticalization of the Future Tense Forms in 16th Century Romanian', *Revue roumaine de linguistique* 56: 421–40.

NILSSON, E. (1969). *Les Termes relatifs et les propositions relatives en roumain moderne: étude de syntaxe descriptive*. Lund: C. W. K. Gleerup.

ONU, L. (1958). 'Unele probleme ale imperfectului românesc', in *Omagiu lui Iorgu Iordan cu prilejul împlinirii a 70 de ani*. Bucharest: Editura Academiei Române, 645–60.

ONU, L. (1959). 'L'Origine de l'accusatif roumain avec P(R)E', in I. Coteanu, I. Iordan, and A. Rosetti (eds), *Récueil d'études romanes*. Bucharest: Editura Academiei Române, 187–209.

ONU, L. (1996). 'Tipologia conjunctivului românesc', in M. Iliescu, and S. Sora (eds), 85–92.

ORTMANN, A., and POPESCU, A. (2000). 'Romanian Definite Articles are not Clitics', in B. Gerlach, and J. Grijzenhout (eds), *Clitics in Phonology, Morphology and Syntax*. Amsterdam: John Benjamins, 295–324.

OUHALLA, J. (2009). 'Variation and Change in Possessive Noun Phrases', *Brill's Annual of Afroasiatic Languages and Linguistics* 9, 1: 1–29.

PANĂ DINDELEGAN, G. (1968). 'Regimul sintactic al verbelor în limba română veche', *Studii și cercetări lingvistice* 19: 265–96.

PANĂ DINDELEGAN, G. (1982). 'Structura sintactică Nominal + Adverb (sau Adjectiv) + Supin', *Limba română* 31: 5–14.

PANĂ DINDELEGAN, G. (1985). 'Preliminarii la semantica modalizatorilor', *Analele Universității București. Limba și literatura română* 34: 15–28.

PANĂ DINDELEGAN, G. (1987). *Aspecte ale dinamicii sistemului morfologic verbal (perioada de după 1880)*. Bucharest: Tipografia Universității din București.
PANĂ DINDELEGAN, G. (1992). *Sintaxă și semantică. Clase de cuvinte și forme gramaticale cu dublă natură*. Tipografia Universității București.
PANĂ DINDELEGAN, G. (1994). 'Pronumele *o* cu valoare neutră și funcția cliticelor în limba română', *Limbă și literatură* I: 9–16.
PANĂ DINDELEGAN, G. (1999 [1976]). *Sintaxa grupului verbal*. Brașov: Aula.
PANĂ DINDELEGAN, G. (2002). 'Formații substantivale recente și rolul "clasificatorilor" în actualizarea lor contextuală', in G. Pană Dindelegan (ed.), 31–46.
PANĂ DINDELEGAN, G. (ed.) (2002). *Aspecte ale dinamicii limbii române actuale*. Bucharest: Editura Universității din București.
PANĂ DINDELEGAN, G. (2003). *Elemente de gramatică. Dificultăți, controverse, noi interpretări*. Bucharest: Humanitas Educațional.
PANĂ DINDELEGAN, G. (ed.) (2004). *Tradiție și inovație în studiul limbii române*. Bucharest: Editura Universității din București.
PANĂ DINDELEGAN, G. (ed.) (2005). *Limba română. Structură și funcționare*. Bucharest: Editura Universității din București.
PANĂ DINDELEGAN, G. (ed.) (2006). *Limba română. Aspecte sincronice și diacronice*. Bucharest: Editura Universității din București.
PANĂ DINDELEGAN, G. (2007a). 'Reflecții pe marginea a două tipare flexionare nominale: (*ea / a)Ø— -le* vs. *-u/ŭ/Ø— -uri*', in S. Reinheimer Rîpeanu and I. Vintilă-Rădulescu (eds), 425–34.
PANĂ DINDELEGAN, G. (2007b), *Din nou despre grupul prepozițional (GPrep). Prepozițiile calității*, în *Limba română azi*. Iași: Editura Universității 'Alexandru Ion Cuza', 213–22.
PANĂ DINDELEGAN, G. (ed.) (2008). *Limba română. Dinamica limbii, dinamica interpretării*. Bucharest: Editura Universității din București.
PANĂ DINDELEGAN, G. (2008a). 'Clase sintactice și sintactico-semantice de verbe', in GALR I, 332–58.
PANĂ DINDELEGAN, G. (2008b). 'Productivitatea conjugărilor; fluctuații între clase', in GALR I, 556–62.
PANĂ DINDELEGAN, G. (2008c). 'Construcții pasive și construcții impersonale', in GALR II, 133–47.
PANĂ DINDELEGAN, G. (2008d). 'Construcții reflexive și construcții reciproce', in GALR II, 148–71.
PANĂ DINDELEGAN, G. (2008e). 'Predicatul', in GALR II, 241–66.
PANĂ DINDELEGAN, G. (2008f). 'Numele predicativ', in GALR II, 267–95.
PANĂ DINDELEGAN, G. (2008g). 'Complementul predicativ al obiectului', in GALR II, 296–300.
PANĂ DINDELEGAN, G. (2008h). 'Tipuri de gramaticalizare. Pe marginea utilizărilor gramaticalizate ale prepozițiilor *de* și *la*', in G. Pană Dindelegan (ed.), 227–39.
PANĂ DINDELEGAN, G. (2008i). 'Concurența *-(ț)iune* ~ *-(ț)ie*; stadiul actual al fenomenului', *Studii și cercetări lingvistice* 59: 489–501.
PANĂ DINDELEGAN, G. (ed.) (2009). *Dinamica limbii române actuale—Aspecte gramaticale și discursive*. Bucharest: Editura Academiei Române.
PANĂ DINDELEGAN, G. (2009a). 'Din nou despre dativul posesiv din grupul verbal. Observații asupra limbii române vechi', *Limba română* 58: 173–82.
PANĂ DINDELEGAN, G. (2009b). 'Trăsături flexionare ale substantivului în româna actuală', in G. Pană Dindelegan (ed.), 3–32.
PANĂ DINDELEGAN, G. (2009c). 'Morfosintaxă și semantică: pe marginea cazului simbolizat ca X', in R. Zafiu, B. Croitor, and A.-M. Mihail (eds), 207–14.
PANĂ DINDELEGAN, G. (2010). 'Verbele *denumirii* și relația cu alte verbe care primesc două complemente—cu privire specială la limba veche', in R. Zafiu, A. Dragomirescu, and A. Nicolae (eds), 141–9.
PANĂ DINDELEGAN, G. (2011). 'Din istoria supinului românesc', in R. Zafiu, C. Ușurelu, and H. Bogdan Oprea (eds), 119–30.
PANĂ DINDELEGAN, G. (2012). 'Distribuția diftongilor *ĕa, ŏa* și poziția lor în sistemul limbii', in M. Constantinescu, G. Stoica, O. Uță Bărbulescu, and R. Zafiu (eds), *Modernitate și*

interdisciplinaritate în cercetarea lingvistică. Omagiu doamnei profesor Liliana Ionescu-Ruxăndoiu. Bucharest: Editura Universității din București, 405–12.

PANCHEVA, R. (2004). 'Balkan Possessive Clitics: The Problem of Case and Category', in O. Miseska Tomić (ed.), 175–215.

PAPAHAGI, T. (1963). *Dicționarul dialectului aromân: general și etimologic.* Bucharest: Editura Academiei.

PASCU, G. (1916). *Sufixele românești.* Bucharest: Edițiunea Academiei Române.

PĂTRUȚ, I. (1957). 'Sur le genre "neutre" en roumain', in *Mélanges linguistiques.* Bucarest: Éditions de l'Académie Roumaine, 291–301.

PHARIES, D. (1997). 'Adverbial Expressions Signifying Bodily Movements and Postures in Hispano-Romance', *Hispanic Review* 4: 391–414.

PHILIPPIDE, A. (2011 [1893–1932]). *Istoria limbii române*, G. Ivănescu, C.-G. Pamfil, and L. Botoșineanu (eds). Iași: Polirom.

PÎRVULESCU, M. (2006). 'Agreement Paradigms across Moods and Tenses', in J.-P. Montreuil, and C. Nishida (eds), *New Perspectives in Romance Linguistics.* Philadelphia: John Benjamins, 229–45.

PÎRVULESCU, M., and ROBERGE, Y. (2000). 'The Syntax and Morphology of Romanian Imperatives', in V. Motapanyane (ed.), 295–312.

PLANGG, G. A., and ILIESCU, M. (eds) (1987). *Akten der Theodor Gartner-Tagung* (Rätoromanisch und Rumänisch), in VIII / Innsbruck 1985, Institut für Romanistik der Leopold-Franzens-Universität, Innsbruck.

POMIAN, I. (2008). *Construcții complexe în sintaxa limbii române.* Pitești: Paralela 45.

POPA, I. C. (2007). 'Les "Verba dicendi" *a spune* et *a zice*', *Studii și cercetări lingvistice* 58: 349–62.

POPESCU-MARIN, M. (ed.) (2007). *Formarea cuvintelor în limba română din secolele al XVI-lea–al XVIII-lea.* Bucharest: Editura Academiei Române.

POSNER, R. (1996). *The Romance Languages.* Cambridge: Cambridge University Press.

POSTAL, P. M. (1971). *Cross-Over Phenomena.* New York: Holt, Rinehart and Winston.

PRICE, G. (2008). *A Comprehensive French Grammar.* Oxford: Blackwell Publishing.

PRINCE, E. F. (1978). 'A Comparison of WH-Clefts and *it*-Clefts in Discourse', *Language* 54: 883–906.

PUȘCARIU, S. (1905). *Etymologisches Wörterbuch der rumänischen Sprache. I: Lateinisches Element.* Heidelberg: K. Winter.

PUȘCARIU, S. (1940). *Limba română. I. Privire generală.* Bucharest: Fundația pentru Literatură și Artă 'Regele Carol II'.

RADFORD, A. (2009). *An Introduction to English Sentence Structure.* Cambridge: Cambridge University Press.

RALLI PATRAS, A. (2008). 'Compound Markers and Parametric Variation', *Language Typology and Universals* 61: 19–38.

RAUH WUPPERTAL, G. (1994). 'Prépositions et rôles: points de vue syntaxique et sémantique', *Langage* 113, 45–78.

RĂDULESCU, M. (1985). 'Observații asupra unor adverbe de timp provenite din substantive în limba română', *Studii și cercetări lingvistice* 36: 246–50.

RĂDULESCU, M. (1992). 'Note despre complementul indirect în genitiv și regentul său', *Limba română* 41: 95–99.

RĂDULESCU SALA, M. (2008). 'Complementul de agent', in GALR II, 454–62.

REBOTIER, A. (2009). 'Le Futur de l'allemand en comparaison avec les langues romanes: esquisse d'une définition d'une catégorie translinguistique de futur', *Faits de langues* 33: 69–78.

REINHEIMER, S. (1965). 'Schiță de descriere structurală a verbelor de mișcare', *Studii și cercetări lingvistice* 16: 519–29.

REINHEIMER, S., and TASMOWSKI, L. (2005). *Pratique des langues romanes. II. Les pronoms personnels.* Paris: L'Hartamann.

REINHEIMER RÎPEANU, S. (1974). *Les Dérivés parasynthétiques dans les langues romanes: roumain, italien, français, espagnol.* The Hague, Paris: Mouton.

REINHEIMER RÎPEANU, S. (1993). *Structuri morfosintactice de bază în limbile romanice*. Bucharest: Tipografia Universității din București.
REINHEIMER RÎPEANU, S. (1998). 'Împrumutul latinesc în limbile romanice: Verbul', *Studii și cercetări lingvistice* 49: 283–95.
REINHEIMER RÎPEANU, S. (2000). 'Le Présomptif roumain: marqueur évidentiel et épistémique', in M. Coene, W. De Mulder, P. Dendale, and Y. D'Hulst (eds), 481–91.
REINHEIMER RÎPEANU, S. (2001). *Lingvistica romanică*. Bucharest: All.
REINHEIMER RÎPEANU, S. (2004). 'Intensification et atténuation en roumain: les adverbes *cam, mai, prea, și, tot*', *Travaux et documents* 24: 225–46.
REINHEIMER RÎPEANU, S. (2005). 'Roum. *tot*, marqueur aspectuel', in M. Coene, and L. Tasmowski (eds), 173–91.
REINHEIMER RÎPEANU, S. (2010). 'Le Roumain *și* adverbial dans le groupe verbal', in M. Iliescu, H. Siller-Runggaldier, and P. Danler (eds), 539–48.
REINHEIMER RÎPEANU, S., and LEAHU, S. (1983). 'Rom. *pe dibuite*—sp. *a tientas*', *Studii și cercetări lingvistice* 34: 451–3.
REINHEIMER RÎPEANU, S., and VINTILĂ-RĂDULESCU, I. (eds) (2007). *Limba română, limbă romanică. Omagiu acad. Marius Sala, la împlinirea a 75 de ani*. Bucharest: Editura Academiei Române.
RENZI, L. (1968). 'Mama, tata, nene, ecc: il sistema delle allocuzioni inverse in rumeno', *Cultura Neolatina* 28: 89–99.
RENZI, L. (1991 [1989]). 'Considerazioni tipologiche sul rumeno', in H. Stammerjohann (ed.), *Analyse et synthèse dans les langues romanes et slaves*. Tübingen: Gunter Narr, 21–5.
RENZI, L. (1993). 'L'articolo posposto rumeno in diacronia e in sincronia', *Revue roumaine de linguistique* 38: 307–23.
RENZI, L. (1994). *Nuova introduzione alla filologia romanza*. Bologna: il Mulino.
RENZI, L. (2002–2003). 'Italiano e romeno', *Dacoromania* 7–8: 197–208.
RENZI, L. (2010). 'La flessione casuale nei pronomi dal latino alle lingue romanze', *Revue de linguistique romane* 74: 27–59.
RENZI, L., and ANDREOSE, A. (2003). *Manuale di linguistica e filologia romanza*. Bologna: il Mulino.
RENZI, L., SALVI, G., and CARDINALETTI, A. (eds) (2001). *Grande grammatica italiana di consultazione*. I-III. Bologna: il Mulino.
REW. MEYER-LÜBKE, W. (1935). *Romanisches etymologisches Wörterbuch*. Heidelberg: Dritte Auflage.
RIVIÈRE, N. (1990). 'Le Participe passé est-il verbe ou adjectif?', *Travaux de linguistique et de philologie* 28: 131–69.
RIZESCU, I. (1959). 'Note asupra pronumelui personal aton în dativ', *Limba română* 7: 18–22.
RIZESCU, I. (1962). 'Observații asupra propozițiilor subordonate relative din *Carte cu învățătură* (1581)', *Studii și cercetări lingvistice* 13: 45–58.
RIZESCU, I. (2007). 'Propozițiile coordonate', in M. Avram (ed.), *Sintaxa limbii române în secolele al XVI-lea–al XVIII-lea*. Bucharest: Editura Academiei Române.
RIZZI, L. (1982). *Issues in Italian Syntax*. Dordrecht: Foris Publications.
RIZZI, L. (1997). 'The Fine Structure of the Left Periphery', in L. Haegeman (ed.), *Elements of Grammar*. Dordrecht: Kluwer Academic Publishers, 281–337.
ROBERTS, I. (2010). *Agreement and Head Movement: Clitics, Incorporation and Defective Goals*. Cambridge, MA: MIT Press.
ROBERTS, I., and ROUSSOU, A. (2003). *Syntactic change: A Minimalist Approach to Grammaticalization*. Cambridge: Cambridge University Press.
ROCCI, A. (2000). 'L'Interprétation épistémique du futur en italien et en français: une analyse procédurale', *Cahiers de linguistique française* 22: 241–74.
ROEGIEST, E. (1981). 'Constructions adjectivales transformées dans les langues romanes', *Revue roumaine de linguistique* 26: 415–33.
ROEGIEST, E. (1987). 'Le Double objet direct du roumain et les universaux du langage', in G. A. Plangg, and M. Iliescu (eds), 349–62.

ROEGIEST, E. (1996). 'L'Objet direct en roumain: variation actantielle, agentivité, topicalité', in M. Iliescu, and S. Sora (eds), 162–73.

ROHLFS, G. (1968). *Grammatica storica della lingua italiana e dei suoi dialetti*. II *Morfologia*. Turin: Einaudi.

ROORYCK, J. (2000). *Configurations of Sentential Complementation: Perspectives from Romance Languages*. London: Routledge.

ROSETTI, A. (1986). *Istoria limbii române*. I. *De la origini până la începutul secolului al XVII-lea*. Bucharest: Editura Ştiinţifică şi Enciclopedică.

ROSS, J R. (1986). *Infinite Syntax*. Norwood, NJ: Ablex.

ROTHSTEIN, S. (2003). 'Secondary Predication and Aspectual Structure', in E. Lang, C. Maienborn, and C. Fabricius-Hansen (eds), *Modifying Adjuncts*. Berlin: Mouton de Gruyter, 551–90.

ROTHSTEIN, S. (2006). 'Secondary Predication', in M. Everaert, H. van Riemsdijk, R. Goedemans, and B. Hollebrandse (eds), 209–33.

ROTHSTEIN, B., and THIEROFF, R. (eds) (2010). *Mood in the Languages of Europe*. Amsterdam / Philadelphia: John Benjamins.

ROUSSOU, A. (2010). 'Selecting Complementizers', *Lingua* 120, 3: 582–603.

ROWLETT, P. (2007). 'Cinque's Functional Verbs in French', *Language Sciences* 29, 6: 755–86.

RUSSU, I. I. (1981). *Etnogeneza românilor. Fondul autohton traco-dacic şi componenta latino-romanică*. Bucharest: Editura Ştiinţifică şi Enciclopedică.

SALA, M. (2006 [1998]). *De la latină la română*. Bucharest: Univers Enciclopedic.

SALA, M. (2010). 'Romanian', *Revue belge de philologie et d'histoire* 88: 841–72.

SALVI, G. (2011). 'Morphosyntactic Persistence', in M. Maiden, J. C. Smith, and A. Ledgeway (eds), 318–81.

SALVI, G., and VANELLI, L. (2004). *Nuova grammatica italiana*. Bologna: il Mulino.

SÁNCHEZ MIRET, F. (2006). 'Productivity of the Weak Verbs in Romanian', *Folia linguistica* 40: 29–50.

SANDFELD, K. (1930). *Linguistique balkanique*. Paris: Champion.

SANDFELD, K. (1970). *Syntaxe du français contemporain*. Paris: Honoré Champion.

SANDFELD, K., and OLSEN, H. (1936, 1960, 1962). *Syntaxe roumaine* I. Paris: E. Droz. II, III. Copenhague: Munksgaard.

SARAMANDU, N. (2008). *La Romanité orientale*. Bucharest: Editura Academiei Române, Tübingen: Gunter Narr.

SĂVESCU CIUCIVARA, O. (2011). *A Syntactic Analysis of Pronominal Clitic Clusters in Romance: The View from Romanian*. Bucharest: Editura Universităţii din Bucureşti.

SCHULTE, K. (2007). *Prepositional Infinitives in Romance: A Usage-Based Approach to Syntactic Change*. Bern: Peter Lang Publishing.

SCHWARZE, C. (2009). 'On the Development of Latin -*sk*- to French and Italian—Lexicalization, Reanalysis and Spreading', *Italian Journal of Linguistics / Rivista di Linguistica* 21, 2: 343–82.

SCIDA, E. (2004). *The Inflected Infinitive in Romance Languages*. New York / London: Routledge.

SCRIPNIC, G. (2010). 'L'Étude de l'adverbe chipurile en tant que marqueur évidentiel', in R. Zafiu, A. Dragomirescu, and A. Nicolae (eds), 151–60.

SERIANNI, L. (1997). *Italiano*. Milano: Garzanti.

SHOPEN, T. (ed.) (2007 [1985]). *Language Typology and Syntactic Description*. II. *Complex constructions*. III. *Grammatical Categories and the Lexicon*. Cambridge: Cambridge University Press.

SHORT, D. (1993). 'Sorbian', in B. Comrie, and G. G. Corbett (eds), *The Slavonic Language*. London / New York: Routledge, 593–685.

SIEGEL, L. (2009). 'Mood Selection in Romance and Balkan', *Lingua* 119: 1859–82.

ŠIMÍK, R. (2011). *Modal Existential Wh-Constructions*. LOT: Utrecht.

SLEEMAN, P. (1996). *Licensing Empty Nouns in French*. The Hague: Holland Academic.

SLEEMAN, P. (2008). 'Prenominal and Postnominal Reduced Relative Clauses: Arguments against Unitary Analyses', *Bucharest Working Papers in Linguistics* 11, 1: 5–16.

SOARE, E. (2002). *Participes, nominalisation et catégories mixtes: le supin roumain*. Ph.D. Thesis, Paris, Université Paris 7 / 'Denis Diderot'.

SOARE, E. (2007). 'Morphsyntactic Mismatches Revised: The Case of Romanian Supine', *Acta Linguistica Hungarica* 54: 1–19.

SOLÀ, J., LLORET, M. R., MASCARÓ, J., and PÉREZ SALDANYA, M. (eds) (2008). *Gramática del catala contemporani*. I-III. Barcelona: Empúries.

SORNICOLA, R. (2011). 'Romance Linguistics and Historical Linguistics: Reflections on Synchrony and Diachrony', in M. Maiden, J. C. Smith, and A. Ledgeway (eds), 1–49.

SQUARTINI, M. (2005). 'L'evidenzialità in rumeno e nelle altre lingue romanze', *Zeitschrift für romanische Philologie* 121: 246–68.

SQUARTINI, M. (2008). 'Lexical vs. Grammatical Evidentiality in French and Italian', *Linguistics* 46: 917–47.

SQUARTINI, M., and BERTINETTO, P. M. (2000). 'The Simple and Compound Past in Romance Languages', in Ö. Dahl (ed.), 403–40.

STAN, C. (2003). *Gramatica numelor de acțiune din limba română*. Bucharest: Editura Universității din București.

STAN, C. (2005). *Categoria cazului*. Bucharest: Editura Universității din București.

STAN, C. (2007). 'Notă gramaticală: conjuncția ca (...) să', *Studii și cercetări lingvistice* 58: 451–8.

STAN, C. (2010a). 'L'articolo indefinito in rumeno', in M. Iliescu, H. Siller-Runggaldier, and P. Danler (eds) 6: 565–72.

STAN, C. (2010b). 'On the Grammaticality Status of Numerals in Romanian', *Revue roumaine de linguistique* 55: 237–46.

STAN, C. (2012a). 'Ortografia și ortoepia limbii române în secolele al XIX-lea–al XX-lea', in G. Chivu, G. Pană Dindelegan, A. Dragomirescu, I. Nedelcu, and I. Nicula (eds), 1–33.

STAN, C. (2012b). *O sintaxă diacronică a limbii române vechi*. Bucharest: Editura Universității din București.

STAN, C. (2012c). 'Sulla sintassi dei sintagmi nominali con più determinanti nel rumeno', in *Actes du XXVIe Congrès International de Linguistique et de Philologie Romanes*. Valencia 2010. Berlin / New York: De Gruyter, to appear by June 2013).

STAN, C., ZAFIU, R, and NICOLAE, A. (eds) (2007). *Studii lingvistice. Omagiu profesoarei Gabriela Pană Dindelegan la aniversare*. Bucharest: Editura Universității din București.

STASSEN, L. (2005). 'Comparative Constructions', in WALS, 490–3.

STATI, S. (1989). 'Rumänisch: Syntax', in G. Holtus, M. Metzeltin, and C. Schmitt (eds), *Die einzelnen romanischen Sprachen und Sprachgebiete von der Renaissance bis zur Gegenwart Rumänisch, Dalmatisch / Istroromanisch, Friulisch, Ladinisch*. III. Bündnerromanisch, Tubingen: Max Niemeyer, 114–26.

STOICHIȚOIU ICHIM, A. (2006). *Creativitate lexicală în româna actuală*. Bucharest: Editura Universității din București.

STONE, G. (1993). 'Czech' in B. Comrie, and G. G. Corbett (eds), 455–532.

SUZUKI, S. (2010). *Costituenti a sinistra in italiano e in romeno. Analisi sincronica e diacronica in relazione ai clitici e agli altri costituenti maggiori*. Firenze: Accademia della Crusca.

SVENONIUS, P. (2008). 'Complex Predicates and the Functional Sequence', in P. Svenonius, and I. Tolskaya (eds), *Troms Working Papers on Language & Linguistics*. CASTL, Troms, 47–88.

SZABOLCSI, A. (1984). 'The Possessor that Ran Away from Home', *The Linguistic Review* 3, 1: 69–102.

SZABOLCSI, A. (1994) 'The Noun Phrase', in K. Ferenc, and K. É. Kiss (eds), *Syntax and Semantics 27: The Syntactic Structure of Hungarian*. New York: Academic Press, 179–275.

ȘERBĂNESCU, A. (2000). 'Dative Possessive Revisited', in L. Tasmowski (ed.), 133–147.

ȘERBĂNESCU, A. (2002). *Întrebarea. Teorie și practică*. Iași: Polirom.

ȘIADBEI, I. (1930). 'Le Sort du prétérit roumain', *Romania* 56: 331–60.

TALMY, L. (1985). 'Lexicalization Patterns: Semantic Structure in Lexical Forms', in T. Shopen (ed.), 36–149.

TALMY, L. (2007). 'Lexical Typologies', in T. Shopen (ed.), 66–168.

TANNEN, D. (ed.) (1981). *Spoken and Written Language*. Norwood, NJ: Ablex.

TASMOWSKI, L. (1990). 'Les Démonstratifs français et roumains dans la phrase et dans le texte', *Langages* 97: 82–99.

TASMOWSKI, L. (ed.) (2000). *The Expression of Possession in Romance and Germanic Languages*. Cluj: Clusium.

TASMOWSKI, L., and PANĂ DINDELEGAN, G. (2009). 'Deux clitiques datifs possessifs en roumain?', in S. Reinheimer Rîpeanu (ed.), *Studia lingvistica in honorem Mariæ Manoliu*. Bucharest, Editura Universității din București: 335–48.

TASMOWSKI, L., and REINHEIMER RÎPEANU, S. (2003). 'Quelques adverbes roumains "de temps" dans une perspective comparative', *Revue roumaine de linguistique* 48: 163–71.

TASMOWSKI-DE RYCK, L. (1987). 'La Réduplication clitique en roumain', in G. A. Plangg, and M. Iliescu (eds), 377–99.

TASMOWSKI-DE RYCK, L. (1994). 'Câteva observații privind folosirea articolului definit și a articolului adjectival', *Limbă și literatură* II: 14–19.

TASMOWSKI-DE RYCK, L. (2000). *Trăsături neașteptate ale limbii române*. Bucharest: Editura Academiei Române.

TĂNASE-DOGARU, M. (2009). *The Category of Number: Its Relevance for the Syntax and Semantic Typology of the Nominal Phrase*. Bucharest: Editura Universității din București.

TDRG. (1903, 1911, 1924). TIKTIN, H. *Rumänisch-deutsches Wörterbuch*. Bucharest: Staatsdrückerei.

TDRG³ (2000, 2003, 2005) P. Miron and E. Lüder (eds), Cluj Napoca: Clusium.

THEODORESCU, M. (1978a). 'Imperfectul indicativului, Perfectul indicativului, Mai-mult-ca-perfectul indicativului', in F. Dimitrescu (ed.), 302–13.

THEODORESCU, M. (1978b). 'Condiționalul', in F. Dimitrescu (ed.), 320–2.

THIEROFF, R. (2010). 'Moods, Moods, Moods', in B. Rothstein and R. Thieroff (eds), 1–29.

THOM, F. (1987). *La Langue de bois*. Paris: Julliard.

TICIO, M. E. (2010). *Locality Domains in the Spanish Determiner Phrase*. Dordrecht: Springer.

TIGĂU, A. M. (2011). *Syntax & Semantics of the Direct Object in Romance and Germanic Languages*. Bucharest: Editura Universității din București.

TIMOTIN, E. (2000a). 'Pasivul românesc în textele originale din secolul al XVI-lea', *Studii și cercetări lingvistice* 51: 225–31.

TIMOTIN, E. (2000b). 'Modalități de exprimare a pasivului în dialectele românești sud-dunărene', *Studii și cercetări lingvistice* 51: 481–90.

TODI, A. (2001). *Elemente de sintaxă românească veche*. Pitești: Editura Paralela 45.

TODORAN, R. (1982). 'Participiile scurte (*văst, vint* etc.)', *Contribuții lingvistice* 22: 60–8.

TOMA, E. (1978). 'Adverbul', in F. Dimitrescu (ed.), 338–48.

TOMESCU, D. (1998). *Gramatica numelor proprii în limba română*. Bucharest: All Educational.

TRUSWELL, R. (2004). 'Non-Restrictive Adjective Interpretation and Association with Focus', in R. Ashdowne, and T. Finbow (eds), *Oxford University Working Papers in Linguistics, Philology and Phonetics* 9: 133–54.

URICARU, L. (2003). *Temporalitate și limbaj*. Bucharest: Allfa.

URITESCU, D. (2007). 'Dans la perspective de l'Atlas de Crișana (I). Le participe passé daco-roumain en -*ă*: mythe roumain ou innovation d'une langue romane?', in S. Reinheimer Rîpeanu, and I. Vintilă-Rădulescu (eds), 555–66.

VAN DE VELDE, D. (1996). 'La Détermination des noms abstraits', in N. Flaux, M. Glatigny, and D. Samain (eds), 275–87.

VAN LANGENDONCK, W., and VAN BELLE, W. (eds) (1998). *The Dative*. Amsterdam / New York: John Benjamins.

VAN PETEGHEM, M. (1991). *Les Phrases copulatives dans les langues romanes*. Wilhelmsfeld: Gottfried Egert.

VAN PETEGHEM, M. (1994a). '*Alt(ul)* vs. *un alt(ul)*: un calc servil sau o nouă distincție semantică?', *Limba română* (Chișinău) 5–6: 121–8.

VAN PETEGHEM, M. (1994b). 'Altul vs. celălalt: la limita între referința hotărâtă și nehotărâtă', *Limbă și literatură* II: 20–8.

VAN PETEGHEM, M. (2007). 'Sur un cas particulier de la possession inaliénable en roumain: la construction *mă doare capul*', in A. Cuniță, C. Lupu, and L. Tasmowski (eds), *Studii de lingvistică și filologie romanică: hommages offerts à Sanda Reinheimer Rîpeanu*. Bucharest: Editura Universității din București: 572–82.

VAN PETEGHEM, M. (2009). 'Sur le subordonnant comparatif dans les langues romanes', *Langages* 174, 2: 99–112.

VAN RIEMSDIJK, H. (1990). 'Functional Prepositions', in H. Pinkster, and I. Genée (eds), *Unity in Diversity*. Dordrecht: Foris, 229–41.

VAN RIEMSDIJK, H. (ed.) (1999). *Clitics in the Languages of Europe*. Berlin / New York: Mouton de Gruyter.

VAN RIEMSDIJK, H. (2006). 'Free Relatives', in M. Everaert, H. van Riemsdijk, R. Goedemans, and B. Hollebrandse (eds), *The Blackwell Companion to Syntax*. II. Oxford: Blackwell Publishing Ltd, 338–82.

VASILEANU, M. (2009). 'Locuțiunile pronominale alocutive. Utilizarea în limba română actuală', in G. Pană Dindelegan (ed.), 195–204.

VASILESCU, A. (2007a). 'Reciprocul', in C. Stan, R. Zafiu, and A. Nicolae (eds), 221–7.

VASILESCU, A. (2007b). 'Sistemul pronominal românesc', in G. Pană Dindelegan (ed.), *Limba română. Stadiul actual al cercetării*. Bucharest: Editura Universității din București, 213–25.

VASILESCU, A. (2008a). 'Pronumele', in GALR I, 181–288.

VASILESCU, A. (2008b). 'Tipuri de enunțuri în funcție de scopul comunicării', in GALR II, 31–44.

VASILESCU, A. (2008c). 'Dialogul', in GALR II, 819–58.

VASILESCU, A. (2009a) '*Cel*: categorie semilexicală', in R. Zafiu, B. Croitor, and A.-M. Mihail (eds), 265–87.

VASILESCU, A. (2009b). 'Strategii pragmatice de reluare, gramaticalizate ca relații apozitive de tip GN1–GN2', *Limba română* 58: 275–84.

VASILESCU, A. (2009c). 'Elemente de dinamică discursivă a pronumelui', in G. Pană Dindelegan (ed.). 115–62.

VASILESCU, A. (2010). '*Iar*—operator pragmatic', in R. Zafiu, A. Dragomirescu, and A. Nicolae (eds), 341–55.

VASILIU, E., and IONESCU-RUXĂNDOIU, L. (1986). *Limba română în secolele al XII-lea–al XV-lea (fonetică—fonologie—gramatică)*. Bucharest: Tipografia Universității București.

VASILIU, L. (1965). 'Acordul în caz al atributului adjectival în limba secolelor al XVI-lea, al XVIII-lea', in *Omagiu lui Alexandru Rosetti la 70 de ani*. Bucharest: Editura Academiei Române, 979–83.

VASILIU, L. (2007). 'Corespondența timpurilor', in M. Avram (ed.), 298–316.

VENDLER, Z. (1967). 'Verbs and Times', *The Philosophical Review* 66, 2: 143–60.

VIȘAN, R. (2002). 'Observații asupra sintaxei exclamativelor cu *ce, ce de, cât* și *cum* în română', in G. Pană Dindelegan (ed.), *Perspective actuale în studiul limbii române*. Bucharest: Editura Universității din București, 415–25.

VIȘAN, R. (2004). 'Aspecte ale sintaxei construcțiilor afective N *de* N în română. Observații asupra acordului', in G. Pană Dindelegan (ed.), 675–82.

VULPE, M. (1980). *Subordonarea în frază în dacoromâna vorbită*. Bucharest: Editura Științifică și Enciclopedică.

VULPE, M. (1987). 'Sur une particularité régionale dans l'emploi des indéfinis', *Revue roumaine de linguistique* 32: 303–7.

VULPE, M. (1993). 'Sur le dialogue reproduit dans la narration orale', in H. Löffler (ed.), *Dialoganalyse* IV, I. Tübingen: Niemeyer, 265–73.

VULPE, M. (2006 [1963]). 'Repartiția geografică a construcțiilor cu infinitivul și cu conjunctivul în limba română', *Opera lingvistică*. II. Cluj-Napoca: Editura Clusium, 193–226.

WADE, T. (2011). *A Comprehensive Russian Grammar*. Oxford: Blackwell.

WALS. H, M., DRYER, M. S., GIL, D., and COMRIE, B. (eds) (2005). *The World Atlas of Language Structures*. Oxford: Oxford University Press.

WEINRICH, H. (1964). *Tempus: Besprochene und erzählte Welt*. Stuttgart: Kohlhammer.

WHEELER, M., YATES, A., and DOLS, N. (1999). *Catalan: A Comprehensive Grammar*. London: Routledge.
WILMET, M. (2003). *Grammaire critique du français*. Bruxelles: Duculot.
WINKLER, S. (2005). *Ellipsis and Focus in Generative Grammar*. Berlin: Mouton de Gruyter.
ZAFIU, R. (2002). 'Evidenţialitatea în limba română actuală', in G. Pană Dindelegan (ed.), 127–44.
ZAFIU, R. (2004). 'Observaţii asupra anaforei în limba română actuală', in G. Pană Dindelegan (ed.), 239–52.
ZAFIU, R. (2005). 'Conjuncţiile adversative din limba română: tipologie şi niveluri de incidenţă', in G. Pană Dindelegan (ed.), 243–58.
ZAFIU, R. (2006). 'Observaţii asupra originii şi a evoluţiei adverbului modal *poate*', in M. Sala (ed.), *Studii de gramatică şi de formare a cuvintelor*. Bucharest: Editura Academiei Române: 478–90.
ZAFIU, R. (2008a). 'Gerunziul', in GALR I, 525–43.
ZAFIU, R. (2008b). 'Afirmaţia', in GALR II, 671–79.
ZAFIU, R. (2008c). 'Negaţia', in GALR II, 680–702.
ZAFIU, R. (2008d). 'Modalizarea', in GALR II, 702–26.
ZAFIU, R. (2009). 'Interpretări gramaticale ale prezumtivului', in R. Zafiu, B. Croitor, and A.-M. Mihail (eds), 289–305.
ZAFIU, R. (2010). 'L'Évolution des connecteurs adversatifs du roumain en perspective romane', in M. Iliescu, H. Siller-Runggaldier, and P. Danler (eds), 603–12.
ZAFIU, R., CROITOR, B., and MIHAIL, A.-M. (eds) (2009). *Studii de gramatică. Omagiu doamnei profesoare Valeria Guţu Romalo*. Bucharest: Editura Universităţii din Bucureşti.
ZAFIU, R., DRAGOMIRESCU, A., and NICOLAE, A. (eds) (2010). *Limba română: controverse, delimitări, noi ipoteze*. Bucharest: Editura Universităţii din Bucureşti.
ZAFIU, R., DRAGOMIRESCU, A., and NICOLAE, A. (eds) (2012). *Limba română: Direcţii actuale în cercetarea lingvistică*. I Bucharest: Editura Universităţii din Bucureşti.
ZAFIU, R., STOICA, G., and CONSTANTINESCU, M. (eds) (2009). *Limba română: teme actuale*. Bucharest: Editura Universităţii din Bucureşti.
ZAFIU, R., UŞURELU, C., and BOGDAN OPREA, H. (eds) (2011). *Limba română: ipostaze ale variaţiei lingvistice*. Bucharest, Editura Universităţii din Bucureşti.
ZAMFIR, D.-M. (2005, 2007). *Morfologia verbului în dacoromâna veche (secolele al XVI-lea–al XVII-lea)*. I, II. Bucharest: Editura Academiei Române.
ZANUTTINI, R. (1997). *Negation and Clausal Structure: A Comparative Study of Romance Languages*. Oxford: Oxford University Press.
ZWICKY, A. M., and PULLUM, G. K. (1983). 'Cliticization vs. Inflection: *English N'T*', *Language* 59, 3: 502–13.

Index

adjacency (constraint) 142, 158, 213, 214, 266, 267, 297, 298, 299, 300, 306, 311, 312, 325, 338, 339, 342, 346, 373, 376, 384, 388, 389, 390, 391, 392, 406, 471, 510, 541
adjective, adjectival phrase 160, 161, 164, 167, 231, 241, 245, 356, 360, 361, 410–31, 436, 450, 534–5, 573, 589
   inflectional classes 411–4
   invariable 291, 412, 413, 617
   participial (see participle, adjectival)
   semantic classes 417–20
      qualifying 417, 428, 429, 431, 378
      relative 312, 316, 417, 418–9, 427, 431
      reference-modifying 417, 419–20, 427, 428, 590
   transitive 424
adjunct
   additive negative 430, 474, 475, 477
   additive positive 248, 430, 474, 475
   aspectual 206
   comitative 114, 515
   concessive 31, 50, 52, 54, 248, 475, 480–1
   conditional 50, 430, 475, 480–1, 547, 550
   connective 474, 482–3
   directional 135
   instrument 248, 425, 474
   locative 206, 241, 425, 474
   manner 248, 425, 474, 475
   purpose 213, 241, 425, 474, 476, 479–80
   quantity 262, 331, 444, 475
   reason 228, 248, 425, 430, 474, 479
   restrictive 241, 242
   result 242, 425, 444, 476, 477, 481
   speech act-related 481
   substractive 430, 474, 475
   temporal 228, 242, 248, 262, 425, 475, 478–9, 206
address 590–6
   reversed form 594–5, 598
adverb, adverbial phrase 143, 239, 432–50, 570
   adverbial formative 439
   adverbial noun 437
   focusing 333, 446–7, 477–8, 568, 574, 575
   formal classification
      compound 432, 434–6
      simple 432, 435
      suffixed 432–4
   pro-forms / substitute 163, 168, 435
   semantic classes 440–442
      concession 441
      condition 441
      indefinite 52, 436
      manner 440, 448–9
      modal 163, 164, 197, 440, 445, 581–2, 583
      neutral affirmation and negation 441, 564, 565
      quantifying 440
      setting (temporal, locative) 440–1, 449
adverbialization 232, 233
agglutination 612, 618
agreement 26, 100, 101, 104, 107, 118, 126, 160, 169, 181, 191, 192, 197–200, 203, 207, 222, 226, 227, 228, 229, 231, 240, 247, 253, 256, 258, 260, 261, 266, 293, 296, 297, 310, 311, 315, 318, 322, 324, 330, 331, 335, 336, 339, 341, 343, 360, 369, 370, 374, 375, 376, 378, 394, 403, 404, 410, 411, 439, 498, 526–36, 581, 594
   adjectival 534–5
   anaphoric 535–6
   by attraction 527
   DP-internal 526–8
   grammatical / formal 528, 533, 536
   lexical 81
   referential 529
   semantic 526, 528, 539
   subject–predicate 282, 528–32, 579
   with coordinated DPs 532–5
alphabet
   Cyrillic 5
   Latin 5, 14
   transitional 5
anacoluthon 118
analogy, analogical form 26, 27, 30, 32, 34, 35, 37, 224, 263, 309, 310, 320, 380, 402, 405, 618
anaphora, anaphorics 84, 105, 107, 112, 113, 117, 138, 139, 180, 181, 292, 299, 300, 355, 376, 380, 396, 403, 404, 407, 430, 488, 489, 495, 496, 514, 523, 526, 537, 573, 574, 584–90, 597
   discourse 585, 586–7
   referential 587–8
   semantic 588–9
   syntactic 585–6
   zero anaphora 584, 586, 587, 589
apodosis 52, 480
apposition 366–9, 370, 378, 384, 395, 426, 429, 485, 590
   chained 368
   classifying 368
   identifying 368
   multiple 368
   of equivalence 368
   qualifying 368
   simple 368
   summarizing 368

Aromanian / Macedo-Romanian 1, 4, 8, 35, 113, 138, 142, 190, 211, 212, 222, 224, 233, 243, 273, 292, 319, 320, 322, 343, 433, 435, 440, 442, 484
article
　article-like ending 280, 290, 323, 344, 382, 443, 463–5
　definite article deletion 128, 158, 285–91, 459–60
　definite enclitic article 234, 255, 258, 263, 264, 266, 267, 274, 277, 280–1, 298, 300, 304, 318, 319, 323, 324, 330, 335, 348, 349, 359, 373, 376, 377, 380, 410, 413, 416, 431, 437, 459, 460, 590
　indefinite proclitic article 186, 263, 280–1, 291–4, 304, 305, 328, 376
　partitive 285, 293
aspect
　aspectual periphrases 64–5, 208
　aspectual verbs 191, 196–7, 200, 221, 237, 238, 516
　inchoative 55
　perfective vs. imperfective 55
　prospective 55
　punctual vs. durative (continuous) 55
　resultative 55
　tense-aspect system 55, 98
　terminative 55
augmentative 414, 602–3
auxiliary 37, 38, 39, 40, 41, 42, 191–4, 546, 550
　auxiliary dislocation 193
　auxiliary inversion 38, 40, 42, 212
　auxiliary selection 74, 97, 229
　phonological reduction 37, 38, 39, 40
　semi-auxiliary 81

Balkan Sprachbund / Balkan linguistic union 1, 7, 8, 30, 40, 41, 45, 47, 61, 68, 138, 142, 151, 163, 190, 194, 200, 203, 221, 222, 257, 262, 263, 273, 286, 294, 310, 343, 344, 375, 377, 381, 398, 435, 440, 467, 469, 475, 479, 480, 484, 487, 511, 562, 568, 572

case 255, 261–73, 291, 295, 315
　analytical case marking (functional prepositions A, LA; proclitic morpheme LUI; AL) 153, 163, 262, 264, 265–71, 279, 312, 339, 375, 454, 455, 456
　accusative 68, 70, 71, 81, 88, 89, 91, 99, 107, 114, 120, 129, 152, 158, 261–2, 290, 322, 341, 351, 380, 381, 383, 385, 387, 388, 392, 399, 400, 455, 458, 459, 485, 505, 507, 569, 615
　　accusative diagnostic 261
　　neuter accusative 162, 398, 408, 588
　　possessive accusative 190, 283
　dative 67, 68, 88, 89, 99, 107, 120, 149, 152, 158, 162, 185, 187, 189–90, 262–72, 290, 350, 351, 354, 380, 381, 383, 385, 387, 388, 392, 399, 400, 422–3, 443–4, 455, 459, 485, 569
　　ethic dative 152, 397, 408
　　locative dative 151
　　neuter dative 152, 398, 408
　　possessive dative 67, 134, 147, 151, 175, 176, 182, 183–9, 190, 282

genitive 158, 162, 179, 187, 188, 234, 262–72, 280, 282, 285, 290, 312, 317, 335, 340, 349, 347, 352, 354, 355, 357, 366, 370, 372, 381, 423–4, 456, 459, 535–6, 614
nominative 100, 101, 160, 379, 261–2, 290, 380, 381, 485, 615
　possessive nominative 283
synthetic case marking 262–5, 375
strong case marking 154
unmarked case form 68, 71, 98, 145, 262, 263, 272, 322, 459
vocative 272–3, 341, 375, 414, 547, 590–6, 598
causative
　alternation 76, 96, 98
　construction 48
　verb 69–70, 92, 93, 96, 141, 164, 201, 178, 429
cleft 539
　pseudo-cleft 144, 488–9, 512, 532, 539, 574
　inverted 532
classifier 369–70
clitic 39
　adverbial 31, 38, 42, 159, 192, 195, 207, 213, 223, 234, 246, 447–8, 450, 560
　adnominal possessive clitic 335, 343–7, 349, 377
　clitic climbing 115, 183, 191–4, 195, 196, 199, 203, 219, 220, 238, 387, 577, 580
　clitic clusters 392–4
　clitic deletion 388
　clitic doubling 67, 68, 113, 126, 127, 129, 134, 136–9, 140, 144, 151, 153, 154–6, 157, 161, 166, 174, 202, 233, 270, 279, 338 342, 346, 376, 394–5, 408, 542, 571, 585
　clitic resumption 139, 571, 572
　clitic reduplication 387
　mesoclitics 391, 392
　pronominal 20, 31, 36, 37, 42, 88–9, 91, 99, 107, 112, 120, 126, 127, 129, 142, 145, 157, 162, 174, 191, 193, 213, 217, 218, 222, 233, 246, 247, 261, 311, 381–92, 443–4, 560, 569, 584
　　bound 382, 388, 391, 399, 443
　　dative/genitive 385, 389
　　doubly realized 201
　　free 382, 388, 399, 443
　　locative 381
　　nominative 104, 381
　　partitive 135, 381
　　reflexive 77, 94, 152, 174, 175, 176, 178, 179, 180, 181, 345, 399, 400, 577, 585
　with neutral value 138
cognate object 74, 76, 98
collocation / frozen phrase / idiomatic structure 128, 175, 200, 221, 284, 294, 328, 432, 434, 438, 439, 441, 443, 454, 471, 550, 563
comparative construction 131, 162, 360, 364, 366, 503–13
　comparative complement 425, 444, 461, 504–6, 508–9
　comparative marker / comparator 504–8, 513

Index 651

derived-case comparative 506, 507, 513
   proportional structure 510
   reduced comparative clause 504–5
complement
   obligatory adverbial complement 444
   of an adjective 49, 361, 422–5
      clausal 425
      dative / indirect 422–3
      direct object 424
      genitive 423–4
      prepositional 241, 424
   of an adverb 442–4
      dative / indirect 443–4
      prepositional 442–3
   of a noun 244, 349–55
   of a preposition 347–8, 357, 359, 446, 458, 462
complement / argument clause 466–73, 556
   headless 466
complementizer 30, 43, 44, 51, 84, 85, 116–7, 123, 124, 139, 141, 143, 145, 158, 163, 165, 174, 202, 213, 214–5, 351, 358, 367, 445, 463, 466–73, 475, 511, 546, 555, 557, 563, 567, 569, 578, 580, 581
   complementizer deletion 466, 511, 544
   complementizer-trace effect 544
   complex complementizer 470, 569
   multifunctional complementizer 472, 512
complex predicate 115, 118, 191–201, 203, 207, 208, 211, 238, 387, 560–1, 577, 579
compounding 434, 606, 612–20
   compound lexemes 278, 300, 454, 612, 613, 618–9
   neo-classical compounds 619, 620
   sentence-like compounds 616
   syntactic compound 612
concord (see agreement)
conditional 24, 46, 575
   perfect 24, 42, 191, 480, 512
   present 24, 41–2
      present conditional periphrasis 41
      synthetic conditional 41
   values and uses 50–3, 387
conjunction
   coordinating (see coordination)
   multifunctional 475, 506, 512, 513
   subordinating 30, 253, 365, 472, 473–83, 505, 516
consonants 9–11
   new consonants 10
construct state 341
control 101–4, 105, 124, 180, 191, 216, 222, 237, 238, 239, 580
   obligatory control 47, 48, 50, 191–5, 200–1, 203, 584
   non-obligatory control 47, 48, 50
   second-position / Wackernagel clitic 343, 344, 377
conversion 615
coordination 180, 195, 197, 249, 267, 293, 343, 514–25, 532–5, 543–4, 547, 549, 567, 584, 586
   adversative 514, 517–8, 522
   asymmetry 523, 525
   conjunctive 514–6, 521, 532, 542
   conclusive 514, 520–1, 522
   disjunctive 334, 514, 517, 521, 533
   end-attachment coordination 525
   pseudo-coordination 516

Danubian Latin 1, 2, 8, 224, 319, 320
degree markers (see intensity)
deixis, deictics 201, 294, 310, 348, 380, 396, 397, 398, 402, 403, 408, 557–8, 588
demonstrative 111, 125, 130, 132, 134, 138, 145, 167, 265, 271, 286, 294–300, 301, 306, 307, 308, 309, 310, 311, 312, 314, 318, 338, 342, 345, 373, 374, 376, 377, 379, 380, 394, 405, 437, 493, 494, 526, 555, 570, 584, 586, 587, 588, 589, 591
   demonstrative resumption 572
   long form 295, 296, 298, 311, 373
   short form 295, 296, 311
dependent-marking 67, 189, 202
derivational morphology 433, 599–606, 611, 619
   back-formation 599, 605–6
   parasynthetic 599, 605
   suffixation 599–604, 606
   prefixation 599, 604–5, 606
determiner 186, 227, 234, 258, 265, 285–319, 371, 437 (*see also* demonstrative)
   alternative determiners 300–6, 372, 376
   freestanding CEL 280, 309–18, 319, 324, 326, 372, 376
   identity determiners 306–9, 372, 376
dicendi / saying verbs 66, 71, 106, 121, 148, 154, 367, 436, 450, 471, 551, 553
dialectal separation 4, 8, 135, 212
Differential Object Marking 130, 202
diminutive 12, 414, 434, 602, 603, 604, 606
diphthong 11–2, 384, 388
diphthongization 12, 389, 390
direct object 66, 68, 69, 70, 72, 98, 125–44, 166, 170, 174, 202, 205, 214, 223, 244, 358, 394, 395, 485, 569, 571, 574–5
   doubling 136–9 (*see also* clitic doubling)
   direct object marker 126, 128–35, 137, 202, 279, 454, 455, 505, 571
double definite / polydefinite structure 291, 297, 306, 309, 318–9, 345, 377

ellipsis 131, 180, 198, 239, 300, 301, 302, 303, 304, 339, 384, 480, 503, 505, 506, 518, 521, 525, 544, 545, 549, 550, 564, 576, 579, 581, 589, 617
   gapping 518, 519, 525
   nominal ellipsis 227, 299, 305, 306, 311, 316, 317, 335, 339, 370–4, 430–1
   sluicing 525
   VP-ellipsis 372
exclamative clause / sentence 548–50, 566–7, 596
expletive 106–8, 109, 138, 139, 173, 201, 203, 396, 398, 408

factitive (see causative)
focus, focalization 91, 92, 117, 124, 148, 152, 286, 299, 318, 356, 374, 378, 446–7, 458, 538, 539, 540, 543, 547, 568, 574–5, 596, 597
  contrastive 122, 123, 374, 568, 574, 597

gender 273, 291, 295, 336, 345, 375
  feminine 255, 275–6
  gender-changing suffix 258
  masculine 255, 274
  neuter 255, 256–8, 276–7, 287, 375
    inflectional ending -*uri* 257, 261, 276
generic reading / sentence 31, 56, 108, 109, 112, 126, 131, 134, 144, 172, 201, 239, 269, 270, 290, 355, 397, 491
gerund / present participle 18, 85, 99, 115, 125, 140, 141, 142, 149, 160, 165, 167, 180, 201, 206, 207, 209, 210, 233, 245–53, 364, 437, 503
  accusative with gerund 99, 250, 254
  adjectival 246–7, 311
  in periphrastic forms 40, 42, 47, 53, 65, 208, 247–8
  inflectional marking 245
  negative 246, 448, 559
  subject of gerund 103, 124, 247, 249
  verbal 246–7
grammaticalization 24, 30, 31, 37, 38, 39, 40, 41, 55, 59, 129, 135, 157, 191, 193, 195, 196, 200, 201, 203, 252, 257, 265, 268, 269, 286, 293, 310, 311, 315, 321, 327, 375, 394, 415, 416, 474, 493, 496, 504, 507, 520, 577, 580, 589

head-marking 67, 127, 202
host 183, 185, 186, 188, 190, 193, 203, 311, 344, 381, 383, 384, 387, 388, 464
  phonological 382, 393
  syntactic 382
hyponymy 612

imperative (mood) 20, 21, 23, 24, 35–37, 546, 547, 555, 556, 575
  unpredictable forms 37
  values and uses 54–5
imperative clause / sentence 206, 214–5, 217, 243, 245, 546–7
impersonal construction 82, 102–3, 106–7, 163, 164, 173–4, 203, 228, 239, 240, 242, 244, 245, 576, 579, 581
  impersonal-reflexive 100, 108, 109, 111, 115, 179, 577
  impersonal-passive (see pasive)
  impersonalization 173, 174, 203
inclussive word 528–9
indicative 24
  absolute / deictic tenses 55
  compound / analytic past 24, 37–8, 191, 229
    aspectual values 59–60
    temporal values 57–8

epistemic future (see presumptive)
future 24, 38–40, 191, 546, 575, 580
  colloquial future 38
  future perfect 24, 40, 41
    future perfect periphrasis 40
    temporal values 62
  future in the past 24, 40
    aspectual values 62
    temporal values 62
  invariable particle o 40
  modal values 63
  regional future 38
  standard future 38
  temporal values 62
  imperfect 24, 32–3, 480, 512
    aspectual values 60–1
    imperfect periphrasis 32
    modal values 61, 575
    temporal values 60
  pluperfect 24, 34–5
    aspectual values 62
    pluperfect periphrasis 35
    temporal values 61–2
  present indicative 18, 21, 25–9, 546, 556–7
    aspectual values 57
    modal values 57
    temporal values 55–7
  relative / anaphoric tenses 55
  simple past 21, 33–4
    aspectual values 59–60
    temporal values 58–9
  values and uses 43–5
indirect object 66, 148–57, 161, 166, 205, 394, 395, 473, 569, 571, 575
  doubling 154–6 (*see also* clitic doubling)
  obligatory 148
  optional 148
infectum 25
infinitive, infinitival clause 20, 24, 48, 115, 119, 125, 140, 149, 158, 160, 164, 180, 194–5, 200, 201, 206, 209, 211–22, 233, 242, 243, 250, 357, 358, 546, 565, 579, 581
  accusative with infinitive 85, 99, 142, 250
  in periphrastic forms 20, 37, 39, 41, 42, 191, 208, 212
  infinitival marker 115, 125, 158, 211, 212–5, 238, 252, 378
  infinitive suffix 18, 211, 212
  long / nominalized infinitive 24, 212, 214, 215–6, 233, 253, 283, 351, 356
  perfect infinitive 206, 220, 253
  personal / inflected 102
  short / verbal infinitive 212, 214, 215–6, 233, 253, 487, 576, 577, 578
  subject of infinitive 102, 124, 218
  subjunctive–infinitive competition 47, 164, 191, 203, 211, 220, 221–2

with imperative value 214–5, 217
inflection 611, 620
   internal 407, 616
   loss of inflection 271, 272, 297, 359, 490, 526, 527
intensifier
   modal 540
   negative 540, 566
intensity 186, 232, 314, 315, 339, 344, 366, 410, 415–7, 439, 510, 615
   absolute superlative 415, 416, 436
   comparative of superiority 415
   comparative of inferiority 415
   comparative of equality 415
   relative superlative of inferiority 415, 416
   relative superlative of superiority 415, 416
interjection 546, 547, 550, 584, 592, 596
internal argument 65, 72
interrogative clause / sentence 46, 47, 539–46
   alternative interrogative 117, 539, 544–5, 556
   echo questions 539, 545–6, 596
   direct 569
      partial 556
   indirect interrogative / question 165, 351, 471, 486–7, 488, 491, 495, 512, 569
   multiple question 542, 543
   polar interrogative 539–40
   rhetorical question 566
   tag questions 539, 545, 596
   wh-interrogative 539, 540–4, 568–9
intonation 51, 54, 537, 538, 539, 540, 541, 545, 546, 547, 548, 549, 551, 553, 555, 557, 571, 574, 590, 592, 596, 597
intransitive verbs 72–82, 174
   copula 70, 71, 78–82, 98–9, 108, 114, 161, 162, 228, 232, 236, 239, 267, 348, 445, 500, 532, 533, 583
      aspectual and modal values 79–80, 161
   Experiencer 72, 82–95, 99
      psych verbs 73, 92–5, 110, 142, 173, 178
      verbs of perception 82–8, 115, 140, 151, 189, 203, 249, 250, 251, 254, 471
      verbs of physical sensation 88–91, 111, 142
   impersonal 72, 104, 106–7, 114, 115, 116, 117, 142, 178, 197, 199, 228, 577, 580, 581
   unaccusative vs unergative 70–8, 96, 97, 98, 99, 100, 108, 111, 164, 173, 178, 230, 240, 283
      syntactic diagnostics 73, 97, 98, 201, 230
   with symmetric arguments 72, 73, 151, 176
island
   adjunct island 543–4
   complex NP constraint 543–4
   coordinate structure constraint 543–4
   island constraint 543–4, 596
   wh-island 543–4
Istro-Romanian 1, 4, 8, 41, 222, 292, 433, 436

juxtaposition 334, 523, 615, 617

Megleno-Romanian 1, 4, 8, 35, 211, 212, 222, 233, 273, 292, 433, 440
mixed category 206, 208, 209, 222, 231, 232, 233, 237, 253, 254, 335
modality 40, 575–84
   deontic 116, 445, 561, 575, 576, 577, 578, 580, 582, 583
   dynamic 561, 575, 576, 577, 578, 580, 581
   epistemic 41, 98, 116, 130, 445, 566, 575, 576, 577, 578, 579, 580, 581, 582, 583, 584, 597
   evaluation 445
   evidential 42, 438, 471, 578, 580, 581, 582, 584
   necessity 39, 578
   obligation 575, 578, 582
   permission 576, 582
   possibility 576, 583
   volitional 575
modal verbs 52, 115, 140, 191, 194–7, 208, 221, 228, 237, 575–81
modal existential construction (see relative infinitival)
modifier
   of an adjective 420–2
   of an adverb 442
   of a noun 227, 236, 246, 249, 258 263, 280, 282, 283, 284, 289, 291, 312, 426–8
      restrictive 355–60, 427, 437
      non-restrictive 360–5, 427, 437, 446
   of a preposition 458
monophtongization / monophtongation 212, 609
mood 575
mood selection 467–8, 476, 480–1, 512, 567
morphophonological alternation 11, 12, 18, 26, 28, 29, 98, 258, 262, 271, 274, 275, 276, 279, 338, 375, 410, 411, 431, 607–11
motion verbs 48, 95–7, 151, 203, 213, 434, 436, 450

n-word 558, 562, 563, 564, 597
negation 39, 42, 558–67, 597
   covert 565
   double 558, 561, 562, 565
   false negation
      double 565–6
      expletive 51, 566–7
   simple 558, 562
      constituent 558, 567
      sentential 558–61, 567
   multiple negation 562–4
   negative marker 31, 39, 42, 191, 196, 199, 213, 217, 223, 234, 238, 246, 558, 559, 560, 561, 562, 566, 567, 597
   prefixal negative marker 207, 559, 560, 566
negative concord 562–4, 597
nominalization 212, 216, 283, 284, 328, 340, 352, 364, 372, 601
nominativus pendens 118
noun, noun phrase 255–378
   abstract 128, 211, 215, 260, 329, 533, 536

noun, noun phrase (*cont.*)
  bare noun 111–2, 127, 128, 161, 167, 281, 285, 293–4, 344, 347, 376, 532, 533, 536, 571
  collective 282, 329, 376, 528, 530, 602, 606
  common 273, 278, 286, 528
  compound nouns 278
  countable vs uncountable 258–61, 280, 281, 293
  deadjectival 283–4, 349–352
  deverbal 283–4, 349–52, 457
  inflectional classes 273–7
  invariable 260, 264
  irregular inflection 277–8
  mass 128, 260, 261, 276, 280–1, 293, 329, 376, 533, 536
  measure DP 530–1
  picture noun 284–5, 352–3, 376
  proper name 167, 271, 272, 279–80, 286, 289, 290, 312, 313, 319, 369–70, 376, 528
  qualitative DP 531–2
  relational 282–3, 349, 353–5
  semantic-grammatical classes 278–85
non-finite clause 115–6, 140, 163, 164, 204–54, 358, 364, 473
  lexical subject of non-finite forms 101–104, 124, 204, 253
number 255, 279, 291, 295
  plural 111, 128, 258, 259, 270, 397, 461–2
  pluralia tantum 260, 261
  singular 258
  singularia tantum 260
numeral 270, 319–28, 527
  cardinal 269, 292, 302, 303, 319–23, 377
  ordinal 319, 323–5
numerical expression 377
  adverbial 319
  collective 319, 325–7
  distributive 319, 325
  fractional 319, 327
  multiplicative 319, 327

objective predicative complement 135, 159, 166–9, 202, 262, 428, 429, 498
obviation 48
orthography 5, 7, 9, 11, 12, 14–6, 17, 20, 27, 28, 32, 287, 288, 289, 321, 330, 451, 607, 612, 613

participle 21, 116, 125, 149, 160, 201, 206, 207, 209, 210, 222–33, 284, 355, 358, 364, 436, 438
  active 164
  adjectival 164, 223, 232, 311, 411, 448, 526
  adjectivization 73, 97, 98, 104, 230
  in periphrastic forms 37, 40, 42, 126, 191, 192, 194, 207, 220, 223, 226
  negative 559
  subject of participle 104, 124
  suffixal marker 33, 222, 224, 225

partitive 113, 135–6, 162, 281, 285, 305, 331, 333, 456, 529–30, 587 (*see also* article, partitive; clitic, partitive; quantifier, partitive; preposition, partitive)
pseudopartitive 281, 331, 456
passive 76, 100, 129, 144, 164, 169–73, 222, 240, 241, 579
  be-passive 87, 169–73, 203, 206, 207, 219, 226–7
  by-phrase 88, 103, 170–1, 206, 284, 352
  impersonal-passive 108–9, 119–20, 170, 172, 227
  passivization 91, 145, 147, 159, 166, 169, 173, 174, 196, 198, 202
  se-passive / reflexive-passive 87, 115, 130, 169–73, 179, 203, 219, 249, 577
perfectum 25, 33, 34, 223
phonological change / evolution 27, 40, 259
phonological system 7–11
pied-piping 496, 543, 596
possession 95, 176, 183, 282, 284, 335–349
  alienable 184
  inalienable 88–9, 121, 183, 184, 188, 190, 349, 355
possessive adjective 125, 163, 183, 188, 189, 282, 285, 312, 335–40, 346, 349, 353, 354, 374, 381, 535
possessive affix 263, 264, 271, 335, 341–3, 354
possessive object 89, 179, 189–90
possesse-subject language 335, 377
possessor deletion 348
possessor-subject language 335
post-consonantal glide [ʲ] 8
predicate inversion 365–6, 456
predicative position 163, 165, 188, 305, 338, 339, 354, 415, 417, 418, 420, 429, 485, 533, 535, 589
prefix 521, 558
preposition, prepositional phrase 157, 158, 159, 170–1, 207, 234, 238, 240, 269, 270, 294, 334, 344, 350, 354, 356, 360, 363, 425, 451–65, 505
  collocated 451–2
  comparative preposition 87
  compound 451–2
  coordinated 521–2
  functional 254, 268, 279, 335, 376, 454–7
  lexical 213, 214, 241, 254, 346–7, 452–4
  of quality 71, 142, 162, 167, 168, 249, 461
  partitive 113, 135
  simple 451–2
  subcategorized / selected 209, 254, 457–8
preposition stranding 159, 202, 496, 596
prepositional object 69, 157–9, 237, 244, 569
presumptive 24, 42
  perfect 24, 41
  present / epistemic future 24, 40–1
  values and uses 53–4
pro-drop 101, 104–11, 125, 201, 528, 538, 586, 596
productivity 20, 21, 98, 256, 620
pronominalization 370–4
pronoun 52, 379–409

emphatic 379
    intensifier / emphatic pronoun 177, 356, 379, 396, 400, 404–6, 409, 526
    personal 337, 379–398, 312, 408, 586
    politeness 379, 401–4, 409, 529
    possessive 526
    reciprocal 179, 180, 182, 307, 407–8, 409
    reflexive 379, 340, 399–401, 409 (*see also* clitic, reflexive)
        reflexive particle 338
pronunciation 16
protasis 50, 52
punctuation 17, 157
purpose value 49, 50, 214, 357

quantifier 258, 269, 281, 289, 293, 303, 319–335, 371, 372, 376, 437
    adverbial 332, 440
    indefinite 280, 328–9, 373, 376, 377
    interrogative 331–2
    multiplicative 333
    negative 330
    null 334
    partitive 135
    pseudo-quantified NP 332
    quantificational nouns 330–1

raising 81, 84, 99, 117–8, 140–2, 191, 197–200, 202, 203, 213, 228, 238, 239, 240, 249, 250, 579, 581
    right node raising 525
reciprocal construction 147, 176, 179–82, 203
    reciprocal device 179
reflexive construction 147, 174–9, 203
    reflexive doubling 174, 179
    reflexivization device 174
relative clause 31, 47, 114–5, 139, 145, 156, 158, 165, 168, 249, 250, 268, 269, 270, 357, 359, 473, 483–97, 556, 569, 574
    headed 317–8, 365, 484, 491
    headless / free 156, 165, 350, 353, 462, 473, 484–5, 486, 491, 493, 512
    integrated 485
    pseudo-relative 471
    reduced relative clause 236
    relative infinitival construction 207, 218–9, 487–8, 512
    relativizer 483, 495
    relativizer deletion 483–4
    supplementary 485–6
remnant 299, 317, 370, 371, 372–4, 378
reported speech 43, 139, 146–7, 551–8
    direct speech 551–3, 557, 596
    free indirect style 557
    indirect speech 553, 596
    quotation indicator 552–3
rich inflection 104, 528, 536
Romanian / Daco-Romanian

Common Romanian / Proto-Romanian / Primitive Romanian 4
emergence 2
genealogical definition 1
history of writing 5
periodization 3–5
speaking area 1
specific features 3, 4, 7, 12, 16–7, 35, 40, 50, 67, 104, 124–5, 127, 130, 140, 154, 159, 163, 178, 194, 200, 211, 256, 258, 265, 273, 275, 285, 286, 292, 293, 294, 298, 322, 329, 347, 356, 360, 362, 363, 378, 381, 409, 416, 427, 429, 431, 434, 436, 437, 440, 450, 453, 460, 467, 475, 480, 487, 509, 549, 555, 558, 559, 562, 571, 574, 577, 604, 609, 610, 614

secondary object 69, 98, 144–8, 170, 202, 205, 223, 227, 262 (*see also* double object verbs)
secondary predicate 84–5, 85–6, 99, 140, 185, 249, 250, 340, 429, 497–503
    adjunct 500–1
    complement 500–1
    depictive 498–500, 512
    resultative 498–500, 512
semivowels 8–9
sequence of tenses 63, 98
Slavic influence 2, 3, 10, 11, 22, 64, 169, 174, 192, 194, 256, 261, 273, 319, 320, 322, 394, 426, 432, 434, 442, 454, 475, 558, 599, 604, 605, 606, 610, 613, 618, 619
stacking 422, 439, 442, 488
stress 13, 19, 20, 22, 25, 26, 32, 33, 34, 299, 381, 539, 546, 574, 597, 607, 608, 610, 611
    secondary stress 13
strong verbal forms 19, 26, 29, 34, 223, 224, 225
subdialects 6
    northern varietis 21, 35, 38, 59, 220, 222, 224, 266, 442
    southern varieties 6, 26, 32, 59, 101, 266, 448, 558
subject 71, 72, 100–25, 170, 359, 485
    doubly realized 112–3
    generic subject 102, 108–9, 173, 201
    internal subject 110
    null pronominal subject (see pro-drop)
    null subject doubling 573
    postverbal subject 100, 101, 102, 103, 104, 106, 107, 111, 119–21, 122, 124, 125, 142, 157, 170, 172, 186, 201, 216, 228, 239, 244, 294, 568, 570–1, 579
    prepositional subject 113–4
    subject–predicate inversion 539, 540, 596
    subjectless verbs 98, 99, 100, 106, 109–11, 157
        (*see also* impersonal construction and verb, impersonal)
subjective predicative complement 78, 86, 87, 159, 160–6, 203, 294, 428, 498, 574
subjunctive 24, 43, 44, 119, 142, 197–201, 206, 210–1, 484, 511, 512, 547, 555, 556–7, 576, 578, 579, 581
    in periphrastic forms 37, 39, 40, 208, 211

subjunctive (*cont.*)
  perfect subjunctive 24, 191
    perfect subjunctive periphrasis 31
    present-past distinction 60
  present subjunctive 18, 21, 24, 29–33
  subjunctive marker 29, 30, 31, 46, 50, 116, 125, 212, 387, 476, 483, 511, 540, 550, 559–60
  subjunctive periphrases 43
  subjunctive with imperative value 36, 546, 575
  values and uses 45–50
subordination 206, 466–97, 586
substantivization 232–3, 247, 303, 316, 365, 430–1
substratum 2, 3, 10, 256, 261, 286, 320, 333, 380, 604
sum pro habeo 163, 186, 188, 190, 203
superiority effect 543
supine 115, 119, 125, 140, 149, 158, 160, 164, 191, 196–7, 200, 201, 206, 208, 209, 210, 228, 233–45, 283, 356, 357, 358, 416, 436, 438, 448, 450, 546, 573, 580
  negative 234, 436, 559
  nominal 234–5, 254
  nominal-verbal 235, 254
  subject of supine 103, 124, 233, 243
  supine marker 115, 228, 238, 240, 254
  supine–infinitive–subjunctive competition 202, 211, 233, 244–5, 254
  verbal 234–5, 254
  with imperative value 243, 245
suffix
  derivational 599–604, 605, 606
  supplementary 19, 21, 22, 25, 26, 98
suppletion, suppletive form 23, 28, 30, 33, 98, 292, 376, 380, 381, 405, 408
syncretism 21, 23, 26, 29, 34, 55, 98, 101, 113, 135, 169, 210, 233, 234, 253, 256, 260, 261, 262, 263, 258, 273, 274, 275, 276, 277, 280, 286, 291, 337, 345, 352, 375, 380, 381, 383, 384, 401, 411, 413, 526

Thraco-Dacian (see substratum)
topicalization 117, 122, 148, 243, 254, 568, 570–3, 597
  fronting 143, 537, 540, 545, 570–1, 574, 577, 579, 582, 597
  left-dislocation 91, 243, 356, 537, 571–2, 574, hanging topic 118, 142, 243, 254, 572–3
  right-dislocation 537, 573

torna, torna, fratre 2
tough-construction 200, 203, 240
transitive verbs 65–72, 73, 93, 108, 125, 169, 174, 229
  double object verbs 66–70, 98, 144, 166, 392 (*see also* secondary object)
  complex transitive verbs with an objective predicative complement 70–2, 98, 159, 500
  null object transitive verbs / transitive absolute 108, 126, 164, 174, 229, 230
triphthongs 12

variation
  morphological 19, 21, 36, 256, 260, 275, 277, 342, 375, 414, 452–3, 463–5
  syntactic 69, 94, 146, 149, 150, 153, 159, 175, 221, 250, 263, 268, 270, 370, 386
verb 18–99
  analytic forms / periphrases 24, 37–43, 207, 447–8, 449, 450
  inflectional classes 18–23, 98, 212
  irregular verbs 23, 26, 28, 37, 38, 98
  reciprocal verbs 180, 351
  reflexive verbs 77, 81, 93, 94, 98, 108, 110, 155, 173, 178, 179
  synthetic / simple forms 24–37
vowel 7–8
  prothetic vowel 388
  thematic vowel 24, 25, 27, 28
  vowel harmony 611
  vowels specific to Romanian 8

word order 113, 119–25, 142–4, 147–8, 157, 165–6, 168, 201–2, 232, 239, 251–2, 263, 291, 294, 295, 296, 297, 298, 299, 300, 302, 305, 306, 308, 311, 316, 317, 329, 338, 342, 343, 344, 355, 356, 360, 361, 362, 363, 369, 378, 386, 387, 389, 391, 392, 393, 400, 406, 408, 413, 423, 426, 427, 428, 431, 447–9, 457, 458, 467, 469–70, 483, 508–9, 512, 513, 537, 538, 549, 559–61, 568–70, 574 (*see also* adjacency and subject, postverbal subject)
weak verbal forms 19, 26, 19, 34, 223, 224, 225
wh-movement 497–8, 512, 543
wh-word/phrase 117, 268, 270, 358, 359, 365, 367, 373, 446, 486, 488, 489–96, 512, 535, 541, 542, 545, 548, 549, 568–9